GABRIEL MANT

THE SOUTH AMERICAN FOOTBALL YEARBOOK

2015-2016

British Library Cataloguing in Publication Data
A catalogue record for this book is available from the British Library

ISBN: 978-1-86223-318-8

72 St. Peter's Avenue, Cleethorpes, N.E. Lincolnshire, DN35 8HU, England

Web site www.soccer-books.co.uk
e-mail info@soccer-books.co.uk

Printed in the UK by 4edge Ltd.

Dear Readers,

The 2014-2015 season in South America began with the various countries coming to terms with the events of the 2014 FIFA World Cup finals tournament. This period was particularly difficult for Brazil, the hosts, who were originally favourites to achieve a record 6th victory but crashed out at the semi-final stage in a most ignominious way imaginable against the ultimate winners, Germany. Trailing 5-0 at half-time (and slightly lucky the deficit wasn't greater!), Brazil failed to rally in the second half and eventually lost by a humiliating 1-7 scoreline to send their country into shock.

To make things even worse for the Brazilians, their arch-rivals Argentina were the ones to save face for CONMEBOL countries as they reached the Final itself and only narrowly lost to the Germans by a solitary goal.In the aftermath, the Brazilian coach, Luiz Felipe Scolari resigned and was surprisingly replaced by Carlos Caetano Bledorn Verri (better known by his nickname as a player, "Dunga") who himself had been ousted as coach following Brazil's failure in the 2010 World Cup Finals! The initial adverse public reaction to this appointment largely evaporated thanks to a 10-match winning run by the 'Seleção', although it should be noted that all these victories came in friendly matches.

Despite the fact that Argentina had only narrowly lost the Final, Alejandro Sabella, nonetheless, resigned as coach and was replaced by Gerardo Martino who had recently left FC Barcelona. Argentina will hope that Martino's experience of working with Lionel Messi can help the 'little genius' replicate his Barça form when playing for his country!

Uruguay, the third of the top CONMEBOL triumvirate, retained their coach Oscar Tabarez, but the retirement of veteran striker Diego Forlán has reduced their options in attack. Luckily for Uruguay, in Suárez and Cavani they already boast two of the most highly-rated strikers in the world so their team shouldn't be weakened too much.

At club level, the Argentinians achieved a clean sweep in the continental competitions with CA San Lorenzo winning the Copa Libertadores for the first time in the club's history and CA River Plate Buenos Aires winning the Copa Sudamericana, also for the first time. In the Copa Libertadores there were no great upsets but Club Bolívar La Paz from Bolivia performed exceptionally well to reach the semi-finals despite the fact that football in their country is not highly rated at present.

The Centennial 45th edition of the Copa America is, extraordinarily, expected to be held in the USA during June 2016, marking the first time this competition will have been held outside of South America. This is in spite of the fact that the final stages of the 44th edition were being played in Chile when this yearbook was being prepared for press! Interestingly, host cities have not yet been selected for the 45th edition, nor a TV deal signed, but it is hoped that the current corruption scandal enveloping FIFA will not affect CONMEBOL's plans to hold the competition one hundred years after it commenced.

As usual, this new edition contains detailed statistics for the 2014-2015 football season throughout South America, at both club level and international level. Complete statistics for the 2015 Copa América are also included in this yearbook. Enjoy the read!

The Author

ABBREVIATIONS

GK	Goalkeeper	**Ape**	Apertura
DF	Defender	**Cla**	Clausura
MF	Midfielder		
FW	Forward	**M**	Matches played
DOB	Date of birth	**G**	Goals

(F) International friendly matches
(CA) 2015 Copa América

FIFA COUNTRY CODES – SOUTH AMERICA

Argentina	**ARG**	Ecuador	**ECU**
Bolivia	**BOL**	Paraguay	**PAR**
Brazil	**BRA**	Peru	**PER**
Chile	**CHI**	Uruguay	**URU**
Colombia	**COL**	Venezuela	**VEN**

FIFA COUNTRY CODES – EUROPE

Austria	**AUT**	Netherlands	**NED**
Belgium	**BEL**	Portugal	**POR**
Bulgaria	**BUL**	Russia	**RUS**
Croatia	**CRO**	Spain	**ESP**
England	**ENG**	Sweden	**SWE**
France	**FRA**	Switzerland	**SUI**
Germany	**GER**	Turkey	**TUR**
Greece	**GRE**	Ukraine	**UKR**
Italy	**ITA**	Wales	**WAL**

FIFA COUNTRY CODES – NORTH & CENTRAL AMERICA

Costa Rica	**CRC**	Mexico	**MEX**
Guatemala	**GUA**	Panama	**PAN**
Honduras	**HON**	United States of America	**USA**

FIFA COUNTRY CODES – AFRICA

Angola	**ANG**	Nigeria	**NGA**
Cameroon	**CMR**		

FIFA COUNTRY CODES – ASIA

Australia	**AUS**	Saudi Arabia	**KSA**
China P.R.	**CHN**	Thailand	**THA**
Japan	**JPN**	United Arab Emirates	**UAE**
Qatar	**QAT**		

SUMMARY

COPA AMÉRICA 2015

The 2015 Copa América, organized by CONMEBOL, South America's football governing body, was the 44th edition of the Copa América and took place in Chile between the dates of 11 June to 4 July 2015. Twelve teams competed, the ten members of CONMEBOL and two guests from CONCACAF, Mexico and Jamaica (invited for the first time to compete).

The draw of the tournament was held on 24 November 2014 in Viña del Mar, The 12 teams were drawn into three groups of four, after being divided into four pots according to their FIFA World Rankings as of 23 October 2014 (as shown in brackets):

Pot A: Chile (13, hosts), Argentina (2), Brazil (6).
Pot B: Colombia (3), Uruguay (8), Mexico (17).
Pot C: Ecuador (27), Peru (54), Paraguay (76).
Pot D: Venezuela (85), Bolivia (103), Jamaica (113).

After the draw, the composition of the four groups were as follows:

Group A	Group B	Group C
Chile	Argentina	Brazil
Ecuador	Paraguay	Peru
Mexico	Uruguay	Colombia
Bolivia	Jamaica	Venezuela

Uruguay were the defending champions, but were eliminated by the hosts in the quarter–finals. Chile won their first title in history by defeating Argentina in the final on a penalty shootout after a goalless draw. Chile is qualified for the 2017 FIFA Confederations Cup in Russia.

List of venues:

City	Stadium	Capacity
Antofagasta	Estadio Regional Calvo y Bascuñán de Antofagasta	21,170
Concepción	Estadio Municipal "Alcaldesa Ester Roa Rebolledo"	30,448
La Serena	Estadio La Portada	18,243
Rancagua	Estadio El Teniente	13,849
Santiago	Estadio Nacional "Julio Martínez Prádanos"	48,745
Santiago	Estadio Monumental "David Arellano"	47,347
Temuco	Estadio Municipal "Germán Becker"	18,413
Valparaíso	Estadio "Elías Figueroa"	21,113
Viña del Mar	Estadio Sausalito	22,360

FINAL TOURNAMENT

(teams in bold are qualified for the 2th Round)

GROUP A

11.06.2015	Santiago	Chile - Ecuador	2-0(0-0)
12.06.2015	Viña del Mar	Mexico - Bolivia	0-0
15.06.2015	Valparaíso	Ecuador - Bolivia	2-3(0-3)
15.06.2015	Santiago	Chile - Mexico	3-3(2-2)
19.06.2015	Rancagua	Mexico - Ecuador	1-2(0-1)
19.06.2015	Santiago	Chile - Bolivia	5-0(2-0)

FINAL STANDINGS

1.	**Chile**	3	2	1	0	10	-	3	7
2.	**Bolivia**	3	1	1	1	3	-	7	4
3.	Ecuador	3	1	0	2	4	-	6	3
4.	Mexico	3	0	2	1	4	-	5	2

GROUP B

13.06.2015	Antofagasta	Uruguay - Jamaica	1-0(0-0)
13.06.2015	La Serena	Argentina - Paraguay	2-2(2-0)
16.06.2015	Antofagasta	Paraguay - Jamaica	1-0(1-0)
16.06.2015	La Serena	Argentina - Uruguay	1-0(0-0)
20.06.2015	La Serena	Uruguay - Paraguay	1-1(1-1)
20.06.2015	Viña del Mar	Argentina - Jamaica	1-0(1-0)

FINAL STANDINGS

1.	**Argentina**	3	2	1	0	4	-	2	7
2.	**Paraguay**	3	1	2	0	4	-	3	5
3.	**Uruguay**	3	1	1	1	2	-	2	4
4.	Jamaica	3	0	0	3	0	-	3	0

GROUP C

14.06.2015	Rancagua	Colombia - Venezuela	0-1(0-0)
14.06.2015	Temuco	Brazil - Peru	2-1(1-1)
17.06.2015	Santiago	Brazil - Colombia	0-1(0-1)
17.06.2015	Valparaíso	Peru - Venezuela	1-0(0-0)
21.06.2015	Temuco	Colombia - Peru	0 0
21.06.2015	Santiago	Brazil - Venezuela	2-1(1-0)

FINAL STANDINGS

1.	**Brazil**	3	2	0	1	4 - 3	6
2.	**Peru**	3	1	1	1	2 - 2	4
3.	**Colombia**	3	1	1	1	1 - 1	4
4.	Venezuela	3	1	0	2	2 - 3	3

RANKING OF THIRD PLACED TEAMS

1.	**Uruguay**	3	1	1	1	2 - 2	4
2.	**Colombia**	3	1	1	1	1 - 1	4
3.	Ecuador	3	1	0	2	4 - 6	3

QUARTER-FINALS

24.06.2015	Santiago	Chile - Uruguay	1-0(0-0)
25.06.2015	Temuco	Bolivia - Peru	1-3(0-2)
26.06.2015	Viña del Mar	Argentina - Colombia	0-0; 5-4 pen
27.06.2015	Concepción	Brazil - Paraguay	1-1(1-0,1-1); 3-4 pen

SEMI-FINALS

29.06.2015	Santiago	Chile - Peru	2-1(1-0)
30.06.2015	Concepción	Argentina - Paraguay	6-1(2-1)

3rd PLACE PLAY-OFF

03.07.2015	Concepción	Peru - Paraguay	2-0(0-0)

FINAL

04.07.2015, Estadio Nacional "Julio Martínez Prádanos", Santiago; Attendance: 45,693
Referee: Wilmar Alexander Roldán Pérez (Colombia)

CHILE - ARGENTINA **0-0; 4-1 on penalties**

CHI: Claudio Andrés Bravo Muñoz, Jorge Luis Valdivia Toro (75.Matías Ariel Fernández Fernández), Arturo Erasmo Vidal Pardo, Mauricio Aníbal Isla Isla, Marcelo Alfonso Díaz Rojas, Gary Alexis Medel Soto, Francisco Andrés Silva Gajardo, Charles Mariano Aránguiz Sandoval, Jean André Emanuel Beausejour Coliqueo, Alexis Alejandro Sánchez Sánchez, Eduardo Jesús Vargas Rojas (95.Ángelo José Henríquez Iturra). Trainer: Jorge Luis Sampaoli Moya (Argentina).

ARG: Sergio Germán Romero, Pablo Javier Zabaleta Girod, Martín Gastón Demichelis, Nicolás Hernán Gonzalo Otamendi, Faustino Marcos Alberto Rojo, Javier Alejandro Mascherano, Lucas Rodrigo Biglia, Ángel Fabián Di María Hernández (29.Ezequiel Iván Lavezzi), Javier Matías Pastore (81.Éver Maximiliano David Banega), Lionel Andrés Messi, Sergio Leonel Agüero del Castillo (74.Gonzalo Gerardo Higuaín). Trainer: Gerardo Daniel Martino.

Penalties: Matías Ariel Fernández Fernández 1-0; Lionel Andrés Messi 1-1; Arturo Erasmo Vidal Pardo 2-1; Gonzalo Gerardo Higuaín (missed); Charles Mariano Aránguiz Sandoval 3-1; Éver Maximiliano David Banega (saved); Alexis Alejandro Sánchez Sánchez 4-1.

Best goalscorers: José Paolo Guerrero Gonzales (Peru) & Eduardo Jesús Vargas Rojas (Chile) – 4 goals each

2015 COPA AMÉRICA SQUADS

ARGENTINA

	Name	DOB	Club	M	G
		Goalkeepers			
1	Sergio Germán Romero	22.02.1987	UC Sampdoria Genoa (ITA)	6	0
12	Nahuel Ignacio Guzmán	10.02.1986	CF Tigres de la UA de Nuevo León	0	0
23	Mariano Gonzalo Andújar	30.07.1983	SSC Napoli (ITA)	0	0
23	Agustín Federico Marchesín*	16.03.1988	Club Santos Laguna Torreón (MEX)	0	0
		Defenders			
2	Ezequiel Marcelo Garay González	10.10.1986	FK Zenit St. Petersburg (RUS)	4	0
3	Facundo Sebastián Roncaglia	10.02.1987	Genoa CFC (ITA)	1	0
4	Pablo Javier Zabaleta Girod	16.01.1985	Manchester City FC (ENG)	5	0
13	Milton Óscar Casco	11.04.1988	CA Newell's Old Boys Rosario	0	0
15	Martín Gastón Demichelis	20.12.1980	Manchester City FC (ENG)	3	0
16	Faustino Marcos Alberto Rojo	20.03.1990	Manchester United FC (ENG)	6	1
17	Nicolás Hernán Gonzalo Otamendi	12.02.1988	Valencia CF (ESP)	5	0
		Midfielders			
5	Fernando Rubén Gago	10.04.1986	CA Boca Juniors Buenos Aires	1	0
6	Lucas Rodrigo Biglia	30.01.1986	SS Lazio Roma (ITA)	6	0
7	Ángel Fabián Di María Hernández	14.02.1988	Manchester United FC (ENG)	6	2
8	Roberto Maximiliano Pereyra	07.01.1991	Juventus FC Torino (ITA)	2	0
14	Javier Alejandro Mascherano	08.06.1984	FC Barcelona (ESP)	6	0
19	Éver Maximiliano David Banega	29.06.1988	Sevilla FC (ESP)	5	0
20	Érik Manuel Lamela	04.03.1992	Tottenham Hotspur FC London (ENG)	1	0
21	Javier Matías Pastore	20.06.1989	Paris Saint-Germain FC (FRA)	6	1
		Forwards			
9	Gonzalo Gerardo Higuaín	10.12.1987	SSC Napoli (ITA)	4	2
10	Lionel Andrés Messi	24.06.1987	FC Barcelona (ESP)	6	1
11	Sergio Leonel Agüero del Castillo	02.06.1988	Manchester City FC (ENG)	5	3
18	Carlos Alberto Martínez Tévez	05.02.1984	Juventus FC Torino (ITA)	4	0
22	Ezequiel Iván Lavezzi	03.05.1985	Paris Saint-Germain FC (FRA)	2	0
		Trainer			
Gerardo Daniel Martino		20.11.1962			

**Please note: Agustín Federico Marchesín was called up to the Argentina squad for the 2015 Copa América after Mariano Andújar suffered a hand injury midway through the tournament.*

BOLIVIA

	Name	DOB	Club	M	G
		Goalkeepers			
1	Romel Javier Quiñónez Suárez	25.06.1992	Club Bolívar La Paz	4	0
12	José Feliciano Peñarrieta Flores	18.11.1988	Club Atletico Petrolero del Gran Chaco Yacuiba	0	0
23	Hugo Suárez Vaca	07.11.1982	CSCD Blooming Santa Cruz	0	0
		Defenders			
2	Edemir Rodríguez Mercado	21.10.1984	Club Bolívar La Paz	1	0
4	Alejandro Leonel Morales Pinedo	02.09.1988	CSCD Blooming Santa Cruz	4	0
5	Ronald Eguino Segovia	20.02.1988	Club Bolívar La Paz	0	0
16	Ronald Raldes Balcazar	20.04.1981	CD Oriente Petrolero Santa Cruz	4	1
17	Marvin Orlando Bejarano Jiménez	06.03.1988	CD Oriente Petrolero Santa Cruz	3	0
21	Cristian Michael Coimbra Arias	11.09.1989	CSCD Blooming Santa Cruz	3	0
22	Edward Mauro Zenteno Álvarez	05.12.1984	Club Jorge Wilstermann Cochabamba	3	0
		Midfielders			
3	Alejandro Saúl Chumacero Bracamonte	22.04.1991	Club The Strongest La Paz	4	0
6	Danny Brayhan Bejarano Yañez	03.01.1994	CD Oriente Petrolero Santa Cruz	3	0
8	Martin Ramiro Guillermo Smedberg-Dalence	10.05.1984	IFK Göteborg (SWE)	4	1
10	Pablo Daniel Escobar Olivetti	23.02.1979	Club The Strongest La Paz	3	0
11	Damián Emmanuel Lizio	30.06.1989	O'Higgins FC Rancagua (CHI)	3	0
13	Damir Miranda Mercado	16.10.1985	Club Bolívar La Paz	2	0
14	Miguel Ángel Hurtado Suárez	04.07.1985	CSCD Blooming Santa Cruz	3	0
15	Sebastián Gamarra Ruíz	15.01.1997	Milan AC (ITA)	0	0
20	Jhasmani Campos Dávalos	10.05.1988	Club Bolívar La Paz	1	0
		Forwards			
7	Alcides Peña Jiménez	14.01.1989	CD Oriente Petrolero Santa Cruz	1	0
9	Marcelo Moreno Martins	18.06.1987	Changchun Yatai FC (CHN)	4	2
18	Ricardo Pedriel Suárez	19.01.1987	Mersin İdmanyurdu SK (TUR)	4	0
19	Wálter Veizaga Argote	22.04.1986	Club The Strongest La Paz	1	0
		Trainer			
	Mauricio Ronald Soria Portillo	01.06.1966			

BRAZIL

	Name	DOB	Club	M	G
		Goalkeepers			
1	Jéfferson de Oliveira Galvão	02.01.1983	Botafogo de FR Rio de Janeiro	4	0
12	Norberto Murara Neto	19.07.1989	AC Fiorentina (ITA)	0	0
23	Marcelo Grohe	13.01.1987	Grêmio Foot-Ball Porto Alegrense	0	0
		Defenders			
2	Daniel Alves da Silva	06.05.1983	FC Barcelona (ESP)	4	0
3	João Miranda de Souza Filho	07.09.1984	Clube Atlético de Madrid (ESP)	4	0
4	David Luiz Moreira Marinho	22.04.1987	Paris Saint-Germain FC (FRA)	2	0
6	Filipe Luís Kasmirski	09.08.1985	Chelsea FC London (ENG)	4	0
13	Marcos Aoás Corrêa „Marquinhos III"	14.05.1994	Paris Saint-Germain FC (FRA)	1	0
14	Thiago Emiliano da Silva	22.09.1984	Paris Saint-Germain FC (FRA)	3	1
15	Geferson Cerqueira Teles	13.05.1994	SC Internacional Porto Alegre	0	0
16	Fábio Henrique Tavares "Fabinho"	23.10.1993	AS Monaco FC (FRA)	0	0
		Midfielders			
5	Fernando Luiz Rosa „Fernandinho"	04.05.1985	Manchester City FC (ENG)	4	0
7	Douglas Costa de Souza	14.09.1990	FK Shakhtar Donetsk (UKR)	3	1
8	Elias Mendes Trindade	16.05.1985	SC Corinthians Paulista São Paulo	4	0
11	Roberto Firmino Barbosa de Oliveira	02.10.1991	1899 Hoffenheim (GER)	4	1
17	Frederico Rodrigues de Paula Santos "Fred III"	05.03.1993	FK Shakhtar Donetsk (UKR)	2	0
18	Everton Augusto de Barros Ribeiro	10.04.1989	Al Ahli Dubai Club (UAE)	2	0
19	Willian Borges da Silva	09.08.1988	Chelsea FC London (ENG)	4	0
21	Philippe Coutinho Correia	12.06.1992	Liverpool FC (ENG)	3	0
22	Carlos Henrique Casemiro	23.02.1992	FC do Porto (POR)	0	0
		Forwards			
9	Diego Tardelli Martins	10.05.1985	Shandong Luneng Taishan FC (CHN)	4	0
10	Neymar da Silva Santos Júnior	05.02.1992	FC Barcelona (ESP)	2	1
20	Robson de Souza "Robinho"	25.01.1984	Santos FC	2	1
		Trainer			
	Carlos Caetano Bledorn Verri "Dunga"	31.10.1963			

CHILE

	Name	DOB	Club	M	G
		Goalkeepers			
1	Claudio Andrés Bravo Muñoz	13.04.1983	FC Barcelona (ESP)	6	0
12	Paulo Andrés Garcés Contreras	02.08.1984	CSD Colo-Colo Santiago	0	0
23	Johnny Cristián Herrera Muñoz	09.05.1981	Club Universidad de Chile Santiago	0	0
		Defenders			
2	Eugenio Esteban Mena Reveco	18.07.1988	Cruzeiro EC Belo-Horizonte (BRA)	4	0
3	Miiko Martín Albornoz Inola	30.11.1990	Hannover'96	2	0
4	Mauricio Aníbal Isla Isla	12.06.1988	Queen's Park Rangers FC London (ENG)	6	1
6	José Pedro Fuenzalida Gana	22.02.1985	CA Boca Juniors Buenos Aires (ARG)	0	0
13	José Manuel Rojas Bahamondes	23.06.1983	Club Universidad de Chile Santiago	1	0
17	Gary Alexis Medel Soto	03.08.1987	FC Internazionale Milano (ITA)	6	1
18	Gonzalo Alejandro Jara Reyes	29.08.1985	1.FSV Mainz 05 (GER)	4	0
		Midfielders			
5	Francisco Andrés Silva Gajardo	11.02.1986	Club Brugge KV (BEL)	1	0
8	Arturo Erasmo Vidal Pardo	22.05.1987	Juventus FC Torino (ITA)	6	3
10	Jorge Luis Valdivia Toro	19.01.1983	SE Palmeiras São Paulo (BRA)	6	0
14	Matías Ariel Fernández Fernández	15.05.1986	AC Fiorentina Firenze (ITA)	4	0
15	Jean André Emanuel Beausejour Coliqueo	01.06.1984	CSD Colo-Colo Santiago	4	0
16	David Marcelo Pizarro Cortés	11.02.1979	AC Fiorentina Firenze (ITA)	4	0
19	Felipe Alejandro Gutiérrez Leiva	08.10.1990	FC Twente Enschede (NED)	1	0
20	Charles Mariano Aránguiz Sandoval	17.04.1989	SC Internacional Porto Alegre (BRA)	6	2
21	Marcelo Alfonso Díaz Rojas	30.12.1986	Hamburger SV (GER)	6	0
		Forwards			
7	Alexis Alejandro Sánchez Sánchez	19.12.1988	Arsenal FC London (ENG)	6	1
9	Mauricio Ricardo Pinilla Ferrera	04.02.1984	Atalanta Bergamasca Calcio (ITA)	2	0
11	Eduardo Jesús Vargas Rojas	20.11.1989	Queen's Park Rangers FC London (ENG)	6	4
22	Ángelo José Henríquez Iturra	13.04.1994	GNK Dinamo Zagreb (CRO)	2	0
		Trainer			
	Jorge Luis Sampaoli Moya (Argentina)	13.03.1960			

COLOMBIA

	Name	DOB	Club	M	G
			Goalkeepers		
1	Ramírez David Ospina	31.08.1988	Arsenal FC London (ENG)	4	0
12	Camilo Andrés Vargas Gil	09.03.1989	Club Atlético Nacional Medellín	0	0
23	Cristian Harson Bonilla Garzón	02.06.1993	CD La Equidad Seguros Bogotá	0	0
			Defenders		
2	Cristián Eduardo Zapata Valencia	30.09.1986	Milan AC (ITA)	4	0
3	Pedro Camilo Franco Ulloa	23.04.1991	Beşiktaş JK Istanbul (TUR)	0	0
4	Santiago Arias Naranjo	13.01.1992	PSV Eindhoven (NED)	2	0
7	Pablo Estifer Armero	02.11.1986	CR Flamengo Rio de Janeiro (BRA)	3	0
13	Darwin Zamir Andrade Marmolejo	11.02.1991	Újpest FC (HUN)	0	0
14	Carlos Enrique Valdés Parra	22.05.1985	Club Nacional de Football Montevideo (URU)	0	0
22	Jeison Fabián Murillo Cerón	27.05.1992	Granada CF (ESP)	4	1
18	Juan Camilo Zúñiga Mosquera	14.12.1986	SSC Napoli (ITA)	3	0
			Midfielders		
5	Edwin Armando Valencia Rodríguez	29.03.1985	Santos FC (BRA)	3	0
6	Carlos Alberto Sánchez Moreno	06.02.1986	Aston Villa FC Birmingham (ENG)	3	0
8	Edwin Andrés Cardona Bedoya	08.12.1992	CF Monterrey (MEX)	2	0
10	James David Rodríguez Rubio	12.07.1991	Real Madrid CF (ESP)	4	0
11	Juan Guillermo Cuadrado Bello	26.05.1988	Chelsea FC London (ENG)	4	0
15	Alexander Mejía Sabalsa	07.09.1988	CF Monterrey (MEX)	3	0
			Forwards		
9	Radamel Falcao García Zárate	10.02.1986	Manchester United FC (ENG)	4	0
16	Segundo Víctor Ibarbo Guerrero	19.05.1990	AS Roma (ITA)	3	0
17	Carlos Arturo Bacca Ahumada	31.12.1984	Sevilla FC (ESP)	2	0
19	Teófilo Antonio Gutiérrez Roncancio	17.05.1985	CA River Plate Buenos Aires (ARG)	4	0
20	Luis Fernando Muriel Fruto	18.04.1991	UC Sampdoria Genoa (ITA)	1	0
21	Jackson Arley Martínez Valencia	03.10.1986	FC do Porto (POR)	3	0
			Trainer		
	José Néstor Pékerman (Argentina)	03.09.1949			

ECUADOR

	Name	DOB	Club	M	G
		Goalkeepers			
1	Daniel Librado Azcona Salinas	18.01.1984	CSD Independiente del Valle Sangolquí	0	0
12	Esteban Javier Dreer	11.11.1981	CS Emelec Guayaquil	0	0
23	Alexander Domínguez Carabalí	05.06.1987	LDU de Quito	3	0
		Defenders			
2	Arturo Rafael Mina Meza	08.10.1990	CSD Independiente del Valle Sangolquí	1	0
3	Frickson Rafael Erazo Vivero	05.05.1988	Grêmio Foot-Ball Porto Alegrense (BRA)	2	0
4	Juan Carlos Paredes Reasco	08.07.1987	Watford FC (ENG)	3	0
10	Walter Orlando Ayoví Corozo	11.08.1979	CF Pachuca (MEX)	3	0
16	Mario Alberto Pineida Martínez	06.07.1992	CSD Independiente del Valle Sangolquí	0	0
18	Óscar Dalmiro Bagüí Angulo	10.12.1982	CS Emelec Guayaquil	0	0
20	John William Narváez Arroyo	12.06.1991	CS Emelec Guayaquil	0	0
21	Gabriel Eduardo Achilier Zurita	24.03.1985	CS Emelec Guayaquil	3	0
		Midfielders			
5	Alex Renato Ibarra Mina	20.01.1991	SBV Vitesse Arnhem (NED)	3	0
6	Christian Fernando Noboa Tello	09.04.1985	PAOK Thessaloníki (GRE)	3	0
7	Jefferson Antonio Montero Vite	01.09.1989	Swansea City AFC (WAL)	3	0
11	Juan Ramón Cazares Sevillano	03.04.1992	CA Banfield (ARG)	2	0
14	Osbaldo Lupo Lastra García	10.08.1983	CS Emelec Guayaquil	2	0
15	Pedro Ángel Quiñónez Rodríguez	04.03.1986	CS Emelec Guayaquil	2	0
19	Pedro Sebastián Larrea Arellano	21.05.1986	LDU de Loja	0	0
22	Jonathan David González Valencia	07.03.1995	Club Universidad de Guadalajara (MEX)	0	0
		Forwards			
8	Miller Alejandro Bolaños Reasco	01.06.1990	CS Emelec Guayaquil	3	2
9	Fidel Francisco Martínez Tenorio	15.02.1990	Club Universidad de Guadalajara (MEX)	3	0
13	Enner Remberto Valencia Lastra	11.04.1989	West Ham United FC London (ENG)	3	2
17	Daniel Patricio Angulo Arroyo	16.11.1986	CSD Independiente del Valle Sangolquí	1	0
		Trainer			
	Gustavo Domingo Quinteros Desabato (Bolivia)	15.02.1965			

JAMAICA

	Name	DOB	Club	M	G
		Goalkeepers			
1	Duwayne Oriel Kerr	16.01.1987	Sarpsborg 08 FF (NOR)	2	0
12	Dwayne St. Aubyn Miller	14.07.1987	Syrianska FC Södertälje (SWE)	1	0
23	Ryan Thompson	07.01.1985	Pittsburgh Riverhounds (USA)	0	0
		Defenders			
2	Daniel Gordon	16.01.1985	Karlsruher SC (GER)	0	0
3	Michael Anthony James Hector	19.07.1992	Reading FC London (ENG)	3	0
4	Westley Nathan Morgan	21.01.1984	Leicester City FC (ENG)	3	0
19	Adrian Joseph Mariappa	03.10.1986	Crystal Palace FC London (ENG)	3	0
20	Kemar Michael Lawrence	17.09.1992	New York Red Bulls (USA)	3	0
21	Jermaine Taylor	14.01.1985	Houston Dynamo (USA)	1	0
		Midfielders			
5	Lancelot Laing	28.02.1988	FC Edmonton (CAN)	3	0
8	Hughan Edwards Gray	25.03.1987	Waterhouse FC Kingston	0	0
10	Joel Joshua Frederick Melvin McAnuff	09.11.1981	Leyton Orient FC London (ENG)	3	0
15	JeVaughn Watson	22.10.1983	FC Dallas (USA)	2	0
16	Joel Valentino Grant	27.08.1987	Yeovil Town FC (ENG)	0	0
17	Rodolph William Austin	01.06.1985	Leeds United FC (ENG)	3	0
18	Simon Jonathan Dawkins	01.12.1987	Derby County FC (ENG)	3	0
22	Garath James McCleary	15.05.1987	Reading FC London (ENG)	3	0
		Forwards			
6	Deshorn Brown	22.12.1990	Vålerenga Fotball Oslo (NOR)	3	0
7	Romeo Ovando Parkes	11.11.1990	AD Isidro Metapán (SLV)	0	0
9	Giles Gordon Barnes	05.08.1988	Houston Dynamo (USA)	3	0
11	Darren Mattocks	02.09.1990	Vancouver Whitecaps FC (CAN)	2	0
13	Dino Williams	31.03.1990	Montego Bay United FC	0	0
14	Allan Ottey	18.12.1992	Montego Bay United FC	0	0
		Trainer			
Winfried Schäfer (Germany)		10.01.1950			

MEXICO

	Name	DOB	Club	M	G
		Goalkeepers			
1	José de Jesús Corona Rodríguez	26.01.1981	Cruz Azul FC Ciudad de México	3	0
12	Alfredo Talavera Díaz	18.09.1982	Deportivo Toluca FC	0	0
23	Édgar Melitón Hernández Cabrera	15.10.1982	CD Tiburones Rojos de Veracruz	0	0
		Defenders			
2	Julio César Domínguez Juárez	08.11.1987	Cruz Azul FC Ciudad de México	3	0
3	Hugo Ayala Castro	31.03.1987	CF Tigres de la UA de Nuevo León	3	0
4	Rafael Márquez Álvarez	13.02.1979	Hellas Verona FC (ITA)	1	0
13	Carlos Joel Salcedo Hernández	29.09.1993	CD Guadalajara	1	0
14	Juan Carlos Valenzuela Hernández	15.05.1984	CSD Atlas de Guadalajara	2	0
15	Gerardo Flores Zúñiga	05.02.1986	Cruz Azul FC Ciudad de México	3	0
16	Adrián Alexei Aldrete Rodríguez	14.06.1988	Club Santos Laguna Torreón	2	0
21	George Ulises Corral Ang	18.07.1990	Querétaro FC	0	0
22	Efraín Velarde Calvillo	18.04.1986	CF Monterrey	1	0
		Midfielders			
5	Juan Carlos Medina Alonso	22.08.1983	CSD Atlas de Guadalajara	3	0
6	Javier Güémez López	17.10.1991	Club Tijuana Xoloitzcuintles de Caliente	3	0
7	Jesús Manuel Corona Ruíz	06.01.1993	FC Twente Enschede (NED)	3	0
8	Marco Jhonfai Fabián de la Mora	21.07.1989	CD Guadalajara	1	0
10	Luis Arturo Montes Jiménez	15.05.1986	Club León FC	1	0
11	Javier Ignacio Aquino Carmona	11.02.1990	Rayo Vallecano de Madrid (ESP)	3	0
17	Mario Humberto Osuna Pereznúñez	20.08.1988	Querétaro FC	1	0
		Forwards			
9	Raúl Alonso Jiménez Rodríguez	05.05.1991	Club Atlético de Madrid (ESP)	3	2
18	Enrique Alejandro Esqueda Tirado	19.04.1988	CF Tigres de la UA de Nuevo León	0	0
19	Vicente José Matías Vuoso	03.11.1981	Chiapas FC Tuxtla Gutiérrez	3	2
20	Eduardo Herrera Aguirre	25.07.1988	Club UNAM Ciudad de México	2	0
		Trainer			
	Miguel Ernesto Herrera Aguirre	18.03.1968			

PARAGUAY

	Name	DOB	Club	M	G
		Goalkeepers			
1	Justo Wilmar Villar Viveros	30.06.1977	CSD Colo-Colo Santiago (CHI)	4	0
12	Joel Alberto Silva Estigarribia	13.01.1989	Club Guaraní Asunción	2	0
23	Alfredo Ariel Aguilar	18.07.1986	Club Guaraní Asunción	0	0
		Defenders			
2	Iván Rodrigo Piris Leguizamón	10.03.1989	Udinese Calcio (ITA)	4	0
3	Marcos Antonio Cáceres Centurión	05.05.1986	CA Newell's Old Boys Rosario (ARG)	3	0
4	Pablo César Aguilar Benítez	02.04.1987	CF América Ciudad de México (MEX)	5	0
5	Bruno Amílcar Valdez	06.10.1992	Club Cerro Porteño Asunción	4	0
6	Miguel Ángel Ramón Samudio	24.08.1986	CF América Ciudad de México (MEX)	3	0
14	Paulo César da Silva Barrios	01.02.1980	Deportivo Toluca FC (MEX)	6	0
19	Fabián Cornelio Balbuena González	23.08.1991	Club Libertad Asunción	0	0
		Midfielders			
13	Richard Ortíz Busto	22.05.1988	Deportivo Toluca FC (MEX)	4	0
15	Víctor Javier Cáceres Centurión	25.03.1985	CR Flamengo Rio de Janeiro (BRA)	5	0
16	Osmar de la Cruz Molinas González	03.05.1985	Club Libertad Asunción	2	0
17	Osvaldo David Martínez Arce	08.04.1986	CF América Ciudad de México	2	0
20	Néstor Ezequiel Ortigoza	07.10.1984	CA San Lorenzo de Almagro (ARG)	4	0
21	Óscar David Romero Villamayor	04.07.1992	Racing Club de Avellaneda (ARG)	3	0
22	Eduardo Lorenzo Aranda	28.01.1985	Club Olimpia Asunción	2	0
		Forwards			
7	Raúl Marcelo Bobadilla	18.06.1987	FC Augsburg (GER)	6	0
8	Lucas Ramón Barrios Cáceres	13.11.1984	Montpellier Hérault SC (FRA)	4	3
9	Roque Luis Santa Cruz Cantero	16.08.1981	Cruz Azul FC Ciudad de México (MEX)	5	0
10	Derlis Alberto González Galeano	20.03.1994	FC Basel (SUI)	5	1
11	Édgar Milciades Benítez Santander	08.11.1987	Deportivo Toluca FC (MEX)	6	1
18	Nelson Antonio Haedo Valdéz	28.11.1983	Eintracht Frankfurt (GER)	5	1
		Trainer			
	Ramón Ángel Díaz (Argentina)	29.08.1959			

PERU

	Name	DOB	Club	M	G
		Goalkeepers			
1	Pedro David Quiroz Gallese	23.04.1990	Club Juan Aurich de Chiclayo	6	0
12	Diego Alonso Roberto Penny	22.04.1984	Club Sporting Cristal Lima	0	0
23	Salomón Alexis Libman Pastor	25.02.1984	CSCD Universidad César Vallejo Trujillo	0	0
		Defenders			
2	Jair Edson Céspedes Zegarra	22.05.1984	Club Juan Aurich de Chiclayo	0	0
3	Hansell Argenis Riojas La Rosa	15.10.1991	CSCD Universidad César Vallejo Trujillo	0	0
4	Pedro Paulo Requena Cisneros	24.01.1991	CSCD Universidad César Vallejo Trujillo	0	0
5	Carlos Augusto Zambrano Ochandarte	10.07.1989	SG Eintracht Frankfurt (GER)	5	0
15	Christian Guillermo Martín Ramos Garagay	04.11.1988	Club Juan Aurich de Chiclayo	2	0
17	Luis Jan Piers Advíncula Castrillón	02.03.1990	Vitória FC Setúbal (POR)	6	0
19	Víctor Yoshimar Yotún Flores	07.04.1990	Malmö FF (SWE)	6	0
		Midfielders			
6	Juan Manuel Vargas Risco	05.10.1983	AC Fiorentina Firenze (ITA)	6	0
7	Cristopher Paolo César Hurtado Huertas	27.07.1990	FC Paços de Ferreira (POR)	4	0
8	Christian Alberto Cueva Bravo	23.11.1991	Club Alianza Lima	6	1
13	Edwin Retamoso Palomino	23.02.1982	Asociación Civil Real Atlético Garcilaso	1	0
16	Carlos Augusto Lobatón Espejo	06.02.1980	Club Sporting Cristal Lima	5	0
20	Joel Melchor Sánchez Alegría	11.07.1989	CD Universidad San Martín de Porres	4	0
21	Josepmir Aarón Ballón Villacorta	21.03.1988	Club Sporting Cristal Lima	5	0
22	Carlos Antonio Ascues Ávila	06.06.1992	FCB Melgar Arequipa	6	0
		Forwards			
9	José Paolo Guerrero Gonzales	01.01.1984	SC Corinthians Paulista São Paulo (BRA)	6	4
10	Jefferson Agustín Farfán Guadalupe	26.10.1984	FC Schalke 04 Gelsenkirchen (GER)	4	0
11	José Yordy Reyna Serna	17.09.1993	RasenBallsport Leipzig (GER)	4	0
14	Claudio Miguel Pizarro Bosio	03.10.1978	FC Bayern München (GER)	4	1
18	André Martín Carrillo Díaz	14.06.1991	Sporting Clube de Portugal Lisboa (POR)	4	1
		Trainer			
	Ricardo Alberto Gareca Nardi (Argentina)	10.02.1958			

URUGUAY

	Name	DOB	Club	M	G
			Goalkeepers		
1	Néstor Fernando Muslera Micol	16.06.1986	Galatasaray SK Istanbul (TUR)	4	0
12	Rodrigo Martín Muñoz Salomón	22.01.1982	Club Libertad Asunción (PAR)	0	0
23	Martín Andrés Silva Leites	25.03.1983	CR Vasco da Gama Rio de Janeiro (BRA)	0	0
			Defenders		
2	José María Giménez de Vargas	20.01.1995	Club Atlético de Madrid (ESP)	4	1
3	Diego Roberto Godín Leal	16.02.1986	Club Atlético de Madrid (ESP)	3	0
4	Jorge Ciro Fucile Perdomo	19.11.1984	Club Nacional de Football Montevideo	1	0
6	Álvaro Daniel Pereira Barragán	28.01.1985	Club Estudiantes de La Plata (ARG)	3	0
13	Gastón Alexis Silva Perdomo	05.03.1994	Torino FC (ITA)	0	0
16	Victorio Maximiliano Pereira Páez	08.06.1984	Sport Lisboa e Benfica (POR)	4	0
18	Mathías Corujo Díaz	08.05.1986	Club Universidad de Chile Santiago (CHI)	0	0
19	Sebastián Coates Nion	07.10.1990	Sunderland AFC (ENG)	1	0
			Midfielders		
5	Carlos Andrés Sánchez Arcosa	02.12.1984	CA River Plate Buenos Aires (ARG)	4	0
7	Cristian Gabriel Rodríguez Barotti	30.09.1985	Grêmio Foot-Ball Porto Alegrense (BRA)	4	1
10	Giorgian Daniel De Arrascaeta Benedetti	01.05.1994	EC Cruzeiro Belo Horizonte (BRA)	1	0
14	Marcelo Nicolás Lodeiro Benítez	21.03.1989	CA Boca Juniors Buenos Aires (ARG)	2	0
15	Ricardo Guzmán Pereira Méndez	16.05.1991	Club Universidad de Chile Santiago (CHI)	0	0
17	Egidio Raúl Arévalo Ríos	01.01.1982	CF Tigres de la UA de Nuevo León	4	0
20	Álvaro Rafael González Luengo	29.10.1984	Torino FC (ITA)	4	0
			Forwards		
8	Abel Mathías Hernández Platero	08.08.1990	Hull City AFC (ENG)	3	0
9	Diego Alejandro Rolán Silva	24.03.1993	FC Girondins de Bordeaux (FRA)	4	0
11	Christian Ricardo Stuani Curbelo	12.10.1986	RCD Espanyol Barcelona (ESP)	2	0
21	Edinson Roberto Cavani Gómez	14.02.1987	Paris Saint-Germain FC (FRA)	4	0
22	Jonathan Javier Rodríguez Portillo	06.07.1993	Sport Lisboa e Benfica (POR)	1	0
		Trainer			
	Óscar Wáshington Tabárez Sclavo	03.03.1947			

VENEZUELA

	Name	DOB	Club	M	G
		Goalkeepers			
1	Alain Baroja Méndez	23.10.1989	Caracas FC	3	0
12	Daniel Hernández Santos	21.10.1985	CD Tenerife (ESP)	0	0
23	Wuilker Fariñez Aray	15.02.1998	Caracas FC	0	0
		Defenders			
2	Wilker José Ángel Romero	18.03.1993	Deportivo Táchira FC San Cristóbal	0	0
3	Andrés José Túñez Arceo	15.03.1987	Buriram United FC (THA)	3	0
4	Oswaldo Augusto Vizcarrondo Araujo	31.05.1984	FC Nantes (FRA)	3	0
5	Fernando Gabriel Amorebieta Mardaras	29.03.1985	Middlesbrough FC (ENG)	2	0
6	Gabriel Alejandro Cichero Konarek	25.04.1985	AC CD Mineros de Guayana Puerto Ordaz	3	0
16	Roberto José Rosales Altuve	20.11.1988	Málaga CF (ESP)	3	0
20	Grenddy Adrián Perozo Rincón	28.02.1986	AC Ajaccio	0	0
		Midfielders			
8	Tomás Eduardo Rincón Hernández	13.01.1988	Genoa CFC (ITA)	3	0
10	Ronald Alejandro Vargas Aranguren	02.12.1986	Balıkesirspor Kulübü (TUR)	3	0
11	César Eduardo González Amais	01.10.1982	Deportivo Táchira FC San Cristóbal	2	0
13	Luis Manuel Seijas Gunther	23.06.1986	Independiente Santa Fe	3	0
14	Franklin José Lucena Peña	20.02.1981	Deportivo La Guaira Caracas	1	0
15	Alejandro Abraham Guerra Morales	09.07.1985	CA Nacional Medellín (COL)	3	0
18	Juan Fernando Arango Sáenz	17.05.1980	Club Tijuana Xoloitzcuintles de Caliente (MEX)	3	0
19	Rafael Eduardo Acosta Cammarota	13.02.1989	AC CD Mineros de Guayana Puerto Ordaz	0	0
		Forwards			
7	Nicolás Ladislao Fedor Flores	19.08.1985	Rayo Vallecano de Madrid (ESP)	2	1
9	José Salomón Rondón Giménez	16.09.1989	FK Zenit St. Petersburg (RUS)	3	1
17	Josef Alexander Martínez Mencia	19.05.1993	Torino FC (ITA)	2	0
21	Gelmin Javier Rivas Boada	23.03.1989	Deportivo Táchira FC San Cristóbal	0	0
22	Jhon Eduard Murillo Romaña	04.06.1995	Zamora FC Barinas	0	0
		Trainer			
	Noel Sanvicente Bethelmy	21.12.1964			

SOUTH AMERICAN CLUB COMPETITIONS 2014

COPA LIBERTADORES 2014

The 2014 Copa Libertadores de América (officially called „2014 Copa Bridgestone Libertadores de América“ for sponsorship reasons) was the 55th edition of the Copa Libertadores, CONMEBOL's and South Americas most important club tournament.

List of participating clubs:

Argentina (5 teams)	Club Atlético Vélez Sarsfield Buenos Aires Club Atlético Newell's Old Boys Rosario Club Atlético San Lorenzo de Almagro Arsenal de Sarandí Fútbol Club Club Atlético Lanús
Bolivia (3 teams)	Club Bolívar La Paz Club The Strongest La Paz Club Deportivo Oriente Petrolero Santa Cruz de la Sierra
Brazil (6 teams)	Clube Atlético Mineiro Belo Horizonte (*title holders*) Cruzeiro Esporte Clube Belo Horizonte Clube de Regatas do Flamengo Rio de Janeiro Grêmio Foot-Ball Porto Alegrense Clube Atlético Paranaense Curitiba Botafogo de Futebol e Regatas Rio de Janeiro
Chile (3 teams)	Club Unión Española Santiago O'Higgins Fútbol Club Rancagua Club Universidad de Chile Santiago
Colombia (3 teams)	Club Atlético Nacional Medellín Asociación Deportivo Cali Santa Fe CD Bogotá
Ecuador (3 teams)	Club Sport Emelec Guayaquil Club Social y Deportivo Independiente Sangolquí Sociedad Deportivo Quito
Paraguay (3 teams)	Club Cerro Porteño Asunción Club Nacional Asunción Club Guaraní Asunción
Peru (3 teams)	Universitario de Deportes Lima Asociación Civil Real Atlético Garcilaso Club Sporting Cristal Lima
Uruguay (3 teams)	Club Atlético Peñarol Montevideo Defensor Sporting Club Montevideo Club Nacional de Football Montevideo
Venezuela (3 teams)	Zamora Fútbol Club Deportivo Anzoátegui SC Puerto La Cruz Caracas Fútbol Club
Mexico (3 teams)	Club Santos Laguna Torreón Club León FC Club Atlético Monarcas Morelia

PRELIMINARY ROUND

28.01.2014, Estadio Morelos, Morelia; Attendance: 24,031
Referee: Juan Ernesto Soto Arevalo (Venezuela)
Club Atlético Monarcas Morelia - Santa Fe CD Bogotá 2-1(1-0)
CA Monarcas: Carlos Felipe Rodríguez Rangel, Felipe Abdiel Baloy Ramírez, Joel Adrián Huiqui Andrade, Ignacio González Espinoza, Christian de Jesús Valdéz Loaiza, Rodrigo Salinas Dorantes (16.Armando Cipriano Zamorano Flores), Carlos Adrián Morales Higuera, Aldo Leao Ramírez Sierra, Héctor Raúl Mancilla Garcés, Duvier Orlando Riascos Barahona (57.Egidio Raúl Arévalo Ríos), Jefferson Antonio Montero Vite (62.Jorge Alejandro Zárate). Trainer: Eduardo de la Torre Menchaca.
Santa Fe: Camilo Andrés Vargas Gil, Sergio Andrés Otálvaro Botero, José Julián de la Cuesta Herrera, Francisco Javier Meza Palma, Yerry Fernando Mina González (46.Jefferson Cuero Castro), Édison Vicente Méndez Méndez, Omar Sebastián Pérez, Luis Manuel Seijas Gunther, Daniel Alejandro Torres Rojas, Wilder Andrés Medina Tamayo (81.Sergio Darío Herrera Month), Luis Carlos Arias (68.José Yulián Anchico Patiño). Trainer: Wilson Jaime Gutiérrez Cardona.
Goals: Héctor Raúl Mancilla Garcés (26), Armando Cipriano Zamorano Flores (65) / Omar Sebastián Pérez (84).

04.02.2014, Estadio „Nemesio Camacho“ [El Campín], Bogotá; Attendance: 27,566
Referee: Raúl Orosco Delgadillo (Bolivia)
Santa Fe CD Bogotá - Club Atlético Monarcas Morelia 1-0(0-0)
Santa Fe: Camilo Andrés Vargas Gil, Sergio Andrés Otálvaro Botero, José Julián de la Cuesta Herrera, Francisco Javier Meza Palma, Édison Vicente Méndez Méndez, Omar Sebastián Pérez (84.José Yulián Anchico Patiño), Luis Manuel Seijas Gunther [*sent off 60*], Daniel Alejandro Torres Rojas, Wilder Andrés Medina Tamayo (75.Silvio Augusto González), Jonathan Copete Valencia, Jefferson Cuero Castro (64.Luis Carlos Arias). Trainer: Wilson Jaime Gutiérrez Cardona.
CA Monarcas: Carlos Felipe Rodríguez Rangel, Joel Adrián Huiqui Andrade (90.Ever Arsenio Guzmán Zavala), Ignacio González Espinoza, Carlos Adrián Morales Higuera, Héctor Reynoso López, Egidio Raúl Arévalo Ríos, Aldo Leao Ramírez Sierra [*sent off 52*], Armando Cipriano Zamorano Flores (74.Francisco Javier Acuña Víctor), Jorge Alejandro Zárate (83.Luis Ángel Morales Rojas), Héctor Raúl Mancilla Garcés, Duvier Orlando Riascos Barahona. Trainer: Eduardo de la Torre Menchaca.
Goals: José Julián de la Cuesta Herrera (58).
[Santa Fe CD Bogotá won on away goals rule (2-2 on aggregate)]

28.01.2014, Estadio „Ramón Tahuichi Aguilera“, Santa Cruz de la Sierra; Attendance: 19,884
Referee: Enrique Cáceres Villafante (Paraguay)
Club Deportivo Oriente Petrolero Santa Cruz de la Sierra – 1-0(1-0)
Club Nacional de Football Montevideo
Oriente Petrolero: Carlos Erwin Arias Égüez, Ronald Raldés Balcazar, Mariano Sebastián Brau, Miguel Ángel Hoyos Guzmán, Marvin Orlando Bejarano Jiménez, Wilder Zabala Perrogón (68.Rodrigo Mauricio Vargas Castillo), Alejandro Meleán Villarroel (84.Ronald Lázaro García Justiniano), Gualberto Olmos Mojica, Danny Bryan Bejarano Yañez, Juan Quero Barraso, Yasmani Georges Duk Arandia (74.Fernando Javier Saucedo Pereyra). Trainer: Tabaré Abayubá Silva Aguilar (Uruguay).
Nacional: Gustavo Adolfo Munúa Vera, Andrés Scotti Ponce de León, Pablo Álvarez Menéndez, Juan Manuel Díaz Martínez, Guillermo Daniel de los Santos Viana, Maximiliano Matías Calzada Fuentes (84.Álvaro Alexander Recoba Rivero), Rafael García Casanova, Gonzalo Ramos Deféminis (46.Paulo Rinaldo Cruzado Durand), Carlos María de Pena Bonino (62.Gastón Rodrigo Pereiro López), Iván Daniel Alonso Vallejo, Richard Aníbal Porta Candelaresi. Trainer: Gerardo Cono Pelusso Boyrie.
Goal: Gualberto Olmos Mojica (32).

04.02.2014, Estadio Gran Parque Central, Montevideo; Attendance: 23,991

Club Nacional de Football Montevideo – 2-0(1-0)
Club Deportivo Oriente Petrolero Santa Cruz de la Sierra

Nacional: Gustavo Adolfo Munúa Vera, Andrés Scotti Ponce de León, Pablo Álvarez Menéndez, Juan Manuel Díaz Martínez, Jorge Winston Curbelo Garis, Paulo Rinaldo Cruzado Durand (85.Rafael García Casanova), Maximiliano Matías Calzada Fuentes (68.Álvaro Alexander Recoba Rivero), Nicolás Santiago Prieto Larrea, Carlos María de Pena Bonino, Iván Daniel Alonso Vallejo, Richard Aníbal Porta Candelaresi (46.Gastón Rodrigo Pereiro López). Trainer: Gerardo Cono Pelusso Boyrie.

Oriente Petrolero: Carlos Erwin Arias Égüez, Ronald Raldés Balcazar, Mariano Sebastián Brau [*sent off 63*], Miguel Ángel Hoyos Guzmán, Marvin Orlando Bejarano Jiménez, Wilder Zabala Perrogón (46.Alcides Peña Jiménez), Alejandro Meleán Villarroel, Gualberto Olmos Mojica, Danny Bryan Bejarano Yañez, Juan Quero Barraso (61.Rodrigo Mauricio Vargas Castillo), Yasmani Georges Duk Arandia (65.Ronny Fernando Montero Martínez). Trainer: Tabaré Abayubá Silva Aguilar (Uruguay).

Goals: Iván Daniel Alonso Vallejo (18), Carlos María de Pena Bonino (73).

[Club Nacional de Football Montevideo won 2-1 on aggregate]

29.01.2014, Estadio Nacional, Lima; Attendance: 23,752
Referee: Enrique Roberto Osses Zencovich (Chile)

Club Sporting Cristal Lima - Clube Atlético Paranaense Curitiba 2-1(1-0)

Sporting Cristal: Diego Alonso Penny Valdez, Víctor Yoshimar Yotún Flores (66.Paolo Giancarlo de la Haza Urquiza), Marcos Armando Ortíz Lovera, Alexis Cossío Zamora, Adan Adolfo Balbín Silva, Marcos Abner Delgado Ocampo, Carlos Augusto Lobatón Espejo (85.Maximiliano Ezequiel Núñez), Jorge Luis Cazulo, Horacio Martín Calcaterra, Irven Beybe Ávila Acero, Leandro Luján Leguizamón (76.Douglas Junior Ross Santillana). Trainer: Daniel Héctor Ahmed (Argentina).

Atlético Paranaense: Wéverton Pereira da Silva, Manoel Messias Silva Carvalho, Sueliton Pereira de Aguiar (63.Douglas Coutinho Gomes de Souza), Cleberson Martins de Souza, Paulo Henrique Dias da Cruz, José Luis dos Santos Pinto "Zezinho" (66.Francisco Mérida Pérez „Fran Mérida"), João Paulo da Silva, Deivid Willian da Silva, Natanael Batista Pimienta, Éderson Alves Ribeiro Silva, Marcelo Cirino da Silva (80.Nathan Allan de Souza). Trainer: Miguel Portugal. Trainer: Miguel Angel Portugal Vicario (Spain).

Goals: Irven Beybe Ávila Acero (29), Carlos Augusto Lobatón Espejo (61 penalty) / Éderson Alves Ribeiro Silva (54 penalty).

05.02.2014, Estádio Vila Capanema, Curitiba; Attendance: 9,156
Referee: Antonio Javier Arias Alvarenga (Paraguay)

Clube Atlético Paranaense Curitiba - Club Sporting Cristal Lima 2-1(0-0,2-1,2-1); 5-4 on penalties

Atlético Paranaense: Wéverton Pereira da Silva, Manoel Messias Silva Carvalho, Sueliton Pereira de Aguiar (81.Nathan Allan de Souza), Cleberson Martins de Souza, Paulo Henrique Dias da Cruz (70.Thiago Rodrigues da Silva "Mosquito"), José Luis dos Santos Pinto "Zezinho", Deivid Willian da Silva, Natanael Batista Pimienta, Éderson Alves Ribeiro Silva, Marcelo Cirino da Silva, Douglas Coutinho Gomes de Souza (46.Francisco Mérida Pérez „Fran Mérida"). Trainer: Miguel Portugal. Trainer: Miguel Angel Portugal Vicario (Spain).

Sporting Cristal: Diego Alonso Penny Valdez, Víctor Yoshimar Yotún Flores (56.Maximiliano Ezequiel Núñez), Marcos Armando Ortíz Lovera, Alexis Cossío Zamora [*sent off 66*], Adan Adolfo Balbín Silva, Marcos Abner Delgado Ocampo, Carlos Augusto Lobatón Espejo, Jorge Luis Cazulo, Horacio Martín Calcaterra, Irven Beybe Ávila Acero (72.Luis Jan Piers Advíncula Castrillón), Leandro Luján Leguizamón (36.Pedro Jesús Aquino Sánchez). Trainer: Daniel Héctor Ahmed (Argentina).

Goals: Manoel Messias Silva Carvalho (61), Éderson Alves Ribeiro Silva (90+7 penalty) / Irven Beybe Ávila Acero (62).

Penalties: Éderson Alves Ribeiro Silva 1-0; Carlos Augusto Lobatón Espejo 1-1; Deivid Willian da Silva (missed); Jorge Luis Cazulo 1-2; Francisco Mérida Pérez „Fran Mérida" 2-2; Luis Jan Piers Advíncula Castrillón 2-3; Nathan Allan de Souza (missed); Marcos Abner Delgado Ocampo (missed);

Natanael Batista Pimienta 3-3; Horacio Martín Calcaterra (missed); Thiago Rodrigues da Silva "Mosquito" 4-3; Maximiliano Ezequiel Núñez 4-4; Manoel Messias Silva Carvalho 5-4; Pedro Jesús Aquino Sánchez (missed).
[Clube Atlético Paranaense Curitiba won 5-4 on penalties (after 3-3 on aggregate)]

29.01.2014, Estadio Olímpico „Atahualpa", Quito; Attendance: 4,123
Referee: Wilmar Alexander Roldán Pérez (Colombia)
Sociedad Deportivo Quito - Botafogo de FR Rio de Janeiro 1-0(1-0)
Deportivo Quito: Rolando Ramírez Estupiñán, Luis Manuel Romero Véliz, Víctor Javier Chinga Solís, Gregory Gerardo Gonzáles Vanegas, Miguel Ángel Bravo Prado (67.Christian Rolando Lara Anangonó), Edder Fabián Fuertes Bravo, Carlos Alfredo Feraud Silva (90+2.Dennys Andrés Quiñónez Espinoza), Edison Fernando Vega Obando, Omar Santiago Andrade Terán, Walter Richard Calderón Carcelén, Víctor Manuel Estupiñán Mairongo (79.Jonathan Alberto Hansen). Trainer: Juan Carlos Garay.
Botafogo: Jefferson de Oliveira Galvão, Fabian Guedes „Bolívar", Júlio César Coelho de Moraes Junior, Edílson Mendes Guimarães, Matheus Dória Macedo, Jorge Wagner Goés Conceição (90.Renato Dirnei Florêncio Santos), Marcelo de Mattos Terra, Rodrigo Ribeiro Souto, Marcelo Nicolás Lodeiro Benítez, Gabriel Girotto Franco (70.Wallyson Ricardo Maciel Monteiro), Juan Carlos Ferreyra (75.Constantino Pereira Filho „Elias"). Trainer: Eduardo Pedro Hungaro.
Goal: Víctor Manuel Estupiñán Mairongo (18).

05.02.2014, Estádio „Jornalista Mário Filho" [Maracanã], Rio de Janeiro; Attendance: 45,154
Referee: Silvio Aníbal Trucco (Argentina)
Botafogo de FR Rio de Janeiro - Sociedad Deportivo Quito 4-0(1-0)
Botafogo: Jefferson de Oliveira Galvão, Fabian Guedes „Bolívar", Júlio César Coelho de Moraes Junior, Edílson Mendes Guimarães, Matheus Dória Macedo, Jorge Wagner Goés Conceição (85.Rodrigo Ribeiro Souto), Marcelo de Mattos Terra, Marcelo Nicolás Lodeiro Benítez, Gabriel Girotto Franco, Juan Carlos Ferreyra (66.Constantino Pereira Filho „Elias"), Wallyson Ricardo Maciel Monteiro (82.Henrique Almeida Caixeta Nascentes). Trainer: Eduardo Pedro Hungaro.
Deportivo Quito: Rolando Ramírez Estupiñán, Fernando Martín Bonjour, Luis Manuel Romero Véliz, Víctor Javier Chinga Solís, Benito Freddy Olivo González (46.Miguel Ángel Bravo Prado), Carlos Alfredo Feraud Silva (82.Santiago Damián Morales Montenegro), Edison Fernando Vega Obando, Carlos Eduardo Vayas Vivanco, Omar Santiago Andrade Terán, Walter Richard Calderón Carcelén, Víctor Manuel Estupiñán Mairongo (54.Christian Rolando Lara Anangonó). Trainer: Juan Carlos Garay.
Goals: Wallyson Ricardo Maciel Monteiro (36, 66, 79), Henrique Almeida Caixeta Nascentes (90+1).
[Botafogo de FR Rio de Janeiro won 4-1 on aggregate]

30.01.2014, Estadio Nacional „Julio Martínez Prádanos", Santiago; Attendance: 34,569
Referee: Martín Emilio Vázquez Broquetas (Uruguay)
Club Universidad de Chile Santiago - Club Guaraní Asunción 1-0(0-0)
Universidad: Luis Antonio Marín Barahona, Matías Nicolás Caruzzo, Osvaldo Alexis González Sepúlveda, José Manuel Rojas Bahamondes, Roberto Andrés Cereceda Guajardo (80.Luciano Civelli), Gustavo Rubén Lorenzetti Espinosa, Ramón Ignacio Fernández (90.Isaac Alejandro Díaz Lobos), Sebastián Martínez Muñoz, Rodrigo Nicanor Mora Núñez, Patricio Rodolfo Rubio Pulgar, Rubén Ignacio Farfan Arancibia (46.Francisco Fernando Castro Gamboa). Trainer: Cristián Andrés Romero Godoy.
Guaraní: Alfredo Ariel Aguilar, Julio César Cáceres López, Tomás Javier Bartomeús, Luis Alberto Cabral Vásquez, Édgar Manuel Aranda, Iván Emmanuel González Ferreira, Ramón Darío Ocampo (79.Eduardo Javier Filippini), Miguel Ángel Paniagua Rivarola, Jorge Darío Mendoza Torres (80.Marcelo José Palau Balzaretti), Federico Javier Santander Mereles (60.Luis Eladio de La Cruz), Fernando Fabián Fernández Acosta. Trainer: Fernando Jubero (Spain).
Goal: Rodrigo Nicanor Mora Núñez (63).

06.02.2014, Estadio Defensores del Chaco, Asunción; Attendance: 4,410
Referee: Pablo Daniel Díaz (Argentina)
Club Guaraní Asunción - Club Universidad de Chile Santiago 2-3(1-0)
Guaraní: Alfredo Ariel Aguilar, Julio César Cáceres López, Tomás Javier Bartomeús, Luis Alberto Cabral Vásquez, Édgar Manuel Aranda, Iván Emmanuel González Ferreira, Ramón Darío Ocampo, Miguel Ángel Paniagua Rivarola (56.Marcelo José Palau Balzaretti), Jorge Darío Mendoza Torres, César Augusto Caicedo Solís (62.Jorge Daniel Benítez Guillen), Fernando Fabián Fernández Acosta (76.Federico Javier Santander Mereles). Trainer: Fernando Jubero (Spain).
Universidad: Luis Antonio Marín Barahona, Matías Nicolás Caruzzo, Osvaldo Alexis González Sepúlveda, José Manuel Rojas Bahamondes, Roberto Andrés Cereceda Guajardo, Juan Rodrigo Rojas Ovelar, Ramón Ignacio Fernández (89.César Alexis Cortés Pinto), Sebastián Martínez Muñoz (67.Gustavo Rubén Lorenzetti Espinosa), Rodrigo Nicanor Mora Núñez (56.Isaac Alejandro Díaz Lobos), Patricio Rodolfo Rubio Pulgar, Francisco Fernando Castro Gamboa. Trainer: Cristián Andrés Romero Godoy.
Goals: Fernando Fabián Fernández Acosta (39), Jorge Daniel Benítez Guillen (64) / Ramón Ignacio Fernández (52), Isaac Alejandro Díaz Lobos (74), Patricio Rodolfo Rubio Pulgar (90+1).
[Club Universidad de Chile Santiago won 4-2 on aggregate]

30.01.2014, Estadio Olímpico de la UCV, Caracas; Attendance: 12,602
Referee: Víctor Hugo Carrillo Casanova (Peru)
Caracas FC - Club Atlético Lanús 0-2(0-1)
Caracas FC: Alain Baroja Méndez, Andrés Elionai Sánchez León, Francisco Carabalí Terán, Rubert José Quijada Fasciana, Ricardo Andreutti Jordán (79.Felix Manuel Cásseres), Roberto Raúl Tucker, Bladimir Alejandro Morales Duarte, Wuiswell Anderson Isea Fernández, Rómulo Otero Vásquez (59.Luis González), Emilio Rentería García (67.Dany Curé), Edder José Farías. Trainer: Eduardo José Saragó Carbón.
CA Lanús: Agustín Federico Marchesín, Paolo Duval Goltz, Maximiliano Nicolás Velázquez, Carlos Luciano Araujo, Carlos Roberto Izquierdoz, Leandro Daniel Somoza, Diego Hernán González, Víctor Hugo Ayala Núñez (89.Jorge Alberto Ortíz), Óscar Junior Benítez (75.Ismael Alfonso Blanco), Lautaro Germán Acosta, Santiago Martín Silva Olivera. Trainer: Guillermo Barros Schelotto.
Goals: Paolo Duval Goltz (18, 86 penalty).

06.02.2014, Estadio Ciudad de Lanús „Néstor Díaz Pérez“, Lanús; Attendance: 19,789
Referee: Sandro Meira Ricci (Brazil)
Club Atlético Lanús - Caracas FC 1-0(0-0)
CA Lanús: Agustín Federico Marchesín, Paolo Duval Goltz, Maximiliano Nicolás Velázquez, Carlos Luciano Araujo, Carlos Roberto Izquierdoz, Leandro Daniel Somoza, Diego Hernán González (76.Jorge Alberto Ortíz), Víctor Hugo Ayala Núñez (85.Fernando Omar Barrientos), Óscar Junior Benítez (64.Jorge Rolando Pereyra Díaz), Lautaro Germán Acosta, Santiago Martín Silva Olivera. Trainer: Guillermo Barros Schelotto.
Caracas FC: Alain Baroja Méndez, Andrés Elionai Sánchez León, Rubert José Quijada Fasciana, Jefre José Vargas Belisario, César Alexander González (57.Luis González), Ricardo Andreutti Jordán, Roberto Raúl Tucker, Bladimir Alejandro Morales Duarte (80.José Enrique Caraballo Rosal), Rómulo Otero Vásquez, Edder José Farías (72.Wuiswell Anderson Isea Fernández), Dany Curé. Trainer: Eduardo José Saragó Carbón.
Goal: Víctor Hugo Ayala Núñez (70).
[Club Atlético Lanús won 3-0 on aggregate]

GROUP STAGE

Each group winner and runner-up advanced to the Round of 16.

GROUP 1

11.02.2014, Estadio Monumental, Lima
Referee: Roddy Alberto Zambrano Olmedo (Ecuador)
Universitario de Deportes Lima - CA Vélez Sarsfield Buenos Aires 0-1(0-0)
Universitario: José Aurelio Carvallo Alonso, Fernando Nicolás Alloco Romano, Dalton Moreira Neto (68.Josimar Hugo Vargas García), Diego Armando Chávez Ramos (73.Cris Robert Martínez Escobar), Rainer Torres Salas, Sebastián Luna, Ángel Elías Romero Iparraguirre, Edwin Alexi Gómez Gutiérrez, Christofer Gonzáles Crespo, Carlos Dante Olascuaga Viera (46.Luis Gabriel García Uribe), Raúl Mario Ruidíaz Misitich. Trainer: Ángel David Comizzo (Argentina).
Vélez Sarsfield: Carlos Sebastián Sosa Silva, Sebastián Enrique Domínguez, Emiliano Ramiro Papa, Fernando Omar Tobío, Alejandro Ariel Cabral (80.Jorge Iván Correa), Fabián Andrés Cubero, Héctor Miguel Canteros (90+1.Leandro Luis Desábato), Agustín Leonel Allione, Lucas Daniel Romero, Lucas David Pratto, Mauro Matías Zárate (83.Federico Nahuel Vázquez). Trainer: José Oscar Flores.
Goal: Héctor Miguel Canteros (80).

13.02.2014, Estádio Vila Capanema, Curitiba
Referee: Daniel Adan Fedorczuk Betancour (Uruguay)
Clube Atlético Paranaense Curitiba - Club The Strongest La Paz 1-0(1-0)
Atlético Paranaense: Wéverton Pereira da Silva, Manoel Messias Silva Carvalho, Sueliton Pereira de Aguiar, Cleberson Martins de Souza, Paulo Henrique Dias da Cruz, Francisco Mérida Pérez „Fran Mérida“ (65.Claudio Matías Mirabaje Correa), João Paulo da Silva, Deivid Willian da Silva, Natanael Batista Pimienta, Éderson Alves Ribeiro Silva (86.Adriano Leite Ribeiro), Thiago Rodrigues da Silva "Mosquito" (64.Bruno Pereira Mendes). Trainer: Miguel Portugal. Trainer: Miguel Angel Portugal Vicario (Spain).
The Strongest: Andrés Martín Jemio Portugal, Enrique Parada Salvatierra, Nelvin Solíz Escalante (80.Jair Alexander Reinoso Moreno), Marcos Israel Barrera, Jeferson Lopes Faustino, Pablo Daniel Escobar Olivetti, Ernesto Rubén Cristaldo Santa Cruz, Víctor Hugo Melgar Bejarano, Raúl Castro Peñaloza, José Gabriel Ríos Banegas (88.Luis Hernán Melgar Ortíz), Boris Xavier Alfaro Chong. Trainer: Eduardo Andrés Villegas Camara.
Goal: Paulo Henrique Dias da Cruz (23).

20.02.2014, Estadio „Hernando Siles“, La Paz
Referee: Julio Quintana Rodríguez (Paraguay)
Club The Strongest La Paz - Universitario de Deportes Lima 1-0(0-0)
The Strongest: Gustavo Adolfo Fernández Pedraza, Enrique Parada Salvatierra, Nelvin Solíz Escalante, Marcos Israel Barrera, Jeferson Lopes Faustino, Alejandro Saúl Chumacero Bracamonte, Pablo Daniel Escobar Olivetti, Diego Horacio Wayar Cruz (76.Diego Armando Chávez Ramos), Raúl Castro Peñaloza, José Gabriel Ríos Banegas (60.Ernesto Rubén Cristaldo Santa Cruz), Boris Xavier Alfaro Chong (90+1.Víctor Hugo Melgar Bejarano). Trainer: Eduardo Andrés Villegas Camara.
Universitario: José Aurelio Carvallo Alonso, Néstor Alonso Duarte Carassa, Fernando Nicolás Alloco Romano, Diego Armando Chávez Ramos, Rainer Torres Salas (75.Cris Robert Martínez Escobar), Sebastián Luna, Ángel Elías Romero Iparraguirre, Luis Gabriel García Uribe (66.Josimar Hugo Vargas García), Edwin Alexi Gómez Gutiérrez, Carlos Dante Olascuaga Viera (83.Gonzalo Maldonado Lostaunau), Raúl Mario Ruidíaz Misitich. Trainer: Ángel David Comizzo (Argentina).
Goal: Diego Horacio Wayar Cruz (70).

25.02.2014, Estadio „José Amalfitani“, Buenos Aires
Referee: Roberto Carlos Silvera Calcerrada (Uruguay)
CA Vélez Sarsfield Buenos Aires - Clube Atlético Paranaense Curitiba 2-0(1-0)
Vélez Sarsfield: Carlos Sebastián Sosa Silva, Sebastián Enrique Domínguez, Emiliano Ramiro Papa, Fernando Omar Tobío, Alejandro Ariel Cabral (70.Jorge Iván Correa), Fabián Andrés Cubero, Héctor Miguel Canteros, Agustín Leonel Allione, Lucas Daniel Romero, Lucas David Pratto (86.Ramiro Julián Cáseres), Mauro Matías Zárate (76.Brian Federico Ferreira). Trainer: José Oscar Flores.
Atlético Paranaense: Wéverton Pereira da Silva, Manoel Messias Silva Carvalho, Sueliton Pereira de Aguiar, Dráusio Luis Salla Gil, Paulo Henrique Dias da Cruz, Francisco Mérida Pérez „Fran Mérida“ (57.Thiago Rodrigues da Silva "Mosquito"), Claudio Matías Mirabaje Correa, João Paulo da Silva (65.Bruno Pereira Mendes), Deivid Willian da Silva, Natanael Batista Pimienta, Éderson Alves Ribeiro Silva (83.Adriano Leite Ribeiro). Trainer: Miguel Portugal. Trainer: Miguel Angel Portugal Vicario (Spain).
Goals: Fernando Omar Tobío (37), Lucas David Pratto (78).

11.03.2014, Estadio „Hernando Siles“, La Paz
Referee: Julio Alberto Bascuñán González (Chile)
Club The Strongest La Paz - CA Vélez Sarsfield Buenos Aires 2-0(0-0)
The Strongest: Daniel Vaca Tasca, Enrique Parada Salvatierra, Nelvin Solíz Escalante (64.Jair Alexander Reinoso Moreno), Marcos Israel Barrera, Jeferson Lopes Faustino, Alejandro Saúl Chumacero Bracamonte, Pablo Daniel Escobar Olivetti (89.Diego Armando Chávez Ramos), Ernesto Rubén Cristaldo Santa Cruz, Diego Horacio Wayar Cruz, Raúl Castro Peñaloza (86.Víctor Hugo Melgar Bejarano), Boris Xavier Alfaro Chong. Trainer: Eduardo Andrés Villegas Camara.
Vélez Sarsfield: Alan Joaquín Aguerre, Juan Alberto Sabiá, Facundo Cardozo (72.Lautaro Daniel Gianetti), Leonardo Gabriel Rolón, Gonzalo Rubén Piovi, Matías Pérez Acuña, Jorge Iván Correa, Leandro Luis Desábato, Brian Federico Ferreira (61.Leonardo Enrique Villalba), Leandro Vera (75.Federico Nahuel Vázquez), Roberto Antonio Nanni. Trainer: José Oscar Flores.
Goals: Pablo Daniel Escobar Olivetti (55 penalty, 76).

13.03.2014, Estadio Monumental, Lima
Referee: Imer Lemuel Machado Barrera (Colombia)
Universitario de Deportes Lima - Clube Atlético Paranaense Curitiba 0-1(0-0)
Universitario: José Aurelio Carvallo Alonso, Néstor Alonso Duarte Carassa, Dalton Moreira Neto, Diego Armando Chávez Ramos, Antonio Emiliano Gonzáles Canchari, Sebastián Luna, Ángel Elías Romero Iparraguirre (46.Josimar Hugo Vargas García), Edwin Alexi Gómez Gutiérrez (70.Joaquín Aldaír Aguirre Luza), Christofer Gonzáles Crespo, Carlos Dante Olascuaga Viera (46.Aurelio Saco-Vértiz Figari), Raúl Mario Ruidíaz Misitich. Trainer: Carlos Jeanpierre Silvestri Saux.
Atlético Paranaense: Wéverton Pereira da Silva, Manoel Messias Silva Carvalho, Sueliton Pereira de Aguiar, Cleberson Martins de Souza, Paulo Henrique Dias da Cruz, Claudio Matías Mirabaje Correa, Deivid Willian da Silva (44.João Paulo da Silva), Natanael Batista Pimienta, Éderson Alves Ribeiro Silva, Bruno Pereira Mendes (66.Felipe de Oliveira Silva), Douglas Coutinho Gomes de Souza (74.Francisco Mérida Pérez „Fran Mérida“). Trainer: Miguel Portugal. Trainer: Miguel Angel Portugal Vicario (Spain).
Goal: Néstor Alonso Duarte Carassa (67 own goal).

18.03.2014, Estadio „José Amalfitani", Buenos Aires
Referee: Juan Ernesto Soto Arevalo (Venezuela)
CA Vélez Sarsfield Buenos Aires - Club The Strongest La Paz 2-0(0-0)
Vélez Sarsfield: Carlos Sebastián Sosa Silva, Sebastián Enrique Domínguez, Emiliano Ramiro Papa, Facundo Cardozo, Alejandro Ariel Cabral (83.Leandro Luis Desábato), Fabián Andrés Cubero, Héctor Miguel Canteros (75.Roberto Antonio Nanni), Agustín Leonel Allione (63.Jorge Iván Correa), Lucas Daniel Romero, Lucas David Pratto, Mauro Matías Zárate. Trainer: José Oscar Flores.
The Strongest: Daniel Vaca Tasca, Enrique Parada Salvatierra, Nelvin Solíz Escalante, Marcos Israel Barrera, Jeferson Lopes Faustino, Alejandro Saúl Chumacero Bracamonte, Pablo Daniel Escobar Olivetti, Ernesto Rubén Cristaldo Santa Cruz (82.Jair Alexander Reinoso Moreno), Raúl Castro Peñaloza, Boris Xavier Alfaro Chong (75.Víctor Hugo Melgar Bejarano), Diego Armando Chávez Ramos (72.Diego Bejarano Ibáñez). Trainer: Eduardo Andrés Villegas Camara.
Goals: Lucas David Pratto (78), Jorge Iván Correa (80).

20.03.2014, Estádio Vila Capanema, Curitiba
Referee: Patricio Antonio Polic Orellana (Chile)
Clube Atlético Paranaense Curitiba - Universitario de Deportes Lima 3-0(1-0)
Atlético Paranaense: Wéverton Pereira da Silva, Manoel Messias Silva Carvalho, Sueliton Pereira de Aguiar, Cleberson Martins de Souza, Paulo Henrique Dias da Cruz, Claudio Matías Mirabaje Correa (59.Felipe de Oliveira Silva), João Paulo da Silva, Natanael Batista Pimienta, Éderson Alves Ribeiro Silva, Bruno Pereira Mendes (76.Crislan Henrique da Silva de Souza), Douglas Coutinho Gomes de Souza (80.Francisco Mérida Pérez „Fran Mérida"). Trainer: Miguel Portugal. Trainer: Miguel Angel Portugal Vicario (Spain).
Universitario: José Aurelio Carvallo Alonso, Néstor Alonso Duarte Carassa, Dalton Moreira Neto, Diego Armando Chávez Ramos, Antonio Emiliano Gonzáles Canchari, Sebastián Luna (69.Carlos Dante Olascuaga Viera), Edwin Alexi Gómez Gutiérrez, Josimar Hugo Vargas García, Christofer Gonzáles Crespo, Raúl Mario Ruidíaz Misitich, Cris Robert Martínez Escobar (78.Joaquín Aldaír Aguirre Luza). Trainer: Carlos Jeanpierre Silvestri Saux.
Goals: Dalton Moreira Neto (10 own goal), Felipe de Oliveira Silva (61), Éderson Alves Ribeiro Silva (84).

26.03.2014, Estádio Vila Capanema, Curitiba
Referee: Wilmar Alexander Roldán Pérez (Colombia)
Clube Atlético Paranaense Curitiba - CA Vélez Sarsfield Buenos Aires 1-3(0-1)
Atlético Paranaense: Wéverton Pereira da Silva, Manoel Messias Silva Carvalho (31.Dráusio Luis Salla Gil), Sueliton Pereira de Aguiar, Cleberson Martins de Souza, Paulo Henrique Dias da Cruz, Claudio Matías Mirabaje Correa (63.Felipe de Oliveira Silva), João Paulo da Silva, Natanael Batista Pimienta, Éderson Alves Ribeiro Silva, Bruno Pereira Mendes (46.Marcelo Cirino da Silva), Douglas Coutinho Gomes de Souza. Trainer: Miguel Portugal. Trainer: Miguel Angel Portugal Vicario (Spain).
Vélez Sarsfield: Carlos Sebastián Sosa Silva, Sebastián Enrique Domínguez, Emiliano Ramiro Papa [*sent off 90*], Fernando Omar Tobío, Alejandro Ariel Cabral (66.Héctor Miguel Canteros), Fabián Andrés Cubero, Jorge Iván Correa (79.Facundo Cardozo), Leandro Luis Desábato, Agustín Leonel Allione, Lucas Daniel Romero, Lucas David Pratto (86.Roberto Antonio Nanni). Trainer: José Oscar Flores.
Goals: Dráusio Luis Salla Gil (53) / Agustín Leonel Allione (6), Lucas David Pratto (59), Héctor Miguel Canteros (90+2).
Please note: Francisco Mérida Pérez „Fran Mérida" was sent off (51) on the bench.

27.03.2014, Estadio Monumental, Lima
Referee: José Hernando Buitrago Arango (Colombia)
Universitario de Deportes Lima - Club The Strongest La Paz 3-3(2-1)
Universitario: José Aurelio Carvallo Alonso, Néstor Alonso Duarte Carassa, Dalton Moreira Neto, Diego Armando Chávez Ramos, Joaquín Aldaír Aguirre Luza, Antonio Emiliano Gonzáles Canchari, Edwin Alexi Gómez Gutiérrez (82.Carlos Dante Olascuaga Viera; 90+2.Cris Robert Martínez Escobar), Josimar Hugo Vargas García, Christofer Gonzáles Crespo, Roberto Siucho Neyra (59.Miguel Ángel Torres Quintana), Raúl Mario Ruidíaz Misitich. Trainer: José Guillermo del Solar Alvarez-Calderón.
The Strongest: Daniel Vaca Tasca, Enrique Parada Salvatierra, Nelvin Solíz Escalante (75.José Gabriel Ríos Banegas), Marcos Israel Barrera, Jeferson Lopes Faustino, Alejandro Saúl Chumacero Bracamonte, Pablo Daniel Escobar Olivetti, Ernesto Rubén Cristaldo Santa Cruz, Diego Bejarano Ibáñez (63.Diego Armando Chávez Ramos), Raúl Castro Peñaloza, Boris Xavier Alfaro Chong (21.Jair Alexander Reinoso Moreno). Trainer: Eduardo Andrés Villegas Camara.
Goals: Raúl Mario Ruidíaz Misitich (28), Christofer Gonzáles Crespo (37), Edwin Alexi Gómez Gutiérrez (56 penalty) / Diego Armando Chávez Ramos (32 own goal), Ernesto Rubén Cristaldo Santa Cruz (65), Jair Alexander Reinoso Moreno (89).

08.04.2014, Estadio „José Amalfitani“, Buenos Aires
Referee: Carlos Ulloa (Chile)
CA Vélez Sarsfield Buenos Aires - Universitario de Deportes Lima 1-0(0-0)
Vélez Sarsfield: Carlos Sebastián Sosa Silva, Sebastián Enrique Domínguez, Juan Alberto Sabiá (79.Eros Medaglia), Facundo Cardozo, Alejandro Ariel Cabral, Fabián Andrés Cubero, Jorge Iván Correa (65.Agustín Leonel Allione), Leandro Luis Desábato, Brian Federico Ferreira (71.Lucas David Pratto), Roberto Antonio Nanni, Ramiro Julián Cáseres. Trainer: José Oscar Flores.
Universitario: José Aurelio Carvallo Alonso, Néstor Alonso Duarte Carassa, Werner Luis Schuler Gamarra, Diego Armando Chávez Ramos, Miguel Ángel Torres Quintana (72.Joaquín Aldaír Aguirre Luza), Antonio Emiliano Gonzáles Canchari, Ángel Elías Romero Iparraguirre (72.Roberto Siucho Neyra), Edwin Alexi Gómez Gutiérrez, Josimar Hugo Vargas García, Christofer Gonzáles Crespo, Raúl Mario Ruidíaz Misitich. Trainer: José Guillermo del Solar Alvarez-Calderón.
Goal: Roberto Antonio Nanni (51).

08.04.2014, Estadio „Hernando Siles“, La Paz
Referee: Roddy Alberto Zambrano Olmedo (Ecuador)
Club The Strongest La Paz - Clube Atlético Paranaense Curitiba 2-1(1-1)
The Strongest: Daniel Vaca Tasca, Enrique Parada Salvatierra, Nelvin Solíz Escalante (70.Ernesto Rubén Cristaldo Santa Cruz; 88.José Gabriel Ríos Banegas), Jeferson Lopes Faustino, Alejandro Saúl Chumacero Bracamonte, Pablo Daniel Escobar Olivetti, Diego Bejarano Ibáñez, Diego Horacio Wayar Cruz, Raúl Castro Peñaloza, Jair Alexander Reinoso Moreno (90+1.Walter Veizaga Argote), Daniel Andrés Chávez Betancourt. Trainer: Eduardo Andrés Villegas Camara.
Atlético Paranaense: Wéverton Pereira da Silva, Manoel Messias Silva Carvalho, Sueliton Pereira de Aguiar, Cleberson Martins de Souza, Paulo Henrique Dias da Cruz (85.Crislan Henrique da Silva de Souza), Claudio Matías Mirabaje Correa (67.Marcos Guilherme de Almeida Santos Matos), João Paulo da Silva, Natanael Batista Pimienta, Adriano Leite Ribeiro, Éderson Alves Ribeiro Silva (53.José Luis dos Santos Pinto "Zezinho"), Marcelo Cirino da Silva. Trainer: Miguel Portugal. Trainer: Miguel Angel Portugal Vicario (Spain).
Goals: Manoel Messias Silva Carvalho (39 own goal), Nelvin Solíz Escalante (54) / Adriano (45+2).

FINAL STANDINGS

1.	**CA Vélez Sarsfield Buenos Aires**	6	5	0	1	9 - 3	15
2.	**Club The Strongest La Paz**	6	3	1	2	8 - 7	10
3.	Clube Atlético Paranaense Curitiba	6	3	0	3	7 - 7	9
4.	Universitario de Deportes Lima	6	0	1	5	3 - 10	1

GROUP 2

11.02.2014, Estádio „Jornalista Mário Filho" [Maracanã], Rio de Janeiro; Attendance: 28,116
Referee: Roberto Carlos Silvera Calcerrada (Uruguay)
Botafogo de FR Rio de Janeiro - CA San Lorenzo de Almagro 2-0(1-0)
Botafogo: Jefferson de Oliveira Galvão, Fabian Guedes „Bolívar", Júlio César Coelho de Moraes Junior, Edílson Mendes Guimarães, Matheus Dória Macedo, Jorge Wagner Goés Conceição, Marcelo de Mattos Terra, Marcelo Nicolás Lodeiro Benítez (90+1.Júnior César Eduardo Machado), Gabriel Girotto Franco, Juan Carlos Ferreyra (70.Henrique Almeida Caixeta Nascentes), Wallyson Ricardo Maciel Monteiro (87.Mario Ariel Bolatti). Trainer: Eduardo Pedro Hungaro.
San Lorenzo: Sebastián Alberto Torrico, Mauro Cetto, Santiago Juan Gentiletti Selak, Emanuel Matías Más, Ignacio Piatti (75.Héctor Villalba), Néstor Ezequiel Ortigoza, Juan Ignacio Mercier, Enzo Kalinski (64.Leandro Atilio Romagnoli), Julio Alberto Buffarini, Nicolás Blandi (64.Mauro Matos), Ángel Correa. Trainer: Edgardo Bauza.
Goals: Juan Carlos Ferreyra (29), Wallyson Ricardo Maciel Monteiro (51).

18.02.2014, Estadio Rumiñahui, Sangolquí
Referee: Raúl Orosco Delgadillo (Bolivia)
CSD Independiente Sangolquí - Club Unión Española Santiago 2-2(1-0)
Independiente: Librado Rodrigo Azcona, Christian Washington Núñez Medina, Andrés Lamas Bervejillo, Mario Alberto Pineida Martínez, Luis Fernando León Bermeo (87.Armando Julian Solís Quentero), Henry Geovanny León León (78.Julio Eduardo Angulo Medina), Fernando Alexander Guerrero Vásquez, Mario Enrique Rizotto Vázquez (78.Jefferson Gabriel Orejuela Izquierdo), Jonathan David González Valencia, Daniel Patricio Angulo Arroyo, Junior Nazareno Sornoza Moreira. Trainer: Pablo Eduardo Repetto Aquino (Uruguay).
Unión Española: Diego Ignacio Sánchez Carvajal, Sebastián Miguel Miranda Córdova, Jorge Enrique Ampuero Cabello, Matías Cristóbal Navarrete Fuentes, Mario Ignacio Larenas Díaz (33.Patricio Elías Vidal), Cristian Manuel Chávez (85.Oscar Ignacio Hernández Polanco), Luis Antonio Pavez Contreras, Matías Daniel Campos Toro, Lorenzo Abel Faravelli, Gustavo Javier Canales [*sent off 74*], Sebastián Oscar Jaime (72.Carlos Daniel Salom Zulema). Trainer: José Luis Sierra Pando.
Goals: Junior Nazareno Sornoza Moreira (30 penalty), Fernando Alexander Guerrero Vásquez (57) / Sebastián Oscar Jaime (53), Cristian Manuel Chávez (58).

26.02.2014, Estadio Santa Laura-Universidad SEK, Independencia
Referee: Juan Ernesto Soto Arevalo (Venezuela)
Club Unión Española Santiago - Botafogo de FR Rio de Janeiro 1-1(0-0)
Unión Española: Diego Ignacio Sánchez Carvajal, Sebastián Miguel Miranda Córdova, Jorge Enrique Ampuero Cabello, Nicolás Berardo, Matías Cristóbal Navarrete Fuentes, Cristian Manuel Chávez, Luis Antonio Pavez Contreras, Matías Daniel Campos Toro, Lorenzo Abel Faravelli, Carlos Daniel Salom Zulema, Sebastián Oscar Jaime. Trainer: José Luis Sierra Pando.
Botafogo: Jefferson de Oliveira Galvão, Fabian Guedes „Bolívar", Júlio César Coelho de Moraes Junior, Edílson Mendes Guimarães, Matheus Dória Macedo, Jorge Wagner Goés Conceição (79.Henrique Almeida Caixeta Nascentes), Marcelo de Mattos Terra, Marcelo Nicolás Lodeiro Benítez, Gabriel Girotto Franco (59.Mario Ariel Bolatti), Juan Carlos Ferreyra, Wallyson Ricardo Maciel Monteiro (88.Daniel Correa Freitas). Trainer: Eduardo Pedro Hungaro.
Goals: Cristian Manuel Chávez (74) / Juan Carlos Ferreyra (86).

27.02.2014, Estadio „Pedro Bidegain", Buenos Aires
Referee: Enrique Cáceres Villafante (Paraguay)
CA San Lorenzo de Almagro - CSD Independiente Sangolquí 1-0(0-0)
San Lorenzo: Sebastián Alberto Torrico, Santiago Juan Gentiletti Selak, Carlos Enrique Valdéz Parra, Emanuel Matías Más, Ignacio Piatti (83.Nicolás Blandi), Néstor Ezequiel Ortigoza, Juan Ignacio Mercier, Julio Alberto Buffarini, Mauro Matos, Héctor Villalba (67.Leandro Atilio Romagnoli), Ángel Correa (75.Leandro Alexis Navarro). Trainer: Edgardo Bauza.
Independiente: Librado Rodrigo Azcona, Christian Washington Núñez Medina, Andrés Lamas Bervejillo, Mario Alberto Pineida Martínez, Luis Fernando León Bermeo, Henry Geovanny León León (76.Jefferson Gabriel Orejuela Izquierdo), Fernando Alexander Guerrero Vásquez (37.Armando Julian Solís Quentero), Mario Enrique Rizotto Vázquez, Jonathan David González Valencia, Daniel Patricio Angulo Arroyo, Junior Nazareno Sornoza Moreira (72.Julio Eduardo Angulo Medina). Trainer: Pablo Eduardo Repetto Aquino (Uruguay).
Goal: Ángel Correa (55).

12.03.2014, Estadio „Pedro Bidegain", Buenos Aires
Referee: Darío Agustín Ubríaco Medero (Uruguay)
CA San Lorenzo de Almagro - Club Unión Española Santiago 1-1(1-0)
San Lorenzo: Sebastián Alberto Torrico, Santiago Juan Gentiletti Selak, Carlos Enrique Valdéz Parra, Emanuel Matías Más, Ignacio Piatti (65.Héctor Villalba), Néstor Ezequiel Ortigoza, Juan Ignacio Mercier, Leandro Atilio Romagnoli (77.Leandro Alexis Navarro), Julio Alberto Buffarini, Mauro Matos (70.Nicolás Blandi), Ángel Correa. Trainer: Edgardo Bauza.
Unión Española: Diego Ignacio Sánchez Carvajal, Sebastián Miguel Miranda Córdova (63.Dagoberto Alexis Currimilla Gómez), Jorge Enrique Ampuero Cabello, Nicolás Berardo, Matías Cristóbal Navarrete Fuentes, Cristian Manuel Chávez, Luis Antonio Pavez Contreras, Matías Daniel Campos Toro (76.Patricio Elías Vidal), Lorenzo Abel Faravelli, Gustavo Javier Canales, Carlos Daniel Salom Zulema (55.Sebastián Oscar Jaime). Trainer: José Luis Sierra Pando.
Goals: Mauro Matos (20) / Gustavo Javier Canales (83).

12.03.2014, Estadio Rumiñahui, Sangolquí
Referee: Manuel Alejandro Garay Evia (Peru)
CSD Independiente Sangolquí - Botafogo de FR Rio de Janeiro 2-1(1-0)
Independiente: Librado Rodrigo Azcona, Christian Washington Núñez Medina, Andrés Lamas Bervejillo, Mario Alberto Pineida Martínez (88.Armando Julian Solís Quentero), Luis Fernando León Bermeo (79.Gabriel Jhon Córtez Casierra), Henry Geovanny León León (71.Julio Eduardo Angulo Medina), Fernando Alexander Guerrero Vásquez, Mario Enrique Rizotto Vázquez, Jonathan David González Valencia, Daniel Patricio Angulo Arroyo, Junior Nazareno Sornoza Moreira. Trainer: Pablo Eduardo Repetto Aquino (Uruguay).
Botafogo: Jefferson de Oliveira Galvão, Fabian Guedes „Bolívar" [*sent off 74*], Júlio César Coelho de Moraes Junior, Edílson Mendes Guimarães [*sent off 74*], Matheus Dória Macedo, Jorge Wagner Goés Conceição, Marcelo de Mattos Terra, Marcelo Nicolás Lodeiro Benítez (90.Mario Ariel Bolatti), Gabriel Girotto Franco, Juan Carlos Ferreyra (82.Lucas Rios Marques), Wallyson Ricardo Maciel Monteiro (79.André Luiz Bahia Santos Viana). Trainer: Eduardo Pedro Hungaro.
Goals: Christian Washington Núñez Medina (26), Junior Nazareno Sornoza Moreira (90) / Fabian Guedes „Bolívar" (59).

18.03.2014, Estádio „Jornalista Mário Filho“ [Maracanã], Rio de Janeiro
Referee: Darío Agustín Ubríaco Medero (Uruguay)
Botafogo de FR Rio de Janeiro - CSD Independiente Sangolquí 1-0(1-0)
Botafogo: Jefferson de Oliveira Galvão, Lucas Rios Marques (83.Júnior César Eduardo Machado), Júlio César Coelho de Moraes Junior, Dankler Luis de Jesús Pereira, Matheus Dória Macedo, Jorge Wagner Goés Conceição, Marcelo de Mattos Terra, Marcelo Nicolás Lodeiro Benítez, Gabriel Girotto Franco (75.Mario Ariel Bolatti), Juan Carlos Ferreyra, Wallyson Ricardo Maciel Monteiro (63.Alcides de Souza Faria Júnior „Cidinho“). Trainer: Eduardo Pedro Hungaro.
Independiente: Librado Rodrigo Azcona, Christian Washington Núñez Medina, Andrés Lamas Bervejillo (89.Julio Eduardo Angulo Medina), Mario Alberto Pineida Martínez, Luis Fernando León Bermeo, Henry Geovanny León León (82.Jefferson Gabriel Orejuela Izquierdo), Fernando Alexander Guerrero Vásquez (82.Armando Julian Solís Quentero), Mario Enrique Rizotto Vázquez, Jonathan David González Valencia, Daniel Patricio Angulo Arroyo, Junior Nazareno Sornoza Moreira. Trainer: Pablo Eduardo Repetto Aquino (Uruguay).
Goal: Juan Carlos Ferreyra (2).

20.03.2014, Estadio Santa Laura-Universidad SEK, Independencia
Referee: José Hernando Buitrago Arango (Colombia)
Club Unión Española Santiago - CA San Lorenzo de Almagro 1-0(0-0)
Unión Española: Diego Ignacio Sánchez Carvajal, Jorge Enrique Ampuero Cabello, Dagoberto Alexis Currimilla Gómez, Nicolás Berardo, Matías Cristóbal Navarrete Fuentes, Cristian Manuel Chávez (90+1.Gonzalo Andrés Villagra Lira), Luis Antonio Pavez Contreras, Matías Daniel Campos Toro (68.Carlos Daniel Salom Zulema), Lorenzo Abel Faravelli, Gustavo Javier Canales, Sebastián Oscar Jaime. Trainer: José Luis Sierra Pando.
San Lorenzo: Sebastián Alberto Torrico, Mauro Cetto [*sent off 53*], Santiago Juan Gentiletti Selak, Fabricio Bautista Fontanini, Emanuel Matías Más, Néstor Ezequiel Ortigoza, Juan Ignacio Mercier, Julio Alberto Buffarini, Mauro Matos (61.Ignacio Piatti), Nicolás Blandi, Héctor Villalba (76.Leandro Atilio Romagnoli). Trainer: Edgardo Bauza.
Goal: Gustavo Javier Canales (66).

27.03.2014, Estadio Olímpico „Atahualpa“, Quito
Referee: Carlos Arecio Amarilla Demarqui (Paraguay)
CSD Independiente Sangolquí - CA San Lorenzo de Almagro 1-1(0-0)
Independiente: Librado Rodrigo Azcona, Christian Washington Núñez Medina, Andrés Lamas Bervejillo, Mario Alberto Pineida Martínez, Luis Fernando León Bermeo (81.Gabriel Jhon Córtez Casierra), Henry Geovanny León León (68.Armando Julian Solís Quentero), Fernando Alexander Guerrero Vásquez, Mario Enrique Rizotto Vázquez, Jonathan David González Valencia (75.Julio Eduardo Angulo Medina), Daniel Patricio Angulo Arroyo, Junior Nazareno Sornoza Moreira. Trainer: Pablo Eduardo Repetto Aquino (Uruguay).
San Lorenzo: Sebastián Alberto Torrico, Santiago Juan Gentiletti Selak, Fabricio Bautista Fontanini, Emanuel Matías Más, Ignacio Piatti, Juan Ignacio Mercier, Leandro Atilio Romagnoli (75.Néstor Ezequiel Ortigoza), Enzo Kalinski, Julio Alberto Buffarini, Nicolás Blandi (85.Mauro Matos), Ángel Correa (80.Juan Ignacio Cavallaro). Trainer: Edgardo Bauza.
Goals: Junior Nazareno Sornoza Moreira (90+5 penalty) / Nicolás Blandi (58).

02.04.2014, Estádio „Jornalista Mário Filho“ [Maracanã], Rio de Janeiro
Referee: Daniel Adan Fedorczuk Betancour (Uruguay)
Botafogo de FR Rio de Janeiro - Club Unión Española Santiago 0-1(0-0)
Botafogo: Jefferson de Oliveira Galvão, Fabian Guedes „Bolívar“, Lucas Rios Marques, Júlio César Coelho de Moraes Junior (90+2.Renato Dirnei Florêncio Santos), Matheus Dória Macedo, Jorge Wagner Goés Conceição, Marcelo de Mattos Terra (78.Daniel Correa Freitas), Mario Ariel Bolatti, Marcelo Nicolás Lodeiro Benítez, Wallyson Ricardo Maciel Monteiro, Henrique Almeida Caixeta Nascentes (66.Ronieri da Silva Pinto „Ronny“). Trainer: Eduardo Pedro Hungaro.
Unión Española: Diego Ignacio Sánchez Carvajal, Jorge Enrique Ampuero Cabello, Dagoberto Alexis Currimilla Gómez, Nicolás Berardo, Matías Cristóbal Navarrete Fuentes, Cristian Manuel Chávez (63.Diego Scotti Ponce De León), Luis Antonio Pavez Contreras, Matías Daniel Campos Toro, Lorenzo Abel Faravelli (82.Gonzalo Andrés Villagra Lira), Gustavo Javier Canales, Sebastián Oscar Jaime (82.Patricio Elías Vidal). Trainer: José Luis Sierra Pando.
Goal: Gustavo Javier Canales (71 penalty).

09.04.2014, Estadio „Pedro Bidegain“, Buenos Aires
Referee: Juan Ernesto Soto Arevalo (Venezuela)
CA San Lorenzo de Almagro - Botafogo de FR Rio de Janeiro 3-0(1-0)
San Lorenzo: Sebastián Alberto Torrico, Santiago Juan Gentiletti Selak, Carlos Enrique Valdéz Parra, Emanuel Matías Más (85.Leandro Alexis Navarro), Ignacio Piatti, Néstor Ezequiel Ortigoza, Juan Ignacio Mercier, Julio Alberto Buffarini, Mauro Matos, Héctor Villalba (66.Juan Ignacio Cavallaro), Ángel Correa (73.Fernando Elizari). Trainer: Edgardo Bauza.
Botafogo: Jefferson de Oliveira Galvão, Fabian Guedes „Bolívar“, Lucas Rios Marques, Júlio César Coelho de Moraes Junior, Matheus Dória Macedo, Jorge Wagner Goés Conceição, Marcelo Nicolás Lodeiro Benítez, Airton Ribeiro Santos (55.Mario Ariel Bolatti), Gabriel Girotto Franco (55.Henrique Almeida Caixeta Nascentes), Juan Carlos Ferreyra, Wallyson Ricardo Maciel Monteiro (79.Fabiano Nascimento Vieira de Menezes). Trainer: Eduardo Pedro Hungaro.
Goals: Héctor Villalba (28), Ignacio Piatti (53, 88).

09.04.2014, Estadio Santa Laura-Universidad SEK, Independencia
Referee: Julio Quintana Rodríguez (Paraguay)
Club Unión Española Santiago - CSD Independiente Sangolquí 4-5(1-1)
Unión Española: Diego Ignacio Sánchez Carvajal, Jorge Enrique Ampuero Cabello, Dagoberto Alexis Currimilla Gómez, Nicolás Berardo, Matías Cristóbal Navarrete Fuentes, Cristian Manuel Chávez (67.Gonzalo Andrés Villagra Lira), Diego Scotti Ponce De León, Matías Daniel Campos Toro (81.Carlos Daniel Salom Zulema), Lorenzo Abel Faravelli, Gustavo Javier Canales, Sebastián Oscar Jaime. Trainer: José Luis Sierra Pando.
Independiente: Librado Rodrigo Azcona, Christian Washington Núñez Medina, Andrés Lamas Bervejillo (88.Julio Eduardo Angulo Medina), Mario Alberto Pineida Martínez, Luis Fernando León Bermeo, Henry Geovanny León León (69.Gabriel Jhon Córtez Casierra), Fernando Alexander Guerrero Vásquez, Mario Enrique Rizotto Vázquez, Jonathan David González Valencia, Daniel Patricio Angulo Arroyo, Junior Nazareno Sornoza Moreira (81.Jefferson Gabriel Orejuela Izquierdo). Trainer: Pablo Eduardo Repetto Aquino (Uruguay).
Goals: Matías Daniel Campos Toro (10, 59), Luis Fernando León Bermeo (65 own goal), Gustavo Javier Canales (72 penalty) / Daniel Patricio Angulo Arroyo (11, 48, 57, 75), Junior Nazareno Sornoza Moreira (77 penalty).

FINAL STANDINGS

1.	**Club Unión Española Santiago**	6	2	3	1	10	-	9	9
2.	**CA San Lorenzo de Almagro**	6	2	2	2	6	-	5	8
3.	CSD Independiente Sangolquí	6	2	2	2	10	-	10	8
4.	Botafogo de FR Rio de Janeiro	6	2	1	3	5	-	7	7

GROUP 3

12.02.2014, Estadio „Pascual Guerrero", Cali
Referee: Paulo César de Oliveira (Brazil)
Asociación Deportivo Cali - Club Cerro Porteño Asunción 1-0(0-0)
Deportivo: Faryd Aly Camilo Mondragón, Víctor Hugo Giraldo López, Luis Miguel Payares Blanco, Fainer Torijano Cano, Jhon Eduis Viáfara Mina, Vladimir Marín Rios, Andrés Eduardo Pérez Gutiérrez, Christian Camilo Marrugo Rodríguez (59.Carlos Augusto Rivas Murillo), Carlos David Lizarazo Landázury (74.Gustavo Adolfo Bolívar Zapata), Gustavo Leonardo Cuellar Gallego, Robin Ariel Ramírez González (81.Harrison Arley Mojica Betancourt). Trainer: Leonel de Jesús Álvarez Zuleta.
Cerro Porteño: Roberto Júnior Fernández Torres, Carlos Bonet Cáceres, Luis Carlos Cardozo Espillaga, Matías Corujo Díaz, Danilo Fabián Ortíz Soto, Junior Osmar Ignacio Alonso Mujica, Julio Daniel Dos Santos Rodríguez (79.Daniel González Güiza), Fidencio Oviedo Domínguez, Óscar David Romero Villamayor (79.Rodolfo Vicente Gamarra Varela), Guillermo Alexis Beltrán Paredes, Ángel Rodrigo Romero Villamayor (88.Iván Arturo Torres Riveros). Trainer: Francisco Javier Arce Rolón.
Goal: Jhon Eduis Viáfara Mina (72).

13.02.2014, Estadio Ciudad de Lanús „Néstor Díaz Pérez", Lanús
Referee: Óscar Maldonado Urey (Bolivia)
Club Atlético Lanús - O'Higgins FC Rancagua 0-0
CA Lanús: Agustín Federico Marchesín, Paolo Duval Goltz, Maximiliano Nicolás Velázquez, Carlos Luciano Araujo, Carlos Roberto Izquierdoz, Leandro Daniel Somoza, Diego Hernán González (86.Fernando Omar Barrientos), Víctor Hugo Ayala Núñez, Óscar Junior Benítez (75.Alejandro Daniel Silva González), Lautaro Germán Acosta (46.Ismael Alfonso Blanco), Santiago Martín Silva Olivera. Trainer: Guillermo Barros Schelotto.
O'Higgins: Paulo Andrés Garcés Contreras, Albert Alejandro Acevedo Vergara, Yerson Flavio Opazo Riquelme (67.Pablo Nicolás Vargas Romero), Eduardo Alejandro López (90.Juan Manuel Cobo Gálvez), Benjamin Fernando Vidal Allendes, Luis Pedro Figueroa Sepúlveda, Braulio Antonio Leal Salvo, Pedro Pablo Hernández, Gonzalo Felipe Barriga Ahumada (77.Gastón Andrés Lezcano), César Nicolás Fuentes González, Pablo Ignacio Calandria. Trainer: Manuel Eduardo Berizzo (Argentina).

19.02.2014, Estadio Monumental „David Arellano", Santiago
Referee: Ricardo Marques Ribeiro (Brazil)
O'Higgins FC Rancagua - Asociación Deportivo Cali 1-0(0-0)
O'Higgins: Paulo Andrés Garcés Contreras, Albert Alejandro Acevedo Vergara, Yerson Flavio Opazo Riquelme, Eduardo Alejandro López, Benjamin Fernando Vidal Allendes, Luis Pedro Figueroa Sepúlveda, Braulio Antonio Leal Salvo, Pedro Pablo Hernández, Gonzalo Felipe Barriga Ahumada (80.Gastón Andrés Lezcano), César Nicolás Fuentes González, Pablo Ignacio Calandria (67.Diego Gonzalo Cháves de Miquelerena). Trainer: Manuel Eduardo Berizzo (Argentina).
Deportivo: Faryd Aly Camilo Mondragón, Mauricio Ferney Casierra, Víctor Hugo Giraldo López, Luis Miguel Payares Blanco, Fainer Torijano Cano, Jhon Eduis Viáfara Mina (76.Gustavo Adolfo Bolívar Zapata), Andrés Eduardo Pérez Gutiérrez, Christian Camilo Marrugo Rodríguez (55.Carlos David Lizarazo Landázury), Néstor Abrahan Camacho Ledesma (71.Carlos Augusto Rivas Murillo), Gustavo Leonardo Cuellar Gallego, Robin Ariel Ramírez González. Trainer: Leonel de Jesús Álvarez Zuleta.
Goal: Yerson Flavio Opazo Riquelme (83).

26.02.2014, Estadio „General Pablo Rojas“, Asunción
Referee: Héber Roberto Lopes (Brazil)
Club Cerro Porteño Asunción - Club Atlético Lanús 3-1(0-0)
Cerro Porteño: Roberto Júnior Fernández Torres, Carlos Bonet Cáceres (88.Víctor Hugo Mareco), Luis Carlos Cardozo Espillaga, Matías Corujo Díaz, Danilo Fabián Ortíz Soto, Junior Osmar Ignacio Alonso Mujica, Julio Daniel Dos Santos Rodríguez, Fidencio Oviedo Domínguez, Óscar David Romero Villamayor (90+1.Guillermo Alexis Beltrán Paredes), Daniel González Güiza (75.Rodolfo Vicente Gamarra Varela), Ángel Rodrigo Romero Villamayor [*sent off 66*]. Trainer: Francisco Javier Arce Rolón.
CA Lanús: Agustín Federico Marchesín, Paolo Duval Goltz, Maximiliano Nicolás Velázquez, Carlos Luciano Araujo, Matías Alfredo Martínez (75.Ismael Alfonso Blanco), Leandro Daniel Somoza, Jorge Alberto Ortíz, Diego Hernán González (75.Víctor Hugo Ayala Núñez), Óscar Junior Benítez, Santiago Martín Silva Olivera, Jorge Rolando Pereyra Díaz (65.Lucas Santiago Melano). Trainer: Guillermo Barros Schelotto.
Goals: Daniel González Güiza (46), Julio Daniel Dos Santos Rodríguez (50, 55 penalty) / Jorge Alberto Ortíz (59).

13.03.2014, Estadio Monumental „David Arellano“, Santiago
Referee: Martín Emilio Vázquez Broquetas (Uruguay)
O'Higgins FC Rancagua - Club Cerro Porteño Asunción 2-2(1-0)
O'Higgins: Paulo Andrés Garcés Contreras, Albert Alejandro Acevedo Vergara, Eduardo Alejandro López, Benjamin Fernando Vidal Allendes, Luis Pedro Figueroa Sepúlveda, Braulio Antonio Leal Salvo [*sent off 62*], Pedro Pablo Hernández, Gonzalo Felipe Barriga Ahumada (64.Yerson Flavio Opazo Riquelme), Pablo Nicolás Vargas Romero, César Nicolás Fuentes González, Pablo Ignacio Calandria (85.Diego Gonzalo Cháves de Miquelerena). Trainer: Manuel Eduardo Berizzo (Argentina).
Cerro Porteño: Roberto Júnior Fernández Torres, Carlos Bonet Cáceres, Luis Carlos Cardozo Espillaga, Matías Corujo Díaz, Danilo Fabián Ortíz Soto (68.Diego Armando Godoy Vásquez), Junior Osmar Ignacio Alonso Mujica, Julio Daniel Dos Santos Rodríguez, Fidencio Oviedo Domínguez, Óscar David Romero Villamayor, Guillermo Alexis Beltrán Paredes (87.Juan José Franco Arrellaga), Rodolfo Vicente Gamarra Varela (79.Epifiano Ariel García Duarte). Trainer: Francisco Javier Arce Rolón.
Goals: Eduardo Alejandro López (35), Luis Pedro Figueroa (46) / Rodolfo Vicente Gamarra Varela (54), Julio Daniel Dos Santos Rodríguez (77).

13.03.2014, Estadio „Pascual Guerrero“, Cali
Referee: Leandro Pedro Vuaden (Brazil)
Asociación Deportivo Cali - Club Atlético Lanús 2-1(0-1)
Deportivo: Faryd Aly Camilo Mondragón, Mauricio Ferney Casierra, Víctor Hugo Giraldo López, Diego Armando Amaya Solano, Luis Antonio Calderón Orozco, Jhon Eduis Viáfara Mina, Andrés Eduardo Pérez Gutiérrez, Carlos David Lizarazo Landázury (77.Luis Miguel Payares Blanco), Cristian Andrés Higuita Beltrán (58.Christian Camilo Marrugo Rodríguez), Robin Ariel Ramírez González, Sergio Esteban Romero Méndez (46.Yerson Candelo Miranda). Trainer: Héctor Fabio Cárdenas Berrío.
CA Lanús: Agustín Federico Marchesín [*sent off 90+5*], Paolo Duval Goltz, Maximiliano Nicolás Velázquez (80.Nicolás Pasquini), Carlos Luciano Araujo, Carlos Roberto Izquierdoz, Leandro Daniel Somoza, Diego Hernán González, Víctor Hugo Ayala Núñez, Óscar Junior Benítez (88.Jorge Rolando Pereyra Díaz), Lautaro Germán Acosta, Ismael Alfonso Blanco. Trainer: Guillermo Barros Schelotto.
Goals: Jhon Eduis Viáfara Mina (62), Carlos David Lizarazo Landázury (73 penalty) / Lautaro Germán Acosta (19).

20.03.2014, Estadio Ciudad de Lanús „Néstor Díaz Pérez“, Lanús
Referee: Daniel Adan Fedorczuk Betancour (Uruguay)
Club Atlético Lanús - Asociación Deportivo Cali 2-0(2-0)
CA Lanús: Esteban Maximiliano Andrada, Paolo Duval Goltz, Maximiliano Nicolás Velázquez, Carlos Luciano Araujo, Carlos Roberto Izquierdoz, Leandro Daniel Somoza, Víctor Hugo Ayala Núñez, Fernando Omar Barrientos (62.Jorge Alberto Ortíz), Lautaro Germán Acosta (66.Alejandro Daniel Silva González), Santiago Martín Silva Olivera (90.Óscar Junior Benítez), Jorge Rolando Pereyra Díaz. Trainer: Guillermo Barros Schelotto.
Deportivo: Faryd Aly Camilo Mondragón, Mauricio Ferney Casierra, Víctor Hugo Giraldo López, Diego Armando Amaya Solano, Fainer Torijano Cano, Jhon Eduis Viáfara Mina (73.Carlos David Lizarazo Landázury), Andrés Eduardo Pérez Gutiérrez, Christian Camilo Marrugo Rodríguez, Gustavo Leonardo Cuellar Gallego (78.Cristian Andrés Higuita Beltrán), Yerson Candelo Miranda (58.Carlos Augusto Rivas Murillo), Robin Ariel Ramírez González. Trainer: Héctor Fabio Cárdenas Berrío.
Goals: Jorge Rolando Pereyra Díaz (2), Maximiliano Nicolás Velázquez (4).

20.03.2014, Estadio „General Pablo Rojas“, Asunción
Referee: Víctor Hugo Carrillo Casanova (Peru)
Club Cerro Porteño Asunción - O'Higgins FC Rancagua 2-1(2-1)
Cerro Porteño: Roberto Júnior Fernández Torres, Carlos Bonet Cáceres, Luis Carlos Cardozo Espillaga, Matías Corujo Díaz, Danilo Fabián Ortíz Soto, Junior Osmar Ignacio Alonso Mujica, Julio Daniel Dos Santos Rodríguez, Fidencio Oviedo Domínguez, Óscar David Romero Villamayor (77.Diego Armando Godoy Vásquez), Daniel González Güiza (46.Rodolfo Vicente Gamarra Varela), Ángel Rodrigo Romero Villamayor (87.Guillermo Alexis Beltrán Paredes). Trainer: Francisco Javier Arce Rolón.
O'Higgins: Paulo Andrés Garcés Contreras, Mariano Esteban Uglessich, Albert Alejandro Acevedo Vergara, Yerson Flavio Opazo Riquelme (70.Juan Manuel Cobo Gálvez), Benjamin Fernando Vidal Allendes, Luis Pedro Figueroa Sepúlveda (27.Gastón Andrés Lezcano), Pedro Pablo Hernández, Gonzalo Felipe Barriga Ahumada (76.Diego Gonzalo Cháves de Miquelerena), Pablo Nicolás Vargas Romero, César Nicolás Fuentes González, Pablo Ignacio Calandria. Trainer: Manuel Eduardo Berizzo (Argentina).
Goals: Daniel González Güiza (2), Julio Daniel Dos Santos Rodríguez (7 penalty) / Pablo Ignacio Calandria (9 penalty).

26.03.2014, Estadio „Pascual Guerrero“, Cali
Referee: Roberto García Orozco (Mexico)
Asociación Deportivo Cali - O'Higgins FC Rancagua 1-1(0-0)
Deportivo: Luis Alfonso Hurtado Osorio, Mauricio Ferney Casierra (62.Vladimir Marín Rios), Víctor Hugo Giraldo López, Luis Miguel Payares Blanco, Fainer Torijano Cano, Christian Camilo Marrugo Rodríguez (59.Carlos Augusto Rivas Murillo), Carlos David Lizarazo Landázury, Gustavo Leonardo Cuellar Gallego, Yerson Candelo Miranda (75.Néstor Abrahan Camacho Ledesma), Cristian Andrés Higuita Beltrán, Robin Ariel Ramírez González. Trainer: Héctor Fabio Cárdenas Berrío.
O'Higgins: Paulo Andrés Garcés Contreras, Mariano Esteban Uglessich, Albert Alejandro Acevedo Vergara, Yerson Flavio Opazo Riquelme, Benjamin Fernando Vidal Allendes, Luis Pedro Figueroa Sepúlveda (79.Juan Eduardo Fuentes), Pedro Pablo Hernández, Gonzalo Felipe Barriga Ahumada (73.Gastón Andrés Lezcano), Pablo Nicolás Vargas Romero, César Nicolás Fuentes González, Pablo Ignacio Calandria (89.Carlos Humberto Escobar Ortíz). Trainer: Manuel Eduardo Berizzo (Argentina).
Goals: Néstor Abrahan Camacho Ledesma (90+2) / Yerson Flavio Opazo Riquelme (56).

27.03.2014, Estadio Ciudad de Lanús „Néstor Díaz Pérez“, Lanús
Referee: Roberto Carlos Silvera Calcerrada (Uruguay)
Club Atlético Lanús - Club Cerro Porteño Asunción 2-0(0-0)
CA Lanús: Esteban Maximiliano Andrada, Paolo Duval Goltz, Maximiliano Nicolás Velázquez, Carlos Luciano Araujo, Carlos Roberto Izquierdoz, Leandro Daniel Somoza, Jorge Alberto Ortíz (83.Fernando Omar Barrientos), Diego Hernán González (79.Víctor Hugo Ayala Núñez), Óscar Junior Benítez, Santiago Martín Silva Olivera, Jorge Rolando Pereyra Díaz (89.Jorge Vidal Valdéz Chamorro). Trainer: Guillermo Barros Schelotto.
Cerro Porteño: Roberto Júnior Fernández Torres, Carlos Bonet Cáceres (82.Guillermo Alexis Beltrán Paredes), Luis Carlos Cardozo Espillaga, Matías Corujo Díaz, Danilo Fabián Ortíz Soto, Junior Osmar Ignacio Alonso Mujica, Julio Daniel Dos Santos Rodríguez, Fidencio Oviedo Domínguez, Óscar David Romero Villamayor (66.Diego Armando Godoy Vásquez), Daniel González Güiza, Ángel Rodrigo Romero Villamayor (71.Rodolfo Vicente Gamarra Varela). Trainer: Francisco Javier Arce Rolón.
Goals: Carlos Luciano Araujo (71), Óscar Junior Benítez (89).

08.04.2014, Estadio „General Pablo Rojas“, Asunción
Referee: Darío Agustín Ubríaco Medero (Uruguay)
Asociación Deportivo Cali - Club Cerro Porteño Asunción 3-2(2-1)
Deportivo: Roberto Júnior Fernández Torres, Carlos Bonet Cáceres (69.César Iván Benítez León), Luis Carlos Cardozo Espillaga, Matías Corujo Díaz, Danilo Fabián Ortíz Soto, Junior Osmar Ignacio Alonso Mujica, Julio Daniel Dos Santos Rodríguez, Jonathan Santana Gehre (56.William Candia), Óscar David Romero Villamayor, Daniel González Güiza (65.Rodolfo Vicente Gamarra Varela), Ángel Rodrigo Romero Villamayor. Trainer: Francisco Javier Arce Rolón.
Cerro Porteño: Faryd Aly Camilo Mondragón, Víctor Hugo Giraldo López, Luis Miguel Payares Blanco, Fainer Torijano Cano, Jhon Eduis Viáfara Mina (58.Carlos Augusto Rivas Murillo), Vladimir Marín Rios, Andrés Eduardo Pérez Gutiérrez [*sent off 79*], Christian Camilo Marrugo Rodríguez, Néstor Abrahan Camacho Ledesma (62.Yerson Candelo Miranda), Gustavo Leonardo Cuellar Gallego (83.Cristian Andrés Higuita Beltrán), Robin Ariel Ramírez González. Trainer: Héctor Fabio Cárdenas Berrío.
Goals: Matías Corujo Díaz (37), Daniel González Güiza (44), Julio Daniel Dos Santos Rodríguez (79 penalty) / Christian Camilo Marrugo Rodríguez (11), Carlos Augusto Rivas Murillo (61).

08.04.2014, Estadio El Teniente, Rancagua
Referee: Wilton Pereira Sampaio (Brazil)
O'Higgins FC Rancagua - Club Atlético Lanús 0-0
O'Higgins: Paulo Andrés Garcés Contreras, Mariano Esteban Uglessich, Albert Alejandro Acevedo Vergara (81.Gastón Andrés Lezcano), Yerson Flavio Opazo Riquelme, Luis Pedro Figueroa Sepúlveda, Braulio Antonio Leal Salvo (89.Osmán Alexis Huerta Cabezas), Pedro Pablo Hernández [*sent off 88*], Gonzalo Felipe Barriga Ahumada (69.Diego Gonzalo Cháves de Miquelerena), Pablo Nicolás Vargas Romero, César Nicolás Fuentes González, Pablo Ignacio Calandria. Trainer: Manuel Eduardo Berizzo (Argentina).
CA Lanús: Agustín Federico Marchesín, Maximiliano Nicolás Velázquez, Carlos Luciano Araujo, Carlos Roberto Izquierdoz, Facundo Daniel Monteseirín, Leandro Daniel Somoza, Jorge Alberto Ortíz, Diego Hernán González, Víctor Hugo Ayala Núñez (90+4.Nicolás Pasquini), Óscar Junior Benítez (90+2.Ismael Alfonso Blanco), Santiago Martín Silva Olivera [*sent off 86*]. Trainer: Guillermo Barros Schelotto.

FINAL STANDINGS

1.	**Club Cerro Porteño Asunción**	6	3	1	2	10	-	9		10
2.	**Club Atlético Lanús**	6	2	2	2	6	-	5		8
3.	O'Higgins FC Rancagua	6	1	4	1	5	-	5		7
4.	Asociación Deportivo Cali	6	2	1	3	6	-	8		7

GROUP 4

11.02.2014, Estadio „Agustín Tovar", Barinas
Referee: Mauro Vigliano (Argentina)
Zamora FC - Clube Atlético Mineiro Belo Horizonte 0-1(0-0)
Zamora: Yáñez Alexis Angulo Vallejo, Hugo Emilio Soto Miranda, Carlos Javier López, Luis Carlos Ovalle Victoria, Jonathan Joan España Santiago, Ynmer Eliécer González Alseco (67.John Eduardo Murillo Romaña), Arles Eduardo Flores Crespo, Luis Humberto Vargas Archila, Pedro Antonio Ramírez Paredes (79.Pierre Alexandre Pluchino Galuppo), Juan Manuel Falcón Jiménez, Ricardo Clarke (61.Jhoan Manuel Arenas Delgado). Trainer: Noel Sanvicente Bethelmy.
Atlético Mineiro: Victor Leandro Bagy, Leonardo Fabiano Silva e Silva, Réver Humberto Alves Araújo, Marcos Luis Rocha de Aquino, Ronaldo de Assis Moreira „Ronaldinho" (89.Lucas Cândido Silva), Lucas Pierre Santos Oliveira, Josué Anunciado de Oliveira, Jesús Alberto Dátolo, Diego Tardelli Martins (90+1.Adolfo Rosinei Nascimento), João Alves de Assis Silva "Jô", Luiz Fernando Pereira da Silva "Fernandinho" (90+1.Sosthenes José Santos Salles „Neto Berola"). Trainer: Paulo Autuori de Mello.
Goal: João Alves de Assis Silva "Jô" (87).

11.02.2014, Estadio „Nemesio Camacho" [El Campín], Bogotá
Referee: Germán Raúl Delfino (Argentina)
Santa Fe CD Bogotá - Club Nacional Asunción 3-1(0-0)
Santa Fe: Camilo Andrés Vargas Gil, Sergio Andrés Otálvaro Botero, José Julián de la Cuesta Herrera (85.Fram Enrique Pacheco Cardona), Francisco Javier Meza Palma, Édison Vicente Méndez Méndez, José Yulián Anchico Patiño (82.Yerry Fernando Mina González), Omar Sebastián Pérez, Daniel Alejandro Torres Rojas, Wilder Andrés Medina Tamayo (68.Jefferson Cuero Castro), Luis Carlos Arias, Jonathan Copete Valencia. Trainer: Wilson Jaime Gutiérrez Cardona.
Nacional: Ignacio Oscar Don, José Leonardo Cáceres Ovelar, David Bernardo Mendoza Ayala, Raúl Eduardo Piris, Ramón David Coronel Gómez, Marcos Benjamín Melgarejo (73.Alejandro Nicolás Martínez Ramos), Marcos Antonio Riveros Krayacich, Derlis Ricardo Orué Acevedo (63.Hugo Américo Lusardi Morínigo), Silvio Gabriel Torales, Julián Alfonso Benítez Franco (89.Julio Eduardo Santa Cruz Cantero), Freddy José Bareiro Gamarra. Trainer: Gustavo Eliseo Morínigo Vázquez.
Goals: Édison Vicente Méndez Méndez (57), Daniel Alejandro Torres Rojas (58), Jonathan Copete Valencia (80) / Alejandro Nicolás Martínez Ramos (77 penalty).

20.02.2014, Estadio Defensores del Chaco, Asunción
Referee: Christian Fred Ferreyra Fernández (Uruguay)
Club Nacional Asunción - Zamora FC 1-0(0-0)
Nacional: Ignacio Oscar Don, José Leonardo Cáceres Ovelar, David Bernardo Mendoza Ayala, Raúl Eduardo Piris, Ramón David Coronel Gómez, Hugo Américo Lusardi Morínigo (67.Derlis Ricardo Orué Acevedo), Marcos Benjamín Melgarejo (81.Julio Eduardo Santa Cruz Cantero), Marcos Antonio Riveros Krayacich, Silvio Gabriel Torales, Julián Alfonso Benítez Franco, Freddy José Bareiro Gamarra (85.Fabián Cornelio Balbuena González). Trainer: Gustavo Eliseo Morínigo Vázquez.
Zamora: Yáñez Alexis Angulo Vallejo, Hugo Emilio Soto Miranda, Carlos Javier López, Luis Carlos Ovalle Victoria, Jonathan Joan España Santiago, Ynmer Eliécer González Alseco (75.Pierre Alexandre Pluchino Galuppo), Arles Eduardo Flores Crespo (46.Óscar Xavier Noriega Medrano; 62.Jhoan Manuel Arenas Delgado), Luis Humberto Vargas Archila, Pedro Antonio Ramírez Paredes, Juan Manuel Falcón Jiménez, Ricardo Clarke. Trainer: Noel Sanvicente Bethelmy.
Goal: Marcos Benjamín Melgarejo (9).

26.02.2014, Estádio Independência, Belo Horizonte
Referee: Daniel Adan Fedorczuk Betancour (Uruguay)
Clube Atlético Mineiro Belo Horizonte - Santa Fe CD Bogotá 2-1(0-0)
Atlético Mineiro: Victor Leandro Bagy, Leonardo Fabiano Silva e Silva, Nicolás Hernán Otamendi, Marcos Luis Rocha de Aquino, Ronaldo de Assis Moreira „Ronaldinho" (89.Leandro Donizete Gonçalves da Silva), Lucas Pierre Santos Oliveira, Josué Anunciado de Oliveira (59.Guilherme Milhomen Gusmão), Jesús Alberto Dátolo, Diego Tardelli Martins, João Alves de Assis Silva "Jô", Luiz Fernando Pereira da Silva "Fernandinho" (76.Sosthenes José Santos Salles „Neto Berola"). Trainer: Paulo Autuori de Mello.
Santa Fe: Camilo Andrés Vargas Gil, José Julián de la Cuesta Herrera, Juan Daniel Roa Reyes (90+1.Sergio Darío Herrera Month), Francisco Javier Meza Palma, Dairon Mosquera Chaverra, Édison Vicente Méndez Méndez, José Yulián Anchico Patiño, Omar Sebastián Pérez, Daniel Alejandro Torres Rojas, Wilder Andrés Medina Tamayo [*sent off 45*], Jefferson Cuero Castro (75.Luis Carlos Arias). Trainer: Wilson Jaime Gutiérrez Cardona.
Goals: João Alves de Assis Silva "Jô" (61), Sosthenes José Santos Salles „Neto Berola" (86) / Omar Sebastián Pérez (59).

12.03.2014, Estadio „Agustín Tovar", Barinas
Referee: Roddy Alberto Zambrano Olmedo (Ecuador)
Zamora FC - Santa Fe CD Bogotá 2-1(0-0)
Zamora: Yáñez Alexis Angulo Vallejo, Hugo Emilio Soto Miranda, Carlos Javier López, Luis Carlos Ovalle Victoria, Jonathan Joan España Santiago, Arles Eduardo Flores Crespo (83.Jhoan Manuel Arenas Delgado), Luis Humberto Vargas Archila, Pedro Antonio Ramírez Paredes, Juan Manuel Falcón Jiménez, John Eduardo Murillo Romaña (67.Ynmer Eliécer González Alseco), Ricardo Clarke (78.Pierre Alexandre Pluchino Galuppo). Trainer: Noel Sanvicente Bethelmy.
Santa Fe: Camilo Andrés Vargas Gil, José Julián de la Cuesta Herrera, Juan Daniel Roa Reyes, Francisco Javier Meza Palma, Édison Vicente Méndez Méndez, Omar Sebastián Pérez, Luis Manuel Seijas Gunther (63.David Arturo Ferreira Rico), Daniel Alejandro Torres Rojas, Hugo Alejandro Acosta Cáceres, Sergio Darío Herrera Month (68.Jonathan Copete Valencia), Jefferson Cuero Castro. Trainer: Wilson Jaime Gutiérrez Cardona.
Goals: Pedro Antonio Ramírez Paredes (58 penalty), Juan Manuel Falcón Jiménez (83) / Jonathan Copete Valencia (71).

12.03.2014, Estadio „Antonio Oddone Sarubbi", Ciudad del Este
Referee: Patricio Hernán Loustau (Argentina)
Club Nacional Asunción - Clube Atlético Mineiro Belo Horizonte 2-2(1-2)
Nacional: Ignacio Oscar Don, José Leonardo Cáceres Ovelar, David Bernardo Mendoza Ayala, Fabián Cornelio Balbuena González, Ramón David Coronel Gómez, Marcos Benjamín Melgarejo (76.Julio Eduardo Santa Cruz Cantero), Marcos Antonio Riveros Krayacich, Derlis Ricardo Orué Acevedo (59.Hugo Américo Lusardi Morínigo), Silvio Gabriel Torales, Julián Alfonso Benítez Franco (87.Alejandro Nicolás Martínez Ramos), Freddy José Bareiro Gamarra. Trainer: Gustavo Eliseo Morínigo Vázquez.
Atlético Mineiro: Victor Leandro Bagy, Leonardo Fabiano Silva e Silva, Nicolás Hernán Otamendi, Marcos Luis Rocha de Aquino, Ronaldo de Assis Moreira „Ronaldinho" (82.Adolfo Rosinei Nascimento), Lucas Pierre Santos Oliveira, Josué Anunciado de Oliveira (59.Leandro Donizete Gonçalves da Silva), Jesús Alberto Dátolo (70.Alex da Silva), Diego Tardelli Martins, João Alves de Assis Silva "Jô", Luiz Fernando Pereira da Silva "Fernandinho". Trainer: Paulo Autuori de Mello.
Goals: Marcos Benjamín Melgarejo (8), Silvio Gabriel Torales (86 penalty) / Josué Anunciado de Oliveira (21), João Alves de Assis Silva "Jô" (26).

18.03.2014, Estadio „Nemesio Camacho“ [El Campín], Bogotá
Referee: Óscar Maldonado Urey (Bolivia)
Santa Fe CD Bogotá - Zamora FC 2-2(1-1)
Santa Fe: Camilo Andrés Vargas Gil, Sergio Andrés Otálvaro Botero (55.José Yulián Anchico Patiño), José Julián de la Cuesta Herrera, Francisco Javier Meza Palma, Héctor Antonio Urrego Hurtado, Édison Vicente Méndez Méndez, Omar Sebastián Pérez, Daniel Alejandro Torres Rojas, Luis Carlos Arias, Jonathan Copete Valencia (60.Jefferson Cuero Castro), Darío Andrés Rodríguez Parra (46.Silvio Augusto González). Trainer: Wilson Jaime Gutiérrez Cardona.
Zamora: Yáñez Alexis Angulo Vallejo, Hugo Emilio Soto Miranda, Layneker Evelio Zafra Martínez, Carlos Javier López, Jonathan Joan España Santiago, Ynmer Eliécer González Alseco, Arles Eduardo Flores Crespo, Luis Humberto Vargas Archila, Pedro Antonio Ramírez Paredes (79.Víctor Alfonso Pérez Zabala), Juan Manuel Falcón Jiménez (85.Pierre Alexandre Pluchino Galuppo), Ricardo Clarke (67.Jhoan Manuel Arenas Delgado). Trainer: Noel Sanvicente Bethelmy.
Goals: Omar Sebastián Pérez (25, 87) / Juan Manuel Falcón Jiménez (45+2, 72).

19.03.2014, Estádio Independência, Belo Horizonte
Referee: Omar Andres Ponce Manzo (Ecuador)
Clube Atlético Mineiro Belo Horizonte - Club Nacional Asunción 1-1(1-1)
Atlético Mineiro: Victor Leandro Bagy, Leonardo Fabiano Silva e Silva, Nicolás Hernán Otamendi, Marcos Luis Rocha de Aquino, Ronaldo de Assis Moreira „Ronaldinho“, Lucas Pierre Santos Oliveira (84.Guilherme Milhomen Gusmão), Josué Anunciado de Oliveira (67.Leandro Donizete Gonçalves da Silva), Jesús Alberto Dátolo, Diego Tardelli Martins, João Alves de Assis Silva "Jô", Luiz Fernando Pereira da Silva "Fernandinho" (38.Sosthenes José Santos Salles „Neto Berola“). Trainer: Paulo Autuori de Mello.
Nacional: Ignacio Oscar Don, José Leonardo Cáceres Ovelar, David Bernardo Mendoza Ayala, Fabián Cornelio Balbuena González, Ramón David Coronel Gómez, Marcos Benjamín Melgarejo (83.Alejandro Nicolás Martínez Ramos), Marcos Antonio Riveros Krayacich, Derlis Ricardo Orué Acevedo, Silvio Gabriel Torales, Julián Alfonso Benítez Franco (65.Raúl Eduardo Piris), Freddy José Bareiro Gamarra (54.Julio Eduardo Santa Cruz Cantero). Trainer: Gustavo Eliseo Morínigo Vázquez.
Goals: Ronaldo de Assis Moreira „Ronaldinho“ (19 penalty) / Marcos Antonio Riveros Krayacich (36).

25.03.2014, Estadio „Agustín Tovar“, Barinas
Referee: Diego Hernán Abal (Argentina)
Zamora FC - Club Nacional Asunción 2-0(0-0)
Zamora: Yáñez Alexis Angulo Vallejo, Hugo Emilio Soto Miranda, Carlos Javier López, Luis Carlos Ovalle Victoria, Jonathan Joan España Santiago, Ynmer Eliécer González Alseco (81.Layneker Evelio Zafra Martínez), Arles Eduardo Flores Crespo, Luis Humberto Vargas Archila, Pedro Antonio Ramírez Paredes (90+3.Jhoan Manuel Arenas Delgado), Juan Manuel Falcón Jiménez, Ricardo Clarke (52.John Eduardo Murillo Romaña). Trainer: Noel Sanvicente Bethelmy.
Nacional: Ignacio Oscar Don, José Leonardo Cáceres Ovelar, David Bernardo Mendoza Ayala, Fabián Cornelio Balbuena González, Ramón David Coronel Gómez, Marcos Benjamín Melgarejo, Marcos Antonio Riveros Krayacich, Derlis Ricardo Orué Acevedo (66.Alejandro Nicolás Martínez Ramos), Silvio Gabriel Torales, Juan David Argüello Arias (28.Julio Eduardo Santa Cruz Cantero), Julián Alfonso Benítez Franco (80.Hugo Américo Lusardi Morínigo). Trainer: Gustavo Eliseo Morínigo Vázquez.
Goals: Juan Manuel Falcón Jiménez (57), John Eduardo Murillo Romaña (64).

03.04.2014, Estadio „Nemesio Camacho“ [El Campín], Bogotá
Referee: Saúl Laverni (Argentina)
Santa Fe CD Bogotá - Clube Atlético Mineiro Belo Horizonte 1-1(0-1)
Santa Fe: Camilo Andrés Vargas Gil, José Julián de la Cuesta Herrera, Francisco Javier Meza Palma, Dairon Mosquera Chaverra, Édison Vicente Méndez Méndez (88.Fram Enrique Pacheco Cardona), David Arturo Ferreira Rico (46.Luis Carlos Arias), José Yulián Anchico Patiño, Daniel Alejandro Torres Rojas, Sergio Darío Herrera Month (46.Wilder Andrés Medina Tamayo), Jonathan Copete Valencia, Jefferson Cuero Castro. Trainer: Wilson Jaime Gutiérrez Cardona.
Atlético Mineiro: Victor Leandro Bagy, Leonardo Fabiano Silva e Silva, Nicolás Hernán Otamendi, Marcos Luis Rocha de Aquino, Ronaldo de Assis Moreira „Ronaldinho“, Lucas Pierre Santos Oliveira, Jesús Alberto Dátolo, Leandro Donizete Gonçalves da Silva (83.Marion Silva Fernandes), Diego Tardelli Martins (60.Alex da Silva), João Alves de Assis Silva "Jô", Guilherme Milhomen Gusmão (75.Sosthenes José Santos Salles „Neto Berola“). Trainer: Paulo Autuori de Mello.
Goals: Jefferson Cuero Castro (63) / Guilherme Milhomen Gusmão (7).

10.04.2014, Estadio Defensores del Chaco, Asunción
Referee: Martín Emilio Vázquez Broquetas (Uruguay)
Club Nacional Asunción - Santa Fe CD Bogotá 3-2(1-1)
Nacional: Ignacio Oscar Don, José Leonardo Cáceres Ovelar, David Bernardo Mendoza Ayala, Raúl Eduardo Piris, Ramón David Coronel Gómez, Hugo Américo Lusardi Morínigo (54.Fabián Cornelio Balbuena González), Marcos Antonio Riveros Krayacich, Derlis Ricardo Orué Acevedo, Silvio Gabriel Torales, Julián Alfonso Benítez Franco (75.Juan David Argüello Arias), Freddy José Bareiro Gamarra (72.Julio Eduardo Santa Cruz Cantero). Trainer: Gustavo Eliseo Morínigo Vázquez.
Santa Fe: Camilo Andrés Vargas Gil, José Julián de la Cuesta Herrera, Rafael Enrique Pérez Almeida, Juan Daniel Roa Reyes, Dairon Mosquera Chaverra, Édison Vicente Méndez Méndez (46.Jefferson Cuero Castro), José Yulián Anchico Patiño (74.Omar Sebastián Pérez), Luis Manuel Seijas Gunther (61.Luis Carlos Arias), Daniel Alejandro Torres Rojas, Wilder Andrés Medina Tamayo, Jonathan Copete Valencia. Trainer: Wilson Jaime Gutiérrez Cardona.
Goals: Julián Alfonso Benítez Franco (38), Freddy José Bareiro Gamarra (47), Silvio Gabriel Torales (83) / Wilder Andrés Medina Tamayo (30, 81 penalty).

10.04.2014, Estádio Independência, Belo Horizonte
Referee: Roberto Tobar Vargas (Chile)
Clube Atlético Mineiro Belo Horizonte - Zamora FC 1-0(1-0)
Atlético Mineiro: Giovanni Aparecido Adriano dos Santos, Leonardo Fabiano Silva e Silva, Nicolás Hernán Otamendi, Marcos Luis Rocha de Aquino (46.Claudinei Junio de Souza), Alex da Silva, Lucas Pierre Santos Oliveira, Leandro Donizete Gonçalves da Silva, Diego Tardelli Martins (67.Marion Silva Fernandes), João Alves de Assis Silva "Jô", Guilherme Milhomen Gusmão, Sosthenes José Santos Salles „Neto Berola“ (55.Luiz Fernando Pereira da Silva "Fernandinho"). Trainer: Paulo Autuori de Mello.
Zamora: Yáñez Alexis Angulo Vallejo, Hugo Emilio Soto Miranda (63.Layneker Evelio Zafra Martínez), Carlos Javier López, Luis Carlos Ovalle Victoria, Jonathan Joan España Santiago [*sent off 73*], Arles Eduardo Flores Crespo (73.Jhoan Manuel Arenas Delgado), Pedro Antonio Ramírez Paredes, Luis Carlos Melo Salcedo, Juan Manuel Falcón Jiménez, John Eduardo Murillo Romaña (46.Pierre Alexandre Pluchino Galuppo), Ricardo Clarke. Trainer: Noel Sanvicente Bethelmy.
Goal: João Alves de Assis Silva "Jô" (9).

FINAL STANDINGS

1.	**Clube Atlético Mineiro Belo Horizonte**	6	3	3	0	8	-	5	12
2.	**Club Nacional Asunción**	6	2	2	2	8	-	10	8
3.	Zamora FC	6	2	1	3	6	-	6	7
4.	Santa Fe CD Bogotá	6	1	2	3	10	-	11	5

GROUP 5

12.02.2014, Estadio Huancayo, Huancayo
Referee: José Ramón Argote Vega (Venezuela)
Asociación Civil Real Atlético Garcilaso - Cruzeiro EC Belo Horizonte 2-1(0-1)
Real Atlético: Juan Miguel Pretel Sánchez, Jhoel Alexander Herrera Zegarra, Cristian Antonio García González (41.Ezequiel David Brítez), Jaime Rodolfo Huerta Boggiano, Gonzalo Matías Maulella Rodríguez, César Andrés Ortíz Castillo, Edwin Retamoso Palomino, Carlos Javier Flores Córdova, Víctor Ramón Ferreira Barrios, Ramón Rodríguez del Solar, Alfredo Sebastián Ramúa (86.Hugo Alexis Ademir Ángeles Chávez). Trainer: Fredy Manuel García Loayza.
Cruzeiro: Fábio Deivson Lopes Maciel, Egidio de Araujo Pereira Júnior, Marcos Venâncio de Albuquerque „Ceará", Bruno Rodrigo Fenelon Palomo, Anderson Vital da Silva „Dedé", Éverton de Barros Ribeiro, Elierce Barbosa de Souza, Lucas Silva Borges, Marcelo Moreno Martins (70.Júlio César Baptista), Dagoberto Pelentier (66.Willian Gomes de Siqueira), Ricardo Goulart Pereira (66.Paulo César Fonseca do Nascimento „Tinga"). Trainer: Marcelo de Oliveira Santos.
Goals: Ezequiel David Brítez (52), Ramón Rodríguez del Solar (62) / Bruno Rodrigo Fenelon Palomo (20).

13.02.2014, Estadio Nacional „Julio Martínez Prádanos", Santiago
Referee: Enrique Cáceres Villafante (Paraguay)
Club Universidad de Chile Santiago - Defensor Sporting Montevideo 1-0(0-0)
Universidad: Jhonny Cristián Herrera Muñoz, Matías Nicolás Caruzzo, Osvaldo Alexis González Sepúlveda, José Manuel Rojas Bahamondes, Roberto Andrés Cereceda Guajardo (63.César Alexis Cortés Pinto), Gustavo Rubén Lorenzetti Espinosa, Juan Rodrigo Rojas Ovelar, Ramón Ignacio Fernández, Rodrigo Nicanor Mora Núñez (72.Isaac Alejandro Díaz Lobos), Patricio Rodolfo Rubio Pulgar, Francisco Fernando Castro Gamboa (82.Rubén Ignacio Farfan Arancibia). Trainer: Cristián Andrés Romero Godoy.
Defensor: Martín Nicolás Campaña Delgado, Pablo César Pintos Cabral (46.Ramón Ginés Arias Quinteros), Roberto Fabián Herrera Rosas, Nicolás Correa Risso, Matías Daniel Malvino Gómez, Andrés Nicolás Olivera, Andrés José Fleurquin Rubio, Leonardo Javier Pais Corbo, Federico Gino Acevedo Fagundez (70.Mathías Adolfo Cardaccio Alaguich), Mario Ignacio Regueiro Pintos (80.Giorgian Daniel de Arrascaeta Benedetti), Matías Damián Alonso Vallejo. Trainer: Fernando Darío Curutchet Godoy.
Goal: Gustavo Rubén Lorenzetti Espinosa (82).

19.02.2014, Estadio „Luis Franzini", Montevideo
Referee: Roddy Alberto Zambrano Olmedo (Ecuador)
Defensor Sporting Montevideo - Asociación Civil Real Atlético Garcilaso 4-1(1-1)
Defensor: Martín Nicolás Campaña Delgado, Roberto Fabián Herrera Rosas, Nicolás Correa Risso, Matías Daniel Malvino Gómez, Emilio Enrique Zeballos Gutiérrez, Andrés Nicolás Olivera, Mathías Adolfo Cardaccio Alaguich (72.Juan Carlos Amado Alanís), Andrés José Fleurquin Rubio, Felipe Gedoz da Conceição (88.Matías Damián Alonso Vallejo), Giorgian Daniel de Arrascaeta Benedetti, Ignacio Risso Thomasset (85.Adrián Nicolás Luna Retamar). Trainer: Fernando Darío Curutchet Godoy.
Real Atlético: Juan Miguel Pretel Sánchez, Jhoel Alexander Herrera Zegarra, Jaime Rodolfo Huerta Boggiano, Ezequiel David Brítez, Gonzalo Matías Maulella Rodríguez, César Andrés Ortíz Castillo, Edwin Retamoso Palomino, Carlos Javier Flores Córdova (71.Anderson Denyro Cueto Sánchez), Víctor Ramón Ferreira Barrios, Ramón Rodríguez del Solar (77.Digno Javier González Sosa), Alfredo Sebastián Ramúa [*sent off 65*]. Trainer: Fredy Manuel García Loayza.
Goals: Nicolás Correa Risso (35), Felipe Gedoz da Conceição (46), Andrés Nicolás Olivera (69, 86) / Alfredo Sebastián Ramúa (20).

25.02.2014, Estádio Mineirão, Belo Horizonte
Referee: Saúl Laverni (Argentina)
Cruzeiro EC Belo Horizonte - Club Universidad de Chile Santiago 5-1(3-0)
Cruzeiro: Fábio Deivson Lopes Maciel, Egidio de Araujo Pereira Júnior, Marcos Venâncio de Albuquerque „Ceará", Bruno Rodrigo Fenelon Palomo, Anderson Vital da Silva „Dedé", Éverton de Barros Ribeiro (78.Elierce Barbosa de Souza), Rodrigo de Souza Fonseca, Lucas Silva Borges, Marcelo Moreno Martins (64.Willian Gomes de Siqueira), Dagoberto Pelentier (75.Johnath Marlone Azevedo da Silva), Ricardo Goulart Pereira. Trainer: Marcelo de Oliveira Santos.
Universidad: Jhonny Cristián Herrera Muñoz, Matías Nicolás Caruzzo, Osvaldo Alexis González Sepúlveda, José Manuel Rojas Bahamondes (36.Igor Lichnovsky Osorio), Roberto Andrés Cereceda Guajardo, Gustavo Rubén Lorenzetti Espinosa, Juan Rodrigo Rojas Ovelar, Sebastián Martínez Muñoz, Enzo Hernán Gutiérrez Lencinas (70.Rodrigo Nicanor Mora Núñez), Patricio Rodolfo Rubio Pulgar (54.Ramón Ignacio Fernández), Francisco Fernando Castro Gamboa. Trainer: Cristián Andrés Romero Godoy.
Goals: Ricardo Goulart Pereira (33), Dagoberto Pelentier (38), Ricardo Goulart Pereira (42, 84), Willian Gomes de Siqueira (89) / Gustavo Rubén Lorenzetti Espinosa (65).

11.03.2014, Estadio „Luis Franzini", Montevideo
Referee: Diego Hernán Abal (Argentina)
Defensor Sporting Club Montevideo - Cruzeiro EC Belo Horizonte 2-0(0-0)
Defensor: Martín Nicolás Campaña Delgado, Roberto Fabián Herrera Rosas, Ramón Ginés Arias Quinteros [*sent off 68*], Matías Daniel Malvino Gómez, Emilio Enrique Zeballos Gutiérrez, Andrés Nicolás Olivera (70.Nicolás Correa Risso), Mathías Adolfo Cardaccio Alaguich, Andrés José Fleurquin Rubio, Felipe Gedoz da Conceição (82.Leonardo Javier Pais Corbo), Giorgian Daniel de Arrascaeta Benedetti, Ignacio Risso Thomasset (61.Matías Damián Alonso Vallejo). Trainer: Fernando Darío Curutchet Godoy.
Cruzeiro: Fábio Deivson Lopes Maciel, Egidio de Araujo Pereira Júnior, Marcos Venâncio de Albuquerque „Ceará", Bruno Rodrigo Fenelon Palomo, Anderson Vital da Silva „Dedé", Éverton de Barros Ribeiro (79.Paulo César Fonseca do Nascimento „Tinga"), Nílton Ferreira Júnior, Rodrigo de Souza Fonseca (74.Johnath Marlone Azevedo da Silva), Marcelo Moreno Martins (58.Willian Gomes de Siqueira), Dagoberto Pelentier, Ricardo Goulart Pereira. Trainer: Marcelo de Oliveira Santos.
Goals: Felipe Gedoz da Conceição (63, 77).

11.03.2014, Estadio Huancayo, Huancayo
Referee: Wilmar Alexander Roldán Pérez (Colombia)
Asociación Civil Real Atlético Garcilaso - Universidad de Chile Santiago 1-2(1-1)
Real Atlético: Diego Martín Carranza Fernández, Jhoel Alexander Herrera Zegarra, Jaime Rodolfo Huerta Boggiano (55.Anderson Denyro Cueto Sánchez), Ezequiel David Brítez, Gonzalo Matías Maulella Rodríguez, Iván Diego Santillán Atoche, César Andrés Ortíz Castillo, Edwin Retamoso Palomino, Carlos Javier Flores Córdova (80.Digno Javier González Sosa), Víctor Ramón Ferreira Barrios [*sent off 90+2*], Ramón Rodríguez del Solar. Trainer: Fredy Manuel García Loayza.
Universidad: Luis Antonio Marín Barahona, Matías Nicolás Caruzzo, Osvaldo Alexis González Sepúlveda, José Manuel Rojas Bahamondes, Roberto Andrés Cereceda Guajardo (86.Igor Lichnovsky Osorio [*sent off 90+2*]), Gustavo Rubén Lorenzetti Espinosa, Juan Rodrigo Rojas Ovelar, Ramón Ignacio Fernández, Sebastián Martínez Muñoz, Enzo Hernán Gutiérrez Lencinas (78.Patricio Rodolfo Rubio Pulgar), Rodrigo Nicanor Mora Núñez (64.Isaac Alejandro Díaz Lobos). Trainer: Cristián Andrés Romero Godoy.
Goals: Víctor Ramón Ferreira Barrios (36) / Ramón Ignacio Fernández (39), Enzo Hernán Gutiérrez Lencinas (76).

18.03.2014, Estadio Santa Laura-Universidad SEK, Independencia
Referee: Antonio Javier Arias Alvarenga (Paraguay)
Universidad de Chile Santiago - Asociación Civil Real Atlético Garcilaso 1-0(0-0)
Universidad: Jhonny Cristián Herrera Muñoz, Matías Nicolás Caruzzo, Osvaldo Alexis González Sepúlveda, José Manuel Rojas Bahamondes, Roberto Andrés Cereceda Guajardo, Gustavo Rubén Lorenzetti Espinosa, Juan Rodrigo Rojas Ovelar, Ramón Ignacio Fernández (83.Fabián Alejandro Carmona Fredes), Sebastián Martínez Muñoz (46.Francisco Fernando Castro Gamboa), Enzo Hernán Gutiérrez Lencinas (63.Isaac Alejandro Díaz Lobos), Rodrigo Nicanor Mora Núñez. Trainer: Cristián Andrés Romero Godoy.
Real Atlético: Diego Martín Carranza Fernández, Jhoel Alexander Herrera Zegarra, Cristian Antonio García González (85.Anderson Denyro Cueto Sánchez), Ezequiel David Brítez, Gonzalo Matías Maulella Rodríguez, Iván Diego Santillán Atoche, César Andrés Ortíz Castillo, Edwin Retamoso Palomino, Carlos Javier Flores Córdova, Ramón Rodríguez del Solar (37.Jahirsino Julio Baylón Iglesias), Alfredo Sebastián Ramúa. Trainer: Fredy Manuel García Loayza.
Goal: Jhonny Cristián Herrera Muñoz (61 penalty).

20.03.2014, Estádio Mineirão, Belo Horizonte
Referee: Mauro Vigliano (Argentina)
Cruzeiro EC Belo Horizonte - Defensor Sporting Club Montevideo 2-2(1-0)
Cruzeiro: Fábio Deivson Lopes Maciel, Egidio de Araujo Pereira Júnior, Marcos Venâncio de Albuquerque „Ceará", Bruno Rodrigo Fenelon Palomo, Anderson Vital da Silva „Dedé", Éverton de Barros Ribeiro (69.Willian Gomes de Siqueira), Nílton Ferreira Júnior [*sent off 45+2*], Lucas Silva Borges, Júlio César Baptista, Dagoberto Pelentier (46.Rodrigo de Souza Fonseca), Ricardo Goulart Pereira (90+1.José Élber Pimentel da Silva). Trainer: Marcelo de Oliveira Santos.
Defensor: Martín Nicolás Campaña Delgado, Roberto Fabián Herrera Rosas, Nicolás Correa Risso, Matías Daniel Malvino Gómez [*sent off 45+2*], Emilio Enrique Zeballos Gutiérrez, Mathías Adolfo Cardaccio Alaguich, Andrés José Fleurquin Rubio (83.Juan Carlos Amado Alanís), Felipe Gedoz da Conceição (76.Adrián Nicolás Luna Retamar), Giorgian Daniel de Arrascaeta Benedetti, Federico Gino Acevedo Fagundez, Matías Damián Alonso Vallejo (46.Gastón Alexis Silva Perdomo). Trainer: Fernando Darío Curutchet Godoy.
Goals: Éverton de Barros Ribeiro (45+4), Júlio César Baptista (62) / Felipe Gedoz da Conceição (65), Emilio Enrique Zeballos Gutiérrez (90+3).

01.04.2014, Estadio Huancayo, Huancayo
Referee: Julio Quintana Rodríguez (Paraguay)
Asociación Civil Real Atlético Garcilaso - Defensor Sporting Montevideo 0-2(0-0)
Real Atlético: Diego Martín Carranza Fernández, Jhoel Alexander Herrera Zegarra, Cristian Antonio García González (61.Cristian Sergio Vildoso Valverde), Jaime Rodolfo Huerta Boggiano (71.Anderson Denyro Cueto Sánchez), Ezequiel David Brítez, Gonzalo Matías Maulella Rodríguez, Iván Diego Santillán Atoche, César Andrés Ortíz Castillo, Ramón Rodríguez del Solar, Jahirsino Julio Baylón Iglesias (81.Digno Javier González Sosa), Alfredo Sebastián Ramúa. Trainer: Fredy Manuel García Loayza.
Defensor: Martín Nicolás Campaña Delgado, Pablo César Pintos Cabral, Roberto Fabián Herrera Rosas (72.Ramón Ginés Arias Quinteros), Nicolás Correa Risso, Gastón Alexis Silva Perdomo, Andrés José Fleurquin Rubio, Juan Carlos Amado Alanís, Felipe Gedoz da Conceição (87.Lucas Elías Morales Villalba), Giorgian Daniel de Arrascaeta Benedetti, Federico Gino Acevedo Fagundez, Matías Damián Alonso Vallejo (69.José Enrique Etcheverry Mendoza). Trainer: Fernando Darío Curutchet Godoy.
Goals: Juan Carlos Amado Alanís (50), Giorgian Daniel de Arrascaeta Benedetti (53).

03.04.2014, Estadio Nacional „Julio Martínez Prádanos", Santiago
Referee: Germán Raúl Delfino (Argentina)
Club Universidad de Chile Santiago - Cruzeiro EC Belo Horizonte 0-2(0-2)
Universidad: Jhonny Cristián Herrera Muñoz, Matías Nicolás Caruzzo [*sent off 84*], Osvaldo Alexis González Sepúlveda, José Manuel Rojas Bahamondes, Roberto Andrés Cereceda Guajardo, Gustavo Rubén Lorenzetti Espinosa, Juan Rodrigo Rojas Ovelar, Ramón Ignacio Fernández, Sebastián Martínez Muñoz (46.Francisco Fernando Castro Gamboa), Rodrigo Nicanor Mora Núñez (66.Rubén Ignacio Farfan Arancibia), Patricio Rodolfo Rubio Pulgar. Trainer: Cristián Andrés Romero Godoy.
Cruzeiro: Fábio Deivson Lopes Maciel, Marcos Venâncio de Albuquerque „Ceará", Miguel Ángel Samudio [*sent off 87*], Bruno Rodrigo Fenelon Palomo, Anderson Vital da Silva „Dedé", Éverton de Barros Ribeiro (81.Luan Michel de Louzã), Henrique Pacheco de Lima, Lucas Silva Borges, Júlio César Baptista, Dagoberto Pelentier (70.Willian Gomes de Siqueira), Ricardo Goulart Pereira (61.Elierce Barbosa de Souza). Trainer: Marcelo de Oliveira Santos.
Goals: Bruno Rodrigo Fenelon Palomo (16), Miguel Ángel Samudio (39).

09.04.2014, Estádio Mineirão, Belo Horizonte
Referee: Adrián Alexander Vélez Londoño (Colombia)
Cruzeiro EC Belo Horizonte - Asociación Civil Real Atlético Garcilaso 3-0(3-0)
Cruzeiro: Fábio Deivson Lopes Maciel, Egidio de Araujo Pereira Júnior, Bruno Rodrigo Fenelon Palomo, Anderson Vital da Silva „Dedé", Mayke Rocha de Oliveira, Éverton de Barros Ribeiro (86.Alisson Euler de Freitas Castro), Henrique Pacheco de Lima, Lucas Silva Borges, Júlio César Baptista, Dagoberto Pelentier (79.Humberlito Borges Teixeira), Ricardo Goulart Pereira (72.José Élber Pimentel da Silva). Trainer: Marcelo de Oliveira Santos.
Real Atlético: Juan Miguel Pretel Sánchez, Jhoel Alexander Herrera Zegarra, Cristian Antonio García González (37.Carlos Javier Flores Córdova), Jaime Rodolfo Huerta Boggiano (46.Juan Diego Lojas Solano), Ezequiel David Brítez, Gonzalo Matías Maulella Rodríguez, Iván Diego Santillán Atoche, César Andrés Ortíz Castillo, Edwin Retamoso Palomino, Ramón Rodríguez del Solar, Alfredo Sebastián Ramúa (80.Digno Javier González Sosa). Trainer: Fredy Manuel García Loayza.
Goals: Ricardo Goulart Pereira (23), Bruno Rodrigo Fenelon Palomo (26), Júlio César Baptista (41).

09.04.2014, Estadio „Luis Franzini", Montevideo
Referee: Patricio Hernán Loustau (Argentina)
Defensor Sporting Montevideo - Club Universidad de Chile Santiago 1-1(0-1)
Defensor: Martín Nicolás Campaña Delgado, Roberto Fabián Herrera Rosas, Nicolás Correa Risso, Matías Daniel Malvino Gómez, Emilio Enrique Zeballos Gutiérrez, Andrés José Fleurquin Rubio, Leonardo Javier Pais Corbo (54.Andrés Nicolás Olivera), Felipe Gedoz da Conceição (67.Juan Carlos Amado Alanís), Giorgian Daniel de Arrascaeta Benedetti, Federico Gino Acevedo Fagundez, Ignacio Risso Thomasset (54.Matías Damián Alonso Vallejo). Trainer: Fernando Darío Curutchet Godoy.
Universidad: Jhonny Cristián Herrera Muñoz, Osvaldo Alexis González Sepúlveda, Roberto Andrés Cereceda Guajardo, Igor Lichnovsky Osorio, Gustavo Rubén Lorenzetti Espinosa, Ramón Ignacio Fernández, Bryan Alfonso Cortés Carvajal, Sebastián Martínez Muñoz, Patricio Rodolfo Rubio Pulgar (90.Luciano Civelli [*sent off 90+3*]), Isaac Alejandro Díaz Lobos (74.Rodrigo Nicanor Mora Núñez), Francisco Fernando Castro Gamboa (67.Sebastián Andrés Ubilla Cambón). Trainer: Cristián Andrés Romero Godoy.
Goals: Matías Damián Alonso Vallejo (56) / Ramón Ignacio Fernández (38).

FINAL STANDINGS

1.	**Defensor Sporting Club Montevideo**	6	3	2	1	11	-	5	11
2.	**Cruzeiro EC Belo Horizonte**	6	3	1	2	13	-	7	10
3.	Club Universidad de Chile Santiago	6	3	1	2	6	-	9	10
4.	Asociación Civil Real Atlético Garcilaso	6	1	0	5	4	-	13	3

GROUP 6

13.02.2014, Estadio Gran Parque Central, Montevideo
Referee: Antonio Javier Arias Alvarenga (Paraguay)
Club Nacional de Football Montevideo - Grêmio Foot-Ball P. Alegrense 0-1(0-0)
Nacional: Gustavo Adolfo Munúa Vera, Andrés Scotti Ponce de León, Pablo Álvarez Menéndez, Juan Manuel Díaz Martínez, Jorge Winston Curbelo Garis, Paulo Rinaldo Cruzado Durand (81.Víctor Hugo Dorrego Coito), Maximiliano Matías Calzada Fuentes, Nicolás Santiago Prieto Larrea, Carlos María de Pena Bonino (74.Álvaro Alexander Recoba Rivero), Gastón Rodrigo Pereiro López (73.Juan Cruz Mascia Paysée), Iván Daniel Alonso Vallejo. Trainer: Gerardo Cono Pelusso Boyrie.
Grêmio: Marcelo Grohe, Luiz Rhodolfo Dini Gaioto, Marcos Rogério Ricci Lopes „Pará", Werley Ananias da Silva, Wendell Nascimento Borges, Cristian Miguel Riveros Núñez, José Roberto da Silva Júnior „Zé Roberto" (90+4.Maximiliano Rodríguez Maeso), Edimo Ferreira Campos „Edinho", Ramiro Moschen Benetti (86.Leonardo David de Moura „Léo Gago"), Luan Guilherme de Jesús Vieira (90+1.Matheus Simonete Bressanelli „Bressan"), Hernán Barcos. Trainer: Enderson Alves Moreira.
Goal: Cristian Miguel Riveros Núñez (68).

13.02.2014, Estadio „Atanasio Girardot", Medellín
Referee: Julio Alberto Bascuñán González (Chile)
Club Atlético Nacional Medellín - CA Newell's Old Boys Rosario 1-0(0-0)
Atlético Nacional: Luis Enrique Martínez Rodríguez, Alejandro Bernal Rios, Farid Alfonso Díaz Rhenals (65.Juan David Valencia Hinestroza), Oscar Fabián Murillo Murillo, Daniel Eduardo Bocanegra Ortíz, John Stefan Medina Ramírez, Sherman Andrés Cárdenas Estupiñán, Alexander Mejía Sabalsa, Edwin Andrés Cardona Bedoya, Juan Pablo Ángel Arango (54.Jefferson Andrés Duque Montoya), Orlando Enrique Berrío Meléndez (76.Jhon Edwar Valoy Riascos). Trainer: Juan Carlos Osorio Arbelaez.
Old Boys: Nahuel Ignacio Guzmán, Marcos Antonio Cáceres Centurión, Víctor Rubén López, Milton Óscar Casco, Maximiliano Rubén Rodríguez, Lucas Ademar Bernardi (85.Alexis Nicolás Castro), Diego Mateo Alustiza, Éver Maximiliano David Banega, Raúl Hernán Villalba, David Sergio Trezeguet (66.Fabián Nicolás Muñoz), Víctor Alberto Figueroa. Trainer: Alfredo Jesús Berti.
Goal: Edwin Andrés Cardona Bedoya (80).

25.02.2014, Arena do Grêmio, Porto Alegre
Referee: Patricio Antonio Polic Orellana (Chile)
Grêmio Foot-Ball Porto Alegrense - Club Atlético Nacional Medellín 3-0(1-0)
Grêmio: Marcelo Grohe, Luiz Rhodolfo Dini Gaioto, Marcos Rogério Ricci Lopes „Pará", Werley Ananias da Silva, Wendell Nascimento Borges, Cristian Miguel Riveros Núñez (90+1.Maximiliano Rodríguez Maeso), José Roberto da Silva Júnior „Zé Roberto" (74.Eduardo Pereira Rodrigues „Dudu"), Edimo Ferreira Campos „Edinho", Ramiro Moschen Benetti, Luan Guilherme de Jesús Vieira (85.Alan Nahuel Ruíz), Hernán Barcos. Trainer: Enderson Alves Moreira.
Atlético Nacional: Luis Enrique Martínez Rodríguez, Alejandro Bernal Rios, Oscar Fabián Murillo Murillo, Daniel Eduardo Bocanegra Ortíz, John Stefan Medina Ramírez, Sherman Andrés Cárdenas Estupiñán, Alexander Mejía Sabalsa, Juan David Valencia Hinestroza, Edwin Andrés Cardona Bedoya, Orlando Enrique Berrío Meléndez (68.Farid Alfonso Díaz Rhenals), Fernando Uribe Hincapié (60.Santiago Tréllez Vivero). Trainer: Juan Carlos Osorio Arbelaez.
Goals: Luan Guilherme de Jesús Vieira (28), Ramiro Moschen Benetti (64), Alan Nahuel Ruíz (88).

27.02.2014, Estadio „Marcelo Bielsa“, Rosario
Referee: Enrique Roberto Osses Zencovich (Chile)
CA Newell's Old Boys Rosario - Club Nacional de Football Montevideo 4-0(2-0)
Old Boys: Nahuel Ignacio Guzmán, Gabriel Iván Heinze, Marcos Antonio Cáceres Centurión, Víctor Rubén López, Milton Óscar Casco, Maximiliano Rubén Rodríguez, Lucas Ademar Bernardi (68.Horacio De Dios Orzán), Diego Mateo Alustiza, Éver Maximiliano David Banega, Víctor Alberto Figueroa (72.Martín Tonso), Fabián Nicolás Muñoz (78.David Sergio Trezeguet). Trainer: Alfredo Jesús Berti.
Nacional: Gustavo Adolfo Munúa Vera, Andrés Scotti Ponce de León, Juan Manuel Díaz Martínez, Jorge Winston Curbelo Garis, Guillermo Daniel de los Santos Viana, Ignacio María González Gatti, Paulo Rinaldo Cruzado Durand (57.Nicolás Santiago Prieto Larrea), Hugo Diego Arismendi Ciapparetta, Carlos María de Pena Bonino, Iván Daniel Alonso Vallejo (57.Santiago Damián García Correa), Renato César Pérez (82.Gastón Rodrigo Pereiro López). Trainer: Gerardo Cono Pelusso Boyrie.
Goals: Maximiliano Rubén Rodríguez (12), Jorge Winston Curbelo Garis (45+1 own goal), Lucas Ademar Bernardi (53), Horacio De Dios Orzán (86).

11.03.2014, Estadio „Atanasio Girardot“, Medellín
Referee: Marco Antonio Rodríguez Moreno (Mexico)
Club Atlético Nacional Medellín - Club Nacional Montevideo 2-2(0-2)
Atlético Nacional: Luis Enrique Martínez Rodríguez, Alejandro Bernal Rios [*sent off 1*], Farid Alfonso Díaz Rhenals (69.Santiago Tréllez Vivero), Oscar Fabián Murillo Murillo, Daniel Eduardo Bocanegra Ortíz, John Stefan Medina Ramírez, Sherman Andrés Cárdenas Estupiñán, Alexander Mejía Sabalsa, Edwin Andrés Cardona Bedoya, Juan Pablo Ángel Arango (24.Jhon Edwar Valoy Riascos), Luis Alfonso Páez Restrepo (46.Jefferson Andrés Duque Montoya). Trainer: Juan Carlos Osorio Arbelaez.
Nacional: Jorge Rodrigo Bava, Pablo Álvarez Menéndez, Jorge Winston Curbelo Garis, Luis Alfonso Espino García (38.Ismael Benegas Arévalos), Ignacio María González Gatti, Hugo Diego Arismendi Ciapparetta (66.Jonathan Alberto Píriz Palacio), Maximiliano Matías Calzada Fuentes, Rafael García Casanova, Carlos María de Pena Bonino, Víctor Hugo Dorrego Coito, Santiago Damián García Correa (82.Alexander Jesús Medina Reobasco). Trainer: Gerardo Cono Pelusso Boyrie.
Goals: Daniel Eduardo Bocanegra Ortíz (70, 90+1) / Carlos María de Pena Bonino (3), Santiago Damián García Correa (18).

13.03.2014, Arena do Grêmio, Porto Alegre
Referee: Carlos Arecio Amarilla Demarqui (Paraguay)
Grêmio Foot-Ball Porto Alegrense - CA Newell's Old Boys Rosario 0-0
Grêmio: Marcelo Grohe, Luiz Rhodolfo Dini Gaioto, Marcos Rogério Ricci Lopes „Pará“, Werley Ananias da Silva, Wendell Nascimento Borges, Cristian Miguel Riveros Núñez (60.Eduardo Pereira Rodrigues „Dudu“), José Roberto da Silva Júnior „Zé Roberto“ (68.Alan Nahuel Ruíz), Edimo Ferreira Campos „Edinho“, Ramiro Moschen Benetti, Luan Guilherme de Jesús Vieira (77.Maximiliano Rodríguez Maeso), Hernán Barcos. Trainer: Enderson Alves Moreira.
Old Boys: Nahuel Ignacio Guzmán, Gabriel Iván Heinze, Marcos Antonio Cáceres Centurión, Víctor Rubén López, Milton Óscar Casco, Maximiliano Rubén Rodríguez, Lucas Ademar Bernardi (80.Alexis Nicolás Castro), Éver Maximiliano David Banega (73.Horacio De Dios Orzán), Raúl Hernán Villalba, Víctor Alberto Figueroa, Ezequiel Ponce (71.David Sergio Trezeguet). Trainer: Alfredo Jesús Berti.

18.03.2014, Estadio Gran Parque Central, Montevideo
Referee: Raúl Orosco Delgadillo (Bolivia)
Club Nacional Montevideo - Club Atlético Nacional Medellín 0-1(0-0)
Nacional: Jorge Rodrigo Bava, Andrés Scotti Ponce de León, Pablo Álvarez Menéndez, Jorge Winston Curbelo Garis, Jonathan Alberto Píriz Palacio (77.Juan Manuel Díaz Martínez), Maximiliano Matías Calzada Fuentes, Rafael García Casanova (72.Nicolás Santiago Prieto Larrea), Carlos María de Pena Bonino, Gastón Rodrigo Pereiro López, Juan Cruz Mascia Paysée, Renato César Pérez (58.Iván Daniel Alonso Vallejo). Trainer: Gerardo Cono Pelusso Boyrie.
Atlético Nacional: Franco Armani, Farid Alfonso Díaz Rhenals (83.Diego Alejandro Arias Hincapié), Oscar Fabián Murillo Murillo, Daniel Eduardo Bocanegra Ortíz, John Stefan Medina Ramírez, Diego Arturo Peralta González, Sherman Andrés Cárdenas Estupiñán (86.Jhon Edwar Valoy Riascos), Alexander Mejía Sabalsa, Juan David Valencia Hinestroza, Edwin Andrés Cardona Bedoya, Jefferson Andrés Duque Montoya (75.Álvaro Francisco Nájera Gil). Trainer: Juan Carlos Osorio Arbelaez.
Goal: Edwin Andrés Cardona Bedoya (63).

19.03.2014, Estadio „Marcelo Bielsa“, Rosario
Referee: Carlos Alfredo Vera Rodríguez (Ecuador)
CA Newell's Old Boys Rosario - Grêmio Foot-Ball Porto Alegrense 1-1(0-0)
Old Boys: Nahuel Ignacio Guzmán, Gabriel Iván Heinze, Marcos Antonio Cáceres Centurión, Víctor Rubén López, Milton Óscar Casco, Maximiliano Rubén Rodríguez, Lucas Ademar Bernardi (89.Alexis Nicolás Castro), Éver Maximiliano David Banega (72.Horacio De Dios Orzán), Raúl Hernán Villalba, Víctor Alberto Figueroa, Ezequiel Ponce (71.David Sergio Trezeguet). Trainer: Alfredo Jesús Berti.
Grêmio: Marcelo Grohe, Luiz Rhodolfo Dini Gaioto, Marcos Rogério Ricci Lopes „Pará“ (89.Everaldo Stum), Werley Ananias da Silva, Wendell Nascimento Borges, Cristian Miguel Riveros Núñez, Edimo Ferreira Campos „Edinho“ (82.Alan Nahuel Ruíz), Eduardo Pereira Rodrigues „Dudu“, Ramiro Moschen Benetti, Luan Guilherme de Jesús Vieira, Hernán Barcos. Trainer: Enderson Alves Moreira.
Goals: Maximiliano Rubén Rodríguez (78) / Luiz Rhodolfo Dini Gaioto (90+1).

26.03.2014, Estadio Centenario, Montevideo
Referee: Patricio Antonio Polic Orellana (Chile)
Club Nacional de Football Montevideo - CA Newell's Old Boys Rosario 2-4(1-1)
Nacional: Jorge Rodrigo Bava [*sent off 81*], Andrés Scotti Ponce de León, Juan Manuel Díaz Martínez, Jorge Winston Curbelo Garis, Guillermo Daniel de los Santos Viana, Paulo Rinaldo Cruzado Durand, Maximiliano Matías Calzada Fuentes, Rafael García Casanova [*sent off 72*], Henry Damián Giménez Báez (59.Gastón Rodrigo Pereiro López), Juan Cruz Mascia Paysée (75.Santiago Damián García Correa), Renato César Pérez (66.Ignacio María González Gatti). Trainer: Gerardo Cono Pelusso Boyrie.
Old Boys: Nahuel Ignacio Guzmán, Gabriel Iván Heinze, Marcos Antonio Cáceres Centurión, Víctor Rubén López, Milton Óscar Casco, Lucas Ademar Bernardi, Alexis Nicolás Castro (67.Fabián Nicolás Muñoz), Éver Maximiliano David Banega (85.Horacio De Dios Orzán), Raúl Hernán Villalba, Víctor Alberto Figueroa, Ezequiel Ponce (66.David Sergio Trezeguet). Trainer: Alfredo Jesús Berti.
Goals: Juan Cruz Mascia Paysée (11), Andrés Scotti Ponce de León (60 penalty) / Alexis Nicolás Castro (21), Marcos Antonio Cáceres Centurión (53), D. Trezeguet (74, 90).

02.04.2014, Estadio „Atanasio Girardot“, Medellín
Referee: Enrique Cáceres Villafante (Paraguay)
Club Atlético Nacional Medellín - Grêmio Foot-Ball Porto Alegrense 0-2(0-0)
Atlético Nacional: Franco Armani, Alexis Héctor Henríquez Charales (62.Orlando Enrique Berrío Meléndez), Farid Alfonso Díaz Rhenals (80.Luis Alfonso Páez Restrepo), Oscar Fabián Murillo Murillo, Daniel Eduardo Bocanegra Ortíz, John Stefan Medina Ramírez, Sherman Andrés Cárdenas Estupiñán, Alexander Mejía Sabalsa, Juan David Valencia Hinestroza, Edwin Andrés Cardona Bedoya, Juan Pablo Ángel Arango (59.Jefferson Andrés Duque Montoya). Trainer: Juan Carlos Osorio Arbelaez.
Grêmio: Marcelo Grohe, Luiz Rhodolfo Dini Gaioto, Marcos Rogério Ricci Lopes „Pará“, Werley Ananias da Silva, Wendell Nascimento Borges, Cristian Miguel Riveros Núñez, Edimo Ferreira Campos „Edinho“, Eduardo Pereira Rodrigues „Dudu“ (90.Pedro Tonon Geromel), Ramiro Moschen Benetti, Luan Guilherme de Jesús Vieira (83.Alan Nahuel Ruíz), Hernán Barcos (90+2.Leonardo David de Moura „Léo Gago“). Trainer: Enderson Alves Moreira.
Goals: Eduardo Pereira Rodrigues „Dudu“ (52), Hernán Barcos (69).

10.04.2014, Arena do Grêmio, Porto Alegre
Referee: Óscar Maldonado Urey (Bolivia)
Grêmio Foot-Ball P. Alegrense - Club Nacional de Football Montevideo 1-0(1-0)
Grêmio: Marcelo Grohe, Luiz Rhodolfo Dini Gaioto, Marcos Rogério Ricci Lopes „Pará“, Werley Ananias da Silva, Wendell Nascimento Borges, Cristian Miguel Riveros Núñez, Edimo Ferreira Campos „Edinho“ (46.Jean Alexandre Deretti), Eduardo Pereira Rodrigues „Dudu“ (72.Maximiliano Rodríguez Maeso), Ramiro Moschen Benetti, Alan Nahuel Ruíz (86.Lucas Coelho), Hernán Barcos. Trainer: Enderson Alves Moreira.
Nacional: Gustavo Adolfo Munúa Vera, Andrés Scotti Ponce de León (52.Sebastián Coates Nion), Juan Manuel Díaz Martínez, Jonathan Alberto Píriz Palacio, Guillermo Daniel de los Santos Viana, Luis Alfonso Espino García, Hugo Diego Arismendi Ciapparetta (46.Maximiliano Matías Calzada Fuentes), Nicolás Santiago Prieto Larrea, Víctor Hugo Dorrego Coito, Iván Daniel Alonso Vallejo, Santiago Damián García Correa (82.Juan Cruz Mascia Paysée). Trainer: Gerardo Cono Pelusso Boyrie.
Goal: Hernán Barcos (12 penalty).

10.04.2014, Estadio „Marcelo Bielsa“, Rosario
Referee: Antonio Javier Arias Alvarenga (Paraguay)
CA Newell‘s Old Boys Rosario - Club Atlético Nacional Medellín 1-3(1-2)
Old Boys: Nahuel Ignacio Guzmán, Víctor Rubén López [*sent off 5*], Milton Óscar Casco, Guillermo Luis Ortíz, Maximiliano Rubén Rodríguez (37.Alexis Nicolás Castro), Lucas Ademar Bernardi, Diego Mateo Alustiza, Éver Maximiliano David Banega (64.Ezequiel Ponce), Raúl Hernán Villalba (17.Horacio De Dios Orzán), David Sergio Trezeguet, Víctor Alberto Figueroa. Trainer: Alfredo Jesús Berti.
Atlético Nacional: Franco Armani, Farid Alfonso Díaz Rhenals, Oscar Fabián Murillo Murillo, Daniel Eduardo Bocanegra Ortíz, John Stefan Medina Ramírez, Diego Alejandro Arias Hincapié (56.Diego Arturo Peralta González), Sherman Andrés Cárdenas Estupiñán (78.Jairo Fabián Palomino Sierra), Alexander Mejía Sabalsa, Juan David Valencia Hinestroza, Edwin Andrés Cardona Bedoya [*sent off 5*], Santiago Tréllez Vivero (46.Orlando Enrique Berrío Meléndez). Trainer: Juan Carlos Osorio Arbelaez.
Goals: Milton Óscar Casco (16) / Santiago Tréllez Vivero (7), Sherman Andrés Cárdenas Estupiñán (13), Orlando Enrique Berrío Meléndez (54).

FINAL STANDINGS

1.	**Grêmio Foot-Ball Porto Alegrense**	6	4	2	0	8	-	1	14
2.	**Club Atlético Nacional Medellín**	6	3	1	2	7	-	8	10
3.	CA Newell‘s Old Boys Rosario	6	2	2	2	10	-	7	8
4.	Club Nacional de Football Montevideo	6	0	1	5	4	-	13	1

12.02.2014, Estadio León, León
Referee: José Hernando Buitrago Arango (Colombia)
Club León FC - CR do Flamengo Rio de Janeiro 2-1(1-1)
León: William Paul Yarbrough Story, Rafael Márquez Álvarez, José Jonny Magallón Oliva, Juan Ignacio González Ibarra (41.Franco Faustino Arizala Hurtado), Edwin William Hernández Herrera, Luis Arturo Montes Jiménez, Eisner Iván Loboa Balanta (90+2.Fernando Navarro Morán), Carlos Alberto Peña Rodríguez, José Juan Vázquez Gómez, Mauro Boselli, Matías Britos Cardoso. Trainer: Christian Gustavo Matosas Paidón (Uruguay).
Flamengo: Luiz Felipe Ventura dos Santos, Leonardo da Silva Moura „Léo Moura", André Clarindo dos Santos, Wallace Reis da Silva, Samir Caetano de Souza Santos, Elano Ralph Blumer (75.Luiz Philipe Lima de Oliveira "Muralha"), Éverton Cardoso da Silva (67.Paulo Luiz Beraldo Santos "Paulinho"), Víctor Javier Cáceres Centurión, Lucas Andrés Mugni (83.Alecsandro Barbosa Felisbino), Mauricio Azevedo Alves „Amaral" [*sent off 12*], Hernane Vidal de Souza. Trainer: Jaime de Almeida Filho.
Goals: Mauro Boselli (31 penalty), Franco Faustino Arizala Hurtado (67) / Víctor Javier Cáceres Centurión (42).

13.02.2014, Estadio „George Capwell", Guayaquil
Referee: Patricio Antonio Polic Orellana (Chile)
CS Emelec Guayaquil - Club Bolívar La Paz 2-1(1-1)
Emelec: Esteban Javier Dreer, Jorge Daniel Guagua Tamayo, Gabriel Eduardo Achilier Zurita, Oscar Dalmiro Bagüi Angulo, Carlos Enrique Vera Morán, Fernando Agustín Giménez Solís, Pedro Angel Quiñónez Rodríguez (46.Fernando Vicente Gaibor Orellana), Ángel Israel Mena Delgado (88.Eddy Roy Corozo Olaya), Miller Alejandro Bolaños Reascos, Denis Andrés Stracqualursi, Marcos Jackson Caicedo Caicedo (66.Luis Miguel Escalada). Trainer: Gustavo Domingo Quinteros Desabato (Bolivia).
Bolívar: Romel Javier Quiñónez Suárez, Nelson David Cabrera Báez, Edemir Rodríguez Mercado, Luis Alberto Gutiérrez Herrera, Walter Alberto Flores Condarco, Juan Miguel Callejón Bueno, Damir Miranda Mercado (85.Jaime Darío Arrascaita Iriondo), Rudy Alejandro Cardozo Fernández (87.José Luis Sánchez Capdevila), César Gerardo Yecerotte Soruco, Ricardo Pedriel Suárez, William Ferreira Martínez. Trainer: Vladimir Soria Camacho.
Goals: Ángel Israel Mena Delgado (11), Fernando Agustín Giménez Solís (73) / Juan Miguel Callejón Bueno (9).

19.02.2014, Estadio „Hernando Siles", La Paz
Referee: Manuel Alejandro Garay Evia (Peru)
Club Bolívar La Paz - Club León FC 1-1(0-1)
Bolívar: Romel Javier Quiñónez Suárez, Nelson David Cabrera Báez, Luis Alberto Gutiérrez Herrera, Walter Alberto Flores Condarco, Juan Miguel Callejón Bueno, Damir Miranda Mercado (67.Lorgio Álvarez Roca), Rudy Alejandro Cardozo Fernández, Juan Carlos Arce Justiniano, César Gerardo Yecerotte Soruco, Ricardo Pedriel Suárez (62.Jaime Darío Arrascaita Iriondo), William Ferreira Martínez. Trainer: Vladimir Soria Camacho.
León: William Paul Yarbrough Story, Rafael Márquez Álvarez, José Jonny Magallón Oliva, Juan Ignacio González Ibarra, Luis Arturo Montes Jiménez, José María Cárdenas López, Elias Hernán Hernández Jacuinde (58.Franco Faustino Arizala Hurtado), Eisner Iván Loboa Balanta, Carlos Alberto Peña Rodríguez (71.Aldo Paúl Rocha González), José Juan Vázquez Gómez, Mauro Boselli (81.Matías Britos Cardoso). Trainer: Christian Gustavo Matosas Paidón (Uruguay).
Goals: Juan Miguel Callejón Bueno (66) / Mauro Boselli (2).

26.02.2014, Estádio „Jornalista Mário Filho“ [Maracanã], Rio de Janeiro
Referee: Néstor Fabián Pitana (Argentina)
CR do Flamengo Rio de Janeiro - CS Emelec Guayaquil 3-1(1-0)
Flamengo: Luiz Felipe Ventura dos Santos, Leonardo da Silva Moura „Léo Moura“, André Clarindo dos Santos, Wallace Reis da Silva, Samir Caetano de Souza Santos, Elano Ralph Blumer (68.Alecsandro Barbosa Felisbino), Éverton Cardoso da Silva, Víctor Javier Cáceres Centurión, Lucas Andrés Mugni (46.Gabriel Santana Pinto), Luiz Philipe Lima de Oliveira "Muralha" (83.Antonio Filipe Gonzaga de Aquino „Feijão“), Hernane Vidal de Souza. Trainer: Jaime de Almeida Filho.
Emelec: Esteban Javier Dreer, Jorge Daniel Guagua Tamayo, Gabriel Eduardo Achilier Zurita [*sent off 73*], Oscar Dalmiro Bagüi Angulo, Cristian Javier Nasuti Matovelle, Fernando Agustín Giménez Solís, Pedro Angel Quiñónez Rodríguez, Ángel Israel Mena Delgado (76.Diego Armando Corozo Castillo), Fernando Vicente Gaibor Orellana, Denis Andrés Stracqualursi (81.Luis Miguel Escalada), Marcos Jackson Caicedo Caicedo. Trainer: Gustavo Domingo Quinteros Desabato (Bolivia).
Goals: Elano Ralph Blumer (10), Hernane Vidal de Souza (54), Éverton Cardoso da Silva (81) / Luis Miguel Escalada (87).

11.03.2014, Estadio „George Capwell“, Guayaquil
Referee: José Ramón Argote Vega (Venezuela)
CS Emelec Guayaquil - Club León FC 2-1(1-1)
Emelec: Esteban Javier Dreer, Jorge Daniel Guagua Tamayo, Oscar Dalmiro Bagüi Angulo, Cristian Javier Nasuti Matovelle, Diego Armando Corozo Castillo (56.José Luis Quiñónez Quiñónez), Fernando Agustín Giménez Solís (5.Luis Miguel Escalada), Pedro Angel Quiñónez Rodríguez, Ángel Israel Mena Delgado, Osbaldo Lupo Lastra García, Denis Andrés Stracqualursi, Marcos Jackson Caicedo Caicedo (86.Eddy Roy Corozo Olaya). Trainer: Gustavo Domingo Quinteros Desabato (Bolivia).
León: William Paul Yarbrough Story, Rafael Márquez Álvarez, José Jonny Magallón Oliva, Juan Ignacio González Ibarra, Edwin William Hernández Herrera (46.José María Cárdenas López), Luis Arturo Montes Jiménez, Elias Hernán Hernández Jacuinde (71.Miguel Sabah Rodríguez), Carlos Alberto Peña Rodríguez, José Juan Vázquez Gómez, Matías Britos Cardoso (61.Franco Faustino Arizala Hurtado), Nelson Sebastián Maz Rosano. Trainer: Christian Gustavo Matosas Paidón (Uruguay).
Goals: Luis Miguel Escalada (15, 60) / Carlos Alberto Peña Rodríguez (21).

12.03.2014, Estádio „Jornalista Mário Filho“ [Maracanã], Rio de Janeiro
Referee: Enrique Roberto Osses Zencovich (Chile)
CR do Flamengo Rio de Janeiro - Club Bolívar La Paz 2-2(0-0)
Flamengo: Luiz Felipe Ventura dos Santos, Wallace Reis da Silva, João Paulo Gomes da Costa, Leonardo Moreira Morais "Leo" (46.Paulo Luiz Beraldo Santos "Paulinho"), Samir Caetano de Souza Santos, Elano Ralph Blumer (63.Alecsandro Barbosa Felisbino), Éverton Cardoso da Silva, Víctor Javier Cáceres Centurión (90+1.Carlos Eduardo Marques), Luiz Philipe Lima de Oliveira "Muralha", Hernane Vidal de Souza, Gabriel Santana Pinto. Trainer: Jaime de Almeida Filho.
Bolívar: Romel Javier Quiñónez Suárez, Nelson David Cabrera Báez, Edemir Rodríguez Mercado, Luis Alberto Gutiérrez Herrera, Walter Alberto Flores Condarco, Juan Miguel Callejón Bueno (71.Ricardo Pedriel Suárez), José Luis Sánchez Capdevila, Damir Miranda Mercado (71.Rudy Alejandro Cardozo Fernández), Juan Carlos Arce Justiniano, César Gerardo Yecerotte Soruco (21.Eduardo Moya Castillo), William Ferreira Martínez. Trainer: Francisco Xabier Azkargorta Uriarte (Spain).
Goals: Éverton Cardoso da Silva (54, 65) / José Luis Sánchez Capdevila (52), Ricardo Pedriel Suárez (72).

19.03.2014, Estadio León, León
Referee: Diego Edgardo Ceballos (Argentina)
Club León FC - CS Emelec Guayaquil 3-0(1-0)
León: William Paul Yarbrough Story, Rafael Márquez Álvarez, José Jonny Magallón Oliva, Juan Ignacio González Ibarra, Edwin William Hernández Herrera, Luis Arturo Montes Jiménez, Elias Hernán Hernández Jacuinde (68.Eisner Iván Loboa Balanta), Carlos Alberto Peña Rodríguez, José Juan Vázquez Gómez, Mauro Boselli (66.Miguel Sabah Rodríguez), Matías Britos Cardoso (84.Mauricio Castañeda Mendoza). Trainer: Christian Gustavo Matosas Paidón (Uruguay).
Emelec: Esteban Javier Dreer, Jorge Daniel Guagua Tamayo, Gabriel Eduardo Achilier Zurita, Oscar Dalmiro Bagüi Angulo, Pedro Angel Quiñónez Rodríguez, José Luis Quiñónez Quiñónez, Ángel Israel Mena Delgado, Miller Alejandro Bolaños Reascos (68.Marcos Jackson Caicedo Caicedo), Osbaldo Lupo Lastra García [*sent off 45+3*], Luis Miguel Escalada (46.Eddy Roy Corozo Olaya), Denis Andrés Stracqualursi. Trainer: Gustavo Domingo Quinteros Desabato (Bolivia).
Goals: Matías Britos Cardoso (19), José Juan Vázquez Gómez (81 penalty), Carlos Alberto Peña Rodríguez (85).

19.03.2014, Estadio „Hernando Siles", La Paz
Referee: Mario Alberto Díaz de Vivar Bogado (Paraguay)
Club Bolívar La Paz - CR do Flamengo Rio de Janeiro 1-0(1-0)
Bolívar: Romel Javier Quiñónez Suárez, Lorgio Álvarez Roca, Nelson David Cabrera Báez, Luis Alberto Gutiérrez Herrera, Walter Alberto Flores Condarco, Juan Miguel Callejón Bueno (81.Leonel Justiniano Araúz), José Luis Sánchez Capdevila, Damir Miranda Mercado, Juan Carlos Arce Justiniano (71.Damián Emanuel Lizio), César Gerardo Yecerotte Soruco (52.Jaime Darío Arrascaita Iriondo), William Ferreira Martínez. Trainer: Francisco Xabier Azkargorta Uriarte (Spain).
Flamengo: Luiz Felipe Ventura dos Santos, Leonardo da Silva Moura „Léo Moura", André Clarindo dos Santos (83.Alecsandro Barbosa Felisbino), Wallace Reis da Silva, Samir Caetano de Souza Santos, Carlos Eduardo Marques (71.Lucas Andrés Mugni), Éverton Cardoso da Silva, Mauricio Azevedo Alves „Amaral", Luiz Philipe Lima de Oliveira "Muralha", Hernane Vidal de Souza, Gabriel Santana Pinto (46.Paulo Luiz Beraldo Santos "Paulinho"). Trainer: Jaime de Almeida Filho.
Goal: Juan Carlos Arce Justiniano (4 penalty).

26.03.2014, Estadio León, León
Referee: Marlon Giovanny Escalante Álvarez (Venezuela)
Club León FC - Club Bolívar La Paz 0-1(0-0)
León: William Paul Yarbrough Story, Rafael Márquez Álvarez, José Jonny Magallón Oliva (37.Eisner Iván Loboa Balanta), Juan Ignacio González Ibarra, Edwin William Hernández Herrera, Luis Arturo Montes Jiménez, Elias Hernán Hernández Jacuinde (69.Franco Faustino Arizala Hurtado), Carlos Alberto Peña Rodríguez (88.Miguel Sabah Rodríguez), José Juan Vázquez Gómez, Mauro Boselli, Matías Britos Cardoso. Trainer: Christian Gustavo Matosas Paidón (Uruguay).
Bolívar: Romel Javier Quiñónez Suárez, Eduardo Moya Castillo, Nelson David Cabrera Báez, Ronald Eguino Segovia, Luis Alberto Gutiérrez Herrera, Damián Emanuel Lizio (89.Jaime Darío Arrascaita Iriondo), Walter Alberto Flores Condarco (54.Lorgio Álvarez Roca), Juan Miguel Callejón Bueno (82.Juan Carlos Arce Justiniano), José Luis Sánchez Capdevila, Damir Miranda Mercado, William Ferreira Martínez. Trainer: Francisco Xabier Azkargorta Uriarte (Spain).
Goal: William Ferreira Martínez (69).

02.04.2014, Estadio „George Capwell", Guayaquil
Referee: Julio Alberto Bascuñán González (Chile)
CS Emelec Guayaquil - CR do Flamengo Rio de Janeiro 1-2(0-1)
Emelec: Esteban Javier Dreer, Jorge Daniel Guagua Tamayo, Oscar Dalmiro Bagüi Angulo, Cristian Javier Nasuti Matovelle, Jhon William Narváez, Fernando Agustín Giménez Solís (79.Javier Isidro Charcopa Alegria), Pedro Angel Quiñónez Rodríguez, Ángel Israel Mena Delgado, Eddy Roy Corozo Olaya (31.Marcos Jackson Caicedo Caicedo), Marcos Gustavo Mondaini (46.Miller Alejandro Bolaños Reascos), Denis Andrés Stracqualursi. Trainer: Gustavo Domingo Quinteros Desabato (Bolivia).
Flamengo: Luiz Felipe Ventura dos Santos, Wallace Reis da Silva, João Paulo Gomes da Costa, Welinton Souza Silva (79.Anderson Sebastião Cardoso "Chicão"), Samir Caetano de Souza Santos, Éverton Cardoso da Silva (80.Guilherme Negueba Ferreira Pinto), Mauricio Azevedo Alves „Amaral", Luiz Philipe Lima de Oliveira "Muralha" (59.Wheidson Roberto dos Santos "Recife"), Alecsandro Barbosa Felisbino, Paulo Luiz Beraldo Santos "Paulinho", Gabriel Santana Pinto. Trainer: Jaime de Almeida Filho.
Goals: Denis Andrés Stracqualursi (65 penalty) / Alecsandro Barbosa Felisbino (8 penalty), Paulo Luiz Beraldo Santos "Paulinho" (90+2).

09.04.2014, Estádio „Jornalista Mário Filho" [Maracanã], Rio de Janeiro
Referee: Diego Hernán Abal (Argentina)
CR do Flamengo Rio de Janeiro - Club León FC 2-3(2-2)
Flamengo: Luiz Felipe Ventura dos Santos, Leonardo da Silva Moura „Léo Moura", André Clarindo dos Santos (72.Guilherme Negueba Ferreira Pinto), Wallace Reis da Silva, Samir Caetano de Souza Santos, Elano Ralph Blumer (12.Gabriel Santana Pinto), Éverton Cardoso da Silva, Mauricio Azevedo Alves „Amaral", Luiz Philipe Lima de Oliveira "Muralha", Alecsandro Barbosa Felisbino, Paulo Luiz Beraldo Santos "Paulinho" (84.Nixson Darlanio Reis Cardoso). Trainer: Jaime de Almeida Filho.
León: William Paul Yarbrough Story, Rafael Márquez Álvarez, José Jonny Magallón Oliva, Juan Ignacio González Ibarra, Edwin William Hernández Herrera, Luis Arturo Montes Jiménez, Elias Hernán Hernández Jacuinde (90+1.Iván Carlos Pineda Vásquez), Carlos Alberto Peña Rodríguez (85.Aldo Paúl Rocha González), José Juan Vázquez Gómez, Mauro Boselli, Franco Faustino Arizala Hurtado (83.Luis Antonio Delgado Tapia). Trainer: Christian Gustavo Matosas Paidón (Uruguay).
Goals: André Clarindo dos Santos (29), Alecsandro Barbosa Felisbino (34) / Franco Faustino Arizala Hurtado (20), Mauro Boselli (30), Carlos Alberto Peña Rodríguez (83).

09.04.2014, Estadio „Hernando Siles", La Paz
Referee: Mauro Vigliano (Argentina)
Club Bolívar La Paz - CS Emelec Guayaquil 2-1(1-0)
Bolívar: Romel Javier Quiñónez Suárez, Nelson David Cabrera Báez, Ronald Eguino Segovia, Luis Alberto Gutiérrez Herrera, Walter Alberto Flores Condarco (83.Lorgio Álvarez Roca), Juan Miguel Callejón Bueno (75.Jaime Darío Arrascaita Iriondo), José Luis Sánchez Capdevila, Damir Miranda Mercado, Juan Carlos Arce Justiniano (87.Damián Emanuel Lizio), César Gerardo Yecerotte Soruco, William Ferreira Martínez. Trainer: Francisco Xabier Azkargorta Uriarte (Spain).
Emelec: Esteban Javier Dreer, Gabriel Eduardo Achilier Zurita, Oscar Dalmiro Bagüi Angulo, Cristian Javier Nasuti Matovelle, Jhon William Narváez, Fernando Agustín Giménez Solís, Pedro Angel Quiñónez Rodríguez, Ángel Israel Mena Delgado (78.Luis Miguel Escalada), Miller Alejandro Bolaños Reascos (65.Javier Isidro Charcopa Alegria), Eddy Roy Corozo Olaya (46.Marcos Jackson Caicedo Caicedo), Denis Andrés Stracqualursi. Trainer: Gustavo Domingo Quinteros Desabato (Bolivia).
Goals: William Ferreira Martínez (1), Juan Miguel Callejón Bueno (50) / Luis Miguel Escalada (87).

FINAL STANDINGS

1.	**Club Bolívar La Paz**	6	3	2	1	8	-	6	11
2.	**Club León FC**	6	3	1	2	10	-	7	10
3.	CR do Flamengo Rio de Janeiro	6	2	1	3	10	-	10	7
4.	CS Emelec Guayaquil	6	2	0	4	7	-	12	6

GROUP 8

11.02.2014, Estadio Corona, Torreón
Referee: Adrián Alexander Vélez Londoño (Colombia)
Club Santos Laguna Torreón - Arsenal de Sarandí FC 1-0(1-0)
Santos: Oswaldo Javier Sánchez Ibarra, Rafael Alejandro Figueroa Gómez, Jonathan Leonardo Lacerda Araujo, Néstor Alejandro Araujo Razo, José Javier Abella Fanjul, Juan Pablo Rodríguez Guerrero, Mauro Emiliano Cejas (64.Sergio Ceballos Herrera), Ribair Rodríguez Pérez, Néstor Calderón Enríquez, Oribe Peralta Morones (86.Eduardo Herrera Aguirre), Carlos Darwin Quintero Villalba (80.Andrés Yair Rentería Morelo). Trainer: Pedro Miguel Faria Caixinha (Portugal).
Arsenal: Cristian Daniel Campestrini, Mariano Raúl Echeverría, Eduardo Javier Casais, Damián Alfredo Pérez, Martín Hugo Nervo, Martín Rolle (83.Emilio José Zelaya), Iván José Marcone, Federico Freire (64.Franco Zuculini), Mauricio Ezequiel Sperdutti (72.Ramiro Ángel Carrera), Milton Joel Caraglio, Julio César Furch. Trainer: Gustavo Julio Alfaro.
Goals: Oribe Peralta Morones (18).

12.02.2014, Estadio „José Antonio Anzoátegui", Puerto la Cruz
Referee: Diego Jefferson Lara León (Ecuador)
Deportivo Anzoátegui SC Puerto La Cruz - CA Peñarol Montevideo 1-1(1-0)
Deportivo Anzoátegui: Edixson Antonio González Peroza, Johnny Jair Mirabal Arboleda, Alejandro Enrique Cichero Konarek, Carlos Javier Lujano Sánchez, Oscar Ezequiel Jonathan Parnisari, Rolando Emilio Escobar Batista, Evelio De Jesús Hernández Guedez [*sent off 81*], Ricardo Manuel Cardoso Martins (72.Robert Enrique Hernández Aguado), Emanuel Calzadilla, Edwin Enrique Aguilar Samaniego (82.Jaime José Moreno Ciorciari), Framber Johan Villegas Sangronis (85.Ronald Steve Ramírez Molina). Trainer: Juvencio Betancourt.
Peñarol: Juan Guillermo Castillo Iriarte, Damián Macaluso Rojas, Octavio Darío Rodríguez Peña, Carlos Adrián Valdéz Suárez, Pablo Martín Lima Olid, Héctor Baltasar Silva Cabrera (66.Emiliano Albín Antognazza), Sergio Daniel Orteman Rodríguez, Jorge Marcelo Rodríguez Núñez (86.Cristopher Paolo César Hurtado Huertas), Antonio Pacheco D'Agosti (59.Jonathan Javier Rodríguez Portillo), Marcel Novick Rattich, Marcelo Danubio Zalayeta. Trainer: Jorge Daniel Fossati Lurachi.
Goals: Framber Johan Villegas Sangronis (38) / Marcelo Danubio Zalayeta (78).

18.02.2014, Estadio Centenario, Montevideo
Referee: Héber Roberto Lopes (Brazil)
CA Peñarol Montevideo - Club Santos Laguna Torreón 0-2(0-0)
Peñarol: Juan Guillermo Castillo Iriarte, Damián Macaluso Rojas (73.Héctor Baltasar Silva Cabrera), Octavio Darío Rodríguez Peña, Carlos Adrián Valdéz Suárez, Emiliano Albín Antognazza, Sergio Daniel Orteman Rodríguez, Jorge Marcelo Rodríguez Núñez (59.Cristopher Paolo César Hurtado Huertas), Luís Bernardo Aguiar Burgos, Antonio Pacheco D'Agosti (64.Jonathan Javier Rodríguez Portillo), Marcelo Danubio Zalayeta, Mauro Raúl Fernández. Trainer: Jorge Daniel Fossati Lurachi.
Santos: Oswaldo Javier Sánchez Ibarra, Rafael Alejandro Figueroa Gómez, Jonathan Leonardo Lacerda Araujo, Oswaldo Alanís Pantoja, José Javier Abella Fanjul, Juan Pablo Rodríguez Guerrero, Mauro Emiliano Cejas (78.Sergio Ceballos Herrera), Ribair Rodríguez Pérez, Néstor Calderón Enríquez, Oribe Peralta Morones (90.Néstor Alejandro Araujo Razo), Carlos Darwin Quintero Villalba (85.Andrés Yair Rentería Morelo). Trainer: Pedro Miguel Faria Caixinha (Portugal).
Goals: Jonathan Leonardo Lacerda Araujo (53), José Javier Abella Fanjul (90).

25.02.2014, Estadio „Julio Humberto Grondona", Sarandí
Referee: Víctor Hugo Carrillo Casanova (Peru)
Arsenal de Sarandí FC - Deportivo Anzoátegui SC Puerto La Cruz 3-0(2-0)
Arsenal: Cristian Daniel Campestrini, Diego Luis Braghieri, Mariano Raúl Echeverría, Damián Alfredo Pérez, Martín Hugo Nervo, Franco Zuculini (61.Julián Cardozo), Matías Ariel Sánchez, Iván José Marcone, Ramiro Ángel Carrera (56.Martín Rolle), Milton Joel Caraglio, Julio César Furch (71.Emilio José Zelaya). Trainer: Gustavo Julio Alfaro.
Deportivo Anzoátegui: Edixson Antonio González Peroza, Johnny Jair Mirabal Arboleda, Alejandro Enrique Cichero Konarek, Carlos Javier Lujano Sánchez, Oscar Ezequiel Jonathan Parnisari, Rolando Emilio Escobar Batista, José David Moreno Chacón (55.Ronald Steve Ramírez Molina), Ricardo Manuel Cardoso Martins, Emanuel Calzadilla [*sent off 45*], Edwin Enrique Aguilar Samaniego (77.Jaime José Moreno Ciorciari), Framber Johan Villegas Sangronis (71.Robert Enrique Hernández Aguado). Trainer: Juvencio Betancourt.
Goals: Julio César Furch (15), Ramiro Ángel Carrera (42), Milton Joel Caraglio (50).

11.03.2014, Estadio „José Antonio Anzoátegui", Puerto la Cruz
Referee: Raúl Orosco Delgadillo (Bolivia)
Deportivo Anzoátegui SC P. La Cruz - Club Santos Laguna Torreón 1-1(0-0)
Deportivo Anzoátegui: Edixson Antonio González Peroza, Johnny Jair Mirabal Arboleda, Alejandro Enrique Cichero Konarek, Edgar José Mendoza Acosta, Oscar Ezequiel Jonathan Parnisari, Rolando Emilio Escobar Batista, José David Moreno Chacón, Evelio De Jesús Hernández Guedez, Ricardo Manuel Cardoso Martins (74.Robert Enrique Hernández Aguado), Framber Johan Villegas Sangronis (59.Manuel Alejandro Arteaga Rubianes), Jaime José Moreno Ciorciari (85.Edwin Enrique Aguilar Samaniego). Trainer: Juvencio Betancourt.
Santos: Oswaldo Javier Sánchez Ibarra, Jonathan Leonardo Lacerda Araujo, Oswaldo Alanís Pantoja, Néstor Alejandro Araujo Razo, José Javier Abella Fanjul, Juan Pablo Rodríguez Guerrero, Mauro Emiliano Cejas (46.Javier Antonio Orozco Peñuelas), Ribair Rodríguez Pérez (80.Rodolfo Salinas Ortíz), Oribe Peralta Morones, Carlos Darwin Quintero Villalba, Andrés Yair Rentería Morelo (57.Néstor Calderón Enríquez). Trainer: Pedro Miguel Faria Caixinha (Portugal).
Goals: Manuel Alejandro Arteaga Rubianes (71) / Oribe Peralta Morones (62).

13.03.2014, Estadio „Julio Humberto Grondona", Sarandí
Referee: Sandro Meira Ricci (Brazil)
Arsenal de Sarandí FC - CA Peñarol Montevideo 1-0(1-0)
Arsenal: Cristian Daniel Campestrini, Diego Luis Braghieri, Damián Alfredo Pérez, Martín Hugo Nervo, Leandro Martín González Pírez, Franco Zuculini (70.Fausto Emanuel Montero), Matías Ariel Sánchez (74.Matías Ezequiel Zaldivia), Iván José Marcone, Ramiro Ángel Carrera, Milton Joel Caraglio, Julio César Furch (81.Mauricio Ezequiel Sperdutti). Trainer: Gustavo Julio Alfaro.
Peñarol: Juan Guillermo Castillo Iriarte, Octavio Darío Rodríguez Peña [*sent off 90+2*], Carlos Adrián Valdéz Suárez, Emiliano Albín Antognazza, Joe Emerson Bastos Bizera (11.Jonathan Alexis Sandoval Rojas), Cristopher Paolo César Hurtado Huertas, Jorge Marcelo Rodríguez Núñez, Luís Bernardo Aguiar Burgos, Marcel Novick Rattich (68.Antonio Pacheco D'Agosti), Marcelo Danubio Zalayeta, Javier Fabián Toledo (57.Jonathan Javier Rodríguez Portillo). Trainer: Jorge Daniel Fossati Lurachi.
Goal: Julio César Furch (3).

18.03.2014, Estadio Corona, Torreón
Referee: Wilson Lamouroux Riveros (Colombia)
Club Santos Laguna Torreón - Deportivo Anzoátegui SC P. La Cruz 3-0(1-0)
Santos: Oswaldo Javier Sánchez Ibarra, Rafael Alejandro Figueroa Gómez, Jonathan Leonardo Lacerda Araujo, Oswaldo Alanís Pantoja, José Javier Abella Fanjul, Juan Pablo Rodríguez Guerrero, Ribair Rodríguez Pérez (69.Rodolfo Salinas Ortíz; 82.Sergio Ceballos Herrera), Oribe Peralta Morones, Carlos Darwin Quintero Villalba (78.Osmar Mares Martínez), Javier Antonio Orozco Peñuelas, Andrés Yair Rentería Morelo. Trainer: Pedro Miguel Faria Caixinha (Portugal).
Deportivo Anzoátegui: Edixson Antonio González Peroza, Johnny Jair Mirabal Arboleda, Alejandro Enrique Cichero Konarek, Oscar Ezequiel Jonathan Parnisari, Rolando Emilio Escobar Batista (71.Edwin Enrique Aguilar Samaniego), Jhonny José Francisco González Barreto, Evelio De Jesús Hernández Guedez, Ricardo Manuel Cardoso Martins (60.Robert Enrique Hernández Aguado), Emanuel Calzadilla (46.José David Moreno Chacón), Framber Johan Villegas Sangronis, Jaime José Moreno Ciorciari. Trainer: Juvencio Betancourt.
Goals: Andrés Yair Rentería Morelo (12), Javier Antonio Orozco Peñuelas (55), Oribe Peralta Morones (65).

19.03.2014, Estadio Centenario, Montevideo
Referee: Wilton Pereira Sampaio (Brazil)
CA Peñarol Montevideo - Arsenal de Sarandí FC 2-1(0-0)
Peñarol: Danilo Emanuel Lerda, Damián Macaluso Rojas, Carlos Adrián Valdéz Suárez, Washington Emilio MacEachen Vázquez (78.Javier Fabián Toledo), Jorge Nicolás Raguso Sánchez (61.Jorge Marcelo Rodríguez Núñez), Cristopher Paolo César Hurtado Huertas, Luís Bernardo Aguiar Burgos, Antonio Pacheco D'Agosti (61.Hernán Novick Rattich), Marcel Novick Rattich, Marcelo Danubio Zalayeta, Jonathan Javier Rodríguez Portillo. Trainer: Jorge Daniel Fossati Lurachi.
Arsenal: Cristian Daniel Campestrini, Diego Luis Braghieri, Damián Alfredo Pérez, Martín Hugo Nervo, Leandro Martín González Pírez, Franco Zuculini (66.Emilio José Zelaya), Matías Ariel Sánchez (82.Julio César Furch), Iván José Marcone, Ramiro Ángel Carrera, Mauricio Ezequiel Sperdutti (72.Matías Ezequiel Zaldivia), Milton Joel Caraglio. Trainer: Gustavo Julio Alfaro.
Goals: Luís Bernardo Aguiar Burgos (69), Jonathan Javier Rodríguez Portillo (81) / Iván José Marcone (53).

25.03.2014, Estadio Corona, Torreón
Referee: Leandro Pedro Vuaden (Brazil)
Club Santos Laguna Torreón - CA Peñarol Montevideo 4-1(1-1)
Santos: Oswaldo Javier Sánchez Ibarra, Rafael Alejandro Figueroa Gómez, Jonathan Leonardo Lacerda Araujo, Oswaldo Alanís Pantoja, José Javier Abella Fanjul, Juan Pablo Rodríguez Guerrero, Ribair Rodríguez Pérez (80.Néstor Alejandro Araujo Razo), Oribe Peralta Morones (85.Eduardo Herrera Aguirre), Carlos Darwin Quintero Villalba, Javier Antonio Orozco Peñuelas (72.Sergio Ceballos Herrera), Andrés Yair Rentería Morelo. Trainer: Pedro Miguel Faria Caixinha (Portugal).
Peñarol: Juan Guillermo Castillo Iriarte, Damián Macaluso Rojas (24.Octavio Darío Rodríguez Peña), Carlos Adrián Valdéz Suárez (65.Emiliano Albín Antognazza), Jonathan Alexis Sandoval Rojas, Joe Emerson Bastos Bizera, Jorge Nicolás Raguso Sánchez, Jorge Marcelo Rodríguez Núñez, Luís Bernardo Aguiar Burgos, Antonio Pacheco D'Agosti (72.Carlos Rodrigo Núñez Techera), Sebastián Gerardo Píriz Ribas, Javier Fabián Toledo. Trainer: Jorge Daniel Fossati Lurachi.
Goals: Carlos Darwin Quintero Villalba (8), Javier Antonio Orozco Peñuelas (58), Carlos Darwin Quintero Villalba (78), Andrés Yair Rentería Morelo (79) / Javier Fabián Toledo (1).

26.03.2014, Estadio „José Antonio Anzoátegui“, Puerto la Cruz
Referee: Ricardo Marques Ribeiro (Brazil)
Deportivo Anzoátegui SC Puerto La Cruz - Arsenal de Sarandí FC 1-3(0-1)
Deportivo Anzoátegui: Edixson Antonio González Peroza, Johnny Jair Mirabal Arboleda (69.Ricardo Manuel Cardoso Martins), Juan José Fuenmayor Núñez, Alejandro Enrique Cichero Konarek, Diego Jesús Araguainamo Guacarán, Rolando Emilio Escobar Batista, José David Moreno Chacón, Evelio De Jesús Hernández Guedez, Manuel Alejandro Arteaga Rubianes (79.Edwin Enrique Aguilar Samaniego), Framber Johan Villegas Sangronis, Jaime José Moreno Ciorciari (63.Oscar Alberto Briceño Bueno). Trainer: Juvencio Betancourt.
Arsenal: Cristian Daniel Campestrini, Mariano Raúl Echeverría, Eduardo Javier Casais, Martín Hugo Nervo, Matías Ezequiel Zaldivia, Leandro Martín González Pírez, Gastón Rubén Esmerado, Martín Rolle, Matías Ariel Sánchez (70.Fausto Emanuel Montero), Mauricio Ezequiel Sperdutti (55.Ramiro Ángel Carrera), Milton Joel Caraglio (79.Julio César Furch). Trainer: Gustavo Julio Alfaro.
Goals: Rolando Emilio Escobar Batista (55) / Matías Ariel Sánchez (35), Martín Rolle (64), Matías Ezequiel Zaldivia (90+2).

10.04.2014, Estadio „Julio Humberto Grondona“, Sarandí
Referee: Marcelo Henrique (Brazil)
Arsenal de Sarandí FC - Club Santos Laguna Torreón 3-0(1-0)
Arsenal: Óscar Alejandro Limia Rodríguez, Diego Luis Braghieri, Mariano Raúl Echeverría, Daniel Alejandro Rosero Valencia, Federico Emanuel Milo, Gastón Rubén Esmerado, Matías Ariel Sánchez, Federico Freire (79.Nicolás Diego Aguirre), Julián Cardozo (75.Franco Zuculini), Emilio José Zelaya (82.Martín Rolle), Milton Joel Caraglio. Trainer: Gustavo Julio Alfaro.
Santos: Julio José González Vela Alvizu, Osmar Mares Martínez (57.José de la Tejera Farias), Jonathan Leonardo Lacerda Araujo, Néstor Alejandro Araujo Razo, Sergio Ceballos Herrera, Rodolfo Salinas Ortíz, Mauro Emiliano Cejas (76.Ulises Rivas Gilio), Marc Crosas Luque, Néstor Calderón Enríquez (58.Jesús Alonso Escoboza Lugo), Eduardo Herrera Aguirre, Walter Gael Sandoval Contreras. Trainer: Pedro Miguel Faria Caixinha (Portugal).
Goals: Emilio José Zelaya (20), Mariano Raúl Echeverría (54), Emilio José Zelaya (73).

10.04.2014, Estadio Centenario, Montevideo
Referee: Diego Mirko Haro Sueldo (Peru)
CA Peñarol Montevideo - Deportivo Anzoátegui SC Puerto La Cruz 1-1(1-0)
Peñarol: Danilo Emanuel Lerda, Pablo Martín Lima Olid, Héctor Baltasar Silva Cabrera (80.Jonathan Javier Rodríguez Portillo), Emiliano Albín Antognazza (68.Fabián Larry Estoyanoff Poggio), Jonathan Alexis Sandoval Rojas, Joe Emerson Bastos Bizera, Washington Emilio MacEachen Vázquez, Jorge Nicolás Raguso Sánchez, Sergio Daniel Orteman Rodríguez, Mauro Raúl Fernández, Hober Gabriel Leyes Viera (71.Javier Fabián Toledo). Trainer: Jorge Daniel Fossati Lurachi.
Deportivo Anzoátegui: Richard Alejandro Ruíz Ruíz, Pablo Jesús Camacho Figueira, Carlos Javier Lujano Sánchez, Edgar José Mendoza Acosta, Diego Jesús Araguainamo Guacarán, José David Moreno Chacón, Diego Silva (46.Alejandro Antonio Carrera Gómez), Ricardo Manuel Cardoso Martins, Robert Enrique Hernández Aguado (87.Gabriel José Boggio Bernal), Edwin Enrique Aguilar Samaniego (81.Luis José Castillo Patiño), Oscar Alberto Briceño Bueno. Trainer: Juvencio Betancourt.
Goals: Héctor Baltasar Silva Cabrera (8) / Edwin Enrique Aguilar Samaniego (64).

FINAL STANDINGS

1.	**Club Santos Laguna Torreón**	6	4	1	1	11	-	5	13
2.	**Arsenal de Sarandí FC**	6	4	0	2	11	-	4	12
3.	CA Peñarol Montevideo	6	1	2	3	5	-	10	5
4.	Deportivo Anzoátegui SC Puerto La Cruz	6	0	3	3	4	-	12	3

ROUND OF 16

16.04.2014, Estadio León, León
Referee: Carlos Arecio Amarilla Demarqui (Paraguay)
Club León FC - Club Bolívar La Paz **2-2(1-1)**
León: William Paul Yarbrough Story, José Jonny Magallón Oliva, Juan Ignacio González Ibarra [*sent off 79*], Edwin William Hernández Herrera, Fernando Navarro Morán, Luis Arturo Montes Jiménez, Elias Hernán Hernández Jacuinde (76.Eisner Iván Loboa Balanta), Carlos Alberto Peña Rodríguez (65.Matías Britos Cardoso), José Juan Vázquez Gómez, Mauro Boselli, Franco Faustino Arizala Hurtado (76.José María Cárdenas López). Trainer: Christian Gustavo Matosas Paidón (Uruguay).
Bolívar: Romel Javier Quiñónez Suárez, Nelson David Cabrera Báez, Ronald Eguino Segovia (74.Lorgio Álvarez Roca), Luis Alberto Gutiérrez Herrera, Walter Alberto Flores Condarco, Juan Miguel Callejón Bueno (76.Erwin Mario Saavedra Flores), José Luis Sánchez Capdevila, Damir Miranda Mercado, Juan Carlos Arce Justiniano (84.Rudy Alejandro Cardozo Fernández), César Gerardo Yecerotte Soruco, William Ferreira Martínez. Trainer: Francisco Xabier Azkargorta Uriarte (Spain).
Goals: Luis Arturo Montes Jiménez (20), Mauro Boselli (85) / Juan Miguel Callejón Bueno (44), Juan Carlos Arce Justiniano (70).

22.04.2014, Estadio „Hernando Siles", La Paz
Referee: Adrián Alexander Vélez Londoño (Colombia)
Club Bolívar La Paz - Club León FC **1-1(1-1)**
Bolívar: Romel Javier Quiñónez Suárez, Nelson David Cabrera Báez, Ronald Eguino Segovia, Luis Alberto Gutiérrez Herrera, Walter Alberto Flores Condarco, Juan Miguel Callejón Bueno (71.Erwin Mario Saavedra Flores), José Luis Sánchez Capdevila, Damir Miranda Mercado, Juan Carlos Arce Justiniano (90+4.Jaime Darío Arrascaita Iriondo), César Gerardo Yecerotte Soruco (81.Lorgio Álvarez Roca), William Ferreira Martínez. Trainer: Francisco Xabier Azkargorta Uriarte (Spain).
León: William Paul Yarbrough Story, Rafael Márquez Álvarez [*sent off 77*], José Jonny Magallón Oliva, Edwin William Hernández Herrera (77.José María Cárdenas López), Fernando Navarro Morán, Luis Arturo Montes Jiménez, Carlos Alberto Peña Rodríguez (73.Eisner Iván Loboa Balanta), José Juan Vázquez Gómez, Mauro Boselli, Franco Faustino Arizala Hurtado, Matías Britos Cardoso (61.Miguel Sabah Rodríguez). Trainer: Christian Gustavo Matosas Paidón (Uruguay).
Goals: Ronald Eguino Segovia (35) / Franco Faustino Arizala Hurtado (5).
[Club Bolívar La Paz won on away goals rule (3-3 on aggregate)]

16.04.2014, Estadio Ciudad de Lanús „Néstor Díaz Pérez", Lanús
Referee: Patricio Antonio Polic Orellana (Chile)
Club Atlético Lanús - Club Santos Laguna Torreón **2-1(0-0)**
CA Lanús: Agustín Federico Marchesín, Maximiliano Nicolás Velázquez, Carlos Luciano Araujo, Matías Alfredo Martínez, Facundo Daniel Monteseirín, Jorge Alberto Ortíz, Diego Hernán González, Víctor Hugo Ayala Núñez, Marcos Emanuel Astina (76.Alejandro Daniel Silva González), Lautaro Germán Acosta (63.Óscar Junior Benítez), Ismael Alfonso Blanco (77.Lucas Santiago Melano). Trainer: Guillermo Barros Schelotto.
Santos: Oswaldo Javier Sánchez Ibarra, Rafael Alejandro Figueroa Gómez, Jonathan Leonardo Lacerda Araujo, Oswaldo Alanís Pantoja, José Javier Abella Fanjul, Sergio Ceballos Herrera, Juan Pablo Rodríguez Guerrero, Mauro Emiliano Cejas (77.Rodolfo Salinas Ortíz), Oribe Peralta Morones (90+1.Javier Antonio Orozco Peñuelas), Carlos Darwin Quintero Villalba, Andrés Yair Rentería Morelo (77.Jesús Alonso Escoboza Lugo). Trainer: Pedro Miguel Faria Caixinha (Portugal).
Goals: Facundo Daniel Monteseirín (65), Matías Alfredo Martínez (90+4) / Carlos Darwin Quintero Villalba (57).

23.04.2014, Estadio Corona, Torreón
Referee: Darío Agustín Ubríaco Medero (Uruguay)
Club Santos Laguna Torreón - Club Atlético Lanús 0-2(0-1)
Santos: Oswaldo Javier Sánchez Ibarra, Rafael Alejandro Figueroa Gómez (46.Mauro Emiliano Cejas), Jonathan Leonardo Lacerda Araujo, Oswaldo Alanís Pantoja, José Javier Abella Fanjul, Sergio Ceballos Herrera, Juan Pablo Rodríguez Guerrero (81.Eduardo Herrera Aguirre), Oribe Peralta Morones, Carlos Darwin Quintero Villalba, Javier Antonio Orozco Peñuelas (55.Ribair Rodríguez Pérez), Andrés Yair Rentería Morelo [*sent off 74*]. Trainer: Pedro Miguel Faria Caixinha (Portugal).
CA Lanús: Agustín Federico Marchesín, Paolo Duval Goltz, Maximiliano Nicolás Velázquez, Carlos Luciano Araujo, Carlos Roberto Izquierdoz, Leandro Daniel Somoza, Diego Hernán González (90.Fernando Omar Barrientos), Víctor Hugo Ayala Núñez, Óscar Junior Benítez (80.Alejandro Daniel Silva González), Lautaro Germán Acosta (57.Jorge Vidal Valdéz Chamorro), Ismael Alfonso Blanco. Trainer: Guillermo Barros Schelotto.
Goals: Ismael Alfonso Blanco (28), Paolo Duval Goltz (50 penalty).
[Club Atlético Lanús won 4-1 on aggregate]

16.04.2014, Estádio Mineirão, Belo Horizonte
Referee: Daniel Adan Fedorczuk Betancour (Uruguay)
Cruzeiro EC Belo Horizonte - Club Cerro Porteño Asunción 1-1(0-1)
Cruzeiro: Fábio Deivson Lopes Maciel, Marcos Venâncio de Albuquerque „Ceará" (58.Mayke Rocha de Oliveira), Miguel Ángel Samudio, Bruno Rodrigo Fenelon Palomo, Anderson Vital da Silva „Dedé", Éverton de Barros Ribeiro, Henrique Pacheco de Lima, José Élber Pimentel da Silva (42.Humberlito Borges Teixeira), Lucas Silva Borges, Júlio César Baptista (76.Johnath Marlone Azevedo da Silva), Willian Gomes de Siqueira. Trainer: Marcelo de Oliveira Santos.
Cerro Porteño: Roberto Júnior Fernández Torres, Carlos Bonet Cáceres, Luis Carlos Cardozo Espillaga, Matías Corujo Díaz, Danilo Fabián Ortíz Soto, Junior Osmar Ignacio Alonso Mujica, Julio Daniel Dos Santos Rodríguez, Fidencio Oviedo Domínguez, Óscar David Romero Villamayor (83.William Candia), Daniel González Güiza (83.Iván Arturo Torres Riveros), Ángel Rodrigo Romero Villamayor (88.Guillermo Alexis Beltrán Paredes). Trainer: Francisco Javier Arce Rolón.
Goals: Miguel Ángel Samudio (90+3) / Ángel Rodrigo Romero Villamayor (31).

30.04.2014, Estadio „General Pablo Rojas", Asunción
Referee: Darío Agustín Ubríaco Medero (Uruguay)
Club Cerro Porteño Asunción - Cruzeiro EC Belo Horizonte 0-2(0-0)
Cerro Porteño: Roberto Júnior Fernández Torres, Carlos Bonet Cáceres, Luis Carlos Cardozo Espillaga, Matías Corujo Díaz [*sent off 84*], Danilo Fabián Ortíz Soto, Junior Osmar Ignacio Alonso Mujica (82.Rodolfo Vicente Gamarra Varela), Julio Daniel Dos Santos Rodríguez, Fidencio Oviedo Domínguez, Óscar David Romero Villamayor, Daniel González Güiza [*sent off 85 on the bench*] (73.Guillermo Alexis Beltrán Paredes), Ángel Rodrigo Romero Villamayor (70.Diego Armando Godoy Vásquez). Trainer: Francisco Javier Arce Rolón.
Cruzeiro: Fábio Deivson Lopes Maciel, Marcos Venâncio de Albuquerque „Ceará", Miguel Ángel Samudio, Bruno Rodrigo Fenelon Palomo [*sent off 78*], Anderson Vital da Silva „Dedé", Éverton de Barros Ribeiro, Henrique Pacheco de Lima, Lucas Silva Borges, Júlio César Baptista (62.Humberlito Borges Teixeira; 82.Leonardo Renan Simões de Lacerda "Léo"), Ricardo Goulart Pereira, Willian Gomes de Siqueira (62.Dagoberto Pelentier). Trainer: Marcelo de Oliveira Santos.
Goals: Anderson Vital da Silva „Dedé" (79), Dagoberto Pelentier (90+3).
[Cruzeiro EC Belo Horizonte won 3-1 on aggregate]

17.04.2014, Estadio „Hernando Siles“, La Paz
Referee: Marcelo Henrique (Brazil)
Club The Strongest La Paz - Defensor Sporting Club Montevideo 2-0(0-0)
The Strongest: Daniel Vaca Tasca, Nelvin Solíz Escalante, Marcos Israel Barrera, Jeferson Lopes Faustino, Alejandro Saúl Chumacero Bracamonte, Pablo Daniel Escobar Olivetti, Diego Bejarano Ibáñez, Diego Horacio Wayar Cruz (53.Luis Hernán Melgar Ortíz), Raúl Castro Peñaloza, Jair Alexander Reinoso Moreno, Daniel Andrés Chávez Betancourt (59.Jair Torrico Camacho). Trainer: Eduardo Andrés Villegas Camara.
Defensor: Martín Nicolás Campaña Delgado, Roberto Fabián Herrera Rosas, Nicolás Correa Risso, Matías Daniel Malvino Gómez, Emilio Enrique Zeballos Gutiérrez, Mathías Adolfo Cardaccio Alaguich (76.Andrés José Fleurquin Rubio), Leonardo Javier Pais Corbo, Felipe Gedoz da Conceição (70.Adrián Nicolás Luna Retamar), Giorgian Daniel de Arrascaeta Benedetti (82.Juan Carlos Amado Alanís), Federico Gino Acevedo Fagundez, Matías Damián Alonso Vallejo. Trainer: Fernando Darío Curutchet Godoy.
Goals: Jair Alexander Reinoso Moreno (68), Raúl Castro Peñaloza (77).

29.04.2014, Estadio „Luis Franzini“, Montevideo
Referee: Antonio Javier Arias Alvarenga (Paraguay)
Defensor Sporting Club Montevideo - Club The Strongest La Paz 2-0(0-0,2-0,2-0); 4-2 on penalties
Defensor: Martín Nicolás Campaña Delgado, Roberto Fabián Herrera Rosas, Nicolás Correa Risso, Matías Daniel Malvino Gómez, Emilio Enrique Zeballos Gutiérrez, Mathías Adolfo Cardaccio Alaguich, Andrés José Fleurquin Rubio, Leonardo Javier Pais Corbo (53.Andrés Nicolás Olivera), Felipe Gedoz da Conceição (80.Adrián Nicolás Luna Retamar), Giorgian Daniel de Arrascaeta Benedetti, Ignacio Risso Thomasset (61.Matías Damián Alonso Vallejo). Trainer: Fernando Darío Curutchet Godoy.
The Strongest: Daniel Vaca Tasca, Nelvin Solíz Escalante (81.Boris Xavier Alfaro Chong), Marcos Israel Barrera, Jeferson Lopes Faustino, Alejandro Saúl Chumacero Bracamonte, Pablo Daniel Escobar Olivetti, Ernesto Rubén Cristaldo Santa Cruz, Diego Bejarano Ibáñez, Raúl Castro Peñaloza, Jair Alexander Reinoso Moreno (63.Víctor Hugo Melgar Bejarano), Daniel Andrés Chávez Betancourt (89.Luis Hernán Melgar Ortíz). Trainer: Eduardo Andrés Villegas Camara.
Goals: Giorgian Daniel de Arrascaeta Benedetti (59), Andrés Nicolás Olivera (64).
Penalties: Matías Damián Alonso Vallejo 1-0; Ernesto Rubén Cristaldo Santa Cruz (missed); Matías Daniel Malvino Gómez 2-0; Marcos Israel Barrera (missed); Andrés José Fleurquin Rubio (missed); Boris Xavier Alfaro Chong 2-1; Adrián Nicolás Luna Retamar 3-1; Raúl Castro Peñaloza 3-2; Andrés Nicolás Olivera 4-2.
[Defensor Sporting Club Montevideo won 4-2 on penalties (after 2-2 on aggregate)]

23.04.2014, Estadio Defensores del Chaco, Asunción
Referee: Héber Roberto Lopes (Brazil)
Club Nacional Asunción - CA Vélez Sarsfield Buenos Aires 1-0(0-0)
Nacional: Ignacio Oscar Don, José Leonardo Cáceres Ovelar, David Bernardo Mendoza Ayala, Raúl Eduardo Piris, Ramón David Coronel Gómez, Marcos Benjamín Melgarejo (86.Hugo Américo Lusardi Morínigo), Marcos Antonio Riveros Krayacich, Derlis Ricardo Orué Acevedo (75.Julio Eduardo Santa Cruz Cantero), Silvio Gabriel Torales, Julián Alfonso Benítez Franco, Freddy José Bareiro Gamarra (90+2.Juan David Argüello Arias). Trainer: Gustavo Eliseo Morínigo Vázquez.
Vélez Sarsfield: Carlos Sebastián Sosa Silva, Sebastián Enrique Domínguez, Fernando Omar Tobío, Facundo Cardozo, Alejandro Ariel Cabral, Fabián Andrés Cubero, Héctor Miguel Canteros, Jorge Iván Correa (85.Leonardo Enrique Villalba), Agustín Leonel Allione (72.Roberto Antonio Nanni), Lucas Daniel Romero, Lucas David Pratto. Trainer: José Oscar Flores.
Goal: Julián Alfonso Benítez Franco (86).

29.04.2014, Estadio „José Amalfitani“, Buenos Aires
Referee: Sandro Meira Ricci (Brazil)
CA Vélez Sarsfield Buenos Aires - Club Nacional Asunción 2-2(0-0)
Vélez Sarsfield: Carlos Sebastián Sosa Silva, Sebastián Enrique Domínguez, Fernando Omar Tobío (85.Yamil Rodrigo Asad), Facundo Cardozo (61.Roberto Antonio Nanni), Alejandro Ariel Cabral, Fabián Andrés Cubero, Héctor Miguel Canteros [*sent off 87*], Jorge Iván Correa, Lucas Daniel Romero [*sent off 78*], Lucas David Pratto, Mauro Matías Zárate. Trainer: José Oscar Flores.
Nacional: Ignacio Oscar Don, José Leonardo Cáceres Ovelar, David Bernardo Mendoza Ayala, Raúl Eduardo Piris, Ramón David Coronel Gómez, Marcos Benjamín Melgarejo (88.Juan David Argüello Arias), Marcos Antonio Riveros Krayacich, Derlis Ricardo Orué Acevedo, Silvio Gabriel Torales, Julián Alfonso Benítez Franco (62.Fabián Cornelio Balbuena González), Freddy José Bareiro Gamarra (83.Julio Eduardo Santa Cruz Cantero). Trainer: Gustavo Eliseo Morínigo Vázquez.
Goals: Jorge Iván Correa (74, 84) / Silvio Gabriel Torales (78 penalty), Derlis Ricardo Orué Acevedo (90+3).
[Club Nacional Asunción won 3-2 on aggregate]

23.04.2014, Estadio „Pedro Bidegain“, Buenos Aires
Referee: Enrique Roberto Osses Zencovich (Chile)
CA San Lorenzo de Almagro - Grêmio Foot-Ball Porto Alegrense 1-0(0-0)
San Lorenzo: Sebastián Alberto Torrico, Santiago Juan Gentiletti Selak, Carlos Enrique Valdéz Parra, Emanuel Matías Más, Ignacio Piatti (69.Walter Kanneman), Néstor Ezequiel Ortigoza, Juan Ignacio Mercier, Julio Alberto Buffarini, Mauro Matos, Héctor Villalba (76.Juan Ignacio Cavallaro), Ángel Correa (83.Fernando Elizari). Trainer: Edgardo Bauza.
Grêmio: Marcelo Grohe, Pedro Tonon Geromel, Marcos Rogério Ricci Lopes „Pará“, Werley Ananias da Silva, Cristian Miguel Riveros Núñez, José Roberto da Silva Júnior „Zé Roberto“ (86.Maximiliano Rodríguez Maeso), Edimo Ferreira Campos „Edinho“, Leonardo David de Moura „Léo Gago“ (83.Breno Lorran da Silva Talvares), Eduardo Pereira Rodrigues „Dudu“, Ramiro Moschen Benetti (57.Luan Guilherme de Jesús Vieira), Hernán Barcos. Trainer: Enderson Alves Moreira.
Goal: Ángel Correa (51).

30.04.2014, Arena do Grêmio, Porto Alegre
Referee: Roberto Carlos Silvera Calcerrada (Uruguay)
Grêmio Foot-Ball Porto Alegrense - CA San Lorenzo de Almagro 1-0(0-0,1-0,1-0); 2-4 on penalties
Grêmio: Marcelo Grohe, Pedro Tonon Geromel, Marcos Rogério Ricci Lopes „Pará“ (80.Lucas Coelho), Werley Ananias da Silva, Wendell Nascimento Borges, Cristian Miguel Riveros Núñez, José Roberto da Silva Júnior „Zé Roberto“ (60.Rodrigo Eduardo Costa Marinho “Rodriguinho”), Edimo Ferreira Campos „Edinho“, Eduardo Pereira Rodrigues „Dudu“, Luan Guilherme de Jesús Vieira (64.Maximiliano Rodríguez Maeso), Hernán Barcos. Trainer: Enderson Alves Moreira.
San Lorenzo: Sebastián Alberto Torrico, Santiago Juan Gentiletti Selak, Carlos Enrique Valdéz Parra, Emanuel Matías Más, Ignacio Piatti, Néstor Ezequiel Ortigoza, Juan Ignacio Mercier, Julio Alberto Buffarini, Mauro Matos, Héctor Villalba (69.Gonzalo Sebastián Prósperi), Ángel Correa (74.Fernando Elizari; 90+2.Nicolás Blandi). Trainer: Edgardo Bauza.
Goal: Eduardo Pereira Rodrigues „Dudu“ (83).
Penalties: Hernán Barcos (missed); Néstor Ezequiel Ortigoza 0-1; Cristian Miguel Riveros Núñez 1-1; Mauro Matos 1-2; Maximiliano Rodríguez Maeso (missed); Nicolás Blandi 1-3; Rodrigo Eduardo Costa Marinho “Rodriguinho” 2-3; Julio Alberto Buffarini 2-4.
[CA San Lorenzo de Almagro won 4-2 on penalties (after 1-1 on aggregate)]

23.04.2014, Estadio „Atanasio Girardot", Medellín
Referee: Martín Emilio Vázquez Broquetas (Uruguay)
Club Atlético Nacional Medellín - Atlético Mineiro Belo Horizonte 1-0(0-0)
Atlético Nacional: Franco Armani, Alexis Héctor Henríquez Charales, Álvaro Francisco Nájera Gil, Alejandro Bernal Rios (58.Diego Alejandro Arias Hincapié), Farid Alfonso Díaz Rhenals, Oscar Fabián Murillo Murillo, Daniel Eduardo Bocanegra Ortíz, Sherman Andrés Cárdenas Estupiñán, Alexander Mejía Sabalsa, Juan David Valencia Hinestroza, Jefferson Andrés Duque Montoya (70.Santiago Tréllez Vivero). Trainer: Juan Carlos Osorio Arbelaez.
Atlético Mineiro: Victor Leandro Bagy, Emerson Conçeiçao, Leonardo Fabiano Silva e Silva, Réver Humberto Alves Araújo, Nicolás Hernán Otamendi, Ronaldo de Assis Moreira „Ronaldinho" (85.Guilherme Milhomen Gusmão), Lucas Pierre Santos Oliveira, Leandro Donizete Gonçalves da Silva, Diego Tardelli Martins, João Alves de Assis Silva "Jô", Luiz Fernando Pereira da Silva "Fernandinho" (82.Marion Silva Fernandes). Trainer: Paulo Autuori de Mello.
Goal: Sherman Andrés Cárdenas Estupiñán (90+1).

01.05.2014, Estádio Independência, Belo Horizonte
Referee: Patricio Hernán Loustau (Argentina)
Atlético Mineiro Belo Horizonte - Club Atlético Nacional Medellín 1-1(1-0)
Atlético Mineiro: Victor Leandro Bagy, Emerson Conçeiçao, Leonardo Fabiano Silva e Silva, Nicolás Hernán Otamendi, Alex da Silva, Ronaldo de Assis Moreira „Ronaldinho", Lucas Pierre Santos Oliveira (73.Réver Humberto Alves Araújo), Leandro Donizete Gonçalves da Silva, Diego Tardelli Martins (73.Guilherme Milhomen Gusmão), João Alves de Assis Silva "Jô", Luiz Fernando Pereira da Silva "Fernandinho" (80.Marion Silva Fernandes). Trainer: Levir Culpi.
Atlético Nacional: Franco Armani, Alexis Héctor Henríquez Charales, Alejandro Bernal Rios (75.Álvaro Francisco Nájera Gil), Farid Alfonso Díaz Rhenals (81.Diego Alejandro Arias Hincapié), Oscar Fabián Murillo Murillo, Daniel Eduardo Bocanegra Ortíz, Diego Arturo Peralta González (58.Jefferson Andrés Duque Montoya), Sherman Andrés Cárdenas Estupiñán, Alexander Mejía Sabalsa, Juan David Valencia Hinestroza, Edwin Andrés Cardona Bedoya. Trainer: Juan Carlos Osorio Arbelaez.
Goals: Luiz Fernando Pereira da Silva "Fernandinho" (20) / Jefferson Andrés Duque Montoya (87).
[Club Atlético Nacional Medellín won 2-1 on aggregate]

24.04.2014, Estadio „Julio Humberto Grondona", Sarandí
Referee: Víctor Hugo Carrillo Casanova (Peru)
Arsenal de Sarandí FC - Club Unión Española Santiago 0-0
Arsenal: Cristian Daniel Campestrini, Diego Luis Braghieri, Mariano Raúl Echeverría [*sent off 87*], Damián Alfredo Pérez, Martín Hugo Nervo, Martín Rolle (67.Franco Zuculini), Matías Ariel Sánchez, Iván José Marcone, Federico Freire, Mauricio Ezequiel Sperdutti (73.Julio César Furch), Milton Joel Caraglio (80.Emilio José Zelaya). Trainer: Martín Palermo.
Unión Española: Diego Ignacio Sánchez Carvajal, Jorge Enrique Ampuero Cabello, Dagoberto Alexis Currimilla Gómez, Nicolás Berardo, Matías Cristóbal Navarrete Fuentes, Cristian Manuel Chávez, Luis Antonio Pavez Contreras, Diego Scotti Ponce De León, Matías Daniel Campos Toro (66.Patricio Elías Vidal), Gustavo Javier Canales, Sebastián Oscar Jaime. Trainer: José Luis Sierra Pando.

30.04.2014, Estadio Santa Laura-Universidad SEK, Independencia
Referee: Ricardo Marques Ribeiro (Brazil)
Club Unión Española Santiago - Arsenal de Sarandí FC 0-1(0-0)
Unión Española: Diego Ignacio Sánchez Carvajal, Jorge Enrique Ampuero Cabello, Dagoberto Alexis Currimilla Gómez, Nicolás Berardo (81.Carlos Daniel Salom Zulema), Matías Cristóbal Navarrete Fuentes, Cristian Manuel Chávez, Luis Antonio Pavez Contreras (68.Lorenzo Abel Faravelli), Diego Scotti Ponce De León, Matías Daniel Campos Toro, Gustavo Javier Canales, Sebastián Oscar Jaime. Trainer: José Luis Sierra Pando.
Arsenal: Cristian Daniel Campestrini, Diego Luis Braghieri, Damián Alfredo Pérez, Martín Hugo Nervo, Leandro Martín González Pírez, Matías Ariel Sánchez (63.Nicolás Diego Aguirre), Iván José Marcone, Federico Freire (87.Matías Ezequiel Zaldivia), Mauricio Ezequiel Sperdutti, Milton Joel Caraglio, Julio César Furch (77.Emilio José Zelaya). Trainer: Martín Palermo.
Goal: Diego Luis Braghieri (66).
[Arsenal de Sarandí FC won 1-0 on aggregate]

QUARTER-FINALS

07.05.2014, Estadio Defensores del Chaco, Asunción
Referee: Wilmar Alexander Roldán Pérez (Colombia)
Club Nacional Asunción - Arsenal de Sarandí FC 1-0(1-0)
Nacional: Ignacio Oscar Don, José Leonardo Cáceres Ovelar, David Bernardo Mendoza Ayala, Raúl Eduardo Piris, Ramón David Coronel Gómez, Marcos Benjamín Melgarejo (65.Fabián Cornelio Balbuena González), Marcos Antonio Riveros Krayacich, Derlis Ricardo Orué Acevedo, Silvio Gabriel Torales, Julián Alfonso Benítez Franco (88.Hugo Américo Lusardi Morínigo), Freddy José Bareiro Gamarra. Trainer: Gustavo Eliseo Morínigo Vázquez.
Arsenal: Cristian Daniel Campestrini, Diego Luis Braghieri, Damián Alfredo Pérez, Martín Hugo Nervo, Leandro Martín González Pírez, Matías Ariel Sánchez (63.Nicolás Diego Aguirre), Iván José Marcone [*sent off 90+5*], Federico Freire (75.Franco Zuculini), Mauricio Ezequiel Sperdutti, Milton Joel Caraglio, Julio César Furch (88.Emilio José Zelaya). Trainer: Martín Palermo.
Goal: Derlis Ricardo Orué Acevedo (35).

14.05.2014, Estadio „Julio Humberto Grondona“, Sarandí
Referee: Leandro Pedro Vuaden (Brazil)
Arsenal de Sarandí FC - Club Nacional Asunción 0-0
Arsenal: Cristian Daniel Campestrini (90+1.Óscar Alejandro Limia Rodríguez), Diego Luis Braghieri, Mariano Raúl Echeverría, Damián Alfredo Pérez, Martín Hugo Nervo, Nicolás Diego Aguirre, Iván José Marcone, Federico Freire (70.Martín Rolle), Mauricio Ezequiel Sperdutti, Milton Joel Caraglio, Julio César Furch (74.Emilio José Zelaya). Trainer: Martín Palermo.
Nacional: Ignacio Oscar Don, José Leonardo Cáceres Ovelar, David Bernardo Mendoza Ayala, Raúl Eduardo Piris, Ramón David Coronel Gómez, Marcos Benjamín Melgarejo (82.Julio Eduardo Santa Cruz Cantero), Marcos Antonio Riveros Krayacich, Derlis Ricardo Orué Acevedo, Silvio Gabriel Torales, Julián Alfonso Benítez Franco (64.Fabián Cornelio Balbuena González), Freddy José Bareiro Gamarra (89.Marcos David Miers). Trainer: Gustavo Eliseo Morínigo Vázquez.
[Club Nacional Asunción won 1-0 on aggregate]

07.05.2014, Estadio „Pedro Bidegain", Buenos Aires
Referee: Antonio Javier Arias Alvarenga (Paraguay)
CA San Lorenzo de Almagro - Cruzeiro EC Belo Horizonte 1-0(0-0)
San Lorenzo: Sebastián Alberto Torrico, Santiago Juan Gentiletti Selak, Carlos Enrique Valdéz Parra, Emanuel Matías Más (81.Leandro Alexis Navarro), Ignacio Piatti, Néstor Ezequiel Ortigoza, Juan Ignacio Mercier, Julio Alberto Buffarini, Mauro Matos, Héctor Villalba (83.Fernando Elizari), Ángel Correa (73.Walter Kanneman). Trainer: Edgardo Bauza.
Cruzeiro: Fábio Deivson Lopes Maciel, Marcos Venâncio de Albuquerque „Ceará", Miguel Ángel Samudio, Leonardo Renan Simões de Lacerda "Léo", Anderson Vital da Silva „Dedé", Éverton de Barros Ribeiro, Henrique Pacheco de Lima, Lucas Silva Borges, Júlio César Baptista (69.Humberlito Borges Teixeira), Ricardo Goulart Pereira, Willian Gomes de Siqueira (69.Dagoberto Pelentier). Trainer: Marcelo de Oliveira Santos.
Goal: Santiago Juan Gentiletti Selak (64).

14.05.2014, Estádio Mineirão, Belo Horizonte
Referee: Martín Emilio Vázquez Broquetas (Uruguay)
Cruzeiro EC Belo Horizonte - CA San Lorenzo de Almagro 1-1(0-1)
Cruzeiro: Fábio Deivson Lopes Maciel, Marcos Venâncio de Albuquerque „Ceará", Miguel Ángel Samudio (33.Egidio de Araujo Pereira Júnior), Bruno Rodrigo Fenelon Palomo, Anderson Vital da Silva „Dedé", Éverton de Barros Ribeiro, Henrique Pacheco de Lima, Nílton Ferreira Júnior (46.Dagoberto Pelentier), Júlio César Baptista (57.Ricardo Goulart Pereira), Marcelo Moreno Martins, Willian Gomes de Siqueira. Trainer: Marcelo de Oliveira Santos.
San Lorenzo: Sebastián Alberto Torrico, Santiago Juan Gentiletti Selak, Carlos Enrique Valdéz Parra, Emanuel Matías Más, Ignacio Piatti (68.Walter Kanneman), Néstor Ezequiel Ortigoza, Juan Ignacio Mercier, Julio Alberto Buffarini, Mauro Matos, Héctor Villalba (76.Enzo Kalinski), Ángel Correa (60.Leandro Atilio Romagnoli [*sent off 77*]). Trainer: Edgardo Bauza.
Goals: Bruno Rodrigo Fenelon Palomo (70) / Ignacio Piatti (9).
[CA San Lorenzo de Almagro won 2-1 on aggregate]

08.05.2014, Estadio Ciudad de Lanús „Néstor Díaz Pérez", Lanús
Referee: Víctor Hugo Carrillo Casanova (Peru)
Club Atlético Lanús - Club Bolívar La Paz 1-1(1-0)
CA Lanús: Agustín Federico Marchesín, Paolo Duval Goltz, Maximiliano Nicolás Velázquez, Carlos Luciano Araujo, Carlos Roberto Izquierdoz, Leandro Daniel Somoza, Diego Hernán González, Víctor Hugo Ayala Núñez, Óscar Junior Benítez, Marcos Emanuel Astina (65.Bruno Leonel Vides), Ismael Alfonso Blanco. Trainer: Guillermo Barros Schelotto.
Bolívar: Romel Javier Quiñónez Suárez, Nelson David Cabrera Báez, Ronald Eguino Segovia, Luis Alberto Gutiérrez Herrera, Walter Alberto Flores Condarco, Juan Miguel Callejón Bueno (75.Erwin Mario Saavedra Flores), José Luis Sánchez Capdevila, Damir Miranda Mercado, Juan Carlos Arce Justiniano (85.Rudy Alejandro Cardozo Fernández), César Gerardo Yecerotte Soruco, William Ferreira Martínez. Trainer: Francisco Xabier Azkargorta Uriarte (Spain).
Goals: Óscar Junior Benítez (7) / William Ferreira Martínez (90+1).

15.05.2014, Estadio „Hernando Siles", La Paz
Referee: Roddy Alberto Zambrano Olmedo (Ecuador)
Club Bolívar La Paz - Club Atlético Lanús 1-0(0-0)
Bolívar: Romel Javier Quiñónez Suárez, Nelson David Cabrera Báez, Ronald Eguino Segovia, Luis Alberto Gutiérrez Herrera, Walter Alberto Flores Condarco, Juan Miguel Callejón Bueno (81.Lorgio Álvarez Roca), José Luis Sánchez Capdevila (86.Rudy Alejandro Cardozo Fernández), Damir Miranda Mercado, Juan Carlos Arce Justiniano (90+1.Jaime Darío Arrascaita Iriondo), César Gerardo Yecerotte Soruco, William Ferreira Martínez. Trainer: Francisco Xabier Azkargorta Uriarte (Spain).
CA Lanús: Agustín Federico Marchesín, Paolo Duval Goltz, Maximiliano Nicolás Velázquez, Carlos Luciano Araujo, Carlos Roberto Izquierdoz [*sent off 59*], Leandro Daniel Somoza (84.Ismael Alfonso Blanco), Jorge Alberto Ortíz (55.Lautaro Germán Acosta), Diego Hernán González (78.Alejandro Daniel Silva González), Víctor Hugo Ayala Núñez, Óscar Junior Benítez, Santiago Martín Silva Olivera. Trainer: Guillermo Barros Schelotto.
Goal: Juan Carlos Arce Justiniano (87).
[Club Bolívar La Paz won 2-1 on aggregate]

08.05.2014, Estadio „Atanasio Girardot", Medellín
Referee: Néstor Fabián Pitana (Argentina)
Club Atlético Nacional Medellín - Defensor Sporting Club Montevideo 0-2(0-0)
Atlético Nacional: Franco Armani, Alejandro Bernal Rios (72.Wilder Andrés Guisao Correa), Farid Alfonso Díaz Rhenals, Oscar Fabián Murillo Murillo, Daniel Eduardo Bocanegra Ortíz (79.Jhon Edwar Valoy Riascos), Diego Arturo Peralta González, Sherman Andrés Cárdenas Estupiñán, Alexander Mejía Sabalsa, Juan David Valencia Hinestroza, Edwin Andrés Cardona Bedoya [*sent off 86*], Jefferson Andrés Duque Montoya (81.Juan Pablo Ángel Arango). Trainer: Juan Carlos Osorio Arbelaez.
Defensor: Martín Nicolás Campaña Delgado, Roberto Fabián Herrera Rosas (67.Gastón Alexis Silva Perdomo), Nicolás Correa Risso, Matías Daniel Malvino Gómez, Emilio Enrique Zeballos Gutiérrez, Mathías Adolfo Cardaccio Alaguich, Andrés José Fleurquin Rubio, Leonardo Javier Pais Corbo, Felipe Gedoz da Conceição (54.Andrés Nicolás Olivera), Giorgian Daniel de Arrascaeta Benedetti (72.Adrián Nicolás Luna Retamar), Matías Damián Alonso Vallejo. Trainer: Fernando Darío Curutchet Godoy.
Goals: Leonardo Javier Pais Corbo (77), Andrés Nicolás Olivera (82).

15.05.2014, Estadio Centenario, Montevideo
Referee: Enrique Roberto Osses Zencovich (Chile)
Defensor Sporting Club Montevideo - Club Atlético Nacional Medellín 1-0(0-0)
Defensor: Martín Nicolás Campaña Delgado, Roberto Fabián Herrera Rosas, Nicolás Correa Risso, Matías Daniel Malvino Gómez, Emilio Enrique Zeballos Gutiérrez, Mathías Adolfo Cardaccio Alaguich (45+2.Juan Carlos Amado Alanís), Andrés José Fleurquin Rubio, Leonardo Javier Pais Corbo, Felipe Gedoz da Conceição (85.Gastón Alexis Silva Perdomo), Giorgian Daniel de Arrascaeta Benedetti, Matías Damián Alonso Vallejo (67.Andrés Nicolás Olivera). Trainer: Fernando Darío Curutchet Godoy.
Atlético Nacional: Franco Armani, Alexis Héctor Henríquez Charales, Álvaro Francisco Nájera Gil, Alejandro Bernal Rios (72.Luis Alfonso Páez Restrepo), Oscar Fabián Murillo Murillo (58.Fernando Uribe Hincapié), Daniel Eduardo Bocanegra Ortíz, Sherman Andrés Cárdenas Estupiñán, Alexander Mejía Sabalsa, Juan David Valencia Hinestroza, Jhon Edwar Valoy Riascos, Jefferson Andrés Duque Montoya (58.Juan Pablo Ángel Arango). Trainer: Juan Carlos Osorio Arbelaez.
Goal: Andrés Nicolás Olivera (88).
[Defensor Sporting Club Montevideo won 3-0 on aggregate]

SEMI-FINALS

22.07.2014, Estadio Defensores del Chaco, Asunción
Referee: Víctor Hugo Carrillo Casanova (Peru)
Club Nacional Asunción - Defensor Sporting Club Montevideo 2-0(1-0)
Nacional: Ignacio Oscar Don, José Leonardo Cáceres Ovelar, David Bernardo Mendoza Ayala, Raúl Eduardo Piris, Ramón David Coronel Gómez, Marcos Benjamín Melgarejo (84.Cecilio Andrés Domínguez Ruiz), Marcos Antonio Riveros Krayacich, Derlis Ricardo Orué Acevedo, Silvio Gabriel Torales, Julián Alfonso Benítez Franco (77.Fabián Cornelio Balbuena González), Brian Guillermo Montenegro Martínez (88.Hugo Américo Lusardi Morínigo). Trainer: Gustavo Eliseo Morínigo Vázquez.
Defensor: Martín Nicolás Campaña Delgado, Roberto Fabián Herrera Rosas, Nicolás Correa Risso, Matías Daniel Malvino Gómez, José Enrique Etcheverry Mendoza, Mathías Adolfo Cardaccio Alaguich, Leonardo Javier Pais Corbo (55.Andrés Nicolás Olivera), Juan Carlos Amado Alanís (80.Adrián Nicolás Luna Retamar), Felipe Gedoz da Conceição, Giorgian Daniel de Arrascaeta Benedetti, Matías Damián Alonso Vallejo (67.Joaquín Antonio Boghossián Lorenzo). Trainer: Fernando Darío Curutchet Godoy.
Goals: Brian Guillermo Montenegro Martínez (35), Derlis Ricardo Orué Acevedo (69).

29.07.2014, Estadio Centenario, Montevideo
Referee: Ricardo Marques Ribeiro (Brazil)
Defensor Sporting Club Montevideo - Club Nacional Asunción 1-0(0-0)
Defensor: Martín Nicolás Campaña Delgado, Roberto Fabián Herrera Rosas, Nicolás Correa Risso, Ramón Ginés Arias Quinteros, Matías Daniel Malvino Gómez, Andrés Nicolás Olivera, Mathías Adolfo Cardaccio Alaguich (46.Adrián Nicolás Luna Retamar), Andrés José Fleurquin Rubio, Felipe Gedoz da Conceição (83.Francisco Fernando Castro Gamboa), Giorgian Daniel de Arrascaeta Benedetti, Ignacio Risso Thomasset (86.Joaquín Antonio Boghossián Lorenzo). Trainer: Fernando Darío Curutchet Godoy.
Nacional: Ignacio Oscar Don, José Leonardo Cáceres Ovelar, David Bernardo Mendoza Ayala, Raúl Eduardo Piris, Ramón David Coronel Gómez, Marcos Benjamín Melgarejo, Marcos Antonio Riveros Krayacich, Derlis Ricardo Orué Acevedo (84.Marcos David Miers), Silvio Gabriel Torales, Julián Alfonso Benítez Franco (57.Fabián Cornelio Balbuena González), Brian Guillermo Montenegro Martínez (61.Freddy José Bareiro Gamarra). Trainer: Gustavo Eliseo Morínigo Vázquez.
Goal: Adrián Nicolás Luna Retamar (55).
[Club Nacional Asunción won 2-1 on aggregate]

23.07.2014, Estadio „Pedro Bidegain", Buenos Aires
Referee: José Hernando Buitrago Arango (Colombia)
CA San Lorenzo de Almagro - Club Bolívar La Paz 5-0(2-0)
San Lorenzo: Sebastián Alberto Torrico, Mauro Cetto, Santiago Juan Gentiletti Selak, Emanuel Matías Más, Ignacio Piatti, Néstor Ezequiel Ortigoza, Juan Ignacio Mercier, Leandro Atilio Romagnoli (62.Pablo Cesar Barrientos), Julio Alberto Buffarini, Mauro Matos (62.Martín Cauteruccio Rodríguez), Héctor Villalba (77.Gonzalo Alberto Verón). Trainer: Edgardo Bauza.
Bolívar: Romel Javier Quiñónez Suárez, Nelson David Cabrera Báez, Ronald Eguino Segovia, Luis Alberto Gutiérrez Herrera, Walter Alberto Flores Condarco, Juan Miguel Callejón Bueno (75.Erwin Mario Saavedra Flores), José Luis Sánchez Capdevila, Damir Miranda Mercado (46.José Luis Chávez Sánchez), Juan Carlos Arce Justiniano, César Gerardo Yecerotte Soruco, Óscar Eduardo Rodas Vargas (46.Carlos Vicente Tenorio Medina). Trainer: Francisco Xabier Azkargorta Uriarte (Spain).
Goals: Mauro Matos (5), Emanuel Matías Más (27), Juan Ignacio Mercier (69), Julio Alberto Buffarini (73), Emanuel Matías Más (87).

30.07.2014, Estadio „Hernando Siles“, La Paz
Referee: Carlos Alfredo Vera Rodríguez (Ecuador)
Club Bolívar La Paz - CA San Lorenzo de Almagro 1-0(0-0)
Bolívar: Romel Javier Quiñónez Suárez, Lorgio Álvarez Roca, Nelson David Cabrera Báez, Ronald Eguino Segovia (66.César Gerardo Yecerotte Soruco), Luis Alberto Gutiérrez Herrera, José Luis Chávez Sánchez, Juan Miguel Callejón Bueno (77.Óscar Eduardo Rodas Vargas), José Luis Sánchez Capdevila, Víctor Andrés Córdoba Córdoba (66.Rudy Alejandro Cardozo Fernández), Carlos Vicente Tenorio Medina, Juan Carlos Arce Justiniano. Trainer: Francisco Xabier Azkargorta Uriarte (Spain).
San Lorenzo: Sebastián Alberto Torrico, Mauro Cetto (76.Fabricio Bautista Fontanini), Gonzalo Sebastián Prósperi, Santiago Juan Gentiletti Selak, Emanuel Matías Más, Ignacio Piatti (65.Walter Kanneman), Néstor Ezequiel Ortigoza, Juan Ignacio Mercier, Leandro Atilio Romagnoli (71.Pablo Cesar Barrientos), Nicolás Blandi, Héctor Villalba. Trainer: Edgardo Bauza.
Goal: César Gerardo Yecerotte Soruco (90+1).
[CA San Lorenzo de Almagro won 5-1 on aggregate]

FINAL

06.08.2014, Estadio Defensores del Chaco, Asunción
Referee: Wilmar Alexander Roldán Pérez (Colombia)
Club Nacional Asunción - CA San Lorenzo de Almagro 1-1(0-0)
Nacional: Ignacio Oscar Don, José Leonardo Cáceres Ovelar, David Bernardo Mendoza Ayala, Raúl Eduardo Piris, Ramón David Coronel Gómez (71.Julio Eduardo Santa Cruz Cantero), Marcos Benjamín Melgarejo, Derlis Ricardo Orué Acevedo (71.Hugo Américo Lusardi Morínigo), Silvio Gabriel Torales, Juan David Argüello Arias, Julián Alfonso Benítez Franco (63.Cecilio Andrés Domínguez Ruiz), Freddy José Bareiro Gamarra. Trainer: Gustavo Eliseo Morínigo Vázquez.
San Lorenzo: Sebastián Alberto Torrico, Santiago Juan Gentiletti Selak, Fabricio Bautista Fontanini, Emanuel Matías Más, Ignacio Piatti, Néstor Ezequiel Ortigoza (86.Enzo Kalinski), Juan Ignacio Mercier, Leandro Atilio Romagnoli (77.Pablo Cesar Barrientos), Julio Alberto Buffarini, Mauro Matos, Héctor Villalba (71.Gonzalo Alberto Verón). Trainer: Edgardo Bauza.
Goals: Julio Eduardo Santa Cruz Cantero (90+2) / Mauro Matos (64).

13.08.2014, Estadio „Pedro Bidegain“, Buenos Aires
Referee: Sandro Meira Ricci (Brazil)
CA San Lorenzo de Almagro - Club Nacional Asunción 1-0(1-0)
San Lorenzo: Sebastián Alberto Torrico, Mauro Cetto, Santiago Juan Gentiletti Selak, Emanuel Matías Más, Néstor Ezequiel Ortigoza, Juan Ignacio Mercier, Leandro Atilio Romagnoli (88.Walter Kanneman), Julio Alberto Buffarini, Mauro Matos, Martín Cauteruccio Rodríguez (66.Gonzalo Alberto Verón), Héctor Villalba (82.Enzo Kalinski). Trainer: Edgardo Bauza.
Nacional: Ignacio Oscar Don, José Leonardo Cáceres Ovelar, David Bernardo Mendoza Ayala, Raúl Eduardo Piris, Ramón David Coronel Gómez, Marcos Benjamín Melgarejo (88.Hugo Américo Lusardi Morínigo), Marcos Antonio Riveros Krayacich, Derlis Ricardo Orué Acevedo (57.Brian Guillermo Montenegro Martínez), Silvio Gabriel Torales, Julián Alfonso Benítez Franco (85.Julio Eduardo Santa Cruz Cantero), Freddy José Bareiro Gamarra. Trainer: Gustavo Eliseo Morínigo Vázquez.
Goal: Néstor Ezequiel Ortigoza (35 penalty).

Copa Libertadores Winner 2014: **Club Atlético San Lorenzo de Almagro (Argentina)**

Best Goalscorer: Julio Daniel dos Santos Rodríguez (Club Cerro Porteño Asunción) & Andrés Nicolás Olivera (Defensor SC Montevideo) – each 5 goals

COPA LIBERTADORES (1960-2013) TABLE OF HONOURS		
1960	Club Atlético Peñarol Montevideo	(URU)
1961	Club Atlético Peñarol Montevideo	(URU)
1962	Santos Futebol Clube	(BRA)
1963	Santos Futebol Clube	(BRA)
1964	Club Atlético Independiente Avellaneda	(ARG)
1965	Club Atlético Independiente Avellaneda	(ARG)
1966	Club Atlético Peñarol Montevideo	(URU)
1967	Racing Club Avellaneda	(ARG)
1968	Club Estudiantes de La Plata	(ARG)
1969	Club Estudiantes de La Plata	(ARG)
1970	Club Estudiantes de La Plata	(ARG)
1971	Club Nacional de Football Montevideo	(URU)
1972	Club Atlético Independiente Avellaneda	(ARG)
1973	Club Atlético Independiente Avellaneda	(ARG)
1974	Club Atlético Independiente Avellaneda	(ARG)
1975	Club Atlético Independiente Avellaneda	(ARG)
1976	Cruzeiro Esporte Clube Belo Horizonte	(BRA)
1977	Club Atlético Boca Juniors Buenos Aires	(ARG)
1978	Club Atlético Boca Juniors Buenos Aires	(ARG)
1979	Club Olimpia Asunción	(PAR)
1980	Club Nacional de Football Montevideo	(URU)
1981	Clube de Regatas do Flamengo Rio de Janeiro	(BRA)
1982	Club Atlético Peñarol Montevideo	(URU)
1983	Grêmio Foot-Ball Porto Alegrense	(BRA)
1984	Club Atlético Independiente Avellaneda	(ARG)
1985	Asociación Atlética Argentinos Juniors Buenos Aires	(ARG)
1986	Club Atlético River Plate Buenos Aires	(ARG)
1987	Club Atlético Peñarol Montevideo	(URU)
1988	Club Nacional de Football Montevideo	(URU)
1989	Atlético Nacional Medellín	(COL)
1990	Club Olimpia Asunción	(PAR)
1991	Club Social y Deportivo Colo-Colo Santiago	(CHI)
1992	São Paulo Futebol Clube	(BRA)
1993	São Paulo Futebol Clube	(BRA)
1994	Club Atlético Vélez Sársfield Buenos Aires	(ARG)
1995	Grêmio Foot-Ball Porto Alegrense	(BRA)
1996	Club Atlético River Plate Buenos Aires	(ARG)
1997	Cruzeiro Esporte Clube Belo Horizonte	(BRA)
1998	Club de Regatas Vasco da Gama Rio de Janeiro	(BRA)
1999	Sociedade Esportiva Palmeiras São Paulo	(BRA)
2000	Club Atlético Boca Juniors Buenos Aires	(ARG)
2001	Club Atlético Boca Juniors Buenos Aires	(ARG)
2002	Club Olimpia Asunción	(PAR)
2003	Club Atlético Boca Juniors Buenos Aires	(ARG)
2004	Corporación Deportiva Once Caldas Manizales	(COL)
2005	São Paulo Futebol Clube	(BRA)
2006	Sport Club Internacional Porto Alegre	(BRA)
2007	Club Atlético Boca Juniors Buenos Aires	(ARG)
2008	Liga Deportiva Universitaria Quito	(ECU)
2009	Club Estudiantes de La Plata	(ARG)
2010	Sport Club Internacional Porto Alegre	(BRA)
2011	Santos Futebol Clube	(BRA)
2012	Sport Club Corinthians Paulista São Paulo	(BRA)
2013	Clube Atlético Mineiro Belo Horizonte	(BRA)
2014	Club Atlético San Lorenzo de Almagro	(ARG)

COPA SUDAMERICANA 2014

The 2014 Copa Sudamericana (officially called „2014 Copa Total Sudamericana de Clubes“ for sponsorship reasons) was the 13th edition of the CONMEBOL‘s and South Americas second most important club tournament.

List of participating clubs:

Argentina (6+1 teams)	Club Atlético Lanús Club Atlético River Plate Buenos Aires Club Atlético Boca Juniors Buenos Aires Club Estudiantes de La Plata Club de Gimnasia y Esgrima La Plata Club Deportivo Godoy Cruz Mendoza Club Atlético Rosario Central
Bolivia (4 teams)	CD San José Oruro CD Jorge Wilsterman Cochabamba Club Atlético Nacional Potosí CD Universitario San Francisco Xavier Sucre
Brazil (8 teams)	EC Vitória Salvador de Bahia Goiás EC Goiânia São Paulo Futebol Clube Esporte Clube Bahia Salvador SC Internacional Porto Alegre Criciúma Esporte Clube Fluminense FC Rio de Janeiro Sport Club do Recife
Chile (4 teams)	CD Iquique CD Cobresal El Salvador Club Deportivo Universidad Católica Santiago CD Huachipato Talcahuano
Colombia (4 teams)	Club Atlético Nacional Medellín Asociación Deportivo Cali CD Los Millonarios Bogotá Águilas Pereira FC
Ecuador (4 teams)	Club Sport Emelec Guayaquil CSD Independiente Del Valle Sangolquí CD Universidad Católica Quito Barcelona SC Guayaquil
Paraguay (4 teams)	Club Cerro Porteño Asunción Club Libertad Asunción Club General Díaz Luque Club Deportivo Capiatá

Peru (4 teams)	Club Alianza Lima CSCD Universidad César Vallejo Trujillo CCD Universidad Técnica de Cajamarca Club Inti Gas Deportes Ayacucho
Uruguay (4 teams)	Danubio FC Montevideo Club Atlético River Plate Montevideo Club Atlético Peñarol Montevideo CA Rentistas Montevideo
Venezuela (4 teams)	Caracas FC Deportivo Anzoátegui SC Puerto La Cruz Trujillanos Fútbol Club Deportivo La Guaira Caracas

PRELIMINARY ROUND – FIRST STAGE

19.08.2014, Estadio CAP, Talcahuano
Referee: Pablo Díaz (Argentina)
CD Huachipato Talcahuano - CD San José Oruro 3-1(1-0)
Huachipato: Miguel Hernán Jiménez Aracenna, Omar Jesús Merlo, Esteban Eduardo González Herrera, Leandro Javier Delgado Plenkovich, Claudio Andrés Muñoz Carrillo, Leandro Ezquerra De León (86.Daniel Alejandro Rodríguez Mellado), Martín Vladimir Rodríguez Torrejon, Leonardo Nicolás Povea Pérez (59.Matías Alberto Sánchez Herrera), Bryan Alfonso Vejar Utreras, Lucas Simón García (77.Angelo Zagal), Andrés Alejandro Vílches Araneda. Trainer: Mario Alfredo Salas Saieg.
San José: Carlos Emilio Lampe Porras, Arnaldo Andrés Vera Chamorro, Ariel Juárez Montaño, Juan Gabriel Valverde Rivera, Delio Ramon Ojeda Ferreira (34.Limbert Méndez Rocha), Mario Alberto Ovando Padilla, Abdón Reyes Cardozo, Ronald Puma Caballero (66.Juan Eduardo Fierro Ribera), Luis Alberto Closa González, Mario Leonardi Parrado Alanez (56.Miguel Oswaldo Loaiza Tardio), Mauro Sergio Bustamante. Trainer: Miguel Ángel Zahzú (Argentina).
Goals: Andrés Alejandro Vílches Araneda (1), Leandro Javier Delgado Plenkovich (47), Andrés Alejandro Vílches Araneda (73) / Mauro Sergio Bustamante (51 penalty).

26.08.2014, Estadio "Jesús Bermúdez", Oruro
Referee: Ulises Luis Arnaldo Mereles Abraham (Paraguay)
CD San José Oruro - CD Huachipato Talcahuano 2-3(0-2)
San José: Carlos Emilio Lampe Porras, Arnaldo Andrés Vera Chamorro (46.Ronald Puma Caballero), Wilder Zabala Perrogón (42.Gil Antonio Parada Velarde), Juan Gabriel Valverde Rivera, Mario Alberto Ovando Padilla, Limbert Méndez Rocha, Abdón Reyes Cardozo, Miguel Oswaldo Loaiza Tardio, Luis Alberto Closa González (46.Mario Leonardi Parrado Alanez), Cristián Omar Díaz, Mauro Sergio Bustamante. Trainer: Miguel Ángel Zahzú (Argentina).
Huachipato: Miguel Hernán Jiménez Aracenna, Omar Jesús Merlo, Esteban Eduardo González Herrera, Claudio Andrés Muñoz Carrillo, Carlos Felipe Ignacio Espinosa Contreras, Leandro Ezquerra De León, Martín Vladimir Rodríguez Torrejon (73.Camilo Pontoni), Leonardo Nicolás Povea Pérez (85.Jair Castro Morales), Bryan Alfonso Vejar Utreras, Lucas Simón García (76.Daniel Alejandro Rodríguez Mellado), Andrés Alejandro Vílches Araneda. Trainer: Mario Alfredo Salas Saieg.
Goals: Cristián Omar Díaz (47 penalty, 90+1) / Lucas Simón García (18), Carlos Felipe Ignacio Espinosa Contreras (33 penalty), Leonardo Nicolás Povea Pérez (83).
[CD Huachipato Talcahuano won 6-3 on aggregate]

19.08.2014, Estadio Olímpico Patria, Sucre
Referee: Mario Díaz de Vivar (Paraguay)
CD Universitario San Francisco Xavier Sucre - CD Iquique 2-0(1-0)
Universitario: Juan Carlos Robles Rodríguez, Alan Loras Vélez, Ezequiel Nicolás Filipetto, Ramiro Daniel Ballivián, Mauricio Saucedo Guardia, Carlos Oswaldo Camacho Suárez, Alejandro René Bejarano Sajama, Federico Silvestre (83.Jorge Ignacio Cuéllar Rojas), Rubén de la Cuesta Vera, Claudio Ezequiel Mosca (46.Martín Adrián Palavicini López), Ignacio Rodríguez Ortiz „Nacho Rodríguez" (63.Diego Aroldo Cabrera Flores). Trainer: Javier Vega.
CD Iquique: Brayan Cortés Fernández, Boris Alexis Rieloff Venegas, Mauricio Alejandro Zenteno Morales, Cristian Javier Báez, Rafael Antonio Caroca Cordero, Mauricio José Yedro (85.Exequiel Emanuel Benavídez), Rodrigo Ezequiel Díaz Rengo, Marcelo Pablo Jorquera Silva, Alberto Martín Gómez (84.José Luis Silva Araya), Misael Aldair Dávila Carvajal a (71.Walter Daniel Mazzolatti Rivarola), Francisco Fernando Castro Gamboa. Trainer: Héctor Hernán Pinto Lara.
Goals: Alejandro René Bejarano Sajama (22), Martín Adrián Palavicini López (74).

26.08.2014, Estadio Tierra de Campeones, Iquique
Referee: Fernando Martín Falce Langone (Uruguay)
CD Iquique - CD Universitario San Francisco Xavier Sucre 1-0(0-0)
CD Iquique: Rodrigo Felipe Naranjo López, Boris Alexis Rieloff Venegas (55.José Luis Silva Araya), Mauricio Alejandro Zenteno Morales, Cristian Javier Báez, Rafael Antonio Caroca Cordero, Rodrigo Ezequiel Díaz Rengo, Marcelo Pablo Jorquera Silva (78.Abraham Ismael Vargas Araya), Manuel Arturo Villalobos Salvo, Alberto Martín Gómez, Misael Aldair Dávila Carvajal (56.Walter Daniel Mazzolatti Rivarola), Francisco Fernando Castro Gamboa. Trainer: Héctor Hernán Pinto Lara.
Universitario: Juan Carlos Robles Rodríguez, Alan Loras Vélez, Ezequiel Nicolás Filipetto [*sent off 46*], Ramiro Daniel Ballivián, Mauricio Saucedo Guardia (73.Diego Gabriel Rivero Cortéz), Carlos Oswaldo Camacho Suárez, Alejandro René Bejarano Sajama, Federico Silvestre, Rubén de la Cuesta Vera, Rolando Ribera Menacho (49.Jorge Ignacio Cuéllar Rojas), Ignacio Rodríguez Ortiz „Nacho Rodríguez" (80.Claudio Ezequiel Mosca). Trainer: Javier Vega.
Goal: Walter Daniel Mazzolatti Rivarola (68).
[CD Universitario San Francisco Xavier Sucre won 2-1 on aggregate]

19.08.2014, Estadio "Luis Franzini", Montevideo
Referee: Diego Ceballos (Argentina)
CA Rentistas Montevideo - Club Cerro Porteño Asunción 0-2(0-1)
Rentistas: Stéfano José Perdomo Pereyra, Ignacio Ithurralde Sáez, Nicolás Alejandro Rodríguez Charquero (46.Anderson Silva de França), Mario Sebastián Ramírez Silva, Jorge Nicolás Raguso Sánchez (45+1.Hugo Maximiliano Soria Sánchez), Erick Cathriel Cabaco Almada, Gonzalo Javier Bazallo Strada, Víctor Hugo Dorrego Coito, José Pablo Varela Rebollo (71.Guillermo Maidana Revetría), Miguel David Terans Pérez, Gustavo Javier Alles Villa. Trainer: Adolfo Barán Flis.
Cerro Porteño: Diego Daniel Barreto Cáceres, Carlos Bonet Cáceres, Víctor Hugo Mareco, Danilo Fabián Ortíz Soto, Junior Osmar Ignacio Alonso Mujica, Julio Daniel Dos Santos Rodríguez (90+3.Epifiano Ariel García Duarte), Miguel Ángel Paniagua Rivarola, Fidencio Oviedo Domínguez, Óscar David Romero Villamayor, Mauricio Ezequiel Sperdutti (68.Rodolfo Vicente Gamarra Varela), José María Ortigoza Ortíz (78.Bruno Amilcar Valdez). Trainer: Francisco Javier Arce Rolón.
Goals: Óscar David Romero Villamayor (27), Julio Daniel Dos Santos Rodríguez (90+1).

26.08.2014, Estadio „General Pablo Rojas“, Asunción
Referee: Néstor Fabián Pitana (Argentina)
Club Cerro Porteño Asunción - CA Rentistas Montevideo 0-1(0-1)
Cerro Porteño: Diego Daniel Barreto Cáceres, Carlos Bonet Cáceres, Víctor Hugo Mareco, Danilo Fabián Ortíz Soto, Junior Osmar Ignacio Alonso Mujica, Miguel Ángel Paniagua Rivarola, Fidencio Oviedo Domínguez, Óscar David Romero Villamayor (90+2.Jonathan Santana Gehre), Miguel Ángel Almirón Rejala (46.Julio Daniel Dos Santos Rodríguez), Mauricio Ezequiel Sperdutti (61.Rodolfo Vicente Gamarra Varela), José María Ortigoza Ortíz. Trainer: Roberto Ismael Torres Báez.
Rentistas: Stéfano José Perdomo Pereyra, Ignacio Ithurralde Sáez, Mario Sebastián Ramírez Silva, Erick Cathriel Cabaco Almada (83.Luciano Barboza de Jesús "Cafú"), Anderson Silva de França, Gonzalo Javier Bazallo Strada, Andrés Silva Cáceres (73.Guillermo Maidana Revetría), Hugo Maximiliano Soria Sánchez, Víctor Hugo Dorrego Coito (60.Danilo Erardo Cócaro Díaz), Miguel David Terans Pérez, Gustavo Javier Alles Villa. Trainer: Adolfo Barán Flis.
Goal: Gustavo Javier Alles Villa (11).
[Club Cerro Porteño Asunción won 2-1 on aggregate]

19.08.2014, Estadio "Hernán Ramírez Villegas", Pereira
Referee: Péricles Bassols Pegado Cortez (Brazil)
Águilas Pereira FC - CS Emelec Guayaquil 1-1(0-1)
Águilas Pereira: David González Giraldo, Javier López Rodríguez, Fabio Darío Rodríguez Mejía, Hanyer Luis Mosquera Córdoba, Carlos Mario Arboleda Ampudia, John Javier Restrepo Pérez, Yohn Géiler Mosquera Martínez (71.Boris Yasser Polo Mosquera), Edinson Manuel Palomino Marrugo, Cleider Leandro Alzáte Correa, Brayan Edinson Angulo Mosquera (46.Diego Andrés Álvarez Sánchez), Johan Jorge Fano (73.Silvio Augusto González). Trainer: Jorge Luis Bernal Caviedes.
Emelec: Esteban Javier Dreer, Jorge Daniel Guagua Tamayo, Gabriel Eduardo Achilier Zurita, Oscar Dalmiro Bagüi Angulo, Pedro Angel Quiñónez Rodríguez, José Luis Quiñónez Quiñónez, Ángel Israel Mena Delgado (88.David Alejandro Noboa Tello), Miller Alejandro Bolaños Reascos, Fernando Agustín Giménez Solís, Marcos Gustavo Mondaini (71.Javier Isidro Charcopa Alegria), Luis Miguel Escalada (79.Emanuel Herrera). Trainer: Gustavo Domingo Quinteros Desabato (Bolivia).
Goals: Diego Andrés Álvarez Sánchez (90+1) / Ángel Israel Mena Delgado (40).

26.08.2014, Estadio „George Capwell“, Guayaquil
Referee: Mauro Vigliano (Argentina)
CS Emelec Guayaquil - Águilas Pereira FC 2-1(1-0)
Emelec: Esteban Javier Dreer, Jorge Daniel Guagua Tamayo, Gabriel Eduardo Achilier Zurita, Oscar Dalmiro Bagüi Angulo, Fernando Agustín Giménez Solís, Pedro Angel Quiñónez Rodríguez (67.Marcos Gustavo Mondaini), José Luis Quiñónez Quiñónez, Ángel Israel Mena Delgado, Miller Alejandro Bolaños Reascos, Osbaldo Lupo Lastra García, Luis Miguel Escalada (67.Emanuel Herrera; 70.Javier Isidro Charcopa Alegria). Trainer: Gustavo Domingo Quinteros Desabato (Bolivia).
Águilas Pereira: Osvaldo Andrés Cabral, Samuel Antonio Vanegas Luna, Javier López Rodríguez, Fabio Darío Rodríguez Mejía (46.Edinson Manuel Palomino Marrugo), Carlos Mario Arboleda Ampudia, Elvis David Mosquera Valdés, John Javier Restrepo Pérez, Yohn Géiler Mosquera Martínez, Cleider Leandro Alzáte Correa (89.Diego Andrés Álvarez Sánchez), Johan Jorge Fano, Silvio Augusto González (76.Hanyer Luis Mosquera Córdoba). Trainer: Jorge Luis Bernal Caviedes.
Goals: Fernando Agustín Giménez Solís (3, 90+3) / Johan Jorge Fano (59).
[CS Emelec Guayaquil won 3-2 on aggregate]

19.08.2014, Estadio Olímpico Atahualpa, Quito
Referee: Jorge Alejandro Mancilla (Bolivia)
CD Universidad Católica Quito – 1-1(1-0)
Deportivo Anzoátegui SC Puerto La Cruz
Universidad Católica: Hernán Ismael Galíndez, Mariano Esteban Uglessich, Henry Junior Cangá Ortíz, Jorge Andrés Mendoza Uza, Wilmar Pascual Meneses Borja (72.Elvis Adán Patta Quintero), Alejandro Gabriel Espinosa Borja, Jesi Alexander Godoy Quiñónes, Carlos Luis Moyano Moran (60.Facundo Martin Martinez Montagnoli), Henry Leonel Patta Quintero (86.Bryan David Sánchez Congo), Armando Lenin Wila Canga, Diego Fernando Benítez Quintena. Trainer: Luis Gustavo Soler Magadán (Argentina).
Deportivo Anzoátegui: Edixson Antonio González Peroza, Juan José Fuenmayor Núñez, William Alexander Díaz Gutiérrez, Richard Emmanuel Badillo Pérez, Rolando Emilio Escobar Batista, José David Moreno Chacón (73.Edgar José Mendoza Acosta), Evelio De Jesús Hernández Guedez, Leopoldo Rafael Jiménez González (81.Ricardo Manuel Cardoso Martins), Robert Enrique Hernández Aguado, David Alejandro Zalzman, Alexander José Rondón Heredia (49.Manuel Alejandro Arteaga Rubianes). Trainer: Dickson Ruberth Morán Puelo.
Goals: Henry Leonel Patta Quintero (35) / Manuel Alejandro Arteaga Rubianes (54).

26.08.2014, Estadio "José Antonio Anzoátegui", Puerto la Cruz
Referee: Miguel Santiváñez de la Cruz (Peru)
Deportivo Anzoátegui SC Puerto La Cruz – 1-1(1-0,1-1,1-1);
CD Universidad Católica Quito 4-5 on penalties
Deportivo Anzoátegui: Edixson Antonio González Peroza, Juan José Fuenmayor Núñez, William Alexander Díaz Gutiérrez, Richard Emmanuel Badillo Pérez, Rolando Emilio Escobar Batista (83.Leopoldo Rafael Jiménez González), José David Moreno Chacón, Evelio De Jesús Hernández Guedez, Ricardo Manuel Cardoso Martins, Robert Enrique Hernández Aguado, David Alejandro Zalzman (59.Edwin Enrique Aguilar Samaniego), Manuel Alejandro Arteaga Rubianes. Trainer: Dickson Ruberth Morán Puelo.
Universidad Católica: Hernán Ismael Galíndez, Mariano Esteban Uglessich, Henry Junior Cangá Ortíz, Wilmar Pascual Meneses Borja (80.Esteban Santiago de la Cruz Santacruz), Alejandro Gabriel Espinosa Borja (31.Facundo Martin Martinez Montagnoli), Jesi Alexander Godoy Quiñónes, Carlos Luis Moyano Moran (46.Elvis Adán Patta Quintero), Jonathan Bladimir Carabalí Palacios, Henry Leonel Patta Quintero, Armando Lenin Wila Canga, Diego Fernando Benítez Quintena. Trainer: Luis Gustavo Soler Magadán (Argentina).
Goals: Rolando Emilio Escobar Batista (33) / Armando Lenin Wila Canga (86 penalty).
Penalties: Evelio De Jesús Hernández Guedez (missed); Facundo Martin Martinez Montagnoli (missed); Edwin Enrique Aguilar Samaniego 1-0; Henry Leonel Patta Quintero 1-1; Robert Enrique Hernández Aguado (missed); Jonathan Bladimir Carabalí Palacios 1-2; Ricardo Manuel Cardoso Martins 2-2; Diego Fernando Benítez Quintena 2-3; Manuel Alejandro Arteaga Rubianes 3-3; Armando Lenin Wila Canga (missed); Juan José Fuenmayor Núñez 4-3; Jesi Alexander Godoy Quiñónes 4-4; José David Moreno Chacón (missed); Mariano Esteban Uglessich 4-5.
[CD Universidad Católica Quito won 5-4 on penalties (after 2-2 on aggregate)]

20.08.2014, Estadio „Feliciano Cáceres", Luque
Referee: Andrés Cunha (Uruguay)
Club General Díaz Luque - CD Cobresal El Salvador 2-1(1-1)
General Díaz: Bernardo David Medina, Gustavo Ariel Toranzo, Alejandro David Bernal, Ángel Osmar Vera Escobar, Pedro Julián Chávez Ruíz, Cristian Martínez Medina, Cristian Gustavo Sosa Ledesma, Blas Antonio Cáceres (83.Diego Javier Doldán Zacarías), Carlos Alberto Vera Segovia (56.Víctor Sócrates Michael Genés Espínola), Roberto Carlos Gamarra Acosta, César Augusto Caicedo Solís (46.Alberto Cirilo Contrera Jiménez). Trainer: Humberto García Ramírez.
Cobresal: Nicolás Miroslav Peric Villarreal, Miguel Andres Escalona Armijo, Alexis Alejandro Salazar Villarroel, Johan Patricio Fuentes Muñoz (68.Juan Pablo Miño Peña), Víctor Hugo Sarabia Aguilar (90+1.Carlos Felipe Herrera Contreras), Mariano Néstor Torres, Hans Francisco Salinas Flores, Patricio Felipe Jérez Aguayo, Rodrigo Andrés Ureña Reyes, Cristian Rolando Ledesma Núñez (71.Ever Milton Cantero Benítez), Jorge Matías Donoso Garáte. Trainer: José Miguel Cantillana Galeas.
Goals: Gustavo Ariel Toranzo (13), Roberto Carlos Gamarra Acosta (70) / Patricio Felipe Jérez Aguayo (27).

27.08.2014, Estadio El Cobre, El Salvador
Referee: Gery Vargas (Bolivia)
CD Cobresal El Salvador - Club General Díaz Luque 2-2(1-2)
Cobresal: Nicolás Miroslav Peric Villarreal, Rolando Marciano Bogado, Miguel Andres Escalona Armijo (42.Ever Milton Cantero Benítez), Alexis Alejandro Salazar Villarroel, Mariano Néstor Torres, Víctor Hugo Sarabia Aguilar, Hans Francisco Salinas Flores, Patricio Felipe Jérez Aguayo, Rodrigo Andrés Ureña Reyes (46.Johan Patricio Fuentes Muñoz), Cristian Rolando Ledesma Núñez, Jorge Matías Donoso Garáte (70.Carlos Humberto Escobar Ortíz). Trainer: José Miguel Cantillana Galeas.
General Díaz: Bernardo David Medina, Gustavo Ariel Toranzo [*sent off 37*], Alejandro David Bernal, Ángel Osmar Vera Escobar [*sent off 37*], Pedro Julián Chávez Ruíz, Cristian Martínez Medina, Cristian Gustavo Sosa Ledesma [*sent off 64*], Alberto Cirilo Contrera Jiménez (74.Carlos Alberto Vera Segovia), Blas Antonio Cáceres, Víctor Sócrates Michael Genés Espínola (42.Alberto Espinola Giménez), Roberto Carlos Gamarra Acosta (53.Marco Antonio Gamarra Arbiniagaldez). Trainer: Humberto García Ramírez.
Goals: Jorge Matías Donoso Garáte (24), Johan Patricio Fuentes Muñoz (86) / Roberto Carlos Gamarra Acosta (3), Víctor Sócrates Michael Genés Espínola (33).
[Club General Díaz Luque won 4-3 on aggregate]

20.08.2014, Estadio „Víctor Agustín Ugarte", Potosí
Referee: Roddy Alberto Zambrano Olmedo (Ecuador)
CA Nacional Potosí - Club Libertad Asunción 1-0(1-0)
Nacional: Carlos Alberto Barahona Angulo, Rony Jiménez Mendoza, Eliseo Isaias Dury Gómez, Ignacio Awad García Justiniano, Anderson Raimundo da Silva (89.Claudio Rubén Centurión), Juan Pablo Sánchez Chanevy, Leonel Justiniano Araúz, Rolando Elmer Choque Calisaya (65.Juan Pablo Alemán), Werther Thiers Charles da Silva (75.Héctor Ariel Calderón Llave), Erlan Gastón Mealla Anachuri, Walter Humberto Rioja Ugarte. Trainer: Marcos Rodolfo Ferrufino Estévez.
Libertad: Rodrigo Martin Muñóz Salomón, Gustavo Ramón Mencia Ávalos, Pedro Juan Benítez Domínguez, Adalberto Román Benítez, Jorge Luis Moreira Ferreira, Ismael Benegas, Claudio David Vargas Villalba (65.Dionisio Ismael Pérez Mambreani), Sergio Daniel Aquino, Jorge Daniel González Marquet (81.Jorge Eduardo Recalde Ramírez), Osmar de la Cruz Molinas González, Hernán Rodrigo López Mora (90.Iván Rodrigo Ramírez Segovia). Trainer: Pedro Alcides Sarabia Achucarro.
Goal: Werther Thiers Charles da Silva (10).

27.08.2014, Estadio „Dr. Nicolás Léoz“, Asunción
Referee: Martín Emilio Vázquez Broquetas (Uruguay)
Club Libertad Asunción - CA Nacional Potosí 3-0(2-0)
Libertad: Rodrigo Martin Muñóz Salomón, Gustavo Ramón Mencia Ávalos, Pedro Juan Benítez Domínguez, Adalberto Román Benítez, Jorge Luis Moreira Ferreira, Sergio Daniel Aquino, Jorge Daniel González Marquet (76.Néstor Abraham Camacho Ledesma), Osmar de la Cruz Molinas González, Jorge Eduardo Recalde Ramírez (89.Claudio David Vargas Villalba), Hernán Rodrigo López Mora, Dionisio Ismael Pérez Mambreani (51.Antonio Bareiro Álvarez). Trainer: Pedro Alcides Sarabia Achucarro.
Nacional: Carlos Alberto Barahona Angulo, Rony Jiménez Mendoza, Claudio Rubén Centurión, Eliseo Isaias Dury Gómez, Juan Pablo Alemán (79.Héctor Ariel Calderón Llave), Ignacio Awad García Justiniano, Anderson Raimundo da Silva, Juan Pablo Sánchez Chanevy (85.Rolando Elmer Choque Calisaya), Leonel Justiniano Araúz, Werther Thiers Charles da Silva, Walter Humberto Rioja Ugarte (46.Erlan Gastón Mealla Anachuri). Trainer: Marcos Rodolfo Ferrufino Estévez.
Goals: Hernán Rodrigo López Mora (4 penalty, 40), Antonio Bareiro Álvarez (89).
[Club Libertad Asunción won 3-1 on aggregate]

20.08.2014, Estadio Olímpico de la UCV, Caracas
Referee: Diego Haro (Peru)
Deportivo La Guaira Caracas - Club Atlético Nacional Medellín 1-1(0-0)
La Guaira: Renny Vicente Vega Hernández, Antonio José Boada Figueroa, Edwar Segundo Bracho Suárez, Franklin José Lucena Peña, Óscar Constantino González, Arquímedes José Figuera Salazar, Javier Alfonso García, Luciano Nahuel Ursino Pegolo, Armando José Carrillo Dangond (58.Framber Johan Villegas Sangronis), Imanol Iriberri (87.Enson Jesús Rodríguez Mesa), Charlis José Ortíz García (90+3.Adalberto Peñaranda Maestre). Trainer: Leonardo Alberto González Antequera.
Atlético Nacional: Franco Armani, Alexis Héctor Henríquez Charales, Álvaro Francisco Nájera Gil (72.Wilder Andrés Guisao Correa), Alejandro Bernal Rios, Daniel Eduardo Bocanegra Ortíz, Alejandro Abraham Guerra Morales (59.Sherman Andrés Cárdenas Estupiñán), Alexander Mejía Sabalsa, Juan David Valencia Hinestroza, Edwin Andrés Cardona Bedoya, Luis Carlos Ruíz Morales, Jonathan Copete Valencia (89.Farid Alfonso Díaz Rhenals). Trainer: Juan Carlos Osorio Arbelaez.
Goals: Framber Johan Villegas Sangronis (65) / Edwin Andrés Cardona Bedoya (82 penalty).

27.08.2014, Estadio „Atanasio Girardot“, Medellín
Referee: Omar Andrés Ponce Manzo (Ecuador)
Club Atlético Nacional Medellín - Deportivo La Guaira Caracas 1-0(0-0)
Atlético Nacional: Franco Armani, Alexis Héctor Henríquez Charales, Álvaro Francisco Nájera Gil (46.Diego Arturo Peralta González), Alejandro Bernal Rios, Daniel Eduardo Bocanegra Ortíz, Sherman Andrés Cárdenas Estupiñán (69.Alejandro Abraham Guerra Morales), Alexander Mejía Sabalsa [*sent off 42*], Juan David Valencia Hinestroza, Wilder Andrés Guisao Correa, Luis Carlos Ruíz Morales (59.Edwin Andrés Cardona Bedoya), Jonathan Copete Valencia. Trainer: Juan Carlos Osorio Arbelaez.
La Guaira: Renny Vicente Vega Hernández, Antonio José Boada Figueroa, Edwar Segundo Bracho Suárez, Franklin José Lucena Peña, Óscar Constantino González, Arquímedes José Figuera Salazar, Javier Alfonso García (66.Enson Jesús Rodríguez Mesa), Luciano Nahuel Ursino Pegolo, Armando José Carrillo Dangond (56.Imanol Iriberri), Charlis José Ortíz García, Framber Johan Villegas Sangronis (80.Adalberto Peñaranda Maestre). Trainer: Leonardo Alberto González Antequera.
Goal: Luis Carlos Ruíz Morales (53).
[Club Atlético Nacional Medellín won 2-1 on aggregate]

20.08.2014, Estadio Centenario, Montevideo
Referee: Wilton Pereira Sampaio (Brazil)
CA Peñarol Montevideo - CD Jorge Wilsterman Cochabamba 2-0(1-0)
Peñarol: Pablo Alejandro Migliore, Damián Macaluso Rojas, Carlos Adrián Valdéz Suárez (62.Sergio Daniel Orteman Rodríguez), Carlos Andrés Rodales Ramírez, Diogo Silvestre Bittencourt, Gonzalo Viera Davyt, Jorge Marcelo Rodríguez Núñez, Antonio Pacheco D'Agosti (76.Alejandro Daniel Silva González), Sebastián Gerardo Píriz Ribas, Marcelo Danubio Zalayeta (71.Juan Manuel Olivera López), Jonathan Javier Rodríguez Portillo. Trainer: Jorge Daniel Fossati Lurachi.
Jorge Wilsterman: Matías Ezequiel Dituro, Christian Israel Vargas Claros, Enrique David Díaz Velázquez, Juan Carlos Zampiery Rivarola, José Carlos Barba Paz, Adán Alexis Félix Bravo (90+1.Óscar Alberto Díaz Acosta), Roly Desiderio Sejas Muñoz, Juan Pablo Aponte Gutiérrez, Augusto Andaveris Iriondo, Carlos Ariel Neumann Torres, Rodrigo Vargas Touchard (71.Félix Quero López). Trainer: Julio César Baldivieso Rico.
Goals: Jorge Marcelo Rodríguez Núñez (11), Jonathan Javier Rodríguez Portillo (85).

28.08.2014, Estadio „Félix Capriles", Cochabamba
Referee: Julio Quintana Rodríguez (Paraguay)
CD Jorge Wilsterman Cochabamba - CA Peñarol Montevideo 0-4(0-1)
Jorge Wilsterman: Matías Ezequiel Dituro, Christian Israel Vargas Claros, Enrique David Díaz Velázquez, Juan Carlos Zampiery Rivarola (77.José Carlos Barba Paz), Adán Alexis Félix Bravo (55.Gianakis Suárez Tan Wing), Roly Desiderio Sejas Muñoz, Juan Pablo Aponte Gutiérrez, Augusto Andaveris Iriondo, Carlos Ariel Neumann Torres, Félix Quero López (46.Carlos Eduardo Vargas Menacho), Rodrigo Vargas Touchard. Trainer: Julio César Baldivieso Rico.
Peñarol: Pablo Alejandro Migliore, Damián Macaluso Rojas, Carlos Adrián Valdéz Suárez, Carlos Andrés Rodales Ramírez, Diogo Silvestre Bittencourt, Alejandro Daniel Silva González, Gonzalo Viera Davyt, Jorge Marcelo Rodríguez Núñez, Sebastián Gerardo Píriz Ribas (73.Sergio Daniel Orteman Rodríguez), Marcelo Danubio Zalayeta (66.Juan Manuel Olivera López), Jonathan Javier Rodríguez Portillo (81.Carlos Rodrigo Núñez Techera). Trainer: Jorge Daniel Fossati Lurachi.
Goals: Diogo Silvestre Bittencourt (23), Jonathan Javier Rodríguez Portillo (69 penalty), Juan Manuel Olivera López (78 penalty), Damián Macaluso Rojas (83).
[CA Peñarol Montevideo won 6-0 on aggregate]

20.08.2014, Estadio "Héroes de San Ramón", Cajamarca
Referee: Julio Bascuñán González (Chile)
CCD Universidad Técnica de Cajamarca - Asociación Deportivo Cali 0-0
Universidad Técnica: Daniel Andrés Ferreyra, Manuel Alejandro Corrales González, Rafael Nicanor Farfán Quispe, Giancarlo Carmona Maldonado, Roberto Merino Ramírez (64.Marcio Andre Valverde Zamora), Jean Carlo Tragodara Gálves (41.Víctor Raúl Rojas García), Juan José Barros Araújo, Reimond Orangel Manco Albarracín (90.Jean Pierre Archimbaud Arriarán), Johan Joussep Sotil Eche, Gianfranco Alberto Labarthe Tomé, Mauro Adrián Vila Wilkins. Trainer: José Eugenio Hernández Sarmiento (Colombia).
Deportivo Cali: Luis Alfonso Hurtado Osorio, Víctor Hugo Giraldo López, Cristian Javier Nasuti Matovelle, Frank Yusty Fabra Palacios, Germán Mera Cáceres, Helibelton Palacios Zapata, Gustavo Adolfo Bolívar Zapata, Juan David Cabezas Nuñez, Carlos David Lizarazo Landázury (73.Yerson Candelo Miranda), Carlos Augusto Rivas Murillo (84.Jhon Eduis Viáfara Mina), Sergio Darío Herrera Month (68.Luis Fernando Mosquera Alomia). Trainer: Héctor Fabio Cárdenas Berrío.

28.08.2014, Estadio Olímpico "Pascual Guerrero", Cali
Referee: Jesús Valenzuela (Venezuela)
Asociación Deportivo Cali - CCD Universidad Técnica de Cajamarca 3-0(2-0)
Deportivo Cali: Luis Alfonso Hurtado Osorio, Cristian Javier Nasuti Matovelle, Frank Yusty Fabra Palacios, Germán Mera Cáceres, Helibelton Palacios Zapata, Andrés Eduardo Pérez Gutiérrez, Miguel Eduardo Caneo, Juan David Cabezas Nuñez, Yerson Candelo Miranda (73.Víctor Hugo Giraldo López), Carlos Augusto Rivas Murillo (57.Luis Fernando Mosquera Alomia), Sergio Darío Herrera Month (72.Robin Ariel Ramírez González). Trainer: Héctor Fabio Cárdenas Berrío.
Universidad Técnica: Daniel Andrés Ferreyra, Raúl Hannes Alemán Mostorino (46.Roberto Merino Ramírez), Manuel Alejandro Corrales González, Víctor Raúl Rojas García, Rafael Nicanor Farfán Quispe, Giancarlo Carmona Maldonado, Marcio Andre Valverde Zamora (46.Reimond Orangel Manco Albarracín), Juan José Barros Araújo, Johan Joussep Sotil Eche, Gianfranco Alberto Labarthe Tomé (72.Jean Pierre Archimbaud Arriarán), Mauro Adrián Vila Wilkins. Trainer: José Eugenio Hernández Sarmiento (Colombia).
Goals: Cristian Javier Nasuti Matovelle (4), Carlos Augusto Rivas Murillo (24), Cristian Javier Nasuti Matovelle (68).
[Asociación Deportivo Cali won 3-0 on aggregate]

21.08.2014, Estadio "San Carlos de Apoquindo", Santiago
Referee: Enrique Patricio Cáceres Villafañe (Paraguay)
CD Universidad Católica Santiago - CA River Plate Montevideo 0-1(0-0)
Universidad Católica: Franco Costanzo, Matías Cahais, Alfonso Cristián Parot Rojas (67.José Luis Muñoz Muñoz), Cristián Andrés Álvarez Valenzuela, Erick Antonio Pulgar Farfán, Mark Dennis González Hoffmann (51.Gonzalo Alfredo Sepúlveda Domínguez), Fernando Patricio Cordero Fonseca, Michael Fabián Ríos Ripoll (78.Darío Bottinelli), Claudio Elias Sepúlveda Castro, David Antonio Llanos Almonacid, Álvaro Sebastián Ramos Sepúlveda. Trainer: Julio César Falcioni (Argentina).
River Plate: Alison Nicola Pérez Barone, Williams Guillermo Martínez Fracchia, Claudio Herrera Casanova, Cristian Mario González Aidinovich, Diego Manuel Rodríguez Da Luz, Gabriel Marques de Andrade Pinto (85.Ángel Leonardo Rodríguez Güelmo), Claudio Gastón Innella Alderete, Fernando Gorriarán Fontes (67.Robert Mario Flores Bistolfi), Cristian Rafael Techera Cribelli, Michael Nicolás Santos Rosadilla (88.Walter Vaz Correa), Leandro Joaquín Rodríguez Telechea. Trainer: Jorge Guillermo Almada Álves.
Goal: Michael Nicolás Santos Rosadilla (76).

27.08.2014, Estadio „Luis Franzini", Montevideo
Referee: Víctor Hugo Carrillo Casanova (Peru)
CA River Plate Montevideo - CD Universidad Católica Santiago 3-0(0-0)
River Plate: Alison Nicola Pérez Barone, Williams Guillermo Martínez Fracchia, Claudio Herrera Casanova, Cristian Mario González Aidinovich, Diego Manuel Rodríguez Da Luz, Gabriel Marques de Andrade Pinto, Claudio Gastón Innella Alderete (84.Ángel Leonardo Rodríguez Güelmo), Fernando Gorriarán Fontes (62.Robert Mario Flores Bistolfi), Cristian Rafael Techera Cribelli, Michael Nicolás Santos Rosadilla, Leandro Joaquín Rodríguez Telechea (46.Santiago Damián García Correa). Trainer: Jorge Guillermo Almada Álves.
Universidad Católica: Franco Costanzo, Alfonso Cristián Parot Rojas [*sent off 60*], Cristián Andrés Álvarez Valenzuela, Stéfano Magnasco Galindo, Erick Antonio Pulgar Farfán, Mark Dennis González Hoffmann (73.José Luis Muñoz Muñoz), Fernando Patricio Cordero Fonseca (54.Mauro Iván Óbolo), Michael Fabián Ríos Ripoll (62.Darío Bottinelli [*sent off 89*]), Claudio Elias Sepúlveda Castro, David Antonio Llanos Almonacid, Álvaro Sebastián Ramos Sepúlveda. Trainer: Julio César Falcioni (Argentina).
Goals: Michael Nicolás Santos Rosadilla (69), Santiago Damián García Correa (87), Cristian Rafael Techera Cribelli (90+2).
[CA River Plate Montevideo won 4-0 on aggregate]

21.08.2014, Estadio Monumental „Isidro Romero Carbo“, Guayaquil
Referee: Adrián Vélez (Colombia)
Barcelona SC Guayaquil - Club Alianza Lima 3-0(1-0)
Barcelona SC: Máximo Orlando Banguera Valdivieso, Luis Armando Checa Villamar, Geovanny Enrique Nazareno Simisterra, Franco Peppino, Pedro Pablo Velasco Arboleda, Alex Leonardo Bolaños Reascos, Mario Roberto Martínez Hernández, Flavio David Caicedo Gracia (88.Matías Damián Oyola), Federico Gastón Nieto (73.Ismael Blanco), Christian Andrés Suárez Valencia (69.Ely Jair Esterilla Castro), Cristian Anderson Penilla Caicedo. Trainer: Rubén Jorge Israel (Uruguay).
Alianza: George Patrick Forsyth Sommer, Walter Fernando Ibáñez Costa, Roberto Efraín Koichi Aparicio Mori, Jorge Luis Molina Cabrera (61.Victor Andrés Cedrón Zurita), Roberto Carlos Guizasola La Rosa, Luis Enrique Trujillo Ortíz, Pablo Nicolas Míguez Farre, Paulo César Albarracín García, Basilio Gabriel Costa Heredia (62.Wilmer Alexander Aguirre Vásquez), Julio César Landauri Ventura (81.Mauricio Alejandro Montes Sanguinetti), Mauro Guevgeozián Crespo. Trainer: Guillermo Óscar Sanguinetti Giordano (Uruguay).
Goals: Cristian Anderson Penilla Caicedo (31), Pedro Pablo Velasco Arboleda (66), Ismael Blanco (90+1).

27.08.2014, Estadio „Alejandro Villanueva“, Lima
Referee: Imer Lemuel Machado Barrera (Colombia)
Club Alianza Lima - Barcelona SC Guayaquil 0-0
Alianza: George Patrick Forsyth Sommer, Walter Fernando Ibáñez Costa, Roberto Efraín Koichi Aparicio Mori, Luis Enrique Trujillo Ortíz, Josimar Jair Atoche Bances [*sent off 80*], Roberto Carlos Guizasola La Rosa, Paulo César Albarracín García (64.Victor Andrés Cedrón Zurita), Basilio Gabriel Costa Heredia (72.Mauricio Alejandro Montes Sanguinetti), Julio César Landauri Ventura, Wilmer Alexander Aguirre Vásquez (86.Jorge Luis Molina Cabrera), Mauro Guevgeozián Crespo. Trainer: Guillermo Óscar Sanguinetti Giordano (Uruguay).
Barcelona SC: Damián Enrique Lanza Moyano, Luis Armando Checa Villamar, Geovanny Enrique Nazareno Simisterra, Franco Peppino, Pedro Pablo Velasco Arboleda, Matías Damián Oyola, Alex Leonardo Bolaños Reascos, Mario Roberto Martínez Hernández (72.Flavio David Caicedo Gracia), Ismael Blanco, Christian Andrés Suárez Valencia (65.Michael Jackson Quiñónez Cabeza), Cristian Anderson Penilla Caicedo (77.Jeison Alfonso Domínguez Quiñónez). Trainer: Rubén Jorge Israel (Uruguay).
[Barcelona SC Guayaquil won 3-0 on aggregate]

21.08.2014, Estadio "José Alberto Pérez", Valera
Referee: Wilson Lamouroux (Colombia)
Trujillanos FC - CSD Independiente Del Valle Sangolquí 0-1(0-0)
Trujillanos FC: Héctor Eduardo Pérez Cuevas, Luigi José Erazo Villamizar [*sent off 90+1*], Edixon Bladimir Cuevas Tirado, Mayker José González Montilla, Erlys Jordano Vásquez Carrero, Jarol Herrera Martínez, Argenis José Gómez Ortega, Maurice Jesús Cova Sánchez (71.Sergio Alberto Alvarez Castellano), Gerardo José Mendoza (71.Johan José Osorio Paredes), Fredys Enrique Arrieta Fontalvo (80.Luis Miguel Rivas Rodríguez), James Fernando Cabezas Mairongo. Trainer: Horacio Ignacio Matuszyczk (Argentina).
Independiente Del Valle: Librado Rodrigo Azcona, Christian Washington Núñez Medina, Mario Alberto Pineida Martínez, Luis Fernando León Bermeo, Fernando Alexander Guerrero Vásquez (88.Luis Alberto Caicedo Medina), Mario Enrique Rizotto Vázquez, Jonathan David González Valencia, Jefferson Gabriel Orejuela Izquierdo (77.Gabriel Jhon Córtez Casierra), Arturo Rafael Mina Meza, Daniel Patricio Angulo Arroyo, Junior Nazareno Sornoza Moreira (82.Julio Eduardo Angulo Medina). Trainer: Pablo Eduardo Repetto Aquino (Uruguay).
Goal: Daniel Patricio Angulo Arroyo (78).

27.08.2014, Estadio Municipal „General Rumiñahui", Sangolquí
Referee: Henry Gambetta Ávalos (Peru)
CSD Independiente Del Valle Sangolquí - Trujillanos FC 1-1(0-0)
Independiente Del Valle: Librado Rodrigo Azcona, Christian Washington Núñez Medina, Mario Alberto Pineida Martínez, Luis Fernando León Bermeo, Gabriel Jhon Córtez Casierra, Fernando Alexander Guerrero Vásquez, Jonathan David González Valencia (73.Julio Eduardo Angulo Medina), Jefferson Gabriel Orejuela Izquierdo (43.Gabriel Jhon Córtez Casierra), Arturo Rafael Mina Meza, Daniel Patricio Angulo Arroyo, Junior Nazareno Sornoza Moreira (64.Armando Julian Solís Quentero). Trainer: Pablo Eduardo Repetto Aquino (Uruguay).
Trujillanos FC: Leandro Díaz Prado, Edixon Bladimir Cuevas Tirado, Mayker José González Montilla, Erlys Jordano Vásquez Carrero, Adolfo Perozo Oberto (44.Johan José Osorio Paredes), Jarol Herrera Martínez [*sent off 1*], Argenis José Gómez Ortega, Maurice Jesús Cova Sánchez, Gerardo José Mendoza (65.Arnaldo del Valle Aranda Rodríguez), Fredys Enrique Arrieta Fontalvo (73.Sergio Alberto Alvarez Castellano), James Fernando Cabezas Mairongo. Trainer: Horacio Ignacio Matuszyczk (Argentina).
Goals: Armando Julian Solís Quentero (90) / Sergio Alberto Alvarez Castellano (90+1).
[CSD Independiente Del Valle Sangolquí won 2-1 on aggregate]

21.08.2014, Estadio „Feliciano Cáceres", Luque
Referee: Roberto Tobar Vargas (Chile)
Club Deportivo Capiatá - Danubio FC Montevideo 3-1(1-0)
Deportivo Capiatá: Tobías Antonio Vargas Insfrán, Arturo David Aquino, Jorge Rodrigo Paredes, Néstor Fabián González, Derlis Fabián Ortíz Rodríguez, Carlos Gabriel Ruíz Peralta (78.Arnaldo Javier Pereira Vera), Blas Bernardo Irala Rojas, Óscar Ramón Ruíz Roa (84.Raúl Basilio Román Garay), Ángel David Martínez, Ricardo Javier Ortíz Pineda (66.Víctor Hugo Ayala Ojeda), Fabio Escobar Benítez. Trainer: Héctor Marecos.
Danubio: Salvador Ichazo Fernández, Emiliano Daniel Velázquez Maldonado, Luis Leandro Sosa Otermin, Guillermo Gastón Cotugno Lima, Fabricio Orosmán Formiliano Duarte, Federico Ricca Rostagnol, Mathías Nicolás De Los Santos Aguirre, Juan Ignacio González Brazeiro (55.Pablo Martín Silvera Duarte), Emiliano Michael Ghan Carranza (46.Néstor Fabián Canobbio Bentaberry), Matías Gastón Castro, Santiago Emiliano González Areco (64.Paul Matías Zunino Escudero). Trainer: Leonardo Alfredo Ramos Giro.
Goals: Fabio Escobar Benítez (16 penalty, 50 penalty), Blas Bernardo Irala Rojas (68) / Paul Matías Zunino Escudero (81).

28.08.2014, Estadio "Luis Franzini", Montevideo
Referee: Germán Delfino (Argentina)
Danubio FC Montevideo - Club Deportivo Capiatá 2-2(1-0)
Danubio: Salvador Ichazo Fernández, Luis Leandro Sosa Otermin (60.Santiago Emiliano González Areco), Guillermo Gastón Cotugno Lima, Fabricio Orosmán Formiliano Duarte, Federico Ricca Rostagnol [*sent off 35*], Mathías Nicolás De Los Santos Aguirre, Camilo Sebastián Mayada Mesa, Juan Ignacio González Brazeiro (55.Pablo Martín Silvera Duarte), Gonzalo Federico González Pereyra (71.Nicolás Milesi van Lommel), Ernesto Antonio Farías, Matías Gastón Castro. Trainer: Leonardo Alfredo Ramos Giro.
Deportivo Capiatá: Tobías Antonio Vargas Insfrán, Arturo David Aquino, Jorge Rodrigo Paredes, Néstor Fabián González, Derlis Fabián Ortíz Rodríguez [*sent off 64*], Carlos Gabriel Ruíz Peralta, Blas Bernardo Irala Rojas, Óscar Ramón Ruíz Roa (82.Víctor Hugo Ayala Ojeda), Ángel David Martínez (87.Arnaldo Javier Pereira Vera), Ricardo Javier Ortíz Pineda, Fabio Escobar Benítez (88.Cristian Ariel López Leiva). Trainer: Héctor Marecos.
Goals: Ernesto Antonio Farías (15 penalty), Matías Gastón Castro (78) / Fabio Escobar Benítez (46, 62 penalty).
[Club Deportivo Capiatá won 5-3 on aggregate]

21.08.2014, Estadio Ciudad de Cumaná, Ayacucho
Referee: Diego Jefferson Lara León (Ecuador)
Club Inti Gas Deportes Ayacucho - Caracas FC 0-1(0-0)
Inti Gas: Mario Eduardo Villasanti Adorno, Jeickson Gustavo Reyes Aparcana, Amilton Jair Prado, Raúl Penalillo Cotito, Óscar Alexander Guerra Maldonado, Yoshiro Abelardo Salazar Flores (60.Andrés Felipe Arroyave Cartagena), Wadid Jesús Arismendi Lazo (73.Henry Jorge Colán Díaz), Paolo Pablo César Joya Ricci, Carlos Alberto Orejuela Pita, Fernando Oliveira de Avila, Carlos Jairzinho Gonzáles Ávalos. Trainer: Carlos Fabián Leeb (Argentina).
Caracas FC: Alain Baroja Méndez, Roberto Raúl Tucker, Andrés Elionai Sánchez León, Francisco Carabalí Terán [*sent off 90+4*], Jefre José Vargas Belisario (84.Wuiliyhon Vivas Trejo), Miguel Ángel Mea Vitali, Giácomo di Georgi Zerill, Ricardo Andreutti Jordán, Rómulo Otero Vásquez (76.Rubert José Quijada Fasciana), Luis González (61.Dany Curé), Jhonder Leonel Cadíz Fernández. Trainer: Eduardo José Saragó Carbón.
Goal: Dany Curé (82).

28.08.2014, Estadio Olímpico de la UCV, Caracas
Referee: Luis Sánchez (Colombia)
Caracas FC - Club Inti Gas Deportes Ayacucho 1-0(1-0)
Caracas FC: Alain Baroja Méndez, Roberto Raúl Tucker, Andrés Elionai Sánchez León, Rubert José Quijada Fasciana, Jefre José Vargas Belisario, Miguel Ángel Mea Vitali, Giácomo di Georgi Zerill, Ricardo Andreutti Jordán, Rómulo Otero Vásquez (53.Luis González), Dany Curé (86.Robert Alexander Garcés Sánchez), Jhonder Leonel Cadíz Fernández (80.Omar Alfonso Perdomo Teheran). Trainer: Eduardo José Saragó Carbón.
Inti Gas: Mario Eduardo Villasanti Adorno, Jeickson Gustavo Reyes Aparcana, Amilton Jair Prado (46.Francesco do Santos Aldair Recalde Sánchez), Raúl Penalillo Cotito, Óscar Alexander Guerra Maldonado, Brayan Gustavo Arana (46.Wadid Jesús Arismendi Lazo), Yoshiro Abelardo Salazar Flores (46.Carlos Alberto Orejuela Pita), Henry Jorge Colán Díaz, Paolo Pablo César Joya Ricci, Fernando Oliveira de Avila, Carlos Jairzinho Gonzáles Ávalos. Trainer: Carlos Fabián Leeb (Argentina).
Goal: Rubert José Quijada Fasciana (10).
[Caracas FC won 2-0 on aggregate]

21.08.2014, Estadio „Nemesio Camacho" [El Campín], Bogotá
Referee: José Ramón Argote Vega (Venezuela)
CD Los Millonarios Bogotá - CSCD Universidad César Vallejo Trujillo 1-2(1-2)
Los Millonarios: Luis Enrique Delgado Mantilla, Román Torres Morcillo, Oswaldo José Henríquez Bocanegra, Andrés Felipe Cadavid Cardona, Lewis Alexander Ochoa Cassiani, Álex Díaz Díaz (61.Javier Arley Reina Calvo), Fabián Andrés Vargas Rivera, Rafael Fernando Robayo Marroquín, Mayer Andrés Candelo García, Fernando Uribe Hincapié (70.Anderson Daniel Plata Guillén), Jhonatan Alexander Agudelo Velásquez. Trainer: Juan Manuel Lillo Díez (Spain).
Universidad: Salomón Alexis Libman Pastor, Emiliano José Ciucci, Luís Felipe Cardoza Zuñiga, John Christopher Hinostroza Guzmán (65.Jesús Branco Geraldo Serrano Aguirre), Jesús Rabanal Dávila, Pedro Paulo Requena Cisneros, Donald Diego Millán Rodríguez (86.Luis Carlos Tejada Hansell), Ronald Jonathan Quinteros Sánchez (83.Atilio Muente Gionti), Juan Gustavo Morales Coronado, Daniel Mackensi Chávez Castillo, Andy Robert Pando García. Trainer: Franco Enrique Navarro Monteyro.
Goals: Fernando Uribe Hincapié (44) / Andy Robert Pando García (2, 39).

28.08.2014, Estadio Mansiche, Trujillo
Referee: Carlos Ulloa (Chile)
CSCD Universidad César Vallejo Trujillo - CD Los Millonarios Bogotá 2-2(2-1)
Universidad: Salomón Alexis Libman Pastor, Emiliano José Ciucci, Luís Felipe Cardoza Zuñiga, John Christopher Hinostroza Guzmán (70.Atilio Muente Gionti), Jesús Rabanal Dávila, Pedro Paulo Requena Cisneros, Donald Diego Millán Rodríguez (76.Luis Carlos Tejada Hansell), Ronald Jonathan Quinteros Sánchez (61.Jesús Branco Geraldo Serrano Aguirre), Juan Gustavo Morales Coronado, Daniel Mackensi Chávez Castillo, Andy Robert Pando García. Trainer: Franco Enrique Navarro Monteyro.
Los Millonarios: Luis Enrique Delgado Mantilla, Román Torres Morcillo, Oswaldo José Henríquez Bocanegra, Andrés Felipe Cadavid Cardona, Lewis Alexander Ochoa Cassiani (84.Yuber Alberto Asprilla Viera), Álex Díaz Díaz (74.Javier Arley Reina Calvo), Fabián Andrés Vargas Rivera, Rafael Fernando Robayo Marroquín (58.Andy Jorman Polo Andrade), Mayer Andrés Candelo García, Fernando Uribe Hincapié, Jhonatan Alexander Agudelo Velásquez. Trainer: Juan Manuel Lillo Díez (Spain).
Goals: Ronald Jonathan Quinteros Sánchez (2, 18) / Fernando Uribe Hincapié (34), Jhonatan Alexander Agudelo Velásquez (66).
[CSCD Universidad César Vallejo Trujillo won 4-3 on aggregate]

PRELIMINARY ROUND – SECOND STAGE

27.08.2014, Estádio Beira-Rio, Porto Alegre; Attendance: 9,368
Referee: Christian Ferreyra (Uruguay)
SC Internacional Porto Alegre - EC Bahia Salvador 0-2(0-1)
Internacional: Nelson de Jesús da Silva "Dida", Ernando Rodrigues Lopes, Alan Luciano Ruschel, Paulo Marcos De Jesus Ribeiro "Paulão", Cláudio Winck Neto, Ygor Maciel Santiago (46.Leandro Joaquim Ribeiro), Alex Raphael Meschini (68.Alan Patrick Lourenço), Charles Mariano Aránguiz Sandoval, Wellington Aparecido Martins, Wanderson Ferreira de Oliveira „Valdivia", Wellington Pereira do Nascimento "Wellington Paulista". Trainer: Abel Carlos da Silva Braga.
Bahia: Marcelo Lomba do Nascimento, Cristian Chagas Tarouco „Titi", Diego Macedo Prado dos Santos (88.Leandro Fahel Matos), Lucas Silva Fonseca, Roniery Ximenis Sousa Silva, Anderson Ferreira da Silva "Pará", Rafael Miranda da Conceição, Leonardo David de Moura "Léo Gago", Emanuel Adrian Biancucchi Cuccitini (71.Rhayner Santos Nascimento), Henrique Almeida Caixeta Nascentes, Rafael Lima Pereira "Rafinha" (80.Guilherme Oliveira Santos). Trainer: Gilson Kleina.
Goals: Lucas Silva Fonseca (42), Diego Macedo Prado dos Santos (46).

04.09.2014, Arena Fonte Nova, Salvador; Attendance: 3,969
Referee: Marcelo de Lima Henrique (Brazil)
EC Bahia Salvador - SC Internacional Porto Alegre 1-1(0-1)
Bahia: Marcelo Lomba do Nascimento, Cristian Chagas Tarouco „Titi", Diego Macedo Prado dos Santos (78.Rafael Lima Pereira "Rafinha"), Lucas Silva Fonseca, Roniery Ximenis Sousa Silva, Anderson Ferreira da Silva "Pará", Rafael Miranda da Conceição, Leonardo David de Moura "Léo Gago", Leandro Fahel Matos, Rhayner Santos Nascimento (68.Guilherme Oliveira Santos), Welker Marçal Almeida "Kieza" (72.Henrique Almeida Caixeta Nascentes). Trainer: Gilson Kleina.
Internacional: Nelson de Jesús da Silva "Dida", Fabrício dos Santos Silva, Ernando Rodrigues Lopes, Paulo Marcos De Jesus Ribeiro "Paulão", Gilberto Moraes Junior, Alex Raphael Meschini, Willians Domingos Fernandes (46.Alan Patrick Lourenço), Wellington Aparecido Martins (79.Leandro Joaquim Ribeiro), Eduardo Colcenti Antunes "Eduardo Sasha" (63.Wanderson Ferreira de Oliveira „Valdivia"), Rafael Martiniano de Miranda Moura, Wellington Pereira do Nascimento "Wellington Paulista". Trainer: Abel Carlos da Silva Braga.
Goals: Henrique Almeida Caixeta Nascentes (78) / Diego Macedo Prado dos Santos (45 own goal).
[EC Bahia Salvador won 3-1 on aggregate]

28.08.2014, Estádio Ilha do Retiro, Recife; Attendance: 8,320
Referee: Óscar Maldonado Urey (Bolivia)
Sport Club do Recife - EC Vitória Salvador de Bahia 0-1(0-1)
SC Recife: Alessandro Beti Rosa "Magrão", Severino dos Ramos Durval da Silva, Patric Cabral Lalau, Ewerton Ribeiro Páscoa (35.Oswaldo Alfredo de Lima Gonçalves), Renê Rodrigues Martins, Wendell Geraldo Maurício e Silva, Ibson Barreto da Silva, Ananias Eloi Castro Monteiro (59.Mike dos Santos Nenatarvicius), Francisco Rithely da Silva Sousa, Euvaldo José de Aguiar Neto "Neto Baiano", Felipe Azevedo dos Santos (38.Diego de Souza Andrade). Trainer: Eduardo Baptista.
Vitória: Roberto Júnior Fernández Torres, Ednei Barbosa de Souza, Ayrton Luiz Ganino, Joéliton Lima Santos „Mansur", Luiz Gustavo Tavares Conde, Márcio José Oliveira "Marcinho", Richarlyson Barbosa Felisbino, José Welison da Silva, Guillermo Alexis Beltrán Paredes (67.Marcelo Machado dos Santos), Marcos Júnior Lima dos Santos (46.Vinícius Santos Silva), Willie Hortencio Barbosa (74.Telmário de Araújo Sacramento "Dinei"). Trainer: Ney Franco da Silveira Júnior.
Goal: Guillermo Alexis Beltrán Paredes (9).

03.09.2014, Estádio „Manoel Barradas“, Salvador; Attendance: 2,592
Referee: Leandro Pedro Vuaden (Brazil)
EC Vitória Salvador de Bahia - Sport Club do Recife 2-1(1-0)
Vitória: Roberto Júnior Fernández Torres, Roger Carvalho (15.Ednei Barbosa de Souza), Severino do Ramos Clementino da Silva „Nino“, Joéliton Lima Santos „Mansur“, Luiz Gustavo Tavares Conde, Márcio José Oliveira "Marcinho", Adriano Bispo dos Santos, Richarlyson Barbosa Felisbino, Guillermo Alexis Beltrán Paredes, Marcos Júnior Lima dos Santos (58.Edno Roberto Cunha), Willie Hortencio Barbosa (46.Luis Enrique Cáceres). Trainer: Ney Franco da Silveira Júnior.
SC Recife: Alessandro Beti Rosa "Magrão", Severino dos Ramos Durval da Silva, Patric Cabral Lalau, Luiz Antonio Linhares Garcia "Ferron", Renê Rodrigues Martins, Danilo Carvalho Barcelos (64.Erico Francisco de Oliveira Junior), Wendell Geraldo Maurício e Silva, Ibson Barreto da Silva (76.Mike dos Santos Nenatarvicius), Francisco Rithely da Silva Sousa, Euvaldo José de Aguiar Neto "Neto Baiano", Felipe Azevedo dos Santos. Trainer: Eduardo Baptista.
Goals: Willie Hortencio Barbosa (21), Márcio José Oliveira "Marcinho" (73) / Francisco Rithely da Silva Sousa (50).
[EC Vitória Salvador de Bahia won 3-1 on aggregate]

28.08.2014, Estádio do Maracanã, Rio de Janeiro; Attendance: 6,314
Referee: Enrique Patricio Cáceres Villafañe (Paraguay)
Fluminense FC Rio de Janeiro - Goiás EC Goiânia 2-1(2-0)
Fluminense: Kléver Rodrigo Gomes Ruffino [*sent off 60*], Bruno Vieira do Nascimento, Edson Felipe da Cruz, Elivélton Viana dos Santos, Marlon Santos da Silva Barbosa, Cícero Santos (46.Wagner Ferreira dos Santos), Darío Leonardo Conca, Jean Raphael Vanderlei Moreira, Francisco Souza dos Santos "Chiquinho", Frederico Chaves Guedes „Fred“ (72.Carlos Henrique dos Santos Souza), Rafael Augusto Sóbis do Nascimento (62.Felipe Garcia dos Prazeres). Trainer: Cristóvão Borges dos Santos.
Goiás: Renan Brito Soares, Leonardo Henrique Veloso "Leo Veloso" (64.Assuério Barbosa de Sousa Junior), Valmir Lucas de Oliveira, Jackson de Souza, Moisés Francisco Dallazen (37.Murilo Henrique Pereira Rocha), Felipe Francisco Macedo, David França Oliveira e Silva, Tiago Real do Prado (76.Lucas Pedro Alves de Lima), Thiago Henrique Mendes Ribeiro, Rubens Raimundo da Silva "Esquerdinha", Erik Nascimento de Lima. Trainer: Sebastião Ricardo Drubscky de Campos.
Goals: Edson Felipe da Cruz (28, 33) / Erik Nascimento de Lima (90+3).

03.09.2014, Estádio Serra Dourada, Goiânia; Attendance: 11,024
Referee: Francisco Carlos Nascimento (Brazil)
Goiás EC Goiânia - Fluminense FC Rio de Janeiro 1-0(0-0)
Goiás: Renan Brito Soares, Leonardo Henrique Veloso "Leo Veloso", Valmir Lucas de Oliveira (63.Rodrigo Baldasso Da Costa), Jackson de Souza, Felipe Francisco Macedo, David França Oliveira e Silva, Tiago Real do Prado (89.Liniker da Silva Moreira), Thiago Henrique Mendes Ribeiro, Murilo Henrique Pereira Rocha, Rubens Raimundo da Silva "Esquerdinha" (90+5.Welinton Junior Ferreira dos Santos), Erik Nascimento de Lima. Trainer: Sebastião Ricardo Drubscky de Campos.
Fluminense: Felipe Garcia dos Prazeres, Carlos Henrique dos Santos Souza, Bruno Vieira do Nascimento (56.Wálter Da Silva), Carlos Andrade Souza "Carlinhos" (45+1.Robert Kenedy Nunes do Nascimento), Elivélton Viana dos Santos [*sent off 61*], Rodrigo Oliveira de Bittencourt „Diguinho“, Cícero Santos, Darío Leonardo Conca, Jean Raphael Vanderlei Moreira, Francisco Souza dos Santos "Chiquinho", Frederico Chaves Guedes „Fred“ (63.Marlon Santos da Silva Barbosa). Trainer: Cristóvão Borges dos Santos.
Goal: Erik Nascimento de Lima (47).
[Goiás EC Goiânia won on away goals rule (2-2 on aggregate)]

03.09.2014, Estadio "Juan Carmelo Zerillo", La Plata; Attendance: 19,786
Referee: Diego Hernán Abal (Argentina)
Club de Gimnasia y Esgrima La Plata - Club Estudiantes de La Plata 0-0
Gimnasia y Esgrima: Fernando Monetti, Lucas Matías Licht, Juan Leandro Quiroga, Osvaldo Rubén Barsottini, Facundo Julián Oreja, Omar Heber Pouso Osores (63.Dardo Federico Miloc), Álvaro Fernández Gay, Ignacio Fernández (71.Ezequiel Augusto Bonifacio Moreno), Jorge Luis Rojas Meza (59.Walter Ariel Bou), Javier Osvaldo Mendoza, Pablo Ezequiel Vegetti Pfaffen. Trainer: Pedro Antonio Troglio.
Estudiantes: Agustín Silva, Leandro Desábato, Germán Davíd Ré (37.Pablo Mauricio Rosales), Jonathan Ariel Schunke, Román Fernando Martínez, Leonardo Rafael Jara, Gastón Gil Romero, Carlos Joaquín Correa (90+1.Gabriel Maximiliano Graciani), Diego Daniel Vera Méndez, Carlos Daniel Auzqui (79.Ezequiel Cerutti), Guido Marcelo Carrillo. Trainer: Mauricio Andrés Pellegrino.

16.09.2014, Estadio Ciudad de La Plata, La Plata; Attendance: 32,666
Referee: Néstor Fabián Pitana (Argentina)
Club Estudiantes de La Plata - Club de Gimnasia y Esgrima La Plata 1-0(0-0)
Estudiantes: Agustín Silva, Leandro Desábato, Jonathan Ariel Schunke, Pablo Mauricio Rosales, Israel Alejandro Damonte, Román Fernando Martínez, Leonardo Rafael Jara, Carlos Joaquín Correa (63.Matias Aguirregaray Guruceaga), Diego Daniel Vera Méndez (71.Ezequiel Cerutti), Carlos Daniel Auzqui (85.Leonardo Sebastián Prediger), Guido Marcelo Carrillo. Trainer: Mauricio Andrés Pellegrino.
Gimnasia y Esgrima: Fernando Monetti, Lucas Matías Licht [*sent off 90+3*], Juan Leandro Quiroga, Osvaldo Rubén Barsottini, Facundo Julián Oreja (84.Nery Antonio Cardozo Escobar), Omar Heber Pouso Osores (68.Walter Ariel Bou), Álvaro Fernández Gay, Ignacio Fernández, Jorge Luis Rojas Meza, Javier Osvaldo Mendoza (74.Diego Oscar Nicolaievsky), Pablo Ezequiel Vegetti Pfaffen. Trainer: Pedro Antonio Troglio.
Goal: Diego Daniel Vera Méndez (49).
[Club Estudiantes de La Plata won 1-0 on aggregate]

03.09.2014, Estadio Malvinas Argentinas, Mendoza; Attendance: 28,451
Referee: Silvio Trucco (Argentina)
CD Godoy Cruz Mendoza - CA River Plate Buenos Aires 0-1(0-0)
Godoy Cruz: Sebastián Emanuel Moyano, Rolando García Guerreño, Sergio Ezequiel Velázquez, Esteban Rodrigo Burgos, Sergio Daniel López (60.Gonzalo Gabriel Cabrera Giordano), Diego Martín Rodríguez Berrini, Luis Jérez Silva, Fernando Zuqui, Daniel Alberto González (73.José Luis Fernández), Rubén Darío Ramírez, Jaime Javier Ayoví Corozo (56.Juan Fernando Garro). Trainer: Carlos Alberto Mayor.
River Plate: Marcelo Alberto Barovero, Bruno Saúl Urribarri, Gabriel Iván Mercado (58.Augusto Jorge Mateo Solari), José Ramiro Funes Mori, Germán Alejo Pezzela, Leonardo Nicolás Pisculichi, Ariel Mauricio Rojas, Carlos Andrés Sánchez Arcosa, Claudio Matías Kranevitter, Rodrigo Nicanor Mora Núñez (85.Sebastián Driussi), Lucas Boyé (57.Tomás Martínez). Trainer: Marcelo Daniel Gallardo.
Goal: Germán Alejo Pezzela (90+1).

17.09.2014, Estadio Monumental „Antonio Vespucio Liberti“, Buenos Aires; Attendance: 36,807
Referee: Saúl Laverni (Argentina)
CA River Plate Buenos Aires - CD Godoy Cruz Mendoza 2-0(2-0)
River Plate: Marcelo Alberto Barovero, Gabriel Iván Mercado, José Ramiro Funes Mori, Germán Alejo Pezzela, Leonardo Nicolás Pisculichi (64.Tomás Martínez), Leonel Jesús Vangioni, Ariel Mauricio Rojas, Carlos Andrés Sánchez Arcosa (83.Augusto Jorge Mateo Solari), Claudio Matías Kranevitter, Teófilo Antonio Gutiérrez Roncancio, Rodrigo Nicanor Mora Núñez (64.Lucas Boyé). Trainer: Marcelo Daniel Gallardo.
Godoy Cruz: Sebastián Emanuel Moyano, Guillermo Cosaro (46.José Luis Fernández), Sergio Ezequiel Velázquez, Esteban Rodrigo Burgos, Sergio Daniel López (46.Claudio Ezequiel Aquino), Diego Martín Rodríguez Berrini, Luis Jérez Silva, Fernando Zuqui, Daniel Alberto González (69.Jonathan Daniel Chávez), Rubén Darío Ramírez, Leandro Miguel Fernández. Trainer: Carlos Alberto Mayor.
Goals: Rodrigo Nicanor Mora Núñez (27, 31).
[CA River Plate Buenos Aires won 3-0 on aggregate]

04.09.2014, Estadio “Dr. Lisandro de la Torre” [Gigante de Arroyito], Rosario; Attendance: 25,073
Referee: Mauro Vigliano (Argentina)
CA Rosario Central - CA Boca Juniors Buenos Aires 1-1(0-1)
Rosario Central: Maurico Ariel Caranta, Paulo Andrés Ferrari, Alejandro César Donatti [*sent off 90+1*], Rafael Marcelo Delgado, Tomás Berra, Damián Marcelo Musto, Leonel Jonás Aguirre Avalo, Fernando Omar Barrientos (78.Walter Iván Montoya), Antonio César Medina (46.Pablo Ignacio Becker), Washington Sebastián Abreu Gal, Walter Rubén Acuña (69.José Adolfo Valencia Arrechea). Trainer: Miguel Ángel Russo.
Boca Juniors: Agustín Ignacio Orión, Daniel Alberto Díaz, Mariano Raúl Echeverría, Lucas Leandro Marín, Gonzalo Pablo Castellani (87.Pablo Martín Ledesma), Nicolás Carlos Colazo, Cristian Damián Erbes, César Marcelo Meli, Luciano Acosta (62.Federico Gastón Carrizo), Andrés Eliseo Chávez (70.Juan Manuel Martínez), Jonathan Calleri. Trainer: Rodolfo Martín Arruabarrena.
Goals: Pablo Ignacio Becker (90+5) / Lucas Leandro Marín (36).

18.09.2014, Estadio „Alberto J. Armando“, Buenos Aires; Attendance: 37,689
Referee: Diego Hernán Abal (Argentina)
CA Boca Juniors Buenos Aires - CA Rosario Central 3-0(1-0)
Boca Juniors: Agustín Ignacio Orión, Daniel Alberto Díaz, Mariano Raúl Echeverría, Lucas Leandro Marín, Fernando Rubén Gago, Nicolás Carlos Colazo, Cristian Damián Erbes, Federico Gastón Carrizo (66.Emanuel Mariano Insúa), César Marcelo Meli (82.José Pedro Fuenzalida Gana), Andrés Eliseo Chávez, Jonathan Calleri (75.Emanuel Gigliotti). Trainer: Rodolfo Martín Arruabarrena.
Rosario Central: Maurico Ariel Caranta, Paulo Andrés Ferrari, Rafael Marcelo Delgado, Lucas Acevedo [*sent off 36*], Tomás Berra, Damián Marcelo Musto, Leonel Jonás Aguirre Avalo (68.Hernán Nicolás Encina), Fernando Omar Barrientos, Nery Andrés Domínguez, Washington Sebastián Abreu Gal, Walter Rubén Acuña (54.Pablo Ignacio Becker). Trainer: Miguel Ángel Russo.
Goals: Andrés Eliseo Chávez (20, 70), José Pedro Fuenzalida Gana (83).
[CA Boca Juniors Buenos Aires won 4-1 on aggregate]

10.09.2014, Estadio „Atanasio Girardot“, Medellín
Referee: Juan Ernesto Soto Arévalo (Venezuela)
Club Atlético Nacional Medellín - Club General Díaz Luque 0-2(0-2)
Atlético Nacional: Franco Armani, Alexis Héctor Henríquez Charales, Álvaro Francisco Nájera Gil (58.Alejandro Bernal Rios), Farid Alfonso Díaz Rhenals, Daniel Eduardo Bocanegra Ortíz, Diego Arturo Peralta González, Sherman Andrés Cárdenas Estupiñán, Edwin Andrés Cardona Bedoya, Sebastián Pérez Cardona, Juan Pablo Ángel Arango (46.Wilder Andrés Guisao Correa), Luis Carlos Ruíz Morales. Trainer: Juan Carlos Osorio Arbelaez.
General Díaz: Bernardo David Medina, Dionisio Mereles Ovelar, Alejandro David Bernal, Alberto Espinola Giménez, Pedro Julián Chávez Ruíz (80.Víctor Hugo Dávalos Aguirre), Cristian Martínez Medina, Alberto Cirilo Contrera Jiménez, Blas Antonio Cáceres (71.Marco Antonio Gamarra Arbiniagaldez), Marcos Antonio Pfingst, Roberto Carlos Gamarra Acosta, Diego Javier Doldán Zacarías (60.Carlos Alberto Vera Segovia). Trainer: Humberto García Ramírez.
Goals: Pedro Julián Chávez Ruíz (16), Blas Antonio Cáceres (25).

25.09.2014, Estadio „Feliciano Cáceres“, Luque
Referee: Julio Bascuñán González (Chile)
Club General Díaz Luque - Club Atlético Nacional Medellín 1-3(0-1)
General Díaz: Bernardo David Medina, Marco Antonio Gamarra Arbiniagaldez (39.Diego Javier Doldán Zacarías), Dionisio Mereles Ovelar, Alejandro David Bernal, Alberto Espinola Giménez, Pedro Julián Chávez Ruíz, Cristian Martínez Medina, Alberto Cirilo Contrera Jiménez (61.Víctor Sócrates Michael Genés Espínola), Blas Antonio Cáceres, Marcos Antonio Pfingst (80.Carlos Alberto Vera Segovia), Roberto Carlos Gamarra Acosta. Trainer: Humberto García Ramírez.
Atlético Nacional: Franco Armani, Álvaro Francisco Nájera Gil, Alejandro Bernal Rios (70.Sherman Andrés Cárdenas Estupiñán), Farid Alfonso Díaz Rhenals (70.Miller Stiwar Mosquera Cabrera), Oscar Fabián Murillo Murillo, Daniel Eduardo Bocanegra Ortíz, Alexander Mejía Sabalsa, Edwin Andrés Cardona Bedoya [*sent off 28*], Wilder Andrés Guisao Correa, Jonathan Copete Valencia (57.Alejandro Abraham Guerra Morales), Santiago Tréllez Vivero. Trainer: Juan Carlos Osorio Arbelaez.
Goals: Roberto Carlos Gamarra Acosta (58) / Edwin Andrés Cardona Bedoya (12), Wilder Andrés Guisao Correa (61), Santiago Tréllez Vivero (87).
[Club Atlético Nacional Medellín won on away goals rule (3-3 on aggregate)]

11.09.2014, Estadio Monumental „Isidro Romero Carbo“, Guayaquil
Referee: Patricio Hernán Loustau (Argentina)
Barcelona SC Guayaquil - Club Libertad Asunción 1-0(1-0)
Barcelona SC: Máximo Orlando Banguera Valdivieso, José Luis Perlaza Napa, Luis Armando Checa Villamar, Geovanny Enrique Nazareno Simisterra, Pedro Pablo Velasco Arboleda, Matías Damián Oyola, Michael Jackson Quiñónez Cabeza (57.Flavio David Caicedo Gracia), Alex Leonardo Bolaños Reascos (73.Mario Roberto Martínez Hernández), Ismael Blanco, Cristian Anderson Penilla Caicedo, Ely Jair Esterilla Castro (62.Christian Andrés Suárez Valencia). Trainer: Rubén Jorge Israel (Uruguay).
Libertad: Rodrigo Martin Muñóz Salomón, Gustavo Ramón Mencia Ávalos, Pedro Juan Benítez Domínguez, Jorge Luis Moreira Ferreira (46.Ismael Benegas), Fabián Cornelio Balbuena González, Claudio David Vargas Villalba, Sergio Daniel Aquino, Jorge Daniel González Marquet (85.Néstor Abraham Camacho Ledesma), Osmar de la Cruz Molinas González, Hernán Rodrigo López Mora, Antonio Bareiro Álvarez (64.Dionisio Ismael Pérez Mambreani). Trainer: Pedro Alcides Sarabia Achucarro.
Goal: Ismael Blanco (14).

17.09.2014, Estadio „Dr. Nicolás Léoz“, Asunción
Referee: Marcelo de Lima Henrique (Brazil)
Club Libertad Asunción - Barcelona SC Guayaquil 2-0(2-0)
Libertad: Rodrigo Martin Muñóz Salomón, Pedro Juan Benítez Domínguez, Jorge Luis Moreira Ferreira, Ismael Benegas, Fabián Cornelio Balbuena González, Claudio David Vargas Villalba (77.Antonio Bareiro Álvarez), Sergio Daniel Aquino, Jorge Daniel González Marquet, Osmar de la Cruz Molinas González, Hernán Rodrigo López Mora (90+3.Adalberto Román Benítez), Dionisio Ismael Pérez Mambreani (68.Jorge Eduardo Recalde Ramírez). Trainer: Pedro Alcides Sarabia Achucarro.
Barcelona SC: Máximo Orlando Banguera Valdivieso, José Luis Perlaza Napa, Luis Armando Checa Villamar, Geovanny Enrique Nazareno Simisterra, Pedro Pablo Velasco Arboleda, Michael Jackson Quiñónez Cabeza (63.Christian Andrés Suárez Valencia), Alex Leonardo Bolaños Reascos [*sent off 90+1*], Flavio David Caicedo Gracia [*sent off 86*], Ismael Blanco, Cristian Anderson Penilla Caicedo (83.Washington Wilfrido Vera Gines), Ely Jair Esterilla Castro (46.Brayan José de la Torre Martínez). Trainer: Rubén Jorge Israel (Uruguay).
Goals: Hernán Rodrigo López Mora (7), Jorge Daniel González Marquet (43).
[Club Libertad Asunción won 2-1 on aggregate]

16.09.2014, Estadio Municipal „General Rumiñahui”, Sangolquí
Referee: José Hernando Buitrago Arango (Colombia)
CSD Independiente Del Valle Sangolquí - Club Cerro Porteño Asunción 1-0(0-0)
Independiente Del Valle: Librado Rodrigo Azcona, Christian Washington Núñez Medina, Mario Alberto Pineida Martínez, Luis Fernando León Bermeo, Gabriel Jhon Córtez Casierra, Fernando Alexander Guerrero Vásquez, Mario Enrique Rizotto Vázquez (61.Jefferson Gabriel Orejuela Izquierdo), Jonathan David González Valencia, Arturo Rafael Mina Meza, Daniel Patricio Angulo Arroyo (75.Richard Aníbal Porta Candelaresi), Junior Nazareno Sornoza Moreira (90.Armando Julian Solís Quentero). Trainer: Pablo Eduardo Repetto Aquino (Uruguay).
Cerro Porteño: Diego Daniel Barreto Cáceres, Carlos Bonet Cáceres, Víctor Hugo Mareco, Danilo Fabián Ortíz Soto, Junior Osmar Ignacio Alonso Mujica, Julio Daniel Dos Santos Rodríguez, Miguel Ángel Paniagua Rivarola, Fidencio Oviedo Domínguez, Óscar David Romero Villamayor (86.Sergio Ismael Díaz Velázquez), José María Ortigoza Ortíz, Rodolfo Vicente Gamarra Varela (72.Mauricio Ezequiel Sperdutti). Trainer: Leonardo Rubén Astrada (Argentina).
Goal: Arturo Rafael Mina Meza (55).

23.09.2014, Estadio Defensores del Chaco, Asunción
Referee: Daniel Adán Fedorczuk Betancour (Uruguay)
Club Cerro Porteño Asunción - CSD Independiente Del Valle Sangolquí 3-0(1-0)
Cerro Porteño: Diego Daniel Barreto Cáceres, Carlos Bonet Cáceres, Víctor Hugo Mareco, César Iván Benítez León (62.Junior Osmar Ignacio Alonso Mujica), Bruno Amilcar Valdez, Julio Daniel Dos Santos Rodríguez, Fidencio Oviedo Domínguez, Óscar David Romero Villamayor, Daniel González Güiza (79.Rodolfo Vicente Gamarra Varela), Mauricio Ezequiel Sperdutti (71.Miguel Ángel Paniagua Rivarola), José María Ortigoza Ortíz. Trainer: Leonardo Rubén Astrada (Argentina).
Independiente Del Valle: Librado Rodrigo Azcona, Christian Washington Núñez Medina (77.Armando Julian Solís Quentero), Mario Alberto Pineida Martínez, Luis Fernando León Bermeo, Gabriel Jhon Córtez Casierra (69.Julio Eduardo Angulo Medina), Fernando Alexander Guerrero Vásquez, Mario Enrique Rizotto Vázquez, Jonathan David González Valencia, Arturo Rafael Mina Meza, Daniel Patricio Angulo Arroyo [*sent off 20*], Junior Nazareno Sornoza Moreira (32.Richard Aníbal Porta Candelaresi). Trainer: Pablo Eduardo Repetto Aquino (Uruguay).
Goals: José María Ortigoza Ortíz (34), Víctor Hugo Mareco (55), Daniel González Güiza (65).
[Club Cerro Porteño Asunción won 3-1 on aggregate]

16.09.2014, Estadio Deportivo Capiatá, Capiatá
Referee: José Jaime Jordán Gallardo (Bolivia)
Club Deportivo Capiatá - Caracas FC 1-1(1-0)
Deportivo Capiatá: Tobías Antonio Vargas Insfrán [*sent off 90+3*], Arturo David Aquino, Jorge Rodrigo Paredes, Néstor Fabián González, Carlos Gabriel Ruíz Peralta (76.Milciades Daniel Silva), Blas Bernardo Irala Rojas, Óscar Ramón Ruíz Roa, Ángel David Martínez, Ricardo Javier Ortíz Pineda (87.Raúl Basilio Román Garay), Fabio Escobar Benítez, Cristian Ariel López Leiva (70.Julio César Irrazábal León). Trainer: Héctor Marecos.
Caracas FC: Alain Baroja Méndez, Roberto Raúl Tucker, Andrés Elionai Sánchez León, Francisco Carabalí Terán, Jefre José Vargas Belisario, Miguel Ángel Mea Vitali, Giácomo di Georgi Zerill, Ricardo Andreutti Jordán (85.Cristian Leonardo Flores Calderón), Rómulo Otero Vásquez, Dany Curé (73.Edder José Farías), Jhonder Leonel Cadíz Fernández (60.Luis González). Trainer: Eduardo José Saragó Carbón.
Goals: Cristian Ariel López Leiva (41) / Rómulo Otero Vásquez (89).

24.09.2014, Estadio Olímpico de la UCV, Caracas
Referee: Víctor Hugo Carrillo Casanova (Peru)
Caracas FC - Club Deportivo Capiatá 1-3(0-1)
Caracas FC: Alain Baroja Méndez, Roberto Raúl Tucker, Andrés Elionai Sánchez León (71.Luis González), Rubert José Quijada Fasciana, Jefre José Vargas Belisario (68.Francisco Carabalí Terán), Miguel Ángel Mea Vitali, Giácomo di Georgi Zerill, Rómulo Otero Vásquez, Robert Alexander Garcés Sánchez (46.Cristian Leonardo Flores Calderón), Edder José Farías, Dany Curé [*sent off 59*]. Trainer: Eduardo José Saragó Carbón.
Deportivo Capiatá: Antonio Alejandro Franco Arza, Arturo David Aquino, Jorge Rodrigo Paredes, Néstor Fabián González, Carlos Gabriel Ruíz Peralta (84.Gustavo Alberto Velázquez Núñez), Blas Bernardo Irala Rojas, Óscar Ramón Ruíz Roa (74.Víctor Hugo Ayala Ojeda), Ángel David Martínez, Ricardo Javier Ortíz Pineda, Fabio Escobar Benítez, Cristian Ariel López Leiva (81.Alfredo David Rojas). Trainer: Héctor Marecos.
Goals: Cristian Leonardo Flores Calderón (49) / Carlos Gabriel Ruíz Peralta (27, 47), Óscar Ramón Ruíz Roa (68).
[Club Deportivo Capiatá won 4-2 on aggregate]

16.09.2014, Estadio Centenario, Montevideo
Referee: Roddy Alberto Zambrano Olmedo (Ecuador)
CA Peñarol Montevideo - Asociación Deportivo Cali 2-2(0-0)
Peñarol: Pablo Alejandro Migliore, Octavio Darío Rodríguez Peña, Carlos Adrián Valdéz Suárez, Carlos Andrés Rodales Ramírez (62.Alejandro Daniel Silva González), Diogo Silvestre Bittencourt (71.Hernán Novick Rattich), Gonzalo Viera Davyt, Jorge Marcelo Rodríguez Núñez, Antonio Pacheco D'Agosti, Sebastián Gerardo Píriz Ribas, Marcelo Danubio Zalayeta, Carlos Rodrigo Núñez Techera (81.Juan Manuel Olivera López). Trainer: Jorge Daniel Fossati Lurachi.
Deportivo Cali: Luis Alfonso Hurtado Osorio, Cristian Javier Nasuti Matovelle, Frank Yusty Fabra Palacios, Germán Mera Cáceres, Helibelton Palacios Zapata, Andrés Eduardo Pérez Gutiérrez, Luis Fernando Mosquera Alomia (73.Víctor Hugo Giraldo López), Juan David Cabezas Nuñez, Yerson Candelo Miranda, Carlos Augusto Rivas Murillo (85.Miguel Ángel Murillo García), Sergio Darío Herrera Month (77.Jhon Eduis Viáfara Mina). Trainer: Héctor Fabio Cárdenas Berrío.
Goals: Carlos Rodrigo Núñez Techera (47), Marcelo Danubio Zalayeta (57) / Sergio Darío Herrera Month (53), Carlos Augusto Rivas Murillo (68).

24.09.2014, Estadio Olímpico "Pascual Guerrero", Cali
Referee: Antonio Javier Arias Alvarenga (Paraguay)
Asociación Deportivo Cali - CA Peñarol Montevideo 0-1(0-1)
Deportivo Cali: Luis Alfonso Hurtado Osorio, Cristian Javier Nasuti Matovelle, Frank Yusty Fabra Palacios, Germán Mera Cáceres, Helibelton Palacios Zapata, Jhon Eduis Viáfara Mina (64.Víctor Hugo Giraldo López), Andrés Eduardo Pérez Gutiérrez, Luis Fernando Mosquera Alomia (43.Carlos David Lizarazo Landázury), Yerson Candelo Miranda, Carlos Augusto Rivas Murillo, Sergio Darío Herrera Month (78.Miguel Ángel Murillo García). Trainer: Héctor Fabio Cárdenas Berrío.
Peñarol: Pablo Alejandro Migliore, Octavio Darío Rodríguez Peña, Carlos Adrián Valdéz Suárez, Carlos Andrés Rodales Ramírez, Diogo Silvestre Bittencourt, Gonzalo Viera Davyt, Jorge Marcelo Rodríguez Núñez, Antonio Pacheco D'Agosti (57.Sergio Daniel Orteman Rodríguez), Sebastián Gerardo Píriz Ribas, Marcelo Danubio Zalayeta (71.Alejandro Daniel Silva González), Jonathan Javier Rodríguez Portillo (87.Juan Manuel Olivera López). Trainer: Jorge Daniel Fossati Lurachi.
Goal: Marcelo Danubio Zalayeta (10).
[CA Peñarol Montevideo won 3-2 on aggregate]

17.09.2014, Estadio Olímpico Patria, Sucre; Attendance: 16,000
Referee: Péricles Bassols Pegado Cortez (Brazil)
CD Universitario San Francisco Xavier Sucre – 2-2(0-0)
CSCD Universidad César Vallejo Trujillo
Universitario: Juan Carlos Robles Rodríguez, Alan Loras Vélez, Ramiro Daniel Ballivián, Jorge Ignacio Cuéllar Rojas, Mauricio Saucedo Guardia (59.Claudio Ezequiel Mosca), Carlos Oswaldo Camacho Suárez, Alejandro René Bejarano Sajama, Federico Silvestre, Rubén de la Cuesta Vera, Lucas Ramón Ojeda Villanueva, Martín Adrián Palavicini López. Trainer: Javier Vega.
Universidad: Salomón Alexis Libman Pastor, Emiliano José Ciucci, Luís Felipe Cardoza Zuñiga, John Christopher Hinostroza Guzmán (81.Atilio Muente Gionti), Jesús Rabanal Dávila, Pedro Paulo Requena Cisneros, Donald Diego Millán Rodríguez, Ronald Jonathan Quinteros Sánchez (63.William Medardo Chiroque Tavara), Juan Gustavo Morales Coronado, Daniel Mackensi Chávez Castillo (75.Jesús Branco Geraldo Serrano Aguirre), Andy Robert Pando García. Trainer: Franco Enrique Navarro Monteyro.
Goals: Ramiro Daniel Ballivián (71), Carlos Oswaldo Camacho Suárez (90+4) / Andy Robert Pando García (50), Daniel Mackensi Chávez Castillo (56).

23.09.2014, Estadio Mansiche, Trujillo
Referee: Adrián Vélez (Colombia)
CSCD Universidad César Vallejo Trujillo – 3-0(0-0)
CD Universitario San Francisco Xavier Sucre
Universidad: Salomón Alexis Libman Pastor, Emiliano José Ciucci, Luís Felipe Cardoza Zuñiga, John Christopher Hinostroza Guzmán (72.Atilio Muente Gionti), Jesús Rabanal Dávila (46.Jesús Branco Geraldo Serrano Aguirre), Pedro Paulo Requena Cisneros, Donald Diego Millán Rodríguez, Ronald Jonathan Quinteros Sánchez, Juan Gustavo Morales Coronado, Daniel Mackensi Chávez Castillo, Andy Robert Pando García (72.Luis Carlos Tejada Hansell). Trainer: Franco Enrique Navarro Monteyro.
Universitario: Juan Carlos Robles Rodríguez, Alan Loras Vélez, Ezequiel Nicolás Filipetto, Ramiro Daniel Ballivián, Carlos Oswaldo Camacho Suárez (86.Jorge Enrique Flores Yrahory), Alejandro René Bejarano Sajama, Federico Silvestre, Rubén de la Cuesta Vera, Claudio Ezequiel Mosca, Lucas Ramón Ojeda Villanueva, Ignacio Rodríguez Ortiz „Nacho Rodríguez" (69.Martín Adrián Palavicini López). Trainer: Javier Vega.
Goals: Donald Diego Millán Rodríguez (56), Andy Robert Pando García (62), Daniel Mackensi Chávez Castillo (81).
[CSCD Universidad César Vallejo Trujillo won 5-2 on aggregate]

17.09.2014, Estadio CAP, Talcahuano
Referee: Andrés Cunha (Uruguay)
CD Huachipato Talcahuano - CD Universidad Católica Quito 2-0(1-0)
Huachipato: Miguel Hernán Jiménez Aracenna, Omar Jesús Merlo, Esteban Eduardo González Herrera, Claudio Andrés Muñoz Carrillo, Carlos Felipe Ignacio Espinosa Contreras (85.Matías Alberto Sánchez Herrera), Leandro Ezquerra De León, Martín Vladimir Rodríguez Torrejon (90+1.Nicolás Ignacio Crovetto Aqueveque), Leonardo Nicolás Povea Pérez, Bryan Alfonso Vejar Utreras, Lucas Simón García (41.Angelo Zagal), Andrés Alejandro Vílches Araneda. Trainer: Mario Alfredo Salas Saieg.
Universidad Católica: Hernán Ismael Galíndez, Mariano Esteban Uglessich, Deison Adolfo Méndez Rosero, Henry Junior Cangá Ortíz, Facundo Martin Martinez Montagnoli, Elvis Adán Patta Quintero, Jesi Alexander Godoy Quiñónes, Jonathan Bladimir Carabalí Palacios (56.Jonathan Oswaldo de la Cruz Valverde), Henry Leonel Patta Quintero (66.Bryan David Sánchez Congo), Armando Lenin Wila Canga, Diego Fernando Benítez Quintena. Trainer: Luis Gustavo Soler Magadán (Argentina).
Goals: Andrés Alejandro Vílches Araneda (12, 48).

24.09.2014, Estadio Olímpico Atahualpa, Quito
Referee: José Ramón Argote Vega (Venezuela)
CD Universidad Católica Quito - CD Huachipato Talcahuano 1-0(1-0)
Universidad Católica: Hernán Ismael Galíndez, Deison Adolfo Méndez Rosero (55.Alejandro Gabriel Espinosa Borja), Henry Junior Cangá Ortíz, Wilmar Pascual Meneses Borja, Facundo Martin Martinez Montagnoli, Elvis Adán Patta Quintero (66.Armando Lenin Wila Canga), Jonathan Oswaldo de la Cruz Valverde (76.Carlos Luis Moyano Moran), Jesi Alexander Godoy Quiñónes, Henry Leonel Patta Quintero, Diego Fernando Benítez Quintena, Bryan David Sánchez Congo. Trainer: Luis Gustavo Soler Magadán (Argentina).
Huachipato: Miguel Hernán Jiménez Aracenna, Omar Jesús Merlo, Esteban Eduardo González Herrera, Claudio Andrés Muñoz Carrillo, Carlos Felipe Ignacio Espinosa Contreras, Leandro Ezquerra De León (69.Francisco Esteban Arrué Pardo), Martín Vladimir Rodríguez Torrejon, Angelo Zagal (64.Matías Alberto Sánchez Herrera), Leonardo Nicolás Povea Pérez (83.Nicolás Ignacio Crovetto Aqueveque), Bryan Alfonso Vejar Utreras, Andrés Alejandro Vílches Araneda. Trainer: Mario Alfredo Salas Saieg.
Goal: Facundo Martin Martinez Montagnoli (33 penalty).
[CD Huachipato Talcahuano won 2-1 on aggregate]

18.09.2014, Estadio „George Capwell“, Guayaquil
Referee: Julio Bascuñán González (Chile)
CS Emelec Guayaquil - CA River Plate Montevideo 2-1(1-0)
Emelec: Esteban Javier Dreer, Gabriel Eduardo Achilier Zurita, Oscar Dalmiro Bagüi Angulo, Jhon William Narváez, Pedro Angel Quiñónez Rodríguez, José Luis Quiñónez Quiñónez, Ángel Israel Mena Delgado, Miller Alejandro Bolaños Reascos, Fernando Agustín Giménez Solís, Osbaldo Lupo Lastra García (77.Emanuel Herrera), Marcos Gustavo Mondaini (86.Mauro Raúl Fernández). Trainer: Gustavo Domingo Quinteros Desabato (Bolivia).
River Plate: Alison Nicola Pérez Barone, Williams Guillermo Martínez Fracchia, Claudio Herrera Casanova [*sent off 75*], Cristian Mario González Aidinovich, Diego Manuel Rodríguez Da Luz, Gabriel Marques de Andrade Pinto, Claudio Gastón Innella Alderete (72.Ángel Leonardo Rodríguez Güelmo), Fernando Gorriarán Fontes (63.Robert Mario Flores Bistolfi), Cristian Rafael Techera Cribelli, Michael Nicolás Santos Rosadilla, Leandro Joaquín Rodríguez Telechea (77.Luis Alberto Torrecilla Michelle). Trainer: Jorge Guillermo Almada Álves.
Goals: Marcos Gustavo Mondaini (26), Miller Alejandro Bolaños Reascos (47) / Michael Nicolás Santos Rosadilla (73 penalty).

25.09.2014, Estadio „Luis Franzini", Montevideo
Referee: Diego Ceballos (Argentina)
CA River Plate Montevideo - CS Emelec Guayaquil 1-1(1-1)
River Plate: Alison Nicola Pérez Barone, Williams Guillermo Martínez Fracchia, Luis Alberto Torrecilla Michelle, Cristian Mario González Aidinovich, Diego Manuel Rodríguez Da Luz (67.Flavio Armando Córdoba Rodríguez), Gabriel Marques de Andrade Pinto, Ángel Leonardo Rodríguez Güelmo (46.Robert Mario Flores Bistolfi), Fernando Gorriarán Fontes, Cristian Rafael Techera Cribelli, Leandro Joaquín Rodríguez Telechea, Alexander Mauricio Rosso Génova (54.Santiago Damián García Correa). Trainer: Jorge Guillermo Almada Álves.
Emelec: Esteban Javier Dreer, Gabriel Eduardo Achilier Zurita [*sent off* 82], Oscar Dalmiro Bagüi Angulo, Jhon William Narváez, Pedro Angel Quiñónez Rodríguez, José Luis Quiñónez Quiñónez, Ángel Israel Mena Delgado (90+1.Javier Isidro Charcopa Alegria), Miller Alejandro Bolaños Reascos (83.Jorge Daniel Guagua Tamayo), Fernando Agustín Giménez Solís, Osbaldo Lupo Lastra García, Marcos Gustavo Mondaini (72.Emanuel Herrera). Trainer: Gustavo Domingo Quinteros Desabato (Bolivia).
Goals: Leandro Joaquín Rodríguez Telechea (34) / Ángel Israel Mena Delgado (26).
[CS Emelec Guayaquil won 3-2 on aggregate]

28.09.2014, Estádio "Heriberto Hülse", Criciúma; Attendance: 7,271
Referee: Julio Bascuñán González (Chile)
Criciúma Esporte Clube - São Paulo FC 2-1(2-1)
Criciúma: Bruno Brigido de Oliveira, Alcides Eduardo Mendes de Araújo Alves, Ronaldo Luiz Alves, Giovanni Palmieri dos Santos, Luís Felipe Dias do Nascimento, Sérgio Antônio Borges Júnior "Serginho", Paulo César Baier (86.Michael Vinicius Silva de Morais), João Vitor Lima Gomes, Wellington Bruno da Silva (68.Rafael Eduardo Costa), Silvio José Cardoso Reis Junior "Silvinho" (78.Mauro Job Pontes Júnior "Maurinho"), Lucca Borges de Brito. Trainer: Wilson Waterkemper "Wilsão".
São Paulo: Rogério Ceni, Édson José da Silva, Álvaro Daniel Pereira Barragán, Jonathan Doin „Paulo Miranda", Lucas Cavalcante Silva Afonso "Lucão", Michel Fernandes Bastos, Maicon Thiago Pereira de Souza (62.Gabriel Boschilia), Húdson Rodrigues dos Santos, Josef de Souza Dias, Alexandre Rodrigues da Silva „Alexandre Pato", Ademilson Braga Bispo Junior (71.Ewandro Felipe de Lima Costa). Trainer: Muricy Ramalho.
Goals: Silvio José Cardoso Reis Junior "Silvinho" (15), Lucca (42) / Alexandro Pato (26).

04.09.2014, Estádio „Cícero Pompeu de Toledo" [Morumbi], São Paulo; Attendance: 10,140
Referee: Ricardo Marques Ribeiro (Brazil)
São Paulo FC - Criciúma Esporte Clube 2-0(2-0)
São Paulo: Rogério Ceni, Édson José da Silva, Jonathan Doin „Paulo Miranda", Rafael Tolói, Ricardo Izecson dos Santos Leite "Kaká" (78.Gabriel Boschilia), Michel Fernandes Bastos, Denílson Pereira Neves, Josef de Souza Dias, Paulo Henrique Chagas de Lima „Ganso", Alan Kardec de Souza Pereira Junior, Osvaldo Lourenço Filho (78.Reinaldo Manoel da Silva). Trainer: Muricy Ramalho.
Criciúma: Rodrigo José Galatto, Alcides Eduardo Mendes de Araújo Alves, Ronaldo Luiz Alves, Giovanni Palmieri dos Santos (85.Ronaldo Cesar Mendes de Medeiros), Luís Felipe Dias do Nascimento, Sérgio Antônio Borges Júnior "Serginho", Cléber Santana Loureiro, João Vitor Lima Gomes, Wellington Bruno da Silva (46.Rodrigo De Souza Cardoso), Silvio José Cardoso Reis Junior "Silvinho", Lucca Borges de Brito (72.Rafael Eduardo Costa). Trainer: Gilmar del Pozzo.
Goals: Édson José da Silva (32), Ricardo Izecson dos Santos Leite "Kaká" (40).
[São Paulo FC won 3-2 on aggregate]

ROUND OF 16

30.09.2014, Estádio „Cícero Pompeu de Toledo“ [Morumbi], São Paulo
Referee: Christian Ferreyra (Uruguay)
São Paulo FC - CD Huachipato Talcahuano 1-0(0-0)
São Paulo: Rogério Ceni, Édson José da Silva, Álvaro Daniel Pereira Barragán, Jonathan Doin „Paulo Miranda“, Auro Alvaro da Cruz Junior (30.Lucas Cavalcante Silva Afonso "Lucão"; 74.Húdson Rodrigues dos Santos), Michel Fernandes Bastos, Denílson Pereira Neves, Josef de Souza Dias, Luís Fabiano Clemente [*sent off 33*], Alexandre Rodrigues da Silva „Alexandre Pato“ (58.Alan Kardec de Souza Pereira Junior), Osvaldo Lourenço Filho. Trainer: Muricy Ramalho.
Huachipato: Miguel Hernán Jiménez Aracenna, Omar Jesús Merlo, Esteban Eduardo González Herrera, Claudio Andrés Muñoz Carrillo, Francisco Esteban Arrué Pardo (61.Carlos Felipe Ignacio Espinosa Contreras), Leandro Ezquerra De León (80.Camilo Pontoni), Martín Vladimir Rodríguez Torrejon (69.Angelo Zagal), Leonardo Nicolás Povea Pérez, Bryan Alfonso Vejar Utreras, Matías Alberto Sánchez Herrera, Andrés Alejandro Vílches Araneda. Trainer: Mario Alfredo Salas Saieg.
Goal: Michel Fernandes Bastos (55).

15.10.2014, Estadio CAP, Talcahuano
Referee: Antonio Javier Arias Alvarenga (Paraguay)
CD Huachipato Talcahuano - São Paulo FC 2-3(1-2)
Huachipato: Miguel Hernán Jiménez Aracenna, Omar Jesús Merlo, Esteban Eduardo González Herrera (46.Martín Vladimir Rodríguez Torrejon), Claudio Andrés Muñoz Carrillo, Francisco Esteban Arrué Pardo, Leandro Ezquerra De León (59.Matías Alberto Sánchez Herrera), Juan Carlos Espinoza Reyes, Angelo Zagal, Leonardo Nicolás Povea Pérez (41.Carlos Felipe Ignacio Espinosa Contreras), Bryan Alfonso Vejar Utreras, Andrés Alejandro Vílches Araneda. Trainer: Mario Alfredo Salas Saieg.
São Paulo: Rogério Ceni, Antônio Carlos dos Santos Aguiar, Édson José da Silva, Álvaro Daniel Pereira Barragán, Jonathan Doin „Paulo Miranda“, Michel Fernandes Bastos, Denílson Pereira Neves [*sent off 37*], Húdson Rodrigues dos Santos, Paulo Henrique Chagas de Lima „Ganso“ (87.Gabriel Boschilia), Alexandre Rodrigues da Silva „Alexandre Pato“ (34.Osvaldo Lourenço Filho; 72.Lucas Cavalcante Silva Afonso "Lucão"), Alan Kardec de Souza Pereira Junior. Trainer: Muricy Ramalho.
Goals: Andrés Alejandro Vílches Araneda (20), Angelo Zagal (87) / Michel Fernandes Bastos (9), Paulo Henrique Chagas de Lima „Ganso“ (22), Gabriel Boschilia (89).
[São Paulo FC won 4-2 on aggregate]

01.10.2014, Estadio „George Capwell“, Guayaquil
Referee: Óscar Maldonado Urey (Bolivia)
CS Emelec Guayaquil - Goiás EC Goiânia 1-0(0-0)
Emelec: Esteban Javier Dreer, Oscar Dalmiro Bagüi Angulo, Jhon William Narváez, Jordan Andrés Jaime Plata (54.Javier Isidro Charcopa Alegria), Fernando Agustín Giménez Solís (83.Emanuel Herrera), Pedro Angel Quiñónez Rodríguez (71.Robert Javier Burbano Cobeña), José Luis Quiñónez Quiñónez, Ángel Israel Mena Delgado, Miller Alejandro Bolaños Reascos, Osbaldo Lupo Lastra García, Marcos Gustavo Mondaini. Trainer: Gustavo Domingo Quinteros Desabato (Bolivia).
Goiás: Renan Brito Soares, Leonardo Henrique Veloso "Leo Veloso", Pedro Henrique Pereira da Silva „Pedrão“, Jackson de Souza, Felipe Francisco Macedo (83.Rodrigo Baldasso Da Costa), David França Oliveira e Silva, Willian José de Souza „Amaral“, Tiago Real do Prado, Thiago Henrique Mendes Ribeiro, Rubens Raimundo da Silva "Esquerdinha" (77.Ramón Rodrigo de Freitas), Erik Nascimento de Lima. Trainer: Sebastião Ricardo Drubscky de Campos.
Goal: Emanuel Herrera (86).

15.10.2014, Estádio Serra Dourada, Goiânia; Attendance: 25,741
Referee: Wilmar Alexander Roldán Pérez (Colombia)
Goiás EC Goiânia - CS Emelec Guayaquil **1-0(1-0,1-0,1-0); 5-6 on penalties**

Goiás: Renan Brito Soares, Leonardo Henrique Veloso "Leo Veloso" (78.Lucas Pedro Alves de Lima), Pedro Henrique Pereira da Silva „Pedrão", Jackson de Souza, Felipe Francisco Macedo, David França Oliveira e Silva (58.Ramón Rodrigo de Freitas), Willian José de Souza „Amaral", Tiago Real do Prado (67.Bruno Menezes Soares "Bruno Mineiro"), Thiago Henrique Mendes Ribeiro, Rubens Raimundo da Silva "Esquerdinha", Erik Nascimento de Lima. Trainer: Sebastião Ricardo Drubscky de Campos.
Emelec: Esteban Javier Dreer, Gabriel Eduardo Achilier Zurita, Oscar Dalmiro Bagüi Angulo, Jhon William Narváez, Pedro Angel Quiñónez Rodríguez (86.Fernando Vicente Gaibor Orellana), José Luis Quiñónez Quiñónez, Ángel Israel Mena Delgado, Miller Alejandro Bolaños Reascos, Fernando Agustín Giménez Solís, Osbaldo Lupo Lastra García, Emanuel Herrera (66.Marcos Gustavo Mondaini). Trainer: Gustavo Domingo Quinteros Desabato (Bolivia).
Goal: Erik Nascimento de Lima (19).
Penalties: Thiago Henrique Mendes Ribeiro 1-0; Miller Alejandro Bolaños Reascos 1-1; Lucas Pedro Alves de Lima 2-1; Ángel Israel Mena Delgado (missed); Bruno Menezes Soares "Bruno Mineiro" (missed); Marcos Gustavo Mondaini 2-2; Jackson de Souza 3-2; Oscar Dalmiro Bagüi Angulo 3-3; Erik Nascimento de Lima 4-3; José Luis Quiñónez Quiñónez 4-4; Rubens Raimundo da Silva "Esquerdinha" 5-4; Fernando Vicente Gaibor Orellana 5-5; Pedro Henrique Pereira da Silva „Pedrão" (missed); Fernando Agustín Giménez Solís 5-6.
[CS Emelec Guayaquil won 6-5 on penalties (after 1-1 on aggregate)]

01.10.2014, Arena Fonte Nova, Salvador
Referee: Carlos Arecio Amarilla Demarqui (Paraguay)
EC Bahia Salvador - CSCD Universidad César Vallejo Trujillo **2-0(0-0)**
Bahia: Marcelo Lomba do Nascimento, Cristian Chagas Tarouco „Titi", Demerson Bruno Costa, Diego Macedo Prado dos Santos (71.Marcos Aurélio de Oliveira Lima), Railan dos Santos Reis, Anderson Ferreira da Silva "Pará", Leonardo David de Moura "Léo Gago", Leandro Fahel Matos, Emanuel Adrian Biancucchi Cuccitini (80.William Silva Gomes Barbio), Welker Marçal Almeida "Kieza", Rafael Lima Pereira "Rafinha" (46.Maximiliano Daniel Biancucchi Cuccittini). Trainer: Gilson Kleina.
Universidad: Salomón Alexis Libman Pastor, Emiliano José Ciucci [*sent off 63*], Luís Felipe Cardoza Zuñiga, John Christopher Hinostroza Guzmán (68.Jesús Branco Geraldo Serrano Aguirre), Jesús Martín Álvarez Hurtado, Pedro Paulo Requena Cisneros, Donald Diego Millán Rodríguez, Ronald Jonathan Quinteros Sánchez, Juan Gustavo Morales Coronado, Daniel Mackensi Chávez Castillo, Andy Robert Pando García (81.Luis Carlos Tejada Hansell). Trainer: Franco Enrique Navarro Monteyro.
Goals: Cristian Chagas Tarouco „Titi" (64), William Silva Gomes Barbio (79).

15.10.2014, Estadio Mansiche, Trujillo
Referee: Carlos Alfredo Vera Rodríguez (Ecuador)
CSCD Universidad César Vallejo Trujillo - EC Bahia Salvador **2-0(0-0,2-0,2-0); 7-6 on penalties**
Universidad: Salomón Alexis Libman Pastor, Luís Felipe Cardoza Zuñiga, Atilio Muente Gionti, Jesús Rabanal Dávila, Jeremy Martín Rostaing Verástegui (72.Luis Carlos Tejada Hansell), Donald Diego Millán Rodríguez, William Medardo Chiroque Tavara, Ronald Jonathan Quinteros Sánchez (86.Niger Josset Vega Argomedo [*sent off 90+3*]), Juan Gustavo Morales Coronado, Daniel Mackensi Chávez Castillo, Andy Robert Pando García. Trainer: Franco Enrique Navarro Monteyro.
Bahia: Marcelo Lomba do Nascimento, Cristian Chagas Tarouco „Titi", Lucas Silva Fonseca, Railan dos Santos Reis, Anderson Ferreira da Silva "Pará", Leonardo David de Moura "Léo Gago", Leandro Fahel Matos, Uelliton da Silva Vieira, Marcos Aurélio de Oliveira Lima, Welker Marçal Almeida "Kieza" (72.Henrique Almeida Caixeta Nascentes), Rafael Lima Pereira "Rafinha" (79.William Silva Gomes Barbio). Trainer: Gilson Kleina.
Goals: Ronald Jonathan Quinteros Sánchez (82), William Medardo Chiroque Tavara (90).

Penalties: Luis Carlos Tejada Hansell 1-0; Marcos Aurélio de Oliveira Lima 1-1; Daniel Mackensi Chávez Castillo (missed); Lucas Silva Fonseca (missed); William Medardo Chiroque Tavara 2-1; Henrique Almeida Caixeta Nascentes 2-2; Andy Robert Pando García 3-2; Cristian Chagas Tarouco „Titi" 3-3; Donald Diego Millán Rodríguez 4-3; Leonardo David de Moura "Léo Gago" 4-4; Jesús Rabanal Dávila (missed); Uelliton da Silva Vieira (missed); Atilio Muente Gionti (missed); Anderson Ferreira da Silva "Pará" (missed); Juan Gustavo Morales Coronado 5-4; William Silva Gomes Barbio 5-5; Luís Felipe Cardoza Zuñiga 6-5; Railan dos Santos Reis 6-6; Salomón Alexis Libman Pastor 7-6; Marcelo Lomba do Nascimento (missed).
[CSCD Universidad César Vallejo Trujillo won 7-6 on penalties (after 2-2 on aggregate)]

01.10.2014, Estadio „Atanasio Girardot", Medellín
Referee: Carlos Alfredo Vera Rodríguez (Ecuador)
Club Atlético Nacional Medellín - EC Vitória Salvador de Bahia 2-2(1-1)
Atlético Nacional: Franco Armani, Álvaro Francisco Nájera Gil, Alejandro Bernal Rios, Farid Alfonso Díaz Rhenals (71.Miller Stiwar Mosquera Cabrera), Oscar Fabián Murillo Murillo, Daniel Eduardo Bocanegra Ortíz, Alejandro Abraham Guerra Morales, Alexander Mejía Sabalsa, Wilder Andrés Guisao Correa, Luis Carlos Ruíz Morales (79.Santiago Tréllez Vivero), Jonathan Copete Valencia (58.Sherman Andrés Cárdenas Estupiñán). Trainer: Juan Carlos Osorio Arbelaez.
Vitória: Roberto Júnior Fernández Torres, Severino do Ramos Clementino da Silva „Nino", Ednei Barbosa de Souza, Joéliton Lima Santos „Mansur", Luiz Gustavo Tavares Conde, Adriano Bispo dos Santos, Luís Bernardo Aguiar Burgos, José Welison da Silva (21.William Henrique Rodrigues da Silva), Edno Roberto Cunha, Guillermo Alexis Beltrán Paredes, Marcos Júnior Lima dos Santos (62.Elosman Euller Silva Cavalcante). Trainer: Ney Franco da Silveira Júnior.
Goals: Daniel Eduardo Bocanegra Ortíz (3), Luis Carlos Ruíz Morales (65 penalty) / Ednei Barbosa de Souza (45), William Henrique (48).

16.10.2014, Estádio „Manoel Barradas", Salvador
Referee: Diego Hernán Abal (Argentina)
EC Vitória Salvador de Bahia - Club Atlético Nacional Medellín 0-1(0-0)
Vitória: Roberto Júnior Fernández Torres, Ricardo Martins de Araújo „Kadu", Roger Carvalho, Severino do Ramos Clementino da Silva „Nino", Joéliton Lima Santos „Mansur", Luiz Gustavo Tavares Conde (88.William Henrique Rodrigues da Silva), Márcio José Oliveira "Marcinho" (73.Luís Bernardo Aguiar Burgos), Richarlyson Barbosa Felisbino (73.Marcos Júnior Lima dos Santos), Telmário de Araújo Sacramento "Dinei", Edno Roberto Cunha, Vinícius Santos Silva. Trainer: Ney Franco da Silveira Júnior.
Atlético Nacional: Franco Armani, Alexis Héctor Henríquez Charales, Álvaro Francisco Nájera Gil, Alejandro Bernal Rios (55.Alexander Mejía Sabalsa), Farid Alfonso Díaz Rhenals, Oscar Fabián Murillo Murillo, Daniel Eduardo Bocanegra Ortíz, Sherman Andrés Cárdenas Estupiñán, Wilder Andrés Guisao Correa, Luis Carlos Ruíz Morales (80.Santiago Tréllez Vivero), Jonathan Copete Valencia (60.Edwin Andrés Cardona Bedoya). Trainer: Juan Carlos Osorio Arbelaez.
Goal: Daniel Eduardo Bocanegra Ortíz (70).
[Club Atlético Nacional Medellín won 3-2 on aggregate]

14.10.2014, Estadio Defensores del Chaco, Asunción
Referee: Darío Agustín Ubriaco Medero (Uruguay)
Club Cerro Porteño Asunción - CA Lanús 2-1(0-0)
Cerro Porteño: Diego Daniel Barreto Cáceres, Carlos Bonet Cáceres, Víctor Hugo Mareco, César Iván Benítez León, Danilo Fabián Ortíz Soto, Julio Daniel Dos Santos Rodríguez, Fidencio Oviedo Domínguez, Óscar David Romero Villamayor, Mauricio Ezequiel Sperdutti (74.Miguel Ángel Paniagua Rivarola), José María Ortigoza Ortíz (81.Jonathan Fabbro), Sergio Ismael Díaz Velázquez (57.Rodolfo Vicente Gamarra Varela). Trainer: Leonardo Rubén Astrada (Argentina).
CA Lanús: Matías Alejandro Ibáñez Basualdo, Maximiliano Nicolás Velázquez (78.Nicolás Pasquini), Carlos Luciano Araujo, Diego Luis Braghieri, Matías Alfredo Martínez, Leandro Daniel Somoza, Jorge Alberto Ortíz, Diego Hernán González, Iván Gonzalo Bella (60.Silvio Ezequiel Romero), Santiago Martín Silva Olivera, Lucas Santiago Melano (87.Víctor Hugo Ayala Núñez). Trainer: Guillermo Barros Schelotto.
Goals: Óscar David Romero Villamayor (61, 63) / Santiago Martín Silva Olivera (72).

21.10.2014, Estadio Ciudad de Lanús „Néstor Díaz Pérez“, Lanús
Referee: Roddy Alberto Zambrano Olmedo (Ecuador)
CA Lanús - Club Cerro Porteño Asunción 1-1(1-1)
CA Lanús: Agustín Federico Marchesín, Maximiliano Nicolás Velázquez (81.Nicolás Pasquini), Carlos Luciano Araujo (65.Jorge Vidal Valdéz Chamorro), Diego Luis Braghieri, Gustavo Raúl Gómez Portillo, Leandro Daniel Somoza, Jorge Alberto Ortíz, Víctor Hugo Ayala Núñez, Santiago Martín Silva Olivera, Silvio Ezequiel Romero, Lucas Santiago Melano (56.Óscar Junior Benítez). Trainer: Guillermo Barros Schelotto.
Cerro Porteño: Diego Daniel Barreto Cáceres, Carlos Bonet Cáceres, Víctor Hugo Mareco, César Iván Benítez León, Bruno Amilcar Valdez, Julio Daniel Dos Santos Rodríguez, Fidencio Oviedo Domínguez, Óscar David Romero Villamayor, Daniel González Güiza (69.Rodolfo Vicente Gamarra Varela), Mauricio Ezequiel Sperdutti (56.Miguel Ángel Paniagua Rivarola), José María Ortigoza Ortíz (81.Jonathan Fabbro). Trainer: Leonardo Rubén Astrada (Argentina).
Goals: Diego Luis Braghieri (38) / Óscar David Romero Villamayor (1).
[Club Cerro Porteño Asunción won 3-2 on aggregate]

14.10.2014, Estadio Ciudad de La Plata, La Plata
Referee: Enrique Roberto Osses Zencovich (Chile)
Club Estudiantes de La Plata - CA Peñarol Montevideo 2-1(1-0)
Estudiantes: Hilario Bernardo Navarro, Leandro Desábato, Jonathan Ariel Schunke, Matias Aguirregaray Guruceaga, Román Fernando Martínez, Leonardo Rafael Jara, Gastón Gil Romero, Carlos Joaquín Correa, Diego Daniel Vera Méndez, Carlos Daniel Auzqui (68.Ezequiel Cerutti), Guido Marcelo Carrillo. Trainer: Mauricio Andrés Pellegrino.
Peñarol: Pablo Alejandro Migliore, Damián Macaluso Rojas, Octavio Darío Rodríguez Peña, Carlos Adrián Valdéz Suárez, Diogo Silvestre Bittencourt, Alejandro Daniel Silva González (82.Jonathan Alexis Sandoval Rojas), Jorge Marcelo Rodríguez Núñez, Antonio Pacheco D'Agosti (68.Sergio Daniel Orteman Rodríguez), Nahitan Michel Nández Acosta, Marcelo Danubio Zalayeta, Juan Manuel Olivera López (59.Fabián Larry Estoyanoff Poggio). Trainer: Jorge Daniel Fossati Lurachi.
Goals: Carlos Joaquín Correa (11), Guido Marcelo Carrillo (90+4 penalty) / Fabián Larry Estoyanoff Poggio (63).

22.10.2014, Estadio Centenario, Montevideo
Referee: Leandro Pedro Vuaden (Brazil)
CA Peñarol Montevideo - Club Estudiantes de La Plata **2-1(2-0,2-1,2-1); 1-3 on penalties**

Peñarol: Pablo Alejandro Migliore, Damián Macaluso Rojas, Carlos Adrián Valdéz Suárez, Diogo Silvestre Bittencourt, Alejandro Daniel Silva González (76.Fabián Larry Estoyanoff Poggio), Gonzalo Viera Davyt, Jorge Marcelo Rodríguez Núñez, Antonio Pacheco D'Agosti (67.Sergio Daniel Orteman Rodríguez), Sebastián Gerardo Píriz Ribas, Marcelo Danubio Zalayeta (81.Carlos Rodrigo Núñez Techera), Jonathan Javier Rodríguez Portillo. Trainer: Jorge Daniel Fossati Lurachi.
Estudiantes: Hilario Bernardo Navarro, Leandro Desábato, Jonathan Ariel Schunke, Matias Aguirregaray Guruceaga (63.Pablo Mauricio Rosales), Román Fernando Martínez, Leonardo Rafael Jara, Gastón Gil Romero, Carlos Joaquín Correa (81.Israel Alejandro Damonte), Diego Daniel Vera Méndez, Carlos Daniel Auzqui (46.Ezequiel Cerutti), Guido Marcelo Carrillo. Trainer: Mauricio Andrés Pellegrino.
Goals: Gonzalo Viera Davyt (22), Jonathan Javier Rodríguez Portillo (45+3) / Guido Marcelo Carrillo (71).
Penalties: Ezequiel Cerutti 0-1; Sergio Daniel Orteman Rodríguez 1-1; Guido Marcelo Carrillo 1-2; Carlos Rodrigo Núñez Techera (missed); Israel Alejandro Damonte (missed); Fabián Larry Estoyanoff Poggio (missed); Pablo Mauricio Rosales 1-3; Jorge Marcelo Rodríguez Núñez (missed).
[Club Estudiantes de La Plata won 3-1 on penalties (after 3-3 on aggregate)]

15.10.2014, Estadio „Alberto J. Armando", Buenos Aires
Referee: Sandro Meira Ricci (Brazil)
CA Boca Juniors Buenos Aires - Club Deportivo Capiatá **0-1(0-1)**

Boca Juniors: Agustín Ignacio Orión, Mariano Raúl Echeverría, Lucas Leandro Marín, Lisandro Magallán Orueta, Gonzalo Pablo Castellani (55.Luciano Acosta), Nicolás Carlos Colazo (71.Emanuel Mariano Insúa), Cristian Damián Erbes, César Marcelo Meli, Juan Manuel Martínez (65.Emanuel Gigliotti), Andrés Eliseo Chávez, Jonathan Calleri. Trainer: Rodolfo Martín Arruabarrena.
Deportivo Capiatá: Antonio Alejandro Franco Arza, Arnaldo Javier Pereira Vera, Arturo David Aquino, Néstor Fabián González, Carlos Gabriel Ruíz Peralta, Blas Bernardo Irala Rojas, Óscar Ramón Ruíz Roa, Ángel David Martínez, Ricardo Javier Ortíz Pineda (90+3.Jorge Luis Candia), Fabio Escobar Benítez (88.Nelson Darío Figueredo Genés), Cristian Ariel López Leiva (52.Julio César Irrazábal León). Trainer: Héctor Marecos.
Goal: Óscar Ramón Ruíz Roa (43).

23.10.2014, Estadio „Feliciano Cáceres", Luque
Referee: Wilmar Alexander Roldán Pérez (Colombia)
Club Deportivo Capiatá - CA Boca Juniors Buenos Aires **0-1(0-0,0-1,0-1); 3-4 on penalties**

Deportivo Capiatá: Antonio Alejandro Franco Arza, Arnaldo Javier Pereira Vera, Arturo David Aquino, Gustavo Alberto Velázquez Núñez [*sent off 65*], Néstor Fabián González, Carlos Gabriel Ruíz Peralta (78.Nelson Darío Figueredo Genés), Blas Bernardo Irala Rojas, Óscar Ramón Ruíz Roa (90+2.Julio César Irrazábal León), Ángel David Martínez, Ricardo Javier Ortíz Pineda (83.Jorge Luis Candia), Fabio Escobar Benítez. Trainer: Héctor Marecos.
Boca Juniors: Agustín Ignacio Orión, Juan Daniel Forlín (70.Luciano Acosta), Claudio Daniel Pérez, Lisandro Magallán Orueta, Fernando Rubén Gago, José Pedro Fuenzalida Gana, Nicolás Carlos Colazo, Federico Gastón Carrizo (61.Juan Manuel Martínez), César Marcelo Meli (77.Emanuel Gigliotti), Andrés Eliseo Chávez, Jonathan Calleri. Trainer: Rodolfo Martín Arruabarrena.
Goal: Jonathan Calleri (73).
Penalties: Emanuel Gigliotti 0-1; Fabio Escobar Benítez 1-1; Claudio Daniel Pérez (missed); Néstor Fabián González 2-1; Fernando Rubén Gago 2-2; Blas Bernardo Irala Rojas (missed); Nicolás Carlos Colazo (missed); Julio César Irrazábal León (missed); Andrés Eliseo Chávez 2-3; Ángel David Martínez 3-3; Agustín Ignacio Orión 3-4; Arturo David Aquino (missed).

[CA Boca Juniors Buenos Aires won 4-3 on penalties (after 1-1 on aggregate)]

16.10.2014, Estadio „Dr. Nicolás Léoz", Asunción
Referee: Víctor Hugo Carrillo Casanova (Peru)
Club Libertad Asunción - CA River Plate Buenos Aires 1-3(1-0)
Libertad: Rodrigo Martin Muñóz Salomón, Pedro Juan Benítez Domínguez (45.Gustavo Ramón Mencia Ávalos), Jorge Luis Moreira Ferreira (69.Néstor Abraham Camacho Ledesma), Ismael Benegas, Fabián Cornelio Balbuena González, Claudio David Vargas Villalba, Sergio Daniel Aquino, Jorge Daniel González Marquet, Osmar de la Cruz Molinas González, Hernán Rodrigo López Mora, Dionisio Ismael Pérez Mambreani (62.Antonio Bareiro Álvarez). Trainer: Pedro Alcides Sarabia Achucarro.
River Plate: Marcelo Alberto Barovero, Jonathan Ramón Maidana, Gabriel Iván Mercado, José Ramiro Funes Mori, Germán Alejo Pezzela, Leonardo Daniel Ponzio, Leonardo Nicolás Pisculichi (78.Augusto Jorge Mateo Solari), Ariel Mauricio Rojas, Carlos Andrés Sánchez Arcosa, Rodrigo Nicanor Mora Núñez (73.Giovanni Pablo Simeone), Lucas Boyé (62.Sebastián Driussi). Trainer: Marcelo Daniel Gallardo.
Goals: Claudio David Vargas Villalba (45+1) / Carlos Andrés Sánchez Arcosa (60), Sebastián Driussi (71), Giovanni Pablo Simeone (75).

22.10.2014, Estadio Monumental „Antonio Vespucio Liberti", Buenos Aires
Referee: José Hernando Buitrago Arango (Colombia)
CA River Plate Buenos Aires - Club Libertad Asunción 2-0(1-0)
River Plate: Marcelo Alberto Barovero, Gabriel Iván Mercado, José Ramiro Funes Mori, Germán Alejo Pezzela, Leonardo Daniel Ponzio, Leonel Jesús Vangioni, Ariel Mauricio Rojas (61.Tomás Martínez), Carlos Andrés Sánchez Arcosa (68.Augusto Jorge Mateo Solari), Teófilo Antonio Gutiérrez Roncancio (60.Giovanni Pablo Simeone), Sebastián Driussi, Lucas Boyé. Trainer: Marcelo Daniel Gallardo.
Libertad: Rodrigo Martin Muñóz Salomón, Adalberto Román Benítez, Jorge Luis Moreira Ferreira, Ismael Benegas, Fabián Cornelio Balbuena González, Claudio David Vargas Villalba (54.Iván Rodrigo Ramírez Segovia), Sergio Daniel Aquino, Jorge Daniel González Marquet, Néstor Abraham Camacho Ledesma (77.Jorge Eduardo Recalde Ramírez), Hernán Rodrigo López Mora (66.Dionisio Ismael Pérez Mambreani), Antonio Bareiro Álvarez [*sent off 23*]. Trainer: Pedro Alcides Sarabia Achucarro.
Goals: Gabriel Iván Mercado (41), Giovanni Pablo Simeone (90+1).
[CA River Plate Buenos Aires won 5-1 on aggregate]

QUARTER-FINALS

29.10.2014, Estadio „Atanasio Girardot“, Medellín
Referee: Héber Roberto Lopes (Brazil)
Club Atlético Nacional Medellín – 1-0(0-0)
CSCD Universidad César Vallejo Trujillo
Atlético Nacional: Franco Armani, Alexis Héctor Henríquez Charales, Álvaro Francisco Nájera Gil, Alejandro Bernal Rios, Farid Alfonso Díaz Rhenals, Daniel Eduardo Bocanegra Ortíz, Sherman Andrés Cárdenas Estupiñán (86.José Hárrison Otálvaro Arce), Alexander Mejía Sabalsa, Wilder Andrés Guisao Correa (68.Jhon Edwar Valoy Riascos), Luis Carlos Ruíz Morales (76.Santiago Tréllez Vivero), Jonathan Copete Valencia. Trainer: Juan Carlos Osorio Arbelaez.
Universidad: Salomón Alexis Libman Pastor, Luis Alberto Guadalupe Rivadeneyra, Atilio Muente Gionti, Jesús Martín Álvarez Hurtado, Jesús Rabanal Dávila, Donald Diego Millán Rodríguez (87.Jeremy Martín Rostaing Verástegui), William Medardo Chiroque Tavara, Ronald Jonathan Quinteros Sánchez, Juan Gustavo Morales Coronado, Daniel Mackensi Chávez Castillo, Andy Robert Pando García (68.Luis Carlos Tejada Hansell). Trainer: Franco Enrique Navarro Monteyro.
Goal: Alejandro Bernal Rios (56).

05.11.2014, Estadio Mansiche, Trujillo
Referee: Mauro Vigliano (Argentina)
CSCD Universidad César Vallejo Trujillo – 0-1(0-0)
Club Atlético Nacional Medellín
Universidad: Salomón Alexis Libman Pastor, Emiliano José Ciucci, Luís Felipe Cardoza Zuñiga [*sent off 67*], Jesús Rabanal Dávila, Jeremy Martín Rostaing Verástegui, Donald Diego Millán Rodríguez, William Medardo Chiroque Tavara, Ronald Jonathan Quinteros Sánchez, Juan Gustavo Morales Coronado, Daniel Mackensi Chávez Castillo, Andy Robert Pando García (74.Luis Carlos Tejada Hansell). Trainer: Franco Enrique Navarro Monteyro.
Atlético Nacional: Franco Armani, Alexis Héctor Henríquez Charales, Álvaro Francisco Nájera Gil, Alejandro Bernal Rios, Farid Alfonso Díaz Rhenals, Daniel Eduardo Bocanegra Ortíz (62.Elkin Darío Calle Grajales), Sherman Andrés Cárdenas Estupiñán, Alexander Mejía Sabalsa [*sent off 76*], Edwin Andrés Cardona Bedoya (86.Jonathan Copete Valencia), Wilder Andrés Guisao Correa, Luis Carlos Ruíz Morales (82.Miller Stiwar Mosquera Cabrera). Trainer: Juan Carlos Osorio Arbelaez.
Goal: Edwin Andrés Cardona Bedoya (80).
[Club Atlético Nacional Medellín won 2-0 on aggregate]

29.10.2014, Estadio Ciudad de La Plata, La Plata
Referee: Diego Hernán Abal (Argentina)
Club Estudiantes de La Plata - CA River Plate Buenos Aires 1-2(1-0)
Estudiantes: Hilario Bernardo Navarro, Leandro Desábato, Jonathan Ariel Schunke, Pablo Mauricio Rosales, Israel Alejandro Damonte (72.Leandro Damián Benítez), Román Fernando Martínez (23.Carlos Daniel Auzqui; 77.Ezequiel Cerutti), Leonardo Rafael Jara, Gastón Gil Romero, Carlos Joaquín Correa, Diego Daniel Vera Méndez, Guido Marcelo Carrillo. Trainer: Mauricio Andrés Pellegrino.
River Plate: Marcelo Alberto Barovero, Jonathan Ramón Maidana, Gabriel Iván Mercado, José Ramiro Funes Mori, Leonardo Daniel Ponzio, Leonardo Nicolás Pisculichi (86.Augusto Jorge Mateo Solari), Leonel Jesús Vangioni (51.Éder Fabián Álvarez Balanta), Ariel Mauricio Rojas, Carlos Andrés Sánchez Arcosa [*sent off 84*], Teófilo Antonio Gutiérrez Roncancio, Rodrigo Nicanor Mora Núñez (80.Sebastián Driussi). Trainer: Marcelo Daniel Gallardo.
Goals: Diego Daniel Vera Méndez (45+1) / Rodrigo Nicanor Mora Núñez (52), Carlos Andrés Sánchez Arcosa (71).

06.11.2014, Estadio Monumental „Antonio Vespucio Liberti", Buenos Aires
Referee: Néstor Fabián Pitana (Argentina)
CA River Plate Buenos Aires - Club Estudiantes de La Plata 3-2(1-1)
River Plate: Marcelo Alberto Barovero, Jonathan Ramón Maidana, Gabriel Iván Mercado, José Ramiro Funes Mori, Leonardo Daniel Ponzio, Leonardo Nicolás Pisculichi (78.Tomás Martínez), Leonel Jesús Vangioni, Ariel Mauricio Rojas (90+2.Giovanni Pablo Simeone), Augusto Jorge Mateo Solari, Teófilo Antonio Gutiérrez Roncancio, Rodrigo Nicanor Mora Núñez (77.Lucas Boyé). Trainer: Marcelo Daniel Gallardo.
Estudiantes: Hilario Bernardo Navarro, Leandro Desábato, Jonathan Ariel Schunke (66.Ezequiel Cerutti), Matias Aguirregaray Guruceaga (61.Ernesto Goñi Ameijenda), Pablo Mauricio Rosales, Leonardo Rafael Jara, Gastón Gil Romero, Carlos Joaquín Correa, Diego Daniel Vera Méndez, Carlos Daniel Auzqui (81.Leandro Damián Benítez), Guido Marcelo Carrillo. Trainer: Mauricio Andrés Pellegrino.
Goals: Teófilo Antonio Gutiérrez Roncancio (1), Rodrigo Nicanor Mora Núñez (60), José Ramiro Funes Mori (62) / Diego Daniel Vera Méndez (41), Guido Marcelo Carrillo (50 penalty).
[CA River Plate Buenos Aires won 5-3 on aggregate]

30.10.2014, Estádio „Cícero Pompeu de Toledo" [Morumbi], São Paulo
Referee: Enrique Patricio Cáceres Villafañe (Paraguay)
São Paulo FC - CS Emelec Guayaquil 4-2(3-0)
São Paulo: Rogério Ceni, Édson José da Silva, Álvaro Daniel Pereira Barragán, Jonathan Doin „Paulo Miranda" (90+1.Auro Alvaro da Cruz Junior), Ricardo Izecson dos Santos Leite "Kaká" (79.Osvaldo Lourenço Filho), Michel Fernandes Bastos, Maicon Thiago Pereira de Souza (46.Antônio Carlos dos Santos Aguiar), Húdson Rodrigues dos Santos, Josef de Souza Dias, Paulo Henrique Chagas de Lima „Ganso", Alan Kardec de Souza Pereira Junior. Trainer: Muricy Ramalho.
Emelec: Esteban Javier Dreer, Gabriel Eduardo Achilier Zurita, Oscar Dalmiro Bagüi Angulo, Jhon William Narváez, Fernando Agustín Giménez Solís, Pedro Angel Quiñónez Rodríguez (78.Fernando Vicente Gaibor Orellana), José Luis Quiñónez Quiñónez, Ángel Israel Mena Delgado, Miller Alejandro Bolaños Reascos, Osbaldo Lupo Lastra García, Emanuel Herrera (78.Luis Miguel Escalada). Trainer: Gustavo Domingo Quinteros Desabato (Bolivia).
Goals: Michel Fernandes Bastos (11), Hudson (35), Alan Kardec de Souza Pereira Junior (44), Antônio Carlos dos Santos Aguiar (69) / Miller Alejandro Bolaños Reascos (47), Ángel Israel Mena Delgado (54).

05.11.2014, Estadio „George Capwell", Guayaquil
Referee: Enrique Roberto Osses Zencovich (Chile)
CS Emelec Guayaquil - São Paulo FC 3-2(1-2)
Emelec: Esteban Javier Dreer, Gabriel Eduardo Achilier Zurita, Oscar Dalmiro Bagüi Angulo, Jhon William Narváez (86.Javier Isidro Charcopa Alegria), Fernando Agustín Giménez Solís, Pedro Angel Quiñónez Rodríguez (46.Fernando Vicente Gaibor Orellana), José Luis Quiñónez Quiñónez, Ángel Israel Mena Delgado, Miller Alejandro Bolaños Reascos, Osbaldo Lupo Lastra García, Emanuel Herrera (46.Marcos Gustavo Mondaini). Trainer: Gustavo Domingo Quinteros Desabato (Bolivia).
São Paulo: Rogério Ceni, Édson José da Silva, Álvaro Daniel Pereira Barragán (68.Ademilson Braga Bispo Junior), Jonathan Doin „Paulo Miranda", Ricardo Izecson dos Santos Leite "Kaká" (83.Osvaldo Lourenço Filho), Michel Fernandes Bastos, Denílson Pereira Neves, Húdson Rodrigues dos Santos, Josef de Souza Dias, Paulo Henrique Chagas de Lima „Ganso", Alan Kardec de Souza Pereira Junior (89.Lucas Cavalcante Silva Afonso "Lucão"). Trainer: Muricy Ramalho.
Goals: Miller Alejandro Bolaños Reascos (1, 48 penalty, 52 penalty) / Alan Kardec de Souza Pereira Junior (28), Paulo Henrique Chagas de Lima „Ganso" (39).
[São Paulo FC won 6-5 on aggregate]

30.10.2014, Estadio „Alberto J. Armando“, Buenos Aires
Referee: Víctor Hugo Carrillo Casanova (Peru)
CA Boca Juniors Buenos Aires - Club Cerro Porteño Asunción 1-0(0-0)
Boca Juniors: Agustín Ignacio Orión, Juan Daniel Forlín, Claudio Daniel Pérez, Lucas Leandro Marín, Fernando Rubén Gago, José Pedro Fuenzalida Gana (57.Juan Manuel Martínez), Nicolás Carlos Colazo, César Marcelo Meli, Adrián Andrés Cubas, Andrés Eliseo Chávez (90+2.Federico Gastón Carrizo), Jonathan Calleri (75.Emanuel Gigliotti). Trainer: Rodolfo Martín Arruabarrena.
Cerro Porteño: Diego Daniel Barreto Cáceres, Carlos Bonet Cáceres, Víctor Hugo Mareco, César Iván Benítez León, Bruno Amilcar Valdez, Julio Daniel Dos Santos Rodríguez, Miguel Ángel Paniagua Rivarola, Fidencio Oviedo Domínguez, Óscar David Romero Villamayor (71.Mauricio Ezequiel Sperdutti), Daniel González Güiza (69.Rodolfo Vicente Gamarra Varela), José María Ortigoza Ortíz. Trainer: Leonardo Rubén Astrada (Argentina).
Goal: Emanuel Gigliotti (82).

06.11.2014, Estadio Defensores del Chaco, Asunción
Referee: Martín Emilio Vázquez Broquetas (Uruguay)
Club Cerro Porteño Asunción - CA Boca Juniors Buenos Aires 1-4(1-1)
Cerro Porteño: Diego Daniel Barreto Cáceres, Carlos Bonet Cáceres, Víctor Hugo Mareco, César Iván Benítez León, Bruno Amilcar Valdez, Julio Daniel Dos Santos Rodríguez (46.Jonathan Fabbro), Fidencio Oviedo Domínguez, Óscar David Romero Villamayor, Daniel González Güiza, Mauricio Ezequiel Sperdutti (46.Rodolfo Vicente Gamarra Varela; 62.Sergio Ismael Díaz Velázquez), José María Ortigoza Ortíz. Trainer: Leonardo Rubén Astrada (Argentina).
Boca Juniors: Agustín Ignacio Orión, Juan Daniel Forlín, Claudio Daniel Pérez, Lucas Leandro Marín, Fernando Rubén Gago, José Pedro Fuenzalida Gana, Nicolás Carlos Colazo, Cristian Damián Erbes (78.Adrián Andrés Cubas), César Marcelo Meli, Andrés Eliseo Chávez (89.Emanuel Mariano Insúa), Jonathan Calleri (72.Emanuel Gigliotti). Trainer: Rodolfo Martín Arruabarrena.
Goals: Daniel González Güiza (27) / Jonathan Calleri (9), Andrés Eliseo Chávez (66), Emanuel Gigliotti (73), Andrés Eliseo Chávez (85).
[CA Boca Juniors Buenos Aires won 5-1 on aggregate]

SEMI-FINALS

19.11.2014, Estadio „Atanasio Girardot", Medellín
Referee: Daniel Adán Fedorczuk Betancour (Uruguay)
Club Atlético Nacional Medellín - São Paulo FC **1-0(1-0)**
Atlético Nacional: Franco Armani, Alexis Héctor Henríquez Charales, Álvaro Francisco Nájera Gil, Farid Alfonso Díaz Rhenals, Oscar Fabián Murillo Murillo, Diego Alejandro Arias Hincapié, Edwin Andrés Cardona Bedoya, Sebastián Pérez Cardona, Luis Carlos Ruíz Morales (59.Wilder Andrés Guisao Correa), Orlando Enrique Berrío Meléndez (75.Sherman Andrés Cárdenas Estupiñán), Jonathan Copete Valencia (68.Juan David Valencia Hinestroza). Trainer: Juan Carlos Osorio Arbelaez.
São Paulo: Rogério Ceni, Édson José da Silva, Rafael Tolói, Ricardo Izecson dos Santos Leite "Kaká" (68.Osvaldo Lourenço Filho), Michel Fernandes Bastos, Denílson Pereira Neves, Húdson Rodrigues dos Santos, Josef de Souza Dias, Paulo Henrique Chagas de Lima „Ganso", Luís Fabiano Clemente (80.Alexandre Rodrigues da Silva „Alexandre Pato"), Alan Kardec de Souza Pereira Junior (43.Álvaro Daniel Pereira Barragán). Trainer: Muricy Ramalho.
Goal: Luis Carlos Ruíz Morales (34).

26.11.2014, Estádio „Cícero Pompeu de Toledo" [Morumbi], São Paulo
Referee: Roddy Alberto Zambrano Olmedo (Ecuador)
São Paulo FC - Club Atlético Nacional Medellín **1-0(0-0,1-0,1-0); 1-4 on penalties**
São Paulo: Rogério Ceni, Édson José da Silva, Álvaro Daniel Pereira Barragán (83.Osvaldo Lourenço Filho), Rafael Tolói, Ricardo Izecson dos Santos Leite "Kaká" (80.Alan Kardec de Souza Pereira Junior), Michel Fernandes Bastos, Denílson Pereira Neves, Húdson Rodrigues dos Santos, Josef de Souza Dias, Paulo Henrique Chagas de Lima „Ganso", Luís Fabiano Clemente. Trainer: Muricy Ramalho.
Atlético Nacional: Franco Armani, Alexis Héctor Henríquez Charales, Álvaro Francisco Nájera Gil (75.Jonathan Copete Valencia), Farid Alfonso Díaz Rhenals (66.Alejandro Bernal Rios), Oscar Fabián Murillo Murillo, Daniel Eduardo Bocanegra Ortíz, Diego Alejandro Arias Hincapié (56.Juan David Valencia Hinestroza), Alexander Mejía Sabalsa, Edwin Andrés Cardona Bedoya, Luis Carlos Ruíz Morales, Orlando Enrique Berrío Meléndez. Trainer: Juan Carlos Osorio Arbelaez.
Goals: Paulo Henrique Chagas de Lima „Ganso" (53).
Penalties: Daniel Eduardo Bocanegra Ortíz 0-1; Alan Kardec de Souza Pereira Junior (missed); Juan David Valencia Hinestroza 0-2; Rogério Ceni 1-2; Edwin Andrés Cardona Bedoya 1-3; Rafael Tolói (missed); Luis Carlos Ruíz Morales 1-4.
[Club Atlético Nacional Medellín won 4-1 on penalties (after 1-1 on aggregate)]

20.11.2014, Estadio „Alberto J. Armando", Buenos Aires; Attendance: 50.000
Referee: Silvio Trucco (Argentina)
CA Boca Juniors Buenos Aires - CA River Plate Buenos Aires **0-0**
Boca Juniors: Agustín Ignacio Orión, Daniel Alberto Díaz, Juan Daniel Forlín, Lucas Leandro Marín, Fernando Rubén Gago, Nicolás Carlos Colazo, Cristian Damián Erbes, César Marcelo Meli, Juan Manuel Martínez (31.José Pedro Fuenzalida Gana), Andrés Eliseo Chávez, Jonathan Calleri (72.Emanuel Gigliotti). Trainer: Rodolfo Martín Arruabarrena.
River Plate: Marcelo Alberto Barovero, Jonathan Ramón Maidana (75.Germán Alejo Pezzela), Gabriel Iván Mercado, José Ramiro Funes Mori, Leonardo Daniel Ponzio, Leonardo Nicolás Pisculichi (85.Augusto Jorge Mateo Solari), Leonel Jesús Vangioni, Ariel Mauricio Rojas, Carlos Andrés Sánchez Arcosa, Teófilo Antonio Gutiérrez Roncancio, Giovanni Pablo Simeone (65.Lucas Boyé). Trainer: Marcelo Daniel Gallardo.

27.11.2014, Estadio Monumental „Antonio Vespucio Liberti", Buenos Aires; Attendance: 65.250
Referee: Germán Delfino (Argentina)
CA River Plate Buenos Aires - CA Boca Juniors Buenos Aires 1-0(1-0)
River Plate: Marcelo Alberto Barovero, Gabriel Iván Mercado, José Ramiro Funes Mori, Germán Alejo Pezzela, Leonardo Daniel Ponzio, Leonardo Nicolás Pisculichi (84.Augusto Jorge Mateo Solari), Leonel Jesús Vangioni, Ariel Mauricio Rojas, Carlos Andrés Sánchez Arcosa, Teófilo Antonio Gutiérrez Roncancio, Rodrigo Nicanor Mora Núñez (87.Fernando Ezequiel Cavenaghi). Trainer: Marcelo Daniel Gallardo.
Boca Juniors: Agustín Ignacio Orión, Daniel Alberto Díaz [*sent off 90+5*], Juan Daniel Forlín, Lucas Leandro Marín, Fernando Rubén Gago (41.José Pedro Fuenzalida Gana; 68.Andrés Eliseo Chávez), Nicolás Carlos Colazo, Cristian Damián Erbes (86.Gonzalo Pablo Castellani), Federico Gastón Carrizo, César Marcelo Meli, Emanuel Gigliotti, Jonathan Calleri. Trainer: Rodolfo Martín Arruabarrena.
Goal: Leonardo Nicolás Pisculichi (16).
[CA River Plate Buenos Aires won 1-0 on aggregate]

FINAL

03.12.2014, Estadio „Atanasio Girardot", Medellín; Attendance: 44,412
Referee: Ricardo Marques Ribeiro (Brazil)
Club Atlético Nacional Medellín - CA River Plate Buenos Aires 1-1(1-0)
Atlético Nacional: Franco Armani, Alexis Héctor Henríquez Charales, Alejandro Bernal Rios (37.Alejandro Abraham Guerra Morales), Farid Alfonso Díaz Rhenals, Oscar Fabián Murillo Murillo, Daniel Eduardo Bocanegra Ortíz, Alexander Mejía Sabalsa, Edwin Andrés Cardona Bedoya, Luis Carlos Ruíz Morales, Orlando Enrique Berrío Meléndez (71.Wilder Andrés Guisao Correa), Jonathan Copete Valencia (59.Sebastián Pérez Cardona). Trainer: Juan Carlos Osorio Arbelaez.
River Plate: Marcelo Alberto Barovero, José Ramiro Funes Mori, Germán Alejo Pezzela, Emanuel Mammana (61.Augusto Jorge Mateo Solari), Leonardo Daniel Ponzio, Leonardo Nicolás Pisculichi (76.Claudio Matías Kranevitter), Leonel Jesús Vangioni, Ariel Mauricio Rojas, Carlos Andrés Sánchez Arcosa, Teófilo Antonio Gutiérrez Roncancio, Rodrigo Nicanor Mora Núñez (67.Fernando Ezequiel Cavenaghi). Trainer: Marcelo Daniel Gallardo.
Goals: 1-0 Orlando Enrique Berrío Meléndez (34), 1-1 Leonardo Nicolás Pisculichi (65).

10.12.2014, Estadio Monumental „Antonio Vespucio Liberti", Buenos Aires
Referee: Darío Agustín Ubriaco Medero (Uruguay)
CA River Plate Buenos Aires - Club Atlético Nacional Medellín 2-0(0-0)
River Plate: Marcelo Alberto Barovero, Gabriel Iván Mercado, José Ramiro Funes Mori, Germán Alejo Pezzela, Leonardo Daniel Ponzio (82.Claudio Matías Kranevitter), Leonardo Nicolás Pisculichi (90.Sebastián Driussi), Leonel Jesús Vangioni, Ariel Mauricio Rojas, Carlos Andrés Sánchez Arcosa, Teófilo Antonio Gutiérrez Roncancio (80.Fernando Ezequiel Cavenaghi), Rodrigo Nicanor Mora Núñez. Trainer: Marcelo Daniel Gallardo.
Atlético Nacional: Franco Armani, Alexis Héctor Henríquez Charales, Álvaro Francisco Nájera Gil (65.Oscar Fabián Murillo Murillo), Alejandro Bernal Rios, Farid Alfonso Díaz Rhenals (66.Wilder Andrés Guisao Correa), Daniel Eduardo Bocanegra Ortíz, Alexander Mejía Sabalsa, Juan David Valencia Hinestroza, Edwin Andrés Cardona Bedoya, Luis Carlos Ruíz Morales, Orlando Enrique Berrío Meléndez (73.Sherman Andrés Cárdenas Estupiñán). Trainer: Juan Carlos Osorio Arbelaez.
Goals: 1-0 Gabriel Iván Mercado (54), 2-0 Germán Alejo Pezzela (58).

Copa Sudamericana Winner 2014: **CA River Plate Buenos Aires**

Best Goalscorer: Miller Alejandro Bolaños Reasco (Club Sport Emelec Guayaquil) & Andrés Alejandro Vilches Araneda (CD Huachipato) – both 5 goals

COPA SUDAMERICANA (2002-2014) TABLE OF HONOURS		
2002	Club Atlético San Lorenzo de Almagro Buenos Aires	(ARG)
2003	Club Sportivo Cienciano de Cuzco	(PER)
2004	Club Atlético Boca Juniors Buenos Aires	(ARG)
2005	Club Atlético Boca Juniors Buenos Aires	(ARG)
2006	Club de Fútbol Pachuca	(MEX)
2007	Arsenal Fútbol Club de Sarandí	(ARG)
2008	Sport Club Internacional Porto Alegre	(BRA)
2009	Liga Deportiva Universitaria Quito	(ECU)
2010	Club Atlético Independiente Avellaneda	(ARG)
2011	CFP de la Universidad de Chile Santiago	(CHI)
2012	São Paulo Futebol Clube	(BRA)
2013	Club Atlético Lanús	(ARG)
2014	Club Atlético River Plate Buenos Aires	(ARG)

RECOPA SUDAMERICANA 2014

The Recopa Sudamericana is an annual football competition disputed between the reigning champions of the previous year's Copa Libertadores and the Copa Sudamericana. Previously, the Recopa Sudamericana was contested between the Copa Libertadores winner and the Supercopa „João Havelange" (created 1988) champion until the Supercopa was disbanded 1997.

The 2014 edition was disputed between Clube Atlético Mineiro Belo Horizonte (2013 Copa Libertadores winner) and Club Atlético Lanús (2013 Copa Sudamericana winner).

16.07.2014, Estadio Ciudad de Lanús, Lanús
Referee: Antonio Javier Arias Alvarenga (Paraguay)
Club Atlético Lanús - Clube Atlético Mineiro Belo Horizonte 0-1(0-0)
CA Lanús: Agustín Federico Marchesín, Carlos Luciano Araujo, Gustavo Raúl Gómez Portillo, Diego Luis Braghieri, Maximiliano Nicolás Velázquez (Cap), Diego Hernán González, Leandro Daniel Somoza, Óscar Junior Benítez (76.Alejandro Daniel Silva González), Víctor Hugo Ayala Núñez (64.Jorge Alberto Ortíz), Lucas Santiago Melano (56.Lautaro Germán Acosta), Santiago Martín Silva Olivera. Trainer: Guillermo Barros Schelotto.
Atlético Mineiro: Victor Leandro Bagy, Marcos Luis Rocha de Aquino, Leonardo Fabiano Silva e Silva (Cap), Jemerson de Jesus Nascimento, Emerson da Conceição, Lucas Pierre Santos Oliveira, Leandro Donizete Gonçalves da Silva, Ronaldo de Assis Moreira "Ronaldinho" (46.Guilherme Milhomen Gusmão), Maicosuel Reginaldo de Matos, Diego Tardelli Martins, André Felipe Ribeiro de Souza (46.João Alves de Assis Silva "Jô"). Trainer: Levir Culpi.
Goal: 0-1 Diego Tardelli Martins (65).

23.07.2014, Estádio Mineirão, Belo Horizonte; Attendance: 54,786
Referee: Roberto Carlos Silvera Calcerrada (Uruguay)
Clube Atlético Mineiro Belo Horizonte - Club Atlético Lanús 4-3(2-2,2-3)
Atlético Mineiro: Victor Leandro Bagy, Marcos Luis Rocha de Aquino, Réver Humberto Alves Araújo, Leonardo Fabiano Silva e Silva (Cap), Emerson da Conceição, Lucas Pierre Santos Oliveira, Leandro Donizete Gonçalves da Silva, Ronaldo de Assis Moreira "Ronaldinho" (64.Luan Madson Gedeão de Paiva), Maicosuel Reginaldo de Matos (76.Guilherme Milhomen Gusmão), Diego Tardelli Martins (88.Jesús Alberto Dátolo), João Alves de Assis Silva "Jô". Trainer: Levir Culpi.
CA Lanús: Agustín Federico Marchesín, Carlos Luciano Araujo (74.Lucas Santiago Melano), Gustavo Raúl Gómez Portillo (106.Óscar Junior Benítez), Diego Luis Braghieri, Maximiliano Nicolás Velázquez (Cap), Diego Hernán González, Leandro Daniel Somoza, Jorge Alberto Ortíz (105.Nicolás Pasquini), Víctor Hugo Ayala Núñez, Lautaro Germán Acosta [*sent off 117*], Santiago Martín Silva Olivera. Trainer: Guillermo Barros Schelotto.
Goals: 1-0 Diego Tardelli Martins (6 penalty), 1-1 Víctor Hugo Ayala Núñez (8), 1-2 Santiago Martín Silva Olivera (25), 2-2 Maicosuel Reginaldo de Matos (37), 2-3 Lautaro Germán Acosta (90+3), 3-3 Gustavo Raúl Gómez Portillo (102 own goal), 4-3 Víctor Hugo Ayala Núñez (111 own goal).

2014 Recopa Sudamericana Winner: **Clube Atlético Mineiro Belo Horizonte**

RECOPA SUDAMERICANA (1989-2014) TABLE OF HONOURS		
1989	Club Nacional de Football Montevideo	(URU)
1990	Club Atlético Boca Juniors Buenos Aires	(ARG)
1991	Club Olimpia Asunción[(1)]	(PAR)
1992	Club Social y Deportivo Colo Colo Santiago	(CHI)
1993	São Paulo Futebol Clube	(BRA)
1994	São Paulo Futebol Clube	(BRA)
1995	Club Atlético Independiente Avellaneda	(ARG)
1996	Grêmio Foot-Ball Porto Alegrense	(BRA)
1997	Club Atlético Vélez Sarsfield Buenos Aires	(ARG)
1998	Cruzeiro Esporte Clube Belo Horizonte	(BRA)
1999	*No competition*	
2000	*No competition*	
2001	*No competition*	
2002	*No competition*	
2003	Club Olimpia Asunción	(PAR)
2004	Club Sportivo Cienciano de Cuzco	(PER)
2005	Club Atlético Boca Juniors Buenos Aires	(ARG)
2006	Club Atlético Boca Juniors Buenos Aires	(ARG)
2007	Sport Club Internacional Porto Alegre	(BRA)
2008	Club Atlético Boca Juniors Buenos Aires	(ARG)
2009	Liga Deportiva Universitaria Quito	(ECU)
2010	Liga Deportiva Universitaria Quito	(ECU)
2011	Sport Club Internacional Porto Alegre	(BRA)
2012	Santos Futebol Clube	(BRA)
2013	Sport Club Corinthians Paulista São Paulo	(BRA)
2014	Clube Atlético Mineiro Belo Horizonte	(BRA)

[(1)]No final match disputed. Club Olimpia Asunción won both Copa Libertadores and the Supercopa „João Havelange“ and was declared Recopa winners.

NATIONAL ASSOCIATIONS

The South American Football Confederation, commonly known as CONMEBOL, but also known as CSF (from Spanish: Confederación Sudamericana de Fútbol) is the continental governing body of association football in South America and it is one of FIFA's six continental confederations. CONMEBOL - the oldest continental confederation in the world, having its headquarters located in Luque (Paraguay) - is responsible for the organization and governance of South American football's major international tournaments. With only 10 member football associations, it has the fewest members of all the confederations in FIFA. This 10 member associations are as follows:

Argentina **Bolivia** **Brazil** **Chile** **Colombia**

Ecuador **Paraguay** **Peru** **Uruguay** **Venezuela**

ARGENTINA

The Country:
República Argentina (Argentine Republic)
Capital: Buenos Aires
Surface: 2,766,890km²
Inhabitants: 42,669,500
Time: UTC-3

The FA:
Asociación del Fútbol Argentino
Viamonte 1366/76 Buenos Aires 1053
Year of Formation: 1893
Member of FIFA since: 1912
Member of CONMEBOL since: 1916
Internet: www.afa.org.ar

NATIONAL TEAM RECORDS	
First international match:	20.07.1902, Montevideo: Uruguay – Argentina 0-6
Most international caps:	Javier Adelmar Zanetti – 145 caps (1994-2011)
Most international goals:	Gabriel Omar Batistuta – 56 goals (78 caps, 1991-2002)

OLYMPIC GAMES 1900-2012
1928 (Runenrs-up), 1960, 1964, 1988, 1996 (Runners-up), **2004 & 2008 (Winners)**
FIFA CONFEDERATIONS CUP 1992-2013
1992 (Winners), 1995 (Runners-up), 2005 (Runners-up).

COPA AMÉRICA	
1916	Runners-up
1917	Runners-up
1919	3rd Place
1920	Runners-up
1921	**Winners**
1922	4th Place
1923	Runners-up
1924	Runners-up
1925	**Winners**
1926	Runners-up
1927	**Winners**
1929	**Winners**
1935	Runners-up
1937	**Winners**
1939	Withdrew
1941	**Winners**
1942	Runners-up
1945	**Winners**
1946	**Winners**
1947	**Winners**
1949	Withdrew
1953	Withdrew
1955	**Winners**
1956	3rd Place
1957	**Winners**
1959	**Winners**
1959E	Runners-up
1963	3rd Place
1967	Runners-up
1975	Round 1
1979	Round 1
1983	Round 1
1987	4th Place
1989	3rd Place
1991	**Winners**
1993	**Winners**
1995	Quarter-Finals
1997	Quarter-Finals
1999	Quarter-Finals
2001	Withdrew
2004	Runners-up
2007	Runners-up
2011	Quarter-Finals
2015	Runners-up

FIFA WORLD CUP	
1930	Final Tournament (Runners-up)
1934	Final Tournament (1st Round)
1938	Withdrew
1950	Withdrew
1954	Withdrew
1958	Final Tournament (Group Stage)
1962	Final Tournament (Group Stage)
1966	Final Tournament (Quarter-Finals)
1970	Qualifiers
1974	Final Tournament (2nd Round)
1978	**Final Tournament (Winners)**
1982	Final Tournament (2nd Round)
1986	**Final Tournament (Winners)**
1990	Final Tournament (Runners-up)
1994	Final Tournament (2nd Round of 16)
1998	Final Tournament (Quarter-Finals)
2002	Final Tournament (Group Stage)
2006	Final Tournament (Quarter-Finals)
2010	Final Tournament (Quarter-Finals)
2014	Final Tournament (Runners-up)

PANAMERICAN GAMES	
1951	**Winners**
1955	**Winners**
1959	**Winners**
1963	Runners-up
1967	Round 1
1971	**Winners**
1975	3rd Place
1979	3rd Place
1983	Round 1
1987	3rd Place
1991	Did not enter
1995	**Winners**
1999	Did not enter
2003	**Winners**
2007	Round 1
2011	Runners-up

PANAMERICAN CHAMPIONSHIP	
1952	Did not enter
1956	Runners-up
1960	**Winners**

ARGENTINIAN CLUB HONOURS IN SOUTH AMERICAN CLUB COMPETITIONS:

COPA LIBERTADORES 1960-2014
CA Independiente Avellaneda (1964, 1965, 1972, 1973, 1974, 1975, 1984)
Racing Club Avellaneda (1967)
Club Estudiantes de La Plata (1968, 1969, 1970, 2009)
CA Boca Juniours Buenos Aires (1977, 1978, 2000, 2001, 2003, 2007)
AA Argentinos Juniors Bunoes Aires (1985)
CA River Plate Buenos Aires (1986, 1996)
CA Vélez Sársfield Buenos Aires (1994)
CA San Lorenzo de Almagro (2014)
COPA SUDAMERICANA 2002-2014
CA San Lorenzo de Almagro (2002)
CA Boca Juniours Buenos Aires (2004, 2005)
Arsenal Fútbol Club de Sarandí (2007)
CA Independiente Avellaneda (2010)
CA Lanús (2013)
CA River Plate Buenos Aires (2014)
RECOPA SUDAMERICANA 1989-2014
CA Boca Juniors Buenos Aires (1990, 2005, 2006, 2008)
CA Independiente Avellaneda (1995)
CA Vélez Sarsfield Buenos Aires (1997)
COPA CONMEBOL 1992-1999
CA Rosario Central (1995)
CA Lanús (1996)
CA Talleres Córdoba (1999)
SUPERCUP „JOÃO HAVELANGE" 1988-1997*
Racing Club Avellaneda (1988)
CA Boca Juniours Buenos Aires (1989)
CA Independiente Avellaneda (1994, 1995)
CA Vélez Sársfield Buenos Aires (1996)
CA River Plate Buenos Aires (1997)
COPA MERCOSUR 1998-2001**
CA San Lorenzo de Almagro (2001)

**Contested betwenn winners of all previous editions of the Copa Libertadores*

***Contested between teams belonging countries from the southern part of South America (Argentina, Brazil, Chile, Paraguay and Uruguay).*

NATIONAL COMPETITIONS
TABLE OF HONOURS

NATIONAL CHAMPIONS
1891-2014

The Amateur Era in Argentine football lasted between 1891 and 1934 and it was the first league tournament outside the United Kingdom. Between 1912-1914 (FAF = Federación Argentina de Football) and 1919-1926 (AAM = Asociación Amateurs de Football), other rival Football Associations organized their own amateur championships, but this associations were not recognized by the FIFA.

	Argentinean Amateur Championship
1891	Saint Andrew's Old Caledonians
1892	*No competition*
1893	Lomas Athletic Club Buenos Aires
1894	Lomas Athletic Club Buenos Aires
1895	Lomas Athletic Club Buenos Aires
1896	Lomas Academy Buenos Aires
1897	Lomas Athletic Club Buenos Aires
1898	Lomas Athletic Club Buenos Aires
1899	Belgrano Athletic Club
1900	Buenos Aires English High School*
1901	Alumni Athletic Club
1902	Alumni Athletic Club
1903	Alumni Athletic Club
1904	Belgrano Athletic Club
1905	Alumni Athletic Club
1906	Alumni Athletic Club
1907	Alumni Athletic Club
1908	Belgrano Athletic Club
1909	Alumni Athletic Club
1910	Alumni Athletic Club
1911	Alumni Athletic Club
1912	Quilmes Atlético Club / Club Porteño (FAF)
1913	Racing Club de Avellaneda / Club Estudiantes de La Plata (FAF)
1914	Racing Club de Avellaneda / Club Porteño (FAF)
1915	Racing Club de Avellaneda
1916	Racing Club de Avellaneda
1917	Racing Club de Avellaneda
1918	Racing Club de Avellaneda
1919	Club Atlético Boca Juniors Buenos Aires / Racing Club de Avellaneda (AAM)
1920	Club Atlético Boca Juniors Buenos Aires / Club Atlético River Plate Buenos Aires (AAM)
1921	Club Atlético Huracán Buenos Aires / Racing Club de Avellaneda (AAM)
1922	Club Atlético Huracán Buenos Aires / Club Atlético Independiente Avellaneda (AAM)
1923	Club Atlético Boca Juniors Buenos Aires / Club Atlético San Lorenzo de Almagro (AAM)
1924	Club Atlético Boca Juniors Buenos Aires / Club Atlético San Lorenzo de Almagro (AAM)
1925	Club Atlético Huracán Buenos Aires / Racing Club de Avellaneda (AAM)
1926	Club Atlético Boca Juniors Buenos Aires / Club Atlético Independiente Avellaneda (AAM)

1927	Club Atlético San Lorenzo de Almagro
1928	Club Atlético Huracán Buenos Aires
1929	Club de Gimnasia y Esgrima La Plata
1930	Club Atlético Boca Juniors Buenos Aires
1931	Club Atlético Estudiantil Porteño
1932	Club Sportivo Barracas Bolívar
1933	Club Sportivo Dock Sud Avellaneda
1934	Club Atlético Estudiantil Porteño

**became later Alumni Athletic Club*

The best teams played since 1931 for the Professional League, founded in 1931. Between 1967 and 1985 two championships were played:

Metropolitano (=Met; First Division) with the club teams based in the Metropolitan area.

Nacional (=Nac) played with teams from all regions.

Between 1985/1986 and 1990/1991, the League played on European style, with autumn-spring seasons.

Since 1991/1992, two championships were played: **Apertura** (=Ape) is the initial championship of the League; **Clausura** (=Cla) is the last championship of the League.

	Argentinean Professional Championship
1931	Club Atlético Boca Juniors Buenos Aires
1932	Club Atlético River Plate Buenos Aires
1933	Club Atlético San Lorenzo de Almagro
1934	Club Atlético Boca Juniors Buenos Aires
1935	Club Atlético Boca Juniors Buenos Aires
1936	Club Atlético River Plate Buenos Aires
1937	Club Atlético River Plate Buenos Aires
1938	Club Atlético Independiente Avellaneda
1939	Club Atlético Independiente Avellaneda
1940	Club Atlético Boca Juniors Buenos Aires
1941	Club Atlético River Plate Buenos Aires
1942	Club Atlético River Plate Buenos Aires
1943	Club Atlético Boca Juniors Buenos Aires
1944	Club Atlético Boca Juniors Buenos Aires
1945	Club Atlético River Plate Buenos Aires
1946	Club Atlético San Lorenzo de Almagro
1947	Club Atlético River Plate Buenos Aires
1948	Club Atlético Independiente Avellaneda
1949	Racing Club de Avellaneda
1950	Racing Club de Avellaneda
1951	Racing Club de Avellaneda
1952	Club Atlético River Plate Buenos Aires
1953	Club Atlético River Plate Buenos Aires
1954	Club Atlético Boca Juniors Buenos Aires
1955	Club Atlético River Plate Buenos Aires
1956	Club Atlético River Plate Buenos Aires
1957	Club Atlético River Plate Buenos Aires
1958	Racing Club de Avellaneda
1959	Club Atlético San Lorenzo de Almagro
1960	Club Atlético Independiente Avellaneda
1961	Racing Club de Avellaneda

1962	Club Atlético Boca Juniors Buenos Aires	
1963	Club Atlético Independiente Avellaneda	
1964	Club Atlético Boca Juniors Buenos Aires	
1965	Club Atlético Boca Juniors Buenos Aires	
1966	Racing Club de Avellaneda	
1967	Met:	Club Estudiantes de La Plata
	Nac:	Club Atlético Independiente Avellaneda
1968	Met:	Club Atlético San Lorenzo de Almagro
	Nac:	Club Atlético Vélez Sársfield Buenos Aires
1969	Met:	Club Atlético Chacarita Juniors San Martín
	Nac:	Club Atlético Boca Juniors Buenos Aires
1970	Met:	Club Atlético Independiente Avellaneda
	Nac:	Club Atlético Boca Juniors Buenos Aires
1971	Met:	Club Atlético Independiente Avellaneda
	Nac:	Club Atlético Rosario Central
1972	Met:	Club Atlético San Lorenzo de Almagro
	Nac:	Club Atlético San Lorenzo de Almagro
1973	Met:	Club Atlético Huracán Buenos Aires
	Nac:	Club Atlético Rosario Central
1974	Met:	Club Atlético Newell's Old Boys Rosario
	Nac:	Club Atlético San Lorenzo de Almagro
1975	Met:	Club Atlético River Plate Buenos Aires
	Nac:	Club Atlético River Plate Buenos Aires
1976	Met:	Club Atlético Boca Juniors Buenos Aires
	Nac:	Club Atlético Boca Juniors Buenos Aires
1977	Met:	Club Atlético River Plate Buenos Aires
	Nac:	Club Atlético Independiente Avellaneda
1978	Met:	Quilmes Atlético Club
	Nac:	Club Atlético Independiente Avellaneda
1979	Met:	Club Atlético River Plate Buenos Aires
	Nac:	Club Atlético River Plate Buenos Aires
1980	Met:	Club Atlético River Plate Buenos Aires
	Nac:	Club Atlético Rosario Central
1981	Met:	Club Atlético Boca Juniors Buenos Aires
	Nac:	Club Atlético River Plate Buenos Aires
1982	Nac:	Club Ferro Carril Oeste Buenos Aires
	Met:	Club Estudiantes de La Plata
1983	Nac:	Club Estudiantes de La Plata
	Met:	Club Atlético Independiente Avellaneda
1984	Nac:	Club Ferro Carril Oeste Buenos Aires
	Met:	Asociación Atlética Argentinos Juniors Buenos Aires
1985	Nac:	Asociación Atlética Argentinos Juniors Buenos Aires
1985/1986	Club Atlético River Plate Buenos Aires	
1986/1987	Club Atlético Rosario Central	
1987/1988	Club Atlético Newell's Old Boys Rosario	
1988/1989	Club Atlético Independiente Avellaneda	
1989/1990	Club Atlético River Plate Buenos Aires	
1990/1991	Club Atlético Newell's Old Boys Rosario	
1991/1992	Ape:	Club Atlético River Plate Buenos Aires
	Cla:	Club Atlético Newell's Old Boys Rosario
1992/1993	Ape:	Club Atlético Boca Juniors Buenos Aires
	Cla:	Club Atlético Vélez Sársfield Buenos Aires

1993/1994	Ape:	Club Atlético River Plate Buenos Aires
	Cla:	Club Atlético Independiente Avellaneda
1994/1995	Ape:	Club Atlético River Plate Buenos Aires
	Cla:	Club Atlético San Lorenzo de Almagro
1995/1996	Ape:	Club Atlético Vélez Sársfield Buenos Aires
	Cla:	Club Atlético Vélez Sársfield Buenos Aires
1996/1997	Ape:	Club Atlético River Plate Buenos Aires
	Cla:	Club Atlético River Plate Buenos Aires
1997/1998	Ape:	Club Atlético River Plate Buenos Aires
	Cla:	Club Atlético Vélez Sársfield Buenos Aires
1998/1999	Ape:	Club Atlético Boca Juniors Buenos Aires
	Cla:	Club Atlético Boca Juniors Buenos Aires
1999/2000	Ape:	Club Atlético River Plate Buenos Aires
	Cla:	Club Atlético River Plate Buenos Aires
2000/2001	Ape:	Club Atlético Boca Juniors Buenos Aires
	Cla:	Club Atlético San Lorenzo de Almagro
2001/2002	Ape:	Racing Club de Avellaneda
	Cla:	Club Atlético River Plate Buenos Aires
2002/2003	Ape:	Club Atlético Independiente Avellaneda
	Cla:	Club Atlético River Plate Buenos Aires
2003/2004	Ape:	Club Atlético Boca Juniors Buenos Aires
	Cla:	Club Atlético River Plate Buenos Aires
2004/2005	Ape:	Club Atlético Newell's Old Boys Rosario
	Cla:	Club Atlético Vélez Sársfield Buenos Aires
2005/2006	Ape:	Club Atlético Boca Juniors Buenos Aires
	Cla:	Club Atlético Boca Juniors Buenos Aires
2006/2007	Ape:	Club Estudiantes de La Plata
	Cla:	Club Atlético San Lorenzo de Almagro
2007/2008	Ape:	Club Atlético Lanús
	Cla:	Club Atlético River Plate Buenos Aires
2008/2009	Ape:	Club Atlético Boca Juniors Buenos Aires
	Cla:	Club Atlético Vélez Sársfield Buenos Aires
2009/2010	Ape:	Club Atlético Banfield
	Cla:	Asociación Atlética Argentinos Juniors Buenos Aires
2010/2011	Ape:	Club Estudiantes de La Plata
	Cla:	Club Atlético Vélez Sársfield Buenos Aires
2011/2012	Ape:	CA Boca Juniors Buenos Aires
	Cla:	Arsenal FC de Sarandí
2012/2013	Ini:	Club Atlético Vélez Sársfield Buenos Aires
	Fin:	Club Atlético Newell's Old Boys Rosario
2013/2014	Ini:	Club Atlético San Lorenzo de Almagro
	Fin:	CA River Plate Buenos Aires
2014	Tra:	Racing Club de Avellaneda

TOP SCORERS
1891-2014

	Argentinean Amateur Championship	
1891	F. Archer (Buenos Aires & Rosario railway)	7
1892	*No competition*	
1893	William Leslie (Lomas AC Buenos Aires)	7
1894	James Gifford (Flores Athletic Club)	4
1895	*Not awarded*	
1896	T. F. Allen (Flores Athletic Club), Juan O. Anderson (Lomas AC Buenos Aires)	7
1897	William Stirling (Lomas AC Buenos Aires)	20
1898	T. F. Allen (Lanús Athletic)	11
1899	Percy Hooton (Belgrano AC)	3
1900	Spencer Leonard (Buenos Aires English High School)	8
1901	Herbert Dorning (Belgrano AC)	5
1902	Jorge Gibson Brown (Alumni AC)	11
1903	Jorge Gibson Brown (Alumni AC)	12
1904	Alfredo Carr Brown (Alumni AC)	11
1905	Tristán González (CA Estudiantes Buenos Aires), Carlos Lett (Alumni AC)	12
1906	Eliseo Brown (Alumni AC), Percy Hooton (Quilmes AC), Henry Lawrie (Lomas AC Buenos Aires), C. H. Whaley (Belgrano AC)	8
1907	Eliseo Brown (Alumni AC)	24
1908	Eliseo Brown (Alumni AC)	19
1909	Eliseo Brown (Alumni AC)	17
1910	Watson Hutton & Arnold Pencliff (Alumni AC)	13
1911	Ricardo S. Malbrán (San Isidro AC), Ricardo S. Malbrán (Alumni AC), Antonio Piaggio (Club Porteño)	10
1912	Alberto Bernardino Ohaco (Racing Club de Avellaneda) Enrique Colla (CA Independiente Avellaneda)/FAF	9 12
1913	Alberto Bernardino Ohaco (Racing Club de Avellaneda) Guillermo Dannaher (CA Argentino de Quilmes)/FAF	20 16
1914	Alberto Bernardino Ohaco (Racing Club de Avellaneda) Norberto Carabelli (Club Hispano Argentino)/FAF	20 11
1915	Alberto Bernardino Ohaco (Racing Club de Avellaneda)	31
1916	Marius Hiller (Club de Gimnasia y Esgrima La Plata)	16
1917	Alberto Andrés Marcovecchio (Racing Club de Avellaneda)	18
1918	Albérico Zabaleta (Racing Club de Avellaneda)	13
1919	Alfredo Garassino, Alfredo Martín (CA Boca Juniors Buenos Aires) Alberto Andrés Marcovecchio (Racing Club de Avellaneda)/AAM	6 12
1920	Fausto Lucarelli (CA Banfield) Santiago Carreras (CA Vélez Sársfield Buenos Aires)/AAM	15 19
1921	Guillermo Dannaher (CA Huracán Buenos Aires) Albérico Zabaleta (Racing Club de Avellaneda)/AAM	23 32
1922	J. Clarke (Sportivo Palermo), Domingo Alberto Tarasconi (CA Boca Juniors) Manuel Seoane (CA Independiente Avellaneda)/AAM	11 55
1923	Domingo Alberto Tarasconi (CA Boca Juniors Buenos Aires) Martín Barceló (Racing Club de Avellaneda)/AAM	40 15
1924	Domingo Alberto Tarasconi (CA Boca Juniors Buenos Aires) Ricardo Lucarelli (Sportivo Buenos Aires), Luis Ravaschino (CA Independiente Avellaneda)/AAM	16 15
1925	José Gaslini (CA Chacarita Juniors San Martín) Alberto Bellomo (Estudiantes de La Plata)/AAM	16 16

1926	Roberto Eugenio Cerro (CA Boca Juniors Buenos Aires) Manuel Seoane (CA Independiente Avellaneda)/AAM	20 29
1927	Domingo Alberto Tarasconi (CA Boca Juniors Buenos Aires)	32
1928	Roberto Eugenio Cerro (CA Boca Juniors Buenos Aires)	32
1929	Juan Bautista Cortesse (CA San Lorenzo de Almagro), Manuel Seoane (CA Independiente Avellaneda)	13
1930	Roberto Eugenio Cerro (CA Boca Juniors Buenos Aires)	37
1931	Julio Ciancia (Club Almagro)	14
1932	Juan Carlos Irurieta (CA All Boys Buenos Aires)	23
1933	A. Lorenzo (CA Barracas Central Buenos Aires)	16
1934	C. Maseda (CA Argentino de Quilmes), Domingo Alberto Tarasconi (Club General San Martín)	16
	Argentinean Professional Championship	
1931	Alberto Máximo Zozaya (Club Estudiantes de La Plata)	33
1932	Bernabé Ferreyra (CA River Plate Buenos Aires)	43
1933	Francisco Antonio Varallo (CA Boca Juniors Buenos Aires)	34
1934	Evaristo Vicente Barrera (Racing Club de Avellaneda)	34
1935	Agustín Cosso (CA Vélez Sársfield Buenos Aires)	33
1936	Evaristo Vicente Barrera (Racing Club de Avellaneda)	33
1937	Arsenio Pastor Erico (CA Independiente Avellaneda)	47
1938	Arsenio Pastor Erico (CA Independiente Avellaneda)	43
1939	Arsenio Pastor Erico (CA Independiente Avellaneda)	40
1940	Delfín Benítez Cáceres (Racing Club de Avellaneda) Isidro Lángara Galarraga (CA San Lorenzo de Almagro)	33
1941	José Canteli (CA Newell's Old Boys Rosario)	30
1942	Rinaldo Fioramonte Martino (CA San Lorenzo de Almagro)	25
1943	Luis Arrieta (CA Lanús), Ángel Amadeo Labruna (CA River Plate Buenos Aires), Raúl Frutos (CA Platense)	23
1944	Atilio Mellone (CA Huracán Buenos Aires)	26
1945	Ángel Amadeo Labruna (CA River Plate Buenos Aires)	25
1946	Mario Emilio Heriberto Boyé Auterio (CA Boca Juniors Buenos Aires)	24
1947	Alfredo Di Stéfano Laulhé (CA River Plate Buenos Aires)	27
1948	Benjamín Santos (CA Rosario Central)	27
1949	Llamil Simes (Racing Club de Avellaneda), Juan José Pizzuti (CA Banfield)	26
1950	Mario Papa (CA San Lorenzo de Almagro)	24
1951	Júlio Carlos Santiago Vernazza (CA River Plate Buenos Aires)	22
1952	Eduardo Ricagni (CA Huracán Buenos Aires)	28
1953	Juan José Pizzuti (Racing Club de Avellaneda), Juan Benavidez (CA San Lorenzo de Almagro)	22
1954	Angel Antonio Berni Gómez (PAR, CA San Lorenzo de Almagro), Norberto Conde (CA Vélez Sársfield Buenos Aires), José Borello (CA Boca Juniors Buenos Aires)	19
1955	Oscar Massei (CA Rosario Central)	21
1956	Juan Alberto Castro (CA Rosario Central), Ernesto Grillo (CA Independiente Avellaneda)	17
1957	Roberto Zárate (CA River Plate Buenos Aires)	22
1958	José Francisco Sanfilippo (CA San Lorenzo de Almagro)	28
1959	José Francisco Sanfilippo (CA San Lorenzo de Almagro)	31
1960	José Francisco Sanfilippo (CA San Lorenzo de Almagro)	34
1961	José Francisco Sanfilippo (CA San Lorenzo de Almagro)	26

1962	Luis Artime (CA River Plate Buenos Aires)		28
1963	Luis Artime (CA River Plate Buenos Aires)		26
1964	Héctor Rodolfo Veira (CA San Lorenzo de Almagro)		17
1965	Juan Carlos Carone (CA Vélez Sársfield Buenos Aires)		19
1966	Luis Artime (CA Independiente Avellaneda)		23
1967	Met:	Bernardo Acosta (CA Lanús)	18
	Nac:	Luis Artime (CA Independiente Avellaneda)	11
1968	Met:	Alfredo Domingo Obberti (CA Los Andes)	13
	Nac:	Omar Wehbe (CA Vélez Sársfield Buenos Aires)	13
1969	Met:	Walter Machado (Racing Club de Avellaneda)	14
	Nac:	Rodolfo José Fischer (CA San Lorenzo de Almagro), Carlos Bulla (CA Platense)	14
1970	Met:	Oscar Antonio Más (CA River Plate Buenos Aires)	16
	Nac:	Carlos Arcecio Bianchi (CA Vélez Sársfield Buenos Aires)	18
1971	Met:	Carlos Arcecio Bianchi (CA Vélez Sársfield Buenos Aires)	36
	Nac:	Alfredo Domingo Obberti (CA Newell's Old Boys Rosario), José Luñíz (Centro Juventud Antoniana Salta)	10
1972	Met:	Miguel Ángel Brindisi (CA Huracán Buenos Aires)	21
	Nac:	Carlos Manuel Morete (CA River Plate Buenos Aires)	14
1973	Met:	Oscar Antonio Más (CA River Plate Buenos Aires), Hugo Alberto Curioni (CA Boca Juniors Buenos Aires), Ignacio Peña (Club Estudiantes de La Plata)	17
	Nac:	Juan Gómez Voglino (CA Atlanta Buenos Aires)	18
1974	Met:	Carlos Manuel Morete (CA River Plate Buenos Aires)	18
	Nac:	Mario Alberto Kempes (CA Rosario Central)	25
1975	Met:	Héctor Horacio Scotta (CA San Lorenzo de Almagro)	28
	Nac:	Héctor Horacio Scotta (CA San Lorenzo de Almagro)	32
1976	Met:	Mario Alberto Kempes (CA Rosario Central)	21
	Nac:	Norberto Eresumo (San Lorenzo de Mar del Plata), Luis Ludueña (CA Talleres Córdoba), Víctor Marchetti (CA Unión de Santa Fé)	12
1977	Met:	Carlos Álvarez (AA Argentinos Juniors Buenos Aires)	27
	Nac:	Alfredo Letanú (Club Estudiantes de La Plata)	13
1978	Met:	Diego Armando Maradona (AA Argentinos Juniors Buenos Aires), Luis Andreucci (Quilmes AC)	22
	Nac:	José Omar Reinaldi (CA Talleres Córdoba)	18
1979	Met:	Diego Armando Maradona (AA Argentinos Juniors Buenos Aires), Sergio Élio Fortunato (Club Estudiantes de La Plata)	14
	Nac:	Diego Armando Maradona (AA Argentinos Juniors Buenos Aires)	12
1980	Met:	Diego Armando Maradona (AA Argentinos Juniors Buenos Aires)	25
	Nac:	Diego Armando Maradona (AA Argentinos Juniors Buenos Aires)	17
1981	Met:	Raúl Chaparro (Instituto Atlético Central Córdoba)	20
	Nac:	Carlos Arcecio Bianchi (CA Vélez Sársfield Buenos Aires)	15
1982	Nac:	Miguel Juárez (Club Ferro Carril Oeste Buenos Aires)	22
	Met:	Carlos Manuel Morete (CA Independiente Avellaneda)	20
1983	Nac:	Armando Mario Husillos (Club Social y Deportivo Loma Negra Olavarría)	11
	Met:	Víctor Rogelio Ramos (CA Newell's Old Boys Rosario)	30
1984	Nac:	Pedro Pablo Pasculli (AA Argentinos Juniors Buenos Aires)	9
	Met:	Enzo Francescoli Uriarte (URU, CA River Plate Buenos Aires)	24
1985	Nac:	Jorge Alberto Comas Romero (CA Vélez Sársfield Buenos Aires)	12
1985/1986	Enzo Francescoli Uriarte (URU, CA River Plate Buenos Aires)		25
1986/1987	Omar Arnaldo Palma (CA Rosario Central)		20

1987/1988	José Luis Rodríguez (Club Social, Deportivo y Cultural Español Buenos Aires)		18
1988/1989	Oscar Alberto Dertycia Álvarez (AA Argentinos Juniors Buenos Aires), Néstor Raúl Gorosito (CA San Lorenzo de Almagro)		20
1989/1990	Ariel Osvaldo Cozzoni (CA Newell's Old Boys Rosario)		23
1990/1991	Esteban Fernando González Sánchez (CA Vélez Sársfield Buenos Aires)		18
1991/1992	Ape:	Ramón Ángel Díaz (CA River Plate Buenos Aires)	14
	Cla:	Darío Oscar Scotto (CA Platense), Diego Fernando Latorre (CA Boca Juniors Buenos Aires)	9
1992/1993	Ape:	Alberto Federico Acosta (CA San Lorenzo de Almagro)	12
	Cla:	Rubén Fernando da Silva Echeverrito (URU, CA River Plate Buenos Aires)	13
1993/1994	Ape:	Sergio Daniel Martínez Alzuri (URU, CA Boca Juniors Buenos Aires)	12
	Cla:	Marcelo Fabian Espina (CA Platense), Marcelo Fabian Espina (CA River Plate Buenos Aires)	11
1994/1995	Ape:	Enzo Francescoli Uriarte (URU, CA River Plate Buenos Aires)	12
	Cla:	José Oscar Flores (CA Vélez Sársfield Buenos Aires)	14
1995/1996	Ape:	José Luis Calderón (Club Estudiantes de La Plata)	13
	Cla:	Ariel Maximiliano López (CA Lanús)	13
1996/1997	Ape:	Gustavo Enrique Reggi (CA Newell's Old Boys Rosario)	11
	Cla:	Sergio Daniel Martínez Alzuri (URU, CA Boca Juniors Buenos Aires)	15
1997/1998	Ape:	Rubén Fernando da Silva Echeverrito (URU, CA Rosario Central)	15
	Cla:	Roberto Carlos Sosa (Club de Gimnasia y Esgrima La Plata)	16
1998/1999	Ape:	Martín Palermo (CA Boca Juniors Buenos Aires)	20
	Cla:	José Luis Calderón (CA Independiente Avellaneda)	17
1999/2000	Ape:	Javier Pedro Saviola Fernández (CA River Plate Buenos Aires)	15
	Cla:	Oscar Esteban Fuertes (CA Colón)	17
2000/2001	Ape:	Juan Pablo Ángel (COL, CA River Plate Buenos Aires)	13
	Cla:	Bernardo Daniel Romeo (CA San Lorenzo de Almagro)	15
2001/2002	Ape:	Martín Alejandro Cardetti (CA River Plate Buenos Aires)	17
	Cla:	Fernando Ezequiel Cavenaghi (CA River Plate Buenos Aires)	15
2002/2003	Ape:	Néstor Andrés Silvera (CA Independiente Avellaneda)	16
	Cla:	Luciano Gabriel Figueroa Herrera (CA Rosario Central)	17
2003/2004	Ape:	Ernesto Antonio Farías (Club Estudiantes de La Plata)	12
	Cla:	Rolando David Zárate Riga (CA Vélez Sársfield Buenos Aires)	13
2004/2005	Ape:	Lisandro López (Racing Club de Avellaneda)	12
	Cla:	Hugo Mariano Pavone (Club Estudiantes de La Plata)	16
2005/2006	Ape:	Javier Edgardo Bustamante Cámpora (CA Tiro Federal Argentino Rosario)	13
	Cla:	Gonzalo Vargas Abella (URU, Club de Gimnasia y Esgrima La Plata)	12
2006/2007	Ape:	Mauro Matías Zárate (CA Vélez Sársfield Buenos Aires), Rodrigo Sebastián Palacio (CA Boca Juniors Buenos Aires)	12
	Cla:	Martín Palermo (CA Boca Juniors Buenos Aires)	11
2007/2008	Ape:	Germán Gustavo Denis (CA Independiente Avellaneda)	18
	Cla:	Darío Cvitanich (CA Banfield)	13
2008/2009	Ape:	José Gustavo Sand (CA Lanús)	15
	Cla:	José Gustavo Sand (CA Lanús)	13
2009/2010	Ape:	Santiago Martín Silva Olivera (URU, CA Banfield)	14
	Cla:	Mauro Boselli (Club Estudiantes de La Plata)	13
2010/2011	Ape:	Santiago Martín Silva Olivera (URU, CA Vélez Sársfield Buenos Aires) Denis Stracqualursi (CA Tigre Victoria)	11
	Cla:	Javier Edgardo Cámpora Bustamante (CA Huracán Buenos Aires) Teófilo Antonio Gutiérrez Rocancio (Racing Club de Avellaneda)	11
2011/2012	Ape:	Rubén Darío Ramírez (CD Godoy Cruz Mendoza)	12
	Cla:	Carlos Ariel Luna (CA Tigre Victoria)	12

2012/2013	Ini:	Facundo Ferreyra (CA Vélez Sársfield Buenos Aires) Ignacio Martín Scocco (CA Newell's Old Boys Rosario)	13
	Fin:	Emanuel Gigliotti (CA Colón de Santa Fé) Ignacio Martín Scocco (CA Newell's Old Boys Rosario)	11
2013/2014	Ini:	César Emanuel Pereyra (CA Belgrano Córdoba)	10
	Fin:	Mauro Matías Zárate (CA Vélez Sársfield Buenos Aires)	13
2014	Tra:	Lucas David Pratto (CA Vélez Sársfield Buenos Aires) Maximiliano Rubén Rodríguez (CA Newell's Old Boys Rosario) Silvio Ezequiel Romero (CA Lanús)	11

NATIONAL CHAMPIONSHIP
Primera División 2014
(08.08.2014 - 14.12.2014)

Torneo de Transición 2014
Torneo "Doctor Ramón Carrillo"

No teams were relegated this season. The league will get expanded to 30 teams in the new 2015 Primera División!!!

Results

Round 1 [08-13.08.2014]
CD Godoy Cruz - CA Banfield 3-0(2-0)
Rosario Central - Quilmes AC 3-1(0-1)
Defensa y Justicia - Racing Club 1-3(0-2)
Independiente - Atlético Rafaela 3-0(1-0)
Boca Juniors - Newell's Old Boys 0-1(0-1)
Gimnasia y Esgrima - River Plate 1-1(0-0)
Arsenal FC - Estudiantes 2-1(1-1)
CA Tigre - Vélez Sársfield 0-1(0-0)
CA Lanús – CA Belgrano Córdoba 1-0(1-0)
CA San Lorenzo - Olimpo 2-0(1-0) [01.10.]

Round 2 [15-18.08.2014]
Newell's Old B. - Gimnasia y Esgrima 1-1(0-0)
Olimpo - CA Tigre 2-1(2-0)
CA Banfield - Defensa y Justicia 2-3(0-1)
Vélez Sársfield - Arsenal FC 2-1(1-0)
Estudiantes - Independiente 1-0(1-0)
Racing Club - CA San Lorenzo 2-0(1-0)
River Plate - Rosario Central 2-0(1-0)
CA Belgrano Córdoba - Boca Juniors 0-1(0-0)
Quilmes AC - CD Godoy Cruz 2-2(1-0)
Atlético Rafaela - CA Lanús 2-1(1-0)

Round 3 [22-24.08.2014]
Arsenal FC - Olimpo 1-0(1-0)
CA Tigre - Racing Club 4-0(2-0)
Gimnasia y Esgrima - Rosario Central 1-2(1-1)
Newell's Old Boys – CA Belgrano 3-3(1-0)
Independiente - Vélez Sársfield 0-4(0-0)
CA San Lorenzo - CA Banfield 0-2(0-0)
CA Lanús - Estudiantes 2-1(1-0)
Defensa y Justicia - Quilmes AC 1-1(1-1)
Boca Juniors - Atlético Rafaela 0-3(0-1)
CD Godoy Cruz - River Plate 0-4(0-3)

Round 4 [26-28.08.2014]
CA Belgrano - Gimnasia y Esgrima 0-0
Olimpo - Independiente 1-2(0-0)
Racing Club - Arsenal FC 1-0(0-0)
Rosario Central - CD Godoy Cruz 0-1(0-0)
Atlético Rafaela - Newell's Old Boys 2-3(0-3)
River Plate - Defensa y Justicia 3-0(2-0)
Estudiantes - Boca Juniors 3-1(3-0)
CA Banfield - CA Tigre 1-0(1-0)
Vélez Sársfield - CA Lanús 1-0(0-0)
Quilmes AC - CA San Lorenzo 0-3(0-2)

Round 5 [30.08.-01.09.2014]
Gimnasia y Esgrima - CD Godoy Cruz 2-0(1-0)
Defensa y Justicia - Rosario Central 1-3(0-0)
Newell's Old Boys - Estudiantes 1-0(0-0)
CA Belgrano - Atlético Rafaela 3-0(1-0)
Independiente - Racing Club 2-1(2-1)
Boca Juniors - Vélez Sársfield 3-1(0-1)
CA San Lorenzo - River Plate 1-3(1-1)
CA Lanús - Olimpo 1-1(1-0)
Arsenal FC - CA Banfield 1-0(0-0)
CA Tigre - Quilmes AC 0-0

Round 6 [06-08.09.2014]
Atlético Rafaela - Gimnasia y Esgrima 2-0(1-0)
Vélez Sársfield - Newell's Old Boys 0-0
Estudiantes - CA Belgrano Córdoba 3-1(1-0)
CA Banfield - Independiente 0-1(0-0)
Rosario Central - CA San Lorenzo 1-1(1-1)
CD Godoy Cruz - Defensa y Justicia 1-1(0-0)
Racing Club - CA Lanús 1-3(1-2)
River Plate - CA Tigre 2-0(1-0)
Olimpo - Boca Juniors 0-1(0-0)
Quilmes AC - Arsenal FC 4-0(1-0)

Round 7 [12-15.09.2014]
Gimnasia y Esg. - Defensa y Justicia 0-3(0-1)
CA San Lorenzo - CD Godoy Cruz 2-1(0-1)
CA Tigre - Rosario Central 4-1(2-1)
Atlético Rafaela - Estudiantes 1-0(0-0)
Independiente - Quilmes AC 5-3(1-1)
CA Lanús - CA Banfield 1-0(0-0)
CA Belgrano - Vélez Sársfield 1-0(1-0)
Newell's Old Boys - Olimpo 1-0(0-0)
Boca Juniors - Racing Club 1-2 [25.09.]
Arsenal FC - River Plate 1-1(0-0) [25.09.]

Round 8 [19-22.09.2014]
Quilmes AC - CA Lanús 0-2(0-2)
Estudiantes - Gimnasia y Esgrima 0-0
Olimpo - CA Belgrano Córdoba 1-0(0-0)
Vélez Sársfield - Atlético Rafaela 0-0
Rosario Central - Arsenal FC 3-1(0-1)
CA Banfield - Boca Juniors 1-1(0-0)
River Plate - Independiente 4-1(2-0)
Defensa y Justicia - CA San Lorenzo 1-3(1-1)
Racing Club - Newell's Old Boys 1-1(1-1)
CD Godoy Cruz - CA Tigre 4-3(1-2) [15.10.]

Round 9 [26-29.09.2014]
Estudiantes - Vélez Sársfield 3-2(0-1)
Atlético Rafaela - Olimpo 0-0
Independiente - Rosario Central 2-0(0-0)
CA San Lorenzo - Gimnasia y Esg. 0-2(0-1)
CA Tigre - Defensa y Justicia 2-1(0-0)
CA Belgrano Córdoba - Racing Club 1-4(1-2)
Boca Juniors - Quilmes AC 1-0(0-0)
CA Lanús - River Plate 1-1(1-0)
Arsenal FC - CD Godoy Cruz 3-0(3-0)
Newell's Old Boys - CA Banfield 0-3(0-2)

Round 10 [03-06.10.2014]
Gimnasia y Esgrima - Vélez Sársfield 2-0(2-0)
CA Banfield - CA Belgrano Córdoba 2-2(1-0)
CA San Lorenzo - CA Tigre 0-2(0-1)
Defensa y Justicia - Arsenal FC 2-1(0-0)
Olimpo - Estudiantes 1-2(0-1)
Quilmes AC - Newell's Old Boys 1-1(1-1)
River Plate - Boca Juniors 1-1(0-1)
Racing Club - Atlético Rafaela 0-2(0-0)
Rosario Central - CA Lanús 1-2(0-1)
CD Godoy Cruz - Independiente 2-2(2-1)

Round 11 [10-13.10.2014]
CA Tigre - Gimnasia y Esgrima 1-0(0-0)
CA Lanús - CD Godoy Cruz 3-3(1-0)
Vélez Sársfield - Olimpo 4-1(2-1)
CA Belgrano Córdoba - Quilmes AC 1-1(0-0)
Estudiantes - Racing Club 0-4(0-2)
Atlético Rafaela - CA Banfield 2-2(2-1)
Independiente - Defensa y Justicia 1-1(0-0)
Boca Juniors - Rosario Central 2-1(0-1)
Newell's Old Boys - River Plate 0-1(0-0)
Arsenal FC - CA San Lorenzo 0-0

Round 12 [17-20.10.2014]
Gimnasia y Esgrima - Olimpo 0-0
Quilmes AC - Atlético Rafaela 0-0
CA Banfield - Estudiantes 1-1(1-0)
CA San Lorenzo - Independiente 1-2(0-1)
Defensa y Justicia - CA Lanús 1-2(1-2)
Rosario Central - Newell's Old Boys 2-0(2-0)
Racing Club - Vélez Sársfield 2-0(2-0)
River Plate - CA Belgrano Córdoba 3-0(1-0)
CD Godoy Cruz - Boca Juniors 2-3(1-1)
CA Tigre - Arsenal FC 1-1(0-0)

Round 13 [24-27.10.2014]
CA Belgrano - Rosario Central 1-0(1-0)
Independiente - CA Tigre 3-1(2-1)
Vélez Sársfield - CA Banfield 1-0(0-0)
Newell's Old Boys - CD Godoy Cruz 2-2(1-1)
Olimpo - Racing Club 1-1(0-1)
Estudiantes - Quilmes AC 1-0(0-0)
CA Lanús - CA San Lorenzo 1-0(1-0)
Boca Juniors - Defensa y Justicia 2-0(2-0)
Atlético Rafaela - River Plate 1-2(1-0)
Arsenal FC - Gimnasia y Esgrima 1-0(1-0)

Round 14 [31.10.-02.11.2014]
CA Banfield - Olimpo 3-0(1-0)
CD Godoy Cruz - CA Belgrano 1-3(1-0)
Gimnasia y Esgrima - Racing Club 0-1(0-0)
Quilmes AC - Vélez Sársfield 2-1(2-0)
Rosario Central - Atlético Rafaela 0-2(0-1)
CA San Lorenzo - Boca Juniors 2-0(0-0)
CA Tigre - CA Lanús 3-0(0-0) [12.11.]
River Plate - Estudiantes 0-1(0-1) [13.11.]
Arsenal FC - Independiente 1-1(1-0) [13.11.]
Defensa y Jst. - Newell's O.B. 1-0(0-0) [20.11.]

Round 15 [07-10.11.2014]
CA Lanús - Arsenal FC 3-2(1-2)
Atlético Rafaela - CD Godoy Cruz 3-4(1-3)
Olimpo - Quilmes AC 2-1(2-0)
CA Belgrano - Defensa y Justicia 3-0(0-0)
Independiente - Gimnasia y Esgrima 0-1(0-0)
Estudiantes - Rosario Central 1-0(1-0)
Racing Club - CA Banfield 1-0(1-0)
Boca Juniors - CA Tigre 2-0(0-0)
Vélez Sársfield - River Plate 1-1(1-1)
Newell's Old Boys - CA San Lorenzo 3-1(1-0)

Round 16 [14-17.11.2014]
Defensa y Justicia - Atlético Rafaela 2-1(0-0)
Rosario Central - Vélez Sársfield 0-0
Gimnasia y Esgrima - CA Banfield 1-1(0-0)
CA San Lorenzo - CA Belgrano 4-0(3-0)
Quilmes AC - Racing Club 0-1(0-0)
CD Godoy Cruz - Estudiantes 1-1(1-0)
CA Tigre - Newell's Old Boys 1-2(1-2)
River Plate - Olimpo 1-1(1-0)
Arsenal FC - Boca Juniors 1-1(0-0)
Independiente - CA Lanús 4-1(2-1)

Round 17 [21-24.11.2014]
CA Banfield - Quilmes AC 3-1(1-1)
Atlético Rafaela - CA San Lorenzo 2-0(0-0)
Olimpo - Rosario Central 1-1(1-0)
Vélez Sársfield - CD Godoy Cruz 1-4(1-2)
CA Lanús - Gimnasia y Esgrima 2-0(1-0)
CA Belgrano Córdoba - CA Tigre 1-2(1-0)
Estudiantes - Defensa y Justicia 0-0
Boca Juniors - Independiente 3-1(1-0)
Racing Club - River Plate 1-0(1-0)
Newell's Old Boys - Arsenal FC 2-4(1-1)

Round 18 [28.11.-01.12.2014]
Gimnasia y Esgrima - Quilmes AC 3-0(1-0)
Defensa y Justicia - Vélez Sársfield 0-2(0-1)
CA San Lorenzo - Estudiantes 4-0(0-0)
Independiente - Newell's Old Boys 1-0(0-0)
Rosario Central - Racing Club 0-3(0-1)
CA Tigre - Atlético Rafaela 3-1(1-1)
River Plate - CA Banfield 3-2(0-1)
CA Lanús - Boca Juniors 2-2(2-0)
CD Godoy Cruz - Olimpo 0-3(0-3)
Arsenal FC - CA Belgrano Córdoba 0-2(0-0)

Round 19 [05-07.12.2014]
Estudiantes - CA Tigre 4-2(1-1)
Vélez Sársfield - CA San Lorenzo 0-2(0-0)
Atlético Rafaela - Arsenal FC 1-6(0-3)
Olimpo - Defensa y Justicia 0-0
CA Banfield - Rosario Central 2-3(0-1)
CA Belgrano Córdoba - Independiente 4-0(2-0)
Newell's Old Boys - CA Lanús 0-0
Boca Juniors - Gimnasia y Esgrima 0-2(0-1)
Racing Club - Godoy Cruz 1-0(0-0) [14.12.]
Quilmes AC - River Plate 0-1(0-0) [14.12.]

Final Standings

1.	**Racing Club de Avellaneda**	19	13	2	4	30 - 16	41
2.	CA River Plate Buenos Aires	19	11	6	2	34 - 13	39
3.	CA Lanús	19	10	5	4	28 - 23	35
4.	CA Independiente Avellaneda	19	10	3	6	31 - 29	33
5.	CA Boca Juniors Buenos Aires	19	9	4	6	25 - 23	31
6.	Club Estudiantes de La Plata	19	9	4	6	23 - 23	31
7.	CA Tigre Victoria	19	8	2	9	30 - 26	26
8.	CA San Lorenzo de Almagro	19	8	2	9	26 - 22	26
9.	Arsenal FC de Sarandí	19	7	5	7	27 - 25	26
10.	CA Belgrano Córdoba	19	7	4	8	26 - 26	25
11.	CA Vélez Sársfield Buenos Aires	19	7	4	8	21 - 22	25
12.	CA Newell's Old Boys Rosario	19	6	7	6	21 - 24	25
13.	AMSD Atlético de Rafaela	19	7	4	8	25 - 29	25
14.	Club de Gimnasia y Esgrima La Plata	19	6	6	7	16 - 15	24
15.	CA Rosario Central	19	6	3	10	21 - 28	21
16.	CD Godoy Cruz Mendoza	19	5	6	8	31 - 39	21
17.	CA Banfield	19	5	5	9	25 - 25	20
18.	CSD Defensa y Justicia Florencio Varela	19	5	5	9	19 - 30	20
19.	Club Olimpo de Bahía Blanca	19	4	7	8	15 - 22	19
20.	Quilmes AC	19	2	6	11	17 - 31	12

Racing Club de Avellaneda, CA River Plate Buenos Aires, CA Boca Juniors Buenos Aires and CA San Lorenzo de Almagro qualified for the 2015 Copa Libertadores (second stage).

Club Estudiantes de La Plata qualified for the 2015 Copa Libertadores (first stage).

CA River Plate Buenos Aires, CA Lanús, CA Independiente Avellaneda, CA Tigre Victoria, Arsenal FC de Sarandí and CA Belgrano Córdoba qualified for the 2015 Copa Sudamericana.

Top goalscorers:

11 goals:	**Lucas David Pratto**	**(CA Vélez Sársfield Buenos Aires)**
	Maximiliano Rubén Rodríguez	**(CA Newell's Old Boys Rosario)**
	Silvio Ezequiel Romero	**(CA Lanús)**
10 goals:	Gustavo Leonardo Bou	(Racing Club de Avellaneda)
	Teófilo Antonio Gutiérrez Roncancio	(CA River Plate Buenos Aires)
	Federico Andrés Mancuello	(CA Independiente Avellaneda)

ARSENAL FÚTBOL CLUB DE SARANDÍ

Foundation date: January 11, 1957
Address: Juan Díaz de Solís 3660, CP: 1872, Sarandí, Avellaneda, Buenos Aires
Stadium: Estadio „Julio H. Grondona“, Buenos Aires - Capacity: 16,300

THE SQUAD

	DOB	M	G
Goalkeepers:			
Esteban Maximiliano Andrada	26.01.1991	18	-
Mauricio Hernán Aquino	27.10.1993	-	-
Óscar Alejandro Limia Rodríguez	16.07.1975	2	-
René Daniel Moyano	26.03.1995	-	-
Defenders:			
Cristian Chimino	09.02.1988	4	1
Marcos Curado	09.05.1995	-	-
Jorge Wiston Curbelo Garis (URU)	21.12.1981	9	-
Federico Emanuel Milo	10.01.1992	1	-
Martín Hugo Nervo	06.01.1991	19	1
Juan Cruz Randazzo	11.03.1994	-	-
José Ignacio San Román Canciani	17.08.1988	18	-
Daniel Alejandro Rosero Valencia (COL)	06.10.1993	-	-
Matias Sarulyte	13.03.1989	10	1
Matías Ezequiel Zaldivia	22.01.1991	9	-
Midfielders:			
Nicolás Diego Aguirre	27.06.1990	14	1
Brahian Milton Alemán Athaydes (URU)	22.12.1989	19	9
Jorge Gabriel Báez Mendoza (PAR)	23.10.1990	2	-
Julián Cardozo	02.01.1991	5	-
Ramiro Ángel Carrera	24.10.1993	17	4
Gastón Rubén Esmerado	08.02.1978	-	-
Hernán Daniel Fredes	27.03.1987	17	-
Federico Freire	06.11.1990	-	-
Leandro Godoy	09.12.1994	2	1
Iván José Marcone	03.06.1988	14	-
Damián Alfredo Pérez	22.12.1988	18	-
Matías Zaldivar	04.08.1995	-	-
Forwards:			
Pablo Burzio	03.12.1992	12	-
Milton Aaron Céliz	25.07.1992	12	-
Sebastián Alberto Palacios	20.01.1992	17	2
Enzo Enrico Prono Zelaya (PAR)	27.06.1991	-	-
Lucas Ramón Pugh	01.01.1994	1	-
Federico Iván Rasic	24.03.1992	6	-
Carlos Bryan Schmidt	19.11.1995	1	-
Emilio José Zelaya	30.07.1987	18	7
Trainer:			
Martín Palermo [as of 15.04.2014]	07.11.1973	19	

ASOCIACIÓN MUTUAL SOCIAL Y DEPORTIVA ATLÉTICO DE RAFAELA

Foundation date: January 13, 1907
Address: Calle Fernando Dentesano 455, 2300 Rafaela, Provincia de Santa Fe
Stadium: Estadio Rafaela (Nuevo Monumental), Rafaela - Capacity: 16,000

THE SQUAD

	DOB	M	G
Goalkeepers:			
Esteban Néstor Conde Quintana (URU)	04.03.1983	19	-
Carlos Alberto De Giorgi	23.04.1984	-	-
Rodrigo Manera	05.04.1991	-	-
Guillermo Enrique Sara	30.09.1987	-	-
Axel Werner	28.02.1996	-	-
Defenders:			
Rodrigo Colombo	19.11.1992	-	-
Martín Damián Díaz Pena (URU)	17.03.1988	5	-
Jonathan Ferrari	08.05.1987	11	-
Mauricio Sebastián Gómez Castro (URU)	16.04.1992	9	1
Lucas Nahuel Kruspzky	06.04.1992	6	-
Dimas Morales	22.06.1994	-	-
Alexis Jorge Niz	17.05.1988	4	-
Joel Sacks	10.04.1989	17	1
Midfielders:			
Adrián Jesús Bastía	20.12.1978	18	1
Rodrigo Leonel Depetris	05.05.1990	12	1
Juan Manuel Eluchans	14.04.1980	15	2
Guillermo Matías Fernández	11.10.1991	17	3
Marcos Fissore	08.08.1992	1	-
Matías Óscar Fissore	21.09.1990	9	-
Pablo Gaitán	09.05.1992	-	-
Diego Armando Montiel	22.04.1996	8	1
Pablo José Pavetti	20.03.1991	-	-
Germán Ezequiel Rodríguez Rojas	05.01.1990	13	1
Pablo Nicolás Royón Silvera (URU)	28.01.1991	14	1
Walter Omar Serrano	02.07.1986	14	1
Sergio Javier Vittor	09.06.1989	19	3
Forwards:			
Lucas Albertengo	30.01.1991	19	4
Federico Rafael González	06.01.1987	19	2
Franco Marcelo Jominy	28.08.1994	-	-
Nicolás Orsini	12.09.1994	11	3
Ignacio Pussetto	21.12.1995	3	-
Mauro Daniel Quiroga	07.12.1989	1	-
Trainer:			
Roberto Néstor Sensini [as of 08.06.2014]	12.10.1966	19	

CLUB ATLÉTICO BANFIELD BUENOS AIRES

Foundation date: January 21, 1896
Address: Avenida Valentín Vergara 1635/55, Banfield 1828, Lomas de Zamora, Provincia de B. Aires
Stadium: Estadio "Florencio Solá", Banfield - Capacity: 34,901

THE SQUAD

	DOB	M	G
Goalkeepers:			
Alejandro Alcayaga	14.06.1993	-	-
Enrique Alberto Bologna Gómez	13.02.1982	-	-
César Pablo Rigamonti	07.04.1987	-	-
Gaspar Andrés Servio	09.03.1992	19	-
Defenders:			
Gonzalo Bettini	26.09.1992	10	-
Nicolás Alexis Bianchi Arce	28.01.1987	15	-
José Ricardo Devaca Sánchez (PAR)	18.09.1982	2	-
Marco di Menno Stavrón	06.01.1993	-	-
Fabián Ariel Noguera	20.03.1993	12	-
Adrián Antonio Reta	11.03.1992	-	-
Jorge Agustín Rodriguez	15.09.1995	2	-
Favio Aarón Segovia	12.01.1989	-	-
Nicolás Alejandro Tagliafico	31.08.1992	14	-
Gustavo Ariel Toledo	19.09.1989	19	-
Midfielders:			
Nicolás Santiago Bertolo	02.01.1986	11	-
Juan Ramón Cazares Sevillano (ECU)	03.04.1992	10	-
Emanuel Cecchini	24.12.1996	-	-
Juan Alberto Cuéllar	05.05.1996	-	-
Nicolás Mario Domingo	08.04.1985	18	-
Walter Daniel Erviti Roldán	12.06.1980	17	-
Carlos Agustín Farías	25.12.1987	1	-
Agustin Fontana	11.06.1996	1	-
Lihué Darío Prichoda	26.06.1989	5	-
Jonathan Iván Requena	11.06.1996	6	-
Iván Rossi	01.11.1993	-	-
Enzo Gabriel Trinidad	19.09.1996	9	-
Mariano Nahuel Yeri	12.09.1991	12	-
Omar Zarif	02.09.1978	4	-
Forwards:			
Mauricio Gabriel Asenjo	23.07.1994	5	-
Leandro Chetti	23.05.1993	9	-
Juan Ezequiel García	09.10.1991	4	-
Ricardo Daniel Noir Meyer	26.02.1987	17	-
Santiago Gabriel Salcedo González (PAR)	06.09.1981	19	-
Emiliano Franco Terzaghi	06.03.1993	12	-
Claudio Villagra	02.01.1996	1	-
Trainer:			
Matías Jesús Almeyda [as of 04.2013]	21.12.1973	19	

CLUB ATLÉTICO BELGRANO CÓRDOBA

Foundation date: March 19, 1905
Address: Calle Dr. Arturo Orgaz 510, Barrio Alberdi 5000, Ciudad de Córdoba
Stadium: Estadio „Julio César Villagra" [El Gigante de Alberdi], Córdoba - Capacity: 28,000

THE SQUAD

	DOB	M	G
Goalkeepers:			
Lucas Mauricio Acosta	12.03.1995	-	-
Pablo Heredia	11.06.1990	4	-
Juan Carlos Olave	21.02.1976	16	-
Defenders:			
Federico Hernán Álvarez	07.08.1994	12	-
Lucas Elio Aveldaño	19.07.1985	17	1
Pier Miqueas Barrios	01.07.1990	15	1
Nicolás Ferreyra	30.03.1993	5	-
Christian Franco Lema	12.09.1990	18	-
Marcos Rivadero	09.10.1992	5	-
Renzo Saravia	16.06.1993	8	-
Carlos Daniel Soto	20.01.1984	1	-
Gastón Alejandro Turus	27.05.1980	2	-
Midfielders:			
Gabriel Alanis	16.03.1994	3	-
Guillermo Martín Farré	16.08.1981	18	-
Esteban Nicolás González Rojas	16.09.1978	11	-
Nahuel Isaías Luján	23.08.1995	1	-
Osvaldo César Mansanelli	29.08.1980	10	-
Lucas Joaquín Parodi Cuello	30.11.1990	5	-
Lucas Abel Pittinari	30.11.1991	9	-
Emiliano Rigoni	04.02.1993	16	3
Jorge Luis Velázquez	07.09.1982	17	2
Lucas Manuel Zelarrayán	20.06.1992	19	4
Forwards:			
Jerry Ricardo Bengtson Bodden (HON)	08.04.1987	8	1
Julio César Furch	29.07.1989	18	8
Fernando Andrés Márquez	10.12.1987	11	3
César Emanuel Pereyra	23.11.1981	14	3
Trainer:			
Ricardo Zielinski [as of 01.01.2011]	14.10.1959	19	

CLUB ATLÉTICO BOCA JUNIORS BUENOS AIRES

Foundation date: April 3, 1905
Address: Brandsen 805, C1161AAQ, La Boca, Buenos Aires
Stadium: Estadio „Alberto J. Armando“ [La Bombonera], Buenos Aires - Capacity: 49,000

THE SQUAD			
	DOB	**M**	**G**
Goalkeepers:			
Sebastián Ezequiel D'Angelo	14.01.1989	-	-
Agustín Ignacio Orión	26.06.1981	18	-
Emanuel Tripodi	07.08.1981	1	-
Manuel Vicentini	19.04.1990	-	-
Defenders:			
Guillermo Enio Burdisso	26.09.1988	1	-
Daniel Alberto "Catá" Díaz	13.03.1979	10	1
Mariano Raúl Echeverría	27.05.1981	13	2
Juan Daniel Forlín	10.01.1988	5	-
Hernán Gustavo Grana	12.04.1985	5	-
Emanuel Mariano Insúa	10.04.1991	12	1
Juan Cruz Komar	13.08.1996	1	-
Lisandro Magallán Orueta	27.09.1993	9	1
Lucas Leandro Marín	22.01.1992	13	1
Claudio Daniel Pérez	26.12.1985	5	-
Nahuel Alejandro Zárate	27.01.1993	4	-
Midfielders:			
Joel Acosta	16.01.1991	1	-
Luciano Acosta	01.05.1994	9	-
Federico Bravo	05.10.1993	8	-
Federico Gastón Carrizo	17.05.1991	19	1
Gonzalo Pablo Castellani	10.08.1987	14	-
Nicolás Carlos Colazo	08.07.1990	10	-
Franco Cristaldo	15.08.1996	3	-
Adrián Andrés Cubas	22.05.1996	7	-
Cristian Damián Erbes	06.01.1990	10	-
José Pedro Fuenzalida Gana (CHI)	22.02.1985	12	-
Fernando Rubén Gago	10.04.1986	10	1
Pablo Martín Ledesma	04.02.1984	2	-
César Marcelo Meli	20.06.1992	10	1
Leonardo Gabriel Suárez	30.03.1996	2	-
Matías Gastón Zaragoza	20.09.1995	-	-
Forwards:			
Jonathan Calleri	23.09.1993	14	6
Andrés Eliseo Chávez	21.03.1991	11	2
Emanuel Gigliotti	20.05.1987	16	5
Juan Manuel Martínez	21.10.1985	9	3
Yamil Jorge Gonzalo Romero	11.07.1995	-	-
Trainer:			
Carlos Arcecio Bianchi [01.01.2013-28.08.2014; Sacked]	29.04.1949	4	
Rodolfo Martín Arruabarrena [as of 29.08.2014]	20.07.1975	15	

CLUB SOCIAL Y DEPORTIVO DEFENSA Y JUSTICIA FLORENCIO VARELA

Foundation date: March 20, 1935
Address: Avenida San Martín 360 Florencio Varela, 1888 Florencio Varela, Provincia de Buenos Aires
Stadium: Estadio „ Norberto Tito Tomaghello", Florencio Varela - Capacity: 8,000

THE SQUAD

	DOB	M	G
Goalkeepers:			
Gabriel Arias	13.09.1987	1	-
Juan Ignacio Dobboletta	06.01.1993	-	-
Diego Fernando Pellegrino	31.03.1986	19	-
Defenders:			
Carlos Damián Casteglione	09.05.1980	9	-
Pablo Timoteo De Miranda	24.02.1986	8	-
Emir Saúl Faccioli	05.08.1989	7	-
Damián Alberto Martínez	31.01.1990	17	-
Carlos Javier Matheu	13.05.1984	7	-
Federico Maya	06.10.1993	-	-
Juan Andrés Tejera Arachichu (URU)	26.07.1983	14	-
Luciano Germán Vella	13.04.1981	10	-
Javier Orlando Yacuzzi	15.08.1979	9	1
Midfielders:			
Mariano Barbieri	29.11.1990	19	2
Leandro Rodrigo Becerra	26.01.1984	1	-
Marcelo Nicolás Benítez	13.01.1991	13	1
Miguel Nicolás Bertocchi	09.06.1989	14	1
Washington Fernando Camacho Martínez (URU)	08.04.1986	18	4
Brian Leonel Fernández	26.09.1994	14	4
Nicolás Emanuel Fernández	08.02.1996	-	-
Leandro Ariel Fioravanti	16.03.1992	5	-
Axel Fernando Juárez	29.07.1990	2	-
Leonardo Emanuel Landriel	14.07.1994	-	-
Nery Leyes	05.09.1989	13	-
Ciro Pablo Rius Aragallo	27.09.1984	19	1
Emilio Mathias Tellechea Zas (URU)	05.07.1987	12	2
Diego Sebastián Venturi	10.04.1993	-	-
Diego Nicolás Villar	25.04.1982	3	-
Diego Hernán Yacob	13.07.1991	6	-
Forwards:			
Kevin Emanuel Cassoratti	06.10.1996	-	-
Maximiliano Gauto González (PAR)	1995	-	-
Leandro González	14.10.1985	15	-
Julio César Rodríguez Giménez	05.12.1990	8	3
Trainer:			
Darío Javier Franco Gatti [as of 08.06.2014]	17.01.1969		

CLUB ESTUDIANTES DE LA PLATA

Foundation date: August 4, 1905
Address: Estudiantes La Plata, Avenida 53 Centro N°620 B1900BAZ, La Plata
Stadium: Estadio Ciudad de La Plata, La Plata - Capacity: 53,000

THE SQUAD

	DOB	M	G
Goalkeepers:			
Nahuel Hernán Losada	17.04.1993	-	-
Hilario Bernardo Navarro	14.11.1980	5	-
Agustín Silva	28.06.1989	14	-
Defenders:			
Matias Aguirregaray Guruceaga (URU)	01.04.1989	14	2
Leandro Desábato	24.01.1979	14	1
Ernesto Goñi Ameijenda (URU)	13.01.1985	9	1
Gabriel Maximiliano Graciani	28.11.1992	11	-
Maximiliano Fernando Oliva	16.03.1990	5	-
Matías Exequiel Orihuela Bonino	17.02.1992	2	-
Matías Isidoro Presentado	13.08.1992	15	-
Germán Davíd Ré	02.11.1981	8	-
Pablo Rosales	10.03.1992	10	-
Jonathan Ariel Schunke	22.02.1987	15	2
Luciano Andrés Vargas	28.01.1994	-	-
Midfielders:			
Leandro Damián Benítez	05.04.1981	5	-
Carlos Joaquín Correa	13.08.1994	15	2
Israel Alejandro Damonte	06.01.1982	5	-
Gastón Gil Romero	06.05.1993	12	-
Leonardo Rafael Jara	20.05.1991	15	-
Julián Augusto Marchioni	11.03.1993	1	-
Román Fernando Martínez	27.03.1983	12	2
Franco Piergiacomi	22.01.1992	-	-
Leonardo Sebastián Prediger	04.09.1986	15	-
Gabriel Nicolás Seijas	24.03.1994	1	-
Forwards:			
Federico Marcelo Anselmo	17.04.1994	1	-
Carlos Daniel Auzqui	16.09.1991	14	-
Mauricio Nicolás Carrasco	24.09.1987	6	-
Guido Marcelo Carrillo	25.05.1991	16	5
Ezequiel Cerutti	17.01.1992	16	2
Leonardo Fabián Marinucci	28.02.1993	1	-
Juan Manuel Olivera López (URU)	14.08.1981	-	-
Diego Daniel Vera Méndez (URU)	05.01.1985	16	4
Trainer:			
Mauricio Andrés Pellegrino [as of 10.04.2013]	05.10.1971	19	

CLUB DE GIMNASIA Y ESGRIMA LA PLATA

Foundation date: June 3, 1887
Address: Calle 4 N° 979, 1900 La Plata, Provincia de Buenos Aires
Stadium: Estadio "Juan Carmelo Zerillo", La Plata - Capacity: 24,544

THE SQUAD

	DOB	M	G
Goalkeepers:			
Yair Iván Bonnin	20.09.1990	-	-
Fernando Monetti	21.02.1989	19	-
Defenders:			
Osvaldo Rubén Barsottini	25.08.1981	16	1
Ezequiel Augusto Bonifacio Moreno	09.05.1994	9	-
Maximiliano Coronel	28.04.1989	5	-
Lucas Matías Licht	06.04.1981	18	2
Facundo Julián Oreja	14.06.1982	17	1
Oliver Páz Benítez	07.06.1991	13	-
Juan Leandro Quiroga	20.04.1982	12	-
Facundo Urquiza	10.06.1992		-
Midfielders:			
David Andrés Distéfano	10.07.1987	3	-
Álvaro Fernández Gay (URU)	11.10.1985	17	1
Ignacio Fernández	12.01.1990	17	1
Ariel Matías García	22.10.1991	2	-
Maximiliano Gorgerino	19.02.1993	1	-
Ignacio Jaúregui	02.08.1995	1	-
Ignacio Lachalde	06.05.1994	2	-
Javier Osvaldo Mendoza	02.09.1992	19	1
Maximiliano Eduardo Meza	15.12.1992	7	-
Dardo Federico Miloc	16.10.1990	16	-
Diego Oscar Nicolaievsky	20.04.1993	7	-
Juan Pablo Pocholo	15.04.1994	1	-
Omar Heber Pouso Osores (URU)	28.02.1980	12	-
Jorge Luis Rojas Meza (PAR)	07.01.1993	16	2
Forwards:			
Gustavo Leonardo Bou	18.02.1990	-	-
Walter Ariel Bou	25.08.1993	8	-
Nery Antonio Cardozo Escobar (PAR)	26.05.1989	9	-
Leandro Nicolás Contin	07.12.1995	-	-
Joaquín Romea	03.03.1993	-	-
Pablo Ezequiel Vegetti Pfaffen	15.10.1988	17	7
Trainer:			
Pedro Antonio Troglio	28.07.1965	19	

CLUB DEPORTIVO GODOY CRUZ

Foundation date: June 21, 1921
Address: Calle Balcarce 477, CP 5501 Godoy Cruz, Mendoza,
Stadium: Estadio Malvinas Argentinas, Mendoza - Capacity: 48,000

THE SQUAD

	DOB	M	G
Goalkeepers:			
Sebastián Emanuel Moyano	26.08.1990	19	-
Roberto Ramírez	07.07.1996	1	-
Rodrigo Rey	08.03.1991	-	-
Defenders:			
Juan Ignacio Alvacete	12.01.1991	4	-
Juan Manuel Barrera	28.06.1991	-	-
Esteban Rodrigo Burgos	09.01.1992	7	-
Lucas Esteban Ceballos Maiz	03.01.1987	18	-
Matías Gabriel Contreras	18.11.1994	-	-
Guillermo Cosaro	07.07.1989	13	2
Rolando García Guerreño (PAR)	10.02.1990	15	1
Ángel González	16.05.1994	-	-
Leandro Sebastián Olivares	15.05.1992	7	-
Sergio Ezequiel Velázquez	12.09.1990	5	-
Midfielders:			
Víctor Emanuel Aguilera	11.06.1989	4	-
Fabricio Angileri	15.03.1991	6	-
Claudio Ezequiel Aquino	24.07.1991	15	3
Gonzalo Gabriel Cabrera Giordano	15.01.1989	8	1
Jonathan Daniel Chávez	08.01.1989	2	-
Armando Enrique Cooper (PAN)	26.11.1987	1	-
José Luis Fernández	26.10.1987	15	1
Santiago Alejandro Gallucci Otero	08.03.1991	-	-
Emanuel García	08.07.1993	-	-
Daniel Alberto González	26.01.1991	13	-
Luis Jérez Silva	20.02.1989	9	1
Federico Eduardo Lértora	05.07.1990	9	-
Sergio Daniel López	04.01.1989	9	1
Gabriel Óscar Moyano Agüero	28.07.1992	-	-
Diego Martín Rodríguez Berrini (URU)	04.09.1989	18	1
Fernando Zuqui	27.11.1981	18	1
Forwards:			
Jaime Javier Ayoví Corozo (ECU)	21.02.1988	13	9
Leandro Miguel Fernández	12.03.1991	14	3
Juan Fernando Garro	24.11.1992	6	-
Rubén Darío Ramírez	17.10.1982	17	7
Rodrigo Javier Salinas	04.06.1986	-	-
Trainer:			
Carlos Alberto Mayor [18.07.-02.11.2014; Sacked]	05.10.1965	14	
Daniel Walter Oldrá [as of 03.11.2014]	15.03.1967	5	

CLUB ATLÉTICO INDEPENDIENTE AVELLANEDA

Foundation date: January 1, 1905
Address: Avenida Mitre 470, 1870 Avellaneda, Provincia de Buenos Aires
Stadium: Estadio "Libertadores de América", Avellaneda - Capacity: 52,853

THE SQUAD

	DOB	M	G
Goalkeepers:			
Facundo Andrés Daffonchio	02.02.1990	-	-
Alan Gustavo Depotte	18.05.1993	-	-
Marcelo Germán Montoya	23.01.1983	-	-
Diego Martín Rodríguez	25.06.1989	19	3
Defenders:			
Rafael Victoriano Barrios	23.05.1993	4	-
Néstor Ariel Breitenbruch	13.09.1995	9	-
Víctor Leandro Cuesta	19.11.1988	16	1
Sergio Daniel Escudero	12.04.1983	3	-
Nicolás Nicolás Figal	03.04.1994	13	-
Rodrigo Miguel Moreira	15.07.1996	1	-
Sergio Maximiliano Ojeda	04.01.1992	4	-
Juan Manuel Martínez Trejo	12.01.1992	-	-
Cristian Alberto Tula	28.01.1978	11	-
Gabriel Gustavo Vallés	31.05.1986	1	-
Julián Alberto Velázquez	23.10.1990	-	-
Lucas Villalba	19.08.1994	15	-
Alexis Joel Zárate	08.05.1994	12	1
Midfielders:			
Víctor Emanuel Aguilera	11.06.1989	5	-
Franco Bellocq	15.10.1993	13	-
Rodrigo Gómez	02.01.1993	4	-
Federico Insúa	03.01.1980	1	-
Juan Martín Lucero	30.11.1991	15	4
Federico Andrés Mancuello	26.03.1989	19	10
Jesús David José Méndez	01.08.1984	12	1
Leonel Ariel Miranda	07.01.1994	-	-
Fabián Ariel Monserrat	25.06.1992	-	-
Daniel Gastón Montenegro	28.03.1979	18	2
Cristian Jonatan Ortíz	20.08.1992	-	-
Guillermo Fabián Pereira	16.01.1994	-	-
Jorge Iván Pérez	23.05.1990		-
Matiás Pisano	13.12.1991	16	1
Marcelo Leonel Vidal	15.01.1991	5	-
Forwards:			
Martín Nicolás Benítez	17.06.1994	8	-
Jonathan José Cañete	12.07.1996	-	-
Maximiliano Francisco Herrera	08.01.1993	-	-
Cristian Jonatan Ortíz	22.09.1983	12	5
Francisco Andrés Pizzini	19.09.1993	14	1
Claudio Maximiliano Riaño	04.08.1988	13	2
Agustin Eloy Rodríguez	05.03.1993	-	-
Patricio Vidal	08.04.1992	-	-
Trainer:			
Jorge Francisco Almirón Quintana [as of 18.07.2014]	19.06.1971	19	

CLUB ATLÉTICO LANÚS

Foundation date: January 3, 1915
Address: Calle 9 de Julio N°1680, B1824KJL Lanús, Provincia de Buenos Aires
Stadium: Estadio Ciudad de Lanús „Néstor Díaz Pérez", Lanús - Capacity: 46,619

THE SQUAD			
	DOB	**M**	**G**
Goalkeepers:			
Aín Acosta Luna	09.09.1994	-	-
Nicolás Avellaneda	24.02.1993	-	-
Matías Alejandro Ibáñez Basualdo	16.12.1986	3	-
Agustín Federico Marchesín	16.03.1988	16	-
Defenders:			
Carlos Luciano Araujo	19.11.1981	19	-
César Gabriel Borda	19.04.1993	-	-
Diego Luis Braghieri	23.02.1987	15	-
Gustavo Raúl Gómez Portillo (PAR)	06.06.1993	15	-
Matías Alfredo Martínez	24.03.1988	5	1
Facundo Daniel Monteseirín	12.03.1995	6	-
Marcos Ariel Pinto	25.01.1994	1	-
Maximiliano Nicolás Velázquez	14.03.1980	13	-
Midfielders:			
Lautaro Germán Acosta	14.03.1988	18	5
Marcos Emanuel Astina	21.01.1996	3	-
Víctor Hugo Ayala Núñez (PAR)	01.01.1988	16	3
Iván Gonzalo Bella	13.09.1989	4	-
Óscar Junior Benítez	14.01.1993	12	-
Maximiliano Cáceres	08.05.1995	-	-
Walter Hernán Gallardo	24.01.1993	-	-
Diego Hernán González	09.02.1988	16	2
Juan Miguel Jaime	01.01.1993	-	-
Jorge Alberto Ortíz	20.06.1984	12	-
Nicolás Pasquini	01.02.1991	11	1
Leandro Daniel Somoza	26.01.1981	17	-
Jorge Vidal Valdéz Chamorro	26.05.1994	8	1
Forwards:			
Ignacio Bailone	20.01.1994	-	-
Lucas Santiago Melano	01.03.1993	9	-
Silvio Ezequiel Romero	22.07.1988	19	11
Andrés Leonardo Sena	30.11.1990	-	-
Santiago Martín Silva Olivera (URU)	09.12.1980	18	1
Trainer:			
Guillermo Barros Schelotto [as of 01.07.2012]	04.05.1973	19	

CLUB ATLÉTICO NEWELL'S OLD BOYS ROSARIO

Foundation date: November 3, 1903
Address: Parque de la Independencia 2000, Rosario, Santa Fe
Stadium: Estadio „Marcelo Bielsa", Rosario - Capacity: 38,095

THE SQUAD

	DOB	M	G
Goalkeepers:			
Lucas Adrián Hoyos	29.04.1989	1	-
Óscar Alfredo Ustari	03.07.1986	19	-
Defenders:			
Enzo Beloso	20.02.1994	-	-
Marcos Antonio Cáceres Centurión (PAR)	05.05.1986	7	-
Gastón Claudio Corvalán	23.03.1989	10	-
Cristian Alberto Díaz	26.05.1989	15	-
Franco Nicolás Escobar	21.02.1995	-	-
Lorenzo Abel Faravelli	29.03.1993	11	1
Leandro Sebastián Fernández	30.01.1983	19	1
Leonel Hernán González	15.03.1994	-	-
Víctor Rubén López	19.12.1978	16	2
Guillermo Luis Ortíz	09.08.1992	6	-
Maximiliano Iván Pollachi	04.01.1995	-	-
Carlos Leonel Torres	20.10.1994	-	-
Jonathan Nahuel Valle	26.01.1993	-	-
Midfielders:			
José Vicente Agüero	22.02.1993	-	-
Lucas Ademar Bernardi	27.09.1977	19	-
Facundo Nicolás Bustamente	05.11.1995	3	-
Milton Óscar Casco	11.04.1988	11	-
Alexis Nicolás Castro	23.01.1984	3	-
Victor Alberto Figueroa	29.09.1983	16	-
Eugenio Horacio Isnaldo	07.01.1994	5	-
Diego Mateo Alustiza	07.08.1978	9	-
Fabián Nicolás Muñoz	03.11.1991	3	-
Horacio De Dios Orzán	14.04.1988	8	-
Maximiliano Rubén Rodríguez	02.01.1981	17	11
Iván Silva Ezequiel	22.01.1994	3	-
Martín Tonso	19.10.1989	7	-
Juan Ignacio Vieyra	20.04.1992	4	-
Raúl Hernán Villalba	30.11.1989	14	-
Forwards:			
Hernán Alexis Altolaguirre	19.02.1993	-	-
Leandro Figueroa	28.03.1993	3	-
Francisco David Fydriszewski	13.04.1993	7	-
Lucas Nicolás Giovagnoli	04.02.1994	-	-
Ezequiel Ponce	29.03.1997	2	-
Ignacio Martín Scocco	29.05.1985	12	3
Mauricio Tévez	31.07.1996	15	2
Trainer:			
Gustavo Daniel Raggio [as of 10.06.2014]	27.10.1971	19	

CLUB OLIMPO DE BAHÍA BLANCA

Foundation date: October 15, 1910
Address: Calle Sarmiento 52, 8000 Bahía Blanca, Provincia de Buenos Aires
Stadium: Estadio "Roberto Natalio Carminatti", Bahía Blanca - Capacity: 20,000

THE SQUAD

	DOB	M	G
Goalkeepers:			
Nereo Champagne	20.01.1985	19	-
Ignacio Torres	01.11.1993	-	-
Ezequiel Héctor Viola	01.09.1987	-	-
Defenders:			
David Eduardo Achucarro Trinidad	05.01.1991	5	-
Emanuel Bilbao	03.11.1989	-	-
Iván Alejandro Furios	20.05.1979	15	-
Adrián Nahuel Martínez	13.02.1992	16	3
Néstor Emanuel Moiraghi	19.04.1985	17	1
Lucas Ezequiel Orozco	15.04.1995	-	-
Ezequiel Jonathan Oscar Parnisari	01.06.1990	9	-
Juan Ignacio Sills	04.05.1987	18	1
Cristian Damián Villanueva	25.12.1983	16	-
Midfielders:			
Jonathan Matías Blanco	29.04.1987	16	4
Juan Manuel Cobo Gálvez	26.11.1984	12	1
Orlando Gabriel Gaona Lugo (PAR)	25.07.1990	12	-
Leonardo Roque Albano Gil	31.05.1991	18	-
José Roberto Lincopán	25.08.1991	2	-
Jacobo Guillermo Mansilla	15.06.1987	10	-
Gustavo Andrés Oberman	25.03.1985	-	-
Juan Manuel Olivares	14.07.1988	12	-
Alejandro Otero	06.07.1993	1	-
Diego Sosa	24.10.1991	2	-
Davíd Alejandro Vega	17.11.1980	11	-
Forwards:			
Miguel Ángel Borja Hernández (COL)	26.01.1993	16	3
Mauricio Andrés Cuero Castillo (COL)	28.01.1993	17	1
Javier Walter Soñer	19.03.1995	-	-
Joaquín Susvielles	28.01.1991	5	-
Gabriel Carlos Tellas	10.08.1992	-	-
Lucas Leonel Vera Piris	02.01.1994	-	-
Norberto Ezequiel Vidal	02.08.1995	5	-
Agustin Vuletich	03.11.1991	9	1
Trainer:			
Walter Osvaldo Perazzo Otero [as of 05.04.2012]	02.08.1962	19	

QUILMES ATLÉTICO CLUB

Year of Formation: November 27, 1897
Address: Calle Guido y Calle General Paz 1878, Quilmes, Provincia de Buenos Aires
Stadium: Estadio Centenario „Dr. José Luis Meiszner“, Quilmes - Capacity: 30,200

THE SQUAD			
	DOB	**M**	**G**
Goalkeepers:			
Walter Daniel Benítez	19.01.1993	13	-
Silvio Marcos Dulcich Arias	01.10.1981	6	-
Marcos Ignacio Ledesma	15.09.1996	-	-
Defenders:			
Alan Alegre	03.02.1991	11	1
Leonardo Ramón Alvarado	28.02.1992	-	-
Leonel Bontempo	01.11.1992	14	-
Christopher Alejandro Cabral	03.08.1993	1	-
Mauro Joel Carli	19.10.1986	15	-
Brian Federico Cucco Ballarini	22.01.1989	3	-
Sebastián Rodrigo Martínez Aguirre (URU)	11.04.1983	13	1
Lucas Suárez	17.03.1995	10	-
Midfielders:			
Rodrigo Braña	07.03.1979	9	-
Nicolás Alejandro Cabrera	05.06.1984	13	-
Emiliano Carrasco	29.05.1992	11	1
Franco Emmanuel Cáseres	04.03.1993	3	-
Arnaldo González	13.05.1989	10	1
Nicolás Mauricio López	18.03.1994	13	1
Santiago Gabriel Martínez Pintos (URU)	30.07.1991	7	-
Matías Morales	05.07.1991	4	-
Lucas Emmanuel Pérez Godoy	30.06.1993	3	-
Sebastián Ariel Romero Salvatore	27.04.1978	13	-
Brian Óscar Sarmiento	22.04.1990	12	3
Adrián Miguel Scifo	10.10.1987	12	1
Jonathan Fabián Zacaría	06.02.1990	16	1
Forwards:			
Flavio Germán Ciampichetti	07.03.1988	-	-
Leonel Maximiliano Demelchori	08.12.1994	1	-
Diego Gaspar Diellos	24.09.1993	-	-
Néstor Adrián Fernández Palacios	04.08.1992	15	2
Sergio Gabriel Hipperdinger	30.10.1989	7	-
Francisco Ilarregui	06.05.1997	4	1
Gonzalo Martín Klusener	21.101.983	19	4
Miguel Eduardo Montaño Bejarano (COL)	25.06.1991	3	-
Lucas Giuliano Passerini	16.07.1994	1	-
Genaro Vuanello	02.02.1992	1	-
Trainer:			
Pablo Javier Quatrocchi [09.06.-05.12.2014]	19.01.1974	19	

RACING CLUB DE AVELLANEDA

Foundation date: March 25, 1903
Address: Avenida Presidente Bartolome Mitre N°934, B1870AAW Avellaneda
Stadium: Estadio „Presidente Juan Domingo Perón", Avellaneda - Capacity: 51,389

THE SQUAD	DOB	M	G
Goalkeepers:			
Nelson Martín Ibáñez	13.11.1980	2	-
Juan Agustín Musso	06.05.1994	-	-
Diego Sebastián Saja	05.06.1979	18	-
Defenders:			
Nelson Fernando Acevedo	11.07.1988	14	-
Yonathan Emanuel Cabral	10.05.1992	16	-
Gastón Matías Campi	06.04.1991	1	-
Ricardo Gastón Díaz	13.03.1988	19	1
Alejandro García	26.02.1991	-	-
José Luis Gómez	13.09.1993	-	-
Leandro Damián Marcelo Grimi	09.02.1985	17	-
Luciano Lollo	29.03.1987	19	1
Matías Alfredo Martínez	24.03.1988	-	-
Iván Alexis Pillud	24.04.1986	12	-
Nicolás Gabriel Sánchez	04.02.1986	6	-
Esteban Ariel Saveljich	20.05.1991	-	-
Germán Ariel Voboril	05.05.1987	3	-
Midfielders:			
Marcos Javier Acuña	28.10.1991	16	2
Pablo Andrés Alvarado	27.02.1986	-	-
Luciano Román Aued	01.03.1987	16	-
Mauro Bazán	27.04.1993	-	-
Adrián Ricardo Centurión	19.01.1993	17	3
Francisco Cerro	09.02.1988	6	-
Ezequiel Alejandro Melillo	05.08.1993	-	-
Nicolás Adrián Oroz	01.04.1994	3	-
Matías Peréz Guedes	18.08.1991	-	-
Michael Leonel Pierce	28.07.1993	-	-
Ezequiel Videla Greppi	19.01.1987	17	-
Diego Nicolás Villar	25.04.1982	5	-
Forwards:			
Gustavo Leonardo Bou	18.02.1990	15	10
Facundo Andrés Castillón	21.08.1985	9	1
Facundo Alfredo Castro	28.02.1996	2	-
Gabriel Agustín Hauche	27.11.1986	13	5
Guillermo Fernando Hauche	31.03.1993	1	-
Diego Alberto Milito	12.06.1979	17	6
Wason Liberado Rentería Cuesta (COL)	04.07.1985	2	-
Trainer:			
Diego Martín Cocca [as of 08.06.2014]	02.11.1972	19	

CLUB ATLÉTICO RIVER PLATE

Foundation date: May 25, 1901
Address: Av. Presidente José Figueroa Alcorta 7597, Núñez 1428, Capital Federal, Buenos Aires
Stadium: Estadio Monumental „Antonio Vespucio Liberti", Buenos Aires - Capacity: 64,000

THE SQUAD			
	DOB	**M**	**G**
Goalkeepers:			
Marcelo Alberto Barovero	18.02.1984	18	-
Julio César Chiarini	04.03.1982	2	-
Nicolás Rodríguez	12.05.1993	-	-
Defenders:			
Éder Fabián Álvarez Balanta (COL)	28.02.1993	2	-
Víctor Cabrera	07.02.1993	-	-
José Ramiro Funes Mori	05.03.1991	17	2
Jonathan Ramón Maidana	29.04.1985	15	-
Emanuel Mammana	10.02.1996	2	-
Gabriel Iván Mercado	18.03.1987	16	1
Germán Alejo Pezzela	27.06.1991	10	1
Bruno Saúl Urribarri	06.11.1986	2	-
Leandro Vega	27.05.1996	-	-
Midfielders:			
Emiliano Germán Agüero	21.01.1995	-	-
Martín Sebastián Aguirre	14.09.1981	-	-
Adrián Ezequiel Cirigliano	24.01.1992	2	-
Osmar Daniel Ferreyra	09.01.1983	5	-
Claudio Matías Kranevitter	21.05.1993	6	-
Tomás Martínez	07.03.1995	8	-
Leonardo Nicolás Pisculichi	18.01.1984	16	5
Leonardo Daniel Ponzio	29.01.1982	10	-
Guido Rodríguez	12.04.1994	7	-
Ariel Mauricio Rojas	16.01.1986	16	2
Carlos Andrés Sánchez Arcosa	02.12.1984	16	5
Augusto Jorge Mateo Solari	03.01.1992	10	-
Leonel Jesús Vangioni	05.05.1987	15	1
Forwards:			
Lucas Boyé	28.02.1996	17	1
Fernando Ezequiel Cavenaghi	21.09.1983	3	2
Sebastián Driussi	09.02.1996	10	-
Teófilo Antonio Gutiérrez Roncancio (COL)	27.05.1985	13	10
Juan Cruz Kaprof	12.03.1995	2	-
Rodrigo Nicanor Mora Núñez (URU)	29.10.1987	17	4
Giovanni Pablo Simeone	05.07.1995	7	-
Trainer:			
Marcelo Daniel Gallardo [as of 06.06.2014]	18.01.1976	19	

CLUB ATLÉTICO ROSARIO CENTRAL

Foundation date: December 24, 1889
Address: Calle 4 N° 979, 1900 La Plata, Provincia de Buenos Aires
Stadium: Estadio "Dr. Lisandro de la Torre" [Gigante de Arroyito], Rosario - Capacity: 41,654

THE SQUAD	DOB	M	G
Goalkeepers:			
Maurico Ariel Caranta	31.07.1978	18	-
Juan Manuel García	08.07.1988	1	-
Jeremías Ledesma	13.02.1993	-	-
Defenders:			
Lucas Acevedo	08.11.1991	9	2
Tomás Berra	19.02.1991	13	-
Franco Emanuel Cervi	26.05.1994	3	-
Rafael Marcelo Delgado	13.01.1990	14	2
Alejandro César Donatti	24.10.1986	13	-
Paulo Andrés Ferrari	04.01.1982	18	-
Elias José Gómez	09.06.1994	7	-
Yeimar Pastor Gómez Andrade (COL)	30.06.1992	4	-
Fernando Piñero	16.02.1993	1	-
Nahuel Quiroga	05.08.1991	-	-
Midfielders:			
Leonel Jonás Aguirre Avalo	05.03.1992	15	-
Fernando Omar Barrientos	17.11.1991	17	1
Hernán Nicolás Da Campo	06.08.1994	2	-
Nery Andrés Domínguez	09.04.1990	12	1
Hernán Nicolás Encina	03.11.1982	10	-
Jesús Alfredo Fared	25.03.1994	1	-
Federico Jesús Flores	18.05.1992	-	-
Maximiliano David González	12.03.1994	-	-
Lucas Lazo Benítez	31.01.1989	2	1
Walter Iván Montoya	21.07.1993	8	-
Damián Marcelo Musto	09.06.1987	16	1
Víctor Ezequiel Salazar	26.05.1993	2	-
Forwards:			
Washington Sebastián Abreu Gallo (URU)	17.10.1976	11	1
Walter Rubén Acuña	04.03.1992	10	3
Pablo Ignacio Becker	29.04.1992	16	-
Marcelo Javier Correa	23.10.1992	3	-
Antonio César Medina	18.12.1984	11	1
Rodrigo Javier Migone	06.06.1996	2	-
Franco Niell	22.05.1983	12	4
José Adolfo Valencia Arrechea (COL)	18.12.1991	14	4
Trainer:			
Miguel Ángel Russo [06.07.2012-28.11.2014; Resigned]	09.04.1956	18	
Hugo Aníbal Galloni [as of 28.11.2014]	15.06.1965	1	

CLUB ATLÉTICO SAN LORENZO DE ALMAGRO

Foundation date: April 1, 1908
Address: Calle Varela N°2680 C1437BJH, Cd. Buenos Aires
Stadium: Estadio „Pedro Bidegain", Nueva Pompeya, Buenos Aires - Capacity: 39,494

THE SQUAD

	DOB	M	G
Goalkeepers:			
Leonardo Neoren Franco	20.05.1977	-	-
Sebastián Alberto Torrico	22.02.1980	19	-
Defenders:			
Ramiro Arias	06.01.1993	2	-
Matías Catalán	19.08.1992	9	-
Mauro Cetto	14.04.1982	9	1
Fabricio Bautista Fontanini	30.03.1990	7	-
Emanuel Matías Más	15.01.1989	19	1
Gonzalo Sebastián Prósperi	03.06.1985	5	-
Facundo Tomás Quignón	02.05.1993	3	-
Mario Alberto Yepes Díaz (COL)	13-01.1976	6	-
Midfielders:			
Alejandro Brian Barbaro	20.01.1992	-	-
Pablo Cesar Barrientos	17.01.1985	11	1
Julio Alberto Buffarini	18.08.1988	17	1
Juan Ignacio Cavallaro	28.06.1994	8	1
Gabriel Esparza	30.01.1993	2	-
Enzo Kalinski	10.03.1987	14	1
Walter Kanneman	14.03.1991	18	-
Juan Ignacio Mercier	02.02.1980	15	1
Claudio Matías Mirabaje Correa (URU)	06.03.1989	-	-
Leandro Alexis Navarro	16.03.1992	-	-
Néstor Ezequiel Ortigoza (PAR)	07.10.1984	14	6
Leandro Atilio Romagnoli	17.03.1981	8	-
Forwards:			
Nicolás Blandi	13.01.1990	14	-
Martín Cauteruccio Rodríguez (URU)	14.04.1987	18	3
Rodrigo Contreras	27.10.1995	-	-
Mauro Matos	06.08.1982	15	4
Gonzalo Alberto Verón	24.12.1989	15	2
Héctor Villalba	26.07.1994	15	3
Trainer:			
Edgardo Bauza [as of 26.12.2013]	26.01.1958	19	

CLUB ATLÉTICO TIGRE VICTORIA

Foundation date: August 3, 1902
Address: Guido Spano 1053 y Presidente Perón, Victoria 1644 , San Fernando, Prov. de Buenos Aires
Stadium: Estadio „José Dellagiovanna“ [Monumental de Victoria], Victoria - Capacity: 26,282

THE SQUAD

	DOB	M	G
Goalkeepers:			
Javier Hernán García	29.01.1987	19	-
Nicolás Gastón Navarro	25.03.1985	-	-
Defenders:			
Juan Carlos Blengio	26.06.1980	19	1
Ignacio Bonadio	27.07.1993	1	-
Pablo Domingo Cáceres Rodríguez (URU)	22.04.1985	15	-
Ignacio Canuto	20.02.1986	17	-
Erik Fernando Godoy	16.08.1993	16	1
Santiago Izaguirre	30.07.1994	-	-
Nicolás Pantaleone	18.02.1993	1	-
Sebastián Ariel Silguero	01.01.1992	1	-
Lucas Vesco	28.01.1991	-	-
Midfielders:			
Walter Aníbal Acevedo	16.02.1986	6	-
Joaquín Arzura	18.05.1993	17	1
Facundo Daniel Bertoglio	30.06.1990	14	2
Emiliano Nahuel Ellacopoulos	14.01.1992	3	-
Martín Sebastián Galmarini	28.02.1982	16	-
Kevin Fabián Emiliano Itabel	20.08.1993	17	3
Lucas Janson	16.08.1994	2	-
Lucas Ariel Menossi	11.07.1992	3	-
Gabriel Martín Peñalba	23.09.1984	17	2
Sebastián Rusculleda	28.04.1985	3	-
Facundo Sánchez	07.03.1990	10	2
Pablo Ernesto Vitti	09.07.1985	7	2
Lucas Daniel Wilchez	31.08.1983	18	3
Forwards:			
Leandro Julián Garate	02.09.1993	7	2
Leandro Leguizamón	04.12.1988	5	-
Carlos Ariel Luna	17.01.1982	18	7
Sebastián Rincón Lucumí (COL)	14.01.1994	15	4
Trainer:			
Fabián Leonardo Alegre [10.09.2013-01.09.2014]	28.08.1966	5	
Gustavo Julio Alfaro [as of 05.09.2014]	14.08.1962	14	

CLUB ATLÉTICO VÉLEZ SÁRSFIELD BUENOS AIRES

Foundation date: January 1, 1910
Address: Avenida Dr. Juan Bautista Justo N°9200, C1408AKU, Ciudad de Buenos Aires
Stadium: Estadio „José Amalfitani", Buenos Aires - Capacity: 49,540

THE SQUAD			
	DOB	**M**	**G**
Goalkeepers:			
Alan Joaquín Aguerre	23.08.1990		-
Carlos Sebastián Sosa Silva (URU)	19.08.1986	19	-
Gonzalo Javier Yordán	20.03.1994		-
Defenders:			
Emiliano Javier Amor	16.05.1995	2	-
Facundo Cardozo	06.04.1995	11	-
Sebastián Enrique Domínguez	29.07.1980	18	1
Lautaro Daniel Gianetti	13.11.1993	-	-
Fausto Grillo	20.02.1993	4	-
Eric Emmanuel Jeréz	20.08.1994	-	-
Matías Pérez Acuña	09.02.1994	12	-
Gonzalo Rubén Piovi	08.09.1994	-	-
Leonardo Gabriel Rolón	19.01.1995	16	1
Midfielders:			
Yamil Rodrigo Asad	27.07.1994	13	-
Alejandro Ariel Cabral	11.09.1987	17	-
Iván Chacón	06.12.1994	-	-
Lucio Compagnucci	23.02.1996	1	-
Jorge Iván Correa	04.05.1993	9	1
Fabián Andrés Cubero	21.12.1978	16	1
Leandro Luis Desábato	30.03.1990	12	-
Brian Federico Ferreira	24.05.1994	11	1
Tiago Flores	07.05.1995	1	-
Sebastián Alejandro Martelli	13.03.1996	4	-
Emiliano Ramiro Papa	19.04.1982	19	-
Lucas Daniel Romero	18.04.1994	16	1
Jairo David Vélez Cedeño (COL)	21.04.1995	1	-
Leandro Vera	21.02.1994	1	-
Leonardo Enrique Villalba	29.09.1994	4	-
Forwards:			
Milton Joel Caraglio	01.12.1988	19	2
Ramiro Julián Cáseres	09.01.1994	10	1
Roberto Antonio Nanni	20.08.1981	6	-
Lucas David Pratto	04.06.1988	17	11
Federico Nahuel Vázquez	31.03.1993	3	-
Trainer:			
José Oscar Flores [as of 26.12.2013]	16.05.1971	19	

SECOND LEVEL
Primera B Nacional 2014

Zone A

1.	CA Colón de Santa Fé (*Promoted*)	20	8	7	5	25 - 15	31
2.	CA San Martín de San Juan (*Promoted*)	20	9	4	7	21 - 12	31
3.	AA Argentinos Juniors Buenos Aires (*Promoted*)	20	9	4	7	17 - 14	31
4.	CA Nueva Chicago Mataderos (*Promotion Play-off*)	20	7	9	4	20 - 16	30
5.	CA Aldovisi Mar del Plata (*Promotion Play-off*)	20	8	6	6	21 - 18	30
6.	CA Gymnasia y Esgrima de Jujuy (*Promotion Play-off*)	20	7	9	4	19 - 16	30
7.	CA Boca Unidos Corrientes	20	7	6	7	18 - 20	27
8.	Instituto Atlético Central Córdoba	20	6	7	7	23 - 27	25
9.	CA Douglas Haig Pergamino	20	6	7	7	16 - 21	25
10.	CD Guaraní Antonio Franco Posadas	20	4	6	10	16 - 27	18
11.	Club Ferro Carril Oeste Buenos Aires	20	3	7	10	11 - 21	16

Zone A Promotion Play-off:

1.	CA Nueva Chicago Mataderos (*Promoted*)	2	1	1	0	1 - 0	4
2.	CA Aldovisi Mar del Plata (*Promoted*)	2	1	1	0	1 - 0	4
3.	CA Gymnasia y Esgrima de Jujuy	2	0	0	2	0 - 2	0

Zone B

1.	CA Unión de Santa Fé (*Promoted*)	20	12	5	3	33 - 16	41
2.	Club Mutual Crucero del Norte Garupá (*Promoted*)	20	10	3	7	22 - 14	33
3.	CA Temperley (*Promoted*)	20	10	2	8	22 - 26	32
4.	CA Sarmiento Junín (*Promoted*)	20	7	9	4	22 - 17	30
5.	CA Tucumán San Miguel (*Promotion Play-off*)	20	8	5	7	27 - 21	29
6.	CA Huracán Buenos Aires (*Promotion Play-off*)	20	8	5	7	26 - 21	29
7.	Club y Biblioteca Ramón Santamarina Tandil	20	6	6	8	21 - 27	24
8.	CA Patronato de la Juventud Católica Paraná	20	5	7	8	15 - 18	22
9.	CS Independiente Rivadavia Mendoza	20	6	4	10	16 - 22	22
10.	CA All Boys Buenos Aires	20	5	7	8	11 - 20	22
11.	Sportivo Belgrano San Francisco	20	4	5	11	18 - 31	17

Zone B Promotion Play-off:

14.12.2014, Estadio Malvinas Argentinas, Mendoza; Referee: Germán Raúl Delfino
CA Huracán Buenos Aires - CA Tucumán San Miguel 4-1(0-0,1-1)
CA Huracán Buenos Aires promoted to the 2015 Primera División.

NATIONAL TEAM
INTERNATIONAL MATCHES
(16.07.2014 – 15.07.2015)

03.09.2014	Düsseldirf	Germany - Argentina	2-4(0-2)	(F)
11.10.2014	Beijing	Brazil - Argentina	2-0(1-0)	(F)
14.10.2014	Hong Kong	Hong Kong - Argentina	0-7(0-3)	(F)
12.11.2014	London	Argentina - Croatia	2-1(0-1)	(F)
18.11.2014	Manchester	Argentina - Portugal	0-1(0-0)	(F)
28.03.2015	Landover	El Salvador - Argentina	0-2(0-0)	(F)
31.03.2015	East Rutherford	Argentina - Ecuador	2-1(1-1)	(F)
06.06.2015	San Juan	Argentina - Bolivia	5-0(3-0)	(F)
13.06.2015	La Serena	Argentina - Paraguay	2-2(2-0)	(CA)
16.06.2015	LA Serena	Argentina – Uruguay	1-0(0-0)	(CA)
20.06.2015	Viña del Mar	Argentina - Jamaica	1-0(1-0)	(CA)
24.06.2015	Viña del Mar	Argentina – Colombia	5-4 pen	(CA)
29.06.2015	Concepción	Argentina - Paraguay	6-1(2-1)	(CA)
04.07.2015	Santiago	Chile - Argentina	4-1 pen	(CA)

03.09.2014, Friendly International
Esprit Arena, Düsseldorf; Attendance: 51,132
Referee: Björn Kuipers (Netherlands)

GERMANY - ARGENTINA **2-4(0-2)**

ARG: Sergio Germán Romero (80.Mariano Gonzalo Andújar), Pablo Javier Zabaleta Girod (77.Hugo Armando Campagnaro), Martín Gastón Demichelis, Federico Fernández, Faustino Marcos Alberto Rojo, Javier Alejandro Mascherano, Lucas Rodrigo Biglia, Enzo Nicolás Pérez (46.Augusto Matías Fernández), Ángel Fabián Di María Hernández (86.Ricardo Gabriel Álvarez), Sergio Leonel Agüero del Castillo (83.Osvaldo Nicolás Fabián Gaitán), Érik Manuel Lamela (68.Fernando Rubén Gago). Trainer: Gerardo Daniel Martino.
Goals: Sergio Leonel Agüero del Castillo (20), Érik Manuel Lamela (40), Federico Fernández (47), Ángel Fabián Di María Hernández (50).

11.10.2014, Friendly International
Beijing National Stadium, Beijing (China P.R.); Attendance: 52,313
Referee: Fan Qi (China P.R.)

BRAZIL - ARGENTINA **2-0(1-0)**

ARG: Sergio Germán Romero, Pablo Javier Zabaleta Girod, Martín Gastón Demichelis, Federico Fernández, Faustino Marcos Alberto Rojo, Javier Alejandro Mascherano, Ángel Fabián Di María Hernández, Roberto Maximiliano Pereyra (76.Enzo Nicolás Pérez), Lionel Andrés Messi, Sergio Leonel Agüero del Castillo (61.Gonzalo Gerardo Higuaín), Érik Manuel Lamela (61.Javier Matías Pastore). Trainer: Gerardo Daniel Martino.

14.10.2014, Friendly International
Hong Kong Stadium, Hong Kong; Attendance: 20,230
Referee: Yuichi Nishimura (Japan)

HONG KONG - ARGENTINA **0-7(0-3)**

ARG: Nahuel Ignacio Guzmán (46.Agustín Federico Marchesín), Facundo Sebastián Roncaglia (60.Pablo Javier Zabaleta Girod), Nicolás Hernán Gonzalo Otamendi, Santiago Vergini, Fernando Rubén Gago (73.Javier Alejandro Mascherano), Enzo Nicolás Pérez (73.Roberto Maximiliano Pereyra), Leonel Jesús Vangioni, Osvaldo Nicolás Fabián Gaitán (73.Ángel Fabián Di María Hernández), Javier Matías Pastore (60.Lionel Andrés Messi), Éver Maximiliano David Banega, Gonzalo Gerardo Higuaín. Trainer: Gerardo Daniel Martino.
Goals: Éver Maximiliano David Banega (19), Gonzalo Gerardo Higuaín (42), Osvaldo Nicolás Fabián

Gaitán (44), Gonzalo Gerardo Higuaín (54), Lionel Andrés Messi (66), Osvaldo Nicolás Fabián Gaitán (72), Lionel Andrés Messi (84).

12.11.2014, Friendly International
Boleyn Ground, London (England); Attendance: 12,000
Referee: Andre Marriner (England)
ARGENTINA - CROATIA 2-1(0-1)
ARG: Sergio Germán Romero, Pablo Javier Zabaleta Girod, Cristian Daniel Ansaldi (77.Jonathan Cristian Silva), Federico Julián Fazio, Santiago Vergini, Javier Alejandro Mascherano, Enzo Nicolás Pérez, Ángel Fabián Di María Hernández (77.Érik Manuel Lamela), Éver Maximiliano David Banega (71.Roberto Maximiliano Pereyra), Lionel Andrés Messi, Sergio Leonel Agüero del Castillo (62.Carlos Alberto Martínez Tévez). Trainer: Gerardo Daniel Martino.
Goals: Cristian Daniel Ansaldi (49), Lionel Andrés Messi (57 penalty).

18.11.2014, Friendly International
Old Trafford, Manchester (England); Attendance: 41,233
Referee: Martin Atkinson (England)
ARGENTINA - PORTUGAL 0-1(0-0)
ARG: Nahuel Ignacio Guzmán, Martín Gastón Demichelis, Facundo Sebastián Roncaglia, Cristian Daniel Ansaldi (73.Jonathan Cristian Silva), Nicolás Hernán Gonzalo Otamendi, Javier Alejandro Mascherano, Lucas Rodrigo Biglia, Ángel Fabián Di María Hernández (61.Érik Manuel Lamela), Javier Matías Pastore (73.Roberto Maximiliano Pereyra), Lionel Andrés Messi (46.Osvaldo Nicolás Fabián Gaitán), Gonzalo Gerardo Higuaín (61.Carlos Alberto Martínez Tévez). Trainer: Gerardo Daniel Martino.

28.03.2015, Friendly International
Fedex Field, Landover (United States); Attendance: 53,968
Referee: Mario Alberto Escobar Toca (Guatemala)
EL SALVADOR - ARGENTINA 0-2(0-0)
ARG: Nahuel Ignacio Guzmán, Pablo Javier Zabaleta Girod, Mateo Pablo Musacchio, Lucas Alfonso Orbán, Ramiro Funes Mori, Ángel Fabián Di María Hernández (73.Federico Andrés Mancuello), Éver Maximiliano David Banega, Roberto Maximiliano Pereyra, Carlos Alberto Martínez Tévez (78.Javier Matías Pastore), Gonzalo Gerardo Higuaín, Ezequiel Iván Lavezzi. Trainer: Gerardo Daniel Martino.
Goals: Néstor Raúl Renderos López (54 own goal), Federico Andrés Mancuello (88).

31.03.2015, Friendly International
MetLife Stadium, East Rutherford (United States); Attendance: 48,000
Referee: Silviu Petrescu (Canada)
ARGENTINA - ECUADOR 2-1(1-1)
ARG: Sergio Germán Romero, Ezequiel Marcelo Garay González, Facundo Sebastián Roncaglia, Nicolás Hernán Gonzalo Otamendi, Faustino Marcos Alberto Rojo, Javier Alejandro Mascherano, Lucas Rodrigo Biglia, Ángel Fabián Di María Hernández (79.Ezequiel Iván Lavezzi), Javier Matías Pastore (79.Éver Maximiliano David Banega), Federico Andrés Mancuello (46.Roberto Maximiliano Pereyra), Sergio Leonel Agüero del Castillo (75.Carlos Alberto Martínez Tévez). Trainer: Gerardo Daniel Martino.
Goals: Sergio Leonel Agüero del Castillo (8), Javier Matías Pastore (58).

06.06.2015, Friendly International
Estadio San Juan del Bicentenario, San Juan; Attendance: 18,000
Referee: Jorge Luis Osorio Reyes (Chile)
ARGENTINA - BOLIVIA 5-0(3-0)
ARG: Sergio Germán Romero (46.Nahuel Ignacio Guzmán), Ezequiel Marcelo Garay González, Facundo Sebastián Roncaglia (60.Milton Óscar Casco), Nicolás Hernán Gonzalo Otamendi (60.Martín Gastón Demichelis), Faustino Marcos Alberto Rojo, Fernando Rubén Gago, Ángel Fabián Di María Hernández, Javier Matías Pastore, Éver Maximiliano David Banega, Sergio Leonel Agüero del Castillo (60.Gonzalo Gerardo Higuaín), Ezequiel Iván Lavezzi (60.Érik Manuel Lamela). Trainer: Gerardo Daniel Martino.
Goals: Ángel Fabián Di María Hernández (25), Sergio Leonel Agüero del Castillo (29 penalty, 31, 51), Ángel Fabián Di María Hernández (55 penalty).

13.06.2015, 44th Copa América, Group Stage
Estadio La Portada, La Serena (Chile); Attendance: 16,281
Referee: Wilmar Alexander Roldán Pérez (Colombia)
ARGENTINA - PARAGUAY 2-2(2-0)
ARG: Sergio Germán Romero, Ezequiel Marcelo Garay González, Facundo Sebastián Roncaglia, Nicolás Hernán Gonzalo Otamendi, Faustino Marcos Alberto Rojo, Javier Alejandro Mascherano, Ángel Fabián Di María Hernández, Javier Matías Pastore (75.Carlos Alberto Martínez Tévez), Éver Maximiliano David Banega (80.Lucas Rodrigo Biglia), Lionel Andrés Messi, Sergio Leonel Agüero del Castillo (76.Gonzalo Gerardo Higuaín). Trainer: Gerardo Daniel Martino.
Goals: Sergio Leonel Agüero del Castillo (28), Lionel Andrés Messi (35 penalty).

16.06.2015, 44th Copa América, Group Stage
Estadio La Portada, La Serena (Chile); Attendance: 17,014
Referee: Sandro Meira Ricci (Brazil)
ARGENTINA – URUGUAY 1-0(0-0)
ARG: Sergio Germán Romero, Pablo Javier Zabaleta Girod, Ezequiel Marcelo Garay González, Nicolás Hernán Gonzalo Otamendi, Faustino Marcos Alberto Rojo, Javier Alejandro Mascherano, Lucas Rodrigo Biglia, Ángel Fabián Di María Hernández (89.Roberto Maximiliano Pereyra), Javier Matías Pastore (79.Éver Maximiliano David Banega), Lionel Andrés Messi, Sergio Leonel Agüero del Castillo (82.Carlos Alberto Martínez Tévez). Trainer: Gerardo Daniel Martino.
Goal: Sergio Leonel Agüero del Castillo (56).

20.06.2015, 44th Copa América, Group Stage
Estadio Sausalito, Viña del Mar (Chile); Attendance: 21,083
Referee: Julio Bascuñán (Chile)
ARGENTINA - JAMAICA 1-0(1-0)
ARG: Sergio Germán Romero, Pablo Javier Zabaleta Girod, Martín Gastón Demichelis, Ezequiel Marcelo Garay González, Faustino Marcos Alberto Rojo, Javier Alejandro Mascherano, Lucas Rodrigo Biglia, Ángel Fabián Di María Hernández (84.Érik Manuel Lamela), Javier Matías Pastore (59.Roberto Maximiliano Pereyra), Lionel Andrés Messi, Gonzalo Gerardo Higuaín (72.Carlos Alberto Martínez Tévez). Trainer: Gerardo Daniel Martino.
Goal: Gonzalo Gerardo Higuaín (10).

26.06.2015, 44th Copa América, Quarter-Finals
Estadio Sausalito, Viña del Mar (Chile); Attendance: 21,508
Referee: Roberto García Orozco (Mexico)
ARGENTINA - COLOMBIA **0-0; 5-4 on penalties**
ARG: Sergio Germán Romero, Pablo Javier Zabaleta Girod, Ezequiel Marcelo Garay González, Nicolás Hernán Gonzalo Otamendi, Faustino Marcos Alberto Rojo, Javier Alejandro Mascherano, Lucas Rodrigo Biglia, Ángel Fabián Di María Hernández (87.Ezequiel Iván Lavezzi), Javier Matías Pastore (77.Éver Maximiliano David Banega), Lionel Andrés Messi, Sergio Leonel Agüero del Castillo (73.Carlos Alberto Martínez Tévez). Trainer: Gerardo Daniel Martino.
Penalties: Lionel Andrés Messi, Ezequiel Marcelo Garay González, Éver Maximiliano David Banega, Ezequiel Iván Lavezzi, Lucas Rodrigo Biglia (missed), Faustino Marcos Alberto Rojo (missed), Carlos Alberto Martínez Tévez.

30.06.2015, 44th Copa América, Semi-Finals
Estadio Municipal „Alcaldesa Ester Roa Rebolledo", Concepción (Chile); Attendance: 29,205
Referee: Sandro Meira Ricci (Brazil)
ARGENTINA - PARAGUAY **6-1(2-1)**
ARG: Sergio Germán Romero, Pablo Javier Zabaleta Girod, Martín Gastón Demichelis, Nicolás Hernán Gonzalo Otamendi, Faustino Marcos Alberto Rojo, Javier Alejandro Mascherano (77.Fernando Rubén Gago), Lucas Rodrigo Biglia, Ángel Fabián Di María Hernández, Javier Matías Pastore (73.Éver Maximiliano David Banega), Lionel Andrés Messi, Sergio Leonel Agüero del Castillo (81.Gonzalo Gerardo Higuaín). Trainer: Gerardo Daniel Martino.
Goals: Faustino Marcos Alberto Rojo (15), Javier Matías Pastore (27), Ángel Fabián Di María Hernández (47, 53), Sergio Leonel Agüero del Castillo (80), Gonzalo Gerardo Higuaín (83).

04.07.2015, 44th Copa América, Final
Estadio Nacional "Julio Martínez Prádanos", Santiago; Attendance: 45,693
Referee: Wilmar Alexander Roldán Pérez (Colombia)
CHILE - ARGENTINA **0-0; 4-1 on penalties**
ARG: Sergio Germán Romero, Pablo Javier Zabaleta Girod, Martín Gastón Demichelis, Nicolás Hernán Gonzalo Otamendi, Faustino Marcos Alberto Rojo, Javier Alejandro Mascherano, Lucas Rodrigo Biglia, Ángel Fabián Di María Hernández (29.Ezequiel Iván Lavezzi), Javier Matías Pastore (81.Éver Maximiliano David Banega), Lionel Andrés Messi, Sergio Leonel Agüero del Castillo (74.Gonzalo Gerardo Higuaín). Trainer: Gerardo Daniel Martino.
Penalties: Lionel Andrés Messi, Gonzalo Gerardo Higuaín (missed), Éver Maximiliano David Banega (saved).

NATIONAL TEAM PLAYERS 2014/2015			
Name [Club 2014/2015]	DOB	Caps	Goals

(Caps and goals at 05.07.2015)

Goalkeepers

Name [Club]	DOB	Caps	Goals
Mariano Gonzalo ANDÚJAR [2014/2015: SSC Napoli (ITA)]	30.07.1983	**11**	**0**
Nahuel Ignacio GUZMÁN [2014/2015: CF Tigres de la UA de Nuevo León (MEX)]	10.02.1986	**4**	**0**
Agustín Federico MARCHESÍN [2014: CA Lanús]	16.03.1988	**2**	**0**
Sergio Germán ROMERO [2014/2015: UC Sampdoria Genoa (ITA)]	22.02.1987	**65**	**0**

Defenders

Name [Club]	DOB	Caps	Goals
Cristian Daniel ANSALDI [2014/2015: Club Atlético de Madrid (ESP)]	20.09.1986	**5**	**1**
Hugo Armando CAMPAGNARO [2014/2015: FC Internazionale Milano (ITA)]	27.06.1980	**17**	**0**
Milton Óscar CASCO [2015: CA Newell's Old Boys Rosario]	11.04.1988	**1**	**0**
Martín Gastón DEMICHELIS [2014/2015: Manchester City FC (ENG)]	20.12.1980	**48**	**2**
Federico Julián FAZIO [2014/2015: Tottenham Hotspur FC London (ENG)]	17.03.1987	**3**	**0**
Federico FERNÁNDEZ [2014/2015: Swansea City AFC (ENG)]	21.02.1989	**32**	**3**
Ramiro José FUNES Mori [2015: CA River Plate Buenos Aires]	05.03.1991	**1**	**0**
Ezequiel Marcelo GARAY González [2014/2015: FK Zenit St. Petersburg (RUS)]	10.10.1986	**31**	**0**
Mateo Pablo MUSACCHIO [2014/2015: Villarreal CF (ESP)]	26.08.1990	**3**	**0**
Lucas Alfonso ORBÁN [2014/2015: Valencia CF (ESP)]	03.02.1989	**2**	**0**
Nicolás Hernán Gonzalo OTAMENDI [2014/2015: Valencia CF (ESP)]	12.02.1988	**25**	**1**
Faustino Marcos Alberto ROJO [2014/2015: Manchester United FC (ENG)]	20.03.1990	**38**	**2**
Facundo Sebastián RONCAGLIA [2014/2015: Genoa CFC (ITA)]	10.02.1987	**6**	**0**
Jonathan Cristian SILVA [2014/2015: Sporting Clube de Portugal Lisboa (POR)]	29.06.1994	**2**	**0**
Leonel Jesús VANGIONI [2014/2015: CA River Plate Buenos Aires]	05.05.1987	**3**	**0**
Santiago VERGINI [2014/2015: Sunderland AFC (ENG)]	03.08.1988	**3**	**0**
Pablo Javier ZABALETA Girod [2014/2015: Manchester City FC (ENG)]	16.01.1985	**53**	**0**

Midfielders

Player	Date of birth	Caps	Goals
Ricardo Gabriel ÁLVAREZ [2014/2015: Sunderland AFC (ENG)]	12.04.1988	**9**	**1**
Éver Maximiliano David BANEGA [2014/2015: Sevilla FC (ESP)]	29.06.1988	**34**	**3**
Lucas Rodrigo BIGLIA [2014/2015: SS Lazio Roma (ITA)]	30.01.1986	**35**	**0**
Ángel Fabián DI MARÍA Hernández [2014/2015: Manchester United FC (ENG)]	14.02.1988	**66**	**15**
Augusto Matías FERNÁNDEZ [2014/2015: Real Club Celta de Vigo (ESP)]	10.04.1986	**10**	**1**
Fernando Rubén GAGO [2014/2015: CA Boca Juniors Buenos Aires]	10.04.1986	**59**	**0**
Osvaldo Nicolás Fabián GAITÁN [2014/2015: Sport Lisboa e Benfica (POR)]	23.02.1988	**9**	**2**
Érik Manuel LAMELA [2014/2015: Tottenham Hotspur FC London (ENG)]	04.03.1992	**12**	**1**
Federico Andrés MANCUELLO [2015: CA Independiente Avellaneda]	26.03.1989	**2**	**1**
Javier Alejandro MASCHERANO [2014/2015: FC Barcelona (ESP)]	08.06.1984	**117**	**3**
Javier Matías PASTORE [2014/2015: Paris Saint-Germain FC (FRA)]	20.06.1989	**25**	**2**
Enzo Nicolás PÉREZ [2014: Sport Lisboa e Benfica (POR)]	22.06.1986	**15**	**1**
Roberto Maximiliano PEREYRA [2014/2015: Juventus FC Torino (ITA)]	07.01.1991	**8**	**0**

Forwards

Player	Date of birth	Caps	Goals
Sergio Leonel AGÜERO Del Castillo [2014/2015: Manchester City FC (ENG)]	02.06.1988	**66**	**29**
Gonzalo Gerardo HIGUAÍN [2014/2015: SSC Napoli (ITA)]	10.12.1987	**52**	**25**
Ezequiel Iván LAVEZZI [2014/2015: Paris Saint-Germain FC (FRA)]	03.05.1985	**42**	**4**
Lionel Andrés MESSI [2014/2015: FC Barcelona (ESP)]	24.06.1987	**103**	**46**
Carlos Alberto Martínez TÉVEZ [2014/2015: Juventus FC Torino (ITA)]	05.02.1984	**72**	**13**

National coaches

Coach	Date of birth	Record
Gerardo Daniel MARTINO	20.11.1962	14 M; 9 W; 3 D; 2 L; 32-10

BOLIVIA

The Country:
Estado Plurinacional de Bolivia (Plurinational State of Bolivia) Capital: Sucre Surface: 1,098,581 km² Inhabitants: 10,556,102 Time: UTC-4

The FA:
Federación Boliviana de Fútbol Av. Libertador Bolívar 1168, Cochabamba Year of Formation: 1925 Member of FIFA since: 1926 Member of CONMEBOL since: 1926 Internet: www.fbf.com.bo

NATIONAL TEAM RECORDS	
First international match:	12.10.1926, Santiago: Chile – Bolivia 7-1
Most international caps:	Marco Antonio Sandy Sansusty (1993-2003) – 93 caps
Most international goals:	Joaquín Botero Vaca – 20 goals (48 caps; 1999-2009)

OLYMPIC GAMES 1900-2012
None
FIFA CONFEDERATIONS CUP 1992-2013
1999

COPA AMÉRICA	
1916	Did not enter
1917	Did not enter
1919	Did not enter
1920	Did not enter
1921	Did not enter
1922	Did not enter
1923	Did not enter
1924	Did not enter
1925	Did not enter
1926	5th Place
1927	4th Place
1929	Withdrew
1935	Withdrew
1937	Withdrew
1939	Withdrew
1941	Withdrew
1942	Withdrew
1945	6th Place
1946	6th Place
1947	7th Place
1949	4th Place
1953	6th Place
1955	Withdrew
1956	Withdrew
1957	Withdrew
1959	7th Place
1959E	Withdrew
1963	**Winners**
1967	6th Place
1975	1st Round
1979	1st Round
1983	1st Round
1987	1st Round
1989	1st Round
1991	1st Round
1993	1st Round
1995	Quarter-Finals
1997	Runners-up
1999	1st Round
2001	1st Round
2004	1st Round
2007	1st Round
2011	1st Round
2015	Quarter-Finals

FIFA WORLD CUP	
1930	Final Tournament (Group Stage)
1934	Did not enter
1938	Did not enter
1950	Final Tournament (Group Stage)
1954	Did not enter
1958	Did not enter
1962	Qualifiers
1966	Qualifiers
1970	Qualifiers
1974	Qualifiers
1978	Qualifiers
1982	Qualifiers
1986	Qualifiers
1990	Qualifiers
1994	Final Tournament (Group Stage)
1998	Qualifiers
2002	Qualifiers
2006	Qualifiers
2010	Qualifiers
2014	Qualifiers
PANAMERICAN GAMES	
1951	Did not enter
1955	Did not enter
1959	Did not enter
1963	Did not enter
1967	Did not enter
1971	Did not enter
1975	2nd Round
1979	Did not enter
1983	Did not enter
1987	Did not enter
1991	Did not enter
1995	Did not enter
1999	Did not enter
2003	Did not enter
2007	4th Place
2011	Did not enter
PANAMERICAN CHAMPIONSHIP	
1952	Did not enter
1956	Did not enter
1960	Did not enter

BOLIVIAN CLUB HONOURS IN SOUTH AMERICAN CLUB COMPETITIONS:

COPA LIBERTADORES 1960-2014
None
COPA SUDAMERICANA 2002-2014
None
RECOPA SUDAMERICANA 1989-2014
None
COPA CONMEBOL 1992-1999
None
SUPERCUP „JOÃO HAVELANGE" 1988-1997*
None
COPA MERCONORTE 1998-2001**
None

**Contested betwenn winners of all previous editions of the Copa Libertadores*

***Contested between teams belonging countries from the northern part of South America (Bolivia, Colombia, Ecuador, Peru and Venezuela);*

NATIONAL COMPETITIONS TABLE OF HONOURS

NATIONAL CHAMPIONS 1914-2014	
	La Paz League
1914	Club The Strongest La Paz
1915	Colegio Militar La Paz
1916-1	Club The Strongest La Paz
1916-2	Club The Strongest La Paz
1917	Club The Strongest La Paz
1918	*No competition*
1919	*No competition*
1920	*No competition*
1921	*No competition*
1922	Club The Strongest La Paz
1923	Club The Strongest La Paz
1924	Club The Strongest La Paz
1925	Club The Strongest La Paz
1926	*No competition*
1927	Nimbles Sport La Paz
1928	Colegio Militar La Paz
1929	CD Universitario La Paz
1930	Club The Strongest La Paz
1931	Nimbles Sport La Paz
1932	Club Bolívar La Paz
1933	*No competition*
1934	*No competition*
1935	Club The Strongest La Paz
1936	Ayacucho La Paz
1937	Club Bolívar La Paz
1938	Club The Strongest La Paz
1939	Club Bolívar La Paz

1940	Club Bolívar La Paz
1941	Club Bolívar La Paz
1942	Club Bolívar La Paz
1943	Club The Strongest La Paz
1944	Deportivo Ferroviario de La Paz
1945	Club The Strongest La Paz
1946	Club The Strongest La Paz
1947	CD Lítoral La Paz
1948	CD Lítoral La Paz
1949	CD Lítoral La Paz
1950	Club Bolívar La Paz
1951	Club Always Ready La Paz
1952	Club The Strongest La Paz
1953	Club Bolívar La Paz
	Torneo Integrado (La Paz & Cochabamba & Oruro)
1954	CD Lítoral La Paz
1955	CS San José Oruro
1956	Club Bolívar La Paz
1957	Club Always Ready La Paz
	Torneo Nacional / Copa Simón Bolívar*
1958	Club Jorge Wilstermann Cochabamba
1959	Club Jorge Wilstermann Cochabamba
1960	Club Jorge Wilstermann Cochabamba
1961	Deportivo Municipal La Paz
1962	*No competition*
1963	Club Aurora Cochabamba
1964	Club The Strongest La Paz
1965	Deportivo Municipal La Paz
1966	Club Bolívar La Paz
1967	Club Jorge Wilstermann Cochabamba
1968	Club Bolívar La Paz
1969	CD Universitario La Paz
1970	CD Chaco Petrolero La Paz
1971	CD Oriente Petrolero Santa Cruz de la Sierra
1972	Club Jorge Wilstermann Cochabamba
1973	Club Jorge Wilstermann Cochabamba
1974	Club The Strongest La Paz
1975	CD Guabirá Montero
1976	Club Bolívar La Paz
	Professional National League
1977	Club The Strongest La Paz
1978	Club Bolívar La Paz
1979	CD Oriente Petrolero Santa Cruz de la Sierra
1980	Club Jorge Wilstermann Cochabamba
1981	Club Jorge Wilstermann Cochabamba
1982	Club Bolívar La Paz
1983	Club Bolívar La Paz
1984	CSCD Blooming Santa Cruz de la Sierra
1985	Club Bolívar La Paz
1986	Club The Strongest La Paz
1987	Club Bolívar La Paz
1988	Club Bolívar La Paz

	CHAMPIONS		CUP WINNERS**
1989	Club The Strongest La Paz		Escuela „Enrique Happ“ Cochabamba
1990	CD Oriente Petrolero Santa Cruz de la Sierra		Club Universidad Santa Cruz
1991	Club Bolívar La Paz		Escuela „Enrique Happ“ Cochabamba
1992	Club Bolívar La Paz		Escuela „Enrique Happ“ Cochabamba
1993	Club The Strongest La Paz		Real Santa Cruz FC
1994	Club Bolívar La Paz		Club Stormers Sucre
1995	CD San José Oruro		Deportivo Municipal La Paz
1996	Club Bolívar La Paz		CSCD Blooming Santa Cruz de la Sierra
1997	Club Bolívar La Paz		Club Bamin Real Potosí
1998	CSCD Blooming Santa Cruz de la Sierra		Club Unión Central Tarija
1999	CSCD Blooming Santa Cruz de la Sierra		Atlético Pompeya
2000	Club Jorge Wilstermann Cochabamba		Club Universidad Iberoamericana
2001	CD Oriente Petrolero Santa Cruz de la Sierra		CD San José Oruro
2002	Club Bolívar La Paz		Club Aurora Cochabamba
2003	Ape:	Club The Strongest La Paz	La Paz FC
	Cla:	Club The Strongest La Paz	
2004	Ape:	Club Bolívar La Paz	Club Destroyers Santa Cruz de la Sierra
	Cla:	CD Oriente Petrolero Santa Cruz de la Sierra	
2005	TA:	Club Bolívar La Paz	CD Universitario Sucre
	Ape:	CSCD Blooming Santa Cruz de la Sierra	
2006	Ape:	Club Bolívar La Paz	Municipal Real Mamoré Trinidad
	Cla:	Club Jorge Wilstermann Cochabamba	
2007	Ape:	Club Bamin Real Potosí	CD Guabirá Montero
	Cla:	CD San José Oruro	
2008	Ape:	CD Universitario Sucre	CA Nacional Potosí
	Cla:	Club Aurora Cochabamba	
2009	Ape:	Club Bolívar La Paz	CD Guabirá Montero
	Cla:	CSCD Blooming Santa Cruz de la Sierra	
2010	Ape:	Club Jorge Wilstermann Cochabamba	CA Nacional Potosí
	Cla:	CD Oriente Petrolero Santa Cruz de la Sierra	
2011	TA	Club Bolívar La Paz	-
2011/2012	Ape:	Club The Strongest La Paz	*No competition*
	Cla:	Club The Strongest La Paz	
2012/2013	Ape:	Club The Strongest La Paz	*No competition*
	Cla:	Club Bolívar La Paz	
2013/2014	Ape:	Club The Strongest La Paz	*No competition*
	Cla:	CD Universitario Sucre	
2014/2015	Ape:	Club Bolívar La Paz	*No competition*
	Cla:	Club Bolívar La Paz	

**between 1960 and 1976, the final play-offs for the Torneo Nacional was known as „Copa Simón Bolívar“.*

***The National Cup competition was reintroduced in 1989 as the Second League championship, whose winner were promoted to the First League.*
In 2005 and 2011, the first half season was called „Torneo Adecuación".

	BEST GOALSCORERS		
1977	Jesús Reynaldo Hurtado (Club Bolívar La Paz)		28
1978	Jesús Reynaldo Hurtado (Club Bolívar La Paz)		39
1979	Raúl Horacio Baldessari (ARG, CSCD Blooming Santa Cruz de la Sierra)		31
1980	Juan Carlos Sánchez (ARG, CD Guabirá Montero)		21
1981	Juan Carlos Sánchez (ARG, CSCD Blooming Santa Cruz de la Sierra)		30
1982	Raúl Horacio Baldessari (ARG, CD Oriente Petrolero Santa Cruz de la Sierra)		25
1983	Juan Carlos Sánchez (ARG, CSCD Blooming Santa Cruz de la Sierra)		30
1984	Víctor Hugo Antelo (CD Oriente Petrolero Santa Cruz de la Sierra)		38
1985	Víctor Hugo Antelo (CD Oriente Petrolero Santa Cruz de la Sierra)		37
1986	Jesús Reynaldo Hurtado (Club The Strongest La Paz)		36
1987	Fernando Salinas (Club Bolívar La Paz)		28
1988	Fernando Salinas (Club Bolívar La Paz)		17
1989	Víctor Hugo Antelo (Real Santa Cruz FC)		22
1990	Juan Carlos Sánchez (ARG, CD San José Oruro)		20
1991	Carlos Da Silva (BRA, CD Oriente Petrolero Santa Cruz de la Sierra) Jorge Hirano Matsumoto (PER, Club Bolívar La Paz) Jasson Rodrigues (BRA, CD Chaco Petrolero La Paz)		19
1992	Álvaro Guillermo Peña (CD San José Oruro)		32
1993	Víctor Hugo Antelo (CD San José Oruro)		20
1994	Oscar Osmar González (ARG, Club Independiente Petrolero Sucre)		23
1995	Juan Berthy Suárez (CD Guabirá Montero)		29
1996	Sergio João (BRA, Club Stormers Sucre)		17
1997	Víctor Hugo Antelo (CSCD Blooming Santa Cruz de la Sierra)		24
1998	Víctor Hugo Antelo (CSCD Blooming Santa Cruz de la Sierra)		31
1999	Víctor Hugo Antelo (CSCD Blooming Santa Cruz de la Sierra)		31
2000	Daniel Alejandro Delfino (ARG, Club The Strongest La Paz)		28
2001	José Alfredo Castillo (CD Oriente Petrolero Santa Cruz de la Sierra)		42
2002	Joaquín Botero Vaca (Club Bolívar La Paz)		49
2003	Ape:	Thiago Leitão Polieri (Club Jorge Wilstermann Cochabamba)	19
	Cla:	Miguel Ángel Mercado Melgar (Club Bolívar La Paz)	18
2004	Ape:	José Martín Menacho Aguilera (Club Bamin Real Potosí)	15
	Cla:	Pablo Daniel Escobar Olivetti (PAR, CD San José Oruro)	17
2005	TA:	Rubén Darío Aguilera Ferreira (PAR, CD San José Oruro)	21
	Ape:	Juan Matías Fischer (ARG, Club Bolívar La Paz)	16
2006	Ape:	Cristino Alfredo Jara Mereles (Club Bamin Real Potosí)	16
	Cla:	Cristino Alfredo Jara Mereles (Club Bamin Real Potosí)	19
2007	Ape:	Hernán Boyero (ARG, CSCD Blooming Santa Cruz de la Sierra) Lizandro Moyano (ARG, CD San José Oruro)	12
	Cla:	Juan Alberto Maraude (ARG, Municipal Real Mamoré Trinidad)	14
2008	Ape:	Anderson Aparecido Gonzaga (BRA, CSCD Blooming Santa Cruz de la Sierra)	16
	Cla:	Hernán Boyero (ARG, CSCD Blooming Santa Cruz de la Sierra) Martín Adrian Palavicini López (CD San José Oruro)	6
2009	Ape:	William Ferreira Martínez (URU, Club Bolívar La Paz)	16

	Cla:	Cristián Omar Díaz (ARG, CD San José Oruro) William Ferreira Martínez (URU, Club Bolívar La Paz) Pastór Torrez (Club Bamin Real Potosí)	9
2010	Ape:	Cristián Omar Díaz (ARG, CD San José Oruro)	18
	Cla:	William Ferreira Martínez (URU, Club Bolívar La Paz)	14
2011	TA:	Juan Alberto Maraude (ARG, Municipal Real Mamoré Trinidad)	19
2011/2012	Ape:	William Ferreira Martínez (URU, Club Bolívar La Paz)	16
	Cla:	Carlos Enrique Saucedo Urgel (CD San José Oruro)	17
2012/2013	Ape:	Carlos Enrique Saucedo Urgel (CD San José Oruro)	24
	Cla:	William Ferreira Martínez (URU, Club Bolívar La Paz) Juan Eduardo Fierro Ribera (CD Universitario Sucre)	17
2013/2014	Ape:	Carlos Enrique Saucedo Urgel (CD San José Oruro) José Marcelo Gomes (BRA, CD San José Oruro)	16
	Cla:	Carlos Ariel Neumann (PAR, CD San José Oruro)	18
2014/2015	Ape:	Juan Miguel Callejón Bueno (ESP, Club Bolívar La Paz)	15
	Cla:	Martín Adrián Palavicini (ARG, CD Universitario Sucre)	13

NATIONAL CHAMPIONSHIP
Liga de Fútbol Profesional Boliviano
Primera División de Bolivia 2014/2015

Torneo Apertura 2014

Results

Round 1 [09-10.08.2014]
Club The Strongest - Sport Boys Warnes 1-0
Universitario Sucre - Universitario Pando 3-0
Real Potosí - Oriente Petrolero 0-0
CD San José - Club Bolívar 1-0
Jorge Wilstermann - CA Petrolero 2-2
CSCD Blooming - CA Nacional Potosí 2-0

Round 2 [15-18.08.2014]
CD San José - Club The Strongest 3-3
Universitario Sucre - Jorge Wilstermann 0-2
Sport Boys Warnes - Real Potosí 1-1
CA Nacional Potosí - Club Bolívar 0-2
Oriente Petrolero - Universitario UA Pando 2-0
CSCD Blooming - CA Petrolero 1-0

Round 3 [23-24.08.2014]
CA Petrolero - Club Bolívar 1-1
Universitario Sucre - CSCD Blooming 0-1
Sport Boys Warnes - Universitario Pando 1-3
Real Potosí - Club The Strongest 1-0
Jorge Wilstermann - Oriente Petrolero 2-0
CD San José - CA Nacional Potosí 1-0 [17.09.]

Round 4 [30-31.08.2014]
Club The Strongest - Universitario Pando 3-1
Sport Boys Warnes - Jorge Wilstermann 1-1
CA Petrolero - CA Nacional Potosí 1-5
Real Potosí - CD San José 3-0
Universitario Sucre - Club Bolívar 1-2
Oriente Petrolero - CSCD Blooming 2-0

Round 5 [13-15.09.2014]
Club Bolívar - Oriente Petrolero 4-0
CD San José - CA Petrolero 4-1
CA Nacional Potosí - Universitario Sucre 3-0
Universitario UA Pando - Real Potosí 0-0
CSCD Blooming - Sport Boys Warnes 2-2
Jorge Wilstermann - Club The Strongest 1-1

Round 6 [20-21.09.2014]
Club The Strongest - CSCD Blooming 4-0
Universitario Sucre - CA Petrolero 4-3
Universitario UA Pando - CD San José 1-2
Sport Boys Warnes - Club Bolívar 5-0
Real Potosí - Jorge Wilstermann 1-0
Oriente Petrolero - CA Nacional Potosí 2-0

Round 7 [24-25.09.2014]
CA Nacional Potosí - Sport Boys Warnes 0-0
CSCD Blooming - Real Potosí 3-1
Jorge Wilstermann - Universitario Pando 3-0
CA Petrolero - Oriente Petrolero 1-1
CD San José - Universitario Sucre 3-1 [29.10.]
Club Bolívar - Club The Strongest 4-2 [29.10.]

Round 8 [28.09.2014]
Club The Strongest - CA Nacional Potosí 2-0
Real Potosí - Club Bolívar 1-0
Sport Boys Warnes - CA Petrolero 1-2
Universitario UA Pando - CSCD Blooming 2-2
Jorge Wilstermann - CD San José 2-1
Oriente Petrolero - Universitario Sucre 4-0

Round 9 [01-02.10.2014]
CA Petrolero - Club The Strongest 2-1
CD San José - Oriente Petrolero 3-0
Club Bolívar - Universitario UA Pando 4-0
CA Nacional Potosí - Real Potosí 1-0
Universitario Sucre - Sport Boys Warnes 1-0
CSCD Blooming - Jorge Wilstermann 1-1

Round 10 [05-06.10.2014]
Club The Strongest - Universitario Sucre 0-1
Sport Boys Warnes - Oriente Petrolero 1-1
Universitario Pando - CA Nacional Potosí 1-0
Jorge Wilstermann - Club Bolívar 0-0
CSCD Blooming - CD San José 3-1
Real Potosí - CA Petrolero 2-3

Round 11 [18-19.10.2014]
CA Petrolero - Universitario UA Pando 2-1
Club Bolívar - CSCD Blooming 4-3
CA Nacional Potosí - Jorge Wilstermann 1-2
CD San José - Sport Boys Warnes 2-0
Universitario Sucre - Real Potosí 0-0
Oriente Petrolero - Club The Strongest 2-0

Round 12 [22-23.10.2014]
CA Petrolero - Jorge Wilstermann 1-1
Universitario Pando - Universitario Sucre 2-3
Club Bolívar - CD San José 6-1
Sport Boys Warnes - Club The Strongest 1-1
CA Nacional Potosí - CSCD Blooming 0-0
Oriente Petrolero - Real Potosí 2-1

Round 13 [25-27.10.2014]
Club Bolívar - CA Nacional Potosí 3-3
Real Potosí - Sport Boys Warnes 1-0
Universitario UA Pando - Oriente Petrolero 0-1
Jorge Wilstermann - Universitario Sucre 2-1
Club The Strongest - CD San José 1-0
CA Petrolero - CSCD Blooming 0-1

Round 14 [01-02.11.2014]
Universitario Pando - Sport Boys Warnes 0-0
Club The Strongest - Real Potosí 0-2
CSCD Blooming - Universitario Sucre 1-2
CA Nacional Potosí - CD San José 2-0
Club Bolívar - CA Petrolero 2-0
Oriente Petrolero - Jorge Wilstermann 2-0

Round 15 [05-06.11.2014]
Sport Boys Warnes - CA Nacional Potosí 1-1
Real Potosí - CSCD Blooming 1-1
Universitario Sucre - CD San José 1-0
Oriente Petrolero - CA Petrolero 4-0
Universitario Pando - Jorge Wilstermann 1-2
Club The Strongest - Club Bolívar 1-1 [26.11.]

Round 16 [08-09.11.2014]
CA Petrolero - CD San José 3-0
Sport Boys Warnes - CSCD Blooming 1-1
Club The Strongest - Jorge Wilstermann 4-1
Real Potosí - Universitario UA Pando 1-0
Universitario Sucre - CA Nacional Potosí 2-1
Oriente Petrolero - Club Bolívar 1-0

Round 17 [12-13.11.2014]
Club Bolívar - Sport Boys Warnes 5-1
CA Nacional Potosí - Oriente Petrolero 1-0
CSCD Blooming - Club The Strongest 0-1
CD San José - Universitario UA Pando 2-1
Jorge Wilstermann - Real Potosí 1-0
CA Petrolero - Universitario Sucre 2-1 [16.11.]

Round 18 [22-23.11.2014]
CD San José - Real Potosí 6-2
Jorge Wilstermann - Sport Boys Warnes 1-2
CA Nacional Potosí - CA Petrolero 3-1
Universitario Pando - Club The Strongest 1-3
Club Bolívar - Universitario Sucre 2-1
CSCD Blooming - Oriente Petrolero 3-2

Round 19 [29-30.11.2014]
CA Petrolero - Sport Boys Warnes 0-0
CD San José - Jorge Wilstermann 2-0
CA Nacional Potosí - Club The Strongest 1-3
Club Bolívar - Real Potosí 6-1
CSCD Blooming - Universitario UA Pando 3-0
Universitario Sucre - Oriente Petrolero 0-2

Round 20 [06-07.12.2014]
Sport Boys Warnes - Universitario Sucre 1-1
Club The Strongest - CA Petrolero 4-0
Universitario UA Pando - Club Bolívar 0-2
Real Potosí - CA Nacional Potosí 2-2
Jorge Wilstermann - CSCD Blooming 1-1
Oriente Petrolero - CD San José 1-0

Round 21 [13-14.12.2014]
CA Nacional Potosí - Universitario Pando 3-2
CA Petrolero - Real Potosí 2-0
CD San José - CSCD Blooming 2-0
Universitario Sucre - Club The Strongest 3-2
Club Bolívar - Jorge Wilstermann 1-0
Oriente Petrolero - Sport Boys Warnes 3-0

Round 22 [21.12.2014]
Real Potosí - Universitario Sucre 2-0 [10.12.]
Sport Boys Warnes - CD San José 2-0 [17.12.]
Universitario UA Pando - CA Petrolero 2-0
Jorge Wilstermann - CA Nacional Potosí 5-2
Club The Strongest - Oriente Petrolero 2-1
CSCD Blooming - Club Bolívar 0-3

Final Standings

1.	**Club Bolívar La Paz**	22	14	4	4	52	-	23	46
2.	CD Oriente Petrolero Santa Cruz de la Sierra	22	13	3	6	33	-	18	42
3.	Club The Strongest La Paz	22	11	4	7	39	-	26	37
4.	CD Jorge Wilsterman Cochabamba	22	9	7	6	30	-	25	34
5.	CD San José Oruro	22	11	1	10	34	-	31	34
6.	CSCD Blooming Santa Cruz de la Sierra	22	8	7	7	29	-	30	31
7.	Club Bamin Real Potosí	22	8	6	8	23	-	28	30
8.	CD Universitario Sucre	22	9	2	11	26	-	35	29
9.	Club Atlético Nacional Potosí	22	7	5	10	29	-	32	26
10.	Club Atlético Petrolero del Gran Chaco Yacuiba	22	7	5	10	27	-	41	26
11.	Sport Boys Warnes	22	3	11	8	21	-	28	20
12.	Club Universitario de la Universidad Amazónica de Pando Cobija	22	3	3	16	18	-	42	12

Top goalscorers:

15 goals:	**Juan Miguel Callejón Bueno (ESP)**	**(Club Bolívar La Paz)**
12 goals:	Carlos Vicente Tenorio Medina (ECU)	(Club Bolívar La Paz)
9 goals:	Sergio Oscar Almirón (ARG)	(CSCD Blooming Santa Cruz de la Sierra)

Torneo Clausura 2015

Results

Round 1 [16-18.01.2015]
Club The Strongest - CA Nacional Potosí 2-2
Universitario UA Pando - Oriente Petrolero 1-6
CA Petrolero - Universitario Sucre 3-0
CD San José - Jorge Wilstermann 1-1
Real Potosí - Club Bolívar 0-2
CSCD Blooming - Sport Boys Warnes 2-0

Round 2 [23-25.01.2015]
Universitario Sucre - Real Potosí 1-0
Sport Boys Warnes - Club The Strongest 1-2
CSCD Blooming - Universitario UA Pando 1-1
CA Nacional Potosí - CD San José 2-3
Club Bolívar - Oriente Petrolero 2-1
Jorge Wilstermann - CA Petrolero 0-0

Round 3 [28-29.01.2015]
Universitario UA Pando - Club Bolívar 1-2
Real Potosí - Jorge Wilstermann 1-1
Club The Strongest - CSCD Blooming 1-1
CA Petrolero - CA Nacional Potosí 0-0
CD San José - Sport Boys Warnes 2-1
Oriente Petrolero - Universitario Sucre 2-2

Round 4 [31.01-01.02.2015]
Club The Strongest - Universitario Pando 5-0
CA Nacional Potosí - Real Potosí 2-2
Jorge Wilstermann - Oriente Petrolero 1-1
Universitario Sucre - Club Bolívar 2-2
CSCD Blooming - CD San José 2-2
Sport Boys Warnes - CA Petrolero 1-2

Round 5 [06-08.02.2015]
Real Potosí - Sport Boys Warnes 2-0
Universitario Pando - Universitario Sucre 1-0
Oriente Petrolero - CA Nacional Potosí 2-2
CA Petrolero - CSCD Blooming 0-0
Club Bolívar - Jorge Wilstermann 1-0
Club The Strongest - CD San José 1-0 [13.04.]

Round 6 [10-12.02.2015]
CD San José - Universitario UA Pando 6-0
CSCD Blooming - Real Potosí 3-0
Sport Boys Warnes - Oriente Petrolero 0-2
Jorge Wilstermann - Universitario Sucre 1-0
CA Nacional Potosí - Club Bolívar 1-2
Club The Strongest - CA Petrolero 4-2 [25.03.]

Round 7 [19.02.2015]
Universitario Pando - Jorge Wilstermann 1-1
Club Bolívar - Sport Boys Warnes 5-0
Universitario Sucre - CA Nacional Potosí 2-1
Or. Petrolero - CSCD Blooming 1-0 [25.02.]
Real Potosí - Club The Strongest 1-2 [11.03.]
CA Petrolero - CD San José 0-0 [31.03.]

Round 8 [21-22.02.2015]
CA Petrolero - Universitario UA Pando 2-2
CD San José - Real Potosí 0-2
Sport Boys Warnes - Universitario Sucre 2-1
CA Nacional Potosí - Jorge Wilstermann 0-1
Club The Strongest - Oriente Petrolero 4-3
CSCD Blooming - Club Bolívar 1-0

Round 9 [27.02.-01.03.2015]
Jorge Wilstermann - Sport Boys Warnes 1-0
Universitario Sucre - CSCD Blooming 1-3
Real Potosí - CA Petrolero 1-0
Universitario Pando - CA Nacional Potosí 2-0
Club Bolívar - Club The Strongest 1-1
Oriente Petrolero - CD San José 4-0

Round 10 [06-08.03.2015]
Sport Boys Warnes - CA Nacional Potosí 0-0
CA Petrolero - Oriente Petrolero 1-1
CD San José - Club Bolívar 0-2
Real Potosí - Universitario UA Pando 6-0
CSCD Blooming - Jorge Wilstermann 0-0
The Strongest – Universit. Sucre 3-0 [01.04.]

Round 11 [13-15.03.2015]
Universitario Pando - Sport Boys Warnes 1-3
Club Bolívar - CA Petrolero 4-1
Universitario Sucre - CD San José 0-0
CA Nacional Potosí - CSCD Blooming 1-0
Jorge Wilstermann - Club The Strongest 1-0
Oriente Petrolero - Real Potosí 1-1

Round 12 [18.03.2015]
Universitario Sucre - CA Petrolero 1-2
Sport Boys Warnes - CSCD Blooming 1-1
Club Bolívar - Real Potosí 2-1
Oriente Petrolero - Universitario UA Pando 3-0
Nacional Potosí - The Strongest 4-3 [29.04.]
Jorge Wilstermann - CD San José 2-0 [29.04.]

Round 13 [21-22.03.2015]
CA Petrolero - Jorge Wilstermann 1-2
Universitario UA Pando - CSCD Blooming 2-2
Club The Strongest - Sport Boys Warnes 6-2
CD San José - CA Nacional Potosí 1-0
Real Potosí - Universitario Sucre 0-2
Oriente Petrolero - Club Bolívar 3-0

Round 14 [03-05.04.2015]
CA Nacional Potosí - CA Petrolero 0-0
Universitario Sucre - Oriente Petrolero 1-2
Jorge Wilstermann - Real Potosí 2-0
Club Bolívar - Universitario UA Pando 4-0
CSCD Blooming - Club The Strongest 2-1
Sport Boys Warnes - CD San José 3-2 [13.05.]

Round 15 [11-12.04.2015]
Club Bolívar – Universit. Sucre 3-0 (awarded)
CD San José - CSCD Blooming 2-2
Universitario Pando - Club The Strongest 2-2
CA Petrolero - Sport Boys Warnes 2-1
Real Potosí - CA Nacional Potosí 0-1
Oriente Petrolero - Jorge Wilstermann 2-0

Round 16 [17-19.04.2015]
CSCD Blooming - CA Petrolero 3-0
Sport Boys Warnes - Real Potosí 1-2
CD San José - Club The Strongest 1-2
Jorge Wilstermann - Club Bolívar 1-1
CA Nacional Potosí - Oriente Petrolero 1-0
Univ. Sucre - Universitario Pando 9-1 [19.05.]

Round 17 [22.04.2015]
CA Petrolero - Club The Strongest 3-2 [08.04.]
Universitario UA Pando - CD San José 0-2
Club Bolívar - CA Nacional Potosí 3-1
Real Potosí - CSCD Blooming 3-0
Oriente Petrolero - Sport Boys Warnes 3-1
Univ. Sucre - Jorge Wilstermann 2-1 [13.05.]

Round 18 [25-26.04.2015]
CD San José - CA Petrolero 1-1
CA Nacional Potosí - Universitario Sucre 0-1
Jorge Wilstermann - Universitario Pando 1-0
Club The Strongest - Real Potosí 3-0
Sport Boys Warnes - Club Bolívar 3-2
CSCD Blooming - Oriente Petrolero 2-1

Round 19 [01-04.05.2015]
Club Bolívar - CSCD Blooming 4-3
Universitario Sucre - Sport Boys Warnes 2-0
Universitario UA Pando - CA Petrolero 0-0
Real Potosí - CD San José 2-0
Jorge Wilstermann - CA Nacional Potosí 2-2
Oriente Petrolero - Club The Strongest 0-0

Round 20 [06-07.05.2015]
Sport Boys Warnes - Jorge Wilstermann 0-1
CA Petrolero - Real Potosí 0-1
Club The Strongest - Club Bolívar 1-0
CA Nacional Potosí - Universitario Pando 3-0
CD San José - Oriente Petrolero 4-1
CSCD Blooming - Universitario Sucre 2-0

Round 21 [10.05.2015]
Universitario UA Pando - Real Potosí 0-3
Club Bolívar - CD San José 1-0
Jorge Wilstermann - CSCD Blooming 1-0
CA Nacional Potosí - Sport Boys Warnes 1-1
Oriente Petrolero - CA Petrolero 0-0
Universitario Sucre - Club The Strongest 0-1

Round 22 [17.05.2015]
Sport Boys Warnes - Universitario Pando 3-0
CA Petrolero - Club Bolívar 1-1
Club The Strongest - Jorge Wilstermann 2-2
CD San José - Universitario Sucre 6-0
Real Potosí - Oriente Petrolero 2-0
CSCD Blooming - CA Nacional Potosí 2-0

Final Standings

1.	**Club Bolívar La Paz**	22	14	4	4	44 - 22	46
2.	Club The Strongest La Paz	22	12	6	4	48 - 28	42
3.	CD Jorge Wilsterman Cochabamba	22	10	9	3	23 - 15	39
4.	CSCD Blooming Santa Cruz de la Sierra	22	9	8	5	32 - 22	35
5.	CD Oriente Petrolero Santa Cruz de la Sierra	22	9	7	6	39 - 25	34
6.	Club Bamin Real Potosí	22	10	3	9	30 - 23	33
7.	CD San José Oruro	22	7	6	9	33 - 29	27
8.	Club Atlético Petrolero del Gran Chaco Yacuiba	22	5	11	6	21 - 25	26
9.	CD Universitario Sucre	22	7	3	12	27 - 36	24
10.	Club Atlético Nacional Potosí	22	5	8	9	24 - 29	23
11.	Sport Boys Warnes	22	5	3	14	24 - 42	18
12.	Club Universitario de la Universidad Amazónica de Pando Cobija	22	2	6	14	15 - 64	12

Top goalscorers:

13 goals:	**Martín Adrián Palavicini (ARG)**	(CD Universitario Sucre)
11 goals:	Hugo Christophe Bargas (ARG)	(CSCD Blooming Santa Cruz de la Sierra)
9 goals:	Gilbert Álvarez Vargas	(Club Bamin Real Potosí)
	Juan Miguel Callejón Bueno (ESP)	(Club Bolívar La Paz)
	Yasmani Georges Duk Arandia	(CD Oriente Petrolero Santa Cruz)

Aggregate Table 2014/2015

1.	Club Bolívar La Paz	44	28	8	8	96 - 45	92
2.	Club The Strongest La Paz	44	23	10	11	87 - 54	79
3.	CD Oriente Petrolero Santa Cruz de la Sierra	44	22	10	12	72 - 43	76
4.	CD Jorge Wilsterman Cochabamba	44	19	16	9	53 - 40	73
5.	CSCD Blooming Santa Cruz de la Sierra	44	17	15	12	61 - 52	66
6.	Club Bamin Real Potosí	44	18	9	17	53 - 51	63
7.	CD San José Oruro	44	18	7	19	67 - 62	61
8.	CD Universitario Sucre	44	16	5	23	53 - 71	53
9.	Club Atlético Petrolero del Gran Chaco Yacuiba	44	12	16	16	48 - 66	52
10.	Club Atlético Nacional Potosí	44	12	13	19	53 - 61	49
11.	Sport Boys Warnes	44	8	14	22	45 - 70	38
12.	Club Universitario de la Universidad Amazónica de Pando Cobija	44	5	9	30	33 - 106	24

Club Bolívar La Paz, Club The Strongest La Paz and CD Oriente Petrolero Santa Cruz de la Sierra qualified for the 2016 Copa Libertadores.

Club Bolívar La Paz, CD Jorge Wilsterman Cochabamba, CSCD Blooming Santa Cruz de la Sierra and Club Bamin Real Potosí qualified for the 2016 Copa Sudamericana.

Relegation Table

The team which will be relegated is determined on average points taking into account results of the last two seasons (Apertura & Clausura 2013/2014, Apertura & Clausura 2014/2015).

Pos	Team	Ape & Cla 2013/2014	Ape & Cla 2014/2015	Total		Aver
		P	P	P	M	
1.	Club Bolívar La Paz	76	92	168	88	1.9091
2.	Club The Strongest La Paz	85	79	164	88	1.8636
3.	CD San José Oruro	80	61	141	88	1.6023
4.	CD Oriente Petrolero Santa Cruz de la Sierra	58	76	134	88	1.5227
5.	CD Jorge Wilsterman Cochabamba	61	73	134	88	1.5227
6.	Club Bamin Real Potosí	67	63	130	88	1.4772
7.	CD Universitario Sucre	71	53	124	88	1.4091
8.	CSCD Blooming Santa Cruz de la Sierra	43	63	109	88	1.2386
9.	Club Atlético Petrolero del Gran Chaco Yacuiba	-	52	52	44	1.1818
10.	Club Atlético Nacional Potosí	52	49	101	88	1.1477
11.	Sport Boys Warnes *(Relegation Play-Off)*	50	38	88	88	1.0000
12.	Club Universitario de la Universidad Amazónica de Pando Cobija *(Relegated)*	-	24	24	44	0.5455

Promotion/Relegation Play-Offs (31.05.-07.06.2015)

Club Atlético Bermejo - Sport Boys Warnes	3-1(0-1)
Sport Boys Warnes - Club Atlético Bermejo	4-1(1-0)
Club Atlético Bermejo - Sport Boys Warnes	0-2(0-0)

Sport Boys Warnes qualified for the next season's first level.

CLUB SOCIAL, CULTURAL Y DEPORTIVO BLOOMING SANTA CRUZ DE LA SIERRA

Foundation date: May 1, 1946
Address: Km. 6,5 Carretera al Norte, Santa Cruz
Stadium: Estadio „Ramón "Tahuichi" Aguilera“, Santa Cruz de la Sierra – Capacity: 40,000

THE SQUAD

	DOB	Ape		Cla	
		M	G	M	G
Goalkeepers:					
Jorge Araúz		-	-	-	-
Eder Jordán Pereyra	17.06.1985	5	-	7	-
Hugo Súarez Vaca	07.02.1982	17	-	14	-
Braulio Uraezaña Cuñaendi	26.03.1995	-	-	-	-
Pedro Daniel Viera Pereyra	01.08.1990	-	-	-	-
Defenders:					
Martin Ángel Aguirre Schmidt (ARG)	10.02.1984	3	-		
Oscar Añez Urachianta	23.07.1990	12	-	8	-
Cristhian Michael Coimbra Arias	31.12.1988	10	-	18	1
Raúl René Gonzáles Guzmán	08.04.1988	-	-	-	-
Miguel Ángel Hurtado Suárez	04.07.1985	16	-	15	-
Dustin Maldonado Antelo	18.03.1990	9	-	5	-
Alejandro Leonel Morales Pinedo	09.02.1988	18	-	15	-
Pablo Elías Pedraza Bustos	10.03.1995	14	-	6	-
Federico Hernán Pereyra (ARG)	04.01.1989	18	2	15	4
Herman Fernando Pérez Ipamo	27.05.1990	-	-		
Jesús Manuel Sagredo	10.03.1994	-	-	-	-
Carlos Hugo Tordoya Pizarro	31.07.1987	19	-	11	-
Moisés Villarroel Angulo	27.08.1998	1	-	14	1
Midfielders:					
Cristián Paul Arano	23.02.1995	-	-	9	-
Luis Daniel Arroyo Cabrera	17.01.1991	-	-	-	-
Joel Bejarano Azogue	21.03.1996	-	-	3	-
Jonathan Wilson Claure Beltrán	1995	-	-	-	-
Osvaldo Junior Daza		-	-	-	-
Helmut Enrique Gutiérrez Zapana	02.07.1987	14	-	13	-
Matías Joel Manzano (ARG)	17.06.1986	19	3	12	3
Mauro Darío Marrone (ARG)	23.06.1986	20	-	19	-
Martín Hernán Minadevino (ARG)	17.08.1983	18	2	14	1
Santos Rodrigo Navarro Arteaga	20.11.1990	-	-		
Ronald Rea Romero	29.03.1989	-	-		
José Manuel Sagredo Chávez	10.03.1994	-	-	-	-
Didi Torrico Camacho	18.05.1988	20	2	17	2
Joselito Vaca Velasco	12.08.1982	21	3	18	1
Forwards:					
Sergio Óscar Almirón (ARG)	20.09.1985	19	9	16	3
Sergio Álvarez	14.11.1994	1	-	3	-
Hugo Christophe Bargas (ARG)	22.10.1986			18	11
Alexis Alfredo Carrasco Sanguino	11.02.1995	2	-		
Vladimir Castellón Colque	08.12.1989	11	1	-	-
Ángel Cuellar Tuero	24.06.1990	-	-	-	-
Jorge Pereira da Silva „Jorghino" (BRA)	04.12.1985	-	-		
Carlos Hugo Moreno Mercado	07.01.1997	-	-	-	-
Dennis Franklin Pinto Saavedra	25.08.1995	-	-	-	-
Pablo Antonio Salinas Menacho	07.08.1979	18	7	15	4
Yovani Sosa		-	-	-	-
Leonardo Vaca Gutiérrez	24.11.1995	-	-	7	-
Trainer:					
Mauricio Ronald Soria Portillo [07.04.-14.12.2014]	01.06.1966	21			
Fernando Suárez [Caretaker]		1			
Erwin Sánchez Freking [as of 01.01.2015]	19.10.1969			22	

CLUB BOLÍVAR LA PAZ

Foundation date: April 12, 1925
Address: Calle 17 de Obrajes, La Paz
Stadium: Estadio „Hernando Siles Zuazo“, La Paz – Capacity: 42,000

THE SQUAD

	DOB	Ape		Cla	
		M	G	M	G
Goalkeepers:					
Romel Javier Quiñónez Suárez	25.06.1992	18	-	20	-
Widen Rojas Jou	01.04.1993	-	-	-	-
Guillermo Viscarra Bruckner	07.02.1993	5	-	1	-
Defenders:					
Lorgio Álvarez Roca	29.06.1978	15	-	6	-
Nelson David Cabrera Báez (PAR)	22.04.1983	17	3	19	6
Ronald Eguino Segovia	20.02.1988	18	1	19	1
Luis Alberto Gutiérrez Herrera	15.01.1985	20	-	17	1
Edemir Rodríguez Mercado	21.10.1986	-	-	11	1
Luis Francisco Rodríguez Zegada	22.08.1994	11	1	12	-
Ricardo Hugo Sagardia Medrano	01.03.1995	3	-	4	-
Stalin Taborga Cortéz	13.02.1994	-	-	-	-
Midfielders:					
Kevin Alcántara Saavedra	10.07.1996	-	-	-	-
Jaime Darío Arrascaita Iriondo	02.09.1993	-	-	6	-
Remy Balcázar	13.06.1995	-	-	-	-
Jhasmani Campos Dávalos	10.05.1988			16	3
José Luis Sánchez Capdevila (ESP)	12.02.1981	18	4	11	2
Rudy Alejandro Cardozo Fernández	14.02.1990	7	2	-	-
José Luis Chávez Sánchez	18.05.1986	14	-	13	-
Víctor Andrés Córdoba Córdoba (COL)	08.11.1987	6	-	9	-
Walter Alberto Flores Condarco	29.10.1978	17	-	18	-
Juan Miguel Callejón Bueno (ESP)	11.02.1987	21	15	18	9
Damir Miranda Mercado	06.10.1985	16	-	15	5
Erwin Mario Saavedra Flores	22.02.1996	21	-	17	2
Miguel Gerardo Suárez Savino	01.06.1993	1	-		
Forwards:					
Luis Alberto Alí Vega	17.04.1994	1	-	8	1
Juan Carlos Arce Justiniano	10.04.1985	21	5	10	2
Jhamil Bejarano		-	-	-	-
Leandro Marcelo Maygua Ríos	12.09.1992	15	3	11	2
Óscar Eduardo Rodas Vargas (COL)	14.07.1987	14	4		
Carlos Vicente Tenorio Medina (ECU)	14.05.1979	21	12	12	4
César Gerardo Yecerotte Soruco (ARG)	28.08.1988	7	1	16	2
Trainer:					
Francisco Xabier Azkargorta Uriarte (ESP) [as of 27.02.2014]	26.09.1952	4			
Vladimir Soria Camacho [Caretaker]	15.07.1964	1			
Francisco Xabier Azkargorta Uriarte (ESP) [as of 27.02.2014]		17		22	

CLUB JORGE WILSTERMAN COCHABAMBA

Year of Formation: November 24, 1949
Address: Calle Ecuador 673, Cochabamba
Stadium: Estadio „Félix Capriles“, Cochabamba – Capacity: 32,000

THE SQUAD

	DOB	Ape		Cla	
		M	G	M	G
Goalkeepers:					
Denis Cartagena Leaño	17.09.1987	-	-		
Matías Ezequiel Dituro (ARG)	08.05.1987	21	2	22	2
Yadin Salazar Caballero	26.03.1982	1	-	-	-
Cristian Germán Salinas Fuentes	09.11.1993	-	-	-	-
Gustavo Salvatierra García		-	-	-	-
Defenders:					
Jorge Miguel Ayala Quintana	27.11.1988	6	-	1	-
José Carlos Barba Paz	21.04.1985	19	-	7	-
Enrique David Díaz Velázquez (URU)	04.09.1982	20	1	20	1
Sergio Daniel Garzón Garzón	16.02.1991	1	-	-	-
Brian Alejandro Hinojosa Pinto		1	-	1	-
Iván Enrique Huayhuata Romero	09.03.1989			17	1
Pablo Antonio Laredo Pardo				-	-
Juan Sebastian Reyes Farell	1996	1	-	-	-
Amilcar Alvaro Sánchez Guzmán	23.01.1991	16	-	18	1
Christian Israel Vargas Claros	08.09.1983	18	1	10	-
Juan Carlos Zampiery Rivarola	28.09.1989	17	-	19	-
Edward Mauro Zenteno Álvarez	05.12.1984	12	-	20	1
Oscar Julio Zenteno Álvarez	07.12.1989	-	-	-	-
Midfielders:					
Juan Pablo Aponte Gutiérrez	18.05.1992	15	1	16	-
Martín Rodrigo Belfortti Rodríguez (ARG)	04.07.1981	-	-	-	-
Adán Alexis Félix Bravo (ARG)	15.09.1984	9	2	3	-
José Fabricio Bustamante		-	-	-	-
Michael Fernando Castellón Escaler	16.04.1996	2	-	7	-
Marcelo Raúl Flores	17.10.1993	-	-	-	-
José Marcelo Gomes (BRA)	24.11.1981	-	-	-	-
David Osvaldo Medina Aguirre	06.08.1986	-	-	-	-
Marco Antonio Rivero Montaño	14.02.1992	1	-	-	-
Ronald Segovia Calzadilla	17.01.1985	15	-	8	-
Roly Desiderio Sejas Muñoz	31.05.1986	11	-	13	-
Gianakis Suárez Tan Wing	26.09.1991	8	-	3	-
Antonio Thomaz Santos de Barros (BRA)	27.01.1986	16	3	18	2
Mariano Néstor Torres (ARG)	19.05.1987			18	4
Edson Marcelo Zenteno Álvarez	12.08.1978	12	-	2	-
Forwards:					
Augusto Andaveris Iriondo	05.05.1979	15	1	17	2
Óscar Alberto Díaz Acosta	22.10.1985	20	8	21	4
Brayan López Peña	27.09.1990	-	-	-	-
José Luis Mendoza Amador	07.05.1994	-	-	-	-
Carlos Ariel Neumann Torres (PAR)	03.01.1986	-	-	19	3
Gabriel Olivera		1	-	-	-
Brian Olmos		1	-	-	-
Félix Quero López (ESP)	07.09.1982	3	-	-	-
Carlos Eduardo Vargas Menacho	26.02.1987	8	1	4	-
Rodrigo Vargas Touchard	01.09.1989	12	2	21	2
Trainer:					
Julio César Baldivieso Rico [01.07.-31.12.2014]	02.12.1971	22			
Juan Manuel Llop (ARG) [as of 01.01.2015]	01.06.1963			22	

CLUB ATLÉTICO NACIONAL POTOSÍ

Foundation date: March 24, 1942
Address: Pasaje Bulevar Edificio Potosi no.2425
Stadium: Estadio „Víctor Agustín Ugarte", Potosí – Capacity: 30,000

THE SQUAD

	DOB	Ape M	Ape G	Cla M	Cla G
Goalkeepers:					
Carlos Alberto Barahona Angulo (COL)	20.01.1980	19	-	10	-
Carlos Leonel Navarro Flores	14.05.1994	-	-	-	-
Diego Zamora Roca	12.09.1993	3	-	13	-
Defenders:					
Juan Pablo Alemán	04.05.1990	19	2	16	1
Rodrigo Borda Quispe	11.02.1992			14	1
Claudio Rubén Centurión (PAR)	21.07.1983	12	1	-	-
Eliseo Isaias Dury Gómez	16.10.1990	22	1	22	3
Douglas Rodolfo Ferrufino Rojas	18.12.1991			2	-
Ignacio Awad García Justiniano	20.08.1986	19	2	20	-
Iván Enrique Huayhuata Romero	09.03.1989	-	-		
Rony Jiménez Mendoza	12.04.1989	21	1	22	-
Armin Oliva Porcel	03.03.1992	-	-	-	-
José Antonio Revuelta	25.04.1988	-	-	-	-
Ronald Rodríguez Cabrera	11.06.1989	-	-	-	-
Marco Antonio Salazar	12.06.1985	-	-	-	-
Midfielders:					
Anderson Raimundo da Silva (BRA)	02.02.1980	17	8	18	2
Rodrigo Ayrton Arias Banegas	04.11.1990	-	-	-	-
Pedro Mauricio Baldivieso Ferrufino	22.07.1996	-	-		
Jaime Cardozo Tahua	16.10.1981	-	-	-	-
Werther Thiers Charles da Silva (BRA)	11.03.1984	17	3	20	4
Rolando Elmer Choque Calisaya	23.05.1993	19	-	12	-
Andrés Fernando Irahola Zallez	01.11.1991	7	1	9	-
Leonel Justiniano Araúz	02.07.1992	22	5	20	4
Wilber Mendoza	03.03.1992	2	-	-	-
Maximiliano Iván Ortíz Cuello (ARG)	11.10.1989	12	-	-	-
Rubén Ángel Panozo	10.12.1999	1	-	-	-
Luis Fernando Pavia				1	-
Roberto Paz Jiménez	19.02.1991	5	-	6	-
Juan Pablo Sánchez Chanevy	08.07.1982	19	-	12	-
Sergio Eduardo Torrez Quiróz	14.02.1981	-	-	-	-
Forwards:					
Diego Fernando Ardaya Serrate	09.04.1991	4	-	-	-
José Antonio Ayala Pacheco (PAR)	08.04.1992			11	2
Sergio Nicolás Bubas (ARG)	23.04.1989			20	6
Héctor Ariel Calderón Llave	03.11.1992	13	1	10	-
Davor Alfredo Cardozo Montaño	23.04.1988	-	-	-	-
Jorge Daniel Detona (ARG)	21.05.1986	3	-	-	-
Erlan Gastón Mealla Anachuri	03.09.1988	20	3	21	1
Pastor Monrroy Fuentes				9	-
José Leandro Padilla Abunter	21.01.1985	-	-	-	-
Diego Franz Quiñonez Suárez	30.11.1993	-	-	-	-
Walter Humberto Rioja Ugarte	23.04.1986	20	1	15	-
Jeison Siquita Toledo	20.01.1992	7	-	-	-
Trainer:					
Marcos Rodolfo Ferrufino Estévez [20.02.2014-23.03.2015]	25.04.1963	22		8	
Miguel Ángel Zahzú (ARG) [as of 26.02.2015]				14	

CLUB DEPORTIVO ORIENTE PETROLERO
SANTA CRUZ DE LA SIERRA

Foundation date: November 5, 1955
Address: Av. Monseñor Costas No.50 - Barrio San Antonio, Santa Cruz de la Sierra
Stadium: Estadio „Ramón "Tahuichi" Aguilera", Santa Cruz de la Sierra – Capacity: 40,000

THE SQUAD

	DOB	Ape		Cla	
		M	G	M	G
Goalkeepers:					
Oscar Luis Antelo Justiniano	18.06.1979	-	-	-	-
Alex Arancibia Chávez	28.01.1990	7	-	4	-
Marcos Ariel Argüello (ARG)	28.07.1981			17	-
Carlos Erwin Arias Égüez	18.02.1980	16	-	2	-
Luiz Fernando Gutiérrez Pimentel		-	-	-	-
Juan David Pedraza Cuellar				-	-
Defenders:					
Joel Fernando Alba				2	-
Carlos Enrique Añez Oliva	06.07.1995	19	-	16	2
Marvin Orlando Bejarano Jiménez	06.03.1988	12	-	17	1
Mariano Sebastián Brau (ARG)	10.07.1982	18	-	19	2
Rubén Darío Carballo Ortíz	03.01.1991	-	-	2	1
Alvaro Christian Córtez Parada		-	-	-	-
Diego Aroldo Cuéllar Tomichá	18.03.1994	-	-	-	-
Raúl Andrés Cuesta Martínez	23.07.1988	7	-	-	-
Alejandro Meleán Villarroel	16.07.1987	22	6	19	4
Yussein Yeltsin Monasterio Miashiro		-	-	-	-
Ronny Fernando Montero Martínez	15.05.1991	2	-	3	-
Gustavo Olguin Mancilla	13.11.1994	-	-		
Jorge Antonio Ortíz Ortíz	01.06.1984	5	-	15	1
Ronald Raldés Balcazar	20.04.1981	19	-	19	-
Midfielders:					
Danny Bryan Bejarano Yañez	03.01.1994	20	-	19	1
Jonathan Delgadillo Vargas	05.06.1993	-	-	-	-
Yasmani Georges Duk Arandia	01.03.1988	8	3	18	9
Brahian Égüez Flores		-	-	1	-
Matías Sebastián García (ARG)	16.01.1983	12	1		
Ronald Lázaro García Justiniano	17.12.1980	2	-	4	-
Diego Josué Hoyos Carrillo	29.09.1992	-	-	5	-
Rodrigo Alejandro Lafuente López	03.01.1991	-	-	-	-
Pedro Luis Laserna Vargas				1	-
Juan Carlos Maldonado (ARG)	07.09.1986			-	-
Alan Jorge Mercado Berthalet		9	-	14	1
Gualberto Olmos Mojica	07.10.1984	20	4	17	4
Juan Alexis Ribera Castillo				1	-
Fernando Javier Saucedo Pereyra	15.03.1990	17	-	-	-
Carlos Augusto Serrano Borja	22.06.1993	-	-	1	-
Diego Terrazas Pérez	23.02.1987	-	-	-	-
Thiago dos Santos Ferreira (BRA)	14.05.1984	21	4	16	2
Mateo Henrique Zoch Méndez		-	-	-	-
Forwards:					
Carmelo Algarañaz Añez	27.01.1996			2	-
Pedro Jesús Azogue Rojas	06.12.1994	13	-	18	-
Elder Cuéllar Yabeta	15.06.1994	-	-	-	-
Grover Cuéllar	09.05.1988	-	-	-	-
Richar Mariano Estigarribia Ortega (PAR)	15.08.1992	16	5	3	-
Danilo Javier Peinado Lerena (URU)	15.02.1985			8	-
Alcides Peña Jiménez	14.01.1989	19	5	18	4
Diego Armando Rodríguez Campos	28.08.1993	2	-	2	1
Carlos Enrique Saucedo Urgel	11.09.1979			17	6
Rodrigo Mauricio Vargas Castillo	19.10.1994	19	5	8	-
Trainer:					
Eduardo Andrés Villegas Camara [01.07.-31.12.2014]	29.03.1964	22			
David Avilés [01.01.-19.01.2015; Caretaker]				1	
José Horacio Basualdo (ARG) [20.01.-08.03.2015]	20.06.1963			9	
David Avilés [as of 09.03.2015]				12	

CLUB ATLÉTICO PETROLERO DEL GRAN CHACO YACUIBA

Foundation date: September 4, 2000
Address: 27 de Mayo 1 entre Ballivian y Avaroa, Yacuiba
Stadium: Estadio Provincial de Yacuiba, Yacuiba – Capacity: 30,000

THE SQUAD

	DOB	Ape		Cla	
		M	G	M	G
Goalkeepers:					
Christian Chilo Rojas	12.03.1994			1	-
Jorge Luis Flores Alcoba	13.12.1988	6	-	4	-
José Feliciano Peñarrieta Flores	18.11.1988	16	-	19	-
Luis Carlos Poquiviqui		-	-		
Defenders:					
Santos Amador Quispe	06.04.1982	18	-	16	1
Jaime Durán Gómez (MEX)	02.12.1981			10	-
Jesús Carlos Flores Vaca	10.04.1996	5	-	3	-
Jorge Samuel Flores Seas		6	-	5	-
Luis Alejandro Flores Gumile	17.12.1994			2	-
Omar Alejandro Flores Serrano (MEX)	06.05.1979			11	-
Faustino Abraham García Justiniano	15.02.1984	1	-	-	-
Gerson Luis García Gálvez	24.04.1985	15	1	19	-
Luis Enrique Hurtado Badani	27.09.1993	9	-	14	-
Omar Jesús Morales Paz	18.01.1988	18	4	7	3
Gustavo Olguin Mancilla	13.11.1994			11	2
Juan Camilo Ríos Arboleda (COL)	04.12.1987	20	2	15	-
Alahin Saavedra Suruy		2	-	-	-
Midfielders:					
Jorge Marco Andia Pizarro	08.02.1988	15	-	4	-
Paul Jorge Burton Salvatierra	25.06.1992	17	-	18	-
Nicolás Marcelo Canalis (ARG)	25.07.1985	11	1	-	-
Jorge Nicolás Díaz (ARG)	29.08.1986	7	-	-	-
Aldo Vladimir Gallardo	07.10.1985	11	-	13	1
Jesús Ronald Gallegos Vera	06.09.1982	19	1	14	-
José María Méndez				14	-
Frank Ernesto Oni Iriarte	28.12.1989	7	-	-	-
Aldo Peña Dorado	26.07.1982	2	-	-	-
Jaime Robles Céspedes	02.02.1978	19	3	17	3
Diego Andrés Vacca Moreno (COL)	10.05.1986	13	2	-	-
Forwards:					
Edwin Alpire Parra	1987	13	1	11	1
Kevin Benítez León	30.09.1994			12	2
Jorge Céspedes Vargas	14.07.1990	11	-	17	1
Juan Eduardo Fierro Ribera	23.06.1988			16	3
Ignacio Martínez Vela	27.01.1993	18	5	14	2
Jorge Hernán Orgaz Cuenca	02.03.1996	6	1	-	-
Álex Fernando Pontons Paz	26.11.1994			7	-
Jeison Arley Quiñónes Angulo (COL)	17.09.1986	19	6	3	2
Pablo Zeballos Bejarano				6	-
Trainer:					
Milton Maygua Herrera [01.07.-11.08.2014]	18.09.1970	1			
David De La Torre (MEX) [12.08.2014-05.04.2015]		21		12	
Alfredo Cristino Jara Mereles (PAR) [as of 06.04.2015]	02.05.1963			10	

CLUB BAMIN REAL POTOSÍ

Foundation date: October 20, 1941
Address: Calle Final Bustillos s/n (Industrias Potosí), Potosí
Stadium: Estadio „Víctor Agustín Ugarte", Potosí – Capacity: 18,000

THE SQUAD

	DOB	Ape		Cla	
		M	G	M	G
Goalkeepers:					
Franz Elmer Arias Fernández	30.01.1986	-	-	-	-
Denis Cartagena Leaño	17.09.1987			2	-
Cristian Céspedes		-	-	-	-
Henry Williams Lapczyk Vera (PAR)	17.04.1978	11	-	20	-
José Osbaldo Nova Anhel	16.05.1994			-	-
Jorge Esteban Ruth Cruz	26.12.1982	11	-	-	-
Defenders:					
Diego Marcelo Blanco Vallejos	10.03.1988	15	1	1	-
Juan Enrique Bustillos Bozo	17.05.1988			-	-
Fabricio Campos Davalos	10.09.1994	-	-	-	-
Luis Miguel Garnica Chávez	27.08.1992	-	-	7	-
Alberto Justiniano Gonzáles	24.04.1994	6	-	-	-
Daniel Mancilla Duran	17.12.1991	9	-	11	-
Alejandro Méndez Chávez	11.01.1992	-	-	-	-
Jorge Antonio Ortuño	14.01.1994	-	-	-	-
Mauricio Simon Panozo Veizaga	03.07.1991	-	-	-	-
Luis Carlos Paz Yabeta	16.05.1986	15	1	11	1
Alan Brian Peredo Salazar		-	-	-	-
Carlos Fernando Ponce	15.05.1987	13	-	3	-
Juan Pablo Rioja		15	-	8	-
Ronald Taylor Rivero Khun	29.01.1980	16	-	21	-
Juan Carlos Sánchez Ampuero	01.03.1985	9	1	20	1
Jorge Leonardo Toco Arredondo	13.01.1992			3	-
Saúl Torres Rojas	22.03.1990	6	1	17	1
José Daniel Zabala Negrete	01.01.1993	-	-		
Mauro Andrés Zanotti (ARG)	14.01.1985	18	-	5	-
Midfielders:					
Jon Paulo Acchura Parraga	01.08.1993	-	-	9	-
Victor Hugo Angola Cadima	14.08.1986	-	-	-	-
Ariel Cirilo Alejandro Aragón (ARG)	22.10.1982	-	-		
Carlos Alberto Arias Gutiérrez	24.01.1981	-	-	-	-
Rodrigo Fabián Ávila Solíz	01.01.1995	-	-	4	-
Álvaro Miguel Berrios		-	-	2	-
Fernando Ariel Brandán (ARG)	15.11.1980	15	-	-	-
Edgar Marcelo Escalante Mojica	13.03.1986	20	-	19	4
Dino Huallpa Mendoza	04.09.1988	13	-	11	1
Carlos Mustafa Kassab Mendoza	09.03.1991	-	-	-	-
Milton Erik Melgar Cuellar	20.11.1986	-	-	-	-
Juan Miguel Noe Siles	29.01.1988	3	-	-	-
Eduardo Fabiano Ortíz Cuéllar	07.05.1980	14	-	18	-
Darwin Peña Arce	08.08.1977	20	2	18	5
Osmar Martín Rivas (PAR)	27.03.1985	-	-	-	-
Erwin Junior Sánchez Paniagua				7	-
Forwards:					
Jenry Alaca Maconde	14.11.1986	-	-	17	1
Gilbert Álvarez Vargas	07.04.1992			22	9
Aldair Jonathan Berrios Arana	30.07.1994	-	-	-	-
Martín Blanco (ARG)	02.06.1991	15	4	15	1
Freddy Chispas Arias	10.06.1984	-	-	-	-
Álvaro Edil Espindola Rivera	26.09.1993	6	-	-	-
Carlos Daniel Hidalgo Cadena (COL)	25.04.1986			11	1
Leonardo Fabián Piris (ARG)	01.04.1990			4	-
Pablo Osvaldo Vázquez Micieli (ARG)	29.07.1982	20	8		
Iván Jamilton Adán Zerda (ARG)	17.11.1989	14	1	20	4
Trainer:					
Víctor Hugo Andrada Canalis (ARG) [07.04.-30.11.2014]	25.12.1958	19			
Juan Miguel Noe Siles [30.11.-31.12.2014; Caretaker]	29.01.1988	3			
Jose Alberto Rossi (ARG) [as of 01.01.2015]				22	

CLUB DEPORTIVO SAN JOSÉ ORURO

Foundation date: March 19, 1942

Address: Caro entre 6 de Agosto y Potosi No. 448, Oruro

Stadium: Estadio „Jesús Bermúdez“, Oruro – Capacity: 28,000

THE SQUAD

	DOB	Ape		Cla	
		M	G	M	G
Goalkeepers:					
Jesús Enrique Careaga Guzmán				-	-
Rubén Escobar Fernández (PAR)	06.02.1991			-	-
Carlos Emilio Lampe Porras	17.03.1987	19	-	21	-
Sergio Ariel Matinella (ARG)	11.02.1984	3	-		
David Patiño Gutiérrez	10.06.1996	-	-	-	-
Roberto Carlos Rivas Rivera	09.06.1985	-	-	1	-
Defenders:					
Marcelo Francisco Estrada Baya	30.12.1992	-	-	-	-
Jasson Martín Fernández Mollo				-	-
Douglas Rodolfo Ferrufino Rojas	18.12.1991	-	-		
Luis Ariel Jaldin Torrico		-	-	-	-
Ariel Juárez Montaño	23.06.1988	20	1	18	2
Miguel Ángel Juárez Montaño	26.03.1988			2	-
Erwin Melgar Melgar	26.02.1987	-	-		
Delio Ramon Ojeda Ferreira (PAR)	25.09.1985	18	2	12	1
Diego Jhosimar Prado Tupa	29.06.1986	9	-	15	-
Luis Aníbal Torrico Valverde	14.09.1986	13	2	21	3
Juan Gabriel Valverde Rivera	24.06.1990	19	3	12	-
Arnaldo Andrés Vera Chamorro (PAR)	22.01.1980	11	-	16	-
Wilder Zabala Perrogón	31.12.1982	18	2	11	1
Midfielders:					
Sebastián Darío Carrizo (ARG)	25.02.1978	-	-	-	-
Luis Alberto Closa González (PAR)	10.03.1984	10	1	-	-
Antonio Fernández Rodríguez	04.06.1997	1	-	-	-
Kevin Aquilino Fernández				5	-
Álex Gutiérrez				-	-
Mijael Huanca Camacho	23.04.1993	1	-	6	1
Leandro Ferreira Pessoa (BRA)	15.07.1986			-	-
Miguel Oswaldo Loaiza Tardio	13.02.1983	18	4	11	1
Darwin Jesús Lora Vidaurre	10.07.1986	6	-	13	-
Limbert Méndez Rocha	18.08.1982	1	-	-	-
Juan Carlos Morales		1	-	2	-
Mario Alberto Ovando Padilla	10.11.1985	18	-	16	-
Gil Antonio Parada Velarde	28.05.1991	9	3	1	-
Mario Leonardi Parrado Alanez	05.10.1993	13	-	12	-
Ronald Puma Caballero	23.05.1980	13	-	16	7
Abdón Reyes Cardozo	15.10.1981	19	2	16	2
Javier Sebastián Robles (ARG)	18.01.1985			11	2
Antonio Armando Torrez Serrano	05.03.1988	-	-	-	-
Erland Urgel Valencia	17.03.1987	-	-	-	-
Ricardo Verduguez	28.07.1989	16	1	11	1
Forwards:					
Carlos Arroyo		1	-	1	-
Mauro Sergio Bustamante (ARG)	23.06.1991	19	8	15	6
José Luis Contaja	26.06.1987			1	-
Miguel Ángel Cuéllar	25.01.1982			11	2
Cristián Omar Díaz (ARG)	03.11.1986	10	1		
Juan Eduardo Fierro Ribera	23.06.1988	-	-		
José Carlos Muñóz López	21.09.1994	14	2	9	-
Angel Reinaldo Orué Echeverría (PAR)	05.01.1989			5	1
Nelson Sossa Chávez	14.03.1986	5	2	12	3
Marcelo Zamorano	02.06.1996	1	-	1	-
Trainer:					
Teodoro Cárdenas [10.08.2014; Caretaker]		1			
Miguel Ángel Zahzú (ARG) [11.08.-26.10.2014]		12			
Teodoro Cárdenas [29.10.2014-14.03.2015]		9		10	
Néstor Rolando Clausen (ARG) [15.03.-27.04.2015]	29.09.1962			8	
Mario Rolando Ortega [as of 28.04.2015]	12.09.1965			4	

CLUB SPORT BOYS WARNES

Year of Formation: August 17, 1954

Address: *Not available*

Stadium: Estadio „Samuel Vaca Jiménez", Warnes – Capacity: 18,000

THE SQUAD

	DOB	Ape		Cla	
		M	G	M	G
Goalkeepers:					
Sergio Daniel Galarza Soliz	25.08.1975	9	-	-	-
Miguel Angel Mercado Mole	08.12.1988	14	-	19	-
Saidt Mustafá	11.09.1989	-	-	3	-
Luis Miguel Romero Kolque	04.08.1996			-	-
Defenders:					
Rolando Barra Pinedo	10.03.1987	15	1	13	-
Mario Alberto Cuéllar Saavedra	05.05.1989	12	-	18	-
Juan Pablo Fernández Méndez	07.02.1982	5	-	10	1
Héctor Luis Gaitán (ARG)	09.02.1987	6	-	1	-
Miguel Ángel Hoyos Guzmán	11.03.1981	15	-	-	-
Luis Gerardo Ibañez (ARG)	02.11.1987			5	-
Daniel Manjón Montero	19.02.1990	11	-	10	-
Erwin Melgar Melgar	26.02.1987			2	-
Carlos Enrique Mendoza Loayza	19.10.1992	11	-	16	-
Herman Fernando Pérez Ipamo	27.05.1990			-	-
Miguel Ángel Rimba de la Barra	20.01.1990	-	-	-	-
Rosauro Rivero Céspedes	08.09.1982	16	1	19	-
Álvaro José Solíz Vaca	19.06.1992	1	-	-	-
Ronald Lorgio Suárez Saucedo	05.12.1990	-	-	-	-
Midfielders:					
Maximiliano Gabriel Andrada (ARG)	05.10.1985	20	2	2	-
Marco Antonio Barrios	23.02.1995	-	-	16	-
Ariel Arnaldo Gómez		1	-	3	-
Jesús Alejandro Gómez Lanza	18.07.1979	15	-	10	1
Olvis Justiniano Cuellar	21.10.1988	12	-	11	-
Sergio Ciro Justiniano		-	-		
Leandro Ferreira Pessoa (BRA)	15.07.1986	22	1	4	1
Luis Antonio Liendo Asbún	25.02.1978	-	-	-	-
Cristhian Machado Pinto	20.06.1990	10	-	-	-
Santos Rodrigo Navarro Arteaga	20.11.1990			8	-
Daner Jesús Pachi Bozo	01.04.1984	-	-	-	-
Julio César Pérez Peredo	24.10.1991	17	2	5	-
Carlos Enrique Pinto Medina		-	-	9	-
Thaigo Leitão Polieri (BRA)	12.06.1978	-	-	-	-
Ronald Rea Romero	29.03.1989			14	1
Juan Francisco Rivero		1	-	1	-
Sergio Fabián Rosado Moscoso	07.06.1993	-	-	-	-
Cristian Manuel Salvatierra Arroyo	26.01.1990			1	-
Forwards:					
Gilbert Álvarez Vargas	07.04.1992	-	-		
Anderson Aparecido Gonzaga Martins "Anderson Gonzaga" (BRA)	29.12.1983	22	4	18	4
José Alfredo Castillo Parada	09.02.1983	14	4	13	6
Eduardo Farias Machado de Salles Filho (BRA)	06.04.1990			16	1
Cristian Gastón Fabbiani (ARG)	09.03.1983	8	-		
Juan Carlos Galvis Claure	08.02.1987	14	-	17	1
Limberg Gutiérrez Mariscal	19.11.1977	2	1	-	-
Delfin Manrique Manrique		5	1	8	2
Marcos Emanuel Ovejero (ARG)	23.11.1986	18	4	15	2
Reinaldo Parada Pérez	17.01.1995	10	-	12	3
Elvis Uriona Escobar	03.12.1984	-	-	5	-
Trainer:					
Néstor Rolando Clausen (ARG) [01.01.-05.10.2014]	29.09.1962	10			
Víctor Hugo Antelo Bárba [06.10.-31.12.2014]	02.11.1964	12			
Celso Rafael Ayala Gavilán (PAR) [01.01.-19.03.2015]	20.08.1970			10	
Víctor Hugo Antelo Bárba [as of 20.03.2015]	02.11.1964			12	

CLUB THE STRONGEST LA PAZ

Foundation date: April 8, 1908
Address: Calle Colón No. 512 esq. Comercio, La Paz
Stadium: Estadio „Hernando Siles Zuazo", La Paz – Capacity: 42,000

THE SQUAD

	DOB	Ape M	Ape G	Cla M	Cla G
Goalkeepers:					
Gustavo Adolfo Fernández Pedraza	23.08.1986	-	-	-	-
Andrés Martín Jemio Portugal (ARG)	06.07.1976	-	-	-	-
Daniel Vaca Tasca	11.03.1978	21	1	16	-
Marco Daniel Vaca Vélez	10.03.1990	2	-	6	-
Defenders:					
Abraham Cabrera Scarpin	20.02.1991	2	-	13	3
Germán Martín Centurión Marecos (PAR)	05.05.1980			14	-
David Rafael Checa Padilla	28.05.1993	8	1	4	-
Ernesto Rubén Cristaldo Santa Cruz (PAR)	16.03.1984	16	4	14	5
Luis Fernando Marteli Dias (BRA)	08.02.1986	20	-	16	2
Nelvin Solíz Escalante	03.11.1989	10	1	11	5
Jair Torrico Camacho	02.08.1986	15	-	17	-
Luis Aníbal Torrico Valverde	14.09.1986	-	-		
Walter Veizaga Argote	22.04.1986	9	-	16	-
Midfielders:					
Maximiliano Bajter Ugollini (URU)	01.03.1986	15	3	9	3
Raúl Castro Peñaloza	19.08.1988	19	-	19	1
Alejandro Saúl Chumacero Bracamonte	22.04.1991	18	2	18	6
Daniel Coca Hurtado	19.02.1995	-	-	-	-
Marcos Antonio León	22.10.1995	4	-	1	-
Sacha Silvestre Lima Castedo	17.08.1981	-	-	-	-
Luis Hernán Melgar Ortíz	22.02.1983	18	7	17	3
Victor Hugo Melgar Bejarano	23.02.1988	2	-	5	-
Enrique Parada Salvatierra	04.11.1981	15	-	10	-
Marco David Paz Alvarez	29.07.1979	17	-	3	-
Miguel Alejandro Quiroga Castillo	15.09.1991	4	-	9	1
Forwards:					
Freddy Alessandro Abastoflór Molina	10.01.1993	1	-	-	-
Daniel Andrés Chávez Betancourt	13.01.1990	11	-	3	-
Bernardo Nicolás Cuesta (ARG)	20.12.1988			13	3
Pablo Daniel Escobar Olivetti	12.07.1978	19	8	16	7
Abel Rodrigo Méndez (ARG)	27.10.1992	17	4	11	-
Rodrigo Luis Ramallo Cornejo	19.10.1990	20	8	18	4
José Gabriel Ríos Banegas	20.03.1986	1	-	13	2
Diego Horacio Wayar Cruz	15.10.1993	17	-	10	-
Trainer:					
Néstor Oscar Craviotto (ARG) [01.07.2014-10.04.2015]	03.10.1946	21		14	
Arturo Andrés Norambuena Ardiles (CHI) [Caretaker for Round 16]	24.11.1971	1			
Juan Carlos Paz García [as of 11.04.2015]				8	

CLUB DEPORTIVO UNIVERSITARIO SAN FRANCISCO XAVIER DE SUCRE

Foundation date: April 5, 1962
Address: Calle Olañeta 45, Sucre
Stadium: Estadio Olímpico Patria, Sucre – Capacity: 32,000

THE SQUAD

	DOB	Ape		Cla	
		M	G	M	G
Goalkeepers:					
Raúl Arturo Cano Salinas	22.01.1990	2	-	1	-
Luis Eduardo Galarza Solíz	14.05.1985	-	-	-	-
Raúl Alejandro Olivares Gálvez (CHI)	17.04.1988			9	-
Juan Marcelo Robledo Pizarro (ARG)	03.12.1978	19	-	1	-
Juan Carlos Robles Rodríguez	25.01.1985	2	-	11	-
Defenders:					
Ramiro Daniel Ballivián	08.04.1992	6	-	17	-
Alejandro René Bejarano Sajama (ARG)	21.06.1984	17	-	14	1
Carlos Oswaldo Camacho Suarez	05.02.1986	11	-	16	-
Jorge Ignacio Cuéllar Rojas	29.04.1991	18	-	17	-
Kevin Yamil Espada				1	-
Elmer Ferrufino Orellano	29.10.1987	-	-	-	-
Ezequiel Nicolás Filipetto (ARG)	09.12.1987	19	-	15	-
Leandro Gareca Fernández	23.01.1991	-	-	6	-
Jorge Ignacio González Barón (URU)	22.12.1983			-	-
Sergio Oliver Rappu		-	-	-	-
Oscar Leandro Ribera Guzman	11.02.1992	14	-	2	-
Luis Yamil Tapia				-	-
José Daniel Zabala Negrete	01.01.1993			2	-
Midfielders:					
Pedro Mauricio Baldivieso Ferrufino	22.07.1996			3	1
Jorge Enrique Flores Yrahory	01.02.1994	14	1	15	-
Alan Loras Vélez	07.04.1986	17	-	20	-
Rolando Ribera Menacho	13.03.1983	20	-	13	1
Diego Gabriel Rivero Cortéz	16.06.1991	18	4	4	-
Ludwing Jorge Rojas Osorio	08.06.1990			7	-
Rubén de la Cuesta Vera „Rubén" (ESP)	11.09.1981	18	2	12	-
Diego Aldair Sandoval Caballero	22.07.1991	4	-	3	-
Federico Silvestre (ARG)	06.10.1987	11	2	11	-
Miguel Gerardo Suárez Savino	01.06.1993			9	1
Cristian Jhamil Urdininea Zambrana	06.01.1993	1	-	9	-
Darlon Zárate	29.11.1994	-	-	-	-
Forwards:					
Cristhian Alexseis Arabe Pedraza	25.12.1991	6	-	2	-
Bryan Bonilla				3	-
Diego Aroldo Cabrera Flores	13.08.1982	3	1	-	-
David Leonardo Castro Cortés (COL)	12.05.1989			16	4
Álvaro Delgadillo Pacheco	30.08.1993	-	-	-	-
Harold Rodrigo Guzmán		-	-	-	-
José Miguel Justiniano				1	-
Richar Luis Mercado Corozo (ECU)	20.12.1986			6	1
Claudio Ezequiel Mosca (ARG)	02.04.1991	19	2		
Ignacio Rodríguez Ortiz „Nacho Rodríguez" (ESP)	06.11.1982	5	-		
Lucas Ramón Ojeda Villanueva	01.02.1986	7	-	-	-
Martín Adrián Palavicini López (ARG)	15.08.1977	15	6	19	13
Edson Rigoberto Pérez Torres	16.12.1992	-	-	9	-
Mauricio Saucedo Guardia	14.08.1985	19	6	13	4
Pastor Buenaventura Tórrez Quiróz	27.08.1990	16	2	3	-
Trainer:					
Javier Vega [01.01.2013-06.12.2014]		20			
Diego Aroldo Cabrera Flores [07-31.12.2014; Caretaker]	13.08.1982	2			
Julio César Baldivieso Rico [as of 01.01.2015]	02.12.1971			22	

CLUB UNIVERSITARIO DE PANDO

Foundation date: March 5, 1995
Address: *Not available*
Stadium: Estadio Universidad Amazónica de Pando, Pando – Capacity: 4,000

THE SQUAD

	DOB	Ape M	Ape G	Cla M	Cla G
Goalkeepers:					
Favio Gabriel Gómez (ARG)	29.03.1984	13	-	5	-
Rider Melgar	18.08.1995	9	-	11	-
Luis Carlos Poquiviqui				6	-
Defenders:					
Óscar Nadin Díaz González (PAR)	29.01.1984			6	-
Gustavo León Trujillo	15.01.1990	13	1	16	2
Manolo Mirlo López	22.07.1990	11	-	15	-
Roberto Carlos López	07.04.1998	1	-	10	-
Miguel Ortíz Pereyra	06.07.1982	11	1	14	-
Miguel David Paredes	01.06.1998	3	-	4	-
Paulo Henrique Moreira (BRA)		20	4	18	2
Luis Gatty Ribeiro Roca	01.11.1979	8	-	-	-
Carlos Daniel Roca	11.05.1997	14	-	4	-
Andrés Felipe Salinas Rodríguez (COL)	11.06.1986	12	1		-
Hermán Solíz Salvatierra	14.07.1982	19	-	1	-
Jammel Soria Oliveira		5	-	-	-
Stalin Taborga Cortez	13.02.1994			10	-
Julio César Villa				1	-
Midfielders:					
Oscar Antonio Areco	24.07.1990	12	-		
David Beimar Beyuma				2	-
Agustín Goñi (ARG)	05.05.1981	12	-		
Ángelo Albert Da Silva Guaqui		1	-	7	-
Brandon Luis Iñiguez Herrera	25.02.1993			1	-
Brayan Íñiguez Herrera	25.03.1992			11	-
Erick Gabriel Iragua Párraga	30.11.1995			10	-
Andrés Jiménez Pérez	08.07.1985	14	-	22	-
Jorge Mauricio Roca		5	-	-	-
Jorge Hugo Rojas				7	1
Limberg Salas Vargas	24.02.1983	12	-	-	-
Nicolás Suárez Vaca	23.12.1978	18	-	16	1
Pedro Fernando Taborga Bascope		11	-	17	2
Felipe Santiago Villalba	14.03.1985			11	1
Carlos Andrés Zabala Negrete	19.05.1994	15	-	9	-
Forwards:					
Jehanamed Castedo Silva	04.04.1990	18	5	11	1
Adrián Cuéllar Paredes	08.09.1982	12	-	4	-
Moisés Michel Guaqui	09.05.1996	1	-	4	-
Rogerio Inacio „Leilao" (BRA)	03.08.1980	18	4	14	2
Enzo Damián Maidana (ARG)	02.01.1990			20	3
Rodrigo Noe Mejido Cruz	06.05.1995	1	-	4	-
Sebastián Yeri Molina Ribera	20.11.1990	4	-	-	-
Denis Auder Moroña Von-Boeck				2	-
Oscar Toluba				-	-
Juan Pablo Zabala Rodríguez		8	1	3	-
Trainer:					
Miguel Ángel Mercado Melgar [01.07.-12.10.2014]	30.08.1975	10			
Sergio Apaza [14.10.-23.11.2014]	22.12.1955	8			
Claudio Marrupe (ARG) [24.11.2014-20.03.2015]	26.12.1960	4		9	
José Luis Ortíz Melgar [as of 21.03.2015]	17.11.1985			13	

SECOND LEVEL
Segunda División - Liga Nacional „B“ "Simón Bolívar" 2014/2015

First Stage

Please note: Top-2 of each group qualified for the final Stage (Hexagonal Final).

Grupo A

1.	CD Guabirá Montero	8	5	2	1	17	-	6	17
2.	Club Destroyers Santa Cruz de la Sierra	8	4	3	1	22	-	5	15
3.	Universitario del Beni Trinidad	8	4	2	2	12	-	10	14
4.	El Torno FC	8	3	1	4	18	-	14	10
5.	Real Mapajo Cobija	8	0	0	8	2	-	36	0

Grupo B

1.	Club Unión Maestranza de Viacha	8	6	1	1	16	-	7	19
2.	Escuela de Fútbol Ramiro Castillo El Alto	8	4	1	3	18	-	11	13
3.	Club Aurora Cochabamba	8	3	3	2	10	-	9	12
4.	Escuela de Fútbol Enrique Happ Shinahota	8	3	2	3	12	-	9	11
5.	Oruro Royal Club	8	0	1	7	7	-	27	1

Grupo C

1.	Club Atlético Bermejo	8	7	1	0	26	-	6	22
2.	Club Atlético Ciclón de Tarija	8	5	1	2	24	-	12	16
3.	Club Fancesa Sucre	8	4	2	2	21	-	15	14
4.	Club 10 de Noviembre Wilstermann Cooperativas Potosí	8	1	0	7	13	-	20	3
5.	Club Quebracho Villamontes	8	1	0	7	15	-	46	3

Hexagonal Final

1.	Club Atlético Ciclón de Tarija (*Promoted*)	10	6	3	1	21	-	12	21
2.	Club Atlético Bermejo (*Promotion/Relegation Play-off*)	10	6	1	3	15	-	11	19
3.	CD Guabirá Montero	10	4	3	3	18	-	14	15
4.	Escuela de Fútbol Ramiro Castillo El Alto	10	4	1	5	21	-	22	13
5.	Club Destroyers Santa Cruz de la Sierra	10	3	3	4	14	-	18	12
6.	Club Unión Maestranza de Viacha	10	1	1	8	11	-	23	4

NATIONAL TEAM
INTERNATIONAL MATCHES
(16.07.2014 – 15.07.2015)

07.09.2014	Fort Lauderdale	Bolivia - Ecuador	0-4(0-2)	(F)
10.09.2014	Denver	Bolivia - Mexico	0-1(0-1)	(F)
14.10.2014	Antofagasta	Chile - Bolivia	2-2(1-1)	(F)
18.11.2014	La Paz	Bolivia - Venezuela	3-2(1-1)	(F)
06.06.2015	San Juan	Argentina - Bolivia	5-0(3-0)	(F)
12.06.2015	Viña del Mar	Mexico - Bolivia	0-0	(CA)
15.06.2015	Valparaíso	Ecuador - Bolivia	2-3(0-3)	(CA)
19.06.2015	Santiago	Chile - Bolivia	5-0(2-0)	(CA)
25.06.2015	Temuco	Bolivia - Peru	1-3(0-2)	(CA)

07.09.2014, Friendly International
Lockhart Stadium, Fort Lauderdale (United States); Attendance: 10,000
Referee: Valdin Legister (Jamaica)

BOLIVIA - ECUADOR 0-4(0-2)

BOL: Romel Javier Quiñónez Suárez, Ronald Raldes Balcázar, Ronald Eguino Segovia, Marvin Orlando Bejarano Jiménez, Alejandro Meleán Villarroel, Ramiro Daniel Ballivian (46.Rodrigo Luis Ramallo Cornejo), Gualberto Mojica Olmos (46.Leandro Marcelo Maygua Ríos), José Luis Chávez Sánchez (76.Alejandro Saúl Chumacero Bracamonte), Raúl Castro Peñaloza (63.Rudy Alejandro Cardozo Fernández), Carlos Enrique Saucedo Urgel (46.Daniel Chávez Betancourt), Pedro Jesús Azogue Rojas (46.Danny Brayhan Bejarano Yañez). Trainer: Francisco Xabier Azcargorta Uriarte (Spain).

10.09.2014, Friendly International
Dick's Sporting Goods Park, Denver (United States); Attendance: 18,136
Referee: Chris Penso (United States)

BOLIVIA - MEXICO 0-1(0-1)

BOL: Daniel Vaca Tasca, Ronald Raldes Balcázar, Ronald Eguino Segovia, Marvin Orlando Bejarano Jiménez, Alejandro Meleán Villarroel (46.Alejandro Saúl Chumacero Bracamonte), José Luis Chávez Sánchez, Rudy Alejandro Cardozo Fernández (46.Gualberto Mojica Olmos), Danny Brayhan Bejarano Yañez (46.Damir Miranda Mercado), Leandro Marcelo Maygua Ríos (76.Mario Alberto Ovando Padilla), Carlos Enrique Saucedo Urgel (64.Rodrigo Luis Ramallo Cornejo), Daniel Chávez Betancourt (46.Ramiro Daniel Ballivian). Trainer: Francisco Xabier Azcargorta Uriarte (Spain).
Sent off: Ramiro Daniel Ballivian (89).

14.10.2014, Friendly International
Estadio Regional "Calvo y Bascuñán", Antofagasta; Attendance: 14,000
Referee: Pablo Díaz (Argentina)

CHILE - BOLIVIA 2-2(1-1)

BOL: Romel Javier Quiñónez Suárez, Ronald Raldes Balcázar, Edward Mauro Zenteno Álvarez, Alejandro Leonel Morales Pinedo, Martin Ramiro Guillermo Smedberg-Dalence (80.Augusto Andaveris Iriondo), Alejandro Meleán Villarroel, Damián Emmanuel Lizio (71.Juan Carlos Zampiery Rivarola), Miguel Ángel Hurtado Suárez (90+5.Ronald Eguino Segovia), Juan Carlos Arce Justiniano (65.Rudy Alejandro Cardozo Fernández; 90+2.Luis Alberto Gutiérrez Herrera), Carlos Enrique Saucedo Urgel (85.Gualberto Mojica Olmos), Pedro Jesús Azogue Rojas. Trainer: Francisco Xabier Azcargorta Uriarte (Spain).
Goals: Carlos Enrique Saucedo Urgel (14, 51).
Sent off: Edward Mauro Zenteno Álvarez (89).

18.11.2014, Friendly International
Estadio „Hernándo Siles Zuazo", La Paz; Attendance: n/a
Referee: Eduardo Gamboa Latourniere (Chile)
BOLIVIA - VENEZUELA 3-2(1-1)
BOL: Romel Javier Quiñónez Suárez, Ronald Raldes Balcázar, Luis Alberto Gutiérrez Herrera, Alejandro Leonel Morales Pinedo, Alejandro Meleán Villarroel (68.José Luis Chávez Sánchez), Damián Emmanuel Lizio (José Vaca Velasco), Miguel Ángel Hurtado Suárez, Alejandro Saúl Chumacero Bracamonte (46.Damir Miranda Mercado), Juan Carlos Arce Justiniano, Carlos Enrique Saucedo Urgel (84.Rodrigo Mauricio Vargas Castillo), Rodrigo Luis Ramallo Cornejo (46.Marcelo Moreno Martins). Trainer: Francisco Xabier Azcargorta Uriarte (Spain).
Goals: Ronald Raldes Balcázar (41), Damián Emmanuel Lizio (53), Juan Carlos Arce Justiniano (87).

06.06.2015, Friendly International
Estadio San Juan del Bicentenario, San Juan; Attendance: 18,000
Referee: Jorge Luis Osorio Reyes (Chile)
ARGENTINA - BOLIVIA 5-0(3-0)
BOL: Romel Javier Quiñónez Suárez, Edemir Rodríguez Mercado (46.Miguel Ángel Hurtado Suárez), Ronald Eguino Segovia (46.Wálter Veizaga Argote), Edward Mauro Zenteno Álvarez, Alejandro Leonel Morales Pinedo, Martin Ramiro Guillermo Smedberg-Dalence, Damián Emmanuel Lizio (57.Jhasmani Campos Dávalos), Pablo Daniel Escobar Olivetti (70.Marvin Orlando Bejarano Jiménez), Danny Brayhan Bejarano Yañez, Sebastián Gamarra Ruíz (46.Ronald Raldes Balcázar), Marcelo Moreno Martins (66.Ricardo Pedriel Suárez). Trainer: Mauricio Ronald Soria Portillo.

12.06.2015, 44th Copa América, Group Stage
Estadio Sausalito, Viña del Mar (Chile); Attendance: 14,987
Referee: Enrique Patricio Cáceres Villafañe (Paraguay)
MEXICO - BOLIVIA 0-0
BOL: Romel Javier Quiñónez Suárez, Ronald Raldes Balcázar, Edward Mauro Zenteno Álvarez, Alejandro Leonel Morales Pinedo, Martin Ramiro Guillermo Smedberg-Dalence, Jhasmani Campos Dávalos (71.Pablo Daniel Escobar Olivetti), Miguel Ángel Hurtado Suárez, Alejandro Saúl Chumacero Bracamonte, Danny Brayhan Bejarano Yañez, Marcelo Moreno Martins, Ricardo Pedriel Suárez (85.Marvin Orlando Bejarano Jiménez). Trainer: Mauricio Ronald Soria Portillo.

15.06.2015, 44th Copa América, Group Stage
Estadio "Elías Figueroa", Valparaíso (Chile); Attendance: 5,982
Referee: Joel Antonio Aguilar Chicas (El Salvador)
ECUADOR - BOLIVIA 2-3(0-3)
BOL: Romel Javier Quiñónez Suárez, Ronald Raldes Balcázar, Edward Mauro Zenteno Álvarez, Alejandro Leonel Morales Pinedo, Martin Ramiro Guillermo Smedberg-Dalence, Damián Emmanuel Lizio (72.Marvin Orlando Bejarano Jiménez), Miguel Ángel Hurtado Suárez, Alejandro Saúl Chumacero Bracamonte, Danny Brayhan Bejarano Yañez, Marcelo Moreno Martins (88.Damir Miranda Mercado), Ricardo Pedriel Suárez (57.Cristian Michael Coimbra Arias). Trainer: Mauricio Ronald Soria Portillo.
Goals: Ronald Raldes Balcázar (4), Martin Ramiro Guillermo Smedberg-Dalence (17), Marcelo Moreno Martins (42 penalty).

19.06.2015, 44th Copa América, Group Stage
Estadio Nacional "Julio Martínez Prádanos", Santiago; Attendance: 45,601
Referee: Andrés Cunha (Uruguay)

CHILE - BOLIVIA 5-0(2-0)

BOL: Romel Javier Quiñónez Suárez, Ronald Raldes Balcázar, Edemir Rodríguez Mercado (46.Marvin Orlando Bejarano Jiménez), Cristian Michael Coimbra Arias, Alejandro Leonel Morales Pinedo, Martin Ramiro Guillermo Smedberg-Dalence, Alejandro Saúl Chumacero Bracamonte, Pablo Daniel Escobar Olivetti (61.Damián Emmanuel Lizio), Marcelo Moreno Martins, Ricardo Pedriel Suárez, Wálter Veizaga Argote (46.Damir Miranda Mercado).Trainer: Mauricio Ronald Soria Portillo.

25.06.2015, 44th Copa América, Quarter-Finals
Estadio Municipal "Germán Becker", Temuco (Chile); Attendance: 16,872
Referee: Wilmar Alexander Roldán Pérez (Colombia)

BOLIVIA - PERU 1-3(0-2)

BOL: Romel Javier Quiñónez Suárez, Ronald Raldes Balcázar, Edward Mauro Zenteno Álvarez, Cristian Michael Coimbra Arias, Alejandro Leonel Morales Pinedo (46.Damián Emmanuel Lizio), Martin Ramiro Guillermo Smedberg-Dalence, Miguel Ángel Hurtado Suárez (46.Pablo Daniel Escobar Olivetti), Alejandro Saúl Chumacero Bracamonte, Danny Brayhan Bejarano Yañez, Marcelo Moreno Martins, Alcides Peña Jiménez (68.Ricardo Pedriel Suárez). Trainer: Mauricio Ronald Soria Portillo.
Goal: Marcelo Moreno Martins (84 penalty).

NATIONAL TEAM PLAYERS 2014/2015			
Name	**DOB**	**Caps**	**Goals**
[Club 2014/2015]			

(Caps and goals at 05.07.2015)

Goalkeepers

Romel Javier QUIÑÓNEZ Suárez [2014/2015: Club Bolívar La Paz]	25.06.1992	**12**	**0**
Daniel VACA Tasca [2014: Club The Strongest La Paz]	03.11.1978	**9**	**0**

Defenders

Ramiro Daniel BALLIVIÁN [2014: CD Universitario San Francisco Xavier Sucre]	08.04.1992	**2**	**0**
Marvin Orlando BEJARANO Jiménez [2014/2015: CD Oriente Petrolero Santa Cruz de la Sierra]	06.03.1988	**23**	**0**
Cristian Michael COIMBRA Arias [2015: CSCD Blooming Santa Cruz de la Sierra]	11.09.1989	**3**	**0**
Ronald EGUINO Segovia [2014/2015: Club Bolívar La Paz]	20.02.1988	**9**	**0**
Luis Alberto GUTIÉRREZ Herrera [2014: Club Bolívar La Paz]	15.01.1985	**41**	**0**
Miguel Ángel HURTADO Suárez [2014/2015: CSCD Blooming Santa Cruz de la Sierra]	04.07.1985	**6**	**0**
Leandro Marcelo MAYGUA Ríos [2014: Club Bolívar La Paz]	12.09.1992	**4**	**0**
Alejandro MELEÁN Villarroel [2014: CD Oriente Petrolero Santa Cruz de la Sierra]	16.06.1987	**9**	**0**

Alejandro Leonel MORALES Pinedo [2014/2015: CSCD Blooming Santa Cruz de la Sierra]	02.09.1988	**7**	**0**
Ronald RALDES Balcazar [2014/2015: CD Oriente Petrolero Santa Cruz de la Sierra]	20.04.1981	**86**	**2**
Edemir RODRÍGUEZ Mercado [2015: Club Bolívar La Paz]	21.10.1984	**16**	**0**
Juan Carlos ZAMPIERY Rivarola [2014: Club Jorge Wilstermann Cochabamba]	28.09.1989	**1**	**0**
Edward Mauro ZENTENO Álvarez [2014/2015: Club Jorge Wilstermann Cochabamba]	05.12.1984	**19**	**0**

Midfielders

Pedro Jesús AZOGUE Rojas [2014: CD Oriente Petrolero Santa Cruz de la Sierra]	06.12.1994	**9**	**0**
Danny Brayhan BEJARANO Yañez [2014/2015: CD Oriente Petrolero Santa Cruz de la Sierra]	03.01.1994	**13**	**0**
Jhasmani CAMPOS Dávalos [2015: Club Bolívar La Paz]	10.05.1988	**28**	**2**
Rudy Alejandro CARDOZO Fernández [2014: Club Bolívar La Paz]	14.02.1990	**33**	**4**
Raúl CASTRO Peñaloza [2014: Club The Strongest La Paz]	19.08.1989	**1**	**0**
Daniel Andrés CHÁVEZ Betancourt [2014: Club The Strongest La Paz]	13.01.1990	**4**	**0**
José Luis CHÁVEZ Sánchez [2014: Club Bolívar La Paz]	18.05.1986	**24**	**1**
Alejandro Saúl CHUMACERO Bracamonte [2014/2015: Club The Strongest La Paz]	22.04.1991	**25**	**1**
Pablo Daniel ESCOBAR Olivetti [2015: Club The Strongest La Paz]	23.02.1979	**20**	**3**
Sebastián GAMARRA Ruíz [2015: Milan AC (ITA)]	15.01.1997	**1**	**0**
Damián Emmanuel LIZIO [2014/2015: O'Higgins FC Rancagua (CHI)]	30.06.1989	**6**	**1**
Damir MIRANDA Mercado [2014/2015: Club Bolívar La Paz]	16.10.1985	**6**	**0**
Gualberto MOJICA Olmos [2014: CD Oriente Petrolero Santa Cruz de la Sierra]	07.10.1984	**30**	**3**
Mario Alberto OVANDO Padilla [2014: CD San José Oruro]	09.11.1985	**1**	**0**
Martin Ramiro Guillermo SMEDBERG-DALENCE [2014/2015: IFK Göteborg (SWE)]	10.05.1984	**6**	**1**
Joselito VACA Velasco [2014: CSCD Blooming Santa Cruz de la Sierra]	12.08.1982	**55**	**2**
Wálter VEIZAGA Argote [2015: Club The Strongest La Paz]	22.04.1986	**12**	**0**

Forwards			
Augusto ANDAVERIS Iriondo [2014: Club Jorge Wilsterman Cochabamba]	05.05.1979	**21**	**1**
Juan Carlos ARCE Justiniano [2014: Club Bolívar La Paz]	10.04.1985	**44**	**6**
Marcelo MORENO Martins [2014: Cruzeiro EC Belo Horizonte (BRA); 02.2015-> Changchun Yatai FC (CHN)]	18.06.1987	**54**	**14**
Ricardo PEDRIEL Suárez [2015: Mersin İdmanyurdu SK (TUR)]	19.01.1987	**19**	**3**
Alcides PEÑA Jiménez [2015: CD Oriente Petrolero Santa Cruz de la Sierra]	14.01.1989	**15**	**1**
Rodrigo Luis RAMALLO Cornejo [2014: Club The Strongest La Paz]	14.10.1990	**4**	**0**
Carlos Enrique SAUCEDO Urgel [2014: Deportivo Saprissa San Juan (CRC)]	11.09.1979	**12**	**7**
Rodrigo Mauricio VARGAS Castillo [2014: CD Oriente Petrolero Santa Cruz de la Sierra:]	19.10.1994	**3**	**0**

National coaches		
Francisco Xabier AZCARGORTA Uriarte (Spain)	26.09.1953	21 M; 4 W; 8 D; 9 L; 23-40
[also national coach between 29.01.1993 – 21.09.1994; Complete records: 58 M; 13 W; 23 D; 22 L; 62-79]		
Mauricio Ronald SORIA Portillo	01.06.1966	5 M; 1 W; 1 D; 3 L; 4-15

BRAZIL

The Country:
República Federativa do Brasil (Federative Republic of Brazil)
Capital: Brasilia
Surface: 8,514,877 km²
Inhabitants: 202,768,562 (estimated 2014)
Time: UTC-2 to -4

The FA:
Confederação Brasileira de Futebol, Rua Victor Civita 66, Bloco 1 - Edifício 5-5 Andar Barra da Tijuca 22775-044 Rio de Janeiro
Year of Formation: 1914
Member of FIFA since: 1923
Member of CONMEBOL since: 1916
Internet: www.cbf.com.br

NATIONAL TEAM RECORDS	
First international match:	20.09.1914, Buenos Aires: Argentina – Brazil 3-0
Most international caps:	Marcos Evangelista de Morais „Cafu" – 142 caps (1990-2006)
Most international goals:	Edson Arantes do Nascimento „Pelé" – 77 goals (92 caps, 1957-1971)

OLYMPIC GAMES 1900-2012
1952, 1960, 1964, 1968, 1972, 1976, 1984&1988 (Runners-up), 1996 (3rd Place), 2000, 2008 (3rd Place), 2012 (Runners-up)
FIFA CONFEDERATIONS CUP 1992-2013
1997 (Winners), 1999 (Runners-up), 2001, 2003, **2005 (Winners)**, **2009 (Winners)**, **2013 (Winners)**

COPA AMÉRICA	
1916	3rd Place
1917	3rd Place
1919	**Winners**
1920	3rd Place
1921	Runners-up
1922	**Winners**
1923	4th Place
1924	Withdrew
1925	Runners-up
1926	Withdrew
1927	Withdrew
1929	Withdrew
1935	Withdrew
1937	Runners-up
1939	Withdrew
1941	Withdrew
1942	3rd Place
1945	Runners-up
1946	Runners-up
1947	Withdrew
1949	**Winners**
1953	Runners-up
1955	Withdrew
1956	4th Place
1957	Runners-up
1959	Runners-up
1959E	3rd Place
1963	4th Place
1967	Withdrew
1975	Semi-Finals
1979	Semi-Finals
1983	Runners-up
1987	Round 1
1989	**Winners**
1991	Runners-up
1993	Quarter-Finals
1995	Runners-up
1997	**Winners**
1999	**Winners**
2001	Quarter-Finals
2004	**Winners**
2007	**Winners**
2011	Quarter-Finals
2015	Quarter-Finals

FIFA WORLD CUP	
1930	Final Tournament (1st Round)
1934	Final Tournament (1st Round)
1938	Final Tournament (3rd Place)
1950	Final Tournament (Runners-up)
1954	Final Tournament (Quarter-Finals)
1958	**Final Tournament (Winners)**
1962	**Final Tournament (Winners)**
1966	Final Tournament (Group Stage)
1970	**Final Tournament (Winners)**
1974	Final Tournament (4th Place)
1978	Final Tournament (3rd Place)
1982	Final Tournament (2nd Round)
1986	Final Tournament (Quarter-Finals)
1990	Final Tournament (2nd Round of 16)
1994	**Final Tournament (Winners)**
1998	Final Tournament (Runners-up)
2002	**Final Tournament (Winners)**
2006	Final Tournament (Quarter-Finals)
2010	Final Tournament (Quarter-Finals)
2014	Final Tournament (4th Place)

PANAMERICAN GAMES	
1951	Withdrew
1955	-
1959	Runners-up
1963	**Winners**
1967	-
1971	-
1975	**Winners**
1979	**Winners**
1983	Runners-up
1987	**Winners**
1991	-
1995	Quarter-Finals
1999	-
2003	Runners-up
2007	Round 1
2011	-

PANAMERICAN CHAMPIONSHIP	
1952	**Winners**
1956	**Winners**
1960	Runners-up

BRAZILIAN CLUB HONOURS IN SOUTH AMERICAN CLUB COMPETITIONS:

COPA LIBERTADORES 1960-2014
Santos Futebol Clube (1962, 1963, 2011)
Cruzeiro Esporte Clube Belo Horizonte (1976, 1997)
Clube de Regatas do Flamengo Rio de Janeiro (1981)
Grêmio Foot-Ball Porto Alegrense (1983, 1995)
São Paulo Futebol Clube (1992, 1993, 2005)
Club de Regatas Vasco da Gama Rio de Janeiro (1998)
Sociedade Esportiva Palmeiras São Paulo (1999)
Sport Club Internacional Porto Alegre (2006, 2010)
Sport Club Corinthians Paulista São Paulo (2012)
Clube Atletico Mineiro Belo Horizonte (2013)
COPA SUDAMERICANA 2002-2014
Sport Club Internacional Porto Alegre (2008)
São Paulo Futebol Clube (2012)
RECOPA SUDAMERICANA 1989-2014
São Paulo Futebol Clube (1993, 1994)
Grêmio Foot-Ball Porto Alegrense (1996)
Cruzeiro Esporte Clube Belo Horizonte (1998)
Sport Club Internacional Porto Alegre (2007, 2011)
Santos Futebol Clube (2012)
Sport Club Corinthians Paulista São Paulo (2013)
Clube Atletico Mineiro Belo Horizonte (2014)
COPA CONMEBOL 1992-1999
Clube Atlético Mineiro (1992, 1997)
Botafogo de Futebol e Regatas Rio de Janeiro (1993)
São Paulo Futebol Clube (1994)
Santos Futebol Clube (1998)
SUPERCUP „JOÃO HAVELANGE“ 1988-1997*
Cruzeiro Esporte Clube Belo Horizonte (1991, 1992)
São Paulo Futebol Clube (1993)
COPA MERCOSUR 1998-2001**
Sociedade Esportiva Palmeiras São Paulo (1998)
Clube de Regatas do Flamengo Rio de Janeiro (1999)
Club de Regatas Vasco da Gama Rio de Janeiro (2000)

**Contested betwenn winners of all previous editions of the Copa Libertadores*

*** Contested between teams belonging countries from the southern part of South America (Argentina, Brazil, Chile, Paraguay and Uruguay).*

NATIONAL COMPETITIONS
TABLE OF HONOURS

	CHAMPIONS	CUP WINNERS
1959	-	Esporte Clube Bahia
1960	-	SE Palmeiras São Paulo
1961	-	Santos FC
1962	-	Santos FC
1963	-	Santos FC
1964	-	Santos FC
1965	-	Santos FC
1966	-	Cruzeiro EC Belo Horizonte
1967	-	SE Palmeiras São Paulo
1968	-	Botafogo de FR Rio de Janeiro
1969	-	-
1970	-	-
1971	Clube Atlético Mineiro	-
1972	SE Palmeiras São Paulo	-
1973	SE Palmeiras São Paulo	-
1974	CR Vasco da Gama Rio de Janeiro	-
1975	SC Internacional Porto Alegre	-
1976	SC Internacional Porto Alegre	-
1977	São Paulo FC	-
1978	Guarani FC Campinas	-
1979	SC Internacional Porto Alegre	-
1980	CR Flamengo Rio de Janeiro	-
1981	Grêmio Foot-Ball Porto Alegrense	-
1982	CR Flamengo Rio de Janeiro	-
1983	CR Flamengo Rio de Janeiro	-
1984	Fluminense FC Rio de Janeiro	-
1985	Coritiba FC	-
1986	São Paulo FC	-
1987	Sport Club do Recife	-
1988	Esporte Clube Bahia	-
1989	CR Vasco da Gama Rio de Janeiro	Grêmio Foot-Ball Porto Alegrense
1990	SC Corinthians Paulista São Paulo	CR Flamengo Rio de Janeiro
1991	São Paulo FC	Criciúma EC
1992	CR Flamengo Rio de Janeiro	SC Internacional Porto Alegre
1993	SE Palmeiras São Paulo	Cruzeiro EC Belo Horizonte
1994	SE Palmeiras São Paulo	Grêmio Foot-Ball Porto Alegrense
1995	Botafogo de FR Rio de Janeiro	SC Corinthians Paulista São Paulo
1996	Grêmio Foot-Ball Porto Alegrense	Cruzeiro EC Belo Horizonte
1997	CR Vasco da Gama Rio de Janeiro	Grêmio Foot-Ball Porto Alegrense
1998	SC Corinthians Paulista São Paulo	SE Palmeiras São Paulo
1999	SC Corinthians Paulista São Paulo	EC Juventude Caxias do Sul
2000	CR Vasco da Gama Rio de Janeiro	Cruzeiro EC Belo Horizonte
2001	Clube Atlético Paranaense Curitiba	Grêmio Foot-Ball Porto Alegrense
2002	Santos FC	SC Corinthians Paulista São Paulo
2003	Cruzeiro EC Belo Horizonte	Cruzeiro EC Belo Horizonte
2004	Santos FC	EC Santo André
2005	SC Corinthians Paulista São Paulo	Paulista FC São Paulo

2006	São Paulo FC	CR Flamengo Rio de Janeiro
2007	São Paulo FC	Fluminense FC Rio de Janeiro
2008	São Paulo FC	Sport Club do Recife
2009	CR Flamengo Rio de Janeiro	SC Corinthians Paulista São Paulo
2010	Fluminense FC Rio de Janeiro	Santos FC
2011	SC Corinthians Paulista São Paulo	CR Vasco da Gama Rio de Janeiro
2012	Fluminense FC Rio de Janeiro	SE Palmeiras São Paulo
2013	Cruzeiro EC Belo Horizonte	CR Flamengo Rio de Janeiro
2014	Cruzeiro EC Belo Horizonte	Clube Atlético Mineiro Belo Horizonte

	BEST GOALSCORERS	
1971	Dario José dos Santos (Clube Atlético Mineiro)	17
1972	Dario José dos Santos (Clube Atlético Mineiro) Pedro Virgilio Rocha Franchetti (São Paulo FC)	17
1973	Ramón da Silva Ramos (Santa Cruz FC Recife)	21
1974	Carlos Roberto de Oliveira „Roberto Dinamite“ (CR Vasco da Gama)	16
1975	Flávio Almeida da Fonseca „Flávio Minuano“ (SC Internacional Porto Alegre)	16
1976	Dario José dos Santos (SC Internacional Porto Alegre)	16
1977	José Reinaldo de Lima (Clube Atlético Mineiro)	28
1978	Paulo Luiz Massariol „Paulinho“ (CR Vasco da Gama)	19
1979	César Martins de Oliveira (América FC Rio de Janeiro) Roberto César Itacaramby (Cruzeiro EC Belo Horizonte)	12
1980	Arthur Antunes Coimbra „Zico“ (CR Flamengo Rio de Janeiro)	21
1981	João Batista Nunes de Oliveira (CR Flamengo Rio de Janeiro)	16
1982	Arthur Antunes Coimbra „Zico“ (CR Flamengo Rio de Janeiro)	21
1983	Sérgio Bernardino „Serginho“ (Santos FC)	22
1984	Carlos Roberto de Oliveira „Roberto Dinamite“ (CR Vasco da Gama)	16
1985	Edmar Bernardes dos Santos (Guarani FC Campinas)	20
1986	Antônio de Oliveira Filho „Careca“ (São Paulo FC)	25
1987	Luís Antônio Corréa da Costa „Müller“ (São Paulo FC)	25
1988	Nílson Esídio Mora (SC Internacional Porto Alegre)	15
1989	Túlio Humberto Pereira Costa (Goiás EC Goiânia)	11
1990	Charles Fabian Figueiredo Santos (Esporte Clube Bahia)	11
1991	Paulo César Vieira Rosa „Paulinho“ (Santos FC)	15
1992	José Roberto Gama de Oliveira „Bebeto“ (CR Vasco da Gama)	18
1993	Alexandre da Silva „Guga“ (Santos FC)	14
1994	Márcio Amoroso dos Santos (Guarani FC Campinas) Túlio Humberto Pereira Costa (Botafogo de FR Rio de Janeiro)	19
1995	Túlio Humberto Pereira Costa (Botafogo de FR Rio de Janeiro)	23
1996	Renaldo Lopes da Cruz (Clube Atlético Mineiro) Arílson de Paula Nunes „Paulo Nunes“ (Grêmio Foot-Ball Porto Alegrense)	16
1997	Edmundo Alves de Souza Neto (CR Vasco da Gama)	29
1998	Paulo Sergio Rosa „Viola“ (Santos FC)	21
1999	Guilherme de Cássio Alves (Clube Atlético Mineiro)	28
2000	Elpídio Barbosa Conceição „Dill“ (Goiás EC Goiânia) Magno Alves de Araújo (Fluminense FC Rio de Janeiro) Romário de Souza Faria (CR Vasco da Gama)	20
2001	Romário de Souza Faria (CR Vasco da Gama)	21
2002	Luís Fabiano Clemente (São Paulo FC) Rodrigo Fabri (Grêmio Foot-Ball Porto Alegrense)	19
2003	Editácio Vieira de Andrade „Dimba“ (Goiás EC Goiânia)	31

2004	Washington Stecanela Cerqueira (Clube Atlético Paranaense Curitiba)	34
2005	Romário de Souza Faria (CR Vasco da Gama)	22
2006	Rodrigo de Souza Cardoso (Goiás EC Goiânia)	17
2007	Josiel da Rocha (Paraná Clube Curitiba)	20
2008	Keirrison de Souza Carneiro (Coritiba FC) Washington Stecanela Cerqueira (Fluminense FC Rio de Janeiro) Kléber João Boas Pereira (Santos FC)	21
2009	Adriano Leite Ribeiro (CR Flamengo Rio de Janeiro) Diego Tardelli Martins (Clube Atlético Mineiro)	19
2010	Jonas Gonçalves Oliveira (Grêmio Foot-Ball Porto Alegrense)	23
2011	Humberlito Borges Teixeira (Santos FC)	23
2012	Frederico Chaves Guedes "Fred" (Fluminense FC Rio de Janeiro)	20
2013	Éderson Alves Ribeiro Silva (Clube Atlético Paranaense Curitiba)	21
2014	Frederico Chaves Guedes "Fred" (Fluminense FC Rio de Janeiro)	18

NATIONAL CHAMPIONSHIP
Campeonato Brasileiro Série A 2014
(19.04.- 07.12.2014)

Results

Round 1 [19-20.04.2014]

Fluminense - Figueirense 3-0(2-0)
SC Internacional - EC Vitória 1-0(1-0)
Chapecoense - Coritiba FC 0-0
São Paulo FC - Botafogo 3-0(2-0)
Atlético Paranaense - Grêmio 1-0(1-0)
Atlético Mineiro - Corinthians 0-0
EC Bahia - Cruzeiro EC 1-2(0-0)
Flamengo - Goiás EC 0-0
Santos FC - SC do Recife 1-1(0-0)
Criciúma EC - SE Palmeiras 1-2(1-0)

Round 2 [26-27.04.2014]

Coritiba FC - Santos FC 0-0
SE Palmeiras - Fluminense 0-1(0-1)
Botafogo - SC Internacional 2-2(0-2)
Corinthians - Flamengo 2-0(1-0)
Cruzeiro EC - São Paulo FC 1-1(0-0)
EC Vitória - Atlético Paranaense 2-2(2-0)
SC do Recife - Chapecoense 2-1(2-1)
Grêmio - Atlético Mineiro 2-1(2-0)
Figueirense - EC Bahia 0-2(0-1)
Goiás EC - Criciúma EC 1-0(0-0)

Round 3 [03-04.05.2014]

São Paulo FC - Coritiba FC 2-2(1-1)
Santos FC - Grêmio 0-0
Atlético Paranaense - Cruzeiro EC 2-3(2-1)
Fluminense - EC Vitória 1-2(0-0)
Flamengo - SE Palmeiras 4-2(1-2)
EC Bahia - Botafogo 1-0(0-0)
SC Internacional - SC do Recife 2-1(2-0)
Criciúma EC - Figueirense 1-0(1-0)
Atlético Mineiro - Goiás EC 0-1(0-0)
Chapecoense - Corinthians 0-1(0-0)

Round 4 [10-11.05.2014]

SE Palmeiras - Goiás EC 2-0(2-0)
SC Internacional - Atlético Paranaense 2-1(0-0)
Botafogo - Criciúma EC 6-0(1-0)
Fluminense - Flamengo 2-0(1-0)
São Paulo FC - Corinthians 1-1(0-0)
Atlético Mineiro - Cruzeiro EC 2-1(0-1)
Chapecoense - Grêmio 1-2(0-1)
Coritiba FC - SC do Recife 0-1(0-0)
EC Bahia - EC Vitória 1-1(0-1)
Figueirense - Santos FC 0-2(0-1)

Round 5 [15-18.05.2014]
Goiás EC - Botafogo 2-0(0-0)
Cruzeiro EC - Coritiba FC 3-2(2-1)
Flamengo - São Paulo FC 0-2(0-1)
Corinthians - Figueirense 0-1(0-0)
Atlético Paranaense - Chapecoense 1-1(0-0)
Grêmio - Fluminense 1-0(1-0)
Santos FC - Atlético Mineiro 1-2(1-0)
EC Vitória - SE Palmeiras 0-1(0-0)
Criciúma EC - SC Internacional 0-0
SC do Recife - EC Bahia 1-0(0-0) [05.06.]

Round 6 [22-23.05.2014]
Flamengo - EC Bahia 1-1(1-0)
Coritiba FC - SC Internacional 1-1(0-1)
Cruzeiro EC - SC do Recife 2-0(0-0)
Criciúma EC - Chapecoense 1-0(1-0)
Fluminense - São Paulo FC 5-2(1-2)
Corinthians - Atlético Paranaense 1-1(0-0)
Grêmio - Botafogo 2-1(1-1)
SE Palmeiras - Figueirense 1-0(1-0)
Goiás EC - Santos FC 2-2(1-2)
EC Vitória - Atlético Mineiro 2-3(0-2)

Round 7 [24-25.05.2014]
EC Bahia - Fluminense 0-1(0-1)
São Paulo FC - Grêmio 1-0(0-0)
SC do Recife - Corinthians 1-4(1-2)
Santos FC - Flamengo 0-0
Atlético Paranaense - Coritiba FC 2-0(0-0)
Figueirense - Goiás EC 0-1(0-1)
Botafogo - EC Vitória 1-1(1-0)
Atlético Mineiro - Criciúma EC 0-0
SC Internacional - Cruzeiro EC 1-3(1-1)
Chapecoense - SE Palmeiras 2-0(1-0)

Round 8 [29-30.05.2014]
SC do Recife - Grêmio 0-0
SE Palmeiras - Botafogo 0-2(0-0)
Criciúma EC - Coritiba FC 1-0(0-0)
SC Internacional - Chapecoense 2-0(1-0)
Goiás EC - EC Vitória 0-0
Corinthians - Cruzeiro EC 1-0(0-0)
Atlético Paranaense - São Paulo FC 2-2(1-0)
Atlético Mineiro - Fluminense 2-0(0-0)
Flamengo - Figueirense 1-1(1-1)
EC Bahia - Santos FC 0-2(0-0)

Round 9 [31.05.-01.06.2014]
São Paulo FC - Atlético Mineiro 2-1(1-0)
Coritiba FC - Goiás EC 3-0(3-0)
EC Vitória - SC do Recife 0-1(0-0)
Cruzeiro EC - Flamengo 3-0(3-0)
Grêmio - SE Palmeiras 0-0
Chapecoense - EC Bahia 2-1(0-0)
Fluminense - SC Internacional 1-1(1-1)
Santos FC - Criciúma EC 2-0(2-0)
Figueirense - Atlético Paranaense 1-3(0-1)
Botafogo - Corinthians 1-0(1-0) [11.10.]

Round 10 [17-18.07.2014]
SC do Recife - Botafogo 1-0(1-0)
Coritiba FC - Figueirense 0-2(0-1)
Grêmio - Goiás EC 0-0
Flamengo - Atlético Paranaense 1-2(1-1)
EC Bahia - São Paulo FC 0-2(0-2)
Criciúma EC - Fluminense 3-2(1-0)
Corinthians - SC Internacional 2-1(2-0)
Santos FC - SE Palmeiras 2-0(1-0)
Cruzeiro EC - EC Vitória 3-1(0-0)
Chapecoense - CA Mineiro 1-1(1-0) [07.08.]

Round 11 [19-20.07.2014]
São Paulo FC - Chapecoense 0-1(0-0)
Atlético Mineiro - EC Bahia 1-1(0-1)
Figueirense - Grêmio 0-1(0-1)
Botafogo - Coritiba FC 1-0(1-0)
SE Palmeiras - Cruzeiro EC 1-2(0-2)
EC Vitória - Corinthians 0-0
SC Internacional - Flamengo 4-0(2-0)
Fluminense - Santos FC 1-0(0-0)
Atlético Paranaense - Criciúma EC 2-0(0-0)
Goiás EC - SC do Recife 0-0

Round 12 [26-27.07.2014]
Santos FC - Chapecoense 3-0(1-0)
Cruzeiro EC - Figueirense 5-0(1-0)
Criciúma EC - EC Vitória 1-3(0-1)
EC Bahia - SC Internacional 0-1(0-0)
SC do Recife - Atlético Mineiro 2-1(0-0)
Corinthians - SE Palmeiras 2-0(0-0)
Atlético Paranaense - Fluminense 0-3(0-2)
Goiás EC - São Paulo FC 2-1(1-0)
Flamengo - Botafogo 1-0(1-0)
Grêmio - Coritiba FC 2-3(0-0)

Round 13 [02-03.08.2014]
Botafogo - Cruzeiro EC 1-1(1-0)
São Paulo FC - Criciúma EC 1-1(0-0)
EC Vitória - Grêmio 2-1(0-1)
SE Palmeiras - EC Bahia 1-1(0-0)
Coritiba FC - Corinthians 0-0
Figueirense - SC do Recife 3-0(1-0)
Chapecoense - Flamengo 1-0(1-0)
Fluminense - Goiás EC 2-0(2-0)
Atlético Mineiro - Atlético Paranaense 3-1(1-0)
SC Internacional - Santos FC 1-0(0-0)

Round 14 [09-10.08.2014]
EC Bahia - Goiás EC 1-0(1-0)
Criciúma EC - Cruzeiro EC 0-0
Fluminense - Coritiba FC 1-1(1-0)
Flamengo - SC do Recife 1-0(0-0)
Santos FC - Corinthians 0-1(0-0)
Atlético Paranaense - Botafogo 2-0(1-0)
SC Internacional - Grêmio 2-0(0-0)
São Paulo FC - EC Vitória 3-1(3-1)
Atlético Mineiro - SE Palmeiras 2-1(1-0)
Chapecoense - Figueirense 0-1(0-0)

Round 15 [16-17.08.2014]
Goiás EC - SC Internacional 0-1(0-0)
Corinthians - EC Bahia 1-1(1-1)
SE Palmeiras - São Paulo FC 1-2(0-0)
Coritiba FC - Flamengo 0-1(0-1)
Cruzeiro EC - Santos FC 3-0(1-0)
EC Vitória - Chapecoense 0-0
Grêmio - Criciúma EC 2-0(1-0)
Botafogo - Fluminense 2-0(0-0)
SC do Recife - Atlético Paranaense 1-1(1-1)
Figueirense - Atlético Mineiro 2-2(1-1)

Round 16 [21-22.08.2014]
SC do Recife - SE Palmeiras 2-1(2-1)
Santos FC - Atlético Paranaense 2-0(1-0)
Figueirense - Botafogo 1-0(1-0)
Coritiba FC - EC Vitória 2-0(1-0)
EC Bahia - Criciúma EC 0-0
Flamengo - Atlético Mineiro 2-1(0-1)
SC Internacional - São Paulo FC 0-1(0-1)
Chapecoense - Fluminense 1-0(0-0)
Corinthians - Goiás EC 5-2(1-1)
Cruzeiro EC - Grêmio 1-0(0-0)

Round 17 [23-24.08.2014]
Botafogo - Chapecoense 1-0(1-0)
Atlético Mineiro - SC Internacional 1-0(0-0)
SE Palmeiras - Coritiba FC 1-0(1-0)
Fluminense - SC do Recife 4-0(2-0)
São Paulo FC - Santos FC 2-1(1-0)
EC Vitória - Figueirense 0-1(0-0)
Grêmio - Corinthians 2-1(0-0)
Criciúma EC - Flamengo 0-2(0-0)
Atlético Paranaense - EC Bahia 0-0
Goiás EC - Cruzeiro EC 0-1(0-1)

Round 18 [30-31.08.2014]
SE Palmeiras - SC Internacional 0-1(0-1)
Cruzeiro EC - Chapecoense 4-2(0-1)
Botafogo - Santos FC 1-0(0-0)
SC do Recife - Criciúma EC 2-0(0-0)
Corinthians - Fluminense 1-1(0-1)
Coritiba FC - Atlético Mineiro 0-0
Figueirense - São Paulo FC 1-1(0-0)
EC Vitória - Flamengo 1-2(1-1)
Grêmio - EC Bahia 1-0(0-0)
Goiás EC - Atlético Paranaense 3-1(2-0)

Round 19 [06-07.09.2014]
Flamengo - Grêmio 0-1(0-0)
Santos FC - EC Vitória 3-1(0-0)
Chapecoense - Goiás EC 0-0
Fluminense - Cruzeiro EC 3-3(2-2)
São Paulo FC - SC do Recife 2-0(2-0)
Atlético Mineiro - Botafogo 1-0(0-0)
Criciúma EC - Corinthians 0-0
Atlético Paranaense - SE Palmeiras 1-1(1-0)
EC Bahia - Coritiba FC 0-0
SC Internacional - Figueirense 2-3(2-0)

Round 20 [11-12.09.2014]
SE Palmeiras - Criciúma EC 1-0(0-0)
Grêmio - Atlético Paranaense 1-0(0-0)
Figueirense - Fluminense 1-1(1-0)
SC do Recife - Santos FC 3-1(1-1)
Coritiba FC - Chapecoense 3-0(2-0)
Botafogo - São Paulo FC 2-4(2-3)
EC Vitória - SC Internacional 2-0(1-0)
Goiás EC - Flamengo 1-0(0-0)
Corinthians - Atlético Mineiro 1-0(1-0)
Cruzeiro EC - EC Bahia 2-1(0-1)

Round 21 [13-14.09.2014]
Fluminense - SE Palmeiras 3-0(2-0)
Chapecoense - SC do Recife 3-1(1-0)
Santos FC - Coritiba FC 2-1(2-0)
Flamengo - Corinthians 1-0(0-0)
São Paulo FC - Cruzeiro EC 2-0(1-0)
EC Bahia - Figueirense 3-0(2-0)
SC Internacional - Botafogo 2-0(1-0)
Atlético Paranaense - EC Vitória 2-0(1-0)
Atlético Mineiro - Grêmio 0-0
Criciúma EC - Goiás EC 1-0(0-0)

Round 22 [18-19.09.2014]
Cruzeiro EC - Atlético Paranaense 2-0(1-0)
EC Vitória - Fluminense 3-1(0-1)
SC do Recife - SC Internacional 0-0
Figueirense - Criciúma EC 1-1(0-1)
Botafogo - EC Bahia 2-3(2-1)
SE Palmeiras - Flamengo 2-2(0-2)
Coritiba FC - São Paulo FC 3-1(0-1)
Corinthians - Chapecoense 1-1(1-0)
Goiás EC - Atlético Mineiro 2-3(0-3)
Grêmio - Santos FC 0-0

Round 23 [20-21.09.2014]
Atlético Paranaense - SC Internacional 0-1(0-0)
Criciúma EC - Botafogo 1-1(0-1)
Flamengo - Fluminense 1-1(1-1)
SC do Recife - Coritiba FC 1-0(0-0)
Corinthians - São Paulo FC 3-2(1-2)
Cruzeiro EC - Atlético Mineiro 2-3(1-2)
EC Vitória - EC Bahia 2-1(1-1)
Santos FC - Figueirense 3-1(1-1)
Grêmio - Chapecoense 1-0(1-0)
Goiás EC - SE Palmeiras 6-0(4-0)

Round 24 [25-26.09.2014]
Coritiba FC - Cruzeiro EC 1-2(0-2)
SC Internacional - Criciúma EC 3-0(1-0)
EC Bahia - SC do Recife 1-0(0-0)
Chapecoense - Atlético Paranaense 3-0(1-0)
Fluminense - Grêmio 0-0
São Paulo FC - Flamengo 2-2(1-1)
Figueirense - Corinthians 1-0(0-0)
Botafogo - Goiás EC 1-0(0-0)
SE Palmeiras - EC Vitória 2-0(1-0)
Atlético Mineiro - Santos FC 3-2(2-0)

Round 25 [27-28.09.2014]
SC do Recife - Cruzeiro EC 0-0
Chapecoense - Criciúma EC 1-1(1-0)
São Paulo FC - Fluminense 1-3(0-0)
Botafogo - Grêmio 0-2(0-0)
Atlético Paranaense - Corinthians 1-0(1-0)
Atlético Mineiro - EC Vitória 2-0(0-0)
EC Bahia - Flamengo 2-1(1-0)
Santos FC - Goiás EC 2-0(1-0)
SC Internacional - Coritiba FC 4-2(3-1)
Figueirense - SE Palmeiras 3-1(0-1)

Round 26 [03-05.10.2014]
SE Palmeiras - Chapecoense 4-2(0-1)
Flamengo - Santos FC 0-1(0-1)
Fluminense - EC Bahia 1-1(1-0)
Coritiba FC - Atlético Paranaense 1-0(0-0)
EC Vitória - Botafogo 2-1(0-0)
Grêmio - São Paulo FC 0-1(0-0)
Corinthians - SC do Recife 3-0(1-0)
Cruzeiro EC - SC Internacional 2-1(2-0)
Criciúma EC - Atlético Mineiro 3-1(2-1)
Goiás EC - Figueirense 1-0(1-0)

Round 27 [09-10.10.2014]
Botafogo - SE Palmeiras 0-1(0-0)
São Paulo FC - Atlético Paranaense 1-0(1-0)
Coritiba FC - Criciúma EC 1-0(1-0)
EC Vitória - Goiás EC 2-2(2-0)
Cruzeiro EC - Corinthians 0-1(0-0)
Grêmio - SC do Recife 2-0(1-0)
Figueirense - Flamengo 1-2(0-1)
Fluminense - Atlético Mineiro 0-0
Santos FC - EC Bahia 1-0(1-0)
Chapecoense - SC Internacional 5-0(2-0)

Round 28 [11-12.10.2014]
Corinthians - Botafogo 1-1(1-0) [01.06.]
Goiás EC - Coritiba FC 3-0(2-0)
SE Palmeiras - Grêmio 2-1(0-0)
Flamengo - Cruzeiro EC 3-0(1-0)
Atlético Mineiro - São Paulo FC 1-0(0-0)
EC Bahia - Chapecoense 0-1(0-1)
SC Internacional - Fluminense 2-1(0-0)
SC do Recife - EC Vitória 1-2(1-2)
Atlético Paranaense - Figueirense 3-0(0-0)
Criciúma EC - Santos FC 3-0(2-0)

Round 29 [18-19.10.2014]
Fluminense - Criciúma EC 4-2(1-1)
São Paulo FC - EC Bahia 2-1(1-0)
Goiás EC - Grêmio 0-0
Atlético Mineiro - Chapecoense 1-0(1-0)
SE Palmeiras - Santos FC 1-3(0-2)
Atlético Paranaense - Flamengo 2-1(2-1)
SC Internacional - Corinthians 1-2(0-2)
Figueirense - Coritiba FC 4-0(1-0)
Botafogo - SC do Recife 1-1(0-1)
EC Vitória - Cruzeiro EC 0-1(0-0)

Round 30 [22-23.10.2014]
EC Bahia - Atlético Mineiro 1-1(0-0)
Flamengo - SC Internacional 2-0(0-0)
Corinthians - EC Vitória 2-1(1-0)
Cruzeiro EC - SE Palmeiras 1-1(0-0)
Criciúma EC - Atlético Paranaense 0-1(0-0)
Coritiba FC - Botafogo 2-0(1-0)
Grêmio - Figueirense 1-0(1-0)
Santos FC - Fluminense 0-1(0-0)
Chapecoense - São Paulo FC 0-0
SC do Recife - Goiás EC 0-1(0-0)

Round 31 [25-27.10.2014]
Fluminense - Atlético Paranaense 2-1(0-0)
SE Palmeiras - Corinthians 1-1(1-0)
Figueirense - Cruzeiro EC 1-1(0-1)
Coritiba FC - Grêmio 1-1(1-0)
Atlético Mineiro - SC do Recife 3-2(1-1)
EC Vitória - Criciúma EC 3-1(0-0)
Chapecoense - Santos FC 1-1(0-1)
Botafogo - Flamengo 2-1(1-0)
SC Internacional - EC Bahia 2-0(2-0)
São Paulo FC - Goiás EC 3-0(2-0)

Round 32 [01-02.11.2014]
Grêmio - EC Vitória 1-0(1-0)
Goiás EC - Fluminense 0-2(0-1)
Corinthians - Coritiba FC 2-2(0-2)
SC do Recife - Figueirense 1-0(0-0)
Santos FC - SC Internacional 1-2(0-1)
Cruzeiro EC - Botafogo 2-1(2-0)
Criciúma EC - São Paulo FC 1-2(0-1)
Flamengo - Chapecoense 3-0(0-0)
Atlético Paranaense - Atlético Mineiro 1-0(1-0)
EC Bahia - SE Palmeiras 0-1(0-1)

Round 33 [08-09.11.2014]
SE Palmeiras - Atlético Mineiro 0-2(0-1)
Coritiba FC - Fluminense 1-0(1-0)
Botafogo - Atlético Paranaense 0-2(0-1)
SC do Recife - Flamengo 2-2(0-2)
EC Vitória - São Paulo FC 1-2(0-1)
Grêmio - SC Internacional 4-1(1-0)
Figueirense - Chapecoense 1-0(0-0)
Corinthians - Santos FC 1-0(1-0)
Cruzeiro EC - Criciúma EC 3-1(0-1)
Goiás EC - EC Bahia 3-0(0-0)

Round 34 [15-16.11.2014]
Fluminense - Botafogo 1-0(0-0)
Criciúma EC - Grêmio 0-3(0-2)
Flamengo - Coritiba FC 3-2(1-0)
Santos FC - Cruzeiro EC 0-1(0-0)
Atlético Paranaense - SC do Recife 0-1(0-0)
EC Bahia - Corinthians 1-2(0-1)
SC Internacional - Goiás EC 1-0(0-0)
São Paulo FC - SE Palmeiras 2-0(1-0)
Atlético Mineiro - Figueirense 1-1(0-1)
Chapecoense - EC Vitória 0-1(0-0)

Round 35 [19-21.11.2014]
São Paulo - SC Internacional 1-1(0-1) [13.11.]
Botafogo - Figueirense 0-1(0-0)
Atlético Paranaense - Santos FC 1-1(0-1)
EC Vitória - Coritiba FC 1-1(1-1)
Criciúma EC - EC Bahia 0-1(0-0)
Goiás EC - Corinthians 0-1(0-1)
SE Palmeiras - SC do Recife 0-2(0-0)
Atlético Mineiro - Flamengo 4-0(2-0)
Fluminense - Chapecoense 1-4(0-0)
Grêmio - Cruzeiro EC 1-2(1-0)

Round 36 [22-23.11.2014]
SC Internacional - Atlético Mineiro 2-1(1-1)
EC Bahia - Atlético Paranaense 1-2(0-0)
Flamengo - Criciúma EC 1-1(1-0)
SC do Recife - Fluminense 2-2(2-1)
Santos FC - São Paulo FC 0-1(0-0)
Cruzeiro EC - Goiás EC 2-1(1-1)
Figueirense - EC Vitória 2-0(1-0)
Corinthians - Grêmio 1-0(0-0)
Coritiba FC - SE Palmeiras 2-0(0-0)
Chapecoense - Botafogo 2-0(0-0)

Round 37 [29-30.11.2014]
SC Internacional - SE Palmeiras 3-1(1-1)
Criciúma EC - SC do Recife 2-2(0-1)
Flamengo - EC Vitória 4-0(1-0)
Fluminense - Corinthians 5-2(1-1)
São Paulo FC - Figueirense 1-1(0-0)
Santos FC - Botafogo 2-0(0-0)
Chapecoense - Cruzeiro EC 1-1(1-0)
Atlético Paranaense - Goiás EC 1-0(0-0)
EC Bahia - Grêmio 1-0(1-0)
Atlético Mineiro - Coritiba FC 1-2(0-1)

Round 38 [06-07.12.2014]
Corinthians - Criciúma EC 2-1(1-0)
Figueirense - SC Internacional 1-2(0-0)
Botafogo - Atlético Mineiro 0-0
SC do Recife - São Paulo FC 1-0(1-0)
SE Palmeiras - Atlético Paranaense 1-1(1-1)
Coritiba FC - EC Bahia 3-2(1-2)
Cruzeiro EC - Fluminense 2-1(1-1)
EC Vitória - Santos FC 0-1(0-0)
Grêmio - Flamengo 1-1(0-1)
Goiás EC - Chapecoense 4-2(2-1)

Final Standings

1.	**Cruzeiro EC Belo Horizonte**	38	24	8	6	67	-	38	80
2.	São Paulo Futebol Clube	38	20	10	8	59	-	40	70
3.	SC Internacional Porto Alegre	38	21	6	11	53	-	41	69
4.	SC Corinthians Paulista São Paulo	38	19	12	7	49	-	31	69
5.	Clube Atlético Mineiro Belo Horizonte	38	17	11	10	51	-	38	62
6.	Fluminense FC Rio de Janeiro	38	17	10	11	61	-	42	61
7.	Grêmio Foot-Ball Porto Alegrense	38	17	10	11	36	-	24	61
8.	Clube Atlético Paranaense Curitiba	38	15	9	14	43	-	42	54
9.	Santos Futebol Clube	38	15	8	15	42	-	35	53
10.	CR Flamengo Rio de Janeiro	38	14	10	14	46	-	47	52
11.	Sport Club do Recife	38	14	10	14	36	-	46	52
12.	Goiás EC Goiânia	38	13	8	17	38	-	40	47
13.	Figueirense FC Florianópolis	38	13	8	17	37	-	47	47
14.	Coritiba Foot Ball Club	38	12	11	15	42	-	45	47
15.	Associação Chapecoense de Futebol	38	11	10	17	39	-	44	43
16.	SE Palmeiras São Paulo	38	11	7	20	34	-	59	40
17.	EC Vitória Salvador de Bahia (*Relegated*)	38	10	8	20	37	-	54	38
18.	Esporte Clube Bahia Salvador (*Relegated*)	38	9	10	19	31	-	43	37
19.	Botafogo de FR Rio de Janeiro (*Relegated*)	38	9	7	22	31	-	48	34
20.	Criciúma Esporte Clube (*Relegated*)	38	7	11	20	28	-	56	32

Top goalscorers:

18 goals:	**Frederico Chaves Guedes "Fred"**	**(Fluminense FC Rio de Janeiro)**
16 goals:	José Henrique da Silva Dourado	(SE Palmeiras São Paulo)
	Ricardo Goulart Pereira	(Cruzeiro EC Belo Horizonte)
15 goals:	Marcelo Martins Moreno (BOL)	(Cruzeiro EC Belo Horizonte)
14 goals:	Hernán Barcos (ARG)	(Grêmio Foot-Ball Porto Alegrense)

Qualified for the 2015 Copa Libertadores (First Stage):
SC Corinthians Paulista São Paulo

Qualified for the 2015 Copa Libertadores (Group Stage):
Cruzeiro EC Belo Horizonte, São Paulo Futebol Clube, SC Internacional Porto Alegre, Clube Atlético Mineiro Belo Horizonte (as 2014 Copa do Brasil winner)

NATIONAL CUP
Copa do Brasil Final 2014 (Copa Sadia)

12.11.2014, Estádio Independência, Belo Horizonte; Attendance: 18,578
Referee: Marcelo de Lima Henrique (Rio de Janeiro)
Clube Atlético Mineiro Belo Horizonte - Cruzeiro EC Belo Horizonte 2-0(1-0)
Atlético Mineiro: Victor Leandro Bagy, Leonardo Fabiano Silva e Silva, Marcos Luis Rocha de Aquino, Douglas dos Santos Justino de Melo, Jemerson de Jesus Nascimento, Josué Anunciado de Oliveira, Jesús Alberto Dátolo, Leandro Donizete, Gonçalves da Silva, Diego Tardelli Martins, Luan Madson Gedeão de Paiva (70.Marion Silva Fernandes), Carlos Alberto Carvalho da Silva Junior. Trainer: Levir Culpi.
Cruzeiro: Fábio Deivson Lopes Maciel, Miguel Ángel Samudio, Bruno Rodrigo Fenelon Palomo, Leonardo Renan Simões de Lacerda "Léo", Mayke Rocha de Oliveira, Éverton de Barros Ribeiro (70.Júlio César Baptista), Henrique Pacheco de Lima, Lucas Silva Borges (46.Nílton Ferreira Júnior), Marcelo Moreno Martins, Ricardo Goulart Pereira (70.Dagoberto Pelentier), Willian Gomes de Siqueira. Trainer: Marcelo de Oliveira Santos.
Goals: 1-0 Luan Madson Gedeão de Paiva (8), 2-0 Jesús Alberto Dátolo (58).

26.11.2014, Estádio "Governador Magalhães Pinto" [Mineirão], Belo Horizonte; Attendance: 39,786
Referee: Luiz Flávio de Oliveira (São Paulo)
Cruzeiro EC Belo Horizonte - Clube Atlético Mineiro Belo Horizonte 0-1(0-1)
Cruzeiro: Fábio Deivson Lopes Maciel, Egidio de Araujo Pereira Júnior, Marcos Venâncio de Albuquerque "Ceará" (78.Júlio César Baptista), Bruno Rodrigo Fenelon Palomo, Leonardo Renan Simões de Lacerda "Léo", Éverton de Barros Ribeiro, Henrique Pacheco de Lima (46.Willian Roberto de Farias), Nílton Ferreira Júnior, Marcelo Moreno Martins, Ricardo Goulart Pereira, Willian Gomes de Siqueira (63.Dagoberto Pelentier). Trainer: Marcelo de Oliveira Santos.
Atlético Mineiro: Victor Leandro Bagy, Leonardo Fabiano Silva e Silva, Marcos Luis Rocha de Aquino, Douglas dos Santos Justino de Melo, Jemerson de Jesus Nascimento, Jesús Alberto Dátolo, Leandro Donizete Gonçalves da Silva [*sent off 85*], Rafael de Souza Pereira „Rafael Carioca" (71.Lucas Pierre Santos Oliveira), Diego Tardelli Martins (88.Eduardo Henrique da Silva), Luan Madson Gedeão de Paiva (32.Maicosuel Reginaldo de Matos), Carlos Alberto Carvalho da Silva Junior. Trainer: Levir Culpi.
Goals: 0-1 Diego Tardelli Martins (45+2).

Copa do Brasil Winner 2014: **Clube Atlético Mineiro Belo Horizonte**

CLUBE ATLÉTICO MINEIRO BELO HORIZONTE

Foundation date: March 25, 1908
Address: Av Olegario Maciel, 1516 , Bairro Centro, Belo Horizonte, MG CEP: 30180-110
Stadium: Estádio Independência, Belo Horizonte – Capacity: 23,018

THE SQUAD

		DOB	M	G
	Goalkeepers:			
Giovanni	Giovanni Aparecido Adriano dos Santos	05.02.1987	5	-
Lee	Lee Winston Leandro da Silva Oliveira	09.03.1988	-	-
Rodolfo	Rodolfo Pereira de Castro	12.04.1995	-	-
Uilson	Uilson Pedruzzi de Oliveira	28.04.1994	2	-
Victor	Victor Leandro Bagy	21.01.1983	32	-
	Defenders:			
Alex	Alex da Silva	15.05.1994	22	-
Donato	Donato Antonio Silva Neto	07.02.1994	1	-
Douglas Santos	Douglas dos Santos Justino de Melo	22.03.1994	13	1
Edcarlos	Edcarlos Conceição Santos		17	-
Emerson	Emerson dos Santos Silva	03.05.1983	-	-
Emerson	Emerson da Conceição	23.02.1986	17	-
Eron	Eron Santos Lourençc	17.01.1992	-	-
Gabriel	Gabriel Costa França	14.03.1995	-	-
Jemerson	Jemerson de Jesus Nascimento	24.08.1992	22	-
Leonardo Silva	Leonardo Fabiano Silva e Silva	22.06.1979	24	3
Marcos Rocha	Marcos Luis Rocha de Aquino	11.12.1988	20	-
Míchel Macedo	Míchel Macedo Rocha Machado	15.02.1990	-	-
	Nicolás Hernán Otamendi (ARG)	12.02.1988	5	-
Réver	Réver Humberto Alves Araújo	04.01.1985	7	1
Tiago	Tiago Pagnussat	17.06.1990	5	2
	Midfielders:			
Botelho	Pedro Roberto Silva Botelho	14.12.1989	11	1
Claudinei	Claudinei Junio de Souza	08.10.1988	7	-
Daniel Abelha	Daniel de Oliveira Sertanejo „Daniel Abelha“	04.11.1994	1	-
	Jesús Alberto Dátolo (ARG)	19.05.1984	27	5
Dodo	Raphael Guimaraes de Paula „Dodo“	05.09.1994	8	4
Eduardo	Eduardo Henrique da Silva	17.05.1995	12	-
Fillipe Soutto	Fillipe Soutto Mayor Nogueira Ferreira	11.03.1991	3	-
Josué	Josué Anunciado de Oliveira	19.07.1979	23	1
Leandro Donizete	Leandro Donizete Gonçalves da Silva	18.05.1985	22	-
Leonan	Leonan José Valandro Gomes	20.10.1995	-	-
Lucas Cândido	Lucas Cândido Silva	25.12.1993	-	-
Maicosuel	Maicosuel Reginaldo de Matos	16.06.1986	15	1
Marcos Vinicius	Marcos Vinicius dos Santos Silva	24.02.1994	-	-
Paulinho	Paulo Modesto Da Silva Júnior "Paulinho"	07.01.1993	2	-
Pierre	Lucas Pierre Santos Oliveira	19.01.1982	21	-
Rafael Carioca	Rafael de Souza Pereira „Rafael Carioca"	18.06.1989	9	-
Ronaldinho	Ronaldo de Assis Moreira "Ronaldinho"	21.03.1980	2	-
Rosinei	Adolfo Rosinei Nascimento	03.05.1983	4	-
	Forwards:			
André	André Felipe Ribeiro de Souza	27.09.1990	20	3
Carlos	Carlos Alberto Carvalho da Silva Junior	15.08.1995	22	5
Cesinha	Cesar Fernando Silva dos Santos „Cesinha“	29.11.1989	6	-
Diego Tardelli	Diego Tardelli Martins	10.05.1985	24	10
Fernandinho	Luiz Fernando Pereira da Silva "Fernandinho"	25.11.1985	6	1
Guilherme	Guilherme Milhomen Gusmão	22.10.1988	21	3
Jô	João Alves de Assis Silva "Jô"	20.03.1987	16	-
Luan	Luan Madson Gedeão de Paiva	11.08.1990	20	5
Marion	Marion Silva Fernandes	07.09.1991	21	1
Neto Berola	Sosthenes José Santos Salles „Neto Berola“	18.11.1987	2	-
	Trainer:			
Paulo Autuori	Paulo Autuori de Mello [01.01.-24.04.2014]	25.08.1956	1	
Levir Culpi	Levir Culpi [as of 25.04.2014]	28.02.1953	37	

CLUBE ATLÉTICO PARANAENSE CURITIBA

Foundation date: May 26, 1924

Address: Rua Petit Carneiro 57, Bairro Água Verde 80240-050, Curitiba, Paraná

Stadium: Estádio "Joaquim Américo Guimarães" [Arena da Baixada] – Capacity: 43,000

THE SQUAD

		DOB	M	G
	Goalkeepers:			
Macanhan	Lucas Macanhan Ferreira	25.06.1994	-	-
Renan Rocha	Renan Nelson Rocha	25.03.1987	-	-
Rodolfo	Rodolfo Alves de Melo	19.03.1991	-	-
Santos	Aderbar Melo dos Santos Neto	17.03.1990	4	-
Wéverton	Wéverton Pereira da Silva	13.12.1987	35	-
	Defenders:			
Cleberson	Cleberson Martins de Souza	17.08.1992	34	5
Dráusio	Dráusio Luis Salla Gil	21.08.1991	9	1
Gustavo	Gustavo Franchin Schiavolin	19.02.1982	16	-
Leo Pereira	Leonardo Pereira „Leo Pereira"	31.01.1996	14	-
Lucão	Lucas Alves de Araujo "Lucão"	22.07.1992	-	-
Manoel	Manoel Messias Silva Carvalho	26.02.1990	-	-
Mario Sérgio	Mario Sérgio Gomes de Souza	16.01.1992	15	-
Natanael	Natanael Batista Pimienta	25.12.1990	31	-
	Lucas René Olaza Catrofe (URU)	21.07.1994	6	-
Potiguar	Ricardo César Dantas da Silva „Potiguar"	13.08.1992	1	1
Rafael Zuchi	Rafael Henrique Zuchi	11.06.1994	-	-
Sidcley	Sidcley Ferreira Pereira	13.05.1993	7	-
Sueliton	Sueliton Pereira de Aguiar	19.08.1986	30	-
Willian	Willian Pereira da Rocha	01.04.1989	11	-
	Midfielders:			
Bady	Renato Escobar Baruffi "Bady"	27.04.1989	26	3
Carlos Alberto	Carlos Alberto da Silva Gonçalves Júnior	22.02.1988	1	-
Deivid	Deivid Willian da Silva	18.01.1989	33	-
Dellatorre	Guilherme Augusto Alves Dellatorre	01.05.1992	18	3
Derley	Wanderley de Jesús Sousa "Derley"	02.08.1986	1	-
Felipe	Felipe de Oliveira Silva	28.05.1990	3	-
Fran Mérida	Francisco Mérida Pérez „Fran Mérida" (ESP)	04.03.1990	-	-
Hernani	Hernani Azevedo Junior	27.03.1994	15	-
João Paulo	João Paulo da Silva	22.02.1985	15	-
Jonatan Lucca	Jonatan Lucca	02.06.1994	-	-
Marcos Guilherme	Marcos Guilherme de Almeida Santos Matos	05.08.1995	36	3
Nathan	Nathan Allan de Souza	13.03.1996	11	-
Otávio	Otávio Henrique Passos Santos	04.05.1994	17	-
Paulinho Dias	Paulo Henrique Dias da Cruz	13.05.1988	23	1
Zé Paulo	José Paulo de Oliveira Pinto "Zé Paulo"	26.03.1994	1	-
	Forwards:			
Bruno Furlan	Bruno de Oliveira Furlan	09.07.1992	1	-
Bruno Mendes	Bruno Pereira Mendes	02.08.1994	3	-
Cléo	Cléverson Gabriel Córdova "Cléo"	09.08.1985	20	9
Douglas Coutinho	Douglas Coutinho Gomes de Souza	08.02.1994	28	7
Dominic Vinicius	Dominic Vinicius Eberechukwu Uzoukwu	05.01.1995	-	-
Éderson	Éderson Alves Ribeiro Silva	13.03.1989	12	1
Guilherme Schettine	Guilherme Schettine Guimarães	10.10.1995	-	-
Marcelo	Marcelo Cirino da Silva	22.01.1991	33	5
Marco Damasceno	Marco Gabriel Damasceno Alves	11.04.1996	3	-
Mosquito	Thiago Rodrigues da Silva "Mosquito"	06.01.1996	11	1
Pedro Paulo	Pedro Paulo Alves Vieira dos Reis	10.02.1994	2	-
	Trainer:			
	Miguel Angel Portugal Vicario (ESP)	28.11.1955	5	
Leandro Ávila	Leandro Corona Ávila [Caretaker]	06.04.1971	4	
Dorival	Dorival Guidoni Júnior	28.05.1972	8	
Leandro Ávila	Leandro Corona Ávila [Caretaker]		21	

ESPORTE CLUBE BAHIA SALVADOR

Foundation date: January 1, 1931
Address: Avenida Octávio Mangabeira 41715-000, Salvador, Bahia
Stadium: Complexo Esportivo Cultural "Professor Octávio Mangabeira Itaipava" [Arena Fonte Nova], Salvador – Capacity: 51,708

THE SQUAD

		DOB	M	G
	Goalkeepers:			
Douglas Pires	Douglas Moreira Pires	30.01.1991	2	-
Guido	Guido Menezes Barreto de Andrade	18.02.1994	-	-
Marcelo Lomba	Marcelo Lomba do Nascimento	18.12.1986	37	-
	Defenders:			
Adaílton	Adaílton José dos Santos Filho	16.04.1983	3	-
Anderson Conceição	Anderson Conceição Benedito	24.10.1989	0	-
Ávine	Ávine Júnior Cardoso	21.02.1988	-	-
Demerson	Demerson Bruno Costa	16.03.1986	28	1
Pará	Anderson Ferreira da Silva "Pará"	23.08.1995	20	1
Rafael Galhardo	Rafael Galhardo de Souza	30.10.1991	5	1
Railan	Railan dos Santos Reis	01.09.1994	19	1
Raul	Raul Diogo Souza Rocha	09.11.1985	1	-
Robson	Robson Januário de Paula	14.02.1994	-	-
Roniery	Roniery Ximenis Sousa Silva	23.11.1987	17	-
Titi	Cristian Chagas Tarouco „Titi"	12.03.1988	24	1
	Midfielders:			
Alessandro	Alessandro Nunes Nascimento	02.03.1982	1	-
Anderson Talisca	Anderson Souza Conceição „Anderson Talisca"	01.02.1994	9	2
	Emanuel Adrian Biancucchi Cuccitini (ARG)	28.07.1988	23	2
Bruno Paulista	Bruno Jacinto da Silva "Bruno Paulista"	21.08.1995	8	-
Diego Felipe	Diego Felipe Coutinho	06.01.1989	-	-
Erick	Erick Luis Palma do Santos	16.07.1992	1	-
Fahel	Leandro Fahel Matos	15.08.1981	25	3
Feijão	Antonio Filipe Gonzaga de Aquino "Feijão"	08.04.1994	5	-
Guilherme Santos	Guilherme Oliveira Santos	05.02.1988	25	2
Hélder	Hélder De Paula Santos	20.06.1984	1	-
Jacó	*Sorry, complete name not available*	27.02.1996	1	-
Léo Gago	Leonardo David de Moura "Léo Gago"	17.02.1983	15	-
Lincoln	Lincoln Cássio de Souza Soares	22.01.1979	9	1
Lucas Fonseca	Lucas Silva Fonseca	02.08.1985	22	-
	Wilson Omar Pittoni Rodríguez (PAR)	14.08.1985	7	-
Rafael Miranda	Rafael Miranda da Conceição	11.08.1984	30	1
Romulo	Romulo José Pacheco da Silva	27.10.1995	3	1
Uelliton	Uelliton da Silva Vieira	28.08.1987	19	-
	Forwards:			
	Maximiliano Daniel Biancucchi Cuccittini (ARG)	15.09.1984	22	3
Branquinho	Wellington Clayton Gonçalves dos Santos "Branquinho"	02.01.1983	11	1
Diego Macedo	Diego Macedo Prado dos Santos	08.05.1987	14	-
Henrique	Henrique Almeida Caixeta Nascentes	27.05.1991	25	2
Ítalo Melo	Ítalo Melo Oliveira	25.02.1993	-	-
Jeam	Eugenio de Oliveira "Jeam"	01.10.1994	7	-
Kieza	Welker Marçal Almeida "Kieza"	24.09.1986	19	6
Marcos Aurélio	Marcos Aurélio de Oliveira Lima	10.02.1984	13	1
Potita	Alessander Asloquer „Potita"	30.07.1984	3	-
Rafinha	Rafael Lima Pereira "Rafinha"	01.04.1993	19	-
Rhayner	Rhayner Santos Nascimento	05.09.1990	12	-
William Barbio	William Silva Gomes Barbio	22.10.1992	25	-
	Trainer:			
Marquinhos Santos	Cristóvão Borges dos Santos Marcos Vinícius dos Santos Gonçalves "Marquinhos Santos"	24.05.1979	12	
Gilson Kleina	Gilson Kleina	30.03.1968	21	
Charles	Charles Fabian Figueiredo Santos	12.04.1968	5	

BOTAFOGO DE FUTEBOL E REGATAS RIO DE JANEIRO

Foundation date: August 12, 1904
Address: Av. Venceslau Brás, 72 - Botafogo Rio de Janeiro, CEP 22290-140
Stadium: Estadio "Jornalista Mário Filho" [Maracanã], Rio de Janeiro – Capacity: 78,838

THE SQUAD

		DOB	M	G
	Goalkeepers:			
Andrey	Andrey da Silva Ventura	17.07.1993	4	-
Helton Leite	Helton Brant Aleixo Leite	02.11.1990	3	-
Jefferson	Jefferson de Oliveira Galvão	02.01.1983	27	-
Luís Guilherme	Luís Guilherme Loreno Marcelino Alves	04.06.1992	-	-
Renan	Renan dos Santos	18.05.1989	4	-
Saulo	Saulo Ferreira Silva	20.04.1995	-	-
	Defenders:			
André Bahia	André Luiz Bahia Santos Viana	24.11.1983	25	1
Bolívar	Fabian Guedes „Bolívar"	16.08.1980	24	1
Dankler	Dankler Luis de Jesús Pereira	24.01.1992	17	-
Edílson	Edílson Mendes Guimarães	27.07.1986	17	2
Igor Rabello	Igor Rabello da Costa	28.04.1995	-	-
Jonh Lennon	Jonh Lennon Silva Santos	29.12.1991	-	-
Júlio César	Júlio César Coelho de Moraes Junior	15.06.1982	13	-
Júnior César	Júnior César Eduardo Machado	09.04.1982	31	-
Lucas	Lucas Rios Marques	26.03.1988	11	-
Matheus Menezes	Matheus Menezes Jacomo	12.01.1991	4	-
	Midfielders:			
Airton	Airton Ribeiro Santos	21.02.1990	24	-
Andreazzi	Mauricio Andreazzi Pereira	09.05.1994	7	-
	Mario Ariel Bolatti (ARG)	17.02.1985	26	2
Carlos Alberto	Carlos Alberto Gomes de Jesús	11.12.1984	13	-
Cidinho	Alcides de Souza Faria Júnior „Cidinho"	28.01.1993	-	-
Daniel	Daniel Correa Freitas	12.01.1994	13	5
Dedé	André Luiz Leocadio de Paula „Dedé"	12.01.1994	-	-
Dória	Matheus Dória Macedo	08.11.1994	10	-
Fabiano	Fabiano Nascimento Vieira de Menezes	02.02.1992	6	-
Gabriel	Gabriel Girotto Franco	10.07.1992	33	-
Gegê	Geirton Marques Aires „Gegê"	28.01.1994	9	-
João Gabriel	João Gabriel dos Santos Neves	07.02.1991	2	-
Jorge Wágner	Jorge Wagner Goés Conceição	17.11.1978	8	-
	Marcelo Nicolás Lodeiro Benítez (URU)	21.03.1989	3	-
Lucas Zen	Lucas de Lacerda Lima Gonçalves „Lucas Zen"	17.06.1991	-	-
Marcelo Mattos	Marcelo de Mattos Terra	10.02.1984	5	-
	Luis Alberto Ramírez Lucay (PER)	10.11.1984	16	1
Régis	Régis Ribeiro de Souza	03.06.1989	13	-
Renato	Renato Dirnei Florêncio Santos	15.05.1979	-	-
Rodrigo Souto	Rodrigo Ribeiro Souto	09.09.1983	13	-
Ronny	Ronieri da Silva Pinto „Ronny"	19.08.1991	2	-
Sidney	Sidney de Freitas Pages	28.01.1994	5	-
Vinicius	Vinicius Rodolfo de Souza Oliveira	27.03.1995	-	-
	Forwards:			
Alex	Alexssander Medeiros de Azeredo	21.08.1990	-	-
Bruno Correa	Bruno César Correa	22.03.1986	7	-
Emerson	Marcio Passos de Albuquerque "Emerson"	06.12.1978	15	6
	Juan Carlos Ferreyra (ARG)	12.09.1983	10	-
Jóbson	Jóbson Leandro Pereira de Oliveira	15.02.1988	8	-
Maikon	Maikon Alves de Aquino	14.05.1993	2	-
Murilo	Murilo de Souza Costa	31.10.1994	11	-
Rogério	José Rogério de Oliveira Melo	24.12.1990	17	2
Sassá	Luis Ricardo Alves "Sassá"	11.01.1994	2	-
Wallyson	Wallyson Ricardo Maciel Monteiro	17.10.1988	25	4
Yuri Mamute	Yuri Souza Almeida "Yuri Mamute"	07.05.1995	17	-
	Pablo Daniel Zeballos Ocampos (PAR)	04.03.1986	30	6
Yguinho	Ygor Lopes Silvestre	20.02.1993	-	-
	Trainer:			
Vágner Mancini	Vágner do Carmo Mancini	24.10.1966	38	

ASSOCIAÇÃO CHAPECOENSE DE FUTEBOL

Foundation date: May 10, 1973
Address: Rua Clevelandia 807E, Bairro Centro 89801-560, Chapecó
Stadium: Arena Condá, Chapecó - Capacity: 22,600

THE SQUAD

		DOB	M	G
	Goalkeepers:			
Danilo	Marcos Danilo Padilha	31.07.1985	37	-
Lauro	Lauro Júnior Batista da Cruz	03.09.1980	-	-
Nivaldo	Jóse Nivaldo Martins Constante	19.03.1974	2	-
Silvio	Silvio Silas da Silva Walenga	11.10.1988	-	-
	Defenders:			
Alemão	Fagner Ironi Daponte "Alemão"	18.10.1990	3	-
Bruno Collaço	Bruno Bairros Collaço	08.03.1990	1	-
Danny Morais	Danny Bittencourt Moraes	29.06.1985	1	-
Douglas Grolli	Douglas Ricardo Grolli	05.10.1989	19	2
Ednei	Ednei Ferreira de Oliveira	30.11.1985	16	-
Fabiano	Fabiano Leismann	18.11.1991	31	-
Fabinho Gaúcho	Fábio Sangurgo da Porcinuncula "Fabinho Gaúcho"	01.08.1982	-	-
Jailton	Jailton de Campos dos Santos	09.03.1986	19	1
Jussandro	Jussandro Pimenta Matos	11.03.1992	5	-
	Enrique Gabriel Meza Brítez (PAR)	28.11.1985	4	-
Neuton	Neuton Sergio Piccoli	14.03.1990	9	-
Rafael Lima	Rafael Ramos de Lima	08.03.1986	32	-
Rodrigo Biro	Rodrigo Pereira Lima "Rodrigo Biro"	18.11.1986	21	-
Tiago Saletti	Tiago Saletti	29.01.1983	2	-
	Midfielders:			
Abuda	Jucimar Lima Pacheco "Abuda"	22.01.1989	23	2
André Paulinho	André Luiz Paulino de Souza Motta	14.03.1985	7	-
Bruno Silva	Bruno Cesar Pereira da Silva	03.08.1986	20	3
Camilo	Fernando Camilo Farias	09.03.1986	25	4
Dedé	Derivaldo Beserra Cavalcante "Dedé"	31.05.1987	19	1
Diones	Diones Coelho da Costa	21.06.1985	21	2
Hyoran	Hyoran Kaue Dalmoro	25.05.1993	4	-
Júnior Timbó	Jorge de Araújo Soares Júnior "Júnior Timbó"	14.11.1990	2	-
Neném	Odair Souza "Neném"	04.02.1982	15	1
Regis	Regis Augusto Salmazzo	30.11.1992	5	-
Ricardo Conceição	Ricardo Renato Conceição	16.07.1984	19	2
Wanderson	Wanderson Pereira Rodrigues	06.10.1980	30	-
Willian Arão	Willian Souza Arão da Silva	03.12.1993	2	-
Zezinho	José Luis dos Santos Pinto "Zezinho"	14.03.1992	17	1
	Forwards:			
Alemão	José Carlos Tofolo Júnior "Alemão"	02.03.1989	1	1
Bérgson	Bérgson Gustavo Silveira da Silva	09.02.1991	7	-
Bruno Rangel	Bruno Rangel Domingues	11.12.1981	20	3
Fabinho	Fabio da Silva Alves "Fabinho"	11.06.1986	25	-
Leandro	Leandro Marcos Pereira	13.07.1991	24	10
Mailson	Mailson Francisco de Farías	23.12.1990	4	-
Rodrigo Gral	Rodrigo Gral	21.02.1977	-	-
Roni	Ronieli Gomes dos Santos "Roni"	25.04.1991	5	-
Rychely	Rychely Cantanhede de Oliveira	06.08.1987	2	-
Tiago Luis	Tiago Luis Martins	13.03.1989	25	5
Wescley	Wescley Gomes dos Santos	11.10.1991	1	-
Yuri	Marcos Yuri Goncalves da Silva de Souza	28.06.1994	4	-
Yuri Mamute	Yuri Souza Almeida "Yuri Mamute"	07.05.1995	-	-
	Trainer:			
Gilmar	Gilmar del Pozzo	01.09.1969	18	
Jorginho	Jorge Luís da Silva „Jorginho"	22.03.1965	17	
Celso Rodrigues	Celso Rodrigues		3	

SPORT CLUB CORINTHIANS PAULISTA SÃO PAULO

Foundation date: September 1, 1910
Address: Rua São Jorge, 777 São Paulo, CEP 03087-000
Stadium: Arena Corinthians, São Paulo - Capacity: 47,605

THE SQUAD				
		DOB	**M**	**G**
Goalkeepers:				
Cássio	Cássio Ramos	06.06.1987	35	-
Danilo Fernandes	Danilo Fernandes Batista	03.04.1988	-	-
Júlio César	Júlio César de Souza Santos	27.10.1984	-	-
Matheus Caldeira	Matheus Caldeira Vidotto de Olivcria	10.04.1993	-	-
Walter	Walter Leandro Capeloza Artune	18.11.1987	4	-
Defenders:				
Anderson Martins	Anderson Vieira Martins	21.08.1987	17	1
Cléber	Cléber Janderson Pereira Reis	05.12.1990	15	-
Fábio Santos	Fábio Santos Romeu	16.09.1985	35	4
Fágner	Fágner Conserva Lemos	11.06.1989	35	2
Felipe Monteiro	Felipe Augusto de Almeida Monteiro	16.05.1989	11	-
Ferrugem	Weverton Almeida Santos "Ferrugem"	28.03.1988	6	-
Gil	Carlos Gilberto Nascimento Silva "Gil"	12.06.1987	34	4
Guilherme Andrade	Guilherme Andrade da Silva	31.01.1989	6	-
Pedro Henrique	Pedro Henrique Ribeiro Gonçalves	02.10.1995	-	-
Uendel	Uendel Pereira Gonçalves	08.10.1988	6	-
Midfielders:				
Bruno Henrique	Bruno Henrique Corsini	21.10.1989	25	1
Danilo	Danilo Gabriel de Andrade	11.06.1979	23	2
Elías	Elías Mendes Trindade	16.05.1985	24	3
Guilherme	Guilherme dos Santos Torres	05.04.1991	5	1
Guilherme Lopes	Guilherme Antonio Arana Lopes	14.04.1997	-	-
Jádson	Jádson Rodrigues da Silva	05.10.1983	30	4
	Marcelo Nicolás Lodeiro Benítez (URU)	21.03.1989	7	-
Luciano	Luciano da Rocha Neves	18.05.1993	33	6
Petros	Petros Matheus dos Santos Araujo	29.05.1989	28	2
Ralf	Ralf de Souza Teles	09.06.1984	30	-
Renato Augusto	Renato Soares de Oliveira Augusto	08.02.1988	30	1
	Ángel Rodrigo Romero Villamayor (PAR)	04.07.1992	21	-
Zé Paulo	José Paulo de Oliveira Pinto "Zé Paulo"	26.03.1994	2	-
Forwards:				
	José Paulo Guerrero Gonzales (PER)	01.01.1984	28	12
Gustavo Tocantins	Gustavo Henrique Barbosa Freire "Gustavo Tocantins"	11.01.1996	4	-
Malcom	Malcom Filipe Silva de Oliveira	26.02.1997	20	2
Paulo Victor	Paulo Victor de Menezes Melo	29.05.1993	1	-
Romarinho	Romário Ricardo da Silva "Romarinho"	12.12.1990	17	3
Trainer:				
Mano Menezes	Luiz Antônio Venker de Menezes "Mano Menezes"	11.06.1962	38	

CORITIBA FOOT BALL CLUB

Foundation date: October 12, 1909

Address: Rua Ubaldino do Amaral 37, Bairro Alto da Glória 80060-190, Curitiba, Paraná

Stadium: Estádio „Major Antônio Couto Pereira" - Capacity: 37,182

THE SQUAD

		DOB	M	G
	Goalkeepers:			
Rafael Martins	Rafael Martins Claro dos Santos	29.11.1991	-	-
Vaná	Vanailson Luciano de Souza Alves "Vaná"	25.04.1991	-	-
Vanderlei	Vanderlei Farias da Silva	01.02.1984	38	-
	Defenders:			
Bonfim	Rafael de Jesus Bonfim	24.07.1991	2	-
Carlinhos	Carlos Emiliano Pereira "Carlinhos"	29.11.1986	28	1
Ceará	Walisson Moreira Farias Maia "Ceará"	21.08.1991	-	-
Dener	Dener Assunção Braz	28.06.1991	6	-
Ivan	Ivan Aparecido Martins	25.08.1992	2	-
Leandro Almeida	Leandro Almeida da Silva	14.03.1987	31	3
Lucas Claro	Luccas Claro dos Santos	20.10.1991	31	2
Maranhão	Wanderson Cavalcante Melo "Maranhão"	26.07.1994	-	-
Moacir	Moacir Costa da Silva	14.02.1986	3	-
Norberto Neto	Norberto Pereira Marinho Neto	19.07.1990	30	1
Reginaldo	Reginaldo Lopes de Jesus	22.02.1993	8	-
Victor Ferraz	Victor Ferraz Macedo	14.01.1988	5	-
Welinton Souza	Welinton Souza Silva	10.04.1989	20	-
	Midfielders:			
Alex	Alexsandro de Souza „Alex"	14.09.1977	26	6
Baraka	Andres Fernandes Gonçalves^"Baraka"	21.07.1986	16	-
Chico	Luis Franco Grando "Chico"	02.02.1987	9	1
Denner	Denner Nascimento da Luz	06.05.1994	6	1
Djair	Djair Veiga Francisco Junior	10.02.1991	-	-
Dudu	Luiz Eduardo Figueiredo „Dudu"	12.05.1991	24	3
Élber	José Élber Pimentel da Silva	27.05.1992	17	-
Geraldo	Hermenegildo da Costa Paulo Bartolomeu "Geraldo" (ANG)	23.11.1991	15	-
Germano	Germano Borovicz Cardoso Schweger	21.03.1981	12	1
Gil	José Gildeixon Clemente de Paiva „Gil"	03.09.1987	15	-
Hélder	Hélder de Paula Santos	20.06.1984	21	2
Luizinho	Luiz Guilherme Dornelles „Luizinho"	04.05.1992	-	-
Misael	Misael Bueno	15.07.1994	-	-
Róbson	Róbson Michael Signorini	10.11.1987	30	3
Sérgio Manoel	Sérgio Manoel Barbosa Santos	08.09.1989	10	-
Zé Rafael	José Rafael Vivian „Zé Rafael"	16.06.1993	3	-
	Forwards:			
Anderson Aquino	Anderson Angus Aquino	18.02.1986	1	-
Deivid	Deivid de Souza	22.10.1979	-	-
Douglas	Douglas Felisbino de Oliveira	16.01.1995	3	-
Jajá	Avelino Jackson De Coelho "Jajá"	28.02.1986	7	-
	Diederrick Joël Tagueu Tadjo (CMR)	06.12.1993	20	8
Júlio César	Júlio César da Silva De Souza	26.02.1980	11	-
Keirrison	Keirrison de Souza Carneiro	03.12.1988	16	3
	Hernán Alejandro Martinuccio (ARG)	16.12.1987	13	2
Roni	Ronei Gleison Rodrigues dos Reis "Roni"	26.01.1991	6	-
Rosinei	Rosinei Adolfo	03.05.1983	12	-
Zé Eduardo	José Eduardo Bischofe de Almeida "Zé Eduardo"	29.10.1987	32	5
	Trainer:			
Celso Roth	Celso Juarez Roth	30.11.1957	38	

CRICIÚMA ESPORTE CLUBE

Foundation date: May 13, 1947
Address: Rua Treze de Maio, Bairro Comerciário 88802-290, Criciúma, Santa Catarina
Stadium: Estádio "Heriberto Hülse", Criciúma - Capacity: 28,749

THE SQUAD

		DOB	M	G
Goalkeepers:				
Bruno	Bruno Brigido de Oliveira	09.03.1991	19	-
Edson Mardden	Edson Mardden Alves Pereira	12.12.1991	3	-
Luiz Silva	Luiz da Silva Filho	07.02.1983	15	-
Rodrigo Galatto	Rodrigo José Galatto	10.04.1983	3	-
Defenders:				
Alcides	Alcides Eduardo Mendes de Araújo Alves	13.03.1985	2	-
Bruno Cortês	Bruno Cortês Barbosa	11.03.1987	21	-
Eduardo Santos	Carlos Eduardo Santos Oliveira	20.11.1986	25	1
Eli Sabiá	Eli Sabia Filho	31.08.1988	-	-
	Sergio Daniel Escudero (ARG)	12.04.1983	8	-
Ezequiel	Ezequiel Jacinto de Biasi	22.02.1993	2	-
Fábio Ferreira	Fábio Ferreira da Silva	23.10.1984	30	1
Giovanni	Giovanni Palmieri dos Santos	03.06.1989	26	-
Gualberto	Gualberto Luís da Silva Júnior	08.04.1990	14	-
Iago Maidana	Iago Justen Maidana Martins	06.02.1996	3	-
Joílson	Joílson de Jesús Cardoso	25.05.1991	10	1
Luís Felipe	Luís Felipe Dias do Nascimento	08.04.1991	10	1
Maicon	Maicon da Silva Macedo	22.05.1988	5	-
Rafael	Rafael Pereira dos Santos	18.11.1984	8	-
Rogério	Rogério Rodrigues da Silva	14.03.1984	-	-
Rômulo	Rômulo Rafael da Silva	24.06.1993	1	-
Ronaldo Alves	Ronaldo Luiz Alves	09.07.1989	12	1
Rafael Donato	Rafael Ferreira Donato	17.03.1989	-	-
Midfielders:				
Andrew	Andrew Lucas Balbino Drummond	15.09.1996	2	-
Cléber Santana	Cléber Santana Loureiro	27.06.1981	20	1
Cleiton	Cleiton Viana da Costa	31.12.1995	-	-
Everton	Francisco Everton de Almeida Andrade	08.08.1984	1	-
Higor	Higor Rodrigues Barbosa Leite	02.06.1993	1	-
João Vitor	João Vitor Lima Gomes	01.06.1988	32	-
Luizinho Mello	Luis Eduardo Mello "Luizinho Mello"	13.03.1993	-	-
Lulinha	Luis Marcelo Morais dos Reis "Lulinha"	10.04.1990	1	-
Martinez	Luiz Fernando Martinez	21.04.1980	11	-
Maylson	Maylson Barbosa Teixeira	06.03.1989	4	-
Paulo Baier	Paulo César Baier	25.10.1974	22	4
Rafael Costa	Rafael Eduardo Costa	19.01.1991	10	-
Ricardinho	Ricardo de Souza Silva "Ricardinho"	10.06.1985	13	-
Rodrigo Souza	Rodrigo de Souza Foneca	27.10.1987	24	1
Roger Gaúcho	Roger Roberto dos Santos "Roger Gaúcho"	30.03.1986	5	-
Ruan	Ruan Luiz Santos da Costa	15.04.1995	-	-
Serginho	Sérgio Antônio Borges Júnior "Serginho"	04.08.1986	26	2
Silvinho	Silvio José Cardoso Reis Junior "Silvinho"	01.07.1990	22	3
Forwards:				
Barreto	Gustavo Bonatto Barreto	10.12.1995	3	-
Bruno Lopes	Bruno Henrique Lopes	19.05.1995	21	-
Cristiano	Cristiano Lopes	24.06.1988	2	-

Danilo Alves	Danilo Almeida Alves	11.04.1991	5	-
Douglas	Douglas de Oliveira	30.01.1986	3	-
Gabriel	Gabriel Moraes Rufino	22.04.1995	2	-
Gustavo	Gustavo Henrique da Silva Sousa	29.03.1994	7	-
Kalil	Leonardo Kalil Abdala	10.04.1996	1	-
Lucca	Lucca Borges de Brito	14.02.1990	26	5
Maurinho	Mauro Job Pontes Júnior "Maurinho"	10.12.1989	11	-
Michael	Michael Vinicius Silva de Morais	19.04.1993	3	-
Rodrigo Silva	Rodrigo Daniel Lopes da Silva	15.06.1983	2	-
Roger	Roger Krug Guedes	02.10.1996	1	1
Ronaldo Mendes	Ronaldo Cesar Mendes de Medeiros	16.08.1992	1	-
Souza	Rodrigo De Souza Cardoso	04.03.1982	13	6
Vitor	Vitor Michels Geremias	23.07.1993	1	-
Wellington Bruno	Wellington Bruno da Silva	25.04.1986	9	-
Zé Carlos	José Carlos Ferreira Filho "Zé Carlos"	24.04.1983	9	-
Trainer:				
Caio Júnior	Luiz Carlos Saroli "Caio Júnior"	08.03.1965	2	
Wagner Lopes	Wagner Lopes (JPN)	29.01.1969	15	
Gilmar	Gilmar del Pozzo	01.09.1969	14	
Toninho Cecílio	Antônio Jorge Cecílio Sobrinho "Toninho Cecílio"	27.05.1967	7	

CRUZEIRO ESPORTE CLUBE BELO HORIZONTE

Foundation date: January 2, 1921
Address: Rua Guajajaras, 1722 , Bairro Barro Preto, Belo Horizonte, CEP 30180-101
Stadium: Estádio „Governador Magalhães Pinto“ [Mineirão], Belo Horizonte – Capacity: 62,547

THE SQUAD

		DOB	M	G
	Goalkeepers:			
Alan	Alan José Bernardon	22.06.1994	-	-
Elisson	Elisson Aparecido Rosa	26.03.1987	1	-
Fábio	Fábio Deivson Lopes Maciel	30.09.1980	36	-
Rafael	Rafael Pires Monteiro	23.06.1989	1	-
	Defenders:			
Alex Flávio	Alex Flávio Santos Luz	21.01.1993	-	-
Breno	Breno Gonçalves Lopes	28.09.1990	1	-
Bruno Almeida	Bruno Edgar Silva Almeida	18.03.1994	1	-
Bruno Rodrigo	Bruno Rodrigo Fenelon Palomo	12.04.1985	11	-
Ceará	Marcos Venâncio de Albuquerque "Ceará"	16.06.1980	17	-
Dedé	Anderson Vital da Silva „Dedé“	01.07.1988	21	2
Egidio	Egidio de Araujo Pereira Júnior	16.06.1986	31	1
Éverton Ribeiro	Éverton de Barros Ribeiro	10.04.1989	31	6
Léo	Leonardo Renan Simões de Lacerda “Léo”	30.01.1988	29	2
Manoel	Manoel Messias Silva Carvalho	26.02.1990	13	1
Mayke	Mayke Rocha de Oliveira	10.11.1992	30	-
	Miguel Ángel Samudio (PAR)	24.08.1986	9	-
Wallace	Wallace Fortuna dos Santos	14.10.1994	3	-
	Midfielders:			
Alisson	Alisson Euler de Freitas Castro	25.06.1993	15	3
Élber	José Élber Pimentel da Silva	27.05.1992	1	-
Eurico	Eurico Nicolau de Lima Neto	16.04.1994	3	-
Henrique	Henrique Pacheco de Lima	16.05.1985	30	-
Hugo Ragelli	Hugo Ragelli Oliveira Andrade	02.05.1995	1	1
Judivan	Judivan Flor da Silva	21.05.1995	2	-
Luan	Luan Michel de Louzã	21.09.1988	4	-
Lucas Silva	Lucas Silva Borges	16.02.1993	26	1
Marlone	Johnath Marlone Azevedo da Silva	02.04.1992	13	-
Nilton	Nílton Ferreira Júnior	21.04.1987	26	3
Ricardo Goulart	Ricardo Goulart Pereira	05.05.1991	26	15
Souza	Elierce Barbosa de Souza	08.03.1988	5	1
Tinga	Paulo César Fonseca do Nascimento "Tinga"	13.01.1978	6	-
Willian	Willian Roberto de Farias	06.06.1989	14	-
	Forwards:			
Borges	Humberlito Borges Teixeira	05.10.1980	10	2
Dagoberto	Dagoberto Pelentier	22.03.1983	21	3
Júlio Baptista	Júlio César Baptista	01.10.1981	14	4
Marquinhos	Marcos Antônio da Silva Gonçalves “Marquinhos”	19.10.1989	18	4
	Hernán Alejandro Martinuccio (ARG)	16.12.1987	1	-
	Marcelo Moreno Martins (BOL)	18.06.1987	32	15
Neilton	Neilton Meira Mestzk	17.02.1994	1	-
Willian	Willian Gomes de Siqueira	19.11.1986	27	1
	Trainer:			
Marcelo	Marcelo de Oliveira Santos	04.03.1955	38	

FIGUEIRENSE FUTEBOL CLUBE FLORIANÓPOLIS

Foundation date: June 12, 1921

Address: Rua Humaitá 194, Bairro Estreito, 88070-730 Florianópolis

Stadium: Estádio „Orlando Scarpelli“,Florianópolis – Capacity: 19,908

THE SQUAD

		DOB	M	G
	Goalkeepers:			
Alex Rafael	Alex Roberto Santana Rafael	10.11.1989	-	-
Alvino Neto	Alvino Volpi Neto	01.08.1992	-	-
Jean	Jean Carlos Drosny	30.01.1994	6	-
Júnior Oliveira	Jucemar de Oliveira Cordeiro Júnior	02.01.1990	-	-
Luan Polli	Luan Polli Gomes	06.04.1993	1	-
Neneca	Anderson Soares da Silva "Neneca"	11.09.1980	-	-
Tiago Volpi	Tiago Luis Volpi	19.12.1990	37	-
	Defenders:			
Artur	José Artur Barbosa de Oliveira	22.10.1984	3	-
Bruno Alves	Bruno Fabiano Alves	16.04.1991	-	-
Ivan	Ivan Saraiva de Souza	18.01.1982	1	-
Kléber	Kléber de Carvalho Corrêa	01.04.1980	4	-
Marquinhos Pedroso	Marcos Garbellotto Pedroso "Marquinhos Pedroso"	04.10.1993	11	-
Nirley	Nirley da Silva Fonseca	09.04.1988	24	-
Raul	Raul Michel Melo da Silva	04.11.1989	3	-
Thiago Heleno	Thiago Heleno Henrique Ferreira	17.09.1988	33	2
William	William Cordeiro Melo	15.07.1993	8	-
	Midfielders:			
Bruno Santos	Bruno Antonio dos Santos	13.06.1995	-	-
	Roberto Andrés Cereceda Guajardo (CHI)	10.10.1984	18	-
Dener	Dener Gonçalves Pinheiro	12.04.1995	10	-
Felipe	Felipe de Oliveira Silva	28.05.1990	14	-
França	Welington Wildy Muniz dos Santos "França"	21.04.1991	15	1
Giovanni Augusto	Giovanni Augusto Oliveira Cardoso	05.09.1989	24	4
Guilherme Lazaroni	Guilherme Henrique dos Reis Lazaroni	18.11.1992	6	-
Hiroshi	Josemar Guimarães da Silva "Hiroshi"	20.02.1986	-	-
Jefferson	Jefferson Nogueira Junior	22.01.1994	15	1
Leandro Silva	Leandro da Silva	22.09.1988	23	-
Leonardo	Leonardo Santos Lisboa	01.06.1994	13	1
Luan	Luan José Nidezielski	11.02.1991	14	-
Marco Antonio	Marco Antonio Miranda Filho	09.11.1984	32	3
Marcos Assunção	Marcos dos Santos Assunção	25.07.1976	2	-
Marquinhos	Marcos Roberto da Silva Barbosa "Marquinhos"	21.10.1982	25	1
Nem	Rogisvaldo João dos Santos "Nem"	12.10.1987	10	-
Paulo Roberto	Paulo Roberto da Silva	06.03.1987	26	-
Rivaldo	Rivaldo Barbosa de Souza	25.08.1985	16	-
Vitor Júnior	Vitor Silva Assis de Oliveira Júnior	15.09.1986	7	-
Yago	Yago Felipe da Costa Rocha	13.02.1995	5	-
	Forwards:			
Ciro	Ciro Henrique Alves Ferreira E Silva	18.04.1989	-	-
Cleitinho	Clayton da Silveira da Silva „Cleitinho“	23.10.1995	22	5
Denilson	Denilson Luis Marques de Souza	25.11.1988	-	-
Dudu	Luiz Eduardo dos Santos Gonzaga "Dudu"	21.04.1990	7	-
Everaldo	Everaldo Stum	05.07.1991	24	6
Éverton Santos	Éverton Leandro dos Santos Pinto	14.10.1986	6	-
	Bruno Fornaroli Mezza (URU)	07.09.1987	-	-
Jonatan	Jonatan Ponciano Silva	30.08.1991	2	-
Lucio Maranhão	Lucielmo Palhano Soares "Lucio Maranhão"	28.09.1988	1	-
Marcão	Marcos Assis Santana "Marcão"	25.09.1985	21	5
Mazola	Marcelino Júnior Lopes Arruda "Mazola"	08.05.1989	10	3
Pablo	Pablo Felipe Teixeira	23.06.1992	19	4
Ricardo Bueno	Ricardo Bueno da Silva	15.08.1987	12	-
Wesley	Wesley Barbosa de Morais	10.11.1981	-	-
William Pottker	William de Oliveira Pottker	22.12.1993	1	-
	Trainer:			
Vinícius Eutrópio	Vinícius Soares Eutrópio	27.06.1966	2	
Guto Ferreira	Augusto Sérgio Ferreira "Guto Ferreira"	07.09.1965	9	
Argel	Argélico Fucks	04.09.1974	27	

CLUBE DE REGATAS DO FLAMENGO RIO DE JANEIRO

Foundation date: November 15, 1895

Address: Av. Borges de Medeiros, 997, Gávea, Rio de Janeiro, CEP 22430-041

Stadium: Estadio "Jornalista Mário Filho" [Maracanã], Rio de Janeiro – Capacity: 78,838

THE SQUAD

		DOB	M	G
	Goalkeepers:			
César	César Bernardo Dutra	27.01.1992	1	-
Daniel	Daniel Miller Tenenbaum	19.04.1995	-	-
Felipe	Luiz Felipe Ventura dos Santos	22.02.1984	8	-
Joao Kuspiosz	Joao Paulo Kuspiosz	10.10.1994	1	-
Paulo Victor	Paulo Victor Mileo Vidotti	12.01.1987	29	-
	Defenders:			
Anderson Pico	Anderson da Silveira Ribeiro "Anderson Pico"	04.11.1988	9	1
André Santos	André Clarindo dos Santos	08.03.1983	8	-
Chicão	Anderson Sebastião Cardoso "Chicão"	03.06.1981	18	-
Digão	Rodrigo Longo Freitas „Digão"	12.03.1993	-	-
	Frickson Rafael Erazo Vivero (ECU)	05.05.1988	2	-
Fernando	Fernando Fernandes Rodrigues	19.03.1993	1	-
João Paulo	João Paulo Gomes da Costa	01.07.1986	27	-
Leo	Leonardo Moreira Morais "Leo"	03.10.1991	3	-
Leó Moura	Leonardo da Silva Moura „Léo Moura"	23.10.1978	33	1
Marcelo	Marcelo Augusto Mathias da Silva	26.08.1991	17	1
Rodrigo Frauches	Rodrigo Frauches de Souza Santos	28.09.1992	-	-
Samir	Samir Caetano de Souza Santos	05.12.1994	17	1
Wallace	Wallace Reis da Silva	26.12.1987	31	1
	Midfielders:			
Amaral	Mauricio Azevedo Alves "Amaral"	01.05.1988	14	-
	Víctor Javier Cáceres Centurión (PAR)	25.03.1985	20	-
	Héctor Miguel Canteros (ARG)	15.03.1989	24	2
Elano	Elano Ralph Blumer	14.06.1981	4	-
Éverton	Éverton Cardoso da Silva	11.12.1988	28	5
Gabriel	Gabriel Santana Pinto	06.01.1990	21	3
Jorge	Jorge Marco de Oliveira Moraes	28.03.1996	-	-
Luiz Antônio	Luiz Antônio de Souza Soares	11.03.1991	27	1
Márcio Araújo	Márcio Rodrigues Araújo	11.06.1984	32	2
Mattheus	Mattheus de Andrade Gama Oliveira	07.07.1994	2	-
	Lucas Andrés Mugni (ARG)	12.01.1992	25	2
Muralha	Luiz Philipe Lima de Oliveira "Muralha"	21.01.1993	8	-
Pablo	Pablo Andrade Plaza da Silva	15.02.1994	-	-
Recife	Wheidson Roberto dos Santos "Recife"	14.10.1994	6	-
Wheidson	Wheidson dos Santos	14.10.1994	-	-
	Forwards:			
Alecsandro	Alecsandro Barbosa Felisbino	04.02.1981	24	7
Arthur	Arthur Caíque do Nascimento Cruz	15.06.1992	12	-
Darlan	Darlan Martins Benvindo	27.02.1994	-	-
Eduardo	Eduardo Alves da Silva	25.02.1983	18	8
Élton	Élton Rodrigues Brandão	01.08.1985	12	2
Hernane	Hernane Vidal de Souza	08.04.1986	1	-
Igor Sartori	Igor Torres Sartori	08.01.1993	5	-
Negueba	Guilherme Negueba Ferreira Pinto	07.04.1992	10	-
Nixson	Nixson Darlanio Reis Cardoso	20.07.1992	16	6
Paulinho	Paulo Luiz Beraldo Santos "Paulinho"	14.06.1988	13	2
	Trainer:			
Jaime	Jaime de Almeida Filho	17.05.1953	4	
Ney Franco	Ney Franco da Silveira Júnior	22.07.1966	7	
Luxemburgo	Vanderlei Luxemburgo da Silva	10.05.1952	27	

FLUMINENSE FOOTBALL CLUB RIO DE JANEIRO

Foundation date: July 21, 1902
Address: Rua Álvaro Chaves, 41, Laranjeiras, Rio de janeiro, CEP 22231-220
Stadium: Estadio "Jornalista Mário Filho" [Maracanã], Rio de Janeiro – Capacity: 78,838

THE SQUAD

		DOB	M	G
Goalkeepers:				
Diego Cavalieri	Diego Cavalieri	01.12.1982	32	-
Felipe	Felipe Garcia dos Prazeres	02.09.1977	3	-
Júlio César	Júlio César Jacobi	02.09.1986	-	-
Kléver	Kléver Rodrigo Gomes Ruffino	20.06.1989	3	-
Marcos	Marcos Felipe de Freitas Monteiro	13.04.1996	-	-
Defenders:				
Bruno	Bruno Vieira do Nascimento	30.08.1985	29	-
Carlinhos	Carlos Andrade Souza "Carlinhos"	23.01.1987	26	-
Edson	Edson Felipe da Cruz	01.07.1991	17	3
Elivélton	Elivélton Viana dos Santos	10.05.1992	25	1
Fabrício	Fabrício Silva Dornellas	20.02.1990	5	-
Fernando Neto	Fernando José da Cunha Neto	27.01.1993	4	-
Gerson	Gerson Santos da Silva	20.07.1997	-	-
Guilherme Mattis	Guilherme Cruz de Mattis	12.09.1990	9	-
Gum	Wellington Pereira Rodrigues „Gum"	04.01.1986	15	-
Henrique	Carlos Henrique dos Santos Souza	02.05.1983	11	-
Marlon	Marlon Santos da Silva Barbosa	07.09.1995	20	-
Renato	José Renato da Silva Júnior	19.01.1990	-	-
Ronan	Ronan Queiroz de Paula Afonso	29.08.1994	1	-
Wellington Carvalho	Wellington Carvalho dos Santos	15.02.1993	-	-
Wellington Silva	Wellington do Nascimento Silva	06.03.1988	2	-
Midfielders:				
Chiquinho	Francisco Souza dos Santos "Chiquinho"	27.07.1989	26	1
Cícero	Cícero Santos	26.08.1984	20	6
	Darío Leonardo Conca (ARG)	11.05.1983	37	9
Diguinho	Rodrigo Oliveira de Bittencourt „Diguinho"	20.03.1983	20	-
Gustavo	Gustavo Henrique Furtado Scarpa	05.01.1994	6	-
Higor	Higor Rodrigues Barbosa Leite	02.06.1993	-	-
Jean	Jean Raphael Vanderlei Moreira	24.06.1986	35	2
Rafinha	Rafael Gimenes da Silva "Rafinha"	05.08.1993	11	-
Robert	Robert Gonçalves Santos	28.09.1996	-	-
	Edwin Armando Valencia Rodríguez (COL)	29.03.1985	19	-
Wagner	Wagner Ferreira dos Santos	29.01.1985	31	7
Willian	Willian Osmar de Oliveira Silva	16.05.1993	-	-
Forwards:				
Biro Biro	Diego Santos Gama Camillo "Biro Biro"	22.11.1994	5	-
Fred	Frederico Chaves Guedes „Fred"	03.10.1983	28	18
Kenedy	Robert Kenedy Nunes do Nascimento	08.02.1996	20	2
Matheus Carvalho	Matheus Thiago de Carvalho	11.03.1992	2	1
Michael	Michael Vinicius Silva de Morais	19.04.1993	1	-
Rafael Sóbis	Rafael Augusto Sóbis do Nascimento	17.06.1985	31	3
Samuel Rosa	Samuel Rosa Gonçalves	25.02.1991	1	-
Wálter	Wálter Da Silva	22.07.1989	23	2
Trainer:				
Cristóvão	Cristóvão Borges dos Santos	09.06.1959	38	

GOIÁS ESPORTE CLUBE GOIÂNIA

Foundation date: April 6, 1943

Address: Avenida Edmundo Pinheiro de Abreu 721, Setor Bela Vista, 74823-030 Goiânia, Goiás

Stadium: Estádio Serra Dourada, Goiânia - Capacity: 50,049

THE SQUAD				
		DOB	**M**	**G**
	Goalkeepers:			
Edson	Edson Pereira Lisboa	24.09.1985	3	-
Harlei	Harlei de Menezes Silva	30.03.1972	-	-
Paulo Henrique	Paulo Henrique Alves de Faria	12.05.1994	-	-
Renan	Renan Brito Soares	24.01.1985	35	-
	Defenders:			
Alex Alves	Alex Alves Cardoso	25.08.1992	10	1
Clayton Sales	Clayton Sales Paulino	24.02.1993	1	-
Felipe	Felipe Francisco Macedo	27.03.1994	18	-
Jackson Souza	Jackson de Souza	01.05.1990	34	4
Leo Veloso	Leonardo Henrique Veloso "Leo Veloso"	29.05.1987	11	-
Lima	Lucas Pedro Alves de Lima	10.10.1991	22	-
Mario	Mario Sergio Valerio	26.04.1994	-	-
Moisés	Moisés Francisco Dallazen	09.08.1990	12	-
Pedrão	Pedro Henrique Pereira da Silva „Pedrão"	18.12.1992	23	-
Rodrigo	Rodrigo Baldasso Da Costa	27.08.1980	8	-
Tulio	Tulio Rocha Lima	24.06.1993	-	-
Valmir Lucas	Valmir Lucas de Oliveira	12.01.1989	10	-
Wallinson	Wallinson Ricardo Inácio Xavier	16.06.1989	-	-
	Midfielders:			
Amaral	Willian José de Souza „Amaral"	07.10.1986	31	2
David	David França Oliveira e Silva	29.05.1982	34	4
João Paulo	João Paulo Mior	08.03.1991	5	-
Juliano	Juliano Real Pacheco	06.04.1990	4	-
Liniker	Liniker da Silva Moreira	08.03.1993	7	-
Murilo	Murilo Henrique Pereira Rocha	20.11.1994	13	-
Paulo Henrique	Paulo Oliveira da Silva "Paulo Henrique"	12.01.1993	-	-
Ramón	Ramón Rodrigo de Freitas	07.04.1983	33	3
Thiago Mendes	Thiago Henrique Mendes Ribeiro	15.03.1992	34	3
Tiago Real	Tiago Real do Prado	16.01.1989	31	-
Vitor	Cícero Vitor dos Santos Júnior	29.07.1982	5	-
	Forwards:			
Araújo	Clemerson de Araújo Soares	08.08.1977	4	-
Assuério	Assuério Barbosa de Sousa Junior	24.02.1993	9	-
Bruno Mineiro	Bruno Menezes Soares "Bruno Mineiro"	02.02.1983	17	2
Danilo Cezario	Danilo Lopes Cezario	25.04.1991	8	1
Erik	Erik Nascimento de Lima	18.07.1994	34	12
Esquerdinha	Rubens Raimundo da Silva "Esquerdinha"	10.10.1989	29	2
Felipe	Felipe Saturnino Gomes	10.08.1995	9	-
Leo	Leonardo Bonatini Lohner Maia „Leo"	28.03.1994	1	-
Rychely	Rychely Cantanhede de Oliveira	06.08.1987	1	-
Samuel Rosa	Samuel Rosa Gonçalves	25.02.1991	20	2
Welinton	Welinton Junior Ferreira dos Santos	08.06.1993	15	1
	Trainer:			
Ricardo Drubscky	Sebastião Ricardo Drubscky de Campos [as of 14.06.2014]	20.01.1962	38	

GRÊMIO FOOT-BALL PORTO ALEGRENSE

Foundation date: September 15, 1903
Address: Rua Largo dos Campeões, 1, Porto Alegre (RS), CEP 9088 – 0440
Stadium: Arena do Grêmio, Porto Alegre – Capacity: 55,662

THE SQUAD

		DOB	M	G
	Goalkeepers:			
Busatto	Gustavo Busatto	23.10.1990	1	-
Follmann	Jakson Ragnar Follmann	14.03.1992	-	-
Leonardo	Leonardo Cesar Jardim	20.03.1995	-	-
Marcelo Grohe	Marcelo Grohe	13.01.1987	35	-
Tiago Machowski	Tiago Machowski	16.05.1993	3	-
	Defenders:			
Bressan	Matheus Simonete Bressanelli „Bressan“	15.01.1993	18	-
Fábio Aurélio	Fábio Aurélio Rodrigues	24.09.1979	-	-
Gabriel	Gabriel Rodrigues dos Santos	28.02.1989	-	-
Geromel	Pedro Tonon Geromel	21.09.1985	24	-
	Matías Nicolas Rodríguez (ARG)	14.04.1986	8	-
Moisés	Moisés Francisco Dallazen	09.08.1990	1	-
Pará	Marcos Rogério Ricci Lopes "Pará"	14.02.1986	33	-
Rafael Thyere	Rafael Thyere de Albuquerque Marques	17.05.1993	1	-
Rhodolfo	Luiz Rhodolfo Dini Gaioto	11.08.1986	24	2
Saimon	Saimon Pains Tormen	03.03.1991	5	-
Wendell	Wendell Nascimento Borges	20.07.1993	2	-
Werley	Werley Ananias da Silva	05.09.1988	13	-
	Midfielders:			
	Alan Nahuel Ruíz (ARG)	19.08.1993	22	4
Breno	Breno Lorran da Silva Talvares	16.03.1995	8	-
Careca	Nicolas Mores da Cruz „Careca“	18.05.1997	1	-
Dudu	Eduardo Pereira Rodrigues „Dudu“	07.01.1992	35	3
Edinho	Edimo Ferreira Campos „Edinho“	15.01.1983	10	-
Erik	Erik Roberto Silva do Nascimento	02.02.1995	3	-
Fellipe Bastos	Fellipe Ramos Ignez Bastos	01.02.1990	22	-
Giuliano	Giuliano Victor de Paula	31.05.1990	17	1
Guilherme	Guilherme da Silva Amorim Marcondes	30.04.1993	-	-
Jean Deretti	Jean Alexandre Deretti	01.05.1993	1	-
Leandro Porto	Leandro Porto Torma	23.11.1994	-	-
Léo Gago	Leonardo David de Moura "Léo Gago"	17.02.1983	1	-
Liverson	Liverson Renan Varante dos Santos	20.02.1997	-	-
Marquinhos Pedroso	Marcos Garbellotto Pedroso „Marquinhos Pedroso"	04.10.1993	1	-
Matheus Biteco	Matheus Bitencourt da Silva „Matheus Biteco“	28.06.1995	17	-
	Maximiliano Rodríguez Maeso (URU)	02.10.1990	4	1
Ramiro	Ramiro Moschen Benetti	22.05.1993	1	-
	Cristian Miguel Riveros Núñez (PAR)	16.10.1982	23	2
Rodriguinho	Rodrigo Eduardo Costa Marinho "Rodriguinho"	27.03.1988	11	2
Walace	Walace Souza Silva	04.04.1995	19	-
Zé Roberto	José Roberto da Silva Júnior "Zé Roberto"	06.07.1974	31	-
	Forwards:			
Balbino	Anderson Balbino Assis	19.01.1997	-	-
	Hernán Barcos (ARG)	11.04.1984	32	14
Everaldo	Everaldo Stum	05.06.1991	-	-
Everton	Everton Sousa Soares	22.03.1996	7	-
Fernandinho	Luiz Fernando Pereira da Silva „Fernandinho“	25.11.1985	13	-
Kléber	Kléber Giacomace de Souza Freitas	12.08.1983	2	-
Luan	Luan Guilherme de Jesús Vieira	27.03.1993	28	4
Lucas Coelho	Lucas Coelho	20.07.1994	18	2
Marcos Paulo	Marcos Paulo Carvalho Inez	27.09.1994	-	-
Mamute	Yuri Souza Almeida „Mamute“	07.05.1995	31	-
Paulinho	Paulo Roberto Moccelin "Paulinho"	16.03.1994	-	-
Ronan	Ronan Jeronimo	22.04.1995	2	-
	Trainer:			
Enderson Moreira	Enderson Alves Moreira [16.12.2013-27.07.2014]	28.09.1971	12	
Felipão	Luiz Felipe Scolari „Felipão“ [as of 28.07.2014]	09.11.1948		

SPORT CLUB INTERNACIONAL PORTO ALEGRE

Foundation date: April 4, 1909

Address: Av. Padre Cacique, 891, Menino Deus, Porto Alegre, CEP 90810-240

Stadium: Estádio "José Pinheiro Borda" [Beira_Rio], Porto Alegre – Capacity: 50,128

THE SQUAD

		DOB	M	G
	Goalkeepers:			
Agenor	Agenor Detofol	11.12.1989	-	-
Alisson	Alisson Ramses Becker	02.10.1992	11	-
Dida	Nelson de Jesús da Silva "Dida"	10.07.1973	27	-
Muriel	Muriel Gustavo Becker	14.02.1987	1	-
	Defenders:			
Alan	Alan Henrique Costa	31.10.1990	10	-
Carlinhos	Carlos Vinicius Santos de Jesus "Carlinhos"	22.06.1994	-	-
Cláudio Winck	Cláudio Winck Neto	15.04.1994	12	2
Diogo Mateus	Diogo Mateus de Almeida Rodrigues Maciel	13.02.1993	7	-
Ernando	Ernando Rodrigues Lopes	17.04.1988	29	-
Fabrício	Fabrício dos Santos Silva	11.01.1987	34	3
Gilberto	Gilberto Moraes Junior	07.03.1993	14	-
Índio	Marcos Antônio de Lima „Índio“	14.02.1975	1	-
Juan	Juan Silveira dos Santos	01.02.1979	21	-
Matheus Bertotto	Matheus Hanauer Bertotto	15.06.1993	9	-
Paulão	Paulo Marcos De Jesus Ribeiro "Paulão"	25.02.1986	23	3
Tales	Talles Henrique da Cunha Carmo	13.03.1989	-	-
Wellington Silva	Wellington do Nascimento Silva	06.03.1988	14	2
	Midfielders:			
Alan Patrick	Alan Patrick Lourenço	13.05.1991	24	2
Alan Ruschel	Alan Luciano Ruschel	23.08.1989	5	-
Alex	Alex Raphael Meschini	25.03.1982	28	5
Andrigo	Andrigo Oliveira de Araújo	27.02.1995	-	-
	Charles Mariano Aránguiz Sandoval (CHI)	17.04.1989	24	6
	Andrés Nicolás D'Alessandro (ARG)	15.04.1981	33	6
Eduardo Sasha	Eduardo Colcenti Antunes "Eduardo Sasha"	24.02.1992	12	4
Geferson	Geferson Cerqueira Teles	13.05.1994	-	-
Gladstony	Gladstony Estevan Paulino da Silva	05.08.1993	1	-
Gustavo	Gustavo Henrique Ferrareis	02.01.1996	2	-
Jair	Jair Rodrigues Júnior	26.08.1994	1	-
João Afonso	João Afonso Crispim	09.02.1995	1	-
	Carlos Martín Luque (ARG)	01.03.1993	1	-
Nathan Indio	Nathan dos Santos Custódio "Nathan Indio"	16.09.1993	-	-
Otávio	Otávio Rotunno Rojas Lima	09.02.1993	6	-
Taiberson Ruan	Taiberson Ruan Menezes Nunes	18.11.1993	5	1
Valdivia	Wanderson Ferreira de Oliveira „Valdivia"	04.10.1994	27	2
Wellington	Wellington Aparecido Martins	28.01.1991	19	1
Wellington Paulista	Wellington Pereira do Nascimento "Wellington Paulista"	22.04.1983	26	3
Willians	Willians Domingos Fernandes	29.01.1986	28	-
Ygor	Ygor Maciel Santiago	01.06.1984	14	-
	Forwards:			
Aylon	Aylon Darwin Tavella	07.04.1992	2	-
Bruno Gomes	Bruno Gomes de Oliveira Conceiçao	19.07.1996	-	-
Jorge Henrique	Jorge Henrique de Souza	23.04.1982	19	2
Leandro	Leandro Joaquim Ribeiro	13.01.1995	5	-
Maurides	Maurides Roque Junior	10.03.1994	1	-
Nilmar	Nilmar Honorato da Silva	14.07.1984	8	2
Rafael Moura	Rafael Martiniano de Miranda Moura	23.05.1983	26	8
	Trainer:			
Abel Braga	Abel Carlos da Silva Braga [as of 13.12.2013]	01.09.1952		

SOCIEDADE ESPORTIVA PALMEIRAS SÃO PAULO

Foundation date: August 26, 1914
Address: Rua Turiaçu 1840, Perdizes 05005-000, São Paulo
Stadium: Estádio Municipal "Paulo Machado de Carvalho" [Pacaembu] / Allianz Parque [Palestra Itália Arena], São Paulo – Capacity: 37,730 / 43,600

THE SQUAD

		DOB	M	G
	Goalkeepers:			
Bruno	Bruno Cortez Cardoso	27.06.1984	1	-
Deola	Eliton Deola	19.04.1983	5	-
Fabio	Fabio Szymonek	11.05.1990	18	-
Fernando Prass	Fernando Büttenbender Prass	09.07.1978	15	-
Jaílson	Jaílson Marcelino dos Santos	20.07.1981	-	-
Neneca	Anderson Soares da Silva "Neneca"	11.09.1980	-	-
Vinicius	Vinicius Silvestre da Costa	28.03.1994	-	-
	Defenders:			
Bruno César	Bruno César Zanaki	03.11.1988	7	-
Gabriel Dias	Gabriel Dias de Oliveira	10.05.1994	5	-
João Pedro	João Pedro Maturano dos Santos	15.11.1996	17	1
Juninho	Evanildo Borges Barbosa Junior "Juninho"	11.01.1990	23	1
Lúcio	Lucimar da Silva Ferreira"Lúcio"	08.05.1978	25	2
Tiago	Tiago dos Santos Alves	29.05.1984	3	-
Thiago Martins	Thiago Martins	17.03.1995	-	-
	Fernando Omar Tobio (ARG)	18.10.1989	18	1
Victor Luís	Victor Luís Chuab Zamblauskas	23.06.1993	28	1
	Mauricio Bernardo Victorino Dansilio (URU)	11.10.1982	7	-
Welder	Welder da Silva Marçal	16.01.1991	6	-
Wellington Silva	Wellington Silva Pinto	30.09.1991	5	-
William	William Matheus Da Silva	02.04.1990	6	-
	Midfielders:			
Alan Kardec	Alan Kardec de Souza Pereira Junior	12.01.1989	1	1
	Agustin Leonel Allione (ARG)	28.10.1994	15	-
Bernardo	Bernardo Vieira de Souza	20.05.1990	8	-
Bruninho	Bruno Felipe Lima Teixeira "Bruninho"	18.09.1992	3	-
Chico	Francisco Manoel Marino Clavero "Chico"	29.01.1993	2	-
Eduardo Júnior	Eduardo José Barbosa da Silva Junior	03.09.1995	1	-
	Sebastián Eguren Ledesma (URU)	08.01.1981	5	-
Felipe Menezes	Felipe Jácomo Menezes	20.01.1988	15	-
Guilherme	Guilherme Pereira dos Santos Dias	04.12.1995	-	-
Josimar	Josimar Rosado da Silva Tavares	18.08.1986	10	-
Leo Cunha	Leonardo Augusto Cunha de Lima "Leo Cunha"	22.08.1995	-	-
Marcelo Oliveira	Marcelo Oliveira Ferreira	29.03.1987	28	-
Matheus Sales	Matheus de Sales Cabral	13.05.1995	-	-
Mazinho	Anderson Soares da Silva "Mazinho"	16.10.1987	11	1
	William Gabriel Mendieta Pintos (PAR)	09.01.1989	11	-
Nathan	Nathan Raphael Pelae Cardoso	13.05.1995	12	-
Patrick Vieira	Patrick Marins Vieira	11.01.1993	5	-
Renatinho	Renato Augusto Santos Junior "Renatinho"	29.10.1992	25	1
	Jorge Luis Valdivia Toro (CHI)	19.10.1983	17	-
Wendel	Wendel Santana Pereira Santos	08.10.1981	15	-
Wesley	Wesley Lopes Beltrame	24.06.1987	26	2
	Forwards:			
	Jonathan Ezequiel Cristaldo (ARG)	05.03.1989	16	2
Diogo	Diogo Luis Santo	26.05.1987	23	1
Erik	Erik Mendes Gonçalves	21.02.1994	3	-
Fernando	Fernando José Gomes Júnior	15.09.1994	-	-
Henrique	Guilherme Pereira dos Santos Dias "Henrique"	15.09.1989	33	16
Leandro	Weverson Leandro Oliveira Moura	12.05.1993	17	1
Marquinhos	Marcos Gabriel do Nascimento "Marquinhos"	21.07.1990	8	1
Miguel Bianconi	Miguel Antonio Bianconi Kohl	14.05.1992	1	-
	Pablo Nicolás Mouche (ARG)	11.10.1987	17	2
Rodolfo	Rodolfo Freitas da Silva	04.10.1993	2	-
Serginho	Sergio Ricardo dos Santos Junior "Serginho"	03.12.1990	2	-
Washington	Washington Santana da Silva	20.01.1989	5	-
	Trainer:			
Gilson Kleina	Gilson Kleina [19.09.2012-08.05.2014]	30.03.1968	3	
Alberto Valentim	Alberto Valentim do Carmo Neto [09-20.05.2014]	22.03.1975	2	
	Ricardo Alberto Gareca Nardi (ARG) [as of 21.05.2014]	10.02.1958	33	

SANTOS FUTEBOL CLUBE

Foundation date: April 14, 1912
Address: Rua Princesa Isabel, 77, Vila Belmiro, Santos, CEP 11075-501
Stadium: Estádio „Urbano Caldeira“ [Vila Belmiro], Santos – Capacity: 16,798

THE SQUAD

		DOB	M	G
	Goalkeepers:			
Aranha	Mário Lúcio Duarte Costa „Aranha“	17.11.1980	33	-
Gabriel	Gabriel Bordinhão Gasparotto	09.02.1993	11	-
Vladimir	Vladimir Orlando Cardoso de Araújo Filho	16.07.1989	5	-
	Defenders:			
Bruno Peres	Bruno da Silva Peres	01.03.1990	2	-
Bruno Uvini	Bruno Uvini Bortolanca	03.06.1991	11	2
Caju	Wanderson de Jesus Martis “Caju”	17.07.1995	11	-
Cicinho	Neuciano de Jesus Gusmão “Cicinho”	26.12.1988	33	-
Daniel Guedes	Daniel Guedes da Silva	02.04.1994	2	-
David	David Braz de Oliveira Filho	21.05.1987	30	3
Edu Dracena	Eduardo Luiz Abonízio de Souza „Edu Dracena“	18.05.1981	19	-
Emerson	Emerson Palmieri dos Santos	13.03.1994	3	-
Geuvânio	Geuvânio Santos Silva	05.04.1992	24	5
Gustavo Vernes	Gustavo Henrique Vernes	24.03.1993	-	-
Jubal	Jubal Rocha Mendes Júnior	29.08.1993	8	-
Léo	Leonardo Lourenço Bastos „Léo“	06.07.1975	-	-
	Eugenio Estenan Mena Reveco (CHI)	18.07.1988	15	-
Nailson	Nailson Fernando Medeiros	24.02.1994	1	-
Neto	Hélio Hermito Zampier Neto	16.08.1985	11	-
Paulo	Paulo Ricardo Ferreira	13.07.1994	1	-
Victor Ferraz	Victor Ferraz Macedo	14.01.1988	5	-
Zé Carlos	José Carlos Cracco Neto „Zé Carlos“	16.05.1994	15	-
	Midfielders:			
Alan	Alan Santos da Silva	24.04.1991	15	1
Alison	Alison Lopes Ferreira	01.03.1993	23	1
Anderson Carvalho	Anderson de Carvalho Santos	20.05.1990	-	-
Arouca	Marcos Arouca da Silva	11.08.1986	33	1
Cícero	Cícero Santos	26.08.1984	6	2
Leandro	Leandro Cordeiro de Lima Silva	25.09.1993	8	-
Lucas Lima	Lucas Rafael Araújo Lima	09.07.1990	35	3
Lucas Otávio	Lucas Otávio Veiga Lopes	09.10.1994	-	-
Renato	Carlos Renato de Abreu	09.06.1978	10	-
	Patricio Julián Rodríguez (ARG)	04.05.1990	6	-
Serginho	Sergio Antonio Soler de Oliveira Junior “Serginho”	15.03.1995	5	-
Souza	Elierce Barbosa de Souza	08.03.1988	18	-
Thiago Maia	Thiago Maia Alencar	23.03.1997	-	-
Victor Andrade	Victor Andrade Santos	30.09.1995	2	-
	Forwards:			
Diego Cardoso	Diego Cardoso Nogueira	06.03.1994	6	2
Gabriel Barbosa	Gabriel Barbosa Almeida	30.08.1996	20	7
Giva	Givanildo Pulgas da Silva „Giva“	03.01.1993	2	-
Jorge	Jorge Eduardo Pedro Junior	08.09.1994	8	-
Leandro Damião	Leandro Damião da Silva dos Santos	22.07.1989	26	6
Rildo	Rildo de Andrade Felicissimo	20.03.1989	22	1
Robinho	Robson de Souza ”Robinho”	25.01.1984	16	4
Stéfano Yuri	Stéfano Yuri Gonçalves Almeida	27.04.1994	8	-
Thiago Ribeiro	Thiago Ribeiro Cardoso	24.02.1986	22	4
	Trainer:			
Oswaldo de Oliveira	Oswaldo de Oliveira Filho [11.12.2013-01.09.2014]	05.12.1950	18	
Enderson Moreira	Enderson Alves Moreira [as of 03.09.2014]	28.09.1971	20	

SÃO PAULO FUTEBOL CLUBE

Foundation date: January 25, 1930
Address: Praça Roberto Gomes Pedrosa, 1, São Paulo, CEP 05653-070
Stadium: Estádio „Cícero Pompeu de Toledo“ [Morumbi], São Paulo – Capacity: 67,428

THE SQUAD				
Goalkeepers:				
Dênis	Denis César de Matos „Dênis“	14.04.1987	3	-
Leo	Leonardo da Silva Vieira "Leo"	22.09.1990	-	-
Renan Ribeiro	Renan Ribeiro	23.03.1990	-	-
Rogério Ceni	Rogério Ceni	22.01.1973	35	8
Defenders:				
Antônio Carlos	Antônio Carlos dos Santos Aguiar	22.06.1983	19	2
Auro	Auro Alvaro da Cruz Junior	23.01.1996	12	-
Douglas	Douglas Pereira dos Santos	06.08.1990	10	1
Édson Silva	Édson José da Silva	09.05.1986	23	4
Lucão	Lucas Cavalcante Silva Afonso “Lucão”	23.03.1996	9	-
Lucas Possignolo	Lucas Possignolo	11.05.1994	-	-
Paulo Miranda	Jonathan Doin "Paulo Miranda"	16.08.1988	14	-
Reinaldo	Reinaldo Manoel da Silva	28.09.1989	18	-
Rodrigo Caio	Rodrigo Caio Coquete Russo	17.08.1993	8	-
	Clemente Juan Rodríguez (ARG)	31.07.1981	-	-
Rafael Tolói	Rafael Tolói	10.10.1990	17	1
Midfielders:				
Alan Kardec	Alan Kardec de Souza Pereira Junior	12.01.1989	27	8
Boschilia	Gabriel Boschilia	05.03.1996	18	1
Denilson	Denílson Pereira Neves	16.02.1988	28	-
Ewandro	Ewandro Felipe de Lima Costa	15.03.1996	4	-
Ganso	Paulo Henrique Chagas de Lima "Ganso"	12.10.1989	34	5
Húdson	Húdson Rodrigues dos Santos	30.01.1988	19	-
João Schmidt	João Felipe Schmidt Urbano	19.05.1993	-	-
Kaká	Ricardo Izecson dos Santos Leite “Kaká”	22.04.1982	19	2
Maicon	Maicon Thiago Pereira de Souza	14.09.1985	19	1
Michel Bastos	Michel Fernandes Bastos	02.08.1983	19	1
	Álvaro Daniel Pereira Barragán (URU)	28.11.1985	21	-
Souza	Josef de Souza Dias	11.02.1989	33	3
Forwards:				
Ademilson	Ademilson Braga Bispo Junior	09.01.1994	15	1
Alexandre Pato	Alexandre Rodrigues da Silva	02.09.1989	29	9
Luis Fabiano	Luís Fabiano Clemente	08.11.1980	23	9
Luiz Ricardo	Luiz Ricardo Silva Umbelino	21.01.1984	3	-
Osvaldo	Osvaldo Lourenço Filho	11.04.1987	32	-
	Dorlan Mauricio Pabón Ríos (COL)	24.01.1988	7	1
Welliton	Welliton Soares de Morais	22.10.1986	-	-
Trainer:				
Muricy Ramalho	Muricy Ramalho [as of 09.09.2013]	30.11.1955	38	

SPORT CLUB DO RECIFE

Foundation date: May 13, 1905

Address: Avenida Sport Club do Recife, Bairro Madalena 50750-221, Recife

Stadium: Estádio "Adelmar da Costa Carvalho" [Ilha do Retiro], Recife - Capacity: 35,020

THE SQUAD

		DOB	M	G
	Goalkeepers:			
Flávio	Flávio Henrique Ferreira Dos Santos Junior	18.05.1993	-	-
Magrão	Alessandro Beti Rosa "Magrão"	09.04.1977	38	-
Saulo	Saulo Araújo Fontes	02.04.1989	-	-
	Defenders:			
Danilo Barcelos	Danilo Carvalho Barcelos	17.08.1991	22	3
Durval	Severino dos Ramos Durval da Silva	11.07.1980	35	1
Ewerton Páscoa	Ewerton Ribeiro Páscoa	14.03.1989	17	1
Ferron	Luiz Antonio Linhares Garcia "Ferron"	11.11.1985	13	-
Henrique Mattos	Henrique Mendonça de Mattos	25.07.1990	9	-
Igor	Igor Fernandes da Silva Araujo	06.06.1992	5	-
Leandro Vicentin	Leandro Vicentin Fernandes	28.07.1994	-	-
Marcelo Cordeiro	Marcelo Cordeiro de Souza	12.04.1981	-	-
	Enrique Gabriel Meza Brítez (PAR)	28.11.1985	-	-
Oswaldo	Oswaldo Alfredo de Lima Gonçalves	27.12.1992	7	-
Patric	Patric Cabral Lalau	25.03.1989	34	7
Renê	Renê Rodrigues Martins	14.09.1992	38	-
Welton	Welton Heleno dos Santos	17.06.1992	-	-
	Midfielders:			
Aílton	Aílton do Nascimento Correia	13.10.1984	6	-
Ananias	Ananias Eloi Castro Monteiro	20.01.1989	22	2
Augusto	Augusto Cesar dos Santos Moreira	16.08.1992	15	1
Bileu	Josileudo Rodrigues de Araújo "Bileu"	28.03.1989	-	-
Diego Souza	Diego de Souza Andrade	17.06.1985	18	4
Felipe Azevedo	Felipe Azevedo dos Santos	10.01.1987	30	3
	Robert Mario Flores Bistolfi (URU)	13.05.1986	1	-
Hyago	Hyago de Oliveira Silva	22.04.1995	-	-
Ibson	Ibson Barreto da Silva	07.11.1983	15	-
Joelinton	Joelinton Cassio Apolinário de Lira	14.08.1996	7	2
Regis	Regis Augusto Salmazzo	30.11.1992	6	1
Renan Oliveira	Renan Henrique Oliveira Vieira	29.12.1989	8	-
Rithely	Francisco Rithely da Silva Sousa	27.01.1991	35	2
Rodrigo Mancha	Rodrigo Marcos dos Santos "Rodrigo Mancha"	16.06.1986	17	1
Ronaldo	Ronaldo Henrique Ferreira da Silva	27.06.1994	10	-
Vitor	Cícero Vitor dos Santos Júnior	29.07.1982	8	-
Wendel	Wendell Geraldo Maurício e Silva	08.04.1992	30	-
Willian	Willian Osmar de Oliveira Silva	16.05.1993	7	-
Zé Mário	José Mário de Bona "Zé Mário"	20.02.1992	14	-
	Forwards:			
Bruninho	Bruno Cardoso Gonçalves Santos "Bruninho"	25.02.1990	1	-
James	James Dean Araujo de Lima	22.07.1997	1	-
Leonardo	Leonardo Gonçalves Silva	26.10.1982	7	-
Mike	Mike dos Santos Nenatarvicius	08.03.1993	12	3
Neto	Antonio Francisco Moura Neto	06.08.1996	2	-
Neto Baiano	Euvaldo José de Aguiar Neto "Neto Baiano"	17.09.1982	24	4
Pelezinho	Érico Francisco de Oliveira Junior "Pelezinho"	22.07.1993	14	-
	Trainer:			
Eduardo Baptista	Eduardo Baptista [as of 14.02.2014]		38	

ESPORTE CLUBE VITÓRIA SALVADOR

Foundation date: May 13, 1899
Address: Rua Artêmio Castro Valente 1, Bairro Nossa Senhora da Vitória, 41750-240 Salvador, Bahia
Stadium: Estádio "Manoel Barradas" [Barradão] - Capacity: 35,632

THE SQUAD

		DOB	M	G
	Goalkeepers:			
	Roberto Júnior Fernández Torres (PAR)	29.03.1988	15	-
Fernando	Fernando Miguel Kaufmann	02.02.1985	-	-
Gustavo	Luis Gustavo de Almeida Pinto	10.03.1993	1	-
	Defenders:			
Ayrton	Ayrton Luiz Ganino	19.04.1985	16	2
Dão	Dannyu Francisco dos Santos "Dão"	28.10.1984	4	-
Defendi	Rodrigo Defendi	17.06.1986	1	-
Ednei	Ednei Barbosa de Souza	05.07.1990	4	-
Euller	Elosman Euller Silva Cavalcante	04.01.1995	9	-
Guilherme	Victor Guilherme da Silva Cavalcante	13.05.1994	-	-
Juan	Juan Maldonado Jaimez Junior	06.02.1982	23	-
Kadu	Ricardo Martins de Araújo „Kadu"	20.07.1986	27	3
Luiz Gustavo	Luiz Gustavo Tavares Conde	12.02.1994	22	1
Mansur	Joéliton Lima Santos „Mansur"	17.04.1993	14	-
Matheus	Matheus Salustiano Pires	19.04.1993	2	-
Nino	Severino do Ramos Clementino da Silva „Nino"	10.01.1986	22	-
Roger Carvalho	Roger Carvalho	10.12.1986	18	-
Romário	Romário Da Silva Santos	18.12.1993	-	-
Tarracha	Danilo Vettori Amaro „Tarracha"	22.09.1984	7	-
Vinícius	Vinícius Santos Silva	03.08.1993	19	1
	Midfielders:			
Adriano	Adriano Bispo dos Santos	29.05.1987	14	-
	Luís Bernardo Aguiar Burgos (URU)	17.11.1985	9	-
	Luis Enrique Cáceres (PAR)	16.04.1988	25	1
Darlan	Darlan Bispo Damasceno	21.07.1994	-	-
	Damián Ariel Escudero (ARG)	20.04.1987	10	-
Felipe	Felipe Tertuliano de Lima	18.01.1991	-	-
Hugo	Hugo Henrique Assis do Nascimento	27.10.1980	3	-
Josa	Joseilson Batista dos Santos "Josa"	24.09.1984	7	-
José Welison	José Welison da Silva	11.03.1995	21	1
Leo	Leonardo de Sousa Pereira "Leo"	03.02.1995	-	-
Léo Costa	Leonardo Fabricio Soares da Costa "Léo Costa"	03.03.1986	5	-
Marcelo	Marcelo Machado dos Santos	29.05.1994	3	-
Marcinho	Márcio José Oliveira "Marcinho"	20.07.1984	23	3
Marquinhos	Marcos Antônio da Silva Gonçalves "Marquinhos"	19.10.1989	6	2
Mauri	Mauri Franco Barbosa da Silva	06.03.1993	2	-
Neto Coruja	Ismael Soares Bastos Neto „Neto Coruja"	07.02.1987	11	-
Nickson	Nickson Gabriel Reis Silva	26.08.1997	1	-
Richarlyson	Richarlyson Barbosa Felisbino	27.12.1982	24	1
Vander	Vander Luiz Silva Souza	17.04.1990	1	-
	Forwards:			
Adaílton	Adaílton dos Santos da Silva	06.12.1990	-	-
Alan Pinheiro	Alan Lopes Pinheiro	13.05.1992	1	-
Alemão	José Carlos Tofolo Júnior "Alemão"	02.03.1989	11	-
	Guillermo Alexis Beltrán Paredes (PAR)	26.04.1984	12	-
Caio	Caio Canedo Corrêa	09.08.1990	18	5

Dinei	Telmário de Araújo Sacramento "Dinei"	11.11.1983	31	8
Edno	Edno Roberto Cunha	31.05.1983	14	5
Marcos Júnior	Marcos Júnior Lima dos Santos	19.01.1993	6	-
Souza	Rodrigo De Souza Cardoso	04.03.1982	5	1
William Henrique	William Henrique Rodrigues da Silva	28.01.1992	22	1
Willie	Willie Hortencio Barbosa	15.05.1993	16	1
Wilson	Wilson Rodrigues de Moura Junior	31.01.1984	24	-
	Trainer:			
Ney Franco	Ney Franco da Silveira Júnior [03.09.2013-12.05.2014]	22.07.1966	4	
Jorginho	Jorge Luís da Silva "Jorginho" [23.05.-21.08.2014]	22.03.1965	12	
Ney Franco	Ney Franco da Silveira Júnior [as of 22.08.2014]	22.07.1966	22	

Campeonato Brasileiro Série B 2014

1.	Joinville Esporte Clube (*Promoted*)	38	21	7	10	54	-	33	70
2.	Associação Atlética Ponte Preta Campinas (*Promoted*)	38	19	12	7	61	-	38	69
3.	CR Vasco da Gama Rio de Janeiro (*Promoted*)	38	16	15	7	50	-	36	63
4.	Avaí FC Florianópolis (*Promoted*)	38	18	8	12	47	-	40	62
5.	América FC Mineiro Belo Horizonte	38	20	7	11	59	-	39	61
6.	Boa Esporte Clube Varginha	38	18	5	15	51	-	48	59
7.	Atlético Clube Goianiense	38	17	8	13	54	-	49	59
8.	Ceará Sporting Club Fortaleza	38	16	9	13	58	-	53	57
9.	Santa Cruz FC Recife	38	14	13	11	51	-	38	55
10.	Sampaio Corrêa FC São Luís	38	13	14	11	54	-	46	53
11.	Paraná Clube Curitiba	38	13	12	13	45	-	43	51
12.	Luverdense Esporte Clube Lucas de Rio Verde	38	15	5	18	40	-	46	50
13.	Clube Náutico Capibaribe Recife	38	14	8	16	40	-	47	50
14.	ABC Futebol Clube Natal	38	14	6	18	34	-	40	48
15.	Oeste Futebol Clube Itápolis	38	12	12	14	39	-	48	48
16.	Clube Atlético Bragantino Bragança Paulista	38	13	7	18	45	-	55	46
17.	América Futebol Clube de Natal (*Relegated*)	38	12	7	19	44	-	53	43
18.	Associação Desportiva Recreativa e Cultural Icasa Juazeiro do Norte (*Relegated*)	38	11	10	17	34	-	43	43
19.	Vila Nova FC Goiânia (*Relegated*)	38	10	2	26	35	-	70	32
20.	Associação Portuguesa de Desportos São Paulo (*Relegated*)	38	4	13	21	29	-	59	25

Promoted for the 2015 Série B season:
Macaé Esporte FC
Paysandu Sport Club Belém
Mogi Mirim Esporte Clube

THE STATE CHAMPIONSHIPS 2014

Acre

Acre State Championship winners:

1919	Rio Branco FC
1920	Ypiranga SC Rio Branco
1921	Rio Branco FC
1922	Rio Branco FC
1923	*Not known*
1924	*Not known*
1925	*Not known*
1926	*Not known*
1927	*Not known*
1928	Rio Branco FC
1929	*Not known*
1930	Associação Atlética Militar Rio Branco
1931	*Not known*
1932	*Not known*
1933	*Not known*
1934	*Not known*
1935	Rio Branco FC
1936	Rio Branco FC
1937	Rio Branco FC
1938	Rio Branco FC
1939	Rio Branco FC
1940	Rio Branco FC
1941	Rio Branco FC
1942	Rio Branco FC
1943	Rio Branco FC
1944	Rio Branco FC
1945	Rio Branco FC
1946	Rio Branco FC
1947	Rio Branco FC
1948	América FC Rio Branco
1949	América FC Rio Branco
1950	Rio Branco FC
1951	Rio Branco FC
1952	Atlético Acreano Rio Branco
1953	Atlético Acreano Rio Branco
1954	Independência FC Rio Branco
1955	Rio Branco FC
1956	Rio Branco FC
1957	Rio Branco FC
1958	Independência FC Rio Branco
1959	Independência FC Rio Branco
1960	Independência FC Rio Branco
1961	Rio Branco FC
1962	Rio Branco FC & Atlético Acreano Rio Branco
1963	Independência FC Rio Branco
1964	Rio Branco FC
1965	AD Vasco da Gama Rio Branco
1966	AC Juventus Rio Branco

1967	Grêmio Atlético Sampaio Rio Branco
1968	Atlético Acreano Rio Branco
1969	AC Juventus Rio Branco
1970	Independência FC Rio Branco
1971	Rio Branco FC
1972	Independência FC Rio Branco
1973	Rio Branco FC
1974	Independência FC Rio Branco
1975	AC Juventus Rio Branco
1976	AC Juventus Rio Branco
1977	AC Juventus Rio Branco
1978	Rio Branco FC
1979	Rio Branco FC
1980	AC Juventus Rio Branco
1981	AC Juventus Rio Branco
1982	AC Juventus Rio Branco
1983	Rio Branco FC
1984	AC Juventus Rio Branco
1985	Independência FC Rio Branco
1986	Rio Branco FC
1987	Atlético Acreano Rio Branco
1988	Independência FC Rio Branco
1989	AC Juventus Rio Branco
1990	AC Juventus Rio Branco
1991	Atlético Acreano Rio Branco
1992	Rio Branco FC
1993	Independência FC Rio Branco
1994	Rio Branco FC
1995	AC Juventus Rio Branco
1996	AC Juventus Rio Branco
1997	Rio Branco FC
1998	Independência FC Rio Branco
1999	AD Vasco da Gama Rio Branco
2000	Rio Branco FC
2001	AD Vasco da Gama Rio Branco
2002	Rio Branco FC
2003	Rio Branco FC
2004	Rio Branco FC
2005	Rio Branco FC
2006	AD Senador Guiomard
2007	Rio Branco FC
2008	Rio Branco FC
2009	AC Juventus Rio Branco
2010	Rio Branco FC
2011	Rio Branco FC
2012	Rio Branco FC
2013	Plácido de Castro FC
2014	Rio Branco FC

Acre State League (Campeonato Acriano) 2014

First Stage

1.	Atlético Acreano Rio Branco	14	11	3	0	29	-	9	36
2.	Rio Branco Football Club	14	9	3	2	27	-	7	30
3.	Plácido de Castro Futebol Clube	14	8	1	5	28	-	13	25
4.	Galvez Esporte Clube	14	5	4	5	26	-	23	19
5.	Associação Desportiva Vasco da Gama Rio Branco	14	4	3	7	28	-	29	15
6.	Náuas Esporte Clube Cruzeiro do Sul	14	4	3	7	19	-	27	15
7.	Alto Acre Futebol Club	14	3	2	9	15	-	39	11
8.	Andirá Esporte Clube (*Relegated*)	14	2	1	11	11	-	36	7

Top-4 qualified for the semi-finals.

Semi-Finals (01-05.06.2014)

Galvez Esporte Clube - Atlético Acreano Rio Branco	0-1	1-1
Plácido de Castro Futebol Clube - Rio Branco Football Club	0-1	1-1

Final (08–11.06.2014)

Rio Branco Football Club - Atlético Acreano Rio Branco	1-1
Atlético Acreano Rio Branco - Rio Branco Football Club	2-2; 2-3 pen

Acre State Championship Winners 2014: **Rio Branco Football Club**

Alagoas

Alagoas State Championship winners:

1927	Clube de Regatas Maceió
1928	Centro Sportivo Alagoano Maceió
1929	Centro Sportivo Alagoano Maceió
1930	Clube de Regatas Maceió
1931	*No competition*
1932	*No competition*
1933	Centro Sportivo Alagoano Maceió
1934	*No competition*
1935	Centro Sportivo Alagoano Maceió
1936	Centro Sportivo Alagoano Maceió
1937	Clube de Regatas Maceió
1938	Clube de Regatas Maceió
1939	Clube de Regatas Maceió
1940	Clube de Regatas Maceió
1941	Centro Sportivo Alagoano Maceió
1942	Centro Sportivo Alagoano Maceió
1943	*No competition*
1944	Centro Sportivo Alagoano Maceió
1945	Santa Cruz FC Maceió
1946	EC Barroso Maceió
1947	EC Alexandria Maceió
1948	Santa Cruz FC Maceió
1949	Centro Sportivo Alagoano Maceió
1950	Clube de Regatas Maceió
1951	Clube de Regatas Maceió
1952	Centro Sportivo Alagoano Maceió
1953	Agremiação Sportiva Arapiraquense
1954	Ferroviário AC Maceió
1955	Centro Sportivo Alagoano Maceió
1956	Centro Sportivo Alagoano Maceió
1957	Centro Sportivo Alagoano Maceió
1958	Centro Sportivo Alagoano Maceió
1959	Centro Sportivo Capelense
1960	Centro Sportivo Alagoano Maceió
1961	Clube de Regatas Maceió
1962	Centro Sportivo Capelense
1963	Centro Sportivo Alagoano Maceió
1964	Clube de Regatas Maceió
1965	Centro Sportivo Alagoano Maceió
1966	Centro Sportivo Alagoano Maceió
1967	Centro Sportivo Alagoano Maceió
1968	Centro Sportivo Alagoano Maceió
1969	Clube de Regatas Maceió
1970	Clube de Regatas Maceió

1971	Centro Sportivo Alagoano Maceió
1972	Clube de Regatas Maceió
1973	Clube de Regatas Maceió
1974	Centro Sportivo Alagoano Maceió
1975	Centro Sportivo Alagoano Maceió
1976	Clube de Regatas Maceió
1977	Clube de Regatas Maceió
1978	Clube de Regatas Maceió
1979	Clube de Regatas Maceió
1980	Centro Sportivo Alagoano Maceió
1981	Centro Sportivo Alagoano Maceió
1982	Centro Sportivo Alagoano Maceió
1983	Clube de Regatas Maceió
1984	Centro Sportivo Alagoano Maceió
1985	Centro Sportivo Alagoano Maceió
1986	Clube de Regatas Maceió
1987	Clube de Regatas Maceió
1988	Centro Sportivo Alagoano Maceió
1989	Centro Sportivo Capelense
1990	Centro Sportivo Alagoano Maceió
1991	Centro Sportivo Alagoano Maceió
1992	Clube de Regatas Maceió
1993	Clube de Regatas Maceió
1994	Centro Sportivo Alagoano Maceió
1995	Clube de Regatas Maceió
1996	Centro Sportivo Alagoano Maceió
1997	Centro Sportivo Alagoano Maceió
1998	Centro Sportivo Alagoano Maceió
1999	Centro Sportivo Alagoano Maceió
2000	Agremiação Sportiva Arapiraquense
2001	Agremiação Sportiva Arapiraquense
2002	Clube de Regatas Maceió
2003	Agremiação Sportiva Arapiraquense
2004	SC Corinthians Alagoano Maceió
2005	Agremiação Sportiva Arapiraquense
2006	Associação Atlética Coruripe
2007	Associação Atlética Coruripe
2008	Centro Sportivo Alagoano Maceió
2009	Agremiação Sportiva Arapiraquense
2010	Murici Futebol Clube
2011	Agremiação Sportiva Arapiraquense
2012	Clube de Regatas Brasil Maceió
2013	Clube de Regatas Brasil Maceió
2014	Associação Atlética Coruripe

Alagoas State League (Campeonato Alagoano) 2014

First Stage (Copa Alagoas)

1.	Agremiação Sportiva Arapiraquense	7	5	1	1	14 - 8	16
2.	Associação Atlética Santa Rita	7	4	3	0	11 - 5	15
3.	Associação Atlética Coruripe	7	2	3	2	12 - 10	9
4.	Murici Futebol Clube	7	2	3	2	8 - 8	9
5.	Clube Sociedade Esportiva Palmeira dos Índios	7	2	2	3	13 - 13	8
6.	Sport Club Penedense	7	2	2	3	6 - 9	8
7.	Centro Esportibo Olhodagüense	7	1	3	3	4 - 9	6
8.	Comercial Futebol Clube Viçosa	7	1	1	5	5 - 11	4

Top-4 teams qualified for the Semi-Finals.
Clube de Regatas Brasil Maceió (as title holders) and Centro Sportivo Alagoano Maceió were qualified directly for the Seond Stage.

Semi-Finals (05-09.02.2014)

Murici Futebol Clube - Agremiação Sportiva Arapiraquense	3-1(1-1)	0-1(0-1)
Associação Atlética Coruripe - Associação Atlética Santa Rita	2-1(0-0)	1-3(0-2)

Final (13-15.02.2014)

Murici Futebol Clube - Associação Atlética Santa Rita	1-0(1-0)
Associação Atlética Santa Rita - Murici Futebol Clube	0-1(0-0)

Second Stage (Copa Maceió)

Grupo A

1.	Clube de Regatas Brasil Maceió	10	6	3	1	15 - 5	21
2.	Agremiação Sportiva Arapiraquense	10	6	1	3	19 - 13	19
3.	Clube Sociedade Esportiva Palmeira dos Índios	10	6	0	4	15 - 14	18
4.	Associação Atlética Santa Rita	10	2	5	3	11 - 15	11
5.	Comercial Futebol Clube Viçosa	10	1	4	5	9 - 19	7

Grupo B

1.	Associação Atlética Coruripe	10	5	2	3	15 - 10	17
2.	Murici Futebol Clube	10	4	2	4	12 - 11	14
3.	Centro Sportivo Alagoano Maceió	10	3	3	4	17 - 13	12
4.	Centro Esportibo Olhodagüense	10	2	3	5	9 - 15	9
5.	Sport Club Penedense	10	2	3	5	13 - 20	9

Semi-Finals (17-19.04.2014)

Murici Futebol Clube - Associação Atlética Coruripe	0-0	0-1(0-0)
Agremiação Sportiva Arapiraquense - Clube de Regatas Brasil Maceió	0-2(0-1)	2-0(1-0)

Final (26.04.-01.05.2014)

Associação Atlética Coruripe - Clube de Regatas Brasil Maceió	2-1(1-1)
Clube de Regatas Brasil Maceió - Associação Atlética Coruripe	0-0

Alagoas State Championship Winners 2014: **Associação Atlética Coruripe**

Amapá State Championship winners:

1944	Esporte Clube Macapá
1945	Amapá Clube Macapá
1946	Esporte Clube Macapá
1947	Esporte Clube Macapá
1948	Esporte Clube Macapá
1949	*No competition*
1950	Amapá Clube Macapá
1951	Amapá Clube Macapá
1952	Trem Desportivo Clube Macapá
1953	Amapá Clube Macapá
1954	Esporte Clube Macapá
1955	Esporte Clube Macapá
1956	Esporte Clube Macapá
1957	Esporte Clube Macapá
1958	Esporte Clube Macapá
1959	Esporte Clube Macapá
1960	Santana Esporte Clube
1961	Santana Esporte Clube
1962	Santana Esporte Clube
1963	CEA Clube
1964	Juventus
1965	Santana Esporte Clube
1966	Juventus
1967	Juventus
1968	Santana Esporte Clube
1969	Esporte Clube Macapá
1970	SER São José Macapá
1971	SER São José Macapá
1972	Santana Esporte Clube
1973	Amapá Clube Macapá
1974	Esporte Clube Macapá
1975	Amapá Clube Macapá
1976	Ypiranga Clube Macapá
1977	Guarany
1978	Esporte Clube Macapá
1979	Amapá Clube Macapá

1980	Esporte Clube Macapá
1981	Esporte Clube Macapá
1982	Independente Esporte Clube Santana
1983	Independente Esporte Clube Santana
1984	Trem Desportivo Clube Macapá
1985	Santana Esporte Clube
1986	Esporte Clube Macapá
1987	Amapá Clube Macapá
1988	Amapá Clube Macapá
1989	Independente Esporte Clube Santana
1990	Amapá Clube Macapá
1991	Esporte Clube Macapá
1992	Ypiranga Clube Macapá
1993	SER São José Macapá
1994	Ypiranga Clube Macapá
1995	Independente Esporte Clube Santana
1996	*No competition*
1997	Ypiranga Clube Macapá
1998	Aliança
1999	Ypiranga Clube Macapá
2000	Santos Futebol Clube Macapá
2001	Independente Esporte Clube Santana
2002	Ypiranga Clube Macapá
2003	Ypiranga Clube Macapá
2004	Ypiranga Clube Macapá
2005	SER São José Macapá
2006	SER São José Macapá
2007	Trem Desportivo Clube Macapá
2008	Cristal Atlético Clube Macapá
2009	SER São José Macapá
2010	Trem Desportivo Clube Macapá
2011	Trem Desportivo Clube Macapá
2012	Oratório Recreativo Clube Macapá
2013	Santos Futebol Clube Macapá
2014	Santos Futebol Clube Macapá

Amapá State League (Campeonato Amapaense) 2014

First Stage

1. Santos Futebol Clube Macapá	3	2	1	0	5 - 1	7
2. Esporte Clube Macapá	3	1	1	1	1 - 3	4
3. São Paulo Futebol Clube Macapá	3	1	0	2	2 - 3	3
4. Santana Esporte Clube	3	0	2	1	2 - 3	2

Top-2 teams qualified for the first stage finals.

Final (26.04.2014)

Santos Futebol Clube Macapá - Esporte Clube Macapá 3-1(2-0)

Santos Futebol Clube Macapá, as winner of the first stage were qualified for the State League Final.

Second Stage

1. Santos Futebol Clube Macapá	3	3	0	0	4 - 1	9
2. São Paulo Futebol Clube Macapá	3	2	0	1	5 - 4	6
3. Esporte Clube Macapá	3	1	0	2	3 - 3	3
4. Santana Esporte Clube	3	0	0	3	1 - 5	0

Top-2 teams qualified for the second stage finals.

Final (17.05.2014)

Santos Futebol Clube Macapá - São Paulo Futebol Clube Macapá 2-0(1-0)

State League Final

Santos Futebol Clube Macapá, as winner of both stages were state champions, no final match needed.

Amapá State Championship Winners 2014: **Santos Futebol Clube Macapá**

Amazonas

Amazonas State Championship winners:

1914	Manaus Athletic Club Manaus
1915	Manaus Athletic Club Manaus
1916	Nacional Futebol Clube Manaus
1917	Nacional Futebol Clube Manaus
1918	Nacional Futebol Clube Manaus
1919	Nacional Futebol Clube Manaus
1920	Nacional Futebol Clube Manaus
1921	Atlético Rio Negro Clube Manaus
1922	Nacional Futebol Clube Manaus
1923	Nacional Futebol Clube Manaus
1924	*No competition*
1925	*No competition*
1926	*No competition*
1927	Atlético Rio Negro Clube Manaus
1928	Cruzeiro do Sul Futebol Clube Manaus
1929	Manaus Sporting Club Manaus
1930	Cruzeiro do Sul Futebol Clube Manaus
1931	Atlético Rio Negro Clube Manaus
1932	Atlético Rio Negro Clube Manaus
1933	Nacional Futebol Clube Manaus
1934	União Esportiva Portuguesa Manaus
1935	União Esportiva Portuguesa Manaus
1936	Nacional Futebol Clube Manaus
1937	Nacional Futebol Clube Manaus
1938	Atlético Rio Negro Clube Manaus
1939	Nacional Futebol Clube Manaus
1940	Atlético Rio Negro Clube Manaus
1941	Nacional Futebol Clube Manaus
1942	Nacional Futebol Clube Manaus
1943	Atlético Rio Negro Clube Manaus
1944	Olímpico Clube Manaus
1945	Nacional Futebol Clube Manaus
1946	Nacional Futebol Clube Manaus
1947	Olímpico Clube Manaus
1948	Nacional Fast Club Manaus
1949	Nacional Fast Club Manaus
1950	Nacional Futebol Clube Manaus
1951	América Futebol Clube Manaus
1952	América Futebol Clube Manaus
1953	América Futebol Clube Manaus
1954	América Futebol Clube Manaus
1955	Nacional Fast Club Manaus
1956	Auto Esporte Clube Manaus
1957	Nacional Futebol Clube Manaus
1958	Santos Futebol Clube Manaus
1959	Auto Esporte Clube Manaus
1960	Nacional Fast Club Manaus
1961	São Raimundo Esporte Clube Manaus
1962	Atlético Rio Negro Clube Manaus
1963	Nacional Futebol Clube Manaus
1964	Nacional Futebol Clube Manaus
1965	Atlético Rio Negro Clube Manaus
1966	São Raimundo Esporte Clube Manaus
1967	Olímpico Clube Manaus
1968	Nacional Futebol Clube Manaus
1969	Nacional Futebol Clube Manaus
1970	Nacional Fast Club Manaus
1971	Nacional Fast Club Manaus
1972	Nacional Futebol Clube Manaus
1973	Associação Atlética Rodoviária Manaus
1974	Nacional Futebol Clube Manaus
1975	Atlético Rio Negro Clube Manaus
1976	Nacional Futebol Clube Manaus
1977	Nacional Futebol Clube Manaus
1978	Nacional Futebol Clube Manaus
1979	Nacional Futebol Clube Manaus
1980	Nacional Futebol Clube Manaus
1981	Nacional Futebol Clube Manaus
1982	Atlético Rio Negro Clube Manaus
1983	Nacional Futebol Clube Manaus
1984	Nacional Futebol Clube Manaus
1985	Nacional Futebol Clube Manaus
1986	Nacional Futebol Clube Manaus
1987	Atlético Rio Negro Clube Manaus
1988	Atlético Rio Negro Clube Manaus
1989	Atlético Rio Negro Clube Manaus
1990	Atlético Rio Negro Clube Manaus
1991	Nacional Futebol Clube Manaus
1992	Sul América Esporte Clube Manaus
1993	Sul América Esporte Clube Manaus
1994	América Futebol Clube Manaus
1995	Nacional Futebol Clube Manaus
1996	Nacional Futebol Clube Manaus
1997	São Raimundo Esporte Clube Manaus
1998	São Raimundo Esporte Clube Manaus
1999	São Raimundo Esporte Clube Manaus
2000	Nacional Futebol Clube Manaus
2001	Atlético Rio Negro Clube Manaus
2002	Nacional Futebol Clube Manaus
2003	Nacional Futebol Clube Manaus
2004	São Raimundo Esporte Clube Manaus
2005	Grêmio Atlético Coariense Coari
2006	São Raimundo Esporte Clube Manaus
2007	Nacional Futebol Clube Manaus
2008	Holanda Esporte Clube Manaus
2009	América Futebol Clube Manaus
2010	Peñarol Atlético Clube Itacoatiara
2011	Peñarol Atlético Clube Itacoatiara
2012	Nacional Futebol Clube Manaus
2013	Princesa do Solimões EC Manacapuru
2014	Nacional Futebol Clube Manaus

Amazonas State Championship (Campeonato Amazonense) 2014

First Stage – Taça Estado do Amazonas

Grupo A

1.	Princesa do Solimões Esporte Clube Manacapuru	4	3	1	0	8 - 3	10
2.	Nacional Fast Clube Manaus	4	3	0	1	14 - 7	9
3.	Manaus Futebol Clube	4	1	2	1	9 - 7	5
4.	Esporte Clube Iranduba da Amazônia	4	1	0	3	5 - 9	3
5.	Sul América Esporte Clube Manaus	4	0	1	3	2 - 12	1

Grupo B

1.	Nacional Futebol Clube Manaus	4	3	0	1	10 - 4	9
2.	AR Clube Nacional Borbense	4	2	2	0	7 - 5	8
3.	Peñarol Atlético Clube Itacoatiara	4	1	2	1	4 - 4	5
4.	Holanda Esporte Clube Rio Preto da Eva	4	0	2	2	1 - 5	2
5.	São Raimundo Esporte Clube	4	0	2	2	1 - 5	2

Top-2 of each group qualified for the semi-finals.

Semi-Finals (02-05.03.2014)

AR Clube Nacional Borbense - Princesa do Solimões Esporte Clube Manacapuru	2-1	1-3
Nacional Fast Clube Manaus - Nacional Futebol Clube Manaus	4-2	0-0

Final (15-22.03.2014)

Nacional Fast Clube Manaus - Princesa do Solimões Esporte Clube Manacapuru	0-0	0-0

Princesa do Solimões Esporte Clube Manacapuru, as winner of the first stage were qualified for the State League Final.

Second Stage - Taça Cidade de Manaus

Grupo A

1.	Princesa do Solimões Esporte Clube Manacapuru	5	5	0	0	11 - 4	15
2.	Manaus Futebol Clube	5	2	1	2	6 - 9	7
3.	Nacional Fast Clube Manaus	5	1	3	1	9 - 9	6
4.	Esporte Clube Iranduba da Amazônia	5	1	2	2	3 - 5	5
5.	Sul América Esporte Clube Manaus	5	1	0	4	2 - 10	3

Grupo B

1.	Nacional Futebol Clube Manaus	5	2	2	1	8 - 4	8
2.	Peñarol Atlético Clube Itacoatiara	5	2	2	1	9 - 6	8
3.	AR Clube Nacional Borbense	5	2	1	2	7 - 6	7
4.	São Raimundo Esporte Clube	5	2	0	3	8 - 9	6
5.	Holanda Esporte Clube Rio Preto da Eva	5	1	1	3	5 - 6	4

Top-2 of each group qualified for the semi-finals.

Semi-Finals (19-27.04.2014)

Manaus Futebol Clube - Nacional Futebol Clube Manaus	0-2	1-3
Peñarol Atlético Clube Itacoatiara - Princesa do Solimões EC Manacapuru	1-4	1-1

Final (03-11.05.2014)

Nacional Futebol Clube Manaus - Princesa do Solimões EC Manacapuru	2-1	2-1

Nacional FC Manaus, as winner of the second stage were qualified for the State League Final.

State League Final (18-24.05.2014)

Nacional Futebol Clube Manaus - Princesa do Solimões EC Manacapuru	0-2
Princesa do Solimões EC Manacapuru - Nacional Futebol Clube Manaus	1-5

Amazonas State Championship Winners 2014: **Nacional Futebol Clube Manaus**

Bahia

Bahia State Championship winners:

Year	Winner	Year	Winner
1905	Clube Internacional de Cricket Salvador	1961	Esporte Clube Bahia Salvador
1906	Clube de Natação e Regatas São Salvador	1962	Esporte Clube Bahia Salvador
1907	Clube de Natação e Regatas São Salvador	1963	Fluminense Futebol Clube Feira de Santana
1908	Esporte Clube Vitória Salvador	1964	Esporte Clube Vitória Salvador
1909	Esporte Clube Vitória Salvador	1965	Esporte Clube Vitória Salvador
1910	Sport Club Santos Dumont Salvador	1966	Associação Desportiva Leônico Salvador
1911	Sport Club Bahia Salvador	1967	Esporte Clube Bahia Salvador
1912	Atlético Futebol Clube Salvador	1968	Galícia Esporte Clube Salvador
1913	Fluminense Futebol Clube Salvador	1969	Fluminense Futebol Clube Feira de Santana
1914	Sport Club Internacional Salvador	1970	Esporte Clube Bahia Salvador
1915	Fluminense Futebol Clube Salvador	1971	Esporte Clube Bahia Salvador
1916	Sport Club República Salvador	1972	Esporte Clube Vitória Salvador
1917	Sport Club Ypiranga Salvador	1973	Esporte Clube Bahia Salvador
1918	Sport Club Ypiranga Salvador	1974	Esporte Clube Bahia Salvador
1919	Sport Club Botafogo Salvador	1975	Esporte Clube Bahia Salvador
1920	Sport Club Ypiranga Salvador	1976	Esporte Clube Bahia Salvador
1921	Sport Club Ypiranga Salvador	1977	Esporte Clube Bahia Salvador
1922	Sport Club Botafogo Salvador	1978	Esporte Clube Bahia Salvador
1923	Sport Club Botafogo Salvador	1979	Esporte Clube Bahia Salvador
1924	Associação Atlética da Bahia Salvador	1980	Esporte Clube Vitória Salvador
1925	Sport Club Ypiranga Salvador	1981	Esporte Clube Bahia Salvador
1926	Sport Club Botafogo Salvador	1982	Esporte Clube Bahia Salvador
1927	Clube Bahiano de Tênis Salvador	1983	Esporte Clube Bahia Salvador
1928	Sport Club Ypiranga Salvador	1984	Esporte Clube Bahia Salvador
1929	Sport Club Ypiranga Salvador	1985	Esporte Clube Vitória Salvador
1930	Sport Club Botafogo Salvador	1986	Esporte Clube Bahia Salvador
1931	Esporte Clube Bahia Salvador	1987	Esporte Clube Bahia Salvador
1932	Sport Club Ypiranga Salvador	1988	Esporte Clube Bahia Salvador
1933	Esporte Clube Bahia Salvador	1989	Esporte Clube Vitória Salvador
1934	Esporte Clube Bahia Salvador	1990	Esporte Clube Vitória Salvador
1935	Sport Club Botafogo Salvador	1991	Esporte Clube Bahia Salvador
1936	Esporte Clube Bahia Salvador	1992	Esporte Clube Vitória Salvador
1937	Galícia Esporte Clube Salvador	1993	Esporte Clube Bahia Salvador
1938	1/ Esporte Clube Bahia Salvador	1994	Esporte Clube Bahia Salvador
1938	2/ Sport Club Botafogo Salvador	1995	Esporte Clube Vitória Salvador
1939	Sport Club Ypiranga Salvador	1996	Esporte Clube Vitória Salvador
1940	Esporte Clube Bahia Salvador	1997	Esporte Clube Vitória Salvador
1941	Galícia Esporte Clube Salvador	1998	Esporte Clube Bahia Salvador
1942	Galícia Esporte Clube Salvador	1999	Esporte Clube Bahia Salvador & Esporte Clube Vitória Salvador (shared)
1943	Galícia Esporte Clube Salvador		
1944	Esporte Clube Bahia Salvador	2000	Esporte Clube Vitória Salvador
1945	Esporte Clube Bahia Salvador	2001	Esporte Clube Bahia Salvador
1946	Associação Desportiva Guarany Salvador	2002	Palmeiras do Nordeste Feira de Santana
1947	Esporte Clube Bahia Salvador	2002	Esporte Clube Vitória Salvador
1948	Esporte Clube Bahia Salvador	2003	Esporte Clube Vitória Salvador
1949	Esporte Clube Bahia Salvador	2004	Esporte Clube Vitória Salvador
1950	Esporte Clube Bahia Salvador	2005	Esporte Clube Vitória Salvador
1951	Sport Club Ypiranga Salvador	2006	Colo-Colo de Futebol e Regatas Ilhéus
1952	Esporte Clube Bahia Salvador	2007	Esporte Clube Vitória Salvador

1953	Esporte Clube Vitória Salvador
1954	Esporte Clube Bahia Salvador
1955	Esporte Clube Vitória Salvador
1956	Esporte Clube Bahia Salvador
1957	Esporte Clube Vitória Salvador
1958	Esporte Clube Bahia Salvador
1959	Esporte Clube Bahia Salvador
1960	Esporte Clube Bahia Salvador
2008	Esporte Clube Vitória Salvador
2009	Esporte Clube Vitória Salvador
2010	Esporte Clube Vitória Salvador
2011	Associação Desportiva Bahia de Feira
2012	Esporte Clube Bahia Salvador
2013	Esporte Clube Vitória Salvador
2014	Esporte Clube Bahia Salvador

Bahia State Championship (Campeonato Baiano) 2014

First Stage

1.	Serrano Sport Club Vitória da Conquista	8	5	1	2	14	-	9	16
2.	Esporte Clube Jacuipense Riachão do Jacuípe	8	4	4	0	13	-	5	16
3.	Sociedade Desportiva Juazeirense	8	4	3	1	15	-	13	15
4.	Galícia Esporte Clube Salvador	8	4	2	2	12	-	5	14
5.	Catuense Futebol S/A Alagoinhas	8	3	3	2	15	-	10	12
6.	Associação Desportiva Bahia de Feira	8	1	5	2	7	-	9	8
7.	Feirense Futebol Clube Santa Maria da Feira	8	1	2	5	11	-	18	5
8.	Juazeiro Social Clube (*Relegated*)	8	1	2	5	7	-	15	5
9.	Botafogo Sport Club Salvador (*Relegated*)	8	1	2	5	9	-	20	5

Top-5 qualified for the Second Stage.

Second Stage

Three teams entered in the second stage the competition: Esporte Clube Bahia, Esporte Clube Vitória Salvador and EC Primeiro Passo Vitória da Conquista. Top-2 teams of each were qualified for the semi-finals

Grupo 1

1.	Esporte Clube Vitória Salvador	8	6	1	1	18	-	8	19
2.	EC Primeiro Passo Vitória da Conquista	8	3	3	2	18	-	11	12
3.	Galícia Esporte Clube Salvador	8	3	3	2	11	-	8	12
4.	Esporte Clube Jacuipense Riachão do Jacuípe	8	2	2	4	13	-	12	8

Grupo 2

1.	Esporte Clube Bahia Salvador	8	5	2	1	13	-	8	17
2.	Serrano Sport Club Vitória da Conquista	8	2	1	5	7	-	20	7
3.	Sociedade Desportiva Juazeirense	8	1	3	4	12	-	15	6
4.	Catuense Futebol S/A Alagoinhas	8	1	3	4	8	-	18	6

Semi-Finals (26-30.03.2014)

EC Primeiro Passo Vitória da Conquista - Esporte Clube Vitória Salvador	1-2(1-0)	0-6(0-3)
Serrano Sport Club Vitória da Conquista - Esporte Clube Bahia Salvador	1-1(1-0)	0-1(0-1)

Third place play-off (03-06.04.2014)

Serrano SC Vitória da Conquista - EC Primeiro Passo Vitória da Conquista	2-1(2-1)	2-3(2-0)

Finals (06-13.04.2014)

Esporte Clube Bahia Salvador - Esporte Clube Vitória Salvador	2-0(1-0)
Esporte Clube Vitória Salvador - Esporte Clube Bahia Salvador	2-2(0-2)

Bahia State Championship Winners 2014: **Esporte Clube Bahia Salvador**

Ceará

Ceará State Championship winners:

1914	Rio Branco Foot-ball Club Fortaleza
1915	Ceará Sporting Club Fortaleza
1916	Ceará Sporting Club Fortaleza
1917	Ceará Sporting Club Fortaleza
1918	Ceará Sporting Club Fortaleza
1919	Ceará Sporting Club Fortaleza
1920	Fortaleza Esporte Clube
1921	Fortaleza Esporte Clube
1922	Ceará Sporting Club Fortaleza
1923	Fortaleza Esporte Clube
1924	Fortaleza Esporte Clube
1925	Ceará Sporting Club Fortaleza
1926	Fortaleza Esporte Clube
1927	Fortaleza Esporte Clube
1928	Fortaleza Esporte Clube
1929	Maguari Esporte Clube Fortaleza
1930	Orion Futebol Clube Fortaleza
1931	Ceará Sporting Club Fortaleza
1932	Ceará Sporting Club Fortaleza
1933	Fortaleza Esporte Clube
1934	Fortaleza Esporte Clube
1935	América Futebol Clube Fortaleza
1936	Maguari Esporte Clube Fortaleza
1937	Fortaleza Esporte Clube
1938	Fortaleza Esporte Clube
1939	Ceará Sporting Club Fortaleza
1940	Tramways Sport Club Fortaleza
1941	Ceará Sporting Club Fortaleza
1942	Ceará Sporting Club Fortaleza
1943	Maguari Esporte Clube Fortaleza
1944	Maguari Esporte Clube Fortaleza
1945	Ferroviário Atlético Clube Fortaleza
1946	Fortaleza Esporte Clube
1947	Fortaleza Esporte Clube
1948	Ceará Sporting Club Fortaleza
1949	Fortaleza Esporte Clube
1950	Ferroviário Atlético Clube Fortaleza
1951	Ceará Sporting Club Fortaleza
1952	Ferroviário Atlético Clube Fortaleza
1953	Fortaleza Esporte Clube
1954	Fortaleza Esporte Clube
1955	Calouros do Ar Futebol Clube Fortaleza
1956	Gentilândia Atlético Clube Fortaleza
1957	Ceará Sporting Club Fortaleza
1958	Ceará Sporting Club Fortaleza
1959	Fortaleza Esporte Clube
1960	Fortaleza Esporte Clube
1961	Ceará Sporting Club Fortaleza
1962	Ceará Sporting Club Fortaleza
1963	Ceará Sporting Club Fortaleza
1964	Fortaleza Esporte Clube Fortaleza
1965	Fortaleza Esporte Clube

1966	América Futebol Clube Fortaleza
1967	Fortaleza Esporte Clube
1968	Ferroviário Atlético Clube Fortaleza
1969	Fortaleza Esporte Clube
1970	Ferroviário Atlético Clube Fortaleza
1971	Ceará Sporting Club Fortaleza
1972	Ceará Sporting Club Fortaleza
1973	Fortaleza Esporte Clube
1974	Fortaleza Esporte Clube
1975	Ceará Sporting Club Fortaleza
1976	Ceará Sporting Club Fortaleza
1977	Ceará Sporting Club Fortaleza
1978	Ceará Sporting Club Fortaleza
1979	Ferroviário Atlético Clube Fortaleza
1980	Ceará Sporting Club Fortaleza
1981	Ceará Sporting Club Fortaleza
1982	Fortaleza Esporte Clube
1983	Fortaleza Esporte Clube
1984	Ceará Sporting Club Fortaleza
1985	Fortaleza Esporte Clube
1986	Ceará Sporting Club Fortaleza
1987	Fortaleza Esporte Clube
1988	Ferroviário Atlético Clube Fortaleza
1989	Ceará Sporting Club Fortaleza
1990	Ceará Sporting Club Fortaleza
1991	Fortaleza Esporte Clube
1992	Fortaleza Esporte Clube
	Ceará Sporting Club Fortaleza
	Associação Esportiva Tiradentes Fortaleza
	Icasa Esporte Clube Juazeiro do Norte
1993	Ceará Sporting Club Fortaleza
1994	Ferroviário Atlético Clube Fortaleza
1995	Ferroviário Atlético Clube Fortaleza
1996	Ceará Sporting Club Fortaleza
1997	Ceará Sporting Club Fortaleza
1998	Ceará Sporting Club Fortaleza
1999	Ceará Sporting Club Fortaleza
2000	Fortaleza Esporte Clube
2001	Fortaleza Esporte Clube
2002	Ceará Sporting Club Fortaleza
2003	Fortaleza Esporte Clube
2004	Fortaleza Esporte Clube
2005	Fortaleza Esporte Clube
2006	Ceará Sporting Club Fortaleza
2007	Fortaleza Esporte Clube
2008	Fortaleza Esporte Clube
2009	Fortaleza Esporte Clube
2010	Fortaleza Esporte Clube
2011	Ceará Sporting Club Fortaleza
2012	Ceará Sporting Club Fortaleza
2013	Ceará Sporting Club Fortaleza
2014	Ceará Sporting Club Fortaleza

Please note: 1992 - four winners (shared).

Ceará State Championship (Campeonato Cearense) 2014

First Stage

1.	Fortaleza Esporte Clube	16	13	3	0	48 - 14	42
2.	Guarani Esporte Clube Juazeiro do Norte	16	7	5	4	17 - 18	26
3.	Horizonte Futebol Clube	16	6	7	3	26 - 18	25
4.	Associação Desportiva Recreativa Cultural Icasa	16	6	6	4	18 - 19	24
5.	Quixadá Futebol Clube	16	7	2	7	25 - 23	23
6.	Itapipoca Esporte Clube	16	5	6	5	19 - 24	21
7.	Ferroviário Atlético Clube Fortaleza (*Relegated*)	16	5	3	8	26 - 25	18
8.	Associação Esportiva Tiradentes (*Relegated*)	16	2	6	8	26 - 32	12
9.	Crato Esporte Clube (*Relegated*)	16	1	2	13	8 - 40	5

Ceará Sporting Club Fortaleza, Guarany Sporting Club Sobral and the Top-6 teams qualified for the Second Stage.

Second Stage

1.	Fortaleza Esporte Clube	10	5	4	1	21 - 12	21
2.	Ceará Sporting Club Fortaleza	10	5	4	1	18 - 9	19
3.	Guarany Sporting Club Sobral	10	3	4	3	15 - 13	13
4.	Associação Desportiva Recreativa Cultural Icasa	10	3	3	4	12 - 14	12
5.	Horizonte Futebol Clube	10	3	2	5	12 - 21	11
6.	Guarani Esporte Clube Juazeiro do Norte	10	0	5	5	8 - 17	6

Top-4 qualified for the Final Stage.

Final Stage - Semi-Finals (06-13.04.2014)

Associação Desportiva Recreativa Cultural Icasa - Fortaleza Esporte Clube	3-1(0-1)	1-3(0-1)
Guarany Sporting Club Sobral - Ceará Sporting Club Fortaleza	2-3(2-1)	2-5(0-1)

Finals (17-24.04.2014)

Fortaleza Esporte Clube - Ceará Sporting Club Fortaleza	0-0
Ceará Sporting Club Fortaleza - Fortaleza Esporte Clube	0-0

Ceará State Championship Winners 2014: **Ceará Sporting Club Fortaleza**

Distrito Federal

Distrito Federal State Championship winners:

1959	GE Brasiliense Núcleo Bandeirante
1960	Defelê Futebol Clube Brasília
1961	Defelê Futebol Clube Brasília
1962	Defelê Futebol Clube Brasília
1963	AE Cruzeiro do Sul Brasília
1964	AA Guanabara Brasília (Am)*
	Rabello Futebol Clube Brasília (Pr)*
1965	Pederneiras FC Brasília (Am)
	Rabello Futebol Clube Brasília (Pr)
1966	AA Guanabara Brasília (Am)
	Rabello Futebol Clube Brasília (Pr)
1967	Rabello Futebol Clube Brasília
1968	Defelê Futebol Clube Brasília
1969	Coenge Futebol Clube Brasília
1970	GE Brasiliense Núcleo Bandeirante
1971	CA Colombo Núcleo Bandeirante
1972	AA Serviço Gráfico Brasília
1973	CEUB Esporte Clube Brasília
1974	Pioneira Futebol Clube Taguatinga
1975	Campineira Brasília
1976	Brasília Esporte Clube
1977	Brasília Esporte Clube
1978	Brasília Esporte Clube
1979	Sociedade Esportiva Gama
1980	Brasília Esporte Clube
1981	Taguatinga Esporte Clube
1982	Brasília Esporte Clube
1983	Brasília Esporte Clube
1984	Brasília Esporte Clube
1985	Sobradinho Esporte Clube

*Am=Amateurs; Pr= Professionals

1986	Sobradinho Esporte Clube
1987	Brasília Esporte Clube
1988	Grêmio Esportivo Tiradentes Brasília
1989	Taguatinga Esporte Clube
1990	Sociedade Esportiva Gama
1991	Taguatinga Esporte Clube
1992	Taguatinga Esporte Clube
1993	Taguatinga Esporte Clube
1994	Sociedade Esportiva Gama
1995	Sociedade Esportiva Gama
1996	Clube de Regatas Guará
1997	Sociedade Esportiva Gama
1998	Sociedade Esportiva Gama
1999	Sociedade Esportiva Gama
2000	Sociedade Esportiva Gama
2001	Sociedade Esportiva Gama
2002	Centro de Futebol do Zico/BSB Brasília
2003	Sociedade Esportiva Gama
2004	Brasiliense Futebol Clube Taguatinga
2005	Brasiliense Futebol Clube Taguatinga
2006	Brasiliense Futebol Clube Taguatinga
2007	Brasiliense Futebol Clube Taguatinga
2008	Brasiliense Futebol Clube Taguatinga
2009	Brasiliense Futebol Clube Taguatinga
2010	Ceilândia Esporte Clube
2011	Brasiliense Futebol Clube Taguatinga
2012	Ceilândia Esporte Clube
2013	Brasiliense Futebol Clube Taguatinga
2014	Associação Atlética Luziânia

Distrito Federal State Championship (Campeonato Brasiliense) 2014

First Stage

1.	Associação Atlética Luziânia	11	7	2	2	11	-	5	23
2.	Brasiliense Futebol Clube Taguatinga	11	6	5	0	14	-	4	23
3.	Brasília Futebol Clube	11	5	5	1	14	-	9	20
4.	Sobradinho Esporte Clube	11	6	1	4	22	-	12	19
5.	Sociedade Esportiva do Gama	11	4	3	4	11	-	9	15
6.	Ceilândia Esporte Clube	11	4	3	4	13	-	12	15
7.	Paracatu Futebol Clube	11	4	2	5	10	-	12	14
8.	Sociedade Esportiva Santa Maria	11	4	2	5	9	-	11	14
9.	Bosque Formosa Esporte Clube	11	4	1	6	16	-	21	13
10.	Sociedade Atlético Ceilandense	11	3	2	6	9	-	18	11
11.	Capital Clube de Futebol Guará (*Relegated*)	11	2	2	7	8	-	15	8
12.	Legião Empreendimentos Esportivos Ltda. Brasília (*Relegated*)	11	1	4	6	10	-	19	7

Top-8 qualified for the Final Stage.

Final Stage

Quarter-Finals (26/28.03.-29/30.04.2014)

Sociedade Esportiva Santa Maria - Associação Atlética Luziânia	0-3(0-2)	0-0
Sociedade Esportiva do Gama - Sobradinho Esporte Clube	2-1(2-0)	0-2(0-0)
Paracatu Futebol Clube - Brasiliense Futebol Clube Taguatinga	w/o*	
Ceilândia Esporte Clube - Brasília Futebol Clube	1-2(0-1)	0-1(0-0)

**Paracatu Futebol Clube withdrew.*

Semi-Finals (26(27.04.-30.04./04.05.2014)

Sobradinho Esporte Clube - Associação Atlética Luziânia	0-0	1-1(0-1)
Brasília Futebol Clube - Brasiliense Futebol Clube Taguatinga	1-0(1-0)	2-2(0-0)

State League Final (10-17.05.2014)

Brasília Futebol Clube - Associação Atlética Luziânia	2-3(1-3)
Associação Atlética Luziânia - Brasília Futebol Clube	0-1(0-0)

Distrito Federal State Championship Winners 2014: **Associação Atlética Luziânia**

Espirito Santo

Espirito Santo State Championship winners:

1930	Rio Branco Atlético Clube Vitória
1931	Santo Antônio Futebol Clube Vitória
1932	Vitória Futebol Clube
1933	Vitória Futebol Clube
1934	Rio Branco Atlético Clube Vitória
1935	Rio Branco Atlético Clube Vitória
1936	Rio Branco Atlético Clube Vitória
1937	Rio Branco Atlético Clube Vitória
1938	Rio Branco Atlético Clube Vitória
1939	Rio Branco Atlético Clube Vitória
1940	Americano Futebol Clube Vitória
1941	Rio Branco Atlético Clube Vitória
1942	Rio Branco Atlético Clube Vitória
1943	Vitória Futebol Clube
1944	Caxias Futebol Clube Vitória
1945	Rio Branco Atlético Clube Vitória
1946	Rio Branco Atlético Clube Vitória
1947	Rio Branco Atlético Clube Vitória
1948	Cachoeiro FC Cachoeiro do Itapemirim
1949	Rio Branco Atlético Clube Vitória
1950	Vitória Futebol Clube
1951	Rio Branco Atlético Clube Vitória
1952	Vitória Futebol Clube
1953	Santo Antônio Futebol Clube Vitória
1954	Santo Antônio Futebol Clube Vitória
1955	Santo Antônio Futebol Clube Vitória
1956	Vitória Futebol Clube
1957	Rio Branco Atlético Clube Vitória
1958	Rio Branco Atlético Clube Vitória
1959	Rio Branco Atlético Clube Vitória
1960	Santo Antônio Futebol Clube Vitória
1961	Santo Antônio Futebol Clube Vitória
1962	Rio Branco Atlético Clube Vitória
1963	Rio Branco Atlético Clube Vitória
1964	Assoc. Desportiva Ferroviária Cariacica
1965	Assoc. Desportiva Ferroviária Cariacica
1966	Rio Branco Atlético Clube Vitória
1967	Assoc. Desportiva Ferroviária Cariacica
1968	Rio Branco Atlético Clube Vitória
1969	Rio Branco Atlético Clube Vitória
1970	Rio Branco Atlético Clube Vitória
1971	Rio Branco Atlético Clube Vitória
1972	Assoc. Desportiva Ferroviária Cariacica

1973	Rio Branco Atlético Clube Vitória
1974	Assoc. Desportiva Ferroviária Cariacica
1975	Rio Branco Atlético Clube Vitória
1976	Vitória Futebol Clube
1977	Assoc. Desportiva Ferroviária Cariacica
1978	Rio Branco Atlético Clube Vitória
1979	Assoc. Desportiva Ferroviária Cariacica
1980	Assoc. Desportiva Ferroviária Cariacica
1981	Assoc. Desportiva Ferroviária Cariacica
1982	Rio Branco Atlético Clube Vitória
1983	Rio Branco Atlético Clube Vitória
1984	Assoc. Desportiva Ferroviária Cariacica
1985	Rio Branco Atlético Clube Vitória
1986	Assoc. Desportiva Ferroviária Cariacica
1987	Guarapari Esporte Clube
1988	Ibiraçu Esporte Clube
1989	Assoc. Desportiva Ferroviária Cariacica
1990	Associação Atlética Colatina
1991	Muniz Freire Futebol Clube
1992	Assoc. Desportiva Ferroviária Cariacica
1993	Linhares Esporte Clube
1994	Assoc. Desportiva Ferroviária Cariacica
1995	Linhares Esporte Clube
1996	Assoc. Desportiva Ferroviária Cariacica
1997	Linhares Esporte Clube
1998	Linhares Esporte Clube
1999	Sociedade Desportiva Serra FC
2000	Assoc. Desportiva Ferroviária Cariacica
2001	Alegrense Futebol Clube
2002	Alegrense Futebol Clube
2003	Sociedade Desportiva Serra FC
2004	Sociedade Desportiva Serra FC
2005	Sociedade Desportiva Serra FC
2006	Vitória Futebol Clube
2007	Linhares Futebol Clube
2008	Sociedade Desportiva Serra FC
2009	Associação Atlética São Mateus
2010	Rio Branco Atlético Clube Vitória
2011	CER Associação Atlética São Mateus
2012	Esporte Clube Aracruz
2013	Assoc. Desportiva Ferroviária Cariacica
2014	Estrela do Norte FC Cachoeiro de Itapemirim

Espirito Santo State Championship (Campeonato Capixaba) 2014

1.	Linhares Futebol Clube	16	9	3	4	28 - 17	30
2.	Centro Educativo Recreativo Associação Atlética São Mateus	16	8	6	2	26 - 11	30
3.	Estrela do Norte Futebol Clube Cachoeiro de Itapemirim	16	8	5	3	22 - 13	29
4.	Castelo Futebol Clube	16	7	6	3	28 - 20	27
5.	Vitória Futebol Clube	16	6	4	6	26 - 23	22
6.	Associação Desportiva Ferroviária Vale do Rio Doce Cariacica	16	6	3	7	21 - 22	21
7.	Real Noroeste Capixaba FC Águia Branca	16	5	6	5	20 - 19	21
8.	Colatina Sociedade Esportiva	16	3	4	9	16 - 33	13
9.	Botafogo Futebol Clube de Jaguaré (*Relegated*)	16	1	1	14	10 - 39	-2

Top-4 qualified for the semi-finals.

Semi-Finals (17/18-24.05.2014)

CER Associação Atlética São Mateus - Estrela do Norte FC Cachoeiro de Itap.	2-1	0-3
Linhares Futebol Clube - Castelo Futebol Clube	0-2	3-1

Espirito Santo Championship Finals (31.05.-07.06.2014)

Estrela do Norte FC Cachoeiro de Itapemirim - Linhares Futebol Clube	0-0
Linhares Futebol Clube - Estrela do Norte FC Cachoeiro de Itapemirim	0-1

Espirito Santo State Championship Winners 2014: **Estrela do Norte Futebol Clube Cachoeiro de Itapemirim**

Goias

Goias State Championship winners:

Amateur Era:

1944	Atlético Clube Goianiense Goiânia
1945	Goiânia Esporte Clube
1946	Goiânia Esporte Clube
1947	Atlético Clube Goianiense Goiânia
1948	Goiânia Esporte Clube
1949	Atlético Clube Goianiense Goiânia
1950	Goiânia Esporte Clube
1951	Goiânia Esporte Clube
1952	Goiânia Esporte Clube
1953	Goiânia Esporte Clube

1954	Goiânia Esporte Clube
1955	Atlético Clube Goianiense Goiânia
1956	Goiânia Esporte Clube
1957	Atlético Clube Goianiense Goiânia
1958	Goiânia Esporte Clube
1959	Goiânia Esporte Clube
1960	Goiânia Esporte Clube
1961	Vila Nova Futebol Clube Goiânia
1962	Vila Nova Futebol Clube Goiânia

Professional Era:

1963	Vila Nova Futebol Clube Goiânia
1964	Atlético Clube Goianiense Goiânia
1965	Anápolis Futebol Clube
1966	Goiás Esporte Clube Goiânia
1967	Clube Recreativo Atlético Catalano
1968	Goiânia Esporte Clube
1969	Vila Nova Futebol Clube Goiânia
1970	Atlético Clube Goianiense Goiânia
1971	Goiás Esporte Clube Goiânia
1972	Goiás Esporte Clube Goiânia
1973	Vila Nova Futebol Clube Goiânia
1974	Goiânia Esporte Clube
1975	Goiás Esporte Clube Goiânia
1976	Goiás Esporte Clube Goiânia
1977	Vila Nova Futebol Clube Goiânia
1978	Vila Nova Futebol Clube Goiânia
1979	Vila Nova Futebol Clube Goiânia
1980	Vila Nova Futebol Clube Goiânia
1981	Goiás Esporte Clube Goiânia
1982	Vila Nova Futebol Clube Goiânia
1983	Goiás Esporte Clube Goiânia
1984	Vila Nova Futebol Clube Goiânia
1985	Atlético Clube Goianiense Goiânia
1986	Goiás Esporte Clube Goiânia
1987	Goiás Esporte Clube Goiânia
1988	Atlético Clube Goianiense Goiânia

1989	Goiás Esporte Clube Goiânia
1990	Goiás Esporte Clube Goiânia
1991	Goiás Esporte Clube Goiânia
1992	Goiatuba Esporte Clube
1993	Vila Nova Futebol Clube Goiânia
1994	Goiás Esporte Clube Goiânia
1995	Vila Nova Futebol Clube Goiânia
1996	Goiás Esporte Clube Goiânia
1997	Goiás Esporte Clube Goiânia
1998	Goiás Esporte Clube Goiânia
1999	Goiás Esporte Clube Goiânia
2000	Goiás Esporte Clube Goiânia
2001	Vila Nova Futebol Clube Goiânia
2002	Goiás Esporte Clube Goiânia
2003	Goiás Esporte Clube Goiânia
2004	Clube Recreativo Atlético Catalano
2005	Vila Nova Futebol Clube Goiânia
2006	Goiás Esporte Clube Goiânia
2007	Atlético Clube Goianiense Goiânia
2008	Itumbiara Esporte Clube
2009	Goiás Esporte Clube Goiânia
2010	Atlético Clube Goianiense Goiânia
2011	Atlético Clube Goianiense Goiânia
2012	Goiás Esporte Clube Goiânia
2013	Goiás Esporte Clube Goiânia
2014	Atlético Clube Goianiense Goiânia

Goias State Championship (Campeonato Goiano) 2014

First Stage

Top-2 of each group qualified for the semi-finals.

Grupo A

1.	Goiás Esporte Clube Goiânia	14	10	4	0	29	-	8	34
2.	Atlético Clube Goianiense Goiânia	14	7	2	5	20	-	13	23
3.	Trindade Atlético Clube	14	6	2	6	19	-	23	20
4.	Clube Recreativo Atlético Catalano (CRAC) Catalão	14	3	6	5	11	-	17	15
5.	Anápolis Futebol Clube (*Relegated*)	14	2	8	4	10	-	12	14

Grupo B

1.	Associação Atlética Anapolina	14	7	0	7	21	-	16	21
2.	Goianésia Esporte Clube	14	6	3	4	18	-	20	21
3.	Associação Atlética Aparecidense	14	4	5	5	14	-	15	17
4.	Grêmio Esportivo Anápolis	14	4	2	8	15	-	25	14
5.	Vila Nova Futebol Clube Goiânia (*Relegated*)	14	3	4	7	11	-	19	13

Semi-Finals (22-30.03.2014)

Atlético Clube Goianiense Goiânia - Goianésia Esporte Clube	1-1(1-1)	1-1(0-1)
Goiás Esporte Clube Goiânia - Goianésia Esporte Clube	3-0(2-0)	3-0(1-0)

Goias Championship Finals (06-13.04.2014)

Atlético Clube Goianiense Goiânia - Goiás Esporte Clube Goiânia	0-0
Goiás Esporte Clube Goiânia - Atlético Clube Goianiense Goiânia	0-1(0-0)

Goias State Championship Winners 2014: **Atlético Clube Goianiense Goiânia**

Maranhão

Maranhão State Championship winners:

1918	Sport Club Luso Brasileiro São Luís
1919	Sport Club Luso Brasileiro São Luís
1920	Football Athletic Club São Luís
1921	Fênix Futebol Clube São Luís
1922	Sport Club Luso Brasileiro São Luís
1923	Sport Club Luso Brasileiro São Luís
1924	Sport Club Luso Brasileiro São Luís
1925	Sport Club Luso Brasileiro São Luís
1926	Sport Club Luso Brasileiro São Luís
1927	Sport Club Luso Brasileiro São Luís
1928	Vasco da Gama Futebol Clube São Luís
1929	*No competition*
1930	Sport Club Sírio São Luís
1931	*No competition*
1932	Tupan Esporte Clube São Luís
1933	Sampaio Corrêa FC São Luís
1934	Sampaio Corrêa FC São Luís
1935	Tupan Esporte Clube São Luís
1936	*No competition*
1937	Maranhão Atlético Clube São Luís
1938	Tupan Esporte Clube São Luís
1939	Maranhão Atlético Clube São Luís
1940	Sampaio Corrêa FC São Luís
1941	Maranhão Atlético Clube São Luís
1942	Sampaio Corrêa FC São Luís
1943	Maranhão Atlético Clube São Luís
1944	Moto Clube São Luís
1945	Moto Clube São Luís
1946	Moto Clube São Luís
1947	Moto Clube São Luís
1948	Moto Clube São Luís
1949	Moto Clube São Luís
1950	Moto Clube São Luís
1951	Maranhão Atlético Clube São
1952	Vitória do Mar Futebol Clube São Luís
1953	Sampaio Corrêa FC São Luís
1954	Sampaio Corrêa FC São Luís
1955	Moto Clube São Luís
1956	Sampaio Corrêa FC São Luís
1957	Ferroviário Esporte Clube São Luís
1958	Ferroviário Esporte Clube São Luís
1959	Moto Clube São Luís
1960	Moto Clube São Luís
1961	Sampaio Corrêa FC São Luís
1962	Sampaio Corrêa FC São Luís
1963	Maranhão Atlético Clube São Luís
1964	Sampaio Corrêa FC São Luís
1965	Sampaio Corrêa FC São Luís
1966	Moto Clube São Luís

1967	Moto Clube São Luís
1968	Moto Clube São Luís
1969	Maranhão Atlético Clube São Luís
1970	Maranhão Atlético Clube São Luís
1971	Ferroviário Esporte Clube São Luís
1972	Sampaio Corrêa FC São Luís
1973	Ferroviário Esporte Clube São Luís
1974	Moto Clube São Luís
1975	Sampaio Corrêa FC São Luís
1976	Sampaio Corrêa FC São Luís
1977	Moto Clube São Luís
1978	Sampaio Corrêa FC São Luís
1979	Maranhão Atlético Clube São Luís
1980	Sampaio Corrêa FC São Luís
1981	Moto Clube São Luís
1982	Moto Clube São Luís
1983	Moto Clube São Luís
1984	Sampaio Corrêa FC São Luís
1985	Sampaio Corrêa FC São Luís
1986	Sampaio Corrêa FC São Luís
1987	Sampaio Corrêa FC São Luís
1988	Sampaio Corrêa FC São Luís
1989	Moto Clube São Luís
1990	Sampaio Corrêa FC São Luís
1991	Sampaio Corrêa FC São Luís
1992	Sampaio Corrêa FC São Luís
1993	Maranhão Atlético Clube São Luís
1994	Maranhão Atlético Clube São Luís
1995	Maranhão Atlético Clube São Luís
1996	Bacabal Esporte Clube
1997	Sampaio Corrêa FC São Luís
1998	Sampaio Corrêa FC São Luís
1999	Maranhão Atlético Clube São Luís
2000	Moto Clube São Luís
2001	Moto Clube São Luís
2002	Sampaio Corrêa FC São Luís
2003	Sampaio Corrêa FC São Luís
2004	Moto Clube São Luís
2005	Sociedade Imperatriz de Desportos
2006	Moto Clube São Luís
2007	Maranhão Atlético Clube São Luís
2008	Moto Clube São Luís
2009	JV Lideral Esporte Clube Imperatriz
2010	Sampaio Corrêa FC São Luís
2011	Sampaio Corrêa FC São Luís
2012	Sampaio Corrêa FC São Luís
2013	Maranhão Atlético Clube São Luís
2014	Sampaio Corrêa FC São Luís

Maranhão State Championship (Campeonato Maranhense) 2014

First Stage

Top-2 of each group qualified for the semi-finals.

Grupo A

1.	Moto Club de São Luís	4	3	0	1	9 - 6	9
2.	Araioses Futebol Clube	4	2	0	2	9 - 6	6
3.	Sociedade Imperatriz de Desportos	4	2	0	2	7 - 6	6
4.	Cordino Esporte Clube Barra do Corda	4	2	0	2	6 - 6	6
5.	São José de Ribamar Esporte Clube	4	1	0	3	2 - 9	3

Grupo B

1.	Sampaio Corrêa Futebol Clube São Luís	4	3	1	0	8 - 1	10
2.	Santa Quitéria Futebol Clube	4	3	0	1	5 - 5	9
3.	Maranhão Atlético Clube São Luís	4	1	2	1	6 - 5	5
4.	Balsas Esporte Clube	4	1	1	2	2 - 3	4
5.	Bacabal Esporte Clube	4	0	0	4	0 - 7	0

Semi-Finals (13-16.02.2014)

Araioses Futebol Clube – Sampaio Corrêa Futebol Clube São Luís	1-2(1-0)	1-3(0-0)
Santa Quitéria Futebol Clube - Moto Club de São Luís	1-0(1-0)	2-3(1-2)

Final (28-31.03.2014)

Moto Club de São Luís - Sampaio Corrêa Futebol Clube São Luís	1-1(1-0)	2-2(0-0)

Sampaio Corrêa Futebol Clube São Luís, as winner of the first stage (better results in the first stage), qualified for the State League Final.

Second Stage

Top-2 of each group qualified for the semi-finals.

Grupo A

1.	Moto Club de São Luís	5	4	0	1	9 - 3	12
2.	Cordino Esporte Clube Barra do Corda	5	4	0	1	11 - 6	12
3.	Sociedade Imperatriz de Desportos	5	3	2	0	9 - 3	11
4.	São José de Ribamar Esporte Clube	5	2	1	2	7 - 4	7
5.	Araioses Futebol Clube	5	2	0	3	4 - 6	6

Grupo B

1.	Sampaio Corrêa Futebol Clube São Luís	5	3	0	2	6 - 2	9
2.	Santa Quitéria Futebol Clube	5	3	0	2	5 - 3	9
3.	Balsas Esporte Clube	5	1	0	4	3 - 14	3
4.	Maranhão Atlético Clube São Luís	5	0	2	3	4 - 7	2
5.	Bacabal Esporte Clube	5	0	1	4	4 - 14	1

Semi-Finals (27.03.-01.04.2014)

Santa Quitéria Futebol Clube - Moto Club de São Luís	1-4(0-2)	3-3(2-1)
Cordino Esporte Clube Barra do Corda - Sampaio Corrêa Futebol Clube São Luís	1-5(0-1)	0-1(0-0)

Final (04-06.04.2014)

Sampaio Corrêa Futebol Clube São Luís - Moto Club de São Luís	2-0(0-0)	0-1(0-1)

Sampaio Corrêa Futebol Clube São Luís, as winner of the second stage, qualified for the State League Final.

State League Final

Sampaio Corrêa Futebol Clube São Luís, as winner of both stages were state champions, no final match needed.

Maranhão State Championship Winners 2014: **Sampaio Corrêa FC São Luís**

Aggregate Table

1.	Sampaio Corrêa Futebol Clube São Luís	17	11	3	3	30	-	10	36
2.	Moto Club de São Luís	17	10	3	4	32	-	21	33
3.	Santa Quitéria Futebol Clube	13	7	1	5	17	-	18	22
4.	Cordino Esporte Clube Barra do Corda	11	7	0	4	18	-	18	21
5.	Sociedade Imperatriz de Desportos	9	5	2	2	16	-	9	17
6.	Araioses Futebol Clube	11	4	0	7	15	-	17	12
7.	São José de Ribamar Esporte Clube	9	3	1	5	9	-	13	10
8.	Balsas Esporte Clube	9	2	1	6	5	-	17	7
9.	Maranhão Atlético Clube São Luís (*Relegated*)	9	1	4	4	10	-	12	7
10.	Bacabal Esporte Clube (*Relegated*)	9	0	1	8	4	-	21	1

Mato Grosso

Mato Grosso State Championship winners:

1943	Mixto Esporte Clube
1944	Americano Futebol Clube Cuiabá
1945	Mixto Esporte Clube Cuiabá
1946	Clube Atlético Matogrossense Cuiabá
1947	Mixto Esporte Clube Cuiabá
1948	Mixto Esporte Clube Cuiabá
1949	Mixto Esporte Clube Cuiabá
1950	Clube Atlético Matogrossense Cuiabá
1951	Mixto Esporte Clube Cuiabá
1952	Mixto Esporte Clube Cuiabá
1953	Mixto Esporte Clube Cuiabá
1954	Mixto Esporte Clube Cuiabá
1955	Clube Atlético Matogrossense Cuiabá
1956	Clube Atlético Matogrossense Cuiabá
1957	Clube Atlético Matogrossense Cuiabá
1958	Clube Esportivo Dom Bosco Cuiabá
1959	Mixto Esporte Clube Cuiabá
1960	Clube Esportivo Dom Bosco Cuiabá
1961	Mixto Esporte Clube Cuiabá
1962	Mixto Esporte Clube Cuiabá
1963	Clube Esportivo Dom Bosco Cuiabá
1964	CE Operário Várzea Grande
1965	Mixto Esporte Clube Cuiabá
1966	Clube Esportivo Dom Bosco Cuiabá
1967	CE Operário Várzea Grande
1968	CE Operário Várzea Grande
1969	Mixto Esporte Clube Cuiabá
1970	Mixto Esporte Clube Cuiabá
1971	Clube Esportivo Dom Bosco Cuiabá
1972	CE Operário Várzea Grande
1973	CE Operário Várzea Grande
1974	Operário Futebol Clube Campo Grande
1975	EC Comercial Campo Grande
1976	Operário Futebol Clube Campo Grande
1977	Operário Futebol Clube Campo Grande
1978	Operário Futebol Clube Campo Grande

1979	Mixto Esporte Clube Cuiabá
1980	Mixto Esporte Clube Cuiabá
1981	Mixto Esporte Clube Cuiabá
1982	Mixto Esporte Clube Cuiabá
1983	CE Operário Várzea Grande
1984	Mixto Esporte Clube Cuiabá
1985	CE Operário Várzea Grande
1986	CE Operário Várzea Grande
1987	CE Operário Várzea Grande
1988	Mixto Esporte Clube Cuiabá
1989	Mixto Esporte Clube Cuiabá
1990	Sinop Futebol Clube
1991	Clube Esportivo Dom Bosco Cuiabá
1992	Sorriso Esporte Clube
1993	Sorriso Esporte Clube
1994	CE Operário Várzea Grande
1995	CE Operário Várzea Grande
1996	Mixto Esporte Clube Cuiabá
1997	CE Operário Várzea Grande
1998	Sinop Futebol Clube
1999	Sinop Futebol Clube
2000	SER Juventude Primavera do Leste
2001	SER Juventude Primavera do Leste
2002	Esporte Clube Operário Várzea Grande
2003	Cuiabá Esporte Clube
2004	Cuiabá Esporte Clube
2005	SE Vila Aurora Rondonópolis
2006	Esporte Clube Operário Várzea Grande
2007	Cacerense Esporte Clube Cáceres
2008	Mixto Esporte Clube Cuiabá
2009	Luverdense EC Lucas do Rio Verde
2010	União Esporte Clube Rondonópolis
2011	Cuiabá Esporte Clube
2012	Luverdense EC Lucas do Rio Verde
2013	Cuiabá Esporte Clube
2014	Cuiabá Esporte Clube

Mato Grosso State Championship (Campeonato Mato-Grossense) 2014

First Stage

Grupo Norte

1.	Luverdense Esporte Clube Lucas do Rio Verde	8	7	0	1	20 - 4	21
2.	Mixto Esporte Clube Cuiabá	8	4	2	2	7 - 7	14
3.	Operário Futebol Clube Ltda. Várzea Grande	8	3	3	2	9 - 7	12
4.	Sinop Futebol Clube	8	2	2	4	5 - 10	8
5.	Mato Grosso Esporte Clube Cuiabá	8	0	1	7	3 - 16	1

Grupo Sul

1.	Rondonópolis Esporte Clube	6	5	1	0	10 - 4	16
2.	União Esporte Clube Rondonópolis	6	3	0	3	9 - 6	9
3.	Cuiabá Esporte Clube	6	2	2	2	4 - 4	8
4.	Cacerense Esporte Clube	6	0	1	5	0 - 9	1

Final Stage

Quarter-Finals (01-12.03.2014)

Operário FC Ltda. Várzea Grande - União Esporte Clube Rondonópolis	1-0(0-0)	1-1(0-0)
Cacerense Esporte Clube - Luverdense Esporte Clube Lucas do Rio Verde	1-0(0-0)	0-2(0-1)
Sinop Futebol Clube - Rondonópolis Esporte Clube	2-2(1-0)	2-2(2-1) 4-3 pen
Cuiabá Esporte Clube - Mixto Esporte Clube Cuiabá	1-0(0-0)	1-1(0-1)

Semi-Finals (16-23.03.2014)

Operário FC Ltda. Várzea Grande - Luverdense EC Lucas do Rio Verde	0-0	0-0; 6-7 pen
Sinop Futebol Clube - Cuiabá Esporte Clube	1-1(1-1)	0-1(0-0)

Mato Grosso Championship Finals (30.03.-06.04.2014)

Cuiabá Esporte Clube - Luverdense Esporte Clube Lucas do Rio Verde	1-0(0-0)
Luverdense Esporte Clube Lucas do Rio Verde - Cuiabá Esporte Clube	0-1(0-1)

Mato Grosso State Championship Winners 2014: **Cuiabá Esporte Clube**

Aggregate Table 2014

1.	Cuiabá Esporte Clube	12	6	4	2	10 - 6	22
2.	Luverdense Esporte Clube Lucas do Rio Verde	14	8	2	4	22 - 7	26
3.	Rondonópolis Esporte Clube	8	5	3	0	14 - 8	18
4.	Operário Futebol Clube Ltda. Várzea Grande	12	4	6	2	11 - 8	18
5.	Mixto Esporte Clube Cuiabá	10	4	3	3	8 - 9	15
6.	Sinop Futebol Clube	12	2	5	5	10 - 16	11
7.	União Esporte Clube Rondonópolis	8	3	1	4	10 - 8	10
8.	Cacerense Esporte Clube	8	1	1	6	1 - 11	4
9.	Mato Grosso Esporte Clube Cuiabá (*Relegated*)	8	0	1	7	3 - 16	1

Mato Grosso do Sul

Mato Grosso do Sul State Championship winners:

1979	Operário Campo Grande
1980	Operário Campo Grande
1981	Operário Campo Grande
1982	Comercial Campo Grande
1983	Operário Campo Grande
1984	Corumbaense Corumbá
1985	Comercial Campo Grande
1986	Operário Campo Grande
1987	Comercial Campo Grande
1988	Operário Campo Grande
1989	Operário Campo Grande
1990	Ubiratan Dourados
1991	Operário Campo Grande
1992	Nova Andradina Nova Andradina
1993	Comercial Campo Grande
1994	Comercial Campo Grande
1995	SER Chapadão
1996	Operário Campo Grande
1997	Operário Campo Grande
1998	Ubiratan Dourados
1999	Ubiratan Dourados
2000	Comercial Campo Grande
2001	Comercial Campo Grande
2002	CENE Campo Grande
2003	SER Chapadão
2004	CENE Campo Grande
2005	CENE Campo Grande
2006	Clube Atlético Coxim
2007	EC Águia Negra Rio Brilhante
2008	Ivinhema Futebol Clube
2009	Clube Esportivo Naviraiense
2010	EC Comercial Campo Grande
2011	CENE Campo Grande
2012	EC Águia Negra Rio Brilhante
2013	CENE Campo Grande
2014	CENE Campo Grande

Mato Grosso do Sul State Championship (Campeonato Sul-Mato-Grossense) 2014

First Stage

Top-4 from each group qualified for the quarter-finals.

Grupo A

1.	Costa Rica Esporte Clube	12	7	3	2	22	-	13	24
2.	Clube Esportivo Nova Esperança (CENE) Campo Grande	12	6	5	1	19	-	10	23
3.	Novoperário Futebol Clube Campo Grande	12	5	5	2	20	-	11	20
4.	Misto Esporte Clube	12	3	4	5	17	-	20	13
5.	Esporte Clube Comercial Campo Grande	12	3	4	5	15	-	18	13
6.	Maracaju Atlético Clube (*Relegated*)	12	2	4	6	13	-	28	10
7.	Escolinha de Futebol Aquidauanense (*Relegated*)	12	2	3	7	14	-	20	9

Grupo B

1.	Clube Esportivo Naviraiense	12	8	2	2	23	-	11	26
2.	Esporte Clube Águia Negra Rio Brilhante	12	7	4	1	18	-	9	25
3.	Ubiratan Esporte Clube Dourados	12	6	3	3	22	-	7	21
4.	Ivinhema Futebol Clube	12	5	1	6	22	-	20	16
5.	Clube Recreativo Desportivo 7 de Setembro Dourados	12	3	5	4	16	-	20	14
6.	Itaporã Futebol Clube (*Relegated*)	12	2	3	7	12	-	29	9
7.	União Recreativo Social Olímpico (URSO) Mundo Novo (*Relegated*)	12	1	2	9	9	-	26	5

Quarter-Finals (16-19.03.2014)

Misto Esporte Clube - Clube Esportivo Naviraiense	1-1(1-0)	2-2(0-1)
Ivinhema Futebol Clube - Costa Rica Esporte Clube	2-1(1-1)	1-0(1-0)
Novoperário FC Campo Grande - Esporte Clube Águia Negra Rio Brilhante	0-2(0-2)	0-2(0-2)
Ubiratan Esporte Clube Dourados - CENE Campo Grande	0-3(0-2)	0-2(0-2)

Semi-Finals (23-30.03.2014)

Ivinhema Futebol Clube - Esporte Clube Águia Negra Rio Brilhante	0-0	0-0
Clube Esportivo Naviraiense - CENE Campo Grande	0-1(0-0)	2-3(1-1)

Mato Grosso do Sul Championship Finals (06-13.04.2014)

Esporte Clube Águia Negra Rio Brilhante - CENE Campo Grande	2-1(1-0)
CENE Campo Grande - Esporte Clube Águia Negra Rio Brilhante	2-0(1-0)

Mato Grosso do Sul State Championship Winners 2014: **Clube Esportivo Nova Esperança Campo Grande**

Minas Gerais

Minas Gerais State Championship winners:

1915	Clube Atlético Mineiro Belo Horizonte
1916	América Futebol Clube Belo Horizonte
1917	América Futebol Clube Belo Horizonte
1918	América Futebol Clube Belo Horizonte
1919	América Futebol Clube Belo Horizonte
1920	América Futebol Clube Belo Horizonte
1922	América Futebol Clube Belo Horizonte
1922	América Futebol Clube Belo Horizonte
1923	América Futebol Clube Belo Horizonte
1924	América Futebol Clube Belo Horizonte
1925	América Futebol Clube Belo Horizonte
1926	Clube Atlético Mineiro Belo Horizonte(1)
	SE Palestra Itália Belo Horizonte(2)
1927	Clube Atlético Mineiro Belo Horizonte
1928	SE Palestra Itália Belo Horizonte
1929	SE Palestra Itália Belo Horizonte
1930	SE Palestra Itália Belo Horizonte
1931	Clube Atlético Mineiro Belo Horizonte
1932	Clube Atlético Mineiro Belo Horizonte(1)
	Villa Nova Atlético Clube Nova Lima(3)
1933	Villa Nova Atlético Clube Nova Lima
1934	Villa Nova Atlético Clube Nova Lima
1935	Villa Nova Atlético Clube Nova Lima
1936	Clube Atlético Mineiro Belo Horizonte
1937	Esporte Clube Siderúrgica Sabará
1938	Clube Atlético Mineiro Belo Horizonte
1939	Clube Atlético Mineiro Belo Horizonte
1940	SE Palestra Itália Belo Horizonte
1941	Clube Atlético Mineiro Belo Horizonte
1942	Clube Atlético Mineiro Belo Horizonte
1943	Cruzeiro Esporte Clube Belo Horizonte
1944	Cruzeiro Esporte Clube Belo Horizonte
1945	Cruzeiro Esporte Clube Belo Horizonte
1946	Clube Atlético Mineiro Belo Horizonte
1947	Clube Atlético Mineiro Belo Horizonte
1964	Esporte Clube Siderúrgica Sabará
1965	Cruzeiro Esporte Clube Belo Horizonte
1966	Cruzeiro Esporte Clube Belo Horizonte
1967	Cruzeiro Esporte Clube Belo Horizonte
1969	Cruzeiro Esporte Clube Belo Horizonte
1969	Cruzeiro Esporte Clube Belo Horizonte
1970	Clube Atlético Mineiro Belo Horizonte
1971	América Futebol Clube Belo Horizonte
1972	Cruzeiro Esporte Clube Belo Horizonte
1973	Cruzeiro Esporte Clube Belo Horizonte
1974	Cruzeiro Esporte Clube Belo Horizonte
1975	Cruzeiro Esporte Clube Belo Horizonte
1976	Clube Atlético Mineiro Belo Horizonte
1977	Cruzeiro Esporte Clube Belo Horizonte
1978	Clube Atlético Mineiro Belo Horizonte
1979	Clube Atlético Mineiro Belo Horizonte
1980	Clube Atlético Mineiro Belo Horizonte
1981	Clube Atlético Mineiro Belo Horizonte
1982	Clube Atlético Mineiro Belo Horizonte
1983	Clube Atlético Mineiro Belo Horizonte
1984	Cruzeiro Esporte Clube Belo Horizonte
1985	Clube Atlético Mineiro Belo Horizonte
1986	Clube Atlético Mineiro Belo Horizonte
1987	Cruzeiro Esporte Clube Belo Horizonte
1988	Clube Atlético Mineiro Belo Horizonte
1989	Clube Atlético Mineiro Belo Horizonte
1990	Cruzeiro Esporte Clube Belo Horizonte
1991	Clube Atlético Mineiro Belo Horizonte
1992	Cruzeiro Esporte Clube Belo Horizonte
1993	América Futebol Clube Belo Horizonte
1994	Cruzeiro Esporte Clube Belo Horizonte
1995	Clube Atlético Mineiro Belo Horizonte
1996	Cruzeiro Esporte Clube Belo Horizonte
1997	Cruzeiro Esporte Clube Belo Horizonte
1998	Cruzeiro Esporte Clube Belo Horizonte

1948	América Futebol Clube Belo Horizonte
1949	Clube Atlético Mineiro Belo Horizonte
1950	Clube Atlético Mineiro Belo Horizonte
1951	Villa Nova Atlético Clube Nova Lima
1952	Clube Atlético Mineiro Belo Horizonte
1953	Clube Atlético Mineiro Belo Horizonte
1954	Clube Atlético Mineiro Belo Horizonte
1955	Clube Atlético Mineiro Belo Horizonte
1956	Clube Atlético Mineiro Belo Horizonte Cruzeiro Esporte Clube Belo Horizonte[(4)]
1957	América Futebol Clube Belo Horizonte
1958	Clube Atlético Mineiro Belo Horizonte
1959	Cruzeiro Esporte Clube Belo Horizonte
1960	Cruzeiro Esporte Clube Belo Horizonte
1961	Cruzeiro Esporte Clube Belo Horizonte
1962	Clube Atlético Mineiro Belo Horizonte
1963	Clube Atlético Mineiro Belo Horizonte

1999	Clube Atlético Mineiro Belo Horizonte
2000	Clube Atlético Mineiro Belo Horizonte
2001	América Futebol Clube Belo Horizonte
2002	AA Caldense Poços de Caldas
2003	Cruzeiro Esporte Clube Belo Horizonte
2004	Cruzeiro Esporte Clube Belo Horizonte
2005	Ipatinga Futebol Clube Ipatinga
2006	Cruzeiro Esporte Clube Belo Horizonte
2007	Clube Atlético Mineiro Belo Horizonte
2008	Cruzeiro Esporte Clube Belo Horizonte
2009	Cruzeiro Esporte Clube Belo Horizonte
2010	Clube Atlético Mineiro Belo Horizonte
2011	Cruzeiro Esporte Clube Belo Horizonte
2012	Clube Atlético Mineiro Belo Horizonte
2013	Clube Atlético Mineiro Belo Horizonte
2014	Cruzeiro Esporte Clube Belo Horizonte

[(1)] Winner of LMDT [Liga Mineira de Desportes Terrestres]
[(2)] Winner of AMET [Associação Mineira de Esportes Terrestres]
[(3)] Winner of AMEG [Associação Mineira de Esportes Geraes]
[(4)] two winners (shared)

Minas Gerais State Championship (Campeonato Mineiro) 2014

First Stage

1.	Cruzeiro Esporte Clube Belo Horizonte	11	9	2	0	24	-	4	29
2.	Clube Atlético Mineiro Belo Horizonte	11	7	2	2	20	-	8	23
3.	América Futebol Clube Belo Horizonte	11	5	3	3	14	-	12	18
4.	Boa Esporte Clube Varginha	11	5	1	5	12	-	14	16
5.	Tupi Football Club Juiz de Fora	11	4	3	4	11	-	11	15
6.	Villa Nova Atlético Clube Nova Lima	11	4	3	4	15	-	17	15
7.	Tombense Futebol Clube	11	3	5	3	11	-	11	14
8.	Associação Atlética Caldense	11	3	4	4	10	-	9	13
9.	União Recreativa dos Trabalhadores Patos de Minas	11	4	0	7	9	-	19	12
10.	Guarani Esporte Clube Divinópolis	11	3	2	6	11	-	14	11
11.	Nacional Esporte Clube Ltda. Nova Serrana *(Relegated)*	11	3	1	7	10	-	17	10
12.	Minas Boca Futebol Ltda Sete Lagoas *(Relegated)*	11	2	2	7	10	-	21	8

Top-4 qualified for the semi-finals.

Semi-Finals (23-30.03.2014)

América FC Belo Horizonte - Clube Atlético Mineiro Belo Horizonte	1-4(0-3)	1-1(1-0)
Boa Esporte Clube Varginha - Cruzeiro Esporte Clube Belo Horizonte	0-1(0-0)	1-2(0-1)

Minas Gerais Championship Finals (06-13.04.2014)

Clube Atlético Mineiro Belo Horizonte - Cruzeiro Esporte Clube Belo Horizonte	0-0
Cruzeiro Esporte Clube Belo Horizonte - Clube Atlético Mineiro Belo Horizonte	0-0

Minas Gerais State Championship Winners 2014: **Cruzeiro Esporte Clube Belo Horizonte**

Pará

Pará State Championship winners:

1908	SA União Sportiva Belém
1909	*No competition*
1910	SA União Sportiva Belém
1911	*No competition*
1912	*No competition*
1913	Clube do Remo Belém
1914	Clube do Remo Belém
1915	Clube do Remo Belém
1916	Clube do Remo Belém
1917	Clube do Remo Belém
1918	Clube do Remo Belém
1919	Clube do Remo Belém
1920	Paysandu Sport Club Belém
1921	Paysandu Sport Club Belém
1922	Paysandu Sport Club Belém
1923	Paysandu Sport Club Belém
1924	Clube do Remo Belém
1925	Clube do Remo Belém
1926	Clube do Remo Belém
1927	Paysandu Sport Club Belém
1928	Paysandu Sport Club Belém
1929	Paysandu Sport Club Belém
1930	Clube do Remo Belém
1931	Paysandu Sport Club Belém
1932	Paysandu Sport Club Belém
1933	Clube do Remo Belém
1934	Paysandu Sport Club Belém
1935	*No competition*
1936	Clube do Remo Belém
1937	Tuna Luso Brasileira Belém
1938	Tuna Luso Brasileira Belém
1939	Paysandu Sport Club Belém
1940	Clube do Remo Belém
1941	Tuna Luso Brasileira Belém
1942	Paysandu Sport Club Belém
1943	Paysandu Sport Club Belém
1944	Paysandu Sport Club Belém
1945	Paysandu Sport Club Belém
1946	*No competition*
1947	Paysandu Sport Club Belém
1948	Tuna Luso Brasileira Belém
1949	Clube do Remo Belém
1950	Clube do Remo Belém
1951	Tuna Luso Brasileira Belém
1952	Clube do Remo Belém
1953	Clube do Remo Belém
1954	Clube do Remo Belém
1955	Tuna Luso Brasileira Belém
1956	Paysandu Sport Club Belém
1957	Paysandu Sport Club Belém
1962	Paysandu Sport Club Belém
1963	Paysandu Sport Club Belém
1964	Clube do Remo Belém
1965	Paysandu Sport Club Belém
1966	Paysandu Sport Club Belém
1967	Paysandu Sport Club Belém
1968	Clube do Remo Belém
1969	Paysandu Sport Club Belém
1970	Tuna Luso Brasileira Belém
1971	Paysandu Sport Club Belém
1972	Paysandu Sport Club Belém
1973	Clube do Remo Belém
1974	Clube do Remo Belém
1975	Clube do Remo Belém
1976	Paysandu Sport Club Belém
1977	Clube do Remo Belém
1978	Clube do Remo Belém
1979	Clube do Remo Belém
1980	Paysandu Sport Club Belém
1981	Paysandu Sport Club Belém
1982	Paysandu Sport Club Belém
1983	Tuna Luso Brasileira Belém
1984	Paysandu Sport Club Belém
1985	Paysandu Sport Club Belém
1986	Clube do Remo Belém
1987	Paysandu Sport Club Belém
1988	Tuna Luso Brasileira Belém
1989	Clube do Remo Belém
1990	Clube do Remo Belém
1991	Clube do Remo Belém
1992	Paysandu Sport Club Belém
1993	Clube do Remo Belém
1994	Clube do Remo Belém
1995	Clube do Remo Belém
1996	Clube do Remo Belém
1997	Clube do Remo Belém
1998	Paysandu Sport Club Belém
1999	Clube do Remo Belém
2000	Paysandu Sport Club Belém
2001	Paysandu Sport Club Belém
2002	Paysandu Sport Club Belém
2003	Clube do Remo Belém
2004	Clube do Remo Belém
2005	Paysandu Sport Club Belém
2006	Paysandu Sport Club Belém
2007	Clube do Remo Belém
2008	Clube do Remo Belém
2009	Paysandu Sport Club Belém
2010	Paysandu Sport Club Belém
2011	Independente Atlético Clube Tucuruí

1958	Tuna Luso Brasileira Belém		2012	Cametá Sport Club
1959	Paysandu Sport Club Belém		2013	Paysandu Sport Club Belém
1960	Clube do Remo Belém		2014	Clube do Remo Belém
1961	Paysandu Sport Club Belém			

Pará State Championship (Campeonato Paraense) 2014

First Phase (Classificação - Taça ACLEP)

1.	Independente Atlético Clube Tucuruí	7	5	0	2	12	-	9	15
2.	Gavião Kyikatejê Futebol Clube	7	4	3	0	9	-	3	15
3.	Águia de Marabá Futebol Clube	7	4	1	2	17	-	12	13
4.	São Raimundo Esporte Clube Santarém	7	3	3	1	9	-	5	12
5.	Parauapebas Futebol Clube	7	3	0	4	10	-	12	9
6.	Castanhal Esporte Clube	7	1	2	4	8	-	11	5
7.	Time Negra Carajás Clube Belém (*Relegated*)	7	0	4	3	8	-	15	4
8.	Tuna Luso Brasileira Belém (*Relegated*)	7	0	3	4	3	-	9	3

Top-2 qualified for the second phase.

Second Phase – First Tournament (Taça Cidade de Belém)

1.	Paysandu Sport Club Belém	7	4	1	2	16	-	8	13
2.	Clube do Remo Belém	7	4	1	2	12	-	6	13
3.	Cametá Sport Club	7	3	2	2	7	-	5	11
4.	Paragominas Futebol Clube	7	2	4	1	9	-	8	10
5.	Independente Atlético Clube Tucuruí	7	1	5	1	5	-	6	8
6.	São Francisco Futebol Clube Rio Branco	7	1	5	1	6	-	11	8
7.	Gavião Kyikatejê Futebol Clube	7	0	5	2	6	-	11	5
8.	Associação Atlética Santa Cruz Salinópolis	7	0	3	4	7	-	13	3

Top-4 qualified for the semi-finals.

Semi-Finals (06-09.02.2014)

Paragominas Futebol Clube - Paysandu Sport Club Belém	1-1	2-2
Cametá Sport Club - Clube do Remo Belém	0-2	1-4

Final (16-23.02.2014)

Paysandu Sport Club Belém - Clube do Remo Belém	0-0
Clube do Remo Belém - Paysandu Sport Club Belém	1-1

Clube do Remo Belém as champions of the First Tournament qualified to the State Championship Finals.

Second Phase – Second Tournament (Taça Estado do Pará)

1.	Paysandu Sport Club Belém	7	4	3	0	15	-	6	15
2.	Clube do Remo Belém	7	3	4	0	13	-	8	13
3.	Independente Atlético Clube Tucuruí	7	4	0	3	10	-	10	12
4.	São Francisco Futebol Clube Rio Branco	7	3	2	2	11	-	9	11
5.	Cametá Sport Club	7	2	3	2	9	-	12	9
6.	Paragominas Futebol Clube	7	2	0	5	8	-	12	6
7.	Associação Atlética Santa Cruz Salinópolis	7	1	3	3	12	-	16	6
8.	Gavião Kyikatejê Futebol Clube	7	0	3	4	8	-	13	3

Top-4 qualified for the semi-finals.

Semi-Finals (20.04.-08.05.2014)

Independente Atlético Clube Tucuruí - Clube do Remo Belém	3-0	0-4
São Francisco Futebol Clube Rio Branco - Paysandu Sport Club Belém	0-1	0-3

Final (23-29.05.2014)

Clube do Remo Belém - Paysandu Sport Club Belém	2-2
Paysandu Sport Club Belém - Clube do Remo Belém	3-3

Paysandu Sport Club Belém as champions of the Second Tournament qualified to the State Championship Finals.

Pará Championship Finals (05-08.06.2014)

Paysandu Sport Club Belém - Clube do Remo Belém	1-4
Clube do Remo Belém - Paysandu Sport Club Belém	0-2

Pará State Championship Winners 2014: **Clube do Remo Belém**

Paraíba

Paraíba State Championship winners:

Liga Desportiva Parahybana:

1919	Palmeiras Sport Club João Pessoa	1930	*No competition*
1920	EC Cabo Branco João Pessoa	1931	EC Cabo Branco João Pessoa
1921	Palmeiras Sport Club João Pessoa	1932	EC Cabo Branco João Pessoa
1922	Pytaguares Futebol Clube João Pessoa	1933	Palmeiras Sport Club João Pessoa
1923	América Football Club João Pessoa	1934	EC Cabo Branco João Pessoa
1924	EC Cabo Branco João Pessoa	1935	Palmeiras Sport Club João Pessoa
1925	América Football Club João Pessoa	1936	Botafogo Futebol Clube João Pessoa
1926	EC Cabo Branco João Pessoa	1937	Botafogo Futebol Clube João Pessoa
1927	EC Cabo Branco João Pessoa	1938	Botafogo Futebol Clube João Pessoa
1928	Palmeiras Sport Club João Pessoa	1939	Auto Esporte Clube João Pessoa
1929	EC Cabo Branco João Pessoa	1940	Treze Futebol Clube Campina Grande

Federação Desportiva de Football

1941	Treze Futebol Clube Campina Grande	1944	Botafogo Futebol Clube João Pessoa
1942	Clube Ástrea João Pessoa	1945	Botafogo Futebol Clube João Pessoa
1943	Clube Ástrea João Pessoa	1946	Felipéia Esporte Clube João Pessoa

Federação Paraíbana de Futebol

1947	Botafogo Futebol Clube João Pessoa	1981	Treze Futebol Clube Campina Grande
1948	Botafogo Futebol Clube João Pessoa	1982	Treze Futebol Clube Campina Grande
1949	Botafogo Futebol Clube João Pessoa	1983	Treze Futebol Clube Campina Grande
1950	Treze Futebol Clube Campina Grande	1984	Botafogo Futebol Clube João Pessoa
1951	*No competition*	1985	*No competition*
1952	Red Cross Football Club João Pessoa	1986	Botafogo Futebol Clube João Pessoa
1953	Botafogo Futebol Clube João Pessoa	1987	Auto Esporte Clube João Pessoa
1954	Botafogo Futebol Clube João Pessoa	1988	Botafogo Futebol Clube João Pessoa
1955	Botafogo Futebol Clube João Pessoa	1989	Treze Futebol Clube Campina Grande
1956	Auto Esporte Clube João Pessoa	1990	Auto Esporte Clube João Pessoa
1957	Botafogo Futebol Clube João Pessoa	1991	Campinense Clube Campina Grande
1958	Auto Esporte Clube João Pessoa	1992	Auto Esporte Clube João Pessoa
1959	Estrela do Mar EC João Pessoa	1993	Campinense Clube Campina Grande
1960	Campinense Clube Campina Grande	1994	Sousa Esporte Clube
1961	Campinense Clube Campina Grande	1995	Santa Cruz Recreativo EC Santa Rita
1962	Campinense Clube Campina Grande	1996	Santa Cruz Recreativo EC Santa Rita
1963	Campinense Clube Campina Grande	1997	Confiança Esporte Clube Sapé
1964	Campinense Clube Campina Grande	1998	Botafogo Futebol Clube João Pessoa
1965	Campinense Clube Campina Grande	1999	Botafogo Futebol Clube João Pessoa
1966	Treze Futebol Clube Campina Grande	2000	Treze Futebol Clube Campina Grande
1967	Campinense Clube Campina Grande	2001	Treze Futebol Clube Campina Grande
1968	Botafogo Futebol Clube João Pessoa	2002	Atlético Cajazeirense de Desportos
1969	Botafogo Futebol Clube João Pessoa	2003	Botafogo Futebol Clube João Pessoa
1970	Botafogo Futebol Clube João Pessoa	2004	Campinense Clube Campina Grande
1971	Campinense Clube Campina Grande	2005	Treze Futebol Clube Campina Grande
1972	Campinense Clube Campina Grande	2006	Treze Futebol Clube Campina Grande
1973	Campinense Clube Campina Grande	2007	Nacional Atlético Clube Patos
1974	Campinense Clube Campina Grande	2008	Campinense Clube Campina Grande
1975	Treze Futebol Clube Campina Grande	2009	Sousa Esporte Clube
	Botafogo Futebol Clube João Pessoa*	2010	Treze Futebol Clube Campina Grande

1976	Botafogo Futebol Clube João Pessoa		2011	Treze Futebol Clube Campina Grande
1977	Botafogo Futebol Clube João Pessoa		2012	Campinense Clube Campina Grande
1978	Botafogo Futebol Clube João Pessoa		2013	Botafogo Futebol Clube João Pessoa
1979	Campinense Clube Campina Grande		2014	Botafogo Futebol Clube João Pessoa
1980	Campinense Clube Campina Grande			

*both teams winners (shared).

Paraíba State Championship (Campeonato Paraibano) 2014

First Stage

1.	Centro Sportivo Paraibano João Pessoa	14	8	5	1	34 - 15	29
2.	Auto Esporte Clube João Pessoa	14	9	1	4	23 - 14	28
3.	Sousa Esporte Clube	14	7	7	0	23 - 10	28
4.	Campinense Clube Campina Grande	14	7	5	2	29 - 12	26
5.	Santa Cruz Recreativo Esporte Clube Santa Rita	14	4	3	7	20 - 19	15
6.	Atlético Cajazeirense de Desportos	14	4	3	7	18 - 25	15
7.	ociedade Esportiva Queimadense (*Relegated*)	14	1	7	6	9 - 17	10
8.	Sport Club Campina Grande (*Relegated*)	14	0	1	13	10 - 54	1

Top-2 qualified for the second stage and semi-finals.

Second Stage

1.	Campinense Clube Campina Grande	14	8	4	2	23 - 11	28
2.	Botafogo Futebol Clube João Pessoa	14	8	3	3	26 - 14	27
3.	Sousa Esporte Clube	14	7	4	3	25 - 20	25
4.	Treze Futebol Clube Campina Grande	14	6	4	4	22 - 14	22
5.	Atlético Cajazeirense de Desportos	14	5	2	7	21 - 29	17
6.	Auto Esporte Clube João Pessoa	14	4	4	6	19 - 19	16
7.	Centro Sportivo Paraibano João Pessoa	14	4	2	8	18 - 25	14
8.	Santa Cruz Recreativo EC Santa Rita	14	2	1	11	18 - 40	7

Top-2 qualified for the semi-finals.

Final Stage

Semi-Finals (15-19.06.2014)

Botafogo Futebol Clube João Pessoa - Centro Sportivo Paraibano João Pessoa	2-1(2-0)	3-1(2-0)
Campinense Clube Campina Grande - Auto Esporte Clube João Pessoa	2-0(0-0)	1-2(1-0)

Paraíba Championship Finals (25-29.06.2014)

Botafogo Futebol Clube João Pessoa - Campinense Clube Campina Grande	3-0(2-0)
Campinense Clube Campina Grande - Botafogo Futebol Clube João Pessoa	0-0

Paraíba State Championship Winners 2014: **Botafogo Futebol Clube João Pessoa**

Paraná

Paraná State Championship winners:

1915	Internacional Futebol Clube Curitiba
1916	Coritiba Foot Ball Club
1917	América Futebol Clube Curitiba
1918	Britânia Sport Club Curitiba
1919	Britânia Sport Club Curitiba
1920	Britânia Sport Club Curitiba
1921	Britânia Sport Club Curitiba
1922	Britânia Sport Club Curitiba
1923	Britânia Sport Club Curitiba
1924	Palestra Itália Futebol Clube Curitiba
1925	Clube Atlético Paranaense Curitiba
1926	Palestra Itália Futebol Clube Curitiba
1927	Coritiba Foot Ball Club
1928	Britânia Sport Club Curitiba
1929	Clube Atlético Paranaense Curitiba
1930	Clube Atlético Paranaense Curitiba
1931	Coritiba Foot Ball Club
1932	Palestra Itália Futebol Clube Curitiba
1933	Coritiba Foot Ball Club
1934	Clube Atlético Paranaense Curitiba
1935	Coritiba Foot Ball Club
1936	Clube Atlético Paranaense Curitiba
1937	Clube Atlético Ferroviário Curitiba
1938	Clube Atlético Ferroviário Curitiba
1939	Coritiba Foot Ball Club
1940	Clube Atlético Paranaense Curitiba
1941	Coritiba Foot Ball Club
1942	Coritiba Foot Ball Club
1943	Clube Atlético Paranaense Curitiba
1944	Clube Atlético Ferroviário Curitiba
1945	Clube Atlético Paranaense Curitiba
1946	Coritiba Foot Ball Club
1947	Coritiba Foot Ball Club
1948	Clube Atlético Ferroviário Curitiba
1949	Clube Atlético Paranaense Curitiba
1950	Clube Atlético Ferroviário Curitiba
1951	Coritiba Foot Ball Club
1952	Coritiba Foot Ball Club
1953	Clube Atlético Ferroviário Curitiba
1954	Coritiba Foot Ball Club
1955	CA Monte Alegre Telêmaco Borba
1956	Coritiba Foot Ball Club
1957	Coritiba Foot Ball Club
1958	Clube Atlético Paranaense Curitiba
1959	Coritiba Foot Ball Club
1960	Coritiba Foot Ball Club
1961	EC Comercial Cornélio Procópio
1962	Londrina de Futebol e Regatas
1963	Grêmio de Esportes Maringá
1964	Grêmio de Esportes Maringá
1965	Clube Atlético Ferroviário Curitiba
1966	Clube Atlético Ferroviário Curitiba
1967	Esporte Clube Água Verde Curitiba
1968	Coritiba Foot Ball Club
1969	Coritiba Foot Ball Club
1970	Clube Atlético Paranaense Curitiba
1971	Coritiba Foot Ball Club
1972	Coritiba Foot Ball Club
1973	Coritiba Foot Ball Club
1974	Coritiba Foot Ball Club
1975	Coritiba Foot Ball Club
1976	Coritiba Foot Ball Club
1977	Grêmio de Esportes Maringá
1978	Coritiba Foot Ball Club
1979	Coritiba Foot Ball Club
1980	Colorado Esporte Clube Curitiba
	Cascavel Esporte Clube Cascavel*
1981	Londrina Esporte Clube
1982	Clube Atlético Paranaense Curitiba
1983	Clube Atlético Paranaense Curitiba
1984	Esporte Clube Pinheiros Curitiba
1985	Clube Atlético Paranaense Curitiba
1986	Coritiba Foot Ball Club
1987	Esporte Clube Pinheiros Curitiba
1988	Clube Atlético Paranaense Curitiba
1989	Coritiba Foot Ball Club
1990	Clube Atlético Paranaense Curitiba
1991	Paraná Clube Curitiba
1992	Londrina Esporte Clube
1993	Paraná Clube Curitiba
1994	Paraná Clube Curitiba
1995	Paraná Clube Curitiba
1996	Paraná Clube Curitiba
1997	Paraná Clube Curitiba
1998	Clube Atlético Paranaense Curitiba
1999	Coritiba Foot Ball Club
2000	Clube Atlético Paranaense Curitiba
2001	Clube Atlético Paranaense Curitiba
2002	Iraty Sport Club
2002	Clube Atlético Paranaense Curitiba**
2003	Coritiba Foot Ball Club
2004	Coritiba Foot Ball Club
2005	Clube Atlético Paranaense Curitiba
2006	Paraná Clube Curitiba
2007	Atlético Clube Paranavaí
2008	Coritiba Foot Ball Club
2009	Clube Atlético Paranaense Curitiba
2010	Coritiba Foot Ball Club
2011	Coritiba Foot Ball Club
2012	Coritiba Foot Ball Club
2013	Coritiba Foot Ball Club
2014	Londrina Esporte Clube

*both teams winners (shared).

**two editions organized in 2002; Clube Atlético Paranaense Curitiba winners of Super Championship

Paraná State Championship (Campeonato Paranaense) 2014

First Stage

1.	Paraná Clube Curitiba	11	5	3	3	15	-	7	18
2.	Coritiba Foot Ball Club	11	5	3	3	14	-	12	18
3.	Maringá Futebol Clube	11	5	2	4	18	-	14	17
4.	Londrina Esporte Clube	11	4	4	3	14	-	10	16
5.	J.Malucelli Futebol S/A Curitiba	11	4	4	3	16	-	14	16
6.	Prudentópolis Futebol Clube	11	4	4	3	11	-	13	16
7.	Rio Branco Sport Club Paranaguá	11	4	4	3	14	-	17	16
8.	Clube Atlético Paranaense Curitiba	11	4	3	4	16	-	14	15
9.	Cianorte Futebol Clube	11	3	5	3	15	-	14	14
10.	Operário Ferroviário EC Ponta Grossa	11	2	7	2	12	-	12	13
11.	Arapongas Esporte Clube	11	2	5	4	11	-	17	11
12.	Toledo Colônia Work	11	1	2	8	12	-	23	5

Top-8 teams qualified for the Second Stage. Places 9-12 qualified for the relegation Play-offs.

Relegation Play-off (Torneio da Morte)

1.	Operário Ferroviário EC Ponta Grossa	6	5	0	1	10	-	3	15
2.	Arapongas Esporte Clube	6	3	1	2	10	-	6	10
3.	Toledo Colônia Work (*Relegated*)	6	2	2	2	7	-	8	8
4.	Cianorte Futebol Clube (*Relegated*)	6	0	1	5	3	-	13	1

Second Stage

Quarter-Finals (16-23.03.2014)

J.Malucelli Futebol S/A Curitiba - Londrina Esporte Clube	1-2(1-1)	0-2(0-0)
Prudentópolis Futebol Clube - Maringá Futebol Clube	3-4(1-3)	0-1(0-0)
Rio Branco Sport Club Paranaguá - Coritiba Foot Ball Club	0-2(0-1)	1-2(1-0)
Clube Atlético Paranaense Curitiba - Paraná Clube Curitiba	1-2(0-1)	2-0(1-0)

Semi-Finals (26.03.-02.04.2014)

Maringá Futebol Clube - Coritiba Foot Ball Club	2-1(2-0)	1-1(0-0)
Clube Atlético Paranaense Curitiba - Londrina Esporte Clube	3-1(0-1)	1-4(1-1)

Paraná Championship Finals (06-13.04.2014)

Londrina Esporte Clube - Maringá Futebol Clube	2-2(1-1)
Maringá Futebol Clube - Londrina Esporte Clube	1-1(1-1,1-1,1-1); 3-4 pen

Paraná State Championship Winners 2014: **Londrina Esporte Clube**

Aggregate Table 2014

1.	Londrina Esporte Clube	17	7	6	4	26 - 18	27
2.	Maringá Futebol Clube	17	8	5	4	24 - 18	29
3.	Coritiba Foot Ball Club	15	7	3	5	25 - 20	24
4.	Clube Atlético Paranaense Curitiba	15	6	3	6	23 - 21	21
5.	Paraná Clube Curitiba	13	6	3	4	17 - 10	21
6.	J.Malucelli Futebol S/A Curitiba	13	4	4	5	17 - 18	16
7.	Prudentópolis Futebol Clube	13	4	4	5	14 - 18	16
8.	Rio Branco Sport Club Paranaguá	13	4	4	5	15 - 21	16
9.	Operário Ferroviário EC Ponta Grossa	17	8	7	3	22 - 15	28
10.	Arapongas Esporte Clube	17	5	6	6	21 - 23	21
11.	Toledo Colônia Work (*Relegated*)	17	3	4	10	19 - 31	13
12.	Cianorte Futebol Clube (*Relegated*)	17	3	6	8	18 - 28	15

Pernambuco

Pernambuco State Championship winners:

1915	Esporte Clube Flamengo Recife
1916	Sport Club do Recife
1917	Sport Club do Recife
1918	América Futebol Clube Recife
1919	América Futebol Clube Recife
1920	Sport Club do Recife
1921	América Futebol Clube Recife
1922	América Futebol Clube Recife
1923	Sport Club do Recife
1924	Sport Club do Recife
1925	Sport Club do Recife
1926	Torre Sport Club Recife
1927	América Futebol Clube Recife
1928	Sport Club do Recife
1929	Torre Sport Club Recife
1930	Torre Sport Club Recife
1931	Santa Cruz Futebol Clube Recife
1932	Santa Cruz Futebol Clube Recife
1933	Santa Cruz Futebol Clube Recife
1934	Clube Náutico Capibaribe Recife
1935	Santa Cruz Futebol Clube Recife
1936	Tramways Sport Club Recife
1937	Tramways Sport Club Recife
1938	Sport Club do Recife
1939	Clube Náutico Capibaribe Recife
1940	Santa Cruz Futebol Clube Recife
1941	Sport Club do Recife
1942	Sport Club do Recife
1943	Sport Club do Recife
1944	América Futebol Clube Recife
1945	Clube Náutico Capibaribe Recife
1946	Santa Cruz Futebol Clube Recife
1947	Santa Cruz Futebol Clube Recife
1948	Sport Club do Recife

1965	Clube Náutico Capibaribe Recife
1966	Clube Náutico Capibaribe Recife
1967	Clube Náutico Capibaribe Recife
1968	Clube Náutico Capibaribe Recife
1969	Santa Cruz Futebol Clube Recife
1970	Santa Cruz Futebol Clube Recife
1971	Santa Cruz Futebol Clube Recife
1972	Santa Cruz Futebol Clube Recife
1973	Santa Cruz Futebol Clube Recife
1974	Clube Náutico Capibaribe Recife
1975	Sport Club do Recife
1976	Santa Cruz Futebol Clube Recife
1977	Sport Club do Recife
1978	Santa Cruz Futebol Clube Recife
1979	Santa Cruz Futebol Clube Recife
1980	Sport Club do Recife
1981	Sport Club do Recife
1982	Sport Club do Recife
1983	Santa Cruz Futebol Clube Recife
1984	Clube Náutico Capibaribe Recife
1985	Clube Náutico Capibaribe Recife
1986	Santa Cruz Futebol Clube Recife
1987	Santa Cruz Futebol Clube Recife
1988	Sport Club do Recife
1989	Clube Náutico Capibaribe Recife
1990	Santa Cruz Futebol Clube Recife
1991	Sport Club do Recife
1992	Sport Club do Recife
1993	Santa Cruz Futebol Clube Recife
1994	Sport Club do Recife
1995	Santa Cruz Futebol Clube Recife
1996	Sport Club do Recife
1997	Sport Club do Recife
1998	Sport Club do Recife

Year	Champion	Year	Champion
1949	Sport Club do Recife	1999	Sport Club do Recife
1950	Clube Náutico Capibaribe Recife	2000	Sport Club do Recife
1951	Clube Náutico Capibaribe Recife	2001	Clube Náutico Capibaribe Recife
1952	Clube Náutico Capibaribe Recife	2002	Clube Náutico Capibaribe Recife
1953	Sport Club do Recife	2003	Sport Club do Recife
1954	Clube Náutico Capibaribe Recife	2004	Clube Náutico Capibaribe Recife
1955	Sport Club do Recife	2005	Santa Cruz Futebol Clube Recife
1956	Sport Club do Recife	2006	Sport Club do Recife
1957	Santa Cruz Futebol Clube Recife	2007	Sport Club do Recife
1958	Sport Club do Recife	2008	Sport Club do Recife
1959	Santa Cruz Futebol Clube Recife	2009	Sport Club do Recife
1960	Clube Náutico Capibaribe Recife	2010	Sport Club do Recife
1961	Sport Club do Recife	2011	Santa Cruz Futebol Clube Recife
1962	Sport Club do Recife	2012	Santa Cruz Futebol Clube Recife
1963	Clube Náutico Capibaribe Recife	2013	Santa Cruz Futebol Clube Recife
1964	Clube Náutico Capibaribe Recife	2014	Sport Club do Recife

Pernambuco State Championship (Campeonato Pernambucano) 2014

First Stage

Pos	Team	P	W	D	L	GF	-	GA	Pts
1.	Salgueiro Atlético Clube	16	10	3	2	23	-	7	36
2.	Central Sport Club Caruaru	16	10	4	2	29	-	14	34
3.	Clube Atlético do Porto Caruaru	16	7	3	6	16	-	12	24
4.	Serra Talhada Futebol Clube	16	5	7	4	18	-	18	22
5.	Associação Acadêmica e Desportiva Vitória das Tabocas Vitória de Santo Antão	16	6	3	7	13	-	15	21
6.	Chã Grande Futebol Clube	16	5	4	7	15	-	18	19
7.	Pesqueira Futebol Clube	16	4	4	8	17	-	21	16
8.	Sociedade Esportiva Ypiranga Futebol Clube Santa Cruz do Capibaribe	16	4	2	10	9	-	24	14
9.	América Futebol Clube Recife	16	3	4	9	12	-	23	13

Top-3 teams qualified for the Second Stage. Places 4-9 played in the Relegation Play-offs.

Second Stage

Pos	Team	P	W	D	L	GF	-	GA	Pts
1.	Clube Náutico Capibaribe Recife	10	6	2	2	19	-	12	20
2.	Sport Club do Recife	10	5	2	3	16	-	7	17
3.	Santa Cruz Futebol Clube	10	4	4	2	23	-	12	16
4.	Salgueiro Atlético Clube	10	4	2	4	9	-	18	14
5.	Central Sport Club Caruaru	10	3	4	3	14	-	12	13
6.	Clube Atlético do Porto Caruaru	10	1	0	9	4	-	24	3

Top-4 qualified for the Semi-Finals.

Relegation Play-offs (Hexagonal de rebaixamento)

Pos	Team	P	W	D	L	GF	-	GA	Pts
1.	Pesqueira Futebol Clube	10	6	2	2	12	-	6	20
2.	Serra Talhada Futebol Clube	10	5	3	2	11	-	10	18
3.	América Futebol Clube Recife	10	4	2	4	7	-	9	14
4.	SE Ypiranga FC Santa Cruz do Capibaribe	10	3	5	2	10	-	6	14
5.	Chã Grande Futebol Clube (*Relegated*)	10	2	5	3	10	-	11	11
6.	AAD Vitória das Tabocas Vitória de Santo Antão (*Relegated*)	10	1	1	8	9	-	17	4

Semi-Finals (06-13.04.2014)

Salgueiro Atlético Clube - Clube Náutico Capibaribe Recife	2-0(1-0)	0-1(0-0) 3-5 pen
Santa Cruz Futebol Clube - Sport Club do Recife	3-0(0-0)	0-1(0-0) 3-5 pen

Third Place Play-off (16-22.04.2014)

Salgueiro Atlético Clube - Santa Cruz Futebol Clube	1-1(1-0)	2-1(1-0)

Pernambuco Championship Final (16-23.05.2014)

Sport Club do Recife - Clube Náutico Capibaribe Recife	2-0(0-0)
Clube Náutico Capibaribe Recife - Sport Club do Recife	0-1(0-0)

Pernambuco State Championship Winners 2014: **Sport Club do Recife**

Piauí

Piauí State Championship winners:

1941	Botafogo Esporte Clube Teresina
1942	Esporte Clube Flamengo Teresina
1943	Esporte Clube Flamengo Teresina
1944	Esporte Clube Flamengo Teresina
1945	Botafogo Esporte Clube Teresina
1946	Botafogo Esporte Clube Teresina
1947	Esporte Clube Flamengo Teresina
1948	Ríver Atlético Clube Teresina
1949	Botafogo Esporte Clube Teresina
1950	Ríver Atlético Clube Teresina
1951	Ríver Atlético Clube Teresina
1952	Ríver Atlético Clube Teresina
1953	Ríver Atlético Clube Teresina
1954	Ríver Atlético Clube Teresina
1955	Ríver Atlético Clube Teresina
1956	Ríver Atlético Clube Teresina
1957	Botafogo Esporte Clube Teresina
1958	Ríver Atlético Clube Teresina
1959	Ríver Atlético Clube Teresina
1960	Ríver Atlético Clube Teresina
1961	Ríver Atlético Clube Teresina
1962	Ríver Atlético Clube Teresina
1963	Ríver Atlético Clube Teresina
1964	Esporte Clube Flamengo Teresina
1965	Esporte Clube Flamengo Teresina
1966	Piauí Esporte Clube Teresina
1967	Piauí Esporte Clube Teresina
1968	Piauí Esporte Clube Teresina
1969	Piauí Esporte Clube Teresina
1970	Esporte Clube Flamengo Teresina
1971	Esporte Clube Flamengo Teresina
1972	Sociedade Esportiva Tiradentes
1973	Ríver Atlético Clube Teresina
1974	Sociedade Esportiva Tiradentes
1975	Ríver Atlético Clube Teresina & Sociedade Esportiva Tiradentes(shared)
1976	Esporte Clube Flamengo Teresina
1977	Ríver Atlético Clube Teresina
1978	Ríver Atlético Clube Teresina
1979	Esporte Clube Flamengo Teresina
1980	Ríver Atlético Clube Teresina
1981	Ríver Atlético Clube Teresina
1982	Sociedade Esportiva Tiradentes
1983	Auto Esporte Clube Teresina
1984	Esporte Clube Flamengo Teresina
1985	Piauí Esporte Clube Teresina
1986	Esporte Clube Flamengo Teresina
1987	Esporte Clube Flamengo Teresina
1988	Esporte Clube Flamengo Teresina
1989	Ríver Atlético Clube Teresina
1990	Sociedade Esportiva Tiradentes
1991	Sociedade Esportiva de Picos
1992	4 de Julho Esporte Clube Piripiri
1993	4 de Julho Esporte Clube Piripiri
1994	Sociedade Esportiva de Picos
1995	Assoc. Atlética Cori-Sabbá Floriano
1996	Ríver Atlético Clube Teresina
1997	Sociedade Esportiva de Picos
1998	Sociedade Esportiva de Picos
1999	Ríver Atlético Clube Teresina
2000	Ríver Atlético Clube Teresina
2001	Ríver Atlético Clube Teresina
2002	Ríver Atlético Clube Teresina
2003	Esporte Clube Flamengo Teresina
2004	Parnahyba Sport Club
2005	Parnahyba Sport Club
2006	Parnahyba Sport Club
2007	Ríver Atlético Clube Teresina
2008	Barras Futebol Clube
2009	Esporte Clube Flamengo Teresina
2010	Comercial Atlético Clube Campo Maior
2011	4 de Julho Esporte Clube Piripiri
2012	Parnahyba Sport Club
2013	Parnahyba Sport Club
2014	Ríver Atlético Clube Teresina

Piauí State Championship (Campeonato Piauiense) 2014

First Stage (Taça Estado do Piauí)

1. Barras Futebol Club	7	3	3	1	11 - 6	12
2. Esporte Clube Flamengo Teresina	7	3	3	1	11 - 9	12
3. Parnahyba Sport Club	7	3	2	2	9 - 6	11
4. Piauí Esporte Clube Teresina	7	3	2	2	13 - 11	11
5. Ríver Atlético Clube Teresina	7	2	5	0	16 - 6	11
6. Associação Atlética Cori-Sabbá Floriano	7	3	1	3	10 - 10	10
7. 4 de Julho Esporte Clube Piripiri	7	1	1	5	7 - 17	4
8. Caiçara Esporte Clube Campo Maior	7	1	1	5	7 - 19	4

Top-4 qualified for the Semi-Finals.

Semi-Finals (15-16.03.2014)

Barras Futebol Club - Piauí Esporte Clube Teresina 1-3(1-1)
Esporte Clube Flamengo Teresina - Parnahyba Sport Club 1-3(1-1)

Final (22.03.2014)

Parnahyba Sport Club - Piauí Esporte Clube Teresina 0-3(0-1)

Piauí Esporte Clube Teresina, as winner of the First Stage were qualified for the state championship finals.

Second Stage (Taça Cidade de Teresina)

1. 4 de Julho Esporte Clube Piripiri	7	4	1	2	12 - 5	13
2. Parnahyba Sport Club	7	4	1	2	14 - 8	13
3. Ríver Atlético Clube Teresina	7	4	0	3	13 - 6	12
4. Esporte Clube Flamengo Teresina	7	4	0	3	9 - 10	12
5. Associação Atlética Cori-Sabbá Floriano	7	3	1	3	8 - 11	10
6. Barras Futebol Club	7	2	2	3	8 - 10	8
7. Piauí Esporte Clube Teresina	7	1	5	1	11 - 12	8
8. Caiçara Esporte Clube Campo Maior	7	0	2	5	2 - 14	2

Top-4 qualified for the Semi-Finals.

Semi-Finals (03-04.05.2014)

4 de Julho Esporte Clube Piripiri - Esporte Clube Flamengo Teresina 1-0(0-0, 0-0)
Parnahyba Sport Club - Ríver Atlético Clube Teresina 1-2(1-0)

Final (10.05.2014)

4 de Julho Esporte Clube Piripiri - Ríver Atlético Clube Teresina 0-2(0-1)

Ríver Atlético Clube Teresina, as winner of the Second Stage were qualified for the state championship finals.

Piauí Championship Finals (18-25.05.2014)

Piauí Esporte Clube Teresina - Ríver Atlético Clube Teresina 2-2(1-2)
Ríver Atlético Clube Teresina - Piauí Esporte Clube Teresina 0-0

Piauí State Championship Winners 2014: **Ríver Atlético Clube Teresina**

Rio de Janeiro

Rio de Janeiro State Championship winners:

1906	Fluminense FC Rio de Janeiro
1907	Fluminense FC Rio de Janeiro & Botafogo FC Rio de Janeiro [shared]
1908	Fluminense FC Rio de Janeiro
1909	Fluminense FC Rio de Janeiro
1910	Botafogo FC Rio de Janeiro
1911	Fluminense FC Rio de Janeiro
1912	Paysandu Cricket Club Rio de Janeiro[(1)]
	Botafogo FC Rio de Janeiro[(2)]
1913	América FC Rio de Janeiro
1914	CR do Flamengo Rio de Janeiro
1915	CR do Flamengo Rio de Janeiro
1916	América FC Rio de Janeiro
1917	Fluminense FC Rio de Janeiro
1918	Fluminense FC Rio de Janeiro
1919	Fluminense FC Rio de Janeiro
1920	CR do Flamengo Rio de Janeiro
1921	CR do Flamengo Rio de Janeiro
1922	América FC Rio de Janeiro
1923	CR Vasco da Gama Rio de Janeiro
1924	CR Vasco da Gama Rio de Janeiro[(3)]
	Fluminense FC Rio de Janeiro[(4)]
1925	CR do Flamengo Rio de Janeiro
1926	São Cristóvão AC Rio de Janeiro
1927	CR do Flamengo Rio de Janeiro
1928	América FC Rio de Janeiro
1929	CR Vasco da Gama Rio de Janeiro
1930	Botafogo FC Rio de Janeiro
1931	América FC Rio de Janeiro
1932	Botafogo FC Rio de Janeiro
1933	Botafogo FC Rio de Janeiro[(4)]
	Bangu Atlético Clube Rio de Janeiro[(5)]
1934	Botafogo FC Rio de Janeiro[(4)]
	CR Vasco da Gama Rio de Janeiro [(5)]
1935	Botafogo FC Rio de Janeiro[(6)]
	América FC Rio de Janeiro[(5)]
1936	CR Vasco da Gama Rio de Janeiro[(6)]
	Fluminense FC Rio de Janeiro[(5)]
1937	Fluminense FC Rio de Janeiro
1938	Fluminense FC Rio de Janeiro
1939	CR do Flamengo Rio de Janeiro
1940	Fluminense FC Rio de Janeiro
1941	Fluminense FC Rio de Janeiro
1942	CR do Flamengo Rio de Janeiro
1943	CR do Flamengo Rio de Janeiro
1944	CR do Flamengo Rio de Janeiro
1945	CR Vasco da Gama Rio de Janeiro
1946	Fluminense FC Rio de Janeiro
1947	CR Vasco da Gama Rio de Janeiro
1948	Botafogo de FR Rio de Janeiro

1958	CR Vasco da Gama Rio de Janeiro
1959	Fluminense FC Rio de Janeiro
1960	América FC Rio de Janeiro
1961	Botafogo de FR Rio de Janeiro
1962	Botafogo de FR Rio de Janeiro
1963	CR do Flamengo Rio de Janeiro
1964	Fluminense FC Rio de Janeiro
1965	CR do Flamengo Rio de Janeiro
1966	Bangu AC Rio de Janeiro
1967	Botafogo de FR Rio de Janeiro
1968	Botafogo de FR Rio de Janeiro
1969	Fluminense FC Rio de Janeiro
1970	CR Vasco da Gama Rio de Janeiro
1971	Fluminense FC Rio de Janeiro
1972	CR do Flamengo Rio de Janeiro
1973	Fluminense FC Rio de Janeiro
1974	CR do Flamengo Rio de Janeiro
1975	Fluminense FC Rio de Janeiro
1976	Fluminense FC Rio de Janeiro
1977	CR Vasco da Gama Rio de Janeiro
1978	CR do Flamengo Rio de Janeiro
1979	CR do Flamengo Rio de Janeiro
	CR do Flamengo Rio de Janeiro*
1980	Fluminense FC Rio de Janeiro
1981	CR do Flamengo Rio de Janeiro
1982	CR Vasco da Gama Rio de Janeiro
1983	Fluminense FC Rio de Janeiro
1984	Fluminense FC Rio de Janeiro
1985	Fluminense FC Rio de Janeiro
1986	CR do Flamengo Rio de Janeiro
1987	CR Vasco da Gama Rio de Janeiro
1988	CR Vasco da Gama Rio de Janeiro
1989	Botafogo de FR Rio de Janeiro
1990	Botafogo de FR Rio de Janeiro
1991	CR do Flamengo Rio de Janeiro
1992	CR Vasco da Gama Rio de Janeiro
1993	CR Vasco da Gama Rio de Janeiro
1994	CR Vasco da Gama Rio de Janeiro
1995	Fluminense FC Rio de Janeiro
1996	CR do Flamengo Rio de Janeiro
1997	Botafogo de FR Rio de Janeiro
1998	CR Vasco da Gama Rio de Janeiro
1999	CR do Flamengo Rio de Janeiro
2000	CR do Flamengo Rio de Janeiro
2001	CR do Flamengo Rio de Janeiro
2002	Fluminense FC Rio de Janeiro
2003	CR Vasco da Gama Rio de Janeiro
2004	CR do Flamengo Rio de Janeiro
2005	Fluminense FC Rio de Janeiro
2006	Botafogo de FR Rio de Janeiro

1949	CR Vasco da Gama Rio de Janeiro		2007	CR do Flamengo Rio de Janeiro
1950	CR Vasco da Gama Rio de Janeiro		2008	CR do Flamengo Rio de Janeiro
1951	Fluminense FC Rio de Janeiro		2009	CR do Flamengo Rio de Janeiro
1952	CR Vasco da Gama Rio de Janeiro		2010	Botafogo de FR Rio de Janeiro
1953	CR do Flamengo Rio de Janeiro		2011	CR do Flamengo Rio de Janeiro
1954	CR do Flamengo Rio de Janeiro		2012	Fluminense FC Rio de Janeiro
1955	CR do Flamengo Rio de Janeiro		2013	Botafogo de FR Rio de Janeiro
1956	CR Vasco da Gama Rio de Janeiro		2014	CR do Flamengo Rio de Janeiro
1957	Botafogo de FR Rio de Janeiro			

(1) champions of LMSA [Liga Metropolitana de Sports Athleticos]
(2) champions of AFRJ [Associação de Football do Rio de Janeiro]
(3) champions of LMDT [Liga Metropolitana de Desportos Terrestres]
(4) champions of AMEA [Associação Metropolitana de Esportes Athleticos]
(5) champions of LCF [Liga Carioca de Futebol]
(6) champions of FMD [Federação Metropolitana de Desportos]
*two editions played in 1979

Rio de Janeiro State Championship (Campeonato Carioca) 2014

First Stage – Taça Guanabara

1.	CR do Flamengo Rio de Janeiro	15	12	2	1	36	-	16	38
2.	Fluminense FC Rio de Janeiro	15	9	4	2	31	-	16	31
3.	CR Vasco da Gama Rio de Janeiro	15	8	5	2	31	-	11	29
4.	Associação Desportiva Cabofriense	15	7	4	4	21	-	20	25
5.	Boavista Sport Club Saquarema	15	7	4	4	20	-	21	25
6.	Friburguense Atlético Clube Nova Friburgo	15	6	4	5	18	-	24	22
7.	Macaé Esporte Futebol Clube	15	5	4	6	22	-	20	19
8.	Nova Iguaçu Futebol Clube	15	4	7	4	20	-	19	19
9.	Botafogo de FR Rio de Janeiro	15	4	5	6	16	-	17	17
10.	Bangu Atlético Clube Rio de Janeiro	15	4	5	6	15	-	19	17
11.	Volta Redonda Futebol Clube	15	4	5	6	15	-	19	17
12.	Madureira Esporte Clube Rio de Janeiro	15	4	3	8	19	-	24	15
13.	Bonsucesso Futebol Clube	15	3	6	6	15	-	18	15
14.	Resende Futebol Clube	15	3	6	6	20	-	24	15
15.	Audax Rio de Janeiro Esporte Clube (*Relegated*)	15	2	5	8	13	-	27	11
16.	Duque de Caxias Futebol Clube (*Relegated*)	15	2	3	10	14	-	31	9

Top-4 teams qualified for the semi-finals.
Promoted for the 2015 season: Barra Mansa Futebol Clube, Esporte Clube Tigres do Brasil Duque de Caxias.

Semi-Finals (26-30.03.2014)

Associação Desportiva Cabofriense - CR do Flamengo Rio de Janeiro	0-3(0-1)	1-3(0-2)
CR Vasco da Gama Rio de Janeiro -	1-1(0-0)	0-1(0-1)

Rio de Janeiro State Championship Finals (06-13.04.2014)

CR Vasco da Gama Rio de Janeiro - CR do Flamengo Rio de Janeiro	1-1(1-0)
CR do Flamengo Rio de Janeiro - CR Vasco da Gama Rio de Janeiro	1-1(0-0)

Rio de Janeiro State Championship Winners 2014: **CR do Flamengo Rio de Janeiro**

Rio Grande Do Norte

Rio Grande do Norte State Championship winners:

1918	*Championship not finished*
1919	América Futebol Clube Natal
1920	América Futebol Clube Natal
1921	Centro Esportivo Natalense Natal
1922	América Futebol Clube Natal
1923	ABC Futebol Clube Natal
1924	Alecrim Futebol Clube Natal
1925	Alecrim Futebol Clube Natal & ABC Futebol Clube Natal [shared]
1926	América Futebol Clube Natal
1927	América Futebol Clube Natal
1928	ABC Futebol Clube Natal
1929	ABC Futebol Clube Natal
1930	América Futebol Clube Natal
1931	América Futebol Clube Natal
1932	ABC Futebol Clube Natal
1933	ABC Futebol Clube Natal
1934	ABC Futebol Clube Natal
1935	ABC Futebol Clube Natal
1936	ABC Futebol Clube Natal
1937	ABC Futebol Clube Natal
1938	ABC Futebol Clube Natal
1939	ABC Futebol Clube Natal
1940	ABC Futebol Clube Natal
1941	ABC Futebol Clube Natal
1942	América Futebol Clube Natal
1943	Santa Cruz Esporte e Cultura Natal
1944	ABC Futebol Clube Natal
1945	ABC Futebol Clube Natal
1946	América Futebol Clube Natal
1947	ABC Futebol Clube Natal
1948	América Futebol Clube Natal
1949	América Futebol Clube Natal
1950	ABC Futebol Clube Natal
1951	América Futebol Clube Natal
1952	América Futebol Clube Natal
1953	ABC Futebol Clube Natal
1954	ABC Futebol Clube Natal
1955	ABC Futebol Clube Natal
1956	América Futebol Clube Natal
1957	América Futebol Clube Natal
1958	ABC Futebol Clube Natal
1959	ABC Futebol Clube Natal
1960	ABC Futebol Clube Natal
1961	ABC Futebol Clube Natal
1962	ABC Futebol Clube Natal
1963	Alecrim Futebol Clube Natal
1964	Alecrim Futebol Clube Natal
1965	ABC Futebol Clube Natal
1966	ABC Futebol Clube Natal
1967	América Futebol Clube Natal
1968	Alecrim Futebol Clube Natal
1969	América Futebol Clube Natal
1970	ABC Futebol Clube Natal
1971	ABC Futebol Clube Natal
1972	ABC Futebol Clube Natal
1973	ABC Futebol Clube Natal
1974	América Futebol Clube Natal
1975	América Futebol Clube Natal
1976	ABC Futebol Clube Natal
1977	América Futebol Clube Natal
1978	ABC Futebol Clube Natal
1979	América Futebol Clube Natal
1980	América Futebol Clube Natal
1981	América Futebol Clube Natal
1982	América Futebol Clube Natal
1983	ABC Futebol Clube Natal
1984	ABC Futebol Clube Natal
1985	Alecrim Futebol Clube Natal
1986	Alecrim Futebol Clube Natal
1987	América Futebol Clube Natal
1988	América Futebol Clube Natal
1989	América Futebol Clube Natal
1990	ABC Futebol Clube Natal
1991	América Futebol Clube Natal
1992	América Futebol Clube Natal
1993	ABC Futebol Clube Natal
1994	ABC Futebol Clube Natal
1995	ABC Futebol Clube Natal
1996	América Futebol Clube Natal
1997	ABC Futebol Clube Natal
1998	ABC Futebol Clube Natal
1999	ABC Futebol Clube Natal
2000	ABC Futebol Clube Natal
2001	Atlético Clube Coríntians Caicó
2002	América Futebol Clube Natal
2003	América Futebol Clube Natal
2004	AC Desportiva Potiguar Mossoró
2005	ABC Futebol Clube Natal
2006	AC Esporte Clube Baraúnas Mossoró
2007	ABC Futebol Clube Natal
2008	ABC Futebol Clube Natal
2009	AS Sociedade Unida Açu
2010	ABC Futebol Clube Natal
2011	ABC Futebol Clube Natal
2012	América Futebol Clube Natal
2013	AC Desportiva Potiguar Mossoró
2014	América Futebol Clube Natal

Rio Grande do Norte State Championship (Campeonato Potiguar) 2014

First Stage (Taça FNF)

Grupo A

1.	Globo Futebol Clube Ceará Mirim	6	2	4	0	9	-	4	10
2.	ABC Futebol Clube Natal	6	2	3	1	8	-	5	9
3.	Alecrim Futebol Clube Natal	6	0	5	1	6	-	8	5
4.	Palmeira Futebol Clube da Una Goianinha (*Relegation Play-off*)	6	0	4	2	5	-	11	4

Grupo B

1.	Associação Cultural EC Baraúnas Mossoró	6	3	3	0	7	-	4	12
2.	Sport Club Santa Cruz	6	3	1	2	11	-	4	10
3.	Atlético Clube Corintians Caicó	6	2	3	1	6	-	9	9
4.	Associação Sportiva Sociedade Unida Açu (*Relegation Play-off*)	6	0	1	5	3	-	10	1

Relegation Play-off (02-05.02.2014)

Associação Sportiva Sociedade Unida Açu - Palmeira FC da Una Goianinha 2-1(0-1) 0-1(0-0)
2-4 pen

First Stage Final (02-06.02.2014)

Globo Futebol Clube Ceará Mirim - Associação Cultural EC Baraúnas Mossoró 0-0 1-1(1-1)
2-0 pen

Second Stage – First Tournament (Taça Rio Grande del Norte)

1.	Globo Futebol Clube Ceará Mirim	7	4	1	2	15	-	8	13
2.	América Futebol Clube Natal	7	4	1	2	15	-	13	13
3.	Alecrim Futebol Clube Natal	7	3	3	1	9	-	6	12
4.	Associação Cultural EC Baraúnas Mossoró	7	2	4	1	9	-	8	10
5.	ABC Futebol Clube Natal	7	2	3	2	9	-	9	9
6.	Atlético Clube Corintians Caicó	7	2	2	3	11	-	13	8
7.	Associação Cultural e Desportiva Potiguar de Mossoró	7	1	2	4	6	-	11	5
8.	Sport Club Santa Cruz	7	0	4	3	6	-	12	4

Globo Futebol Clube Ceará Mirim qualified for the State Championship Final.

Second Stage – Second Tournament (Taça Cidade de Natal)

1.	América Futebol Clube Natal	7	6	1	0	16	-	8	19
2.	ABC Futebol Clube Natal	7	4	0	3	12	-	7	12
3.	Associação Cultural e Desportiva Potiguar de Mossoró	7	3	3	1	11	-	10	12
4.	Alecrim Futebol Clube Natal	7	3	1	3	9	-	8	10
5.	Globo Futebol Clube Ceará Mirim	7	3	1	3	6	-	6	10
6.	Sport Club Santa Cruz	7	2	1	4	6	-	10	7
7.	Atlético Clube Corintians Caicó	7	2	0	5	12	-	17	6
8.	Associação Cultural EC Baraúnas Mossoró	7	1	1	5	9	-	15	4

América Futebol Clube Natal qualified for the State Championship Final.

Rio Grande do Norte Championship Finals (16-30.04.2014)

Globo Futebol Clube Ceará Mirim - América Futebol Clube Natal 1-2(1-0)
América Futebol Clube Natal - Globo Futebol Clube Ceará Mirim 0-0

Rio Grande do Norte State Championship Winners 2014: **América Futebol Clube Natal**

Aggregate Table 2014

1.	América Futebol Clube de Natal	16	11	3	2	33	-	22	36
2.	Globo Futebol Clube Ceará Mirim	16	7	3	6	22	-	16	24
3.	Alecrim Futebol Clube Natal	14	6	4	4	18	-	14	22
4.	ABC Futebol Clube Natal	14	6	3	5	21	-	16	21
5.	Associação Cultural e Desportiva Potiguar de Mossoró	14	4	5	5	17	-	21	17
6.	Atlético Clube Corintians Caicó	14	4	2	8	23	-	30	14
7.	Associação Cultural EC Baraúnas Mossoró	14	3	5	6	18	-	23	14
8.	Sport Club Santa Cruz	14	2	5	7	12	-	22	11
9.	Palmeira Futebol Clube da Una Goianinha	6	0	4	2	5	-	11	4
10.	Associação Sportiva Sociedade Unida Açu (*Relegated*)	6	0	1	5	3	-	10	1

Rio Grande do Sul

1919	Grêmio Esportivo Brasil Pelotas
1920	Guarany Futebol Clube Bagé
1921	Grêmio Foot-ball Porto Alegrense
1922	Grêmio Foot-ball Porto Alegrense
1923	*No competition*
1924	*No competition*
1925	Grêmio Esportivo Bagé
1926	Grêmio Foot-ball Porto Alegrense
1927	Sport Club Internacional Porto Alegre
1928	Sport Club Americano Porto Alegre
1929	Esporte Clube Cruzeiro Porto Alegre
1930	Esporte Clube Pelotas Pelotas
1931	Grêmio Foot-ball Porto Alegrense
1932	Grêmio Foot-ball Porto Alegrense
1933	Sport Club São Paulo Rio Grande
1934	Sport Club Internacional Porto Alegre
1935	Grêmio Atlético Farroupilha Pelotas
1936	Sport Club Rio Grande Rio Grande
1937	Grêmio Foot-ball Santanense
1938	Guarany Futebol Clube Bagé
1939	FC Riograndense Rio Grande
1940	Sport Club Internacional Porto Alegre
1941	Sport Club Internacional Porto Alegre
1942	Sport Club Internacional Porto Alegre
1943	Sport Club Internacional Porto Alegre
1944	Sport Club Internacional Porto Alegre
1945	Sport Club Internacional Porto Alegre
1946	Grêmio Foot-ball Porto Alegrense
1947	Sport Club Internacional Porto Alegre
1948	Sport Club Internacional Porto Alegre
1949	Grêmio Foot-ball Porto Alegrense
1950	Sport Club Internacional Porto Alegre
1951	Sport Club Internacional Porto Alegre
1952	Sport Club Internacional Porto Alegre
1953	Sport Club Internacional Porto Alegre
1954	Sport Club Renner Porto Alegre
1955	Sport Club Internacional Porto Alegre
1956	Grêmio Foot-ball Porto Alegrense
1957	Grêmio Foot-ball Porto Alegrense
1958	Grêmio Foot-ball Porto Alegrense
1959	Grêmio Foot-ball Porto Alegrense
1960	Grêmio Foot-ball Porto Alegrense
1961	Sport Club Internacional Porto Alegre
1962	Grêmio Foot-ball Porto Alegrense
1963	Grêmio Foot-ball Porto Alegrense
1964	Grêmio Foot-ball Porto Alegrense
1965	Grêmio Foot-ball Porto Alegrense
1966	Grêmio Foot-ball Porto Alegrense
1967	Grêmio Foot-ball Porto Alegrense
1968	Grêmio Foot-ball Porto Alegrense
1969	Sport Club Internacional Porto Alegre
1970	Sport Club Internacional Porto Alegre
1971	Sport Club Internacional Porto Alegre
1972	Sport Club Internacional Porto Alegre
1973	Sport Club Internacional Porto Alegre
1974	Sport Club Internacional Porto Alegre
1975	Sport Club Internacional Porto Alegre
1976	Sport Club Internacional Porto Alegre
1977	Grêmio Foot-ball Porto Alegrense
1978	Sport Club Internacional Porto Alegre
1979	Grêmio Foot-ball Porto Alegrense
1980	Grêmio Foot-ball Porto Alegrense
1981	Sport Club Internacional Porto Alegre
1982	Sport Club Internacional Porto Alegre
1983	Sport Club Internacional Porto Alegre
1984	Sport Club Internacional Porto Alegre
1985	Grêmio Foot-ball Porto Alegrense
1986	Grêmio Foot-ball Porto Alegrense
1987	Grêmio Foot-ball Porto Alegrense
1988	Grêmio Foot-ball Porto Alegrense
1989	Grêmio Foot-ball Porto Alegrense
1990	Grêmio Foot-ball Porto Alegrense
1991	Sport Club Internacional Porto Alegre
1992	Sport Club Internacional Porto Alegre
1993	Grêmio Foot-ball Porto Alegrense
1994	Sport Club Internacional Porto Alegre
1995	Grêmio Foot-ball Porto Alegrense
1996	Grêmio Foot-ball Porto Alegrense
1997	Sport Club Internacional Porto Alegre
1998	Esporte Clube Juventude Caxias do Sul
1999	Grêmio Foot-ball Porto Alegrense
2000	SE Recreativa Caxias do Sul
2001	Grêmio Foot-ball Porto Alegrense
2002	Sport Club Internacional Porto Alegre
2003	Sport Club Internacional Porto Alegre
2004	Sport Club Internacional Porto Alegre
2005	Sport Club Internacional Porto Alegre
2006	Grêmio Foot-ball Porto Alegrense
2007	Grêmio Foot-ball Porto Alegrense
2008	Sport Club Internacional Porto Alegre
2009	Sport Club Internacional Porto Alegre
2010	Grêmio Foot-ball Porto Alegrense
2011	Sport Club Internacional Porto Alegre
2012	Sport Club Internacional Porto Alegre
2013	Sport Club Internacional Porto Alegre
2014	Sport Club Internacional Porto Alegre

Rio Grande do Sul State Championship (Campeonato Gaúcho) 2014

First Stage

Grupo 1

1.	Sport Club Internacional Porto Alegre	15	12	2	1	28	-	9	38
2.	Grêmio Esportivo Brasil Pelotas	15	8	5	2	18	-	6	29
3.	Veranópolis EC Recreativo e Cultural	15	5	7	3	16	-	13	22
4.	Esporte Clube Juventude Caxias do Sul	15	5	5	5	16	-	16	20
5.	Esporte Clube São José	15	4	5	6	13	-	17	17
6.	Clube Esportivo Aimoré São Leopoldo	15	4	5	6	17	-	23	17
7.	Clube Esportivo Lajeadense	15	4	4	7	14	-	15	16
8.	Clube Esportivo Bento Gonçalves*	15	4	4	7	16	-	24	13

**3 points deducted*

Grupo 2

1.	Grêmio Foot-ball Porto Alegrense	15	8	5	2	28	-	13	29
2.	Sociedade Esportiva e Recreativa Caxias do Sul	15	8	3	4	23	-	16	27
3.	Esporte Clube Novo Hamburgo	15	6	2	7	16	-	18	20
4.	Esporte Clube Passo Fundo**	15	5	4	6	19	-	22	19
5.	Esporte Clube Cruzeiro Porto Alegre	15	4	7	4	17	-	22	19
6.	Sport Club São Paulo Rio Grande	15	4	5	6	17	-	20	17
7.	Esporte Clube São Luiz	15	2	5	8	13	-	21	11
8.	Esporte Clube Pelotas	15	2	2	11	12	-	28	8

***9 points deducted - Esporte Clube Passo Fundo missed the second stage.*

Top-4 from each group qualified for the second stage.

Second Stage

Quarter-Finals (21-23.03.2014)

SE e Recreativa Caxias do Sul - Veranópolis EC Recreativo e Cultural	2-2(0-2); 9-8 pen
Grêmio Esportivo Brasil Pelotas - Esporte Clube Novo Hamburgo	2-0(1-0)
Sport Club Internacional Porto Alegre - Esporte Clube Cruzeiro Porto Alegre	3-1(1-0)
Grêmio Foot-ball Porto Alegrense - Esporte Clube Juventude Caxias do Sul	3-0(1-0)

Semi-Finals (26.03.2014)

Sport Club Internacional Porto Alegre - SE e Recreativa Caxias do Sul	3-0(2-0)
Grêmio Foot-ball Porto Alegrense - Grêmio Esportivo Brasil Pelotas	2-1(1-0)

Rio Grande do Sul Championship Finals (30.03.-13.04.2014)

Grêmio Foot-ball Porto Alegrense - Sport Club Internacional Porto Alegre	1-2(1-0)
Sport Club Internacional Porto Alegre - Grêmio Foot-ball Porto Alegrense	4-1(1-0)

Rio Grande do Sul State Championship Winners 2014: **Sport Club Internacional Porto Alegre**

Aggregate Table 2014

1.	Sport Club Internacional Porto Alegre	19	16	2	1	40	-	12	50
2.	Grêmio Foot-ball Porto Alegrense	19	10	5	4	35	-	20	35
3.	Grêmio Esportivo Brasil Pelotas	17	9	5	3	21	-	8	32
4.	Sociedade Esportiva e Recreativa Caxias do Sul	17	8	4	5	25	-	21	28
5.	Veranópolis EC Recreativo e Cultural	16	5	8	3	18	-	15	23
6.	Esporte Clube Novo Hamburgo	16	6	2	8	16	-	20	20
7.	Esporte Clube Juventude Caxias do Sul	16	5	5	6	16	-	19	20
8.	Esporte Clube Passo Fundo	15	5	4	6	20	-	23	19
9.	Esporte Clube Cruzeiro Porto Alegre	16	4	7	5	18	-	25	19
10.	Sport Club São Paulo Rio Grande	15	4	5	6	17	-	20	17
11.	Esporte Clube São José	15	4	5	6	13	-	17	17
12.	Clube Esportivo Aimoré São Leopoldo	15	4	5	6	17	-	23	17
13.	Clube Esportivo Lajeadense	15	4	4	7	14	-	15	16
14.	Clube Esportivo Bento Gonçalves (*Relegated*)	15	4	4	7	16	-	24	13
15.	Esporte Clube São Luiz (*Relegated*)	15	2	5	8	13	-	21	11
16.	Esporte Clube Pelotas (*Relegated*)	15	2	2	11	12	-	28	8

Rondônia

Rondonia State Championship winners:

1945	Ypiranga Esporte Clube Porto Velho	1980	Moto Clube Porto Velho
1946	Ferroviário Atlético Clube Porto Velho	1981	Moto Clube Porto Velho
1947	Ferroviário Atlético Clube Porto Velho	1982	CR Flamengo Porto Velho
1948	Ferroviário Atlético Clube Porto Velho	1983	CR Flamengo Porto Velho
1949	Ferroviário Atlético Clube Porto Velho	1984	Ypiranga Esporte Clube Porto Velho
1950	Ferroviário Atlético Clube Porto Velho	1985	CR Flamengo Porto Velho
1951	Ferroviário Atlético Clube Porto Velho	1986	Ferroviário Atlético Clube Porto Velho
1952	Ferroviário Atlético Clube Porto Velho	1987	Ferroviário Atlético Clube Porto Velho
1953	Ypiranga Esporte Clube Porto Velho	1988	*No competition*
1954	Moto Clube Porto Velho	1989	Ferroviário Atlético Clube Porto Velho
1955	Ferroviário Atlético Clube Porto Velho	1990	*No competition*
1956	CR Flamengo Porto Velho	1991	Ji-Paraná Futebol Clube
1957	Ferroviário Atlético Clube Porto Velho	1992	Ji-Paraná Futebol Clube
1958	Ferroviário Atlético Clube Porto Velho	1993	Sociedade Esportiva Ariquemes
1959	Ypiranga Esporte Clube Porto Velho	1994	Sociedade Esportiva Ariquemes
1960	CR Flamengo Porto Velho	1995	Ji-Paraná Futebol Clube
1961	CR Flamengo Porto Velho	1996	Ji-Paraná Futebol Clube
1962	CR Flamengo Porto Velho	1997	Ji-Paraná Futebol Clube
1963	Ferroviário Atlético Clube Porto Velho	1998	Ji-Paraná Futebol Clube
1964	Ypiranga Esporte Clube Porto Velho	1999	Ji-Paraná Futebol Clube
1965	CR Flamengo Porto Velho	2000	Guajará Esporte Clube Guajará-Mirim
1966	CR Flamengo Porto Velho	2001	Ji-Paraná Futebol Clube
1967	CR Flamengo Porto Velho	2002	Centro de Fut. Amazônia Porto Velho
1968	Moto Clube Porto Velho	2003	Sociedade Esportiva União Cacoalense
1969	Moto Clube Porto Velho	2004	Sociedade Esportiva União Cacoalense
1970	Ferroviário Atlético Clube Porto Velho	2005	Vilhena Esporte Clube
1971	Moto Clube Porto Velho	2006	Sport Clube Ulbra Ji-Paraná
1972	Moto Clube Porto Velho	2007	Sport Clube Ulbra Ji-Paraná
1973	São Domingos EC Porto Velho	2008	Sport Clube Ulbra Ji-Paraná
1974	Botafogo Futebol Clube Porto Velho	2009	Vilhena Esporte Clube
1975	Moto Clube Porto Velho	2010	Vilhena Esporte Clube
1976	Moto Clube Porto Velho	2011	Esporte Clube Espigão
1977	Moto Clube Porto Velho	2012	Ji-Paraná Futebol Clube
1978	Ferroviário Atlético Clube Porto Velho	2013	Vilhena Esporte Clube
1979	Ferroviário Atlético Clube Porto Velho	2014	Vilhena Esporte Clube

Rondônia State Championship (Campeonato Rondoniense) 2014

1.	Vilhena Esporte Clube	12	8	2	2	21 - 7	26
2.	Ariquemes Futebol Clube	12	8	2	2	20 - 8	26
3.	Clube Atlético Pimentense Pimenta Bueno	12	6	2	4	22 - 15	20
4.	Rolim de Moura Esporte Clube	12	4	3	5	18 - 21	15
5.	Sociedade Esportiva União Cacoalense	12	4	2	6	21 - 25	14
6.	Sport Club Genus de Porto Velho	12	4	2	6	14 - 20	14
7.	Ji-Paraná Futebol Clube (*Relegated*)	12	1	1	10	9 - 29	4

Top-4 qualified for the semi-finals.

Semi-Finals (10-18.05.2014)

Rolim de Moura Esporte Clube - Vilhena Esporte Clube	0-1	0-2
Clube Atlético Pimentense Pimenta Bueno - Ariquemes Futebol Clube	1-5	1-0

Rondônia State Championship Finals (24-31.05.2014)

Ariquemes Futebol Clube - Vilhena Esporte Clube	0-0
Vilhena Esporte Clube - Ariquemes Futebol Clube	1-0

Rondônia State Championship Winners 2014: **Vilhena Esporte Clube**

Roraima

Roraima State Championship winners:

Amateur Era:

1974	São Francisco Futebol Clube Boa Vista
1975	Atlético Roraima Clube Boa Vista
1976	Atlético Roraima Clube Boa Vista
1977	São Raimundo Esporte Clube Boa Vista
1978	Atlético Roraima Clube Boa Vista
1979	Ríver Esporte Clube Boa Vista
1980	Atlético Roraima Clube Boa Vista
1981	Atlético Roraima Clube Boa Vista
1982	Baré Esporte Clube Boa Vista
1983	Atlético Roraima Clube Boa Vista
1984	Baré Esporte Clube Boa Vista
1985	Atlético Roraima Clube Boa Vista
1986	Baré Esporte Clube Boa Vista
1987	Atlético Roraima Clube Boa Vista
1988	Baré Esporte Clube Boa Vista
1989	Ríver Esporte Clube Boa Vista
1990	Atlético Roraima Clube Boa Vista
1991	Atlético Rio Negro Clube Boa Vista
1992	São Raimundo Esporte Clube Boa Vista
1993	Atlético Roraima Clube Boa Vista
1994	Ríver Esporte Clube Boa Vista

Professional Era:

1995	Atlético Roraima Clube Boa Vista
1996	Baré Esporte Clube Boa Vista
1997	Baré Esporte Clube Boa Vista
1998	Atlético Roraima Clube Boa Vista
1999	Baré Esporte Clube Boa Vista
2000	Atlético Rio Negro Clube Boa Vista
2001	Atlético Roraima Clube Boa Vista
2002	Atlético Roraima Clube Boa Vista
2003	Atlético Roraima Clube Boa Vista
2004	São Raimundo Esporte Clube Boa Vista
2005	São Raimundo Esporte Clube Boa Vista
2006	Baré Esporte Clube Boa Vista
2007	Atlético Roraima Clube Boa Vista
2008	Atlético Roraima Clube Boa Vista
2009	Atlético Roraima Clube Boa Vista
2010	Baré Esporte Clube Boa Vista
2011	AE Real São Luiz do Anauá
2012	São Raimundo Esporte Clube Boa Vista
2013	Náutico Futebol Clube Boa Vista
2014	São Raimundo Esporte Clube Boa Vista

First Stage – Taça Boa Vista

	Team								
1.	São Raimundo Esporte Clube Boa Vista	5	4	1	0	12	-	4	13
2.	Baré Esporte Clube Boa Vista	5	3	0	2	13	-	4	9
3.	Náutico Futebol Clube Boa Vista	5	2	2	1	11	-	7	8
4.	Atlético Roraima Clube Boa Vista	5	1	2	2	8	-	13	5
5.	Atlético Rio Negro Clube Boa Vista	5	2	1	2	7	-	11	4
6.	Grêmio Atlético Sampaio (GAS) Boa Vista	5	0	0	5	4		16	0

São Raimundo Esporte Clube Boa Vista qualified for the State Championship Final.
Places 1-4 qualified for the Second Stage.

Second Stage – Taça Roraima

Semi-Finals (10.05.2014)

Baré Esporte Clube Boa Vista - São Raimundo Esporte Clube Boa Vista 1-3
Náutico Futebol Clube Boa Vista - Atlético Roraima Clube Boa Vista 5-2

Final (14.05.2014)

São Raimundo Esporte Clube Boa Vista - Náutico Futebol Clube Boa Vista 2-1
São Raimundo Esporte Clube Boa Vista qualified for the State Championship Final.

Roraima State Championship Finals (24-31.05.2014)

No final needed. São Raimundo Esporte Clube Boa Vista, as winner of both stages were State Champions.

Roraima State Championship Winners 2014: **São Raimundo Esporte Clube Boa Vista**

Santa Catarina State Championship winners:

1924	Avaí Futebol Clube Florianópolis
1925	Externato Futebol Clube Florianópolis
1926	Avaí Futebol Clube Florianópolis
1927	Avaí Futebol Clube Florianópolis
1928	Avaí Futebol Clube Florianópolis
1929	Caxias Futebol Clube Joinville
1930	Avaí Futebol Clubc Florianópolis
1931	Lauro Müller Futebol Clube Itajaí
1932	Figueirense FC Florianópolis
1933	*Not finished*
1934	CA Catarinense Florianópolis
1935	Figueirense FC Florianópolis
1936	Figueirense FC Florianópolis
1937	Figueirense FC Florianópolis
1938	CIP Futebol Clube Itajaí
1939	Figueirense FC Florianópolis
1940	Ypiranga FC São Francisco do Sul
1941	Figueirense FC Florianópolis
1942	Avaí Futebol Clube Florianópolis
1943	Avaí Futebol Clube Florianópolis
1944	Avaí Futebol Clube Florianópolis
1945	Avaí Futebol Clube Florianópolis
1946	*No competition*
1947	América Futebol Clube Joinville
1948	América Futebol Clube Joinville
1949	Grêmio Esportivo Olímpico Blumenau
1950	Clube Atlético Carlos Renaux Brusque
1951	América Futebol Clube Joinville
1952	América Futebol Clube Joinville
1953	Clube Atlético Carlos Renaux Brusque
1954	Caxias Futebol Clube Joinville
1955	Caxias Futebol Clube Joinville
1956	Clube Atlético Operário Joinville
1957	Hercílio Luz Futebol Clube Tubarão
1958	Hercílio Luz Futebol Clube Tubarão
1959	Paula Ramos EC Florianópolis
1960	Esporte Clube Metropol Criciúma
1961	Esporte Clube Metropol Criciúma
1962	Esporte Clube Metropol Criciúma
1963	Clube Náutico Marcílio Dias Itajaí
1964	Grêmio Esportivo Olímpico Blumenau
1965	Esporte Clube Internacional Lages
1966	SER Perdigão Concórdia
1967	Esporte Clube Metropol Criciúma
1968	Comerciário Esporte Clube Criciúma
1969	Esporte Clube Metropol Criciúma
1970	Esporte Clube Ferroviário Tubarão
1971	América Futebol Clube Joinville
1972	Figueirense FC Florianópolis
1973	Avaí Futebol Clube Florianópolis
1974	Figueirense FC Florianópolis
1975	Avaí Futebol Clube Florianópolis
1976	Joinville Esporte Clube
1977	Ass. Chapecoense de Futebol Chapecó
1978	Joinville Esporte Clube
1979	Joinville Esporte Clube
1980	Joinville Esporte Clube
1981	Joinville Esporte Clube
1982	Joinville Esporte Clube
1983	Joinville Esporte Clube
1984	Joinville Esporte Clube
1985	Joinville Esporte Clube
1986	Criciúma Esporte Clube
1987	Joinville Esporte Clube
1988	Avaí Futebol Clube Florianópolis
1989	Criciúma Esporte Clube
1990	Criciúma Esporte Clube
1991	Criciúma Esporte Clube
1992	Brusque Futebol Clube
1993	Criciúma Esporte Clube
1994	Figueirense FC Florianópolis
1995	Criciúma Esporte Clube
1996	Ass. Chapecoense de Futebol Chapecó
1997	Avaí Futebol Clube Florianópolis
1998	Criciúma Esporte Clube
1999	Figueirense FC Florianópolis
2000	Joinville Esporte Clube
2001	Joinville Esporte Clube
2002	Figueirense FC Florianópolis
2003	Figueirense FC Florianópolis
2004	Figueirense FC Florianópolis
2005	Criciúma Esporte Clube
2006	Figueirense FC Florianópolis
2007	Ass. Chapecoense de Futebol Chapecó
2008	Figueirense FC Florianópolis
2009	Avaí Futebol Clube Florianópolis
2010	Avaí Futebol Clube Florianópolis
2011	Ass. Chapecoense de Futebol Chapecó
2012	Avaí Futebol Clube Florianópolis
2013	Criciúma Esporte Clube
2014	Figueirense FC Florianópolis

Santa Catarina State Championship (Campeonato Catarinense) 2014

First Stage

1.	Clube Atlético Metropolitano Blumenau	9	6	0	3	17	-	12	18
2.	Criciúma Esporte Clube	9	4	4	1	10	-	7	16
3.	Joinville Esporte Clube	9	4	3	2	14	-	8	15
4.	Figueirense Futebol Clube Florianópolis	9	4	3	2	12	-	7	15
5.	Associação Chapecoense de Futebol Chapecó	9	4	3	2	12	-	10	15
6.	Brusque Futebol Clube	9	4	2	3	13	-	7	14
7.	Clube Náutico Marcílio Dias Itajaí	9	2	4	3	11	-	13	10
8.	Avaí Futebol Clube Florianópolis	9	2	1	6	11	-	14	7
9.	Grêmio Esportivo Juventus Jaraguá do Sul	9	2	1	6	10	-	21	7
10.	Clube Atlético Hermann Aichinger Ibirama	9	2	1	6	9	-	20	7

Places 1-4 qualified for the Second Stage (Quadrangular); Places 5-10 qualified for the Relegation Play-offs (Hexagonal de Rebaixamento).

Second Stage

Hexagonal de Rebaixamento

1.	Associação Chapecoense de Futebol Chapecó	10	6	2	2	15	-	7	20
2.	Avaí Futebol Clube Florianópolis	10	5	2	3	19	-	13	17
3.	Clube Náutico Marcílio Dias Itajaí	10	4	3	3	18	-	12	15
4.	Clube Atlético Hermann Aichinger Ibirama	10	4	0	6	10	-	15	12
5.	Brusque Futebol Clube (*Relegated*)	10	3	3	4	10	-	14	12
6.	Grêmio Esportivo Juventus Jaraguá do Sul (*Relegated*)	10	2	2	6	10	-	21	8

Quadrangular

1.	Figueirense Futebol Clube Florianópolis	6	3	2	1	10	-	7	11
2.	Joinville Esporte Clube	6	2	4	0	4	-	2	10
3.	Criciúma Esporte Clube	6	2	1	3	7	-	6	7
4.	Clube Atlético Metropolitano Blumenau	6	0	3	3	2	-	8	3

Top-2 teams qualified for the State Championship finals.

Santa Catarina Championship Finals (06-13.04.2014)

Joinville Esporte Clube - Figueirense Futebol Clube Florianópolis	2-1(1-0)
Figueirense Futebol Clube Florianópolis - Joinville Esporte Clube	2-1(2-0)

Santa Catarina State Championship Winners 2014: **Figueirense FC Florianópolis**

São Paulo State Championship winners:

1902	São Paulo Athletic Club
1903	São Paulo Athletic Club
1904	São Paulo Athletic Club
1905	Clube Atlético Paulistano São Paulo
1906	Sport Club Germânia São Paulo
1907	Sport Club Internacional São Paulo
1908	Clube Atlético Paulistano São Paulo
1909	AA das Palmeiras São Paulo
1910	AA das Palmeiras São Paulo
1911	São Paulo Athletic Club
1912	Sport Club Americano São Paulo
1913	Sport Club Americano São Paulo(1)
	Clube Atlético Paulistano São Paulo(2)
1914	SC Corinthians Paulista São Paulo(1)
	AA São Bento São Paulo (2)
1915	Sport Club Germânia São Paulo(1)
	AA das Palmeiras São Paulo(2)
1916	SC Corinthians Paulista São Paulo(1)
	Clube Atlético Paulistano São Paulo(2)
1917	Clube Atlético Paulistano São Paulo
1918	Clube Atlético Paulistano São Paulo
1919	Clube Atlético Paulistano São Paulo
1920	Palestra Itália São Paulo
1921	Clube Atlético Paulistano São Paulo
1922	SC Corinthians Paulista São Paulo
1923	SC Corinthians Paulista São Paulo
1924	SC Corinthians Paulista São Paulo
1925	AA São Bento São Paulo
1926	Palestra Itália São Paulo(2)
	Clube Atlético Paulistano São Paulo(3)
1927	Palestra Itália São Paulo(2)
	Clube Atlético Paulistano São Paulo(3)
1928	SC Corinthians Paulista São Paulo(2)
	Sport Club Internacional São Paulo(3)
1929	SC Corinthians Paulista São Paulo(2)
	Clube Atlético Paulistano São Paulo(3)
1930	SC Corinthians Paulista São Paulo
1931	São Paulo Futebol Clube
1932	Palestra Itália São Paulo
1933	Palestra Itália São Paulo
1934	Palestra Itália São Paulo
1935	Santos Futebol Clube(1)
	Portuguesa de Desportos São Paulo(2)
1936	Palestra Itália São Paulo(1)
	Portuguesa de Desportos São Paulo(2)
1937	SC Corinthians Paulista São Paulo
1938	SC Corinthians Paulista São Paulo
1939	SC Corinthians Paulista São Paulo
1940	Palestra Itália São Paulo
1941	SC Corinthians Paulista São Paulo

1954	SC Corinthians Paulista São Paulo
1955	Santos Futebol Clube
1956	Santos Futebol Clube
1957	São Paulo Futebol Clube
1958	Santos Futebol Clube
1959	SE Palmeiras São Paulo
1960	Santos Futebol Clube
1961	Santos Futebol Clube
1962	Santos Futebol Clube
1963	SE Palmeiras São Paulo
1964	Santos Futebol Clube
1965	Santos Futebol Clube
1966	SE Palmeiras São Paulo
1967	Santos Futebol Clube
1968	Santos Futebol Clube
1969	Santos Futebol Clube
1970	São Paulo Futebol Clube
1971	São Paulo Futebol Clube
1972	SE Palmeiras São Paulo
1973	Santos Futebol Clube &
	Portuguesa de Desportos São Paulo*
1974	SE Palmeiras São Paulo
1975	São Paulo Futebol Clube
1976	SE Palmeiras São Paulo
1977	SC Corinthians Paulista São Paulo
1978	Santos Futebol Clube
1979	SC Corinthians Paulista São Paulo
1980	São Paulo Futebol Clube
1981	São Paulo Futebol Clube
1982	SC Corinthians Paulista São Paulo
1983	SC Corinthians Paulista São Paulo
1984	Santos Futebol Clube
1985	São Paulo Futebol Clube
1986	Assoc. Atlética Internacional Limeira
1987	São Paulo Futebol Clube
1988	SC Corinthians Paulista São Paulo
1989	São Paulo Futebol Clube
1990	CA Bragantino Bragança Paulista
1991	São Paulo Futebol Clube
1992	São Paulo Futebol Clube
1993	SE Palmeiras São Paulo
1994	SE Palmeiras São Paulo
1995	SC Corinthians Paulista São Paulo
1996	SE Palmeiras São Paulo
1997	SC Corinthians Paulista São Paulo
1998	São Paulo Futebol Clube
1999	SC Corinthians Paulista São Paulo
2000	São Paulo Futebol Clube
2001	SC Corinthians Paulista São Paulo
2002	Ituano Futebol Clube Itu

1942	SE Palmeiras São Paulo	2003	SC Corinthians Paulista São Paulo
1943	São Paulo Futebol Clube	2004	São Caetano Futebol Limitada
1944	SE Palmeiras São Paulo	2005	São Paulo Futebol Clube
1945	São Paulo Futebol Clube	2006	Santos Futebol Clube
1946	São Paulo Futebol Clube	2007	Santos Futebol Clube
1947	SE Palmeiras São Paulo	2008	SE Palmeiras São Paulo
1948	São Paulo Futebol Clube	2009	SC Corinthians Paulista São Paulo
1949	São Paulo Futebol Clube	2010	Santos Futebol Clube
1950	SE Palmeiras São Paulo	2011	Santos Futebol Clube
1951	SC Corinthians Paulista São Paulo	2012	Santos Futebol Clube
1952	SC Corinthians Paulista São Paulo	2013	SC Corinthians Paulista São Paulo
1953	São Paulo Futebol Clube	2014	Ituano Futebol Clube São Paulo

(1) champions of LPF [Liga Paulista de Foot-Ball]
(2) champions of APEA [Associação Paulista de Esportes Atléticos]
(3) champions of LAF [Liga dos Amadores de Futebol]
*shared winners

São Paulo State Championship (Campeonato Paulista) 2014

First Stage

Top-2 of each group qualified for the quarter-finals.

Grupo A

1.	São Paulo Futebol Clube	15	8	3	4	28	-	15	27
2.	Clube Atlético Penapolense	15	6	1	8	14	-	17	19
3.	Clube Atlético Linense	15	5	1	9	9	-	21	16
4.	Comercial Futebol Clube Ribeirão Preto	15	3	3	9	13	-	21	12
5.	Clube Atlético Sorocaba	15	2	5	8	16	-	29	11

Grupo B

1.	Botafogo Futebol Clube Ribeirão Preto	15	9	1	5	23	-	20	28
2.	Ituano Futebol Clube São Paulo	15	8	4	3	16	-	10	28
3.	Sport Club Corinthians Paulista São Paulo	15	7	3	5	24	-	19	24
4.	Grêmio Osasco Audax São Paulo	15	6	5	4	17	-	15	23
5.	Esporte Clube XV de Novembro Piracicaba	15	5	4	6	18	-	18	19

Grupo C

1.	Santos Futebol Clube	15	11	3	1	39	-	16	36
2.	Associação Atlética Ponte Preta	15	8	0	7	17	-	23	24
3.	São Bernardo Futebol Clube	15	6	5	4	23	-	18	23
4.	Associação Portuguesa de Desportos São Paulo	15	6	2	7	23	-	19	20
5.	Paulista Futebol Clube Jundiaí	15	0	4	11	14	-	31	4

Grupo D

1.	Sociedade Esportiva Palmeiras São Paulo	15	11	2	2	27	-	13	35
2.	Clube Atlético Bragantino Bragança	15	7	2	6	17	-	18	23
3.	Rio Claro Futebol Clube	15	5	5	5	29	-	27	20
4.	Mogi Mirim Esporte Clube	15	4	5	6	25	-	30	17
5.	Oeste Futebol Clube Itápolis	15	3	2	10	16	-	28	11

Quarter-Finals (26-28.03.2014)

Santos Futebol Clube - Associação Atlética Ponte Preta	4-0(1-0)
Botafogo Futebol Clube Ribeirão Preto - Ituano Futebol Clube São Paulo	0-0; 1-4 pen
São Paulo Futebol Clube - Clube Atlético Penapolense	0-0; 4-5 pen
Sociedade Esportiva Palmeiras São Paulo - Clube Atlético Bragantino Bragança	2-0

Semi-Finals (30.03.2014)

Santos Futebol Clube - Clube Atlético Penapolense	3-2(1-2)
Sociedade Esportiva Palmeiras São Paulo - Ituano Futebol Clube São Paulo	0-1(0-0)

São Paulo Championship Finals (06-13.04.2014)

Ituano Futebol Clube São Paulo - Santos Futebol Clube	1-0(1-0)
Santos Futebol Clube - Ituano Futebol Clube São Paulo	1-0(1-0,1-0,1-0); 6-7 on penalties

São Paulo State Championship Winners 2014: **Ituano Futebol Clube São Paulo**

Aggregate Table 2014

1.	Ituano Futebol Clube São Paulo	19	10	5	4	18	-	11	35
2.	Santos Futebol Clube	19	14	3	2	46	-	19	45
3.	Sociedade Esportiva Palmeiras São Paulo	17	12	2	3	29	-	14	38
4.	Clube Atlético Penapolense	17	6	2	9	16	-	20	20
5.	Botafogo Futebol Clube Ribeirão Preto	16	9	2	5	23	-	20	29
6.	São Paulo Futebol Clube	16	8	4	4	28	-	15	28
7.	Associação Atlética Ponte Preta	16	8	0	8	17	-	26	24
8.	Clube Atlético Bragantino Bragança	16	7	2	7	17	-	20	23
9.	Sport Club Corinthians Paulista São Paulo	15	7	3	5	24	-	19	24
10.	São Bernardo Futebol Clube	15	6	5	4	23	-	18	23
11.	Grêmio Osasco Audax São Paulo	15	6	5	4	17	-	15	23
12.	Associação Portuguesa de Desportos São Paulo	15	6	2	7	23	-	19	20
13.	Rio Claro Futebol Clube	15	5	5	5	29	-	27	20
14.	Esporte Clube XV de Novembro Piracicaba	15	5	4	6	18	-	18	19
15.	Mogi Mirim Esporte Clube	15	4	5	6	25	-	30	17
16.	Clube Atlético Linense	15	5	1	9	9	-	21	16
17.	Comercial Futebol Clube Ribeirão Preto (*Relegated*)	15	3	3	9	13	-	21	12
18.	Oeste Futebol Clube Itápolis (*Relegated*)	15	3	2	10	16	-	28	11
19.	Clube Atlético Sorocaba (*Relegated*)	15	2	5	8	16	-	29	11
20.	Paulista Futebol Clube Jundiaí (*Relegated*)	15	0	4	11	14	-	31	4

Promoted clubs for the 2015 São Paulo State Championship:
Capivariano Futebol Clube,
Red Bull Futebol e Entretenimento Ltda. Campinas,
Esporte Clube São Bento Sorocaba,
Marilia Atlético Clube.

Sergipe

Sergipe State Championship winners:

1918	Cotinguiba Sport Club Aracaju
1919	*No competition*
1920	Cotinguiba Sport Club Aracaju
1921	Industrial Futebol Clube Aracaju
1922	Club Sportivo Sergipe Aracaju
1923	Cotinguiba Sport Club Aracaju
1924	Club Sportivo Sergipe Aracaju
1925	*No competition*
1926	*No competition*
1927	Club Sportivo Sergipe Aracaju
1928	Club Sportivo Sergipe Aracaju
1929	Club Sportivo Sergipe Aracaju
1930	*No competition*
1931	*No competition*
1932	Club Sportivo Sergipe Aracaju
1933	Club Sportivo Sergipe Aracaju
1934	Palestra Futebol Clube Aracaju
1935	Palestra Futebol Clube Aracaju
1936	Cotinguiba Sport Club Aracaju
1937	Club Sportivo Sergipe Aracaju
1938	*No competition*
1939	Ipiranga Futebol Clube Maruim
1940	Club Sportivo Sergipe Aracaju
1941	Riachuelo Futebol Clube Aracaju
1942	Cotinguiba Sport Club Aracaju
1943	Club Sportivo Sergipe Aracaju
1944	Vasco Esporte Clube Aracaju
1945	Ipiranga Futebol Clube Maruim
1946	Olímpico Futebol Clube Aracaju
1947	Olímpico Futebol Clube Aracaju
1948	Vasco Esporte Clube Aracaju
1949	Palestra Futebol Clube Aracaju
1950	Passagem Futebol Clube Aracaju
1951	Assoc. Desportiva Confiança Aracaju
1952	Cotinguiba Sport Club Aracaju
1953	Vasco Esporte Clube Aracaju
1954	Assoc. Desportiva Confiança Aracaju
1955	Club Sportivo Sergipe Aracaju
1956	Esporte Clube Santa Cruz Estância
1957	Esporte Clube Santa Cruz Estância
1958	Esporte Clube Santa Cruz Estância
1959	Esporte Clube Santa Cruz Estância
1960	Esporte Clube Santa Cruz Estância
1961	Club Sportivo Sergipe Aracaju
1962	Assoc. Desportiva Confiança Aracaju
1963	Assoc. Desportiva Confiança Aracaju
1964	Club Sportivo Sergipe Aracaju
1965	Assoc. Desportiva Confiança Aracaju
1966	América Futebol Clube Propriá
1967	Club Sportivo Sergipe Aracaju
1968	Assoc. Desportiva Confiança Aracaju
1969	Associação Olímpica Itabaiana
1970	Club Sportivo Sergipe Aracaju
1971	Club Sportivo Sergipe Aracaju
1972	Club Sportivo Sergipe Aracaju
1973	Associação Olímpica Itabaiana
1974	Club Sportivo Sergipe Aracaju
1975	Club Sportivo Sergipe Aracaju
1976	Assoc. Desportiva Confiança Aracaju
1977	Assoc. Desportiva Confiança Aracaju
1978	Associação Olímpica Itabaiana
1979	Associação Olímpica Itabaiana
1980	Associação Olímpica Itabaiana
1981	Associação Olímpica Itabaiana
1982	Associação Olímpica Itabaiana & Club Sportivo Sergipe Aracaju [shared]
1983	Assoc. Desportiva Confiança Aracaju
1984	Club Sportivo Sergipe Aracaju
1985	Club Sportivo Sergipe Aracaju
1986	Assoc. Desportiva Confiança Aracaju
1987	Vasco Esporte Clube Aracaju
1988	Assoc. Desportiva Confiança Aracaju
1989	Club Sportivo Sergipe Aracaju
1990	Assoc. Desportiva Confiança Aracaju
1991	Club Sportivo Sergipe Aracaju
1992	Club Sportivo Sergipe Aracaju
1993	Club Sportivo Sergipe Aracaju
1994	Club Sportivo Sergipe Aracaju
1995	Club Sportivo Sergipe Aracaju
1996	Club Sportivo Sergipe Aracaju
1997	Associação Olímpica Itabaiana
1998	Olimpico Lagartense Lagarto
1999	Club Sportivo Sergipe Aracaju
2000	Club Sportivo Sergipe Aracaju
2001	Assoc. Desportiva Confiança Aracaju
2002	Assoc. Desportiva Confiança Aracaju
2003	Club Sportivo Sergipe Aracaju
2004	Assoc. Desportiva Confiança Aracaju
2005	Associação Olímpica Itabaiana
2006	Olímpico Pirambu Futebol Clube
2007	América Futebol Clube Propriá
2008	Assoc. Desportiva Confiança Aracaju
2009	Assoc. Desportiva Confiança Aracaju
2010	Soc. Esportiva River Plate Carmópolis
2011	Soc. Esportiva River Plate Carmópolis
2012	Olímpico Esporte Clube Itabaianinha
2013	Club Sportivo Sergipe Aracaju
2014	Assoc. Desportiva Confiança Aracaju

Sergipe State Championship (Campeonato Sergipano) 2014

First Stage (Copa Governo do Estado de Sergipe)

Group A

1.	Associação Desportiva Socorrense Nossa Senhora do Socorro	6	3	2	1	5 - 3	11
2.	Associação Olímpica de Itabaiana	6	3	1	2	11 - 6	10
3.	Itabaiana Coritiba Foot Ball Clube	6	3	1	2	9 - 10	10
4.	Clube Desportivo de Canindé do São Francisco*	6	1	0	5	5 - 11	-3

**6 points deducted*

Group B

1.	Estanciano Esporte Clube	6	5	0	1	12 - 5	15
2.	Amadense Esporte Clube Tobias Barreto	6	3	2	1	12 - 5	11
3.	Lagarto Futebol Clube	6	2	2	2	7 - 5	8
4.	Olímpico Esporte Clube Itabaianinha	6	0	0	6	0 - 18	0

Semi-Finals (02.02.2014)

AD Socorrense Nossa Senhora do Socorro - Amadense SC Tobias Barreto 0-2(0-1)
Estanciano Esporte Clube - Associação Olímpica de Itabaiana 0-3(0-1)

First Stage Final (07-09.02.2014)

Associação Olímpica de Itabaiana - Amadense SC Tobias Barreto 0-1(0-0) 2-2(1-0)

Copa Governo do Estado de Sergipe winners: **Amadense Esporte Clube Tobias Barreto**

Second Stage

1.	Club Sportivo Sergipe Aracaju	18	13	3	2	46 - 13	42
2.	Associação Desportiva Confiança Aracaju	18	13	2	3	42 - 18	41
3.	Estanciano Esporte Clube	18	12	2	4	33 - 23	38
4.	Associação Desportiva Socorrense Nossa Senhora do Socorro	18	9	3	6	28 - 19	30
5.	Associação Olímpica de Itabaiana	18	9	1	8	25 - 19	28
6.	Lagarto Futebol Clube	18	5	6	7	24 - 29	21
7.	Itabaiana Coritiba Foot Ball Clube	18	6	2	10	19 - 24	20
8.	Amadense Esporte Clube Tobias Barreto	18	5	4	9	20 - 27	19
9.	Clube Desportivo de Canindé do São Francisco	18	5	3	10	26 - 37	18
10.	Olímpico Esporte Clube Itabaianinha	18	0	0	18	0 - 54	0

Top-4 qualified for the semi-finals.

Semi-Finals (15-18.05.2014)

Estanciano Esporte Clube - Associação Desportiva Confiança Aracaju 2-0(0-0) 1-3(1-1)
AD Socorrense Nossa Senhora do Socorro - Club Sportivo Sergipe Aracaju 1-1(0-0) 1-2(1-1)

Sergipe Championship Finals (25.05.-01.06.2014)

AD Socorrense Nossa Senhora do Socorro - AD Confiança Aracaju 0-2(0-0) 1-2(0-2)

Sergipe State Championship Winners 2014: **Associação Desportiva Confiança Aracaju**

Aggregate Table 2014

1.	Associação Desportiva Confiança Aracaju	22	16	2	4	49 - 22	50
2.	Associação Desportiva Socorrense Nossa Senhora do Socorro	22	10	4	8	32 - 25	34
3.	Club Sportivo Sergipe Aracaju	20	13	4	3	48 - 16	43
4.	Estanciano Esporte Clube	20	13	2	5	36 - 26	41
5.	Associação Olímpica de Itabaiana	18	9	1	8	25 - 19	28
6.	Lagarto Futebol Clube	18	5	6	7	24 - 29	21
7.	Itabaiana Coritiba Foot Ball Clube	18	6	2	10	19 - 24	20
8.	Amadense Esporte Clube Tobias Barreto	18	5	4	9	20 - 27	19
9.	Clube Desportivo de Canindé do São Francisco (*Relegated*)	18	5	3	10	26 - 37	18
10.	Olímpico Esporte Clube Itabaianinha (*Relegated*)	18	0	0	18	0 - 54	0

Tocatins

Tocatins State Championship winners:

1993	Tocantinópolis Esporte Clube
1994	União Atlética Araguainense
1995	Intercap Esporte Clube Paraíso
1996	Gurupi Esporte Clube
1997	Gurupi Esporte Clube
1998	Associação Atlética Alvorada
1999	Interporto FC Porto Nacional
2000	Palmas Futebol e Regatas
2001	Palmas Futebol e Regatas
2002	Tocantinópolis Esporte Clube
2003	Palmas Futebol e Regatas
2004	Palmas Futebol e Regatas
2005	Colinas Esporte Clube
2006	Araguaína Futebol e Regatas
2007	Palmas Futebol e Regatas
2008	Tocantins Futebol Clube Palmas
2009	Araguaína Futebol e Regatas
2010	Gurupi Esporte Clube Tocantinópolis
2011	Gurupi Esporte Clube Tocantinópolis
2012	Gurupi Esporte Clube Tocantinópolis
2013	Interporto FC Porto Nacional
2014	Interporto FC Porto Nacional

Tocatins State Championship (Campeonato Tocantinense) 2014

First Stage

1.	Gurupi Esporte Clube Tocantinópolis	14	8	1	5	21	-	14	25
2.	Tocantinópolis Esporte Clube	14	7	3	4	30	-	19	24
3.	Palmas Futebol e Regatas	14	6	6	2	31	-	23	24
4.	Interporto Futebol Clube Porto Nacional	14	6	4	4	18	-	11	22
5.	Tocantins Esporte Clube de Miracema do Tocantins	14	5	4	5	23	-	21	19
6.	Araguaína Futebol e Regatas	14	5	4	5	18	-	21	19
7.	Colinas Esporte Clube (*Relegated*)	14	2	6	6	19	-	34	12
8.	Sport Club Guaraí (*Relegated*)	14	1	4	9	11	-	28	7

Top-4 qualified for the stage finals.

Second Stage

Semi-Finals (17-25.05.2014)

Interporto Futebol Clube Porto Nacional - Gurupi Esporte Clube Tocantinópolis	2-0	1-1
Palmas Futebol e Regatas - Tocantinópolis Esporte Clube	0-0	1-2

Tocatins Championship Finals (31.05.-08.06.2014)

Interporto Futebol Clube Porto Nacional - Tocantinópolis Esporte Clube	1-0
Tocantinópolis Esporte Clube - Interporto Futebol Clube Porto Nacional	1-0

Tocatins State Championship Winners 2013: **Interporto Futebol Clube Porto Nacional**

NATIONAL TEAM INTERNATIONAL MATCHES (16.07.2014 – 15.07.2015)

05.09.2014	Miami Gardens	Brazil - Colombia	1-0(0-0)	(F)
09.09.2014	East Rutherford	Brazil - Ecuador	1-0(1-0)	(F)
11.10.2014	Beijing	Brazil - Argentina	2-0(1-0)	(F)
14.10.2014	Kallang	Japan - Brazil	0-4(0-1)	(F)
12.11.2014	Istanbul	Turkey - Brazil	0-4(0-3)	(F)
18.11.2014	Wien	Austria - Brazil	1-2(0-0)	(F)
26.03.2015	Paris	France - Brazil	1-3(1-1)	(F)
29.03.2015	London	Brazil - Chile	1-0(0-0)	(F)
07.06.2015	São Paulo	Brazil - Mexico	2-0(2-0)	(F)
10.06.2015	Porto Alegre	Brazil - Honduras	1-0(1-0)	(F)
14.06.2015	Temuco	Brazil - Peru	2-1(1-1)	(CA)
17.06.2015	Santiago	Brazil - Colombia	0-1(0-1)	(CA)
21.06.2015	Santiago	Brazil - Venezuela	2-1(1-0)	(CA)
27.06.2015	Concepción	Brazil - Paraguay	3-4 pen	(CA)

05.09.2014, Friendly International
Sun Life Stadium, Miami Gardens (United States); Attendance: 73,479
Referee: Dave Gantar (Canada)
BRAZIL - COLOMBIA 1-0(0-0)
BRA: Jéfferson, Maicon, Miranda, David Luiz (80.Marquinhos III), Filipe Luís, Luiz Gustavo (46.Fernandinho), Ramires (46.Elias), Oscar (72.Philippe Coutinho), Willian (72.Everton Ribeiro), Diego Tardelli (77.Robinho), Neymar (Cap). Trainer: Carlos Caetano Bledorn Verri „Dunga".
Goal: Neymar (83).

09.09.2014, Friendly International
Metlife Stadium, East Rutherford (United States); Attendance: 35,975
Referee: Edwin Jurisevic (United States)
BRAZIL - ECUADOR 1-0(1-0)
BRA: Jéfferson, Danilo I (90.Gil II), Miranda, Marquinhos III, Filipe Luís, Luiz Gustavo (74.Fernandinho), Ramires (69.Elias), Willian (46.Ricardo Goulart), Oscar (46.Everton Ribeiro), Neymar (Cap), Diego Tardelli (67.Philippe Coutinho). Trainer: Carlos Caetano Bledorn Verri „Dunga".
Goal: Willian (30).

11.10.2014, Friendly International
Beijing National Stadium, Beijing (China P.R.); Attendance: 52,313
Referee: Fan Qi (China P.R.)
BRAZIL - ARGENTINA 2-0(1-0)
BRA: Jéfferson, Danilo I, Miranda, David Luiz (90.Gil II), Filipe Luís, Luiz Gustavo, Elias, Willian, Oscar, Neymar (Cap) (90+5.Robinho), Diego Tardelli (82.Kaká). Trainer: Carlos Caetano Bledorn Verri „Dunga".
Goals: Diego Tardelli (28, 64).

14.10.2014, Friendly International
Singapore National Stadium, Kallang (Singapore); Attendance: 51,577
Referee: Ahmad A'Qashah (Singapore)
JAPAN - BRAZIL 0-4(0-1)
BRA: Jéfferson, Danilo I (46.Mário Fernandes), Miranda, Gil II, Filipe Luís, Elias (76.Kaká), Luiz Gustavo (72.Souza III), Oscar (46.Philippe Coutinho), Willian (46.Everton Ribeiro), Neymar (Cap), Diego Tardelli (65.Robinho). Trainer: Carlos Caetano Bledorn Verri „Dunga".

Goals: Neymar (18, 48, 77, 81).

12.11.2014, Friendly International
Şükrü Saracoğlu Stadyumu, Istanbul; Attendance: 50,509
Referee: Ravshan Irmatov (Uzbekistan)
TURKEY - BRAZIL **0-4(0-3)**
BRA: Diego Alves, Danilo I, Miranda, David Luiz, Filipe Luís, Luiz Gustavo (85.Fred III), Fernandinho (73.Casemiro), Willian (77.Douglas Costa), Oscar (73.Philippe Coutinho), Neymar (Cap), Luiz Adriano (73.Roberto Firmino). Trainer: Carlos Caetano Bledorn Verri „Dunga".
Goals: Neymar (20), Semih Kaya (24 own goal), Willian (44), Neymar (60).

18.11.2014, Friendly International
„Ernst Happel"Stadion, Wien; Attendance: 48,500
Referee: William Collum (Scotland)
AUSTRIA - BRAZIL **1-2(0-0)**
BRA: Diego Alves, Danilo I, Miranda (28.Thiago Silva), David Luiz, Filipe Luís, Luiz Gustavo, Fernandinho (82.Casemiro), Willian (63.Douglas Costa), Oscar (77.Fred III), Neymar (Cap) (90+2.Marquinhos III), Luiz Adriano (62.Roberto Firmino). Trainer: Carlos Caetano Bledorn Verri „Dunga".
Goals: David Luiz (64), Roberto Firmino (83).

26.03.2015, Friendly International
Stade de France, Saint-Denis, Paris; Attendance: 81,338
Referee: Nicola Rizzoli (Italy)
FRANCE - BRAZIL **1-3(1-1)**
BRA: Jéfferson, Danilo I, Thiago Silva, Miranda, Filipe Luís, Elias (90+2.Marcelo), Luiz Gustavo (90.Fernandinho), Willian (83.Douglas Costa), Oscar (86.Souza III), Neymar (Cap), Roberto Firmino (88.Luiz Adriano). Trainer: Carlos Caetano Bledorn Verri „Dunga".
Goals: Oscar (40), Neymar (57), Luiz Gustavo (69).

29.03.2015, Friendly International
Emirates Stadium, London (England); Attendance: 60,000
Referee: Martin Atkinson (England)
BRAZIL - CHILE **1-0(0-0)**
BRA: Jéfferson, Danilo I, Thiago Silva, Miranda, Marcelo (76.Filipe Luís), Souza III (60.Elias), Fernandinho, Douglas Costa (62.Willian), Philippe Coutinho (60.Robinho), Neymar (Cap), Luiz Adriano (60.Roberto Firmino). Trainer: Carlos Caetano Bledorn Verri „Dunga".
Goal: Roberto Firmino (71).

07.06.2015, Friendly International
Allianz Parque, São Paulo; Attendance: 45,000
Referee: Julio César Quintana Rodríguez (Paraguay)
BRAZIL - MEXICO **2-0(2-0)**
BRA: Jéfferson, Danilo I (46.Fabinho), Miranda, David Luiz (Cap), Filipe Luís, Fernandinho, Elias (78.Casemiro), Willian (74.Douglas Costa), Philippe Coutinho (70.Everton Ribeiro), Fred III (83.Felipe Ânderson), Diego Tardelli (59.Roberto Firmino). Trainer: Carlos Caetano Bledorn Verri „Dunga".
Goals: Philippe Coutinho (28), Diego Tardelli (37).

10.06.2015, Friendly International
Estádio "José Pinheiro Borba" (Beira-Rio), Porto Alegre; Attendance: n/a
Referee: Gery Vargas (Bolivia)
BRAZIL - HONDURAS 1-0(1-0)
BRA: Jéfferson, Fabinho (75.Marquinhos III), Miranda, David Luiz (Cap) (46.Thiago Silva), Filipe Luís, Casemiro, Fernandinho, Willian (46.Douglas Costa), Philippe Coutinho (46.Neymar), Fred III (81.Elias), Roberto Firmino (71.Robinho). Trainer: Carlos Caetano Bledorn Verri „Dunga".
Goal: Roberto Firmino (33).

14.06.2015, 44th Copa América, Group Stage
Estadio Municipal "Germán Becker", Temuco (Chile); Attendance: 16,342
Referee: Roberto García Orozco (Mexico)
BRAZIL - PERU 2-1(1-1)
BRA: Jéfferson, Daniel Alves, Miranda, David Luiz, Filipe Luís, Fernandinho, Elias, Willian (87.Everton Ribeiro), Fred III (75.Roberto Firmino), Diego Tardelli (66.Douglas Costa), Neymar (Cap). Trainer: Carlos Caetano Bledorn Verri „Dunga".
Goals: Neymar (5), Douglas Costa (90+3).

17.06.2015, 44th Copa América, Group Stage
Estadio "Monumental David Arellano", Santiago (Chile); Attendance: 44,008
Referee: Enrique Roberto Osses Zencovich (Chile)
BRAZIL - COLOMBIA 0-1(0-1)
BRA: Jéfferson, Daniel Alves, Thiago Silva, Miranda, Filipe Luís, Fernandinho, Elias (76.Diego Tardelli), Willian (69.Douglas Costa), Fred III (46.Philippe Coutinho), Roberto Firmino, Neymar (Cap). Trainer: Carlos Caetano Bledorn Verri „Dunga".
Sent off: Neymar (90+4).

21.06.2015, 44th Copa América, Group Stage
Estadio "Monumental David Arellano", Santiago (Chile); Attendance: 33,284
Referee: Enrique Patricio Cáceres Villafañe (Paraguay)
BRAZIL - VENEZUELA 2-1(1-0)
BRA: Jéfferson, Daniel Alves, Thiago Silva, Miranda (Cap), Filipe Luís, Fernandinho, Elias, Willian, Philippe Coutinho (67.Diego Tardelli), Roberto Firmino (67.David Luiz), Robinho (76.Marquinhos III). Trainer: Carlos Caetano Bledorn Verri „Dunga".
Goals: Thiago Silva (9), Roberto Firmino (52).

27.06.2015, 44th Copa América, Quarter-Finals
Estadio Municipal „Alcaldesa Ester Roa Rebolledo", Concepción (Chile); Attendance: 29,276
Referee: Andrés Cunha (Uruguay)
BRAZIL - PARAGUAY 1-1(1-0,1-1); 3-4 on penalties
BRA: Jéfferson, Daniel Alves, Thiago Silva, Miranda (Cap), Filipe Luís, Elias, Fernandinho, Willian (60.Douglas Costa), Philippe Coutinho, Robinho (87.Everton Ribeiro), Roberto Firmino (69.Diego Tardelli). Trainer: Carlos Caetano Bledorn Verri „Dunga".
Goal: Robinho (14).
Penalties: Fernandinho, Everton Ribeiro (missed), Miranda, Douglas Costa (missed), Philippe Coutinho.

NATIONAL TEAM PLAYERS 2014/2015			
Name	**DOB**	**Caps**	**Goals**
[Club 2014/2015]			

(Caps and goals at 05.07.2015)

Goalkeepers

DIEGO ALVES Carreira [2014: Valencia CF (ESP)]	24.06.1985	**9**	**0**
JÉFFERSON de Oliveira Galvão [2014/2015: Botafogo de FR Rio de Janeiro]	02.01.1983	**21**	**0**

Defenders

DANIEL ALVES da Silva [2014/2015: FC Barcelona (ESP)]	06.05.1983	**83**	**6**
Danilo Luiz da Silva „DANILO I" [2014/2015: FC do Porto (POR)]	15.07.1991	**14**	**0**
DAVID LUIZ Moreira Marinho [2014/2015: Paris Saint-Germain FC (FRA)]	22.04.1987	**51**	**3**
Fábio Henrique Tavares "FABINHO" [2014/2015: AS Monaco FC (FRA)]	23.10.1993	**2**	**0**
FILIPE LUÍS Kasmirski [2014/2015: Chelsea FC London (ENG)]	09.08.1985	**18**	**0**
Carlos Gilberto Nascimento Silva "GIL II" [2014: SC Corinthians Paulista São Paulo]	12.06.1987	**3**	**0**
MAICON Douglas Sisenando [2014/2015: AS Roma (ITA)]	26.07.1981	**76**	**7**
MARCELO Vieira da Silva Júnior [2014/2015: Real Madrid CF (ESP)]	12.05.1988	**39**	**4**
MÁRIO Figueira FERNANDES [2014/2015: CSKA Moskva (RUS)]	19.09.1990	**1**	**0**
Marcos Aoás Corrêa „MARQUINHOS III" [2014/2015: Paris Saint-Germain FC (FRA)]	14.05.1994	**6**	**0**
João MIRANDA de Souza Filho [2014/2015: Clube Atlético de Madrid (ESP)]	07.09.1984	**21**	**0**
THIAGO Emiliano da SILVA [2014/2015: Paris Saint-Germain FC (FRA)]	22.09.1984	**59**	**4**

Midfielders

Carlos Henrique CASEMIRO [2014/2015: FC do Porto (POR)]	23.02.1992	**9**	**0**
DOUGLAS COSTA de Souza [2014/2015: FK Shakhtar Donetsk (UKR)]	14.09.1990	**9**	**1**
ELIAS Mendes Trindade [2014/2015: SC Corinthians Paulista São Paulo]	16.05.1985	**25**	**0**
EVERTON Augusto de Barros RIBEIRO [2014: Cruzeiro EC Belo Horizonte; 02.2015-> Al Ahli Dubai Club (UAE)]	10.04.1989	**6**	**0**
FELIPE ANDERSON Pereira Gomes [2014/2015: SS Lazio Roma (ITA)]	15.04.1993	**1**	**0**
Fernando Luiz Rosa „FERNANDINHO“ [2014/2015: Manchester City FC (ENG)]	04.05.1985	**24**	**2**
Frederico Rodrigues de Paula Santos “FRED III” [2014/2015: FK Shakhtar Donetsk (UKR)]	05.03.1993	**6**	**0**
Ricardo Izecson dos Santos Leite “KAKÁ” [2014: São Paulo FC]	22.04.1982	**89**	**29**
LUIZ GUSTAVO Dias [2014/2015: VfL Wolfsburg (GER)]	23.07.1987	**32**	**2**
OSCAR dos Santos Emboaba Júnior [2014/2015: Chelsea FC London (ENG)]	09.09.1991	**45**	**12**
PHILIPPE COUTINHO Correia [2014/2015: Liverpool FC (ENG)]	12.06.1992	**11**	**1**
RICARDO GOULART Pereira [2014: Cruzeiro EC Belo Horizonte]	05.06.1991	**1**	**0**
ROBERTO FIRMINO Barbosa de Oliveira [2014/2015: 1899 Hoffenheim (GER)]	02.10.1991	**10**	**4**
Josef de Souza Dias „SOUZA III“ [2014: São Paulo FC]	11.02.1989	**3**	**0**
WILLIAN Borges da Silva [2014/2015: Chelsea FC London (ENG)]	09.08.1988	**26**	**4**

Forwards

DIEGO TARDELLI Martins [2014: Clube Atlético Mineiro Belo Horizonte; 17.01.2015-> Shandong Luneng Taishan FC (CHN)]	10.05.1985	**14**	**3**
NEYMAR da Silva Santos Júnior [2014/2015: FC Barcelona (ESP)]	05.02.1992	**65**	**44**
Robson de Souza “ROBINHO” [2014/2015: Santos FC]	25.01.1984	**99**	**28**

National coaches

Carlos Caetano Bledorn Verri "DUNGA"	31.10.1963	14 M; 12 W; 1 D; 1 L; 26-6
[also national coach between 16.08.2006 – 02.07.2010; Complete records: 73 M; 53 W; 13 D; 7 L; 149-47]		

CHILE

The Country:
República de Chile (Republic of Chile)
Capital: Santiago
Surface: 756,950 km²
Inhabitants: 18,006,407 [2015 estimate)
Time: UTC -4

The FA:
Federación de Fútbol de Chile
Avenida Quilín No. 5635 - Comuna Peñalolén, Casilla No. 3733 Central de Casillas, Santiago
Year of Formation: 1895
Member of FIFA since: 1913
Member of CONMEBOL since: 1916
Internet: www.anfp.cl

NATIONAL TEAM RECORDS	
First international match:	27.05.1910, Buenos Aires: Argentina – Chile 3-1
Most international caps:	Claudio Andrés BRAVO Muñoz - 95 caps (since 2004)
Most international goals:	José Marcelo Salas Melinao - 37 goals / 71 caps (1994-2007)

OLYMPIC GAMES 1900-2012
1952, 1984, 2000 (3rd Place)

COPA AMÉRICA	
1916	4th Place
1917	4th Place
1919	4th Place
1920	4th Place
1921	Withdrew
1922	5th Place
1923	Withdrew
1924	4th Place
1925	Withdrew
1926	3rd Place
1927	Withdrew
1929	Withdrew
1935	4th Place
1937	5th Place
1939	4th Place
1941	3rd Place
1942	6th Place
1945	3rd Place
1946	5th Place
1947	4th Place
1949	5th Place
1953	4th Place
1955	Runners-up
1956	Runners-up
1957	6th Place
1959	5th Place
1959E	Withdrew
1963	Withdrew
1967	3rd Place
1975	Round 1
1979	Runners-up
1983	Round 1
1987	Runners-up
1989	Round 1
1991	3rd Place
1993	Round 1
1995	Round 1
1997	Round 1
1999	4th Place
2001	Quarter-Finals
2004	Round 1
2007	Quarter-Finals
2011	Quarter-Finals
2015	**Winners**

FIFA WORLD CUP	
1930	Final Tournament (Group Stage)
1934	Withdrew
1938	Withdrew
1950	Final Tournament (Group Stage)
1954	Qualifiers
1958	Qualifiers
1962	Final Tournament (3rd Place)
1966	Final Tournament (Group Stage)
1970	Qualifiers
1974	Final Tournament (Group Stage)
1978	Qualifiers
1982	Final Tournament (Group Stage)
1986	Qualifiers
1990	Disqualified by the FIFA
1994	Banned by the FIFA
1998	Final Tournament (2nd Round of 16)
2002	Qualifiers
2006	Qualifiers
2010	Final Tournament (2nd Round of 16)
2014	Final Tournament (2nd Round of 16)

PANAMERICAN GAMES	
1951	3rd Place
1955	Did not enter
1959	Did not enter
1963	3rd Place
1967	Did not enter
1971	Did not enter
1975	Did not enter
1979	Did not enter
1983	Round 1
1987	Runners-up
1991	Did not enter
1995	Quarter-Finals
1999	Did not enter
2003	Did not enter
2007	Did not enter
2011	Did not enter

PANAMERICAN CHAMPIONSHIP	
1952	Runners-up
1956	6th Place
1960	Did not enter

CHILEAN CLUB HONOURS IN SOUTH AMERICAN CLUB COMPETITIONS:

COPA LIBERTADORES 1960-2014
Club Social y Deportivo Colo-Colo Santiago (1991)
COPA SUDAMERICANA 2002-2014
CFP de la Universidad de Chile (2011)
RECOPA SUDAMERICANA 1989-2014
Club Social y Deportivo Colo-Colo Santiago (1992)
COPA CONMEBOL 1992-1999
None
SUPERCUP „JOÃO HAVELANGE“ 1988-1997*
None
COPA MERCOSUR 1998-2001**
None

**Contested betwenn winners of all previous editions of the Copa Libertadores*
***Contested between teams belonging countries from the southern part of South America (Argentina, Brazil, Chile, Paraguay and Uruguay).*

NATIONAL COMPETITIONS
TABLE OF HONOURS

	CHAMPIONS	CUP WINNERS
1933	CD Magallanes Santiago	-
1934	CD Magallanes Santiago	-
1935	CD Magallanes Santiago	-
1936	Audax CS Italiano Santiago*	-
1937	CSD Colo-Colo Santiago	-
1938	CD Magallanes Santiago	-
1939	CSD Colo-Colo Santiago	-
1940	CFP de la Universidad de Chile	-
1941	CSD Colo-Colo Santiago	-
1942	CD Santiago Morning	-
1943	Club Unión Española Santiago	-
1944	CSD Colo-Colo Santiago	-
1945	CD Green Cross Santiago	-
1946	Audax CS Italiano Santiago	-
1947	CSD Colo-Colo Santiago	-
1948	Audax CS Italiano Santiago	-
1949	CD Universidad Católica Santiago	-
1950	Everton de Viña del Mar	-
1951	Club Unión Española Santiago	-
1952	Everton de Viña del Mar	-
1953	CSD Colo-Colo Santiago	-
1954	CD Universidad Católica Santiago	-
1955	CD Palestino Santiago	-
1956	CSD Colo-Colo Santiago	-
1957	Audax CS Italiano Santiago	-
1958	CD Santiago Wanderers Valparaíso	CSD Colo-Colo Santiago
1959	CFP de la Universidad de Chile	CD Santiago Wanderers Valparaíso
1960	CSD Colo-Colo Santiago	Club de Deportes La Serena

1961	CD Universidad Católica Santiago	CD Santiago Wanderers Valparaíso
1962	CFP de la Universidad de Chile	CD Luis Cruz Martínez Curicó
1963	CSD Colo-Colo Santiago	*No competition*
1964	CFP de la Universidad de Chile	*No competition*
1965	CFP de la Universidad de Chile	*No competition*
1966	CD Universidad Católica Santiago	*No competition*
1967	CFP de la Universidad de Chile	*No competition*
1968	CD Santiago Wanderers Valparaíso	*No competition*
1969	CFP de la Universidad de Chile	*No competition*
1970	CSD Colo-Colo Santiago	*No competition*
1971	CD Unión San Felipe	*No competition*
1972	CSD Colo-Colo Santiago	*No competition*
1973	Club Unión Española Santiago	*No competition*
1974	CD Huachipato Talcahuano	CSD Colo-Colo Santiago
1975	Club Unión Española Santiago	CD Palestino Santiago
1976	Everton de Viña del Mar	*No competition*
1977	Club Unión Española Santiago	*No competition*
1978	CD Palestino Santiago	CD Palestino Santiago
1979	CSD Colo-Colo Santiago	CFP de la Universidad de Chile
1980	CD Cobreloa Calama	CD Municipal Iquique
1981	CSD Colo-Colo Santiago	CSD Colo-Colo Santiago
1982	CD Cobreloa Calama	CSD Colo-Colo Santiago
1983	CSD Colo-Colo Santiago	CD Universidad Católica Santiago
1984	CD Universidad Católica Santiago	Everton de Viña del Mar
1985	CD Cobreloa Calama	CSD Colo-Colo Santiago
1986	CSD Colo-Colo Santiago	CD Cobreloa Calama
1987	CD Universidad Católica Santiago	CD Cobresal El Salvador
1988	CD Cobreloa Calama	CSD Colo-Colo Santiago
1989	CSD Colo-Colo Santiago	CSD Colo-Colo Santiago
1990	CSD Colo-Colo Santiago	CSD Colo-Colo Santiago
1991	CSD Colo-Colo Santiago	CD Universidad Católica Santiago
1992	CD Cobreloa Calama	Club Unión Española Santiago
1993	CSD Colo-Colo Santiago	Club Unión Española Santiago
1994	CFP de la Universidad de Chile	CSD Colo-Colo Santiago
1995	CFP de la Universidad de Chile	CD Universidad Católica Santiago
1996	CSD Colo-Colo Santiago	CSD Colo-Colo Santiago
1997	Ape: CD Universidad Católica Santiago	*No competition*
	Cla: CSD Colo-Colo Santiago	
1998	CSD Colo-Colo Santiago	CFP de la Universidad de Chile
1999	CFP de la Universidad de Chile	*No competition*
2000	CFP de la Universidad de Chile	CFP de la Universidad de Chile
2001	CD Santiago Wanderers Valparaíso	*No competition*
2002	Ape: CD Universidad Católica Santiago	*No competition*
	Cla: CSD Colo-Colo Santiago	
2003	Ape: CD Cobreloa Calama	*No competition*
	Cla: CD Cobreloa Calama	
2004	Ape: CFP de la Universidad de Chile	*No competition*
	Cla: CD Cobreloa Calama	
2005	Ape: Club Unión Española Santiago	*No competition*
	Cla: CD Universidad Católica Santiago	
2006	Ape: CSD Colo-Colo Santiago	*No competition*
	Cla: CSD Colo-Colo Santiago	

2007	Ape:	CSD Colo-Colo Santiago	*No competition*
	Cla:	CSD Colo-Colo Santiago	
2008	Ape:	Everton de Viña del Mar	Universidad de Concepción
	Cla:	CSD Colo-Colo Santiago	
2009	Ape:	CFP de la Universidad de Chile	CD Unión San Felipe
	Cla:	CSD Colo-Colo Santiago	
2010	CD Universidad Católica Santiago		CD Municipal Iquique
2011	Ape:	CFP de la Universidad de Chile	CD Universidad Católica Santiago
	Cla:	CFP de la Universidad de Chile	
2012	Ape:	CFP de la Universidad de Chile	CFP de la Universidad de Chile (2012/2013)
	Cla:	CD Huachipato Talcahuano	
2013	Club Unión Española Santiago		-
2013/2014	Ape:	CD O'Higgins Rancagua	CD Iquique
	Cla:	CSD Colo-Colo Santiago	
2014/2015	Ape:	Club Universidad de Chile	CD Universidad de Concepción
	Cla:	CD Cobresal El Salvador	

**became in January 2007 Audax CS Italiano La Florida.*

	BEST GOALSCORERS	
1933	Luis Carvallo (CSD Colo-Colo Santiago)	9
1934	Carlos Giudice (Audax CS Italiano Santiago)	19
1935	Aurelio Domínguez (CSD Colo-Colo Santiago) Guillermo Ogaz (CD Magallanes Santiago)	12
1936	Hernán Bolaños (CRC, Audax CS Italiano Santiago)	14
1937	Hernán Bolaños (CRC, Audax CS Italiano Santiago)	16
1938	Gustavo Pizarro (Badminton FC Santiago)	17
1939	Alfonso Domínguez (CSD Colo-Colo Santiago)	32
1940	Victor Alonso (CFP de la Universidad de Chile Santiago) Pedro Valenzuela (CD Magallanes Santiago)	20
1941	José Profetta (ARG, Santiago National FC)	19
1942	Domingo Romo (CD Santiago Morning)	16
1943	Luis Machuca (Club Unión Española Santiago) Victor Mancilla (CD Universidad Católica Santiago)	17
1944	Juan Alcantara (CSD Colo-Colo Santiago) Alfonso Domínguez (Audax CS Italiano Santiago)	19
1945	Ubaldo Cruche (URU, CFP de la Universidad de Chile Santiago) Hugo Giorgi (Audax CS Italiano Santiago) Juan Zárate (ARG, CD Green Cross Santiago)	17
1946	Ubaldo Cruche (URU, CFP de la Universidad de Chile Santiago)	25
1947	Apolonides Vera (Santiago National FC)	17
1948	Juan Zárate (ARG, Audax CS Italiano Santiago)	22
1949	Mario Lorca (Club Unión Española Santiago)	20
1950	Félix Díaz (ARG, CD Green Cross Santiago)	21
1951	Rubén Aguilera (CD Santiago Morning) Carlos Tello (Audax CS Italiano Santiago)	21
1952	René Meléndez (Everton de Viña del Mar)	30
1953	Jorge Robledo Oliver (CSD Colo-Colo Santiago)	26
1954	Jorge Robledo Oliver (CSD Colo-Colo Santiago)	25
1955	Nicolas Moreno (ARG, CD Green Cross Santiago)	27
1956	Guillermo Villarroel (CD O'Higgins Rancagua)	19
1957	Gustavo Albella (ARG, CD Green Cross Santiago)	27

1958	Gustavo Albella (ARG, CD Green Cross Santiago) Carlos Verdejo (Club de Deportes La Serena)	23
1959	José Benito Rios (CD O'Higgins Rancagua)	
1960	Juan Falcón (ARG, CD Palestino Santiago)	21
1961	Carlos Campos Sánchez (CFP de la Universidad de Chile Santiago) Honorino Landa Vera (Club Unión Española Santiago)	24
1962	Carlos Campos Sánchez (CFP de la Universidad de Chile Santiago)	34
1963	Luis Hernán Álvarez (CSD Colo-Colo Santiago)	37
1964	Daniel Escudero (Everton de Viña del Mar)	25
1965	Héctor Scandolli (CSD Rangers Talca)	25
1966	Felipe Bracamonte (ARG, CD Unión San Felipe) Carlos Campos Sánchez (CFP de la Universidad de Chile Santiago)	21
1967	Eladio Zarate (PAR, Club Unión Española Santiago)	28
1968	Carlos Enzo Reinoso Valdenegro (Audax CS Italiano Santiago)	21
1969	Eladio Zarate (PAR, Club Unión Española Santiago)	22
1970	Osvaldo Castro Pelayo (Universidad de Concepción)	36
1971	Eladio Zarate (PAR, CFP de la Universidad de Chile Santiago)	25
1972	Fernando Espinoza (CD Magallanes Santiago)	25
1973	Guillermo Yávar (Club Unión Española Santiago)	21
1974	Julio Crisosto (CSD Colo-Colo Santiago)	28
1975	Víctor Pizarro (CD Santiago Morning)	27
1976	Oscar Fabbiani (ARG, CD Palestino Santiago)	23
1977	Oscar Fabbiani (ARG, CD Palestino Santiago)	34
1978	Oscar Fabbiani (ARG, CD Palestino Santiago)	35
1979	Carlos Humberto Caszely Garrido (CSD Colo-Colo Santiago)	20
1980	Carlos Humberto Caszely Garrido (CSD Colo-Colo Santiago)	26
1981	Víctor Cabrera (CD San Luis de Quillota) Carlos Humberto Caszely Garrido (CSD Colo-Colo Santiago) Luis Marcoleta (CD Magallanes Santiago)	20
1982	Jorge Luis Siviero (URU, CD Cobreloa Calama)	18
1983	Washington Oliveira (URU, CD Cobreloa Calama)	29
1984	Víctor Cabrera (CD Regional Atacama Copiapó)	18
1985	Ivo Alexis Basay Hatibovic (CD Magallanes Santiago)	19
1986	Sergio Salgado (CD Cobresal El Salvador)	18
1987	Osvaldo Heriberto Hurtado Galeguillo (CD Universidad Católica Santiago)	21
1988	Gustavo De Luca (ARG, Club de Deportes La Serena) Juan José Oré (PER, CD Municipal Iquique)	18
1989	Rubén Martínez (CD Cobresal El Salvador)	25
1990	Rubén Martínez (CSD Colo-Colo Santiago)	22
1991	Rubén Martínez (CSD Colo-Colo Santiago)	23
1992	Aníbal Segundo González Espinoza (CSD Colo-Colo Santiago)	24
1993	Marco Antonio Figueroa Montero (CD Cobreloa Calama)	18
1994	Alberto Federico Acosta (ARG, CD Universidad Católica Santiago)	33
1995	Gabriel Esteban Caballero Schiker (ARG, Club Deportes Antofagasta) Aníbal Segundo González Espinoza (CD Palestino Santiago)	18
1996	Mario Véner (CD Santiago Wanderers Valparaíso)	30
1997	Ape: David Bisconti (ARG, CD Universidad Católica Santiago)	15
	Cla: Richard Martín Báez Fernández (PAR, Universidad de Chile Santiago) Rubén Vallejos (Club de Deportes Puerto Montt)	10
1998	Pedro Alejandro González Vera (CFP de la Universidad de Chile Santiago)	23
1999	Mario Núñez (CD O'Higgins Rancagua)	34
2000	Pedro Alejandro González Vera (CFP de la Universidad de Chile Santiago)	26

2001	Héctor Santiago Tapia Urdile (CSD Colo-Colo Santiago)		24
2002	Ape:	Sebastián Ignacio González Valdés (CSD Colo-Colo Santiago)	18
	Cla:	Manuel Alejandro Neira Díaz (CSD Colo-Colo Santiago)	14
2003	Ape:	Salvador Cabañas Ortega (PAR, Audax CS Italiano Santiago)	18
	Cla:	Gustavo Javier Biscayzacú Perea (URU, Club Unión Española Santiago)	21
2004	Ape:	Patricio Sebastián Galaz Sepúlveda (CD Cobreloa Calama)	23
	Cla:	Patricio Sebastián Galaz Sepúlveda (CD Cobreloa Calama)	19
2005	Ape:	Joel Estay Silva (Everton de Viña del Mar) Álvaro Gustavo Sarabia Navarro (CD Huachipato Talcahuano) Héctor Raúl Mancilla (CD Cobresal El Salvador)	13
	Cla:	Cristian Antonio Montecinos González (CD Concepción) Gonzalo Antonio Fierro Caniullán (CSD Colo-Colo Santiago) César Díaz (CD Cobresal El Salvador)	13
2006	Ape:	Humberto Andrés Suazo Pontivo (CSD Colo-Colo Santiago)	19
	Cla:	Leonardo Esteban Monje Valenzuela (Universidad de Concepción)	17
2007	Ape:	Humberto Andrés Suazo Pontivo (CSD Colo-Colo Santiago)	18
	Cla:	Carlos Andrés Villanueva Roland (Audax CS Italiano La Florida)	20
2008	Ape:	Lucas Ramón Barrios Arioli (ARG, CSD Colo-Colo Santiago)	19
	Cla:	Lucas Ramón Barrios Arioli (ARG, CSD Colo-Colo Santiago)	18
2009	Ape:	Esteban Efraín Paredes Quintanilla (CD Santiago Morning)	17
	Cla:	Diego Gabriel Rivarola Popón (ARG, CD Santiago Morning)	13
2010	Milovan Petar Mirošević Albornoz (CD Universidad Católica Santiago)		19
2011	Ape:	Matías Héctor Sebastián Urbano (ARG, CD Unión San Felipe)	11
	Cla:	Esteban Efraín Paredes Quintanilla (CSD Colo-Colo Santiago)	14
2012	Ape:	Enzo Hernán Gutiérrez Lencinas (CD O'Higgins Rancagua) Emanuel Herrera (Club Unión Española Santiago) Sebastián Andrés Ubilla Cambón (CD Santiago Wanderers Valparaíso)	11
	Cla:	Sebastián Oscar Jaime (ARG, Club Unión Española Santiago) Carlos Andrés Muñoz Rojas (CSD Colo-Colo Santiago) Jorge Sebastián Sáez (ARG, Audax CS Italiano La Florida)	12
2013	Tra:	Javier Aníbal Elizondo (ARG, CD Antofagasta) Jorge Sebastián Sáez (ARG, Audax CS Italiano La Florida)	14
2013/2014	Ape:	Claudio Luciano Vázquez (ARG, Deportivo Ñublense Chillán)	11
	Cla:	Esteban Efraín Paredes Quintanilla (CSD Colo-Colo Santiago)	16
2014/2015	Ape:	Esteban Efraín Paredes Quintanilla (CSD Colo-Colo Santiago)	12
	Cla:	Jean Paul Jesús Pineda Cortés (CD Unión La Calera) Esteban Efraín Paredes Quintanilla (CSD Colo-Colo Santiago)	11

NATIONAL CHAMPIONSHIP
Campeonato Nacional de Primera División de la Asociación Nacional de Fútbol Profesional 2014/2015
Campeonato Nacional "Scotiabank"

Torneo Apertura 2014

Results

Round 1 [19-20.07.2014]
CD San Marcos - Colo-Colo 1-1(1-0)
Universid. Católica - CD Antofagasta 1-0(1-0)
Santiago Wanderers - AC Barnechea 3-0(2-0)
Audax Italiano - Unión Española 0-1(0-1)
CD Palestino - CD Cobreloa 1-2(0-2)
Unión La Calera - O'Higgins 1-2(0-1)
CD Huachipato - Deportivo Ñublense 3-0(2-0)
CD Iquique - Universidad Concepción 1-1(0-1)
Universidad de Chile - CD Cobresal 3-1(3-0)

Round 2 [25-27.07.2014]
CD Antofagasta - Audax Italiano 0-0
Univ. Concepción - CD Huachipato 0-1(0-0)
O'Higgins - Universidad de Chile 1-3(0-1)
AC Barnechea - Unión La Calera 0-3(0-0)
Unión Española – Universid. Católica 1-0(0-0)
Deportivo Ñublense - CD San Marcos 2-1(0-0)
CD Cobreloa - Santiago Wanderers 1-2(1-1)
CD Cobresal - CD Palestino 0-1(0-0)
Colo-Colo - CD Iquique 2-0(0-0)

Round 3 [01-03.08.2014]
Unión La Calera - CD Antofagasta 3-1(2-1)
CD Palestino - Deportivo Ñublense 2-2(2-0)
Univ. de Chile - Santiago Wanderers 3-2(2-1)
Universidad Católica - CD Cobreloa 5-1(2-1)
O'Higgins - Universidad Concepción 2-2(2-0)
CD San Marcos - Unión Española 2-1(2-1)
CD Huachipato - Colo-Colo 1-3(0-1)
CD Iquique - CD Cobresal 2-2(1-1)
Audax Italiano - AC Barnechea 3-1(3-0)

Round 4 [08-10.08.2014]
Unión Española - Unión La Calera 2-0(0-0)
CD Palestino - Audax Italiano 1-0(0-0)
Deportivo Ñublense – Univ. Católica 2-1(1-0)
CD Antofagasta – Universid. de Chile 0-3(0-1)
Santiago Wanderers - CD Iquique 2-0(1-0)
Colo-Colo - O'Higgins 2-3(2-1)
CD Cobreloa – Universid. Concepción 0-2(0-0)
CD Cobresal - CD Huachipato 2-2(1-0)
AC Barnechea - CD San Marcos 1-0(0-0)

Round 5 [15-17.08.2014]
CD Iquique - Universidad de Chile 2-2(1-1)
CD Huachipato - CD Palestino 2-0(1-0)
Audax Italiano - CD Cobresal 2-2(2-0)
Univers. Concepción - AC Barnechea 3-2(1-2)
Unión La Calera - Deportivo Ñublense 3-2(1-1)
O'Higgins - CD Cobreloa 4-1(3-1)
CD San Marcos - CD Antofagasta 1-0(0-0)
Colo-Colo - Unión Española 2-0(0-0)
Univ. Católica - Santiago Wanderers 0-1(0-1)

Round 6 [22-24.08.2014]
Santiago Wanderers - Audax Italiano 2-2(1-1)
Universidad de Chile - CD Huachipato 2-1(2-0)
Deportivo Ñublense - O'Higgins 1-1(1-0)
Unión Española - Universidad Concepción 0-0
CD Antofagasta - CD Iquique 1-0(0-0)
AC Barnechea - Colo-Colo 0-3(0-1)
CD Cobresal - CD San Marcos 0-0
CD Cobreloa - Unión La Calera 1-1(1-0)
CD Palestino - Universidad Católica 2-1(0-1)

Round 7 [28-31.08.2014]
Unión Española – Universid. de Chile 0-1(0-0)
CD San Marcos - CD Palestino 1-0(0-0)
Colo-Colo - CD Antofagasta 4-0(3-0)
CD Huachipato - Santiago Wanderers 4-0(3-0)
Universidad Católica - O'Higgins 2-2(1-1)
Univ. Concepción - Unión La Calera 1-1(1-0)
CD Cobresal - CD Cobreloa 2-1(1-1)
CD Iquique - AC Barnechea 1-0(0-0)
Audax Italiano - Deportivo Ñublense 0-1(0-1)

Round 8 [12-14.09.2014]
Unión La Calera - CD Iquique 1-1(0-0)
Santiago Wanderers - CD Cobresal 4-1(1-0)
Universid. Católica - CD San Marcos 2-0(0-0)
O'Higgins - Unión Española 1-3(1-1)
CD Palestino - Colo-Colo 1-3(0-2)
CD Cobreloa - Audax Italiano 0-1(0-1)
Deportivo Ñublense - AC Barnechea 0-1(0-0)
CD Antofagasta - CD Huachipato 2-2(0-1)
Univers. de Chile – Univ. Concepción 1-0(1-0)

Round 9 [27-28.09.2014]
Un. Concepción - Santiago Wanderers 1-3(0-0)
Audax Italiano - Universidad de Chile 2-3(1-2)
AC Barnechea - O'Higgins 1-2(0-0)
Unión Española - CD Antofagasta 1-0(0-0)
CD San Marcos - CD Cobreloa 0-1(0-1)
CD Cobresal - Universidad Católica 0-1(0-1)
CD Iquique - CD Palestino 2-4(0-1)
Colo-Colo - Deportivo Ñublense 0-0
Huachipato - Unión La Calera 0-4(0-1) [11.10.]

Round 10 [03-05.10.2014]
Audax Italiano - CD Iquique 2-1(1-1)
Unión La Calera - CD Cobresal 2-1(0-1)
O'Higgins - CD Palestino 0-1(0-1)
Universidad Católica - CD Huachipato 0-3(0-1)
Universidad Concepción - Colo-Colo 0-1(0-0)
CD Cobreloa - AC Barnechea 1-2(0-1)
CD Antofagasta - Deportivo Ñublense 2-0(1-0)
Universid. de Chile - CD San Marcos 2-0(0-0)
S. Wanderers - Unión Españ. 1-0(0-0) [12.10.]

Round 11 [18-20.10.2014]
CD Palestino - Santiago Wanderers 0-1(0-0)
Deportivo Ñublense – Un. Concepción 2-1(1-0)
AC Barnechea - Universidad Católica 1-0(1-0)
CD Iquique - O'Higgins 0-0
CD San Marcos - Unión La Calera 2-1(1-0)
Colo-Colo - Universidad de Chile 2-0(0-0)
CD Cobresal - CD Antofagasta 1-1(0-0)
Unión Española - CD Cobreloa 2-1(0-0)
CD Huachipato - Audax Italiano 1-2(0-1)

Round 12 [24-26.10.2014]
Deportivo Ñublense - Unión Española 3-1(1-1)
Universid. Concepción - CD Cobresal 3-2(1-1)
Santiago Wanderers - CD San Marcos 2-1(2-0)
Universidad Católica - Audax Italiano 2-1(1-1)
O'Higgins - CD Huachipato 3-0(2-0)
Unión La Calera - Colo-Colo 0-2(0-1)
CD Cobreloa - CD Iquique 3-3(2-2)
CD Antofagasta - AC Barnechea 1-1(0-0)
Universidad de Chile - CD Palestino 2-1(2-0)

Round 13 [31.10.-02.11.2014]
Santiago Wanderers - O'Higgins 1-0(0-0)
Universidad de Chile – Univ. Católica 3-0(2-0)
CD Palestino - CD Antofagasta 3-1(2-0)
CD Huachipato - CD Cobreloa 2-0(0-0)
AC Barnechea - Unión Española 1-0(1-0)
CD San Marcos - Universidad Concepción 0-0
CD Cobresal - Colo-Colo 0-1(0-0)
CD Iquique - Deportivo Ñublense 1-1(0-1)
Audax Italiano - Unión La Calera 2-2(2-1)

Round 14 [07-09.11.2014]
O'Higgins - CD San Marcos 3-1(1-1)
Unión Española - CD Iquique 2-5(2-1)
CD Cobreloa - Universidad de Chile 0-4(0-1)
Unión La Calera – Univ. Católica 1-0(1-0)
AC Barnechea - CD Huachipato 3-0(2-0)
CD Antofagasta - Santiago Wanderers 0-2(0-0)
Universid. Concepción - CD Palestino 0-1(0-1)
Deportivo Ñublense - CD Cobresal 2-3(2-2)
Colo-Colo - Audax Italiano 2-1(1-0)

Round 15 [21-23.11.2014]
CD Antofagasta - CD Cobreloa 2-1(1-1)
CD Huachipato - Unión Española 1-3(1-3)
Universidad de Chile - AC Barnechea 1-1(1-0)
CD San Marcos - CD Iquique 1-0 Wert.
Sant. Wanderers - Deportivo Ñublense 2-1(1-0)
Universidad Católica - Colo-Colo 1-2(0-1)
CD Palestino - Unión La Calera 3-2(2-2)
CD Cobresal - O'Higgins 3-1(0-0)
Audax Italiano – Univ. Concepción 4-1(2-0)

Round 16 [28.11.-01.12.2014]
O'Higgins - Audax Italiano 1-1(1-0)
CD Iquique - Universidad Católica 3-2(2-0)
CD San Marcos - CD Huachipato 1-2(0-2)
Univ. Concepción - CD Antofagasta 1-0(0-0)
Deportivo Ñublense – Univ. de Chile 0-3(0-1)
Colo-Colo - CD Cobreloa 4-1(3-0)
Unión La Calera - Santiago Wanderers 0-1(0-0)
AC Barnechea - CD Cobresal 1-3(1-1)
Unión Española - CD Palestino 2-5(2-2)

Round 17 [05-07.12.2014]
CD Cobreloa - Deportivo Ñublense 4-2(1-1)
Univ. Católica – Univers. Concepción 2-2(2-0)
Santiago Wanderers - Colo-Colo 2-0(0-0)
Universid. de Chile - Unión La Calera 1-0(0-0)
CD Huachipato - CD Iquique 5-0(3-0)
CD Cobresal - Unión Española 1-3(1-1)
CD Palestino - AC Barnechea 2-0(0-0)
CD Antofagasta - O'Higgins 2-1(0-1)
Audax Italiano - CD San Marcos 3-0(2-0)

Final Standings

1.	**Club Universidad de Chile Santiago**	17	14	2	1	37	-	13	44
2.	CD Santiago Wanderers Valparaíso	17	14	1	2	31	-	14	43
3.	CSD Colo-Colo Santiago	17	13	2	2	34	-	11	41
4.	CD Palestino Santiago	17	10	1	6	28	-	21	31
5.	CD Huachipato Talcahuano	17	8	2	7	30	-	25	26
6.	Club Unión Española Santiago	17	8	1	8	22	-	24	25
7.	Audax CS Italiano La Florida	17	6	5	6	26	-	21	23
8.	CD O'Higgins Rancagua	17	6	5	6	27	-	25	23
9.	CD Unión La Calera	17	6	4	7	25	-	22	22
10.	Athletic Club Barnechea	17	6	2	9	16	-	26	20
11.	Deportivo Ñublense Chillán	17	5	4	8	21	-	29	19
12.	CD Universidad de Concepción	17	4	6	7	18	-	23	18
13.	CD San Marcos de Arica	17	5	3	9	12	-	21	18
14.	CD Universidad Católica Santiago	17	5	2	10	20	-	25	17
15.	CD Cobresal El Salvador	17	4	5	8	24	-	30	17
16.	CD Iquique	17	3	7	7	22	-	31	16
17.	CD Antofagasta	17	4	4	9	13	-	25	16
18.	CD Cobreloa Calama	17	3	2	12	19	-	39	11

As Apertura champions, Club Universidad de Chile Santiago were qualified for the 2015 Copa Libertadores.

Apertura Liguilla Pre-Libertadores 2014

Semi-Finals (10-14.12.2014)

CD Huachipato Talcahuano - CD Palestino Santiago	1-3(0-2)	0-3(0-1)
Club Unión Española Santiago - CD Santiago Wanderers Valparaíso	2-4(1-1)	3-2(1-1)

Liguilla Finals (17-21.12.2014)

CD Palestino Santiago - CD Santiago Wanderers Valparaíso	3-1(2-0)	6-1(3-1)

CD Palestino Santiago qualified for the 2015 Copa Libertadores.
CD Santiago Wanderers Valparaíso qualified for the 2015 Copa Sudamericana.

<u>Apertura 2014 - Top goalscorers*</u>:

12 goals:	**Esteban Efraín Paredes Quintanilla**	**(CSD Colo-Colo Santiago)**
11 goals:	Roberto Carlos Gutiérrez Gamboa	(CD Santiago Wanderers Valparaíso)
	Patricio Rodolfo Rubio Pulgar	(Club Universidad de Chile Santiago)

**only regular season, no Liguilla goals included!*

Torneo Clausura 2015

Results

Round 1 [02-07.01.2015]
O'Higgins - Unión La Calera 2-1(1-0)
CD Cobresal - Universidad de Chile 1-1(0-0)
Deportivo Ñublense - CD Huachipato 3-1(1-1)
CD Antofagasta - Univ. Católica 2-3(0-2)
Univ. Concepción - CD Iquique 3-1(3-0)
Colo-Colo - CD San Marcos 0-1(0-0)
Unión Española - Audax Italiano 0-2(0-1)
CD Cobreloa - CD Palestino 3-0(1-0)
AC Barnechea - Santiago Wanderers 0-2(0-0)

Round 2 [09-11.01.2015]
CD Huachipato - Univ. Concepción 1-2(0-2)
Audax Italiano - CD Antofagasta 1-1(0-1)
Universidad de Chile - O'Higgins 3-0(1-0)
Unión La Calera - AC Barnechea 3-0(1-0)
CD San Marcos - Deportivo Ñublense 0-0
CD Iquique - Colo-Colo 3-2(0-0)
CD Palestino - CD Cobresal 0-1(0-0)
Univ. Católica - Unión Española 0-0
Santiago Wanderers - CD Cobreloa 0-1(0-1)

Round 3 [16-19.01.2015]
CD Cobreloa - Univ. Católica 1-3(0-1)
Univ. Concepción - O'Higgins 2-1(0-1)
Santiago Wanderers – Univ. de Chile 3-2(1-1)
Unión Española - CD San Marcos 1-2(0-2)
CD Cobresal - CD Iquique 4-2(4-0)
Deportivo Ñublense - CD Palestino 0-3(0-2)
CD Antofagasta - Unión La Calera 3-4(2-2)
Colo-Colo - CD Huachipato 2-2(1-2)
AC Barnechea - Audax Italiano 0-0

Round 4 [30.01.-01.02.2015]
CD Huachipato - CD Cobresal 2-1(1-0)
CD Iquique - Santiago Wanderers 2-1(1-1)
Unión La Calera - Unión Española 2-0(0-0)
Univ. Concepción - CD Cobreloa 3-2(2-2)
Universid. de Chile - CD Antofagasta 1-3(0-1)
Audax Italiano - CD Palestino 1-2(1-0)
CD San Marcos - AC Barnechea 0-0
O'Higgins - Colo-Colo 0-2(0-0)
Univ. Católica - Deportivo Ñublense 2-1(0-1)

Round 5 [03-05.02.2015]
Universidad de Chile - CD Iquique 2-3(0-0)
AC Barnechea - Univ. Concepción 1-2(1-2)
CD Cobresal - Audax Italiano 3-1(0-0)
CD Antofagasta - CD San Marcos 0-2(0-2)
Unión Española - Colo-Colo 1-3(0-1)
Santiago Wanderers - Univ. Católica 2-0(1-0)
CD Cobreloa - O'Higgins 0-0
Deportivo Ñublense - Unión La Calera 1-2(0-1)
CD Palestino - CD Huachipato 1-1(0-1)[25.03.]

Round 6 [07-09.02.2015]
CD Huachipato - Universidad de Chile 2-2(1-1)
Colo-Colo - AC Barnechea 4-1(3-1)
Audax Italiano - Santiago Wanderers 2-1(0-1)
CD San Marcos - CD Cobresal 1-1(0-0)
Univ. Concepción - Unión Española 1-2(0-1)
CD Iquique - CD Antofagasta 1-2(0-1)
Unión La Calera - CD Cobreloa 0-0
Univ. Católica - CD Palestino 3-2(1-1)
O'Higgins - Deportivo Ñublense 1-0(0-0)

Round 7 [13-15.02.2015]
AC Barnechea - CD Iquique 1-0(1-0)
Universid. de Chile - Unión Española 1-2(1-1)
CD Antofagasta - Colo-Colo 1-2(0-1)
Unión La Calera - Univ. Concepción 2-0(0-0)
CD Cobreloa - CD Cobresal 1-3(1-2)
Deportivo Ñublense - Audax Italiano 1-0(0-0)
O'Higgins - Univ. Católica 1-1(1-0)
CD Palestino - CD San Marcos 0-4(0-2)
Santiago Wanderers - CD Huachipato 0-1(0-0)

Round 8 [20-22.02.2015]
AC Barnechea - Deportivo Ñublense 1-3(0-1)
CD San Marcos - Univ. Católica 3-3(2-1)
CD Huachipato - CD Antofagasta 2-0(0-0)
Unión Española - O'Higgins 1-2(1-0)
Univ. Concepción – Univ. de Chile 1-2(0-1)
CD Cobresal - Santiago Wanderers 1-0(0-0)
Colo-Colo - CD Palestino 1-1(0-0)
Audax Italiano - CD Cobreloa 1-0(0-0)
CD Iquique - Unión La Calera 2-1(0-0)

Round 9 [27.02.-02.03.2015]

Santiago Wanderers - Univ. Concepción 0-0
O'Higgins - AC Barnechea 3-1(0-0)
Univ. Católica - CD Cobresal 2-4(1-1)
CD Palestino - CD Iquique 2-2(2-0)
CD Cobreloa - CD San Marcos 1-0(0-0)
Deportivo Ñublense - Colo-Colo 0-1(0-0)
CD Antofagasta - Unión Española 1-2(1-2)
Unión La Calera - CD Huachipato 0-1(0-1)
Universidad de Chile - Audax Italiano 2-3(0-1)

Round 10 [06-08.03.2015]

Unión Española - Santiago Wanderers 2-2(0-1)
AC Barnechea - CD Cobreloa 0-1(0-1)
CD Palestino - O'Higgins 3-3(1-1)
CD Huachipato - Univ. Católica 3-5(2-2)
CD Iquique - Audax Italiano 3-2(3-2)
CD San Marcos – Universid. de Chile 0-1(0-0)
CD Cobresal - Unión La Calera 1-1(1-0)
Deportivo Ñublense - CD Antofagasta 0-1(0-0)
Colo-Colo - Univ. Concepción 3-0(1-0)

Round 11 [13-15.03.2015]

Un. Concepción - Deportivo Ñublense 2-2(2-1)
O'Higgins - CD Iquique 1-0(0-0)
Universidad de Chile - Colo-Colo 1-2(1-0)
CD Cobreloa - Unión Española 1-1(0-1)
CD Antofagasta - CD Cobresal 2-0(2-0)
Univ. Católica - AC Barnechea 5-0(3-0)
Audax Italiano - CD Huachipato 2-2(1-0)
U. La Calera - CD San Marcos 1-4(1-2)[28.03.]
S. Wanderers - CD Palestino 0-3(0-1) [01.04.]

Round 12 [20-22.03.2015]

Audax Italiano - Univ. Católica 1-1(1-1)
AC Barnechea - CD Antofagasta 1-3(1-1)
Unión Española - Deportivo Ñublense 1-1(0-0)
CD Huachipato - O'Higgins 3-2(1-0)
Colo-Colo - Unión La Calera 1-4(0-2)
CD San Marcos - Santiago Wanderers 3-3(0-0)
CD Iquique - CD Cobreloa 0-0
CD Palestino - Universidad de Chile 1-3(0-2)
CD Cobresal - Univ. Concepción 2-1(0-1)

Round 13 [03-05.04.2015]

Colo-Colo - CD Cobresal 1-2(1-1)
Deportivo Ñublense - CD Iquique 2-0(1-0)
O'Higgins - Santiago Wanderers 1-1(1-0)
CD Antofagasta - CD Palestino 1-2(0-0)
Unión La Calera - Audax Italiano 2-2(1-0)
Unión Española - AC Barnechea 2-1(0-1)
Univ. Católica - Universidad de Chile 2-4(0-1)
CD Cobreloa - CD Huachipato 6-0(1-0)
Univ. Concepción - CD San Marcos 3-2(1-0)

Round 14 [10-12.04.2015]

Univ. Católica - Unión La Calera 4-2(3-2)
CD Palestino - Univ. Concepción 3-2(0-2)
Santiago Wanderers - CD Antofagasta 0-2(0-0)
Universidad de Chile - CD Cobreloa 4-0(2-0)
CD Cobresal - Deportivo Ñublense 1-0(1-0)
CD San Marcos - O'Higgins 0-0
Audax Italiano - Colo-Colo 0-1(0-1)
CD Iquique - Unión Española 0-1(0-1)
CD Huachipato - AC Barnechea 4-1(3-0)

Round 15 [17-19.04.2015]

O'Higgins - CD Cobresal 2-0(1-0)
Colo-Colo - Univ. Católica 0-3(0-3)
CD Cobreloa - CD Antofagasta 3-1(2-0)
Unión Española - CD Huachipato 0-1(0-0)
Dep. Ñublense - Santiago Wanderers 1-1(1-0)
Univ. Concepción - Audax Italiano 2-2(2-0)
CD Iquique - CD San Marcos 4-1(2-1)
AC Barnechea - Universidad de Chile 1-4(1-3)
Unión La Calera - CD Palestino 4-0(2-0)

Round 16 [25-26.04.2015]

CD Palestino - Unión Española 2-3(1-2)
Santiago Wanderers - Unión La Calera 4-2(2-1)
CD Antofagasta - Univ. Concepción 0-1(0-1)
CD Huachipato - CD San Marcos 1-0(1-0)
Audax Italiano - O'Higgins 3-0(0-0)
CD Cobreloa - Colo-Colo 0-4(0-0)
Universidad de Chile – Dep. Ñublense 2-1(1-1)
Univ. Católica - CD Iquique 3-3(3-0)
CD Cobresal - AC Barnechea 3-2(1-2)

Round 17 [30.04.-03.05.2015]

AC Barnechea - CD Palestino 2-1(1-0)
Univ. Concepción - Univ. Católica 2-0(2-0)
Colo-Colo - Santiago Wanderers 3-1(1-1)
CD Iquique - CD Huachipato 1-2(1-1)
Unión Española - CD Cobresal 1-1(0-0)
Unión La Calera – Universid. de Chile 2-1(2-0)
O'Higgins - CD Antofagasta 2-2(1-1)
CD San Marcos - Audax Italiano 3-0(1-0)
Deportivo Ñublense - CD Cobreloa 3-2(1-1)

Final Standings

1.	**CD Cobresal El Salvador**	17	10	4	3	29	-	20	34
2.	CSD Colo-Colo Santiago	17	10	2	5	32	-	21	32
3.	CD Huachipato Talcahuano	17	9	4	4	29	-	28	31
4.	CD Universidad Católica Santiago	17	8	5	4	40	-	31	29
5.	CD Unión La Calera	17	8	3	6	33	-	26	27
6.	CD Universidad de Concepción	17	8	3	6	27	-	26	27
7.	Club Universidad de Chile Santiago	17	8	2	7	36	-	27	26
8.	CD San Marcos de Arica	17	6	6	5	26	-	19	24
9.	CD O'Higgins Rancagua	17	6	6	5	21	-	23	24
10.	Club Unión Española Santiago	17	6	5	6	20	-	23	23
11.	Audax CS Italiano La Florida	17	5	6	6	23	-	24	21
12.	CD Iquique	17	6	3	8	27	-	30	21
13.	CD Antofagasta	17	6	2	9	25	-	27	20
14.	CD Cobreloa Calama*	17	6	4	7	22	-	23	19
15.	Deportivo Ñublense Chillán	17	5	4	8	19	-	21	19
16.	CD Palestino Santiago	17	5	4	8	26	-	34	19
17.	CD Santiago Wanderers Valparaíso	17	4	5	8	21	-	26	17
18.	Athletic Club Barnechea	17	2	2	13	13	-	40	8

**3 points deducted*

As Clausura champions, CD Cobresal El Salvador were qualified for the 2016 Copa Libertadores.

Clausura Liguilla

Semi-Finals (09-14.05.2015)

CD O'Higgins Rancagua - CD Universidad Católica Santiago	2-2(0-1)	1-3(1-1)
CD San Marcos de Arica - CD Unión La Calera	1-1(0-0)	1-1(0-0) 4-2 pen

Liguilla Finals (17-20.05.2015)

CD San Marcos de Arica - CD Universidad Católica Santiago	3-1(2-0)	1-3(0-0) 5-6 pen

CD Universidad Católica Santiago qualified for the 2015 Copa Sudamericana.

Clausura 2015 - Top goalscorers*:

11 goals:	**Jean Paul Jesús Pineda Cortés**	**(CD Unión La Calera)**
	Esteban Efraín Paredes Quintanilla	**(CSD Colo-Colo Santiago)**
9 goals:	Gustavo Javier Canales Bustos	(Club Universidad de Chile Santiago)
	Jorge Matías Donoso Garate	(CD Cobresal El Salvador)
	Ever Milton Cantero Benítez (PAR)	(CD Cobresal El Salvador)

**only regular season, no Liguilla goals included!*

Primera División del Fútbol Profesional Chileno
Aggregate Table 2014/2015

1.	CSD Colo-Colo Santiago	34	23	4	7	66	-	32	73
2.	Club Universidad de Chile Santiago	34	22	4	8	73	-	40	70
3.	CD Santiago Wanderers Valparaíso	34	18	6	10	52	-	40	60
4.	CD Huachipato Talcahuano	34	17	6	11	59	-	53	57
5.	CD Cobresal El Salvador	34	14	9	11	53	-	50	51
6.	CD Palestino Santiago	34	15	5	14	54	-	55	50
7.	CD Unión La Calera	34	14	7	13	58	-	48	49
8.	Club Unión Española Santiago	34	14	6	14	42	-	47	48
9.	CD O'Higgins Rancagua	34	12	11	11	48	-	48	47
10.	CD Universidad Católica Santiago	34	13	7	14	60	-	56	46
11.	CD Universidad de Concepción	34	12	9	13	45	-	49	45
12.	Audax CS Italiano La Florida	34	11	11	12	49	-	45	44
13.	CD San Marcos de Arica	34	11	9	14	38	-	40	42
14.	Deportivo Ñublense Chillán	34	10	8	16	40	-	50	38
15.	CD Iquique	34	9	10	15	49	-	61	37
16.	CD Antofagasta	34	10	6	18	38	-	52	36
17.	CD Cobreloa Calama	34	9	6	19	41	-	62	30
18.	Athletic Club Barnechea	34	8	4	22	29	-	66	28

CD Santiago Wanderers Valparaíso, CD Huachipato Talcahuano and CD Universidad de Concepción (as winner of the Copa Chile 2014/2015) were qualified for the 2015 Copa Sudamericana.

Relegation Table

The team which will be relegated is determined on average points taking into account results of the last two seasons (Apertura & Clausura 2013/2014, Apertura & Clausura 2014/2015).

Pos	Team	Ape & Cla 2013/2014	Ape & Cla 2014/2015	Total		Aver
		P	P	P	M	
1.	CSD Colo-Colo Santiago	66	73	68	139	2,044
2.	CD Universidad Católica Santiago	72	45	68	118	1,735
3.	Club Universidad de Chile Santiago	47	70	68	117	1,720
4.	CD O'Higgins Rancagua	69	47	68	116	1,705
5.	CD Palestino Santiago	53	50	68	103	1,514
6.	CD Santiago Wanderers Valparaíso	40	60	68	100	1,470
7.	Club Unión Española Santiago	50	48	68	98	1,441
8.	CD Cobresal El Salvador	45	51	68	96	1,411
9.	CD Huachipato Talcahuano	38	57	68	95	1,397
10.	CD Universidad de Concepción	49	45	68	94	1,382
11.	CD Iquique	51	37	68	88	1,294
12.	CD Unión La Calera	35	49	68	84	1,235
13.	CD San Marcos de Arica	-	42	34	42	1,235
14.	Audax CS Italiano La Florida	36	44	68	80	1,176
15.	CD Antofagasta	44	36	68	80	1,176
16.	Deportivo Ñublense Chillán (*Relegated*)	41	38	68	79	1,161
17.	CD Cobreloa Calama (*Relegated*)	45	30	68	75	1,102
18.	Athletic Club Barnechea (*Relegated*)	-	28	34	28	0,824

NATIONAL CUP
Copa Chile Final 2014/2015

28.03.2015, Estadio Fiscal, Talca; Attendance: 3,360
Referee: Enrique Roberto Osses Zencovich
CD Universidad de Concepción - CD Palestino Santiago 3-2(2-0)
Concepción: Cristián Fernando Muñoz Hoffman, Alexis Machuca, Héctor Eduardo Berríos Ibarra, Felipe Andrés Muñoz Flores, Esteban Flores Martínez, Pedro Emiliano Muñoz Zúñiga (56.Sebastián Alejandro Roco Melgarejo), Michael Antonio Lepe Labraña, Francisco Leoncio Portillo Maidana, Fernando Alejandro Manríquez Hernández, Diego Nicolás Guastavino Bentancor (42.Fabián Raúl Benítez Gómez), Gabriel Alejandro Vargas Venegas (54.Diego Churín Puyo). Trainer: Ronald Hugo Fuentes Núñez.
Palestino: Darío Esteban Melo Pulgar, Germán Lanaro, Alejandro Andrés Contreras Daza (60.Diego Ignacio Torres Quintana), Diego Rosende Lagos, Esteban Andrés Carvajal Tapia, Paulo César Díaz Huincales (46.Diego Gonzalo Cháves de Miquelerena), Alejandro Samuel Márquez Pérez (30.Marcos Daniel Riquelme), Jason Alejandro Silva Pérez, Leonardo Felipe Valencia Rossel, Renato Andrés Ramos Madrigal, Jorge Ricardo Guajardo Neira. Trainer: Pablo Adrián Guede Barrirero (Argentina).
Goals: 1-0 Paulo César Díaz Huincales (4 own goal), 2-0 Gabriel Alejandro Vargas Venegas (10), 3-0 Fernando Alejandro Manríquez Hernández (79), 3-1 Jorge Ricardo Guajardo Neira (81), 3-2 Diego Gonzalo Cháves de Miquelerena (89).

2014/2015 Copa Chile Winners: **CD Universidad de Concepción**

CLUB DE DEPORTES ANTOFAGASTA

Foundation date: May 14, 1966
Address: Calle General Manuel Baquedano 482, Oficina 24-25, 124-0000 Antofagasta
Stadium: Estadio Regional Calvo y Bascuñán, Antofagasta – Capacity: 21,178

THE SQUAD

	DOB	Ape		Cla	
		M	G	M	G
Goalkeepers:					
Nicolás Araya		-	-	-	-
Pablo Fernando Aurrecochea Medina (URU)	08.03.1981	12	-	17	-
Alán Cortés Cornejo	20.12.1996	-	-	-	-
Luis Rodrigo Santelices Tello	29.10.1985	5	-	-	-
Defenders:					
Francisco Alarcón Cruz	14.04.1988	14	-	9	1
Baltazar del Carmen Astorga Quezada	16.06.1982	3	-	2	-
Alejandro Alfredo Delfino (ARG)	18.09.1989	17	-	14	2
Carlos Alberto Escudero Lavado	18.01.1979	-	-	5	-
Ronald Damián González Tabilo	17.10.1990	14	2	16	1
Patricio Andrés Jérez Díaz	26.06.1987	8	-	10	-
Nicolás Patricio Ortíz Vergara	06.04.1984	10	-	-	-
Rodrigo Fabián Riquelme Cabrera (PAR)	01.06.1984			16	4
Midfielders:					
Marcos Sebastián Aguirre (ARG)	30.03.1984			13	2
Cristian Marcelo Álvarez (ARG)	28.09.1992	8	-	8	-
Branco Ampuero Vera	19.07.1993	7	-	14	-
Luis Alberto Cabrera Figueroa	07.01.1994	13	2	15	2
Felipe Andrés Díaz Henríquez	09.08.1983	5	-	3	-
Diego Ismael Ferreira Villa (URU)	04.05.1985	12	-	14	2
Emanuel Giménez (ARG)	19.02.1984	10	-		
Angelo Patricio González Aceituno	02.03.1989	3	-	-	-
Daniel Felipe González Calvo	30.01.1984	3	-		
Osmán Alexis Huerta Cabezas	21.06.1989	9	-		
Felipe Ignacio Muñoz Cáceres	09.04.1996	1	-	-	-
Cristián Manuel Rojas Sanhueza	19.12.1985	1	-	12	-
Forwards:					
Marcos Nikolas Bolados Hidalgo	28.02.1996	14	-	14	3
Nicolás Dávalos Ramos	21.06.1993	4	1	4	-
Javier Aníbal Elizondo (ARG)	31.10.1982	14	4		
Rúben Ignacio Farfan Arancibia	25.09.1991	17	3	16	2
Matías Nicolás Jadue González	16.05.1992	8	-	9	1
Gonzalo Daniel Malán Arenas (URU)	08.04.1988			7	1
Gerson Sebastián Martínez Arredondo	10.01.1989	13	1	12	4
Francisco Javier Sepúlveda Riveros	03.09.1991	6	-	8	-
Trainer:					
Jaime Andrés Vera Rodríguez [01.07.-10.11.2014]	25.03.1963	14			
Sergio Marchant Muñoz [11.11.-31.12.2014]	17.09.1961	3			
José Miguel Cantillana [as of 01.01.2015]	14.10.1965			17	

AUDAX CLUB SPORTIVO ITALIANO LA FLORIDA

Foundation date: November 30, 1910
Address: Enrique Olivares 1003, La Florida, 832-0000 Santiago
Stadium: Estadio Bicentenario Municipal de La Florida – Capacity: 12,000

THE SQUAD	DOB	Ape		Cla	
		M	G	M	G
Goalkeepers:					
Jaime Alejandro Bravo Jeffery	04.04.1982	-	-	12	-
Joaquín Emanuel Muñoz Almarza	28.12.1990	-	-	-	-
Nery Alexis Veloso Espinoza	02.03.1987	17	-	5	-
Defenders:					
Bryan Paul Carrasco Santos	31.01.1991	16	4	17	7
José Raúl Contreras Arrau	23.03.1982	12	-	14	-
Juan Francisco Cornejo Palma	27.02.1990	17	1	17	3
Christian André Jélvez Palacios	22.01.1991	6	-	9	-
Claudio Andrés Meneses Cordero	05.02.1988	11	-	8	-
Rafael Andrés Olarra Guerrero	25.05.1978	10	-	12	-
Nelson Saavedra Sánchez	06.04.1988	3	1	7	1
Sebastián Ignacio Silva Pérez	16.07.1991	9	1	3	-
Sebastián Ignacio Vegas Orellana	04.12.1996	7	-	13	-
Midfielders:					
Osvaldo Javier Bosso Torres	14.10.1993	7	-	8	1
Cristian Ezequiel Canuhé (ARG)	25.08.1987	8	-		
Alexis Nicolás Delgado Navarrete	31.12.1987	-	-	-	-
David Hernán Drocco (ARG)	20.01.1989	15	-	15	-
Jorge Alexis Henríquez Neira	17.06.1994	-	-	3	-
Pablo Darío López (ARG)	04.06.1982	10	-	-	-
Diego Alfonso Valdés Contreras	30.01.1994	15	5	16	2
Forwards:					
Javier Aníbal Elizondo (ARG)	31.10.1982			11	1
Gonzalo Ezequiel Menéndez (ARG)	16.12.1992	1	-	-	-
Felipe Andrés Mora Aliaga	02.08.1993	13	2	12	-
Mauro Andrés Olivi (ARG)	18.03.1983	11	1	12	2
Marcos Sebastián Pol (ARG)	15.03.1988	8	2	10	4
Sergio Henríque Santos Gómes	04.09.1994	-	-	1	-
Diego Alfredo Vallejos Hernández	16.03.1990	17	7	9	1
Iván Gonzalo Vásquez Quilodrán	13.08.1985	15	1	17	-
Domingo Omar Zalazar (ARG)	10.08.1986	8	1	3	-
Trainer:					
Jorge Alberto Pellicer Berceló [as of 01.07.2014]	07.02.1966	17		17	

ATHLETIC CLUB BARNECHEA

Foundation date: December 23, 1929
Address: Avenida Barnechea 413, Santiago de Chile
Stadium: Estadio "San Carlos de Apoquindo", Las Condes, Santiago – Capacity: 12,000

THE SQUAD	DOB	Ape		Cla	
		M	G	M	G
Goalkeepers:					
Jorge Ignacio Manduca Aglieri (ARG)	27.10.1979	14	-	10	-
Gregory Saavedra Morales	11.02.1989	-	-	1	-
Álvaro Luis Salazar Bravo	24.03.1993	4	-	6	-
Defenders:					
Daniel Alejandro Castillo Galindo	24.08.1989	11	-	9	-
Bastián González	06.09.1996			-	-
Gonzalo Lauler Godoy	14.01.1989	8	-	4	-
Sebastián Francisco Javier Montesinos Pezoa	12.03.1986			6	-
Mario Esteban Pardo Acuña	13.05.1988	7	-	12	-
Cristián Eduardo Reynero Cerda	25.08.1979	4	-	9	-
John Antonio Santander Plaza	15.05.1994			14	2
Víctor Nicolás Suárez	20.05.1982	13	-	13	-
Moisés Valentín Vásquez Higuera	02.02.1990	13	-	13	1
Maximiliano Vivianni	12.04.1995			1	-
Midfielders:					
Matias Ignacio Aguilar Brule	05.11.1994	1	-	1	-
Mikel Arguinarena Lara	27.06.1991	7	-	1	-
Ignacio Caroca Cordero	02.11.1993	4	-	5	-
Esteban Cossio	22.05.1997			1	-
David Jonathan Escalante Ríos (ARG)	21.05.1991	4	-	9	1
Daniel Felipe González Calvo	30.01.1984			9	1
Oscar Ignacio Hernández Polanco	07.03.1993	14	1	6	-
Cristian Nicolás Ivanobski (ARG)	11.02.1990	15	2	14	2
Francisco Manuel Levipán Cariqueo	11.06.1993	13	1	12	1
Felipe Sebastián Mancilla Pantoja	30.03.1994	1	-	2	-
Christian Jorge Martínez Muñoz	18.06.1983	10	-	9	-
Nicolás Alexander Maturana Caneo	08.07.1993	9	4		
Joaquín Ignacio Moya Fuentes	13.12.1993	2	-	7	1
Nelson Arnoldo Rebolledo Tapia	14.11.1985	6	-	7	-
Camilo Elías Rencoret Lecaros	23.09.1990	16	-	8	-
Manuel Rivera				1	-
Claudio Simón Riveros Alcapan	28.07.1993	4	-	-	-
Mauricio Orlando Yévenes Saavedra	09.03.1994	2	-	9	1
Forwards:					
José Tomás Arancibia Sánz	22.07.1996			1	1
Jhonny Roberto Contreras Mora	27.10.1994			6	-
Gonzalo Martin De Porras (ARG)	26.07.1984	7	-	4	-
Francisco Javier Ibáñez Campos	13.01.1986	15	5	8	2
Bayron Andrés Oyarzo Muñoz	14.07.1995	1	-	1	-
Francisco Javier Pizarro Cartes	10.05.1989	10	2	10	-
Bibencio Servín Paredes (PAR)	02.11.1984	9	-	-	-
Axl Nicolás Silva Cardenas	09.04.1993	1	-	-	-
Cristóbal Alberto Vergara Maldonado	20.06.1994	10	-	9	-
Trainer:					
Francisco Bozán Santibáñez [as of 24.07.2014]	12.12.1987	17		17	

CLUB DE DEPORTES COBRELOA CALAMA

Foundation date: January 7, 1977
Address: Calel Atacama 1482, 139-0000 Calama
Stadium: Estadio Municipal, Calama – Capacity: 12,000

THE SQUAD

	DOB	Ape		Cla	
		M	G	M	G
Goalkeepers:					
Matías Carrasco		-	-	-	-
Sebastián Andrés Contreras Jofré	01.01.1988	6	-	3	-
Luciano Ramón Palos Ongaro (ARG)	29.11.1979	11	-	14	-
Exequiel Rojas				-	-
Defenders:					
Eric Andrés Ahumada Escobar	14.02.1994	10	-	10	-
Maximiliano Andrés Gálvez Benavides	07.01.1994			-	-
Raúl Matías González Gutiérrez	14.04.1993	1	-	-	-
Rodolfo Antonio González Aránguiz	28.02.1989	14	1	14	1
Marco Hidalgo Zúñiga	06.07.1990	6	-	6	-
Ricardo Julián Martínez Pavón (PAR)	18.02.1984			15	-
Sebastián Alejandro Rocco Melgarejo	26.06.1983	15	2		
Miguel Alejandro Sanhueza Mora	30.08.1991	11	-	15	-
Martín Juan Zbrun (ARG)	27.01.1985			5	-
Midfielders:					
Juan Carlos Araya Díaz	29.08.1994	-	-	-	-
Ángel Martín Cofré Romero	11.07.1994	-	-	-	-
Fernando Nicolás Cornejo Miranda	26.12.1995	14	1	10	-
Gustavo Alberto Cristaldo Britez (PAR)	31.05.1989	6	2	16	4
Cristián Iván Gaitán (ARG)	15.01.1990	10	-	14	1
Paolo Ignacio Gómez	12.08.1993	-	-	-	-
Iván Ledesma	19.07.1995	7	-	4	-
Gabriel Antonio Méndez (ARG)	08.05.1988	15	4		
Felipe Andrés Palacios	22.10.1993	-	-	5	-
Edwin Retamoso Palomino (PER)	23.02.1982	9	-		
Mauricio Ignacio Sánchez Silva	07.01.1996			1	-
Diego Alejandro Silva	11.03.1983	10	2	15	2
Patricio Antonio Troncoso Baeza	10.06.1992	4	-	4	-
Forwards:					
Vildan Andrés Alfaro Paredes	17.04.1995	-	-	-	-
Ángel Santiago Barboza Manzzi (URU)	03.10.1989			15	5
Rodrigo Pablo Gattás Bertoni	02.12.1991	2	-	7	-
Ignacio José Herrera Fernández	30.10.1987	8	-	17	4
José Luis Jiménez Marín	08.08.1983	11	2	12	1
Álvaro Fabián López Ojeda	24.09.1992	2	1	12	2
José Eduardo Pérez Ferrada	28.07.1985	8	1	14	-
Jair Alexander Reinoso Moreno (COL)	07.06.1985	7	3	2	1
Sebastián Nicolás Romero Fernández	25.01.1996	-	-	7	-
Trainer:					
Marcelo Antonio Trobbiani Ughetto (ARG) [15.03.-22.08.2014]	17.02.1955	5			
Pablo Marcelo Trobbiani [23.08.-02.09.2014; Caretaker]	28.12.1976	2			
Luis Fernando Vergara Meylan [12.09.-31.12.2014]	13.05.1970	10			
Marco Antonio Figueroa Montero [as of 01.01.2015]	21.02.1962			17	

CLUB DE DEPORTES COBRESAL EL SALVADOR

Foundation date: May 5, 1979
Address: Avenida Arqueros 2500, 150-8101 El Salvador, Diego de Almagro
Stadium: Estadio El Cobre, El Salvador – Capacity: 20,752

THE SQUAD

	DOB	Ape M	Ape G	Cla M	Cla G
Goalkeepers:					
Jeff Alan Barría Huenchul	11.05.1994			-	-
Fabián Alfredo Cerda Valdés	07.02.1989	3	-		
Sebastián Leonel Cuerdo (ARG)	16.07.1986	-	-	-	-
Eduardo Andrés Miranda Ríos	03.10.1992	-	-	-	-
Nicolás Miroslav Peric Villarreal	19.10.1978	14	-	17	-
Defenders:					
Daniel Andrés Aguilera Godoy	30.07.1988	-	-	-	-
Matías Ignacio Arriagada Maraboli	12.07.1991	-	-	-	-
Rolando Marciano Bogado (PAR)	22.04.1984	12	-		
Diego Andrés Cerón Silva	15.09.1991	1	-	1	-
Miguel Andrés Escalona Armijo	23.03.1990	14	1	15	-
Federico Martorell Rigo (ARG)	26.03.1981			11	1
Alexis Alejandro Salazar Villarroel	03.06.1983	10	1	14	-
Midfielders:					
Augusto Tomás Álvarez (ARG)	01.08.1984			3	-
Mauricio Alejandro Flores Farías	30.10.1996	-	-	-	-
Johan Patricio Fuentes Muñoz	02.09.1984	17	2	16	2
Carlos Felipe Herrera Contreras	06.08.1983	4	-	2	-
Patricio Felipe Jérez Aguayo	29.06.1987	16	-	16	-
Lino Waldemar Maldonado Gárnica	27.07.1990	-	-	1	-
Juan Pablo Miño Peña (ARG)	23.08.1987	16	-	14	-
Diego Andrés Muñoz Tapia	25.12.1989	-	-	-	-
Sebastián José Pérez Hernández	20.01.1995			-	-
Israel Elías Poblete Zúñiga	22.06.1995	1	-	4	-
Flavio Rojas Catalán	16.01.1994	4	-	2	-
Hans Francisco Salinas Flores	23.04.1990	16	3	16	2
Francisco Javier Sánchez Silva	02.06.1985	7	-		
Iván Ignacio Sandoval	22.04.1995			2	1
Víctor Hugo Sarabia Aguilar	27.11.1983	12	1	12	2
Nelson Alejandro Sepúlveda Moya	22.01.1992	9	-	14	1
Mariano Néstor Torres (ARG)	19.05.1987	16	1		
Rodrigo Andrés Ureña Reyes	01.03.1993	14	-	16	-
Felipe Esteban Vásquez Vásquez	09.12.1992	1	-	-	-
Forwards:					
Ever Milton Cantero Benítez (PAR)	03.12.1985	14	4	10	9
Jorge Matías Donoso Garáte	08.07.1986	14	4	16	9
Carlos Humberto Escobar Ortíz	24.12.1989	13	2	17	-
Cristian Rolando Ledesma Núñez (PAR)	11.02.1987	8	5	4	-
Sebastián Zúñiga Fuenzalida	21.06.1990			12	2
Trainer:					
José Miguel Cantillana Galeas [06.03.2013 - 20.10.2014]	14.10.1965	11			
Rubén Vallejos Gajardo [23.10.-28.10.2014; Caretaker]	20.05.1967	1			
Dalcio Víctor Giovagnoli [as of 31.10.2014]	05.06.1963	5			

CLUB SOCIAL Y DEPORTIVO COLO-COLO SANTIAGO

Foundation date: April 19, 1925
Address: Avenida Marathon 5300, Macul, 782-0919 Santiago
Stadium: Estadio Monumental „David Arellano", Santiago – Capacity: 47,017

THE SQUAD

	DOB	Ape		Cla	
		M	G	M	G
Goalkeepers:					
Paulo Andrés Garcés Contreras	02.08.1984	2	-	8	-
José Ignacio González Catalán	02.12.1989	-	-	-	-
Eduardo Eugenio Lobos Landaeta	31.07.1981	-	-		
Pablo César Soto Soto	07.02.1995	-	-	-	-
Justo Wilmar Villar Viveros (PAR)	30.06.1977	16	-	9	-
Defenders:					
Julio Alberto Barroso (ARG)	16.01.1985	17	-	10	-
José Leonardo Cáceres Ovelar (PAR)	28.04.1985			9	-
Hardy Fabián Cavero Vargas	31.05.1996	1	-	1	-
Modou Lamin Jadama (USA)	17.03.1994			-	-
Nicolás Iván Orellana Acuña	03.09.1995	-	-	1	-
Luis Alberto Pavez Muñoz	17.09.1995	10	-	5	-
Camilo Bryan Rodríguez Pedraza	04.03.1995	3	-	10	-
Sebastián Patricio Toro Hormazábal	02.02.1990	5	-		
Christian Alberto Vilches González	13.07.1983	17	1	17	-
Dylan Patricio Zúñiga Valenzuela	26.07.1996	-	-	3	-
Midfielders:					
Jorge Matias Araya Pozo	25.03.1994	-	-	-	-
Jean André Eman Beausejour Coliqueo	01.06.1984	14	3	15	1
Bryan Andrés Carvallo Utreras	15.09.1996	5	-	4	-
Carlos Alfredo Contreras Zambrano	22.01.1995			2	-
Juan Antonio Delgado Baeza	05.03.1993	17	5	15	3
Luciano Javier Díaz Araya	08.05.1998			-	-
Luis Pedro Figueroa Sepúlveda	14.05.1983			10	-
José Pedro Fuenzalida Gana	22.02.1985	2	-		
Jorge Sebastián Matías Lagües Suárez	22.01.1997			1	-
Francisco Antonio Lara Uribe	25.01.1995	-	-	-	-
Claudio Andrés Del Tránsito Maldonado Rivera	03.01.1980	13	-	8	-
Daniel Ignacio Malhué Toro	13.02.1995	-	-	-	-
Ariel Elias Martínez Arce	10.01.1994	-	-	-	-
Esteban Pavez Suazo	01.05.1990	16	2	15	2
Jaime Andrés Zapata Valdés	11.01.1981	13	4	10	2
Emiliano Gabriel Vecchio (ARG)	16.11.1988	17	3	11	3
Forwards:					
Claudio Baeza Baeza	23.12.1993	14	-	16	2
Gonzalo Antonio Fierro Caniullán	21.03.1983	17	2	13	1
Felipe Ignacio Flores Chandia	09.01.1987	17	1	15	5
Esteban Efraín Paredes Quintanilla	01.08.1980	17	12	15	11
Roberto Ignacio Riveros Uribe	27.02.1996			2	-
Humberto Andrés Suazo Pontivo	10.05.1981			10	2
Trainer:					
Héctor Santiago Tapia Urdile [as of 16.10.2013]	30.09.1977	17		17	

CLUB DEPORTIVO HUACHIPATO TALCAHUANO

Foundation date: June 7, 1947
Address: Avenida Desiderio García 909, Las Higueras, 429-0035 Talcahuano
Stadium: Estadio CAP, Talcahuano – Capacity: 10,500

THE SQUAD					
	DOB	Ape*		Cla	
		M	G	M	G
Goalkeepers:					
Franco Antonio Collado Moraleda	20.04.1994			1	-
Miguel Hernán Jiménez Aracenna	12.12.1980	3	-		
Felipe Alejandro Núñez Becerra	25.02.1979			14	-
Guillermo Martín Reyes Maneiro (URU)	10.07.1986	16	-	3	-
Álvaro Sáenz-Laguna Saavedra	04.09.1991	-	-	-	-
Defenders:					
Leandro Javier Delgado Plenkovich	15.07.1982	9	-	16	1
Esteban Eduardo González Herrera	22.05.1982	11	-	12	1
Omar Jesús Merlo (ARG)	12.06.1987	16	2	16	-
Claudio Andrés Muñoz Carrillo	02.12.1984	17	-	17	1
Midfielders:					
Francisco Esteban Arrué Pardo	07.08.1977	11	1	-	-
Jair Castro Morales	28.12.1995	-	-	-	-
Nicolás Ignacio Crovetto Aqueveque	15.03.1986	11	-	15	1
Victor Alejandro Dávila Zavala	04.11.1997	1	-	-	-
Juan Ignacio Duma (ARG)	08.12.1993			4	2
Felipe Ernesto Elgueta Salgado	13.04.1992	3	-	6	-
Carlos Felipe Ignacio Espinosa Contreras	22.11.1982	17	1	15	3
Juan Carlos Espinoza Reyes	05.07.1991	11	1	14	-
Leandro Ezquerra De León (URU)	05.06.1986	19	-	9	1
Kevin Hidalgo Silva	29.07.1995	-	-	-	-
Jimmy Antonio Martínez	26.01.1997	-	-	2	-
Nicolás Arnaldo Núñez Rojas	12.09.1984	14	1	11	1
Camilo Pontoni	29.01.1995	4	-	10	-
Leonardo Nicolás Povea Pérez	26.01.1994	16	-	14	1
Daniel Alejandro Rodríguez Mellado	12.03.1991	4	-	3	-
Martín Vladimir Rodríguez Torrejon	05.08.1994	15	1	11	1
Bryan Alfonso Vejar Utreras	14.07.1995	15	-	11	1-
Forwards:					
Vicente Marcelo Gatica Grandón	11.02.1996	4	-	-	-
Héctor Raúl Mancilla Garcés	12.11.1980			12	6
Martín Molini (ARG)	20.01.1994	-	-	-	-
Matías Alberto Sánchez Herrera	08.05.1990	10	-	1	-
Lucas Simón García (ARG)	01.08.1986	8	10	2	-
Álvaro Mirko Sobarzo Escobar	10.02.1993	-	-	-	-
Andrés Alejandro Vílches Araneda	14.11.1992	19	11	14	8
Angelo Zagal	18.04.1993	12	3	4	1
Trainer:					
Mario Alfredo Salas Saieg [06.12.1013-31.12.2014]	11.10.1967	19			
Hugo Alejandro Héctor Vilches Manuguian [as of 01.01.2015]	27.02.1969			17	

**Matches and goals in 2014 Liguilla Apertura included*

CLUB DEPORTES IQUIQUE

Foundation date: May 21, 1978
Address: Avenida Soldado Pedro Prado con Avenida Tadeo Haenke, Iquique
Stadium: Estadio Tierra de Campeones, Iquique – Capacity: 9,500

THE SQUAD

	DOB	Ape		Cla	
		M	G	M	G
Goalkeepers:					
Alejandro Becerra Soto	15.04.1988	1	-		
Brayan Cortés Fernández	29.05.1995	5	-	3	-
Carlos Felipe González Montero	06.12.1994	1	-	-	-
Rodrigo Felipe Naranjo López	30.08.1979	11	-	14	-
Luis Ignacio Sotomayor Orrego	04.12.1996	-	-	-	-
Defenders:					
Cristian Javier Báez (PAR)	09.04.1990	9	-	10	-
Javier Ignacio Cabezas Cavieres	06.04.1995	-	-	-	-
Marcos Contreras Araya	31.08.1994	-	-	-	-
Michael Jordan Contreras Araya	10.02.1993	6	-	7	1
Walter Daniel Mazzolatti Rivarola (ARG)	25.04.1990	12	1	6	-
Cristián Gonzalo Oviedo Molina	22.05.1980			17	1
Boris Alexis Rieloff Venegas	08.01.1984	14	1	14	-
Sebastián Patricio Toro Hormazábal	02.02.1990			6	-
Mauricio Alejandro Zenteno Morales	21.04.1984	14	1	14	-
Midfielders:					
Exequiel Emanuel Benavídez (ARG)	05.03.1989	9	-		-
Rafael Antonio Caroca Cordero	19.07.1989	17	2	17	1
Álvaro Alejandro Delgado Sciaraffia	13.05.1995	-	-	2	-
Rodrigo Ezequiel Díaz Rengo (ARG)	28.08.1981	12	3		-
Diego Nicolás Fernández Castro	08.03.1998	-	-	-	-
Felipe Herrera Vásquez	20.02.1993	-	-		
Marcelo Pablo Jorquera Silva	13.10.1992	12	-	3	-
Fernando Tomás Lazcano Barros	10.11.1988	11	-	7	-
Jorge Moraga Roble	09.02.1991	2	-	-	-
Javier Enrique Muñoz Calabacero	24.01.1995	2	-	-	-
Brandon Eduardo Olivares Orrego	20.04.1995	-	-		
Christian Andrés Peñaranda Lema	01.10.1995	1	-	-	-
César Ignacio Pinares Tamayo	23.05.1991			15	3
Jonathan Eduardo Rebolledo Ardiles	22.10.1991	7	-	7	-
José Luis Silva Araya	07.01.1991	10	-	-	-
Mauricio José Yedro (ARG)	10.05.1987	14	-	17	-
Forwards:					
Cristian Venancio Bogado Morínigo (PAR)	07.01.1987			16	8
Francisco Fernando Castro Gamboa	04.09.1990	16	3	15	4
Misael Omar Cubillos Ramos	06.02.1996	-	-	-	-
Misael Aldair Dávila Carvajal	17.07.1991	15	1	13	1
Alberto Martín Gómez (ARG)	26.01.1983	11	1	15	3
Kevin Alexander Mellado Torres	17.07.1998	1	-	-	-
Abraham Ismael Vargas Araya	11.05.1993	-	-		
Manuel Arturo Villalobos Salvo	15.10.1980	15	9	16	5
Trainer:					
Héctor Hernán Pinto Lara [01.07.-28.08.2014]	12.06.1951	6			
Erick Guerrero [30.08.-13.10.2014]		4			
Nelson Bonifacio Acosta López (URU) [as of 14.10.2014]	12.06.1944	7		17	

CLUB DEPORTIVO ÑUBLENSE

Foundation date: August 20, 1916
Address: Avenida Bulnes 377, 378-0000 Chillán
Stadium: Estadio Bicentenario Municipal "Nelson Oyarzún", Chillán – Capacity: 12,000

THE SQUAD					
	DOB	Ape		Cla	
		M	G	M	G
Goalkeepers:					
Damián Frascarelli Gutiérrez (URU)	02.06.1985	17	-	17	-
Diego Matias Fuentes Faúndez	03.03.1991	-	-	-	-
Pablo César Reinoso Ojeda	18.12.1985	-	-	-	-
Defenders:					
Gonzalo Damián Godoy Silva (URU)	17.01.1988	13	-	17	-
Javier Andrés González Tupper (VEN)	26.02.1988	1	-	-	-
Maximiliano Isaac González Torres	20.12.1993	-	-	-	-
Orlando Salvador Gutiérrez Leiva	19.08.1989	10	-	8	-
Sebastián Francisco Javier Montesinos Pezoa	12.03.1986	6	1		
Mirko Andrés Opazo Torrejón	09.02.1991	4	-		
Andrés Esteban Reyes Santibañez	26.09.1987	5	-	15	-
José Antonio Rojas Barrera	13.01.1987	15	1	12	-
Benjamín Ignacio Ruíz Herrera	21.08.1981	13	-	15	-
Andrés Ignacio Sepúlveda Berríos	19.03.1993	-	-	-	-
Midfielders:					
Jonathan Josué Cisternas Fernández	16.06.1980	16	2	17	1
Nicolás Emanuel Croce (ARG)	22.07.1985	13	-	12	1
Tomás Lanzini (ARG)	03.06.1991	3	-	8	1
Pablo Alejandro Parra Rubilar	23.07.1994	14	-	7	-
Luis Antonio Pavez Contreras	25.06.1988	9	-	9	-
Octavio Ernesto Pozo Miranda	31.07.1983	13	-	11	1
Mathías Damian Riquero Beretta (URU)	29.08.1982	17	5	17	1
Boris Sagredo Romero	21.03.1989	11	1	8	1
Gonzalo Alfredo Sepúlveda Domínguez	10.11.1988			3	-
Manuel Jesús Silva González	18.03.1988	2	-	2	-
Sebastián Esteban Varas Moreno	01.08.1988	17	8	17	5
Alejandro Gonzalo Vásquez Aguilera	05.07.1984	8	-	6	-
Forwards:					
Marcelo Enrique Ibáñez Hernández	16.01.1993	-	-	-	-
Juan Gonzalo Lorca Donoso	15.01.1985	16	3	13	4
Gabriel Nicolás Rodríguez (ARG)	05.02.1989	10	-	16	3
Damián Gerardo Salvatierra (ARG)	17.11.1984			8	1
Lucas Javier Triviño Toro	26.04.1992	-	-	-	-
Trainer:					
Ivo Alexis Basay Hatibovic [01.07.2014-07.02.2015; Resigned]	13.04.1966	17		5	
Fernando Díaz Seguel [as of 08.02.2015]	27.12.1961			12	

CLUB DEPORTIVO O'HIGGINS RANCAGUA

Foundation date: April 7, 1955
Address: Calle Cuevas 51, 284-0608 Rancagua
Stadium: Estadio El Teniente Codelco, Rancagua – Capacity: 15,600

THE SQUAD

	DOB	Ape		Cla*	
		M	G	M	G
Goalkeepers:					
Jorge Carlos Carranza (ARG)	07.05.1981	13	-	19	-
Roberto Andrés González Beltran	19.05.1976	4	-	-	-
Felipe Ochagavía Eguiguren	16.09.1993	-	-	-	-
Defenders:					
Albert Alejandro Acevedo Vergara	06.05.1983	16	-	17	2
Guillermo Cubillos González	14.01.1995	-	-	4	-
Hugo Patricio Droguett Diocares	02.09.1982			13	-
Hans Alexis Martínez Cabrera	04.01.1987	13	-	14	-
Yerson Flavio Opazo Riquelme	24.12.1984	14	-	18	-
Raúl Andrés Osorio Medina	29.06.1995	-	-	1	-
Brian Nicolás Torrealba Silva	14.07.1997	-	-	-	-
Pablo Nicolás Vargas Romero	15.09.1992	9	-	16	1
Cristhián Andrés Venegas Yáñez	27.05.1993	2	-	-	-
Midfielders:					
Sebastián Céspedes Reyes	18.04.1992	2	-	4	-
Fernando Gastón Elizari (ARG)	05.04.1991	13	1	7	-
Luis Pedro Figueroa Sepúlveda	14.05.1983	7	1		
César Nicolás Fuentes González	12.04.1993	15	1	18	-
Juan Eduardo Fuentes	21.03.1995	11	-	7	-
Luis Humberto Fuentes Jiménez	21.04.1995	1	-	-	-
Diego Ignacio González Reyes	16.01.1991	-	-	-	-
Braulio Antonio Leal Salvo	22.11.1981	15	2	18	2
Santiago Nicolás Lizana Lizana	30.09.1992	5	-	7	-
Damián Emanuel Lizio (ARG)	30.06.1989	14	-	13	1
Eduardo Alejandro López (ARG)	16.06.1989	15	-	15	-
Iván Marcelo Pardo Córdova	10.11.1995	1	-	-	-
Bastián San Juan Martínez	27.04.1994	3	-	8	-
Luís Gabriel Valenzuela Toledo	22.02.1988	16	5	14	1
Juan Antonio Zúñiga Quiroz	05.04.1996	-	-	2	-
Forwards:					
Pablo Ignacio Calandria (ARG)	15.03.1982	-	-	19	10
Diego Gonzalo Cháves de Miquelerena (URU)	14.02.1986	14	3		
Aníbal González Ramírez	08.04.1995	1	-	-	-
César Alejandro González Ramírez	11.01.1997	-	-	-	-
Fabián Marcelo Hormazabal Berríos	26.04.1996			5	-
Gastón Andrés Lezcano	21.11.1986	15	3	14	4
Sebastián Andrés Pinto Perurena	15.02.1986			13	3
Raúl Octavio Rivero Falero (URU)	24.01.1992	16	10		
Trainer:					
Facundo Sava Stell (ARG) [01.07.2014-21.01.2015; Sacked]	07.03.1974	17		3	
Pablo Andrés Sánchez (ARG) [as of 22.01.2015]	03.01.1973			16	

**Matches and goals in 2015 Liguilla Clausura included*

CLUB DEPORTIVO PALESTINO SANTIAGO

Foundation date: August 20, 1920
Address: Avenida El Parrón 999, La Cisterna, 797-0227 Santiago
Stadium: Estadio Municipal de La Cisterna, Santiago – Capacity: 12,000

THE SQUAD					
	DOB	**Ape***		**Cla**	
		M	**G**	**M**	**G**
Goalkeepers:					
Matías Nicolás Herrera Fuentes	07.05.1995			3	-
Iván Ignacio Meirone Macías	28.06.1995	-	-	1	-
Darío Esteban Melo Pulgar	24.03.1994	13	-	13	-
Felipe Alejandro Núñez Becerra	24.02.1979	5	-		
José Antonio Quezada Salazar	17.08.1990	3	-	1	-
Defenders:					
Felipe Manuel Campos Mosqueira	08.11.1993	13	-	10	-
Alejandro Andrés Contreras Daza	03.03.1993	18	3	10	-
Matías Andrés Escudero (ARG)	15.12.1988			13	-
Germán Lanaro (ARG)	21.03.1986	19	3	6	-
Rodrigo Fabián Riquelme Cabrera (PAR)	01.06.1984	7	1		
Diego Rosende Lagos	11.02.1986	14	-	6	-
Bayron Antonio Saavedra Navarro	06.07.1997	1	-	5	-
Midfielders:					
Ignacio Nicolás Ayala Rojas	29.11.1997			2	-
Luis Martín Bevacqua (ARG)	12.06.1989	4	-		
Víctor Félix Campos Olavarría	24.09.1997			1	-
Jonathan Eduardo Cantillana Zorrilla	26.05.1992			11	2
Esteban Andrés Carvajal Tapia	17.11.1988	21	-	9	-
Gabriel Adrián Díaz	17.10.1989	5	-		
Paulo César Díaz Huincales	25.08.1994	18	3	9	3
Carlos Agustín Farías (ARG)	25.12.1987			11	-
Alejandro Samuel Márquez Pérez	31.10.1991	15	1	10	-
Marcelo Alejandro Morales Gonzalez	14.07.1992	2	1	7	2
José Ignacio Sagredo Caruz	25.02.1994	1	-	4	-
Jorge Osvaldo Schwager Navarrete	04.07.1983	8	-	6	-
Jason Alejandro Silva Pérez	13.02.1991	14	1	11	-
Juan Andrés Silva Cárdenas	11.03.1989	9	-	-	-
Sebastián Felipe Silva Lavanderos	01.07.1997			-	-
Diego Ignacio Torres Quintana	31.07.1992	19	1	7	1
Sebastián Antonio Urra Castro	18.07.1995	-	-	-	-
Leonardo Felipe Valencia Rossel	25.04.1991	20	12	11	2
César Valenzuela Martínez	04.09.1992	20	3	16	1
Christopher Veloso	13.07.1996			1	-
Forwards:					
Fabián Antonio Ahumada Astete		1	-	2	1
Diego Gonzalo Cháves de Miquelerena (URU)	14.02.1986			10	5
Matías García	19.04.1993	-	-	-	-
Jorge Ricardo Guajardo Neira	09.05.1994	7	-	9	2
Richard Paredes	1996			1	-
Jorge Maximiliano Piris (ARG)	22.07.1990	3	-		
Renato Andrés Ramos Madrigal	12.02.1979	17	10	9	2
Marcos Daniel Riquelme (ARG)	01.06.1989	14	4	9	3
Matías Leonardo Vidangossy Rebolledo	25.05.1987			13	1
Trainer:					
Pablo Adrián Guede Barrirero (ARG) [as of 01.07.2014]	11.11.1974	21		17	

**Matches and goals in 2014 Liguilla Apertura included*

CLUB DEPORTIVO SAN MARCOS DE ARICA

Foundation date: February 14, 1978
Address: Avenida 18 de Septiembre 2000, Arica
Stadium: Estadio "Carlos Dittborn", Arica – Capacity: 17,786

THE SQUAD

	DOB	Ape M	Ape G	Cla* M	Cla* G
Goalkeepers:					
Pedro Alex Carrizo Córdova	09.07.1977	15	-	16	-
Eduardo Eugenio Lobos Landaeta	30.07.1981			6	-
Zacarías López González	30.06.1998	-	-	-	-
Gastón Ezequiel Monzón (ARG)	13.05.1987	3	-	-	-
Diego Andrés Tapia Rojas	07.05.1995	-	-	-	-
Defenders:					
José Francisco Durán Prieto	20.07.1994	1	-	-	-
Eric Orlando Godoy Zepeda	26.03.1987	-	-	-	-
Carlos Alfredo Labrín Candia	02.12.1990	14	-	20	-
Fernando Nicolás Meza (ARG)	21.03.1990	15	1	21	-
Diego Alejandro Oyarzún Carrasco	19.01.1993	11	-	12	2
José Félix Pedroso Bogarín (PAR)	21.04.1981	-	-	-	-
Romano Rodrigues (BRA)	10.11.1987			2	-
Midfielders:					
Augusto Sebastián Barrios Silva	03.10.1991	17	1	9	1
Daniel Antonio Briceño Jalabert	02.03.1982	6	-	-	-
Marco Tulio Ciani Barillas (GUA)	07.03.1987	7	-	-	-
Miguel Ángel Coronado Contreras	06.02.1987	16	-	14	-
Santiago Dittborn Martínez-Conde	30.10.1992	-	-	2	-
Pablo Ignacio González Reyes	19.11.1986	15	1	21	3
Renato Patricio González De La Hoz	19.02.1990	16	1	21	3
Kevin Andrew Harbottle Carrasco	08.06.1990	17	2	19	6
Claudio Andrés Jopia Arias	17.11.1991	8	-	20	-
Edgardo López	26.05.1994	-	-	-	-
Gustavo Andrés Oberman (ARG)	25.03.1985			13	2
Sebastián Alejandro Rivera Morales	16.06.1988	11	-	19	2
Oscar Fernando Salinas Aguilar	26.06.1988	6	-	4	-
Gabriel Eduardo Sandoval Alarcón	13.03.1984	14	-	21	-
Christopher Singer Ossandón	03.06.1994	-	-	-	-
Washington Leandro Torres	23.05.1984	5	-	3	-
Forwards:					
Jaime Andrés Grondona Bobadilla	15.04.1987	5	-	3	-
Nicolás Estebán Medina Ríos	28.03.1987	7	1	17	2
Juan Carlos Oviedo (ARG)	30.04.1993	1	-	-	-
Leonardo Javier Ramos (ARG)	21.08.1989	8	1	21	9
Emilio Rentería García (VEN)	09.10.1984	17	4	9	2
Trainer:					
Fernando Maximiliano Díaz Seguel [01.07.-03.11.2014]	27.12.1961	13			
Kenny Mamani [06.11.-31.12.2014]		4			
Luis Fernando Vergara Meyland [as of 01.01.2015]	13.05.1970			21	

**Matches and goals in 2015 Liguilla Clausura included*

CLUB DE DEPORTES SANTIAGO WANDERERS S.A.D.P.

Foundation date: August 15, 1892
Address: Calle Independencia 2061, 234-0000 Valparaíso
Stadium: Estadio "Elías Figueroa Brander", Valparaíso – Capacity: 23,000

THE SQUAD	DOB	Ape* M	Ape* G	Cla M	Cla G
Goalkeepers:					
Gabriel Jesús Castellón Velazque	08.09.1993	7	-	1	-
Diego Carlos Figueroa Cobo	21.02.1990	-	-	-	-
Mauricio Alejandro Viana Caamaño (BRA)	14.06.1989	14	-	16	-
Defenders:					
Juan René Abarca Fuentes	07.12.1988	14	-	9	-
Mario López Quintana	07.07.1995	4	-	8	1
Ezequiel Luna (ARG)	19.11.1986	25	2	16	-
Samuel Mendoza Villagran	06.02.1993	-	-	-	-
Óscar Mauricio Opazo Lara	18.10.1990	1	-	14	-
Agustín Hernán Felipe Parra Repetto	10.06.1989	19	-	2	-
Mauricio Prieto Garcés (URU)	26.09.1987	19	1	15	2
Franz Hermann Schulz Ramírez	20.07.1991	13	-	14	1
Midfielders:					
Gonzalo Felipe Barriga Ahumada	21.07.1984	21	1	12	1
Jefferson Alexis Castillo Marin	10.06.1990	-	-	8	-
Jimmy Andrés Cisterna Moya	05.04.1993	8	-	4	-
Kevin Andrés Flores Senecal	01.01.1995	-	-	2	-
Álex Daniel González Arancibia	02.02.1992	-	-	3	-
Giakumis Yaya Kodogiannis Valencia	13.02.1992	5	-	4	-
Marco Antonio Medel de la Fuente	30.06.1989	21	4	7	2
Sebastián Antonio Méndez Plaza	06.06.1986	-	-	6	-
Henry Matías Mier Codina (URU)	02.08.1990	18	3		
Jorge Andrés Ormeño Guerra	14.06.1977	18	-	12	-
Pablo Andrés Tamburrini Bravo	30.01.1990	13	1	14	1
Kevin Douglas Valenzuela Fuentes	30.07.1993	-	-	5	-
Forwards:					
Gastón Andrés Javier Cellerino (ARG)	27.06.1986	16	1	15	8
Ronnie Alan Fernández Sáez	01.02.1992	15	3	16	1
Carlos Gabriel González Espínola (PAR)	04.02.1993			10	-
Roberto Carlos Gutiérrez Gamboa	18.04.1983	17	13		
Jorge Luis Luna (ARG)	14.12.1986	17	10	11	4
Sebastián Tomás Reyes Canelo	06.03.1993	1	-	2	-
Roberto Jesús Saldías Díaz	25.02.1993	1	-	9	-
Juan Carlos Soto Swett	02.07.1994	-	-	-	-
Trainer:					
Emiliano Eduardo Astorga Lobos [as of 01.07.2014]	21.09.1960	21		17	

**Matches and goals in 2014 Liguilla Apertura included*

CLUB UNIÓN ESPAÑOLA SANTIAGO

Foundation date: May 18, 1897
Address: Calle Julio Martínez Pradanos 1365, Independencia, 833-0072 Santiago
Stadium: Estadio „Santa Laura"-Universidad SEK, Santiago – Capacity: 22,000

THE SQUAD

	DOB	Ape*		Cla	
		M	G	M	G
Goalkeepers:					
Cristian Edward Guerra Torres	09.08.1994	-	-	1	-
Walter Limenza	13.11.1997	-	-	-	-
Jonathan Alejandro Salvador Lara	09.09.1991	1	-	-	-
Diego Ignacio Sánchez Carvajal	08.05.1987	18	-	16	-
Milenko Tomas Tadic Peters	10.02.1996	-	-	-	-
Defenders:					
Jorge Enrique Ampuero Cabello	01.07.1986	17	2	14	1
Tomás Pablo Astaburuaga Montoya	11.10.1996	-	-	-	-
Nicolás Berardo (ARG)	26.07.1990	8	1	16	1
Fernando Esteban Cornejo Padilla	13.04.1994	1	-	6	-
Marcos Andrés González Salazar	09.06.1980	16	3	15	-
Cristóbal Alfonso Jiménez Aguilar	15.12.1993	-	-	-	-
Mario Ignacio Larenas Díaz	27.07.1993	16	-	6	-
Matías Cristóbal Navarrete Fuentes	20.01.1992	5	-	-	-
Christopher Ross		-	-	1	-
Midfielders:					
Cristian Manuel Chávez (ARG)	16.06.1986	16	-		
Dagoberto Alexis Currimilla Gómez	26.12.1987	18	2	16	1
Pablo Ignacio Feres García	26.11.1993	-	-	-	-
Jason Flores Abrigo	28.02.1997	3	1	-	-
Pablo Ignacio Galdames Millán	30.12.1996	3	-	13	1
René Martín Lima (ARG)	03.01.1985	17	1	13	-
Sergio Daniel López (ARG)	04.01.1989			13	1
Dante Martínez Jara	18.06.1994	4	-	6	-
Gabriel Antonio Méndez (ARG)	08.05.1988			2	-
Milovan Petar Mirosevic Albornoz	20.07.1980	14	4	14	4
Ángel Muñoz Castro	23.11.1991	2	-	4	-
Diego Scotti Ponce De León (URU)	14.01.1977	7	1	10	1
Gonzalo Andrés Villagra Lira	17.09.1981	18	-	15	-
Forwards:					
Gonzalo Daniel Abán (ARG)	11.06.1987			14	2
Ramsés Maximiliano Bustos Guerrero	13.10.1991	4	-	-	-
Juan Carlos Ferreyra (ARG)	12.09.1983			13	5
Sebastián Oscar Jaime (ARG)	30.01.1987	3	1		
Ramón Alberto Lentini (ARG)	24.10.1988	6	-		
Fabián Saavedra Muñoz	27.01.1992	18	3	7	1
Carlos Daniel Salom Zulema (ARG)	15.04.1987	15	6	16	2
José Luis Sierra Cabrera	24.06.1997	9	1	1	-
Matías Leonardo Vidangossy Rebolledo	25.05.1987	16	-		
Trainer:					
José Luis Sierra Pando [as of 01.01.2011]	05.12.1968	19		17	

**Matches and goals in 2014 Liguilla Apertura included*

CLUB DEPORTIVO UNIÓN LA CALERA

Foundation date: January 26, 1954
Address: Calle Balmaceda 372, La Calera
Stadium: Estadio Municipal „Nicolás Chahuán", La Calera - Capacity: 15,000

THE SQUAD

	DOB	Ape		Cla*	
		M	G	M	G
Goalkeepers:					
José Luis Aguilera Mejías	12.10.1988	-	-	3	-
Cristofer Jesús Fuentes Ramírez	14.03.1997	-	-	-	-
Lucas Raúl Giovini Schiapino (ARG)	13.10.1981	17	-	16	-
Defenders:					
Francisco Bahamondes Galea	07.04.1988	13	1	17	-
Hugo Gabriel Bascuñán Vera	11.01.1985	13	1	2	-
Mario Esteban Berríos Jara	20.08.1981	7	-	19	-
Tomás Patricio Charles (ARG)	12.06.1985	13	1	18	3
Eduardo Ignacio Farías Diaz	01.01.1989	16	-	18	-
Francisco Javier Romero Pérez	20.09.1995			-	-
José Alberto Shaffer (ARG)	16.12.1985	10	-	6	-
Midfielders:					
Roberto Carlos Ávalos Pino	16.06.1980	5	-	-	-
Fabian Alejandro Beas Aranda	13.11.1992	-	-	-	-
Leandro Iván Benegas (ARG)	27.11.1988	15	10		-
Esteban Andrés Bravo Cancino	12.08.1987	11	-	11	-
Luis Ignacio Casanova Sandoval	01.07.1992	12	-	5	-
Cristhian Alejandro Collao Valencia	08.09.1995	-	-	2	-
Eduardo Andrés Mauricio Gaete Erices	15.02.1994	-	-	-	-
Agustín González Tapia (ARG)	30.01.1983	16	1	17	-
Emilio Exequiel Hernández Hernández	14.09.1984	8	2	7	-
Fabián Esteban Pizarro Venenciano	22.07.1996	1	-	-	-
Javier Ignacio Ramírez	27.12.1994	-	-	-	-
Paulo Roberto Rosales (ARG)	10.04.1984	16	1	18	5
Carlos Felipe Sepúlveda Huerta	31.01.1995	2	1	7	-
Jonathan Alfonso Suazo Cuevas	04.08.1989	17	-	15	-
Forwards:					
Humberto Álvarez San Martín	26.04.1987	-	-	-	-
Ramiro Costa (ARG)	21.08.1992			14	2
Leandro Yamil Lima (ARG)	11.08.1994	4	-	-	-
Jean Paul Jesús Pineda Cortés	24.02.1989	17	6	18	11
Francesco Andrés Akermann Silva (VEN)	07.03.1995	2	1	-	-
Michael Andrés Silva Torres	12.03.1988	8	-	17	2
Juan Manuel Tévez (ARG)	28.08.1987	7	-	14	6
Patricio Vidal (ARG)	08.04.1992			15	5
Trainer:					
Ariel Roberto Pereyra Legallais [as of 01.07.2014]	11.11.1973	17		19	

**Matches and goals in 2015 Liguilla Clausura included*

CLUB DEPORTIVO UNIVERSIDAD CATÓLICA SANTIAGO

Foundation date: April 21, 1937
Address: Avenida Andrés Bello 2782, Las Condes, 755-0006 Santiago
Stadium: Estadio "San Carlos de Apoquindo", Santiago – Capacity: 18,000

THE SQUAD

	DOB	Ape		Cla*	
		M	G	M	G
Goalkeepers:					
Fabián Alfredo Cerda Valdes	07.02.1989			4	-
Franco Costanzo (ARG)	05.09.1980	16	-	18	-
Andrés Ignacio Gutiérrez Bascuñán	13.02.1993	-	-	-	-
Claudio Patricio Santis Torrejón	16.10.1992	-	-	-	-
Cristopher Benjamín Toselli Ríos	15.06.1988	1	-	-	-
Miguel Ángel Vargas Mañan	15.06.1996			-	-
Defenders:					
Cristián Andrés Álvarez Valenzuela	20.01.1980	14	-	13	1
Pablo Álvarez Menéndez (URU)	07.02.1985			8	-
Enzo Pablo Andía Roco	16.08.1992	1	-		
Marko Andrés Biskupovic Venturino	30.06.1989	1	-	11	-
Matías Cahais (ARG)	24.12.1987	13	1	1	-
Tomás Costa (ARG)	30.01.1985	12	2	11	-
Walter Fernando Ibáñez Costa (URU)	10.12.1984			15	1
Stéfano Magnasco Galindo	28.09.1992	4	-	9	-
Guillermo Alfonso Maripán Loaysa	06.05.1994	1	-	4	-
Alfonso Cristián Parot Rojas	15.10.1989	14	1	6	-
Erick Antonio Pulgar Farfán	15.01.1994	16	1	19	6
Raimundo Rebolledo	02.05.1996			-	-
Midfielders:					
Darío Bottinelli (ARG)	26.12.1986	15	-	13	3
Fernando Patricio Cordero Fonseca	26.08.1987	14	1	21	1
Juan Pablo Gómez Vidal	11.05.1991	4	-	10	-
Mark Dennis González Hoffmann	10.07.1984	13	3	14	5
Benjamín Kuscevic Jaramillo	02.05.1996	-	-		
Carlos Alberto Lobos Ubilla	21.02.1997	1	-	-	-
Fabián Jorge Manzano Pérez	13.01.1994	6	-	4	-
Fernando Andrés Meneses Cornejo	27.08.1985	4	-		
Michael Fabián Ríos Ripoll	24.04.1985	9	-	17	7
Diego Nicolás Rojas Orellana	15.02.1995	4	-	12	2
Claudio Elias Sepúlveda Castro	19.06.1992	11	-	13	-
Gonzalo Alfredo Sepúlveda Domínguez	10.11.1988	3	-		
Jeisson Andrés Vargas Salazar	15.09.1997	1	-	8	-
Forwards:					
Hugo Andrés Alarcón Abarzua	04.11.1993	-	-	-	-
Ramiro Costa (ARG)	21.08.1992	9	1		
Roberto Carlos Gutiérrez Gamboa	18.04.1983			17	6
David Antonio Llanos Almonacid	27.07.1989	13	4	16	7
José Luis Muñoz Muñoz	24.07.1987	14	3	17	6
Mauro Iván Óbolo (ARG)	28.09.1981	9	1		
Álvaro Sebastián Ramos Sepúlveda	14.04.1992	12	2	13	1
Francisco Sierralta Carvallo	06.05.1997			-	-
Trainer:					
Julio César Falcioni (ARG) [01.07.-26.11.2014]	20.07.1956	15			
Luis Patricio Ormazábal Mozó [27.11.-31.12.2014]	12.02.1979	2			
Mario Alfredo Salas Saieg [as of 01.01.2015]	11.10.1967			21	

**Matches and goals in 2015 Liguilla Clausura included*

CLUB UNIVERSIDAD DE CHILE SANTIAGO

Foundation date: May 24, 1927
Address: Avenida Campo de Deportes 565, Ňuñoa, 775-0332 Santiago
Stadium: Estadio Nacional „Julio Martínez Prádanos", Santiago – Capacity: 77,000

THE SQUAD	DOB	Ape M	Ape G	Cla M	Cla G
Goalkeepers:					
Leandro Cañete Sepúlveda	22.03.1995	-	-	-	-
Nelson Francisco Espinoza Díaz	22.09.1995	-	-	-	-
Jhonny Cristián Herrera Muñoz	09.05.1981	17	-	15	-
Miguel Hernán Jiménez Aracena	12.12.1980			2	-
Luis Antonio Marín Barahona	18.05.1983	-	-		
Defenders:					
Bernardo Humberto Cerezo Rojas	21.01.1995	-	-	-	-
Mathias Corujo Díaz (URU)	08.05.1986	17	4	16	1
Cristián Alejandro Cuevas Jara	02.04.1995	-	-	4	-
Osvaldo Alexis González Sepúlveda	10.08.1984	14	-	12	-
Paulo Cesar Magalhães Lobos	14.12.1989	6	-	9	1
Waldo Alonso Ponce Carrizo	04.12.1982	-	-	2	-
José Manuel Rojas Bahamondes	23.06.1983	14	-	12	-
Cristián Fernando Suárez Figueroa	06.02.1987	17	-	7	1
Benjamin Fernando Vidal Allendes	18.03.1991	9	1	8	-
Midfielders:					
Roberto Andrés Cereceda Guajardo	10.10.1984			1	-
Bryan Alfonso Cortés Carvajal	19.08.1991	-	-	5	-
Rodrigo Eduardo Echeverría Sáez	17.04.1995	-	-	-	-
Gonzalo Alejandro Espinoza Toledo	09.04.1990	12	-	13	1
Ramón Ignacio Fernández (ARG)	03.12.1984	14	2	8	-
Diego García		-	-	-	-
Enzo Hernán Gutiérrez Lencinas	28.05.1986	12	1	10	2
Yerko Bastián Leiva Lazo	14.06.1998	-	-	-	-
Gustavo Rubén Lorenzetti Espinosa (ARG)	10.05.1985	12	-	13	1
Sebastián Martínez Muñoz	06.06.1993	12	-	11	-
Joao Luis Ortíz Pérez	10.02.1991	4	-	7	-
Ricardo Guzmán Pereira Méndez /URU)	16.05.1991	13	-	15	2
Luis Felipe Pinilla	24.09.1997			2	-
Maximiliano Rodríguez Maeso (URU)	02.10.1990			12	2
Sebastián Andrés Ubilla Cambón	09.08.1990	12	5	11	5
Forwards:					
Leandro Iván Benegas (ARG)	27.11.1988			15	8
Gustavo Javier Canales	30.03.1982	15	9	10	9
Fabián Alejandro Carmona Fredes	21.03.1994	5	-	7	3
César Alexis Cortés Pinto	09.01.1984	6	1	8	-
Juan Ignacio Duma (ARG)	08.12.1993	10	-		
Sebastián Gómez Ríos	09.01.1996			-	-
Patricio Rodolfo Rubio Pulgar	18.07.1989	16	11	1	-
Nazareno Damián Solís (ARG)	22.04.1994	-	-		
Bryan Danilo Taiva Lobos	19.03.1995	-	-	-	-
Sebastián Zúñiga Fuenzalida	21.06.1990	-	-		
Trainer:					
Martín Bernardo Lasarte Arróspide (URU) [as of 01.07.2014]	20.03.1961	17		17	

CLUB DEPORTIVO UNIVERSIDAD DE CONCEPCIÓN

Foundation date: August 8, 1994
Address: Calle Beltrán Mathieu 97, Barrio Universitario, 403-0576 Concepción
Stadium: Estadio Municipal „Alcaldesa Ester Roa Rebolledo“ – Capacity: 35,000

THE SQUAD

	DOB	Ape		Cla	
		M	G	M	G
Goalkeepers:					
Pablo Benítez				-	-
Leonardo Hilario Figueroa González	17.03.1992	-	-	3	-
Cristián Fernando Muñoz Hoffman (ARG)	01.07.1977	17	-	14	-
Guillermo Enrique Orellana Riquelme	29.07.1986	-	-	-	-
Defenders:					
Héctor Eduardo Berríos Ibarra	18.10.1986	17	-	15	1
Diego Armando Díaz Ahumada	12.07.1986	-	-	9	-
Esteban Flores Martínez	07.04.1992	16	-	16	-
Alexis Machuca (ARG)	10.05.1990	11	-	11	-
Cristian Javier Magaña Leyton	26.02.1991	-	-	-	-
Felipe Andrés Muñoz Flores	04.04.1985	15	-	13	-
Sebastián Alejandro Roco Melgarejo	26.06.1983			8	1
Sebastián Sánchez				-	-
Midfielders:					
Marcelo Aguirre (ARG)	25.08.1983	10	1	14	3
Fabián Raúl Benítez Gómez (PAR)	27.02.1985	11	-	7	-
Joseph Aníbal Carvallo Torres	01.05.1990	1	-	2	-
Diego Nicolás Guastavino Bentancor (URU)	26.07.1984			9	1
Andrés Roberto Imperiale (ARG)	08.07.1986	12	-		
José Lagos		-	-	1	-
Michael Antonio Lepe Labraña	13.08.1990	2	-	9	2
Fernando Alejandro Manríquez Hernández	01.02.1984	14	-	15	-
Jonathan Manuel Morales (ARG)	21.11.1992	1	-	-	-
Pedro Emiliano Muñoz Zúñiga	09.06.1986	16	4	15	3
Sixto Raimundo Peralta Salso (ARG)	16.04.1979	13	-		
Francisco Leoncio Portillo Maidana (PAR)	24.07.1987	16	1	15	1
Hans Francisco Salinas Flores	23.04.1990			9	2
Forwards:					
Manuel Briones	16.01.1994	-	-		-
Diego Churín Puyo (ARG)	12.01.1989	17	1	12	1
José Huentelaf Santana	22.01.1989	4	1	8	4
Leonardo Esteban Monje Valenzuela	16.03.1981	12	1		
Felipe Andrés Reynero Galarce	14.03.1989	9	-	11	2
Jorge Troncoso Ramírez	14.01.1993	4	-	6	-
Gabriel Alejandro Vargas Venegas	08.12.1983	17	8	15	6
Trainer:					
Pablo Andrés Sánchez (ARG) [01.01.2013-31.12.2014]	03.01.1973	17			

SECOND LEVEL
Campeonato National "Scotiabank" de Primera División B del Fútbol Profesional Chileno
2014/2015

The 14 teams were divided into 2 groups of each 7 clubs as follows:

Zona Norte:
CD Coquimbo Unido
CD Deportes Copiapó
CD La Serena
Everton de Viña del Mar
CD Magallanes Santiago
CD San Luis de Quillota
CD Unión San Felipe

Zona Sur:
CD Provincial Curicó Unido
CS Deportes Concepción
CD Temuco
Deportes Iberia Los Ángeles
CD Lota Schwager Coronel
CSD Rangers Talca
CD Santiago Morning

For each Apertura and Clausura tournament, a single round-robin tournament, called Fase Regional was played between the 7 teams of each zone, followed by a single round-robin tournament, called Fase Nacional between all 14 teams. So each team played 38 matches (6+13 Apertura 2014 & 6+13 Clausura 2015).

Aggregate Table 2014/2015

1.	CD San Luis de Quillota (*Promoted*)	38	24	9	5	61	-	32	81
2.	CD Unión San Felipe	38	22	6	10	80	-	45	72
3.	Everton de Viña del Mar	38	18	8	12	50	-	46	62
4.	CS Deportes Concepción	38	17	7	14	50	-	56	58
5.	CD Deportes Copiapó	38	14	14	10	45	-	46	56
6.	CD Temuco	38	15	9	14	49	-	52	54
7.	Deportes Iberia Los Ángeles	38	15	8	15	47	-	46	53
8.	CD Santiago Morning	38	14	7	17	46	-	44	49
9.	CD Provincial Curicó Unido	38	12	11	15	49	-	48	46
10.	CSD Rangers Talca	38	10	13	15	38	-	48	43
11.	CD La Serena	38	11	10	17	41	-	52	43
12.	CD Magallanes Santiago	38	10	11	17	36	-	48	41
13.	CD Coquimbo Unido	38	9	13	16	52	-	60	40
14.	CD Lota Schwager Coronel (*Relegated*)	38	7	10	21	38	-	59	31

NATIONAL TEAM
INTERNATIONAL MATCHES
(16.07.2014 – 15.07.2015)

06.09.2014	Santa Clara	Chile - Mexico	0-0	(F)
09.09.2014	Fort Lauderdale	Chile - Haiti	1-0(1-0)	(F)
10.10.2014	Valparaíso	Chile - Peru	3-0(2-0)	(F)
14.10.2014	Coquimbo	Chile - Bolivia	2-2(1-1)	(F)
14.11.2014	Talcahuano	Chile - Venezuela	5-0(2-0)	(F)
18.11.2014	Santiago	Chile - Uruguay	1-2(1-1)	(F)
28.01.2015	Rancagua	Chile – United States	3-2(1-2)	(F)
26.03.2015	Sankt Pölten	Iran - Chile	2-0(1-0)	(F)
29.03.2015	London	Brazil - Chile	1-0(0-0)	(F)
05.06.2015	Rancagua	Chile – El Salvador	1-0(1-0)	(F)
11.06.2015	Santiago	Chile - Ecuador	2-0(0-0)	(CA)
15.06.2015	Santiago	Chile – Mexico	3-3(2-2)	(CA)
19.06.2015	Santiago	Chile - Bolivia	5-0(2-0)	(CA)
24.06.2015	Santiago	Chile – Uruguay	1-0(0-0)	(CA)
29.06.2015	Santiago	Chile – Peru	2-1(1-0)	(CA)
04.07.2015	Santiago	Chile - Argentina	4-1 pen	(CA)

06.09.2014, Friendly International
Levi's Stadium, Santa Clara (United States); Attendance: 67,175
Referee: Juan Guzmán (United States)

CHILE - MEXICO 0-0

CHI: Claudio Andrés Bravo Muñoz, Gonzalo Alejandro Jara Reyes, Eugenio Esteban Mena Reveco (56.Miiko Martín Albornoz Inola), Arturo Erasmo Vidal Pardo, Mauricio Aníbal Isla Isla, Marcelo Alfonso Díaz Rojas, Gary Alexis Medel Soto, Francisco Andrés Silva Gajardo, Charles Mariano Aránguiz Sandoval (71.Mauricio Ricardo Pinilla Ferrera), Rodrigo Javier Millar Carvajal, Alexis Alejandro Sánchez Sánchez (85.Juan Antonio Delgado Baeza). Trainer: Jorge Luis Sampaoli Moya (Argentina).

09.09.2014, Friendly International
Lockhart Stadium, Fort Lauderdale (United States); Attendance: 10,000
Referee: Óscar Donaldo Moncada Godoy (Honduras)

CHILE - HAITI 1-0(1-0)

CHI: Johnny Cristián Herrera Muñoz, José Manuel Rojas Bahamondes, Miiko Martín Albornoz Inola, Mauricio Aníbal Isla Isla, Fabián Ariel Orellana Valenzuela (56.Eduardo Jesús Vargas Rojas), Marcelo Alfonso Díaz Rojas (66.Sebastián Ignacio Martínez Muñoz), Gary Alexis Medel Soto, Charles Mariano Aránguiz Sandoval, Rodrigo Javier Millar Carvajal (66.Martín Vladimir Rodríguez Torrejon), Juan Antonio Delgado Baeza (66.Jean André Emanuel Beausejour Coliqueo), Alexis Alejandro Sánchez Sánchez (86.José Pedro Fuenzalida Gana). Trainer: Jorge Luis Sampaoli Moya (Argentina).
Goal: Juan Antonio Delgado Baeza (20).

10.10.2014, Friendly International
Estadio "Elías Figueroa Brander", Valparaíso; Attendance: 17,000
Referee: Julio Quintana Rodríguez (Paraguay)

CHILE - PERU 3-0(2-0)

CHI: Claudio Andrés Bravo Muñoz, Gonzalo Alejandro Jara Reyes, José Manuel Rojas Bahamondes (66.José Pedro Fuenzalida Gana), Arturo Erasmo Vidal Pardo, Mauricio Aníbal Isla Isla, Marcelo Alfonso Díaz Rojas (83.Carlos Emilio Carmona Tello), Gary Alexis Medel Soto (45+1.Francisco Andrés Silva Gajardo), Charles Mariano Aránguiz Sandoval, Jean André Emanuel Beausejour Coliqueo (73.Juan Antonio Delgado Baeza), Alexis Alejandro Sánchez Sánchez, Eduardo Jesús Vargas Rojas

(79.Ángelo José Henríquez Iturra). Trainer: Jorge Luis Sampaoli Moya (Argentina).
Goals: Eduardo Jesús Vargas Rojas (28), Gary Alexis Medel Soto (34), Eduardo Jesús Vargas Rojas (53).

14.10.2014, Friendly International
Estadio Municipal "Francisco Sánchez Rumoroso", Coquimbo; Attendance: 14,000
Referee: Pablo Díaz (Argentina)
CHILE - BOLIVIA 2-2(1-1)
CHI: Johnny Cristián Herrera Muñoz, Gonzalo Alejandro Jara Reyes, Enzo Pablo Roco Roco (56.Eugenio Esteban Mena Reveco), Arturo Erasmo Vidal Pardo, Mauricio Aníbal Isla Isla, Marcelo Alfonso Díaz Rojas (87.Pedro Pablo Hernández), Gary Alexis Medel Soto, Charles Mariano Aránguiz Sandoval (65.Rodrigo Javier Millar Carvajal), Jean André Emanuel Beausejour Coliqueo (57.Juan Antonio Delgado Baeza), Alexis Alejandro Sánchez Sánchez, Eduardo Jesús Vargas Rojas (72.Ángelo José Henríquez Iturra). Trainer: Jorge Luis Sampaoli Moya (Argentina).
Goals: Charles Mariano Aránguiz Sandoval (42), Arturo Erasmo Vidal Pardo (90+1 penalty).

14.11.2014, Friendly International
Estadio CAP, Talcahuano; Attendance: 10,200
Referee: Antonio Javier Arias Alvarenga (Paraguay)
CHILE - VENEZUELA 5-0(2-0)
CHI: Claudio Andrés Bravo Muñoz, Eugenio Esteban Mena Reveco, Igor Lichnovsky Osorio, Jorge Luis Valdivia Toro (77.Pedro Pablo Hernández), Arturo Erasmo Vidal Pardo (76.Rodrigo Javier Millar Carvajal), Mauricio Aníbal Isla Isla, Marcelo Alfonso Díaz Rojas (81.Carlos Emilio Carmona Tello), Gary Alexis Medel Soto, Charles Mariano Aránguiz Sandoval, Alexis Alejandro Sánchez Sánchez (85.Mauricio Ricardo Pinilla Ferrera), Eduardo Jesús Vargas Rojas (77.Fabián Ariel Orellana Valenzuela). Trainer: Jorge Luis Sampaoli Moya (Argentina).
Goals: Alexis Alejandro Sánchez Sánchez (17), Jorge Luis Valdivia Toro (45+1), Eduardo Jesús Vargas Rojas (55), Rodrigo Javier Millar Carvajal (78), Pedro Pablo Hernández (90+3).

18.11.2014, Friendly International
Estadio Monumental "David Arellano", Santiago; Attendance: 40,000
Referee: Carlos Alfredo Vera Rodríguez (Ecuador)
CHILE - URUGUAY 1-2(1-1)
CHI: Claudio Andrés Bravo Muñoz, Gonzalo Alejandro Jara Reyes, Eugenio Esteban Mena Reveco (88.Jean André Emanuel Beausejour Coliqueo), Arturo Erasmo Vidal Pardo, Mauricio Aníbal Isla Isla, Fabián Ariel Orellana Valenzuela, Marcelo Alfonso Díaz Rojas (88.Rodrigo Javier Millar Carvajal), Gary Alexis Medel Soto, Charles Mariano Aránguiz Sandoval, Alexis Alejandro Sánchez Sánchez, Eduardo Jesús Vargas Rojas (70.Mauricio Ricardo Pinilla Ferrera). Trainer: Jorge Luis Sampaoli Moya (Argentina).
Goal: Alexis Alejandro Sánchez Sánchez (28).

28.01.2015, Friendly International
Estadio El Teniente, Rancagua; Attendance: 13,000
Referee: Patricio Hernán Loustau (Argentina)
CHILE – UNITED STATES 3-2(1-2)
CHI: Johnny Cristián Herrera Muñoz, Osvaldo Alexis González Sepúlveda, José Manuel Rojas Bahamondes, Bryan Paul Carrasco Santos, Juan Francisco Cornejo Palma, Erick Antonio Pulgar Farfán, Mark Dennis González Hoffmann (90.Ángelo Nicolás Sagal Tapia), Marco Antonio Medel de la Fuente (79.Paulo César Díaz Huincales), Gonzalo Alejandro Espinoza Toledo (72.Gonzalo Antonio Fierro Caniullán), Diego Alfonso Valdés Contreras (59.Juan Antonio Delgado Baeza), Roberto Carlos Gutiérrez Gamboa (90+3.Andrés Alejandro Vilches Araneda). Trainer: Jorge Luis Sampaoli Moya (Argentina).
Goals: Roberto Carlos Gutiérrez Gamboa (10), Mark Dennis González Hoffmann (66, 75).

26.03.2015, Friendly International
NV Arena, Sankt Pölten (Austria); Attendance: 2,000
Referee: Manuel Schüttengruber (Austria)

IRAN - CHILE 2-0(1-0)

CHI: Claudio Andrés Bravo Muñoz, Gonzalo Alejandro Jara Reyes, Enzo Pablo Roco Roco (63.Gary Alexis Medel Soto), Juan Francisco Cornejo Palma, Erick Antonio Pulgar Farfán (46.Charles Mariano Aránguiz Sandoval), Mark Dennis González Hoffmann (46.Roberto Carlos Gutiérrez Gamboa), Matías Ariel Fernández Fernández, Fabián Ariel Orellana Valenzuela (46.Alexis Alejandro Sánchez Sánchez), José Pedro Fuenzalida Gana (62.Mauricio Aníbal Isla Isla), Rodrigo Javier Millar Carvajal (63.David Marcelo Pizarro Cortés), Eduardo Jesús Vargas Rojas. Trainer: Jorge Luis Sampaoli Moya (Argentina).

29.03.2015, Friendly International
Emirates Stadium, London (England); Attendance: 60,000
Referee: Martin Atkinson (England)

BRAZIL - CHILE 1-0(0-0)

CHI: Claudio Andrés Bravo Muñoz, Gonzalo Alejandro Jara Reyes, Miiko Martín Albornoz Inola, Eugenio Esteban Mena Reveco (82.Mark Dennis González Hoffmann), Arturo Erasmo Vidal Pardo (80.Eduardo Jesús Vargas Rojas), Mauricio Aníbal Isla Isla, Gary Alexis Medel Soto, Charles Mariano Aránguiz Sandoval, Rodrigo Javier Millar Carvajal (74.Juan Francisco Cornejo Palma), Pedro Pablo Hernández, Alexis Alejandro Sánchez Sánchez. Trainer: Jorge Luis Sampaoli Moya (Argentina).

05.06.2015, Friendly International
Estadio El Teniente, Rancagua; Attendance: 14,000
Referee: Fernando Rapallini (Argentina)

CHILE – EL SALVADOR 1-0(1-0)

CHI: Johnny Cristián Herrera Muñoz, Gonzalo Alejandro Jara Reyes, Jorge Luis Valdivia Toro (63.Mauricio Ricardo Pinilla Ferrera), Mauricio Aníbal Isla Isla, Marcelo Alfonso Díaz Rojas (80.Miiko Martín Albornoz Inola), Gary Alexis Medel Soto, Charles Mariano Aránguiz Sandoval, Jean André Emanuel Beausejour Coliqueo (65.Eugenio Esteban Mena Reveco), Felipe Alejandro Gutiérrez Leiva (46.David Marcelo Pizarro Cortés), Alexis Alejandro Sánchez Sánchez, Eduardo Jesús Vargas Rojas (74.Ángelo José Henríquez Iturra). Trainer: Jorge Luis Sampaoli Moya (Argentina).
Goal: Jorge Luis Valdivia Toro (10).

11.06.2015, 44th Copa América, Group Stage
Estadio Nacional "Julio Martínez Prádanos", Santiago; Attendance: 46,000
Referee: Néstor Fabián Pitana (Argentina)

CHILE - ECUADOR 2-0(0-0)

CHI: Claudio Andrés Bravo Muñoz, Gonzalo Alejandro Jara Reyes, Eugenio Esteban Mena Reveco, Jorge Luis Valdivia Toro (68.Matías Ariel Fernández Fernández), Arturo Erasmo Vidal Pardo, Mauricio Aníbal Isla Isla, Marcelo Alfonso Díaz Rojas, Gary Alexis Medel Soto, Charles Mariano Aránguiz Sandoval (85.David Marcelo Pizarro Cortés), Jean André Emanuel Beausejour Coliqueo (46.Eduardo Jesús Vargas Rojas), Alexis Alejandro Sánchez Sánchez. Trainer: Jorge Luis Sampaoli Moya (Argentina).
Goals: Arturo Erasmo Vidal Pardo (66 penalty), Eduardo Jesús Vargas Rojas (83).
Sent off: Matías Ariel Fernández Fernández (90+3).

15.06.2015, 44th Copa América, Group Stage
Estadio Nacional „Julio Martínez Prádanos", Santiago; Attendance: 45,583
Referee: Víctor Hugo Carrillo Casanova (Peru)

CHILE – MEXICO 3-3(2-2)

CHI: Claudio Andrés Bravo Muñoz, Gonzalo Alejandro Jara Reyes, Miiko Martín Albornoz Inola (87.Jean André Emanuel Beausejour Coliqueo), Jorge Luis Valdivia Toro, Arturo Erasmo Vidal Pardo, Mauricio Aníbal Isla Isla, Marcelo Alfonso Díaz Rojas (71.Eugenio Esteban Mena Reveco), Gary Alexis Medel Soto, Charles Mariano Aránguiz Sandoval, Alexis Alejandro Sánchez Sánchez, Eduardo Jesús Vargas Rojas (85.Mauricio Ricardo Pinilla Ferrera). Trainer: Jorge Luis Sampaoli Moya (Argentina).
Goals: Arturo Erasmo Vidal Pardo (21), Eduardo Jesús Vargas Rojas (41), Arturo Erasmo Vidal Pardo (54 penalty).

19.06.2015, 44th Copa América, Group Stage
Estadio Nacional „Julio Martínez Prádanos", Santiago; Attendance: 45,601
Referee: Andrés Cunha (Uruguay)

CHILE - BOLIVIA 5-0(2-0)

CHI: Claudio Andrés Bravo Muñoz, Gonzalo Alejandro Jara Reyes (70.David Marcelo Pizarro Cortés), Jorge Luis Valdivia Toro, Arturo Erasmo Vidal Pardo (46.Matías Ariel Fernández Fernández), Mauricio Aníbal Isla Isla, Marcelo Alfonso Díaz Rojas, Gary Alexis Medel Soto, Charles Mariano Aránguiz Sandoval, Jean André Emanuel Beausejour Coliqueo, Alexis Alejandro Sánchez Sánchez (46.Ángelo José Henríquez Iturra), Eduardo Jesús Vargas Rojas. Trainer: Jorge Luis Sampaoli Moya (Argentina).
Goals: Charles Mariano Aránguiz Sandoval (3), Alexis Alejandro Sánchez Sánchez (37), Charles Mariano Aránguiz Sandoval (66), Gary Alexis Medel Soto (79), Ronald Raldes Balcázar (86 own goal).

24.06.2015, 44th Copa América, Quarter-Finals
Estadio Nacional „Julio Martínez Prádanos", Santiago; Attendance: 45,304
Referee: Sandro Meira Ricci (Brazil)

CHILE - URUGUAY 1-0(0-0)

CHI: Claudio Andrés Bravo Muñoz, Gonzalo Alejandro Jara Reyes, Eugenio Esteban Mena Reveco, Jorge Luis Valdivia Toro (85.David Marcelo Pizarro Cortés), Arturo Erasmo Vidal Pardo, Mauricio Aníbal Isla Isla, Marcelo Alfonso Díaz Rojas (71.Matías Ariel Fernández Fernández), Gary Alexis Medel Soto, Charles Mariano Aránguiz Sandoval, Alexis Alejandro Sánchez Sánchez, Eduardo Jesús Vargas Rojas (71.Mauricio Ricardo Pinilla Ferrera). Trainer: Jorge Luis Sampaoli Moya (Argentina).
Goal: Mauricio Aníbal Isla Isla (81).

29.06.2015, 44th Copa América, Semi-Finals
Estadio Nacional „Julio Martínez Prádanos", Santiago; Attendance: 45,651
Referee: José Ramón Argote Vega (Venezuela)

CHILE - PERU 2-1(1-0)

CHI: Claudio Andrés Bravo Muñoz, José Manuel Rojas Bahamondes, Miiko Martín Albornoz Inola (46.Eugenio Esteban Mena Reveco), Jorge Luis Valdivia Toro (86.Felipe Alejandro Gutiérrez Leiva), Arturo Erasmo Vidal Pardo, Mauricio Aníbal Isla Isla, Marcelo Alfonso Díaz Rojas (46.David Marcelo Pizarro Cortés), Gary Alexis Medel Soto, Charles Mariano Aránguiz Sandoval, Alexis Alejandro Sánchez Sánchez, Eduardo Jesús Vargas Rojas. Trainer: Jorge Luis Sampaoli Moya (Argentina).
Goals: Eduardo Jesús Vargas Rojas (42, 64).

04.07.2015, 44th Copa América, Final
Estadio Nacional "Julio Martínez Prádanos", Santiago; Attendance: 45,693
Referee: Wilmar Alexander Roldán Pérez (Colombia)
CHILE - ARGENTINA **0-0; 4-1 on penalties**
CHI: Claudio Andrés Bravo Muñoz, Jorge Luis Valdivia Toro (75.Matías Ariel Fernández Fernández), Arturo Erasmo Vidal Pardo, Mauricio Aníbal Isla Isla, Marcelo Alfonso Díaz Rojas, Gary Alexis Medel Soto, Francisco Andrés Silva Gajardo, Charles Mariano Aránguiz Sandoval, Jean André Emanuel Beausejour Coliqueo, Alexis Alejandro Sánchez Sánchez, Eduardo Jesús Vargas Rojas (95.Ángelo José Henríquez Iturra). Trainer: Jorge Luis Sampaoli Moya (Argentina).
Penalties: Matías Ariel Fernández Fernández, Arturo Erasmo Vidal Pardo, Charles Mariano Aránguiz Sandoval, Alexis Alejandro Sánchez Sánchez.

NATIONAL TEAM PLAYERS 2014/2015			
Name	**DOB**	**Caps**	**Goals**
[Club 2014/2015]			

(Caps and goals at 05.07.2015)

Goalkeepers

Claudio Andrés BRAVO Muñoz [2014/2015: FC Barcelona (ESP)]	13.04.1983	**95**	**0**
Johnny Cristian HERRERA Muñoz [2014/2015: Club Universidad de Chile Santiago]	09.05.1981	**12**	**0**

Defenders

Miiko Martín ALBORNOZ Inola [2014/2015: Hannover'96]	30.11.1990	**8**	**1**
Juan Francisco CORNEJO Palma [2014/2015: Audax CS Italiano La Florida]	27.02.1990	**3**	**0**
Paulo César DÍAZ Huincales [2015: CD Palestino Santiago]	24.03.1994	**1**	**0**
Gonzalo Antonio FIERRO Caniullán [2015: CSD Colo-Colo Santiago]	21.03.1983	**24**	**1**
Osvaldo Alexis GONZÁLEZ Sepúlveda [2015: Club Universidad de Chile Santiago]	10.08.1984	**14**	**0**
Mauricio Aníbal ISLA Isla [2014/2015: Queen's Park Rangers FC London (ENG), on loan]	12.06.1988	**66**	**3**
Gonzalo Alejandro JARA Reyes [2014/2015: 1.FSV Mainz 05 (GER)]	29.08.1985	**80**	**3**
Igor LICHNOVSKY Osorio [2014/2015: FC do Porto (POR)]	07.03.1994	**1**	**0**
Gary Alexis MEDEL Soto [2014/2015: FC Internazionale Milano (ITA)]	03.08.1987	**80**	**7**
Eugenio Esteban MENA Reveco [2014: Santos FC (BRA); 01.2015-> Cruzeiro EC Belo-Horizonte (BRA)]	18.07.1988	**39**	**3**
Erick Antonio PULGAR Farfán [2015: CD Universidad Católica Santiago]	15.01.1994	**2**	**0**
Enzo Pablo ROCO Roco [*called earlier Enzo Pablo Andía Roco*] [2014/2015: Elche CF (ESP)]	16.08.1992	**6**	**1**
José Manuel ROJAS Bahamondes [2014/2015: Club Universidad de Chile Santiago]	23.06.1983	**24**	**1**

Midfielders			
Charles Mariano ARÁNGUIZ Sandoval [2014/2015: SC Internacional Porto Alegre (BRA)]	17.04.1989	**40**	**6**
Jean André Emanuel BEAUSEJOUR Coliqueo [2014/2015: CSD Colo-Colo Santiago]	01.06.1984	**70**	**6**
Carlos Emilio CARMONA Tello [2014/2015: Atalanta Bergamasca Calcio (ITA)]	21.02.1987	**47**	**1**
Bryan Paul CARRASCO Santos [2014/2015: Audax CS Italiano La Florida]	31.01.1991	**4**	**1**
Marcelo Alfonso DÍAZ Rojas [2014: FC Basel (SUI); 02.02.2015-> Hamburger SV (GER)]	30.12.1986	**38**	**1**
Gonzalo Alejandro ESPINOZA Toledo [2014/2015: Club Universidad de Chile Santiago]	09.04.1990	**1**	**0**
Matías Ariel FERNÁNDEZ Fernández [2014/2015: AC Fiorentina Firenze (ITA)]	15.05.1986	**65**	**14**
José Pedro FUENZALIDA Gana [2014/2015: CA Boca Juniors Buenos Aires (ARG)]	22.02.1985	**26**	**1**
Mark Dennis GONZÁLEZ Hoffmann [2015: CD Universidad Católica Santiago]	10.07.1984	**51**	**6**
Felipe Alejandro GUTIÉRREZ Leiva [2014/2015: FC Twente Enschede (NED)]	08.10.1990	**24**	**1**
Pedro Pablo HERNÁNDEZ [2014/2015: RC Celta de Vigo (ESP)]	24.10.1986	**4**	**3**
Sebastián Ignacio MARTÍNEZ Muñoz [2014/2015: Club Universidad de Chile Santiago]	06.06.1993	**1**	**0**
Marco Antonio MEDEL de la Fuente [2015: CD Santiago Wanderers]	06.06.1989	**1**	**0**
Rodrigo Javier MILLAR Carvajal [2014/2015: Atlas FC Guadalajara (MEX)]	03.11.1981	**36**	**3**
David Marcelo PIZARRO Cortés [2014/2015: AC Fiorentina Firenze (ITA)]	11.02.1979	**46**	**2**
Martín Vladimir RODRÍGUEZ Torrejon [2014: CD Huachipato]	05.08.1994	**1**	**0**
Ángelo Nicolás SAGAL Tapia [2014/2015: CD Huachipato]	05.08.1994	**1**	**0**
Francisco Andrés SILVA Gajardo [2014/2015: Club Brugge KV (BEL)]	11.02.1986	**18**	**0**
Diego Alfonso VALDÉS Contreras [2015: Audax CS Italiano La Florida]	30.01.1994	**1**	**0**
Jorge Luis VALDIVIA Toro [2014/2015: SE Palmeiras São Paulo (BRA)]	19.01.1983	**68**	**7**
Arturo Erasmo VIDAL Pardo [2014/2015: Juventus FC Torino (ITA)]	22.05.1987	**69**	**12**

Forwards

Juan Antonio DELGADO Baeza [2014/2015: CSD Colo-Colo Santiago]	05.03.1993	**5**	**1**
Roberto Carlos GUTIÉRREZ Gamboa [2015: CD Universidad Católica Santiago]	18.04.1983	**6**	**3**
Ángelo José HENRÍQUEZ Iturra [2014/2015: GNK Dinamo Zagreb (CRO)]	13.04.1994	**8**	**2**
Fabián Ariel ORELLANA Valenzuela [2014/2015: RC Celta de Vigo (ESP)]	27.01.1986	**30**	**2**
Mauricio Ricardo PINILLA Ferrera [2014: Genoa CFC (ITA); 01.2015-> Atalanta Bergamasca Calcio (ITA)]	04.02.1984	**36**	**6**
Alexis Alejandro SÁNCHEZ Sánchez [2014/2015: Arsenal FC London (ENG)]	19.12.1988	**86**	**27**
Eduardo Jesús VARGAS Rojas [2014/2015: Queen's Park Rangers FC London (ENG), on loan]	20.11.1989	**48**	**22**
Andrés Alejandro VILCHES Araneda [2015: CD Huachipato]	14.01.1992	**1**	**0**

National coaches

Jorge Luis SAMPAOLI Moya (Argentina)	09.11.1948	39 M; 24 W; 8 D; 7 L; 79-35

COLOMBIA

The Country:
República de Colombia (Republic of Colombia) Capital: Bogotá Surface: 1,141,748 km² Inhabitants: 48,014,026 Time: UTC-5

The FA:
Federación Colombiana de Fútbol Avenida 32 No. 16-22 Piso 4°, Apdo Aéreo, 17602 Santa Fé de Bogotá D.C. Year of Formation: 1924 Member of FIFA since: 1936 Member of CONMEBOL since: 1936 Internet: fcf.com.co

NATIONAL TEAM RECORDS	
First international match:	10.02.1938, Ciudad de Panamá: Mexico – Colombia 3-1
Most international caps:	Carlos Alberto Valderrama Palacio – 111 caps (1985-1998)
Most international goals:	Arnoldo Alberto Iguarán Zúñiga – 25 goals / 68 caps (1979-1993) Radamel Falcao García Zárate - 25 goals / 61 caps (since 2007)

OLYMPIC GAMES 1900-2012
1968, 1972, 1980, 1992
FIFA CONFEDERATIONS CUP 1992-2013
2003

COPA AMÉRICA	
1916	Did not enter
1917	Did not enter
1919	Did not enter
1920	Did not enter
1921	Did not enter
1922	Did not enter
1923	Did not enter
1924	Did not enter
1925	Did not enter
1926	Did not enter
1927	Did not enter
1929	Did not enter
1935	Did not enter
1937	Did not enter
1939	Did not enter
1941	Did not enter
1942	Did not enter
1945	5th Place
1946	Withdrew
1947	8th Place
1949	8th Place
1953	Withdrew
1955	Withdrew
1956	Withdrew
1957	5th Place
1959	Withdrew
1959E	Withdrew
1963	7th Place
1967	Qualifying Round
1975	Runners-up
1979	Round 1
1983	Round 1
1987	3rd Place
1989	Round 1
1991	4th Place
1993	3rd Place
1995	3rd Place
1997	Quarter-Finals
1999	Quarter-Finals
2001	**Winners**
2004	4th Place
2007	Round 1
2011	Quarter-Finals
2015	Quarter-Finals

FIFA WORLD CUP	
1930	Did not enter
1934	Did not enter
1938	Withdrew
1950	Did not enter
1954	Did not enter
1958	Qualifiers
1962	Final Tournament (Group Stage)
1966	Qualifiers
1970	Qualifiers
1974	Qualifiers
1978	Qualifiers
1982	Qualifiers
1986	Qualifiers
1990	Final Tournament (2nd Round of 16)
1994	Final Tournament (Group Stage)
1998	Final Tournament (Group Stage)
2002	Qualifiers
2006	Qualifiers
2010	Qualifiers
2014	Final Tournament (Quarter-Finals)

PANAMERICAN GAMES	
1951	Did not enter
1955	Did not enter
1959	Did not enter
1963	Did not enter
1967	Round 1
1971	Runners-up
1975	Did not enter
1979	Did not enter
1983	Did not enter
1987	Round 1
1991	Did not enter
1995	3rd Place
1999	Did not enter
2003	4th Place
2007	Round 1
2011	Did not enter

PANAMERICAN CHAMPIONSHIP	
1952	Did not enter
1956	Did not enter
1960	Did not enter

COLOMBIAN CLUB HONOURS IN SOUTH AMERICAN CLUB COMPETITIONS:

COPA LIBERTADORES 1960-2014
Corporación Deportiva Atlético Nacional Medellín (1989) Corporación Deportiva Once Caldas Manizales (2004)
COPA SUDAMERICANA 2002-2014
None
RECOPA SUDAMERICANA 1989-2014
None
COPA CONMEBOL 1992-1999
None
SUPERCUP „JOÃO HAVELANGE“ 1988-1997*
None
COPA MERCONORTE 1998-2001**
Corporación Deportiva Atlético Nacional Medellín (1998, 2000) Corporación Deportiva América de Cali (1999) Club Deportivo Los Millonarios Bogotá (2001)

**Contested betwenn winners of all previous editions of the Copa Libertadores*

***Contested between teams belonging countries from the northern part of South America (Bolivia, Colombia, Ecuador, Peru and Venezuela);*

NATIONAL COMPETITIONS
TABLE OF HONOURS

NATIONAL CHAMPIONS 1948-2014	
1948	Independiente Santa Fé Bogotá[(1)]
1949	CD Los Millonarios Bogotá
1950	CD Once Caldas Manizales
1951	CD Los Millonarios Bogotá
1952	CD Los Millonarios Bogotá
1953	CD Los Millonarios Bogotá
1954	CD Atlético Nacional Medellín
1955	CD Independiente Medellín
1956	Deportes Quindío Armenia
1957	CD Independiente Medellín
1958	Independiente Santa Fé Bogotá
1959	CD Los Millonarios Bogotá
1960	Independiente Santa Fé Bogotá
1961	CD Los Millonarios Bogotá
1962	CD Los Millonarios Bogotá
1963	CD Los Millonarios Bogotá
1964	CD Los Millonarios Bogotá
1965	Asociación Deportivo Cali
1966	Independiente Santa Fé Bogotá
1967	Asociación Deportivo Cali
1968	AD Unión Magdalena Santa Marta
1969	Asociación Deportivo Cali
1970	Asociación Deportivo Cali
1971	Independiente Santa Fé Bogotá
1972	CD Los Millonarios Bogotá
1973	CD Atlético Nacional Medellín

1974		Asociación Deportivo Cali
1975		Independiente Santa Fé Bogotá
1976		CD Atlético Nacional Medellín
1977		CDPJ Atlético Junior Barranquilla
1978		CD Los Millonarios Bogotá
1979		CD América de Cali
1980		CDPJ Atlético Junior Barranquilla
1981		CD Atlético Nacional Medellín
1982		CD América de Cali
1983		CD América de Cali
1984		CD América de Cali
1985		CD América de Cali
1986		CD América de Cali
1987		CD Los Millonarios Bogotá
1988		CD Los Millonarios Bogotá
1989		*Championship cancelled*
1990		CD América de Cali
1991		CD Atlético Nacional Medellín
1992		CD América de Cali
1993		CDPJ Atlético Junior Barranquilla
1994		CD Atlético Nacional Medellín
1995		CDPJ Atlético Junior Barranquilla(2)
1995/1996		Asociación Deportivo Cali
1996/1997		CD América de Cali
1998		Asociación Deportivo Cali
1999		CD Atlético Nacional Medellín
2000		CD América de Cali
2001		CD América de Cali
2002	Ape:	CD América de Cali
	Fin:	CD Independiente Medellín
2003	Ape:	CD Once Caldas Manizales
	Fin:	CC Deportes Tolima
2004	Ape:	CD Independiente Medellín
	Fin:	CDPJ Atlético Junior Barranquilla
2005	Ape:	CD Atlético Nacional Medellín
	Fin:	Asociación Deportivo Cali
2006	Ape:	Asociación Deportivo Pasto
	Fin:	CN Cúcuta Deportivo
2007	Ape:	CD Atlético Nacional Medellín
	Fin:	CD Atlético Nacional Medellín
2008	Ape:	Boyacá Chicó FC Tunja
	Fin:	CD América de Cali
2009	Ape:	CD Once Caldas Manizales
	Fin:	CD Independiente Medellín
2010	Ape:	CDP Junior Barranquilla
	Fin:	CD Once Caldas Manizales
2011	Ape:	CD Atlético Nacional Medellín
	Fin:	CDP Junior Barranquilla
2012	Ape:	Santa Fe CD Bogotá
	Fin:	CD Los Millonarios Bogotá
2013	Ape:	CD Atlético Nacional Medellín
	Fin:	CD Atlético Nacional Medellín

2014	Ape:	CD Atlético Nacional Medellín
	Fin:	Santa Fe CD Bogotá

[(1)]became Santa Fe CD Bogotá.
[(2)]became CDP Junior Barranquilla.

	BEST GOALSCORERS	
1948	Alfredo Castillo (ARG, CD Los Millonarios Bogotá)	31
1949	Pedro Cabillón (ARG, CD Los Millonarios Bogotá)	42
1950	Casimiro Ávalos (PAR, CSDC de Pereira)	27
1951	Alfredo Stéfano Di Stéfano Laulhé (ARG, CD Los Millonarios Bogotá)	31
1952	Alfredo Stéfano Di Stéfano Laulhé (ARG, CD Los Millonarios Bogotá)	19
1953	Mario Garelli (ARG, Deportes Quindío Armenia)	20
1954	Carlos Alberto Gambina (ARG, CD Atlético Nacional Medellín)	21
1955	Felipe Marino (ARG, CD Independiente Medellín)	22
1956	Jaime Gutiérrez (Deportes Quindío Armenia)	21
1957	José Vicente Grecco (ARG, CD Independiente Medellín)	30
1958	José Americo Montanini (ARG, Club Atlético Bucaramanga CD)	36
1959	Felipe Marino (ARG, CN Cúcuta Deportivo)	35
1960	Walter Marcolini (ARG, Asociación Deportivo Cali)	30
1961	Alberto Perazzo (ARG, Independiente Santa Fé Bogotá)	32
1962	José Omar Verdún (URU, CN Cúcuta Deportivo)	36
1963	Omar Lorenzo Devanni (ARG, Club Atlético Bucaramanga CD) José Omar Verdún (URU, CN Cúcuta Deportivo)	36
1964	Omar Lorenzo Devanni (ARG, AD Unión Magdalena Santa Marta / Club Atlético Bucaramanga CD)	28
1965	Perfecto Rodríguez (ARG, CD Independiente Medellín)	38
1966	Omar Lorenzo Devanni (ARG, Independiente Santa Fé Bogotá)	31
1967	José María Ferrero (ARG, CD Los Millonarios Bogotá)	38
1968	José María Ferrero (ARG, CD Los Millonarios Bogotá)	32
1969	Hugo Horacio Londero (ARG, CD América de Cali)	25
1970	José María Ferrero (ARG, CN Cúcuta Deportivo) Walter Sosa (URU, Independiente Santa Fé Bogotá)	27
1971	Hugo Horacio Londero (ARG, CN Cúcuta Deportivo) Apolinar Paniagua (PAR, CSDC de Pereira)	30
1972	Hugo Horacio Londero (ARG, CN Cúcuta Deportivo)	27
1973	Nelson Silva Pacheco (URU, CN Cúcuta Deportivo)	36
1974	Víctor Ephanor (BRA, CDPJ Atlético Junior Barranquilla)	33
1975	Jorge Ramón Cáceres (ARG, CSDC de Pereira)	35
1976	Miguel Ángel Converti (ARG, CD Los Millonarios Bogotá)	33
1977	Oswaldo Marcial Palavecino (ARG, CD Atlético Nacional Medellín)	33
1978	Oswaldo Marcial Palavecino (ARG, CD Atlético Nacional Medellín)	36
1979	Juan José Irigiyon (ARG, CD Los Millonarios Bogotá)	36
1980	Sergio Cierra (ARG, CSDC de Pereira)	26
1981	Víctor Hugo Del Río (ARG, CC Deportes Tolima)	29
1982	Miguel Oswaldo González (ARG, Club Atlético Bucaramanga CD)	27
1983	Hugo Ernesto Gottardi (ARG, Independiente Santa Fé Bogotá)	29
1984	Hugo Ernesto Gottardi (ARG, Independiente Santa Fé Bogotá)	23
1985	Miguel Oswaldo González (ARG, Club Atlético Bucaramanga CD)	34
1986	Hugo Ramón Sosa (ARG, CD Independiente Medellín)	23
1987	Jorge Orlando Aravena Plaza (CHI, Asociación Deportivo Cali)	23
1988	Sergio Angulo Bolaños (Independiente Santa Fé Bogotá)	29

1989	Héctor Gerardo Móndez (URU, CSDC de Pereira)		17
1990	Antony Wílliam de Ávila Charris (CD América de Cali)		25
1991	Sergio Angulo Bolaños (CDPJ Atlético Junior Barranquilla)		30
1992	John Jairo Tréllez (CD Atlético Nacional Medellín)		25
1993	Miguel Guerrero (CDPJ Atlético Junior Barranquilla)		34
1994	Rubén Darío Hernández (CD Atlético Nacional Medellín / CSDC de Pereira / CD América de Cali)		32
1995	Iván René Valenciano Pérez (CDPJ Atlético Junior Barranquilla)		24
1995/1996	Iván René Valenciano Pérez (CDPJ Atlético Junior Barranquilla)		36
1996/1997	Hamilton Ricard Cuesta (Asociación Deportivo Cali)		36
1998	Víctor Manuel Bonilla Hinestroza (Asociación Deportivo Cali)		37
1999	Sergio Galván Rey (ARG, CD Once Caldas Manizales)		26
2000	Carlos Alberto Castro (CD Los Millonarios Bogotá)		24
2001	Carlos Alberto Castro (CD Los Millonarios Bogotá) Jorge Horacio Serna Castañeda (CD Independiente Medellín)		29
2002	Ape:	Luis Fernando Zuleta (AD Unión Magdalena Santa Marta)	13
	Fin:	Orlando Enrique Ballesteros Santos (Club Atlético Bucaramanga CD) Milton Fabián Rodríguez Suárez (CSDC de Pereira)	13
2003	Ape:	Arnulfo Valentierra Cuero (CD Once Caldas Manizales)	13
	Fin:	Léider Calimenio Preciado Guerrero (Asociación Deportivo Cali)	17
2004	Ape:	Sergio Darío Herrera Month (CD América de Cali)	13
	Fin:	Leonardo Fabio Moreno Cortés (CD América de Cali) Léider Calimenio Preciado Guerrero (Independiente Santa Fé Bogotá)	15
2005	Ape:	Víctor Hugo Aristizábal Posada (CD Atlético Nacional Medellín)	16
	Fin:	Jémerson Rentería (Independiente Santa Fé Bogotá) Hugo Rodallega Martínez (Asociación Deportivo Cali)	12
2006	Ape:	Jorge Moreno (CN Cúcuta Deportivo)	15
	Fin:	Diego Álvarez (CD Independiente Medellín) John Jairo Charria Escobar (CC Deportes Tolima)	11
2007	Ape:	Fredy Henkyer Montero Muñoz Jr. (CD Atlético Huila Neiva) Sergio Galván Rey (CD Atlético Nacional Medellín)	13
	Fin:	Dayro Mauricio Moreno Galindo (CD Once Caldas Manizales)	16
2008	Ape:	Iván Velásquez (Deportes Quindío Armenia) Miguel Eduardo Caneo (ARG, Boyacá Chicó FC Tunja)	13
	Fin:	Fredy Henkyer Montero Muñoz Jr. (Asociación Deportivo Cali)	16
2009	Ape:	Teófilo Antonio Gutiérrez Rocancio (CDP Junior Barranquilla)	16
	Fin:	Jackson Arley Martínez Valencia (CD Independiente Medellín)	18
2010	Ape:	Carlos Arturo Bacca Ahumada (CDP Junior Barranquilla) Carlos Alveiro Rentería Cuesta (CD La Equidad Seguros Bogotá)	12
	Fin:	Wilder Andrés Medina Tamayo (CC Deportes Tolima)	17
2011	Ape:	Carlos Alveiro Rentería Cuesta (CD Atlético Nacional Medellín)	12
	Fin:	Carlos Arturo Bacca Ahumada (CDP Junior Barranquilla)	12
2012	Ape:	Robin Ariel Ramírez González (CC Deportes Tolima)	13
	Fin:	Henry Javier Hernández Álvarez (CN Cúcuta Deportivo)	9
2013	Ape:	Wilder Andrés Medina Tamayo (Santa Fe CD Bogotá)	12
	Fin:	Dayro Mauricio Moreno Galindo (CD Los Millonarios Bogotá) Luis Carlos Ruiz Morales (CDP Junior Barranquilla)	16
2014	Ape:	Dayro Mauricio Moreno Galindo (CD Los Millonarios Bogotá)	13
	Fin:	Germán Ezequiel Cano (ARG, CD Independiente Medellín)	16

NATIONAL CHAMPIONSHIP
PRIMERA A 2014

Torneo Apertura - Liga Postobón I

Results

Round 1 [24-26.01.2014]
La Equidad - Alianza Petrolera 1-1(1-1)
Santa Fe - Itagüi FC 3-0(2-0)
Uniautónoma FC - Deportes Tolima 3-2(0-1)
Envigado FC - Los Millonarios 1-2(0-2)
Once Caldas - Fortaleza FC 3-1(1-0)
Atlético Huila - CDP Junior 2-3(0-1)
Deportivo Pasto - Patriotas FC 3-1(2-0)
Atlético Nacional – Indep. Medellín 3-1(1-0)
Boyacá Chicó FC - Deportivo Cali 2-1(1-0)

Round 2 [31.01.-02.02.2014]
Patriotas FC - Once Caldas 0-0
Indep. Medellín - Deportivo Pasto 2-0(1-0)
Alianza Petrolera - Boyacá Chicó FC 1-2(1-0)
CDP Junior - Uniautónoma FC 1-1(1-0)
Fortaleza FC - Santa Fe 1-2(1-0)
Deportes Tolima - Envigado FC 2-4(1-2)
Itagüi FC - Atlético Huila 2-1(1-1)
Los Millonarios - La Equidad 0-1(0-1)
Deportivo Cali - Atlético Nacional 0-3(0-2)

Round 3 [04-06.02.2014]
Once Caldas - Independiente Medellín 2-2(2-2)
Envigado FC - Uniautónoma FC 1-0(0-0)
La Equidad - Deportes Tolima 0-2(0-1)
Deportivo Pasto - Deportivo Cali 1-1(0-0)
Santa Fe - Patriotas FC 1-0(0-0)
Atlético Nacional - Alianza Petrolera 5-1(2-0)
Atlético Huila - Fortaleza FC 3-1(3-1)
Boyacá Chicó FC - Los Millonarios 1-0(0-0)
CDP Junior - Itagüi FC 2-0(0-0)

Round 4 [08-10.02.2014]
Envigado FC - La Equidad 1-3(1-0)
Independiente Medellín - Santa Fe 0-2(0-2)
Deportivo Cali - Once Caldas 0-1(0-1)
Uniautónoma FC - Itagüi FC 1-1(0-1)
Alianza Petrolera - Deportivo Pasto 1-1(0-0)
Los Millonarios - Atlético Nacional 3-1(2-0)
Deportes Tolima - Boyacá Chicó FC 1-0(0-0)
Patriotas FC - Atlético Huila 3-1(1-0)
Fortaleza FC - CDP Junior 0-0

Round 5 [14-16.02.2014]
Boyacá Chicó FC - Envigado FC 2-0(2-0)
Atlético Huila – Indep. Medellín 1-1(0-1)
La Equidad - Uniautónoma FC 0-0
Deportivo Pasto - Los Millonarios 1-1(1-1)
Itagüi FC - Fortaleza FC 2-1(1-0)
Santa Fe - Deportivo Cali 0-0
Once Caldas - Alianza Petrolera 2-1(2-0)
CDP Junior - Patriotas FC 1-0(1-0)
Atlético Nacional - Deportes Tolima 2-0(1-0)

Round 6 [18-20.02.2014]
Uniautónoma FC - Fortaleza FC 0-1(0-0)
La Equidad - Boyacá Chicó FC 1-0(1-0)
Alianza Petrolera - Santa Fe 1-2(1-0)
Patriotas FC - Itagüi FC 1-0(0-0)
Los Millonarios - Once Caldas 1-1(1-0)
Envigado FC - Atlético Nacional 2-3(2-1)
Deportes Tolima - Deportivo Pasto 1-1(0-0)
Independiente Medellín - CDP Junior 2-2(1-0)
Depor.Cali - Atlético Huila 1-0(1-0) [05.03.]

Round 7 [22-23.02.2014]
Fortaleza FC - Patriotas FC 2-2(1-2)
Atlético Huila - Alianza Petrolera 3-0(1-0)
Santa Fe - Los Millonarios 0-1(0-1)
Boyacá Chicó FC - Uniautónoma FC 3-2(2-0)
Atlético Nacional - La Equidad 1-2(0-0)
Deportivo Pasto - Envigado FC 1-2(0-0)
Itagüi FC - Independiente Medellín 1-1(0-0)
Once Caldas - Deportes Tolima 3-0(1-0)
CDP Junior - Deportivo Cali 1-0(0-0)

Round 8 [25-27.02.2014]
Uniautónoma FC - Patriotas FC 2-0(1-0)
Los Millonarios - Atlético Huila 2-2(0-2)
Independiente Medellín - Fortaleza FC 3-3(1-1)
Envigado FC - Once Caldas 2-1(1-0)
La Equidad - Deportivo Pasto 1-1(1-0)
Alianza Petrolera - CDP Junior 1-0(0-0)
Deportivo Cali - Itagüi FC 2-3(1-0)
Deportes Tolima - Santa Fe 0-0 [06.03.]
Boyacá Chicó - Atlético Nac. 1-2(0-2) [07.03.]

Round 9 [01-02.03.2014]
Fortaleza FC - La Equidad 1-1(1-0)
Patriotas FC - Boyacá Chicó FC 2-1(1-0)
Indep. Medellín - Atlético Nacional 0-2(0-2)
Deportes Tolima - Atlético Huila 1-1(1-1)
Itagüi FC - Envigado FC 1-0(0-0)
Alianza Petrolera - Once Caldas 0-2(0-0)
Deportivo Cali - Deportivo Pasto 2-2(1-1)
Los Millonarios - Santa Fe 2-1(1-0)
Uniautónoma - CDP Junior 1-2(1-0) [27.03.]

Round 10 [10-13.03.2014]
Atlético Nac. - Uniautónoma 3-1(1-0) [04.03.]
Fortaleza FC - Deportivo Cali 0-0
Deportivo Pasto - Boyacá Chicó FC 0-0
CDP Junior - Los Millonarios 0-1(0-0)
Itagüi FC - Alianza Petrolera 1-2(0-1)
Once Caldas - La Equidad 0-0
Atlético Huila - Deportes Tolima 2-0(1-0)
Patriotas FC - Independiente Medellín 1-0(1-0)
Santa Fe - Envigado FC 0-1(0-1) [26.03.]

Round 11 [14-16.03.2014]
Atlético Nacional - Deportivo Pasto 1-1(1-1)
Alianza Petrolera - Fortaleza FC 1-0(0-0)
Boyacá Chicó FC - Once Caldas 1-1(0-0)
La Equidad - Santa Fe 0-2(0-0)
Deportivo Cali - Patriotas FC 2-1(1-0)
Envigado FC - Atlético Huila 2-0(0-0)
Los Millonarios - Itagüi FC 3-0(2-0)
Uniautónoma FC – Indep. Medellín 4-2(2-0)
Deportes Tolima - CDP Junior 3-1(1-0)

Round 12 [21-23.03.2014]
Atlético Huila - La Equidad 0-1(0-0)
Itagüi FC - Deportes Tolima 1-0(0-0)
Santa Fe - Boyacá Chicó FC 0-0
Patriotas FC - Alianza Petrolera 3-3(2-1)
Once Caldas - Atlético Nacional 0-0
Deportivo Pasto - Uniautónoma FC 4-0(1-0)
Indep. Medellín - Deportivo Cali 2-0(1-0)
CDP Junior - Envigado FC 1-0(0-0)
Fortaleza FC - Los Millonarios 0-1(0-1)

Round 13 [28-30.03.2014]
Deportivo Pasto - Once Caldas 3-2(2-1)
Alianza Petrolera – Indep. Medellín 2-1(0-0)
Los Millonarios - Patriotas FC 4-0(2-0)
Boyacá Chicó FC - Atlético Huila 1-0(0-0)
Atlético Nacional - Santa Fe 2-2(0-1)
Envigado FC - Itagüi FC 1-0(1-0)
La Equidad - CDP Junior 0-1(0-1)
Deportes Tolima - Fortaleza FC 1-1(1-0)
Uniautónoma FC - Deportivo Cali 0-2(0-1)

Round 14 [01-03.04.2014]
Atlético Huila - Atlético Nac. 2-0(1-0) [26.03.]
Santa Fe - Deportivo Pasto 3-2(2-2)
Indep. Medellín - Los Millonarios 2-1(0-0)
Once Caldas - Uniautónoma FC 3-1(2-0)
CDP Junior - Boyacá Chicó FC 2-1(0-0)
Deportivo Cali - Alianza Petrolera 1-2(0-1)
Itagüi FC - La Equidad 3-1(1-0)
Fortaleza FC - Envigado FC 2-1(0-1)
Patriotas FC - Deportes Tolima 1-2(1-1)

Round 15 [05-06.04.2014]
Deportivo Pasto - Atlético Huila 5-1(3-0)
Los Millonarios - Deportivo Cali 1-0(1-0)
Uniautónoma FC - Alianza Petrolera 0-2(0-0)
Atlético Nacional - CDP Junior 1-0(0-0)
La Equidad - Fortaleza FC 1-1(0-1)
Once Caldas - Santa Fe 1-1(0-0)
Boyacá Chicó FC - Itagüi FC 0-1(0-0)
Envigado FC - Patriotas FC 2-2(2-1)
Deportes Tolima – Indep. Medellín 1-1(1-1)

Round 16 [08-10.04.2014]
Alianza Petrolera - Los Millonarios 2-1(1-0)
CDP Junior - Deportivo Pasto 1-0(0-0)
Fortaleza FC - Boyacá Chicó FC 0-0
Patriotas FC - La Equidad 1-2(0-2)
Atlético Huila - Once Caldas 2-0(0-0)
Deportivo Cali - Deportes Tolima 2-0(2-0)
Indep. Medellín - Envigado FC 3-2(0-2)
Santa Fe - Uniautónoma FC 2-2(0-1) [16.04.]
Itagüi FC - Atlético Nacional 1-1(1-0) [16.04.]

Round 17 [11-13.04.2014]
Deportivo Pasto - Itagüi FC 1-2(1-1)
Boyacá Chicó FC - Patriotas FC 3-0(1-0)
Once Caldas - CDP Junior 3-0(0-0)
Uniautónoma FC - Los Millonarios 1-0(0-0)
Deportes Tolima - Alianza Petrolera 1-2(0-0)
La Equidad - Independiente Medellín 2-1(1-0)
Santa Fe - Atlético Huila 2-1(1-0)
Envigado FC - Deportivo Cali 3-1(1-0)
Atlético Nacional - Fortaleza FC 4-3(2-0)

Round 18 [19-20.04.2014]
Atlético Huila - Uniautónoma FC 1-1(1-1)
Los Millonarios - Deportes Tolima 3-1(1-1)
Patriotas FC - Atlético Nacional 2-1(1-0)
Itagüi FC - Once Caldas 2-2(1-2)
Deportivo Cali - La Equidad 1-0(0-0)
Indep. Medellín - Boyacá Chicó FC 2-1(1-0)
Alianza Petrolera - Envigado FC 0-2(0-0)
CDP Junior - Santa Fe 2-1(0-0)
Fortaleza FC - Deportivo Pasto 4-1(2-0)

Final Standings

1.	CD Atlético Nacional Medellín	18	10	4	4	35	-	22	34
2.	CD Los Millonarios Bogotá	18	10	3	5	27	-	15	33
3.	CDP Junior Barranquilla	18	10	3	5	20	-	17	33
4.	Santa Fe CD Bogotá	18	8	6	4	24	-	16	30
5.	CD Once Caldas Manizales	18	7	8	3	27	-	17	29
6.	Envigado FC	18	9	1	8	27	-	24	28
7.	Itagüí FC	18	8	4	6	21	-	23	28
8.	CD La Equidad Seguros Bogotá	18	7	6	5	17	-	17	27
9.	CD Alianza Petrolera Barrancabermeja	18	8	3	7	23	-	28	27
10.	Boyacá Chicó FC Tunja	18	7	4	7	19	-	16	25
11.	CD Independiente Medellín	18	5	6	7	26	-	30	21
12.	Asociación Deportivo Pasto	18	4	8	6	28	-	26	20
13.	CD Atlético Huila Neiva	18	5	4	9	23	-	26	19
14.	Asociación Deportivo Cali	18	5	4	9	16	-	22	19
15.	CD Patriotas FC Tunja	18	5	4	9	20	-	30	19
16.	Fortaleza FC Zipaquira	18	3	8	7	22	-	26	17
17.	Uniautónoma FC Barranquilla	18	4	5	9	20	-	30	17
18.	CC Deportes Tolima	18	4	5	9	18	-	28	17

Top-8 qualified for the Play-offs.

Play-offs

Quarter-Finals [25.04.-04.05.2014]

Envigado FC - CD Atlético Nacional Medellín	1-4(0-2)	1-2(1-0)
CD Once Caldas Manizales - Santa Fe CD Bogotá	1-4(1-3)	2-1(1-0)
Itagüí FC - CDP Junior Barranquilla	1-1(0-0)	1-2(1-0)
CD La Equidad Seguros Bogotá - CD Los Millonarios Bogotá	0-1(0-0)	1-1(0-0)

Semi-Finals [07-11.05.2014]

Santa Fe CD Bogotá - CD Atlético Nacional Medellín	1-0(1-0)	0-2(0-1)
CDP Junior Barranquilla - CD Los Millonarios Bogotá	0-0	5-4 pen

Liga Postobón I Final

18.05.2014, Estadio Metropolitano "Roberto Meléndez", Attendance: 44,000
Referee: Luis Sánchez González
CDP Junior Barranquilla - CD Atlético Nacional Medellín 1-0(0-0)
Junior: Mario Sebastián Viera Galaín (Cap), Andrés Felipe Correa Osorio, William José Tesillo Gutiérrez, César Augusto Fawcett Lebolo, Vladimir Javier Hernández Rivero (87.Martín Enrique Arzuaga Coronel), Luis Manuel Narváez Pitalúa, Jossymar Andrés Gómez Pereira (73.Maicol Balanta Peña), Jhonny Alexander Vásquez Salazar, Guillermo León Celis Montiel, Luis Enrique Quiñónes García (80.Jorge Andrés Aguirre Restrepo), José Edison Toloza Colorado. Trainer: Julio Avelino Comesaña (Uruguay).
Atlético Nacional: Franco Armani, Oscar Fabián Murillo Murillo, Álvaro Francisco Nájera Gil, Juan David Valencia Hinestroza, Alexis Héctor Henríquez Charales, Farid Alfonso Díaz Rhenals (77.Sebastián Pérez Cardona), Edwin Andrés Cardona Bedoya, Alexander Mejía Sabalsa (Cap), Wilder Andrés Guisao Correa, Diego Alejandro Arias Hincapié (57.Jhon Edwar Valoy Riascos), Luis Alfonso Páez Restrepo (66.Santiago Tréllez Vivero). Trainer: Juan Carlos Osorio Arbelaez.
Goal: 1-0 José Edison Toloza Colorado (55).

21.05.2014, Estadio "Atanasio Girardot", Medellín; Attendance: 40,051
Referee: Ímer Lemuel Machado Barrera
CD Atlético Nacional Medellín - CDP Junior Barranquilla 2-1(1-1,2-1,2-1);
4-2 on penalties
Atlético Nacional: Franco Armani, Alexis Héctor Henríquez Charales (Cap) (46.Wilder Andrés Guisao Correa), Alejandro Bernal Rios, Farid Alfonso Díaz Rhenals (64.Jhon Edwar Valoy Riascos), Oscar Fabián Murillo Murillo, Daniel Eduardo Bocanegra Ortíz, Jairo Fabián Palomino Sierra (75.Juan Pablo Ángel Arango), Sherman Andrés Cárdenas Estupiñán, Juan David Valencia Hinestroza, Edwin Andrés Cardona Bedoya, Jefferson Andrés Duque Montoya. Trainer: Juan Carlos Osorio Arbelaez.
Junior: Mario Sebastián Viera Galaín (Cap), Samuel Antonio Vanegas Luna, César Augusto Fawcett Lebolo (84.Andrés Felipe González Ramírez), Juan Guillermo Domínguez Cabeza, William José Tesillo Gutiérrez, Jhonny Alexander Vásquez Salazar, Luis Manuel Narváez Pitalúa, Jossymar Andrés Gómez Pereira, Guillermo León Celis Montiel, Jorge Andrés Aguirre Restrepo (72.Jhonny Albeiro Ramírez Lozano), José Edison Toloza Colorado (39.Maicol Balanta Peña). Trainer: Julio Avelino Comesaña (Uruguay).
Goals: 1-0 Alexis Héctor Henríquez Charales (2), 1-1 José Edison Toloza Colorado (17), 2-1 Jhon Edwar Valoy Riascos (90+3).
Penalties: Juan Guillermo Domínguez Cabeza 0-1; Juan David Valencia Hinestroza 1-1; Mario Sebastián Viera Galaín (missed); Edwin Andrés Cardona Bedoya 2-1; Luis Manuel Narváez Pitalúa 2-2; Daniel Eduardo Bocanegra Ortíz 3-2; Jhonny Alexander Vásquez Salazar (missed); Alejandro Bernal Rios 4-2.

2014 Campeonato Apertura Champions: **CD Atlético Nacional Medellín**

Top goalscorers:

13 goals:	**Dayro Mauricio Moreno Galindo**	**(CD Los Millonarios Bogotá)**
11 goals:	Germán Ezequiel Cano (ARG)	(CD Independiente Medellín)
10 goals:	Carlos Alveiro Rentería Cuesta	(CD Patriotas FC Tunja)
	Óscar Eduardo Rodas Vargas	(Envigado FC)
9 goals:	Ayron del Valle Rodríguez	(CD Alianza Petrolera)

Torneo Finalización - Liga Postobón II

Ítagüi FC was expelled from Itagüí in May 2014 and moved to the city of Pereira due to financial supporting problems. As result the team changed its name to Águilas Pereira FC.

Results

Round 1 [18-20.07.2014]
Patriotas FC - Deportivo Pasto 3-0(2-0)
Deportivo Cali - Boyacá Chicó FC 0-1(0-0)
Los Millonarios - Envigado FC 2-1(2-0)
Indep. Medellín - Atlético Nacional 1-0(0-0)
Deportes Tolima - Uniautónoma FC 2-0(2-0)
Fortaleza FC - Once Caldas 0-1(0-0)
Águilas Pereira - Santa Fe 2-1(2-1) [03.09.]
CDP Junior - Atlético Huila 4-3(2-2) [03.09.]
Alianza Petrol. - La Equidad 3-1(2-0) [04.09.]

Round 2 [26-27.07.2014]
Atlético Huila - Águilas Pereira 1-3(1-0)
Envigado FC - Deportes Tolima 0-0
Uniautónoma FC - CDP Junior 2-4(0-1)
La Equidad - Los Millonarios 0-1(0-0)
Deportivo Pasto - Independiente Medellín 0-0
Once Caldas - Patriotas FC 2-0(2-0)
Santa Fe - Fortaleza FC 2-0(1-0)
Boyacá Chicó FC - Alianza Petrolera 1-0(1-0)
Atlético Nacional - Deportivo Cali 2-2(2-1)

Round 3 [02-03.08.2014]
Fortaleza FC - Atlético Huila 1-1(0-0)
Uniautónoma FC - Envigado FC 0-2(0-0)
Patriotas FC - Santa Fe 0-0
Águilas Pereira - CDP Junior 0-0
Los Millonarios - Boyacá Chicó FC 1-1(0-0)
Alianza Petrolera - Atlético Nacional 1-1(1-1)
Deportivo Cali - Deportivo Pasto 2-0(1-0)
Independiente Medellín - Once Caldas 1-3(0-2)
Deportes Tolima - La Equidad 2-1(0-1)

Round 4 [09-10.08.2014]
Deportivo Pasto - Alianza Petrolera 0-0
Águilas Pereira - Uniautónoma FC 2-0(2-0)
Santa Fe - Independiente Medellín 2-1(2-0)
Atlético Huila - Patriotas FC 4-1(2-0)
La Equidad - Envigado FC 0-1(0-1)
Boyacá Chicó FC - Deportes Tolima 0-1(0-0)
CDP Junior - Fortaleza FC 1-3(0-1)
Atlético Nacional - Los Millonarios 5-0(0-0)
Once Caldas - Deportivo Cali 3-3(2-1)

Round 5 [16-17.08.2014]
Envigado FC - Boyacá Chicó FC 2-2(1-0)
Fortaleza FC - Águilas Pereira 0-2(0-0)
Deportes Tolima - Atlético Nacional 1-1(1-0)
Uniautónoma FC - La Equidad 3-2(1-2)
Los Millonarios - Deportivo Pasto 1-1(1-1)
Alianza Petrolera - Once Caldas 1-0(1-0)
Deportivo Cali - Santa Fe 2-0(1-0)
Patriotas FC - CDP Junior 0-0
Indep. Medellín - Atlético Huila 4-1(2-1)

Round 6 [23-24.08.2014]
Fortaleza FC - Uniautónoma FC 1-1(0-0)
Águilas Pereira - Patriotas FC 2-3(0-1)
Atlético Nacional - Envigado FC 0-1(0-1)
Santa Fe - Alianza Petrolera 0-0
Boyacá Chicó FC - La Equidad 5-1(1-0)
CDP Junior - Independiente Medellín 0-1(0-0)
Atlético Huila - Deportivo Cali 0-1(0-1)
Once Caldas - Los Millonarios 1-1(0-0)
Deportivo Pasto - Deportes Tolima 2-2(0-1)

Round 7 [30.08.-01.09.2014]
Alianza Petrolera - Atlético Huila 0-0
Uniautónoma FC - Boyacá Chicó FC 1-1(0-1)
Patriotas FC - Fortaleza FC 1-0(1-0)
Envigado FC - Deportivo Pasto 1-2(0-2)
Deportivo Cali - CDP Junior 1-0(0-0)
Deportes Tolima - Once Caldas 3-3(0-3)
Indep. Medellín - Águilas Pereira 3-0(0-0)
Los Millonarios - Santa Fe 0-1(0-0)
La Equidad - Atlético Nacional 0-4(0-1)

Round 8 [06-07.09.2014]
Fortaleza FC - Independiente Medellín 2-3(2-1)
Atlético Huila - Los Millonarios 1-0(1-0)
Santa Fe - Deportes Tolima 5-0(2-0)
Patriotas FC - Uniautónoma FC 1-0(1-0)
Once Caldas - Envigado FC 2-1(0-1)
Deportivo Pasto - La Equidad 0-0
CDP Junior - Alianza Petrolera 0-1(0-1)
Atlético Nacional - Boyacá Chicó FC 2-2(1-1)
Águilas Pereira - Deportivo Cali 0-1(0-1)

Round 9 [12-14.09.2014]
Envigado FC - Águilas Pereira 2-0(1-0)
La Equidad - Fortaleza FC 0-0
Deportivo Pasto - Deportivo Cali 2-0(1-0)
Santa Fe - Los Millonarios 4-1(2-0)
Atlético Nacional – Indep. Medellín 1-0(1-0)
Boyacá Chicó FC - Patriotas FC 1-1(1-0)
Once Caldas - Alianza Petrolera 3-0(0-0)
Atlético Huila - Deportes Tolima 0-0
CDP Junior - Uniautónoma FC 3-1(0-1)

Round 10 [20-21.09.2014]
Boyacá Chicó FC - Deportivo Pasto 0-0
Deportes Tolima - Atlético Huila 1-5(1-3)
La Equidad - Once Caldas 2-0(0-0)
Los Millonarios - CDP Junior 0-0
Independiente Medellín - Patriotas FC 3-1(2-0)
Alianza Petrolera - Águilas Pereira 1-0(1-0)
Uniautónoma FC - Atlético Nacional 0-3(0-1)
Envigado FC - Santa Fe 2-2(1-2)
Deportivo Cali - Fortaleza FC 2-0(1-0)

Round 11 [24-25.09.2014]
Fortaleza FC - Alianza Petrolera 2-1(0-0)
Atlético Huila - Envigado FC 1-1(1-0)
CDP Junior - Deportes Tolima 1-0(1-0)
Santa Fe - La Equidad 2-0(1-0)
Indep. Medellín - Uniautónoma FC 1-0(0-0)
Águilas Pereira - Los Millonarios 4-2(2-0)
Patriotas FC - Deportivo Cali 1-0(1-0)
Once Caldas - Boyacá Chicó FC 4-1(2-1)
Deport. Pasto – Atl. Nacional 2-1(1-1) [15.10.]

Round 12 [27-28.09.2014]
La Equidad - Atlético Huila 1-1(1-0)
Uniautónoma FC - Deportivo Pasto 1-1(1-0)
Envigado FC - CDP Junior 1-0(0-0)
Deportes Tolima - Águilas Pereira 2-0(1-0)
Los Millonarios - Fortaleza FC 4-0(1-0)
Alianza Petrolera - Patriotas FC 1-1(0-0)
Atlético Nacional - Once Caldas 0-0
Boyacá Chicó FC - Santa Fe 1-2(1-0)
Deportivo Cali – Indep. Medellín 1-1(1-1)

Round 13 [03-05.10.2014]
Atlético Huila - Boyacá Chicó FC 2-0(1-0)
Águilas Pereira - Envigado FC 1-0(1-0)
Indep. Medellín - Alianza Petrolera 1-2(0-1)
Once Caldas - Deportivo Pasto 1-0(0-0)
Patriotas FC - Los Millonarios 0-3(0-1)
CDP Junior - La Equidad 1-0(1-0)
Deportivo Cali - Uniautónoma FC 0-4(0-3)
Santa Fe - Atlético Nacional 0-1(0-0)
Fortaleza FC - Deportes Tolima 1-1(0-1)

Round 14 [10-12.10.2014]
La Equidad - Águilas Pereira 0-0
Alianza Petrolera - Deportivo Cali 3-1(0-1)
Deportivo Pasto - Santa Fe 1-2(0-0)
Los Millonarios – Indep. Medellín 1-4(1-2)
Uniautónoma FC - Once Caldas 0-0
Envigado FC - Fortaleza FC 0-2(0-1)
Boyacá Chicó FC - CDP Junior 2-0(0-0)
Deportes Tolima - Patriotas FC 1-1(1-0)
Atlético Nacional - Atlético Huila 0-1(0-1)

Round 15 [17-19.10.2014]
Fortaleza FC - La Equidad 3-0(3-0)
Alianza Petrolera - Uniautónoma FC 0-0
Indep. Medellín - Deportes Tolima 2-3(0-1)
Santa Fe - Once Caldas 0-0
Patriotas FC - Envigado FC 2-1(1-0)
Águilas Pereira - Boyacá Chicó FC 3-2(1-1)
Deportivo Cali - Los Millonarios 4-3(1-1)
CDP Junior - Atlético Nacional 0-1(0-1)
Atlético Huila - Deportivo Pasto 3-0(2-0)

Round 16 [24-26.10.2014]
Boyacá Chicó FC - Fortaleza FC 0-0
La Equidad - Patriotas FC 4-2(1-0)
Uniautónoma FC - Santa Fe 1-0(1-0)
Atlético Nacional - Águilas Pereira 2-0(0-0)
Los Millonarios - Alianza Petrolera 2-0(1-0)
Deportivo Pasto - CDP Junior 3-3(1-2)
Once Caldas - Atlético Huila 0-0
Envigado FC – Indep. Medellín 0-1(0-0)
Deportes Tolima - Deportivo Cali 2-3(2-2)

Round 17 [01-02.11.2014]
Águilas Pereira - Deportivo Pasto 2-0(1-0)
Deportivo Cali - Envigado FC 0-0
Independiente Medellín - La Equidad 1-1(1-0)
Fortaleza FC - Atlético Nacional 1-0(1-0)
Patriotas FC - Boyacá Chicó FC 1-0(0-0)
Alianza Petrolera - Deportes Tolima 0-1(0-0)
Los Millonarios - Uniautónoma FC 0-0
Atlético Huila - Santa Fe 1-0(1-0)
CDP Junior - Once Caldas 2-0(1-0)

Round 18 [09.11.2014]
Uniautónoma FC - Atlético Huila 1-0(0-0)
Santa Fe - CDP Junior 1-0(0-0)
Once Caldas - Águilas Pereira 1-2(1-0)
Deportivo Pasto - Fortaleza FC 1-1(1-0)
Atlético Nacional - Patriotas FC 2-0(1-0)
La Equidad - Deportivo Cali 3-2(0-0)
Boyacá Chicó FC – Indep. Medellín 3-1(0-1)
Envigado FC - Alianza Petrolera 2-3(2-1)
Deportes Tolima - Los Millonarios 1-0(1-0)

Final Standings

1.	Santa Fe CD Bogotá	18	9	4	5	24 - 13	31
2.	CD Independiente Medellín	18	9	3	6	29 - 21	30
3.	CD Atlético Nacional Medellín	18	8	5	5	26 - 12	29
4.	Águilas Pereira FC	18	9	2	7	23 - 21	29
5.	CD Once Caldas Manizales	18	7	7	4	24 - 17	28
6.	Asociación Deportivo Cali	18	8	4	6	25 - 25	28
7.	CC Deportes Tolima	18	7	7	4	23 - 25	28
8.	CD Atlético Huila Neiva	18	7	6	5	25 - 18	27
9.	CD Alianza Petrolera Barrancabermeja	18	7	6	5	17 - 16	27
10.	CD Patriotas FC Tunja	18	7	5	6	19 - 24	26
11.	Boyacá Chicó FC Tunja	18	5	7	6	23 - 22	22
12.	CDP Junior Barranquilla	18	6	4	8	19 - 20	22
13.	Fortaleza FC Zipaquira	18	5	6	7	17 - 21	21
14.	Envigado FC	18	5	5	8	18 - 20	20
15.	CD Los Millonarios Bogotá	18	5	5	8	22 - 28	20
16.	Uniautónoma FC Barranquilla	18	4	6	8	15 - 23	18
17.	Asociación Deportivo Pasto	18	3	9	6	15 - 23	18
18.	CD La Equidad Seguros Bogotá	18	3	5	10	16 - 31	14

Top-8 qualified for the Cuadrangulares.

Cuadrangulares

Grupo A [14.11.2014-15.12.2014]
Atlético Nacional - Atlético Huila 1-0(0-0)
Santa Fe - Atlético Nacional 3-2(2-2)
Atlético Huila - Once Caldas 2-1(2-0)
Once Caldas - Santa Fe 0-1(0-0)
Once Caldas - Atlético Nacional 1-0(0-0)
Atlético Huila - Santa Fe 3-3(1-1)
Santa Fe - Atlético Huila 0-0
Atlético Nacional - Once Caldas 1-0(0-0)
Santa Fe - Once Caldas 0-1(0-0)
Atlético Huila - Atlético Nacional 1-0(1-0)
Once Caldas - Atlético Huila 1-2(0-0)
Atlético Nacional - Santa Fe 0-1(0-0)

Grupo B [16.11.2014-13.12.2014]
Indep. Medellín - Deportivo Cali 3-2(2-1)
Águilas Pereira - Deportes Tolima 2-2(0-1)
Deportivo Cali - Águilas Pereira 2-2(1-0)
Deportes Tolima – Indep. Medellín 1-2(1-0)
Deportivo Cali - Deportes Tolima 2-1(0-0)
Indep. Medellín - Águilas Pereira 2-1(1-1)
Deportes Tolima - Deportivo Cali 4-2(2-0)
Águilas Pereira - Indep. Medellín 2-2(0-1)
Águilas Pereira - Deportivo Cali 2-2(1-1)
Indep. Medellín - Deportes Tolima 1-1(1-1)
Deportes Tolima - Águilas Pereira 1-2(1-2)
Deportivo Cali - Indep. Medellín 2-1(1-0)

Grupo A

1. Santa Fe CD Bogotá	6	3	2	1	8 - 6	11
2. CD Atlético Huila Neiva	6	3	2	1	8 - 6	11
3. CD Atlético Nacional Medellín	6	2	0	4	4 - 6	6
4. CD Once Caldas Manizales	6	2	0	4	4 - 6	6

Grupo B

1. CD Independiente Medellín	6	3	2	1	11 - 9	11
2. Asociación Deportivo Cali	6	2	2	2	12 - 13	8
3. Águilas Pereira FC	6	1	4	1	11 - 11	7
4. CC Deportes Tolima	6	1	2	3	10 - 11	5

Please note: winner of each group qualified for the final.

Liga Postobón II Final

17.12.2014, Estadio "Atanasio Girardot", Medellín; Attendance: 40,000
Referee: Ulises Arrieta

CD Independiente Medellín - Santa Fe CD Bogotá 1-2(1-0)

Independiente: Carlos Andrés Bejarano Palacios, Carlos Alberto Valencia Paredes, Hernán Enrique Pertúz Ortega, Andrés Felipe Mosquera Guardia, Vladimir Marín Ríos, Jherson Enrique Córdoba Ospina, Christian Camilo Marrugo Rodríguez, Javier Calle Estrada (76.Elton Martins Da Cruz), Jhon Edison Hernández Montoya, Germán Ezequiel Cano (Cap), Yorleys Mena Palacios. Trainer: Hernán Torres Oliveros.

Santa Fe: Camilo Andrés Vargas Gil (Cap), Sergio Andrés Otálvaro Botero, Yovanny Arrechea Amu, Francisco Javier Meza Palma, Dairon Mosquera Chaverra, Omar Sebastián Pérez (46.Armando Junior Vargas Morales), Luis Manuel Seijas Gunther, Daniel Alejandro Torres Rojas, Wilson David Morelo López (87.Ricardo José Villarraga Marchena), Luis Carlos Arias (80.Yerry Fernando Mina González), Jefferson Cuero Castro. Trainer: Gustavo Adolfo Costas Makeira (Argentina).

Goals: 1-0 Germán Ezequiel Cano (37), 1-1 Francisco Javier Meza Palma (65), 1-2 Wilson David Morelo López (68).

21.12.2014, Estadio "Nemesio Camacho" [El Campín], Bogotá; Attendance: 39,000
Referee: Luis Sánchez González

Santa Fe CD Bogotá - CD Independiente Medellín 1-1(0-0)

Santa Fe: Camilo Andrés Vargas Gil (Cap), Yovanny Arrechea Amu, Juan Daniel Roa Reyes, Francisco Javier Meza Palma, Dairon Mosquera Chaverra, José Yulián Anchico Patiño, Daniel Alejandro Torres Rojas, Armando Junior Vargas Morales, Wilson David Morelo López (86.Yerry Fernando Mina González), Luis Carlos Arias (73.Luis Manuel Seijas Gunther), Jefferson Cuero Castro (90+3.Omar Sebastián Pérez). Trainer: Gustavo Adolfo Costas Makeira (Argentina).

Independiente: Carlos Andrés Bejarano Palacios, Diego Armando Hérner, Carlos Alberto Valencia Paredes, Andrés Felipe Mosquera Guardia, Vladimir Marín Ríos, Jherson Enrique Córdoba Ospina, Christian Camilo Marrugo Rodríguez, Javier Calle Estrada (69.Daniel Hernández), Jhon Edison Hernández Montoya, Germán Ezequiel Cano (Cap), Yorleys Mena Palacios (66.Alfredo José Morelos Avilés). Trainer: Hernán Torres Oliveros.

Goals: 1-0 Luis Carlos Arias (46), 1-1 Andrés Felipe Mosquera Guardia (89).

2014 Campeonato Finalización Champions: **Santa Fe CD Bogotá**

Top goalscorers:

16 goals:	**Germán Ezequiel Cano (ARG)**	**(CD Independiente Medellín)**
14 goals:	Juan Fernando Caicedo Benítez	(CD Atlético Huila Neiva)
10 goals:	Wilson David Morelo López	(Santa Fe CD Bogotá)
	Fernando Uribe Hincapié	(CD Los Millonarios Bogotá)
9 goals:	Johan Leandro Arango Ambuila	(CD Once Caldas Manizales)
	Hernán Hechalar (ARG)	(CD Atlético Huila Neiva)

Aggregate Table 2014

1.	Santa Fe CD Bogotá	48	23	13	12	65	-	42	82
2.	CD Atlético Nacional Medellín	48	24	9	15	75	-	45	81
3.	CD Once Caldas Manizales	44	17	15	12	58	-	45	66
4.	Águilas Pereira FC	44	18	11	15	57	-	58	65
5.	CDP Junior Barranquilla	42	18	10	14	44	-	41	64
6.	CD Independiente Medellín	44	17	12	15	68	-	63	63
7.	CD Los Millonarios Bogotá	40	16	11	13	51	-	44	59
8.	CD Atlético Huila Neiva	42	15	12	15	56	-	50	57
9.	Asociación Deportivo Cali	42	15	10	17	53	-	60	55
10.	CD Alianza Petrolera Barrancabermeja	36	15	9	12	40	-	44	54
11.	CC Deportes Tolima	42	12	14	16	51	-	64	50
12.	Envigado FC	38	14	6	18	47	-	50	48
13.	Boyacá Chicó FC Tunja	36	12	11	13	42	-	38	47
14.	CD Patriotas FC Tunja	36	12	9	15	39	-	54	45
15.	CD La Equidad Seguros Bogotá	38	10	12	16	34	-	50	42
16.	Asociación Deportivo Pasto	36	7	17	12	43	-	49	38
17.	Fortaleza FC Zipaquira	36	8	14	14	40	-	47	38
18.	Uniautónoma FC Barranquilla	36	8	11	17	35	-	53	35

Qualified for the 2015 Copa Libertadores (First Stage):
CD Once Caldas Manizales

Qualified for the 2015 Copa Libertadores (Second Stage):
Santa Fe CD Bogotá, CD Atlético Nacional Medellín

Qualified for the 2015 Copa Sudamericana (First Stage):
Santa Fe CD Bogotá, Águilas Pereira FC, CDP Junior Barranquilla, CC Deportes Tolima

Relegation Table 2014

Relegation was determined by an average of the points obtained in the First Stages of the past six championships (last three seasons: 2011, 2012, 2013).

Pos	Team	2012	2013	2014	Total		Aver
		P	P	P	P	M	
1.	CD Atlético Nacional Medellín	52	69	63	184	108	1.704
2.	Águilas Pereira FC	61	58	57	176	108	1.630
3.	Santa Fe CD Bogotá	52	61	61	174	108	1.611
4.	CD Los Millonarios Bogotá	57	59	53	169	108	1.565
5.	CDP Junior Barranquilla	57	52	55	164	108	1.519
6.	CC Deportes Tolima	65	50	45	160	108	1.481
7.	Asociación Deportivo Cali	49	58	47	154	108	1.426
8.	CD La Equidad Seguros Bogotá	61	45	41	147	108	1.361
9.	CD Once Caldas Manizales	33	56	57	146	108	1.352
10.	Asociación Deportivo Pasto	52	53	38	143	108	1.324
11.	CD Independiente Medellín	43	47	51	141	108	1.306
12.	CD Alianza Petrolera Barrancabermeja	41	38	54	133	108	1.231
13.	Envigado FC	44	39	48	131	108	1.213
14.	Boyacá Chicó FC Tunja	49	34	47	130	108	1.204
15.	CD Atlético Huila Neiva	41	40	46	127	108	1.176
16.	CD Patriotas FC Tunja	44	34	45	123	108	1.139
17.	Uniautónoma FC Barranquilla (*Relegation Play-Off*)	44	34	35	113	108	1.046
18.	Fortaleza FC Zipaquira (*Relegated*)	35	39	38	112	108	1.037

Promotion/Relegation Play-Off

Deportes Quindío Armenia - Uniautónoma FC Barranquilla	0-0	0-2

COPA COLOMBIA
Copa Postobón FINAL 2014

05.12.2014, "Estadio Manuel Murillo Toro", Ibagué;
Referee: Luis Sánchez González
CC Deportes Tolima - Santa Fe CD Bogotá 2-0(0-0)
Deportes Tolima: Leonardo Fabián Burián Castro, Dávinson Álex Monsalve Jiménez, Félix Enrique Noguera, Julian Alveiro Quiñones García, Nicolás Palacios Vidal, Juan Alejandro Mahecha Molina, David Macalister Silva Mosquera (68.Andrés Felipe Ibargüen García), Wilmar Enrique Barrios Teherán, Didier Delgado Delgado, Charles Junior Monsalvo Peralta (82.Héctor Fabián Acuña Maciel), Yimmi Javier Chará Zamora (89.Jhon Fredy Hurtado). Trainer: Alberto Miguel Gamero Morillo.
Santa Fe: Camilo Andrés Vargas Gil, Sergio Andrés Otálvaro Botero, Yovanny Arrechea Amu, José Julián de la Cuesta Herrera, Juan Daniel Roa Reyes, Dairon Mosquera Chaverra, Omar Sebastián Pérez (89.Darío Andrés Rodríguez Parra), Daniel Alejandro Torres Rojas, Wilson David Morelo López, Luis Carlos Arias, Jefferson Cuero Castro (83.Michael Jhon Ander Rangel Valencia). Trainer: Gustavo Adolfo Costas Makeira (Argentina).
Goals: 1-0 Félix Enrique Noguera (80 penalty), 2-0 Yimmi Javier Chará Zamora (86).

12.12.2014, Estadio "Nemesio Camacho" [El Campín], Bogotá;
Referee: Gustavo González
Santa Fe CD Bogotá - CC Deportes Tolima 2-1(1-1)
Santa Fe: Robinson Zapata Rufay, Sergio Andrés Otálvaro Botero (46.Juan Daniel Roa Reyes), José Julián de la Cuesta Herrera (74.Wilson David Morelo López), Francisco Javier Meza Palma, Yerry Fernando Mina González, Omar Sebastián Pérez, Luis Manuel Seijas Gunther (64.Dairon Mosquera Chaverra), Daniel Alejandro Torres Rojas, Wilder Andrés Medina Tamayo, Luis Carlos Arias, Jefferson Cuero Castro. Trainer: Gustavo Adolfo Costas Makeira (Argentina).
Deportes Tolima: Leonardo Fabián Burián Castro, Dávinson Álex Monsalve Jiménez, Félix Enrique Noguera, Julian Alveiro Quiñones García, Nicolás Palacios Vidal, Juan Alejandro Mahecha Molina, David Macalister Silva Mosquera (86.Bréiner Bonilla Montaño), Wilmar Enrique Barrios Teherán, Didier Delgado Delgado, Andrés Felipe Ibargüen García, Wilfrido De La Rosa Mendoza (72.Marco Jhonnier Pérez Murillo [*sent off 90+3*]). Trainer: Alberto Miguel Gamero Morillo.
Goals: 1-0 Luis Carlos Arias (42), 1-1 Andrés Felipe Ibargüen García (44), 2-1 Jefferson Cuero Castro (56).

2014 Copa Colombia Winners: **CC Deportes Tolima**

CLUB DEPORTIVO ALIANZA PETROLERA BARRANCABERMEJA

Foundation date: October 24, 1991
Address: *Not available*
Stadium: Estadio "Álvaro Gómez Hurtado", Floridablanca – Capacity: 10,400

THE SQUAD

	DOB	Ape		Fin	
		M	G	M	G
Goalkeepers:					
Jorge Alberto Henríquez Pérez	23.02.1985	2	-	3	-
Pier Luigi Grazziani Serrano	14.08.1994			-	-
Ricardo Antonio Jérez Figueroa (GUA)	04.02.1986	16	-	15	-
Defenders:					
Felipe Aguilar Mendoza	20.01.1993	13	-	15	-
Andrés Felipe Álvarez Gordón	01.07.1993	13	-	3	-
Juan Guillermo Arboleda Sánchez	28.07.1989	16	1	17	-
Jonathan Ávila Martínez	01.11.1991	9	2	11	-
Deivy Alexander Balanta Abonía	09.02.1993	13	-	14	-
Santiago Cardona Jaramillo	23.02.1989	-	-	-	-
Deiver Andrés Machado Mena	02.09.1993	7	-	17	-
Arnaldo Javier Pereira Vera (PAR)	11.01.1986	8	-		
David Alonso Valencia Figueroa	31.05.1991	9	1	9	1
Midfielders:					
Níver Alejandro Arango Ramírez	06.05.1991	12	-	2	-
Camilo Andrés Ayala Quintero	23.06.1986	13	-	16	-
Nelson Alberto Barahona Collins (PAN)	22.11.1987	16	-	15	-
Rafael Andrés Carrascal Avílez	17.03.1992	16	1	15	-
Víctor Alfonso Castillo Ocoro	10.07.1987	9	1	4	-
Alex Stik Castro Giraldo	08.03.1994	3	-	9	-
Giovanny Martínez Cortés	07.07.1989			6	-
Julio César Mora Bravo	23.06.1988	-	-	-	-
Luis Arturo Muriel Cruz	23.03.1993			1	-
Juan Pablo Nieto Salazar	25.02.1993			6	-
Henry Andrés Rojas Delgado	27.07.1987	13	3	16	1
Daniel Santa Moreno	07.06.1992	11	-	6	-
Forwards:					
Dairon Estibens Asprilla Rivas	25.05.1992	9	2	16	5
Ayron del Valle Rodríguez	27.01.1989	17	9	15	6
Jeison Estupiñán	13.08.1995	3	-	-	-
Juan Sebastián Herrera Sanabria	04.11.1994	13	2	17	3
Wilson Antonio Mena Asprilla	02.07.1987	8	1	2	-
Wilmer Parra Cadena	10.08.1983	2	-		
Trainer:					
Adolfo León Holguín	01.05.1975	18		18	

CLUB DEPORTIVO ATLÉTICO HUILA NEIVA

Foundation date: November 29, 1990
Address: Coliseo Cubierto la Libertad, Carrera 18 N° 18 – 25, Neiva
Stadium: Estadio „Guillermo Plazas Alcid", Neiva – Capacity: 23,000

THE SQUAD

	DOB	Ape		Fin*	
		M	G	M	G
Goalkeepers:					
Carlos Andrés Abella Parra	25.01.1986	1	-	1	-
Ernesto Hernández (URU)	26.07.1985	17	-	23	-
Johan Camilo Lizarralde Pedraza	08.03.1995			-	-
Gustavo Adolfo Sánchez Giraldo	17.01.1996			-	-
Defenders:					
Elacio José Córdoba Mosquera	21.10.1993	-	-	11	-
Carlos Alberto Díaz	28.11.1982	10	1	17	1
Iván Alonso Garrido Pinzón	02.06.1981	14	-	14	-
John Jairo Lozano Castaño	31.07.1984			11	1
Járol Enrique Martínez González	22.03.1987	15	-	7	-
César Augusto Mena Mosquera	15.10.1988	13	-	13	-
Yonatan Yovanny Murillo Alegría	05.07.1992	5	-	19	-
Elvis Yoan Perlaza Lara	07.03.1989			21	-
Midfielders:					
Jean Carlos Becerra Cuello	17.08.1993	13	1	6	-
Marco Antonio Canchila Vásquez	06.01.1981	10	1	6	-
Duberley Cayapú Zapata	10.01.1993	-	-	-	-
Francisco Antonio Córdoba Escarpeta	08.09.1988	5	1		
Hernán Hechalar (ARG)	12.08.1988	17	4	21	9
Juan Carlos Guazá Pedroza	22.08.1980			18	1
John Edward Hernández García	11.01.1991	-	-	-	-
Jefferson Andrés Lerma Solís	25.10.1994	16	3	21	1
Didier Andrés Moreno Asprilla	15.09.1991	11	1	21	-
Dayron Alexander Pérez Calle	24.12.1978	13	-	19	2
Elieser Evangelista Quiñónes Tenorio	07.11.1988	12	2	-	-
César Alexander Quintero Jiménez	09.11.1988			8	-
Bryan Eduardo Urueña Díaz	31.10.1992	2	-		
Forwards:					
Marcelo Raúl Bergese (ARG)	30.04.1985			9	2
Jean Carlos Blanco Becerra	06.04.1992	17	5	20	2
Juan Fernando Caicedo Benítez	13.07.1989			21	14
Cristian Stiven Canga Vargas	23.02.1991	10	1	8	-
Jhony Moisés Cano Barrios	14.06.1989	6	1	4	-
Camilo Javier Mancillo Valencia	26.03.1993	3	-	1	-
Christian de Jesús Mejía Martínez	11.10.1990	10	-		
Janeiler Rivas Palacios	18.05.1988	6	-	-	-
Henry Fabián Solis	11.08.1990	7	-	-	-
César Augusto Valoyes Córdoba	05.01.1984	14	1		
Efraín Viáfara Molina	08.04.1981	4	1		
Didier Jair Viveros Arboleda	12.05.1994	-	-		
Trainer:					
Virgilio Puerto Polanco [27.09.2013-25.08.2014]	10.10.1975	18		6	
Fernando Castro Lozada [as of 26.08.2014]	11.02.1949			18	

**Matches and goals in 2014 Torneo Finalización play-offs included*

CORPORACIÓN DEPORTIVA ATLÉTICO NACIONAL MEDELLÍN

Foundation date: March 7, 1947
Address: Calle 62 N° 44-103, Itagüí
Stadium: Estadio „Atanasio Girardot", Medellín – Capacity: 52,872

THE SQUAD	DOB	Ape*		Fin**	
		M	G	M	G
Goalkeepers:					
Franco Armani (ARG)	16.10.1986	10	-	11	-
Christián Harson Bonilla Garzón	02.06.1993	2	-	2	-
Luis Enrique „Neco" Martínez Rodríguez	11.07.1982	11	-	7	-
Christián Vargas Cortés	16.11.1989	1	-	3	-
Defenders:					
Alejandro Bernal Rios	03.06.1988	10	1	14	-
Elkin Darío Calle Grajales	19.01.1985	11	1	12	1
Farid Alfonso Díaz Rhenals	20.07.1983	16	1	12	-
Alexis Héctor Henríquez Charales	01.02.1983	13	1	11	-
John Stefan Medina Ramírez	14.06.1992	7	-		
Miller Stiwar Mosquera Cabrera	16.07.1992	11	-	16	1
Luis Arturo Muriel Cruz	23.03.1993	-	-		
Oscar Fabián Murillo Murillo	18.04.1988	13	-	13	-
Álvaro Francisco Nájera Gil	25.07.1983	17	1	11	1
Diego Arturo Peralta González	02.01.1985	12	2	9	1
Edison Restrepo Perea	19.12.1996			1	-
César Alexander Quintero Jiménez	29.11.1989	7	-		
Juan David Valencia Hinestroza	15.01.1986	13	5	10	-
Midfielders:					
Daniel Eduardo Bocanegra Ortíz	23.04.1987	9	1	16	3
Sherman Andrés Cárdenas Estupiñán	07.08.1989	13	3	18	3
Edwin Andrés Cardona Bedoya	08.12.1992	17	6	15	4
Alejandro Abraham Guerra Morales	09.07.1985			10	1
Wilder Andrés Guisao Correa	30.07.1991	8	1	20	2
Alexander Mejía Sabalsa	11.07.1988	8	-	11	-
Dayron Alexander Mosquera Mendoza	07.08.1995			1	-
Juan Pablo Nieto Salazar	25.02.1993	-	-		
José Hárrison Otálvaro Arce	28.02.1986			9	-
Jairo Fabián Palomino Sierra	02.08.1988	10	1	-	-
Sebastián Pérez Cardona	29.03.1993	16	1	13	-
Davinson Sánchez Mina	12.06.1996	-	-	2	-
John Henry Sánchez Valencia	15.05.1995	-	-	1	-
Jhon Edwar Valoy Riascos	26.07.1991	17	2	8	-
Forwards:					
Juan Pablo Ángel Arango	24.10.1975	9	5	7	3
Diego Alejandro Arias Hincapié	15.06.1985	17	1	13	-
Orlando Enrique Berrío Meléndez	14.02.1991	9	1	4	1
Juan David Castañeda Muñoz	26.01.1995			-	-
Jonathan Copete Valencia	23.01.1988			16	3
Jefferson Andrés Duque Montoya	17.05.1987	12	3	1	-
Marlos Moreno Durán	20.09.1996			1	-
Luis Alfonso Páez Restrepo	12.10.1986	14	2	11	4
Brayan Andrés Rovira Ferreira	02.12.1996			-	-
Rodin Jair Quiñónes Rentería	30.05.1995	-	-	2	-
Luis Carlos Ruíz Morales	08.01.1987			12	2
Santiago Tréllez Vivero	17.01.1990	14	2	9	-
Fernando Uribe Hincapié	01.01.1988	8	3		
Trainer:					
Juan Carlos Osorio Arbelaez [as of 03.05.2012]	08.06.1962	24		24	

**Matches and goals in 2014 Torneo Apertura play-offs included*
***Matches and goals in 2014 Torneo Finalización play-offs included*

BOYACÁ CHICÓ FÚTBOL CLUB TUNJA

Foundation date: March 26, 2002
Address: Carrera 7 N° 156 - 80 - Torre I - Oficina 1301, Tunja
Stadium: Estadio de La Independencia, Tunja – Capacity: 20,000

THE SQUAD

	DOB	Ape		Fin	
		M	G	M	G
Goalkeepers:					
Sebastián Arango Mercado	27.01.1996			-	-
Breiner Clemente Castillo Caicedo	05.05.1978	18	-		
Eder Aleixo Chaux Ospina	20.12.1991	-	-	17	-
Andrés David Saldarriaga Cardona	18.09.1978	-	-	2	-
Defenders:					
Simone Bruni Zamorano	21.09.1993	-	-	-	-
Juan Cruz Gotta (ARG)	10.07.1990	4	-	-	-
Luis Hernando Mena Sepúlveda	20.05.1994	17	-	1	-
Yoimar Mosquera Murillo	20.09.1993	-	-	2	-
Johnny Javier Mostasilla Ceballos	03.01.1991	16	1	13	1
Pedro Pablo Tavima Alba	16.11.1985	11	-	17	1
Midfielders:					
Yesid Alberto Aponzá Romero	14.01.1992	10	-	-	-
Alexander Felipe Arrieta Hernández	25.05.1993	-	-		
Edwin Ernesto Ávila Peñaranda	24.09.1986	18	1	13	1
Luis Miguel Carabali Guacales	22.09.1990	2	-	-	-
Diego Fernando Chica López	11.02.1981	16	1	17	1
Nicolás Andrés Giraldo Urueta	29.03.1993			7	-
Yeison Stiven Gordillo Vargas	25.06.1992	16	-	15	-
Joan Sebastián Jaramillo Herrera	14.04.1994	9	-	12	-
Juan Alejandro Mahecha Molina	22.07.1987	16	3		
Edwin Dayan Móvil Cabrera	07.05.1986	15	3	17	3
Juan Daniel Murillo Machado	24.09.1987	5	-	4	-
David Ángel Oltolina (ARG)	22.03.1985			7	-
Mateo Palacios Pretel	12.10.1996			1	-
Juan David Pérez Benítez	23.03.1991	17	1	17	7
Leonel Ríos (ARG)	17.11.1982			14	1
Francisco Javier Rodriguez Ibarra	24.06.1987	-	-	17	2
Ronny Rodríguez Peña	26.06.1994			2	-
Javier Andrés Sanguinetti (ARG)	28.08.1990	17	2	18	1
Jonathan Villa Tangarife	14.06.1991	-	-	-	-
Forwards:					
Cristián Alessandrini (ARG)	27.05.1985	6	1		
Juan David Alzáte Calderón	20.01.1984	1	-	2	1
Kevin Benítez León	30.09.1994			1	-
Armando José Carrillo Dangond	03.11.1985	16	4		
Jairo Fernando Castillo Cortés	17.11.1977	11	1	13	3
Goor Edilson Córdoba Mena	10.01.1994	-	-	-	-
Winston Manuel Girón Amaya	28.04.1988	3	-	4	1
Juan Daniel Gómez Herrera	28.04.1995			1	-
Jeferson Alexis Hurtado Valencia	07.06.1994	4	-	-	-
Diego Germán Leguiza (ARG)	23.03.1985			6	-
Rafael Juniór Martínez Barrios	04.12.1989	3	-	1	-
Sergio Andrés Quiñónes Ortíz	15.04.1995			1	-
Trainer:					
Eduardo Pimentel Murcia	18.05.1961	18		18	

CORPORACION CLUB DEPORTES TOLIMA IBAGUÉ

Foundation date: December 18, 1954
Address: Carrera 4 Bis N° 34-60,. Ibagué
Stadium: Estadio „Manuel Murillo Toro", Ibagué – Capacity: 31,000

THE SQUAD

	DOB	Ape M	Ape G	Fin* M	Fin* G
Goalkeepers:					
William Orlando Arias Bermúdez	27.08.1990	-	-	-	-
Leonardo Fabián Burián Castro (URU)	21.01.1984			24	-
Luis Alberto Estacio Valverde	19.04.1980	11	-		
Janer Alberto Serpa Pacheco	12.02.1981	6	-	1	-
Antony Domingo Silva Cano (PAR)	27.02.1984	-	-		
Defenders:					
Omar Antonio Albornoz Contreras	28.09.1995			4	-
Wilmar Enrique Barrios Teherán	17.10.1993	16	-	20	-
Bréiner Bonilla Montaño	21.07.1986	7	2	13	1
Frank Sebastián Lozano Rengifo	22.08.1993	-	-	-	-
Fredy Machado Mosquera	29.04.1988	6	-	-	-
Davinson Alex Monsalve Jiménez	06.09.1984	8	-	18	4
Félix Enrique Noguera	31.03.1987	14	2	19	-
Julian Alveiro Quiñones García	05.11.1989	15	-	18	-
John Alexander Valencia Hinestroza	04.01.1982	12	-	8	-
Midfielders:					
Cesar Andrés Amaya Solano	12.10.1990	9	2	-	-
Danovis Banguero Lerma	27.10.1989	16	3	13	2
Yesus Segundo Cabrera Ramírez	15.09.1990	13	-		
Jhony Moises Cano Barrios	14.07.1989	11	-		
Didier Delgado Delgado	25.07.1992	14	-	14	-
Jhon Fredy Hurtado	23.03.1985	17	-	11	-
Darwin Guillermo López Tobías	10.02.1992	6	-		
Juan Alejandro Mahecha Molina	22.07.1987			17	-
Jonathan Yulián Mejia Chaverra	28.07.1990			13	3
Henry Yoseiner Obando Estacio	05.04.1993	1	-	11	-
Nicolás Palacios Vidal	11.02.1992	7	-		
David Macalister Silva Mosquera	13.12.1986	17	1	15	4
Forwards:					
Héctor Fabián Acuña Maciel (URU)	27.10.1981			17	4
Róbinson Aponzá Carabali	11.04.1989	3	1	6	1
Isaac Enrique Arias Villamíl	08.10.1990	-	-	-	-
Gustavo Cañizalez Amor	17.12.1995	-	-	-	-
Yimmi Javier Chará Zamora	02.04.1991	15	3	20	8
Wilfrido De La Rosa Mendoza	07.02.1993	10	1	14	-
Andrés Felipe Ibargüen García	07.05.1992			16	1
Charles Junior Monsalvo Peralta	06.05.1990	4	3	10	2
Nicolás Palacios Vidal	11.02.1992			14	-
Marco Jhonnier Pérez Murillo	18.09.1990			17	3
Óscar Eduardo Villarreal Rivera	27.03.1981	6	-		
Trainer:					
Carlos César Castro Varón [26.08.2012-10.05.2014]	17.08.1970	18			
Alberto Miguel Gamero Morillo [as of 01.07.2014]	03.02.1964			24	

**Matches and goals in 2014 Torneo Finalización play-offs included*

ASOCIACIÓN DEPORTIVO CALI

Foundation date: November 23, 1912
Address: Calle 34 Norte N°2 BN 75, Cali
Stadium: Estadio Olimpico „Pascal Guerrero" – Capacity: 33,130

THE SQUAD

	DOB	Ape		Fin*	
		M	G	M	G
Goalkeepers:					
Jáiber Damián Cardona Lozano	19.01.1990			2	-
Luis Alfonso Hurtado Osorio	24.01.1994	7	-	13	-
Manuel Fernando Loaiza Quintas	06.04.1995			-	-
Faryd Aly Camilo Mondragón	21.06.1971	5	-	-	-
José Johan Silva Hurtatiz	12.06.1994	6	-	9	-
Johan Wallens Otálvaro	03.08.1992	-	-	-	-
Defenders:					
Diego Armando Amaya Solano	10.11.1985	6	-		
Jeison Andrés Angulo Trujillo	27.06.1996	3	-	6	-
Luis Antonio Calderón Orozco	02.06.1990	10	-	7	-
Frank Yusty Fabra Palacios	22.02.1991			19	1
Mauricio Ferney Casierra	12.08.1985	9	-		
Víctor Hugo Giraldo López	30.09.1985	11	-	20	-
Germán Mera Cáceres	05.03.1990			17	1
Cristian Javier Nasuti Matovelle (ARG)	06.09.1982			18	-
Luis Manuel Orejuela García	20.08.1996	1	-	-	-
Helibelton Palacios Zapata	09.06.1993			20	3
Luis Miguel Payares Blanco	14.01.1990	9	-	3	-
Fáiner Torijano Cano	31.08.1988	13	-	5	1
Gerson Andrés Vidal	04.04.1994	1	-	1	-
Midfielders:					
Gustavo Adolfo Bolívar Zapata	16.04.1985	8	-	6	1
Juan David Cabezas Nuñez	27.02.1991			19	6
Néstor Abrahan Camacho Ledesma (PAR)	15.10.1987	13	1		
Yerson Candelo Miranda	24.02.1992	16	1	22	1
Miguel Eduardo Caneo (ARG)	17.03.1983			14	-
Nilson David Castrillón Burbano	28.01.1996			3	-
Gustavo Leonardo Cuellar Gallego	14.10.1992	10	-		
Daniel Eduardo Giraldo Cárdenas	01.07.1992	-	-		
Cristian Andrés Higuita Beltrán	12.01.1994	10	2	-	-
Carlos David Lizarazo Landázury	26.04.1991	9	1	8	-
Brian Loaiza López	20.06.1995			1	-
Vladimir Marín Rios	26.09.1979	8	-		
Christian Camilo Marrugo Rodríguez	18.07.1985	13	-		
John Stiveen Mendoza Valencia	27.06.1992	5	1		
Luis Fernando Mosquera Alomia	17.08.1986	-	-	9	1
Andrés Eduardo Pérez Gutiérrez	05.09.1980	13	-	18	1
Juan Fernando Quintero Paniagua	18.01.1993	1	-	2	-
Carlos Enrique Renteria Olaya	05.07.1995	2	-	2	1
Carlos Augusto Rivas Murillo	15.04.1994	10	4	19	8
Andrés Felipe Roa Estrada	25.05.1993	-	-		
Sergio Esteban Romero Méndez	22.11.1988	14	1		
Lucas Daniel Scaglia (ARG)	06.05.1987	3	-		
Jhon Eduis Viáfara Mina	27.10.1978	12	-	9	-
Forwards:					
Juan Andrés Balanta Palacios	03.03.1997	1	-	2	-
Rafael Santos Borré Amaury	15.09.1995	1	1	6	2
Jown Anderson Cardona Agudelo	09.01.1995	1	-	-	-
Juan David González Escallón	08.06.1995			1	-
Sergio Darío Herrera Month	15.03.1981			19	3
José David Lloreda Guevara	12.08.1994	2	1		
Harrison Arley Mojica Betancourt	17.02.1993	7	-	-	-
Miguel Ángel Murillo García	19.10.1993	-	-	16	7
Robin Ariel Ramírez González (PAR)	11.11.1989	11	3	3	-
Harold Fernando Reina Figueroa	18.07.1990			5	-
Camilo Andrés Rosero Téllez	16.08.1994			3	-
Albeiro Sánchez	18.11.1997	1	-	2	-
Trainer:					
Héctor Fabio Cárdenas Berrío	28.08.1979	18		24	

**Matches and goals in 2014 Torneo Finalización play-offs included*

ASOCIACIÓN DEPORTIVO PASTO

Foundation date: October 12, 1949

Address: Estadio Departamental Libertad, San Juan de Pasto

Stadium: Estadio Departamental Libertad, Pasto – Capacity: 25,000

THE SQUAD

	DOB	Ape		Fin	
		M	G	M	G
Goalkeepers:					
Lucero Gonzalo Álvarez Martínez (URU)	24.02.1985	18	-		
Juan Guillermo Castillo Iriarte (URU)	17.04.1978			16	-
José Huber Escobar Giraldo	10.09.1987	-	-	1	-
Defenders:					
Arbey Darío Díaz Castillo	02.04.1991	-	-	-	-
Julián Hurtado Izquierdo	24.11.1979			14	-
Luis Alejandro Malagón Liscano	20.02.1991	5	-		
Omar Mancilla Arboleda	05.10.1994	12	-	2	-
Ervin Antonio Maturana Órtiz	05.10.1979	15	2	12	-
John Jairo Montaño Victoria	17.04.1984	16	2	16	2
Juan Carlos Mosquera Gómez	12.10.1982	14	-	3	-
Jesús David Murillo Largacha	18.02.1994	-	-	14	-
Eduard Sneyder Pinzón Oviedo	07.09.1991	9	-	-	-
Hugo Emilio Soto Miranda	28.09.1983			16	-
Jhon Fredy Zea Mosquera	02.11.1983	14	1	-	-
Midfielders:					
Hugo Alejandro Acosta Cáceres	29.01.1991			15	-
Mike Campaz	16.11.1987	15	-	16	-
Nelson Andrés Coral Flórez	01.05.1993	-	-	-	-
Juan Carlos Escobar Rodríguez	30.10.1982	10	-	11	-
Juan Camilo Hernández Jaramillo	20.04.1993			1	-
Víctor Danilo Mejía Mina	04.02.1993	-	-	-	-
Jorge Emanuel Molina (ARG)	04.03.1987	16	1	16	3
Carlos Andrés Mosquera Perea	12.06.1991	4	-	-	-
Luis Carlos Murillo	16.10.1990	9	-		
Juan Sebastián Ospina Colorado	23.06.1993			1	-
Jairo Leonard Patiño Rosero	05.04.1978	1	-	16	1
Kévin Camillo Rendón Guerrero	08.02.1993	12	2	3	1
Jonathan René Rosero Tovar	05.09.1984	-	-	-	-
Eder Brandon Ruales Pazmino	03.01.1990	7	-	4	-
Juan Sebastián Villota Vargas	18.02.1992	15	3	10	-
Víctor Manuel Zapata Mera	01.11.1985	15	3	14	-
Forwards:					
Juan Andrés Arizala Rivero	05.05.1995	1	1	-	-
Bosco Silvio Frontán Vega (URU)	24.03.1984	15	7	18	3
Mauricio Mina Quintero	24.08.1982	9	2	12	1
Andrés Javier Mosquera Murillo	19.09.1989	1	-		
Jorge Andrés Ramírez Frostte (URU)	25.05.1986	7	1	12	2
William Zapata Brand	28.04.1988	12	3	8	1
Trainer:					
Jorge Luis Bernal Caviedes [01.01.-28.05.2014]	27.09.1952	18			
Wilson Jaime Gutiérrez Cardona [29.05.-17.11.2014]	05.05.1971			18	

ENVIGADO FÚTBOL CLUB

Foundation date: Ocotober 14, 1989
Address: Polideportivo Sur Carrera 48 - 46 Sur 150, Envigado
Stadium: Estadio Polideportivo Sur, Envigado – Capacity: 6,000

THE SQUAD

	DOB	Ape*		Fin	
		M	G	M	G
Goalkeepers:					
Breiner Clemente Castillo Caicedo	05.05.1978			15	-
Juan Esteban Jiménez Villada	20.06.1996			-	-
Jefferson Justino Martínez Valverde	16.08.1993	3	-	3	-
Víctor Hugo Soto Azcarate	12.11.1989	17	-		
Defenders:					
Frank Yusty Fabra Palacios	22.02.1991	15	1		
Jefferson José Gómez Genes	22.06.1996			1	-
Freddy Andrés Hurtado Abadía	27.05.1976	15	-	5	-
Nelson Eduardo Lemus Hurtado	15.02.1989	16	1	15	-
Daniel Londoño Castañeda	01.01.1995			15	1
Maximiliano Felipe Montero Rodríguez (URU)	27.08.1988	7	-		
Sergio Andrés Mosquera Zapata	09.02.1994	-	-	-	-
Andrés Felipe Orozco Vásquez	18.03.1979	12	1	16	1
Carlos Andrés Ramírez Aguirre	01.05.1988	14	-	17	-
Juan Camillo Saíz Ortegón	01.03.1992	15	-	7	-
Mateus Andrés Uribe Villa	21.03.1991	16	2	13	1
Midfielders:					
Jonathan Esteban Álvarez Isaza	27.06.1987	17	4	17	3
Yilmar Alonso Angulo González	09.01.1987	15	1	16	-
Kevin Mateo Cardona Bedoya	11.02.1996			2	-
Julián Alonso Figueroa Rentería	29.01.1993	5	-	-	-
Yony Alexander González Copete	11.07.1994	4	-	17	1
Néider Yesid Morantes Londoño	03.08.1975	16	5	11	1
Juan Carlos Quintero Pérez	20.02.1978	17	1	8	-
Nicolás Fernando Rubio Guzmán	29.01.1995	-	-	-	-
Andrés Felipe Tello Muñoz	06.09.1996	4	-	12	1
Forwards:					
Diego Andrés Álvarez Sánchez	23.09.1981	11	-		
Cristian Daniel Arango Duque	09.03.1995	6	1	1	-
Fáider Favio Burbano Castillo	12.06.1992	19	1	9	1
Víctor Javier Cortés	26.02.1976			16	3
Jairo Gabriel Molina Ospino	28.04.1993	2	-	-	-
John Jairo Mosquera	15.01.1988			6	-
Michael Jhon Ander Rangel Valencia	08.03.1991	15	2		
Óscar Eduardo Rodas Vargas	04.06.1987	19	10		
Angelo José Rodríguez Henry	04.04.1989			18	5
Juan Camilo Zapata Londoño	15.04.1994	-	-	11	-
Trainer:					
Juan Carlos Sánchez [as of 16.04.2013]		20		18	

**Matches and goals in 2014 Torneo Apertura play-offs included*

FORTALEZA FÚTBOL CLUB ZIPAQUIRÁ

Foundation date: November 15, 2010

Address: Carrera 14 B Número 119 - 92 Segundo Piso, Bogotá, Soacha

Stadium: Estadio Metropolitano de Techo, Bogotá – Capacity: 10,000

THE SQUAD

	DOB	Ape		Fin	
		M	G	M	G
Goalkeepers:					
Williams Iván Buenaños Mosquera	17.10.1983	1	-	3	-
César Augusto Giraldo Peláez	24.09.1989	-	-		
Andrés Felipe Mosquera Marmolejo	10.09.1991	17	-	15	-
Carlos Andrés Mosquera Marmolejo	21.09.1994			-	-
Defenders:					
Fredy Arizala Segura	20.02.1983			7	-
Néstor Alberto Asprilla Murillo	28.01.1986	-	-	-	-
Deyner Cetré Lizcano	04.10.1986	8	-		
Andrés Correa Valencia	29.01.1994			7	-
Yamith Cuesta Romaña	17.04.1989			15	2
Victor Martin Galain Pecora (URU)	02.03.1989			13	1
Juan Gabriel Galicia Molina	04.04.1986	10	1		
Edgar Francisco Delgado Zúñiga	14.08.1980	-	-	-	-
Diaryn González Mosquera	04.06.1990	15	-	17	-
José Luis Moya Vanegas	02.03.1984	10	-	-	-
Jair Ulices Palacios Silva	30.06.1990	17	3	16	2
Elvis Yohan Perlaza Lara	07.03.1989	14	2		
Pedro Macario Pino Moreno	30.07.1978			11	-
Ómar Alexander Rodríguez	14.09.1981	6	-	-	-
Carlos Gabriel Rodríguez Orantes (PAN)	12.04.1990			8	-
Jonathan Sáenz Álvarez	01.02.1995	1	-	-	-
John Jairo Sandoval Guarín	15.01.1984	11	-		
Midfielders:					
Gerardo Alberto Bedoya Múnera	26.11.1975			11	3
Jhonathan Caicedo Vergara	15.11.1995			11	1
Diego Steven Gómez Maldonado	21.10.1988	6	1	3	-
Juan Carlos Guazá Pedroza	22.08.1980	14	2		
John Alexander Jaramillo Gómez	11.06.1980	16	-	15	-
Johan Ricardo Muñoz Ossa	14.09.1987	7	-	-	-
Hilton Murillo Sanmartín	31.01.1988	-	-	-	-
Juan Gilberto Nuñez Castillo	25.03.1986	6	1	15	3
Fram Enrique Pacheco Cardona	08.11.1990			12	-
Yorman Wilfredo Rueda Muñoz	06.05.1987	9	-		
Norbey Salazar Giraldo	10.11.1987	10	-	12	2
George Saunders	10.06.1989	7	1		
Juan Felipe Torres Lombana	29.10.1994			5	-
Andrés Guillermo Uhía Cuello	19.11.1985	10	-	-	-
Argemiro Vacca Cortés	25.02.1989	14	1	-	-
Forwards:					
Jhon Stiwar García Mena	06.09.1990	11	4	6	-
Malher Tressor Moreno Baldrich	11.01.1979			10	1
Juan Ferney Otero Tovar	26.05.1995			6	-
Jorge Luis Ramos Sánchez	02.10.1992	14	5	16	2
Germán Sosa (ARG)	20.07.1990			6	-
Pedro Javier Velázquez Insfrán (PAR)	13.05.1983	8	-	-	-
Efraín Viáfara Molina	08.04.1981			7	-
Onel Cristóbal Vidal Campaz	26.05.1990			4	-
Jefferson Andrés Viveros Mina	21.12.1988	6	1		
Trainer:					
Alexis Enrique García Vega [as of 02.03.2014]	21.07.1960	18		18	

CORPORACIÓN DEPORTIVA INDEPENDIENTE MEDELLÍN

Foundation date: April 15, 1914
Address: Carrera 74 N° 48-37 C.E. Obelisco Oficina 1037, Medellín
Stadium: Estadio „Atanasio Girardot", Medellín – Capacity: 52,872

THE SQUAD

	DOB	Ape		Fin*	
		M	G	M	G
Goalkeepers:					
Carlos Andrés Bejarano Palacios	29.01.1985	3	-	17	-
Andrés Leandro Castellanos Serrano	09.03.1984	9	-	9	-
Juan David Gómez Gómez	06.01.1996	-	-	-	-
Juan David Valencia Arboleda	19.03.1993	-	-	3	-
Luis Herney Vásquez Caicedo	01.03.1996	7	-	-	-
Defenders:					
Diego Armando Amaya Solano	10.11.1985			1	-
Jorge Enrique Arias De La Hoz	13.12.1992	-	-	-	-
Jherson Enrique Córdoba Ospina	09.02.1988	14	-	23	-
Andrés Correa Valencia	29.01.1994	6	-		
Gilberto García Olarte	27.01.1987	11	1	11	-
Diego Armando Hérner (ARG)	31.07.1983	12	-	11	-
Vladimir Marín Ríos	26.09.1979			19	3
Jefferson Mena Palacios	15.06.1989	11	-	14	1
Jhonny Mena Palacios	27.09.1994	1	-		
Hernán Enrique Pertúz Ortega	31.03.1989	6	-	13	1
Pedro Macario Pino Moreno	30.07.1978	6	-		
Luis Alberto Tipton Palacio	28.07.1992	13	2	8	-
Carlos Alberto Valencia Paredes	28.04.1989			13	-
Midfielders:					
William Francisco Arboleda Perea	08.06.1990	14	-	3	-
Javier Calle Estrada	29.04.1991	2	-	19	6
Julián Guillermo Rojas	23.02.1990			9	-
Amílcar Henríquez (PAN)	02.08.1983	13	1		
Daniel Alejandro Hernández González	10.12.1990			24	1
Giovanni Hernández Soto Prínc	16.06.1976	16	-		
Jhon Edison Hernández Montoya	22.06.1986	16	1	19	2
Christian Camilo Marrugo Rodríguez	18.07.1985			22	2
Jonathan Yulián Mejia Chaverra	28.07.1990	17	3		
Víctor Andrés Moreno Córdoba	23.10.1994	-	-		
Yairo Yesid Moreno Berrío	04.04.1995	1	-	-	-
Dager Yair Palacios Palacios	04.04.1985	7	-		
Cristian Alberto Restrepo González	07.06.1988	6	-	17	-
Forwards:					
Germán Ezequiel Cano (ARG)	02.02.1988	18	11	25	16
Elton Martins Da Cruz (BRA)	04.11.1988			16	1
Leonel Ernesto García Dulce	24.04.1995	1	-	-	-
Yorleys Mena Palacios	20.07.1991	15	6	24	5
Alfredo José Morelos Aviléz	21.06.1996			6	1
Andrés Javier Mosquera Murillo	19.09.1989	11	-	25	1
William Parra Sinisterra	01.03.1995			1	-
Juan Carlos Pereira Díaz	08.02.1993	-	-		
Marco Jhonnier Pérez Murillo	18.09.1990	10	-		
Juan Pablo Pino Puello	30.03.1987	-	-		
Ray Andrés Vanegas Zúñiga	12.03.1993	3	-	3	-
Trainer:					
Pedro Enrique Sarmiento Solís [09.09.2013-21.02.2014]	26.10.1956	6			
Hernán Torres Oliveros [as of 22.02.2014]	18.02.1961	12		26	

**Matches and goals in 2014 Torneo Finalización play-offs included*

ITAGÜÍ FÚTBOL CLUB / ÁGUILAS PEREIRA FÚTBOL CLUB

Foundation date: January 7, 2008 / November 1991
Address: Calle 36 N° 59, 69 Int. 187 Itagüí / Carrera 11 N° 46 - 152 – Maraya, Pereira
Stadium: Estadio Metropolitano Ciudad de Itagüí – Capacity: 12,000 /
Estadio "Hernán Ramírez Villegas", Pereira – Capacity: 30,297

THE SQUAD

	DOB	Ape*		Fin**	
		M	G	M	G
Goalkeepers:					
Osvaldo Andrés Cabral (ARG)	04.06.1985	6	-	16	-
David González Giraldo	20.07.1982	14	-	8	-
Kevin Wilson Piedrahita Velasco (USA)	18.06.1991	-	-	-	-
Defenders:					
Carlos Mario Arboleda Ampudia	08.06.1986	20	-	19	-
Camilo Andrés Ceballos Zapata	15.07.1984	17	4	4	-
Braynner Yezid García Leal	06.09.1986	-	-		
Jair Enrique Iglesias Jiménez	27.03.1988	1	-		
Hanyer Luis Mosquera Córdoba	15.01.1987			8	-
Javier López Rodríguez	30.10.1988	13	-	18	1
Jhonny Mesa Morelos	11.09.1993	5	-	-	-
Andrés Felipe Ortíz Agudelo	20.03.1987	9	-		
Fabio Darío Rodríguez Mejía	03.10.1985	10	-	18	2
Samuel Antonio Vanegas Luna	08.09.1976			22	1
Fabián Alexis Viáfara Alarcón	16.03.1992	1	-	14	-
Anderson Fernan Zapata Diosa	03.12.1984			18	1
Midfielders:					
Cleider Leandro Alzáte Correa	05.02.1988	19	2	18	2
Brayan Edinson Angulo Mosquera	19.07.1993	15	1	16	4
Bréiner Steven Belalcázar Ulabarri	22.09.1984	15	-	3	-
Matías Alejandro Giménez (ARG)	23.12.1984			4	1
Mauricio Gómez Pérez	08.03.1983	-	-	-	-
Juan José Mezú Viáfara	06.01.1989	5	-		
Elvis David Mosquera Valdés	22.01.1991	9	2	7	-
Yohn Géiler Mosquera Martínez	15.04.1989	17	-	20	-
Yonaider Ortega Crespo	22.09.1987	3	-	-	-
Edinson Manuel Palomino Marrugo	30.01.1986	17	2	22	8
Boris Yasser Polo Mosquera	26.05.1991			7	1
John Javier Restrepo Pérez	22.08.1977	16	-	22	-
Andrés Ricaurte Vélez	03.10.1991	-	-	1	-
Juan David Rodríguez Rico	24.09.1992	3	-	2	-
Omar Andrés Rodríguez Martínez	04.03.1981	1	-		
Forwards:					
Diego Andrés Álvarez Sánchez	23.09.1981			19	3
Maicol Balanta Peña	02.01.1990			16	2
David Leonardo Castro Cortés	12.05.1989	15	1	-	-
Johan Jorge Fano (PER)	09.08.1978			20	6
Silvio Augusto González (ARG)	08.06.1980			6	-
Yessi Ferley Mena Palacios	05.07.1989	19	8		
Malher Tressor Moreno Baldrich	11.01.1979	15	2		
Kevin Alfredo Nieto Márquez	24.05.1995			4	-
Juan Guillermo Vélez Córdoba	16.10.1983	3	-	-	-
Trainer:					
Alberto Miguel Gamero Morillo [01.01.-09.05.1964]	03.02.1964	2			
Jorge Luis Bernal Caviedes [03.06.-23.09.2014]	27.09.1952	18		10	
Óscar Héctor Quintabani Faggiolani (ARG) [as of 24.09.2014]	04.06.1950			14	

**Matches and goals in 2014 Torneo Apertura play-offs included*
***Matches and goals in 2014 Torneo Finalización play-offs included*

CORPORACIÓN POPULAR DEPORTIVA JUNIOR BARRANQUILLA

Foundation date: August 7, 1924
Address: Carrera 57 N° 72-56, Barranquilla
Stadium: Estadio Metropolitano "Roberto Meléndez", Barranquilla – Capacity: 60,000

THE SQUAD					
	DOB	Ape*		Fin	
		M	G	M	G
Goalkeepers:					
José Luis Chunga Vega	11.07.1991	-	-	1	-
Sergio Andrés Estrada Peña	30.05.1996			-	-
Carlos Andrés Rodríguez Ibarra	07.05.1983	1	-	-	-
Mario Sebastián Viera Galaín (URU)	07.03.1983	23	-	17	-
Defenders:					
Nery Rubén Bareiro Zorrilla (PAR)	03.03.1988			16	-
Jarlan Junior Barrera Escalona	16.09.1985			13	2
Andrés Felipe Correa Osorio	02.07.1984	18	-	13	1
Juan Guillermo Domínguez Cabeza	17.12.1986	19	2	8	2
César Augusto Fawcett Lebolo	12.08.1984	12	-	-	-
Andrés Felipe González Ramírez	08.01.1984	2	-		
Germán Andrés Gutiérrez Henao	16.01.1980			1	-
Pablo Manuel Maldonado Charris	01.02.1991	-	-	-	-
Oidel Jair Pérez Rivadeneira	29.01.1991			6	-
Jamell Orlando Ramos Hernández	12.10.1981	2	-	-	-
Germán Andrés Rodríguez Henao	16.01.1990			-	-
Kevin David Sandoval Rudas	13.01.1993	-	-		
William José Tesillo Gutiérrez	02.02.1990	24	-	17	-
Samuel Antonio Vanegas Luna	08.09.1976	14	-		
José Iván Vélez Castillo	16.08.1984	-	-	-	-
Midfielders:					
Jorge Andrés Aguirre Restrepo	18.06.1987	10	-	18	8
Matías Ariel Bolatti (ARG)	09.05.1988	12	1		
Guillermo León Celis Montiel	06.05.1993	17	-	11	-
Gustavo Leonardo Cuellar Gallego	14.10.1992			15	-
Álvaro José Domínguez Cabezas	10.06.1981			4	-
Brayner Yesid García Leal	06.09.1986			12	-
Jossymarn Andrés Gómez Pereira	13.08.1987	16	1	12	-
Vladimir Javier Hernández Rivero	08.02.1989	21	3	13	1
Luis Manuel Narváez Pitalúa	11.07.1984	23	-	15	1
Michael Javier Ortega Dieppa	06.04.1991	15	1	6	-
Jhonny Albeiro Ramírez Lozano	23.05.1983	13	-	9	-
Jhonny Alexander Vásquez Salazar	23.06.1987	18	1	5	1
Forwards:					
Martín Enrique Arzuaga Coronel	23.07.1981	16	5		
Maicol Balanta Peña	02.01.1990	7	-		
Luis Carlos de la Hoz Suárez	27.10.1989			7	-
Yessy Ferley Mena Palacios	05.07.1989			17	2
Jorge Miguel Ortega Salinas (PAR)	16.04.1991			4	-
Roberto Andrés Ovelar Maldonado (PAR)	01.02.1985			3	-
Luis Enrique Quiñónes García	26.06.1991	19	3	7	1
Luis Carlos Ruiz Morales	08.01.1987	6	1		
José Edison Toloza Colorado	15.06.1984	16	7		
Trainer:					
Miguel Ángel López Elhall (ARG) [04.06.2013-18.03.2014]	01.03.1942	11			
Julio Avelino Comesaña (URU) [as of 19.03.2014]	10.03.1948	13		18	

**Matches and goals in 2014 Torneo Apertura play-offs included*

CLUB DEPORTIVO LA EQUIDAD SEGUROS

Foundation date: Ocotober 12, 1990
Address: Calle 193 N° 38-20, Bogotá
Stadium: Estadio Metropolitano de Techo, Bogotá – Capacity: 12,000

THE SQUAD

	DOB	Ape*		Fin	
		M	G	M	G
Goalkeepers:					
William David Cuesta Mosquera	19.02.1993	-	-	-	-
Diego Alejandro Novoa Urrego	31.05.1989	20	-	17	-
Cristian Andrés Pinzón Rivera	29.11.1984	-	-	2	-
Esteban Armando Ruíz Molina	15.07.1997			-	-
Defenders:					
Daniel Oswaldo Briceño Bueno	09.06.1985	13	-	12	-
Wilmer Díaz Lucumi	23.06.1978	17	-	9	1
Elvis Javier Gónzalez Herrera	20.02.1982	15	1	17	-
Jerson Andrés Malagón Piracún	26.06.1993	8	-	12	-
Andrés Felipe Murillo Segura	04.0.1996			1	-
Helibelton Palacios Zapata	09.06.1993	15	-		
Geisson Alexander Perea Ocoró	06.08.1991	-	-	-	-
Pedro Paulo Portocarrero Angulo	13.05.1977	10	-	8	-
Amaury Torralvo Polo	12.01.1994	6	-	3	-
Midfielders:					
Jhoan Sebastián Ayala Sanabria	14.09.1995	12	-		
Fernando Nicolás Battiste (ARG)	11.03.1984	18	1	13	-
Francisco Antonio Córdoba Escarpeta	08.09.1988			4	-
Jhon Fredy Duque Arias	04.06.1992			1	-
Jorge Andrés Guillén Ovalle	08.02.1996			3	-
Freddy Hinestroza Arias	05.04.1990	16	2		
Yonni Fernando Hinestroza Lozano	20.08.1984	9	-	13	-
José Manuel Nájera Ríos	03.09.1988	13	-	13	-
Jorge Daniel Núñez Espínola (PAR)	22.09.1984	1	-	-	-
Dager Yair Palacios Palacios	04.04.1985			15	-
Jhon Jairo Valencia Ortíz	27.03.1982	14	-	17	2
Forwards:					
Paulo César Arango Ambuila	27.08.1984	15	-	12	2
Oscar David Barreto Pérez	28.04.1993	8	1	14	2
Esteban Felipe Castañeda Otálvaro	18.12.1991	-	-	-	-
Luis Cuesta Cuesta	11.11.1993	3	-	9	-
Henry Javier Hernández Álvarez	14.05.1982	15	5	7	1
Matías Martín Jones Mourigan (URU)	01.07.1991			7	-
José Alcides Moreno Mora	10.09.1981	16	7	13	1
Lionard Fernando Pajoy Ortíz	07.06.1981	10	-	10	1
Iván David Rivas Mendoza	10.03.1988	13	-	5	-
Leonardo Adrián Villagra Enciso (PAR)	02.09.1990	11	1	14	5
Trainer:					
Néstor William Otero Carvajal [as of 27.12.2012]	18.09.1955	20		18	

**Matches and goals in 2014 Torneo Apertura play-offs included*

CLUB DEPORTIVO LOS MILLONARIOS BOGOTÁ

Foundation date: June 18, 1946
Address: Carrera 50 N° 59-54, Bogotá
Stadium: Estadio „Nemesio Camacho" [El Campín], Bogotá – Capacity: 48,310

THE SQUAD

	DOB	Ape* M	Ape* G	Fin M	Fin G
Goalkeepers:					
Luis Enrique Delgado Mantilla	26.10.1980	17	2	9	1
Mateo Mendoza Valderrama	27.09.1995	-	-	-	-
Nelson Fernando Ramos Betancourt	23.11.1981	5	-	9	-
Brayan Esteban Silva Pinto	04.09.1997			-	-
Defenders:					
Andrés Felipe Cadavid Cardona	28.12.1985	17	1	16	-
Nelson Cuero Betancurt	21.01.1995			2	-
Álex Díaz Díaz	13.01.1989	16	1	11	-
Gabriel Eduardo Díaz Rico	28.01.1996			5	1
Oswaldo José Henríquez Bocanegra	03.10.1989	18	1	7	-
Lewis Alexander Ochoa Cassiani	04.09.1984	15	-	14	-
Román Torres Morcillo (PAN)	20.03.1986	16	1	13	-
Stiven Vega Londoño	22.05.1998			-	-
Midfielders:					
Elkin Blanco Rivas	05.09.1989	4	-		
Mayer Andrés Candelo García	20.02.1977	20	3	18	1
Jorge Andrés Carrascal Guardo	25.05.1998			1	-
Jefferson Marzio Herrera Geves	20.07.1992	3	-	-	-
Dahwling Leudo Cossio	24.07.1989	13	-	10	-
Modeste M'Bami (CMR)	09.10.1982	14	-		
Luis Hernán Mosquera Chamorro	25.05.1989	1	-	16	-
Juan Esteban Ortíz Blandón	29.08.1987	12	-	13	-
José Harrison Otálvaro Arce	28.02.1986	17	2		
Jorge Isaacs Perlaza Angulo	11.10.1984	-	-	-	-
Arturo David Ramírez (ARG)	18.02.1981	-	-		
Javier Arley Reina Calvo	04.01.1989			10	1
Rafael Fernando Robayo Marroquín	24.04.1984	19	1	10	-
Daniel Mauricio Torres González	28.06.1993	2	-	2	-
Fabián Andrés Vargas Rivera	17.04.1980	18	1	17	1
Edson Omar Vásquez Ortega	15.08.1989	18	2	4	1
Wesley Lopes da F. Vargas Silva	10.11.1980	12	1		
Sergio Leonardo Villarreal Ruíz	29.01.1995			2	-
Forwards:					
Jhonatan Alexander Agudelo Velásquez	17.12.1992	5	-	15	2
Cristhian Felipe Alarcón Guarín	29.05.1992	2	-	2	-
Yuber Alberto Asprilla Viera	11.12.1992	5	-	2	-
Dayro Mauricio Moreno Galindo	16.09.1985	21	13		
Sebastián Andrés Pinto Perurena	15.02.1986			4	1
Anderson Daniel Plata Guillén	08.11.1990	5	-	11	1
Andy Jorman Polo Andrade (PER)	29.09.1994			11	2
Fernando Uribe Hincapié	01.01.1988			14	10
Trainer:					
Juan Manuel Lillo Díez (ESP) [04.12.2013-02.09.2014]	03.11.1965	22		7	
Ricardo Gabriel Lunari Del Federico (ARG) [as of 03.09.2014]	06.02.1970			11	

**Matches and goals in 2014 Torneo Apertura play-offs included*

CORPORACIÓN DEPORTIVA ONCE CALDAS MANIZALES

Foundation date: April 16, 1947
Address: Carrera 23 N° 55-81, Puerta 18, Manizales
Stadium: Estadio Palogrande, Manizales – Capacity: 42,553

THE SQUAD

	DOB	Ape* M	Ape* G	Fin** M	Fin** G
Goalkeepers:					
José Fernando Cuadrado Romero	01.06.1985	18	-	21	-
Wanerge Delgado de Armas	10.01.1989	-	-	-	-
Juan Carlos Henao Valencia	30.12.1971	1	-	3	-
Sergio Felipe Román Palacios	21.05.1995	2	-	-	-
Defenders:					
Fernando Martín Bonjour (ARG)	04.09.1985			4	-
Marino García González	28.06.1982	6	-	6	-
Jonathan Lopera Jiménez	02.06.1987	7	1	11	1
José Luis Moreno Peña	22.10.1996			6	1
Hanyer Luis Mosquera Córdoba	15.01.1987	13	1	12	1
Luis Carlos Murillo	16.10.1990			5	-
Fausto Manuel Obeso Pérez	28.08.1988	15	-	16	-
Clemente Palacios Santos	24.10.1993	6	-	6	-
Juan Camilo Pérez Saldarriaga	26.10.1985	19	-	19	-
Marlon Javier Piedrahita Londoño	13.06.1985	19	1	22	1
Edy Rentería Mena	03.10.1993	-	-	-	-
Midfielders:					
Johan Leandro Arango Ambuila	05.02.1991	4	-	9	1
Juan David Cabezas Nuñez	27.02.1991	16	2	14	2
Juan José Castaño Jiménez	14.11.1993	-	-	-	-
Gustavo Culma	20.04.1993	10	2	13	2
Leandro Javier Díaz (ARG)	26.06.1986			5	-
Carlos Alberto Giraldo Quiroga	17.11.1979	16	-	15	-
Hárrison Steve Henao Hurtado	19.12.1987	14	-	12	-
Daniel Alejandro Hernández González	10.12.1990	16	1	14	1
César Augusto Hinestroza Lozano	20.11.1989	1	-	1	-
Santiago Loaiza Valencia	07.09.1993	-	-	-	-
Cristian Fernando Osorio Jaramillo	23.02.1989			1	-
Cristian Andrés Palomeque Valoyes	02.04.1994	12	1	12	1
Patricio Pablo Pérez (ARG)	27.06.1985	16	3	15	3
Carlos Julio Robles Rocha	16.05.1992	8	1	7	-
Sergio Esteban Romero Méndez	22.11.1988			6	-
Forwards:					
César Augusto Arias Moros	02.04.1988	17	7	20	6
Yovanny Arrechea Amu	23.01.1983	6	-	6	-
José Heriberto Izquierdo Mena	07.07.1992	19	7	17	7
Edwards Yesid Jiménez Gómez	14.07.1981	12	2	16	3
Jelinson Mosquera Rodríguez	08.09.1995			1	-
William Enrique Palacio González	21.07.1994	-	-	-	-
Raúl Eduardo Peñaranda Contreras	02.05.1991			1	-
Jaime Andrés Sierra Ramírez	11.04.1986	6	1	11	1
Jhon Fredy Salazar Valencia	01.04.1995			1	-
Trainer:					
José Flabio Torres Sierra	07.12.1970	20		24	

**Matches and goals in 2014 Torneo Apertura play-offs included*
***Matches and goals in 2014 Torneo Finalización play-offs included*

CORPORACIÓN DEPORTIVA PATRIOTAS FUTBOL CLUB TUNJA

Foundation date: February 18, 2003
Address: Calle 19 #9-35 Ofi: 607, Tunja
Stadium: Estadio La Independencia, Tunja – Capacity: 21,000

THE SQUAD

	DOB	Ape M	Ape G	Fin M	Fin G
Goalkeepers:					
Sergio Manuel Gutiérrez Suárez	28.05.1989			-	-
Alejandro Antonio Otero Orejuela	10.02.1984	11	-	5	-
Santiago Quiróz Henao	27.10.1993	-	-	-	-
Nicolas Vikonis Moreau (URU)	06.08.1984	8	-	14	-
Oswaldo Villada Amaya	28.01.1996	-	-	-	-
Defenders:					
Danny Leandro Aguilar Mancilla	25.02.1986	10	-	-	-
Hugo Armando Bolaño Gómez	26.11.1982	14	-		
Jhon Alexander Cano Angulo	20.12.1982			12	-
Nicolás Carreño Suárez	24.07.1993	-	-	5	-
Carlos Alberto Henao Sánchez	03.12.1988			14	-
César Augusto Hinestroza Lozano	20.11.1989			14	-
Aldair Lasso Mulato	07.05.1991	12	-	-	-
Harold Macias Cabrera	12.06.1980			14	1
Luis Alejandro Malagón Liscano	20.02.1991			-	-
Gonzalo Martínez Caicedo	30.11.1975	16	1	11	3
Jesús David Murillo León	17.08.1993	4	-	-	-
Jesús Steven Murillo León	17.08.1993	-	-	-	-
Luis Alberto Nuñez Charales	10.12.1983	15	-		
Clemente Palacios Santos	24.10.1993			3	-
Jeferson Palacios Palacios	16.09.1993			-	-
Andrés Felipe Salinas Rodríguez	11.06.1986	2	1		
Walden Alexis Vargas Castillo	25.11.1984	12	1		
Midfielders:					
Estéfano Arango González	18.01.1994			12	1
Iván Arturo Corredor Hurtado	25.06.1983	-	-	11	-
Jhonatan Estrada Campillo	27.01.1983	18	2	18	4
Raúl Alberto Loaiza Morelos	08.06.1994	15	2	10	-
Leonardo Fávio López Méndez	18.05.1987			1	-
Manuel Emilio Palacios Murillo	13.02.1993	7	1		
Leonardo Rubén Pico Carvajal	04.10.1991	17	-	16	-
Emmanuel Prisco Jaramillo	25.04.1991	14	-		
Avimileth Rivas Quintero	17.10.1984	12	-	13	-
Jonathan Segura	09.07.1990	6	-	10	-
Cristhian Camilo Subero Mier	26.05.1991	-	-	5	1
Larry Vásquez Ortega	19.09.1992	11	1	14	-
Forwards:					
Franco Junior Aliberti Barreto (URU)	16.06.1984	6	-		
Andrés Lizardo Angulo Quiñónes	09.01.1986	-	-	-	-
Maximiliano Brito Hernández (URU)	19.07.1991	10	1		
Robinson Estiven Larrahondo Juanillo	28.04.1993	9	-	-	-
Marcos Antonio Lazaga Dávalos (PAR)	26.02.1983			14	3
Óscar Darío Martínez Pantoja	19.02.1980	4	-	-	-
Maicol Giovanny Medina Medina	04.06.1997			1	-
Carlos Alveiro Rentería Cuesta	04.03.1986	15	10	18	2
Carlos Andrés Rivas Gómez	22.08.1991			15	2
Juan Leandro Vogliotti (ARG)	11.04.1985	1	-		
Trainer:					
Julio Avelino Comesaña (URU) [01.07.2013-01.02.2014]	10.03.1948	2			
Harold Rivera Roa [as of 02.02.2014]	01.05.1974	16		18	

SANTA FE CORPORACIÓN DEPORTIVA BOGOTÁ

Foundation date: February 28, 1941
Address: Calle 64 a Nº 50 b – 08 (Nueva Nomenclatura), Bogotá
Stadium: Estadio „Nemesio Camacho" [El Campín], Bogotá – Capacity: 48,310

THE SQUAD

	DOB	Ape*		Fin**	
		M	G	M	G
Goalkeepers:					
Libis Andrés Arenas Murillo	12.05.1987	-	-	-	-
Camilo Andrés Vargas Gil	09.03.1989	13	-	20	1
Robinson Zapata Rufay	30.09.1978	9	-	6	-
Defenders:					
Jair Arrechea Amú	08.11.1980			9	-
José Julián de la Cuesta Herrera	10.02.1983	14	1	19	-
Francisco Javier Meza Palma	29.08.1991	14	-	24	1
Yerry Fernando Mina González	23.09.1994	16	1	18	2
Dairon Mosquera Chaverra	23.07.1992	16	-	17	-
Sergio Andrés Otálvaro Botero	12.10.1986	11	-	15	-
Rafael Enrique Pérez Almeida	09.01.1990	5	-		
Juan Daniel Roa Reyes	20.08.1991	14	-	23	1
Héctor Antonio Urrego Hurtado	10.11.1992	10	-	-	-
Ricardo José Villarraga Marchena	23.04.1992	1	-	7	-
Midfielders:					
Hugo Alejandro Acosta Cáceres	29.01.1991	1	-		
José Yulián Anchico Patiño	28.05.1984	13	2	16	-
Gerardo Alberto Bedoya Múnera	26.11.1975	-	-		
David Arturo Ferreira Rico	09.08.1979	6	-	3	-
Julián Guillermo Rojas	23.02.1990	6	-		
Juan Sebastián Hernández Obando	24.04.1994	-	-	-	-
Édison Vicente Méndez Méndez	16.03.1979	10	-	-	-
Fram Enrique Pacheco Cardona	08.11.1980	13	-		
Juan Guillermo Pedroza Perdomo	14.04.1993	-	-	-	-
Omar Sebastián Pérez (ARG)	29.03.1981	12	3	21	5
Franco Razzotti Viretto (ARG)	06.02.1985			2	-
Luis Manuel Seijas Gunther (VEN)	23.06.1986	17	2	18	1
Sebastián Enríque Salazar Beltrán	30.09.1995			2	-
Daniel Alejandro Torres Rojas	15.11.1989	14	-	22	1
Forwards:					
Luis Carlos Arias	13.01.1985	16	4	23	6
Juan Fernando Caicedo Benítez	13.07.1989	-	-		
Jonathan Copete Valencia	23.01.1988	15	1		
Jefferson Cuero Castro	15.05.1988	17	3	18	3
Silvio Augusto González (ARG)	08.06.1980	4	2		
Sergio Darío Herrera Month	15.03.1981	12	2		
Wilder Andrés Medina Tamayo	21.02.1981	19	8	11	3
Jhon Fredy Miranda Rada	07.03.1997	-	-	4	-
Wilson David Morelo López	21.05.1987			25	10
Michael Jhon Ander Rangel Valencia	08.03.1991			12	1
Darío Andrés Rodríguez Parra	15.05.1995	6	-	8	-
Armando Junior Vargas Morales	27.12.1988	2	1	10	-
Trainer:					
Gustavo Adolfo Costas Makeira (ARG)	28.02.1963	22		26	

**Matches and goals in 2014 Torneo Apertura play-offs included*
***Matches and goals in 2014 Torneo Finalización play-offs included*

UNIAUTÓNOMA FÚTBOL CLUB BARRANQUILLA

Foundation date: November 1, 2010
Address: Calle 88 No. 47-76 Barranquilla
Stadium: Estadio Metropolitano „Roberto Meléndez" ,Barranquilla – Capacity: 49,612

THE SQUAD

	DOB	Ape		Fin	
		M	G	M	G
Goalkeepers:					
Jafeb José Bonilla Pájaro	16.04.1996	-	-	-	-
Jáiber Damián Cardona Lozano	19.01.1990	12	-		
Carlos Geovanni Chávez Ospina	07.08.1984	6	-	1	-
Carl Stevans de la Cruz Ramírez	25.06.1995	-	-	-	-
Sebastián Alberto López (ARG)	14.09.1985			17	-
Defenders:					
Alonso Antonio Acosta Arrieta	10.02.1989	7	-	15	1
Harold Andres Gómez Muñoz	21.04.1992	2	-	-	-
Harold Macias Cabrera	12.06.1980	15	1		
Leonel Antonio Parris Mitre (PAN)	13.06.1982			3	-
Alexis Rafael Pérez Fontanilla	25.03.1994	16	-	5	-
Carlos Alfredo Saa Posso	12.04.1983	13	-	12	1
James Amilkar Sánchez Altamiranda	04.05.1988			13	-
Nelino José Tapia Gil	01.02.1991	14	-	17	2
Edgar Alonso Zapata Pérez	01.09.1979			4	-
Midfielders:					
José Antonio Amaya Pardo	16.07.1980	3	-	10	1
Estéfano Arango González	18.01.1994	8	-		
Javier Araujo Penaloza	26.12.1984	6	-	-	-
Faber Cañaveral Renteria	31.08.1988	13	-	14	1
James Enrique Castro Maestre	24.11.1984	15	-	10	-
Daniel Machacón Hernández	05.01.1985	14	-	16	-
Giovanny Martínez Cortés	07.07.1989	12	1		
John Edinson Méndez Bettin	10.08.1985	13	2	17	-
Jefferson Eulises Murillo Aguilar	18.01.1992	6	-	-	-
Raúl Murillo Navarro	26.02.1995			-	-
Alan Ferney Navarro Espinosa	08.05.1989	14	6	11	1
Luis Carlos Núñez Arias	22.11.1991	1	-	2	-
Víctor Hugo Ocampo Idárraga	05.05.1993	-	-	1	-
Walmer Pacheco Mejía	16.01.1995			8	-
Alberto Andrés Pardo Zapata	25.03.1996			1	-
Brayan Quiroga	13.04.1995			2	-
Gerson Andrés Rodríguez González	12.08.1994	-	-	-	-
Didier Enríque Roa Obregón	10.09.1989	-	-	-	-
Giovanni Hernández Soto Prínc	16.06.1976			12	-
Forwards:					
Mario Alexander Álvarez Villalba	03.06.1994			-	-
Martín Enrique Arzuaga Coronel	23.07.1981			14	2
Michael David Barrios Puerta	21.04.1991	16	4	17	3
Cristian Luis Fernándes Mejía	10.04.1990	16	3	5	-
José Del Carmen González Joly (PAN)	05.05.1991	1	-		
Mauro Andrés Manotas Pérez	15.07.1995	1	-	11	3
Félix Andrés Micolta Micolta	30.11.1989	11	-		
Alfredo Antonio Padilla Gutiérrez	29.07.1989			6	-
Abel Andrés Quintero Ortíz	07.08.1995			1	-
Jhon Henry Ramírez Pombo	03.09.1985	-	-		
Angelo José Rodríguez Henry	04.04.1989	10	-		
Joao Leandro Rodríguez González	19.05.1996	6	1		
Jefferson Viveros	21.12.1988			4	-
Trainer:					
José Manuel Rodríguez Becerra [01.08.2012-05.04.2014]	08.10.1965	15			
Jaime De La Pava Márquez [06.04.-22.09.2014]	14.04.1967	3		10	
Calixto José Chiquillo Mendoza [as of 23.09.2014]	23.11.1973			8	

SECOND LEVEL
Primera B 2014 - Torneo Postobón

Torneo Apertura

First Stage

1.	Club Atlético Bucaramanga CD	18	10	4	4	22	-	12	34
2.	Llaneros FC Villavicencio	18	9	6	3	23	-	15	33
3.	SAD América de Cali	18	9	5	4	24	-	15	32
4.	Jaguares de Córdoba FC Montería	18	9	4	5	26	-	20	31
5.	Deportes Quindío Armenia	18	8	6	4	23	-	13	30
6.	CN Cúcuta Deportivo	18	9	3	6	20	-	18	30
7.	CF Deportivo Rionegro	18	9	2	7	30	-	25	29
8.	AD Unión Magdalena Santa Marta	18	8	4	6	21	-	22	28
9.	Valledupar FC	18	8	3	7	29	-	18	27
10.	CD Real Cartagena FC	18	7	6	5	24	-	17	27
11.	Universitário de Popayán	18	8	2	8	25	-	25	26
12.	Barranquilla FC	18	5	7	6	18	-	22	22
13.	CD Real Santander Floridablanca	18	6	4	8	21	-	28	22
14.	CC Deportivo Tuluá	18	4	7	7	21	-	26	19
15.	Bogotá FC	18	4	5	9	15	-	27	17
16.	CD Expreso Rojo Zipaquirá	18	3	5	10	17	-	28	14
17.	CS Deportivo y Cultural Pereira	18	3	4	11	18	-	33	13
18.	Depor FC Aguablanca Cali	18	3	3	12	17	-	30	12

Play-offs

Quarter-Finals [17-22.05.2014]

AD Unión Magdalena Santa Marta - Club Atlético Bucaramanga CD	2-1(1-0)	0-1(0-0) 4-5 pen
CF Deportivo Rionegro - Jaguares de Córdoba FC Montería	2-1(2-1)	0-2(0-1)
CN Cúcuta Deportivo - Llaneros FC Villavicencio	0-2(0-2)	1-1(1-0)
Deportes Quindío Armenia - SAD América de Cali	1-1(0-0)	1-3(0-1)

Semi-Finals [28.05.-01.06.2014]

Jaguares de Córdoba FC Montería - Club Atlético Bucaramanga CD	3-0(1-0)	0-3(0-1) 6-5 pen
SAD América de Cali - Llaneros FC Villavicencio	4-0(3-0)	2-2(1-1)

Torneo Apertura Final [04-08.06.2014]

Jaguares de Córdoba FC Montería - SAD América de Cali	4-1(1-0)	1-1(1-1)

2014 Torneo Apertura Champions: **Jaguares de Córdoba FC Montería**

Torneo Finalización

First Stage

	Team	P	W	D	L	GF		GA	Pts
1.	Jaguares de Córdoba FC Montería	18	10	4	4	27	-	18	34
2.	CS Deportivo y Cultural Pereira	18	9	6	3	28	-	15	33
3.	Deportes Quindío Armenia	18	9	6	3	28	-	17	33
4.	CF Deportivo Rionegro	18	9	6	3	26	-	15	33
5.	AD Unión Magdalena Santa Marta	18	9	5	4	32	-	20	32
6.	CN Cúcuta Deportivo	18	9	5	4	21	-	15	32
7.	Club Atlético Bucaramanga CD	18	8	7	3	23	-	19	31
8.	SAD América de Cali	18	8	6	4	25	-	17	30
9.	CD Real Cartagena FC	18	9	3	6	20	-	18	30
10.	CC Deportivo Tuluá	18	8	1	9	21	-	19	25
11.	Valledupar FC	18	7	4	7	16	-	18	25
12.	Llaneros FC Villavicencio	18	6	4	8	25	-	25	22
13.	Universitário de Popayán	18	5	4	9	17	-	29	19
14.	CD Real Santander Floridablanca	18	4	6	8	17	-	24	18
15.	CD Expreso Rojo Zipaquirá	18	3	4	11	11	-	20	13
16.	Depor FC Aguablanca Cali	18	3	4	11	18	-	35	13
17.	Bogotá FC	18	2	5	11	17	-	29	11
18.	Barranquilla FC	18	3	2	13	11	-	30	11

Top-8 qualified for the Cuadrangulares.

Cuadrangulares

Grupo A

	Team	P	W	D	L	GF		GA	Pts
1.	Deportes Quindío Armenia	6	3	1	2	7	-	3	10
2.	CN Cúcuta Deportivo	6	3	1	2	7	-	7	10
3.	Club Atlético Bucaramanga CD	6	3	0	3	6	-	6	9
4.	Jaguares de Córdoba FC Montería	6	2	0	4	5	-	9	6

Grupo B

	Team	P	W	D	L	GF		GA	Pts
1.	CF Deportivo Rionegro	6	3	1	2	9	-	10	10
2.	CS Deportivo y Cultural Pereira	6	2	3	1	10	-	6	9
3.	AD Unión Magdalena Santa Marta	6	1	3	2	8	-	8	6
4.	SAD América de Cali	6	1	3	2	6	-	9	6

Torneo Finalización Final [01-04.12.2014]

CF Deportivo Rionegro - Deportes Quindío Armenia 1-0(0-0) 1-4(1-2)

2014 Torneo Finalización Champions: **Deportes Quindío Armenia**

Primera B 2014 – Finals
[09-14.12.2014]

Deportes Quindío Armenia - Jaguares de Córdoba FC Montería 2-0(0-0) 0-3(0-2)
Jaguares de Córdoba FC Montería promoted to „Primera A“

Aggregate Table 2014

1.	Jaguares de Córdoba FC Montería (*Promoted*)	50	25	9	16	72 - 56	84
2.	Deportes Quindío Armenia (*Promotion/Relegation Play-off*)	48	22	14	12	66 - 42	80
3.	Club Atlético Bucaramanga CD	46	23	11	12	56 - 42	80
4.	CF Deportivo Rionegro	46	23	9	14	69 - 57	78
5.	SAD América de Cali	48	20	17	11	67 - 50	77
6.	CN Cúcuta Deportivo	44	21	10	13	49 - 43	73
7.	AD Unión Magdalena Santa Marta	44	19	12	13	63 - 52	69
8.	Llaneros FC Villavicencio	40	16	12	12	53 - 47	60
9.	CD Real Cartagena FC	36	16	9	11	44 - 35	57
10.	CS Deportivo y Cultural Pereira	42	14	13	15	56 - 54	55
11.	Valledupar FC	36	15	7	14	45 - 36	52
12.	Universitário de Popayán	36	13	6	17	42 - 54	45
13.	CC Deportivo Tuluá	36	12	8	16	42 - 45	44
14.	CD Real Santander Floridablanca	36	10	10	16	38 - 52	40
15.	Barranquilla FC	36	8	9	19	29 - 52	33
16.	Bogotá FC	36	6	10	20	32 - 56	28
17.	CD Expreso Rojo Zipaquirá	36	6	9	21	28 - 48	27
18.	Depor FC Aguablanca Cali	36	6	7	23	35 - 65	25

NATIONAL TEAM
INTERNATIONAL MATCHES
(16.07.2014 – 15.07.2015)

05.09.2014	Miami Gardens	Brazil - Colombia	1-0(0-0)	(F)
10.10.2014	Harrison	Colombia – El Salvador	3-0(1-0)	(F)
14.10.2014	Harrison	Canada - Colombia	0-1(0-0)	(F)
14.11.2014	London	United States - Colombia	1-2(1-0)	(F)
18.11.2014	Ljubljana	Slovenia - Colombia	0-1(0-1)	(F)
26.03.2015	Riffa	Bahrain - Colombia	0-6(0-3)	(F)
30.03.2015	Abu Dhabi	Colombia - Kuwait	3-1(1-1)	(F)
06.06.2015	Buenos Aires	Colombia – Costa Rica	1-0(0-0)	(F)
14.06.2015	Rancagua	Colombia – Venezuela	0-1(0-0)	(CA)
17.06.2015	Santiago	Brazil - Colombia	0-1(0-1)	(CA)
21.06.2015	Temuco	Colombia - Peru	0-0	(CA)
24.06.2015	Viña del Mar	Argentina - Colombia	5-4 pen	(CA)

05.09.2014, Friendly International
Sun Life Stadium, Miami Gardens (United States); Attendance: 73,479
Referee: Dave Gantar (Canada)
BRAZIL - COLOMBIA 1-0(0-0)
COL: David Ospina Ramírez, Cristián Eduardo Zapata Valencia, Pablo Estifer Armero, Carlos Enrique Valdés Parra, Juan Camilo Zúñiga Mosquera (73.Alexander Mejía Sabalza), Carlos Alberto Sánchez Moreno (85.Gustavo Adrián Ramos Vásquez), Aldo Leão Ramírez Sierra (46.Santiago Arias Naranjo), Juan Guillermo Cuadrado Bello, James David Rodríguez Rubio (77.Radamel Falcao García Zárate), Teófilo Antonio Gutiérrez Roncancio (64.Carlos Arturo Bacca Ahumada), Jackson Arley Martínez Valencia (65.Fredy Alejandro Guarín Vásquez). Trainer: José Néstor Pékerman (Argentina).
Sent off: Juan Guillermo Cuadrado Bello (49).

10.10.2014, Friendly International
Red Bull Arena, Harrison (United States); Attendance: 25,189
Referee: Dave Gantar (Canada)
COLOMBIA – EL SALVADOR 3-0(1-0)
COL: Camilo Andrés Vargas Gil, Pablo Estifer Armero, Pedro Camilo Franco Ulloa (61.Jeison Fabián Murillo Cerón), Santiago Arias Naranjo, Éder Fabián Álvarez Balanta, Alexander Mejía Sabalza, James David Rodríguez Rubio (82.Abel Enrique Aguilar Tapias), Edwin Andrés Cardona Bedoya (61.Juan Fernando Quintero Paniagua), Carlos Mario Carbonero Mancilla (72.Yimmi Javier Chará Zamora), Radamel Falcao García Zárate (62.Jackson Arley Martínez Valencia), Carlos Arturo Bacca Ahumada (66.Gustavo Adrián Ramos Vásquez). Trainer: José Néstor Pékerman (Argentina).
Goals: Radamel Falcao García Zárate (8), Carlos Arturo Bacca Ahumada (49, 51).

14.10.2014, Friendly International
Red Bull Arena, Harrison (United States); Attendance: n/a
Referee: Juan Guzmán (United States)
CANADA - COLOMBIA 0-1(0-0)
COL: Camilo Andrés Vargas Gil, Cristián Eduardo Zapata Valencia, Santiago Arias Naranjo, Jeison Fabián Murillo Cerón (86.Carlos Alberto Sánchez Moreno), Juan Camilo Zúñiga Mosquera (67.Pablo Estifer Armero), Alexander Mejía Sabalza, Juan Guillermo Cuadrado Bello, James David Rodríguez Rubio (82.Gustavo Adrián Ramos Vásquez), Carlos Mario Carbonero Mancilla (46.Fredy Alejandro Guarín Vásquez), Radamel Falcao García Zárate (67.Jackson Arley Martínez Valencia), Teófilo Antonio Gutiérrez Roncancio (71.Juan Fernando Quintero Paniagua). Trainer: José Néstor Pékerman (Argentina).

Goal: James David Rodríguez Rubio (75).

14.11.2014, Friendly International
Craven Cottage, London (England); Attendance: 24,235
Referee: Szymon Marciniak (Poland)
UNITED STATES - COLOMBIA 1-2(1-0)
COL: Camilo Andrés Vargas Gil, Pablo Estifer Armero, Pedro Camilo Franco Ulloa, Santiago Arias Naranjo, Jeison Fabián Murillo Cerón, Abel Enrique Aguilar Tapias (74.Edwin Andrés Cardona Bedoya), Carlos Alberto Sánchez Moreno, Juan Guillermo Cuadrado Bello (88.Juan Fernando Quintero Paniagua), James David Rodríguez Rubio, Teófilo Antonio Gutiérrez Roncancio (89.Jackson Arley Martínez Valencia), Carlos Arturo Bacca Ahumada (79.Gustavo Adrián Ramos Vásquez). Trainer: José Néstor Pékerman (Argentina).
Goals: Carlos Arturo Bacca Ahumada (60), Teófilo Antonio Gutiérrez Roncancio (87).

18.11.2014, Friendly International
Stožice Stadium. Ljubljana; Attendance: 15,250
Referee: Andreas Pappas (Greece)
SLOVENIA - COLOMBIA 0-1(0-1)
COL: Camilo Andrés Vargas Gil, Cristián Eduardo Zapata Valencia, Pablo Estifer Armero, Santiago Arias Naranjo (64.Daniel Eduardo Bocanegra Ortíz), Jeison Fabián Murillo Cerón, Abel Enrique Aguilar Tapias (57.Carlos Mario Carbonero Mancilla), Alexander Mejía Sabalza (87.Carlos Alberto Sánchez Moreno), Juan Guillermo Cuadrado Bello (80.Brayan Alexis Angulo León), James David Rodríguez Rubio (73.Yimmi Javier Chará Zamora), Gustavo Adrián Ramos Vásquez, Jackson Arley Martínez Valencia (65.Juan Fernando Quintero Paniagua). Trainer: José Néstor Pékerman (Argentina).
Goal: Gustavo Adrián Ramos Vásquez (43).

26.03.2015, Friendly International
Bahrain National Stadium, Riffa; Attendance: 5,000
Referee: Mohammed Al Hoaish (Saudi Arabia)
BAHRAIN - COLOMBIA 0-6(0-3)
COL: David Ospina Ramírez, Pedro Camilo Franco Ulloa, Daniel Eduardo Bocanegra Ortíz, Jeison Fabián Murillo Cerón (46.Fredy Alejandro Guarín Vásquez), Darwin Zamir Andrade Marmolejo, Abel Enrique Aguilar Tapias (76.John Stefan Medina Ramírez), Carlos Alberto Sánchez Moreno, Juan Guillermo Cuadrado Bello (83.Edwin Andrés Cardona Bedoya), Juan Fernando Quintero Paniagua (63.Johan Andrés Mojica Palacio), Radamel Falcao García Zárate (72.Andrés Jair Rentería Morelo), Carlos Arturo Bacca Ahumada (46.Gustavo Adrián Ramos Vásquez). Trainer: José Néstor Pékerman (Argentina).
Goals: Carlos Arturo Bacca Ahumada (15), Radamel Falcao García Zárate (32, 36), Gustavo Adrián Ramos Vásquez (59), Johan Andrés Mojica Palacio (79), Andrés Jair Rentería Morelo (82).

30.03.2015, Friendly International
"Mohammed Bin Zayed" Stadium, Abu Dhabi (United Arab Emirates); Attendance: 6,000
Referee: Sultan Abdulrazaq Ibrahim Al Marzouqi (United Arab Emirates)
COLOMBIA - KUWAIT 3-1(1-1)
COL: David Ospina Ramírez, Pedro Camilo Franco Ulloa, Daniel Eduardo Bocanegra Ortíz, Darwin Zamir Andrade Marmolejo (68.Andrés Jair Rentería Morelo), Abel Enrique Aguilar Tapias (64.Alexander Mejía Sabalza), Carlos Alberto Sánchez Moreno, Fredy Alejandro Guarín Vásquez, Juan Guillermo Cuadrado Bello (46.Edwin Andrés Cardona Bedoya), Juan Fernando Quintero Paniagua (46.Johan Andrés Mojica Palacio), Radamel Falcao García Zárate, Carlos Arturo Bacca Ahumada (46.Teófilo Antonio Gutiérrez Roncancio). Trainer: José Néstor Pékerman (Argentina).
Goals: Abel Enrique Aguilar Tapias (22), Edwin Andres Cardona Bedoya (69), Radamel Falcao García Zárate (74 penalty).

06.06.2015, Friendly International
Estadio "Diego Armando Maradona", Buenos Aires (Argentina); Attendance: 15,000
Referee: Carlos Arecio Amarilla Demarqui (Paraguay)
COLOMBIA – COSTA RICA 1-0(0-0)
COL: David Ospina Ramírez, Cristián Eduardo Zapata Valencia, Jeison Fabián Murillo Cerón (46.Pedro Camilo Franco Ulloa), Darwin Zamir Andrade Marmolejo, Juan Camilo Zúñiga Mosquera (46.Carlos Enrique Valdés Parra), Carlos Alberto Sánchez Moreno, Edwin Armando Valencia Rodríguez (46.Alexander Mejía Sabalza), Juan Guillermo Cuadrado Bello (77.Edwin Andrés Cardona Bedoya), James David Rodríguez Rubio, Radamel Falcao García Zárate (63.Teófilo Antonio Gutiérrez Roncancio), Jackson Arley Martínez Valencia (63.Carlos Arturo Bacca Ahumada). Trainer: José Néstor Pékerman (Argentina).
Goal: Radamel Falcao García Zárate (47).

14.06.2015, 44th Copa América, Group Stage
Estadio El Teniente, Rancagua (Chile); Attendance: 12,387
Referee: Andrés Cunha (Uruguay)
COLOMBIA – VENEZUELA 0-1(0-0)
COL: David Ospina Ramírez, Cristián Eduardo Zapata Valencia, Pablo Estifer Armero (82.Jackson Arley Martínez Valencia), Jeison Fabián Murillo Cerón, Juan Camilo Zúñiga Mosquera, Carlos Alberto Sánchez Moreno (63.Edwin Andrés Cardona Bedoya), Edwin Armando Valencia Rodríguez, Juan Guillermo Cuadrado Bello, James David Rodríguez Rubio, Radamel Falcao García Zárate, Carlos Arturo Bacca Ahumada (72.Teófilo Antonio Gutiérrez Roncancio). Trainer: José Néstor Pékerman (Argentina).

17.06.2015, 44th Copa América, Group Stage
Estadio Monumental "David Arellano", Santiago (Chile); Attendance: 44,008
Referee: Enrique Roberto Osses Zencovich (Chile)
BRAZIL - COLOMBIA 0-1(0-1)
COL: David Ospina Ramírez, Cristián Eduardo Zapata Valencia, Pablo Estifer Armero, Jeison Fabián Murillo Cerón, Juan Camilo Zúñiga Mosquera, Carlos Alberto Sánchez Moreno, Edwin Armando Valencia Rodríguez (80.Alexander Mejía Sabalza), Juan Guillermo Cuadrado Bello, James David Rodríguez Rubio, Radamel Falcao García Zárate (69.Segundo Víctor Ibarbo Guerrero), Teófilo Antonio Gutiérrez Roncancio (76.Carlos Arturo Bacca Ahumada). Trainer: José Néstor Pékerman (Argentina).
Goal: Jeison Fabián Murillo Cerón (36).
Sent off: Carlos Arturo Bacca Ahumada (90+6).

21.06.2015, 44th Copa América, Group Stage
Estadio Municipal "Germán Becker", Temuco (Chile); Attendance: 17,332
Referee: Néstor Fabián Pitana (Argentina)
COLOMBIA - PERU 0-0
COL: David Ospina Ramírez, Santiago Arias Naranjo, Cristián Eduardo Zapata Valencia, Pablo Estifer Armero (57.Segundo Víctor Ibarbo Guerrero), Jeison Fabián Murillo Cerón, Carlos Alberto Sánchez Moreno, Edwin Armando Valencia Rodríguez (24.Alexander Mejía Sabalza), Juan Guillermo Cuadrado Bello, James David Rodríguez Rubio, Radamel Falcao García Zárate (66.Jackson Arley Martínez Valencia), Teófilo Antonio Gutiérrez Roncancio. Trainer: José Néstor Pékerman (Argentina).

26.06.2015, 44th Copa América, Quarter-Finals
Estadio Sausalito, Viña del Mar (Chile); Attendance: 21,508
Referee: Roberto García Orozco (Mexico)

ARGENTINA - COLOMBIA **0-0; 5-4 on penalties**

COL: David Ospina Ramírez, Santiago Arias Naranjo, Cristián Eduardo Zapata Valencia, Jeison Fabián Murillo Cerón, Juan Camilo Zúñiga Mosquera, Alexander Mejía Sabalza, Juan Guillermo Cuadrado Bello, James David Rodríguez Rubio, Teófilo Antonio Gutiérrez Roncancio (24.Edwin Andrés Cardona Bedoya), Jackson Arley Martínez Valencia (74.Radamel Falcao García Zárate), Segundo Víctor Ibarbo Guerrero (86.Luis Fernando Muriel Fruto). Trainer: José Néstor Pékerman (Argentina).

Penalties: James David Rodríguez Rubio, Radamel Falcao García Zárate, Juan Guillermo Cuadrado Bello, Luis Fernando Muriel Fruto (missed), Edwin Andrés Cardona Bedoya, Juan Camilo Zúñiga Mosquera (saved), Jeison Fabián Murillo Cerón (missed).

NATIONAL TEAM PLAYERS 2014/2015			
Name	DOB	Caps	Goals
[Club 2014/2015]			

(Caps and goals at 05.07.2015)

Goalkeepers

Name [Club]	DOB	Caps	Goals
Ramírez David OSPINA [2014/2015: Arsenal FC London (ENG)]	31.08.1988	**57**	**0**
Camilo Andrés VARGAS Gil [2014: Independiente Santa Fe]	09.03.1989	**4**	**0**

Defenders

Name [Club]	DOB	Caps	Goals
Éder Fabián ÁLVAREZ Balanta [2014: CA River Plate Buenos Aires (ARG)]	26.02.1993	**5**	**0**
Darwin Zamir ANDRADE Marmolejo [2015: Újpest FC (HUN)]	11.02.1991	**3**	**0**
Brayan Alexis ANGULO León [2014: PFC Ludogorets Razgrad (BUL)]	02.11.1989	**1**	**0**
Santiago ARIAS Naranjo [2014/2015: PSV Eindhoven (NED)]	13.01.1992	**16**	**0**
Pablo Estifer ARMERO [2014: Milan AC (ITA); 10.04.2015-> CR Flamengo Rio de Janeiro (BRA), on loan from Udinese Calcio (ITA)]	02.11.1986	**66**	**2**
Daniel Eduardo BOCANEGRA Ortíz [2014/2015: Club Atlético Nacional Medellín]	23.04.1987	**3**	**0**
Pedro Camilo FRANCO Ulloa [2014/2015: Beşiktaş JK Istanbul (TUR)]	23.04.1991	**5**	**0**
John Stefan MEDINA Ramírez [2015: CF Monterrey (MEX)]	14.06.1992	**3**	**0**
Jeison Fabián MURILLO Cerón [2014/2015: Granada CF (ESP)]	27.05.1992	**10**	**1**
Juan Fernando QUINTERO Paniagua [2014/2015: FC do Porto (POR)]	18.01.1993	**13**	**1**
Carlos Enrique VALDÉS Parra [2014: Philadelphia Union (USA); 02.2015-> Club Nacional de Football Montevideo (URU), on loan]	22.05.1985	**17**	**2**

Cristián Eduardo ZAPATA Valencia [2014/2015: Milan AC (ITA)]	30.09.1986	**35**	**0**
Juan Camilo ZÚÑIGA Mosquera [2014/2015: SSC Napoli (ITA)]	14.12.1986	**62**	1

Midfielders

Abel Enrique AGUILAR Tapias [2014/2015: Toulouse FC (FRA)]	06.01.1985	**56**	7
Carlos Mario CARBONERO Mancilla [2014: AC Cesena (ITA)]	25.07.1990	**2**	**0**
Edwin Andrés CARDONA Bedoya [2014: Club Atlético Nacional Medellín; 01.2015-> CF Monterrey (MEX)]	08.12.1992	**7**	1
Juan Guillermo CUADRADO Bello [2014: AC Fiorentina Firenze (ITA); 02.2015-> Chelsea FC London (ENG)]	26.05.1988	**44**	**5**
Freddy Alejandro GUARÍN Vásquez [2014/2015: FC Internazionale Milano (ITA)]	30.06.1986	**56**	**4**
Alexander MEJÍA Sabalsa [2014: CD Atlético Nacional Medellín; 01.2015-> CF Monterrey (MEX)]	07.09.1988	**21**	**0**
Johan Andrés MOJICA Palacio [2015: Real Valladolid CF (ESP)]	21.08.1992	**2**	1
Aldo Leão RAMÍREZ Sierra [2014: Atlas FC Guadalajara (MEX)]	18.04.1981	**30**	1
Andrés Jair RENTERÍA Morelo [2015: Club Santos Laguna Torreón (MEX)]	06.03.1993	**2**	1
James David RODRÍGUEZ Rubio [2014/2015: Real Madrid CF (ESP)]	12.07.1991	**37**	**12**
Carlos Alberto SÁNCHEZ Moreno [2014/2015: Aston Villa FC Birmingham (ENG)]	06.02.1986	**58**	**0**
Edwin Armando VALENCIA Rodríguez [2015: Santos FC (BRA)]	29.03.1985	**19**	**0**

Forwards

Carlos Arturo BACCA Ahumada [2014/2015: Sevilla FC (ESP)]	31.12.1984	**20**	7
Yimmi Javier CHARÁ Zamora [2014: Club Deportes Tolima]	02.04.1991	**2**	**0**
Radamel Falcao GARCÍA Zárate [2014/2015: Manchester United FC (ENG)]	10.02.1986	**61**	**25**
Teófilo Antonio GUTIÉRREZ Roncancio [2014/2015: CA River Plate Buenos Aires (ARG)]	17.05.1985	**44**	**14**
Segundo Víctor IBARBO Guerrero [2015: AS Roma (ITA)]	19.05.1990	**15**	1
Jackson Arley MARTÍNEZ Valencia [2014/2015: FC do Porto (POR)]	03.10.1986	**39**	**10**
Luis Fernando MURIEL Fruto [2015: UC Sampdoria Genoa (ITA)]	18.04.1991	**6**	1
Gustavo Adrián RAMOS Vásquez [2014/2015: BV Borussia Dortmund (GER)]	22.01.1986	**35**	**4**

National Coach

José Néstor PÉKERMAN (Argentina)	03.09.1949	40 M; 26 W; 8 D; 6 L; 72-22

ECUADOR

The Country:
República del Ecuador (Republic of Ecuador) Capital: Quito Surface: 256,370 km² Inhabitants: 15,223,680 Time: UTC-5 to -6

The FA:
Federación Ecuatoriana de Fútbol Avenida Las Aguas y Calle Alianza, P.O. Box 09-01-7447, Guayaquíl Year of Formation: 1925 Member of FIFA since: 1926 Member of CONMEBOL since: 1927 Internet: www.ecuafutbol.org

NATIONAL TEAM RECORDS	
First international match:	08.08.1938, Bogotá: Bolivia – Ecuador 1-1
Most international caps:	Iván Jacinto Hurtado Angulo – 168 caps (1992-2015)
Most international goals:	Agustín Javier Delgado Chalá – 31 goals / 72 caps (1994-2011)

OLYMPIC GAMES 1900-2012
None
FIFA CONFEDERATIONS CUP 1992-2013
None

COPA AMÉRICA	
1916	Did not enter
1917	Did not enter
1919	Did not enter
1920	Did not enter
1921	Did not enter
1922	Did not enter
1923	Did not enter
1924	Did not enter
1925	Did not enter
1926	Did not enter
1927	Did not enter
1929	Did not enter
1935	Did not enter
1937	Did not enter
1939	5th Place
1941	5th Place
1942	7th Place
1945	7th Place
1946	Withdrew
1947	6th Place
1949	7th Place
1953	6th Place
1955	7th Place
1956	Withdrew
1957	7th Place
1959	Withdrew
1959E	4th Place
1963	6th Place
1967	Qualifying Round
1975	Round 1
1979	Round 1
1983	Round 1
1987	Round 1
1989	Round 1
1991	Round 1
1993	4th Place
1995	Round 1
1997	Quarter-Finals
1999	Round 1
2001	Round 1
2004	Round 1
2007	Round 1
2011	Round 1
2015	Round 1

FIFA WORLD CUP	
1930	Did not enter
1934	Did not enter
1938	Did not enter
1950	Withdrew
1954	Did not enter
1958	Did not enter
1962	Qualifiers
1966	Qualifiers
1970	Qualifiers
1974	Qualifiers
1978	Qualifiers
1982	Qualifiers
1986	Qualifiers
1990	Qualifiers
1994	Qualifiers
1998	Qualifiers
2002	Final Tournament (Group Stage)
2006	Final Tournament (2nd Round of 16)
2010	Qualifiers
2014	Final Tournament (Group Stage)
PANAMERICAN GAMES	
1951	Did not enter
1955	Did not enter
1959	Did not enter
1963	Did not enter
1967	Did not enter
1971	Did not enter
1975	Did not enter
1979	Did not enter
1983	Did not enter
1987	Did not enter
1991	Did not enter
1995	Round 1
1999	Did not enter
2003	Did not enter
2007	**Winners**
2011	Group Stage
PANAMERICAN CHAMPIONSHIP	
1952	Did not enter
1956	Did not enter
1960	Did not enter

ECUADORIAN CLUB HONOURS IN SOUTH AMERICAN CLUB COMPETITIONS:

COPA LIBERTADORES 1960-2014
Liga Deportiva Universitaria de Quito (2008)
COPA SUDAMERICANA 2002-2014
Liga Deportiva Universitaria de Quito (2009)
RECOPA SUDAMERICANA 1989-2014
Liga Deportiva Universitaria Quito (2009, 2010)
COPA CONMEBOL 1992-1999
None
SUPERCUP „JOÃO HAVELANGE“ 1988-1997*
None
COPA MERCONORTE 1998-2001**
None

**Contested betwenn winners of all previous editions of the Copa Libertadores*

***Contested between teams belonging countries from the northern part of South America (Bolivia, Colombia, Ecuador, Peru and Venezuela)*

NATIONAL COMPETITIONS
TABLE OF HONOURS

NATIONAL CHAMPIONS 1957-2014	
1957	CS Emelec Guayaquil
1958	*No competition*
1959	*No competition*
1960	Barcelona SC Guayaquil
1961	CS Emelec Guayaquil
1962	CD Everest Guayaquil
1963	Barcelona SC Guayaquil
1964	Sociedad Deportivo Quito
1965	CS Emelec Guayaquil
1966	Barcelona SC Guayaquil
1967	CD El Nacional Quito
1968	Sociedad Deportivo Quito
1969	LDU de Quito
1970	Barcelona SC Guayaquil
1971	Barcelona SC Guayaquil
1972	CS Emelec Guayaquil
1973	CD El Nacional Quito
1974	LDU de Quito
1975	LDU de Quito
1976	CD El Nacional Quito
1977	CD El Nacional Quito
1978	CD El Nacional Quito
1979	CS Emelec Guayaquil
1980	Barcelona SC Guayaquil
1981	Barcelona SC Guayaquil
1982	CD El Nacional Quito
1983	CD El Nacional Quito
1984	CD El Nacional Quito

1985	Barcelona SC Guayaquil
1986	CD El Nacional Quito
1987	Barcelona SC Guayaquil
1988	CS Emelec Guayaquil
1989	Barcelona SC Guayaquil
1990	LDU de Quito
1991	Barcelona SC Guayaquil
1992	CD El Nacional Quito
1993	CS Emelec Guayaquil
1994	CS Emelec Guayaquil
1995	Barcelona SC Guayaquil
1996	CD El Nacional Quito
1997	Barcelona SC Guayaquil
1998	LDU de Quito
1999	LDU de Quito
2000	CD Olmedo Riobamba
2001	CS Emelec Guayaquil
2002	CS Emelec Guayaquil
2003	LDU de Quito
2004	Club Deportivo Cuenca
2005	Ape: LDU de Quito
	Fin: CD El Nacional Quito
2006	CD El Nacional Quito
2007	LDU de Quito
2008	Sociedad Deportivo Quito
2009	Sociedad Deportivo Quito
2010	LDU de Quito
2011	Sociedad Deportivo Quito
2012	Barcelona SC Guayaquil
2013	CS Emelec Guayaquil
2014	CS Emelec Guayaquil

	BEST GOALSCORERS	
1957	Simón Cañarte (Barcelona SC Guayaquil)	4
1960	Enrique Cantos (Barcelona SC Guayaquil)	8
1961	Galo Pinto (CD Everest Guayaquil)	12
1962	Iris López (BRA, Barcelona SC Guayaquil)	9
1963	Carlos Alberto Raffo Vallaco (ARG, CS Emelec Guayaquil)	4
1964	Jorge Valencia (CD América de Manta)	8
1965	Hélio Cruz (BRA, Barcelona SC Guayaquil)	8
1966	Pio Coutinho (BRA, LDU de Quito)	13
1967	Tomás Rodríguez (CD El Nacional Quito)	16
1968	Víctor Manuel Battaini Treglia (URU, Sociedad Deportivo Quito)	19
1969	Francisco Bertocchi (URU, LDU de Quito)	26
1970	Rómulo Dudar Mina (CSD Macará)	19
1971	Alfonso Obregón (PAR, LDU de Portoviejo)	18
1972	Nelson Miranda „Nelsinho“ (BRA, Barcelona SC Guayaquil)	15
1973	Ángel Marín (URU, CD América de Quito)	18
1974	Ángel Luis Liciardi Pasculi (ARG, Club Deportivo Cuenca)	19
1975	Ángel Luis Liciardi Pasculi (ARG, Club Deportivo Cuenca)	36
1976	Ángel Luis Liciardi Pasculi (ARG, Club Deportivo Cuenca)	35

1977	Fabián Paz y Miño (CD El Nacional Quito) Ángel Marín (URU, Sociedad Deportivo Quito)	27
1978	Juan José Pérez (ARG, LDU de Portoviejo)	24
1979	Carlos Horacio Miori (ARG, CS Emelec Guayaquil)	26
1980	Miguel Ángel Gutiérrez (ARG, CD América de Quito)	26
1981	Paulo César Evangelista (BRA, LDU de Quito)	25
1982	José Villafuerte (CD El Nacional Quito)	25
1983	Paulo César Evangelista (BRA, Barcelona SC Guayaquil)	28
1984	Sergio Antonio Saucedo (ARG, Sociedad Deportivo Quito)	25
1985	Juan Carlos de Lima (URU, CD Universidad Católica Quito) Alexander Da Silva „Guga" (BRA, CSD Esmeraldas Petrolero)	24
1986	Juan Carlos de Lima (URU, Sociedad Deportivo Quito)	23
1987	Ermen Benítez (CD El Nacional Quito) Hamilton Cuvi (CD Filanbanco Guayaquil) Waldemar Barreto Victorino (URU, LDU de Portoviejo)	23
1988	Janio Pinto (BRA, LDU de Quito)	18
1989	Ermen Benítez (CD El Nacional Quito)	23
1990	Ermen Benítez (CD El Nacional Quito)	28
1991	Pedro Emir Varela (URU, Delfin SC Manta)	24
1992	Carlos Antonio Muñoz Martínez (Barcelona SC Guayaquil)	19
1993	Diego Rodrigo Herrera (LDU de Quito)	18
1994	Manuel Antonio Uquillas (CD Espoli Quito)	
1995	Manuel Antonio Uquillas (Barcelona SC Guayaquil)	24
1996	Ariel José Graziani Lentini (ARG, CS Emelec Guayaquil)	29
1997	Ariel José Graziani Lentini (ARG, CS Emelec Guayaquil)	24
1998	Jaime Iván Kaviedes Llorenty (CS Emelec Guayaquil)	43
1999	Christian José Botero (ARG, CSD Macará)	25
2000	Alejandro Martín Kenig (ARG, CS Emelec Guayaquil)	25
2001	Carlos Alberto Juárez Devico (ARG, CS Emelec Guayaquil)	17
2002	Christian Gabriel Carnero (ARG, Sociedad Deportivo Quito)	26
2003	Ariel José Graziani Lentini (ARG, Barcelona SC Guayaquil)	23
2004	Ebelio Agustín Ordóñez Martínez (CD El Nacional Quito)	28
2005	Ape: Wilson Segura (LDU de Quito)	21
	Fin: Omar Alfredo Guerra Castilla (SD Aucas Quito)	
2006	Luis Miguel Escalada (ARG, CS Emelec Guayaquil)	29
2007	Juan Carlos Ferreyra (ARG, Club Deportivo Cuenca)	17
2008	Pablo David Palacios Herrería (Barcelona SC Guayaquil)	20
2009	Claudio Daniel Bieler (ARG, LDU de Quito)	22
2010	Jaime Javier Ayoví Corozo (CS Emelec Guayaquil)	23
2011	Arrinton Narciso Mina Villalba (CSD Independiente José Terán Sangolquí)	28
2012	Arrinton Narciso Mina Villalba (Barcelona SC Guayaquil)	30
2013	Federico Gastón Nieto (ARG, Sociedad Deportivo Quito)	29
2014	Armando Lenin Wila Canga (CD Universidad Católica Quito)	20

NATIONAL CHAMPIONSHIP
Campeonato Ecuatoriano de Fútbol 2014
Serie A - Copa Pilsener

Primera Etapa

Results

Round 1 [25-26.01.2014]
CD Universidad Católica - CD Cuenca 1-1(1-1)
Manta FC - LDU Quito 1-0(1-0)
LDU Loja - El Nacional Quito 2-1(1-1)
CSD Independiente - Deportivo Quito 2-0(0-0)
CCD Olmedo - Barcelona SC 2-1(1-0)
CS Emelec - Mushuc Runa SC 1-0(1-0)

Round 2 [29.01.2014]
El Nacional Quito - CCD Olmedo 0-3(0-1)
Mushuc Runa - Universidad Católica 1-2(0-1)
LDU Quito - LDU Loja 2-2(2-0)
Barcelona SC - Manta FC 1-0(1-0)
CD Cuenca - CSD Independiente 1-1(1-0)
Deportivo Quito - CS Emelec 0-0 [26.03.]

Round 3 [01-02.02.2014]
CCD Olmedo - Deportivo Quito 0-0
Universidad Católica - CSD Independ.4-3(2-2)
LDU Quito - El Nacional Quito 1-0(0-0)
Manta FC - Mushuc Runa SC 1-1(0-1)
LDU Loja - Barcelona SC 1-1(1-1)
CS Emelec - CD Cuenca 3-0(2-0)

Round 4 [08-09.02.2014]
El Nacional Quito – Univers. Católica 2-1(1-0)
Mushuc Runa SC - LDU Loja 0-1(0-0)
CSD Independiente - CS Emelec 0-0
Deportivo Quito - Manta FC 1-1(0-0)
Barcelona SC - LDU Quito 0-0
CD Cuenca - CCD Olmedo 1-1(1-0)

Round 5 [14-16.02.2014]
CCD Olmedo - CSD Independiente 0-1(0-0)
LDU Loja - Deportivo Quito 1-0(0-0)
Manta FC - CD Cuenca 2-0(1-0)
El Nacional Quito - Barcelona SC 1-0(0-0)
LDU Quito - Mushuc Runa SC 0-0
CS Emelec - CD Universidad Católica 2-1(2-0)

Round 6 [21-22.02.2014]
Deportivo Quito - LDU Quito 1-1(0-0)
CD Cuenca - LDU Loja 0-1(0-0)
Universidad Católica - CCD Olmedo 1-2(0-1)
CSD Independiente - Manta FC 1-0(1-0)
Mushuc Runa SC - El Nacional Quito 0-1(0-0)
Barcelona SC - CS Emelec 1-2(1-1)

Round 7 [28.02.-01.03.2014]
El Nacional Quito - Deportivo Quito 1-1(1-1)
LDU Quito - CD Cuenca 3-0(1-0)
Barcelona SC - Mushuc Runa SC 3-0(3-0)
Manta FC - CD Universidad Católica 0-1(0-1)
LDU Loja - CSD Independ. 1-2(0-1) [05.03.]
CCD Olmedo - CS Emelec 1-1(1-0) [30.04.]

Round 8 [07-09.03.2014]
CS Emelec - Manta FC 4-1(1-0)
CD Cuenca - El Nacional Quito 1-2(1-2)
CD Universidad Católica - LDU Loja 1-1(1-1)
Mushuc Runa SC - CCD Olmedo 1-0(0-0)
CSD Independiente - LDU Quito 0-0
Deportivo Quito - Barcelona SC 2-1(0-1)

Round 9 [15-16.03.2014]
LDU Loja - CS Emelec 1-2(1-0)
Manta FC - CCD Olmedo 1-1(0-1)
El Nacional - CSD Independiente 2-4(0-1)
LDU Quito - CD Universidad Católica 0-2(0-0)
Mushuc Runa SC - Deportivo Quito 1-0(1-0)
Barcelona SC - CD Cuenca 2-1(0-1)

Round 10 [21-23.03.2014]
CD Cuenca - Mushuc Runa SC 3-2(2-1)
Universid. Católica - Deportivo Quito 1-1(0-1)
Manta FC - El Nacional Quito 1-0(1-0)
CSD Independiente - Barcelona SC 0-0
CCD Olmedo - LDU Loja 0-1(0-0)
CS Emelec - LDU Quito 3-0(2-0)

Round 11 [29-30.03.2014]
LDU Loja - Manta FC 1-0(1-0)
Deportivo Quito - CD Cuenca 3-1(3-0)
El Nacional Quito - CS Emelec 2-0(0-0)
LDU Quito - CCD Olmedo 2-2(1-0)
Mushuc Runa - CSD Independiente 0-1(0-0)
Barcelona SC - Universidad Católica 2-1(0-1)

Round 12 [04-06.04.2014]
CSD Independiente - Mushuc Runa 2-1(0-1)
CD Cuenca - Deportivo Quito 0-1(0-0)
Manta FC - LDU Loja 4-2(1-1)
CS Emelec - El Nacional Quito 5-1(2-0)
Universidad Católica - Barcelona SC 2-0(1-0)
CCD Olmedo - LDU Quito 1-0(0-0)

Round 13 [11-13.04.2014]
LDU Loja - CCD Olmedo 1-0(1-0)
Deportivo Quito – Universid. Católica 0-1(0-0)
Mushuc Runa SC - CD Cuenca 1-1(1-0)
El Nacional Quito - Manta FC 1-2(0-1)
LDU Quito - CS Emelec 0-0
Barcelona SC - CSD Independiente 2-0(0-0)

Round 14 [17-20.04.2014]
Deportivo Quito - Mushuc Runa SC 1-0(0-0)
CS Emelec - LDU Loja 3-1(1-0)
CD Universidad Católica - LDU Quito 3-1(1-0)
CSD Independiente - El Nacional 2-3(1-0)
CD Cuenca - Barcelona SC 0-1(0-1)
CCD Olmedo - Manta FC 0-0

Round 15 [26-27.04.2014]
LDU Loja - CD Universidad Católica 1-0(1-0)
El Nacional Quito - CD Cuenca 1-3(0-1)
Manta FC - CS Emelec 1-3(0-2)
CCD Olmedo - Mushuc Runa SC 2-3(1-0)
LDU Quito - CSD Independiente 3-2(2-1)
Barcelona SC - Deportivo Quito 1-0(0-0)

Round 16 [02-04.05.2014]
Deportivo Quito - El Nacional Quito 3-0(1-0)
CD Cuenca - LDU Quito 0-0
CSD Independiente - LDU Loja 4-0(3-0)
CD Universidad Católica - Manta FC 2-1(2-0)
Mushuc Runa SC - Barcelona SC 0-0
CS Emelec - CCD Olmedo 0-2(0-0)

Round 17 [09-11.05.2014]
LDU Loja - CD Cuenca 2-1(0-1)
Manta FC - CSD Independiente 0-1(0-1)
El Nacional Quito - Mushuc Runa SC 1-1(1-1)
LDU Quito - Deportivo Quito 2-0(0-0)
CCD Olmedo - Universidad Católica 2-0(1-0)
CS Emelec - Barcelona SC 2-0(1-0)

Round 18 [04-06.07.2014]
CD Cuenca - Manta FC 3-0(1-0)
Deportivo Quito - LDU Loja 2-3(2-1)
CSD Independiente - CCD Olmedo 6-0(2-0)
CD Universidad Católica - CS Emelec 0-2(0-1)
Mushuc Runa SC - LDU Quito 1-2(1-2)
Barcelona SC - El Nacional Quito 2-1(2-0)

Round 19 [11-13.07.2014]
CCD Olmedo - CD Cuenca 0-1(0-0)
LDU Loja - Mushuc Runa SC 1-2(1-1)
Universidad Católica - El Nacional 1-3(1-1)
LDU Quito - Barcelona SC 2-1(1-1)
Manta FC - Deportivo Quito 1-1(1-0)
CS Emelec - CSD Independiente 0-0

Round 20 [18-20.07.2014]
Deportivo Quito - CCD Olmedo 2-1(2-0)
CD Cuenca - CS Emelec 1-0(1-0)
CSD Independiente - Universidad Católica 0-0
Mushuc Runa SC - Manta FC 2-1(0-0)
Barcelona SC - LDU Loja 4-0(1-0)
El Nacional Quito - LDU Quito 0-1(0-1)

Round 21 [30.07.2014]
Universidad Católica - Mushuc Runa 0-1(0-0)
CARE Independiente - CD Cuenca 3-0(2-0)
CS Emelec - Deportivo Quito 2-0(2-0)
CCD Olmedo - El Nacional Quito 1-1(0-1)
LDU Loja - LDU Quito 1-0(1-0)
Manta FC - Barcelona SC 1-3(1-2)

Round 22 [03.08.2014]
El Nacional Quito - LDU Loja 2-0(1-0)
LDU Quito - Manta FC 0-2(0-2)
Deportivo Quito - Independiente 1-1(1-0)
CD Cuenca - CD Universidad Católica 2-1(1-1)
Mushuc Runa SC - CS Emelec 1-0(0-0)
Barcelona SC - CCD Olmedo 0-0

Final Standings

1.	CS Emelec Guayaquil	22	13	5	4	35	-	14	44
2.	CARE Independiente del Valle Sangolquí*	22	11	7	4	36	-	18	40
3.	Liga Deportiva Universitaria de Loja	22	11	3	8	25	-	31	36
4.	Barcelona SC Guayaquil	22	10	5	7	26	-	18	35
5.	Liga Deportiva Universitaria de Quito	22	7	8	7	20	-	22	29
6.	CD Universidad Católica Quito	22	8	4	10	26	-	28	28
7.	CD El Nacional Quito	22	8	3	11	26	-	35	27
8.	Sociedad Deportivo Quito	22	6	8	8	20	-	22	26
9.	Club Centro Deportivo Olmedo	22	6	8	8	21	-	24	26
10.	Mushuc Runa SC Ambato	22	7	5	10	19	-	24	26
11.	Manta FC	22	6	5	11	21	-	29	23
12.	Club Deportivo Cuenca	22	6	5	11	21	-	31	23

Please note: CS Emelec Guayaquil qualified for the Championship finals and the 2015 Copa Libertadores second stage.

*On 29.07.2014, CSD Independiente José Terrqan Sangolquí changed its name to Club de Alto Rendimiento Especializado Independiente del Valle Sangolquí

Segunda Etapa

Results

Round 1 [08-10.08.2014]

Deportivo Quito - Mushuc Runa SC 1-1(0-0)
CD Cuenca - El Nacional Quito 2-1(0-1)
LDU Quito - LDU Loja 1-1(0-1)
Manta FC - CARE Independiente 2-3(1-2)
CCD Olmedo - CS Emelec 1-1(0-0)
Barcelona SC - CD Universidad Católica 0-0

Round 2 [13.08.2014]

El Nacional Quito - Manta FC 2-1(2-1)
Mushuc Runa SC - Barcelona SC 2-0(1-0)
CARE Independiente - CCD Olmedo 1-1(0-0)
CS Emelec - CD Cuenca 3-0(2-0)
CD Universidad Católica - LDU Quito 1-2(0-0)
LDU Loja - Deportivo Quito 4-0(0-0)

Round 3 [17.08.2014]

CCD Olmedo - Mushuc Runa SC 1-2(1-1)
Barcelona SC - LDU Loja 3-1(1-1)
LDU Quito - Deportivo Quito 3-0(1-0) [27.08.]
CD Cuenca – Univ. Católica 1-0(0-0) [05.09.]
Manta FC - CS Emelec 1-3(1-1) [10.10.]
El Nacional - Independiente 0-1(0-0) [12.11.]

Round 4 [22-24.08.2014]

LDU Loja - CD Cuenca 1-1(0-1)
CS Emelec - El Nacional Quito 5-0(2-0)
Deportivo Quito - Barcelona SC 1-3(0-0)
Mushuc Runa SC - Manta FC 1-0(0-0)
Univ. Católica - CCD Olmedo 1-0(1-0) [12.10.]
Independiente - LDU Quito 3-1(2-0) [22.10.]

Round 5 [31.08.2014]

El Nacional Quito - Mushuc Runa SC 1-0(0-0)
Manta FC - CD Universidad Católica 1-1(1-1)
CD Cuenca - Deportivo Quito 0-0
CCD Olmedo - LDU Loja 0-0
Barcelona SC - LDU Quito 1-0(1-0)
CARE Independiente - CS Emelec 5-0(3-0)

Round 6 [12-14.09.2014]

Mushuc Runa - CARE Independiente 1-1(0-1)
Universidad Católica - El Nacional 0-2(0-2)
LDU Loja - Manta FC 2-0(1-0)
Deportivo Quito - CCD Olmedo 2-0(2-0)
LDU Quito - CD Cuenca 1-1(0-0)
Barcelona SC - CS Emelec 1-0(0-0)

Round 7 [20-21.09.2014]
Manta FC - Deportivo Quito 1-1(1-1)
El Nacional Quito - LDU Loja 1-1(0-1)
CCD Olmedo - LDU Quito 1-1(0-0)
CD Cuenca - Barcelona SC 0-2(0-1)
CS Emelec - Mushuc Runa SC 3-1(1-0)
Independiente – Un. Católica 4-0(0-0) [29.10.]

Round 8 [26-27.09.2014]
Deportivo Quito - El Nacional Quito 0-4(0-1)
LDU Quito - Manta FC 2-0(1-0)
CD Cuenca - Mushuc Runa SC 1-1(1-0)
LDU Loja - CARE Independiente 0-0
Barcelona SC - CCD Olmedo 2-0(0-0)
Univ. Católica - CS Emelec 2-5(1-3) [22.10.]

Round 9 [01.10.2014]
Mushuc Runa - Universidad Católica 2-0(2-0)
CCD Olmedo - CD Cuenca 2-2(1-1)
Manta FC - Barcelona SC 2-4(1-3)
Independiente - Deportivo Quito 2-0(2-0)
El Nacional Quito - LDU Quito 0-0
CS Emelec - LDU Loja 3-1(2-0) [12.11.]

Round 10 [05.10.2014]
LDU Quito - CS Emelec 2-1(1-0)
Deportivo Quito – Universid. Católica 1-0(0-0)
CD Cuenca - Manta FC 1-0(1-0)
CCD Olmedo - El Nacional Quito 1-2(1-0)
LDU Loja - Mushuc Runa SC 2-1(0-0)
Barcelona SC - CARE Independiente 1-4(0-2)

Round 11 [17-19.10.2014]
CD Universidad Católica - LDU Loja 4-1(1-1)
CARE Independiente - CD Cuenca 4-0(1-0)
El Nacional Quito - Barcelona SC 1-4(0-1)
Manta FC - CCD Olmedo 0-0
Mushuc Runa SC - LDU Quito 1-1(0-0)
CS Emelec - Deportivo Quito 3-0 (awarded)

Round 12 [25-26.10.2014]
LDU Loja - CD Universidad Católica 1-2(1-1)
LDU Quito - Mushuc Runa SC 5-1(3-1)
Deportivo Quito - CS Emelec 2-2(2-0)
CD Cuenca - CARE Independiente 0-1(0-0)
CCD Olmedo - Manta FC 1-0(0-0)
Barcelona SC - El Nacional Quito 1-0(0-0)

Round 13 [01-02.11.2014]
El Nacional Quito - CCD Olmedo 2-1(0-0)
Manta FC - CD Cuenca 2-1(1-0)
Mushuc Runa SC - LDU Loja 1-1(1-0)
CARE Independiente - Barcelona SC 2-1(1-1)
Universid. Católica - Deportivo Quito 1-0(1-0)
CS Emelec - LDU Quito 0-1(0-1)

Round 14 [05.11.2014]
Universidad Católica - Mushuc Runa 1-1(0-1)
LDU Quito - El Nacional Quito 2-1(0-1)
Deportivo Quito - Independiente 3-0(0-0)
Barcelona SC - Manta FC 0-1(0-0)
CD Cuenca - CCD Olmedo 3-1(2-1)
LDU Loja - CS Emelec 0-2(0-1) [03.12.]

Round 15 [09.11.2014]
El Nacional Quito - Deportivo Quito 0-0
CCD Olmedo - Barcelona SC 0-1(0-0)
Manta FC - LDU Quito 3-3(1-0)
Mushuc Runa SC - CD Cuenca 1-2(1-1)
CARE Independiente - LDU Loja 1-1(1-1)
CS Emelec - CD Universidad Católica 2-1(1-0)

Round 16 [14-16.11.2014]
LDU Quito - CCD Olmedo 5-1(0-1)
Deportivo Quito - Manta FC 1-1(1-1)
Barcelona SC - CD Cuenca 2-2(2-1)
Univ. Católica - CARE Independiente 1-2(0-0)
LDU Loja - El Nacional Quito 1-0(0-0)
Mushuc Runa SC - CS Emelec 0-1(0-1)

Round 17 [19.11.2014]
Manta FC - LDU Loja 3-0(1-0)
CARE Independiente - Mushuc Runa 1-0(0-0)
CS Emelec - Barcelona SC 0-1(0-0)
CCD Olmedo - Deportivo Quito 1-0(0-0)
El Nacional - Universidad Católica 1-1(1-0)
CD Cuenca - LDU Quito 1-2(1-1)

Round 18 [23.11.2014]
Deportivo Quito - CD Cuenca 0-0
LDU Quito - Barcelona SC 0-0
CD Universidad Católica - Manta FC 2-1(1-0)
Mushuc Runa SC - El Nacional Quito 1-1(0-1)
LDU Loja - CCD Olmedo 0-3(0-2)
CS Emelec - CARE Independiente 1-0(0-0)

Round 19 [28-30.11.2014]
CD Cuenca - LDU Loja 1-0(0-0)
LDU Quito - CARE Independiente 2-0(1-0)
El Nacional Quito - CS Emelec 0-1(0-0)
CCD Olmedo - Universidad Católica 0-3(0-1)
Manta FC - Mushuc Runa SC 3-0(2-0)
Barcelona SC - Deportivo Quito 1-0(0-0)

Round 20 [05-07.12.2014]
CD Universidad Católica - CD Cuenca 2-1(2-0)
Mushuc Runa SC - CCD Olmedo 1-1(1-1)
CARE Independiente - El Nacional 0-1(0-0)
LDU Loja - Barcelona SC 0-1(0-0)
Deportivo Quito - LDU Quito 2-3(0-1)
CS Emelec - Manta FC 2-1(1-0)

Round 21 [10.12.2014]
LDU Quito - CD Universidad Católica 1-2(0-0)
Deportivo Quito - LDU Loja 3-2(2-2)
Barcelona SC - Mushuc Runa SC 3-0(1-0)
CD Cuenca - CS Emelec 2-1(2-1)
CCD Olmedo - CARE Independiente 2-3(0-1)
Manta FC - El Nacional Quito 2-1(0-1)

Round 22 [14.12.2014]
CARE Independiente - Manta FC 4-0(3-0)
El Nacional Quito - CD Cuenca 2-1(2-1)
Universidad Católica - Barcelona SC 0-1(0-1)
CS Emelec - CCD Olmedo 1-0(0-0)
Mushuc Runa SC - Deportivo Quito 0-0
LDU Loja - LDU Quito 1-0(0-0)

Final Standings

1.	Barcelona SC Guayaquil	22	15	3	4	33	-	16	48
2.	CARE Independiente del Valle Sangolquí	22	14	4	4	42	-	18	46
3.	CS Emelec Guayaquil	22	14	2	6	40	-	22	44
4.	Liga Deportiva Universitaria de Quito	22	11	7	4	38	-	22	40
5.	CD El Nacional Quito	22	8	5	9	23	-	26	29
6.	CD Universidad Católica Quito	22	8	4	10	25	-	30	28
7.	Club Deportivo Cuenca	22	7	7	8	23	-	29	28
8.	Liga Deportiva Universitaria de Loja	22	5	7	10	21	-	31	22
9.	Mushuc Runa SC Ambato	22	4	9	9	19	-	30	21
10.	Manta FC	22	5	5	12	25	-	35	20
11.	Sociedad Deportivo Quito	22	4	8	10	17	-	32	20
12.	Club Centro Deportivo Olmedo	22	3	7	12	18	-	33	16

Please note: Barcelona SC Guayaquil qualified for the Championship finals and the 2015 Copa Libertadores second stage.

Campeonato Ecuatoriano de Fútbol - Final 2014

17.12.2014, Estadio Monumental "Isidro Romero Carbo", Guayaquil; Attendance: 63,686
Referee: Omar Andrés Ponce Manzo

Barcelona SC Guayaquil - CS Emelec Guayaquil 1-1(0-1)

Barcelona: Máximo Orlando Banguera Valdivieso, Luis Armando Checa Villamar, Geovanny Enrique Nazareno Simisterra, Franco Peppino, Pedro Pablo Velasco Arboleda, Matías Damián Oyola, Luis Andrés Caicedo de la Cruz (46.Michael Jackson Quiñónez Cabeza), Alex Leonardo Bolaños Reascos, Gedy Aaron Peñafiel Bruno (46.Ely Jair Esterilla Castro), Ismael Blanco, Christian Andrés Suárez Valencia (90+1.Brayan José de la Torre Martínez). Rubén Jorge Israel (Uruguay).

Emelec: Esteban Javier Dreer, Jorge Daniel Guagua Tamayo, Gabriel Eduardo Achilier Zurita, Oscar Dalmiro Bagüi Angulo, Jhon William Narváez, Fernando Agustín Giménez Solís, Pedro Angel Quiñónez Rodríguez, Ángel Israel Mena Delgado (71.Emanuel Herrera), Miller Alejandro Bolaños Reascos (87.José Luis Quiñónez Quiñónez), Osbaldo Lupo Lastra García, Robert Javier Burbano Cobeña (82.Mauro Raúl Fernández). Trainer: Gustavo Domingo Quinteros Desabato (Bolivia).

Goals: 0-1 Ángel Israel Mena Delgado (19), 1-1 Ismael Blanco (88).

21.12.2014, Estadio "George Capwell", Guayaquil; Attendance: 23,459
Referee: Carlos Alfredo Vera Rodríguez
CS Emelec Guayaquil - Barcelona SC Guayaquil 3-0(1-0)
Emelec: Esteban Javier Dreer, Jorge Daniel Guagua Tamayo, Gabriel Eduardo Achilier Zurita, Oscar Dalmiro Bagüi Angulo, Jhon William Narváez, Fernando Agustín Giménez Solís, Pedro Angel Quiñónez Rodríguez, Ángel Israel Mena Delgado, Miller Alejandro Bolaños Reascos, Osbaldo Lupo Lastra García, Robert Javier Burbano Cobeña (64.Marcos Gustavo Mondaini). Trainer: Gustavo Domingo Quinteros Desabato (Bolivia).
Barcelona: Máximo Orlando Banguera Valdivieso, Luis Armando Checa Villamar, Geovanny Enrique Nazareno Simisterra, Franco Peppino, Pedro Pablo Velasco Arboleda, Matías Damián Oyola, Alex Leonardo Bolaños Reascos [*sent off 10*], Gedy Aaron Peñafiel Bruno (56.Brayan José de la Torre Martínez), Ismael Blanco, Christian Andrés Suárez Valencia (39.Michael Jackson Quiñónez Cabeza), Ely Jair Esterilla Castro (32.Flavio David Caicedo Gracia). Trainer: Rubén Jorge Israel (Uruguay).
Goals: 1-0 Ángel Israel Mena Delgado (22), 2-0 Miller Alejandro Bolaños Reascos (81), 3-0 Miller Alejandro Bolaños Reascos (87).

2014 Campeonato Ecuatoriano de Fútbol / Copa Credife Winners: **CS Emelec Guayaquil**

Aggregate Table 2014

1.	CS Emelec Guayaquil	44	27	7	10	75	-	36	88
2.	CARE Independiente del Valle Sangolquí	44	25	11	8	78	-	36	86
3.	Barcelona SC Guayaquil	44	25	8	11	59	-	34	83
4.	Liga Deportiva Universitaria de Quito	44	18	15	11	58	-	44	69
5.	Liga Deportiva Universitaria de Loja	44	16	10	18	48	-	62	58
6.	CD Universidad Católica Quito	44	16	8	20	51	-	58	56
7.	CD El Nacional Quito	44	16	8	20	49	-	61	56
8.	Club Deportivo Cuenca	44	13	12	19	44	-	60	51
9.	Mushuc Runa SC Ambato	44	11	14	19	38	-	54	47
10.	Sociedad Deportivo Quito	44	10	16	18	37	-	54	46
11.	Manta FC (*Relegated*)	44	11	10	23	46	-	64	43
12.	Club Centro Deportivo Olmedo (*Relegated*)	44	9	15	20	39	-	57	42

CS Emelec Guayaquil, CARE Independiente del Valle Sangolquí and Barcelona SC Guayaquil qualified for the 2015 Copa Libertadores.

CS Emelec Guayaquil, Liga Deportiva Universitaria de Quito, Liga Deportiva Universitaria de Loja and CD Universidad Católica Quito qualified for the 2015 Copa Sudamericana.

Top goalscorers:

20 goals:	**Armando Lenin Wila Canga**	**(CD Universidad Católica)**
19 goals:	Miller Alejandro Bolaños Reasco	(CS Emelec Guayaquil)
17 goals:	Junior Nazareno Sornoza Moreira	(CARE Independiente del Valle Sangolquí)
16 goals:	Daniel Patricio Angulo Arroyo	(CARE Independiente del Valle Sangolquí)
14 goals:	Juan Manuel Cobelli (ARG)	(Club Deportivo Cuenca)
	Ángel Israel Mena Delgado	(CS Emelec Guayaquil)

BARCELONA SPORTING CLUB GUAYAQUIL

Foundation date: May 1, 1925
Address: Ciudadela Bellavista, Estadio Monumental, Guayaquil
Stadium: Estadio Monumental „Isidro Romero Carbo", Guayaquil – Capacity: 57,267

THE SQUAD

	DOB	Pr Et		Sg Et*	
		M	G	M	G
Goalkeepers:					
Máximo Orlando Banguera Valdivieso	16.12.1985	19	-	22	1
Carlos Luis Bone Cagua	05.01.1996			-	-
Bryan Esteban Caicedo Medina	13.07.1994	-	-	-	-
Damián Enrique Lanza Moyano	10.04.1982	3	-	1	-
Ayrton Abel Morales Caballero	19.05.1995			2	-
Defenders:					
Luis Armando Checa Villamar	21.12.1983	21	2	20	-
Geovanny Enrique Nazareno Simisterra	17.01.1988	9	-	24	2
Anderson Rafael Ordóñez Valdez	29.01.1994	1	-	-	-
Juan Carlos Paredes Reasco	08.07.1987	8	-		
Franco Peppino (ARG)	14.06.1982	10	-	14	-
José Luis Perlaza Napa	06.10.1981	14	1	15	2
Pablo Andrés Saucedo	06.03.1982	5	1	1	-
Midfielders:					
Alex Leonardo Bolaños Reascos	22.01.1985	14	-	20	-
Flavio David Caicedo Gracia	28.02.1988	14	-	15	-
Luis Andrés Caicedo de la Cruz	12.05.1979	13	3	13	-
Gerson Jair Cedeño Aspiazu	09.03.1992	-	-	-	-
Brayan José de la Torre Martínez	11.01.1991	8	-	7	-
Emiliano Lionel Díaz (ARG)	05.10.1991	-	-	-	-
Andrés Franzoia (ARG)	21.10.1985	-	-	-	-
Vicente Elias Macías Mosquera	20.01.1995	1	-	-	-
Mario Roberto Martínez Hernández (HON)	30.07.1989	1	-	15	-
Anderson Joffre Mina Mina	15.07.1995	-	-	-	-
Stalin Motta Vaquiro	28.03.1984	15	-	-	-
Matías Damián Oyola (ARG)	15.10.1982	20	4	20	1
Roosevelt Esteban Oyola Zuriaga	06.04.1991	1	-		
Gedy Aaron Peñafiel Bruno	23.10.1995	2	1	11	1
Michael Jackson Quiñónez Cabeza	21.06.1984	6	-	23	-
Luis Fernando Saritama Padilla	20.10.1983	10	-	2	-
Pedro Pablo Velasco Arboleda	26.06.1993	15	-	24	2
Washington Wilfrido Vera Gines	24.04.1994	2	-	1	-
Forwards:					
Alex Javier Ayoví Chila	26.02.1995	1	-	1	-
Ismael Blanco (ARG)	19.01.1983	-	-	20	12
Jeison Alfonso Domínguez Quiñónez	31.05.1995	15	-	6	-
Ely Jair Esterilla Castro	06.02.1993	16	3	21	3
Federico Raúl Laurito (ARG)	18.05.1990	8	1	-	-
Edson Eli Montaño Angulo	15.03.1991	4	-		
Federico Gastón Nieto (ARG)	26.08.1984	14	2	3	2
Cristian Anderson Penilla Caicedo	02.05.1991	20	5	13	1
Alexander Alfonso Pinillo Arce	27.05.1995	5	-	-	-
Carlos Luis Quintero Arroyo	27.09.1982	-	-		
Christian Andrés Suárez Valencia	02.11.1985	4	2	21	6
Trainer:					
Carlos Luis Ischia (ARG) [01.01.-21.05.2014; End of contract]	28.10.1956	17			
Rubén Jorge Israel (URU) [as of 28.05.2014]	08.12.1955	5		24	

**Matches and goals in Championship finals included*

CLUB DEPORTIVO CUENCA

Foundation date: March 4, 1971
Address: Avenida del Estadio y José Peralta, Cuenca
Stadium: Estadio „Alejandro Serrano Aguilar", Cuenca – Capacity: 20,502

THE SQUAD

	DOB	Pr Et M	Pr Et G	Sg Et M	Sg Et G
Goalkeepers:					
Brian Roberto Heras González	17.04.1995	-	-	1	-
Cristhian Rafael Mora Medrano	26.08.1979	13	-	-	-
Hamilton Emanuel Piedra Ordóñez	20.02.1993	9	-	21	-
Defenders:					
Elvis Elber Bone Sánchez	07.04.1983	21	1	17	1
Galo Ricardo Corozo Junco	20.08.1990	16	-	15	-
Jefferson Javier Hurtado Orovio	02.08.1987	9	-	1	-
Jerry Gabriel León Nazareno	22.04.1995	4	-	-	-
Rodrigo Gastón Mieres Pérez (URU)	19.04.1989	15	-	19	-
Eduardo Xavier Morante Rosas	01.06.1987	11	1	2	-
Andrés Eduardo Vélez Mora	16.10.1995	-	-	-	-
Midfielders:					
Xavier Nicolás Abril Aguilar	14.02.1992	3	-	-	-
Freddy Ubeiman Araujo Araujo	10.09.1993	7	1	9	-
Adrián Marcelo Arias Jacóme	15.10.1994	8	-	2	-
Miguel Ángel Bravo Prado	29.10.1986	9	2	14	-
Andrés Sebastián Calle Estrella	27.01.1997			3	-
John Dennis Campoverde Ramírez	18.10.1997	-	-	-	-
Rúben Dario Canga Yánez	07.04.1994	4	-	4	-
Santiago Sebastián Carpio Avíles	06.06.1995	-	-	-	-
Moisés David Corozo Cañizares	20.10.1992	10	-	7	-
Alejandro Javier Frezzotti (ARG)	15.02.1991	17	1	21	1
Alex Efrén González Palma	18.08.1995	1	-	11	2
Jhon Carlos González Palma	21.08.1991	2	-	-	-
Sebastián Emanuel González (ARG)	04.03.1992	17	1	-	-
Juan José Govea Tenorio	27.01.1991	15	1	18	-
Diego Alejandro Jervés Cordóva	15.05.1997	2	-	2	-
Marcos Andres López Cabrera	04.02.1993	20	2	22	2
David Alejandro Matute Novo	13.12.1993	-	-	1	-
Roosevelt Esteban Oyola Zuriaga	06.04.1991	11	-	8	-
David Alejandro Patiño Marín	01.08.1992	-	-	-	-
James Andrés Quiñónez Castillo	27.10.1995	-	-	1	-
Tilmer Josué Renteria Caicedo	12.04.1996	-	-	-	-
Henry Geovanny Rua Quiñonez	08.01.1994	5	-		
Jhon Eryck Valencia Ramírez	07.06.1996	-	-	-	-
Walter Germán Zea Baldeón	07.01.1985	12	-	22	3
Forwards:					
Hugo Christophe Bargas (FRA/ARG)	22.10.1986	4	-	20	3
Juan Manuel Cobelli (ARG)	27.02.1988	15	7	13	7
Joffre Andrés Escobar Moyano	24.10.1996	5	-	1	-
Silvio Patricio Gutiérrez Álvarez	28.02.1993	8	-	19	2
Ronaldo Iván Johnson Mina	15.04.1995	13	2	7	-
José Mauricio Ramírez Lastre	29.03.1994	6	-		
Luis Bernardo Santana Vera	09.07.1991	12	2	21	1
Trainer:					
Roberto Carlos Mario Gómez (ARG) [19.12.2013-02.03.2014;Resigned]	27.02.1957	7			
Guillermo Duró (ARG) [as of 02.03.2014]	14.03.1969	15		22	

SOCIEDAD DEPORTIVO QUITO

Foundation date: February 25, 1955

Address: Avenida República del Salvador 34-399 y Irlanda, Carcelén, Quito

Stadium: Estadio Olímpico Atahualpa, Quito – Capacity: 35,258

THE SQUAD

	DOB	Pr Et M	Pr Et G	Sg Et M	Sg Et G
Goalkeepers:					
Rorys Andrés Aragón Espinoza	28.06.1982	12	-	5	-
Alexi Ever Lemos Castillo	15.12.1989	-	-	-	-
Rolando Ramírez Estupiñán	16.03.1978	10	-	16	-
Defenders:					
Fernando Martín Bonjour (ARG)	04.09.1985	13	1		
Banner Geovanny Caicedo Quiñónez	28.03.1981	3	-		
Christian César Castro Garzón	16.02.1978	-	-	1	-
Roberto Michael Castro Cadena	15.07.1989	8	-	16	1
Víctor Javier Chinga Solís	25.08.1983	3	-	-	-
William Osvaldo España España	01.02.1987	17	-	13	-
Giovanny Patricio Espinoza Pabón	12.04.1977	-	-	-	-
Edder Fabian Fuertes Bravo	27.03.1992	13	-	9	-
Gregory Gerardo Gonzáles Vanegas	16.08.1987	13	1	7	-
Eddie Fernando Guevara Chávez	02.04.1990	-	-	6	-
Luis Manuel Romero Véliz	15.05.1984	15	1	-	-
Carlos Eduardo Vayas Vivanco	09.05.1987	12	-	6	-
Midfielders:					
Cristian Andrés Acosta Congo	04.10.1994			1	-
Omar Santiago Andrade Terán	16.06.1986	10	-		
Michael Steven Arboleda Quiñónez	16.02.1994	3	-	11	-
Luis Alfredo Ayoví Medina	05.05.1993	1	-	4	-
Jairon Enríque Bonett Sulvaran	10.04.1995	10	1	16	1
Jonathan Darwin Borja Colorado	05.04.1994	4	-	1	-
Miguel Ángel Bravo Prado	29.10.1986	2	-		
Ronie Edmundo Carrillo Morales	08.09.1996			1	-
Hugo Franklin Córtez Viveros	10.11.1995			2	-
Richard Santiago Estrella Mejía	15.04.1995	-	-	1	-
Carlos Alfredo Feraud Silva	23.10.1990	15	2	10	1
Golber Enríque Gómez Álvarez	09.02.1995			-	-
Christian Rolando Lara Anangonó	27.04.1990	22	5	21	3
Daniel Antonio Loor Rodríguez	05.02.1996	1	-	-	-
Santiago Damián Morales Montenegro	03.05.1979	10	-	4	-
Luis Gabriel Mosquera Rodríguez	17.01.1992	1	-	-	-
Luis Alberto Motato Zamora	22.06.1995			4	-
Benito Freddy Olivo González	26.11.1982	2	-		
Jefferson David Preciado Arboleda	29.12.1997			-	-
Efrén Vicente Proaño Nazareno	11.07.1992	4	-	20	1
Dennys Andrés Quiñónez Espinoza	12.03.1992	11	-	19	-
Francisco Elías Rojas Mendoza	13.01.1991	2	-		
Edison Fernando Vega Obando	08.03.1990	21	1	19	-
Forwards:					
Walter Richard Calderón Carcelén	17.10.1977	8	-	18	6
José Javier Córtez Arroyo	05.05.1995	6	1	12	2
Alister David de Jesús Borja	17.04.1995	7	1	3	-
Víctor Manuel Estupiñán Mairongo	05.03.1988	18	3	13	-
Carlos Jhon Garcés Acosta	01.03.1990	12	3	-	-
Jonathan Alberto Hansen (ARG)	10.09.1988	12	-	20	2
José Mauricio Ramírez Lastre	29.03.1994	3	-	10	-
Beder Joseph Valencia Angulo	31.10.1995	-	-	-	-
Trainer:					
Juan Carlos Garay [Resigned on 09.08.2014]	15.09.1968	22		1	
Carlos Edmundo Sevilla Dalgo [as of 10.08.2014]	26.08.1950			21	

CLUB DEPORTIVO EL NACIONAL QUITO

Foundation date: June 1, 1964
Address: Yasuni e Isla San Cristóbal, Ciudadela Jipijapa, Quito
Stadium: Estadio Olímpico Atahualpa, Quito – Capacity: 35,258

THE SQUAD

	DOB	Pr Et		Sg Et	
		M	G	M	G
Goalkeepers:					
Adrián Javier Bone Sánchez	08.09.1988	22	-	21	-
Darwin Patricio Cuero Anangono	15.10.1994	-	-	-	-
			-		-
Defenders:					
Banner Geovanny Caicedo Quiñónez	28.03.1981	2	-	20	-
Aníbal Hernán Chalá Ayoví	09.05.1996	13	1	18	-
Edwin Manolo Hurtado Mina	15.10.1982	16	1	13	-
Luis Enrique Lastra Castro	21.01.1990	10	-	-	-
Isaac Bryan Mina Arboleda	17.10.1980	19	-	2	-
Marvin Jonathan Pita Mora	17.04.1985	21	2	19	2
Javier Alejandro Quiñónez Castillo	27.07.1989	7	-	16	-
Jorge David Valencia Quiñónez	22.05.1992	8	1	19	-
Rody Jossephe Zambrano Marcillo	21.02.1993	14	-	10	-
Midfielders:					
Vinicio César Angulo Pata	26.07.1988	11	4	-	-
Fabricio Ildegar Bagui Wila	07.05.1989	4	-	13	-
Dario Darwin Bone Lastre	27.03.1990	7	-	3	-
José Andrés Cárdenas Duque	23.03.1998			-	-
Jairo Víctor Castillo Nazareno	22.05.1991	13	-	9	-
Bagner Samuel Delgado Loor	20.11.1995			-	-
Franklin Joshua Guerra Cedeño	12.04.1992	20	-	20	-
Luis Armando Lastra Salazar	12.11.1994	-	-	-	-
Jhon Jairo Macías Vargas	02.08.1995	2	-	-	-
Ronny Bryan Medina Valencia	09.04.1995	1	-		
Felipe Jonathan Mejía Perlaza	25.02.1995			15	5
Marco Roberto Montaño Díaz	08.09.1992	-	-	13	1
José Alexander Pabón de la Cruz	08.08.1991	1	-	11	-
Nea Fernando Padilla Landazuri	24.03.1995	3	-		
Lenín Guillermo Porozo Quintero	17.07.1990	14	1	2	-
Ángel Marcelo Quiñónez Angulo	02.12.1991			3	-
Walter Wilfrido Reyes Caicedo	25.01.1991	4	1	-	-
Tito Johan Valencia Gómez	05.01.1991	19	1	20	7
Alejandro Javier Villalva Pavón	28.11.1992	17	6	21	4
Forwards:					
Kwame Junior León Valencia	24.12.1990	2	-	-	-
Julián José Mina Salvatierra	29.09.1985	6	-	-	-
Kevin Alexander Minda García	28.03.1996			2	-
Pablo David Palacios Herrería	05.02.1982	18	1	16	2
Miguel Enrique Parrales Vera	26.12.1995	3	1	13	2
Daniel Esteban Samaniego Dávila	27.08.1986	13	1	3	-
Augusto Mercedes Sevillano Hurtado	24.11.1982	2	-	-	-
Carlos Vicente Tenorio Medina	14.05.1979	12	5		
Trainer:					
Carlos Edmundo Sevilla Dalgo [10.03.2013-05.08.2014; End of contract]	26.08.1950	22			
Octavio Zambrano [as of 11.08.2014]	03.02.1958			22	

CLUB SPORT EMELEC GUAYAQUIL

Foundation date: April 29, 1929
Address: General Gómez 1312 y Avenida Quito, Guayaquil
Stadium: Estadio „George Capwell", Guayaquil – Capacity: 21,388

THE SQUAD

	DOB	Pr Et M	Pr Et G	Sg Et* M	Sg Et* G
Goalkeepers:					
Cristian Jonathan Arana Hurtado	03.08.1988	5	-	2	-
Xavier Andrés Cevallos Durán	22.06.1996			-	-
Esteban Javier Dreer (ARG)	11.11.1981	17	-	20	-
Javier Hernán Klimowicz Laganá	10.03.1977	-	-	1	-
Defenders:					
Gabriel Eduardo Achilier Zurita	24.03.1985	17	-	21	-
Oscar Dalmiro Bagüi Angulo	10.12.1982	20	-	19	-
Diego Armando Corozo Castillo	25.12.1990	2	-	-	-
Jorge Daniel Guagua Tamayo	28.09.1981	10	-	17	-
Jordan Andrés Jaime Plata	28.10.1995	3	-	1	-
Jhon William Narváez	12.06.1991	12	-	17	-
Fernando Darío Pinillo Mina	27.03.1991	-	-	-	-
Carlos Enrique Vera Morán	13.07.1995	2	-	-	-
Midfielders:					
Christian Fernando Alemán Alegria	05.02.1996	-	-	1	-
Brayan Dennis Angulo Tenorio	30.11.1995	-	-	7	-
Miller Alejandro Bolaños Reascos	01.06.1990	17	3	18	16
Robert Javier Burbano Cobeña	10.04.1995	18	1	13	-
Marcos Jackson Caicedo Caicedo	10.11.1991	10	3		
Walberto Rolando Caicedo Caicedo	21.08.1992			-	-
Javier Isidro Charcopa Alegria	02.09.1992	11	1	16	1
Eddy Roy Corozo Olaya	28.06.1994	6	-	-	-
Fernando Vicente Gaibor Orellana	08.10.1991	4	-	7	3
Osbaldo Lupo Lastra García	12.06.1985	17	2	20	-
Byron Andrés Mina Cuero	01.08.1991	1	-	6	-
Carlos Alberto Moreno Romaña	04.10.1995			2	-
Cristian Javier Nasuti Matovelle (ARG)	06.09.1982	11	1		
David Alejandro Noboa Tello	16.05.1995	-	-	4	-
José Luis Quiñónez Quiñónez	29.05.1984	15	-	15	-
Pedro Angel Quiñónez Rodríguez	04.03.1986	17	-	18	2
Yorman Michael Valencia Caicedo	18.03.1995	3	-	-	-
Forwards:					
Luis Miguel Escalada	27.02.1986	16	5	11	-
Mauro Raúl Fernández (ARG)	31.03.1991	1	-	10	-
Fernando Agustín Giménez Solís (PAR)	10.07.1984	19	2	20	3
Emanuel Herrera (ARG)	13.04.1987	3	-	14	7
Ángel Israel Mena Delgado	21.01.1988	20	6	20	8
Marcos Gustavo Mondaini (ARG)	14.02.1985	16	5	16	1
Denis Andrés Stracqualursi (ARG)	20.10.1987	13	5	-	-
Trainer:					
Gustavo Domingo Quinteros Desabato (BOL) [as of 08.07.2012]	15.02.1965	22		24	

**Matches and goals in Championship finals included*

CLUB DE ALTO RENDIMIENTO ESPECIALIZADO INDEPENDIENTE DEL VALLE

Foundation date: March 1, 1958
Address: Calle Oinchincha 603 y Calle García Moreno, Sangolquí
Stadium: Estadio Municipal „General Rumiñahui Sangolquí" – Capacity: 7,233

THE SQUAD

	DOB	Pr Et M	Pr Et G	Sg Et M	Sg Et G
Goalkeepers:					
Librado Rodrigo Azcona (PAR)	18.01.1984	22	-	22	-
Johan David Padilla Quiñónez	14.08.1992	-	-	-	-
José Luis Emilio Vizcaíno Ortega	26.05.1994	-	-	-	-
Defenders:					
Andi Didier Caicedo Corozo	16.01.1993	-	-	-	-
Luis Alberto Caicedo Medina	11.05.1992	9	1	14	-
Andrés Lamas Bervejillo (URU)	16.01.1984	16	3		
Luis Fernando León Bermeo	11.04.1993	14	-	20	-
Arturo Rafael Mina Meza	08.10.1990	10	2	20	1
Christian Washington Núñez Medina (URU)	24.09.1982	20	1	17	3
Mario Alberto Pineida Martínez	06.07.1992	16	-	21	-
Midfielders:					
Julio Eduardo Angulo Medina	28.05.1990	19	2	14	-
Abel Alexander Araujo Córtez	15.01.1994	-	-	-	-
Luis Miguel Ayala Brucil	24.09.1993	11	-	15	-
Bryan Alfredo Cabezas Segura	20.03.1997	2	-	4	-
Gabriel Jhon Córtez Casierra	10.10.1995	11	2	3	1
Jonathan David González Valencia	03.07.1995	22	4	17	4
Fernando Alexander Guerrero Vásquez	30.09.1989	20	5	22	5
Henry Geovanny León León	20.04.1983	19	-	21	1
Cristian Andrés Oña Tituaña	30.10.1992	2	-	3	-
Jefferson Gabriel Orejuela Izquierdo	14.02.1993	11	-	13	1
Marco Abel Ramos Preciado	09.07.1992	-	-	-	-
Mario Enrique Rizotto Vázquez (URU)	30.08.1984	20	-	20	3
Juan Diego Rojas Caicedo	23.12.1992	-	-	-	-
Armando Julian Solís Quentero	17.09.1987	14	2	10	3
Forwards:					
Daniel Patricio Angulo Arroyo	16.11.1986	17	6	17	10
Jacson Mauricio Pita Mina	08.12.1995	4	-	-	-
Richard Aníbal Porta Candelaresi (AUS/URU)	01.08.1983			10	2
Junior Nazareno Sornoza Moreira	28.01.1994	21	9	20	8
Nilo Cristian Valencia Caicedo	07.12.1992	6	-	2	-
Trainer:					
Pablo Eduardo Repetto Aquino (URU) [as of 24.09.2012]	14.03.1974	22		22	

LIGA DEPORTIVA UNIVERSITARIA DE LOJA

Foundation date: October 23, 1987
Address: Universidad Nacional de Loja, Loja
Stadium: Estadio Federativo Reina del Cisne, Loja – Capacity: 13,359

THE SQUAD

	DOB	Pr Et M	Pr Et G	Sg Et M	Sg Et G
Goalkeepers:					
Danny Cruzelio Cabezas Vera	04.03.1985	4	-	5	-
Luis Fernando Fernández López	01.07.1978	19	-	18	-
Defenders:					
Darío Javier Aimar Álvarez	05.01.1995			2	-
Robert Abel Arboleda Escobar	22.10.1991	20	1	21	-
Óscar Darío Ayala Ojeda (PAR)	14.03.1980	14	2	9	-
Julio Walberto Ayoví Casierra	30.05.1982	13	-	21	2
Jimmy Bermúdez Valencia	16.12.1987	12	-	1	-
Armando Francisco Gómez Torres	24.01.1984	18	1	16	1
Ángel Fernando Gracia Toral	30.05.1989	1	-	15	-
David Saul Vilela Quiñónez	22.03.1985	3	-	-	-
Midfielders:					
Kener Luis Arce Caicedo	17.06.1988	15	-	14	-
Juan Andrés Armijos Quevedo	06.05.1998			1	-
Dixon Jair Arroyo Espinoza	01.06.1992	13	1	12	1
Byron Esteban Calva Cumbicus	17.08.1993	7	1	6	-
Geovanny Patricio Cumbicus Castillo	25.01.1980	-	-	-	-
Dubar Adrián Enríquez Sánchez	10.08.1992	-	-	-	-
Jover Orlando Espinoza Valencia	05.05.1992	1	-	-	-
Pablo Alejandro Estrella Ordoñez	13.12.1995	4	-	-	-
Jhon Antonio García Figueroa	17.10.1976	14	3	10	-
Fabricio Jonathan Guevara Cangá	16.02.1989	16	-	16	-
Osvaldo Hobecker García	23.03.1984	6	-		
Lenin Michael Infante Santos	21.02.1996	-	-	2	1
Pedro Sebastián Larrea Arellano	21.05.1986	16	2	18	-
Onofre Ramiro Mejía Mero	24.03.1986	2	-	17	-
Robinson Andrés Requene Reasco	01.12.1992	8	-	6	-
Jonny Alexander Uchuari Pintado	19.01.1984	18	6	14	4
Edder Javier Vaca Quinde	25.12.1995			7	-
Forwards:					
Carlos Javier Caicedo Preciado	04.01.1993	-	-	6	-
Danilo Ezequiel Carando (ARG)	05.08.1988	17	3	20	6
Fábio Renato Pereira de Azevedo Lima (BRA)	17.06.1980	17	2	-	-
Iván Jaime Kaviedes Llorentty	24.10.1977	3	-	-	-
Marco Antonio Micolta Quiñónez	05.09.1995	5	-	-	-
Sergio Danilo Mina Jaramillo	12.03.1990	13	2	22	3
Gregoris Antonio Ortíz Espinoza	10.12.1995	13	-	16	1
Juan Carlos Villacrés Espín	30.09.1989	14	1	10	2
Trainer:					
Álex Darío Aguinaga Garzón [01.07.2013-20.03.2014]	09.07.1968	9			
Diego Fernando Ochoa Sánchez [as of 20.03.2014; Caretaker]	16.06.1966	13		22	

LIGA DEPORTIVA UNIVERSITARIA DE QUITO

Foundation date: January 11, 1930
Address: Calle Robles 653 y Avenida Amazonas 41-01, Edif. Proinco, Quito
Stadium: Estadio Casa Blanca, Quito – Capacity: 41,575

THE SQUAD

	DOB	Pr Et M	Pr Et G	Sg Et M	Sg Et G
Goalkeepers:					
Walter Daniel Chávez Solorzano	06.04.1994	-	-	-	-
Alexander Domínguez Carabalí	05.06.1987	15	-	11	-
Leonel Romario Nazareno Delgado	05.08.1994	-	-	-	-
Daniel Jimmy Viteri Vinces	12.12.1981	7	-	11	-
Defenders:					
Gerardo Alcoba Rebollo (URU)	25.11.1984	-	-	19	2
Norberto Carlos Araujo López	13.10.1978	21	-	21	2
Carlos Alexi Arboleda Ruíz	24.01.1991	-	-	1	-
Luciano Balbi (ARG)	04.04.1989	10	-	-	-
Diego Armando Calderón Espinoza	26.10.1986	5	-	7	-
Luis David Canga Sánchez	18.06.1995	22	-	9	2
Jorge Antonio Carcelén Espinoza	01.05.1995			-	-
David Koob Hurtado Arboleda	19.07.1985	9	1	2	-
Kevin Bryan Mercado Mina	28.01.1995	8	-		
Néicer Reasco Yano	23.07.1977	9	-	18	-
Midfielders:					
Hancel Javier Batalla Carreño	09.11.1997	11	-	16	1
Danny Alejandro Cabezas Bazan	29.01.1993	3	-	1	-
José Francisco Cevallos Enriquez Jr.	18.01.1995	3	-	15	-
Gabriel Eduardo Corozo Vásquez	05.01.1995	5	-		
Fernando Roberto Hidalgo Maldonado	20.05.1985	21	2	20	2
Diego Pablo Hurtado Vasconez	29.06.1995	5	-	6	1
Jefferson Alfredo Intriago Mendoza	04.06.1996	14	-	18	-
Anderson Andrés Julio Santos	31.05.1996	-	-	-	-
Eduardo Fabián Ledesma Trinidad (PAR)	07.08.1985	12	-		
Luis Alejandro Luna Quinteros	25.01.1988	5	-	3	-
José Enrique Madrid Orobio	21.04.1988	17	1	19	-
Holger Eduardo Matamoros Chunga	04.01.1985	20	3	14	3
Diego Alberto Morales (ARG)	29.11.1986	15	-	17	6
Luis Fernando Saritama Padilla	20.10.1983	-	-		
Enrique Daniel Vera Torres (PAR)	10.03.1979	19	2	18	1
Forwards:					
Juan Luis Anangonó León	13.04.1989	4	2	21	9
Luis Alberto Bolaños León	27.03.1985	17	2		
Félix Alexander Borja Valencia	02.04.1983	16	2		
Luis Gonzalo Congo Minda	27.02.1989	14	5	19	2
Jonathan Raphael Ramis Persincula (URU)	06.11.1989	-	-	17	6
Trainer:					
Luis Francisco Zubeldía (ARG) [as of 26.11.2013]	13.01.1981	22		22	

MANTA FÚTBOL CLUB

Foundation date: July 27, 1998

Address: Calle 9 y Avenida 3 Edif. Mutualista Pichincha 3er. Piso, Manta

Stadium: Estadio Municipal Jocay, Manta – Capacity: 17,834

THE SQUAD

	DOB	Pr Et		Sg Et	
		M	G	M	G
Goalkeepers:					
Geovanny Francisco Camacho Paredes	15.12.1984	4	-	6	-
Dennis Wilber Corozo Villalva	05.04.1988	19	-	16	-
Jesús Fabricio Zambrano Mantuano	06.03.1995	-	-	-	-
Jean Carlos Zamora Macías	31.05.1993	-	-	-	-
Defenders:					
Xavier Ricardo Arreaga Bermello	28.09.1994	2	-	9	-
Hernán Santiago Calle Tenezaca	25.01.1984	20	-	6	-
Harry Gerson Chérrez Casanova	17.08.1991	-	-	8	-
Alexander Leonardo Mendoza Espinales	17.04.1994	2	-	12	-
Alejandro Javier Rodríguez Morales (URU)	09.07.1986	3	-	16	-
Enrique Romaña Gónzalez (COL)	28.12.1988	10	-	-	-
Ronny Marcelo Santos Mendoza	04.07.1995	2	-	13	-
Jordan Steeven Sierra Flores	23.04.1997	1	-	1	-
Midfielders:					
Miguel Ángel Álvarez Cobeña	07.03.1995	10	-	-	-
Walter Alejandro Busse (ARG)	07.02.1987	-	-	20	1
Santos Fausto Caicedo Manfredi	19.02.1986	1	-	-	-
Diego Steven Cedeño Moreira	23.01.1996	-	-	-	-
Jéfferson Camillo Cuellar Cuenu	22.07.1994	-	-	1	-
Wilson Alfredo Folleco Morales	04.09.1989	14	-	20	-
Jimmy Joao Gómez Medina	25.01.1996	3	-	3	-
Elio Roberto Lastra García	10.08.1983	14	1	15	1
Luis Enrique Loor Solorzano	25.05.1995	3	-	10	1
Ricardo Iván López Mendoza	08.11.1981	18	1	20	1
Diego Armando Macías Gorozabel	21.04.1985	3	-	-	-
Efrén Alexander Mera Moreira	23.06.1985	19	1	22	3
Benito Fredy Olivo González	26.11.1982	12	-	15	-
Jorge Luis Palacios Bravo	10.04.1992	17	7	2	-
Carlos Ariel Recalde González	14.12.1983	8	-		
Raúl Roberto Rivas Acosta	12.01.1989	-	-	-	-
Francisco Elías Rojas Mendoza	13.01.1991	3	1	5	-
Jefferson Alexander Sierra Flores	13.05.1993	13	-	4	-
Arnaldo Andrés Valverde Morante	03.05.1991	9	-	3	-
Jefferson Stalin Villacis López	03.09.1988	14	-	1	-
José Marcelo Zambrano Moncayo	07.08.1984	-	-	-	-
Forwards:					
Miller David Castillo Quiñonez	01.08.1987	15	-	20	11
José Luis Flecha González (PAR)	19.03.1988	1	-	10	1
Alberto Martín Gómez (ARG)	26.01.1983	19	3		
Javier Antonio Grbec (ARG)	24.03.1986	9	1		
Christian Gabriel Márquez Mina	16.11.1980	18	2	9	2
Eduardo Luis Mina Casierra	02.11.1989	6	2	12	3
Jorge Luis Palacios Avila	02.09.1993	4	1	14	-
Jonathan Javier Saltos Mera	19.08.1995	8	-	9	-
Jersón Sloanny Sierra Flores	25.06.1995	2	-	3	-
Jesús Alberto Vélez Mero	17.08.1990	-	-	2	-
Trainer:					
Juan Manuel Llop (ARG) [18.12.2013-14.08.2014; Resigned]	01.06.1963	22		2	
Armando Osma Rueda [15.08.11.10.2014]				8	
Jorge Rolando Alfonso Ávalos [as of 11.10.2014]	26.01.1971			12	

MUSHUC RUNA SPORTING CLUB AMBATO

Foundation date: January 2, 2003
Address: Montalvo Entre 12 de Noviembre y Juan Benigno Vela
Stadium: Estadio Bellavista, Ambato – Capacity: 16,467

THE SQUAD	DOB	Pr Et		Sg Et	
		M	G	M	G
Goalkeepers:					
Sebastián Alberto Blázquez Tosso	27.11.1979	19	-	22	-
Nelson Vinicio Cartagena López	15.04.1986	-	-		
Deny Javier Mideros Valencia	10.07.1993	-	-	-	-
Juan Gabriel Molina Guevara	10.09.1982	4	-	-	-
Defenders:					
Juan Carlos Anangonó Campos	29.03.1989	14	-	22	-
Jesús Fernando Cabezas Cabezas	25.04.1995	16	-	6	-
Jhonny Xavier Gudiño Ramos	10.12.1983	12	-	6	-
Erwin Argenis Moreira Alcívar	15.06.1987	4	1	19	-
Gustavo Nazareno Cortez	01.04.1985	19	1	18	1
Darwin Estuardo Quilumba Diaz	07.12.1988	22	-	12	-
Víctor Andrés Valarezo Ospina	17.05.1988	4	-	11	-
Yery Javier Valencia Perea	13.10.1989	1	-	-	-
Midfielders:					
Christian Santiago Cordero Rodríguez	20.10.1987	17	5	16	1
Cristhian David Cuero Valencia	22.12.1989	15	-	15	1
Silvano de los Santos Estacio Montaño	16.12.1981	4	-	1	-
Jorge Mauricio Folleco Yepez	17.07.1983	7	-	8	-
Fernando Gastón López Hernández (URU)	11.01.1985	14	-	18	1
Danny Gabriel Luna Morán	25.05.1991	3	-	-	-
Rafael Raúl Manosalvas Córdovez	19.12.1981	4	-	-	-
Juan Ignacio Marcarie Carra (ARG)	25.09.1985	14	-	16	2
Christian Serafin Pandi Masabanda	09.06.1986	-	-	1	-
Bryan Javier Rodríguez Estrella	18.01.1990	12	1	-	-
Wellington Eduardo Sánchez Luzuriaga	19.06.1974	4	-	15	1
Kléver José Triviño Zambrano	20.03.1986	9	-	11	-
Edder Javier Vaca Quinde	25.12.1985	1	-		
Ederson Wilmar Valencia Vásquez	18.08.1995	6	-	7	-
Elvis Ernesto Vásquez Benalcazar	24.10.1989	7	-	2	-
William Fernando Viveros Jarrin	19.01.1995			6	-
Rommel Santiago Zura De Jesús	21.11.1983	11	-	15	1
Forwards:					
Federico Almerares (ARG)	02.05.1985	4	-		-
Orlindo Ayoví Caicedo	15.09.1984			8	1
Maximiliano Fabián Barreiro (ARG)	16.03.1985	19	5	19	8
Luis Hernán Batioja Castillo	16.02.1994	3	-	-	-
Gustavo Omar Figueroa Cáceres	30.08.1978	-	-	7	-
Víctor Iván Macías García	01.07.1984	6	-	16	-
Carlos Luis Quintero Arroyo	27.08.1982	14	5		
Edmundo Salomón Zura de Jesús	01.12.1983	18	1	11	1
Trainer:					
César Eduardo Vigevani Martínez [13.12.2012-01.04.2014; Sacked]	1974	11			
Fabián Vicente Burbano Ayala [01.04.-06.04.2014; Caretaker]	12.08.1950	1			
Julio Daniel Asad (ARG) [as of 07.04.2014]	07.06.1953	10		22	

CLUB CENTRO DEPORTIVO OLMEDO

Foundation date: November 11, 1919
Address: Calle Veloz y García Moreno, Edificio Esmeralda 4to Piso, Riobamba
Stadium: Estadio Olímpico de Riobamba, Riobamba – Capacity: 18,936

THE SQUAD

	DOB	Pr Et M	Pr Et G	Sg Et M	Sg Et G
Goalkeepers:					
Guillermo Eduardo Palacios Montaño	14.03.1987	-	-	-	-
Robinson Jeovanny Sánchez Suquillo	25.03.1978	22	-	17	-
Wilmer Fabián Zumba Ramírez	18.12.1978	-	-	6	-
Defenders:					
Vicente Paúl Ambrosi Zambrano	14.10.1980			11	-
Miller Carlos Angulo Bazan	28.05.1993			3	-
Bernardo Javier Chila Ayoví	14.07.1984	12	-	13	1
Marvin Richard Corozo Angulo	13.07.1987	2	-	-	-
Fulton Bienvenido Francis Angulo	22.03.1985	7	-	-	-
Enzo Nicolás González Cruz	15.06.1996	7	-	9	-
Omar Eduardo Ledesma Moyón	04.11.1977	4	-	1	-
Mariano Florencio Mina Orobio	03.03.1979	20	-	20	-
Carlos Daniel Santucho Gradiol (URU)	12.03.1985	17	-	12	-
Midfielders:					
José Luis Ardila Valencia	17.01.1988	20	-	14	1
Romario Javier Caicedo Ante	23.05.1990	22	5	19	-
Andrés Stiven Campas Monroy	05.08.1992	-	-	7	-
Byron Gonzalo Cano Recalde	20.04.1990	14	5	10	1
Erick Leonel Castillo Arroyo	05.02.1995	14	-	15	-
Ángel Lizardo Cheme Ortíz	19.11.1981	10	-	11	-
John Jairo Garcés Pino	28.06.1987	4	-	3	-
Franco Eduardo Mazurek (ARG)	24.09.1993	7	2	17	1
José Ángel Mendoza Nivela	13.12.1995	1	-	-	-
Armando Andrés Monteverde (ARG)	06.03.1985	11	-	14	-
Ricardo Daniel Moreira Cruel	21.12.1995	-	-	1	-
Marco Roberto Mosquera Borja	03.12.1984	20	-	18	-
Jacob Israel Murillo Moncada	31.03.1993	10	2	3	-
Mario David Quiroz Villón	08.09.1982	11	-	1	-
André Aristóteles Skiada Wohigemuth	14.03.1985	-	-	4	1
Andrés Alejandro Vinueza Robalino	30.10.1989	3	-	7	-
Polo Raúl Wila Cangá	09.02.1987	17	-	-	-
Forwards:					
Diego Francisco Avila Murillo	15.11.1993	2	-	4	-
Richard Luis Mercado Corozo	20.12.1986	5	-	-	-
Álvaro Damián Navarro Bica (URU)	28.01.1985			22	8
Carlos Alfredo Orejuela Quiñónez	14.03.1993	8	-	4	-
Cristian Martín Palacios Ferreira (URU)	02.09.1990	20	5	20	3
Marcos Vinicio Romero Nazareno	10.05.1987	-	-	5	-
Franklin Agustín Salas Nárvaez	30.08.1981	2	-	13	2
Willian Gustavo Tixe Naranjo	28.03.1994	1	-	-	-
Luis Alfredo Vila (ARG)	06.03.1992	13	2	-	-
Trainer:					
Gabriel Gustavo Perrone (ARG) [12.12.2013-19.07.2014; Sacked]	15.04.1965	20			
Mario Daniel Saralegui Iriarte (URU) [31.07.-07.10.2014; Resigned]	21.04.1959	2		10	
Héctor Manuel González Ortíz [07.10.-16.11.2014; Sacked]	04.05.1972			6	
Juan Urquiza (ARG) [as of 16.11.2014]				6	

CLUB DEPORTIVO UNIVERSIDAD CATÓLICA QUITO

Foundation date: June 26, 1963
Address: Pasaje Manuela Sáenz 827 y Hénández Girón, Quito
Stadium: Estadio Olímpico Atahualpa, Quito – Capacity: 35,258

THE SQUAD

	DOB	Pr Et M	Pr Et G	Sg Et M	Sg Et G
Goalkeepers:					
Hernán Ismael Galíndez (ARG)	30.03.1987	21	-	20	-
Rodrigo Ramiro Perea Salazar	08.04.1990	1	-	2	-
Defenders:					
Ridder Voltaire Alcívar Cedeño	13.03.1994	7	-	-	-
Henry Junior Cangá Ortíz	20.06.1987	20	1	20	-
Enzo Bernabé Cuesta Valdiviezo	22.02.1996	3	-		
Deison Adolfo Méndez Rosero	27.10.1990	3	-	13	-
Jorge Andrés Mendoza Uza	16.08.1989	18	-	2	1
Wilmar Pascual Meneses Borja	14.12.1995	4	-	11	-
Levis Steeven Segura Quiñónez	20.08.1995			-	-
Mariano Esteban Uglessich	06.11.1981			19	1
Midfielders:					
Diego Fernando Benítez Quintena (URU)	23.01.1988	18	1	16	2
Franklin Alexander Carabalí Carabalí	27.06.1996			-	-
Jonathan Bladimir Carabalí Palacios	18.02.1995	19	-	17	-
Jonathan Oswaldo de la Cruz Valverde	18.07.1992	14	-	17	1
Alejandro Gabriel Espinosa Borja	13.08.1985	22	-	6	-
Jesi Alexander Godoy Quiñónes	15.09.1992	21	-	19	-
Wilmer Javier Godoy Quiñónez	05.11.1993	-	-	8	-
Romario Andrés Ibarra Mina	24.09.1994	18	1	16	3
Renny Salen Jaramillo Barre	12.06.1996			-	-
Jhonathan Jeison Lucas Figueroa	28.01.1996			2	-
Facundo Martin Martinez Montagnoli (URU)	02.04.1983	18	1	20	1
Kleber Andrés Miranda Vargas	15.04.1995	-	-	-	-
Carlos Luis Moyano Moran	28.06.1989	16	-	14	-
Elvis Adán Patta Quintero	17.11.1990	20	2	21	1
Daniel Guillermo Porozo Valencia	20.09.1997	6	-	3	-
Alexander Xavier Ushiña Goyes	26.08.1996	-	-	1	-
Hugo Javier Vélez Benítez	26.05.1986	1	-		
Forwards:					
Jorge Luis Cuesta Valdiviezo	25.02.1992	10	1	-	-
Esteban Santiago de la Cruz Santacruz	23.06.1993			5	-
Cristian Daniel González (ARG)	27.12.1993	4	1		
Henry Leonel Patta Quintero	14.01.1987	20	6	21	6
Bryan David Sánchez Congo	24.04.1993	-	-	13	1
Armando Lenin Wila Canga	12.05.1985	21	12	17	8
Trainer:					
Jorge César Fortunato Celico (ARG) [21.09.2010-05.08.2014] [*Promoted to Director of football for the club*]	13.09.1964	22			
Luis Gustavo Soler Magadán (ARG) [05.08.-07.10.2014; Sacked]	09.06.1951			10	
Jorge César Fortunato Celico (ARG) [as of 07.10.2014]	13.09.1964			12	

SECOND LEVEL
Campeonato Ecuatoriano de Fútbol Serie B 2014 / Copa Pilsener Serie B

Primera Etapa

1.	Liga Deportiva Universitaria de Portoviejo	22	14	2	6	39 - 20	44
2.	CD River Plate Ecuador Guayaquil	22	12	6	4	30 - 18	42
3.	Sociedad Deportiva Aucas	22	12	4	6	32 - 15	40
4.	CSD Macará	22	9	7	6	24 - 16	34
5.	Club Deportivo Técnico Universitario Ambato	22	9	6	7	35 - 23	33
6.	CD Espoli Quito	22	7	9	6	27 - 27	30
7.	Delfín Sporting Club Manta	22	9	3	10	21 - 21	30
8.	Club Deportivo Quevedo	22	7	6	9	24 - 34	27
9.	Club Deportivo Azogues	22	6	8	8	18 - 22	26
10.	Club Deportivo Municipal de Cañar	22	5	6	11	23 - 40	21
11.	CD Universidad Técnica de Cotopaxi Latacunga	22	5	5	12	22 - 41	20
12.	Imbabura SC Ibarra	22	3	6	13	17 - 35	15

Segunda Etapa

1.	Club Deportivo Técnico Universitario Ambato	22	14	2	6	35 - 19	44
2.	Sociedad Deportiva Aucas	22	12	7	3	32 - 17	43
3.	CD River Plate Ecuador Guayaquil	22	10	6	6	32 - 27	36
4.	Imbabura SC Ibarra	22	9	6	7	23 - 23	33
5.	Club Deportivo Quevedo	22	9	5	8	28 - 28	32
6.	Liga Deportiva Universitaria de Portoviejo	22	8	7	7	28 - 28	31
7.	Club Deportivo Azogues	22	7	9	6	28 - 25	30
8.	CSD Macará	22	8	4	10	25 - 25	28
9.	CD Universidad Técnica de Cotopaxi Latacunga	22	8	4	10	34 - 35	28
10.	Delfín Sporting Club Manta	22	6	7	9	22 - 28	25
11.	CD Espoli Quito	22	5	6	11	23 - 29	20
12.	Club Deportivo Municipal de Cañar	22	2	5	15	18 - 43	11

Aggregate Table 2014

1.	Sociedad Deportiva Aucas (*Promoted*)	44	24	11	9	64 - 33	83
2.	CD River Plate Ecuador Guayaquil (*Promoted*)	44	22	12	10	62 - 45	78
3.	Club Deportivo Técnico Universitario Ambato	44	23	8	13	70 - 42	77
4.	Liga Deportiva Universitaria de Portoviejo	44	22	9	13	67 - 48	75
5.	CSD Macará	44	17	11	16	49 - 41	62
6.	Club Deportivo Quevedo	44	16	11	17	52 - 62	59
7.	Club Deportivo Azogues	44	13	17	14	46 - 47	56
8.	Delfín Sporting Club Manta	44	15	10	19	43 - 49	55
9.	CD Espoli Quito	44	12	15	17	50 - 56	50
10.	Imbabura SC Ibarra	44	12	12	20	40 - 58	48
11.	CD Universidad Técnica de Cotopaxi Latacunga (*Relegated*)	44	13	9	22	57 - 77	48
12.	Club Deportivo Municipal de Cañar (*Relegated*)	44	7	11	26	41 - 83	32

NATIONAL TEAM
INTERNATIONAL MATCHES
(16.07.2014 – 15.07.2015)

06.09.2014	Fort Lauderdale	Bolivia - Ecuador	0-4(0-2)	(F)
09.09.2014	East Rutherford	Brazil - Ecuador	1-0(1-0)	(F)
10.10.2014	East Hartford	United States - Ecuador	1-1(1-0)	(F)
14.10.2014	Harrison	El Salvador - Ecuador	1-5(1-3)	(F)
28.03.2015	Los Angeles	Mexico - Ecuador	1-0(1-0)	(F)
31.03.2015	East Rutherford	Argentina - Ecuador	2-1(1-1)	(F)
03.06.2015	Ciudad de Panamá	Panama - Ecuador	1-1(0-0)	(F)
06.06.2015	Portoviejo	Ecuador - Panama	4-0(3-0)	(F)
11.06.2015	Santiago	Chile - Ecuador	2-0(1-0)	(CA)
15.06.2015	Valparaíso	Ecuador - Bolivia	2-3(0-3)	(CA)
19.06.2015	Rancagua	Mexico - Ecuador	1-2(0-1)	(CA)

06.09.2014, Friendly International
Lockhart Stadium, Fort Lauderdale (United States); Attendance: 10,000
Referee: Valdin Legister (Jamaica)
BOLIVIA - ECUADOR **0-4(0-2)**
ECU: Máximo Orlando Banguera Valdivieso, Walter Orlando Ayoví Corozo (86.Cristian Leonel Ramírez Zambrano), Juan Carlos Paredes Reasco, Frickson Rafael Erazo Vivero, Luis David Cangá Sánchez, Segundo Alejandro Castillo Nazareno (71.Carlos Armando Gruezo Arboleda), Christian Fernando Noboa Tello, Alex Renato Ibarra Mina (69.Joao Jimmy Plata Cotera), Fidel Francisco Martínez Tenorio (8.Joao Robin Rojas Mendoza; 77.Junior Nazareno Sornoza Moreira), Juan Ramon Cazares Sevillano, Enner Remberto Valencia Lastra (76.Daniel Patricio Angulo Arroyo). Trainer: Sixto Rafael Vizuete Toapanta.
Goals: Christian Fernando Noboa Tello (9), Juan Ramon Cazares Sevillano (34), Enner Remberto Valencia Lastra (65), Junior Nazareno Sornoza Moreira (84).

09.09.2014, Friendly International
Metlife Stadium, East Rutherford (United States); Attendance: 35,975
Referee: Edwin Jurisevic (United States)
BRAZIL - ECUADOR **1-0(1-0)**
ECU: Alexander Domínguez Carabalí, Walter Orlando Ayoví Corozo, Juan Carlos Paredes Reasco, Frickson Rafael Erazo Vivero, Luis David Cangá Sánchez, Segundo Alejandro Castillo Nazareno, Christian Fernando Noboa Tello, Alex Renato Ibarra Mina (83.Fidel Francisco Martínez Tenorio), Juan Ramon Cazares Sevillano (67.Daniel Patricio Angulo Arroyo), Enner Remberto Valencia Lastra, Junior Nazareno Sornoza Moreira (46.Joao Robin Rojas Mendoza). Trainer: Sixto Rafael Vizuete Toapanta.

10.10.2014, Friendly International
Rentschler Field, East Hartford; Attendance: 36,265
Referee: Roberto Moreno Salazar (Panama)
UNITED STATES - ECUADOR **1-1(1-0)**
ECU: Máximo Orlando Banguera Valdivieso, Walter Orlando Ayoví Corozo, Juan Carlos Paredes Reasco (90+3.Mario Alberto Pineida Martínez), Frickson Rafael Erazo Vivero (86.Luis Fernando León Bermeo), Luis David Cangá Sánchez, Segundo Alejandro Castillo Nazareno (86.Carlos Armando Gruezo Arboleda), Christian Fernando Noboa Tello, Alex Renato Ibarra Mina (44.Jonathan David González Valencia), Juan Ramon Cazares Sevillano (85.Junior Nazareno Sornoza Moreira), Enner Remberto Valencia Lastra, Cristian Anderson Penilla Caicedo (46.Joao Jimmy Plata Cotera). Trainer: Sixto Rafael Vizuete Toapanta.
Goal: Enner Remberto Valencia Lastra (88).

14.10.2014, Friendly International
Red Bull Arena, Harrison (United States); Attendance: n/a
Referee: Edwin Jurisevic (United States)
EL SALVADOR - ECUADOR 1-5(1-3)
ECU: Alexander Domínguez Carabalí, Iván Jacinto Hurtado Angulo (42.Arturo Rafael Mina Meza), Walter Orlando Ayoví Corozo (72.Cristian Anderson Penilla Caicedo), Juan Carlos Paredes Reasco (70.Mario Alberto Pineida Martínez), Frickson Rafael Erazo Vivero, Segundo Alejandro Castillo Nazareno (70.Carlos Armando Gruezo Arboleda), Christian Fernando Noboa Tello, Jonathan David González Valencia (59.Cristian Leonel Ramírez Zambrano), Enner Remberto Valencia Lastra, Joao Jimmy Plata Cotera (72.Jonny Alexander Uchuari Pintado), Junior Nazareno Sornoza Moreira. Trainer: Sixto Rafael Vizuete Toapanta.
Goals: Joao Jimmy Plata Cotera (16), Enner Remberto Valencia Lastra (18), Joao Jimmy Plata Cotera (25), Enner Remberto Valencia Lastra (73), Cristian Anderson Penilla Caicedo (83).

28.03.2015, Friendly International
Memorial Coliseum, Los Angeles (United States); Attendance: 88,409
Referee: Christopher Reid (Belize)
MEXICO - ECUADOR 1-0(1-0)
ECU: Alexander Domínguez Carabalí, Walter Orlando Ayoví Corozo, Juan Carlos Paredes Reasco (83.Joao Robin Rojas Mendoza), Frickson Rafael Erazo Vivero, Arturo Rafael Mina Meza, Luis Antonio Valencia Mosquera, Christian Fernando Noboa Tello, Osbaldo Lupo Lastra García, Jefferson Antonio Montero Vite (44.Ángel Israel Mena Delgado), Felipe Salvador Caicedo Corozo (74.Fidel Francisco Martínez Tenorio), Miller Alejandro Bolaños Reasco. Trainer: Gustavo Domingo Quinteros Desabato (Bolivia).

31.03.2015, Friendly International
MetLife Stadium, East Rutherford (United States); Attendance: 48,000
Referee: Silviu Petrescu (Canada)
ARGENTINA - ECUADOR 2-1(1-1)
ECU: Alexander Domínguez Carabalí, Gabriel Eduardo Achilier Zurita, Walter Orlando Ayoví Corozo, Juan Carlos Paredes Reasco, Frickson Rafael Erazo Vivero, Christian Fernando Noboa Tello, Alex Renato Ibarra Mina (85.Fidel Francisco Martínez Tenorio), Osbaldo Lupo Lastra García (65.Carlos Armando Gruezo Arboleda), Ángel Israel Mena Delgado, Felipe Salvador Caicedo Corozo (70.Jaime Javier Ayoví Corozo), Miller Alejandro Bolaños Reasco. Trainer: Gustavo Domingo Quinteros Desabato (Bolivia).
Goal: Miller Alejandro Bolaños Reasco (24).

03.06.2015, Friendly International
Estadio „Rommel Fernández Gutiérrez“, Ciudad de Panamá; Attendance: 10,000
Referee: Paul Enrique Delgadillo Haro (Mexico)
PANAMA - ECUADOR 1-1(0-0)
ECU: Alexander Domínguez Carabalí, Óscar Dalmiro Bagüí Angulo (71.Mario Alberto Pineida Martínez), Juan Carlos Paredes Reasco, Frickson Rafael Erazo Vivero, Arturo Rafael Mina Meza, Pedro Ángel Quiñónez Rodríguez, Fidel Francisco Martínez Tenorio, Jonathan David González Valencia (74.Juan Ramon Cazares Sevillano), Osbaldo Lupo Lastra García (46.Christian Fernando Noboa Tello), Jaime Javier Ayoví Corozo (45.Jefferson Antonio Montero Vite), Miller Alejandro Bolaños Reasco (61.Enner Remberto Valencia Lastra). Trainer: Gustavo Domingo Quinteros Desabato (Bolivia).
Goal: Fidel Francisco Martínez Tenorio (51).

06.06.2015, Friendly International
Estadio Reales Tamarindos, Portoviejo; Attendance: n/a
Referee: Henry Percy Gambetta Avalos (Peru)

ECUADOR - PANAMA 4-0(3-0)

ECU: Alexander Domínguez Carabalí, Gabriel Eduardo Achilier Zurita, Walter Orlando Ayoví Corozo (46.Óscar Dalmiro Bagüí Angulo), Juan Carlos Paredes Reasco, Frickson Rafael Erazo Vivero (73.Arturo Rafael Mina Meza), Christian Fernando Noboa Tello (73.Jonathan David González Valencia), Osbaldo Lupo Lastra García, Jefferson Antonio Montero Vite (89.John William Narváez Arroyo), Fidel Francisco Martínez Tenorio (64.Juan Ramon Cazares Sevillano), Miller Alejandro Bolaños Reasco, Enner Remberto Valencia Lastra. Trainer: Gustavo Domingo Quinteros Desabato (Bolivia).
Goals: Miller Alejandro Bolaños Reasco (20), Fidel Francisco Martínez Tenorio (31, 40), Jefferson Antonio Montero Vite (52).
Sent off: Arturo Rafael Mina Meza (89).

11.06.2015, 44th Copa América, Group Stage
Estadio Nacional "Julio Martínez Prádanos", Santiago; Attendance: 46,000
Referee: Néstor Fabián Pitana (Argentina)

CHILE - ECUADOR 2-0(1-0)

ECU: Alexander Domínguez Carabalí, Gabriel Eduardo Achilier Zurita, Walter Orlando Ayoví Corozo, Juan Carlos Paredes Reasco, Frickson Rafael Erazo Vivero, Christian Fernando Noboa Tello, Fidel Francisco Martínez Tenorio (79.Alex Renato Ibarra Mina), Osbaldo Lupo Lastra García (68.Pedro Ángel Quiñónez Rodríguez), Jefferson Antonio Montero Vite, Miller Alejandro Bolaños Reasco, Enner Remberto Valencia Lastra. Trainer: Gustavo Domingo Quinteros Desabato (Bolivia).

15.06.2015, 44th Copa América, Group Stage
Estadio "Elías Figueroa", Valparaíso (Chile); Attendance: 5,982
Referee: Joel Antonio Aguilar Chicas (El Salvador)

ECUADOR - BOLIVIA 2-3(0-3)

ECU: Alexander Domínguez Carabalí, Gabriel Eduardo Achilier Zurita, Walter Orlando Ayoví Corozo, Juan Carlos Paredes Reasco (46.Daniel Patricia Angulo Arroyo), Frickson Rafael Erazo Vivero, Christian Fernando Noboa Tello, Pedro Ángel Quiñónez Rodríguez (46.Juan Ramon Cazares Sevillano), Fidel Francisco Martínez Tenorio (46.Alex Renato Ibarra Mina), Jefferson Antonio Montero Vite, Miller Alejandro Bolaños Reasco, Enner Remberto Valencia Lastra. Trainer: Gustavo Domingo Quinteros Desabato (Bolivia).
Goals: Enner Remberto Valencia Lastra (47), Miller Alejandro Bolaños Reasco (80).

19.06.2015, 44th Copa América, Group Stage
Estadio El Teniente, Rancagua (Chile); Attendance: 11,051
Referee: José Ramón Argote Vega (Venezuela)

MEXICO - ECUADOR 1-2(0-1)

ECU: Alexander Domínguez Carabalí, Gabriel Eduardo Achilier Zurita, Walter Orlando Ayoví Corozo, Juan Carlos Paredes Reasco, Arturo Rafael Mina Meza, Christian Fernando Noboa Tello, Alex Renato Ibarra Mina (78.Juan Ramon Cazares Sevillano), Osbaldo Lupo Lastra García, Jefferson Antonio Montero Vite (90+2.Fidel Francisco Martínez Tenorio), Miller Alejandro Bolaños Reasco, Enner Remberto Valencia Lastra. Trainer: Gustavo Domingo Quinteros Desabato (Bolivia).
Goals: Miller Alejandro Bolaños Reasco (26), Enner Remberto Valencia Lastra (57).

NATIONAL TEAM PLAYERS 2014/2015			
Name	**DOB**	**Caps**	**Goals**
[Club 2014/2015]			

(Caps and goals at 05.07.2015)

Goalkeepers

Máximo Orlando BANGUERA Valdivieso [2014: Barcelona SC Guayaquil]	16.12.1985	**27**	**0**
Alexander DOMÍNGUEZ Carabalí [2014/2015: LDU de Quito]	05.06.1987	**30**	**0**

Defenders

Gabriel Eduardo ACHILIER Zurita [2014/2015: CS Emelec Guayaquil]	24.03.1985	**30**	**0**
Walter Orlando AYOVÍ Corozo [2014/2015: CF Pachuca (MEX)]	11.08.1979	**105**	**8**
Óscar Dalmiro BAGÜÍ Angulo [2015: CS Emelec Guayaquil]	10.12.1982	**23**	**0**
Luis David CANGÁ Sánchez [2014: LDU de Quito]	18.06.1995	**3**	**0**
Frickson Rafael ERAZO Vivero [2014: CR Flamengo Rio de Janeiro (BRA); 17.01.2015-> Grêmio Foot-Ball Porto Alegrense (BRA)]	05.05.1988	**50**	**1**
Iván Jacinto HURTADO Angulo [2014/2015: *unattached*]	16.08.1974	**168**	**5**
Luis Fernando LEÓN Bermeo [2014: CSD Independiente del Valle Sangolquí]	11.04.1993	**1**	**0**
Arturo Rafael MINA Meza [2014/2015: CSD Independiente del Valle Sangolquí]	08.10.1990	**5**	**0**
John William NARVÁEZ Arroyo [2015: CS Emelec Guayaquil]	12.06.1991	**1**	**0**
Juan Carlos PAREDES Reasco [2014/2015: Watford FC (ENG)]	08.07.1987	**52**	**0**
Mario Alberto PINEIDA Martínez [2014/2015: CSD Independiente del Valle Sangolquí]	06.07.1992	**3**	**0**
Cristian Leonel RAMÍREZ Zambrano [2014: 1.FC Nürnberg (GER)]	12.08.1994	**4**	**0**

Midfielders			
Segundo Alejandro CASTILLO Nazareno [2014: Al Hilal Saudi FC Riyadh (KSA)]	15.05.1982	**85**	**9**
Juan Ramón CAZARES Sevillano [2014/2015: CA Banfield (ARG)]	03.04.1992	**7**	**1**
Jonathan David GONZÁLEZ Valencia [2014: CSD Independiente del Valle Sangolquí; 01.2015-> Club Universidad de Guadalajara (MEX)]	07.03.1995	**4**	**0**
Carlos Armando GRUEZO Arboleda [2014/2015: VfB Stuttgart (GER)]	19.04.1995	**9**	**0**
Alex Renato IBARRA Mina [2014/2015: SBV Vitesse Arnhem (NED)]	20.01.1991	**26**	**0**
Osbaldo Lupo LASTRA García [2014/2015: CS Emelec Guayaquil]	10.08.1983	**6**	**0**
Ángel Israel MENA Delgado [2015: CS Emelec Guayaquil]	21.01.1988	**2**	**0**
Jefferson Antonio MONTERO Vite [2014/2015: Swansea City AFC (WAL)]	01.09.1989	**49**	**9**
Christian Fernando NOBOA Tello [2014: FK Dinamo Moskva (RUS); 07.01.2015-> PAOK Thessaloníki (GRE)]	09.04.1985	**56**	**3**
Cristian Anderson PENILLA Caicedo [2014: Barcelona SC Guayaquil]	02.05.1991	**2**	**1**
Pedro Ángel QUIÑÓNEZ Rodríguez [2015: CS Emelec Guayaquil]	04.03.1986	**14**	**0**
Joao Robin ROJAS Mendoza [2014/2015: Cruz Azul FC Ciudad de México (MEX)]	14.07.1989	**34**	**2**
Junior Nazareno SORNOZA Moreira [2014: CSD Independiente del Valle Sangolquí]	28.01.1994	**4**	**1**
Jonny Alexander UCHUARI Pintado [2014: LDU de Loja]	19.01.1994	**1**	**0**
Luis Antonio VALENCIA Mosquera [2014/2015: Manchester United FC (ENG)]	04.08.1985	**75**	**8**

Forwards

Daniel Patricio ANGULO Arroyo [2014/2015: CSD Independiente del Valle Sangolquí]	16.11.1986	**3**	**0**
Jaime Javier AYOVÍ Corozo [2015: CD Godoy Cruz Antonio Tomba (ARG)]	21.02.1988	**32**	**9**
Miller Alejandro BOLAÑOS Reasco [2015: CS Emelec Guayaquil]	01.06.1990	**7**	**4**
Felipe Salvador CAICEDO Corozo [2014/2015: RCD Espanyol Barcelona (ESP)]	05.09.1988	**54**	**15**
Fidel Francisco MARTÍNEZ Tenorio [2014/2015: Club Universidad de Guadalajara (MEX)]	15.02.1990	**17**	**5**
Joao Jimmy PLATA Cotera [2014/2015: Real Salt Lake (USA)]	01.03.1992	**4**	**2**
Enner Remberto VALENCIA Lastra [2014/2015: West Ham United FC London (ENG)]	11.04.1989	**22**	**13**

National coaches

Sixto Rafael VIZUETE Toapanta [23.07.2014-28.01.2015]	13.01.1961	4 M; 2 W; 1 D; 1 L; 10-3
Gustavo Domingo QUINTEROS Desabato (Bolivia) [as of 29.01.2015]	15.02.1965	7 M; 2 W; 1 D; 4 L; 10-10

PARAGUAY

The Country:
República del Paraguay (Republic of Paraguay)
Capital: Asunción
Surface: 406,752 km²
Inhabitants: 6,800,284 [estimated 2013]
Time: UTC-4

The FA:
Asociación Paraguaya de Fútbol
Estadio de los Defensores del Chaco, Calle Mayor Martínez, 1393 Asunción
Year of Formation: 1906
Member of FIFA since: 1925
Member of CONMEBOL since: 1921
Internet: www.apf.org.py

NATIONAL TEAM RECORDS	
First international match:	11.05.1919, Asunción: Paraguay - Argentina 1-5
Most international caps:	Paulo César da Silva Barrios - 127 caps (2000-2015)
Most international goals:	Roque Luis Santa Cruz Cantero – 32 goals / 110 caps (1999-2015)

OLYMPIC GAMES 1900-2012
1992, 2004 (Runners-up)

COPA AMÉRICA	
1916	Did not enter
1917	Did not enter
1919	Did not enter
1920	Did not enter
1921	4th Place
1922	Runners-up
1923	3rd Place
1924	3rd Place
1925	3rd Place
1926	4th Place
1927	Withdrew
1929	Runners-up
1935	Withdrew
1937	4th Place
1939	3rd Place
1941	Withdrew
1942	4th Place
1945	Withdrew
1946	3rd Place
1947	Runners-up
1949	Runners-up
1953	**Winners**
1955	5th Place
1956	5th Place
1957	Withdrew
1959	3rd Place
1959E	5th Place
1963	Runners-up
1967	4th Place
1975	Round 1
1979	**Winners**
1983	Semi-Finals
1987	Round 1
1989	4th Place
1991	Round 1
1993	Quarter-Finals
1995	Quarter-Finals
1997	Quarter-Finals
1999	Quarter-Finals
2001	Round 1
2004	Quarter-Finals
2007	Quarter-Finals
2011	Runners-up
2015	4th Place

FIFA WORLD CUP	
1930	Final Tournament (1st Round)
1934	Did not enter
1938	Did not enter
1950	Final Tournament (Group Stage)
1954	Qualifiers
1958	Final Tournament (Group Stage)
1962	Qualifiers
1966	Qualifiers
1970	Qualifiers
1974	Qualifiers
1978	Qualifiers
1982	Qualifiers
1986	Final Tournament (2nd Round of 16)
1990	Qualifiers
1994	Qualifiers
1998	Final Tournament (2nd Round of 16)
2002	Final Tournament (2nd Round of 16)
2006	Final Tournament (Group Stage)
2010	Final Tournament (Quarter-Finals)
2014	Qualifiers

PANAMERICAN GAMES	
1951	5th Place
1955	Did not enter
1959	Did not enter
1963	Did not enter
1967	Did not enter
1971	Did not enter
1975	Did not enter
1979	Did not enter
1983	Did not enter
1987	Round 1
1991	Did not enter
1995	Quarter-Finals
1999	Did not enter
2003	Round 1
2007	Did not enter
2011	Did not enter

PANAMERICAN CHAMPIONSHIP	
1952	Did not enter
1956	Did not enter
1960	Did not enter

PARAGUAYAN CLUB HONOURS IN SOUTH AMERICAN CLUB COMPETITIONS:

COPA LIBERTADORES 1960-2014
Club Olimpia Asunción (1979, 1990, 2002)
COPA SUDAMERICANA 2002-2014
None
RECOPA SUDAMERICANA 1989-2014
Club Olimpia Asunción (1991, 2003)
COPA CONMEBOL 1992-1999
None
SUPERCUP „JOÃO HAVELANGE" 1988-1997*
Club Olimpia Asunción (1990)
COPA MERCONORTE 1998-2001**
None

**Contested betwenn winners of all previous editions of the Copa Libertadores*
***Contested between teams belonging countries from the southern part of South America (Argentina, Brazil, Chile, Paraguay and Uruguay).*

NATIONAL COMPETITIONS TABLE OF HONOURS

NATIONAL CHAMPIONS 1906-2014	
	Amateur Era Championship
1906	Club Guaraní Asunción
1907	Club Guaraní Asunción
1908	*No championship*
1909	Club Nacional Asunción
1910	Club Libertad Asunción
1911	Club Nacional Asunción
1912	Club Olimpia Asunción
1913	Club Cerro Porteño Asunción
1914	Club Olimpia Asunción
1915	Club Cerro Porteño Asunción
1916	Club Olimpia Asunción
1917	Club Libertad Asunción
1918	Club Cerro Porteño Asunción
1919	Club Cerro Porteño Asunción
1920	Club Libertad Asunción
1921	Club Guaraní Asunción
1922	*No championship*
1923	Club Guaraní Asunción
1924	Club Nacional Asunción
1925	Club Olimpia Asunción
1926	Club Nacional Asunción
1927	Club Olimpia Asunción
1928	Club Olimpia Asunción
1929	Club Olimpia Asunción
1930	Club Libertad Asunción
1931	Club Olimpia Asunción
1932	*No championship*

1933	*No championship*
1934	*No championship*
	Professional Era Championship
1935	Club Cerro Porteño Asunción
1936	Club Olimpia Asunción
1937	Club Olimpia Asunción
1938	Club Olimpia Asunción
1939	Club Cerro Porteño Asunción
1940	Club Cerro Porteño Asunción
1941	Club Cerro Porteño Asunción
1942	Club Nacional Asunción
1943	Club Libertad Asunción
1944	Club Cerro Porteño Asunción
1945	Club Libertad Asunción
1946	Club Nacional Asunción
1947	Club Olimpia Asunción
1948	Club Olimpia Asunción
1949	Club Guaraní Asunción
1950	Club Cerro Porteño Asunción
1951	Club Sportivo Luqueño
1952	Club Presidente Hayes Asunción
1953	Club Sportivo Luqueño
1954	Club Cerro Porteño Asunción
1955	Club Libertad Asunción
1956	Club Olimpia Asunción
1957	Club Olimpia Asunción
1958	Club Olimpia Asunción
1959	Club Olimpia Asunción
1960	Club Olimpia Asunción
1961	Club Cerro Porteño Asunción
1962	Club Olimpia Asunción
1963	Club Cerro Porteño Asunción
1964	Club Guaraní Asunción
1965	Club Olimpia Asunción
1966	Club Cerro Porteño Asunción
1967	Club Guaraní Asunción
1968	Club Olimpia Asunción
1969	Club Guaraní Asunción
1970	Club Cerro Porteño Asunción
1971	Club Olimpia Asunción
1972	Club Cerro Porteño Asunción
1973	Club Cerro Porteño Asunción
1974	Club Cerro Porteño Asunción
1975	Club Olimpia Asunción
1976	Club Libertad Asunción
1977	Club Cerro Porteño Asunción
1978	Club Olimpia Asunción
1979	Club Olimpia Asunción
1980	Club Olimpia Asunción
1981	Club Olimpia Asunción
1982	Club Olimpia Asunción
1983	Club Olimpia Asunción

1984	Club Guaraní Asunción
1985	Club Olimpia Asunción
1986	Club Sol de América Asunción
1987	Club Cerro Porteño Asunción
1988	Club Olimpia Asunción
1989	Club Olimpia Asunción
1990	Club Cerro Porteño Asunción
1991	Club Sol de América Asunción
1992	Club Cerro Porteño Asunción
1993	Club Olimpia Asunción
1994	Club Cerro Porteño Asunción
1995	Club Olimpia Asunción
1996	Club Cerro Porteño Asunción
1997	Club Olimpia Asunción
1998	Club Olimpia Asunción
1999	Club Olimpia Asunción
2000	Club Olimpia Asunción
2001	Club Cerro Porteño Asunción
2002	Club Libertad Asunción
2003	Club Libertad Asunción
2004	Club Cerro Porteño Asunción
2005	Club Cerro Porteño Asunción
2006	Club Libertad Asunción
2007	Club Libertad Asunción
2008	Ape: Club Libertad Asunción
	Cla: Club Libertad Asunción
2009	Ape: Club Cerro Porteño Asunción
	Cla: Club Nacional Asunción
2010	Ape: Club Guaraní Asunción
	Cla: Club Libertad Asunción
2011	Ape: Club Nacional Asunción
	Cla: Club Olimpia Asunción
2012	Ape: Club Cerro Porteño Asunción
	Cla: Club Libertad Asunción
2013	Ape: Club Nacional Asunción
	Cla: Club Cerro Porteño Asunción
2014	Ape: Club Libertad Asunción
	Cla: Club Libertad Asunción

	BEST GOALSCORERS	
1935	Pedro Osorio (Club Cerro Porteño Asunción)	18
1936	Flaminio Silva (Club Olimpia Asunción)	36
1937	Francisco Sosa (Club Cerro Porteño Asunción)	21
1938	Martín Flor (Club Cerro Porteño Asunción) Amado Salinas (Club Libertad Asunción)	17
1939	Teófilo Salinas (Club Libertad Asunción)	28
1940	José Vinsac (Club Cerro Porteño Asunción)	30
1941	Benjamín Laterza (Club Cerro Porteño Asunción) Fabio Franco (Club Nacional Asunción)	18
1942	Francisco Sosa (Club Cerro Porteño Asunción)	23
1943	Atilio Mellone (Club Guaraní Asunción)	27

1944	Porfirio Rolón (Club Libertad Asunción) Sixto Noceda (Club Presidente Hayes Asunción)	18
1945	Porfirio Rolón (Club Libertad Asunción)	18
1946	Leocadio Marín (Club Olimpia Asunción)	26
1947	Leocadio Marín (Club Olimpia Asunción)	27
1948	Fabio Franco (Club Nacional Asunción)	24
1949	Darío Jara Saguier (Club Cerro Porteño Asunción)	18
1950	Darío Jara Saguier (Club Cerro Porteño Asunción)	18
1951	Antonio Ramón Gómez (Club Libertad Asunción)	19
1952	Antonio Ramón Gómez (Club Libertad Asunción) Rubén Fernández Real (Club Libertad Asunción)	16
1953	Antonio Acosta (Club Presidente Hayes Asunción)	15
1954	Máximo Rolón (Club Libertad Asunción)	24
1955	Máximo Rolón (Club Libertad Asunción)	25
1956	Máximo Rolón (Club Libertad Asunción)	26
1957	Juan Bautista Agüero (Club Olimpia Asunción)	14
1958	Juan Bautista Agüero (Club Olimpia Asunción)	16
1959	Ramón Rodríguez (Club River Plate Asunción)	17
1960	Benigno Gilberto Penayo (Club Cerro Porteño Asunción)	18
1961	Justo Pastor Leiva (Club Guaraní Asunción)	17
1962	Cecilio Martínez (Club Nacional Asunción)	19
1963	Juan Cabañas (Club Libertad Asunción)	17
1964	Genaro García (Club Guaraní Asunción) A. Jara (Club Sol de América Asunción) Antonio González (Club Rubio Ñu Asunción)	8
1965	Genaro García (Club Guaraní Asunción)	15
1966	Celino Mora (Club Cerro Porteño Asunción)	14
1967	Sebastián Fleitas Miranda (Club Libertad Asunción)	18
1968	Pedro Antonio Cibils (Club Libertad Asunción)	13
1969	Benicio Ferreira (Club Olimpia Asunción)	13
1970	Saturnino Arrúa (Club Cerro Porteño Asunción)	19
1971	Cristóbal Maldonado (Club Libertad Asunción)	11
1972	Saturnino Arrúa (Club Cerro Porteño Asunción)	17
1973	Mario Beron (Club Cerro Porteño Asunción) Clemente Rolón (Club River Plate Asunción)	15
1974	Mario Beron (Club Cerro Porteño Asunción) Fermín Cabrera (Club Sportivo Luqueño)	10
1975	Hugo Enrique Kiesse (Club Olimpia Asunción)	12
1976	Arsenio Meza (Club River Plate Asunción)	11
1977	Gustavo Fanego (Club Guaraní Asunción)	12
1978	Enrique Villalba (Club Olimpia Asunción)	10
1979	Edgar Ozuna (Club Capitán Figari Lambaré)	10
1980	Miguel Michelagnoli (Club Olimpia Asunción)	11
1981	Eulalio Mora (Club Guaraní Asunción)	9
1982	Pedro Fernánez (Club River Plate Asunción)	13
1983	Rafael Bobadilla (Club Olimpia Asunción)	14
1984	Amancio Mereles (Club River Plate Asunción) Milciades Morel (Club Cerro Porteño Asunción)	12
1985	Adriano Samaniego Giménez (Club Olimpia Asunción)	19
1986	Félix Ricardo Torres (Club Sol de América Asunción)	13
1987	Félix Brítez Román (Club Cerro Porteño Asunción)	11
1988	Raúl Vicente Amarilla (Club Olimpia Asunción)	17

1989		Jorge López (Club Sportivo San Lorenzo)	16
1990		Buenaventura Ferreira Gómez (Club Libertad Asunción / Club Cerro Porteño Asunción) Julio César Romero (Club Sportivo Luqueño)	17
1991		Carlos Luis Torres (Club Olimpia Asunción) Lilio Torales (Club Atlético Colegiales)	12
1992		Felipe Nery Franco (Club Libertad Asunción)	13
1993		Francisco Flaminio Ferreira Romero (Club Sportivo Luqueño)	13
1994		Héctor Núñez Bello (URU, Club Cerro Porteño Asunción)	27
1995		Héctor Núñez Bello (URU, Club Cerro Porteño Asunción)	17
1996		Arístides Miguel Rojas Aranda (Club Guaraní Asunción)	22
1997		Luis Molinas (Club Nacional Asunción / Club Atlético Tembetary Yparé)	13
1998		Mauro Antonio Caballero (Club Olimpia Asunción)	21
1999		Paulo Roberto Junges „Gauchinho" (BRA, Club Cerro Porteño Asunción)	22
2000		Francisco Flaminio Ferreira Romero (Club Cerro Porteño Asunción)	23
2001		Mauro Antonio Caballero López (Club Cerro Porteño Asunción / Club Libertad Asunción)	13
2002		Juan Eduardo Samudio Serna (Club Libertad Asunción)	23
2003		Erwin Lorenzo Ávalos (Club Cerro Porteño Asunción)	17
2004		Juan Eduardo Samudio Serna (Club Libertad Asunción)	22
2005		Dante Rafael López Fariña (Club Nacional Asunción / Club Olimpia Asunción)	21
2006		Hernán Rodrigo López Mora (URU, Club Libertad Asunción)	27
2007		Fabio Ramón Ramos Mereles (Club Nacional Asunción) Pablo Daniel Zeballos Ocampos (Club Sol de América Asunción)	15
2008	Ape:	Fabio Escobar Benítez (Club Nacional Asunción)	13
	Cla:	Edgar Benítez Santander (Club Sol de América Asunción)	14
2009	Ape:	Pablo César Leonardo Velázquez Centurión (Club Rubio Ñu Asunción)	16
	Cla:	César Cáceres Cañete (Club Guaraní Asunción)	11
2010	Ape:	Rodrigo Teixeira Pereira (BRA, Club Guaraní Asunción) Pablo Daniel Zeballos Ocampos (Club Cerro Porteño Asunción)	16
	Cla:	Juan Carlos Ferreyra (ARG, Club Olimpia Asunción) Roberto Antonio Nanni (ARG, Club Cerro Porteño Asunción)	12
2011	Ape:	Pablo Daniel Zeballos Ocampos (Club Olimpia Asunción)	13
	Cla:	Freddy José Barreiro Gamarra (Club Cerro Porteño Asunción)	13
2012	Ape:	José María Ortigoza Ortíz (Club Sol de América Asunción)	13
	Cla:	José Ariel Nuñez Portelli (Club Libertad Asunción)	13
2013	Ape:	Julián Alfonso Benítez Franco (Club Nacional Asunción)	13
	Cla:	Hernán Rodrigo López Mora (URU, Club Sportivo Luqueño)	17
2014	Ape:	Hernán Rodrigo López Mora (URU, Club Libertad Asunción) Christian Gilberto Ovelar Rodríguez (Club Sol de América Asunción)	19
	Cla:	Fernando Fabián Fernández Acosta (Club Guaraní Asunción)	17

NATIONAL CHAMPIONSHIP
División Profesional - 2014 Copa TIGO-Visión Banco
Torneo Apertura 2014

Results

Round 1 [14-16.02.2014]
Libertad - Guaraní 2-0(2-0)
3 de Febrero - Deportivo Capiatá 0-0
General Díaz - Olimpia 1-3(0-2)
Nacional - Sportivo Luqueño 3-0(1-0)
Sol de América - Rubio Ñu 2-2(1-1)
12 de Octubre - Cerro Porteño 1-3(0-3)

Round 2 [21-23.02.2014]
Cerro Porteño - 3 de Febrero 2-1(1-0)
Guaraní - Olimpia 2-1(1-0)
Deportivo Capiatá - Sol de América 0-0
Rubio Ñu - Nacional 4-1(1-0)
12 de Octubre - General Díaz 1-1(0-0)
Sportivo Luqueño - Libertad 0-0

Round 3 [28.02.-02.03.2014]
General Díaz - Guaraní 3-1(1-0)
3 de Febrero - 12 de Octubre 3-2(2-1)
Libertad - Rubio Ñu 3-1(2-1)
Nacional - Deportivo Capiatá 3-1(3-0)
Olimpia - Sportivo Luqueño 1-1(1-0)
Sol de América - Cerro Porteño 4-4(1-1)

Round 4 [07-10.03.2014]
12 de Octubre - Sol de América 0-3(0-1)
Cerro Porteño - Nacional 0-1(0-0)
Sportivo Luqueño - Guaraní 1-4(1-1)
3 de Febrero - General Díaz 1-1(1-1)
Rubio Ñu - Olimpia 2-1(1-1)
Deportivo Capiatá - Libertad 1-5(0-3)

Round 5 [14-16.03.2014]
General Díaz - Sportivo Luqueño 0-1(0-0)
Sol de América - 3 de Febrero 1-1(1-1)
Olimpia - Deportivo Capiatá 2-1(2-0)
Guaraní - Rubio Ñu 2-2(1-0)
Nacional - 12 de Octubre 1-0(1-0)
Libertad - Cerro Porteño 3-1(2-1)

Round 6 [21-23.03.2014]
Deportivo Capiatá - Guaraní 0-2(0-0)
Rubio Ñu - Sportivo Luqueño 1-4(1-2)
Sol de América - General Díaz 4-2(2-2)
12 de Octubre - Libertad 1-2(1-0)
Cerro Porteño - Olimpia 2-2(0-1)
3 de Febrero - Nacional 0-2(0-0) [29.05.]

Round 7 [29.03-01.04.2014]
General Díaz - Rubio Ñu 1-1(0-1)
Olimpia - 12 de Octubre 1-1(1-0)
Sportivo Luqueño - Deportivo Capiatá 1-1(1-0)
Libertad - 3 de Febrero 4-1(1-0)
Guaraní - Cerro Porteño 3-0(0-0)
Nacional - Sol de América 2-1(1-1)

Round 8 [04-06.04.2014]
Cerro Porteño - Sportivo Luqueño 0-0
12 de Octubre - Guaraní 2-2(0-0)
Nacional - General Díaz 0-0
Deportivo Capiatá - Rubio Ñu 4-0(1-0)
Sol de América - Libertad 1-1(1-1)
3 de Febrero - Olimpia 1-5(1-4)

Round 9 [12-14.04.2014]
General Díaz - Deportivo Capiatá 1-1(0-0)
Rubio Ñu - Cerro Porteño 3-3(1-1)
Guaraní - 3 de Febrero 2-1(1-1)
Sportivo Luqueño - 12 de Octubre 1-2(1-0)
Olimpia - Sol de América 1-1(1-0)
Libertad - Nacional 1-0(0-0)

Round 10 [19-21.04.2014]
3 de Febrero - Sportivo Luqueño 0-2(0-0)
12 de Octubre - Rubio Ñu 0-3(0-2)
Nacional - Olimpia 0-2(0-2)
Libertad - General Díaz 5-0(1-0)
Sol de América - Guaraní 0-4(0-1)
Cerro Porteño - Deportivo Capiatá 7-0(4-0)

Round 11 [25-27.04.2014]
General Díaz - Cerro Porteño 1-1(1-1)
Rubio Ñu - 3 de Febrero 5-1(3-1)
Guaraní - Nacional 0-4(0-1)
Deportivo Capiatá - 12 de Octubre 2-2(2-1)
Sportivo Luqueño - Sol de América 1-3(0-1)
Olimpia - Libertad 2-1(2-0)

Round 12 [03-04.05.2014]
Sportivo Luqueño - Nacional 1-1(0-0)
Rubio Ñu - Sol de América 0-2(0-1)
Cerro Porteño - 12 de Octubre 4-1(4-1)
Deportivo Capiatá - 3 de Febrero 2-2(0-1)
Guaraní - Libertad 2-4(1-2)
Olimpia - General Díaz 1-0(1-0)

Round 13 [09-10.05.2014]
General Díaz - 12 de Octubre 1-0(0-0)
Libertad - Sportivo Luqueño 3-2(1-1)
Sol de América - Deportivo Capiatá 3-0(1-0)
Olimpia - Guaraní 1-1(1-0)
3 de Febrero - Cerro Porteño 1-1(0-0)
Nacional - Rubio Ñu 0-1(0-1)

Round 14 [13-14.05.2014]
Sportivo Luqueño - Olimpia 1-0(0-0)
Guaraní - General Díaz 2-0(1-0)
12 de Octubre - 3 de Febrero 1-1(0-1)
Rubio Ñu - Libertad 0-1(0-0)
Cerro Porteño - Sol de América 6-3(4-0)
Deportivo Capiatá - Nacional 2-1(1-1) [04.06.]

Round 15 [17-18.05.2014]
Guaraní - Sportivo Luqueño 1-0(1-0)
Olimpia - Rubio Ñu 3-0(3-0)
General Díaz - 3 de Febrero 2-3(1-2)
Libertad - Deportivo Capiatá 0-0
Sol de América - 12 de Octubre 1-1(1-0)
Nacional - Cerro Porteño 2-1(2-0)

Round 16 [24-25.05.2014]
12 de Octubre - Nacional 1-1(1-0)
Rubio Ñu - Guaraní 1-4(1-0)
Deportivo Capiatá - Olimpia 2-0(1-0)
Sportivo Luqueño - General Díaz 0-0
3 de Febrero - Sol de América 0-1(0-1)
Cerro Porteño - Libertad 4-0(2-0)

Round 17 [30.05.-01.06.2014]
Sportivo Luqueño - Rubio Ñu 1-1(1-0)
General Díaz - Sol de América 2-1(0-0)
Nacional - 3 de Febrero 0-0
Guaraní - Deportivo Capiatá 6-0(2-0)
Libertad - 12 de Octubre 1-0(0-0)
Olimpia - Cerro Porteño 0-2(0-1) [19.06.]

Round 18 [06-08.06.2014]
Rubio Ñu - General Díaz 4-0(0-0)
Cerro Porteño - Guaraní 5-5(4-1)
3 de Febrero - Libertad 0-2(0-1)
12 de Octubre - Olimpia 1-1(1-0)
Deportivo Capiatá - Sportivo Luqueño 1-1(0-1)
Sol de América - Nacional 1-1(1-0)

Round 19 [10-12.06.2014]
Guaraní - 12 de Octubre 2-1(1-0)
General Díaz - Nacional 2-0(1-0)
Rubio Ñu - Deportivo Capiatá 1-0(1-0)
Sportivo Luqueño - Cerro Porteño 1-0(1-0)
Olimpia - 3 de Febrero 3-2(1-0)
Libertad - Sol de América 0-0

Round 20 [14-16.06.2014]
Cerro Porteño - Rubio Ñu 1-4(0-1)
Deportivo Capiatá - General Díaz 1-0(0-0)
12 de Octubre - Sportivo Luqueño 1-1(1-1)
3 de Febrero - Guaraní 0-2(0-1)
Sol de América - Olimpia 3-0(1-0)
Nacional - Libertad 1-1(0-0)

Round 21 [20-22.06.2014]
Rubio Ñu - 12 de Octubre 1-2(0-1)
General Díaz - Libertad 0-1(0-0)
Guaraní - Sol de América 3-1(2-0)
Deportivo Capiatá - Cerro Porteño 1-0(1-0)
Sportivo Luqueño - 3 de Febrero 3-2(1-0)
Olimpia - Nacional 2-0(0-0)

Round 22 [26-28.06.2014]
Nacional - Guaraní 2-6(0-1)
12 de Octubre - Deportivo Capiatá 0-2(0-0)
Sol de América - Sportivo Luqueño 0-0
Cerro Porteño - General Díaz 2-1(1-1)
3 de Febrero - Rubio Ñu 1-1(1-1)
Libertad - Olimpia 1-0(0-0)

Final Standings

1.	**Club Libertad Asunción**	22	15	5	2	41	-	17	50
2.	Club Guaraní Asunción	22	14	4	4	56	-	31	46
3.	Club Olimpia Asunción	22	9	6	7	32	-	26	33
4.	Club Cerro Porteño Asunción	22	8	7	7	49	-	38	31
5.	Club Sol de América Asunción	22	7	10	5	36	-	31	31
6.	Club Rubio Ñu Asunción	22	8	6	8	38	-	37	30
7.	Club Nacional Asunción	22	8	6	8	26	-	27	30
8.	Club Sportivo Luqueño	22	6	10	6	23	-	25	28
9.	Club Deportivo Capiatá	22	6	8	8	22	-	37	26
10.	Club General Díaz Luque	22	4	7	11	19	-	34	19
11.	12 de Octubre Football Club Itauguá	22	2	9	11	21	-	38	15
12.	Club Atlético 3 de Febrero Ciudad del Este	22	2	8	12	22	-	44	14

Top goalscorers:

19 goals:	**Hernán Rodrigo López Mora (URU)**	**(Club Libertad Asunción)**
	Christian Gilberto Ovelar Rodríguez	**(Club Sol de América Asunción)**
17 goals:	Jorge Daniel Benítez Guillén	(Club Guaraní Asunción)
14 goals:	Fernando Fabián Fernández Acosta	(Club Guaraní Asunción)
13 goals:	Guillermo Alexis Beltrán Paredes	(Club Cerro Porteño Asunción)

NATIONAL CHAMPIONSHIP
División Profesional - 2014 Copa TIGO-Visión Banco
Torneo Clausura 2014

Results

Round 1 [25-27.07.2014]
Nacional - Deportivo Capiatá 0-3(0-1)
Sol de América - Libertad 2-3(0-1)
Sportivo Luqueño - Rubio Ñu 0-0
12 de Octubre - Guaraní 1-1(0-0)
3 de Febrero - Olimpia 1-3(0-1)
General Díaz - Cerro Porteño 3-2(1-1)

Round 2 [02-03.08.2014]
Deportivo Capiatá - Sol de América 1-1(0-0)
Rubio Ñu - Nacional 1-2(0-1)
3 de Febrero - General Díaz 2-1(2-1)
Libertad - Cerro Porteño 0-0
Guaraní - Sportivo Luqueño 2-0(1-0)
Olimpia - 12 de Octubre 2-0(2-0)

Round 3 [09-10.08.2014]
12 de Octubre - 3 de Febrero 1-1(1-0)
Sol de América - Rubio Ñu 1-0(1-0)
Nacional - Guaraní 0-1(0-0)
Cerro Porteño - Deportivo Capiatá 1-0(1-0)
Sportivo Luqueño - Olimpia 1-1(0-0)
General Díaz - Libertad 0-1(0-1)

Round 4 [15-17.08.2014]
12 de Octubre - General Díaz 3-2(1-1)
Rubio Ñu - Cerro Porteño 0-4(0-0)
Deportivo Capiatá - Libertad 1-0(1-0)
3 de Febrero - Sportivo Luqueño 0-1(0-0)
Guaraní - Sol de América 3-0(0-0)
Olimpia - Nacional 0-1(0-0)

Round 5 [23-24.08.2014]
Nacional - 3 de Febrero 1-0(0-0)
Cerro Porteño - Guaraní 1-4(0-2)
Sportivo Luqueño - 12 de Octubre 2-1(0-0)
Libertad - Rubio Ñu 5-1(2-0)
General Díaz - Deportivo Capiatá 2-0(0-0)
Sol de América - Olimpia 1-2(1-0)

Round 6 [30-31.08.2014]
3 de Febrero - Sol de América 1-1(1-0)
Olimpia - Cerro Porteño 1-0(1-0)
Sportivo Luqueño - General Díaz 1-1(0-0)
Rubio Ñu - Deportivo Capiatá 3-0(0-0)
Guaraní - Libertad 5-1(3-1)
12 de Octubre - Nacional 1-1(1-1) [17.09.]

Round 7 [05-07.09.2014]
General Díaz - Rubio Ñu 2-1(1-1)
Deportivo Capiatá - Guaraní 1-0(1-0)
Libertad - Olimpia 3-1(2-0)
Sol de América - 12 de Octubre 2-3(1-2)
Nacional - Sportivo Luqueño 2-1(2-0) [24.09.]
Cerro Porteño - 3 de Febrero 2-0(2-0) [08.10.]

Round 8 [12-14.09.2014]
12 de Octubre - Cerro Porteño 0-2(0-1)
Olimpia - Deportivo Capiatá 2-0(0-0)
Guaraní - Rubio Ñu 0-0
Sportivo Luqueño - Sol de América 2-0(0-0)
Nacional - General Díaz 2-0(2-0)
3 de Febrero - Libertad 2-0(0-0) [25.09.]

Round 9 [19-21.09.2014]
General Díaz - Guaraní 1-1(1-0)
Deportivo Capiatá - 3 de Febrero 2-3(1-3)
Cerro Porteño - Sportivo Luqueño 4-0(1-0)
Rubio Ñu - Olimpia 0-2(0-0)
Sol de América - Nacional 1-0(0-0)
Libertad - 12 de Octubre 2-0(0-0)

Round 10 [27-29.09.2014]
Olimpia - Guaraní 1-2(1-1)
3 de Febrero - Rubio Ñu 0-0
Sportivo Luqueño - Libertad 1-0(1-0)
Sol de América - General Díaz 0-1(0-0)
Nacional - Cerro Porteño 0-1(0-1)
12 de Octubre - Deportivo Capiatá 2-3(1-2)

Round 11 [01-02.10.2014]
Guaraní - 3 de Febrero 2-3(1-0)
Deportivo Capiatá - Sportivo Luqueño 1-3(1-2)
Libertad - Nacional 0-0
General Díaz - Olimpia 1-1(1-1)
Rubio Ñu - 12 de Octubre 3-1(1-0)
Cerro Porteño - Sol de América 2-0(1-0)

Round 12 [04-06.10.2014]
Olimpia - 3 de Febrero 0-1(0-0)
Deportivo Capiatá - Nacional 2-3(0-1)
Libertad - Sol de América 3-0(0-0)
Rubio Ñu - Sportivo Luqueño 2-2(2-2)
Cerro Porteño - General Díaz 3-1(2-0)
Guaraní - 12 de Octubre 2-1(1-0)

Round 13 [10-12.10.2014]
Sol de América - Deportivo Capiatá 1-1(1-0)
General Díaz - 3 de Febrero 1-0(0-0)
Cerro Porteño - Libertad 2-2(2-2)
Sportivo Luqueño - Guaraní 2-2(0-1)
12 de Octubre - Olimpia 2-1(0-0)
Nacional - Rubio Ñu 2-1(0-1) [29.10.]

Round 14 [17-20.10.2014]
Rubio Ñu - Sol de América 1-1(0-1)
Deportivo Capiatá - Cerro Porteño 1-1(0-1)
Olimpia - Sportivo Luqueño 1-1(0-0)
3 de Febrero - 12 de Octubre 0-2(0-0)
Libertad - General Díaz 6-0(3-0)
Guaraní - Nacional 0-0

Round 15 [24-26.10.2014]
General Díaz - 12 de Octubre 1-0(0-0)
Sol de América - Guaraní 3-1(1-1)
Nacional - Olimpia 0-2(0-1)
Cerro Porteño - Rubio Ñu 1-1(1-1)
Sportivo Luqueño - 3 de Febrero 2-1(0-1)
Libertad - Deportivo Capiatá 2-1(0-1)

Round 16 [02-04.11.2014]
12 de Octubre - Sportivo Luqueño 0-1(0-1)
Deportivo Capiatá - General Díaz 1-1(0-1)
3 de Febrero - Nacional 2-1(1-0)
Olimpia - Sol de América 1-1(0-0)
Rubio Ñu - Libertad 0-3(0-1)
Guaraní - Cerro Porteño 3-4(1-2) [20.11.]

Round 17 [08-09.11.2014]
General Díaz - Sportivo Luqueño 1-2(0-2)
Sol de América - 3 de Febrero 3-2(2-2)
Deportivo Capiatá - Rubio Ñu 2-0(1-0)
Nacional - 12 de Octubre 1-0(1-0)
Cerro Porteño - Olimpia 1-1(1-0)
Libertad - Guaraní 4-1(2-0)

Round 18 [12-13.11.2014]
12 de Octubre - Sol de América 2-4(0-1)
3 de Febrero - Cerro Porteño 0-5(0-3)
Sportivo Luqueño - Nacional 1-1(0-1)
Rubio Ñu - General Díaz 1-1(1-0)
Olimpia - Libertad 0-1(0-0)
Guaraní - Deportivo Capiatá 4-1(1-0)

Round 19 [15-17.11.2014]
General Díaz - Nacional 0-1(0-1)
Sol de América - Sportivo Luqueño 2-0(1-0)
Deportivo Capiatá - Olimpia 0-3(0-0)
Rubio Ñu - Guaraní 1-3(0-2)
Cerro Porteño - 12 de Octubre 4-2(1-1)
Libertad - 3 de Febrero 1-1(0-0)

Round 20 [22-24.11.2014]
Nacional - Sol de América 0-0
Olimpia - Rubio Ñu 0-0
3 de Febrero - Deportivo Capiatá 2-1(2-0)
12 de Octubre - Libertad 0-2(0-2)
Sportivo Luqueño - Cerro Porteño 1-0(0-0)
Guaraní - General Díaz 4-2(2-0)

Round 21 [28-30.11.2014]
General Díaz - Sol de América 1-0(1-0)
Rubio Ñu - 3 de Febrero 1-0(0-0)
Deportivo Capiatá - 12 de Octubre 0-0
Guaraní - Olimpia 4-2(3-0)
Cerro Porteño - Nacional 1-0(1-0)
Libertad - Sportivo Luqueño 1-0(0-0)

Round 22 [04-06.12.2014]
12 de Octubre - Rubio Ñu 1-4(1-1)
Olimpia - General Díaz 1-3(0-1)
3 de Febrero - Guaraní 0-4(0-2)
Sportivo Luqueño - Deportivo Capiatá 0-0
Nacional - Libertad 0-1(0-0)
Sol de América - Cerro Porteño 0-2(0-0)

Final Standings

1.	**Club Libertad Asunción**	22	14	4	4	41	-	18	46
2.	Club Cerro Porteño Asunción	22	13	5	4	43	-	20	44
3.	Club Guaraní Asunción	22	12	5	5	49	-	29	41
4.	Club Sportivo Luqueño	22	9	8	5	24	-	23	35
5.	Club Nacional Asunción	22	9	5	8	18	-	19	32
6.	Club Olimpia Asunción	22	8	6	8	28	-	24	30
7.	Club General Díaz Luque	22	8	5	9	26	-	33	29
8.	Club Atlético 3 de Febrero Ciudad del Este	22	7	4	11	22	-	35	25
9.	Club Sol de América Asunción	22	6	6	10	24	-	32	24
10.	Club Deportivo Capiatá	22	5	6	11	22	-	34	21
11.	Club Rubio Ñu Asunción	22	4	8	10	21	-	33	20
12.	12 de Octubre Football Club Itauguá	22	4	4	14	23	-	41	16

Top goalscorers:

17 goals:	**Fernando Fabián Fernández Acosta**	**(Club Guaraní Asunción)**
11 goals:	Federico Javier Santander Mereles	(Club Guaraní Asunción)
10 goals:	José María Ortigoza Ortíz	(Club Cerro Porteño Asunción)
9 goals:	Christian Gilberto Ovelar Rodríguez	(Club Olimpia Asunción)

Aggregate Table 2014

1.	Club Libertad Asunción	44	29	9	6	82 - 35	96
2.	Club Guaraní Asunción	44	26	9	9	105 - 60	87
3.	Club Cerro Porteño Asunción	44	21	12	11	91 - 58	75
4.	Club Olimpia Asunción	44	15	18	11	47 - 48	63
5.	Club Sportivo Luqueño	44	17	12	15	60 - 50	63
6.	Club Nacional Asunción	44	17	11	16	44 - 46	62
7.	Club Sol de América Asunción	44	13	16	15	60 - 63	55
8.	Club Rubio Ñu Asunción	44	12	14	18	59 - 70	50
9.	Club General Díaz Luque	44	12	12	20	45 - 67	48
10.	Club Deportivo Capiatá	44	11	14	19	44 - 71	47
11.	Club Atlético 3 de Febrero Ciudad del Este	44	9	12	23	44 - 79	39
12.	12 de Octubre Football Club Itauguá	44	6	13	25	44 - 79	31

Club Libertad Asunción qualified for the 2015 Copa Libertadores and 2015 Copa Sudamericana.
Club Guaraní Asunción and Club Cerro Porteño Asunción qualified for the 2015 Copa Libertadores.
Club Olimpia Asunción, Club Sportivo Luqueño and Club Nacional Asunción qualified for the 2015 Copa Sudamericana.

Relegation Table

The team which will be relegated is determined on average points taking into account results of the last six seasons (Apertura & Clausura 2012, Apertura & Clausura 2013, Apertura & Clausura 2014).

Pos	Team	2011	2012	2013	Total		Aver
		P	P	P	P	M	
1.	Club Libertad Asunción	91	75	96	262	132	1.9848
2.	Club Cerro Porteño Asunción	86	87	75	248	132	1.8788
3.	Club Guaraní Asunción	73	77	87	237	132	1.7955
4.	Club Nacional Asunción	77	79	62	218	132	1.6515
5.	Club Olimpia Asunción	79	55	63	197	132	1.4924
6.	Club Sportivo Luqueño	59	54	63	176	132	1.3333
7.	Club Deportivo Capiatá	—	65	47	111	88	1.2614
8.	Club General Díaz Luque	—	61	48	109	88	1.2386
9.	Club Sol de América Asunción	60	46	55	161	132	1.2197
10.	Club Rubio Ñu Asunción	36	50	50	136	132	1.0303
11.	Club Atlético 3 de Febrero Ciudad del Este (*Relegated*)	—	—	39	39	44	0.8864
12.	12 de Octubre Football Club Itauguá (*Relegated*)	—	—	31	31	44	0.7045

CLUB 12 DE OCTUBRE ITAUGUÁ

Foundation date: August 14, 1914
Address: Ruta Mariscal Estigarribia, Km. 30, Itauguá
Stadium: Estadio „ Juan Canuto Pettengill", Itauguá – Capacity: 5,000

THE SQUAD

	DOB	Ape M	Ape G	Cla M	Cla G
Goalkeepers:					
Jorge Candia				2	-
Juanito José Alfonso Guevara	24.06.1990	16	-	16	-
Mario Fleitas				1	-
Arístides Ramón Florentín Ocampos	10.05.1982			4	-
Derlis Venancio Gómez López	02.11.1972	3	-	-	-
Wilson Daniel Quiñonez Amarilla	04.09.1988	3	-		
Defenders:					
Wildo Javier Alonso Jara	30.07.1990	17	1	16	1
Lúcio Ricardo Báez Moninigo	05.02.1991	-	-	-	-
Jorge Luís Caballero Alonzo	10.03.1990	6	-	10	-
Germán Martín Centurión Marecos	05.05.1980	18	1	12	1
Christian Ramón Enciso Barreto	12.05.1991	2	-	-	-
Luis Fernando Gavilán Cardozo	11.01.1991			7	1
César Andrés Godoy Ríos	14.08.1993			3	-
Walter González	12.11.1991	7	-	5	-
Richard Guerrero	09.04.1991	1	-	1	-
Elvis Israel Marecos	15.02.1980	2	-		
Eder Líder Mármol Cuenca	02.10.1985	12	1	-	-
Fidel Miño Cabrera	30.06.1986	5	-		
Francisco Miranda	30.06.1989	10	-	3	-
David Robles				12	1
Enrique Vázquez	01.10.1988	4	-	7	1
Midfielders:					
Juan Gabriel Abente Amarilla	04.03.1984			18	4
Roberto Miguel Acuña Cabello	25.03.1972	8	1		
Martín Benítez				2	-
Héctor Caballero	02.02.1988	10	-	19	-
Yimmy Adán Cano Morínigo	02.06.1986	14	-	17	-
Pedro Julián Chávez Ruiz	29.06.1985	7	1		
Osvaldo Javier Díaz Giménez	22.12.1981	6	-	6	-
Dario Adrián Ferreira Verón	16.02.1991	6	1	1	-
Juan Gauto	29.04.1994	6	1	-	-
Rodrigo Antonio Jacquet	15.12.1993			7	1
Joel David Lesme	17.07.1990	10	2	3	-
Carlos Damián Martínez Arce	28.05.1987	1	-	-	-
Carlos Ariel Recalde González	14.12.1993			3	-
Edgar Arnulfo Robles Coronel	22.11.1977	13	-	-	-
Pablo Rolón	15.04.1995	6	-	16	-
Fabian Ariel Stark Zelaya	30.10.1988			2	-
William Schuster Dornelles da Silva (BRA)	31.05.1987	19	1	14	-
Forwards:					
Jorge Daniel Achucarro	11.06.1981			19	1
Aurelio Acosta	05.02.1990	8	-	13	-

Jorge Manuel Armoa Ayala	11.08.1995	4	-	10	2
Néstor Ayala Villagra	18.02.1983	1	-		-
Rodrigo Bernal González	17.07.1993	1	-	5	-
Santiago Nicolás Caballero	27.03.1988	22	-	9	-
Richar Mariano Estigarribia Ortega	15.08.1982	14	4	2	-
Gerardo Isaac Fleitas				2	-
Tomás Andrés Guzmán Gaetan	07.03.1982	14	5	9	-
Júnior Irala	29.04.1994	1	-	-	-
Javier Benito Lezcano Obregón	24.09.1989	4	-	-	-
Héctor Martínez	31.12.1995	5	-	2	-
Angel Reinaldo Orué Echeverría	05.01.1989	15	2		
Ariel Roa	03.02.1993	7	-	14	2
Gustavo Ariel Santa Cruz González	21.07.1993			15	8
Trainer:					
Estanislao Struway Samaniego [01.01.-07.03.2014]	25.06.1968	4			
Felix Darío León [08.03.-19.06.2014]	05.05.1961	16			
Alicio Ignacio Solalinde Miers [20.06.-04.10.2014]	01.02.1952	2		12	
René Vázquez [05.10.-14.10.2014; Caretaker]				1	
Roque Vicente Yassogna (ARG) [13.10.-03.11.2014; Resigned]				4	
René Vázquez [as of 11.11.2014; Caretaker]				5	

CLUB ATLÉTICO 3 DE FEBRERO CIUDAD DEL ESTE

Foundation date: November 20, 1970
Address: Ruta 7, km 3, Ciudad del Este
Stadium: Estadio „Antonio Oddone Sarubbi“, Ciudad del Este – Capacity: 28,000

THE SQUAD

	DOB	Ape		Cla	
		M	G	M	G
Goalkeepers:					
Roque Alberto Cardozo	16.08.1987	1	-	6	-
Miguel López	07.04.1982	1	-	-	-
Orlando Ramón Rojas Cáceres	14.12.1983	4	-		
Antony Domingo Silva Cano	27.02.1984	16	-	17	-
Defenders:					
Diego Douglas Balbinot (BRA)	07.01.1984	10	1	-	-
Felipe Márcio Dallabrida (BRA)	14.05.1991	2	-		
Edgar Ramón Ferreira Gallas	31.08.1987	10	-	-	-
Ángel Fleitas	18.04.1993	2	-	-	-
Ever Hugo González	11.10.1986	21	1	16	-
Hugo Germán Iriarte (ARG)	26.03.1982			7	-
Jefferson Tiago de Moura Heinemann (BRA)	29.12.1993	1	-		
Ricardo Julián Martínez Pavón	18.02.1984			14	-
Richard José Matto	06.09.1986	12	-	1	-
Ricardo Mazacotte	09.01.1985	8	-	9	-
Juan Melgarejo		3	-	-	-
Wilson Heriberto Méndez Arévalos	25.05.1982	7	-	5	-
Leonardo Martín Miglionico (URU)	31.01.1980			7	1
Aldo David Olmedo Román	25.09.1989			16	-
Reinaldo Román Fernández	23.05.1984	14	-	1	-
Aníbal Ruíz Díaz				3	-

Midfielders:					
Anderson Omar Lima da Rosa „Amaral“ (BRA)	21.07.1989	13	-	3	1
Regis Adair Quaresma de Souza	25.01.1982	-	-	-	-
Rodrigo Ramón Burgos Oviedo	21.06.1989			14	-
Sergio Gustavo Escalante (ARG)	09.03.1986	5	-		
Víctor Sócrates Michael Genes Espínola	29.09.1987	10	-		
César Llamas Cantero	13.07.1985	21	3	20	2
Reinaldo Daniel López Escurra	28.12.1987	8	-	1	-
David Ariel Mendieta Chávez	22.08.1986	16	7	17	3
Raúl Olmedo	04.09.1994	1	-	-	-
Remigio Hernán Pérez Ortíz	12.02.1991			4	1
Juan Pablo Raponi (ARG)	07.05.1982	14	2	4	-
José Domingo Salcedo González	11.09.1983	19	-	18	-
Jorge Martín Salinas	06.05.1992	5	1	20	2
Pedro Agustín Vera Britez	20.04.1984	11	-	17	-
Washington Luis Jesus Veiga de Carvalho (BRA)	15.11.1985	1	-	-	-
Forwards:					
Julio Ramón Aguilar Franco	01.07.1986			3	-
Silvio Allende	02.03.1993	3	-	-	-
Luis Antonio Amarilla Lencina	25.08.1995	5	-		
Marcelo David Baez Casco	14.01.1991	5	-	14	-
Héctor Bustamante				13	-
José Benjamín Cáceres Burgos	04.09.1983			9	-
Cristian Colmán	26.02.1994	19	5	21	8
Johny Costella		1	-	-	-
Eduardo Da Silva	08.01.1994			-	-
Luís Fernando dos Santos (BRA)	22.10.1988	10	-	2	-
Jaime Hinterleitner Schening	03.06.1984	6	-	-	-
Rogério Luis Leichtweis	28.06.1988			14	2
Christian Riveros	09.08.1994	1	-	-	-
Édgar Riveros	13.03.1998	-	-	-	-
Hugo Sebastián Santacruz Villalba	06.02.1989	13	-	6	1
Trainer:					
Márcio Marolla dos Santos (BRA) [01.01.-12.04.2014]		9			
Carlos Alberto Kiese Wiesner [13.04.-31.05.2014]	01.06.1957	8			
Robson Retamozo (BRA) [01.06.-06.06.2014]		1			
Ricardo Mariano Dabrowski (ARG) [07.06.-29.08.2014]	28.03.1961	4		5	
Eduardo Rivera (URU) [as of 30.08.2014]				17	

CLUB CERRO PORTEÑO ASUNCIÓN

Foundation date: October 1, 1912
Address: Avenida 5ta, N° 828 c/ Tacuary, Barrio Obrero, Asunción
Stadium: Estadio „General Pablo Rojas", Asunción – Capacity: 32,000

THE SQUAD

	DOB	Ape M	Ape G	Cla M	Cla G
Goalkeepers:					
Diego Daniel Barreto Cáceres	16.07.1981	11	-	22	-
Roberto Júnior Fernández Torres	29.03.1988	11	-		
Carlos Alberto Gamarra Montanía jr.	06.06.1992	-	-	-	-
Pablo Martín Gavilán	18.07.1989	-	-	-	-
Defenders:					
Junior Osmar Ignacio Alonso Mujica	11.02.1993	17	1	13	1
César Iván Benítez León	28.05.1990	9	-	13	-
Carlos Bonet Cáceres	02.10.1977	13	-	19	-
Osmar Alexis Cantero Guillén	04.01.1995	2	-	-	-
Luis Carlos Cardozo Espillaga	10.10.1988	14	-		
Matías Corujo Díaz (URU)	08.05.1986	11	1		
Carlos González	09.01.1994	1	-	-	-
Víctor Hugo Mareco	26.02.1984	6	-	18	-
Carlos Montiel Cañiza	08.02.1994	1	-	3	-
Danilo Fabián Ortíz Soto	28.07.1992	17	-	13	-
Fidencio Oviedo Domínguez	30.05.1987	17	-	15	-
Carlos Montiel Cañiza	08.02.1994	1	-	3	-
Teodoro Paul Paredes Pavón	01.04.1993	2	-	-	-
Bruno Amilcar Valdez	06.10.1992			16	2
Diego Roberto Vera Cabrera	27.11.1989	8	2	-	-
Diego Francisco Viera Ruiz Díaz	30.04.1991	5	-	-	-
Midfielders:					
Miguel Ángel Almirón Rejala	13.11.1993	12	-	2	-
Willian Benito Candia Garay	27.03.1993	7	-	1	-
Júnior Danilo Coronel Pavón	10.02.1997	-	-	-	-
Julio Daniel Dos Santos Rodríguez	07.05.1983	13	6	20	7
Jonathan Fabbro (ARG)	16.01.1982			7	3
Juan José Franco Arrellaga	10.02.1992	5	-	9	-
Epifiano Ariel García Duarte	02.07.1992	4	-	1	-
Diego Armando Godoy Vásquez	01.04.1992	11	-	5	1
Alexis Joel González Belotto	07.01.1992	1	-	-	-
Santiago Ariel López Stockel	13.03.1996	7	-	-	-
Miguel Ángel Paniagua Rivarola	14.05.1987			14	-
Néstor Javier Ramírez Martínez	15.10.1990	3	-	-	-
Matías Rojas		1	-	-	-
Ángel Rodrigo Romero Villamayor	04.07.1992	12	11		
Óscar David Romero Villamayor	04.07.1992	18	2	20	3
Jonathan Santana Gehre	19.10.1981	10	-	12	-
Iván Arturo Torres Riveros	27.02.1991	6	1	3	-
Forwards:					
Guillermo Alexis Beltrán Paredes	26.04.1984	19	13	13	-
Enrique Javier Borja	30.05.1995	1	-	-	-
Sergio Ismael Díaz Velázquez	06.12.1998	1	-	19	8
Rodolfo Vicente Gamarra Varela	10.12.1988	16	3	9	3
Arnaldo Andrés Giménez Ayala		2	-	-	-
Daniel González Güiza (ESP)	17.08.1980	13	9	19	3
José María Ortigoza Ortíz	01.04.1987			17	10
Mauricio Ezequiel Sperdutti (ARG)	16.02.1986			17	1
Trainer:					
Francisco Javier Arce Rolón [06.03.2013-23.08.2014]	02.04.1971	22		5	
Roberto Ismael Torres Báez [23-27.08.2014; Caretaker]	06.04.1972			-	
Leonardo Rubén Astrada (ARG) [as of 28.08.2014]	06.01.1970			17	

CLUB DEPORTIVO CAPIATÁ

Foundation date: September 4, 2008
Address: Calle La Candelaria, Capiatá
Stadium: Estadio Deportivo, Capiatá – Capacity: 6,000

THE SQUAD

	DOB	Ape		Cla	
		M	G	M	G
Goalkeepers:					
Pablo Fernando Aurrecochea Medina (URU)	08.03.1981	7	-		
Antonio Alejandro Franco Arza	10.07.1991	13	-	9	-
Roberto Jara		3	-	3	-
Elio Martínez				1	-
Moisés Morales Martínez	04.01.1987	-	-	-	-
Tobías Antonio Vargas Insfrán	21.08.1989			10	-
Defenders:					
Máximo Alejandro Aguero Cabañas	27.06.1991	-	-	-	-
Arturo David Aquino	14.09.1982	9	-	12	-
Marcos Arce	03.05.1983	1	-	-	-
Víctor Hugo Ayala Ojeda	05.11.1988	11	-	12	-
Jorge Manuel Balbuena Carreras	07.06.1993			1	-
Diosnel Barreto		1	-	2	-
Jorge Darío Florentín	18.05.1987	2	-	-	-
Néstor Fabián González	09.05.1986	19	-	17	-
Julio César Irrazábal León	25.11.1980			5	-
Darío López Torres				5	1
Alexis Maciel		-	-	-	-
Jorge Martín Núñez Mendoza	22.01.1978	-	-	-	-
Jorge Rodrigo Paredes	23.04.1985	-	-	9	1
Arnaldo Javier Pereira Vera	11.01.1986			7	-
Alfredo David Rojas	30.12.1987	18	-	9	-
Pedro Pablo Sosa		3	-	-	-
Gustavo Alberto Velázquez Núñez	17.12.1987	9	-	7	-
Midfielders:					
Cristian Fernando Andersen Oviedo	03.06.1984	4	1		
Èdgar Enrique Balbuena Zevallos	20.01.1994	7	-	8	-
Jorge Luis Candia	17.03.1986	12	-	9	-
Rodrigo Díaz	13.09.1994	1	-	-	-
Fulvio Ramón Duarte Belotto	04.05.1989	5	-	-	-
Nelson Darío Figueredo Genés	17.12.1984	13	-	9	1
Jhon Steve Florez Guerrero (COL)	17.01.1982	2	-	-	-
Wálter Milcíades Fretes Bogarín	18.05.1982			4	-
Miguel Ángel Godoy Melgarejo	07.05.1983	4	-		
Blas Bernardo Irala Rojas	30.11.1983			13	1
Cristian Ariel López Leiva	31.12.1987	12	2	8	-
Ángel David Martínez	13.04.1989	20	-	19	1
Iván Meza				1	-
Fabián Ocampo				3	-
Reinaldo David Ocampo	06.01.1987			9	5
Derlis Fabián Ortíz Rodríguez	12.12.1986	9	-	7	-
Ricardo Javier Ortíz Pineda	22.08.1983	19	2	17	1
Félix Gustavo Romero Benítez	01.10.1987	18	-		
Carlos Gabriel Ruíz Peralta	17.07.1984			15	1
Óscar Ramón Ruíz Roa	14.05.1991	17	3	15	1

César Agustín Serna Sarabia	20.02.1992	8	-	-	-
Juan Villalba				3	-
Forwards:					
Diego Rubén Alfonso	05.09.1985	2	-	-	-
Jorge Sebastián Ayala Álvarez	04.07.1984			4	-
Lucas Chávez				1	-
Romero Pedro Delvalle	06.01.1994	6	-	-	-
Fabio Escobar Benítez	15.02.1982	18	9	18	7
Hernán Espínola Pacheco	28.04.1987			7	-
Amílcar Javier Franco Cuéllar	06.01.1987			3	-
Julio Galeano				5	-
Francisco Javier García	04.04.1991	11	2		
Porfirio Gauto	23.03.1992			2	-
Alexis López				1	-
Derlis Maidana		1	-	-	-
Bruno Mendieta		2	-	-	-
Raúl Basilio Román Garay	25.10.1977	3	1	10	1
Guillermo Rodríguez	17.10.1986			4	-
Sergio Cirilo Samudio	08.01.1987	11	1		
Jonathan Sánchez	28.02.1996	5	1	1	-
Milciades Daniel Silva	30.09.1985	-	-	1	-
Trainer:					
Mario César Jacquet Martínez [04.03.2013-22.04.2014]	29.07.1946	6			
Héctor Marecos [as of 23.04.2014]		16		22	

CLUB GUARANÍ ASUNCIÓN

Foundation date: October 12, 1903
Address: Avenida Dr. Eusebio Ayala N° 770 y Calle 1811, Barrio Dos Bocas, Asunción
Stadium: Estadio „Rogelio Livieres“, Asunción – Capacity: 6,000

THE SQUAD

	DOB	Ape		Cla	
		M	G	M	G
Goalkeepers:					
Alfredo Ariel Aguilar	18.07.1986	13	-	12	-
Alejandro Daniel Bogado Flecha	28.04.1994	-	-	-	-
Joel Alberto Silva Estigarribia	13.01.1989	9	-	11	-
Defenders:					
Édgar Manuel Aranda	05.09.1983	14	-	13	-
Tomás Javier Bartomeús	27.10.1982	10	-	8	-
Luis Alberto Cabral Vásquez	23.09.1983	22	1	22	2
Julio César Cáceres López	05.10.1979	22	2	18	-
Eric Tomás Cristaldo Paniagua	17.12.1990	8	-	4	-
Eduardo Javier Filippini (ARG)	05.06.1983	15	-	19	1
Adilson Antonio Lezcano	27.12.1994			10	-
Juan Gabriel Patiño Martinez	29.11.1989	1	-	4	-
Armando Marcelo Ruíz Díaz Galeano	14.07.1993	1	-	4	-
Óscar Basilio Velázquez Mendoza	19.04.1990	2	1		
Midfielders:					
Juan José Aguilar Orzusa	24.06.1989	10	1	19	2
Rodrigo Bogarín	24.05.1997			1	-
Luis Eladio de La Cruz	23.03.1991	6	1	13	1
Iván Emmanuel González Ferreira	28.01.1987	21	10	20	7
Luis Armando González Gaona	25.01.1993	-	-		
Marcelo Sebastián González Cabral	27.05.1996			9	1
Jorge Darío Mendoza Torres	15.05.1989	22	1	19	2
Sergio Adrián Mendoza Espinola	27.05.1994	19	2	5	-
Ramón Darío Ocampo (ARG)	21.06.1986	21	1	16	2
Marcelo José Palau Balzaretti (URU)	01.08.1985	19	4	20	3
Miguel Ángel Paniagua Rivarola	14.05.1987	17	1		
Marcelo Miguel Paredes Váldez	04.01.1993	-	-	-	-
Nicolás Riquelme Quintana	31.10.1993	-	-	-	-
Alexis Iván Vargas Artela	05.04.1991	2	-	-	-
Nildo Arturo Viera Recalde	20.03.1993			3	-
Forwards:					
Jorge Daniel Benítez Guillen	02.09.1992	21	17		
Marcos Cabañas González	22.04.1993	-	-	3	-
César Augusto Caicedo Solís	21.10.1994	5	-		
Fernando Fabián Fernández Acosta	08.01.1992	21	14	22	17
Cristian Palacios	19.01.1994	3	-	-	-
Críspulo Guillermo Peña Ayala	21.04.1991	-	-	-	-
Federico Javier Santander Mereles	04.06.1991	3	-	22	11
Trainer:					
Fernando Jubero (ESP)		22		22	

GENERAL DÍAZ FOOTBALL CLUB LUQUE

Foundation date: November 22, 1917
Address: Avenida "General Elizardo Aquino y General Jara Luque", Luque
Stadium: Estadio „General Adrián Jara", Luque – Capacity: 3,500

THE SQUAD

	DOB	Ape M	Ape G	Cla M	Cla G
Goalkeepers:					
Jorge Luis González Cardozo	28.02.1989	6	-	4	-
Bernardo David Medina	14.01.1988	10	-	18	-
Orlando Ramón Rojas Cáceres	14.12.1983			-	-
Mario Alberto Santilli (ARG)	27.06.1984	6	-		
Defenders:					
Lidio Benítez Domínguez	18.07.1978	7	1		
Alejandro David Bernal	09.07.1987	2	-	13	-
Walter Cabrera	01.07.1990	22	-	2	-
Jorge Narciso Cáceres	22.11.1984	8	1	-	-
Víctor Hugo Dávalos Aguirre	03.02.1991	16	-	4	-
Alberto Espinola Giménez	08.02.1991	15	-	13	2
Marco Antonio Gamarra Arbiniagaldez	08.07.1988	16	-	8	-
Julio César González Trinidad	28.06.1992			2	-
Dionisio Mereles Ovelar	23.02.1986	7	1	4	-
Rolando Fidel Sanabria	22.03.1985	6	-	15	-
Gustavo Ariel Toranzo (ARG)	15.09.1987	7	-	17	1
Ángel Osmar Vera Escobar	25.02.1992	8	-	7	-
Midfielders:					
José Luis Ávalos	10.11.1987	2	-	-	-
Wilfrido Manuel Báez	18.06.1994	14	-	12	1
Diego Javier Benítez	18.02.1991	-	-	1	-
Carlos Borja		1	-	-	-
Blas Antonio Cáceres	01.07.1989			15	4
Pedro Julián Chávez Ruíz	29.06.1985			13	2
Alberto Cirilo Contrera Jiménez	14.02.1992			19	2
Oscar Moisés Gamarra	09.09.1986	14	1	3	-
Víctor Sócrates Michael Genés Espínola	29.09.1987			11	-
Luis Armando González Gaona	25.01.1993			2	-
Cristian Martínez Medina	19.05.1983	13	1	16	-
Víctor Hugo Matta	21.04.1990	7	-	3	-
Adilio Fabián Mora López	16.05.1985	4	1	1	-
Reinaldo David Ocampo	06.01.1987	6	1		
Gustavo Ojeda		3	-	-	-
Marcos Antonio Pfingst	29.03.1993	6	1	6	-
Richard Fabián Prieto	25.01.1997			1	-
Ricardo Elías Solís	10.10.1994	7	-	2	-
Cristian Gustavo Sosa Ledesma	08.08.1987			20	1
Eric Valiente		3	-	-	-
Carlos Alberto Vera Segovia	19.05.1983	14	-	15	-
Edgar Catalino Zaracho Zorilla	29.11.1989	6	-	1	-
Forwards:					
Mario Álvarez				5	-
César Augusto Caicedo Solís (COL)	21.10.1994			8	2
Alfredo Virginio Cano Benítez (ARG)	30.08.1982	20	6	-	-
Diego Javier Doldán Zacarías	06.02.1987	17	2	18	3
Julio Sebastián Doldán	15.10.1993	7	-	5	-
Roberto Carlos Gamarra Acosta	11.05.1981			19	6
Jorge Américo Giménez	11.06.1991	10	2	3	2
Sergio Reinaldo Gómez Duarte	18.12.1990	4	-	-	-
Juan Andrés Noguera Ramírez	10.09.1984	10	1	-	-
Francisco Omzi				2	-
Arnaldo Oviedo Villalba	07.09.1990	4	-	-	-
Trainer:					
Humberto García Ramirez	13.05.1974	22		22	

CLUB LIBERTAD ASUNCIÓN

Foundation date: July 30, 1905
Address: Avenida Artigas N° 1030, esq. Cusmanich, Asunción
Stadium: Estadio „Dr. Nicolás Leoz", Asunción – Capacity: 10,000

THE SQUAD

	DOB	Ape		Cla	
		M	G	M	G
Goalkeepers:					
Junior Ramón Balbuena	31.08.1994	-	-	-	-
Rodrigo Martin Muñóz Salomón (URU)	22.01.1982	14	-	15	-
Pablo Andrés Torresagasti	05.08.1980	8	-	7	-
Armando Andrés Vera Amarilla	04.02.1993	-	-	-	-
Defenders:					
Fabián Cornelio Balbuena González	23.08.1991			16	1
Ismael Benegas	01.08.1987			13	3
Alan Max Benítez Domínguez	25.01.1994	3	-	10	1
Pedro Juan Benítez Domínguez	23.03.1981	14	-	10	-
César Coronel Recalde	05.03.1991	1	-	-	-
Carlos Daniel Desvars	26.11.1993	-	-	1	-
Gustavo Raúl Gómez Portillo	06.05.1993	20	4		
Gustavo Ramón Mencia Ávalos	05.07.1988	14	1	15	2
Jorge Luis Moreira Ferreira	01.02.1990	20	1	13	-
Aldo David Olmedo Román	25.09.1989	2	-		
Arnaldo Joel Recalde Ramírez	21.06.1991	9	-	2	-
Jorge Eduardo Recalde Ramírez	08.05.1992	20	4	14	4
Adalberto Román Benítez	11.04.1987	10	-	14	1
Midfielders:					
Sergio Daniel Aquino (ARG)	21.09.1979	21	-	17	-
Ángel María Benítez Argüello	27.01.1996	-	-	-	-
Ángel Rodrigo Cardozo Lucena	19.10.1994	3	-		
Néstor Abraham Camacho Ledesma	15.10.1987			20	7
Blas Yamil Díaz Silva	03.02.1991	-	-	-	-
Jorge Daniel González Marquet	25.03.1988	15	1	21	3
Osmar de la Cruz Molinas González	03.05.1987	19	-	20	-
Iván Rodrigo Ramírez Segovia	08.12.1994	16	1	10	-
Juan Danilo Santacruz González	12.06.1995			13	4
Claudio David Vargas Villalba	15.12.1985	17	3	18	1
Forwards:					
Luis Antonio Amarilla Lencina	25.08.1995			3	-
Antonio Bareiro Álvarez	24.04.1989	17	4	15	3
Rogério Luis Leichtweis	28.06.1988	4	-		
Hernán Rodrigo López Mora (URU)	21.01.1978	20	19	17	7
Manuel José Maciel Fernández	12.02.1984			-	-
Jesús Manuel Medina Maldonado	30.04.1997	-	-	-	-
Brian Guillermo Montenegro Martínez	10.06.1993	19	1		
Dionisio Ismael Pérez Mambreani	13.08.1986	9	-	14	2
Nelson David Romero Cárdenas	18.11.1984	12	1	4	-
Jonathan Ariel Valiente	21.02.1998			4	1
Trainer:					
Pedro Alcides Sarabia Achucarro [as of 02.09.2013]	05.07.1975	22		22	

CLUB NACIONAL ASUNCIÓN

Foundation date: June 5, 1904
Address: Cerro León y Paraguarí, Barrio Obrero, Asunción
Stadium: Estadio „Arsenio Erico", Asunción – Capacity: 4,000

THE SQUAD

	DOB	Ape M	Ape G	Cla M	Cla G
Goalkeepers:					
Óscar Tadeo Agüero Soria	15.06.1980	9	-	5	-
José Coronel	04.02.1993	1	-	-	-
Ignacio Oscar Don (ARG)	28.02.1982	14	-	17	-
Defenders:					
Marco Antonio Acosta Rojas	08.11.1984			14	-
Fabián Cornelio Balbuena González	23.08.1981	16	1		
José Leonardo Cáceres Ovelar	28.04.1985	13	-	18	-
Ramón David Coronel Gómez	31.03.1991	10	1	14	1
Miguel Isaías Jacquet Duarte	20.05.1995	5	-	3	-
Nelson Mazacotte	17.09.1994	1	-	-	-
David Bernardo Mendoza Ayala	10.05.1985	7	-	11	-
Marcos David Miers	24.03.1990	14	-	10	-
Raúl Eduardo Piris	09.12.1980	11	-	18	-
Sandino Sosa Weiberlen	01.03.1991	5	2	7	-
Midfielders:					
José Rodrigo Aguilar	10.12.1993	6	-	2	-
Ángel David Almirón Pereira	05.02.1996	1	-	1	-
Guido Javier Aquino Acuña	12.06.1992	3	-	-	-
Enrique Araújo Álvarez	03.10.1995	16	1	14	-
Juan David Argüello Arias	28.09.1991	12	1	7	-
Julián Alfonso Benítez Franco	06.06.1987	13	3	18	1
Hugo Wilmar Cabrera González	12.03.1994	5	-	3	-
Nicolás Chávez	16.10.1993	1	-	-	-
César Casimiro Florenciáñez Denis	04.03.1992	1	-	-	-
Hugo Américo Lusardi Morínigo	17.08.1982	13	1	18	2
Alejandro Nicolás Martínez Ramos	15.02.1989	10	2		
Marcos Benjamín Melgarejo	03.10.1986	11	1	9	-
Cristian David Mélida Argüello	23.04.1991	1	-	-	-
Derlis Ricardo Orué Acevedo	02.01.1989	13	1	15	1
Marcos Antonio Riveros Krayacich	04.09.1988	13	-	16	-
Luis Fernando Rodríguez Barrios	19.03.1993	6	1	2	-
Alex Junior Rojas Alvarez	01.01.1997			-	-
Carlos Gabriel Ruíz Peralta	17.07.1984	9	-		
Silvio Gabriel Torales	23.09.1991	12	4	18	7
Yony Villasanti	25.06.1996			4	-
Forwards:					
Jorge Daniel Achucarro	11.06.1981	5	-		
Freddy José Bareiro Gamarra	27.03.1982	10	1	18	3
Armando Javier De Giacomi Prantl	02.01.1994			3	-
Douglas Holger Martínez	13.04.1994	2	-	1	-
Brian Guillermo Montenegro Martínez	18.06.1993			2	1
Marcelo Montiel				1	-
Benjamín Salvador Pedrozo Lezcano	01.01.1991	6	1	5	-
Marco Prieto	15.08.1990	10	2	3	-
Julio Eduardo Santa Cruz Cantero	12.05.1990	18	2	17	2
Víctor Gustavo Velázquez	17.04.1991			13	-
Elías Arturo Zimnavonda Méndez	21.01.1996	1	-	-	-
Trainer:					
Gustavo Eliseo Morínigo Vázquez [as of 18.04.2012]	23.01.1977	22		22	

CLUB OLIMPIA ASUNCIÓN

Foundation date: July 25, 1902
Address: Avenida Mariscal López 1499, casi Avenida General M. Santos, Barrio Las Mercedes, Asunción
Stadium: Estadio „Manuel Ferreira", Asunción – Capacity: 15,000

THE SQUAD

	DOB	Ape		Cla	
		M	G	M	G
Goalkeepers:					
Ever Alexis Caballero	27.04.1982	-	-	1	-
Víctor Hugo Centurión Miranda	24.02.1986	22	-	21	-
Carlos María Servín Caballero	24.03.1987			-	-
Defenders:					
Nelson Pablo Benítez (ARG)	24.05.1984	10	-	-	-
Richard Cabrera				2	-
Salustiano Antonio Candia Galeano	08.07.1983			18	-
Orlando Israel Gallardo Noguera	27.06.1994	1	-	-	-
Ronald Renato Huth Manzur	05.10.1989	2	-	-	-
Jonathan Leonardo Lacerda Araujo	07.02.1987			13	1
Julio César Manzur	22.01.1981	20	3	8	-
Ricardo Julián Martínez Pavón	18.02.1984	3	-		
Arturo Luis Mendoza Ayala	02.09.994	7	-	2	-
Gustavo David Noguera Domínguez	07.11.1987	20	-	17	-
Carlos Adalberto Rolón Ibarra	30.06.1992	19	3		
Saúl Savin Salcedo Zárate	29.08.1997			3	-
Richard Adrián Salinas	06.02.1988	11	-	11	-
Midfielders:					
Juan Gabriel Abente Amarilla	04.03.1987	2	-		
Miguel Angel Amado Alanís	28.12.1994	22	-	15	1
César Assia (COL)	15.07.1992	-	-	-	-
Jorge Gabriel Báez Mendoza	23.10.1990	7	-		
Diego Fabián Barreto Lara	31.05.1993	-	-	-	-
Juan Jeremías Bogado Britos	04.07.1995	13	-	13	1
Walter David Clar Fritz	27.09.1994	22	-	22	2
Eduardo Alberto Echeverría Espinola	04.03.1989	-	-		
Carlos Javier Guerreño Otazú	22.12.1995	1	-	14	3
Eduardo Fabián Ledesma Trinidad	07.08.1985			13	-
Ángel Martínez	27.01.1995	5	-	-	-
Fernando Martínez	13.05.1994	2	-	11	-
José Arnulfo Montiel Núñez	19.03.1988			14	-
Aldo Andrés Paniagua Benítez	12.07.1989	10	1	-	-
Carlos Humberto Paredes Monges	16.07.1976	8	1	13	-
Remigio Hernán Pérez Ortíz	12.02.1991	3	-		
Wilson Omar Pittoni Rodríguez	14.08.1985			16	-
Esteban Javier Ramírez Samaniego	17.05.1985	20	4	6	-
Rodrigo Raúl Resquín Jara	23.08.1989	3	-		
Cristian Gustavo Sosa Ledesma	08.08.1987	4	-		
Forwards:					
Carlos Javier Acuña Caballero	23.06.1988			19	5
Jorge Sebastián Ayala Álvarez	04.07.1984	2	-		
Nery Antonio Cardozo Escobar	26.05.1989	18	6		
Diego Omar Centurión	05.06.1982	19	5	7	2
Jorge David Colmán Aguayo	12.12.1997	-	-	-	-

Marcelo Javier Correa (ARG)	23.10.1992	5	-		
Pedro Javier Godoy Agüero	28.06.1995			2	-
Derlis Alberto González Galeano	20.03.1994	20	8		
Wálter Rodrigo González Sosa	21.06.1995	1	-	5	-
Marcos Antonio Lazaga Dávalos	26.02.1983	2	-		
Osmar Leguizamón Pavón	11.05.1994	3	-	3	1
Cristian Gilberto Ovelar	18.01.1986			19	9
Juan Manuel Salgueiro Silva (URU)	03.04.1983			20	3
Trainer:					
Ever Hugo Almeida Almada [Sacked on 10.03.2014]	01.07.1948	4			
Diego Martín Alonso López (URU) [12.03.2014-05.10.2014]	16.04.1975	18		12	
Luis Alberto Monzón León [06-13.10.2014; Caretaker]	26.05.1970			1	
Nery Alberto Pumpido Barrinat (ARG) [as of 14.10.2014]	30.07.1957			9	

CLUB RUBIO ÑU ASUNCIÓN

Foundation date: August 24, 1913
Address: Calle Espíritu Santo y Juana P. Carillo, Barrio Santísima Trinidad, Asunción
Stadium: Estadio La Arboleda, Asunción – Capacity: 5,500

THE SQUAD

	DOB	Ape		Cla	
		M	G	M	G
Goalkeepers:					
Jorge Alberto De Olivera (ARG)	21.08.1982	19	-		
Diego Alejandro Morel Bejarano	15.12.1993	3	-	3	-
Mario Alberto Santilli (ARG)	27.06.1984			12	-
Blas Valenzuela	1991	-	-	8	-
Defenders:					
Wilfrido Guzmán Bazán Arrúa	04.08.1984	-	-	-	-
Denis Ramón Caniza Acuña	29.08.1974	13	-	19	2
Diego Nicolás Ciz Torres (URU)	31.05.1981			19	-
Pablo Esteban Espinoza	21.06.1988	6	1	3	-
Claudio Daniel Estigarribia Balmori	07.03.1992	1	-	5	-
Hugo Rafael Fleytas Báez	23.06.1988	2	-	2	-
Gustavo Giménez	19.06.1987	21	-	9	-
Celso Daniel González Ferreira	18.06.1980	22	1	15	-
Maximiliano Lugo (ARG)	04.12.1989	15	3	19	1
Miller David Mareco Colmán	31.01.1994	1	-	-	-
Rubén Monges Figari	06.02.1993	4	-	-	-
Nelson Ruíz Giménez	27.12.1991	4	-	-	-
Arnaldo Andrés Vera Chamorro	22.01.1980	20	-		
Óscar Basilio Velázquez Mendoza	19.04.1990			12	-
Francisco Miguel Vera González	15.01.1986	10	1	13	-
Midfielders:					
Eduardo Ramon Aveiro Almeida	13.10.1984	1	-		
Ángel Rodrigo Cardozo Lucena	19.10.1994			16	3
Carlos Díaz		-	-	-	-
Julio César Domínguez Castillo	07.04.1992	4	-	16	1
Eduardo Alberto Echeverría Espinola	04.03.1989			1	-
Ángel Daniel Enciso Castillo	10.09.1987			10	-
Sergio Gustavo Escalante (ARG)	09.03.1986			12	2
Diego Antonio Figueredo Matiauda	28.04.1982	20	3	8	-
Alex Garay		5	2	5	-

Marcos Antonio Gimenéz Vera	25.01.1991	3	-	-	-
Osvaldo Hobecker García	23.03.1984			15	2
Alfredo Carlos Alberto Mazacotte	17.11.1987	14	1		-
Juan Nuñez				3	1
David Pereira		2	-	7	-
Daniel Pérez		2	-	-	-
Robert Ayrton Piris Da Mota	26.07.1994	15	-	20	2
Ismael Roa		3	-	4	-
Gustavo Agustín Viera Velázquez	28.08.1995	16	2	2	1
Forwards:					
Wilson Brahian Ayala Vera	29.06.1995	-	-	4	1
Arnulfo Colmán Larrea	31.08.1991	2	1	2	-
Claudio César Correa Cañiza	03.05.1993	22	7		
Walter Silvestre Cubilla (ARG)	05.03.1989	4	1		-
Miguel Ángel Cuéllar	25.01.1982			7	-
Alejandro Damián Da Silva	18.05.1982			20	4
Victor Manuel Gómez	16.10.1983	14	4	-	-
Enzo Damián Maidana (ARG)	02.01.1990	2	-		
Gumercindo Mendieta		3	-	-	-
Jorge Miguel Ortega Salinas	16.04.1991	18	9		
Alfio Oviedo		-	-	4	1
Cristian Santacruz Ojeda	03.06.1991	9	1	7	-
Aquilino Villalba Sanabria	20.09.1983	8	-	-	-
Trainer:					
Pablo Leonardo Caballero Cáceres [01.01.-22.08.2014]	25.06.1972	22		4	
Mario Darío Grana (ARG) [23.08.-17.11.2014]	27.01.1973			15	
Alicio Ignacio Solalinde Miers [as of 18.11.2014]	01.02.1952			3	

CLUB SOL DE AMÉRICA ASUNCIÓN

Foundation date: February 22, 1909
Address: Avenida 5ta y Antequera, Barrio Villa Elisa, Asunción
Stadium: Estadio „Luis Alfonso Giagni", Asunción – Capacity: 5,000

THE SQUAD

	DOB	Ape		Cla	
		M	G	M	G
Goalkeepers:					
Roberto Carlos Acosta Coronel	12.07.1984	8	-	13	-
Óscar Benegas	26.06.1993	-	-	-	-
Gerardo Amilcar Ortíz Zarza	25.03.1989	14	-	9	-
Mario Fabián Ovando Colmán	22.02.1991	-	-	-	-
Defenders:					
Marcos Ramón Acosta Pera	07.10.1987	-	-	7	-
Diego Aguada				5	-
Diego Manuel Arrúa	25.07.1988	9	-	-	-
Celso Cáceres		9	1	15	-
Raúl Alejandro Cáceres Bogado	18.09.1991	22	-	22	-
Pablo Daniel De Muner (ARG)	14.04.1981	3	-		
Adalberto Goiri Sandoval	16.12.1987	16	-	18	1
Claudio Marcelo Morel Rodríguez	02.02.1978			14	-
Adolfo Valdéz	24.07.1991	-	-	-	-
Bruno Amilcar Valdéz	06.10.1992	18	2		
Midfielders:					
Walter Ramón Araujo Molinas	05.09.1995	4	-	4	-
Blas Antonio Cáceres	01.07.1989	10	2		
Diego de Jesús Chamorro Freyre	23.03.1988	11	1		
Luis Rodrigo Daher Benítez (ARG)	25.02.1992	7	-		-
Marcos Duré	18.02.1991	18	2	19	1
Jorge Alejandro Jara González	11.11.1991	13	-	3	-
Rasem Maluff	18.02.1992	-	-	-	-
Alfredo Carlos Alberto Mazacotte	17.11.1987			20	3
Ignacio Miño	18.04.1992	19	6	16	-
Edgardo Orzuza	23.02.1986	19	-	20	-
Aureliano Torres Román	16.06.1982	19	-	22	3
Rodrigo Sebastián Vázquez Maidana (URU)	04.11.1980			7	-
Édgar Villasboa	07.07.1992	6	1	11	2
Forwards:					
Massimiliano Ammendola (ITA)	15.05.1990	3	-	-	-
Pedro Marcelo Arce Meaurio	09.08.1991	6	-	12	1
Claudio César Correa Cañiza	03.05.1993			20	7
Cecilio Andrés Domínguez Ruíz	22.07.1993	20	-	18	3
Lorenzo Rodrigo Frutos	04.06.1989	7	1	11	2
Mario Groménida	05.10.1994	-	-	-	-
Cristian Gilberto Ovelar	18.01.1986	21	19		
Enzo Enrico Prono Zelaya	27.06.1991	9	-		
Diego Vázquez	12.02.1992	10	1	17	1
Osvaldo Vigo	02.04.1993	-	-	5	-
Trainer:					
Roberto Fabián Pompei (ARG) [01.01.-05.10.2014]	14.03.1970	22		12	
Mario César Jacquet Martínez [as of 06.10.2014]	29.07.1946			10	

CLUB SPORTIVO LUQUEÑO

Foundation date: May 1, 1921
Address: Avenida Sportivo Luqueño y Gaspar R. de Francia, Barrio Tercer, Luque
Stadium: Estadio „Feliciano Cáceres“, Luque – Capacity: 25,000

THE SQUAD

	DOB	Ape		Cla	
		M	G	M	G
Goalkeepers:					
Jorge Javier Chena Alonso	31.10.1988	12	-	2	-
Tomás Dionisio Echagüe Coronel	18.09.1996	-	-	-	-
John Alston Hoore Bodden (HON)	03.10.1981			1	-
Rodolfo Fabián Rodríguez Jara	08.03.1987			20	-
Tobías Antonio Vargas Insfrán	21.08.1989	10	-		
Defenders:					
Robert Gustavo Aldama Rodas	03.06.1987	9	-	11	-
José Carlos Báez	10.07.1988	1	-	-	-
José Manuel Babak Wlosek	22.04.1988	-	-		
Oscar Julián Benítez				1	-
Diego Nicolás Ciz (URU)	31.05.1981	20	-		
Juan Marcelo Escobar Chena	03.07.1995	8	-	13	-
Édson Figueiredo (BRA)		-	-	-	-
Aquilino Giménez Gaona	21.04.1993	6	-	8	-
Fredy Aldemar González Fernández	13.04.1996	-	-	-	-
Julio César Irrazábal León	25.11.1980	14	-		
Matías Emanuel Lequi (ARG)	13.05.1981	21	8		
Freddy Alfredo Portillo	23.04.1992	4	-	-	-
Carlos Adalberto Rolón Ibarra	30.06.1992			15	1
Sergio Raúl Vergara Romero	15.12.1988	14	1	20	1
Midfielders:					
Christian Javier Aguada Jacquet	04.05.1993	6	-	14	1
Milton Rodrigo Benítez Lirio	30.03.1986	16	-	16	-
Fúlvio Milciades Chávez	05.07.1993	-	-	1	-
Freddy Javier Coronel Ortíz	22.07.1989	11	-		
Leonardo Delvalle Morel	18.01.1985	19	-	10	1
Guido Di Vanni (ARG)	06.11.1988			17	4
Ángel Daniel Enciso Castillo	10.09.1987	9	-		
Miguel Ángel Godoy Melgarejo	07.05.1983			21	-
Luis Carlos Matto Vera	15.07.1993	-	-	14	-
Luis Alcides Miño Muñoz	08.01.1989	10	-	19	6
Félix Gustavo Romero Benítez	01.10.1987			5	-
Adilson Ruíz	17.11.1983			-	-
Henry Ruíz				1	-
Mario Saldívar	12.09.1990	-	-	13	1
Forwards:					
Derlis Roberto Alegre Amante	10.01.1994	22	2	22	3
Francisco Aldo Barreto Miranda	03.01.1988			3	-
Marcelo Augusto Ferreira Bordón	17.08.1993	12	2	19	2
José Alfredo Leguizamón	24.04.1984	13	-	20	-
Juan Manuel Lucero Campos (ARG)	26.05.1985	9	1		
Manuel José Maciel Fernández	12.02.1984	13	2		
Wilfrido Rivas	12.09.1990	-	-	1	-
Rodrigo Teixeira Pereira	16.06.1978	18	6	19	3
Robert Rodríguez		1	-	-	-
Andrés Walter Rodríguez Ferrando (URU)	21.01.1983			1	-
Hugo Alejandro Serravalle (ARG)	13.03.1984	5	-		
Víctor Gustavo Velázquez	17.04.1991	19	1		
Trainer:					
Alicio Ignacio Solalinde Miers [05.05.2013-09.03.2014]	01.02.1952	4			
Eduardo Rivera (URU) [10.03.-29.08.2014]		18		5	
Daniel Navarro Leguizamón [30.08.-27.09.2014]	16.03.1963			5	
Pablo Leonardo Caballero Cáceres [as of 28.09.2014]	25.06.1972			12	

SECOND LEVEL
División Intermedia 2014
"90 años del Club Tacuary y Homenaje a Don Julián Mora Llanes"

1.	Club Sportivo San Lorenzo (*Promoted*)	30	17	6	7	40	-	20	57
2.	Club Deportivo Santaní (*Promoted*)	30	16	9	5	36	-	22	57
3.	Resistencia Sport Club Asunción	30	13	8	9	34	-	25	47
4.	Club Sportivo Iteño	30	13	8	9	35	-	29	47
5.	Club Deportivo Caaguazú	30	12	8	10	33	-	32	44
6.	Independiente FBC Asunción	30	11	10	9	39	-	34	43
7.	Club Sportivo Trinidense	30	10	12	8	36	-	27	42
8.	Sport Colombia Fernando de la Mora	30	11	9	10	37	-	37	42
9.	Club River Plate Asunción	30	8	15	7	34	-	29	39
10.	Caacupé Football Club	30	10	9	11	32	-	35	39
11.	Club Sportivo Carapeguá	30	8	12	10	30	-	31	36
12.	Tacuary Football Club Asunción	30	9	9	12	36	-	39	36
13.	General Caballero Sport Club Zeballos Cué	30	8	10	12	34	-	36	34
14.	Paranaense FC Ciudad del Este	30	7	9	14	26	-	46	30
15.	Club Cerro Porteño Presidente Franco	30	7	6	17	33	-	51	27
16.	Club Olimpia de Itá	30	6	8	16	23	-	45	26

CHAMPIONSHIP FINAL

01.11.2014, Estadio Defensores del Chaco, Asunción
Referee: Fernando López
Club Sportivo San Lorenzo - Club Deportivo Santaní **1-1(0-0,1-1,1-1); 5-3 on penalties**

2014 Second Level champions: **Club Sportivo San Lorenzo**

Relegation Table

The team which will be relegated is determined on average points taking into account results of the last three seasons (2012, 2013 and 2014).

Pos	Team	2012	2013	2014	Total		Aver
		P	P	P	P	M	
1.	Club Deportivo Santaní	54	34	57	145	90	1,611
2.	Club Sportivo Iteño	-	-	47	47	30	1,566
3.	Club Sportivo Trinidense	46	49	43	138	90	1,533
4.	Independiente FBC Asunción	-	47	44	91	60	1,516
5.	Club Sportivo San Lorenzo	48	30	57	135	90	1,500
6.	Club Deportivo Caaguazú	-	-	45	45	30	1,500
7.	Sport Colombia Fernando de la Mora	43	47	41	131	90	1,455
8.	Tacuary Football Club Asunción	-	48	36	84	60	1,400
9.	Resistencia Sport Club Asunción	40	35	47	122	90	1,355
10.	General Caballero Sport Club Zeballos Cué	42	39	34	115	90	1,277
11.	Caacupé Football Club	-	38	38	76	60	1,266
12.	Club River Plate Asunción	41	33	39	113	90	1,255
13.	Club Sportivo Carapeguá	-	-	36	36	30	1,200
14.	Paranaense FC Ciudad del Este (*Relegated*)	34	40	30	104	90	1,155
15.	Club Cerro Porteño Presidente Franco (*Relegated*)	-	-	29	29	30	0,966
16.	Club Olimpia de Itá (*Relegated*)	-	-	24	24	30	0,800

<u>Promoted for the 2015 División Intermedia</u>:
Club Cristóbal Colón Ñemby
Club Fernando de la Mora Asunción
Club Deportivo Liberación

NATIONAL TEAM INTERNATIONAL MATCHES (16.07.2014 – 15.07.2015)

07.09.2014	Villach	Paraguay – United Arab Emirates	0-0	(F)
10.10.2014	Cheonan	Korea Republic - Paraguay	2-0(2-0)	(F)
14.10.2014	Changsha	China P.R. - Paraguay	2-1(2-0)	(F)
15.11.2014	Luque	Paraguay - Peru	2-1(0-0)	(F)
18.11.2014	Lima	Peru - Paraguay	2-1(0-1)	(F)
26.03.2015	San José	Costa Rica - Paraguay	0-0	(F)
31.03.2015	Kansas City	Mexico - Paraguay	1-0(1-0)	(F)
06.06.2015	Asunción	Paraguay - Honduras	2-2(1-2)	(F)
13.06.2015	La Serena	Argentina - Paraguay	2-2(2-0)	(CA)
16.06.2015	Antofagasta	Paraguay - Jamaica	1-0(1-0)	(CA)
20.06.2015	La Serena	Uruguay - Paraguay	1-1(1-1)	(CA)
27.06.2015	Concepción	Brazil - Paraguay	3-4 pen	(CA)
30.06.2015	Concepción	Argentina - Paraguay	6-1(2-1)	(CA)
03.07.2015	Concepción	Peru - Paraguay	2-0(0-0)	(CA)

07.09.2014, Friendly International
Stadion Villach-Lind, Villach (Austria); Attendance: 1,000
Referee: Harald Lechner (Austria)

PARAGUAY – UNITED ARAB EMIRATES 0-0

PAR: Joel Alberto Silva Estigarribia, Pablo César Aguilar Benítez, Jorge Luis Moreira Ferreira, Gustavo Raúl Gómez Portillo (88.José Leonardo Cáceres Ovelar), Júnior Osmar Ignacio Alonso Mujica, Néstor Ezequiel Ortigoza (74.Silvio Gabriel Torales Castillo), Víctor Javier Cáceres Centurión (68.Jorge Daniel Benítez Guillén), Óscar David Romero Villamayor (61.Miguel Ángel Paniagua Rivarola), Jorge Luis Rojas Mendoza (82.David Ariel Mendieta Chávez), Roque Luis Santa Cruz Cantero, Arnaldo Antonio Sanabria Ayala (58.Derlis Alberto González Galeano). Trainer: Víctor Genés.

10.10.2014, Friendly International
Cheonan Baekseok Stadium, Cheonan; Attendance: 25,156
Referee: Valentin Kovalenko (Uzbekistan)

KOREA REPUBLIC - PARAGUAY 2-0(2-0)

PAR: Antony Domingo Silva Cano, Pablo César Aguilar Benítez, José Leonardo Cáceres Ovelar (46.Julián Alfonso Benítez Franco), Iván Rodrigo Piris Leguizamón, Gustavo Raúl Gómez Portillo, Néstor Ezequiel Ortigoza (46.Jorge Luis Rojas Mendoza), Marcelo Alejandro Estigarribia Balmori (36.David Bernardo Mendoza Ayala), Celso Fabián Ortíz Gamarra (68.Silvio Gabriel Torales Castillo), Marcos Antonio Riveros Krayacich, Roque Luis Santa Cruz Cantero (78.Christian Gilberto Ovelar Rodríguez), Derlis Alberto González Galeano (69.Cecilio Andrés Domínguez Ruíz). Trainer: Víctor Genés.

14.10.2014, Friendly International
He Long Stadium, Changsha; Attendance: 20,000
Referee: Ko Hyung-Jin (Korea Republic)

CHINA P.R. - PARAGUAY 2-1(2-0)

PAR: Joel Alberto Silva Estigarribia (46.Bernardo David Medina), Pablo César Aguilar Benítez, David Bernardo Mendoza Ayala, Luis Carlos Cardozo Espillaga, Iván Rodrigo Piris Leguizamón (46.Gustavo Raúl Gómez Portillo), Marcos Antonio Riveros Krayacich (70.Julián Alfonso Benítez Franco), Silvio Gabriel Torales Castillo (46.Celso Fabián Ortíz Gamarra), Jorge Luis Rojas Mendoza, Roque Luis Santa Cruz Cantero, Christian Gilberto Ovelar Rodríguez (46.Néstor Ezequiel Ortigoza), Derlis Alberto González Galeano (59.Cecilio Andrés Domínguez Ruíz). Trainer: Víctor Genés.

Goal: Néstor Ezequiel Ortigoza (82).

15.11.2014, Friendly International
Estadio "Feliciano Cáceres", Luque; Attendance: n/a
Referee: Ricardo Marques Ribeiro (Brazil)
PARAGUAY - PERU **2-1(0-0)**
PAR: Justo Wilmar Villar Viveros, Paulo César da Silva Barrios, Jorge Luis Moreira Ferreira, Gustavo Raúl Gómez Portillo, Júnior Osmar Ignacio Alonso Mujica, Cristian Miguel Riveros Núñez (85.Marcos Antonio Riveros Krayacich), Víctor Javier Cáceres Centurión (46.Celso Fabián Ortíz Gamarra), Víctor Hugo Ayala Núñez (46.Jorge Luis Rojas Mendoza), Roque Luis Santa Cruz Cantero (81.Derlis Alberto González Galeano), Édgar Milciades Benítez Santander (69.Óscar Ramón Ruíz Roa), Arnaldo Antonio Sanabria Ayala (46.Ángel Rodrigo Romero Villamayor). Trainer: Víctor Genés.
Goals: Ángel Rodrigo Romero Villamayor (70), Derlis Alberto González Galeano (90+2 penalty).

18.11.2014, Friendly International
Estadio Nacional, Lima; Attendance: n/a
Referee: Wilmar Alexander Roldán Pérez (Colombia)
PERU - PARAGUAY **2-1(0-1)**
PAR: Justo Wilmar Villar Viveros, Paulo César da Silva Barrios, Luis Carlos Cardozo Espillaga, Jorge Luis Moreira Ferreira, Iván Rodrigo Piris Leguizamón (84.Derlis Alberto González Galeano), Gustavo Raúl Gómez Portillo (46.Jorge Luis Rojas Mendoza), Cristian Miguel Riveros Núñez (46.Víctor Javier Cáceres Centurión), Celso Fabián Ortíz Gamarra (46.Marcos Antonio Riveros Krayacich), Roque Luis Santa Cruz Cantero, Édgar Milciades Benítez Santander, Ángel Rodrigo Romero Villamayor (67.Óscar Ramón Ruíz Roa). Trainer: Víctor Genés.
Goal: Roque Luis Santa Cruz Cantero (43).
Sent off: Derlis Alberto González Galeano (90).

26.03.2015, Friendly International
Estadio Nacional, San José; Attendance: 31,000
Referee: Jhon Pitti (Panama)
COSTA RICA - PARAGUAY **0-0**
PAR: Justo Wilmar Villar Viveros, Paulo César da Silva Barrios, Pablo César Aguilar Benítez, Marcos Antonio Cáceres Centurión, Miguel Ángel Ramón Samudio, Víctor Javier Cáceres Centurión, Osmar de la Cruz Molinas González (68.Fidencio Oviedo Domínguez), Richard Ortíz Busto, Raúl Marcelo Bobadilla (80.Jorge Luis Rojas Mendoza), Lucas Ramón Barrios Cáceres, Édgar Milciades Benítez Santander (76.Óscar David Romero Villamayor). Trainer: Ramón Ángel Díaz (Argentina).

31.03.2015, Friendly International
Arrowhead Stadium, Kansas City (United States); Attendance: 38,144
Referee: Walter Alexander López Castellanos (Guatemala)
MEXICO - PARAGUAY **1-0(1-0)**
PAR: Justo Wilmar Villar Viveros (30.Antony Domingo Silva Cano), Paulo César da Silva Barrios, Pablo César Aguilar Benítez (65.Marcos Antonio Cáceres Centurión), Jorge Luis Moreira Ferreira (81.Jorge Luis Rojas Mendoza), Iván Rodrigo Piris Leguizamón (46.Miguel Ángel Ramón Samudio), Fabián Cornelio Balbuena González, Fidencio Oviedo Domínguez, Richard Ortíz Busto, Óscar David Romero Villamayor (46.Osvaldo David Martínez Arce), Raúl Marcelo Bobadilla (62.Hernán Arsenio Pérez González), Lucas Ramón Barrios Cáceres. Trainer: Ramón Ángel Díaz (Argentina).

06.06.2015, Friendly International
Estadio Defensores del Chaco, Asunción; Attendance: 9,500
Referee: Fernando Martín Falce Langone (Uruguay)

PARAGUAY - HONDURAS 2-2(1-2)

PAR: Justo Wilmar Villar Viveros, Paulo César da Silva Barrios, Marcos Antonio Cáceres Centurión (68.Bruno Amílcar Valdez), Miguel Ángel Ramón Samudio, Fabián Cornelio Balbuena González, Néstor Ezequiel Ortigoza (46.Osvaldo David Martínez Arce), Víctor Javier Cáceres Centurión, Richard Ortíz Busto (46.Derlis Alberto González Galeano), Nelson Antonio Haedo Valdéz, Roque Luis Santa Cruz Cantero (72.Lucas Ramón Barrios Cáceres), Édgar Milciades Benítez Santander (46.Óscar David Romero Villamayor). Trainer: Ramón Ángel Díaz (Argentina).
Goals: Roque Luis Santa Cruz Cantero (19, 55).
Sent off: Nelson Antonio Haedo Valdéz (51).

13.06.2015, 44th Copa América, Group Stage
Estadio La Portada, La Serena (Chile); Attendance: 16,281
Referee: Wilmar Alexander Roldán Pérez (Colombia)

ARGENTINA - PARAGUAY 2-2(2-0)

PAR: Antony Domingo Silva Cano, Paulo César da Silva Barrios, Pablo César Aguilar Benítez, Marcos Antonio Cáceres Centurión, Miguel Ángel Ramón Samudio, Néstor Ezequiel Ortigoza, Víctor Javier Cáceres Centurión, Richard Ortíz Busto (46.Derlis Alberto González Galeano), Nelson Antonio Haedo Valdéz, Roque Luis Santa Cruz Cantero (79.Lucas Ramón Barrios Cáceres), Raúl Marcelo Bobadilla (66.Édgar Milciades Benítez Santander). Trainer: Ramón Ángel Díaz (Argentina).
Goals: Nelson Antonio Haedo Valdéz (59), Lucas Ramón Barrios Cáceres (89).

16.06.2015, 44th Copa América, Group Stage
Estadio Regional "Calvo y Bascuñán", Antofagasta (Chile); Attendance: 6,099
Referee: Carlos Alfredo Vera Rodríguez (Ecuador)

PARAGUAY - JAMAICA 1-0(1-0)

PAR: Antony Domingo Silva Cano, Paulo César da Silva Barrios, Pablo César Aguilar Benítez, Miguel Ángel Ramón Samudio (77.Iván Rodrigo Piris Leguizamón), Bruno Amílcar Valdez, Néstor Ezequiel Ortigoza, Víctor Javier Cáceres Centurión, Roque Luis Santa Cruz Cantero, Raúl Marcelo Bobadilla (75.Nelson Antonio Haedo Valdéz), Édgar Milciades Benítez Santander (86.Osmar de la Cruz Molinas González), Derlis Alberto González Galeano. Trainer: Ramón Ángel Díaz (Argentina).
Goal: Édgar Milciades Benítez Santander (35).

20.06.2015, 44th Copa América, Group Stage
Estadio La Portada, La Serena (Chile); Attendance: 16,021
Referee: Roberto García Orozco (Mexico)

URUGUAY - PARAGUAY 1-1(1-1)

PAR: Justo Wilmar Villar Viveros, Paulo César da Silva Barrios, Marcos Antonio Cáceres Centurión, Iván Rodrigo Piris Leguizamón, Bruno Amílcar Valdez, Néstor Ezequiel Ortigoza (64.Richard Ortíz Busto), Osmar de la Cruz Molinas González, Nelson Antonio Haedo Valdéz, Raúl Marcelo Bobadilla (68.Derlis Alberto González Galeano), Lucas Ramón Barrios Cáceres (72.Roque Luis Santa Cruz Cantero), Édgar Milciades Benítez Santander. Trainer: Ramón Ángel Díaz (Argentina).
Goal: Lucas Ramón Barrios Cáceres (44).

27.06.2015, 44th Copa América, Quarter-Finals
Estadio Municipal „Alcaldesa Ester Roa Rebolledo", Concepción (Chile); Attendance: 29,276
Referee: Andrés Cunha (Uruguay)

BRAZIL - PARAGUAY 1-1(1-0,1-1); 3-4 on penalties

PAR: Justo Wilmar Villar Viveros, Paulo César da Silva Barrios, Pablo César Aguilar Benítez, Iván Rodrigo Piris Leguizamón, Bruno Amílcar Valdez, Víctor Javier Cáceres Centurión, Eduardo Lorenzo Aranda (77.Osvaldo David Martínez Arce), Nelson Antonio Haedo Valdéz (74.Raúl Marcelo Bobadilla), Roque Luis Santa Cruz Cantero, Édgar Milciades Benítez Santander (84,Óscar David Romero Villamayor), Derlis Alberto González Galeano. Trainer: Ramón Ángel Díaz (Argentina).
Goal: Derlis Alberto González Galeano (72 penalty).
Penalties: Osvaldo David Martínez Arce, Víctor Javier Cáceres Centurión, Raúl Marcelo Bobadilla, Roque Luis Santa Cruz Cantero (missed), Derlis Alberto González Galeano.

30.06.2015, 44th Copa América, Semi-Finals
Estadio Municipal „Alcaldesa Ester Roa Rebolledo", Concepción (Chile); Attendance: 29,205
Referee: Sandro Meira Ricci (Brazil)

ARGENTINA - PARAGUAY 6-1(2-1)

PAR: Justo Wilmar Villar Viveros, Paulo César da Silva Barrios, Pablo César Aguilar Benítez, Iván Rodrigo Piris Leguizamón, Bruno Amílcar Valdez, Víctor Javier Cáceres Centurión, Richard Ortíz Busto, Nelson Antonio Haedo Valdéz (56.Óscar David Romero Villamayor), Roque Luis Santa Cruz Cantero (30.Lucas Ramón Barrios Cáceres), Édgar Milciades Benítez Santander, Derlis Alberto González Galeano (27.Raúl Marcelo Bobadilla). Trainer: Ramón Ángel Díaz (Argentina).
Goal: Lucas Ramón Barrios Cáceres (43).

03.07.2015, 44th Copa América, Third Place Play-off
Estadio Municipal „Alcaldesa Ester Roa Rebolledo", Concepción (Chile); Attendance: 29,143
Referee: Raúl Orosco Delgadillo (Bolivia)

PERU - PARAGUAY 2-0(0-0)

PAR: Justo Wilmar Villar Viveros, Paulo César da Silva Barrios, Pablo César Aguilar Benítez, Marcos Antonio Cáceres Centurión, Miguel Ángel Ramón Samudio, Néstor Ezequiel Ortigoza (64.Richard Ortíz Busto), Víctor Javier Cáceres Centurión (59.Eduardo Lorenzo Aranda), Osvaldo David Martínez Arce (57.Édgar Milciades Benítez Santander), Óscar David Romero Villamayor, Raúl Marcelo Bobadilla, Lucas Ramón Barrios Cáceres. Trainer: Ramón Ángel Díaz (Argentina).

NATIONAL TEAM PLAYERS 2014/2015			
Name	**DOB**	**Caps**	**Goals**
[Club 2014/2015]			

(Caps and goals at 05.07.2015)

Goalkeepers

Bernardo David MEDINA [2014: Club General Díaz Luque]	14.01.1988	**1**	**0**
Antony Domingo SILVA Cano [2014: CA 3 de Febrero Ciudad del Este; 01.2015-> Deportivo Independiente Medellín (COL)]	27.02.1984	**8**	**0**
Joel Alberto SILVA Estigarribia [2014: Club Guaraní Asunción]	13.01.1989	**7**	**0**
Justo Wilmar VILLAR Viveros [2014/2015: CSD Colo-Colo Santiago (CHI)]	30.06.1977	**112**	**0**

Defenders

Pablo César AGUILAR Benítez [2014/2015: CF América Ciudad de México (MEX)]	02.04.1987	**20**	**4**
Júnior Osmar Igancio ALONSO Mujica [2014/2015: Club Cerro Porteño Asunción]	09.02.1993	**6**	**0**
Fabián Cornelio BALBUENA González [2015: Club Libertad Asunción]	23.08.1991	**2**	**0**
José Leonardo CÁCERES Ovelar [2014: Club Nacional Asunción]	28.04.1985	**2**	**0**
Marcos Antonio CÁCERES Centurión [2014/2015: CA Newell's Old Boys Rosario (ARG)]	05.05.1986	**21**	**0**
Luis Carlos CARDOZO Espillaga [2014: CA Monarcas Morelia (MEX)]	10.10.1988	**7**	**0**
Paulo César DA SILVA Barrios [2014/2015: Deportivo Toluca FC (MEX)]	01.02.1980	**127**	**2**
Gustavo Raúl GÓMEZ Portillo [2014/2015: CA Lanús (ARG)]	06.05.1993	**10**	**2**
David Bernardo MENDOZA Ayala [2014/2015: Club Nacional Asunción]	10.05.1985	**2**	**0**
Jorge Luís MOREIRA Ferreira [2014/2015: Club Libertad Asunción]	01.02.1990	**6**	**0**
Iván Rodrigo PIRIS Leguizamón [2014/2015: Udinese Calcio (ITA)]	10.03.1989	**21**	**0**
Miguel Ángel Ramón SAMUDIO [2015: CF América Ciudad de México (MEX)]	24.08.1986	**26**	**1**
Bruno Amílcar VALDEZ [2015: Club Cerro Porteño Asunción]	06.10.1992	**5**	**0**

Midfielders			
Eduardo Lorenzo ARANDA [2015: Club Olimpia Asunción]	28.01.1985	**3**	**0**
Víctor Hugo AYALA Núñez [2014/2015: CA Lanús (ARG)]	01.01.1988	**17**	**0**
Víctor Javier CÁCERES Centurión [2014/2015: CR Flamengo Rio de Janeiro (BRA)]	25.03.1985	**66**	**1**
Marcelo Alejandro ESTIGARRIBIA Balmori [2014: Atalanta Bergamasca Calcio (ITA)]	21.09.1987	**33**	**1**
Osvaldo David MARTÍNEZ Arce [2015: CF América Ciudad de México (MEX)]	08.04.1986	**28**	**1**
David Ariel MENDIETA Chávez [2014: CA 3 de Febrero Ciudad del Este]	22.08.1986	**4**	**0**
Osmar de la Cruz MOLINAS González [2014: Club Libertad Asunción]	03.05.1985	**10**	**0**
Néstor Ezequiel ORTIGOZA [2014/2015: CA San Lorenzo de Almagro (ARG)]	07.10.1984	**26**	**1**
Celso Fabián ORTÍZ Gamarra [2014/2015: AZ'67 Alkmaar (NED)]	26.01.1989	**7**	**0**
Richard ORTÍZ Busto [2015: Deportivo Toluca FC (MEX)]	22.05.1988	**20**	**4**
Fidencio OVIEDO Domínguez [2015: Club Cerro Porteño Asunción]	30.05.1987	**15**	**0**
Miguel Ángel PANIAGUA Rivarola [2014: Club Cerro Porteño Asunción]	14.05.1987	**1**	**0**
Hernán Arsenio PÉREZ González [2013/2014: Real Valladolid CF (ESP)]	25.02.1989	**22**	**1**
Cristian Miguel RIVEROS Núñez [2014: Grêmio Foot-Ball Porto Alegrense (BRA)]	16.10.1982	**90**	**15**
Marcos Antonio RIVEROS Krayacich [2014: Club Nacional Asunción]	04.09.1988	**14**	**1**
Jorge Luis ROJAS Mendoza [2014/2015: Club de Gimnasia y Esgrima La Plata (ARG)]	07.01.1993	**15**	**1**
Óscar David ROMERO Villamayor [2014: Club Cerro Porteño Asunción; 01.2015-> Racing Club de Avellaneda (ARG)]	04.07.1992	**14**	**1**
Óscar Ramón RUÍZ Roa [2014: Club Deportivo Capiatá]	14.05.1991	**2**	**0**
Silvio Gabriel TORALES Castillo [2014: Club Nacional Asunción]	23.09.1991	**7**	**0**

Forwards

Lucas Ramón BARRIOS Cáceres [2014/2015: Montpellier Hérault SC (FRA)]	13.11.1984	**30**	**9**
Édgar Milciades BENÍTEZ Santander [2014/2015: Deportivo Toluca FC (MEX)]	08.11.1987	**47**	**7**
Jorge Daniel BENÍTEZ Guillén [2014: PAE Olympiacos Peiraiás (GRE)]	02.09.1992	**2**	**0**
Julián Alfonso BENÍTEZ Franco [2014: Club Nacional Asunción]	06.06.1987	**4**	**0**
Raúl Marcelo BOBADILLA [2015: FC Augsburg (GER)]	18.06.1987	**8**	**0**
Cecilio Andrés DOMÍNGUEZ Ruíz [2014: Club Sol de América Asunción]	11.08.1994	**2**	**0**
Derlis Alberto GONZÁLEZ Galeano [2014/2015: FC Basel (SUI)]	20.03.1994	**14**	**2**
Christian Gilberto OVELAR Rodríguez [2014: Club Olimpia Asunción]	18.01.1985	**3**	**0**
Ángel Rodrigo ROMERO Villamayor [2014: SC Corinthians Paulista São Paulo]	04.07.1992	**3**	**1**
Arnaldo Antonio SANABRIA Ayala [2014/2015: AS Roma (ITA)]	04.03.1996	**5**	**0**
Roque Luis SANTA CRUZ Cantero [2014: Málaga FC (ESP); 01.2015-> Cruz Azul FC Ciudad de México (MEX)]	16.08.1981	**110**	**32**
Nelson Antonio Haedo VALDÉZ [2015: Eintracht Frankfurt (GER)]	28.11.1983	**73**	**13**

National coaches

Víctor GENÉS [27.07.2013-18.11.2014]	29.06.1971	13 M; 3 W; 4 D; 6 L; 19-22
Ramón Ángel DÍAZ (ARG) [as of 04.12.2014]	29.08.1959	9 M; 1 W; 5 D; 3 L; 8-15

PERU

The Country:
República del Perú (Republic of Peru)
Capital: Lima
Surface: 1,285,216 km²
Inhabitants: 31,151,643
Time: UTC-5

The FA:
Federación Peruana de Fútbol
Avenida Aviación 2085 San Luis, Lima 30
Year of Formation: 1922
Member of FIFA since: 1924
Member of CONMEBOL since: 1925
Internet: www.fpf.com.pe

NATIONAL TEAM RECORDS	
First international match:	01.11.1927, Lima: Peru – Uruguay 0-4
Most international caps:	Roberto Carlos Palacios Mestas – 128 caps (1992-2012)
Most international goals:	Teófilo Juan Cubillas Arizaga – 26 goals / 81 caps (1968-1982)

OLYMPIC GAMES 1900-2012
1936, 1960
FIFA CONFEDERATIONS CUP 1992-2013
None

COPA AMÉRICA	
1916	Did not enter
1917	Did not enter
1919	Did not enter
1920	Did not enter
1921	Did not enter
1922	Did not enter
1923	Did not enter
1924	Did not enter
1925	Did not enter
1926	Did not enter
1927	3rd Place
1929	4th Place
1935	3rd Place
1937	6th Place
1939	**Winners**
1941	4th Place
1942	5th Place
1945	Withdrew
1946	Withdrew
1947	5th Place
1949	3rd Place
1953	5th Place
1955	3rd Place
1956	6th Place
1957	4th Place
1959	4th Place
1959E	Did not enter
1963	5th Place
1967	Withdrew
1975	**Winners**
1979	Semi-Finals
1983	Semi-Finals
1987	Round 1
1989	Round 1
1991	Round 1
1993	Quarter-Finals
1995	Round 1
1997	4th Place
1999	Quarter-Finals
2001	Quarter-Finals
2004	Quarter-Finals
2007	Quarter-Finals
2011	3rd Place
2015	3rd Place

FIFA WORLD CUP	
1930	Final Tournament (Group Stage)
1934	Withdrew
1938	Qualifiers
1950	Withdrew
1954	Withdrew
1958	Qualifiers
1962	Qualifiers
1966	Qualifiers
1970	Final Tournament (Quarter-Finals)
1974	Qualifiers
1978	Final Tournament (2nd Round of 16)
1982	Final Tournament (Group Stage)
1986	Qualifiers
1990	Qualifiers
1994	Qualifiers
1998	Qualifiers
2002	Qualifiers
2006	Qualifiers
2010	Qualifiers
2014	Qualifiers

PANAMERICAN GAMES	
1951	Did not enter
1955	Did not enter
1959	Did not enter
1963	Did not enter
1967	Did not enter
1971	Did not enter
1975	Did not enter
1979	Did not enter
1983	Did not enter
1987	Did not enter
1991	Did not enter
1995	Did not enter
1999	Did not enter
2003	Did not enter
2007	Did not enter
2011	Did not enter

PANAMERICAN CHAMPIONSHIP	
1952	4th Place
1956	4th Place
1960	Did not enter

PERUVIAN CLUB HONOURS IN SOUTH AMERICAN CLUB COMPETITIONS:

COPA LIBERTADORES 1960-2014
None
COPA SUDAMERICANA 2002-2014
Club Sportivo Cienciano Cuzco (2003)
RECOPA SUDAMERICANA 1989-2014
Club Sportivo Cienciano Cuzco (2004)
COPA CONMEBOL 1992-1999
None
SUPERCUP „JOÃO HAVELANGE“ 1988-1997*
None
COPA MERCONORTE 1998-2001**
None

**Contested betwenn winners of all previous editions of the Copa Libertadores*

***Contested between teams belonging countries from the northern part of South America (Bolivia, Colombia, Ecuador, Peru and Venezuela);*

NATIONAL COMPETITIONS
TABLE OF HONOURS

NATIONAL CHAMPIONS 1906-2014	
	Liga Peruana
1912	Lima Cricket and Football Club
1913	Jorge Chávez Nr. 1 Lima
1914	Lima Cricket and Football Club
1915	Sport José Galvez Lima
1916	Sport José Galvez Lima
1917	Sport Juan Bielovucic Lima
1918	Sport Alianza Lima(1)
1919	Sport Alianza Lima
1920	Sport Inca Lima
1921	Sport Progreso Lima
1922	*No competition*
1923	*No competition*
1924	*No competition*
1925	*No competition*
	Amateur Era Championship
1926	Sport Progreso Lima
1927	Club Alianza Lima
1928	Club Alianza Lima
1929	Federación Universitaria Lima(2)
1930	Club Atlético Chalaco Callao
1931	Club Alianza Lima
1932	Club Alianza Lima
1933	Club Alianza Lima
1934	Club Universitario de Deportes Lima
1935	Sport Boys Association Callao
1936	*No competition*
1937	Sport Boys Association Callao
1938	Club Centro Deportivo Municipal Lima

1939	Club Universitario de Deportes Lima
1940	Club Centro Deportivo Municipal Lima
1941	Club Universitario de Deportes Lima
1942	Sport Boys Association Callao
1943	Club Centro Deportivo Municipal Lima
1944	Mariscal Sucre FC Lima
1945	Club Universitario de Deportes Lima
1946	Club Universitario de Deportes Lima
1947	Club Atlético Chalaco Callao
1948	Club Alianza Lima
1949	Club Universitario de Deportes Lima
1950	Club Centro Deportivo Municipal Lima
	Lima & Callao League
1951	Sport Boys Association Callao
1952	Club Alianza Lima
1953	Mariscal Sucre FC Lima
1954	Club Alianza Lima
1955	Club Alianza Lima
1956	Club Sporting Cristal Lima
1957	Club Centro Iqueño Lima
1958	Sport Boys Association Callao
1959	Club Universitario de Deportes Lima
1960	Club Universitario de Deportes Lima
1961	Club Sporting Cristal Lima
1962	Club Alianza Lima
1963	Club Alianza Lima
1964	Club Universitario de Deportes Lima
1965	Club Alianza Lima
	Professional (Descentralizado) Era Championship
1966	Club Universitario de Deportes Lima
1967	Club Universitario de Deportes Lima
1968	Club Sporting Cristal Lima
1969	Club Universitario de Deportes Lima
1970	Club Sporting Cristal Lima
1971	Club Universitario de Deportes Lima
1972	Club Sporting Cristal Lima
1973	Club Atlético Defensor Lima
1974	Club Universitario de Deportes Lima
1975	Club Alianza Lima
1976	Club Sport Unión Huaral
1977	Club Alianza Lima
1978	Club Alianza Lima
1979	Club Sporting Cristal Lima
1980	Club Sporting Cristal Lima
1981	Foot Ball Club Melgar Arequipa
1982	Club Universitario de Deportes Lima
1983	Club Sporting Cristal Lima
1984	Sport Boys Association Callao
1985	Club Universitario de Deportes Lima
1986	Club Deportivo Colegio San Agustín Lima
1987	Club Universitario de Deportes Lima
1988	Club Sporting Cristal Lima

1989	Club Sport Unión Huaral
1990	Club Universitario de Deportes Lima
1991	Club Sporting Cristal Lima
1992	Club Universitario de Deportes Lima
1993	Club Universitario de Deportes Lima
1994	Club Sporting Cristal Lima
1995	Club Sporting Cristal Lima
1996	Club Sporting Cristal Lima
1997	Club Alianza Lima
1998	Club Universitario de Deportes Lima
1999	Club Universitario de Deportes Lima
2000	Club Universitario de Deportes Lima
2001	Club Alianza Lima
2002	Club Sporting Cristal Lima
2003	Club Alianza Lima
2004	Club Alianza Lima
2005	Club Sporting Cristal Lima
2006	Club Alianza Lima
2007	Club Deportivo Universidad San Martín de Porres
2008	Club Deportivo Universidad San Martín de Porres
2009	Club Universitario de Deportes Lima
2010	Club Deportivo Universidad San Martín de Porres
2011	Club Juan Aurich de Chiclayo
2012	Club Sporting Cristal Lima
2013	Club Universitario de Deportes Lima
2014	Club Sporting Cristal Lima

(1)became 1927 Club Alianza Lima

(2)became 1931 Club Universitario de Deportes Lima

	BEST GOALSCORERS	
1928	Carlos Alejandro Villanueva Martinez (Club Alianza Lima)	3
1929	Carlos Cilloniz (Federación Universitaria Lima)	8
1930	Manuel Puente (Club Atlético Chalaco Callao)	3
1931	Carlos Alejandro Villanueva Martinez (Club Alianza Lima)	16
1932	Teodoro Fernández Meyzán (Club Universitario de Deportes Lima)	11
1933	Teodoro Fernández Meyzán (Club Universitario de Deportes Lima)	9
1934	Teodoro Fernández Meyzán (Club Universitario de Deportes Lima)	9
1935	Jorge Alcalde (Sport Boys Association Callao)	5
1936	*No competition*	
1937	Juan Flores (Sport Boys Association Callao)	10
1938	Jorge Alcalde (Sport Boys Association Callao)	8
1939	Teodoro Fernández Meyzán (Club Universitario de Deportes Lima)	15
1940	Teodoro Fernández Meyzán (Club Universitario de Deportes Lima)	15
1941	Jorge Cabrejos (Club Centro Deportivo Municipal Lima)	13
1942	Teodoro Fernández Meyzán (Club Universitario de Deportes Lima)	11
1943	German Cerro (Club Universitario de Deportes Lima)	9
1944	Victor Espinoza (Club Universitario de Deportes Lima)	16
1945	Teodoro Fernández Meyzán (Club Universitario de Deportes Lima)	16
1946	Valeriano López (Sport Boys Association Callao)	22
1947	Valeriano López (Sport Boys Association Callao)	20
1948	Valeriano López (Sport Boys Association Callao)	20
1949	Emilio Salinas (Club Alianza Lima)	18
1950	Alberto Terry Arias-Schreiber (Club Universitario de Deportes Lima)	16
1951	Valeriano López (Sport Boys Association Callao)	31
1952	Emilio Salinas (Club Alianza Lima)	22
1953	Gualberto Blanco (Club Atlético Chalaco Callao)	17
1954	Vicente Villanueva (Club Sporting Tabaco Lima)	
1955	Maximo Mosquera (Club Alianza Lima)	11
1956	Daniel Ruiz (Club Universitario de Deportes Lima)	16
1957	Daniel Ruiz (Club Universitario de Deportes Lima)	20
1958	Juan Joya (Club Alianza Lima)	17
1959	Daniel Ruiz (Club Universitario de Deportes Lima)	28
1960	Fernando Olaechea (Club Centro Iqueño Lima)	18
1961	Alberto Gallardo (Club Sporting Cristal Lima)	18
1962	Alberto Gallardo (Club Sporting Cristal Lima)	22
1963	Pedro Pablo León García (Club Alianza Lima)	13
1964	Ángel Uribe Sánchez (Club Universitario de Deportes Lima)	15
1965	Carlos Urranaga (Club Atlético Defensor Lima)	16
1966	Teófilo Juan Cubillas Arizaga (Club Alianza Lima)	19
1967	Pedro Pablo León García (Club Alianza Lima)	14
1968	Oswaldo Felipe Ramírez Salcedo (Sport Boys Association Callao)	26
1969	Jaime Moreno (Club Centro Deportivo Municipal Lima)	15
1970	Teófilo Juan Cubillas Arizaga (Club Alianza Lima)	22
1971	Manuel Mellan (Club Centro Deportivo Municipal Lima)	25
1972	Francisco González (Club Atlético Defensor Lima)	20
1973	Francisco González (Club Atlético Defensor Lima)	25
1974	Pablo Muchotrigo (Club Sportivo Cienciano Cuzco)	32
1975	José Leyva (Club Alfonso Ugarte Puno)	28
1976	Alejandro Luces (Club Sport Unión Huaral)	17
1977	Freddy Ravello (Club Alianza Lima)	21
1978	Juan José Oré Herrera (Club Universitario de Deportes Lima)	19

1979	José Leyva (Club Alfonso Ugarte Puno)	28
1980	Oswaldo Felipe Ramírez Salcedo (Club Sporting Cristal Lima)	18
1981	José Carranza (Club Alianza Lima)	15
1982	Percy Rojas Montero (Club Universitario de Deportes Lima)	19
1983	Juan Caballero (Club Sporting Cristal Lima)	29
1984	Jaime Drago (Club Universitario de Deportes Lima) Francisco Montero (Club Atlético Torino de Talara)	13
1985	Genaro Neyra (Foot Ball Club Melgar Arequipa)	22
1986	Juvenal Briceño (Foot Ball Club Melgar Arequipa)	16
1987	Fidel Suárez (Club Universitario de Deportes Lima)	20
1988	Alberto Mora (Club Social Deportivo Octavio Espinoza Ica)	15
1989	Carlos Delgado (Club Carlos Mannucci de Trujillo)	14
1990	Cláudio Adalberto Adão (BRA, Sport Boys Association Callao)	31
1991	Horacio Raúl Baldessari Guntero (ARG, Club Sporting Cristal Lima)	25
1992	Marco dos Santos „Marquinho" (BRA, Sport Boys Association Callao)	18
1993	Waldir Alejandro Sáenz Pérez (Club Alianza Lima)	31
1994	Flavio Francisco Maestri Andrade (Club Sporting Cristal Lima)	25
1995	Julio César de Andrade Moura „Julinho" (BRA, Club Sporting Cristal Lima)	23
1996	Waldir Alejandro Sáenz Pérez (Club Alianza Lima)	19
1997	Ricardo Zegarra (Club Alianza Atlético Sullana)	17
1998	Nílson Esídio Mora (BRA, Club Sporting Cristal Lima)	25
1999	Herlyn Ysrael Zuñiga Yañez (Foot Ball Club Melgar Arequipa)	32
2000	José Eduardo Esidio (BRA, Club Universitario de Deportes Lima)	37
2001	Jorge Ramírez (Club Deportivo Wanka Huancayo)	21
2002	Luis Fabián Artime (ARG, Foot Ball Club Melgar Arequipa)	24
2003	Luis Alberto Bonnet (ARG, Club Sporting Cristal Lima)	20
2004	Gabriel García (URU, Foot Ball Club Melgar Arequipa)	35
2005	Miguel Ángel Mostto Fernández-Prada (Club Sportivo Cienciano Cuzco)	18
2006	Miguel Ángel Mostto Fernández-Prada (Club Sportivo Cienciano Cuzco)	22
2007	Johan Javier Fano Espinoza (Club Universitario de Deportes Lima)	19
2008	Miguel Alejandro Ximénez Acosta (URU, Club Sporting Cristal Lima)	32
2009	Richard María Estigarribia (PAR, Total Chalaco FBC Callao)	23
2010	Héber Alberto Arriola (ARG, CD Universidad San Martín de Porres)	24
2011	Luis Carlos Tejada Hansell (PAN, Club Juan Aurich de Chiclayo)	17
2012	Andy Roberto Pando García (Asociación Civil Real Atlético Garcilaso)	27
2013	Víctor Alfonso Rossel Del Mar (CD Unión Comercio Nueva Cajamarca) Raúl Mario Ruidíaz Misitich (Club Universitario de Deportes Lima)	21
2014	Santiago Silva Gerez (URU, CD Universidad San Martín de Porres)	23

Torneo del Inca 2014
(2014 Copa Movistar)
14.02.-21.05.2014

The 2014 Torneo del Inca was the 2nd season of the Peruvian domestic cup. It was played before the start of the national championship 2014. The 16 teams were divided into 2 groups of each 8 teams, the winner of each group being qualified for the final.

Group A

1.	**Club Alianza Lima**	14	7	6	1	20	-	8	27
2.	Club Juan Aurich de Chiclayo	14	7	3	4	32	-	20	24
3.	CSD León de Huánuco	14	6	6	2	20	-	15	24
4.	Club Sporting Cristal Lima	14	5	5	4	26	-	21	20
5.	Asociación Civil Real Atlético Garcilaso	14	5	4	5	20	-	15	19
6.	CD Unión Comercio Nueva Cajamarca	14	3	6	5	15	-	25	15
7.	Club Inti Gas Deportes Ayacucho	14	3	3	8	17	-	31	12
8.	Club Deportivo Comunitario Laboral San Simón	14	2	3	9	10	-	25	9

Group B

1.	**CD Universidad San Martín de Porres**	14	8	1	5	26	-	19	25
2.	CSCD Universidad César Vallejo Trujillo	14	7	3	4	23	-	15	24
3.	Foot Ball Club Melgar Arequipa	14	6	4	4	18	-	11	22
4.	CCD Universidad Técnica de Cajamarca	14	5	5	4	14	-	18	20
5.	CCD Los Caimanes de Puerto Etén	14	4	6	4	16	-	16	18
6.	Deportivo Sport Huancayo	14	4	5	5	16	-	22	17
7.	Club Universitario de Deportes Lima	14	3	6	5	12	-	14	15
8.	Club Sportivo Cienciano Cuzco*	14	3	2	9	9	-	19	7

**4 points deducted - Club Sportivo Cienciano Cuzco will start the 2014 Torneo Apertura with a deduction of 3 points!*

Copa Inca Final 2014

21.05.2014, Estadio "Miguel Grau", Callao; Attendance: 13,239
Referee: Víctor Hugo Carrillo Casanova
Club Alianza Lima - CD Universidad San Martín de Porres **3-3(0-2,2-2,3-3); 5-3 on penalties**

Alianza: Manuel Alexander Heredia Rojas, Walter Fernando Ibáñez Costa, Roberto Efraín Koichi Aparicio Mori, Guillermo Alejandro Guizasola La Rosa (66.Junior Alexander Ponce Pardo), Roberto Carlos Guizasola La Rosa, Pablo Nicolas Míguez Farre, Paulo César Albarracín García, Eduardo Israel Kahn Gómez (46.Mauricio Alejandro Montes Sanguinetti), Josimar Jair Atoche Bances (46.Julio César Landauri Ventura), Wilmer Alexander Aguirre Vásquez, Mauro Guevgeozián Crespo. Trainer: Guillermo Óscar Sanguinetti Giordano.

Universidad San Martín: Pedro David Gallese, Yhirbis Yosec Córdova Guizasola, Josepmir Aaron Ballón Villacorta, Johnnier Esteiner Montaño Caicedo (81.Raziel Samir García Paredes), Carlos Oswaldo Fernández Maldonado, Carlos Ariel Marinelli (34.Paulo Hernán Hinostroza Vásquez), Luis Enrique Álvarez Valdivia, Carlos Antonio Ascues Ávila, Benjamín Ubierna Barandiarán, Luis Alberto Perea Pérez [*sent off 40*], Santiago Silva Gérez (46.Jersson Vásquez Shampiama). Trainer: Julio César Uribe Flores.

Goals: 0-1 Luis Alberto Perea Pérez (16 penalty), 0-2 Santiago Silva Gérez (28), 1-2 Roberto Efraín Koichi Aparicio Mori (85), 2-2 Mauro Guevgeozián Crespo (90+2), 3-2 Mauricio Alejandro Montes Sanguinetti (111), 3-3 Benjamín Ubierna Barandiarán (112).

Penalties: Walter Fernando Ibáñez Costa 1-0; Josepmir Aaron Ballón Villacorta 1-1; Roberto Efraín Koichi Aparicio Mori 2-1; Jersson Vásquez Shampiama 2-2; Junior Alexander Ponce Pardo 3-2; Carlos Oswaldo Fernández Maldonado (missed), Wilmer Alexander Aguirre Vásquez 4-2; Paulo Hernán Hinostroza Vásquez 4-3; Mauro Guevgeozián Crespo 5-3.

NATIONAL CHAMPIONSHIP
Primera División del Perú / Torneo Descentralizado de Fútbol Profesional 2014
(Copa Movistar)

Torneo Apertura

Results

Round 1 [07-09.06.2014]
Real A. Garcilaso - León de Huánuco 3-1(3-0)
Univ.San Martín – Univ.Cesar Vallejo 1-1(0-0)
Juan Aurich - CD San Simón 2-1(1-1)
FBC Melgar - CS Cienciano 0-0
CD Unión Comercio - CCD Los Caimanes 4-0
Club Inti Gas - Alianza Lima 1-1
Universitario Lima - Sport Huancayo 3-0
Universidad Técnica - Sporting Cristal 1-1

Round 2 [13-15.06.2014]
CCD Los Caimanes - Universidad Técnica 0-0
CD San Simón - CD Unión Comercio 0-1
Sport Huancayo - Club Inti Gas 1-3(1-2)
Sporting Cristal - FBC Melgar 1-2(1-0)
Univ. Cesar Vallejo - Juan Aurich 2-0(2-0)
León de Huánuco – Univ. San Martín 1-1(0-1)
CS Cienciano - Universitario Lima 1-2(1-1)
Alianza Lima - Real Atl. Garcilaso 2-0(1-0)

Round 3 [20-22.06.2014]
Univ. Técnica – CD Unión Comercio 1-1(1-0)
FBC Melgar - CCD Los Caimanes 3-0(0-0)
Club Inti Gas - CS Cienciano 3-1(0-1)
Juan Aurich - León de Huánuco 2-1(1-0)
Univ. San Martín - Alianza Lima 1-1(0-0)
Real Atl. Garcilaso - Sport Huancayo 1-2(1-1)
CD San Simón – Univ. Cesar Vallejo 2-1(0-0)
Universitario Lima - Sporting Cristal 0-0

Round 4 [27-29.06.2014]
León de Huánuco - CD San Simón 4-0(1-0)
Sporting Cristal - Club Inti Gas 3-0(2-0)
Univ. Cesar Vallejo – Univ. Técnica 3-0(2-0)
CS Cienciano - Real Atl. Garcilaso 2-0(1-0)
CD Unión Comercio - FBC Melgar 0-2(0-0)
Sport Huancayo – Univ. San Martín 2-4(1-1)
Alianza Lima - Juan Aurich 0-0
Los Caimanes - Universitario Lima 2-4(1-2)

Round 5 [05-06.07.2014]
Real Atl. Garcilaso - Sporting Cristal 2-1(0-0)
FBC Melgar - Universidad Técnica 2-2(1-0)
Univ. San Martín - CS Cienciano 0-1(0-0)
Juan Aurich - Sport Huancayo 6-0(3-0)
Univ. Cesar Vallejo - León Huánuco 3-1(2-0)
Club Inti Gas - CCD Los Caimanes 2-1(2-0)
CD San Simón - Alianza Lima 1-0(0-0)
Universitario Lima - CD Unión Comercio 0-0

Round 6 [11-13.07.2014]
CD Unión Comercio - Club Inti Gas 0-1(0-1)
FBC Melgar - León de Huánuco 1-1(0-1)
Sporting Cristal - Univ. San Martín 0-0
Sport Huancayo - CD San Simón 1-1(0-1)
Univ. Técnica - Universitario Lima 2-1(0-0)
Los Caimanes - Real Atl. Garcilaso 0-1(0-0)
Alianza Lima - Univ. Cesar Vallejo 0-0
CS Cienciano - Juan Aurich 1-1(0-0)

Round 7 [15-17.07.2014]
Univ. San Martín - Los Caimanes 3-1(1-0)
Real Atl. Garcilaso - Unión Comercio 1-0(1-0)
Club Inti Gas - Universidad Técnica 1-1(1-0)
León de Huánuco - Alianza Lima 1-0(0-0)
Univ. Cesar Vallejo - Sport Huancayo 2-0(0-0)
Universitario Lima - FBC Melgar 1-2(1-1)
CD San Simón - CS Cienciano 0-2(0-2)
Juan Aurich - Sporting Cristal 3-4(2-4)

Round 8 [19-21.07.2014]
Sport Huancayo - León de Huánuco 0-1(0-1)
Univ. Técnica - Real Atl. Garcilaso 1-0(1-0)
Universitario Lima - Alianza Lima 1-0(1-0)
CS Cienciano - Univ. Cesar Vallejo 2-0(0-0)
Sporting Cristal - CD San Simón 6-0(2-0)
CCD Los Caimanes - Juan Aurich 0-4(0-1)
Unión Comercio - Univ. San Martín 1-0(0-0)
FBC Melgar - Club Inti Gas 2-2(0-1)

Round 9 [23-27.07.2014]
Alianza Lima - Sport Huancayo 4-3(2-0)
Real Atl. Garcilaso - FBC Melgar 1-1(0-1)
León de Huánuco - CS Cienciano 2-2(1-0)
Univ. San Martín – Univ. Técnica 4-0(3-0)
Univ. Cesar Vallejo - Sporting Cristal 3-2(1-2)
Juan Aurich - CD Unión Comercio 2-1(0-0)
CD San Simón - CCD Los Caimanes 2-4(1-2)
Club Inti Gas - Universitario Lima 2-0(2-0)

Round 10 [29-31.07.2014]
CS Cienciano - Alianza Lima 2-1(1-0)
Los Caimanes - Univ. Cesar Vallejo 1-0(1-0)
Universidad Técnica - Juan Aurich 3-1(1-0)
Universit. Lima - Real Atl. Garcilaso 2-1(2-0)
Unión Comercio - Sport Huancayo 3-0(1-0)
FBC Melgar - Univ. San Martín 2-1(1-0)
Sporting Cristal - León de Huánuco 4-0(2-0)
Inti Gas - CD San Simón 3-2(3-0) [03.08.]

Round 11 [08-10.08.2014]
León de Huánuco - Los Caimanes 1-0(1-0)
Sport Huancayo - CS Cienciano 3-1(3-1)
Juan Aurich - FBC Melgar 3-1(2-1)
Univ. Cesar Vallejo - Unión Comercio 1-0(1-0)
Univ. San Martín - Universitario Lima 3-3(3-1)
Real Atl. Garcilaso - Club Inti Gas 3-0(2-0)
CD San Simón - Universidad Técnica 2-1(0-0)
Alianza Lima - Sporting Cristal 2-1(0-0)

Round 12 [13-14.08.2014]
FBC Melgar - Univ. Cesar Vallejo 2-1(1-1)
Real Atl. Garcilaso - Juan Aurich 2-2(2-0)
Club Inti Gas - Univ. San Martín 2-4(1-2)
CCD Los Caimanes - Alianza Lima 0-0
Universitario Lima - CD San Simón 1-0(0-0)
Sporting Cristal - Sport Huancayo 1-2(1-1)
Unión Comercio - León de Huánuco 1-0(0-0)
Universidad Técnica - CS Cienciano 2-1(1-1)

Round 13 [16-18.08.2014]
Univ. San Martín - Real Atl. Garcilaso 2-0(2-0)
Univ. Cesar Vallejo – Universit. Lima 1-2(0-0)
CD San Simón - FBC Melgar 1-0(0-0)
CS Cienciano - Sporting Cristal 1-1(1-0)
Alianza Lima - CD Unión Comercio 2-2(1-0)
Juan Aurich - Club Inti Gas 4-1(3-0)
Sport Huancayo - CCD Los Caimanes 5-1(3-0)
L. Huánuco – Univ. Técnica 1-0(0-0) [03.09.]

Round 14 [23-24.08.2014]
CCD Los Caimanes - CS Cienciano 2-1(0-1)
CD Unión Comercio - Sporting Cristal 2-0(1-0)
Universitario Lima - León de Huánuco 1-2(0-0)
Club Inti Gas - Univ. Cesar Vallejo 3-3(2-1)
FBC Melgar - Sport Huancayo 2-2(2-2)
Real Atl. Garcilaso - CD San Simón 4-1(2-1)
Univ. San Martín - Juan Aurich 1-2(1-1)
Universidad Técnica - Alianza Lima 0-2(0-1)

Round 15 [30-31.08.2014]
CS Cienciano - CD Unión Comercio 2-1(1-0)
U. Cesar Vallejo - Real Atl. Garcilaso 2-0(1-0)
CD San Simón - Univ. San Martín 0-0
Alianza Lima - FBC Melgar 1-1(0-1)
Juan Aurich - Universitario Lima 2-0(1-0)
Sporting Cristal - CCD Los Caimanes 1-1(0-1)
Sport Huancayo - Universidad Técnica 1-1(1-0)
León de Huánuco - Club Inti Gas 1-1(0-0)

Final Standings

1.	Club Juan Aurich de Chiclayo	15	9	3	3	34	-	18	30
2.	Foot Ball Club Melgar Arequipa	15	6	7	2	23	-	17	25
3.	CSCD Universidad César Vallejo Trujillo	15	7	3	5	23	-	16	24
4.	Club Universitario de Deportes Lima	15	7	3	5	21	-	18	24
5.	Club Inti Gas Deportes Ayacucho	15	6	5	4	25	-	27	23
6.	CSD León de Huánuco	15	6	4	5	18	-	19	22
7.	CD Universidad San Martín de Porres	15	5	6	4	25	-	17	21
8.	CD Unión Comercio Nueva Cajamarca	15	6	3	6	17	-	12	21
9.	Asociación Civil Real Atlético Garcilaso	15	6	2	7	19	-	19	20
10.	Club Sportivo Cienciano Cuzco*	15	6	4	5	20	-	18	19
11.	Club Alianza Lima	15	4	7	4	16	-	14	19
12.	CCD Universidad Técnica de Cajamarca	15	4	6	5	15	-	21	18
13.	Club Sporting Cristal Lima	15	4	5	6	26	-	19	17
14.	Deportivo Sport Huancayo	15	4	3	8	22	-	34	15
15.	Club Deportivo Comunitario Laboral San Simón	15	4	2	9	13	-	30	14
16.	CCD Los Caimanes de Puerto Etén	15	3	3	9	13	-	31	12

*Please note: *Club Sportivo Cienciano Cuzco – 3 points deducted*
Club Juan Aurich de Chiclayo were qualified for the Championship finals.

Torneo Clausura

Results

Round 1 [06-08.09.2014]
León d. Huánuco - Real Atl. Garcilaso 1-1(0-1)
CS Cienciano - FBC Melgar 0-2(0-0)
CD San Simón - Juan Aurich 1-2(0-2)
Sport Huancayo - Universitario Lima 0-1(0-0)
Sporting Cristal - Universidad Técnica 3-2(2-1)
os Caimanes - CD Unión Comercio 1-0(0-0)
Alianza Lima - Club Inti Gas 2-1(1-1) [17.09.]
U. Cesar Vallejo - San Martín 1-0(0-0) [20.11.]

Round 2 [12-14.09.2014]
Univ. Técnica - CCD Los Caimanes 1-1(0-0)
CD Unión Comercio - CD San Simón 3-1(2-1)
Club Inti Gas - Sport Huancayo 1-1(1-0)
Univ. San Martín - León de Huánuco 0-1(0-1)
Juan Aurich - Univ. Cesar Vallejo 1-2(1-1)
FBC Melgar - Sporting Cristal 1-0(0-0)
Real Atl. Garcilaso - Alianza Lima 0-0
Universitario Lima - CS Cienciano 2-0(1-0)

Round 3 [20-21.09.2014]
Sport Huancayo - Real Atl. Garcilaso 3-1(1-0)
CD Unión Comercio – Univ. Técnica 3-0(1-0)
León de Huánuco - Juan Aurich 3-0(2-0)
Univ. Cesar Vallejo - CD San Simón 2-0(1-0)
CS Cienciano - Club Inti Gas 0-0
CCD Los Caimanes - FBC Melgar 0-3(0-0)
Alianza Lima - Univ. San Martín 2-1(1-1)
Sporting Cristal – Univ. Lima 3-0(1-0) [24.09.]

Round 4 [26-28.09.2014]
Univ. San Martín - Sport Huancayo 4-1(1-1)
Univ. Técnica - Univ. Cesar Vallejo 1-0(1-0)
FBC Melgar - CD Unión Comercio 1-0(1-0)
Real Atl. Garcilaso - CS Cienciano 0-2(0-2)
Juan Aurich - Alianza Lima 0-0
CD San Simón - León de Huánuco 2-2(1-1)
Club Inti Gas - Sporting Cristal 3-3(2-1)
Universitario Lima - Los Caimanes 1-0(0-0)

Round 5 [01-02.10.2014]
CCD Los Caimanes - Club Inti Gas 0-0
Unión Comercio – Universit. Lima 2-0(0-0)
Sporting Cristal - Real Atl. Garcilaso 1-1(1-0)
CS Cienciano - Univ. San Martín 3-2(2-0)
Sport Huancayo - Juan Aurich 0-1(0-1)
Universidad Técnica - FBC Melgar 2-0(1-0)
Alianza Lima - CD San Simón 2-0(1-0)
Huánuco - Un. Cesar Vallejo 1-0(1-0) [26.11.]

Round 6 [10-12.10.2014]
CD San Simón - Sport Huancayo 0-1(0-0)
Club Inti Gas - CD Unión Comercio 1-2(1-1)
Real Atl. Garcilaso - Los Caimanes 2-0(0-0)
Univ. Cesar Vallejo - Alianza Lima 2-2(0-1)
León de Huánuco - FBC Melgar 0-1(0-0)
Universitario Lima – Univ. Técnica 3-0(1-0)
Juan Aurich - CS Cienciano 1-0(1-0)
San Martín - Sporting Cristal 0-1(0-1) [05.11.]

Round 7 [16-19.10.2014]
Universidad Técnica - Club Inti Gas 0-1(0-0)
Sporting Cristal - Juan Aurich 4-1(0-1)
CS Cienciano - CD San Simón 2-0(0-0)
FBC Melgar - Universitario Lima 1-1(0-1)
Los Caimanes - Univ. San Martín 4-1(0-1)
Unión Comercio - Real Atl. Garcilaso 2-2(2-1)
Sport Huancayo - Univ. Cesar Vallejo 3-1(1-1)
Alianza Lima - León de Huánuco 2-0(1-0)

Round 8 [21-22.10.2014]
CD San Simón - Sporting Cristal 2-3(0-2)
Univ. San Martín - Unión Comercio 2-1(1-1)
Juan Aurich - CCD Los Caimanes 0-0
Real Atl. Garcilaso – Univ. Técnica 3-0(1-0)
Club Inti Gas - FBC Melgar 2-0(1-0)
León de Huánuco - Sport Huancayo 1-0(0-0)
Univ. Cesar Vallejo - CS Cienciano 3-2(2-2)
Alianza Lima - Universitario Lima 1-0(0-0)

Round 9 [25-27.10.2014]
CS Cienciano - León de Huánuco 4-2(3-2)
Sporting Cristal - Univ. Cesar Vallejo 4-1(4-0)
Sport Huancayo - Alianza Lima 0-1(0-1)
FBC Melgar - Real Atl. Garcilaso 2-2(0-0)
CD Unión Comercio - Juan Aurich 1-0(0-0)
Universitario Lima - Club Inti Gas 1-1(0-0)
CCD Los Caimanes - CD San Simón 0-2(0-0)
Univ. Técnica - Univ. San Martín 1-1(0-1)

Round 10 [01-02.11.2014]
CD San Simón - Club Inti Gas 1-0(1-0)
Real Atl. Garcilaso – Universit. Lima 2-0(0-0)
Univ. San Martín - FBC Melgar 0-2(0-2)
Juan Aurich - Universidad Técnica 2-0(2-0)
Univ. Cesar Vallejo - Los Caimanes 2-3(1-1)
Sport Huancayo - Unión Comercio 2-1(1-0)
León de Huánuco - Sporting Cristal 1-3(1-2)
Alianza Lima - CS Cienciano 5-0(4-0)

Round 11 [06-09.11.2014]
Universidad Técnica - CD San Simón 3-0(1-0)
CS Cienciano - Sport Huancayo 2-0(1-0)
Unión Comercio - Univ. Cesar Vallejo 2-1(1-0)
FBC Melgar - Juan Aurich 1-1(1-0)
Los Caimanes - León de Huánuco 3-2(1-0)
Club Inti Gas - Real Atl. Garcilaso 2-1(1-0)
Universitario Lima - Univ. San Martín 3-1(0-0)
Sport. Cristal - Alianza Lima 3-2(1-1) [21.11.]

Round 12 [11-13.11.2014]
Sport Huancayo - Sporting Cristal 1-2(0-0)
CS Cienciano - Universidad Técnica 1-1(1-1)
León de Huánuco - Unión Comercio 2-0(0-0)
Juan Aurich - Real Atl. Garcilaso 1-0(0-0)
Univ. Cesar Vallejo - FBC Melgar 1-2(1-0)
Alianza Lima - CCD Los Caimanes 3-1(1-1)
CD San Simón - Universitario Lima 1-1(0-0)
Univ. San Martín - Inti Gas 2-1(0-1) [26.11.]

Round 13 [15-18.11.2014]
Sporting Cristal - CS Cienciano 2-0(0-0)
Club Inti Gas - Juan Aurich 3-1(0-0)
Universit. Lima - Univ. Cesar Vallejo 1-2(0-2)
FBC Melgar - CD San Simón 2-1(0-1)
CCD Los Caimanes - Sport Huancayo 0-0
Univ. Técnica - León de Huánuco 0-1(0-0)
Un. Comercio - Alianza Lima 1-0(0-0) [26.11.]
Real A. Garcilaso - San Martín 1-0(1-0)[28.11.]

Round 14 [22-23.11.2014]
CD San Simón - Real Atl. Garcilaso 2-2(2-1)
CS Cienciano - CCD Los Caimanes 0-1(0-0)
Sport Huancayo - FBC Melgar 3-1(1-1)
Univ. Cesar Vallejo - Club Inti Gas 3-0(0-0)
Sporting Cristal - CD Unión Comercio 2-3(1-1)
León de Huánuco - Universitario Lima 2-0(0-0)
Alianza Lima - Universidad Técnica 2-0(1-0)
Juan Aurich - Univ. San Martín 1-1(0-1)

Round 15 [30.11.2014]	
Real Atl. Garcilaso - U. Cesar Vallejo 2-1(1-0)	Universidad Técnica - Sport Huancayo 3-1(2-1)
Univ. San Martín - CD San Simón 6-0(4-0)	FBC Melgar - Alianza Lima 2-3(1-0)
Club Inti Gas - León de Huánuco 5-2(3-1)	Universitario Lima - Juan Aurich 3-1(0-1)
CD Unión Comercio - CS Cienciano 3-0(2-0)	CCD Los Caimanes - Sporting Cristal 1-1(1-1)

Final Standings

1.	Club Sporting Cristal Lima	15	10	3	2	35	-	19	33
2.	Club Alianza Lima	15	10	3	2	27	-	11	33
3.	CD Unión Comercio Nueva Cajamarca	15	9	1	5	24	-	15	28
4.	Foot Ball Club Melgar Arequipa	15	8	3	4	21	-	16	27
5.	CSD León de Huánuco	15	7	2	6	21	-	21	23
6.	Asociación Civil Real Atlético Garcilaso	15	5	6	4	20	-	17	21
7.	Club Universitario de Deportes Lima	15	6	3	6	17	-	17	21
8.	Club Inti Gas Deportes Ayacucho	15	5	5	5	21	-	19	20
9.	CCD Los Caimanes de Puerto Etén	15	5	5	5	15	-	18	20
10.	CSCD Universidad César Vallejo Trujillo	15	6	1	8	22	-	24	19
11.	Club Juan Aurich de Chiclayo	15	5	4	6	13	-	19	19
12.	Deportivo Sport Huancayo	15	5	2	8	16	-	20	17
13.	Club Sportivo Cienciano Cuzco	15	5	2	8	16	-	24	17
14.	CCD Universidad Técnica de Cajamarca	15	4	3	8	14	-	22	15
15.	CD Universidad San Martín de Porres	15	4	2	9	21	-	23	14
16.	Club Deportivo Comunitario Laboral San Simón	15	2	3	10	13	-	31	9

Torneo Clausura Final

04.12.2014, Estadio Monumental UNSA, Arequipa; Attendance: 21,898
Referee: Henry Percy Gambetta Avalos
Club Sporting Cristal Lima - Club Alianza Lima **1-0(0-0)**
Goal: Sergio Rubén Blanco Soto (57).

Club Sporting Cristal Lima were qualified for the Championship finals.

Championship final

14.12.2014, Estadio "Elías Aguirre", Chiclayo; Attendance: 10,002
Referee: Manuel Alejandro Garay Evia
Club Juan Aurich de Chiclayo - Club Sporting Cristal Lima 2-2(0-2)
Juan Aurich: Erick Guillermo Delgado, Edgar Gabriel Balbuena Adorno (70.Harold Oshkaly Cummings Segura), Christian Guillermo Ramos Garagay, Jair Edson Céspedes Zegarra, Josué Daniel Estrada Aguilar, Rodrigo Cuba Piedra (Jorge Luis Bazán Lazarte), Óscar Christopher Vílchez Soto, César Junior Viza Seminario (46.Osmar Noronha Montani), Alfredo Junior Rojas Pajuelo, Hernán Rengifo Trigoso, Germán Ezequiel Pacheco. Trainer: Roberto Orlando Mosquera Vera.
Sporting Cristal: Diego Alonso Penny Valdez, Víctor Yoshimar Yotún Flores, Marcos Armando Ortíz Lovera, Alexís Cossio Zamora, Edinson José Chávez Quiñónez, Paolo Giancarlo de la Haza Urquiza (81.Pedro Jesús Aquino Sánchez), Adán Adolfo Balbín Silva, Carlos Augusto Lobatón Espejo (73.Luis Alfonso Abram Ugarelli), Horacio Martín Calcaterra, Sergio Rubén Blanco Soto, Irven Beybe Ávila Acero (84.Maximiliano Ezequiel Núñez). Trainer: Daniel Héctor Ahmed (Argentina).
Goals: 0-1 Irven Beybe Ávila Acero (24), 0-2 Irven Beybe Ávila Acero (36), 1-2 Christian Guillermo Ramos Garagay (88), 2-2 Germán Ezequiel Pacheco (90+3).

17.12.2014, Estadio Nacional, Lima; Attendance: 30,569
Referee: Víctor Hugo Carrillo Casanova
Club Sporting Cristal Lima - Club Juan Aurich de Chiclayo 0-0
Sporting Cristal: Diego Alonso Penny Valdez, Renzo Revoredo Zuazo, Víctor Yoshimar Yotún Flores, Alexís Cossio Zamora (77.Renzo Santiago Sheput Rodríguez), Edinson José Chávez Quiñónez, Luis Alfonso Abram Ugarelli, Carlos Augusto Lobatón Espejo, Maximiliano Ezequiel Núñez, Jorge Luis Cazulo, Sergio Rubén Blanco Soto, Irven Beybe Ávila Acero. Trainer: Daniel Héctor Ahmed (Argentina).
Juan Aurich: Erick Guillermo Delgado, Edgar Gabriel Balbuena Adorno, Christian Guillermo Ramos Garagay, Harold Oshkaly Cummings Segura, Jair Edson Céspedes Zegarra, Rodrigo Cuba Piedra (57.Jorge Luis Bazán Lazarte), Jair Edson Céspedes Zegarra, Óscar Christopher Vílchez Soto, Alfredo Junior Rojas Pajuelo, Hernán Rengifo Trigoso (75.Osmar Noronha Montani), Germán Ezequiel Pacheco. Trainer: Roberto Orlando Mosquera Vera.

21.12.2014, Estadio Mansiche, Trujillo; Attendance: 18,895
Referee: Miguel Santivañez de la Cruz
Club Sporting Cristal Lima - Club Juan Aurich de Chiclayo 3-2(1-2,2-2)
Sporting Cristal: Diego Alonso Penny Valdez (110.Luis Alexander Araújo Ludeña), Renzo Revoredo Zuazo, Víctor Yoshimar Yotún Flores, Luis Alfonso Abram Ugarelli, Paolo Giancarlo de la Haza Urquiza (56.Renzo Santiago Sheput Rodríguez), Carlos Augusto Lobatón Espejo, Maximiliano Ezequiel Núñez (104.Edinson José Chávez Quiñónez), Jorge Luis Cazulo, Horacio Martín Calcaterra, Sergio Rubén Blanco Soto, Irven Beybe Ávila Acero. Trainer: Daniel Héctor Ahmed (Argentina).
Juan Aurich: Erick Guillermo Delgado, Edgar Gabriel Balbuena Adorno, Christian Guillermo Ramos Garagay, Harold Oshkaly Cummings Segura, Jair Edson Céspedes Zegarra, Rodrigo Cuba Piedra, Óscar Christopher Vílchez Soto (72.Josué Daniel Estrada Aguilar), César Junior Viza Seminario (77.Deyair Reyes Contreras), Alfredo Junior Rojas Pajuelo, Hernán Rengifo Trigoso (80.Osmar Noronha Montani), Germán Ezequiel Pacheco. Trainer: Roberto Orlando Mosquera Vera.
Goals: 0-1 Hernán Rengifo Trigoso (12), 1-1 Irven Beybe Ávila Acero (41), 1-2 César Junior Viza Seminario (43), 2-2 Horacio Martín Calcaterra (67), 3-2 Edinson José Chávez Quiñónez (113).

2014 Torneo Descentralizado de Fútbol Profesional Winners: **Club Sporting Cristal Lima**

Top goalscorers:

23 goals:	Santiago Silva Gerez (URU)	**(Universidad San Martín de Porres)**
17 goals:	Juan Ramón Rodríguez del Solar	(AC Real Atlético Garcilaso)
	Cristian Venancio Bogado Morínigo (PAR)	(Unión Comercio Nueva Cajamarca)
	Bernardo Nicolás Cuesta	(Foot Ball Club Melgar Arequipa)
14 goals:	Raúl Mario Ruidíaz Misitich	(Club Universitario de Deportes Lima)

Aggregate Table 2014

1.	Foot Ball Club Melgar Arequipa*	30	14	10	6	44	-	33	54
2.	Club Alianza Lima	30	14	10	6	43	-	25	52
3.	Club Sporting Cristal Lima	30	14	8	8	61	-	38	50
4.	CD Unión Comercio Nueva Cajamarca	30	15	4	11	41	-	27	49
5.	Club Juan Aurich de Chiclayo	30	14	7	9	47	-	37	49
6.	Club Universitario de Deportes Lima**	30	13	6	11	38	-	35	46
7.	CSD León de Huánuco	30	13	6	11	39	-	40	45
8.	CSCD Universidad César Vallejo Trujillo	30	13	4	13	45	-	40	43
9.	Club Inti Gas Deportes Ayacucho	30	11	10	9	46	-	46	43
10.	Asociación Civil Real Atlético Garcilaso	30	11	8	11	39	-	36	41
11.	Club Sportivo Cienciano Cuzco***	30	11	6	13	36	-	42	36
12.	CD Universidad San Martín de Porres	30	9	8	13	46	-	40	35
13.	CCD Universidad Técnica de Cajamarca	30	8	9	13	29	-	43	33
14.	Deportivo Sport Huancayo	30	9	5	16	38	-	54	32
15.	CCD Los Caimanes de Puerto Etén (*Relegated*)	30	8	8	14	28	-	49	32
16.	Club Deportivo Comunitario Laboral San Simón (*Relegated*)	30	6	5	19	26	-	61	23

** 2 points awarded as 2014 Torneo de Promoción y Reserva champions*
*** 1 point awarded as 2014 Torneo de Promoción y Reserva runners-up*
**** 3 points deducted (Torneo Apertura)*

Relegation Play-off:

04.12.2014, Estadio "Julio Lores Colán", Huaral; Attendance: 14,000
Referee: Luis Ángel Seminario Barrientos
Deportivo Sport Huancayo - CCD Los Caimanes de Puerto Etén **1-0,0-0,0-0)**
Goal: Jankarlo dos Santos Chirinos Tello (119).

Qualified for the 2015 Copa Libertadores:
Club Sporting Cristal Lima, Club Juan Aurich de Chiclayo, Club Alianza Lima
Qualified for the 2015 Copa Sudamericana:
Foot Ball Club Melgar Arequipa, CD Unión Comercio Nueva Cajamarca, Club Universitario de Deportes Lima, CSD León de Huánuco.

Copa Perú Final 2015

15.12.2014, Estadio "Aliardo Soria", Pucallpa
Referee: Víctor Hugo Carrillo Casanova
Club Deportivo Sport Loreto - Unión Fuerza Minera 4-1(1-0)
Goals: 1-0 Diego Mayora (29), 2-0 Diego Mayora (63), 3-0 Edinho Terrones (75), 4-0 Diego Mayora (84), 4-1 John Andersonn Fajardo Pinchi (87).

21.12.2014, Estadio "Guillermo Briceño Rosamedina", Juliaca
Referee: Manuel Alejandro Garay Evia
Unión Fuerza Minera - Club Deportivo Sport Loreto 1-0(0-0)
Goal: 1-0 Walter Portugal (74).

Club Deportivo Sport Loreto promoted for the 2015 Primera División del Perú.

THE CLUBS 2014

CLUB ALIANZA LIMA

Foundation date: February 15, 1901
Address: Calle Jirón Abtao con Avenida Isabel La Católica 821, La Victoria, Lima
Stadium: Estadio „Alejandro Villanueva“, Lima – Capacity: 36,966

THE SQUAD

	DOB	Ape		Cla*	
		M	G	M	G
Goalkeepers:					
George Patrick Forsyth Sommer	20.06.1982	12	-	12	-
Fischer Guevara Urbina	24.07.1979	-	-	5	-
Manuel Alexander Heredia Rojas	09.01.1986	2	-	-	-
Daniel Arturo Prieto Solimano	18.09.1995	-	-	-	-
Gerson Gustavo Valladares Rodríguez	09.09.1995	2	-	-	-
Defenders:					
Roberto Efraín Koichi Aparicio Mori	06.06.1993	12	-	4	-
Miguel Gianpierre Araújo Blanco	24.10.1994	-	-	15	-
José Vladimir Cánova Hernández	30.09.1992	3	-	2	-
Diego Ricardo Donayre Blondet	06.04.1991	1	-		
Guillermo Alejandro Guizasola La Rosa	08.02.1982	8	-	4	-
Walter Fernando Ibáñez Costa (URU)	10.12.1984	15	2	14	2
Diego Alejandro Minaya Naters	01.05.1990	-	-	-	-
Aldair Jean Pierre Ramos Ballarta	12.08.1995	5	-	-	-
Midfielders:					
Paulo César Albarracín García	30.11.1989	8	-	11	-
Josimar Jair Atoche Bances	29.09.1989	11	-	11	-
Bryan Jair Canela Mestanza	20.03.1994	3	-	-	-
Victor Andrés Cedrón Zurita	06.10.1993	11	-	15	2
Basilio Gabriel Costa Heredia (URU)	02.04.1990	15	5	15	7
Christian Alberto Cueva Bravo	23.11.1991	-	-	15	3
Roberto Carlos Guizasola La Rosa	31.08.1984	10	-	14	-
Eduardo Israel Kahn Gómez	01.12.1988	7	1		
Julio César Landauri Ventura	17.04.1986	14	-	15	3
Alexander Ángelo Llanos Calisaya	01.04.1997	2	-	-	-
Pablo Nicolas Míguez Farre (URU)	19.06.1987	12	2	13	2
Jorge Luis Molina Cabrera	05.06.1990	5	-	-	-
Junior Alexander Ponce Pardo	16.02.1994	3	-		
Marco Aldair Rodríguez Iraola	06.08.1994	-	-	-	-
David Torres Fernández	14.11.1994	3	-	-	-
Luis Enrique Trujillo Ortíz	27.12.1990	9	-	14	-
Julio Edson Uribe Elera	09.05.1982	-	-	1	-
Forwards:					
Wilmer Alexander Aguirre Vásquez	10.05.1983	6	1	9	-
Juan Diego Gonzales Vigil Bentin	18.02.1985	5	-	5	-
Gonzalo Martín Guadalupe Martínez	04.12.1994	-	-	2	-
Mauro Guevgeozián Crespo (URU)	10.05.1986	12	1	11	7
Mauricio Alejandro Montes Sanguinetti	22.06.1982	13	3	14	1
Trainer:					
Guillermo Óscar Sanguinetti Giordano (URU) [as of 01.01.2014]	21.06.1966	15		16	

**Matches and goals in Torneo Clausura Final included*

CLUB SPORTIVO CIENCIANO CUZCO

Foundation date: July 8, 1901
Address: Calle Gastón Zapata 446, Cuzco
Stadium: Estadio Garcilaso de la Vega, Cuzco – Capacity: 42,056

THE SQUAD

	DOB	Ape M	Ape G	Cla M	Cla G
Goalkeepers:					
Álex Florencio Buleje Serna	29.03.1992	-	-	-	-
Fischer Guevara Urbina	24.07.1979	-	-		
Diego Eduardo Macedo Tejeda	01.02.1990	-	-	-	-
Diego Hernán Morales López	16.03.1983	15	-	15	-
Defenders:					
Wilmer Santiago Acasiete Ariadela	22.11.1977	9	1	9	-
Javier Alejandro Asenjo Gómez	03.10.1993	12	-	14	-
Juan Augusto Barreda Bellido	20.03.1993	2	-	3	-
Javier Angel Chumpitaz Zea	04.01.1984	12	-	11	-
Vladimir Alexander Hinostroza Moreno	21.12.1993	-	-	-	-
Edison Antony Kuncho Ynchcsana	12.02.1996			-	-
Fernando Octavio Masías Mory	23.01.1978	10	1	12	-
Yoel Alfonso Orosco Sagastegui	08.04.1991	-	-	-	-
Hansell Argenis Riojas La Rosa	15.10.1991	14	-	12	-
Midfielders:					
Wilfredo Junior Baca Ochoa	23.02.1995			4	-
Herbert Luis Castillo Figuero	05.12.1991	15	2	13	1
Renatto Alonso Chira Lora	07.04.1992	3	-	1	-
Gary Jeamsen Correa Gogin	23.05.1990	15	7	15	4
Sidney Enrique Faiffer Ames	12.05.1980	-	-	13	-
Bryan Hermoza Segura	16.06.1995	9	2	5	-
Héctor Martín Icart Atahídes (URU)	01.12.1984	14	-	10	4
Farih Jasauí Peirano	09.09.1991	1	-	-	-
Jesús Molina Flores	03.07.1992	2	-	-	-
Juan Carlos Nakaya Taira	31.12.1983	15	-	12	-
Andrés Ota Tamashiro	06.02.1993	-	-	-	-
Claudio Domingo Rivero Rodríguez (URU)	14.04.1985	12	1	14	-
Jorge Kelvin Robles Patiño	31.01.1994	2	-	4	-
Diego Eduardo Virrueta Candia	07.03.1992	5	-	3	-
Forwards:					
Luis Ricardo Caldas Morales	27.04.1981	-	-	-	-
Rodrigo David Camino Velásquez	29.12.1993	-	-	8	3
Sebastián Capurro Silva	24.01.1990	12	1		
Junior Miguel Castrillón Castillo	10.04.1993	1	-	6	-
Josías Paulo Cardoso Junior "Josías Cardoso"	07.11.1981	10	3		
Manuel Angel Tejada Medina	12.01.1989	12	-	6	-
Miguel Alejandro Ximénez Acosta (URU)	26.08.1977	-	-	14	3
Trainer:					
Mario Roberto Viera Gil (URU)	19.10.1959	15		15	

CLUB INTI GAS DEPORTES AYACUCHO

Foundation date: July 27, 1972
Address: Avenida Machu Picchu, Barrio de Miraflores, San Juan Bautista, Ayacucho
Stadium: Estadio Ciudad de Cumaná, Ayacucho – Capacity: 15,000

THE SQUAD

	DOB	Ape		Cla	
		M	G	M	G
Goalkeepers:					
Gianfranco Castellanos Conde	08.04.1988	-	-	-	-
Mario Eduardo Villasanti Adorno (PAR)	02.07.1991	15	-	15	1
Defenders:					
Dani Marcelino Aliaga Beltrán	24.03.1993	1	-	1	-
Brayan Gustavo Arana	21.01.1994	3	-	4	-
Horacio Cristian Benincasa Olaya	11.04.1994	12	1	11	2
Óscar Alexander Guerra Maldonado	25.03.1985	12	3	13	1
José Luis Honores Valle	22.02.1989	3	-	-	-
Raúl Penalillo Cotito	29.09.1982	14	2	10	-
Amilton Jair Prado	06.05.1979	14	1	14	1
Luis Carlos Prieto Zayas (PAR)	20.04.1988	-	-	14	-
Jeickson Gustavo Reyes Aparcana	09.10.1987	15	1	10	1
Midfielders:					
Wadid Jesús Arismendi Lazo	25.03.1987	8	3	13	2
Iván Aparicio Camarino Conde	21.12.1986	8	-	-	-
Henry Jorge Colán Díaz	13.03.1982	6	-	14	-
Paolo Pablo César Joya Ricci	31.01.1984	15	-	13	1
Joseph Martín Juárez	16.06.1994	6	-	1	-
Damián Oscar Luna (ARG)	21.02.1985	-	-	-	-
Juan Raúl Neira Medina	07.05.1995			1	-
Ricardo Jeremanho Ramos Ramos	29.09.1989	7	-	-	-
Francesco do Santos Aldair Recalde Sánchez	12.01.1991	6	3	8	3
Yoshiro Abelardo Salazar Flores	26.03.1987	14	-	12	2
Forwards:					
Andrés Felipe Arroyave Cartagena (COL)	09.06.1990	12	-	3	-
Jorge Luis Bazán Lazarte	23.03.1991	2	-		
Fernando Oliveira de Avila (BRA)	11.05.1984	13	3	12	1
Jesús Ray Gómez Carreño	29.12.1993			9	-
Carlos Jairzinho Gonzáles Ávalos	20.12.1989	12	3	8	-
Giorman Ronaldo Goyzueta Ronaldo	13.04.1994			5	-
Carlos Alberto Orejuela Pita	04.04.1980	8	5	12	5
Francis Giovanni Ortíz Lovera	01.08.1994	-	-	-	-
Anderson Edwin Sinchitullo Medrano	09.06.1996			-	-
Trainer:					
Carlos Fabián Leeb (ARG) [as of 01.01.2014]	18.07.1968	15		15	

CLUB JUAN AURICH DE CHICLAYO

Foundation date: September 3, 1922
Address: Avenida Miguel Grau 473 Urb. Santa Victoria, Chiclayo
Stadium: Estadio „Capitán Remigio Elías Aguirre Romero“, Chiclayo – Capacity: 24,500

THE SQUAD					
	DOB	Ape		Cla*	
		M	G	M	G
Goalkeepers:					
Erick Guillermo Delgado	30.06.1982	-	-	13	-
Alejandro Christoph Duarte Preus	05.04.1994	-	-	-	-
Juan Gilberto Goyoneche Carrasco	14.10.1985	5	-	5	-
Steven Aldair Rivadeneyra del Villar	02.11.1994	10	-	-	-
Defenders:					
Juan Carlos Arce Ormeño	02.05.1995			-	-
Edgar Gabriel Balbuena Adorno (PAR)	20.11.1980	15	5	15	2
Jair Edson Céspedes Zegarra	22.05.1984	14	1	13	1
Harold Oshkaly Cummings Segura (PAN)	01.03.1992	8	-	10	-
Josué Daniel Estrada Aguilar	07.09.1994	9	-	18	1
Aldair Perleche Romero	04.06.1995			4	-
Christian Guillermo Ramos Garagay	04.11.1988	13	2	14	1
Héctor Aldair Salazar Tejada	19.08.1994	1	-	1	1
Midfielders:					
Segundo Henry Acevedo Arana	18.02.1994	-	-	13	-
Tarek Brahan Carranza Terry	13.02.1992	9	1	11	-
Rodrigo Cuba Piedra	17.05.1992	14	2	8	-
Gino Guerrero Lara	24.10.1992	5	-	-	-
José Miguel Manzaneda Pineda	10.09.1994	5	-	3	-
Juan Carlos Mariño Márquez	02.01.1982	9	-	8	2
Álvaro Eduardo Medrano Chuchuca	23.10.1995	-	-	2	-
Adrián Sneyder Mujica Gamarra	30.12.1995			-	-
Osmar Noronha Montani	17.12.1991	10	1	17	1
Italo Estuard Regalado Algendones	15.09.1995	-	-	-	-
Deyair Reyes Contreras	04.03.1992	5	-	8	-
Alfredo Junior Rojas Pajuelo	01.05.1991	15	-	15	-
Óscar Christopher Vílchez Soto	21.01.1986	15	4	10	-
Yordi Eduardo Vilchez Cienfuegos	13.02.1995	-	-	3	-
César Junior Viza Seminario	03.04.1985	14	1	7	1
Forwards:					
Jorge Luis Bazán Lazarte	23.03.1991	-	-	14	-
Roberto Andrés Ovelar Maldonado (PAR)	01.12.1985	3	1		
Germán Ezequiel Pacheco (ARG)	19.05.1991	15	7	16	2
Hernán Rengifo Trigoso	18.04.1983	15	9	14	4
Sergio Ezequiel Unrein (ARG)	16.06.1991			5	-
Trainer:					
Roberto Orlando Mosquera Vera [as of 02.09.2013]	21.06.1956	15		18	

**Matches and goals in 2014 Championship finals included*

CLUB DEPORTIVO LEÓN DE HUÁNUCO

Foundation date: June 29, 1946
Address: Jr. Dos de Mayo 769, Huánuco
Stadium: Estadio „Heraclio Tapia", Huánuco – Capacity: 20,000

THE SQUAD					
	DOB	Ape		Cla	
		M	G	M	G
Goalkeepers:					
Jesús Eduardo Cisneros Ríos	18.03.1979	9	-	8	-
Eduardo Figueroa Meza	20.07.1995	-	-	-	-
Jorge Eddie Rivera Galindo (COL)	28.10.1978	7	-	8	-
Defenders:					
Juan Manuel Cámara Miranda	21.12.1992	5	-	-	-
Jean-Pierre Cáncar Maccari	08.07.1987	9	-	10	-
Orlando Contreras Collantes	11.06.1982	13	-	7	-
Gianfranco Roberto Espinoza Andrade	26.08.1986	10	1	14	1
John Christian Galliquio Castro	12.01.1979	1	-	13	2
José Diego Gómez Villaizán	10.05.1994	1	-	-	-
Juan Manuel Cámara Miranda	21.12.1992	-	-	-	-
Midfielders:					
Paul Yerson Bashi Quijano	01.04.1993	-	-	-	-
Fernando Alexis Canales Alvarado	13.04.1995	12	1	11	-
Éver Gustavo Chávez Hernández	28.12.1984	12	1	15	1
Christian Alejandro Chui Carcagno	12.08.1987	4	-	-	-
Jean Pierre Fuentes Siguas	18.10.1991	2	-	-	-
Alonso Alejandro Ibáñez Balmaceda	31.08.1995	-	-	-	-
Damián Ismodes Saravia	10.03.1989	12	1	11	1
Khader Jasaui Peirano	17.11.1995	-	-	-	-
César Manuel Medina Lozada	08.05.1991	7	1	11	-
Giovanny Christofer Morales Moreno	10.03.1992	2	-	-	-
Víctor Manuel Peña Espinoza	14.10.1987	15	-	13	2
Henry Edson Quinteros Sánchez	19.10.1977	8	-	8	-
Fabio Ramón Ramos Mereles (PAR)	14.06.1980	8	-	12	-
Ricardo Enrique Salcedo Smith	23.03.1990	14	-	-	-
Anderson Santamaría Bardales	10.01.1992	11	-	13	2
Eduardo Alberto Uribe Oshiro	02.09.1985	5	-	10	-
Renato André Zapata Portilla	16.02.1992	-	-	8	-
Forwards:					
Johan Javier Fano Espinoza	09.08.1978	2	1		
Jarvey Raúl López Bardales	01.09.1992	-	-	-	-
Diego Ariel Manicero (ARG)	24.05.1985	13	3	6	3
Juan Orlando Muriel (ARG)	18.03.1989	9	-	1	-
Carlos Alberto Preciado Benítez	30.03.1985	7	2	13	8
Cristofer Augusto Jesús Soto Gonzáles	06.01.1990	-	-	5	-
Guillermo Tomasevich Castañeda	20.03.1987	11	5	13	-
Trainer:					
Elar Wilmar Valencia Pacheco [01.01.-02.08.2014]	27.10.1961	10			
Marciano Rolando Chilavert González (PAR) [as of 03.08.2014]	22.05.1961	5		15	

CENTRO CULTURAL DEPORTIVO LOS CAIMANES PUERTO ETÉN

Foundation date: May 22, 1957
Address: *Not available*
Stadium: Estadio „Elías Aguirre", Chiclayo – Capacity: 25,000

THE SQUAD	DOB	Ape M	Ape G	Cla M	Cla G
Goalkeepers:					
Julio Américo Aliaga Wong	26.07.1990	-	-	4	-
Maximiliano Lombardi Rodríguez (ARG)	06.01.1980	15	-	12	-
Luis Cristian Ortíz Lovera	09.06.1990	-	-	-	-
Defenders:					
Moisés Cabada Apreciado	02.11.1985	5	-	11	-
Julio José Miguel Jefferson García Escurra	20.04.1994	3	-	-	-
Renzo Junior Guevara Ávalos	02.09.1983	11	-	5	-
Jhonny Javier Lalopú Mera	25.05.1982	9	-	9	-
Renzo Rodrigo Reaños Mina	17.05.1986	-	-	4	-
Enrique „Kike" Rodríguez Castillo	06.09.1991	-	-	7	-
Ricardo Antonio Ronceros Ramos	20.07.1977	11	2	10	1
Nelson Eusebio Semperena González (URU)	19.02.1984	10	-	-	-
Midfielders:					
Christian Edgardo Adrianzen Gómez	21.03.1994	5	-	12	-
Edson Diego Aubert Cervantes	14.11.1988	12	1		
Aderli James Campos Cabrejo	19.09.1988	10	-	2	-
Víctor Johan Carbajal Callirgos	23.06.1988	1	-	1	-
Marco Antonio Casas Fernández	26.05.1979	10	-	1	-
Carlos Roberto Elías Galliani	23.03.1988	2	-	-	-
Mario Augusto Gómez Urbina	27.05.1981	9	-	12	-
Daniel Alexander Hidalgo Guevara	30.08.1982	11	-	13	-
Fidel Alfredo Inolopú Barrera	23.08.1992	-	-	7	-
Maximiliano Lombardi Rodríguez (URU)	11.05.1987	-	-	13	2
Gino Roberto Navarro Lavalle	10.10.1987	7	-	5	-
Ángel Ojeda Allauca	11.08.1992	8	1	13	-
Alexander Gustavo Sánchez Reyes	06.06.1983	-	-	13	1
Juan Pablo Vergara Martínez	24.02.1985	8	1	-	-
Gerardo Sebastián Vonder Putten (URU)	28.02.1988	4	-	10	-
Forwards:					
Saulo Aponte Córdova	03.09.1985	11	-	-	-
Pedro Luis Ascoy Córtez	10.08.1980	-	-	1	-
Roberto Carlos Jiménez Jiménez	17.04.1983	11	7	12	4
Josías Paulo Cardoso Junior (BRA)	07.11.1981	-	-	8	1
Pierre Jonathan Orozco Torrelio	18.05.1987	-	-	-	-
Luis Armando Ovelar Maldonado (PAR)	08.06.1983	10	1	6	1
Janio Carlo Posito Olazábal	10.10.1989	9	-	6	3
Elsar Rodas Mendoza	28.12.1994	15	-	10	1
Nicolás Ignacio Vigneri Cetrulo (URU)	06.07.1983	2	-		
Trainer:					
Teddy Armando Cardama Sinti [01.01.-21.08.2014]	15.08.1966	13			
Claudio Enrique Techera Seoane (URU) [as of 22.08.2014]	11.04.1964	2		15	

FOOT BALL CLUB MELGAR AREQUIPA

Foundation date: March 25, 1915
Address: Calle Consuelo 414, Arequipa
Stadium: Estadio Virgen de Chapi, Arequipa – Capacity: 40,217

THE SQUAD					
	DOB	Ape		Cla	
		M	G	M	G
Goalkeepers:					
Juan Pablo Begazo Valvidia	18.05.1988	1	-	-	-
Leao Butrón Gotuzzo	06.03.1977	14	-	15	-
Jonathan Benito Medina Angulo	29.04.1993	-	-	-	-
Defenders:					
Víctor Julio Rodolfo Balta Mori	30.01.1986	9	-	8	2
Gianmarco Gambetta Sponza	02.05.1991	-	-	1	-
Juan Diego Li Naranjo	16.02.1995	1	-	-	-
Nelinho Minzúm Quina Asín	11.05.1987	15	-	11	-
Willy Alexander Rivas Asin	04.06.1985	11	-	15	-
Édgar Humberto Villamarín Arguedas	01.04.1982	12	-	11	-
Midfielders:					
Patricio Salvatore Arce Cambana	23.02.1993			-	-
Alexis Arias Tuesta	13.12.1995	-	-	6	-
Carlos Javier Beltrán Neroni	18.08.1990	11	-	10	1
Omar Andrés Fernández Frasica	11.02.1993	-	-	15	4
Luis Alberto Hernández Diaz	15.02.1981	12	-	10	-
Alejandro Hohberg González	20.08.1991	9	1	4	1
Lampros Kontogiannis Gómez (MEX)	01.08.1988	10	-	14	-
Nilson Evair Loyola Morales	26.10.1994	-	-	-	-
Donny Renzo Neyra Ferrada	12.01.1984	-	-	13	-
Diego Enrique Pizarro Bosio	14.08.1990	-	-	7	-
Minzún Nelinho Quina Asín	11.05.1987	15	3	14	3
Mario Jorge Soto Weninger	19.04.1987	9	1	2	-
Gustavo Alfonso Torres Quispe	23.07.1995	11	-	5	-
Jorge Johan Vásquez Rosales	08.10.1984	10	1	8	-
Forwards:					
Piero Fernando Alva Niezen	14.02.1979	15	2	13	-
Piero Renzo Chirinos Portugal	27.08.1990	5	-	2	-
Bernardo Nicolás Cuesta (ARG)	20.12.1988	14	8	14	9
José Aurelio Gonzáles Vigil Bentin	01.03.1996			-	-
Kevin Ruíz Rosales	14.02.1995	7	-	1	-
Renzo Renato Valdéz Orihuela	13.11.1990	3	-	-	-
Herlyn Ysrael Zúñiga Yañez	27.08.1976	12	7	10	1
Trainer:					
Juan Máximo Reynoso Guzmán [as of 01.01.2014]	28.12.1969	15		15	

ASOCIACIÓN CIVIL REAL ATLÉTICO GARCILASO CUZCO

Foundation date: July 16, 2009
Address: Calle Huayruru Pata y 24 de Junio
Stadium: Estadio "Inca Garcilaso de la Vega", Cuzco – Capacity: 42,056

THE SQUAD

	DOB	Ape M	Ape G	Cla M	Cla G
Goalkeepers:					
Diego Martín Carranza Fernández	28.08.1981	8	-	11	-
Juan Miguel Pretel Sánchez	05.11.1983	8	-	4	-
Miguel Alberto Taffur Pérez	04.02.1992	-	-	-	-
Defenders:					
Hugo Alexis Ademir Ángeles Chávez	18.12.1993	11	-	2	-
Cristian Antonio García González	02.03.1981	-	-	1	-
Jhoel Alexander Herrera Zegarra	09.07.1980	15	1	12	-
Royer Alberto Holgado Palma	20.09.1994	3	-	-	-
Jaime Rodolfo Huerta Boggiano	08.08.1987	9	-	9	-
Juan Diego Lojas Solano	23.04.1989	13	2	13	-
Gonzalo Matías Maulella Rodríguez (URU)	06.07.1984	15	1	12	-
Diego Alexis Pinto Mamani	09.04.1994	2	-	-	-
Iván Diego Santillán Atoche	06.05.1991	12	1	10	2
Manuel Eduardo Tenchy Ugaz Nemotto	21.06.1981	-	-	9	-
Midfielders:					
Fabrizio Emmanuel Altamirano Espinoza	30.01.1996	3	-	3	1
Edson Diego Aubert Cervantes	14.11.1988	-	-	14	-
Carlos Alberto Barrena Fabián	24.04.1982	-	-	-	-
John Camero Condorpusa	16.04.1993	-	-	-	-
Erick Edgardo Coavoy De la Cruz	22.01.1990	9	-	-	-
Anderson Denyro Cueto Sánchez	24.05.1989	-	-	-	-
Marcos Abner Delgado Ocampo	17.02.1989	-	-	13	1
Carlos Javier Flores Córdova	09.05.1988	15	-	14	1
Sebastian Andrés Lojas Solano	04.07.1995	7	-	4	-
Edson Aldair López Rubina	03.08.1996			4	1
Juan Carlos Jesús Odar Pérez	19.02.1993	-	-	-	-
César Andrés Ortíz Castillo	21.12.1983	13	1	13	2
Alfredo Sebastián Ramúa	04.09.1986	15	2	14	3
Edwin Retamoso Palomino	23.02.1982	2	-		
Ryan Zonath Salazar Rivera	25.02.1981	4	-	-	-
Cristian Sergio Vildoso Valverde	29.01.1979	5	-	5	-
Forwards:					
Cristian Fernando Andersen Oviedo (PAR)	03.06.1984	-	-	3	-
Jairzinho Julio Baylón Iglesias	26.02.1989	5	-		
José Carlos Fernández Piedra	14.05.1983	-	-	12	-
Víctor Ramón Ferreira Barrios (PAR)	09.05.1986	13	2	14	-
Digno Javier González Sosa (PAR)	05.02.1990	2	-		
Iván Cristopher Martínez Saavedra	05.08.1988	2	-	-	-
Ramón Rodríguez del Solar	08.08.1977	14	8	13	9
Trainer:					
Fredy Manuel García Loayza [01.01.2011-28.09.2014]	22.11.1959	15		4	
Luis Alberto Flores Villena [as of 29.09.2014]	18.08.1964			11	

CLUB DEPORTIVO COMUNITARIO LABORAL SAN SIMÓN MOQUEGUA

Foundation date: January 5, 1983
Address: *Not available*
Stadium: Estadio 25 de Noviembre, Moquegua – Capacity: 21,000

THE SQUAD

	DOB	Ape M	Ape G	Cla M	Cla G
Goalkeepers:					
Álvaro Bouroncle Cuentas	16.07.1994	1	-	-	-
Braham Omar Maldonado Romero	25.04.1991	-	-	-	-
Óscar Alfredo Mendoza Ortíz	30.01.1994			1	-
Federico Ariel Nicosia (ARG)	05.02.1990	15	-	14	-
Defenders:					
Jonathan Acasiete Ariadela	11.11.1988	13	-	9	1
David Alonso Díaz Colunga	12.03.1991	8	-	13	-
Óscar Nadin Díaz González (PAR)	29.01.1984	4	-	1	-
Gian Carlo Franco Paredes	12.09.1990	3	-	-	-
Carlos Humberto Jhonifer García Martínez	25.03.1994	8	1	9	-
Nahuel Jesús Guerrero (ARG)	06.07.1987	-	-	4	-
César Manuel Mayuri Lara	04.09.1992	4	-	6	2
José Adolfo Mendoza Zambrano	24.07.1982	10	-	12	-
Luis Arnaldo Molina Leandro	13.09.1991	-	-	-	-
Kerwin Junior Peixoto Chiclayo	21.02.1988	13	-	13	-
Jean Franco Rodríguez Malpartida	31.01.1987	11	3	8	-
Yampol Salvatierra	11.06.1995			1	-
Luis Alfredo Teves Santamaría	03.04.1994	-	-	4	-
Midfielders:					
Karlo Edson Calcina Zúñiga	03.03.1984	-	-	6	-
Nelson Eduardo Chaparro Belapatiño	15.10.1991	-	-	-	-
Diego Iván Chavarri Rodríguez (USA)	07.03.1989	14	2	7	1
César Eduardo García				1	-
Fernando Luis Giarrizzo (ARG)	12.12.1983	-	-	10	-
Paulo Jair Lovera Luna	11.10.1994	13	-	1	-
Neil Jaime Marcos Morán	11.05.1992			14	-
Mauricio Josué Mori Cairo	16.02.1992	3	-	-	-
Junior Stefano Reyna Allie	03.09.1990	2	-	1	-
Jorge Alberto Rodríguez Pisco	15.03.1989	6	-	-	-
Hilden Salas Castillo	19.07.1980	-	-	10	1
Larry Keith Yáñez Zúñiga	28.04.1981	-	-	9	1
Carlos Alberto Zegarra Zamora	02.03.1977	14	2	6	-
Forwards:					
Luis Antonio Fernández Dávila Adams	23.03.1997	-	-	3	-
Daniel Ferreira Caballero	25.09.1982	6	-	-	-
Sergio Ramón Ibarra Guzmán (ARG)	11.01.1973	-	-	6	-
Jesús Eduardo Alberto Rey Estupiñán	09.02.1988	13	1	6	-
Christian César Sánchez Valenzuela	19.09.1982	-	-	-	-
Daniel Alonso Sánchez Albujar	02.05.1990	2	-	1	-
Matías Eric Sen (ARG)	29.10.1991	-	-	14	4
Miguel Ángel Silva	14.09.1988	14	4	7	2
Gustavo Fernando Alfredo Stagnaro Rodriguez	20.01.1989	15	-	12	1
Trainer:					
Edgardo Malvestiti (ARG) [as of 13.05.2014]		15		15	

DEPORTIVO SPORT HUANCAYO

Foundation date: February 7, 2007
Address: Jr. Loreto N° 839 - 2do. Piso - Huancayo
Stadium: Estadio Huancayo, Huancayo – Capacity: 20,000

THE SQUAD					
	DOB	Ape		Cla	
		M	G	M	G
Goalkeepers:					
Joel Ademir Pinto Herrera	05.06.1980	5	-	9	-
Carlos Martín Solís Ugarte	20.09.1990	-	-	-	-
Michael Anthony Sotillo Cañari	29.09.1984	11	-	6	-
Defenders:					
Edson Robert Ávila Armas	06.07.1994	-	-	2	-
Cord Jesús Cleque Sánchez	09.10.1986	15	-	12	-
Manuel Alejandro Contreras Siadén	21.05.1989	14	2	3	-
Anier Alfonso Figueroa Mosquera (COL)	27.07.1987	15	-	13	-
Diego Emanuel González Pereira (ARG)	16.11.1986	-	-	10	-
Rogelio José Gonzáles Cary	12.08.1993	-	-	4	1
Carlos Guillermo Hernández Morán	01.09.1994	9	-	6	-
Juan Francisco Hernández Díaz	24.06.1978	5	-	1	-
Luis Román Ojeda Alva	10.05.1980	6	-	3	-
Renzo Rodrigo Reaños Mina	17.05.1986	2	-		
Midfielders:					
Jhordan Estanis Campos Merino	15.09.1995	3	1	6	1
Yancarlo Victorio Casas Acosta	15.07.1981	10	-	12	-
Iván Christopher Chumpitáz Blas	17.05.1990	11	-	9	-
Ángelo Daniel Cruzado Sifuentes	10.12.1979	12	2	13	2
Blas Ramón López Medez (PAR)	14.03.1984	14	-	12	1
Juan Jerardo Mayo Oliva	15.04.1994	4	-	5	-
Hans Ericsson Paiva Colina	19.01.1986			1	-
Nelson Edil Roque Alburqueque	04.09.1984	6	-	14	1
César Augusto Ruiz Sánchez	10.01.1990	4	-	14	-
Forwards:					
Ronald Céliz Milian	30.08.1983	5	-	11	4
Jankarlo de los Santos Chirinos Tello	30.03.1988	5	-	5	-
Petter Benjamin Joya Casas	11.05.1995	3	-	-	-
Kleyr Vieira dos Santos (BRA)	14.09.1980	14	8	11	5
Daniel Fabio Morales Quispe	28.04.1992	12	2	15	-
Enrique Rafael Narvay (ARG)	26.01.1990	8	1	-	-
Víctor Alonso Rossel Del Mar	05.11.1985	10	5	9	1
Trainer:					
Daniel Córdoba (ARG) [01.01.-20.07.2014]		8			
Marcelo Favio Messina (ARG) [21.07.-04.11.2014]	23.12.1968	7		10	
Walter Orlando Lizarraga (ARG) [as of 05.11.2014]				5	

CLUB SPORTING CRISTAL LIMA

Foundation date: December 13, 1955
Address: Calle 18 s/n, La Florida, Rímac, Lima
Stadium: Estadio "Alberto Gallardo" (ex-San Martín de Porres), Lima – Capacity: 18,000

THE SQUAD

	DOB	Ape M	Ape G	Cla* M	Cla* G
Goalkeepers:					
Luis Alexander Araújo Ludeña	16.01.1981	2	-	2	-
Carlos Alfonso Grados Heredia	15.05.1995	-	-	-	-
Diego Alonso Penny Valdez	22.04.1984	13	-	18	-
Defenders:					
Luis Alfonso Abram Ugarelli	27.02.1996	4	-	17	1
Luis Jan Piers Advíncula Castrillón	02.03.1990	10	2		
Jesús Martín Álvarez Hurtado	26.08.1981	5	-		
Brian Robert Bernaola Acosta	17.01.1995	-	-	-	-
Marcos Armando Ortíz Lovera	27.03.1993	2	-	2	-
Renzo Revoredo Zuazo	11.05.1986	14	-	18	2
Víctor Yoshimar Yotún Flores	07.04.1990	12	-	14	1
Midfielders:					
Pedro Jesús Aquino Sánchez	13.04.1995	8	-	7	-
Adán Adolfo Balbín Silva	13.10.1986	8	-	87	-
Horacio Martín Calcaterra (ARG)	22.02.1989	13	1	18	2
Jorge Luis Cazulo (URU)	14.02.1982	14	1	17	-
Edinson José Chávez Quiñónez	20.11.1993	11	2	19	2
Alexís Cossio Zamora	11.02.1995	8	1	12	1
Luiz Humberto da Silva Silva	28.12.1996	5	1	9	1
Paolo Giancarlo de la Haza Urquiza	30.11.1983	11	-	13	-
Pier Antonio Larrauri Conroy	26.03.1994	4	-	1	-
Carlos Augusto Lobatón Espejo	06.02.1980	13	8	18	5
Maximiliano Ezequiel Núñez (ARG)	17.09.1986	14	4	18	4
Renzo Santiago Sheput Rodríguez	08.11.1990	8	1	15	3
Edison Yeyson Silva Fanarraga	02.05.1994	1	-	-	-
Carlo André Urquiaga Cabrera	12.08.1994	-	-	-	-
Forwards:					
Joazhiño Walhir Arroé Salcedo	05.06.1992	-	-	-	-
Irven Beybe Ávila Acero	02.07.1990	13	4	17	9
Sergio Rubén Blanco Soto (URU)	25.11.1981	-	-	19	9
Leandro Luján Leguizamón (ARG)	04.12.1988	7	-		
Douglas Junior Ross Santillana	19.02.1986	-	-	-	-
Ray Anderson Sandoval Baylón	13.02.1995	4	1	-	-
Alexander Succar Cañote	12.08.1995	2	-	-	-
Trainer:					
Daniel Hector Ahmed (ARG) [as of 01.01.2014]	22.11.1965	15		19	

**Matches and goals in Torneo Clausura Final and Championship finals included*

CLUB DEPORTIVO UNIÓN COMERCIO NUEVA CAJAMARCA

Foundation date: June 15, 1994
Address: Jr. Imperio Nro. 688, Nueva Cajamarca
Stadium: Estadio IPD de Moyobamba, Moyobamba – Capacity: 8,000

THE SQUAD	DOB	Ape M	Ape G	Cla M	Cla G
Goalkeepers:					
Ángel David Azurín Condori	29.05.1991	-	-	-	-
Ronald Pierr Ruíz Ordinola	02.08.1984	15	-	15	-
Defenders:					
Diego Ricardo Donayre Blondet	06.04.1991	-	-	8	-
Ronal Omar Huacca Jurado	20.12.1993	-	-	-	-
Jorge Jair Yglesias Cárdenas	10.02.1981	15	1	11	1
Ederson Leonel Mogollón Flores	04.10.1992	6	-	1	-
Wálter José Moreno Arco	18.05.1978	14	2	12	-
Félix Josimar Uculmana Aliaga	25.02.1991	1	-	-	-
Jaime Vásquez Ramírez	21.02.1991	13	-	3	-
Midfielders:					
Lee Alexander Andonaire Delfín	05.10.1980	1	-	9	-
Roberto Mauro Cantoro (ARG)	01.09.1976	-	-	-	-
Miguel Alexander Carranza Macahuachi	03.11.1995	4	-	7	1
Heiner Jesús Chávez Salazar	05.03.1986	14	-	14	3
José Alberto Corcuera Valdiviezo	06.08.1981	7	-	15	-
Michael Fidel Guevara Legua	10.06.1984	-	-	10	-
Wilber Huaynacari Ríos	26.08.1982	11	-	6	-
Evany Gamal Ángel Machahuay Ruíz	08.03.1996	9	-	5	-
Nicolás Rubén Medina (ARG)	17.02.1982	13	1	15	-
Omar Ernesto Reyes Burga	13.12.1988	8	-	10	-
Yves Patrick Marcos Roach Farfán	07.08.1992	3	-	-	-
Miguel Ángel Trauco Saavedra	25.08.1992	14	-	13	-
Mario Alfonso Velarde Pinto	03.07.1990	15	3	12	-
Nixon Villoslada Avellaneda	21.05.1993	-	-	-	-
Forwards:					
José Antonio Ayala Pacheco (PAR)	08.04.1992	-	-	9	2
Jairzinho Julio Baylón Iglesias	26.02.1989	-	-	3	-
Cristian Venancio Bogado Morínigo (PAR)	07.01.1987	14	6	14	11
Luis Jonathan Laguna Fuentes	24.05.1988	5	-	-	-
Antonio Meza Cuadra Bisso	12.09.1982	14	4	8	3
Joao de Jesús Villamarin Antúnez	10.02.1992	13	-	8	3
Trainer:					
Walter Fernando Aristizábal Serna (COL) [as of 01.01.2014]	13.04.1966	15		15	

CLUB SOCIAL CULTURAL DEPORTIVO UNIVERSIDAD CÉSAR VALLEJO TRUJILLO

Foundation date: January 6, 1996
Address: Avenida Víctor Larco 1700, Trujillo
Stadium: Estadio Mansiche, Trujillo – Capacity: 25,036

THE SQUAD

	DOB	Ape		Cla	
		M	G	M	G
Goalkeepers:					
Eder Alberto Hermoza Guevara	04.04.1990	2	-	2	-
Salomón Alexis Libman Pastor	25.02.1984	13	-	12	-
Regis Martín Quiróz Ampuero	04.08.1994			-	-
Máximo Saúl Rabines Terrones	05.07.1993	-	-	1	-
Defenders:					
Jesús Martín Álvarez Hurtado	26.08.1981	-	-	5	-
Luís Felipe Cardoza Zuñiga (COL)	19.12.1984	13	4	12	2
Luis Alberto Guadalupe Rivadeneyra	03.04.1976	11	-	9	-
Marcos Alfredo Jaunarena Collantes	17.12.1995	1	1	1	-
Atilio Muente Gionti	15.03.1980	5	-	10	1
Jesús Rabanal Dávila	25.12.1984	14	-	7	-
Jeremy Martín Rostaing Verástegui	23.05.1995	10	-	11	-
Jesús Branco Geraldo Serrano Aguirre	24.08.1992	3	-	3	-
Niger Josset Vega Argomedo	06.08.1993	3	-	5	-
Frank Víctor Nayid Vilela	13.03.1993	-	-	-	-
Midfielders:					
William Medardo Chiroque Tavara	10.05.1980	12	-	13	1
Emiliano José Ciucci (ARG)	07.04.1986	10	-	13	3
Carlos Stefano Díez Lino	18.04.1996			-	-
Anthony Manuel Alberto Gordillo Vásquez	30.04.1994	-	-	2	-
John Christopher Hinostroza Guzmán	22.02.1980	9	-	11	-
Eduardo Israel Kahn Gómez	01.12.1988	-	-	11	1
Donald Diego Millán Rodríguez (COL)	21.03.1986			11	1
Juan Gustavo Morales Coronado	06.03.1989	12	-	10	-
Jean Pierre Mikhail Ortíz Montero	15.05.1993	-	-	2	-
Ronald Jonathan Quinteros Sánchez	28.06.1985	13	3	11	-
Pedro Paulo Requena Cisneros	24.01.1991	13	-	-	-
Ángel Bryan Silva Rodríguez	27.08.1994			2	-
Marco Aldair Rodríguez Iraola	06.08.1994	8	-		
Forwards:					
Christian Anthony Buenaño Romero	16.07.1995			2	-
Daniel Mackensi Chávez Castillo	08.01.1988	14	5	13	2
Erick Joel de Jésus Quintana	22.12.1992			2	-
Andy Robert Pando García	28.07.1983	10	-	12	5
Luis Carlos Tejada Hansell (PAN)	28.03.1982	15	6	11	4
Trainer:					
Franco Enrique Navarro Monteyro [as of 01.01.2014]	10.11.1961				

CLUB DEPORTIVO UNIVERSIDAD SAN MARTÍN DE PORRES

Foundation date: January 21, 2004
Address: Avenida Las Calandrias, Santa Anita, Lima
Stadium: Estadio "Alberto Gallardo" (ex-San Martín de Porres), Lima – Capacity: 18,000

THE SQUAD					
	DOB	Ape		Cla	
		M	G	M	G
Goalkeepers:					
Ricardo Daniel Farro Caballero	06.03.1989	-	-	1	-
Pedro David Gallese Quiróz	23.02.1990	15	-	14	-
Mario Fernando Suárez Rodríguez	31.05.1994	-	-	-	-
Renzo John Tueros Guerra	27.01.1995	-	-	-	-
Defenders:					
Carlos Antonio Ascues Avila	19.06.1992	8	1	11	-
Jorge Adolfo Bosmediano Carrasco	16.02.1991	-	-	-	-
Yhirbis Yosec Córdova Guizasola	03.01.1991	8	-	10	1
Aldo Sebastián Corzo Chávez	20.05.1989	11	1	7	-
Carlos Oswaldo Fernández Maldonado	01.11.1984	15	1	12	-
Anthony Belkier Molina Rubio	17.02.1989	14	-	11	-
Jack Robert Safra Montilla	03.02.1992	2	-	2	-
Daniel Aldair Salazar López	08.08.1997			1	-
Jerson Vásquez Shapiama	05.03.1986	10	1	13	1
Midfielders:					
Luis Enrique Álvarez Valdivia	17.05.1990	15	1	11	-
Josepmir Aaron Ballón Villacorta	21.03.1988	12	-	15	-
Juan Paolo Bustamante Requena	24.06.1994	2	-	-	-
Renzo Renato Garcés Mori	12.06.1996	1	-	4	-
Raziel Samir García Paredes	15.02.1994	6	-	7	-
Paulo Hernán Hinostroza Vásquez	21.12.1993	13	-	15	-
Carlos Ariel Marinelli (ARG)	14.03.1982	2	-	3	-
Alejandro Segundo Medina Huáman	15.06.1995	4	-	6	-
Johnnier Esteiner Montaño Caicedo (COL)	14.01.1983	10	-	13	1
Willy Fernando Pretel Santos	20.04.1994			-	-
Claudio Torrejón Tineo	14.05.1993	-	-	1	-
Benjamín Ubierna Barandiarán	22.11.1991	13	1	12	1
Adrián Martín Ugarriza Tello	01.01.1997	5	1	4	-
Forwards:					
Dangelo Josué Artiaga Morales	15.06.1996	2	-	-	-
Luis Enrique Iberico Robalino	06.02.1998	5	-	5	-
Luis Alberto Perea Pérez (COL)	03.09.1986	12	6	15	5
Santiago Silva Gérez (URU)	26.08.1990	15	11	14	12
Trainer:					
Julio César Escoba Uribe Flores [as of 14.05.2013]	09.05.1958	15		15	

CLUB CULTURAL Y DEPORTIVO UNIVERSIDAD TÉCNICA DE CAJAMARCA

Foundation date: July 14, 1964
Address: *Not available*
Stadium: Estadio "Héroes de San Ramón", Cajamarca – Capacity: 18,000

THE SQUAD

	DOB	Ape M	Ape G	Cla M	Cla G
Goalkeepers:					
Daniel Andrés Ferreyra (ARG)	22.01.1982	15	-	15	-
Daniel Alexander Reyes Buenaño	12.12.1987	-	-	-	-
Fernando Junior Sánchez Pichardo	09.12.1992			-	-
Defenders:					
Raúl Hannes Alemán Mostorino	19.07.1979	10	-	8	-
Manuel Alejandro Corrales González	03.09.1982	14	6	12	1
Rafael Nicanor Farfán Quispe	28.12.1975	13	-	10	1
José Luis Granda Bravo	13.04.1992	7	1	8	-
Franco Andrés Pretell Ramírez	19.01.1995	2	-	1	-
Víctor Raúl Rojas García	15.04.1994	12	-	11	-
Walter Ricardo Vílchez Soto	20.02.1982	10	-	11	-
Midfielders:					
Julio Alfredo Acosta Ñique	23.01.1996	5	-	1	-
Jean Pierre Archimbaud Arriarán	16.08.1994	8	-	3	-
Giancarlo Carmona Maldonado	12.10.1985	15	-	11	-
Miguel Ángel Cevasco Abad	27.04.1986	-	-	-	-
Reimond Orangel Manco Albarracín	23.08.1990	11	2	12	-
Roberto Merino Ramírez	19.05.1982	-	-	10	1
Saúl Yonatan Salas Carrillo	10.10.1994	9	-	4	-
Alexander Gustavo Sánchez Reyes	06.06.1983	-	-		
Jean Carlo Tragodara Gálves	16.12.1985	5	-	13	-
Marcio Andre Valverde Zamora	23.10.1987	9	2	15	-
Forwards:					
Juan José Barros Araújo	24.06.1989	6	-	1	-
Gianfranco Alberto Labarthe Tomé	20.09.1984	15	4	9	1
Luciano Félix Leguizamón (ARG)	01.07.1982	-	-	3	1
Diego Antonio Ramírez Cutti	02.11.1994	8	-	4	-
Johan Joussep Sotil Eche	29.08.1982	12	-	10	1
César Augusto Valoyes Córdoba (COL)	05.01.1984	-	-	15	7
Mauro Adrián Vila Wilkins (URU)	25.02.1986	13	-	14	1
Jorge Isaac Vílchez Calla	13.04.1991	7	-	5	-
Trainer:					
Carlos Alberto Galván Méndez (ARG) [27.04.-06.07.2014]	28.10.1973	5			
José Eugenio Hernández Sarmiento (COL) [as of 07.07.2014]	18.03.1956	10		15	

CLUB UNIVERSITARIO DE DEPORTES LIMA

Foundation date: August 7, 1924
Address: Avenida Javier Prado Este, 77 Ate-Vitarte, Lima
Stadium: Estadio Monumental del Perú, Lima – Capacity: 80,093

THE SQUAD

	DOB	Ape M	Ape G	Cla M	Cla G
Goalkeepers:					
Carlos Esteban Cáceda Reyes	27.09.1991	1	-	-	-
José Aurelio Carvallo Alonso	16.03.1986	14	-	15	-
Luis Ricardo Llontop Godeau	02.10.1985		-	1	-
Patrick Sergei Zunczuk Meléndez	21.02.1995	-	-	-	-
Defenders:					
Fernando Nicolás Alloco Romano (ARG)	30.04.1986	-	-	15	1
Diego Armando Chávez Ramos	07.03.1993	-	-	13	1
Dalton Moreira Neto (BRA)	05.02.1990	-	-	-	-
Pedro Alberto Junior Díez Canseco	22.05.1992	-	-	2	-
Néstor Alonso Duarte Carassa	08.09.1990	13	-	5	-
Javier Eduardo Núñez Mendoza	23.01.1997	-	-	-	-
Franco Otarola Moore	07.06.1992	6	-	7	-
Ángel Elías Romero Iparraguirre	09.08.1990	11	1	11	-
Aurelio Saco-Vértiz Figari	30.05.1989	-	-	-	-
Werner Luis Schuler Gamarra	27.07.1990	11	-	1	-
Gonzalo Manuel Soto (ARG)	03.04.1990	-	-	-	-
Midfielders:					
Alvaro Francisco Ampuero García Rosell	25.09.1992	-	-	11	-
José Luis Cáceres Zevallos	25.01.1995			-	-
Cristian Gabriel Dávila Rivaz	06.07.1990	9	1	-	-
Jorge Gabriel Esparza Ariadel	22.06.1993	-	-	-	-
Luis Gabriel García Uribe	05.06.1988	-	-	3	-
Edwin Alexi Gómez Gutiérrez	04.03.1993	12	-	10	1
Antonio Emiliano Gonzáles Canchari	16.05.1986	10	-	10	-
Christofer Gonzáles Crespo	12.10.1992	13	4	7	2
Paulo César Goyoneche Yaranaga	08.04.1993	-	-	-	-
Rafael Nicanor Guarderas Saravia	12.09.1993	6	-	9	-
César Andrés Huamantica Semorile	10.10.1996	-	-	-	-
Giordano Marcos Mendoza Lescano	18.10.1993	6	-	1	-
Gerson André Panduro Alvarado	01.08.1995	-	-	-	-
Andy Maelo Reátegui Castillo	14.06.1995	9	-	12	-
Miguel Ángel Torres Quintana	17.01.1982	7	-	10	1
Rainer Torres Salas	12.01.1980	15	-	11	-
Carlos Iván Uribe Zambrano	25.03.1992	-	-	-	-
Josimar Hugo Vargas García	06.04.1990	14	-	10	-
Forwards:					
Joaquín Aldaír Aguirre Luza	24.07.1995	3	-	3	-
Germán Ariel Alemanno (ARG)	27.09.1983	-	-	15	5
Édison Michael Flores Peralta	14.05.1994	11	1	5	1
Gonzalo Maldonado Lostaunau	18.05.1994	4	-	-	-
Cris Robert Martínez Escobar (PAR)	24.04.1993	10	3	10	-
Carlos Dante Olascuaga Viera	22.07.1992	6	1		
Raúl Mario Ruidíaz Misitich	25.07.1990	15	10	10	4
Roberto Siucho Neyra	07.02.1997	-	-	-	-
Trainer:					
José Guillermo del Solar Alvarez-Calderón [07.03.-04.09.2014]	28.11.1967	15			
Oscar Manuel Ibáñez Holzmann (ARG) [as of 05.09.2014]	08.08.1967			15	

SECOND LEVEL
Segunda División 2014

1.	Club Centro Deportivo Municipal Lima (*Promoted*)	30	18	7	5	49 - 30	61
2.	Club Deportivo Coopsol Lima	30	17	7	6	53 - 26	58
3.	CSD Carlos A. Manucci Trujillo	30	17	5	8	46 - 32	56
4.	CDSC Alianza Universidad de Huánuco	30	15	8	7	51 - 30	53
5.	CDSC Willy Serrato Puse Pimentel	30	12	10	8	44 - 37	46
6.	Club Sport Unión Huaral	30	11	7	12	38 - 37	40
7.	Club Deportivo Defensor San Alejandro	30	10	9	11	37 - 37	39
8.	Club Atlético Minero Matucana	30	10	9	11	30 - 40	39
9.	Club Atlético Torino Talara	30	9	10	11	37 - 34	37
10.	Club Deportivo Alfonso Ugarte Puno(1)	30	11	6	13	36 - 51	35
11.	Club Deportivo Pacifico FC Lima	30	9	8	13	33 - 44	35
12.	Sport Boys Association Callao(2)	30	8	13	9	42 - 47	33
13.	Club Sport Victoria Ica	30	7	10	13	32 - 39	31
14.	CSDC Comerciantes Unidos Cutervo	30	7	9	14	29 - 36	30
15.	José Gálvez FBC Chimbote(3) (*Relegated*)	30	7	10	13	25 - 39	25
16.	Club Deportivo Walter Ormeño de Cañete(2) (*Relegated*)	30	4	9	17	22 - 47	19

Please note:
(1) 4 points deducted.
(2) 2 points deducted.
(3) 6 points deducted.

NATIONAL TEAM
INTERNATIONAL MATCHES
(16.07.2014 – 15.07.2015)

06.08.2014	Lima	Peru - Panama	3-0(1-0)	(F)
05.09.2014	Dubai	Iraq - Peru	0-2(0-2)	(F)
09.09.2014	Doha	Qatar - Peru	0-2(0-0)	(F)
10.10.2014	Valparaíso	Chile - Peru	3-0(2-0)	(F)
14.10.2014	Lima	Peru - Guatemala	1-0(1-0)	(F)
14.11.2014	Luque	Paraguay - Peru	2-1(0-0)	(F)
18.11.2014	Lima	Peru - Paraguay	2-1(0-1)	(F)
31.03.2015	Fort Lauderdale	Peru - Venezuela	0-1(0-0)	(F)
03.06.2015	Lima	Peru - Mexico	1-1(0-0)	(F)
14.06.2015	Temuco	Brazil - Peru	2-1(1-0)	(CA)
18.06.2015	Valparaíso	Peru – Venezuela	1-0(0-0)	(CA)
21.06.2015	Temuco	Colombia - Peru	0-0	(CA)
24.06.2015	Temuco	Bolivia - Peru	1-3(0-2)	(CA)
29.06.2015	Santiago	Chile - Peru	2-1(1-0)	(CA)
03.07.2015	Concepción	Peru - Paraguay	2-0(0-0)	(CA)

06.08.2014, Friendly International
Estadio Nacional, Lima; Attendance: 6,000
Referee: José Luis Espinel Mena (Ecuador)

PERU - PANAMA 3-0(1-0)

PER: Pedro David Quiroz Gallese, Christian Guillermo Martín Ramos Garagay, Víctor Yoshimar Yotún Flores (46.Miguel Ángel Trauco Saavedra), Luis Jan Piers Advíncula Castrillón, Hansell Argenis Riojas La Rosa, Paulo Rinaldo Cruzado Durand (67.Mario Alfonso Velarde Pinto), Josepmir Aarón Ballón Villacorta (86.Benjamín Ubierna Barandiarán), Carlos Antonio Ascues Ávila, Víctor Andrés Cedron Zurita (54.Carlos Jairsinho Gonzáles Ávalos), Christofer Gonzáles Crespo (78.Paulo Hernán Junior Hinostroza Vásquez), Daniel Mackensi Chávez Castillo. Trainer: Pablo Javier Bengoechea Dutra Bruno (Uruguay).

Goals: Carlos Antonio Ascues Ávila (44), Christian Guillermo Martín Ramos Garagay (81), Carlos Antonio Ascues Ávila (90+1).

05.09.2014, Friendly International
"Maktoum Bin Rashid Al Maktoum" Stadium, Dubai (United Arab Emirates); Attendance: 2,000
Referee: Hamad Al Shaikh Hashmi (United Arab Emirates)

IRAQ - PERU 0-2(0-2)

PER: Pedro David Quiroz Gallese, Víctor Yoshimar Yotún Flores (46.Miguel Ángel Trauco Saavedra), Carlos Augusto Zambrano Ochandarte, Luis Jan Piers Advíncula Castrillón, Alexander Martín Marquinho Callens Asín, Paulo Rinaldo Cruzado Durand (62.Mario Alfonso Velarde Pinto), Josepmir Aarón Ballón Villacorta, Carlos Antonio Ascues Ávila (32.Paulo Hernán Junior Hinostroza Vásquez), José Paolo Guerrero Gonzales (66.Benjamín Ubierna Barandiarán), André Martín Carrillo Díaz (81.Pedro Paulo Requena Cisneros), Jean Carlos Francisco Deza Sánchez (54.Daniel Mackensi Chávez Castillo). Trainer: Pablo Javier Bengoechea Dutra Bruno (Uruguay).

Goals: Mustafa Nadhim Jari Al Shabbani (19 own goal), Carlos Augusto Zambrano Ochandarte (26).

Sent off: Carlos Augusto Zambrano Ochandarte (90).

09.09.2014, Friendly International
"Abdullah bin Khalifa Stadium", Doha; Attendance: 4,000
Referee: Ionuţ Marius Avram (Romania)

QATAR - PERU 0-2(0-0)

PER: George Patrick Forsyth Sommer, Víctor Yoshimar Yotún Flores, Luis Jan Piers Advíncula Castrillón (90+2.Pedro Paulo Requena Cisneros), Alexander Martín Marquinho Callens Asín, Hansell Argenis Riojas La Rosa (67.Roberto Efraín Koichi Aparicio Mori), Paulo Rinaldo Cruzado Durand (86.Benjamín Ubierna Barandiarán), Josepmir Aarón Ballón Villacorta, Mario Alfonso Velarde Pinto (77.Paulo Hernán Junior Hinostroza Vásquez), José Paolo Guerrero Gonzales, André Martín Carrillo Díaz (77.Daniel Mackensi Chávez Castillo), Jean Carlos Francisco Deza Sánchez (46.Víctor Andrés Cedron Zurita). Trainer: Pablo Javier Bengoechea Dutra Bruno (Uruguay).
Goals: Alexander Martín Marquinho Callens Asín (84), José Paolo Guerrero Gonzales (88).

10.10.2014, Friendly International
Estadio "Elías Figueroa Brander", Valparaíso; Attendance: n/a
Referee: Julio César Quintana Rodríguez (Paraguay)

CHILE - PERU 3-0(2-0)

PER: Raúl Omar Fernández Valverde, Víctor Yoshimar Yotún Flores, Carlos Augusto Zambrano Ochandarte (74.Josimar Jair Atoche Bances), Luis Jan Piers Advíncula Castrillón, Alexander Martín Marquinho Callens Asín, Paulo Rinaldo Cruzado Durand, Josepmir Aarón Ballón Villacorta, Juan Manuel Vargas Risco (58.Christian Guillermo Martín Ramos Garagay), Carlos Antonio Ascues Ávila, José Paolo Guerrero Gonzales, André Martín Carrillo Díaz (86.Mario Alfonso Velarde Pinto). Trainer: Pablo Javier Bengoechea Dutra Bruno (Uruguay).
Sent off: Paulo Rinaldo Cruzado Durand (39).

14.10.2014, Friendly International
Estadio "Alejandro Villanueva", Lima; Attendance: n/a
Referee: Diego Jefferson Lara León (Ecuador)

PERU - GUATEMALA 1-0(1-0)

PER: Pedro David Quiroz Gallese, Christian Guillermo Martín Ramos Garagay, Víctor Yoshimar Yotún Flores, Luis Jan Piers Advíncula Castrillón, Alexander Martín Marquinho Callens Asín, Josepmir Aarón Ballón Villacorta, Juan Manuel Vargas Risco (57.Cristian Benavente Bristol), Mario Alfonso Velarde Pinto (62.Paulo Hernán Junior Hinostroza Vásquez), Carlos Antonio Ascues Ávila (85.Josimar Jair Atoche Bances), Claudio Miguel Pizarro Bosio, André Martín Carrillo Díaz (72.Irven Beybe Ávila Acero). Trainer: Pablo Javier Bengoechea Dutra Bruno (Uruguay).
Goal: Carlos Antonio Ascues Ávila (35).

14.11.2014, Friendly International
Estadio "Feliciano Cáceres", Luque; Attendance: n/a
Referee: Ricardo Marques Ribeiro (Brazil)

PARAGUAY - PERU 2-1(0-0)

PER: Pedro David Quiroz Gallese, Christian Guillermo Martín Ramos Garagay, Víctor Yoshimar Yotún Flores, Luis Jan Piers Advíncula Castrillón (77.Rodrigo Cuba Piedra), Alexander Martín Marquinho Callens Asín, Josepmir Aarón Ballón Villacorta, Luis Alberto Ramírez Lucay (46.Mario Alfonso Velarde Pinto), Cristopher Paolo César Hurtado Huertas (46.José Yordy Reyna Serna), Carlos Antonio Ascues Ávila (67.Josimar Jair Atoche Bances), José Paolo Guerrero Gonzales (88.Juan Manuel Vargas Risco), André Martín Carrillo Díaz (81.Cristian Benavente Bristol). Trainer: Pablo Javier Bengoechea Dutra Bruno (Uruguay).
Goals: José Paolo Guerrero Gonzales (74).
Sent off: Víctor Yoshimar Yotún Flores (90).

18.11.2014, Friendly International
Estadio Nacional, Lima; Attendance: n/a
Referee: Wilmar Alexander Roldán Pérez (Colombia)

PERU - PARAGUAY 2-1(0-1)

PER: Pedro David Quiroz Gallese, Christian Guillermo Martín Ramos Garagay, Luis Jan Piers Advíncula Castrillón, Iván Diego Santillán Atoche (46.Cristian Benavente Bristol; 84.Miguel Araujo Blanco), Alexander Martín Marquinho Callens Asín, Josepmir Aarón Ballón Villacorta (72.Carlos Antonio Ascues Ávila), Luis Alberto Ramírez Lucay (72.Josimar Jair Atoche Bances), Juan Manuel Vargas Risco, Mario Alfonso Velarde Pinto (46.André Martín Carrillo Díaz), José Paolo Guerrero Gonzales, Jean Carlos Francisco Deza Sánchez (46.José Yordy Reyna Serna). Trainer: Pablo Javier Bengoechea Dutra Bruno (Uruguay).
Goals: Carlos Antonio Ascues Ávila (73, 81).
Sent off: José Paolo Guerrero Gonzales (67), José Yordy Reyna Serna (90).

31.03.2015, Friendly International
Lockhart Stadium, Fort Lauderdale (United States); Attendance: 10,000
Referee: Armando Isaí Castro Oviedo (Honduras)

PERU - VENEZUELA 0-1(0-0)

PER: Pedro David Quiroz Gallese, Christian Guillermo Martín Ramos Garagay, Carlos Augusto Zambrano Ochandarte, Luis Jan Piers Advíncula Castrillón, Jair Edson Céspedes Zegarra, Josepmir Aarón Ballón Villacorta, Cristopher Paolo César Hurtado Huertas (84.Christofer Gonzáles Crespo), Renato Tapia Cortijo, Irven Beybe Ávila Acero (71.Raúl Mario Ruidíaz Misitich), André Martín Carrillo Díaz (71.Cristian Benavente Bristol), Jean Carlos Francisco Deza Sánchez (30.Christian Alberto Cueva Bravo). Trainer: Ricardo Alberto Gareca Nardi (Argentina).

03.06.2015, Friendly International
Estadio Monumental, Lima; Attendance: n/a
Referee: Omar Andrés Ponce Manzo (Ecuador)

PERU - MEXICO 1-1(0-0)

PER: Pedro David Quiroz Gallese, Carlos Augusto Zambrano Ochandarte, Luis Jan Piers Advíncula Castrillón (50.Pedro Paulo Requena Cisneros), Jair Edson Céspedes Zegarra (79.Hansell Argenis Riojas La Rosa), Josepmir Aarón Ballón Villacorta, Carlos Augusto Lobatón Espejo (65.Cristopher Paolo César Hurtado Huertas), Christian Alberto Cueva Bravo (68.José Yordy Reyna Serna), Jefferson Agustín Farfán Guadalupe (73.Claudio Miguel Pizarro Bosio), Joel Melchor Sánchez Alegría, Carlos Antonio Ascues Ávila, José Paolo Guerrero Gonzales. Trainer: Ricardo Alberto Gareca Nardi (Argentina).
Goal: Jefferson Agustín Farfán Guadalupe (62).
Sent off: Pedro Paulo Requena Cisneros (78).

14.06.2015, 44th Copa América, Group Stage
Estadio Municipal "Germán Becker", Temuco (Chile); Attendance: 16,342
Referee: Roberto García Orozco (Mexico)

BRAZIL - PERU 2-1(1-0)

PER: Pedro David Quiroz Gallese, Carlos Augusto Zambrano Ochandarte, Luis Jan Piers Advíncula Castrillón, Josepmir Aarón Ballón Villacorta, Carlos Augusto Lobatón Espejo, Christian Alberto Cueva Bravo (82.José Yordy Reyna Serna), Juan Manuel Vargas Risco (89.Víctor Yoshimar Yotún Flores), Joel Melchor Sánchez Alegría, Jefferson Agustín Farfán Guadalupe (82.André Martín Carrillo Díaz), Carlos Antonio Ascues Ávila, José Paolo Guerrero Gonzales. Trainer: Ricardo Alberto Gareca Nardi (Argentina).
Goal: Christian Alberto Cueva Bravo (2).

18.06.2015, 44th Copa América, Group Stage
Estadio "Elías Figueroa", Valparaíso (Chile); Attendance: 15,542
Referee: Raúl Orosco Delgadillo (Bolivia)

PERU – VENEZUELA 1-0(0-0)

PER: Pedro David Quiroz Gallese, Carlos Augusto Zambrano Ochandarte, Luis Jan Piers Advíncula Castrillón, Josepmir Aarón Ballón Villacorta, Carlos Augusto Lobatón Espejo (46.José Yordy Reyna Serna), Christian Alberto Cueva Bravo (83.Cristopher Paolo César Hurtado Huertas), Juan Manuel Vargas Risco, Joel Melchor Sánchez Alegría, Carlos Antonio Ascues Ávila, José Paolo Guerrero Gonzales, Claudio Miguel Pizarro Bosio (89.Víctor Yoshimar Yotún Flores). Trainer: Ricardo Alberto Gareca Nardi (Argentina).
Goal: Claudio Miguel Pizarro Bosio (72).

21.06.2015, 44th Copa América, Group Stage
Estadio Municipal "Germán Becker", Temuco (Chile); Attendance: 17,332
Referee: Néstor Fabián Pitana (Argentina)

COLOMBIA - PERU 0-0

PER: Pedro David Quiroz Gallese, Carlos Augusto Zambrano Ochandarte, Luis Jan Piers Advíncula Castrillón, Josepmir Aarón Ballón Villacorta, Carlos Augusto Lobatón Espejo, Christian Alberto Cueva Bravo (90.Víctor Yoshimar Yotún Flores), Juan Manuel Vargas Risco, Joel Melchor Sánchez Alegría (81.Cristopher Paolo César Hurtado Huertas), Carlos Antonio Ascues Ávila, José Paolo Guerrero Gonzales, Claudio Miguel Pizarro Bosio (56.Jefferson Agustín Farfán Guadalupe). Trainer: Ricardo Alberto Gareca Nardi (Argentina).

24.06.2015, 44th Copa América, Quarter-Finals
Estadio Municipal "Germán Becker", Temuco (Chile); Attendance: 16,872
Referee: Wilmar Alexander Roldán Pérez (Colombia)

BOLIVIA - PERU 1-3(0-2)

PER: Pedro David Quiroz Gallese, Víctor Yoshimar Yotún Flores, Carlos Augusto Zambrano Ochandarte, Luis Jan Piers Advíncula Castrillón, Edwin Retamoso Palomino, Christian Alberto Cueva Bravo (82.José Yordy Reyna Serna), Juan Manuel Vargas Risco, Carlos Antonio Ascues Ávila, Jefferson Agustín Farfán Guadalupe (77.Cristopher Paolo César Hurtado Huertas), José Paolo Guerrero Gonzales, Claudio Miguel Pizarro Bosio (66.André Martín Carrillo Díaz). Trainer: Ricardo Alberto Gareca Nardi (Argentina).
Goals: José Paolo Guerrero Gonzales (20, 23, 74).

29.06.2015, 44th Copa América, Semi-Finals
Estadio Nacional "Julio Martínez Prádanos", Santiago; Attendance: 45,651
Referee: José Ramón Argote Vega (Venezuela)

CHILE - PERU 2-1(1-0)

PER: Pedro David Quiroz Gallese, Carlos Augusto Zambrano Ochandarte, Luis Jan Piers Advíncula Castrillón, Josepmir Aarón Ballón Villacorta, Carlos Augusto Lobatón Espejo (73.Víctor Yoshimar Yotún Flores), Christian Alberto Cueva Bravo (27.Christian Guillermo Martín Ramos Garagay), Juan Manuel Vargas Risco, Carlos Antonio Ascues Ávila, Jefferson Agustín Farfán Guadalupe, José Paolo Guerrero Gonzales, André Martín Carrillo Díaz (73.Claudio Miguel Pizarro Bosio). Trainer: Ricardo Alberto Gareca Nardi (Argentina).
Goal: Gary Alexis Medel Soto (60 own goal).
Sent off: Carlos Augusto Zambrano Ochandarte (20).

03.07.2015, 44th Copa América, Third Place Play-off
Estadio Municipal „Alcaldesa Ester Roa Rebolledo", Concepción (Chile); Attendance: 29,143
Referee: Raúl Orosco Delgadillo (Bolivia)

PERU - PARAGUAY **2-0(0-0)**

PER: Pedro David Quiroz Gallese, Christian Guillermo Martín Ramos Garagay, Luis Jan Piers Advíncula Castrillón, Josepmir Aarón Ballón Villacorta, Carlos Augusto Lobatón Espejo (57.Víctor Yoshimar Yotún Flores), Christian Alberto Cueva Bravo, Juan Manuel Vargas Risco, Carlos Antonio Ascues Ávila, José Yordy Reyna Serna (84.Joel Melchor Sánchez Alegría), José Paolo Guerrero Gonzales, André Martín Carrillo Díaz (90+1.Cristopher Paolo César Hurtado Huertas). Trainer: Ricardo Alberto Gareca Nardi (Argentina).

Goals: André Martín Carrillo Díaz (48), José Paolo Guerrero Gonzales (89).

NATIONAL TEAM PLAYERS 2014/2015			
Name	**DOB**	**Caps**	**Goals**
[Club 2014/2015]			

(Caps and goals at 05.07.2015)

Goalkeepers

Name	DOB	Caps	Goals
Raúl Omar FERNÁNDEZ Valverde [2014: FC Dallas (USA)]	06.10.1985	**29**	**0**
George Patrick FORSYTH Sommer [2014/2015: Club Alianza Lima]	20.06.1982	**7**	**0**
Pedro David Quiroz GALLESE [2014: CD Universidad San Martín de Porres; 01.2015-> Club Juan Aurich de Chiclayo]	23.04.1990	**13**	**0**

Defenders

Name	DOB	Caps	Goals
Luis Jan Piers ADVÍNCULA Castrillón [2014/2015: Vitória FC Setúbal (POR)]	02.03.1990	**48**	**0**
Roberto Efraín Koichi APARICIO Mori [2014: Club Alianza Lima]	06.06.1993	**2**	**0**
Miguel Gianpirre ARAUJO Blanco [2014: Club Alianza Lima]	24.10.1994	**1**	**0**
Alexander Martín Marquinho CALLENS Asín [2014/2015: Real Sociedad de Fútbol San Sebastián "B"]	04.05.1992	**10**	**1**
Jair Edson CÉSPEDES Zegarra [2015: Club Juan Aurich de Chiclayo]	22.05.1984	**5**	**0**
Rodrigo CUBA Piedra [2014: Club Juan Aurich de Chiclayo]	17.05.1992	**1**	**0**
Hansell Argenis RIOJAS La Rosa [2014: Club Sportivo Cienciano Cuzco; 01.2015-> CD Universidad César Vallejo Trujillo]	15.10.1991	**4**	**0**
Christian Guillermo Martín RAMOS Garagay [2014/2015: Club Juan Aurich de Chiclayo]	04.11.1988	**40**	**1**
Pedro Paulo REQUENA Cisneros [2014/2015: CSCD Universidad César Vallejo Trujillo]	24.01.1991	**3**	**0**
Iván Diego SANTILLÁN Atoche [2014: Asociación Civil Real Atlético Garcilaso]	06.05.1990	**1**	**0**
Víctor Yoshimar YOTÚN Flores [2014: Club Sporting Cristal Lima; 27.01.12015-> Malmö FF (SWE)]	07.04.1990	**45**	**1**
Carlos Augusto ZAMBRANO Ochandarte [2014/2015: SG Eintracht Frankfurt (GER)]	10.07.1989	**35**	**4**

Midfielders			
Carlos Antonio ASCUES Ávila [2014: CD Universidad San Martín de Porres; 01.2015-> FCB Melgar Arequipa]	06.06.1992	**13**	**5**
Josimar Jair ATOCHE Bances [2014: Club Alianza Lima]	29.09.1989	**4**	**0**
Josepmir Aaron BALLÓN Villacorta [2014: Club Universidad San Martín de Porres; 01.2015-> Club Sporting Cristal Lima]	21.03.1988	**41**	**0**
Cristian BENAVENTE Bristol [2014/2015: Real Madrid CF "B" (ESP)]	19.05.1994	**9**	**1**
Víctor Andrés CEDRON Zurita [2014: CD Universidad César Vallejo Trujillo]	06.10.1993	**2**	**0**
Paulo Rinaldo CRUZADO Durand [2014: Club Nacional de Football Montevideo (URU)]	21.09.1984	**44**	**2**
Christian Alberto CUEVA Bravo [2015: Club Alianza Lima]	23.11.1991	**14**	**1**
Christofer GONZÁLES Crespo [2014/2015: Club Universitario de Deportes Lima]	12.10.1992	**5**	**1**
Paulo Hernán Junior HINOSTROZA Vásquez [2014: CD Universidad San Martín de Porres]	21.12.1993	**4**	**0**
Christopher Paolo César HURTADO Huertas [2014/2015: FC Paços de Ferreira (POR)]	27.07.1990	**20**	**2**
Carlos Augusto LOBATÓN Espejo [2014/2015: Club Sporting Cristal Lima]	06.02.1980	**39**	**1**
Luis Alberto RAMÍREZ Lucay [2014: Botafogo FR Rio de Janeiro (BRA), on loan]	10.11.1984	**33**	**2**
Edwin RETAMOSO Palomino [2015: Asociación Civil Real Atlético Garcilaso]	23.02.1982	**12**	**0**
Joel Melchor SÁNCHEZ Alegría [2015: CD Universidad San Martín de Porres]	11.07.1989	**7**	**0**
Renato TAPIA Cortijo [2014/2015: Jong FC Twente Enschede (NED)]	28.07.1995	**1**	**0**
Juan Manuel VARGAS Risco [2014/2015: AC Fiorentina Firenze (ITA)]	05.10.1983	**59**	**4**
Benjamin UBIERNA Barandiarán [2014: CD Universidad San Martín de Porres]	22.11.1991	**3**	**0**
Mario Alfonso VELARDE Pinto [2014/2015: CD Unión Comercio Nueva Cajamarca]	03.07.1990	**8**	**0**

Forwards

Irven Beybe ÁVILA Acero [2014/2015: Club Sporting Cristal Lima]	02.07.1990	**11**	**0**
André Martín CARRILLO Díaz [2014/2015: Sporting Clube de Portugal Lisboa (POR)]	14.06.1991	**27**	**2**
Daniel Mackensi CHÁVEZ Castillo [2014: CSCD Universidad César Vallejo Trujillo]	08.01.1988	**16**	**0**
Jean Carlos Francisco DEZA Sánchez [2014: Montpellier-Hérault SC (FRA); 02.02.2015-> Club Alianza Lima]	09.06.1993	**6**	**0**
Jefferson Agustín FARFÁN Guadalupe [2014/2015: FC Schalke 04 Gelsenkirchen (GER)]	26.10.1984	**69**	**18**
Carlos Jairsinho GONZÁLES Ávalos [2014: Club Sporting Cristal Lima]	20.12.1989	**1**	**0**
José Paolo GUERRERO Gonzales [2014/2015: SC Corinthians Paulista São Paulo (BRA)]	01.01.1984	**63**	**24**
Claudio Miguel PIZARRO Bosio [2014/2015: FC Bayern München (GER)]	03.10.1978	**81**	**20**
José Yordy REYNA Serna [2014: FC Red Bull Salzburg (AUT); 01.2015-> RasenBallsport Leipzig (GER)]	17.09.1993	**13**	**2**
Raúl Mario RUIDÍAZ Misitich [2015: FCB Melgar Arequipa]	25.07.1990	**10**	**0**
Miguel Ángel TRAUCO Saavedra [2014: CD Unión Comercio Nueva Cajamarca]	25.08.1992	**2**	**0**

National Trainers

Pablo Javier BENGOECHEA DUTRA Bruno (Uruguay)	27.06.1965	7 M; 5 W; 0 D; 2 L; 11-6
Ricardo Alberto GARECA Nardi (Argentina)	10.02.1958	8 M; 3 W; 2 D; 3 L; 9-7

URUGUAY

The Country:
República Oriental del Uruguay (Oriental Republic of Uruguay)
Capital: Montevideo
Surface: 176,215 km²
Inhabitants: 3,324,460
Time: UTC-3

The FA:
Asociación Uruguaya de Fútbol
Guayabo 1531, Montevideo 11200
Year of Formation: 1900
Member of FIFA since: 1923
Member of CONMEBOL since: 1916
Internet: www.auf.org.uy

NATIONAL TEAM RECORDS	
First international match:	20.07.1902, Montevideo: Uruguay – Argentina 0-6
Most international caps:	Diego Martín Forlán Corazzo – 112 caps (2002-2014)
Most international goals:	Luis Alberto Suárez Díaz – 43 goals / 82 caps (since 2007)

OLYMPIC GAMES 1900-2012
1924 (Winners), 1928 (Winners)
FIFA CONFEDERATIONS CUP 1992-2009
1997, 2013

COPA AMÉRICA	
1916	**Winners**
1917	**Winners**
1919	Runners-up
1920	**Winners**
1921	3rd Place
1922	3rd Place
1923	**Winners**
1924	**Winners**
1925	Withdrew
1926	**Winners**
1927	Runners-up
1929	3rd Place
1935	**Winners**
1937	3rd Place
1939	Runners-up
1941	Runners-up
1942	**Winners**
1945	4th Place
1946	4th Place
1947	3rd Place
1949	6th Place
1953	3rd Place
1955	4th Place
1956	**Winners**
1957	3rd Place
1959	5th Place
1959E	**Winners**
1963	Withdrew
1967	**Winners**
1975	Semi-Finals
1979	Round 1
1983	**Winners**
1987	**Winners**
1989	Runners-up
1991	Round 1
1993	Quarter-Finals
1995	**Winners**
1997	Round 1
1999	Runners-up
2001	Semi-Finals
2004	3rd Place
2007	Semi-Finals
2011	**Winners**
2015	Quarter-Finals

FIFA WORLD CUP	
1930	**Final Tournament (Winners)**
1934	Withdrew
1938	Did not enter
1950	**Final Tournament (Winners)**
1954	Final Tournament (Semi-Finals)
1958	Qualifiers
1962	Final Tournament (Group Stage)
1966	Final Tournament (Quarter-Finals)
1970	Final Tournament (4th Place)
1974	Final Tournament (Group Stage)
1978	Qualifiers
1982	Qualifiers
1986	Final Tournament (2nd Round of 16)
1990	Final Tournament (2nd Round of 16)
1994	Qualifiers
1998	Qualifiers
2002	Final Tournament (Group Stage)
2006	Qualifiers
2010	Final Tournament (4th Place)
2014	Final Tournament (2nd Round of 16)

PANAMERICAN GAMES	
1951	Did not enter
1955	Did not enter
1959	Did not enter
1963	4th Place
1967	Did not enter
1971	Did not enter
1975	Round 1
1979	Did not enter
1983	**Winners**
1987	Did not enter
1991	Did not enter
1995	Did not enter
1999	Round 1
2003	Did not enter
2007	Did not enter
2011	3rd Place

PANAMERICAN CHAMPIONSHIP	
1952	3rd Place
1956	Did not enter
1960	Did not enter

URUGUAYAN CLUB HONOURS IN SOUTH AMERICAN CLUB COMPETITIONS:

COPA LIBERTADORES 1960-2014
Club Atlético Peñarol Montevideo (1960, 1961, 1966, 1982, 1987) Club Nacional de Football Montevideo (1971, 1980, 1988)
COPA SUDAMERICANA 2002-2014
None
RECOPA SUDAMERICANA 1989-2013
Club Nacional de Football Montevideo (1989)
COPA CONMEBOL 1992-1999
None
SUPERCUP „JOÃO HAVELANGE" 1988-1997*
None
COPA MERCOSUR 1998-2001**
None

**Contested betwenn winners of all previous editions of the Copa Libertadores*

***Contested between teams belonging countries from the southern part of South America (Argentina, Brazil, Chile, Paraguay and Uruguay).*

NATIONAL COMPETITIONS
TABLE OF HONOURS

NATIONAL CHAMPIONS
1900-2014

	THE AMATEUR ERA
	Uruguay Association Foot-ball League
1900	Central Uruguay Railway Cricket Club Montevideo (CURCC)
1901	Central Uruguay Railway Cricket Club Montevideo
1902	Club Nacional de Football Montevideo
1903	Club Nacional de Football Montevideo
1904	*No competition*
1905	Central Uruguay Railway Cricket Club Montevideo
1906	Montevideo Wanderers FC
1907	Central Uruguay Railway Cricket Club Montevideo
	Liga Uruguaya
1908	River Plate FC Montevideo
1909	Montevideo Wanderers FC
1910	River Plate FC Montevideo
1911	Central Uruguay Railway Cricket Club Montevideo
1912	Club Nacional de Football Montevideo
1913	River Plate FC Montevideo
1914	River Plate FC Montevideo
	Asociación Uruguaya de Foot-ball
1915	Club Nacional de Football Montevideo
1916	Club Nacional de Football Montevideo
1917	Club Nacional de Football Montevideo
1918	CA Peñarol Montevideo
1919	Club Nacional de Football Montevideo
1920	Club Nacional de Football Montevideo
1921	CA Peñarol Montevideo
1922	Club Nacional de Football Montevideo
1923	Club Nacional de Football Montevideo
1924	Club Nacional de Football Montevideo
1925	*Championship not finished*
	Consejo Provisorio
1926	CA Peñarol Montevideo
	Asociación Uruguaya de Foot-ball
1927	Rampla Juniors FC Montevideo
1928	CA Peñarol Montevideo
1929	CA Peñarol Montevideo
1930	*No competition*
1931	Montevideo Wanderers FC
	THE PROFESSIONAL ERA
	Asociación Uruguaya de Fútbol
1932	CA Peñarol Montevideo
1933	Club Nacional de Football Montevideo
1934	Club Nacional de Football Montevideo
1935	CA Peñarol Montevideo
1936	CA Peñarol Montevideo
1937	CA Peñarol Montevideo

1938	CA Peñarol Montevideo
1939	Club Nacional de Football Montevideo
1940	Club Nacional de Football Montevideo
1941	Club Nacional de Football Montevideo
1942	Club Nacional de Football Montevideo
1943	Club Nacional de Football Montevideo
1944	CA Peñarol Montevideo
1945	CA Peñarol Montevideo
1946	Club Nacional de Football Montevideo
1947	Club Nacional de Football Montevideo
1948	*Championship not fiished*
1949	CA Peñarol Montevideo
1950	Club Nacional de Football Montevideo
1951	CA Peñarol Montevideo
1952	Club Nacional de Football Montevideo
1953	CA Peñarol Montevideo
1954	CA Peñarol Montevideo
1955	Club Nacional de Football Montevideo
1956	Club Nacional de Football Montevideo
1957	Club Nacional de Football Montevideo
1958	CA Peñarol Montevideo
1959	CA Peñarol Montevideo
1960	CA Peñarol Montevideo
1961	CA Peñarol Montevideo
1962	CA Peñarol Montevideo
1963	Club Nacional de Football Montevideo
1964	CA Peñarol Montevideo
1965	CA Peñarol Montevideo
1966	Club Nacional de Football Montevideo
1967	CA Peñarol Montevideo
1968	CA Peñarol Montevideo
1969	Club Nacional de Football Montevideo
1970	Club Nacional de Football Montevideo
1971	Club Nacional de Football Montevideo
1972	Club Nacional de Football Montevideo
1973	CA Peñarol Montevideo
1974	CA Peñarol Montevideo
1975	CA Peñarol Montevideo
1976	Defensor SC Montevideo
1977	Club Nacional de Football Montevideo
1978	CA Peñarol Montevideo
1979	CA Peñarol Montevideo
1980	Club Nacional de Football Montevideo
1981	CA Peñarol Montevideo
1982	CA Peñarol Montevideo
1983	Club Nacional de Football Montevideo
1984	Central Español FC Montevideo
1985	CA Peñarol Montevideo
1986	CA Peñarol Montevideo
1987	Defensor SC Montevideo
1988	Danubio FC Montevideo
1989	CA Progreso Montevideo

1990	CA Bella Vista Montevideo
1991	Defensor SC Montevideo
1992	Club Nacional de Football Montevideo
1993	CA Peñarol Montevideo
1994	CA Peñarol Montevideo
1995	CA Peñarol Montevideo
1996	CA Peñarol Montevideo
1997	CA Peñarol Montevideo
1998	Club Nacional de Football Montevideo
1999	CA Peñarol Montevideo
2000	Club Nacional de Football Montevideo
2001	Club Nacional de Football Montevideo
2002	Club Nacional de Football Montevideo
2003	CA Peñarol Montevideo
2004	Danubio FC Montevideo
2005	Club Nacional de Football Montevideo
2005/2006	Club Nacional de Football Montevideo
2006/2007	Danubio FC Montevideo
2007/2008	Defensor SC Montevideo
2008/2009	Club Nacional de Football Montevideo
2009/2010	CA Peñarol Montevideo
2010/2011	Club Nacional de Football Montevideo
2011/2012	Club Nacional de Football Montevideo
2012/2013	CA Peñarol Montevideo
2013/2014	Danubio FC Montevideo
2014/2015	Club Nacional de Football Montevideo

	BEST GOALSCORERS	
1932	Juan Labraga (Rampla Juniors FC Montevideo)	17
1933	Juan Young (CA Peñarol Montevideo)	33
1934	Aníbal Ciocca (Club Nacional de Football Montevideo)	13
1935	Antonio Cataldo (Defensor SC Montevideo)	12
1936	Aníbal Ciocca (Club Nacional de Football Montevideo)	14
1937	Horacio Tellechea (CA Peñarol Montevideo)	16
1938	Atilio Ceferino García Pérez (ARG, Club Nacional de Football Montevideo)	20
1939	Atilio Ceferino García Pérez (ARG, Club Nacional de Football Montevideo)	21
1940	Atilio Ceferino García Pérez (ARG, Club Nacional de Football Montevideo)	18
1941	Atilio Ceferino García Pérez (ARG, Club Nacional de Football Montevideo)	23
1942	Atilio Ceferino García Pérez (ARG, Club Nacional de Football Montevideo)	19
1943	Atilio Ceferino García Pérez (ARG, Club Nacional de Football Montevideo)	18
1944	Atilio Ceferino García Pérez (ARG, Club Nacional de Football Montevideo)	21
1945	Nicolás Falero (CA Peñarol Montevideo) Juan Alberto Schiaffino Villano (CA Peñarol Montevideo)	21
1946	Atilio Ceferino García Pérez (ARG, Club Nacional de Football Montevideo)	21
1947	Nicolás Falero (CA Peñarol Montevideo)	17
1948	Óscar Omar Míguez (CA Peñarol Montevideo)	8
1949	Óscar Omar Míguez (CA Peñarol Montevideo)	20
1950	Juan Ramón Orlandi (Club Nacional de Football Montevideo)	14
1951	Juan Eduardo Hohberg (CA Peñarol Montevideo)	17
1952	Jorge Enrico (Club Nacional de Football Montevideo)	15
1953	Juan Eduardo Hohberg (CA Peñarol Montevideo)	17
1954	Juan Romay (CA Peñarol Montevideo)	12
1955	Javier Ambrois (Club Nacional de Football Montevideo)	17
1956	Carlos Carranza (CA Cerro Montevideo)	18
1957	Walter Hernández (Defensor SC Montevideo)	16
1958	Manuel Pedersen (Rampla Juniors FC Montevideo)	12
1959	Víctor Guaglianone (Montevideo Wanderers FC)	13
1960	Ángel Cabrera (CA Peñarol Montevideo)	14
1961	Alberto Spencer Herrera (ECU, CA Peñarol Montevideo)	18
1962	Alberto Spencer Herrera (ECU, CA Peñarol Montevideo)	16
1963	Pedro Virgilio Rocha Franchetti (CA Peñarol Montevideo)	18
1964	Héctor Salva (Rampla Juniors FC Montevideo)	12
1965	Pedro Virgilio Rocha Franchetti (CA Peñarol Montevideo)	15
1966	Araquem De Melo (BRA, Danubio FC Montevideo)	12
1967	Alberto Spencer Herrera (ECU, CA Peñarol Montevideo)	11
1968	Alberto Spencer Herrera (ECU, CA Peñarol Montevideo) Pedro Virgilio Rocha Franchetti (CA Peñarol Montevideo) Ruben García (CA Cerro Montevideo) Ruben Bareño (CA Cerro Montevideo)	8
1969	Luis Artime (ARG, Club Nacional de Football Montevideo)	24
1970	Luis Artime (ARG, Club Nacional de Football Montevideo)	21
1971	Luis Artime (ARG, Club Nacional de Football Montevideo)	16
1972	Juan Carlos Mamelli (Club Nacional de Football Montevideo)	20
1973	Fernando Morena Belora (CA Peñarol Montevideo)	23
1974	Fernando Morena Belora (CA Peñarol Montevideo)	27
1975	Fernando Morena Belora (CA Peñarol Montevideo)	34
1976	Fernando Morena Belora (CA Peñarol Montevideo)	18
1977	Fernando Morena Belora (CA Peñarol Montevideo)	19

1978	Fernando Morena Belora (CA Peñarol Montevideo)	36
1979	Waldemar Barreto Victorino (Club Nacional de Football Montevideo)	19
1980	Jorge Luis Siviero Vlahussich (Institución Atlética Sud América Montevideo)	19
1981	Ruben Walter Paz Márquez (CA Peñarol Montevideo)	17
1982	Fernando Morena Belora (CA Peñarol Montevideo)	17
1983	Roberto Arsenio Luzardo Correa (Club Nacional de Football Montevideo)	13
1984	José Villareal (Central Español FC Montevideo)	18
1985	Antonio Valentín Alzamendi Casas (CA Peñarol Montevideo)	13
1986	Juan Ramón Carrasco Torres (Club Nacional de Football Montevideo) Gerardo Miranda (Defensor SC Montevideo)	11
1987	Gerardo Miranda (Defensor SC Montevideo)	13
1988	Rubén Fernando da Silva Echeverrito (Danubio FC Montevideo)	23
1989	Johnny Miqueiro (CA Progreso Montevideo) Diego Vicente Aguirre Camblor (CA Peñarol Montevideo) Oscar Quagliata (CSD Huracán Buceo)	7
1990	Adolfo Barán (CA Peñarol Montevideo)	13
1991	Julio César Dely Valdés (PAN, Club Nacional de Football Montevideo)	16
1992	Julio César Dely Valdés (PAN, Club Nacional de Football Montevideo)	13
1993	Wilmar Rubens Cabrera Sappa (CSD Huracán Buceo)	12
1994	Darío Debray Silva Pereira (CA Peñarol Montevideo)	19
1995	Juan Antonio González Crespo (Club Nacional de Football Montevideo)	16
1996	Juan Antonio González Crespo (Club Nacional de Football Montevideo)	13
1997	Pablo Javier Bengoechea Dutra (CA Peñarol Montevideo)	10
1998	Jorge Martín Rodríguez Alba (CA River Plate Montevideo) Rubén Sosa Ardáiz (Club Nacional de Football Montevideo)	13
1999	Jorge Gabriel Álvez Fernández (Club Nacional de Football Montevideo)	24
2000	Ernesto Javier Chevantón Espinoza (Danubio FC Montevideo)	33
2001	Eliomar Marcón (BRA, Defensor SC Montevideo)	21
2002	Germán Hornos (Centro Atlético Fénix Montevideo)	25
2003	Alexander Jesús Medina Reobasco (Liverpool FC Montevideo)	22
2004	Alexander Jesús Medina Reobasco (Club Nacional de Football Montevideo) Carlos Éber Bueno Suárez (CA Peñarol Montevideo)	26
2005	Pablo Mariano Granoche Louro (Club Sportivo Miramar Misiones)	16
2005/2006	Pedro Cardoso (Rocha Fútbol Club)	17
2006/2007	Aldo Díaz (Tacuarembó FC)	15
2007/2008	Christian Ricardo Stuani (Danubio FC Montevideo) Richard Aníbal Porta Candelaresi (CA River Plate Montevideo)	19
2008/2009	Líber Quiñones (Racing Club de Montevideo) Antonio Pacheco D'Agosti (CA Peñarol Montevideo)	12
2009/2010	Antonio Pacheco D'Agosti (CA Peñarol Montevideo)	23
2010/2011	Santiago Damián García Correa (Club Nacional de Football Montevideo)	23
2011/2012	Richard Aníbal Porta Candelaresi (Club Nacional de Football Montevideo)	17
2012/2013	Juan Manuel Olivera López (CA Peñarol Montevideo)	18
2013/2014	Héctor Fabián Acuña Maciel (CA Cerro Montevideo)	20
2014/2015	Iván Daniel Alonso Vallejo (Club Nacional de Football Montevideo)	22

NATIONAL CHAMPIONSHIP
Liga Profesional de Primera División 2014/2015
Torneo Uruguayo Copa „Coca-Cola" / Campeonato Uruguayo "Óscar Duque"

Torneo Apertura „Montevideo Capital Iberoamericana de la Cultura" 2013

Results

Round 1 [16-17.08.2014]

CA Rentistas - Tacuarembó FC 1-1(1-0)
Danubio FC - Racing Club 2-4(2-0)
CA Atenas - CA River Plate 1-3(1-1)
CA Peñarol - CA Cerro 3-0(1-0)
Wanderers FC - CCD El Tanque 1-2(0-0)
Rampla Juniors - IA Sud América 1-2(1-0)
CA Fénix - CA Juventud 3-1(0-0)
Club Nacional - Defensor Sporting 5-2(2-1)

Round 2 [22-24.08.2014]

Defensor Sporting - CA Rentistas 1-2(0-0)
Tacuarembó FC - CA Fénix 1-2(0-2)
IA Sud América - Club Nacional 0-1(0-0)
Racing Club - CA Cerro 4-1(2-0)
CA Juventud - CA Peñarol 0-1(0-0)
CCD El Tanque - Rampla Juniors 3-3(1-2)
CA River Plate - Wanderers FC 1-2(0-0)
Danubio FC - CA Atenas 2-0(0-0)

Round 3 [30-31.08.2014]

Club Nacional - CCD El Tanque 1-2(1-2)
CA Fénix - Defensor Sporting 3-4(1-2)
CA Atenas - Racing Club 1-3(0-1)
Wanderers FC - Danubio FC 4-1(3-0)
Rampla Juniors - CA River Plate 0-2(0-0)
CA Rentistas - IA Sud América 3-1(1-0)
CA Cerro - CA Juventud 1-3(0-1)
CA Peñarol - Tacuarembó FC 2-0(1-0)

Round 4 [06-07.09.2014]

Defensor Sporting - CA Peñarol 0-0
IA Sud América - CA Fénix 2-2(0-1)
Danubio FC - Rampla Juniors 5-0(1-0)
Racing Club - CA Juventud 1-1(1-1)
Tacuarembó FC - CA Cerro 4-0(1-0)
CCD El Tanque - CA Rentistas 2-0(1-0)
CA River Plate - Club Nacional 1-3(0-2)
CA Atenas - Wanderers FC 1-0(0-0)

Round 5 [12-14.09.2014]

CA Peñarol - IA Sud América 1-1(1-0)
CA Rentistas - CA River Plate 2-0(0-0)
Wanderers FC - Racing Club 2-3(1-1)
Rampla Juniors - CA Atenas 4-2(1-0)
CA Fénix - CCD El Tanque 1-0(0-0)
CA Cerro - Defensor Sporting 0-3(0-0)
CA Juventud - Tacuarembó FC 4-2(3-1)
Club Nacional - Danubio FC 3-0(2-0)

Round 6 [20-22.09.2014]

IA Sud América - CA Cerro 0-0
CCD El Tanque - CA Peñarol 1-1(1-0)
Racing Club - Tacuarembó FC 1-0(0-0)
Defensor Sporting - CA Juventud 2-0(0-0)
Danubio FC - CA Rentistas 0-3(0-1)
Wanderers FC - Rampla Juniors 0-1(0-0)
CA Atenas - Club Nacional 0-2(0-2)
CA River Plate - CA Fénix 3-1(1-1)

Round 7 [27-28.09.2014]

CA Cerro - CCD El Tanque 0-0
Club Nacional - Wanderers FC 2-0(1-0)
Rampla Juniors - Racing Club 1-2(1-1)
CA Rentistas - CA Atenas 0-3(0-0)
CA Fénix - Danubio FC 0-0
CA Juventud - IA Sud América 1-3(1-1)
Tacuarembó FC - Defensor Sporting 1-4(0-2)
CA Peñarol - CA River Plate 3-1(1-1)

Round 8 [04-05.10.2014]

IA Sud América - Tacuarembó FC 2-1(0-0)
Danubio FC - CA Peñarol 1-1(1-0)
Racing Club - Defensor Sporting 1-6(1-2)
CCD El Tanque - CA Juventud 0-3(0-1)
CA River Plate - CA Cerro 3-0(2-0)
CA Atenas - CA Fénix 3-0(0-0)
Wanderers FC - CA Rentistas 3-2(1-1)
Rampla Juniors - Club Nacional 0-2(0-0)

Round 9 [10-12.10.2014]
CA Peñarol - CA Atenas 4-1(2-0)
CA Rentistas - Rampla Juniors 0-2(0-1)
CA Fénix - Wanderers FC 2-1(1-0)
CA Cerro - Danubio FC 2-0(0-0)
CA Juventud - CA River Plate 0-3(0-2)
Tacuarembó FC - CCD El Tanque 2-3(0-2)
Defensor Sporting - IA Sud América 1-1(0-0)
Club Nacional - Racing Club 2-0(1-0)

Round 10 [18-19.10.2014]
Rampla Juniors - CA Fénix 1-0(1-0)
Wanderers FC - CA Peñarol 2-1(1-0)
Racing Club - IA Sud América 3-2(2-1)
CCD El Tanque - Defensor Sporting 2-1(1-0)
CA River Plate - Tacuarembó FC 2-2(2-0)
Danubio FC - CA Juventud 0-0
Club Nacional - CA Rentistas 2-0(1-0)
CA Atenas - CA Cerro 3-1(2-1)

Round 11 [01-02.11.2014]
Defensor Sporting - CA River Plate 0-2(0-2)
IA Sud América - CCD El Tanque 1-0(0-0)
CA Fénix - Club Nacional 0-3(0-1)
CA Rentistas - Racing Club 1-1(1-1)
CA Cerro - Wanderers FC 2-1(1-0)
CA Juventud - CA Atenas 2-1(2-0)
Tacuarembó FC - Danubio FC 0-0
CA Peñarol - Rampla Juniors 2-3(1-0)

Round 12 [08-09.11.2014]
Racing Club - CCD El Tanque 3-1(1-1)
CA River Plate - IA Sud América 2-1(0-1)
Wanderers FC - CA Juventud 1-0(0-0)
Rampla Juniors - CA Cerro 1-2(1-0)
CA Rentistas - CA Fénix 1-0(0-0)
Danubio FC - Defensor Sporting 2-1(2-1)
CA Atenas - Tacuarembó FC 2-1(1-0)
Club Nacional - CA Peñarol 2-1(0-0)

Round 13 [14-16.11.2014]
Defensor Sporting - CA Atenas 0-2(0-1)
IA Sud América - Danubio FC 0-1(0-1)
CA Peñarol - CA Rentistas 4-0(1-0)
CA Juventud - Rampla Juniors 2-0(1-0)
Tacuarembó FC - Wanderers FC 1-3(1-1)
CCD El Tanque - CA River Plate 1-0(1-0)
CA Fénix - Racing Club 2-3(1-1)
Club Nacional - CA Cerro 1-0(1-0)

Round 14 [21-23.11.2014]
CA Atenas - IA Sud América 0-0
Danubio FC - CCD El Tanque 1-1(0-1)
Wanderers FC - Defensor Sporting 1-1(0-1)
CA Rentistas - CA Cerro 3-1(1-0)
Club Nacional - CA Juventud 4-1(2-1)
Racing Club - CA River Plate 0-2(0-1)
Rampla Juniors - Tacuarembó FC 1-1(0-0)
CA Fénix - CA Peñarol 1-2(1-0)

Round 15 [06-07.12.2014]
CA Juventud - CA Rentistas 3-0(3-0)
IA Sud América - Wanderers FC 1-0(0-0)
CA River Plate - Danubio FC 1-2(0-0)
Tacuarembó FC - Club Nacional 0-1(0-0)
CA Cerro - CA Fénix 1-3(1-1)
Defensor Sporting - Rampla Juniors 2-0(1-0)
CCD El Tanque - CA Atenas 0-0
CA Peñarol - Racing Club 2-3(2-0)

Final Standings

1.	**Club Nacional de Football Montevideo**	15	14	0	1	34 - 7	42
2.	Racing Club de Montevideo	15	10	2	3	32 - 26	32
3.	CA Peñarol Montevideo	15	7	4	4	28 - 16	25
4.	CA River Plate Montevideo	15	8	1	6	26 - 18	25
5.	CCD El Tanque Sisley Montevideo	15	6	5	4	18 - 18	23
6.	Defensor Sporting Club Montevideo	15	6	3	6	28 - 22	21
7.	Institución Atlética Sud América Montevideo	15	5	5	5	17 - 17	20
8.	CA Juventud de Las Piedras	15	6	2	7	21 - 22	20
9.	CA Atenas de San Carlos	15	6	2	7	18 - 20	20
10.	Danubio FC Montevideo	15	5	5	5	18 - 21	20
11.	CA Rentistas Montevideo	15	6	2	7	18 - 24	20
12.	Montevideo Wanderers FC	15	6	1	8	21 - 21	19
13.	CA Fénix Montevideo	15	5	2	8	20 - 26	17
14.	Rampla Juniors FC Montevideo	15	5	2	8	18 - 27	17
15.	CA Cerro Montevideo	15	3	2	10	10 - 31	11
16.	Tacuarembó FC	15	1	4	10	17 - 28	7

Club Nacional de Football Montevideo qualified for the championship semi-finals.

Torneo Clausura „100 años de Sud América“ 2015

Results

Round 1 [14-15.02.2015]

IA Sud América - Rampla Juniors 1-1(1-1)
CCD El Tanque - Wanderers FC 1-0(0-0)
CA River Plate - CA Atenas 2-5(0-2)
CA Cerro - CA Peñarol 0-3(0-0)
Racing Club - Danubio FC 0-1(0-0)
CA Juventud - CA Fénix 1-1(0-0)
Tacuarembó FC - CA Rentistas 0-1(0-1)
Defensor Sporting - Club Nacional 0-0

Round 2 [21-22.02.2015]

CA Fénix - Tacuarembó FC 0-1(0-1)
Club Nacional - IA Sud América 1-2(0-1)
Rampla Juniors - CCD El Tanque 3-2(2-1)
Wanderers FC - CA River Plate 1-1(0-1)
CA Rentistas - Defensor Sporting 2-6(0-2)
CA Cerro - Racing Club 1-0(0-0)
CA Atenas - Danubio FC 3-1(1-1)
CA Peñarol - CA Juventud 4-1(2-0)

Round 3 [07-08.03.2015]

Defensor Sporting - CA Fénix 1-0(0-0)
IA Sud América - CA Rentistas 2-3(1-0)
Danubio FC - Wanderers FC 0-0
Tacuarembó FC - CA Peñarol 1-1(1-1)
Racing Club - CA Atenas 3-2(2-0)
CA River Plate - Rampla Juniors 4-0(4-0)
CA Juventud - CA Cerro 4-3(2-2)
CCD El Tanque - Club Nacional 0-1(0-0)

Round 4 [14-15.03.2015]

CA Fénix - IA Sud América 0-0
Rampla Juniors - Danubio FC 1-2(1-0)
Club Nacional - CA River Plate 1-2(1-2)
Wanderers FC - CA Atenas 1-2(1-1)
CA Juventud - Racing Club 1-0(0-0)
CA Cerro - Tacuarembó FC 2-1(0-0)
CA Rentistas - CCD El Tanque 0-1(0-0)
CA Peñarol - Defensor Sporting 2-0(1-0)

Round 5 [21-22.03.2015]
IA Sud América - CA Peñarol 1-0(1-0)
Defensor Sporting - CA Cerro 1-1(0-0)
Racing Club - Wanderers FC 2-1(0-0)
Danubio FC - Club Nacional 2-1(2-0)
CA River Plate - CA Rentistas 1-0(0-0)
CCD El Tanque - CA Fénix 0-3(0-1)
Tacuarembó FC - CA Juventud 2-1(0-0)
CA Atenas - Rampla Juniors 1-4(1-2) [26.03.]

Round 6 [28-29.03.2015]
CA Rentistas - Danubio FC 1-0(0-0)
CA Peñarol - CCD El Tanque 2-1(2-0)
Tacuarembó FC - Racing Club 1-0(1-0)
CA Juventud - Defensor Sporting 5-0(2-0)
CA Cerro - IA Sud América 2-2(0-1)
CA Fénix - CA River Plate 1-2(0-1)
Rampla Juniors - Wanderers FC 1-3(0-2)
Club Nacional - CA Atenas 5-3(0-0)

Round 7 [04-05.04.2015]
Wanderers FC - Club Nacional 2-0(1-0)
IA Sud América - CA Juventud 1-2(0-0)
Racing Club - Rampla Juniors 0-3(0-0)
CA Atenas - CA Rentistas 1-0(1-0)
Danubio FC - CA Fénix 3-0(1-0)
CA River Plate - CA Peñarol 1-2(0-2)
CCD El Tanque - CA Cerro 1-2(0-1)
Defensor Sporting - Tacuarembó FC 1-0(0-0)

Round 8 [11-12.04.2015]
CA Fénix - CA Atenas 3-2(1-0)
CA Peñarol - Danubio FC 2-3(1-2)
CA Juventud - CCD El Tanque 1-1(1-1)
Defensor Sporting - Racing Club 2-1(1-1)
Tacuarembó FC - IA Sud América 2-2(2-0)
CA Cerro - CA River Plate 2-2(1-2)
CA Rentistas - Wanderers FC 1-1(0-1)
Club Nacional - Rampla Juniors 3-1(3-1)

Round 9 [18-21.04.2015]
Racing Club - Club Nacional 2-4(1-2)
Rampla Juniors - CA Rentistas 1-0(0-0)
IA Sud América - Defensor Sporting 0-0
CA River Plate - CA Juventud 2-0(2-0)
CA Atenas - CA Peñarol 1-1(0-0)
Danubio FC - CA Cerro 1-0(0-0)
CCD El Tanque - Tacuarembó FC 1-1(0-1)
Wanderers FC - CA Fénix 0-1(0-1)

Round 10 [25-26.04.2015]
IA Sud América - Racing Club 3-1(2-0)
CA Peñarol - Wanderers FC 2-1(2-0)
Defensor Sporting - CCD El Tanque 2-2(1-1)
Tacuarembó FC - CA River Plate 1-3(1-1)
CA Juventud - Danubio FC 0-1(0-0)
CA Cerro - CA Atenas 2-1(1-0)
CA Fénix - Rampla Juniors 1-0(1-0)
CA Rentistas - Club Nacional 2-4(1-3)

Round 11 [02-03.05.2015]
Wanderers FC - CA Cerro 4-1(2-1)
Club Nacional - CA Fénix 1-0(1-0)
Racing Club - CA Rentistas 1-4(0-1)
CA Atenas - CA Juventud 0-4(0-1)
Danubio FC - Tacuarembó FC 0-1(0-0)
CA River Plate - Defensor Sporting 1-2(0-0)
CCD El Tanque - IA Sud América 1-1(0-1)
Rampla Juniors - CA Peñarol 0-2(0-1)

Round 12 [16-17.05.2015]
IA Sud América - CA River Plate 0-4(0-1)
Tacuarembó FC - CA Atenas 4-2(1-1)
CA Cerro - Rampla Juniors 2-0(1-0)
CA Fénix - CA Rentistas 4-1(1-0)
Defensor Sporting - Danubio FC 1-1(1-1)
CCD El Tanque - Racing Club 1-3(0-1)
CA Juventud - Wanderers FC 1-0(0-0)
CA Peñarol - Club Nacional 1-1(0-0)

Round 13 [23-24.05.2015]
CA River Plate - CCD El Tanque 4-0(1-0)
CA Rentistas - CA Peñarol 0-2(0-1)
Racing Club - CA Fénix 2-1(2-1)
CA Cerro - Club Nacional 1-0(0-0)
Rampla Juniors - CA Juventud 1-3(0-0)
Wanderers FC - Tacuarembó FC 4-1(1-0)
CA Atenas - Defensor Sporting 1-2(0-2)
Danubio FC - IA Sud América 0-1(0-0)

Round 14 [30-31.05.2015]
CA Juventud - Club Nacional 0-0
Defensor Sporting - Wanderers FC 2-0(1-0)
CA River Plate - Racing Club 1-0(0-0)
CCD El Tanque - Danubio FC 1-0(1-0)
IA Sud América - CA Atenas 1-1(0-1)
Tacuarembó FC - Rampla Juniors 4-2(1-1)
CA Cerro - CA Rentistas 2-0(2-0)
CA Peñarol - CA Fénix 2-0(1-0)

Round 15 [05-07.06.2015]	
Club Nacional - Tacuarembó FC 2-3(1-0)	Racing Club - CA Peñarol 2-2(0-1)
CA Fénix - CA Cerro 3-0(1-0)	CA Rentistas - CA Juventud 1-1(1-1)
Wanderers FC - IA Sud América 1-2(0-2)	Rampla Juniors - Defensor Sporting 0-0
CA Atenas - CCD El Tanque 2-4(1-0)	Danubio FC - CA River Plate 2-0(0-0)

Final Standings

1.	**CA Peñarol Montevideo**	15	9	4	2	28	-	13	31
2.	CA River Plate Montevideo	15	9	2	4	30	-	17	29
3.	Defensor Sporting Club Montevideo	15	7	6	2	20	-	16	27
4.	Danubio FC Montevideo	15	8	2	5	17	-	12	26
5.	CA Juventud de Las Piedras	15	7	4	4	25	-	17	25
6.	Tacuarembó FC	15	7	3	5	23	-	22	24
7.	CA Cerro Montevideo*	15	7	3	5	21	-	23	23
8.	Institución Atlética Sud América Montevideo	15	5	7	3	19	-	19	22
9.	Club Nacional de Football Montevideo	15	6	3	6	24	-	21	21
10.	CA Fénix Montevideo	15	6	2	7	18	-	16	20
11.	CCD El Tanque Sisley Montevideo	15	4	4	7	17	-	25	16
12.	Montevideo Wanderers FC	15	4	3	8	19	-	18	15
13.	CA Atenas de San Carlos	15	4	2	9	27	-	37	14
14.	Rampla Juniors FC Montevideo	15	4	2	9	18	-	28	14
15.	CA Rentistas Montevideo	15	4	2	9	16	-	27	14
16.	Racing Club de Montevideo	15	4	1	10	17	-	28	13

**1 point deducted*

CA Peñarol Montevideo qualified for the championship semi-finals.

Aggregate Table 2014/2015

1.	**Club Nacional de Football Montevideo**	30	20	3	7	58	-	28	63
2.	CA Peñarol Montevideo	30	16	8	6	56	-	29	56
3.	CA River Plate Montevideo	30	17	3	10	56	-	35	54
4.	Defensor Sporting Club Montevideo	30	13	9	8	48	-	38	48
5.	Danubio FC Montevideo	30	13	7	10	34	-	32	46
6.	CA Juventud de Las Piedras	30	13	6	11	46	-	39	45
7.	Racing Club de Montevideo	30	14	3	13	49	-	54	45
8.	Institución Atlética Sud América Montevideo	30	10	12	8	36	-	36	42
9.	CCD El Tanque Sisley Montevideo	30	10	9	11	35	-	43	39
10.	CA Fénix Montevideo	30	11	4	15	38	-	42	37
11.	Montevideo Wanderers FC	30	10	4	16	40	-	39	34
12.	CA Atenas de San Carlos	30	10	4	16	45	-	57	34
13.	CA Rentistas Montevideo	30	10	4	16	34	-	51	34
14.	CA Cerro Montevideo	30	10	5	15	29	-	52	34
15.	Tacuarembó FC	30	8	7	15	40	-	50	31
16.	Rampla Juniors FC Montevideo	30	9	4	17	36	-	55	31

Club Nacional de Football Montevideo qualified for the championship finals.

Club Nacional de Football Montevideo, CA Peñarol Montevideo and CA River Plate Montevideo qualified for the 2016 Copa Libertadores.
Club Nacional de Football Montevideo, Defensor Sporting Club Montevideo, Danubio FC Montevideo and CA Juventud de Las Piedras qualified for the 2015 Copa Sudamericana.

Championship Semi-final

14.06.2015, Estadio Centenario, Montevideo; Attendance: n/a
Referee: Javier Bentancor
Club Nacional de Football Montevideo - CA Peñarol Montevideo 3-2(2-0,2-2)
Nacional: Gustavo Adolfo Munúa Vera (Cap), Sebastián Gorga Nogueira, Diego Fabián Polenta Museti, Luis Alfonso Espino García, Santiago Ernesto Romero Fernández, Gonzalo Fabián Porras Burghi, Hugo Diego Arismendi Ciapparetta (70.Nicolás Santiago Prieto Larrea), Carlos María de Pena Bonino (87.Álvaro Alexánder Recoba Rivero), Sebastián Bruno Fernández Miglierina, Iván Daniel Alonso Vallejo, Leandro Barcía Montero (75.Christian Alejandro Tabó Hornos). Trainer: Álvaro Gutiérrez Felscher.
Peñarol: Pablo Alejandro Migliore, Jonathan Alexis Sandoval Rojas (46.Nahitan Michel Nández Acosta), Carlos Adrián Valdéz Suárez, Washington Emilio MacEachen Vázquez, Diogo Silvestre Bittencourt (46.Hober Gabriel Leyes Viera), Jonathan Urretaviscaya da Luz, Luis Bernardo Aguiar Burgos, Sebastián Gerardo Píriz Ribas, Jorge Marcelo Rodríguez Núñez, Antonio Pacheco D'Agosti (Cap) (75.Hernán Novick Rattich), Marcelo Danubio Zalayeta. Trainer: Pablo Javier Bengoechea Dutra Bruno.
Goals: 1-0 Sebastián Bruno Fernández Miglierina (20), 2-0 Iván Daniel Alonso Vallejo (33), 2-1 Luis Bernardo Aguiar Burgos (69), 2-2 Luis Bernardo Aguiar Burgos (90+2), 3-2 Santiago Ernesto Romero Fernández (109).
Sent off: Juan Manuel Olivera López (67, on the bench), Jorge Marcelo Rodríguez Núñez (84).

Club Nacional de Football Montevideo qualified for the championship finals against the winner of the aggregate table.

Championship final

No final needed after Club Nacional de Football Montevideo were winners of both semi-final and aggregate table.

2014/2015 Primera División Profesional Champions: **Club Nacional de Football Montevideo**

Top goalscorers:

22 goals:	**Iván Daniel Alonso Vallejo**	**(Club Nacional de Football Montevideo)**
21 goals:	Michel Nicolás Santos Rosadilla	(CA River Plate Montevideo)
16 goals:	Yoel Orozmán Burgueño Marcant	(CCD El Tanque Sisley Montevideo)
14 goals:	Lucas Daniel Cavallini (ARG)	(CA Fénix Montevideo)
	Aldo Fabián Díaz	(Tacuarembó FC)

Relegation Table 2014/2015

The relagation was determined after adding points obtained in the two last seasons. Teams promoted this season doubled their points.

Pos	Team	2013/14	2014/15	Total	
		P	P	M	P
1.	Club Nacional de Football Montevideo	57	63	60	120
2.	CA River Plate Montevideo	58	54	60	112
3.	CA Peñarol Montevideo	52	56	60	108
4.	Danubio FC Montevideo	58	46	60	104
5.	Montevideo Wanderers FC	62	34	60	96
6.	Defensor Sporting Club Montevideo	36	48	60	84
7.	Racing Club de Montevideo	39	45	60	84
8.	CA Rentistas Montevideo	45	34	60	79
9.	CA Juventud de Las Piedras	32	45	60	77
10.	Institución Atlética Sud América Montevideo	35	42	60	77
11.	CA Fénix Montevideo	40	37	60	77
12.	CCD El Tanque Sisley Montevideo	33	39	60	72
13.	CA Cerro Montevideo	38	34	60	71
14.	CA Atenas de San Carlos (*Relegated*)	-	34	30	68
15.	Tacuarembó FC (*Relegated*)	-	31	30	62
16.	Rampla Juniors FC Montevideo (*Relegated*)	-	31	30	62

CLUB ATLÉTICO ATENAS SAN CARLOS

Foundation date: May 1, 1928
Address: Avenida Rocha 822, San Carlos
Stadium: Estadio Atenas, San Carlos – Capacity: 6,000

THE SQUAD

	DOB	Ape		Cla	
		M	G	M	G
Goalkeepers:					
Martín Raúl Barlocco Canale	19.12.1977	15	-	10	-
Gastón Hernández Bravo	19.01.1996			-	-
Carlos Ignacio Méndez Cerullo	03.03.1990	-	-	7	-
Defenders:					
Alexandre Pompeu da Silva "Alexandre Caxambu" (BRA)	31.08.1993	4	-	-	-
Gonzalo Gabriel Castillo Cabral	17.10.1990	13	-	13	1
Gérson Fraga Vieira (BRA)	04.10.1992	14	-	12	1
Rodrigo Hernán Petrik Vidal	21.10.1994	6	-	5	-
Gustavo Alejandro Pintos Amaya	12.08.1995			-	-
Gonzalo Fernando Rosa Herrera	30.11.1990	5	-	-	-
Jonathan Sebastián Ruíz Díaz San Emeterio	01.12.1993	9	-	7	-
Maicol Sebastián Santurio Olivera	21.03.1993	2	-	-	-
Héctor Martín Torres Alonso	05.02.1992	12	-	8	-
Midfielders:					
David Michel Acosta Márquez	14.02.1988	13	2	11	3
Óscar Darío Arce Valenzuela (COL)	15.02.1990			7	-
Bartolo Sebastián Cal Farías	29.04.1997	2	-		
Sebastián Andrés Canobra Acosta	03.11.1994			4	-
Carlos Eduardo Keosseian Lagomarsino	18.03.1988	14	2	13	2
Homero Antonio Plada Sequeira	12.05.1995	-	-	-	-
Leandro Sosa Toranza	24.06.1994	14	3	15	3
Federico Nicolás Tabeira Arrúa	08.02.1996	-	-	-	-
Francisco Emiliano Techera Bergalo	16.12.1994			8	-
Guillermo Ramón Trinidad Barbosa	27.09.1988	9	-	15	1
Simón Vanderhoegt Santos	05.06.1986	12	-	8	-
Forwards:					
Alejandro Rafael Acosta Cabrera	02.10.1990	14	1	13	3
José Ignacio Álvarez Medero	27.12.1994	2	-	6	1
Ángel Santiago Barboza Manzzi	03.10.1989	14	10		
Claudio Federico Castellanos Garcia	15.12.1992	11	-	6	1
Santiago Nicolás Charamoni Ferreira	28.01.1994			7	3
Douglas Starnley Ferreira (BRA)	11.02.1993	10	-	3	1
Gonzalo José Latorre	26.04.1996			8	-
Facundo Peraza Fontana	27.07.1992	6	1	14	7
Maximiliano Sigales Straneo	30.09.1993	7	-	6	-
Trainer:					
Edgardo Martín Arias Ferrari [as of 01.07.2014]	17.06.1964	15		15	

CLUB ATLÉTICO CERRO MONTEVIDEO

Foundation date: December 1, 1922
Address: Avenida Grecia 3621, 11600 Montevideo
Stadium: Estadio Monumental „Luis Tróccoli", Montevideo – Capacity: 25,000

THE SQUAD

	DOB	Ape		Fin	
		M	G	M	G
Goalkeepers:					
Jonathan Mathías Cubero Rieta	15.01.1994	5	-	4	-
Pablo Sebastián Fuentes Fraga	18.01.1987	10	-	12	-
Sebastián Medina Ortelli	24.02.1993	1	-	-	-
Defenders:					
Rodrigo Canosa Martínez	10.06.1987	13	-	14	1
Néstor Misael del Río Delgado	23.11.1992	-	-	-	-
Silvio Emiliano Dorrego Coito	30.03.1987			11	-
Lucas Camilo Hernández Perdomo	05.08.1992	7	-	9	1
Rodrigo Andrés Izquierdo Díaz	19.11.1992	3	-	-	-
Daniel Leites	28.02.1982	14	-	-	-
Williams Guillermo Martínez Fracchia	18.12.1982			15	1
Pablo Rodrigo Melo	04.07.1982	11	-	-	-
Maximiliano Rodrigo Pereira Cardozo	25.04.1993	1	-	-	-
Ángelo Pizzorno	21.10.1992			-	-
Andrés Ravecca Cadenas	01.09.1989	13	-	7	-
Nicolás Gabriel Techera Pereira	26.08.1993	4	-	4	-
Midfielders:					
Matías Alberto Abisab Gutíérrez	10.09.1993	14	-	9	-
Edward Andrés Barboza Cubilla	23.07.1994	-	-	-	-
Álvaro Nicolás Brum Martínez	10.04.1987			14	-
Pablo Eduardo Caballero Sebastiani	21.11.1987	10	-		
Jhon Cristián Cossú Sánchez	05.06.1992	6	-	-	-
Juan Ramón Curbelo Garis	02.05.1979	8	1	-	-
Carlos Javier Grossmüller	04.05.1983	9	-		
Gastón Martínez Menéndez	01.12.1989			8	-
Matías Nicolás Masiero Balas	15.01.1988	4	-	-	-
Gonzalo Montes Calderini	22.12.1994	-	-	1	-
Mario Ignacio Regueiro Pintos	14.09.1978	9	3	14	6
Leandro Federico Reymundez Martínez	01.02.1992	1	-		
Rodrigo de Oliveira Longaray (BRA)	12.05.1985	15	-	14	-
Jonathan Ezequiel Rodríguez García	26.03.1993	8	-		
Héctor Baltasar Silva Cabrera	19.11.1984			12	-
José Luis Tancredi Malatez	14.02.1983			12	1
Luis Alfredo Urruti Giménez	11.09.1992	4	-	10	1
Forwards:					
Joaquín Antonio Boghossian	19.06.1987			11	1
Juan Ignacio Delgado Martínez	05.07.1994	6	-		
Aníbal Gabriel Hernández De Los Santos	29.06.1986			12	6
Adrián Eloys Leites López	08.02.1992	2	-	-	-
Joaquin Emanuel Lemos Bellini	27.04.1994	3	-	-	-
Fabián Muñoz Alvarado	15.03.1993	-	-	1	-
Fabricio Damián Núñez Lozano	04.11.1985	12	1		
Walter Horacio Peralta Saracho	03.06.1982	7	1	-	-
Hugo Gabriel Silveira Pereira	23.05.1993	13	4	13	3
Trainer:					
Pablo Martín Rodríguez (ARG) [03.03.-08.09.2014; Resigned]	07.03.1977	4			
Juan Ramón Tejera Pérez [08.09.-24.11.2014; Resigned]	23.02.1956	10			
Juan Santiago Kalemkerian Espeleta [24.11.-27.12.2014; Caretaker]	09.10.1968	1			
Miguel Falero Correa [as of 27.12.2014]	17.05.1957			15	

DANUBIO FÚTBOL CLUB MONTEVIDEO

Foundation date: March 1, 1932
Address: Avenida 8 de Octubre 4584, 12100 Montevideo
Stadium: Estadio Jardines del Hipódromo, Montevideo – Capacity: 18,000

THE SQUAD

	DOB	Ape		Cla	
		M	G	M	G
Goalkeepers:					
Salvador Ichazo Fernández	26.01.1992	15	-		
Facundo Ariel Silva Scheefer	04.07.1996			-	-
Franco Luis Torgnascioli Lagreca	24.08.1990	1	-	15	-
Defenders:					
Carlos Alberto Canobbio Bentaberry	07.01.1982	4	-	-	-
Guillermo Gastón Cotugno Lima	17.03.1995	11	-	1	-
Julio César Ferrón Álvez	12.10.1988	-	-		
Fabricio Orosmán Formiliano Duarte	14.01.1993	14	1	13	1
Cristian Marcelo González Tassano	23.07.1996			9	-
Gianfranco Larrosa Leguizamón	27.04.1996			1	-
Alejandro Agustín Peña Montero	08.03.1989	9	-	5	-
Joaquín Alejandro Pereyra Cantero	10.07.1994			12	-
Federico Ricca Rostagnol	01.12.1994	15	1	14	-
Marcelo Josemir Saracchi Pintos	23.04.1998			-	-
Luis Leandro Sosa Otermin	18.03.1991	7	-	13	1
Emiliano Daniel Velázquez Maldonado	30.04.1994	1	-		
Matías Exequiel Velázquez Maldonado	16.05.1992	4	-	4	-
Midfielders:					
Néstor Fabián Canobbio Bentaberry	08.03.1980	3	-	-	-
Luis Miguel De Los Santos Cáceres	04.03.1993	5	1		
Mathías Nicolás De Los Santos Aguirre	20.01.1991	11	-	7	-
Gastón Faber Chevalier	21.04.1996	5	-	2	-
Gonzalo Federico González Pereyra	07.10.1993	8	-	-	-
Juan Ignacio González Brazeiro	05.11.1993	14	2	13	1
Jadson Viera Castro (BRA)	04.08.1981	3	-	-	-
Camilo Sebastián Mayada Mesa	08.01.1991	11	1		
Nicolás Milesi van Lommel	10.11.1992	6	-	6	-
Hamilton Miguel Pereira Ferrón	26.06.1987			14	2
Emiliano Ezequiel Pessoa González	28.06.1994			2	-
Renzo Daniel Pozzi Palombo	12.10.1984	4	-	3	-
Santiago Andrés Schirone Álvarez	15.02.1996			-	-
Agustín Viana Ache	23.08.1983			9	-
Paul Matías Zunino Escudero	20.04.1990	3	-		
Forwards:					
Adrián Martin Balboa Camacho	19.01.1994	4	-	7	1
Gonzalo Barreto Mastropierro	22.01.1992			10	2
Matías Gastón Castro (ARG)	18.12.1991	15	7	12	2
Ernesto Antonio Farías	29.05.1980	7	1		
Bruno Fornaroli Mezza	07.09.1987			11	3
Emiliano Michael Ghan Carranza	05.06.1996	-	-	3	-
Santiago Emiliano González Areco	11.06.1992	11	1		
Jorge Daniel Gravi Piñeiro	16.01.1994	-	-	10	-
Jonathan Matías Pinto Bermúdez	10.02.1996			2	-
Hugo Horacio Sequeira Soiza	20.09.1995	5	1	2	-
Pablo Martín Silvera Duarte	26.08.1995	10	-	2	-
Marcelo Tabárez Rodríguez	10.02.1993	2	-	6	3
Trainer:					
Leonardo Alfredo Ramos Giro [as of 01.01.2013]	11.09.1969	15		15	

DEFENSOR SPORTING CLUB MONTEVIDEO

Foundation date: March 15, 1913
Address: Avenida 21 de Setiembre N° 2362 Parque Rodó, 1100 Montevideo
Stadium: Estadio „Luis Franzini", Montevideo – Capacity: 18,000

THE SQUAD

	DOB	Ape M	Ape G	Cla M	Cla G
Goalkeepers:					
Martín Nicolás Campaña Delgado	29.05.1989	14	-	15	-
Yonatan Irrazabál Condines	12.02.1988	1	-	-	-
Matías Gastón Rodríguez Olivera	12.02.1994	-	-	-	-
Defenders:					
Ramón Ginés Arias Quinteros	27.07.1992	15	1	12	-
Nicolás Correa Risso	25.12.1983	7	-		
José Enrique Etcheverry Mendoza	10.05.1996	-	-	-	-
Guillermo Fratta Cabrera	19.09.1995			-	-
Roberto Fabián Herrera Rosas	01.03.1989	14	-	9	-
Paolo Mauricio Lemos Merladey	28.12.1995	3	-	4	-
Matías Daniel Malvino Gómez	20.01.1992	2	-		
Lucas Elías Morales Villalba	14.02.1994	8	1	7	-
Andrés Scotti Ponce de León	14.12.1975	10	1	13	-
Mario Pablo Risso Caffiro	31.01.1988			4	-
Mathías Sebastián Suárez Suárez	24.06.1996	1	-	-	-
Midfielders:					
Federico Gino Acevedo Fagundez	26.02.1993	14	1	9	-
Juan Carlos Amado Alanís	28.09.1990	9	-	2	-
Mauro Wilney Arambarri Rosa	30.09.1995	12	-	7	1
Juan Pablo Caffa (ARG)	30.09.1994	8	-		
Mathías Adolfo Cardaccio Alaguich	02.10.1987	-	-	13	1
Facundo Ismael Castro Souto	22.01.1995	5	-	2	-
Giorgian Daniel de Arrascaeta Benedetti	01.06.1994	11	6		
Felipe Gedoz da Conceição (BRA)	12.07.1993	2	1		
Andrés José Fleurquin Rubio	08.02.1975	2	-	2	-
Brian Avelino Lozano Aparicio	23.02.1994	10	2	15	5
Adrián Nicolás Luna Retamar	12.04.1992	15	2	13	5
Leonardo Javier Pais Corbo	07.07.1994	1	-	2	-
Franco Nicolás Pizzichillo	03.01.1996			-	-
Martín Ernesto Rabuñal Rey	22.04.1994	1	-	6	1
Felipe Jorge Rodríguez Valla	26.05.1990			9	1
Emilio Enrique Zeballos Gutiérrez	05.08.1992	10	-	15	1
Forwards:					
Matías Damián Alonso Vallejo	16.04.1985	8	3	7	-
Jaime Báez Stábile	25.04.1995			6	1
Maximiliano Fabián Barreiro (ARG)	16.03.1985			10	-
Rubén Daniel Bentancourt Morales	02.03.1993			8	-
Joaquín Antonio Boghossián Lorenzo	19.06.1987	5	1		
Santiago Nicolás Charamoni Ferreira	28.01.1994	-	-		
Andrés Nicolás Olivera	30.05.1978	7	3	10	-
Ignacio Risso Thomasset	08.10.1977	14	4	10	3
Trainer:					
Fernando Darío Curutchet Godoy [as of 25.11.2013-24.11.2014]	06.10.1960	13			
Heber Silva Cantera [24.11.-31.12.2014; Caretaker]	12.06.1958	2			
José Mauricio Larriera Dibarboure [as of 01.01.2015]	16.08.1970			15	

CENTRO CULTURAL Y DEPORTIVO EL TANQUE SISLEY MONTEVIDEO

Foundation date: March 17, 1955
Address: Santa Mónica 2370, Montevideo
Stadium: Estadio „Víctor Della Valle“, Montevideo – Capacity: 6,000

THE SQUAD	DOB	Ape		Cla	
		M	G	M	G
Goalkeepers:					
Jhonny Alexander da Silva Sosa	21.08.1991	12	-		
Alvaro Marcelo García Zaroba	13.01.1984			3	-
Rubén Darío Silva Silva	19.02.1992	3	-	12	-
Defenders:					
Horacio Joaquín Aguirre Santellán	23.03.1991	15	1	14	-
Ronaldo Alexander Conceiçao Silveira (BRA)	03.04.1987	-	-		
Juan Pablo Fagúndez Duarte	16.07.1985	11	-	12	-
Sergio Andrés Felipe Silva	21.02.1991	9	-	3	-
Julio César Ferrón Alvez	12.10.1988			7	-
Santiago Augusto Fosgt Brehm	17.03.1986	12	-	11	-
Robert Matías González Núñez	23.11.1993	3	-	4	-
Yefferson Moreira Scaraffoni	07.03.1991	14	-	14	1
Juan Pablo Péndola Sellanes	09.09.1980	15	-	10	2
Ronaldo Alexander Conceiçao Silveira (BRA)	03.04.1987			1	-
Midfielders:					
Mathías Alexander Acuña Maciel	28.11.1992	8	1		
Ricardo Andrés Aparicio De la Quintana	10.08.1976	10	-	4	-
Danilo Asconeguy Ruiz	04.09.1986	-	-	-	-
Yoel Orozmán Burgueño Marcant	15.02.1988	15	9	13	7
Alexander Leonel Corro	27.01.1988	2	-	-	-
Claudio Martín Dadomo Minervini	10.02.1982			3	-
Leandro Nicolás Díaz Baffico	24.03.1990			9	-
Pablo Lima Gualco	19.08.1990	10	-	14	1
Gastón Rodrigo Machado López	19.01.1986	7	1	3	-
Gastón Martínez Menéndez	01.12.1989	12	-		
Felipe Jorge Rodríguez Valla	26.05.1990	14	2		
Juan Ignacio Surraco Lamé	14.08.1987			7	-
Diego Viera Moreira	04.06.1994	12	1	10	-
Paul Matías Zunino Escudero	20.04.1990			14	1
Forwards:					
Facundo Barcelo Viera	31.02.1993			11	1
Borys Santiago Barone Grillo	31.05.1994			10	1
Alex Maximiliano Borges Ávila	20.06.1984	2	-	1	-
Franco Sebastián López Taborda	20.10.1992			7	1
Luis Enrique Machado Mora	22.12.1991	2	-		
Miguel Antonio Murillo Rivas (COL)	03.07.1988	12	3	12	1
Brian Matías Uribe	16.08.1991	10	1		
Trainer:					
Raúl Norberto Möller Bartel [09.08.2013-06.04.2015; Resigned]	09.10.1950	15		7	
Julio César Antúnez Amorín [as of 07.04.2015]	09.01.1956			8	

CENTRO ATLÉTICO FÉNIX MONTEVIDEO

Foundation date: July 7, 1916
Address: Avenida Capurro 874, 11200 Montevideo
Stadium: Estadio Parque Capurro, Montevideo – Capacity: 10,000

THE SQUAD

	DOB	Ape M	Ape G	Cla M	Cla G
Goalkeepers:					
Erik Jonathan Acevedo Méndez	26.01.1993	-	-	-	-
Adrián Berbia Pose	12.10.1977	-	-	-	-
Emiliano Darío Denis Figueroa	16.12.1991	-	-	-	-
Víctor Rafael García Muníz	08.12.1989	-	-	2	-
Luis Ángel Mejía Cajar (PAN)	16.03.1991	6	-	13	-
Santiago Andrés Mele Castanero	06.09.1997			-	-
Michel Emanuel Tabárez	29.03.1995	9	-	-	-
Defenders:					
Rodrigo Abascal Barros	14.01.1994			5	-
Juan Daniel Álvez Ortíz	21.08.1983	14	-	15	1
Davies Rúben Banchero Martínez	19.09.1990	1	-	-	-
Facundo Nicolás Bone Vale	16.11.1995	12	2	11	-
Silvio Emiliano Dorrego Coito	30.03.1987	9	-		
Antonio Nicolás Fernández Mozzo	07.08.1985			8	-
Ángelo Emanuel Gabrielli Scaroni	23.09.1992	5	-	8	-
José Ignacio Pallas Martínez	05.01.1983	12	1	14	-
Maximiliano Perg Schneider	16.09.1991	8	-	14	-
Nicolás Sanguinetti Parodi	13.04.1992			-	-
Fabricio Silva Jorge	05.04.1990	12	-	4	-
Leandro Agustín Zazpe Rodríguez	29.04.1994	3	-	1	-
Midfielders:					
Rafael Aranda Brazia	10.04.1992			2	-
Mateo Gastón Carro Gaiza	27.10.1994	1	-	6	1
Leonardo Cecilio Fernández López	08.11.1998			1	-
Raúl Freddy Ferro Olivera	13.01.1983	14	-	12	3
Aníbal Gabriel Hernández De Los Santos	29.06.1986	10	1		
Martín Ricardo Ligüera López	09.11.1980	9	2	13	3
Juan Ángel Neira (ARG)	21.02.1989	8	-		
Agustín Olivera Scalabrini	02.03.1992	1	-	-	-
Gonzalo Sebastián Papa Palleiro	08.05.1989	12	1	14	-
Edgardo Andrés Schetino Yancev	26.05.1994	8	-	11	2
Jonathan Alejandro Siles Cuadro	25.08.1993	1	-	6	-
Jorge Carlos Zambrana Echague	28.03.1986	10	1	-	-
Forwards:					
Franco Acosta Machado	05.03.1996	8	1		
Diego Nicolás Blanco Lemos	19.10.1994	7	-	2	-
Lucas Daniel Cavallini (ARG)	28.12.1992	14	8	13	6
Eric di Paula Lima (BRA)	14.07.1990			2	-
Alexander Jesús Medina Reobasco	08.08.1978	3	1	13	1
Carlos Federico Puppo Gross	06.12.1986			8	-
Cecilio Alfonso Waterman Ruíz (PAN)	13.04.1991	12	2	10	1
Trainer:					
Gustavo Daniel Bueno D'Amico [01.07.-24.11.2014; Resigned]	16.07.1963	14			
Rosario Martínez [as of 24.11.2014]	03.09.1957	1		15	

CLUB ATLÉTICO JUVENTUD DE LAS PIEDRAS

Foundation date: December 24, 1935
Address: Avenida Lavalleja 584, Las Piedras
Stadium: Estadio Parque Artigas, Las Piedras – Capacity: 5,500

THE SQUAD					
	DOB	**Ape**		**Cla**	
		M	**G**	**M**	**G**
Goalkeepers:					
Héctor Fabián Carini Hernández	26.12.1979	13	-	15	-
Gonzalo Adrián Falcón Vitancour	16.11.1996	-	-	-	-
Marcelo Nicolás Marticorena Garguilo	07.07.1993	-	-	-	-
Martín Sebastián Rodríguez Prantl	20.09.1989	4	-	-	-
Defenders:					
Rodrigo Sergio Cabrera Sasía	02.05.1989	14	-	13	-
Mathías Nicolás Céspedes Crause	03.11.1998			-	-
Facundo Jorge Fajardo Puentes	10.08.1994	-	-	2	-
Ismael Fernando Gularte Bustos	12.05.1996			-	-
Luis Fernando Machado Pinto	26.09.1979	8	-	9	-
Enzo Martín Pérez Verdum	25.11.1990			7	-
Matías Omar Pérez Laborda	20.07.1985	15	2	11	3
Diego Martín Rodríguez Telechea	08.01.1991	8	-		
Matías Fernando Soto de Freitas	23.04.1991	3	-	9	-
Midfielders:					
Xavier Miguel Civitate Frascheri	01.02.1991	-	-	-	-
Matías Nicolás Duffard Villarreal	27.04.1989	9	-	13	1
Damián Alejandro Eroza Medeiro	22.03.1993	5	-	9	-
Alex Javier Fernández Aguirre	14.12.1994	5	-	5	-
Christian Marcelo Latorre Long	17.04.1987	6	1	14	1
Pablo Maximiliano Lemos Merladett	17.12.1993			1	-
Federico Damián Millacet Echevarría	21.07.1991	6	1	10	-
Álvaro Damián Pastoriza Catalán	10.01.1987	1	-	2	-
Matías Sebastián Porcari (ARG)	12.04.1986	15	2		
Alejandro Clever Reyes Sosa	01.01.1984	14	-	14	1
Emiliano Romero Clavijo	30.09.1992	14	-	14	-
Sebastián Rosano Escobar	25.05.1987	12	-	2	-
Edison Eliézer Torres Martínez (PAR)	04.04.1983	-	-		
Rodrigo Viega Alves	07.08.1991	14	4	12	1
Forwards:					
Sergio Mathias Agüete Pizzi	02.01.1993	-	-	-	-
Jaime Báez Stábile	25.04.1995	14	5		
Hugo Daniel Cuatrin (ARG)	16.11.1988	9	2	3	-
Marcos Gastón Labandeira Castro	18.01.1995			10	-
Jorge Andrés Martínez Barrios	05.04.1983	4	-	7	1
Cristian Martín Palacios Ferreira	02.09.1990			14	13
Agustín Peraza Fontana	03.06.1994	-	-	-	-
Leonardo Gastón Puerari Torres	23.01.1986	14	3	14	4
Trainer:					
Jorge Antonio Giordano Moreno [as of 04.11.2013]	27.02.1965	15		15	

MONTEVIDEO WANDERERS FÚTBOL CLUB

Foundation date: August 15, 1902
Address: Avenida Agraciada 2871, 11700 Montevideo
Stadium: Estadio Parque „Alfredo Víctor Viera", Montevideo – Capacity: 12,000

THE SQUAD

	DOB	Ape M	Ape G	Cla M	Cla G
Goalkeepers:					
Leonardo Fabián Burian Castro	21.01.1984			12	-
Federico Alfredo Cristóforo Pepe	19.09.1989	15	-	-	-
Ignacio de Arruabarrena Fernández	16.01.1997			-	-
Pablo Emmanuel Silveira De Los Santos	09.01.1994	-	-		
Carlos Leandro Techera Sánchez	28.04.1992			3	-
Defenders:					
Federico Andueza Velazco	25.05.1997			1	-
Federico Barrandeguy Martino	08.05.1996			3	-
Gastón Matías Bueno Sciutto	02.02.1985	12	1	13	-
Luis Manuel Castro Cáceres	27.09.1995	1	-	-	-
Emiliano Mathías Díaz Rondine	29.06.1990	14	-	6	-
Germán Duarte Pistone	19.04.1990	-	-	-	-
Victor Martín Galaín Pecora	02.03.1989			4	1
Emanuel Gularte Méndez	30.09.1995			2	-
Paulo Fabián Lima Simoes	20.01.1992	5	-	8	-
Maximiliano Martín Olivera De Andrea	05.03.1992	14	1	9	1
Matias Quagliotti Ponce de León	17.05.1985	5	2	6	-
Rodrigo Rivero Fernández	27.12.1995			1	-
Alex Silva Quiroga	15.06.1993	13	1	12	-
Midfielders:					
Adrián Nicolás Colombino Rodríguez	12.10.1993	15	1	9	-
Juan Manuel Duarte Genta	15.11.1994	1	-	-	-
Nicolás Andrés Freitas Silva	08.06.1987	13	1		
Yuri León Galli Mora	04.06.1994	12	1	4	-
Franco Guillermo Gentile Rotondaro	19.02.1997	2	-	1	-
Damián González González	05.01.1993	1	-	-	-
Santiago Gabriel Martínez Pintos	30.07.1991			10	1
Leandro Gastón Paiva Santurión	15.02.1994	9	-	7	-
Nicolás Queiros Martínez	07.05.1996			1	-
Leandro Federico Reymundez Martínez	01.02.1992			11	2
Roberto Martín Rivas Tagliabúe	14.03.1992	7	-	7	-
Jonathan Ezequiel Rodríguez García	26.03.1993			3	-
Matías Joaquín Santos Arotegui	11.03.1994	1	-	12	2
Joaquín Azzem Vergés Collazo	01.06.1992			8	1
Forwards:					
Nicolás Gabriel Albarracín Basil	11.06.1993	14	1	11	2
Santiago Bellini Noya	19.09.1993			12	5
Sergio Rubén Blanco Soto	25.11.1981	2	1		
Gerardo Sebastián Gularte Fros	21.05.1990	14	3	3	-
Juan Crúz Mascia Paysée	03.01.1994			8	-
Ramiro Manuel Quintana Hernández	28.08.1994	2	-		
Kevin Federik Ramírez Dutra	01.04.1994	9	1		
Diego Nicolás Riolfo Pérez	08.01.1990	14	3	12	1
Gastón Rodríguez Maeso	23.03.1992	13	4	11	3
Trainer:					
Alfredo Carlos Arias Sánchez [as of 13.12.2011]	28.11.1958	15		15	

CLUB NACIONAL DE FOOTBALL MONTEVIDEO

Foundation date: May 14, 1899
Address: Avenida 8 de Octubre 2847, 11200 Montevideo
Stadium: Estadio Gran Parque Central, Montevideo – Capacity: 22,000

THE SQUAD

	DOB	Ape		Cla	
		M	G	M	G
Goalkeepers:					
Gabriel Araujo Soto	28.03.1993	-	-	-	-
Jorge Rodrigo Bava	02.08.1981	-	-	5	-
Gustavo Adolfo Munúa Vera	27.01.1978	15	-	11	-
Defenders:					
José Manuel Aja Livchich	10.05.1993	3	-	3	-
Carlos Nicolás Cordero Álvarez	09.03.1993			-	-
Guillermo Daniel de los Santos Viana	15.02.1991	4	-	7	-
Juan Manuel Díaz Martínez	28.10.1987	4	-	5	-
Luis Alfonso Espino García	05.01.1992	11	-	10	-
Jorge Ciro Fucile Perdomo	19.11.1984	3	-	4	-
Sebastián Gorga Nogueira	06.04.1994	-	-	10	-
Luis Nicolás Olivera Moreira	17.02.1993			-	-
Diego Fabián Polenta Museti	06.02.1992	11	-	13	-
Carlos Enrique Valdéz Parra (COL)	22.05.1985			8	-
Midfielders:					
Pablo Álvarez Menéndez	07.02.1985	4	-		
Hugo Diego Arismendi Ciapparetta	25.01.1988	11	3	11	2
Maximiliano Matías Calzada Fuentes	21.04.1990	11	-		
Paulo Rinaldo Cruzado Durand (PER)	21.09.1984	1	-		
Carlos María de Pena Bonino	11.03.1992	12	4	13	5
Víctor Hugo Dorrego Coito	09.05.1993			-	-
Rafael García Casanova	06.01.1989	14	-		
Ignacio María „Nacho" González Gatti	14.05.1982	4	-	5	-
Gastón Rodrigo Pereiro López	11.06.1995	14	4	10	2
Gonzalo Fabián Porras Burghi	31.01.1984	14	1	15	-
Nicolás Santiago Prieto Larrea	05.09.1992	-	-	1	-
Gonzalo Ramos Deféminis	16.05.1991	-	-	4	1
Ribair Rodríguez Pérez	04.10.1987			4	-
Santiago Ernesto Romero Fernández	15.02.1990	14	-	9	-
Forwards:					
Iván Daniel Alonso Vallejo	10.04.1979	15	15	12	7
Leandro Barcía Montero	08.10.1992	5	1	13	5
Gonzalo Diego Bueno Bingola	16.01.1993			7	1
Sebastián Bruno Fernández Miglierina	23.05.1985	9	2	12	1
Henry Damián Giménez Báez	13.03.1986	11	1		
Juan Crúz Mascia Paysée	03.01.1994	3	-		
Álvaro Alexánder Recoba Rivero	17.03.1976	11	2	6	-
Christian Alejandro Tabó Hornos	23.11.1993			7	-
Sebastián Taborda Ramos	22.05.1981	3	-	4	-
Trainer:					
Álvaro Gutiérrez Felscher	21.07.1968	15		15	

CLUB ATLÉTICO PEÑAROL MONTEVIDEO

Foundation date: September 28, 1891
Address: Palacio Peñarol „Contador Gastón Güelfi", Avenida Magallanes 1721, 11200 Montevideo
Stadium: Estadio Centenario, Montevideo – Capacity: 65,235

THE SQUAD

	DOB	Ape M	Ape G	Cla M	Cla G
Goalkeepers:					
Washington Omar Aguerre Lima	23.04.1993	2	-	-	-
Thiago Gastón Cardozo	31.07.1996			-	-
Leandro Gelpi Rosales	27.02.1991	-	-	-	-
Gastón Guruceaga Fagundez	15.03.1995			-	-
Pablo Alejandro Migliore	27.01.1982	13	-	15	-
Defenders:					
Emiliano Albín Antognazza	24.01.1989	-	-	5	-
Joe Emerson Bastos Bizera	17.05.1980	4	-	2	-
Diogo Silvestre Bittencourt (BRA)	30.12.1989	12	-	12	1
Pablo Martín Lima Olid	26.03.1981	3	-	-	-
Damián Macaluso Rojas	09.03.1980	9	1	1	-
Washington Emilio MacEachen Vázquez	05.04.1992	1	-	12	1
Carlos Andrés Rodales Ramírez	09.07.1987	11	-	7	-
Gianni Daniel Rodríguez Fernández	07.06.1994			5	-
Octavio Darío Rodríguez Peña	17.09.1974	9	-		
Jonathan Alexis Sandoval Rojas	25.06.1987	-	-	10	1
Alejandro Daniel Silva González	04.09.1989	12	-		
Héctor Baltasar Silva Cabrera	19.11.1984	-	-		
Carlos Adrián Valdéz Suárez	02.05.1983	11	-	13	-
Gonzalo Viera Davyt	08.02.1987	11	-	9	-
Midfielders:					
Luis Bernardo Aguiar Burgos	17.11.1985			14	2
Elbio Maximiliano Álvarez Wallace	13.06.1994	-	-		
Nahitan Michel Nández Acosta	28.12.1995	4	-	5	-
Hernán Novick Rattich	13.12.1988	6	-	10	1
Marcel Novick Rattich	11.10.1983	6	-	2	-
Sergio Daniel Orteman Rodríguez	29.09.1978	7	1		
Antonio Pacheco D'Agosti	11.04.1976	14	5	15	4
Sebastián Gerardo Píriz Ribas	04.03.1990	14	4	13	4
Jorge Marcelo Rodríguez Núñez	13.01.1985	14	3	15	1
Jonathan Urretaviscaya da Luz	19.03.1990			13	7
Forwards:					
Fabián Larry Estoyanoff Poggio	27.09.1982	10	1		
Gonzalo José Latorre	26.04.1996	-	-		
Hober Gabriel Leyes Viera	29.05.1990	-	-	8	2
Carlos Rodrigo Núñez Techera	22.06.1992	6	1		
Juan Manuel Olivera López	14.08.1981	6	1	3	-
Facundo Rodríguez Calleriza	20.08.1995			6	-
Jonathan Javier Rodríguez Portillo	06.07.1993	11	5		
Santiago Silva Gérez	26.08.1990			-	-
Marcelo Danubio Zalayeta	05.12.1978	14	6	15	4
Trainer:					
Jorge Daniel Fossati Lurachi [26.01.-09.11.2014; Resigned]	22.11.1952	12			
Rónald Paolo Montero Iglesias [09.11.-22.12.2014; Caretaker]	03.09.1971	3			
Pablo Javier Bengoechea Dutra Bruno [as of 22.12.2014]	27.06.1965			15	

RAMPLA JUNIORS FÚTBOL CLUB MONTEVIDEO

Foundation date: January 7, 1914
Address: Avenida Grecia 3504, 12300 Montevideo
Stadium: Estadio Olímpico, Montevideo – Capacity: 6,000

THE SQUAD

	DOB	Ape		Cla	
		M	G	M	G
Goalkeepers:					
Gian Carlo Duarte Lualdi	22.03.1997			-	-
Bernardo Enzo Long Baccino	27.09.1989	15	-	12	-
Juan Emilio Marroco Martínez	04.08.1987	-	-	-	-
Danilo Henry Saén Dobinin	03.04.1994	-	-	3	-
Defenders:					
Jorge Luis Anchén Cajiga	17.08.1980	8	-	-	-
Álvaro Maximiliano Arias Invernizzi	03.10.1988	7	-		
Diego Martin Barboza González	09.01.1991	6	-	7	-
Gonzalo Daniel Camargo Pintos	16.02.1991	-	-	-	-
Emiliano Martín García Tellechea	14.01.1990	14	-		
Maximiliano Felipe Montero Rodríguez	27.08.1988	8	-	13	-
Luis Nicolás Olivera Moreira	17.02.1993	-	-		
Pablo Andrés Pereira Errandonea	24.04.1985	7	-	6	-
Jonathan Alberto Píriz Palacio	02.10.1986	5	-	-	-
Alejandro Javier Rodríguez Morales	09.07.1986			13	1
Carlos Daniel Santucho Gradiol	12.03.1985			7	1
Danny Gabriel Tejera Sánchez	14.04.1986	5	-	5	-
César Fabián Vargas Cáceres	09.12.1989	15	-	12	-
Midfielders:					
Gustavo Javier Aprile Retta	10.08.1988	13	2		
Bruno Federico Barreto González	09.05.1989	10	1		
Luis Ezequiel Casaña Rivero	21.12.1992			1	-
Mathias Alberto Choca Usher	20.07.1993	-	-	5	-
Carlos Emanuel Cuello Azambuya	15.08.1994	7	-	10	-
Paul Michael Dzeruvs Sosa	01.11.1988	14	4	10	1
Diego Alejandro Galo Prado	14.03.1994			14	2
Richard Darío Núñez Pereyra	16.02.1976	6	1	14	3
Ángel Piz (ARG)	28.01.1992	2	-	-	-
Marcel Nicolás Román Núñez	07.02.1988	12	-	13	-
Jim Morrison Varela Devotto	16.10.1994			8	-
Diego Gonzalo Vega Martínez	29.06.1992	13	1	7	1
Forwards:					
Camilo Cándido				1	-
Luis Francis D'Albenas Reyes	11.01.1996	9	1	4	-
Leonardo Gabriel Fagundez Fernández (ARG)	24.09.1993			8	-
Luis Enrique Machado Mora	22.12.1991			11	4
Gonzalo Daniel Malán Arenas	08.04.1988	13	7		
Juan Orlando Muriel (ARG)	18.03.1989			9	2
Matías Wolf Rigoleto Arévalo	02.06.1995			1	-
Nicolás Raimondi Schiaffarino	05.09.1984	1	-	3	1
Flavio Andrés Scarone Bruno	13.05.1991	-	-	-	-
Nicolás Ignacio Vigneri Cetrulo	06.07.1983	8	-	-	-
Mauro Adrián Vila Wilkins	25.02.1986			13	2
Trainer:					
Marcelo Saralegui Arregin [01.04.2014-03.01.2015; Resigned]	18.05.1971	15			
Jorge Walter Barrios Balestrasse [04.01.-25.05.2015;	24.01.1961			13	
Nelson Artigas Olveira Romero [as of 26.05.2015]	19.06.1974			2	

RACING CLUB DE MONTEVIDEO

Foundation date: April 6, 1919
Address: Avenida Millán 4712 entre Avenida Sayago y Vedia, 12900 Montevideo
Stadium: Estadio Parque „Osvaldo Roberto", Montevideo – Capacity: 8,500

THE SQUAD

	DOB	Ape		Cla	
		M	G	M	G
Goalkeepers:					
Jorge Walter Contreras Rodríguez	21.09.1971	15	-	10	-
Nicolás Enrique Gentilio Martínez	13.04.1987	-	-	5	-
Diego Melián de León	04.11.1991	-	-	-	-
Defenders:					
Gonzalo Aguilar Camacho	02.08.1987	15	1	15	-
Rodrigo Nicolás Brasesco Pérez	23.01.1986	9	-	9	-
Sebastián Cardozo Coitinho	09.09.1995			5	-
Luciano Rodrigo Domínguez Nunes	08.06.1995	-	-	-	-
Pablo Martín Lacoste Icardi	15.01.1988	7	-	9	-
Damián Alejandro Malrrechaufe Verdún	19.10.1984	14	5		
Franco Gastón Romero Ponte	11.02.1995	-	-	6	-
Darwin Fabián Torres Alonso	16.02.1991	13	-	12	-
Midfielders:					
Carlos Daniel Acosta Alcántara	19.04.1990	11	3	11	-
Gastón Rodrigo Alvíte Duarte	09.03.1996			1	-
Ángel Gabriel Cayetano Pirez	08.01.1991			8	-
Carlos Richard Díaz	04.02.1979	10	-	-	-
Ernesto Simón Dudok Parrilla	14.01.1987	14	1	9	-
Mauro Nahuel Estol Rodríguez	27.01.1995	2	-	4	-
Miguel Agustín Gutiérrez de León	11.02.1992	4	4	11	1
Óscar Javier Méndez Albornoz	05.12.1994			1	-
Ignacio Nicolini Díaz	04.02.1987	15	-	15	-
Juan Pablo Rodríguez Conde	14.06.1982	15	2	14	4
Jesús Emiliano Trinidade Flores	10.07.1993	9	-	10	1
Forwards:					
Mauricio Alfonso Prieto	26.01.1992	11	5	15	7
Gabriel Matías Fernández Leites	13.05.1994	14	5	-	-
Joaquín Jacques	12.02.1993			-	-
Renzo López Patrón	16.04.1994			8	-
Diego Andrés Martiñones Rus	25.01.1985			13	2
Carlos Leonardo Muela Viera	22.06.1991	1	-	1	-
Xavier Páez Freire	11.03.1994	-	-	-	-
Christian Alejandro Tabo Hornos	23.11.1993	15	1		
Diego Martín Zabala Morales	19.09.1991	14	3	15	2
Trainer:					
José Mauricio Larriera Dibarboure [01.01.-20.12.2014; End of contract]	16.08.1970	15			
José Pablo Alonso May [01.01.-06.04.2015; Sacked]	12.02.1960	7			
Darío Larrosa [07.04.-11.04.2015; Caretaker]				1	
Santiago Ostolaza Sosa [as of 12.04.2015]	10.07.1962			7	

CLUB ATLÉTICO RENTISTAS MONTEVIDEO

Foundation date: March 26, 1933
Address: Avenida "General Flores" 4020, Montevideo
Stadium: Estadio Complejo Rentistas, Montevideo – Capacity: 10,600

THE SQUAD

	DOB	Ape		Cla	
		M	G	M	G
Goalkeepers:					
John Alex Faust Acosta	26.09.1990	1	-	-	-
Santiago Morandi Vidal	06.04.1984			7	-
Stéfano José Perdomo Pereyra	21.07.1990	11	-	9	-
Martín Tejera Vázquez	16.02.1991	3	-		
Defenders:					
Erick Cathriel Cabaco Almada	19.04.1995	13	-	6	-
Luciano Barboza de Jesús "Cafú" (BRA)	25.05.1972	6	-	1	-
Ignacio Ithurralde Sáez	30.05.1983	12	1	9	1
Jorge Nicolás Raguso Sánchez	02.01.1992	3	-	4	-
Mario Sebastián Ramírez Silva	18.05.1992	13	-	14	-
Nicolás Alejandro Rodríguez Charquero	22.07.1991	8	-	13	3
Sebastián Daniel Sellanes Averbene	15.01.1992	2	-	9	-
Rubén Martín Sosa Aquino	15.02.1993	3	1	2	-
Midfielders:					
Anderson Silva de França (BRA)	28.08.1982	12	-	7	-
José Miguel Barreto Pérez	09.02.1993	2	-	-	-
Gonzalo Javier Bazallo Strada	29.04.1986	14	-	13	-
Luis Miguel De Los Santos Cáceres	04.03.1993			6	-
Víctor Hugo Dorrego Coito	09.05.1993	7	-		
Emiliano Joaquin Fernández García	12.12.1992	1	-	-	-
Nicolás Andrés Giraldo Urueta (COL)	29.03.1993			3	-
Federico Horacio Laens Martino	14.01.1988	8	2	14	3
Maximiliano Lombardi Rodríguez	11.05.1987			8	3
Alfonso Darío Pereira D'Atri	25.02.1996	-	-	-	-
Lucas Guzmán Rodríguez Cardoso	08.05.1993	1	-	8	-
Andrés Silva Cáceres	17.08.1989	6	-	8	1
Hugo Maximiliano Soria Sánchez	16.02.1990	15	1	14	2
José Pablo Varela Rebollo	29.05.1988	12	1	10	-
Forwards:					
Gustavo Javier Alles Villa	09.04.1989	15	3		
Danilo Erardo Cócaro Díaz	22.08.1991	7	-	11	-
Marcelo Juvenal Fernández García	04.04.1988	10	1	5	-
Guillermo Maidana Revetría	18.01.1988	9	4		
Gastón Javier Palacios Baleirón	26.12.1997			3	-
Richard Aníbal Porta Candelaresi	01.08.1983			12	2
Miguel David Terans Pérez	11.08.1994	12	1	14	-
Trainer:					
Adolfo Barán Flis [as of 01.07.2012-23.12.2014; End of contract]	22.11.1961	15			
Manuel Gregorio Keosseian [as of 01.01.2015]	17.08.1953			15	

CLUB ATLÉTICO RIVER PLATE MONTEVIDEO

Foundation date: May 11, 1932
Address: Avenida 19 de Abril 1145, 11200 Montevideo
Stadium: Estadio Parque „Federico Omar Saroldi“, Montevideo – Capacity: 5,165

THE SQUAD					
	DOB	Ape		Cla	
		M	G	M	G
Goalkeepers:					
Gastón Hernán Olveira Echeverría	21.04.1993	1	-	14	-
Alison Nicola Pérez Barone	05.02.1990	14	-	1	-
Juan Francisco Tinaglini Olariaga	09.11.1998			-	-
Defenders:					
Agustín Ale Perego	19.02.1995	2	-	9	-
Flavio Armando Córdoba Rodríguez (COL)	04.10.1984	3	-	-	-
Gabriel Marques de Andrade Pinto (BRA)	03.03.1988	14	-	15	1
Cristian Mario González Aidinovich	19.12.1976	12	-	9	-
Giovanni Alessandro González Apud	20.09.1994	3	-	-	-
Claudio Herrera Casanova	11.02.1988	14	-	14	-
Williams Guillermo Martínez Fracchia	18.12.1982	10	-		
Diego Manuel Rodríguez Da Luz	08.08.1986	7	-	14	1
Lucas Ruíz Alonso	07.03.1996	1	-	1	-
Luis Alberto Torrecilla Michelle	18.03.1989	8	1	4	-
Midfielders:					
Fabián Andrés Bastidas (USA)	06.10.1993	7	-	4	1
Jonathan Blanes Núñez	10.03.1987	-	-	-	-
Robert Mario Flores Bistolfi	13.05.1986	10	1	8	1
Fernando Gorriarán Fontes	27.11.1994	9	-	12	1
Claudio Gastón Innella Alderete	23.11.1990	8	-	12	-
Cristhian Stivens Maciel Gallo	12.02.1992	1	-		
Marcus Vinícius Vidal Cunha "Marquinhos Carioca" (BRA)	28.05.1992			4	-
Bruno Montelongo Gesta	12.09.1987	6	-	7	1
Heber Ignacio Ratti Guardia	05.04.1994	3	-	4	-
Ángel Leonardo Rodríguez Güelmo	02.12.1992	10	-	13	1
Iván Rodrigo Silva Olivera	23.10.1993			4	1
Forwards:					
Diego Mateo Casas López	04.03.1995	3	-	2	-
Santiago Damián García Correa	14.09.1990	13	2	7	1
Jonathan Alexander Ramírez Silva	18.12.1990	5	1	4	1
Leandro Joaquín Rodríguez Telechea	19.11.1992	13	3	10	6
Alexander Mauricio Rosso Génova	27.02.1993	2	-	9	-
Michael Nicolás Santos Rosadilla	13.03.1993	15	11	14	10
Nicolás Javier Schiappacasse Oliva	12.01.1999			7	1
Cristian Rafael Techera Cribelli	31.05.1992	14	7	6	2
Walter Vaz Correa (FRA)	24.05.1990	2	-	1	-
Trainer:					
Jorge Guillermo Almada Álves [as of 01.07.2011]	18.06.1969	15		15	

INSTITUCIÓN ATLÉTICA SUD AMÉRICA MONTEVIDEO

Foundation date: February 15, 1914
Address: Avenida Domingo Aramburu 16-34, Montevideo
Stadium: Estadio "Parque Carlos Ángel Fossa", Montevideo – Capacity: 6,000

THE SQUAD					
	DOB	Ape		Cla	
		M	G	M	G
Goalkeepers:					
Jorge Luís Fleitas de María	24.01.1993	-	-	-	-
Cono Javier Irazún González	04.12.1986	15	-	15	-
Matías Quintana Caraballo	02.08.1991	-	-	-	-
Defenders:					
Juan Ramón Alsina Kligger	15.11.1989	2	-	9	-
Adrián Argachá González	21.12.1986	14	3	11	-
Álvaro Maximiliano Arias Invernizzi	03.10.1988			1	-
Santiago Nicolás Carrera Sanguinetti	05.03.1994	14	2		
César Alejandro Galván Soler	18.01.1993	-	-	4	-
Edgard Leonardo Martínez Fracchia	26.01.1979	15	-	13	1
Lucas Francesco Mesones Gamarra	04.09.1993	1	-	1	-
Maximiliano Pereiro Zugarramurdi	17.08.1990	14	-	9	-
Julián Ricardo Perujo Airala	23.01.1986			15	-
Jorge Diego Viotti Godoy	27.02.1992	2	-	6	-
Midfielders:					
José Fernando Arismendi Peralta	31.03.1991	7	-	15	3
Jonathan Daniel Barboza Bonilla	02.11.1990			6	-
Emanuel Adrián Centurión (ARG)	25.08.1982	13	-	4	-
Rodrigo Gastón Díaz Rodríguez	04.07.1995	7	-	8	-
Javier Agustín Favarel (ARG)	10.07.1991	-	-	-	-
Maureen Javier Franco Alonso	13.12.1983	13	5	14	7
Federico Gallego Revetria	13.06.1990	14	1		
Diego Gastón López Barrios	23.02.1994			2	-
Agustín Sebastián Miranda Cambón	28.11.1992	2	-	-	-
Fernando Martín Pascual (ARG)	23.02.1991	-	-	-	-
Richard Javier Pellejero Ferreira	30.05.1976	14	-	13	-
Fabián Rodrigo Yantorno Blengio	04.09.1982	8	-	13	-
Forwards:					
Bryan Maximiliano Aldave Benítez	29.09.1983			5	-
Mauricio Sebastián Alonso Pereda	12.02.1994	13	-	13	1
Maico Rodrigo Carneiro	09.02.1993	-	-	-	-
Heber Gastón Colmán Leguisamo	04.04.1989	11	2	14	4
Bruno Rodrigo Giménez Migliónico	05.10.1991	7	-	1	-
Santiago Emiliano González Areco	11.06.1992			-	-
Ángel Emanuel Luna (ARG)	30.01.1989	14	2	14	3
Federico Olivera				-	-
Max Rauhofer Federico	28.10.1990	9	2	2	-
Trainer:					
Jorge Antonio Vivaldo (ARG) [as of 01.07.2014]	16.02.1967	15		15	

TACUAREMBÓ FÚTBOL CLUB

Foundation date: January 3, 1999
Address: Avenida Joaquín Suárez 215, 45000 Tacuarembó
Stadium: Estadio "Inginiero Raúl Goyenola", Tacuarembó – Capacity: 12,000

THE SQUAD

	DOB	Ape M	Ape G	Cla M	Cla G
Goalkeepers:					
Jonathan Sebastián Deniz Machado	23.08.1990	14	-	15	-
Narío Rodrigo dos Santos Freitas	09.04.1993	1	-	-	-
Danilo Nicolás Suárez García da Rosa	07.03.1989	1	-	-	-
Jhonatan Eduardo Vaz Silva Caballero	05.09.1987			-	-
Defenders:					
Luis Felipe Carvalho da Silva	18.09.1993			15	-
Óscar Padula Castro Rodríguez	28.11.1993	9	1	6	-
Álvaro Daniel Duarte Estévez	20.08.1984	3	-	4	-
Carlos Sebastián Dutra Ferreira	06.04.1989	14	-	13	-
Bruno Valentino Fiordelmondo Scheffer	08.01.1987	10	-	-	-
Marcos Rony González Ortega	14.06.1990	-	-	7	-
Lucas Martín López Quintana	05.05.1994	4	-	1	-
Enzo Martín Pérez Verdum	25.11.1990	14	-		-
Néstor Andrés Vilar Cordero	19.10.1993			-	-
Midfielders:					
Alberto Sebastián Assis Silva	04.03.1993	13	-	14	1
Matías Barboza Andrade	12.01.1993	9	-	8	-
Emilio Martín Ferreira Silva	04.10.1991	2	-	13	-
Luis Javier Guarino Moscatelli	16.04.1986	5	2	-	-
Fernando Daniel Lima Pereira	26.05.1991			13	2
Fernando Luna				1	-
Cristhian Stivens Maciel Gallo	12.02.1992			13	-
Gonzalo Píriz González	04.10.1988	-	-	-	-
Pablo Martín Porcile	24.06.1996	8	-	9	1
Cristian Martín Rodríguez Telis	10.02.1985	8	-	7	1
Iván Rodrigo Silva Olivera	23.10.1993	1	-		
Franco Ariel Sosa Portela	12.08.1983	6	-	-	-
Joaquín Azzem Vergés Collazo	01.06.1992	15	1		-
Forwards:					
Ramiro Washington Bruschi Sanguinetti	05.09.1981	7	1		-
Jonathan Alexis de los Santos Rodríguez	26.04.1993	10	2	8	-
Aldo Fabián Díaz	28.05.1975	15	7	14	7
Nicolás Emilio Fagúndez Sequeira	20.02.1986	13	-	15	4
Esteban Ricardo González Maciel	26.01.1991	7	-	13	1
Maickol Pio Martíns Aristegui	29.04.1993	1	-	-	-
Nicolás Andrés Nicolay Aznarez (ARG)	09.10.1979	5	-	-	-
Álvaro Sebastián Sánchez Burgos	04.04.1989	6	1	-	-
Néstor Fabián Silva Fros	17.01.1982	8	1	5	1
Octavio Daniel Siqueira Darriulat	23.01.1987	-	-	14	3
Trainer:					
Jorge Eduardo Moncecchi Pezzatti [01.07.-12.10.2014; Resigned]	23.06.1969	9			
Mario Daniel Saralegui Iriarte [12.10.-29.12.2014; Resigned]	24.04.1959	6			
Jorge Hugo Castelli (ARG) [as of 01.01.2015]	12.05.1946			15	

SECOND LEVEL
Segunda División Profesional 2014/2015

1.	Liverpool FC Montevideo (*Promoted*)	28	17	7	4	69 - 28	58
2.	Club Plaza Colonia de Deportes Colonia del Sacramento (*Promoted*)	28	16	5	7	44 - 37	53
3.	CA Villa Teresa Montevideo	28	13	8	7	43 - 32	47
4.	CA Boston River Montevideo	28	13	5	10	45 - 41	44
5.	Canadian Soccer Club Montevideo	28	12	7	9	39 - 36	43
6.	Central Español FC Montevideo	28	12	7	9	39 - 37	43
7.	CSD Villa Española Montevideo	28	12	6	10	51 - 36	42
8.	Huracán FC Montevideo	28	11	8	9	54 - 48	41
9.	CS Miramar Misiones	28	9	10	9	35 - 30	37
10.	CA Torque Montevideo	28	9	8	11	39 - 49	35
11.	Cerro Largo FC Melo	28	8	8	12	27 - 30	32
12.	CD Maldonado	28	9	4	15	27 - 43	31
13.	CA Progreso Montevideo	28	5	10	13	27 - 42	25
14.	Rocha FC	28	6	7	15	26 - 53	25
15.	CS Cerrito Montevideo (*Relegated*)	28	4	8	16	31 - 54	20

Places 3-6 qualified for the Promotion Play-offs.

Promotion Play-offs

Semi-Finals

Central Español FC Montevideo - CA Villa Teresa Montevideo	1-1(0-1)	1-3(1-0)
Canadian Soccer Club Montevideo - CA Boston River Montevideo	1-2(0-1)	1-2(1-1)

Finals

CA Boston River Montevideo - CA Villa Teresa Montevideo	1-1(1-1)
CA Villa Teresa Montevideo - CA Boston River Montevideo	2-2(1-2); 4-3pen

CA Villa Teresa Montevideo promoted to the 2015/2016 Primera División.

NATIONAL TEAM
INTERNATIONAL MATCHES
(16.07.2014 – 15.07.2015)

05.09.2014	Sapporo	Japan - Uruguay	0-2(0-1)	(F)
09.09.2014	Goyang	Korea Republic - Uruguay	0-1(0-0)	(F)
10.10.2014	Jeddah	Saudi Arabia - Uruguay	1-1(0-0)	(F)
13.10.2014	Muscat	Oman - Uruguay	0-3(0-0)	(F)
13.11.2014	Montevideo	Uruguay – Costa Rica	6-7 pen	(F)
18.11.2014	Santiago	Chile - Uruguay	1-2(1-1)	(F)
28.03.2015	Agadir	Morocco - Uruguay	0-1(0-0)	(F)
06.06.2015	Montevideo	Uruguay - Guatemala	5-1(3-0)	(F)
13.06.2015	Antofagasta	Uruguay - Jamaica	1-0(0-0)	(CA)
16.06.2015	La Serena	Argentina - Uruguay	1-0(0-0)	(CA)
20.06.2015	La Serena	Uruguay - Paraguay	1-1(1-1)	(CA)
24.06.2015	Santiago	Chile - Uruguay	1-0(0-0)	(CA)

05.09.2014, Friendly International
Sapporo Dome, Sapporo; Attendance: 39,294
Referee: Kim Sang-Woo (Korea Republic)
JAPAN - URUGUAY **0-2(0-1)**
URU: Néstor Fernando Muslera Micol, Victorio Maximiliano Pereira Páez (76.Matías Aguirregaray Guruceaga), José Martín Cáceres Silva (84.Camilo Sebastián Mayada Mesa), Diego Roberto Godín Leal, Mathías Corujo Díaz (69.Álvaro Rafael González Luengo), José María Giménez de Vargas, Cristian Gabriel Rodríguez Barotti (73.Álvaro Daniel Pereira Barragán), Egidio Raúl Arévalo Ríos, Marcelo Nicolás Lodeiro Benítez, Edinson Roberto Cavani Gómez (58.Christian Ricardo Stuani Curbelo), Diego Alejandro Rolán Silva (65.Abel Mathías Hernández Platero). Trainer: Óscar Wáshington Tabárez Silva.
Goals: Edinson Roberto Cavani Gómez (34), Abel Mathías Hernández Platero (70).

09.09.2014, Friendly International
Goyang Sports Complex, Goyang; Attendance: n/a
Referee: Ryuji Sato (Japan)
KOREA REPUBLIC - URUGUAY **0-1(0-0)**
URU: Martín Andrés Silva Leites, Victorio Maximiliano Pereira Páez (90+4.Matías Aguirregaray Guruceaga), José Martín Cáceres Silva, Diego Roberto Godín Leal, José María Giménez de Vargas, Cristian Gabriel Rodríguez Barotti (24.Álvaro Daniel Pereira Barragán), Egidio Raúl Arévalo Ríos, Marcelo Nicolás Lodeiro Benítez (62.Giorgian Daniel De Arrascaeta Benedetti), Camilo Sebastián Mayada Mesa (90+1.Mathías Corujo Díaz), Edinson Roberto Cavani Gómez (57.Christian Ricardo Stuani Curbelo), Abel Mathías Hernández Platero (78.Diego Alejandro Rolán Silva). Trainer: Óscar Wáshington Tabárez Silva.
Goal: José María Giménez de Vargas (70).

10.10.2014, Friendly International
"King Abdullah Sports City", Jeddah; Attendance: n/a
Referee: Jamil Juma (Bahrain)
SAUDI ARABIA - URUGUAY **1-1(0-0)**
URU: Néstor Fernando Muslera Micol, Victorio Maximiliano Pereira Páez, Mathías Corujo Díaz (76.Christian Ricardo Stuani Curbelo), Álvaro Daniel Pereira Barragán, Emiliano Daniel Velázquez Maldonado, José María Giménez de Vargas, Cristian Gabriel Rodríguez Barotti (46.Diego Alejandro Rolán Silva), Egidio Raúl Arévalo Ríos (85.Camilo Sebastián Mayada Mesa), Marcelo Nicolás Lodeiro Benítez (62.Giorgian Daniel De Arrascaeta Benedetti), Luis Alberto Suárez Díaz (70.Abel Mathías Hernández Platero), Jonathan Javier Rodríguez Portillo (62.Hugo Diego Arismendi Ciapparetta).

Trainer: Óscar Wáshington Tabárez Silva.
Goal: Hassan Muath Fallatah (47 own goal).

13.10.2014, Friendly International
"Sultan Qaboos" Sports Complex, Muscat; Attendance: n/a
Referee: Marai Al Awaji (Saudi Arabia)
OMAN - URUGUAY 0-3(0-0)
URU: Martín Andrés Silva Leites, Victorio Maximiliano Pereira Páez (70.Mathías Corujo Díaz), Diego Roberto Godín Leal, Gastón Alexis Silva Perdomo, José María Giménez de Vargas, Cristian Gabriel Rodríguez Barotti (46.Gastón Exequiel Ramírez Pereyra), Egidio Raúl Arévalo Ríos (65.Hugo Diego Arismendi Ciapparetta), Marcelo Nicolás Lodeiro Benítez, Giorgian Daniel De Arrascaeta Benedetti (46.Jonathan Javier Rodríguez Portillo), Luis Alberto Suárez Díaz (78.Christian Ricardo Stuani Curbelo), Diego Alejandro Rolán Silva (78.Camilo Sebastián Mayada Mesa). Trainer: Óscar Wáshington Tabárez Silva.
Goals: Luis Alberto Suárez Díaz (57, 66), Jonathan Javier Rodríguez Portillo (87).

13.11.2014, Friendly International
Estadio Centenario, Montevideo: Attendance: n/a
Referee: Germán Delfino (Argentina)
URUGUAY – COSTA RICA 3-3(0-1,3-3); 6-7 on penalties
URU: Néstor Fernando Muslera Micol, Victorio Maximiliano Pereira Páez, Diego Roberto Godín Leal, Álvaro Daniel Pereira Barragán, José María Giménez de Vargas, Cristian Gabriel Rodríguez Barotti (80.Gastón Exequiel Ramírez Pereyra), Egidio Raúl Arévalo Ríos, Marcelo Nicolás Lodeiro Benítez (68.Ricardo Guzmán Pereira Méndez), Carlos Andrés Sánchez Arcosa (80.Mathías Corujo Díaz), Luis Alberto Suárez Díaz, Edinson Roberto Cavani Gómez (71.Jonathan Javier Rodríguez Portillo).Trainer: Óscar Wáshington Tabárez Silva.
Goals: Luis Alberto Suárez Díaz (50), José María Giménez de Vargas (64), Edinson Roberto Cavani Gómez (67).
Penalties: Luis Alberto Suárez Díaz, Jonathan Javier Rodríguez Portillo, Gastón Exequiel Ramírez Pereyra, Mathías Corujo Díaz, Egidio Raúl Arévalo Ríos (missed), Álvaro Daniel Pereira Barragán, Victorio Maximiliano Pereira Páez, Ricardo Guzmán Pereira Méndez (missed).

18.11.2014, Friendly International
Estadio Monumental "David Arellano", Santiago; Attendance: 40,000
Referee: Carlos Alfredo Vera Rodríguez (Ecuador)
CHILE - URUGUAY 1-2(1-1)
URU: Néstor Fernando Muslera Micol, Victorio Maximiliano Pereira Páez (63.Gastón Exequiel Ramírez Pereyra), Diego Roberto Godín Leal, Álvaro Daniel Pereira Barragán, José María Giménez de Vargas, Cristian Gabriel Rodríguez Barotti, Egidio Raúl Arévalo Ríos, Marcelo Nicolás Lodeiro Benítez (63.Mathías Corujo Díaz), Carlos Andrés Sánchez Arcosa (46.Ricardo Guzmán Pereira Méndez), Edinson Roberto Cavani Gómez (80.Álvaro Rafael González Luengo), Diego Alejandro Rolán Silva (84.Jonathan Javier Rodríguez Portillo). Trainer: Óscar Wáshington Tabárez Silva.
Goals: Diego Alejandro Rolán Silva (45+1), Álvaro Rafael González Luengo (80).

28.03.2015, Friendly International
Grand Stade d'Agadir, Agadir; Attendance: 58,000
Referee: Malang Diedhiou (Senegal)
MOROCCO - URUGUAY 0-1(0-0)
URU: Néstor Fernando Muslera Micol, Victorio Maximiliano Pereira Páez, Diego Roberto Godín Leal, Álvaro Daniel Pereira Barragán, José María Giménez de Vargas, Egidio Raúl Arévalo Ríos, Marcelo Nicolás Lodeiro Benítez (70.Álvaro Rafael González Luengo), Carlos Andrés Sánchez Arcosa (80.Ricardo Guzmán Pereira Méndez), Edinson Roberto Cavani Gómez, Diego Alejandro Rolán Silva (70.Giorgian Daniel De Arrascaeta Benedetti), Jonathan Javier Rodríguez Portillo (60.Christian Ricardo Stuani Curbelo). Trainer: Óscar Wáshington Tabárez Silva.

Goal: Edinson Roberto Cavani Gómez (52 penalty).

06.06.2015, Friendly International
Estadio Centenario, Montevideo; Attendance: 18,500
Referee: Patricio Hernán Loustau (Argentina)
URUGUAY - GUATEMALA **5-1(3-0)**
URU: Néstor Fernando Muslera Micol, Victorio Maximiliano Pereira Páez (58.Mathías Corujo Díaz), Diego Roberto Godín Leal, Álvaro Daniel Pereira Barragán, José María Giménez de Vargas, Cristian Gabriel Rodríguez Barotti (46.Giorgian Daniel De Arrascaeta Benedetti), Egidio Raúl Arévalo Ríos, Marcelo Nicolás Lodeiro Benítez (46.Álvaro Rafael González Luengo), Carlos Andrés Sánchez Arcosa (58.Christian Ricardo Stuani Curbelo), Edinson Roberto Cavani Gómez (46.Abel Mathías Hernández Platero), Diego Alejandro Rolán Silva (68.Jonathan Javier Rodríguez Portillo). Trainer: Óscar Wáshington Tabárez Silva.
Goals: Diego Alejandro Rolán Silva (3), Edinson Roberto Cavani Gómez (18, 31 penalty), Giorgian Daniel De Arrascaeta Benedetti (55), Abel Mathías Hernández Platero (57).

13.06.2015, 44th Copa América, Group Stage
Estadio Regional de Antofagasta, Antofagasta (Chile); Attendance: 8,653
Referee: José Ramón Argote Vega (Venezuela)
URUGUAY - JAMAICA **1-0(0-0)**
URU: Néstor Fernando Muslera Micol, Victorio Maximiliano Pereira Páez, Diego Roberto Godín Leal, Álvaro Daniel Pereira Barragán, José María Giménez de Vargas, Cristian Gabriel Rodríguez Barotti (64.Giorgian Daniel De Arrascaeta Benedetti), Egidio Raúl Arévalo Ríos, Marcelo Nicolás Lodeiro Benítez (86.Álvaro Rafael González Luengo), Carlos Andrés Sánchez Arcosa (73.Christian Ricardo Stuani Curbelo), Edinson Roberto Cavani Gómez, Diego Alejandro Rolán Silva. Trainer: Óscar Wáshington Tabárez Silva.
Goal: Cristian Gabriel Rodríguez Barotti (51).

16.06.2015, 44th Copa América, Group Stage
Estadio La Portada, La Serena (Chile); Attendance: n/a
Referee: Sandro Meira Ricci (Brazil)
ARGENTINA - URUGUAY **1-0(0-0)**
URU: Néstor Fernando Muslera Micol, Victorio Maximiliano Pereira Páez, Diego Roberto Godín Leal, Álvaro Daniel Pereira Barragán, José María Giménez de Vargas, Cristian Gabriel Rodríguez Barotti (64.Carlos Andrés Sánchez Arcosa), Álvaro Rafael González Luengo, Egidio Raúl Arévalo Ríos, Marcelo Nicolás Lodeiro Benítez (69.Abel Mathías Hernández Platero), Edinson Roberto Cavani Gómez, Diego Alejandro Rolán Silva. Trainer: Óscar Wáshington Tabárez Silva.

20.06.2015, 44th Copa América, Group Stage
Estadio La Portada, La Serena (Chile); Attendance: 16,021
Referee: Roberto García Orozco (Mexico)
URUGUAY - PARAGUAY **1-1(1-1)**
URU: Néstor Fernando Muslera Micol, Victorio Maximiliano Pereira Páez, Álvaro Daniel Pereira Barragán, Sebastián Coates Nion, José María Giménez de Vargas, Álvaro Rafael González Luengo, Egidio Raúl Arévalo Ríos, Carlos Andrés Sánchez Arcosa (67.Cristian Gabriel Rodríguez Barotti), Edinson Roberto Cavani Gómez, Abel Mathías Hernández Platero (46.Christian Ricardo Stuani Curbelo), Diego Alejandro Rolán Silva. Trainer: Óscar Wáshington Tabárez Silva.
Goal: José María Giménez de Vargas (29).

24.06.2015, 44th Copa América, Quarter-Finals
Estadio "Nacional Julio Martínez Prádanos", Santiago; Attendance: 45,304
Referee: Sandro Meira Ricci (Brazil)

CHILE - URUGUAY **1-0(0-0)**

URU: Néstor Fernando Muslera Micol, Victorio Maximiliano Pereira Páez, Jorge Ciro Fucile Perdomo, Diego Roberto Godín Leal, José María Giménez de Vargas, Cristian Gabriel Rodríguez Barotti, Álvaro Rafael González Luengo, Egidio Raúl Arévalo Ríos, Carlos Andrés Sánchez Arcosa (85.Jonathan Javier Rodríguez Portillo), Edinson Roberto Cavani Gómez, Diego Alejandro Rolán Silva (58.Abel Mathías Hernández Platero). Trainer: Óscar Wáshington Tabárez Silva.
Sent off: Edinson Roberto Cavani Gómez (63), Jorge Ciro Fucile Perdomo (88).

NATIONAL TEAM PLAYERS 2014/2015			
Name	**DOB**	**Caps**	**Goals**
[Club 2014/2015]			

(Caps and goals at 05.07.2015)

Goalkeepers

Name	DOB	Caps	Goals
Néstor Fernando MUSLERA Micol [2014/2015: SK Galatasaray Istanbul (TUR)]	16.06.1986	**72**	**0**
Martín Andrés SILVA Leites [2014: CR Vasco da Gama Rio de Janeiro (BRA)]	25.03.1983	**6**	**0**

Defenders

Name	DOB	Caps	Goals
Matías AGUIRREGARAY Guruceaga [2014: Club Estudiantes de La Plata (ARG)]	01.04.1989	**6**	**0**
José Martín CÁCERES Silva [2014/2015: Juventus FC Torino (ITA)]	07.04.1987	**63**	**1**
Sebastián COATES Nión [2014/2015: Sunderland AFC (ENG)]	07.10.1990	**17**	**1**
José María GIMÉNEZ De Vargas [2014/2015: Club Atlético de Madrid (ESP)]	20.01.1995	**21**	**3**
Diego Roberto GODÍN Leal [2014/2015: Club Atlético de Madrid (ESP)]	16.02.1986	**91**	**4**
Jorge Ciro FUCILE Perdomo [2015: Club Nacional de Football Montevideo]	19.11.1984	**44**	**0**
Victorio Maximiliano PEREIRA Páez [2014/2015: Sport Lisboa e Benfica (POR)]	08.06.1984	**105**	**3**
Gastón Alexis SILVA Perdomo [2014: Torino FC (ITA)]	05.03.1994	**1**	**0**
Emiliano Daniel VELÁZQUEZ Maldonado [2014/2015: Getafe CF (ESP)]	30.04.1994	**1**	**0**

Midfielders

Player	Date of birth	Caps	Goals
Egidio Raúl ARÉVALO Ríos [2014/2015: CF Tigres de la Universidad Autónoma de Nuevo León (MEX)]	01.01.1982	**71**	**0**
Hugo Diego ARISMENDI Ciapparetta [2014: Club Nacional de Football Montevideo]	25.01.1988	**4**	**0**
Mathías CORUJO Díaz [2014/2015: Club Universidad de Chile Santiago (CHI)]	08.05.1986	**7**	**0**
Giorgian Daniel DE ARRASCAETA Benedetti [2014: Defensor Sporting Club Montevideo; 19.01.2015-> EC Cruzeiro Belo Horizonte (BRA)]	01.05.1994	**6**	**1**
Álvaro Rafael GONZÁLEZ Luengo [2014: SS Lazio Roma (ITA); 02.2015-> Torino FC (ITA), on loan]	29.10.1984	**55**	**3**
Marcelo Nicolás LODEIRO Benítez [2014: SC Corinthians Paulista São Paulo (BRA); 02.2015-> CA Boca Juniors Buenos Aires (ARG)]	21.03.1989	**39**	**3**
Camilo Sebastián MAYADA Mesa [2014: Danubio FC Montevideo]	08.01.1991	**4**	**0**
Álvaro Daniel PEREIRA Barragán [2014: São Paulo FC (BRA), on loan; 27.01.2015-> Club Estudiantes de La Plata (ARG), on loan]	28.01.1985	**70**	**6**
Ricardo Guzmán PEREIRA Méndez [2014/2015: Club Universidad de Chile Santiago (CHI)]	16.05.1991	**3**	**0**
Gastón Ezequiel RAMÍREZ Pereyra [2014/2015: Hull City AFC (ENG)]	02.12.1990	**31**	**0**
Cristian Gabriel RODRÍGUEZ Barotti [2014: Club Atlético de Madrid (ESP); 01-03.2015: Parma FC (ITA), on loan; 03.2015-> Grêmio Foot-Ball Porto Alegrense (BRA), on loan]	30.09.1985	**88**	**9**
Jonathan Javier RODRÍGUEZ Portillo [2014: CA Peñarol Montevideo; 02.2015-> Sport Lisboa e Benfica (POR)]	06.07.1993	**7**	**1**
Carlos Andrés SÁNCHEZ Arcosa [2014/2015: CA River Plate Buenos Aires (ARG)]	02.12.1984	**8**	**0**

Forwards

Player	Date of birth	Caps	Goals
Edinson Roberto CAVANI Gómez [2014/2015: Paris Saint-Germain FC (FRA)]	14.02.1987	**76**	**27**
Abel Mathías HERNÁNDEZ Platero [2014/2015: Hull City AFC (ENG)]	08.08.1990	**22**	**9**
Diego Alejandro ROLÁN Silva [2014/2015: FC Girondins de Bordeaux (FRA)]	24.03.1993	**11**	**2**
Christian Ricardo STUANI Curbelo [2014/2015: RCD Espanyol Barcelona (ESP)]	12.10.1986	**22**	**4**
Luis Alberto SUÁREZ Díaz [2014/2015: FC Barcelona (ESP)]	24.01.1987	**82**	**43**

National coaches

Coach	Date of birth	Record
Óscar Wáshington TABÁREZ Silva	03.03.1947	120 M; 58 W; 34 D; 28 L; 203-128
[also national coach between 27.09.1988 – 25.06.1990; Complete records: 154 M; 75 W; 429 D; 37 L; 253-156]		

VENEZUELA

The Country:
República Bolivariana de Venezuela (Bolivarian Republic of Venezuela) Capital: Caracas Surface: 916,445 km² Inhabitants: 30,206,307 Time: UTC-4.30

The FA:
Federación Venezolana de Fútbol Avenida Santos Erminy Ira, Calle las Delicias, Torre, Mega II P.H. Sabana Grande, Caracas 1050 Year of Formation: 1926 Member of FIFA since: 1952 Member of CONMEBOL since: 1952 Internet: www.federacionvenezolanadefutbol.org

NATIONAL TEAM RECORDS	
First international match:	12.02.1938, Ciudad de Panamá: Panama – Venezuela 2-1
Most international caps:	Juan Fernando Arango Sáenz – 127 caps (1999-2015)
Most international goals:	Giancarlo Gregorio Maldonado Marrero – 22 goals / 65 caps (2003-2011) Juan Fernando Arango Sáenz - 22 goals / 127 caps (1999-2015)

OLYMPIC GAMES 1900-2012
1980

COPA AMÉRICA	
1916	Did not enter
1917	Did not enter
1919	Did not enter
1920	Did not enter
1921	Did not enter
1922	Did not enter
1923	Did not enter
1924	Did not enter
1925	Did not enter
1926	Did not enter
1927	Did not enter
1929	Did not enter
1935	Did not enter
1937	Did not enter
1939	Did not enter
1941	Did not enter
1942	Did not enter
1945	Did not enter
1946	Did not enter
1947	Did not enter
1949	Did not enter
1953	Did not enter
1955	Did not enter
1956	Did not enter
1957	Did not enter
1959	Did not enter
1959E	Did not enter
1963	Did not enter
1967	5th Place
1975	Round 1
1979	Round 1
1983	Round 1
1987	Round 1
1989	Round 1
1991	Round 1
1993	Round 1
1995	Round 1
1997	Round 1
1999	Round 1
2001	Round 1
2004	Round 1
2007	Quarter-Finals
2011	4th Place
2015	Round 1

FIFA WORLD CUP	
1930	Did not enter
1934	Did not enter
1938	Did not enter
1950	Did not enter
1954	Did not enter
1958	*Withdrew*
1962	Did not enter
1966	Qualifiers
1970	Qualifiers
1974	Withdrew
1978	Qualifiers
1982	Qualifiers
1986	Qualifiers
1990	Qualifiers
1994	Qualifiers
1998	Qualifiers
2002	Qualifiers
2006	Qualifiers
2010	Qualifiers
2014	Qualifiers

PANAMERICAN GAMES	
1951	4th Place
1955	4th Place
1959	Did not enter
1963	Did not enter
1967	Did not enter
1971	Did not enter
1975	Did not enter
1979	Did not enter
1983	Round 1
1987	Did not enter
1991	Did not enter
1995	Did not enter
1999	Did not enter
2003	Did not enter
2007	Round 1
2011	Did not enter

PANAMERICAN CHAMPIONSHIP	
1952	Did not enter
1956	Did not enter
1960	Did not enter

VENEZUELAN CLUB HONOURS IN SOUTH AMERICAN CLUB COMPETITIONS:

COPA LIBERTADORES 1960-2014
None
COPA SUDAMERICANA 2002-2014
None
RECOPA SUDAMERICANA 1989-2014
None
COPA CONMEBOL 1992-1999
None
SUPERCUP „JOÃO HAVELANGE“ 1988-1997*
None
COPA MERCONORTE 1998-2001**
None

**Contested betwenn winners of all previous editions of the Copa Libertadores*

***Contested between teams belonging countries from the northern part of South America (Bolivia, Colombia, Ecuador, Peru and Venezuela);*

NATIONAL COMPETITIONS TABLE OF HONOURS

	CHAMPIONS	CUP WINNERS[1]
	THE AMATEUR ERA	
1921	Las América FC	-
1922	Centro Atlético SC	-
1923	Las América FC	-
1924	Centro Atlético SC	-
1925	Loyola SC	-
1926	Centro Atlético SC	-
1927	Venzóleo	-
1928	Deportivo Venezuela	-
1929	Deportivo Venezuela	-
1930	Centro Atlético SC	-
1931	Deportivo Venezuela	-
1932	Unión SC	-
1933	Deportivo Venezuela	-
1934	Unión SC	-
1935	Unión SC	-
1936	Dos Caminos SC	-
1937	Dos Caminos SC	-
1938	Dos Caminos SC	-
1939	Unión SC	-
1940	Unión SC	-
1941	Litoral SC	-
1942	Dos Caminos SC	-
1943	Loyola SC	-
1944	Loyola SC	-
1945	Dos Caminos SC	-
1946	Club Deportivo Español	-
1947	Unión SC	-
1948	Loyola SC	-

1949	Dos Caminos SC	-
1950	Unión SC	-
1951	Universidad Central de Venezuela FC	-
1952	La Salle FC	-
1953	Universidad Central de Venezuela FC	-
1954	Deportivo Vasco	-
1955	La Salle FC	-
1956	Banco Obrero	-
	THE PROFESSIONAL ERA	
1957	Universidad Central de Venezuela FC	-
1958	CD Portugués Caracas	-
1959	CD Español	CD Portugués Caracas
1960	CD Portugués Caracas	Banco Agrícola y Pecuario
1961	Deportivo Italia FC Caracas(2)	Deportivo Italia FC Caracas
1962	CD Portugués Caracas	Deportivo Italia FC Caracas
1963	Deportivo Italia FC Caracas	Unión Deportivo Canarias
1964	Deportivo Galicia Caracas(3)	Tiquire Flores FC
1965	Lara FC Barquisimeto	Valencia FC
1966	Deportivo Italia FC Caracas	Deportivo Galicia Caracas
1967	CD Portugués Caracas	Deportivo Galicia Caracas
1968	Unión Deportivo Canarias	Unión Deportivo Canarias
1969	Deportivo Galicia Caracas	Deportivo Galicia Caracas
1970	Deportivo Galicia Caracas	Deportivo Italia FC Caracas
1971	Valencia FC(4)	Estudiantes de Mérida FC
1972	Deportivo Italia FC Caracas	CD Portugués Caracas
1973	Portuguesa FC Acarigua	Portuguesa FC Acarigua
1974	Deportivo Galicia Caracas	*No competition*
1975	Portuguesa FC Acarigua	Estudiantes de Mérida FC
1976	Portuguesa FC Acarigua	Portuguesa FC Acarigua
1977	Portuguesa FC Acarigua	Portuguesa FC Acarigua
1978	Portuguesa FC Acarigua	Valencia FC
1979	Deportivo Táchira FC San Cristóbal(5)	Deportivo Galicia Caracas
1980	Estudiantes de Mérida FC	Atlético Zamora FC Barinas
1981	Deportivo Táchira FC San Cristóbal	Deportivo Galicia Caracas
1982	Club Atlético San Cristóbal	Atlético Zamora FC Barinas
1983	Universidad de Los Andes FC Mérida	*No competitio*
1984	Deportivo Táchira FC San Cristóbal	AC Mineros de Guayana FC Puerto Ordaz
1985	Estudiantes de Mérida FC	Estudiantes de Mérida FC
1986	Unión Atlético Táchira San Cristóbal	Deportivo Táchira FC San Cristóbal
1986/1987	CS Marítimo de Venezuela Caracas	CS Marítimo de Venezuela Caracas (1987)
1987/1988	CS Marítimo de Venezuela Caracas	Caracas FC (1988)
1988/1989	AC Mineros de Guayana FC Puerto Ordaz	CS Marítimo de Venezuela Caracas (1989)
1989/1990	CS Marítimo de Venezuela Caracas	Anzoátegui FC (1990)
1990/1991	Universidad de Los Andes FC Mérida	Internacional de Anzoátegui Puerto La Cruz (1991)
1991/1992	Caracas FC	Trujillanos FC Valera (1992)
1992/1993	CS Marítimo de Venezuela Caracas	*No competition* (1993)
1993/1994	Caracas FC	Caracas FC (1994)
1994/1995	Caracas FC	Caracas FC (1995)
1995/1996	AC Minervén Bolívar FC Ciudad Guayana	Universidad de Los Andes FC Mérida (1996)
1996/1997	Caracas FC	Atlético Zulia FC Maracaibo (1997)

1997/1998	Atlético Zulia FC Maracaibo	*No competition* (1998)
1998/1999	Deportivo Italchacao FC Caracas	*No competition* (1999)
1999/2000	Deportivo Táchira FC San Cristóbal	Caracas FC (2000)
2000/2001	Caracas FC	*No competition* (2001)
2001/2002	Club Nacional Táchira San Cristóbal	*No competition* (2002)
2002/2003	Caracas FC	*No competition* (2003)
2003/2004	Caracas FC	*No competition* (2004)
2004/2005	CD Unión Atlético Maracaibo	*No competition* (2005)
2005/2006	Caracas FC	*No competition* (2006)
2006/2007	Caracas FC	AC Aragua FC Maracay (2007)
2007/2008	Deportivo Táchira FC San Cristóbal	Deportivo Anzoátegui SC Puerto La Cruz (2008)
2008/2009	Caracas FC	Caracas FC (2009)
2009/2010	Caracas FC	Trujillanos FC Valera (2010)
2010/2011	Deportivo Táchira FC San Cristóbal	AC CD Mineros de Guayana Puerto Ordaz (2011)
2011/2012	CD Lara Barquisimeto	Deportivo Anzoátegui SC Puerto La Cruz (2012)
2012/2013	Zamora FC Barinas	Caracas FC (2013)
2013/2014	Zamora FC Barinas	Deportivo La Guaira Caracas (2014)
2014/2015	Deportivo Táchira FC San Cristóbal	

(1)The National Cup had different names over the years: Copa Liga Mayor (1959), Copa Naciones (1960), Copa Caracas (1961-1967), Copa Venezuela (1968-1971), Copa Valencia (1972), Copa Venezuela (1973-today).
(2)changed its name to Deportivo Italchacao FC Caracas between 1998 and 2006.
(3)became 2005 Galicia de Araguay, after moving to Maracay.
(4)became 1997 Carabobo FC Valencia.
(5)called Unión Atlético Táchira San Cristóbal between 1986 and 1999.

	BEST GOALSCORERS	
1957	Marino Araújo „Tonho" (BRA, Universidad Central de Venezuela FC)	12
1958	René Irazque (CD Portugués Caracas)	6
1959	Abel Benítez (ESP, CD Español)	15
1960	José Luis Iglesias (ESP, CD Portugués Caracas)	9
1961	Antonio Rávelo (Banco Agrícola y Pecuario)	11
1962	Jaime Araújo da Silva (BRA, Universidad Central de Venezuela FC)	16
1963	Aldeny Isidro „Nino" (BRA, CD Portugués Caracas)	15
1964	Hélio Rodrigues (BRA, Tiquire Flores FC)	12
1965	Mario Mateo (BRA, Lara FC Barquisimeto) Jorge Horacio Romero (ARG, La Salle FC)	16
1966	Luis De Mouros „Ratto" (BRA, CD Portugués Caracas)	21
1967	João Ramos (CD Portugués Caracas)	18
1968	Raimundo Lima „Raimundinho" (CD Portugués Caracas)	21
1969	Eustaquio Batista (Deportivo Italia FC Caracas) Aurélio dos Santos „Lelo" (Valencia FC)	19
1970	Roland Langón (URU, Deportivo Galicia Caracas)	13
1971	Agostinho Sabara (BRA, Tiquire Aragua FC)	20
1972	Francisco Rodríguez (Anzoátegui FC)	18
1973	José Chiazzaro (URU, Estudiantes de Mérida FC)	14
1974	José Chiazzaro (URU, Estudiantes de Mérida FC) Sergio Hugo Castillo (URU, Anzoátegui FC)	15
1975	Pedro Pascual Peralta (PAR, Portuguesa FC Acarigua)	20

1976	Pedro Pascual Peralta (PAR, Portuguesa FC Acarigua)	25
1977	Jair Ventura Filho „Jairzinho“ (BRA, Portuguesa FC Acarigua) Juan César Silva (Portuguesa FC Acarigua)	20
1978	Jorge Luís Andrade (Universidad de Los Andes FC Mérida)	23
1979	Omar Ferrari (URU, Deportivo Táchira FC San Cristóbal)	15
1980	Walfrido Campos (BRA, Portuguesa FC Acarigua)	12
1981	Rafael Angulo (COL, Deportivo Táchira FC San Cristóbal)	14
1982	Germán Montero (URU, Estudiantes de Mérida FC)	21
1983	Johnny Castellanos (Atlético Zamora FC Barinas)	13
1984	Sérgio Meckler (BRA, Atlético Zamora FC Barinas)	15
1985	Sérgio Meckler (BRA, Deportivo Táchira FC San Cristóbal)	17
1986	Wilton Arreaza (Caracas FC)	8
1986/1987	Johnny Castellanos (Portuguesa FC Acarigua)	16
1987/1988	Miguel Oswaldo González (ARG, Unión Atlético Táchira San Cristóbal)	22
1988/1989	Johnny Castellanos (AC Mineros de Guayana FC Puerto Ordaz)	24
1989/1990	Herbert Márquez (CS Marítimo de Venezuela Caracas)	19
1990/1991	Alexander Bottini (Monagas SC Maturín)	15
1991/1992	Andreas Vogler (GER, Caracas FC)	22
1992/1993	Herbert Márquez (CS Marítimo de Venezuela Caracas)	21
1993/1994	Rodrigo Soto (COL, Trujillanos FC Valera)	20
1994/1995	Rogeiro Da Silva (BRA, Mineros de Guayana FC Puerto Ordaz)	30
1995/1996	José Luis Dolgetta (Caracas FC)	22
1996/1997	Rafael Ernesto Castellín García (Caracas FC)	19
1997/1998	José Luis Dolgetta (Estudiantes de Mérida FC / Caracas FC)	22
1998/1999	Gustavo Fonseca (COL, Internacional Lara FC)	24
1999/2000	Juan García Rivas (Caracas FC)	24
2000/2001	(Estudiantes de Mérida FC)	12
2001/2002	Juan García Rivas (Club Nacional Táchira San Cristóbal)	34
2002/2003	Juan García Rivas (Monagas SC Maturín / AC Mineros de Guayana FC Puerto Ordaz)	19
2003/2004	Juan García Rivas (AC Mineros de Guayana FC Puerto Ordaz)	18
2004/2005	Daniel Delfino (ARG, Carabobo FC Valencia)	19
2005/2006	Juan García Rivas (Deportivo Táchira FC San Cristóbal)	21
2006/2007	Robinson Rentería (COL, Trujillanos FC Valera)	19
2007/2008	Alexander Rondón Heredia (Deportivo Anzoátegui SC Puerto La Cruz)	19
2008/2009	Heatklif Rafael Castillo Delgado (AC Aragua FC Maracay) Daniel Enrique Arismendi (Deportivo Táchira FC San Cristóbal)	17
2009/2010	Norman Freddy Cabrera Valencia (Atlético El Vigía FC)	20
2010/2011	Daniel Enrique Arismendi (Deportivo Anzoátegui SC Puerto La Cruz)	20
2011/2012	Rafael Ernesto Castellín García (CD Lara Barquisimeto)	21
2012/2013	Gabriel Arturo Torres Tejada (Zamora FC Barinas)	20
2013/2014	Juan Manuel Falcón Jiménez (Zamora FC Barinas)	18
2014/2015	Edwin Enrique Aguilar Samaniego (Deportivo Anzoátegui SC Puerto La Cruz)	23

NATIONAL CHAMPIONSHIP
Primera División de Venezuela 2014/2015

Torneo Apertura 2014 – Copa Movilnet

Results

Round 1 [09-10.08.2014]
Aragua FC - Trujillanos FC 1-2
Tucanes de Amazonas - Carabobo FC 1-1
Zulia FC - Deportivo Petare 0-1
Mineros de Guayana - Metropolitanos FC 1-0
Deport. La Guaira - Deportivo Anzoátegui 3-2
Caracas FC - Estudiantes de Mérida 0-1
Deportivo Táchira - Atlético Venezuela 3-0
Portuguesa FC - Llaneros de Guanare 1-0
Zamora FC - CD Lara 1-1

Round 2 [16-17.08.2014]
CD Lara - Deportivo La Guaira 1-1
Metropolitanos FC - Aragua FC 1-1
Estudiantes de Mérida - Zamora FC 1-1
Mineros de Guayana - Portuguesa FC 1-1
Atlético Venezuela - Zulia FC 1-0
Deportivo Petare - Tucanes de Amazonas 1-1
Llaneros de Guanare - Deportivo Táchira 0-2
Carabobo FC – Depor. Anzoátegui 0-0 [08.10.]
Trujillanos FC - Caracas FC 2-1 [12.11.]

Round 3 [23-24.08.2014]
Caracas FC - Metropolitanos FC 3-1 [13.08.]
Deport. La Guaira - Estudiantes de Mérida 1-2
Aragua FC - Mineros de Guayana 2-2
Deportivo Anzoátegui - Deportivo Petare 1-0
Tucanes de Amazonas - Atlético Venezuela 1-0
Zulia FC - Llaneros de Guanare 0-1
CD Lara - Carabobo FC 0-1
Deportivo Táchira - Portuguesa FC 1-1
Zamora FC - Trujillanos FC 0-1 [29.10.]

Round 4 [30-31.08.2014]
Aragua FC - Deportivo Táchira 0-2
Metropolitanos FC - Zamora FC 1-1
Estudiantes de Mérida - CD Lara 1-1
Llaneros de Guanare - Tucanes de Amaz. 0-2
Atlético Venezuela - Deportivo Anzoátegui 1-0
Deportivo Petare - Carabobo FC 1-1
Portuguesa FC - Zulia FC 1-2
Trujillanos FC – Deport. La Guaira 0-1 [10.09.]
Mineros de Guayana - Caracas FC 0-0 [29.10.]

Round 5 [14.09.2014]
Caracas FC - Aragua FC 5-0 [10.09.]
Tucanes de Amazonas - Portuguesa FC 2-0
Carabobo FC - Atlético Venezuela 1-1
Zulia FC - Deportivo Táchira 1-2
Deportivo La Guaira - Metropolitanos FC 3-0
Estudiantes de Mérida - Deportivo Petare 1-1
CD Lara - Trujillanos FC 0-0
Deport. Anzoátegui - Llaneros de Guanare 5-0
Zamora FC - Mineros de Guayana 1-1

Round 6 [20-21.09.2014]
Metropolitanos FC - CD Lara 1-1
Llaneros de Guanare - Carabobo FC 1-2
Trujillanos FC - Estudiantes de Mérida 3-0
Portuguesa FC - Deportivo Anzoátegui 0-0
Atlético Venezuela - Deportivo Petare 0-0
Aragua FC - Zamora FC 2-1
Mineros de Guayana - Deportivo La Guaira 1-2
Deportivo Táchira - Tucanes de Amazonas 4-0
Caracas FC - Zulia FC 4-2 [15.10.]

Round 7 [24-25.09.2014]
Tucanes de Amazonas - Zulia FC 2-0
CD Lara - Mineros de Guayana 3-1
Deportivo Anzoátegui - Deportivo Táchira 1-0
Trujillanos FC - Atlético Venezuela 3-3
Carabobo FC - Portuguesa FC 0-0
Estudiantes de Mérida - Metropolitanos FC 2-2
Deportivo La Guaira - Aragua FC 2-1
Dep. Petare - Llaneros de Guanare 1-1 [11.10.]
Zamora FC - Caracas FC 2-1 [19.11.]

Round 8 [27-28.09.2014]
Metropolitanos FC - Trujillanos FC 4-1
Tucanes de Amazonas - Zamora FC 1-0
Zulia FC - Deportivo Anzoátegui 1-0
Portuguesa FC - Deportivo Petare 0-0
Llaneros de Guanare - Atlético Venezuela 1-0
Mineros de Guayana - Estudiantes Mérida 2-0
Caracas FC - Deportivo La Guaira 2-1
Aragua FC - CD Lara 3-0
Deportivo Táchira - Carabobo FC 1-1

Round 9 [04-05.10.2014]
Deportivo La Guaira - Zamora FC 1-0
Llaneros de Guanare - Metropolitanos FC 2-1
CD Lara - Caracas FC 0-0
Carabobo FC - Zulia FC 1-1
Trujillanos FC - Mineros de Guayana 1-0
Estudiantes de Mérida - Aragua FC 1-3
Atlético Venezuela - Portuguesa FC 2-0
Deportivo Petare - Deportivo Táchira 1-3
Depor. Anzoátegui - Tucanes de Amazonas 2-1

Round 10 [18-19.10.2014]
Deportivo La Guaira - Carabobo FC 1-1
Aragua FC - Zulia FC 4-1
Mineros de Guayana - Deportivo Táchira 2-1
Metropolitanos FC - Portuguesa FC 1-1
Trujillanos FC - Llaneros de Guanare 2-0
Estudiantes de Mérida - Atlético Venezuela 1-2
Caracas FC - Tucanes de Amazonas 5-1
CD Lara - Deportivo Petare 2-0
Zamora FC - Deportivo Anzoátegui 1-1

Round 11 [26.10.2014]
Tucanes de Amazonas - Aragua FC 0-0
Zulia FC - Mineros de Guayana 1-1
Carabobo FC - Zamora FC 2-1
Llaneros de Guanare - Estudiantes Mérida 0-2
Atlético Venezuela - CD Lara 2-2
Deportivo Petare - Deportivo La Guaira 0-0
Deportivo Táchira - Metropolitanos FC 0-1
Portuguesa FC - Trujillanos FC 2-2
Deportivo Anzoátegui - Caracas FC 1-0

Round 12 [01-02.11.2014]
Deportivo La Guaira - Atlético Venezuela 3-1
CD Lara - Llaneros de Guanare 4-2
Metropolitanos FC - Zulia FC 1-0
Trujillanos FC - Deportivo Táchira 1-0
Estudiantes de Mérida - Portuguesa FC 3-1
Mineros de Guayana - Tucanes de Amaz. 0-1
Aragua FC - Deportivo Anzoátegui 3-2
Caracas FC - Carabobo FC 3-2
Zamora FC - Deportivo Petare 0-0

Round 13 [09.11.2014]
Tucanes de Amazonas - Metropolitanos FC 2-1
Zulia FC - Trujillanos FC 0-3
Carabobo FC - Aragua FC 0-0
Llaneros de Guanare - Deportivo La Guaira 1-1
Atlético Venezuela - Zamora FC 1-2
Deportivo Petare - Caracas FC 0-2
Deportivo Táchira - Estudiantes de Mérida 0-0
Portuguesa FC - CD Lara 0-4
Deport. Anzoátegui - Mineros de Guayana 2-3

Round 14 [22-23.11.2014]
Deportivo La Guaira - Portuguesa FC 1-0
Aragua FC - Deportivo Petare 2-1
Trujillanos FC - Tucanes de Amazonas 1-0
Estudiantes de Mérida - Zulia FC 0-0
Mineros de Guayana - Carabobo FC 4-1
CD Lara - Deportivo Táchira 3-3
Caracas FC - Atlético Venezuela 1-0
Zamora FC - Llaneros de Guanare 2-1
Metropolitanos FC - Deportivo Anzoátegui 0-7

Round 15 [29-30.11.2014]
Deportivo Anzoátegui - Trujillanos FC 2-0
Llaneros de Guanare - Caracas FC 0-0
Tucanes de Amaz. - Estudiantes de Mérida 0-1
Zulia FC - CD Lara 0-2
Portuguesa FC - Zamora FC 1-2
Atlético Venezuela - Aragua FC 0-2
Deportivo Petare - Mineros de Guayana 0-0
Carabobo FC - Metropolitanos FC 3-1
Deportivo Táchira - Deportivo La Guaira 0-1

Round 16 [06-07.12.2014]
Deportivo La Guaira - Zulia FC 1-1
CD Lara - Tucanes de Amazonas 1-1
Caracas FC - Portuguesa FC 5-2
Estudiantes de Mérida – Depor. Anzoátegui 2-1
Aragua FC - Llaneros de Guanare 4-2
Mineros de Guayana - Atlético Venezuela 0-0
Metropolitanos FC - Deportivo Petare 0-1
Trujillanos FC - Carabobo FC 2-1
Zamora FC - Deportivo Táchira 2-1

Round 17 [14.12.2014]	
Tucanes de Amaz. - Deportivo La Guaira 0-2	Llaneros de Guanare - Mineros de Guayana 0-1
Zulia FC - Zamora FC 2-2	Atlético Venezuela - Metropolitanos FC 0-0
Deportivo Táchira - Caracas FC 1-1	Deport. Petare - Trujillanos FC 0-3 (Awarded)
Portuguesa FC - Aragua FC 0-2	Carabobo FC - Estudiantes de Mérida 3-2
Deportivo Anzoátegui - CD Lara 1-0	

Final Standings

1.	**Trujillanos FC Valera**	17	11	3	3	27	-	15	36
2.	Deportivo La Guaira Caracas	17	10	5	2	25	-	13	35
3.	Caracas FC	17	9	4	4	33	-	16	31
4.	AC Aragua FC Maracay	17	9	4	4	30	-	22	31
5.	Deportivo Anzoátegui SC Puerto La Cruz	17	8	3	6	28	-	15	27
6.	AC CD Mineros de Guayana Puerto Ordaz	17	6	7	4	20	-	16	25
7.	Tucanes de Amazonas FC Puerto Ayacucho	17	7	4	6	16	-	19	25
8.	CD Lara Barquisimeto	17	5	9	3	25	-	18	24
9.	Carabobo FC Valencia	17	5	9	3	21	-	20	24
10.	Estudiantes de Mérida FC	17	6	6	5	20	-	21	24
11.	Deportivo Táchira FC San Cristóbal	17	6	5	6	24	-	16	23
12.	Zamora FC Barinas	17	5	7	5	19	-	19	22
13.	Atlético Venezuela CF Caracas	17	4	6	7	14	-	20	18
14.	Metropolitanos FC Los Teques Caracas	17	3	6	8	16	-	29	15
15.	Deportivo Petare FC Caracas	17	2	9	6	8	-	17	12
16.	Llaneros de Guanare FC	17	3	3	11	12	-	30	12
17.	Zulia FC Maracaibo	17	2	5	10	12	-	27	11
18.	Portuguesa FC Acarígua	17	1	7	9	11	-	28	10

Trujillanos FC Valera (as winners of the Apertura Championship) were qualified for the Championship finals and for the 2016 Copa Libertadores.

Torneo Clausura 2015 – Copa Movilnet

Results

Round 1 [10-11.01.2015]
Metropolitanos FC - Mineros de Guayana 2-1
Deportivo Petare - Zulia FC 0-0
Carabobo FC - Tucanes de Amazonas 0-1
CD Lara - Zamora FC 1-1
Atlético Venezuela - Deportivo Táchira 2-1
Estudiantes de Mérida - Caracas FC 1-2
Llaneros de Guanare - Portuguesa FC 4-1
Trujillanos FC - Aragua FC 1-1
Deport. Anzoátegui - Deportivo La Guaira 1-0

Round 2 [17-18.01.2015]
Deportivo La Guaira - CD Lara 2-1
Portuguesa FC - Mineros de Guayana 0-1
Tucanes de Amazonas - Deportivo Petare 0-0
Zulia FC - Atlético Venezuela 1-0
Aragua FC - Metropolitanos FC 2-1
Caracas FC - Trujillanos FC 2-1
Deportivo Táchira - Llaneros de Guanare 4-1
Deportivo Anzoátegui - Carabobo FC 4-2
Zamora FC - Estudiantes de Mérida 1-0

Round 3 [24-25.01.2015]
Metropolitanos FC - Caracas FC 0-1
Portuguesa FC - Deportivo Táchira 1-3
Llaneros de Guanare - Zulia FC 2-0
Carabobo FC - CD Lara 0-1
Estudiantes de Mérida – Deport. La Guaira 2-1
Trujillanos FC - Zamora FC 0-1
Mineros de Guayana - Aragua FC 1-2
Deportivo Petare - Deportivo Anzoátegui 0-0
Atlético Venezuela - Tucanes de Amazonas 3-0

Round 4 [31.01.-01.02.2015]
Deportivo Táchira - Aragua FC 3-1 [14.01.]
Deportivo La Guaira - Trujillanos FC 2-1
Tucanes de Amaz. - Llaneros de Guanare 0-0
Zulia FC - Portuguesa FC 2-2
Carabobo FC - Deportivo Petare 0-1
Deportivo Anzoátegui - Atlético Venezuela 0-0
Caracas FC - Mineros de Guayana 1-1
Zamora FC - Metropolitanos FC 4-0
CD Lara - Estudiantes de Mérida 0-0 [04.03.]

Round 5 [08.02.2015]
Metropolitanos FC - Deportivo La Guaira 0-1
Portuguesa FC - Tucanes de Amazonas 4-0
Llaneros de Guanare – Deport. Anzoátegui 2-3
Trujillanos FC - CD Lara 1-1
Mineros de Guayana - Zamora FC 0-0
Atlético Venezuela - Carabobo FC 2-2
Aragua FC - Caracas FC 0-0
Deportivo Táchira - Zulia FC 3-1 [02.04.]
Dep.Petare - Estudiantes de Mérida 0-1 [23.04.]

Round 6 [22.02.2015]
Deportivo Anzoátegui - Portuguesa FC 3-1
CD Lara - Metropolitanos FC 3-1
Carabobo FC - Llaneros de Guanare 4-1
Zulia FC - Caracas FC 1-0
Estudiantes de Mérida - Trujillanos FC 1-0
Deportivo Petare - Atlético Venezuela 1-0
La Guaira - Mineros de Guayana 2-2 [04.04.]
Tucanes de Amaz. – Dep. Táchira 1-0 [05.04.]
Zamora FC - Aragua FC 3-0 [23.04.]

Round 7 [25.02.2015]
Mineros de Guayana - CD Lara 2-2 [15.02.]
Portuguesa FC - Carabobo FC 0-1
Zulia FC - Tucanes de Amazonas 2-0
Atlético Venezuela - Trujillanos FC 1-2
Aragua FC - Deportivo La Guaira 3-2
Llaneros de Guanare - Deportivo Petare 0-1
Metropolitanos FC - Estudiantes de Mérida 2-1
Caracas FC - Zamora FC 1-0 [04.03.]
Deport. Táchira – Dep. Anzoátegui 2-1 [22.04.]

Round 8 [01.03.2015]
Deportivo La Guaira - Caracas FC 1-2 [28.02.]
CD Lara - Aragua FC 2-1
Carabobo FC - Deportivo Táchira 1-1
Trujillanos FC - Metropolitanos FC 1-1
Deportivo Petare - Portuguesa FC 0-1
Atlético Venezuela - Llaneros de Guanare 2-0
Deportivo Anzoátegui - Zulia FC 3-1
Zamora FC - Tucanes de Amazonas 4-0
Est. Mérida - Mineros de Guayana 1-2 [29.04.]

Round 9 [07-08.03.2015]
Deportivo Táchira - Deportivo Petare 3-0
Zamora FC - Deportivo La Guaira 2-1
Metropolitanos FC - Llaneros de Guanare 3-0
Portuguesa FC - Atlético Venezuela 1-1
Tucanes de Amazonas – Dep. Anzoátegui 1-1
Zulia FC - Carabobo FC 1-0
Mineros de Guayana - Trujillanos FC 3-0
Aragua FC - Estudiantes de Mérida 2-2
Caracas FC - CD Lara 1-2

Round 10 [14-15.03.2015]
Deportivo Táchira - Mineros de Guayana 5-2
Tucanes de Amazonas - Caracas FC 0-1
Portuguesa FC - Metropolitanos FC 2-2
Llaneros de Guanare - Trujillanos FC 2-3
Zulia FC - Aragua FC 2-1
Atlético Venezuela - Estudiantes de Mérida 0-1
Deportivo Petare - CD Lara 0-1
Carabobo FC - Deportivo La Guaira 1-2
Dep. Anzoátegui - Zamora FC 1-1 [25.03.]

Round 11 [18.03.2015]
Zamora FC - Carabobo FC 4-2 [28.01.]
CD Lara - Atlético Venezuela 1-1
Aragua FC - Tucanes de Amazonas 3-0
Trujillanos FC - Portuguesa FC 1-0
Caracas FC - Deportivo Anzoátegui 1-0
Estudiant. de Mérida - Llaneros de Guanare 0-0
Metropolitanos FC – Dep. Táchira 2-3 [25.03.]
Dep. La Guaira - Deportivo Petare 1-0 [25.03.]
Mineros de Guayana - Zulia FC 1-0 [25.03.]

Round 12 [22.03.2015]
Tucanes de Amaz. - Mineros de Guayana 1-0
Portuguesa FC - Estudiantes de Mérida 3-1
Zulia FC - Metropolitanos FC 1-2
Carabobo FC - Caracas FC 0-2
Llaneros de Guanare - CD Lara 3-0
Atlético Venezuela - Deportivo La Guaira 1-1
Deportivo Petare - Zamora FC 1-2
Deportivo Táchira - Trujillanos FC 2-1
Deportivo Anzoátegui - Aragua FC 3-2

Round 13 [28-30.03.2015]
Deportivo La Guaira - Llaneros de Guanare 3-0
CD Lara - Portuguesa FC 4-1
Metropolitanos FC - Tucanes de Amazonas 0-0
Trujillanos FC - Zulia FC 1-0
Estudiantes de Mérida - Deportivo Táchira 0-2
Mineros de Guayana – Deport. Anzoátegui 1-3
Caracas FC - Deportivo Petare 1-0
Aragua FC - Carabobo FC 1-1
Zamora FC - Atlético Venezuela 3-0

Round 14 [12.04.2015]
Tucanes de Amazonas - Trujillanos FC 0-0
Portuguesa FC - Deportivo La Guaira 0-0
Llaneros de Guanare - Zamora FC 5-0
Zulia FC - Estudiantes de Mérida 0-1
Atlético Venezuela - Caracas FC 0-1
Deportivo Petare - Aragua FC 1-0
Deportivo Anzoátegui - Metropolitanos FC 3-2
Carabobo FC - Mineros de Guay. 0-1 [18.04.]
Deportivo Táchira - CD Lara 3-0 [29.04.]

Round 15 [18.04.2015]
Mineros de Guayana – Dep. Petare 2-1 [12.03.]
Trujillanos FC - Deportivo Anzoátegui 1-0
Deportivo La Guaira - Deportivo Táchira 1-2
CD Lara - Zulia FC 0-0
Estud. de Mérida - Tucanes de Amazonas 1-1
Caracas FC - Llaneros de Guanare 3-2
Aragua FC - Atlético Venezuela 0-2
Zamora FC - Portuguesa FC 1-0
Metropolitanos FC - Carabobo FC 2-3 [22.04.]

Round 16 [26.04.2015]
Tucanes de Amazonas - CD Lara 0-0
Zulia FC - Deportivo La Guaira 1-0
Deportivo Táchira - Zamora FC 1-0
Portuguesa FC - Caracas FC 0-2
Dep. Anzoátegui - Estudiantes de Mérida 4-3
Llaneros de Guanare - Aragua FC 1-2
Atlético Venezuela - Mineros de Guayana 2-0
Deportivo Petare - Metropolitanos FC 0-1
Carabobo FC - Trujillanos FC 2-0

Round 17 [03.05.2015]
Deport. La Guaira - Tucanes de Amazonas 3-1
Zamora FC - Zulia FC 2-1
Caracas FC - Deportivo Táchira 2-2
Aragua FC - Portuguesa FC 4-0
CD Lara - Deportivo Anzoátegui 3-1
Mineros de Guayana - Llaneros de Guanare 3-1
Metropolitanos FC - Atlético Venezuela 0-0
Trujillanos FC - Deportivo Petare 1-1
Estudiantes de Mérida - Carabobo FC 2-1

Final Standings

1.	**Deportivo Táchira FC San Cristóbal**	17	13	2	2	39 - 16	41
2.	Caracas FC	17	12	3	2	23 - 11	39
3.	Zamora FC Barinas	17	11	3	3	29 - 14	36
4.	Deportivo Anzoátegui SC Puerto La Cruz	17	9	4	4	31 - 23	31
5.	CD Lara Barquisimeto	17	7	7	3	22 - 18	28
6.	AC CD Mineros de Guayana Puerto Ordaz	17	7	4	6	23 - 23	25
7.	Deportivo La Guaira Caracas	17	7	3	7	22 - 19	24
8.	AC Aragua FC Maracay	17	6	4	7	25 - 25	22
9.	Atlético Venezuela CF Caracas	17	5	6	6	17 - 15	21
10.	Zulia FC Maracaibo	17	6	3	8	14 - 18	21
11.	Trujillanos FC Valera	17	5	5	7	15 - 20	20
12.	Metropolitanos FC Los Teques Caracas	17	5	4	8	21 - 26	19
13.	Deportivo Petare FC Caracas	17	4	4	9	7 - 14	16
14.	Tucanes de Amazonas FC Puerto Ayacucho	17	3	7	7	6 - 22	16
15.	Carabobo FC Valencia	17	4	3	10	20 - 26	15
16.	Llaneros de Guanare FC	17	4	2	11	24 - 32	14
17.	Estudiantes de Mérida FC	17	6	4	7	18 - 21	13
18.	Portuguesa FC Acarígua	17	3	4	10	17 - 30	13

Deportivo Táchira FC San Cristóbal (as winners of the Clausura Championship) were qualified for the Championship finals and for the 2016 Copa Libertadores.

Top goalscorers*:

23 goals:	**Edwin Enrique Aguilar Samaniego**	**(Deportivo Anzoátegui SC Puerto La Cruz)**
20 goals:	Gelmin Javier Rivas Boada	(Deportivo Táchira FC San Cristóbal)
17 goals:	Edder José Farías	(Caracas FC)
14 goals:	Jorge Alberto Rojas Méndez	(Deportivo Táchira FC San Cristóbal & Metropolitanos FC Los Teques Caracas)
	Over Felipe García Torres	(Estudiantes de Mérida FC)

**only regular season (Apertura & Clausura)*

Championship final

10.05.2015, Estadio „José Alberto Pérez", Valera; Attendance: 13,145
Referee: Jesús Valenzuela
Trujillanos FC Valera - Deportivo Táchira FC San Cristóbal 0-0
Trujillanos: Leandro Díaz Prado, Manuel Alejandro Granados Asprilla, Luigi José Erazo Villamizar (Cap), Mayker José González Montilla (90.Carlos Enrique Castro), Maurice Jesús Cova Sánchez, Johan José Osorio Paredes, Gerardo José Mendoza (64.Raúl Antonio Vallona Espinoza), Jarol Herrera Martínez, Carlos José Sosa Moreno, Sergio Alberto Alvarez Castellano (65.Irwin Rafael Antón Barroso), Alfredo Antonio Padilla Gutiérrez. Trainer: Horacio Ignacio Matuszyczk (Argentina).
Deportivo Táchira: Alan José Liebeskind Díaz, Carlos Gregorio Rivero González, Carlos Alfredo Salazar Cumaná [*sent off 65*], Carlos Javier López, Yuber Antonio Mosquera Perea, Carlos Javier Lujano Sánchez, Carlos Eduardo Cermeño Uzcategui, César Eduardo González Amais (Cap) (90+3.Agnel José Flores Hernández), Yohandry José Orozco Cujía (77.José Miguel Reyes Marín), José Alí Meza Draegertt (70.Gelmin Javier Rivas Boada). Trainer: Daniel Alejandro Farías Acosta.

16.05.2015, Estadio Polideportivo de Pueblo Nuevo, San Cristóbal; Attendance: 37,365
Referee: José Ramón Argote Vega
Deportivo Táchira FC San Cristóbal - Trujillanos FC Valera 1-0(0-0)
Deportivo Táchira: Alan José Liebeskind Díaz, Gerzon Armando Chacón Varela, Wilker José Ángel Romero, Carlos Javier López, Yuber Antonio Mosquera Perea, Agnel José Flores Hernández (55.José Alí Meza Draegertt), Carlos Eduardo Cermeño Uzcategui, Yohandry José Orozco Cujía (81.Carlos Javier Lujano Sánchez), César Eduardo González Amais (Cap), Jorge Alberto Rojas Méndez, Gelmin Javier Rivas Boada (67.Pablo Fernando Olivera Fernández). Trainer: Daniel Alejandro Farías Acosta.
Trujillanos: Leandro Díaz Prado, Manuel Alejandro Granados Asprilla, Luigi José Erazo Villamizar (Cap), Mayker José González Montilla, Johan José Osorio Paredes, Gerardo José Mendoza (78.Sergio Alberto Alvarez Castellano), Maurice Jesús Cova Sánchez, Jarol Herrera Martínez (64.Raúl Antonio Vallona Espinoza), Carlos José Sosa Moreno, Irwin Rafael Antón Barroso (69.Argenis José Gómez Ortega), Alfredo Antonio Padilla Gutiérrez. Trainer: Horacio Ignacio Matuszyczk (Argentina).
Goal: 1-0 Jorge Alberto Rojas Méndez (75 penalty).

2014/2015 Primera División de Venezuela Winners : **Deportivo Táchira FC San Cristóbal**

Aggregate Table 2014/2015

1.	Caracas FC	34	21	7	6	56	- 27	70
2.	Deportivo Táchira FC San Cristóbal	34	19	7	8	64	- 33	64
3.	Deportivo La Guaira Caracas	34	17	8	9	48	- 33	59
4.	Deportivo Anzoátegui SC Puerto La Cruz	34	17	7	10	59	- 38	58
5.	Zamora FC Barinas	34	16	10	8	48	- 33	58
6.	Trujillanos FC Valera	34	16	8	10	42	- 35	56
7.	AC Aragua FC Maracay	34	15	8	11	55	- 47	53
8.	CD Lara Barquisimeto	34	12	16	6	47	- 36	52
9.	AC CD Mineros de Guayana Puerto Ordaz	34	13	11	10	43	- 39	50
10.	Tucanes de Amazonas FC Puerto Ayacucho	34	10	11	13	22	- 41	41
11.	Atlético Venezuela CF Caracas	34	9	12	13	31	- 35	39
12.	Carabobo FC Valencia	34	9	12	13	41	- 46	39
13.	Estudiantes de Mérida FC	34	12	10	12	38	- 42	46
14.	Metropolitanos FC Los Teques Caracas	34	8	10	16	37	- 55	34
15.	Zulia FC Maracaibo	34	8	8	18	26	- 45	32
16.	Deportivo Petare FC Caracas	34	6	11	15	15	- 31	29
17.	Llaneros de Guanare FC (*Relegated*)	34	7	5	22	36	- 62	26
18.	Portuguesa FC Acarígua (*Relegated*)	34	4	11	19	28	- 58	23

Caracas FC, Deportivo Táchira FC San Cristóbal and Trujillanos FC Valera qualified for the 2016 Copa Libertadores.

Deportivo La Guaira Caracas and Deportivo Anzoátegui SC Puerto La Cruz qualified for the 2015 Copa Sudamericana.

Copa Sudamericana 2015 Play-offs

Quarter-Finals

Estudiantes de Mérida FC - Zamora FC Barinas	1-2(1-1)	2-4(1-2)
Tucanes de Amazonas FC Puerto Ayacucho - Mineros de Guayana Puerto Ordaz	0-0	0-3(0-1)
Atlético Venezuela CF Caracas - CD Lara Barquisimeto	1-0(0-0)	0-2(0-1)
Carabobo FC Valencia - AC Aragua FC Maracay	1-0(1-0)	0-0

Semi-Finals

AC CD Mineros de Guayana Puerto Ordaz - Zamora FC Barinas	2-3(1-1)	2-3(0-0)
Carabobo FC Valencia - CD Lara Barquisimeto	1-0(0-0)	0-1aet 3-1 pen

Zamora FC Barinas and Carabobo FC Valencia qualified for the 2015 Copa Sudamericana.

COPA VENEZUELA FINAL 2014

26.11.2014, Estadio Olimpico de la UCV, Caracas; Attendance: n/a
Referee: José Ramón Argote Vega
Deportivo La Guaira Caracas - Trujillanos FC Valera 1-1(0-1)
La Guaira: Renny Vicente Vega Hernández, Edwar Segundo Bracho Suárez (82.Daniel Eduardo Benítez Pernía), Antonio José Boada Figueroa, Franklin José Lucena Peña (Cap), Óscar Constantino González, Arquímedes José Figuera Salazar, Javier Alfonso García (67.Enson Jesús Rodríguez Mesa), Luciano Nahuel Ursino Pegolo, Framber Johan Villegas Sangronis (62.Armando José Carrillo Dangond), Charlis José Ortíz García, Imanol Iriberri. Trainer: Leonardo Alberto González Antequera.
Trujillanos: Leandro Díaz Prado, Manuel Alejandro Granados Asprilla, Luigi José Erazo Villamizar, Edixon Bladimir Cuevas Tirado (Cap), Mayker José González Montilla, Galileo Antonio Del Castillo Carrasquel (46.Raúl Antonio Vallona Espinoza), Johan José Osorio Paredes, Jarol Herrera Martínez, Argenis José Gómez Ortega (68.Maurice Jesús Cova Sánchez), Fredys Enrique Arrieta Fontalvo (76.Gerardo José Mendoza), James Fernando Cabezas Mairongo. Trainer: Horacio Ignacio Matuszyczk (Argentina).
Goals: 0-1 Fredys Enrique Arrieta Fontalvo (41 penalty), 1-1 Óscar Constantino González (81).

03.12.2014, Estadio "José Alberto Pérez", Valera; Attendance: 19,920
Referee: Jesús Noel Valenzuela Sáez
Trujillanos FC Valera - Deportivo La Guaira Caracas 1-1(0-1,1-1,1-1); 3-4 on penalties
Trujillanos: Leandro Díaz Prado, Carlos Enrique Castro, Luigi José Erazo Villamizar, Edixon Bladimir Cuevas Tirado (Cap), Manuel Alejandro Granados Asprilla (76.Mayker José González Montilla), Jarol Herrera Martínez (68.Maurice Jesús Cova Sánchez), Raúl Antonio Vallona Espinoza (65.Sergio Alberto Alvarez Castellano), Johan José Osorio Paredes, Argenis José Gómez Ortega, Fredys Enrique Arrieta Fontalvo, James Fernando Cabezas Mairongo. Trainer: Horacio Ignacio Matuszyczk (Argentina).
La Guaira: Renny Vicente Vega Hernández (90+3.Luis Carlos Rojas), Edwar Segundo Bracho Suárez, Luis Alfonso Morgillo Marrero, Daniel Eduardo Benítez Pernía, Óscar Constantino González, Charlis José Ortíz García (68.Javier Alfonso García), Franklin José Lucena Peña (Cap), Arquímedes José Figuera Salazar, Luciano Nahuel Ursino Pegolo, Framber Johan Villegas Sangronis (89.Armando José Carrillo Dangond), Imanol Iriberri. Trainer: Leonardo Alberto González Antequera.
Goals: 0-1 Fredys Enrique Arrieta Fontalvo (45), 1-1 Imanol Iriberri (85).
Penalties: Argenis José Gómez Ortega 1-0; Luciano Nahuel Ursino Pegolo 1-1; James Fernando Cabezas Mairongo (missed); Armando José Carrillo Dangond 1-2; Maurice Jesús Cova Sánchez 2-2; Imanol Iriberri 2-3; Sergio Alberto Alvarez Castellano 3-3; Óscar Constantino González 3-4; Fredys Enrique Arrieta Fontalvo (missed).

2014 Copa Venezuela Winners: **Deportivo La Guaira** (qualified for the 2014 Copa Sudamericana)

ASOCIACIÓN CIVIL ARAGUA FÚTBOL CLUB MARACAY

Foundation date: August 20, 2002
Address: Prolongación Avenida Sucre y Avenida Las Delicias, Maracay, Estado Aragua
Stadium: Estadio Olímpico „Hermanos Ghersi Páez“, Maracay – Capacity: 16,000

THE SQUAD

	DOB	Ape		Cla	
		M	G	M	G
Goalkeepers:					
Jean Carlos Issa Venta	19.07.1990	12	-	14	-
Geancarlos Martínez Villarroel	21.05.1979	5	-	3	-
Defenders:					
Rohel Antonio Briceño Carpio	15.03.1984	15	2	6	-
Jaime Andrés Bustamante Suárez (COL)	21.04.1980	15	2	13	-
Jonás Cárdenas	07.08.1995	-	-	-	-
José Ángel Cardoza	07.08.1995			6	-
Francisco Javier Fajardo Gil	08.07.1990	-	-		
Jean Carlos Neto Gaspar	01.10.1981	4	-	5	-
Henry Junior Plazas Mendoza	12.12.1992	5	-	10	1
Loren Walcott Ray Hernández	29.10.1993	13	-	7	-
José Jesús Yégüez Salgado	19.09.1987	2	-		
Carlos Zabala				1	-
Midfielders:					
Luis Felipe Chará Zamora (COL)	06.01.1981	13	-	12	-
Ángel Antonio Chourio Galíndez	04.05.1985			12	1
Francisco Andrés La Mantia Pipaon	24.02.1996	10	-	6	-
Jackson Armando López Osorio	01.08.1990	7	-	5	-
Jesús Alberto Lugo Limpia	14.09.1991	15	6	17	5
José Manuel Manríquez Hernández	19.03.1987	16	2	15	-
Sergio Luis Ortíz	08.05.1995	6	-	8	1
José Mauricio Parra Perdomo	06.02.1990	11	1	8	1
Orlando José Peraza Venegas	19.03.1991	12	-	16	-
Gustavo Adolfo Rojas Rocha	14.01.1982	17	3	16	3
Pedro Jesús Váldes	29.09.1995	-	-	9	-
Forwards:					
Néstor Fabián Bareiro Leguizamón (PAR)	11.12.1983	16	7	15	6
José Castillo	15.02.1994			5	-
Hermes Manuel Palomino Fariñes	04.03.1988	7	1	-	-
Ronaldo José Pérez	14.09.1994	7	-	6	-
Jarín Medardo Quintero León (COL)	19.08.1993	13	5	14	7
Kenny Anthony Romero	03.06.1995	12	-	4	-
Kristian Salas	09.09.1996	-	-	-	-
Trainer:					
Manuel Plasencia Mendoza [as of 01.07.2014]	30.03.1970	17		17	

ATLÉTICO VENEZUELA CLUB DE FÚTBOL CARACAS

Foundation date: July 23, 2009
Address: *Not known*
Stadium: Estadio Nacional "Brígido Iriarte", Caracas – Capacity: 12,500

THE SQUAD	DOB	Ape		Cla	
		M	G	M	G
Goalkeepers:					
Wilver Eduardo Jiménez Herrera	16.03.1990	1	-	-	-
Bryant José Martin Gammiero	02.11.1993	-	-	-	-
Daniel Eduardo Valdés Guerrero	09.04.1985	16	-	17	-
Defenders:					
René Gregorio Flores Navas	29.04.1991	12	-	-	-
Johnny Alberto González Benavente	15.09.1995	9	-	9	-
Kender Gutiérrez	20.10.1994	1	-	4	-
Andrés Eduardo Maldonado Manzini	09.04.1994	-	-	4	-
Daniel Kabir Mustafá (ARG)	02.08.1984	13	2	15	1
Hildemaro Antonio Rosales Castañeda	17.03.1994	-	-	-	-
Jhoel Jesús Salazar Pérez	20.11.1988	5	-	1	-
Luis Torres	12.02.1993	10	-	1	-
Diego Fernando Valdés Parra (COL)	13.08.1981	16	-	15	-
Midfielders:					
Henrys Junior Alcalá Cedeño	25.07.1991	3	-	-	-
Rubén Darío Arocha Hernández	21.04.1987	14	-	16	-
Daniel Alejandro da Silva Deniz	23.06.1990	10	-	8	-
Daniel Ricardo Febles Argüelles	08.02.1992	15	1	14	1
Alexander Abel Molina La Cruz	28.03.1994	6	1	10	-
Guillermo Antonio Octavio Izquierdo	16.07.1989	13	2	11	-
Jairo José Otero Vásquez	11.12.1993	3	-	3	-
Francisco Leandro Parra Guerra	26.04.1986	17	1	16	1
Héctor Enrique Pérez Ramírez	11.10.1986	12	2	13	4
José Piña	05.01.1996	-	-	-	-
Guillermo Abel Ramírez Valdivia	10.11.1989	10	-	16	-
Juan Miguel Tineo Villabón	13.04.1996	10	-	8	-
César José Urpín Díaz	14.08.1994			8	-
Forwards:					
Leonardo Ezequiel Carboni (ARG)	04.11.1984	14	3	16	4
Orangel José Carrero Ibedaca	23.12.1989			1	-
Walter Rangel	21.12.1995			1	-
José Antonio Sojo Perález	18.05.1994	1	-	1	-
Anthony Chelin Uribe Francia	24.10.1990	16	2	14	4
Yeferson José Velasco Leal	13.06.1986	11	-	16	1
Trainer:					
José Hernández [as of 01.01.1912]		17		17	

CARABOBO FÚTBOL CLUB VALENCIA

Foundation date: July 24, 1964
Address: Avenida Bolívar Norte, Valencia
Stadium: Estadio "Misael Delgado", Valencia – Capacity: 10,000

THE SQUAD

	DOB	Ape M	Ape G	Cla M	Cla G
Goalkeepers:					
Joel Graterol	13.02.1997			1	-
José Leonardo Morales Lares	07.07.1978	16	-	16	-
Rafael Quiñones	04.11.1995	1	-	1	-
Defenders:					
Martín Germán Alberich (ARG)	19.05.1989			7	-
José Jesús Acosta Amaiz	28.11.1989	11	-	14	-
Eduard Alexander Bello Gil	20.08.1995	2	-	11	2
Giovanny Dolguetta	28.09.1994	-	-	1	-
Alejandro Fuenmayor	29.08.1996	1	-	3	-
Raudy Javier Guerrero Reyes	19.11.1993	7	-	5	-
Joaquín Adán Lencinas (ARG)	11.05.1988			7	1
Diego Osio	03.01.1997	1	-	-	-
Edwin Peraza Lárez	11.03.1993	16	-		
José Gregorio Peraza	14.04.1994	10	-	14	-
Jorge Enrique Trejo Quintero	29.08.1986	8	-	5	-
Midfielders:					
Mijaíl Alexander Avilés Flores	05.06.1987	10	-	1	-
Juan Carlos Azócar Segura	04.10.1995			8	-
José Balza				1	-
Gleider Caro	17.06.1988	9	1	1	-
Luis Enríque del Pino Mago	15.09.1994			5	-
Robert Alexander Garcés Sánchez	05.04.1993			13	1
Diego Leonardo García Veneri	05.08.1993	15	3	13	2
Luis Jiménez Vivas	28.12.1995	-	-	6	-
José Nicolás Márquez Torres	21.02.1996			2	1
Víctor Alfonso Pérez Zabala	14.02.1990	15	1	3	-
Jesús Alexi Quintero Briceño	13.02.1984	16	1	15	1
José Ramón Reyes Marín	08.11.1994	1	-	-	-
Hermes Aristóteles Romero	18.10.1995	7	1	-	-
Sleyker Alexander Schoonewolff Orozco	16.09.1996	-	-	1	-
Luis Roberto Seijas Gunther	09.04.1989	16	-	17	1
Carlos Adrián Súarez Váldez	26.04.1992	16	2	14	1
Forwards:					
Cristián Alessandrini (ARG)	27.05.1985			9	5
Daniel Enrique Arismendi Marchan	04.07.1982	17	2	5	-
Gustavo González	20.02.1996	13	1	11	1
Javier Andres Jaramillo Rivas	13.08.1996	4	-	-	-
Ángel Nieves		9	1	11	-
Aquiles David Ocanto Querales	18.11.1988	17	6	13	3
Billy David José Palencia Graterol	21.08.1993			3	-
Trainer:					
Jhonny Ferreira [as of 07.06.2013]		17			

CARACAS FÚTBOL CLUB

Foundation date: Ocotober 3, 1989
Address: Cocodrilos Sports Park, Cota 905, Ofoconas del Caracas FC, Caracas
Stadium: Estadio Olímpico de la Universidad Central de Venezuela, Caracas – Capacity: 23,000

THE SQUAD	DOB	Ape		Cla	
		M	G	M	G
Goalkeepers:					
Alain Baroja Méndez	23.10.1989	15	-	16	-
Beycker Eduardo Velásquez	06.10.1996	-	-	-	-
Yhonathan Yustiz	27.01.1992	3	-	1	-
Defenders:					
Marcelo Barreña (ARG)	13.02.1987			11	-
Jesús Blanco	30.11.1994	-	-	-	-
Francisco Carabalí Terán	24.02.1991	13	1	9	-
Eduardo González	25.05.1994			4	-
Carlos Alfredo Hernández Pérez	10.10.1990			1	-
Rubert José Quijada Fasciana	10.02.1989	12	-	16	2
Andrés Elionai Sánchez León	12.12.1987	10	1	16	1
Víctor Manuel Sifontes Antequera	21.10.1993	2	-	3	1
Jefre José Vargas Belisario	29.04.1991	9	-	13	-
Midfielders:					
Ricardo Andreutti Jordán	30.06.1987	17	2	16	-
Felix Manuel Cásseres	13.06.1987	-	-	9	1
Juan Carlos Castellanos Anuel	30.10.1995	1	-		
Giácomo di Georgi Zerill	24.02.1981	15	1	14	-
Diomar Ángel Díaz Calderón	07.03.1990			11	-
Cristian Leonardo Flores Calderón	02.04.1988	10	-	12	-
Leonardo Flores	05.08.1995	4	-	4	-
Robert Alexander Garcés Sánchez	05.04.1993	5	1		
Luis González	22.12.1990	14	1		
Miguel Ángel Mea Vitali	19.02.1981	15	5	15	1
Rómulo Otero Vásquez	09.11.1992	14	6	8	2
Leomar José Pinto Blanco	17.03.1997	4	1	2	-
Daniel Alessandro Saggiomo Mosquera	07.02.1998	1	-	1	-
Roberto Raúl Tucker (ARG)	27.06.1983	16	2		
Wuiliyhon Vivas Trejo	29.09.1993	4	-		
Forwards:					
Fabián Bordagaray (ARG)	15.02.1987			14	1
Jhonder Leonel Cadíz Fernández	29.07.1995	16	3	16	3
Dany Curé	07.04.1990	13	-	9	-
Edder José Farías	12.04.1988	14	6	17	11
Omar Alfonso Perdomo Teheran	03.02.1993	10	2		
Trainer:					
Eduardo José Saragó Carbón [as of 01.07.2013]	11.01.1982	17		17	

CLUB DEPORTIVO LARA BARQUISIMETO

Foundation date: 2006
Address: Avenida Libertador entre Calles 36 y 38, Oficinas del Domo Bolivariano, Barquisimeto, Estado Lara.
Stadium: Estadio Metropolitano de Fútbol de Lara, Barquisimeto – Capacity: 40,312

THE SQUAD

	DOB	Ape		Cla	
		M	G	M	G
Goalkeepers:					
David Ricardo González Herrera	24.03.1986	15	-	17	-
Eduardo José Herrera Alvarado	06.06.1993	2	-	-	-
Defenders:					
Joel Fernando Cáceres Álvarez	15.02.1993	8	1	9	-
Jhon Chancellor	02.01.1992	15	2	15	2
Luis Enrique Colmenarez Gutiérrez	26.09.1988	10	-	2	-
Henry Pernía	09.11.1990	8	-	10	1
José Manuel Rey Cortegoso	20.05.1975	13	-	8	-
Edgardo Rito	17.02.1996	2	-	-	-
Mikel Villanueva Álvarez	14.04.1993	2	-	14	4
Midfielders:					
Daniel José Carrillo Montilla	02.12.1995	1	-	3	1
Oswaldo José Chaurant Arreaza	27.05.1984	14	-	10	-
Juan Carlos Colina Silva	21.10.1986	12	-	13	-
Marlon Antonio Fernández Jiménez	16.01.1986	16	4	3	-
César Iván González Torres	10.10.1987			17	-
Juan Francisco Guerra Piñero	16.02.1987	10	-		
José Luis Marrufo Jiménez	12.05.1996	7	1	5	-
Junior Leonardo Moreno Borrero	20.07.1993	10	-	16	1
Edgar Fernando Pérez Greco	16.02.1982	17	7		
Vicente Antonio Suanno Rodríguez	01.01.1983	9	-	1	-
Ángel Ernesto Urdaneta Buenaño	01.06.1990	4	1	2	-
Ely Antonio Valderrey Medino	29.04.1986			10	-
Renzo José Zambrano	26.08.1994	7	-	15	1
Forwards:					
José Enrique Caraballo Rosal	21.02.1996	11	-	14	1
Heiber Eduardo Díaz Tovar	11.10.1984	9	1	16	7
Darwin de Jesús Gómez Rivas	24.10.1991			12	-
Armando Rafael Maita Urbáez	26.08.1991	15	5	7	1
Léinner Pérez	17.02.1994	4	-	-	-
José Rafael Romo Pérez	06.12.1993	15	2	13	1
Aníbal José Rosales Heregua	29.02.1996	2	-	6	2
Trainer:					
Rafael Edgar Dudamel Ochoa [as of 17.12.2013]	07.01.1973	17		17	

DEPORTIVO ANZOÁTEGUI SPORT CLUB PUERTO LA CRUZ

Foundation date: November 9, 2002

Address: Avenida Américo Vespucio CC Casablanca, of. 6, Lechería, Puerto Ordaz, Estado Anzoátegui

Stadium: Estadio „José Antonio Anzoátegui", Puerto La Cruz – Capacity: 38,000

THE SQUAD					
	DOB	**Ape**		**Cla**	
		M	**G**	**M**	**G**
Goalkeepers:					
Cristhian Flores	06.09.1990	-	-		
Edixson Antonio González Peroza	13.01.1990	16	-	11	-
Richard Alejandro Ruíz Ruíz	28.07.1988	1	-	2	-
César Vásquez				5	-
Defenders:					
Diego Jesús Araguainamo Guacarán	29.09.1994	10	-	11	1
Richard Emmanuel Badillo Pérez	24.09.1989	9	-	13	1
Luis José Caraballo Gamboa	17.07.1996	2	-	-	-
William Alexander Díaz Gutiérrez	31.03.1985	15	2	17	-
Juan José Fuenmayor Núñez	05.09.1979	12	-	14	1
Edgar José Mendoza Acosta	15.06.1991	11	-	4	-
Johnny Jair Mirabal Arboleda	30.06.1990	10	-	16	-
Frederick Rojas				1	-
Midfielders:					
Emanuel Calzadilla	17.02.1993	8	-	4	-
Luis Enríque del Pino Mago	15.09.1994	3	-		
Rolando Emilio Escobar Batista (PAN)	24.10.1981	11	6	13	4
Manuel Fuentes				11	2
Ronald Germán Giraldo Sánchez	16.08.1983	2	-	4	1
Jhonny José Francisco González Barreto	09.08.1979			12	3
Evelio De Jesús Hernández Guedez	18.06.1984	16	2	12	-
Robert Enrique Hernández Aguado	14.09.1993	14	1	1	-
Leopoldo Rafael Jiménez González	22.05.1978	5	-	2	-
Gian Franco Lettieri de Paula	21.07.1994			1	-
Manuel Moisés Medori Martínez	08.02.1991	4	-		
José David Moreno Chacón	31.10.1982	9	-	14	3
Ricardo Manuel Cardoso Martins (POR)	24.01.1990	16	1	16	-
David Alejandro Zalzman	04.03.1996	6	-	10	-
Forwards:					
Edwin Enrique Aguilar Samaniego	07.08.1985	17	13	14	10
Gregory Josué Araque Molina	13.03.1997	1	-	3	1
Manuel Alejandro Arteaga Rubianes	17.06.1994	10	1		
Oscar Alberto Briceño Bueno	06.09.1985	10	1	9	-
Luis José Castillo Patiño	27.02.1992	4	-	12	3
Yohan Cumana	08.03.1996	7	-	-	-
Ever Rodríguez Moreno (COL)	02.08.1991			2	-
Alexander José Rondón Heredia	30.08.1977	5	-	4	-
Trainer:					
Dickson Ruberth Morán Puelo [as of 01.07.2014]	11.08.1973	17		17	

DEPORTIVO LA GUAIRA CARACAS

Foundation date: 2008
Address: Calle La Cinta, Complejo Deportivo Fray Luis, Piso 1, Oficina 02, Caracas
Stadium: Estadio Nacional "Brígido Iriarte", Caracas – Capacity: 12,500

THE SQUAD

	DOB	Ape		Cla	
		M	G	M	G
Goalkeepers:					
Luis Carlos Rojas	30.04.1988	8	-	4	-
Renny Vicente Vega Hernández	04.07.1979	9	-	13	-
Defenders:					
Daniel Eduardo Benítez Pernía	23.09.1987	5	-	13	-
Antonio José Boada Figueroa	17.08.1981	10	-	10	-
Edwar Segundo Bracho Suárez	05.01.1987	10	-	14	-
Pablo Jesús Camacho Figueira	12.12.1990	8	-	4	-
John Chacón				1	-
Francisco Chávez	14.02.1987	1	-	-	-
José Luis Granados Asprilla	22.10.1986			5	1
Óscar Constantino González	25.02.1992	17	2	13	-
Athony Graterol	27.02.1995	8	-	6	-
Franklin José Lucena Peña	20.02.1981	17	2	10	5
Luis Alfonso Morgillo Marrero	15.06.1993	6	-	5	-
César Eduardo Pérez Cumaná	12.05.1993			1	-
Midfielders:					
Arquímedes José Figuera Salazar	06.10.1989	16	2	15	-
Javier Alfonso García	22.04.1987	15	2	14	2
Darwin Jesús González Mendoza	20.05.1994			2	2
Luis González	22.12.1990			12	1
Diego Alejandro Guerrero Corredor	26.06.1986	1	-	3	-
Enson Jesús Rodríguez Mesa	05.09.1989	7	-		
Gabriel Rosa	15.07.1993	1	-	-	-
Luciano Nahuel Ursino Pegolo (ARG)	31.10.1988	16	3	16	2
Yanko Vagovits Suárez	02.02.1996	1	-	2	-
Ely Antonio Valderrey Medino	29.04.1986	8	1		
Forwards:					
Fredys Enrique Arrieta Fontalvo (COL)	20.08.1985			17	7
Néstor Eduardo Canelón Gil	19.08.1991	2	-	-	-
Armando José Carrillo Dangond (COL)	03.11.1985	14	1		
Heatklif Rafael Castillo Delgado	28.11.1979	3	1	-	-
Imanol Iriberri (ARG)	04.03.1987	16	7	16	-
Charlis José Ortíz García	21.07.1986	13	-	10	1
Adalberto Peñaranda Maestre	31.05.1997	11	2	8	1
Edgar Fernando Pérez Greco	16.02.1982			13	-
Julio Armando Ruíz Bolívar	26.01.1996			1	-
Framber Johan Villegas Sangronis	24.02.1986	14	1	9	1
Trainer:					
Leonardo Alberto González Antequera [as of 01.07.2014]	14.07.1972	17		17	

DEPORTIVO PETARE FÚTBOL CLUB CARACAS

Foundation date: August 18, 1948
Address: Calle El Río con Avenida Las Palamas, Edificio Melvin, Boleita Sur, Caracas
Stadium: Estadio Olímpico de la Universidad Central de Venezuela, Caracas – Capacity: 23,000

THE SQUAD					
	DOB	Ape		Cla	
		M	G	M	G
Goalkeepers:					
Keiner Escorcia Ramírez	11.07.1995	-	-	-	-
Eduardo Luis Lima Prado	09.08.1992	10	-		
Giancarlo Schiavone Modica	02.11.1993	7	-	17	-
Defenders:					
Darío Bastardo		9	-	12	-
Henry Leonardo Bautista Blanco	29.08.1983	13	-	17	-
Gabriel Alejandro Benítez D'Andrea	30.09.1993			5	-
Néstor José Gabriel Cova Meneses	02.05.1995			11	1
Jhon Freddy Palacios Ramírez	23.01.1983	13	1		
Juan Pablo Rodríguez Rodríguez	12.05.1994	5	-	5	-
Alexander José Sandoval Hernández	20.11.1988			1	-
Joseph Bryan Sosa Lozano	13.07.1992	15	1	15	-
Leonardo Javier Terán Balaustren	09.03.1993	8	-	16	-
Midfielders:					
Rafael Daniel Arace Gargaro	22.05.1995	14	-	14	-
Francisco Humberto Aristeguieta	01.10.1988	14	-		
Guillermo José Banquez Almario	24.02.1989	15	1		
Cristian Augusto Bravo Sandoval	28.04.1992			7	-
Juan Carlos Castellanos Anuel	30.10.1995			4	-
David Francisco Centeno Bracho	10.04.1992	16	1		
Cristhian Hereira	12.08.1994	3	-	5	-
Richard Yohans López Salas	22.07.1990	6	-	3	-
Luis Alberto Martínez Zapata	07.09.1984	-	-	2	-
Carlos Raúl Pineda González	30.05.1990			5	-
Michel David Quintero García	09.07.1996	2	-	-	-
Alejandro Jávier Valldeperas Pazmiño	09.03.1991	10	-	16	-
Wuiliyhon Vivas Trejo	29.09.1993			14	-
Forwards:					
Franco Renato Arévalo Guerrero	10.01.1990			8	-
José Luís Cassiani Díaz	14.12.1990			4	1
Néstor José Colina Urbáez	18.03.1996	1	-	-	-
Emilio Manuel Garcés Sánchez	30.05.1984	6	-	2	-
Héctor Griders García Mata	19.09.1988	10	-	11	1
Darwin de Jesús Gómez Rivas	24.10.1991	16	2		
Jacobo Salvador Kouffati	30.06.1993	13	1	16	1
Byron Stefano Olaya Morello	12.09.1994			1	-
Juan Carlos Parada	08.03.1988	10	-	15	2
Genlis Alberto Piñeros Novoa	06.07.1989	9	-	12	1
José Francisco Torres Briceño	19.06.1993	11	-		
Trainer:					
Jhon Giraldo [as of 01.07.2014]		17			

DEPORTIVO TÁCHIRA FÚTBOL CLUB SAN CRISTÓBAL

Foundation date: January 1, 1974
Address: Calle 14, entre carreras 20 y 21, N° 20-95, Quinta Chelita, Barrio Obrero, San Cristóbal, Estado Táchira
Stadium: Estadio Polideportivo de Pueblo Nuevo, San Cristóbal – Capacity: 40,500

THE SQUAD

	DOB	Ape		Cla*	
		M	G	M	G
Goalkeepers:					
Andrés Colmenares Sanabria	08.02.1997			-	-
José David Contreras Verna	20.10.1994	15	-	3	-
Alan José Liebeskind Díaz	07.01.1985			16	-
Yerikson Alexander Murillo Rosas	25.09.1994	2	-	-	-
Defenders:					
Wilker José Ángel Romero	18.03.1993	17	3	18	1
Carlos Javier López (ARG)	19.03.1980			18	-
Carlos Javier Lujano Sánchez	14.07.1991	4	-	10	-
Yuber Antonio Mosquera Perea	31.08.1984	16	-	17	1
Carlos Gregorio Rivero González	27.11.1992	17	-	5	-
Carlos Alfredo Salazar Cumaná	15.05.1989	-	-	1	-
Midfielders:					
Carlos Eduardo Cermeño Uzcategui	08.08.1995	10	-	15	-
Gerzon Armando Chacón Varela	27.10.1980	14	-	17	1
Agnel José Flores Hernández	29.05.1989	12	-	13	-
Francisco Javier Flores Sequera	30.04.1990	13	-	8	-
César Eduardo González Amais	01.10.1982	16	6	15	7
Juan Carlos Mora Velasco	01.05.1994			5	-
Marcelo Alexander Moreno Borrero	03.09.1994	1	-	3	-
Yohandry José Orozco Cujía	19.03.1991	16	1	18	2
Jorge Alberto Rojas Méndez	01.10.1977			17	7
Marcos Anibal Sánchez Mullins (PAN)	23.12.1989	7	-		
José Luis Tancredi Malatez (URU)	14.02.1983	14	1		
Jhoan Vargas	06.08.1995			-	-
Romeri Villamizar	06.06.1995	3	-	1	-
Forwards:					
Juan Carlos Azócar Segura	01.10.1995	2	-		
Ronaldo Chacón	18.02.1998	1	-	-	-
José Ali Meza Draegertt	17.04.1991	16	-	15	1
Pablo Fernando Olivera Fernández (URU)	08.12.1987			9	2
Ángel Arturo Osorio Meza	02.01.1990	11	3	6	-
José Miguel Reyes Marín	19.09.1992	16	2	15	5
Gelmin Javier Rivas Boada	23.03.1989	13	7	18	13
Trainer:					
Daniel Alejandro Farías Acosta [as of 01.01.2013]	28.09.1981	17		19	

**Please note: matches and goals in Championship Finals included*

ESTUDIANTES DE MÉRIDA FÚTBOL CLUB

Foundation date: April 14, 1971
Address: Avenida Urdaneta con calle 51, N° 3-14, Edificio Confirmerca, PB. Mérida, Estado Mérida
Stadium: Estadio Olímpico Metropolitano de Mérida, Mérida – Capacity: 42,500

THE SQUAD

	DOB	Ape		Cla	
		M	G	M	G
Goalkeepers:					
Alejandro Araque Peña	14.09.1995	4	-	8	-
Ángel Javier Hernández Gómez	01.07.1980	13	-	9	-
Defenders:					
Héctor Acosta	29.03.1995	8	-	16	-
Marlon Bastardo Castro	05.04.1991	15	1	15	-
Cristian José Bustamante Chaparro	23.09.1988	10	-	1	-
Carlos Enrique de Castro Storace (URU)	19.04.1979	16	1	3	-
Atahualpa Gabriel González Lanz (CRC)	04.05.1977			11	1
Richard Lobo	19.07.1994			1	-
Ángel Emilio Ojeda Pinto	08.07.1982	16	1	10	-
Ronald Steve Ramírez Molina	29.12.1987			3	-
Rubén Rivas		2	-	-	-
Manuel Bernardo Rodríguez Molina	23.01.1980	13	-	3	-
Midfielders:					
Winston Alberto Azuaje Parra	06.04.1993	14	1	12	-
Luis Alexis Barrios Rojas	19.05.1994	10	-	16	1
Luis Blanco Brito	28.02.1993	9	1	17	2
Silvio Briceño				7	-
Javier Ali Guillén Salazar	05.01.1993	16	2	12	-
Oscar Alberto Guillén Contreras	17.05.1995	10	-	14	-
Omar Alberto Labrador Gutíerrez	18.02.1992	3	-	6	-
Yorwin De Jesús Lobo Peña	26.07.1993	-	-		
Rodrigo Morales	05.08.1994	1	-	-	-
Jesús Alejandro Quintero Pérez	21.04.1994	12	1	17	1
Wislintos Rentería Menas	19.06.1984	12	-	8	-
Luis Rivas	09.04.1994	2	-	1	-
Forwards:					
César Augusto Alzate Mesa (COL)	30.09.1989			16	5
Jhon Fernández	29.03.1995	1	-	1	-
Over Felipe García Torres	16.06.1992	17	5	17	9
Jesús Alberto González Quijada	27.08.1987	16	5		
Edixon Mena	19.07.1996	11	-	3	-
Mario Mosquera	23.03.1992	3	-	5	-
Yan Alexander Salazar Marín	18.04.1988	-	-		
Trainer:					
José Francisco Moreno [as of 28.01.2014]		17		17	

METROPOLITANOS FÚTBOL CLUB CARACAS

Foundation date: August 3, 2011

Address: *Not known*

Stadium: Estadio Nacional "Brígido Iriarte", Caracas – Capacity: 12,500

THE SQUAD	DOB	Ape		Cla	
		M	G	M	G
Goalkeepers:					
Yáñez Alexis Angulo Vallejo	21.02.1984			2	-
Víctor Antulio Rivero García	13.02.1980	7	-		
Javier Eduardo Toyo Barcenas	12.10.1977	11	-	15	-
Defenders:					
César Aponte	07.09.1993	1	-	-	-
John Deyvis Ariza Cuello	31.01.1990	7	-	7	-
Gabriel José Boggio Bernal	19.04.1993			11	1
Pascual Calderaro		8	1	3	-
Gabriel Darío Díaz Valdiviezo (ARG)	02.07.1987	5	-		
Javier Alejandro Maldonado Manzini	09.04.1994	5	-	-	-
David Andrew McIntosh Parra	17.02.1973	16	1	16	-
Rafael Loreto Mea Vitali	16.02.1975	9	-	1	-
John Freddy Palacios Ramírez	23.01.1983			13	-
Rennier Alexander Rodríguez González	25.03.1984	10	-	-	-
Carlos Verdú	23.02.1986	12	-	8	1
Juan Pablo Villarroel di Parsia	13.09.1991	7	-	16	-
Midfielders:					
Anderson Johan Arciniegas Torres	07.12.1986	8	1	8	-
Francisco Humberto Aristeguieta Bernardini	01.11.1988			12	-
Guillermo José Banquez Almario	24.02.1989			14	2
Andrés Leonardo Benítez	22.03.1996	5	-	1	-
Daniel Blanco	25.05.1990	11	-	4	-
Engelberth Jose Briceño Avendaño	02.04.1984	10	-	9	-
Jonathan Cabrera				5	-
Jorge Francisco Casanova Canchila	06.07.1984	6	-	1	-
David Francisco Centeno Bracho	10.04.1992			16	3
Sebastián Contreras (ARG)	05.04.1990			13	2
Josué Esqueche		1	-	-	-
Danyelo Esquivel		4	-	10	-
Nelson Hernández	11.02.1993	12	-	4	-
Wuiswell Anderson Isea Fernández	13.09.1982	2	-		
Rodolfo Méndez				2	-
Andrés Gerardo Quintero Vargas	20.06.1989	12	1	3	-
Jorge Alberto Rojas Méndez	01.10.1977	17	7		
Forwards:					
Sergio Nicolás Bubas (ARG)	23.04.1989	17	1		
Armando José Carrillo Dangond (COL)	03.11.1985			17	10
Cristian Alfonso Cásseres Cáceres	29.06.1977	8	2		
Guillermo Orlando Fernández Gagliardi	21.01.1988	6	-	-	-
Omar Alfonso Perdomo Teheran	03.02.1993			4	-
José Antonio Torrealba Acevedo	13.06.1980			15	1
Diego Valdés Giraldo (COL)	29.01.1991			8	1
Trainer:					
Hugo Savarese [as of 01.07.2014]		17		17	

ASOCIACIÓN CIVIL CLUB DEPORTIVO MINEROS DE GUAYANA PUERTO ORDAZ

Foundation date: November 20, 1981
Address: Urbanización Mendoza, Calle Jusepín, Puerto Ordaz, Estado Bolívar
Stadium: Centro Total de Entretenimiento Cachamay, Puerto Ordaz – Capacity: 41,600

THE SQUAD

	DOB	Ape		Cla	
		M	G	M	G
Goalkeepers:					
Eduardo Luis Lima Prado	09.08.1992			-	-
Tito Daniel Rojas Rojas	11.10.1987	4	-		
Luis Enrique Romero Durán	16.11.1990	1	-	6	-
Rafael Enrique Romo Pérez	25.02.1990	12	-	11	-
Defenders:					
Gabriel Alejandro Cichero Konarek	25.04.1984	12	-	9	4
Edixon Vladimir Cuevas Tirado	25.05.1979			13	1
Atahualpa Gabriel González Lanz (CRC)	04.05.1977	1	-		
Arnoldo López	24.11.1994	11	1	13	-
Julio César Machado Cesario	19.06.1982	14	-	13	2
Anthony Matos	10.06.1995	1	-	14	-
Luis Alejandro Parra	15.12.1996	1	-	-	-
Enrique Andrés Rouga Rossi	02.03.1982	7	-	-	-
Luis José Vallenilla Pacheco	13.03.1974	16	2	11	1
José Manuel Velázquez Rodríguez	08.09.1990	11	-	7	-
Midfielders:					
Rafael Eduardo Acosta Cammarota	13.02.1989	9	1	9	-
Overath Breitner da Silva Medina	09.11.1989	16	1		
Alberto Cabello	27.01.1985	10	2	14	3
Édson Castillo	18.05.1994	11	-	7	-
Álvaro Castro	07.02.1994			6	1
Ángel Antonio Chourio Galíndez	04.05.1985	3	-		
Orlando José Cordero Zambrano	24.10.1984	4	1	-	-
Luis Guerra	20.11.1996	10	1	10	1
Edgar Hernán Jiménez González	19.10.1994	14	-	10	-
José Manuel Nájera Ríos (COL)	03.09.1988			3	-
José Gregorio Navarro	02.04.1995			-	-
Louis Ángelo Peña Puentes	25.12.1989	12	1	15	1
Ebby José Pérez Acero	01.03.1991			10	-
Andrés David Sampedro Salazar	12.05.1995	10	-	4	-
Forwards:					
Richard José Blanco Delgado	21.01.1982	14	6	11	1
James Fernando Cabezas Mairongo (COL)	15.06.1984			14	1
Víctor Díaz	23.06.1995	3	-	-	-
Juan José Morales (ARG)	23.03.1982	5	-		
Abraham Moreno		1	-	-	-
Alfredo Navarro	04.08.1986	1	-	-	-
Rubén Rojas	03.07.1992	14	1	12	1
Zamir Valoyes Naboyán	16.03.1986	10	3	16	7
Trainer:					
Richard Alfred Mayela Páez Monzón [10.12.2012-12.09.2014]	31.12.1953	5			
Marcos Mathías [12.09.2014-15.03.2015]	12.05.1970	12		10	
Antonio Franco [as of 16.03.2015]				7	

LLANEROS DE GUANARE FÚTBOL CLUB

Foundation date: August 26, 1984
Address: Avenida José María Vargas, Guanare
Stadium: Estadio „Rafael Calles Pinto“, Guanare – Capacity: 13,000

THE SQUAD

	DOB	Ape M	Ape G	Cla M	Cla G
Goalkeepers:					
Ánibal Bassano (ARG)	21.06.1991	1	-		
Pedro Alejandro Caraballo Ordaz	10.04.1990	4	-	-	-
Cristhian Flores	06.09.1990			3	-
Johel Semidey	13.08.1993	12	-	14	-
Defenders:					
Franko Mauricio Díaz Graterol	06.02.1996	10	-	-	-
Gilber José Guerra Guedez	02.04.1993	4	-	12	-
Jesseuf Gregmar Guzmán Hernández	09.07.1993			5	-
José María Hernández	04.04.1994	1	-		
Douglas Julio	20.04.1993	-	-	10	-
Charles Martínez	30.01.1987	9	1	3	-
Anderson Rafael Orozco Torres	26.02.1984	7	-	14	-
Alexander José Osorio Meza	23.11.1991	9	1	13	-
Anahan Pacheco				2	-
Gilberto Piñero	28.03.1996	2	-	3	-
Nolberto Riascos Segura	17.02.1984	16	-	15	2
Adrián Rodríguez	20.05.1991	4	-	9	-
Darvis Rodríguez	01.07.1994	7	1	-	-
Luis Emilio Sampedro Salazar	10.09.1991	1	-		
Midfielders:					
David Nicolás Altuna (ARG)	22.01.1990	1	-		
Numan Andueza Ramirez				1	-
Jesús Cedeño	16.01.1993	8	1	11	1
Jan Bryan Contreras Soto	21.07.1991			8	2
Carlos Enrique Fernández Carico	01.09.1990	13	-	5	-
Luís Alfredo García Urbano	21.07.1983	8	-	15	2
Freddy Andrey González Sosa	02.10.1993	2	-	-	-
Dhylam Hernández	15.03.1996	1	-	1	-
Junior Alexander Monsalve Miranda	17.01.1994	7	1	6	-
Juan Carlos Mora Velasco	01.05.1994	11	-		
Ronald Erickson Mora	27.08.1983	11	1	17	1
Jonathan Di Marco Rios	19.10.1989	10	-	-	-
José Francisco Torres Briceño	19.06.1993			16	1
Jhoan Vargas	06.08.1995	4	-		-
Forwards:					
Armando José Araque Peña	06.03.1989			12	2
Jesús Hernández	06.01.1993	15	2	-	-
José Martínez	25.02.1998	1	-	-	-
Oscar José Núñez López	12.07.1994	9	-	11	-
Jelson Jesús País Rondón	26.01.1991	7	-	-	-
Andrés Fabián Ponce Núñez	11.11.1996	9	2		
Jaime Ponce		8	2	-	-
Yanowsky Reyes	15.05.1995	10	-	11	4
Leandro Abel Vargas Cruzate	10.03.1979			17	9
Albert Jesús Zambrano Ferrer	01.10.1995	11	-		
Trainer:					
José Francisco González Quijada [01.07.-31.12.2014]	21.07.1971	17			
Fabio Espada (ARG) [01.01.2015-07.03.2015]					

PORTUGUESA FÚTBOL CLUB ACARÍGUA

Foundation date: March 2, 1987
Address: *Not known*
Stadium: Estadio "General José Antonio Páez", Acarígua – Capacity: 18,000

THE SQUAD

	DOB	Ape M	Ape G	Cla M	Cla G
Goalkeepers:					
Alan José Liebeskind Díaz	07.01.1985	15	-		
Argenis Márquez				7	-
Luigi Alfredo Palomino	06.04.1981	2	-	3	-
Eddy Vargas	21.03.1983			7	-
Defenders:					
Gabriel Alejandro Benítez D'Andrea	30.09.1993	1	-		
Luis Ángel Carrillo Campero	01.01.1988	2	-	8	1
Francisco Javier Fajardo Gil	08.07.1990			15	-
Leonardo Falcón	20.08.1988	17	-	15	-
Ángel Enrique Faría Mendoza	28.04.1983	11	-		
Daniel Linarez	23.03.1992	3	-	6	-
Jorge Luna	25.01.1994	4	1	2	-
Jorge Ortíz	23.10.1984	3	-	9	-
José Páez				7	-
Carlos Palma	28.10.1985	11	-	9	-
Carlos Torres Cuevas	24.05.1993	1	-	-	-
Dustin Alexander Váldez Atencio	21.05.1981	13	-		
Midfielders:					
Ángel Oswaldo Cassú Pérez	01.03.1993	4	-	-	-
William Francisco Colina	12.04.1987			4	-
Manuel Cuárez	04.03.1980	8	-	6	-
Heber García	27.03.1997	13	-	9	-
Rafael Augusto García Andrade	27.01.1993			2	-
Luis Andrés González González	27.06.1993	6	-	-	-
Andrés Alejandro Hernández Hernández	21.04.1993	2	-	-	-
Wuiswell Anderson Isea Fernández	13.09.1982			10	-
Bernaldo Manzano	07.06.1990	15	1	16	1
Bladimir Alejandro Morales Duarte	09.04.1983			7	-
Ricardo Piña	13.05.1996	8	-	6	-
Enson Jesús Rodríguez Mesa	05.09.1989			12	5
Alexis Saavedra	24.06.1988	14	1	1	-
Marcos Anibal Sánchez Mullins (PAN)	23.12.1989			9	-
José Torrealba		1	-	-	-
José Javier Villafraz Quintero	01.01.1980	11	1		
Víctor Alfonso Villarreal Pérez	15.09.1988			5	-
Forwards:					
Jean Carlos Alfaro Benítez	10.02.1992	1	-	1	-
Johan José Arrieche	16.07.1992			-	-
Wilber Bravo	04.12.1990	11	1	2	-
Cristian Alfonso Cásseres Cáceres	29.06.1977			15	2
Luis Escobar		1	-	-	-
Tulio Enrique Etchemaite (ARG)	10.07.1987			13	8
José Eduardo Jiménez Gómez	26.12.1993	11	2		
Raigel Alexis Márquez Nieves	04.02.1992	13	2	10	-
Ronaldo Luis Peña Vargas	10.03.1997	4	-	4	-
Cristian Sánchez				1	-
Diego Silva	11.03.1993	5	-	-	-
Guillermo Stradella (ARG)	16.09.1993	12	-	16	-
Leandro Abel Vargas Cruzate (COL)	10.03.1979	8	2		
Trainer:					
Francesco Stifano Garzone [01.07.-30.09.2014]	19.07.1979	8			
Lenín José Bastidas Bello [as of 01.10.2014]	22.09.1980	11			

TRUJILLANOS FÚTBOL CLUB VALERA

Foundation date: August 25, 1981
Address: Tienda „Gol x Gol", Centro Comerical Plaza, Edificio 2, Nivel Plaza, Local P. 102, Valera
Stadium: Estadio „José Alberto Pérez", Valera – Capacity: 20,000

THE SQUAD					
	DOB	**Ape**		**Cla***	
		M	**G**	**M**	**G**
Goalkeepers:					
Leandro Díaz Prado	09.07.1983	15	-	9	-
Roberto de Jesús Olivar Jiménez	20.01.1995	-	-	-	-
Héctor Eduardo Pérez Cuevas	16.06.1991	3	-	10	-
Defenders:					
Arnaldo del Valle Aranda Rodríguez	27.02.1982	5	-	1	-
Carlos Enrique Castro	04.12.1986	15	-	12	-
Edixon Bladimir Cuevas Tirado	20.05.1979	14	-		
Galileo Antonio Del Castillo Carrasquel	01.02.1991	7	-	12	-
Luigi José Erazo Villamizar	13.06.1988	15	-	13	-
Mayker José González Montilla	06.06.1988	12	-	14	-
Manuel Alejandro Granados Asprilla	16.02.1989	4	-	15	-
Adolfo Perozo Oberto	27.06.1989	1	-	2	-
Wilker de Jesús Terán Mendoza	04.01.1996	-	-	-	-
Erlys Jordano Vásquez Carrero	17.04.1993	3	-	-	-
Midfielders:					
Maurice Jesús Cova Sánchez	11.08.1992	16	1	16	-
Argenis José Gómez Ortega	23.11.1987	17	2	15	2
José Freddy Granados Asprilla	08.07.1995	-	-	2	-
Jarol Herrera Martínez	26.05.1984	16	2	18	2
Robert William Mejía Tejada	02.07.1994	-	-	7	-
Gerardo José Mendoza	03.01.1989	12	-	11	-
Johan José Osorio Paredes	03.09.1990	10	2	19	-
Gabriel Rivas				2	-
Luis Miguel Rivas Rodríguez	24.02.1993	2	-	4	-
Carlos José Sosa Moreno	02.08.1995	8	-	13	2
Raúl Antonio Vallona Espinoza	07.09.1984	10	1	14	1
Forwards:					
Sergio Alberto Alvarez Castellano	18.01.1991	15	4	19	3
Irwin Rafael Antón Barroso	10.01.1988	3	1	8	-
José Manuel Araujo	16.01.1994	-	-	2	-
Fredys Enrique Arrieta Fontalvo (COL)	20.08.1985	16	3		
James Fernando Cabezas Mairongo (COL)	15.06.1984	16	10		
Danilo Gambín	15.07.1995	-	-	5	-
Elioscar Lizardo				2	1
Alfredo Antonio Padilla Gutiérrez (COL)	29.07.1989			15	4
Jorge Luis Ruíz	10.01.1989			4	-
Trainer:					
Horacio Ignacio Matuszyczk (ARG)	29.11.1961	17		19	

**Please note: matches and goals in Championship Finals included*

TUCANES DE AMAZONAS FÚTBOL CLUB PUERTO AYACUCHO

Foundation date: 2008
Address: *Not known*
Stadium: Estadio "Antonio José de Sucre", Puerto Ayacucho – Capacity: 10,000

THE SQUAD					
	DOB	Ape		Cla	
		M	G	M	G
Goalkeepers:					
Carlos Alberto Salazar Lugo	20.08.1980	17	-	16	-
Víctor Antulio Rivero García	13.02.1980			1	-
Luis Alberto Terán Guzmán	14.08.1993	-	-		
Defenders:					
Willkhei Acuña Gonzales	23.06.1993			2	-
Javier Enrique Bolivar Quiñones	10.05.1993	14	-	6	-
Leminger Bolivar	18.02.1990	12	-	15	-
Robert Humberto Díaz Villazana	01.02.1993	5	-	10	-
Frank Nedu Ejiofor (NGA)	01.02.1994	4	-	5	-
Orlando José Galindo Seijas	02.10.1985			2	-
Yersón Javier Payema Guarula	23.09.1992	6	-	5	-
Orlando Pérez Cortes	22.01.1984	15	-	14	-
Frank José Presilla Suniaga	28.07.1982	11	-	12	-
Víctor José Valera Pineda	09.09.1984	12	1	16	-
Midfielders:					
Horacio Sebastián Cárdenas Gonzáles	01.07.1994	10	1	7	2
Sergio Sael Golindano Hernández	13.02.1990	17	6	15	-
Umáwali Liborio Guarulla Campos	19.08.1987	10	-	6	-
José Santana Gutiérrez Carreño	15.03.1993	3	-	13	2
Yaniel Hernández	10.06.1997	13	-		
Manuel Moisés Medori Martínez	08.02.1991			7	-
Jackson Muñoz	01.07.1992	12	-	8	1
Kizito Chinonye Obi (NGA)	20.07.1991	16	-	13	-
José Francisco Parada Bonifaz	22.09.1987	13	2	-	-
Hermes Santiago Saliyas Viera	12.02.1993	1	-	-	-
Osmar Alexander Saliyas Viera	12.07.1995	4	-	8	-
José Segura				1	-
Nelson Rolando Suárez Chávez	23.03.1983			4	-
José Gregorio Tividor	01.03.1996	4	-	1	-
Forwards:					
Jhefrey Antonio Araca Salas	1995			1	-
Ever Eleazar Espinoza	16.02.1985	3	-	-	-
Kleudes Karlee García Ramos	31.07.1987			11	-
Ricardo Márquez				9	-
Eliecer Yovanny Mina Arrollo	20.06.1991	7	1	3	-
Kéiner Daniel Pérez Álvarez	08.05.1992	5	1	8	1
Rolando Andrés Ramírez Pizarro	11.01.1988	8	-	2	-
Edgar José Rito Manzanilla	20.06.1988			5	-
Gilson José Salazar Rodríguez	23.01.1989	14	4	11	-
Trainer:					
Jorge Pérez [07.07.-31.12.2014]		17			
Darío Martínez [as of 01.01.2015]				17	

ZAMORA FÚTBOL CLUB BARINAS

Foundation date: February 2, 1977
Address: Barinas 5201, Estado Barinas
Stadium: Estadio „Agustín Tovar", Barinas – Capacity: 27,500

THE SQUAD

	DOB	Ape M	Ape G	Cla M	Cla G
Goalkeepers:					
Álvaro Antonio Forero Rojas	19.12.1991	15	-	11	-
Edward Ibarbo Cadena	03.12.1986	2	-	2	-
Luis Alberto Terán Guzmán	14.08.1993			4	-
Defenders:					
Yordani José Abreu Chourio	27.10.1988	10	-	4	-
Henry Humberto Alzolay Danields	04.06.1993	5	-	-	-
Ángel Enrique Faría Mendoza	28.04.1983			15	-
Moises de Jesús Galezo Villalobos	19.03.1981	12	1	9	1
Ymmer Eliécer González Alseco	08.03.1982	-	-	6	-
Carlos Javier López (ARG)	19.03.1980	8	2		
Edson Jesús Mendoza Tablante	07.02.1993	12	2	-	-
Edwin Peraza Lárez	11.03.1993			10	1
Dustin Alexander Váldez Atencio	21.05.1981			13	-
Rosmel Gabriel Villanueva Parra	16.08.1992	1	-	-	-
Midfielders:					
Jhoan Manuel Arenas Delgado (COL)	16.01.1990	14	1	13	-
Santiago Leonardo Bello Mosteiro	20.05.1984			8	2
Arles Eduardo Flores Crespo	12.04.1991	16	-	15	2
Yaniel Hernández				4	-
Yorwin Lobo	26.07.1993			1	-
César Enrique Martínez Quintero	30.09.1991	8	-	3	2
Luis Carlos Melo Salcedo	18.08.1991	9	-	9	-
Johan Orlando Moreno Vivas	10.06.1991	16	3	7	3
Yordan Hernándo Osorio Paredes	10.05.1994	7	-	12	1
Luis Carlos Ovalle Victoria (PAN)	07.09.1988	11	-	13	1
Gustavo Andrés Páez Martínez	18.04.1990			11	2
Edwin Johán Sierra Rojas	19.04.1993	1	-	-	-
Yeferson Julio Soteldo Martínez	30.06.1996	9	-	14	1
José Daniel Soto Montero	18.05.1994	1	-	-	-
José Angel Torres Rattis	11.01.1988	14	1	5	-
Luis Humberto Vargas Archila	08.01.1988	12	1	14	1
Layneker Evelio Zafra Martínez	23.05.1986	3	-		
Forwards:					
Boris Xavier Alfaro Chong (PAN)	29.10.1988	6	-		
Anthony Miguel Blondell Blondell	17.05.1994	14	2	5	1
Ricardo Clarke (PAN)	27.09.1992	-	-	6	1
Erickson Yirson Gallardo Toro	19.06.1993	3	-	-	-
Domingo Andrés Medina Contreras	11.02.1993	5	-	-	-
John Eduardo Murillo Romaña	21.11.1995	10	2	12	6
Pierre Alexandre Pluchino Galuppo	23.01.1989	7	4	11	3
Eduardo José Sosa Vega	20.06.1996	4	-	-	-
Trainer:					
Juvencio José Betancourt Flores [01.07.-30.09.2014]	23.03.1972	8			
Julio Alberto Quintero [as of 01.10.2014]	31.10.1964	9			

ZULIA FÚTBOL CLUB MARACAIBO

Foundation date: January 16, 2005
Address: C.C Montielco, piso 12 oficina 1-2, Maracaibo
Stadium: Estadio Olímpico „José Encarnación 'Pachencho' Romero", Maracaibo – Capacity: 38,000

THE SQUAD

	DOB	Ape		Cla	
		M	G	M	G
Goalkeepers:					
Luis Eduardo Curiel Riera	28.06.1989	16	-	1	-
Jesús Alfredo Escalona Campos	15.02.1992	1	-	-	-
Xoger Jesús Requena Rangel	19.12.1994	-	-	-	-
Tito Daniel Rojas Rojas	11.10.1987			17	-
Defenders:					
Kerwis Arcides Chirinos Sánchez	25.05.1985	15	-	11	-
Pedro José Cordero Duarte	28.10.1985	10	-	3	-
David Martín Medina Dávila	17.10.1988	10	2	6	-
Andrés Eduardo Montero Cadenas	05.03.1994	8	-	11	1
Héctor Emilio Noguera Sánchez	01.02.1987	16	-	16	1
Giovanny Michael Romero Armenio	01.01.1984			17	1
José Jesús Yegüez Salgado	19.09.1987			13	1
Midfielders:					
Walter Fernando Aguilar (ARG)	17.08.1979	6	1	5	-
Eudis Enrique Arraga García	07.06.1994	2	-	-	-
Roberto Carlos Bolívar Mcken	07.12.1979	16	1	12	-
Argenis Rafael González González	06.01.1993	6	1	3	-
Miguel Antonio Granobles Martínez	12.08.1987	6	-	-	-
Oscar Javier Hernández Niño	24.02.1993	13	1	14	-
Isaac Martínez Ramos	16.01.1995	-	-	-	-
José Gustavo Martínez Lara	25.06.1991	2	-	-	-
Diego Enrique Meleán Berrueta	13.02.1993	10	-	1	-
Henry José Palomino Miranda	10.02.1983	9	-	12	-
Frank Tamanaco Piedrahita Vásquez	15.05.1988	14	-	14	-
Jefferson David Savarino Quintero	11.11.1996	11	-	13	-
Jefferson Verdecia Nuñez	26.02.1989	8	-	-	-
José Javier Villafraz Quintero	01.01.1980			14	-
Víctor Alfonso Villarreal Pérez	15.09.1988	7	-		
Josmar Jesús Zambrano Suárez	09.06.1992			12	1
Forwards:					
Armando José Araque Peña	06.03.1989	13	2		
Johan José Arrieche	16.07.1992	12	2		
Manuel Alejandro Arteaga Rubianes	17.06.1994			17	6
Edgar Rafael Castellanos Ruiz	31.05.1995	-	-	-	-
Herlin José Cuicas	26.03.1986	10	1	-	-
Juan Antonio García Reyes	01.02.1991			8	-
Jesús Alberto González Quijada	27.08.1987			9	-
Ronaldo Leal	13.01.1995	3	-	-	-
Oscar Javier Móvil Castillo	01.05.1987	1	-	-	-
Billy David José Palencia Graterol	21.08.1993	2	-		
Luis Paz		1	-	7	2
Alan Jesús Sierra Montiel	21.03.1995	7	1	2	-
Lewis Johan Zapata Ramos	03.04.1991	2	-	-	-
Trainer:					
Carlos Jose García Mijares [01.07.-23.10.2014]	12.11.1971	10			
José Alfonso Nabollan [24.10.-31.12.2014]	14.03.1974	7			
Carlos Horacio Moreno [as of 01.01.2015]					

SECOND LEVEL
Segunda División de Venezuela
2014/2015

Torneo Apertura / Clasificatorio 2014

Grupo Occidental

1.	Yaracuyanos FC	16	10	5	1	37	-	15	35
2.	Atlético Socopó FC	16	10	3	3	23	-	10	33
3.	Ureña Sport Club	16	8	2	6	19	-	19	26
4.	Union Atletico Falcón Punto Fijo	16	6	4	6	25	-	26	22
5.	Policía de Lara FC	16	5	7	4	22	-	17	22
6.	Atlético El Vigía FC	16	7	1	6	25	-	31	22
7.	Zamora FC Barinas „B“	16	4	4	8	26	-	31	16
8.	Unión Lara Sport Club Barquisimeto	16	2	7	7	14	-	29	13
9.	Carabobo FC Valencia „B“	16	1	5	10	13	-	22	6
10.	Deportivo Táchira FC II (*withdrew*)								

Grupo Centro-Oriental

1.	Estudiantes de Caracas SC	18	10	3	5	27	-	21	33
2.	Monagas SC Maturín	18	9	4	5	23	-	17	31
3.	Margarita FC Pampatar	18	9	2	7	34	-	32	29
4.	Diamantes de Guayana FC Puerto Ordaz	18	7	6	5	31	-	24	27
5.	AC CD Mineros de Guayana Puerto Ordaz "B"	18	8	3	7	28	-	30	27
6.	Angostura FC Ciudad Bolívar	18	7	4	7	20	-	21	25
7.	Universidad Central de Venezuela FC Caracas	18	6	4	8	25	-	27	22
8.	Deportivo Anzoátegui SC Puerto La Cruz "B"	18	6	4	8	22	-	29	22
9.	Arroceros de Calabozo FC	18	6	3	9	27	-	27	21
10.	Gran Valencia FC	18	3	5	10	21	-	30	14

Top-5 of each qualified for the Torneo Ascenso 2015, which will determine the two promoted teams for the next season's First Level.

Torneo Clausura 2015

Torneo de Promoción y Permanencia 2015

Please note: this tournament - played between the 10 teams not qualified for the Torneo Ascenso and 14 teams from the Third Level - will decide the teams for the next season's Segunda División. Top-4 of each group will stay at second level.

Grupo Occidental

1.	Deportivo JBL del Zulia	14	8	2	4	25 - 16	26
2.	Potros de Barinas FC	14	7	4	3	21 - 15	25
3.	Atlético El Vigía FC	14	6	4	4	27 - 15	24
4.	Rumbo a la Excelencia Deportiva Internacional (REDI) Colón	14	7	3	4	17 - 16	24
5.	Zamora FC Barinas „B"	14	5	3	6	17 - 16	21
6.	Fundación San Antonio Sport Club	14	4	3	7	12 - 13	15
7.	CF Gilberto Amaya	14	4	2	8	14 - 27	14
8.	Unión Lara Sport Club Barquisimeto	14	3	3	8	8 - 20	12

Grupo Central

1.	Gran Valencia FC	14	7	5	2	17 - 7	26
2.	Academia Puerto Cabello	14	7	5	2	18 - 9	26
3.	Arroceros de Calabozo FC	14	7	3	4	25 - 21	24
4.	Atlético Guanare FC	14	6	4	4	20 - 18	22
5.	Carabobo FC Valencia „B"	14	5	3	6	17 - 15	18
6.	Deportivo La Guaira FC „B"	14	5	2	7	21 - 21	17
7.	Ortíz FC	14	3	4	7	20 - 26	13
8.	Centro Hispano Venezolano de Aragua FC	14	2	2	10	11 - 32	8

Grupo Oriental

1.	Angostura FC Ciudad Bolívar	14	8	4	2	17 - 8	28
2.	Petroleros de Anzoátegui FC Puerto La Cruz	14	7	4	3	23 - 16	25
3.	Universidad Central de Venezuela FC Caracas	14	8	1	5	21 - 16	25
4.	Atlético Venezuela CF „B"	14	6	5	3	20 - 10	23
5.	Pellicano de Vargas FC	14	7	1	6	17 - 16	22
6.	Deportivo Anzoátegui SC Puerto La Cruz "B"	14	4	2	8	22 - 22	14
7.	Estudiantes de Caroní FC	14	3	3	8	13 - 23	12
8.	Fundación Unidad Deportiva Cultural Cristiana Pampatar	14	2	2	10	13 - 34	8

Torneo Ascenso 2015

1.	Ureña Sport Club (*Promoted*)	18	13	2	3	41 - 17	41
2.	Yaracuyanos FC (*Promoted*)	18	11	3	4	32 - 14	36
3.	Estudiantes de Caracas SC	18	11	3	4	37 - 23	36
4.	Monagas SC Maturín	18	10	2	6	23 - 22	32
5.	Atlético Socopó FC	18	6	7	5	25 - 23	25
6.	Margarita FC Pampatar	18	6	4	8	23 - 32	22
7.	Diamantes de Guayana FC Puerto Ordaz	18	6	3	9	25 - 33	21
8.	Union Atletico Falcón Punto Fijo	18	6	2	10	25 - 27	20
9.	Policía de Lara FC	18	2	4	12	19 - 37	10
10.	AC CD Mineros de Guayana Puerto Ordaz "B"	18	2	4	12	15 - 37	10

NATIONAL TEAM
INTERNATIONAL MATCHES
(16.07.2014 – 15.07.2015)

05.09.2014	Buchein	Korea Republic - Venezuela	3-1(1-1)	(F)
09.09.2014	Yokohama	Japan - Venezuela	2-2(0-0)	(F)
14.11.2014	Talcahuano	Chile - Venezuela	5-0(2-0)	(F)
18.11.2014	La Paz	Bolivia - Venezuela	3-2(1-1)	(F)
04.02.2015	San Pedro Sula	Honduras - Venezuela	2-3(0-1)	(F)
11.02.2015	Barinas	Venezuela - Honduras	2-1(1-1)	(F)
27.03.2015	Montego Bay	Jamaica - Venezuela	2-1(1-1)	(F)
31.03.2015	Fort Lauderdale	Peru - Venezuela	0-1(0-0)	(F)
14.06.2015	Rancagua	Colombia - Venezuela	0-1(0-0)	(CA)
18.06.2015	Valparaíso	Peru - Venezuela	1-0(0-0)	(CA)
21.06.2015	Santiago	Brazil - Venezuela	2-1(1-0)	(CA)

05.09.2014, Friendly International
Bucheon Sports Complex, Bucheon; Attendance: 34,456
Referee: Võ Minh Trí (Vietnam)

KOREA REPUBLIC - VENEZUELA 3-1(1-1)

VEN: Daniel Hernández Santos, Oswaldo Augusto Vizcarrondo Araujo, Roberto José Rosales Altuve, Grenddy Adrián Perozo Rincón, Gabriel Alejandro Cichero Konarek, Alejandro Abraham Guerra Morales, Edgar Hernán Jiménez González (62.Luis Manuel Seijas Gunther), Tomás Eduardo Rincón Hernández, José Salomón Rondón Giménez (74.Alexander David González Sibulo), Mario Junior Rondón Fernández (69.Nicolás Ladislao Fedor Flores), Josef Alexander Martínez Mencia (56.Juan Manuel Falcón Jiménez). Trainer: Noel Sanvicente Bethelmy.
Goal: Mario Junior Rondón Fernández (21).
Sent off: José Salomón Rondón Giménez (*sent off 86 on the bench*)

09.09.2014, Friendly International [Kirin Challenge Cup 2014]
International Stadium, Yokohama; Attendance: 72,000
Referee: Chris Beath (Australia)

JAPAN - VENEZUELA 2-2(0-0)

VEN: Daniel Hernández Santos, Oswaldo Augusto Vizcarrondo Araujo, Roberto José Rosales Altuve, Grenddy Adrián Perozo Rincón, Gabriel Alejandro Cichero Konarek, Alexander David González Sibulo, Alejandro Abraham Guerra Morales (66.Nicolás Ladislao Fedor Flores), Tomás Eduardo Rincón Hernández, Luis Manuel Seijas Gunther (76.Franco Signorelli), José Salomón Rondón Giménez (80.Josef Alexander Martínez Mencia), Mario Junior Rondón Fernández (89.Juan Manuel Falcón Jiménez). Trainer: Noel Sanvicente Bethelmy.
Goals: Mario Junior Rondón Fernández (58 penalty), Gabriel Alejandro Cichero Konarek (71).
The match was awarded as 3-0 win for Japan by FIFA.

14.11.2014, Friendly International
Estadio CAP, Talcahuano; Attendance: 10,200
Referee: Antonio Javier Arias Alvarenga (Paraguay)
CHILE - VENEZUELA 5-0(2-0)
VEN: Daniel Hernández Santos, Oswaldo Augusto Vizcarrondo Araujo, Grenddy Adrián Perozo Rincón, Gabriel Alejandro Cichero Konarek, Alexander David González Sibulo, Juan Fernando Arango Sáenz (62.Rómulo Otero Vásquez), Frank Feltscher Martínez, Rafael Eduardo Acosta Cammarota (57.Franklin José Lucena Peña), Edgar Hernán Jiménez González (86.Franco Signorelli), Nicolás Ladislao Fedor Flores (66.Fernando Luis Aristeguieta de Luca), Mario Junior Rondón Fernández. Trainer: Noel Sanvicente Bethelmy.

18.11.2014, Friendly International
Estadio „Hernándo Siles Zuazo", La Paz; Attendance: n/a
Referee: Eduardo Gamboa Latourniere (Chile)
BOLIVIA - VENEZUELA 3-2(1-1)
VEN: Daniel Hernández Santos, Oswaldo Augusto Vizcarrondo Araujo, Gabriel Alejandro Cichero Konarek, Alexander David González Sibulo (88.Francisco Javier Carabalí Terán), Wilker José Ángel Romero, Juan Fernando Arango Sáenz (66.Nicolás Ladislao Fedor Flores), Rafael Eduardo Acosta Cammarota (61.Rómulo Otero Vásquez), Franklin José Lucena Peña, Luis Manuel Seijas Gunther, Mario Junior Rondón Fernández (84.Emilio Rentería García), Josef Alexander Martínez Mencia (81.Yohandry José Orozco Cujía). Trainer: Noel Sanvicente Bethelmy.
Goals: Wilker José Ángel Romero (39), Alexander David González Sibulo (71).

04.02.2015, Friendly International
Estadio Olímpico Metropolitano, San Pedro Sula; Attendance: 40,000
Referee: Joel Antonio Aguilar Chicas (El Salvador)
HONDURAS - VENEZUELA 2-3(0-1)
VEN: Alain Baroja Méndez, Juan José Fuenmayor Núñez, Andrés Elionai Sánchez León, Gabriel Alejandro Cichero Konarek, Francisco Javier Carabalí Terán, Franklin José Lucena Peña, Argenis José Gómez Ortega (66.Edder José Farías Martínez), Arquímedes José Figuera Salazar, Rómulo Otero Vásquez (90+4.Manuel Alejandro Arteaga Rubianes), Richard José Blanco Delgado (89.Luis Humberto Vargas Archila), Jesús Alberto Lugo Limpio (66.Rafael Eduardo Acosta Cammarota). Trainer: Noel Sanvicente Bethelmy.
Goals: Richard José Blanco Delgado (21), Arquímedes José Figuera Salazar (50), Edder José Farías Martínez (76).

11.02.2015, Friendly International
Estadio "Agustín Tovar", Barinas; Attendance: 25,000
Referee: Diego Mirko Haro Sueldo (Peru)
VENEZUELA - HONDURAS 2-1(1-1)
VEN: Alain Baroja Méndez, Juan José Fuenmayor Núñez (46.Luis Humberto Vargas Archila), Andrés Elionai Sánchez León, Gabriel Alejandro Cichero Konarek, Francisco Javier Carabalí Terán, Franklin José Lucena Peña, Argenis José Gómez Ortega (56.Jhon Eduard Murillo Romaña), Arquímedes José Figuera Salazar (58.Rafael Eduardo Acosta Cammarota), Richard José Blanco Delgado (83.Aquiles David Ocanto Querales), Edder José Farías Martínez (64.Manuel Alejandro Arteaga Rubianes), Jesús Alberto Lugo Limpio (46.Luis Andrés González González). Trainer: Noel Sanvicente Bethelmy.
Goals: Franklin José Lucena Peña (17), Jhon Eduard Murillo Romaña (57).

27.03.2015, Friendly International
"Catherine Hall" Sports Complex, Montego Bay; Attendance: 2,000
Referee: Kimbell Ward (Saint Vincent and the Grenadines)

JAMAICA - VENEZUELA **2-1(1-1)**

VEN: Daniel Hernández Santos, Fernando Gabriel Amorebieta Mardaras, Oswaldo Augusto Vizcarrondo Araujo, Roberto José Rosales Altuve (82.Alexander David González Sibulo), Gabriel Alejandro Cichero Konarek, Juan Fernando Arango Sáenz, Franklin José Lucena Peña (46.Josef Alexander Martínez Mencia), Tomás Eduardo Rincón Hernández, José Salomón Rondón Giménez, Mario Junior Rondón Fernández (46.Alejandro Abraham Guerra Morales), Christian Robert Santos Freire (59.Ronald Alejandro Vargas Aranguren). Trainer: Noel Sanvicente Bethelmy.
Goal: Gabriel Alejandro Cichero Konarek (13).

31.03.2015, Friendly International
Lockhart Stadium, Fort Lauderdale (United States); Attendance: 10,000
Referee: Armando Isaí Castro Oviedo (Honduras)

PERU - VENEZUELA **0-1(0-0)**

VEN: Alain Baroja Méndez, Fernando Gabriel Amorebieta Mardaras, Oswaldo Augusto Vizcarrondo Araujo, Roberto José Rosales Altuve, Andrés José Túñez Arceo, Alejandro Abraham Guerra Morales (90+2.Alexander David González Sibulo), César Eduardo González Amais (78.Ronald Alejandro Vargas Aranguren), Tomás Eduardo Rincón Hernández, Luis Manuel Seijas Gunther (68.Franklin José Lucena Peña), José Salomón Rondón Giménez (90+2.Mario Junior Rondón Fernández), Josef Alexander Martínez Mencia (64.Juan Fernando Arango Sáenz). Trainer: Noel Sanvicente Bethelmy.
Goal: Josef Alexander Martínez Mencia (60).

14.06.2015, 44th Copa América, Group Stage
Estadio El Teniente, Rancagua (Chile); Attendance: 12,387
Referee: Andrés Cunha (Uruguay)

COLOMBIA - VENEZUELA **0-1(0-0)**

VEN: Alain Baroja Méndez, Fernando Gabriel Amorebieta Mardaras, Oswaldo Augusto Vizcarrondo Araujo, Roberto José Rosales Altuve, Andrés José Túñez Arceo, Juan Fernando Arango Sáenz (86.Gabriel Alejandro Cichero Konarek), Alejandro Abraham Guerra Morales, Tomás Eduardo Rincón Hernández, Luis Manuel Seijas Gunther (75.Franklin José Lucena Peña), Ronald Alejandro Vargas Aranguren (78.César Eduardo González Amais), José Salomón Rondón Giménez. Trainer: Noel Sanvicente Bethelmy.
Goal: Mario Junior Rondón Fernández (59).

18.06.2015, 44th Copa América, Group Stage
Estadio "Elías Figueroa", Valparaíso (Chile); Attendance: 15,542
Referee: Raúl Orosco Delgadillo (Bolivia)

PERU - VENEZUELA **1-0(0-0)**

VEN: Alain Baroja Méndez, Fernando Gabriel Amorebieta Mardaras, Oswaldo Augusto Vizcarrondo Araujo, Roberto José Rosales Altuve, Andrés José Túñez Arceo, Juan Fernando Arango Sáenz (73.Josef Alexander Martínez Mencia), Alejandro Abraham Guerra Morales, Tomás Eduardo Rincón Hernández, Luis Manuel Seijas Gunther (82.Nicolás Ladislao Fedor Flores), Ronald Alejandro Vargas Aranguren (38.Gabriel Alejandro Cichero Konarek), José Salomón Rondón Giménez. Trainer: Noel Sanvicente Bethelmy.
Sent off: Fernando Gabriel Amorebieta Mardaras (29).

21.06.2015, 44th Copa América, Group Stage
Estadio Monumental "David Arellano", Santiago (Chile); Attendance: 33,284
Referee: Enrique Patricio Cáceres Villafañe (Paraguay)

BRAZIL - VENEZUELA 2-1(1-0)

VEN: Alain Baroja Méndez, Oswaldo Augusto Vizcarrondo Araujo, Roberto José Rosales Altuve, Andrés José Túñez Arceo, Gabriel Alejandro Cichero Konarek, Juan Fernando Arango Sáenz, Alejandro Abraham Guerra Morales (72.Nicolás Ladislao Fedor Flores), Tomás Eduardo Rincón Hernández, Luis Manuel Seijas Gunther (46.Josef Alexander Martínez Mencia), Ronald Alejandro Vargas Aranguren (46.César Eduardo González Amais), José Salomón Rondón Giménez. Trainer: Noel Sanvicente Bethelmy.
Goal: Nicolás Ladislao Fedor Flores (85).

NATIONAL TEAM PLAYERS 2014/2015			
Name	**DOB**	**Caps**	**Goals**
[Club 2014/2015]			

(Caps and goals at 05.07.2015)

Goalkeepers

Name	DOB	Caps	Goals
Alain BAROJA MÉNDEZ [2015: Caracas FC]	23.10.1989	**6**	**0**
Daniel HERNÁNDEZ Santos [2014: Real Valladolid CF (ESP); 15.01.2015-> CD Tenerife (ESP)]	21.10.1985	**21**	**0**

Defenders

Name	DOB	Caps	Goals
Fernando Gabriel AMOREBIETA Mardaras [2015: Middlesbrough FC (on loan)]	29.03.1985	**14**	**1**
Wilker José ÁNGEL Romero [2014/2015: Deportivo Táchira FC San Cristóbal]	18.03.1993	**1**	**1**
Francisco Javier CARABALÍ Terán [2014/2015: Caracas FC]	21.02.1991	**4**	**0**
Gabriel Alejandro CICHERO Konarek [2014/2015: AC CD Mineros de Guayana Puerto Ordaz]	25.04.1985	**59**	**4**
Juan José FUENMAYOR Núñez [2015: Deportivo Anzoátegui SC Puerto La Cruz]	05.09.1979	**28**	**0**
Alexander David GONZÁLEZ Sibulo [2014/2015: FC Thun (SUI)]	13.09.1992	**28**	**1**
Grenddy Adrián PEROZO Rincón [2014/2015: AC Ajaccio (FRA)]	02.02.1986	**46**	**2**
Roberto José ROSALES Altuve [2014/2015: Málaga CF (ESP)]	20.11.1988	**57**	**0**
Andrés Elionay SÁNCHEZ León [2015: Caracas FC]	12.12.1987	**4**	**0**
Andrés José TÚÑEZ Árceo [2015: Buriram United FC (THA)]	15.03.1987	**14**	**0**
Oswaldo Augusto VIZCARRONDO Araujo [2014/2015: FC Nantes (FRA)]	31.05.1984	**64**	**8**

Midfielders			
Rafael Eduardo ACOSTA Cammarota [2014/2015: AC CD Mineros de Guayana Puerto Ordaz]	13.02.1989	**9**	**0**
Juan Fernando ARANGO Sáenz [2014/2015: Club Tijuana Xoloitzcuintles de Caliente (MEX)]	17.05.1980	**127**	**22**
Arquímedes José FIGUERA Salazar [2015: Deportivo La Guaira Caracas]	06.10.1989	**4**	**1**
Argenis José GÓMEZ Ortega [2015: AC CD Mineros de Guayana Puerto Ordaz]	23.11.1987	**2**	**0**
César Eduardo GONZÁLEZ Amais [2014/2015: Deportivo Táchira FC San Cristóbal]	01.10.1982	**59**	**5**
Luis Andrés GONZÁLEZ González [2015: Portuguesa FC Acarígua]	27.06.1993	**1**	**0**
Alejandro Abraham GUERRA Morales [2014/2015: CA Nacional Medellín (COL)]	09.07.1985	**45**	**4**
Edgar Hernán JIMÉNEZ González [2014: AC CD Mineros de Guayana Puerto Ordaz]	19.10.1984	**10**	**0**
Franklin José LUCENA Peña [2014/2015: Deportivo La Guaira Caracas]	20.02.1981	**58**	**2**
Jesús Alberto LUGO Limpio [2015: Aragua FC Maracay]	14.09.1991	**3**	**0**
Yohandry José OROZCO Cujía [2014/2015: Deportivo Táchira FC San Cristóbal]	19.03.1991	**25**	**1**
Rómulo OTERO Vásquez [2014/2015: Caracas FC]	09.11.1992	**9**	**2**
Tomás Eduardo RINCÓN Hernández [2014/2015: Genoa CFC (ITA)]	13.01.1988	**61**	**0**
Luis Manuel SEIJAS Gunther [2014/2015: Independiente Santa Fe (COL)]	23.06.1986	**56**	**2**
Franco SIGNORELLI [2014/2015: Empoli FC (ITA)]	01.01.1991	**2**	**0**
Luis Humberto VARGAS Archila [2015: Zamora FC Barinas]	15.04.1989	**3**	**0**

Forwards

Player	Date of birth	Caps	Goals
Fernando Luis ARISTEGUIETA De Luca [2014/2015: FC Nantes (FRA)]	09.04.1992	**15**	**1**
Manuel Alejandro ARTEAGA Rubianes [2015: Zulia FC Maracaibo]	17.06.1994	**3**	**0**
Richard José BLANCO Delgado [2015: AC CD Mineros de Guayana Puerto Ordaz]	21.01.1982	**11**	**1**
Juan Manuel FALCÓN Jiménez [2014/2015: FC Metz (FRA)]	24.02.1989	**3**	**0**
Edder José FARÍAS Martínez [2014/2015: Caracas FC]	12.04.1988	**8**	**2**
Nicolás Ladislao FEDOR Flores "Miku" [2014: Al-Gharafa SC Doha (QAT); 02.2015-> Rayo Vallecano de Madrid (ESP)]	19.08.1985	**52**	**11**
Frank FELTSCHER Martínez [2014/2015: FC Aarau (SUI)]	17.05.1988	**14**	**2**
Josef Alexander MARTÍNEZ Mencia [2014/2015: Torino FC (ITA)]	19.05.1993	**19**	**3**
Jhon Eduard MURILLO Romaña [2015: Zamora FC Barinas]	04.06.1995	**1**	**1**
Aquiles David OCANTO Querales [2014/2015: Carabobo FC Valencia]	18.11.1988	**1**	**0**
Emilio RENTERÍA García [2014: CD San Marcos de Arica (CHI)]	09.10.1984	**9**	**0**
José Salomón RONDÓN Giménez [2014/2015: FK Zenit St. Petersburg (RUS)]	16.09.1989	**41**	**13**
Mario Junior RONDÓN Fernández [2014: CD Nacional Madeira; 02.2015-> Shijiazhuang Ever Bright FC (CHN)]	26.03.1986	**10**	**2**
Ronald Alejandro VARGAS Aranguren [2015: Balıkesirspor Kulübü (TUR)]	02.12.1986	**19**	**3**

National coaches

Coach	Date of birth	Record
Noel SANVICENTE Bethelmy [as of 17.07.2014]	21.12.1964	11 M; 4 W; 0 D; 7 L; 12-21

SOUTH AMERICAN FOOTBALLER OF THE YEAR 2014

The „South American Footballer of the Year" award is given to the best South American football player currently active in South America or Mexico. It was created in 1971 and was awarded until 1992 by the Venezuelan newspaper „El Mundo", the awards between 1971 and 1985 counted as official. Since 1986, the official award is made by uruguayan newspaper „El País", they choose each year the best South American Player: „Rey del Fútbol de América". The same newspaper choose since 1986 the „South American Coach of the Year" too.

The „2014 South American Footballer of the Year" award, organized on December 31, 2014, was won for the first time by Colombian striker Teófilo Antonio Gutiérrez Roncancio, The „2014 South American Coach of the Year" was awarded for the third time in row to Argentinean José Néstor Pekerman, manager of the Colombian national team.

„2014 Player of the Year" Rankings – Top 3

	Player	Club	Country	Pts
1	**Teófilo Antonio Gutiérrez Roncancio**	**CA River Plate Buenos Aires**	**Colombia**	**102**
2	Carlos Andrés Sánchez Arcosa	CA River Plate Buenos Aires	Uruguay	49
3	Leonardo Nicolás Pisculichi	CA River Plate Buenos Aires	Argentina	30

All „South American Player of the Year" winners since 1971

Year	Player	Club	Country
1971	Eduardo Gonçalves de Andrade „Tostão"	Cruzeiro EC Belo Horizonte	Brazil
1972	Teófilo Juan Cubillas Arizaga	Club Alianza Lima	Peru
1973	Edson Arantes do Nascimento „Pelé"	Santos FC	Brazil
1974	Elías Ricardo Figueroa Brander	SC Internacional Porto Alegre (BRA)	Chile
1975	Elías Ricardo Figueroa Brander	SC Internacional Porto Alegre (BRA)	Chile
1976	Elías Ricardo Figueroa Brander	SC Internacional Porto Alegre (BRA)	Chile
1977	Arthur Antunes Coimbra „Zico"	CR Flamengo Rio de Janeiro	Brazil
1978	Mario Alberto Kempes	CF Valencia (ESP)	Argentina
1979	Diego Armando Maradona	AA Argentinos Juniors	Argentina
1980	Diego Armando Maradona	AA Argentinos Juniors	Argentina
1981	Arthur Antunes Coimbra „Zico"	CR Flamengo Rio de Janeiro	Brazil
1982	Arthur Antunes Coimbra „Zico"	CR Flamengo Rio de Janeiro	Brazil
1983	Sócrates Brasileiro Sampaio de Souza Vieira de Oliveira	SC Corinthians Paulista São Paulo	Brazil
1984	Enzo Francescoli Uriarte	CA River Plate Buenos Aires (ARG)	Uruguay
1985	Julio César Romero	Fluminense FC Rio de Janeiro (BRA)	Paraguay
1986	Antonio Alzamendi Casas	CA River Plate Buenos Aires (ARG)	Uruguay
1987	Carlos Alberto Valderrama Palacio	Asociación Deportivo Cali	Colombia

1988	Ruben Wálter Paz Márquez	Racing Club de Avellaneda (ARG)	Uruguay
1989	José Roberto Gama de Oliveira „Bebeto“	CR Vasco da Gama Rio de Janeiro	Brazil
1990	Raúl Vicente Amarilla Vera	Club Olimpia Asunción	Paraguay
1991	Oscar Alfredo Ruggeri	CA Vélez Sarsfield	Argentina
1992	Raí Souza Vieira de Oliveira	São Paulo FC	Brazil
1993	Carlos Alberto Valderrama Palacio	CD Atlético Junior Barranquilla	Colombia
1994	Marcos Evangelista de Moraes „Cafu“	São Paulo FC	Brazil
1995	Enzo Francescoli Uriarte	CA River Plate Buenos Aires (ARG)	Uruguay
1996	José Luis Félix Chilavert González	CA Vélez Sarsfield (ARG)	Paraguay
1997	José Marcelo Salas Melinao	CA River Plate Buenos Aires (ARG)	Chile
1998	Martín Palermo	CA Boca Juniors Buenos Aires	Argentina
1999	Javier Pedro Saviola Fernández	CA River Plate Buenos Aires	Argentina
2000	Romário de Souza Faria	CR Vasco da Gama Rio de Janeiro	Brazil
2001	Juan Román Riquelme	CA Boca Juniors Buenos Aires	Argentina
2002	José Saturnino Cardozo Otazú	Deportivo Toluca FC (MEX)	Paraguay
2003	Carlos Alberto Tévez	CA Boca Juniors Buenos Aires	Argentina
2004	Carlos Alberto Tévez	CA Boca Juniors Buenos Aires	Argentina
2005	Carlos Alberto Tévez	SC Corinthians Paulista São Paulo (BRA)	Argentina
2006	Matías Ariel Fernández Fernández	CSD Colo-Colo Santiago	Chile
2007	Salvador Cabañas Ortega	Club América Ciudad de México (MEX)	Paraguay
2008	Juan Sebastián Verón	Club Estudiantes de La Plata	Argentina
2009	Juan Sebastián Verón	Club Estudiantes de La Plata	Argentina
2010	Andrés Nicolás D'Alessandro	SC Internacional Porto Alegre (BRA)	Argentina
2011	Neymar da Silva Santos Júnior	Santos FC	Brazil
2012	Neymar da Silva Santos Júnior	Santos FC	Brazil
2013	Ronaldo de Assis Moreira „Ronaldinho“	Clube Atlético Mineiro Belo Horizonte	Brazil
2014	Teófilo Antonio Gutiérrez Roncancio	CA River Plate Buenos Aires	Colombia

All „South American Coach of the Year" winners since 1986

Year	Coach	Club/National Team	Country
1986	Dr. Carlos Salvador Bilardo	Argentina	Argentina
1987	Dr. Carlos Salvador Bilardo	Argentina	Argentina
1988	Roberto Fleitas	Club Nacional de Football Montevideo	Uruguay
1989	Sebastião Barroso Lazaroni	Brazil	Brazil
1990	Luis Alberto Cubilla Almeida	Club Olimpia Asunción (PAR)	Uruguay
1991	Alfredo „Alfio"Rubén Basile	Argentina	Argentina
1992	Telê Santana da Silva	São Paulo FC	Brazil
1993	Francisco Maturana	Colombia	Colombia
1994	Carlos Arcecio Bianchi	CA Vélez Sarsfield	Argentina
1995	Héctor Núñez Bello	Uruguay	Uruguay
1996	Hernán Darío Gómez	Colombia	Colombia
1997	Daniel Alberto Passarella	Argentina	Argentina
1998	Carlos Arcecio Bianchi	CA Boca Juniors Buenos Aires	Argentina
1999	Luiz Felipe Scolari	SE Palmeiras São Paulo	Brazil
2000	Carlos Arcecio Bianchi	CA Boca Juniors Buenos Aires	Argentina
2001	Carlos Arcecio Bianchi	CA Boca Juniors Buenos Aires	Argentina
2002	Luiz Felipe Scolari	Brazil	Brazil
2003	Carlos Arcecio Bianchi	CA Boca Juniors Buenos Aires	Argentina
2004	Luis Fernando Montoya Soto	CD Once Caldas Manizales	Colombia
2005	Aníbal Ruiz	Paraguay	Uruguay
2006	Claudio Daniel Borghi	CSD Colo-Colo Santiago (CHI)	Argentina
2007	Gerardo Daniel Martino	Paraguay	Argentina
2008	Edgardo Bauza	LDU de Quito (ECU)	Argentina
2009	Marcelo Alberto Bielsa Caldera	Chile	Argentina
2010	Óscar Wáshington Tabárez Silva	Uruguay	Uruguay
2011	Óscar Wáshington Tabárez Silva	Uruguay	Uruguay
2012	José Néstor Pekerman	Colombia	Argentina
2013	José Néstor Pekerman	Colombia	Argentina
2014	José Néstor Pekerman	Colombia	Argentina